D0138797

USEFUL CHECKLISTS, SUMMARIES, AND BOXES

Critical Thinking and *Critical Decisions* Boxes

The Writing and Revising Process: Essays and Paragraphs

Revising Sentences, Words, Punctuation (see also *Critical Decisions* boxes)

Researching and Writing in the Disciplines

The Allyn & Bacon Handbook

Third Edition

Leonard J. Rosen,
Harvard University
Expository Writing Program

Laurence Behrens,
University of California,
Santa Barbara

The NEW third edition offers

Up-to-date information on using electronic resources for research

Emphasis on writing across the curriculum

Increased focus on critical thinking

Fresh, new examples, exercises, and student papers

New appendix on document design

The first handbook built on the underlying themes of critical thinking and writing across the curriculum now moves into the next generation with coverage of electronic research and document design, plus new examples and student papers!

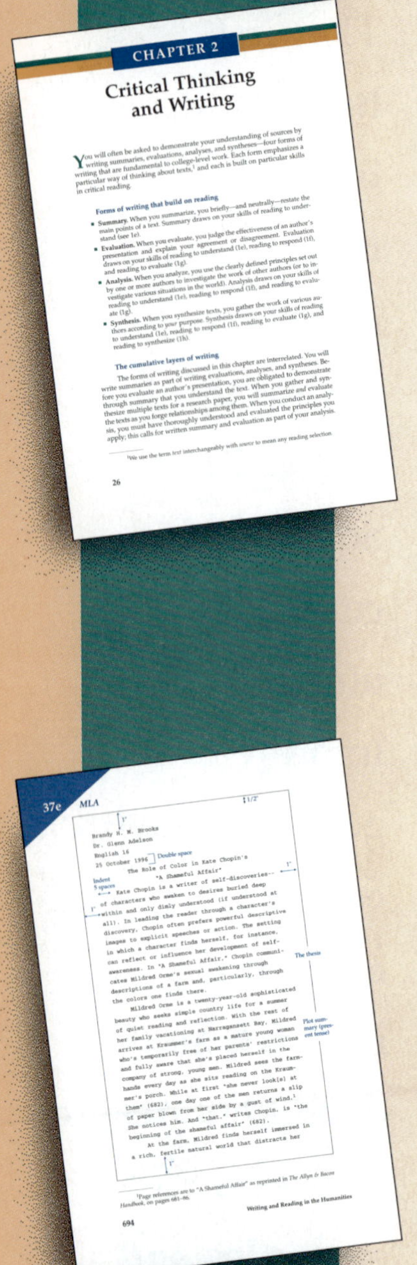

CHAPTER 2

Critical Thinking and Writing

You will often be asked to demonstrate your understanding of sources by writing summaries, evaluations, analyses, and syntheses—four forms of writing that are fundamental to college-level work. Each form emphasizes a particular way of thinking about texts,[1] and each is built on particular skills in critical reading.

Forms of writing that build on reading

- **Summary.** When you summarize, you briefly—and neutrally—restate the main points of a text. Summary draws on your skills of reading to understand (see 1e).
- **Evaluation.** When you evaluate, you judge the effectiveness of an author's presentation and explain your agreement or disagreement. Evaluation draws on your skills of reading to understand (1e), reading to respond (1f), and reading to evaluate (1g).
- **Analysis.** When you analyze, you use the clearly defined principles set out by one or more authors to investigate the work of other authors (or to investigate various situations in the world). Analysis draws on your skills of reading to understand (1e), reading to respond (1f), and reading to evaluate (1g).
- **Synthesis.** When you synthesize texts, you gather the work of various authors according to *your* purpose. Synthesis draws on your skills of reading to understand (1e), reading to respond (1f), reading to evaluate (1g), and reading to synthesize (1h).

The cumulative layers of writing

The forms of writing discussed in this chapter are interrelated. You will write summaries as part of writing evaluations, analyses, and syntheses. Before you evaluate an author's presentation, you are obligated to demonstrate through summary that you understand the text. When you gather and synthesize multiple texts for a research paper, you will summarize *and* evaluate the texts as you forge relationships among them. When you conduct an analysis, you must have thoroughly understood and evaluated the principles you apply; this calls for written summary and evaluation as part of your analysis.

[1]We use the term *text* interchangeably with *source* to mean any reading selection.

26

37e MLA

1/2"

1"

Brandy H. M. Brooks
Dr. Glenn Adelson
English 16
25 October 1996 — Double space
The Role of Color in Kate Chopin's
"A Shameful Affair"

Indent 5 spaces

Kate Chopin is a writer of self-discoveries--
of characters who awaken to desires buried deep
within and only dimly understood (if understood at
all). In leading the reader through a character's
discovery, Chopin often prefers powerful descriptive
images to explicit speeches or action. The setting
in which a character finds herself, for instance,
can reflect or influence her development of self-
awareness. In "A Shameful Affair," Chopin communicates Mildred Orme's sexual awakening through
descriptions of a farm and, particularly, through
the colors one finds there.

The thesis

Mildred Orme is a twenty-year-old sophisticated
beauty who seeks simple country life for a summer
of quiet reading and reflection. With the rest of
her family vacationing at Narragansett Bay, Mildred
arrives at Kraummer's farm as a mature young woman
who's temporarily free of her parents' restrictions
and fully aware that she's placed herself in the
company of strong, young men. Mildred sees the farmhands every day as she sits reading on the Kraummer's porch. While at first "she never look[s] at
them" (682), one day one of the men returns a slip
of paper blown from her side by a gust of wind.[1]
She notices him. And "that," writes Chopin, is "the
beginning of the shameful affair" (682).

Plot summary (present tense)

At the farm, Mildred finds herself immersed in
a rich, fertile natural world that distracts her

1"

[1]Page references are to "A Shameful Affair" as reprinted in *The Allyn & Bacon Handbook*, on pages 681–86.

694 Writing and Reading in the Humanities

The third edition gives students even more help with learning to think, read, and write critically

The Allyn & Bacon Handbook's opening chapters on critical thinking and writing provide a unique foundation for decision-making skills from the invention and planning stage to the designing of sentences.

- *NEW!* **Expanded coverage of critical thinking** in the rhetoric and research sections. **Fresh, new examples and readings** provide continuous illustrations for demonstrating student thinking and writing skills.
- *NEW!* Chapters 3 and 4, "Planning, Developing, and Writing a Draft" and "The Process of Revision," are redeveloped with a **new student paper** example emphasizing how to use critical skills in the composing process.
- *NEW!* **Approximately 50% of all examples, exercises, and student papers are new.** Three new student papers: "Gender Differences in the Computer Industry," "What Do We Want at the Mall?," and "The Role of Color in Kate Chopin's 'A Shameful Affair,'" serve as examples for demonstrating student thinking and writing skills.
- Critical thinking chapters are based on the idea that **writing at the college level is most often a response to reading.** Reading materials here serve as the basis for discussion of ideas in an evolving paper in Chapters 3 and 4.
- Critical Decision boxes throughout the text help students **apply critical thinking skills to using grammar and writing.**
- The text stresses the **recursive nature of writing** and the evolution of a successful paper through a critical thinking and writing process.

The most detailed coverage of electronic resources in any handbook

- *NEW!* Chapter 33, "Understanding the Research Process," presents a **thorough introduction to the Internet** and to using its resources in research.
- *NEW!* **Provides definitions and discusses access and reliability** of resources on the World Wide Web, gopher, ftp (file transfer protocol), and WAIS as well as user groups, listservs, and email.
- *NEW!* Features clear details on how to **locate and evaluate material from the Internet and other online sources.** Includes a step-by-step demonstration on using search words to seek out usable Internet sources, with Web pages replicated to show how to conduct the search process.
- *NEW!* Chapter 36, "Documenting Research," teaches students the conventions of **citing electronic sources using MLA, APA, CBE, and CMS formats.**
- *NEW!* **Three new student papers show examples of electronic and Internet sources in use.**
- *NEW!* A revised Appendix A on Computer Writing updates the discussion on basic techniques for word processing, adding two new subsections on **using disks or networks for collaborative learning and for peer editing.**

The most extensive coverage of argument in any handbook

- An adapted **Toulmin Model of argumentation,** offered since the first edition, helps students develop and support an argument.
- Each cross-curricular chapter reviews **patterns for making arguments in the disciplines.**
- **Two student papers** illustrate the writing process and the development of an argument.

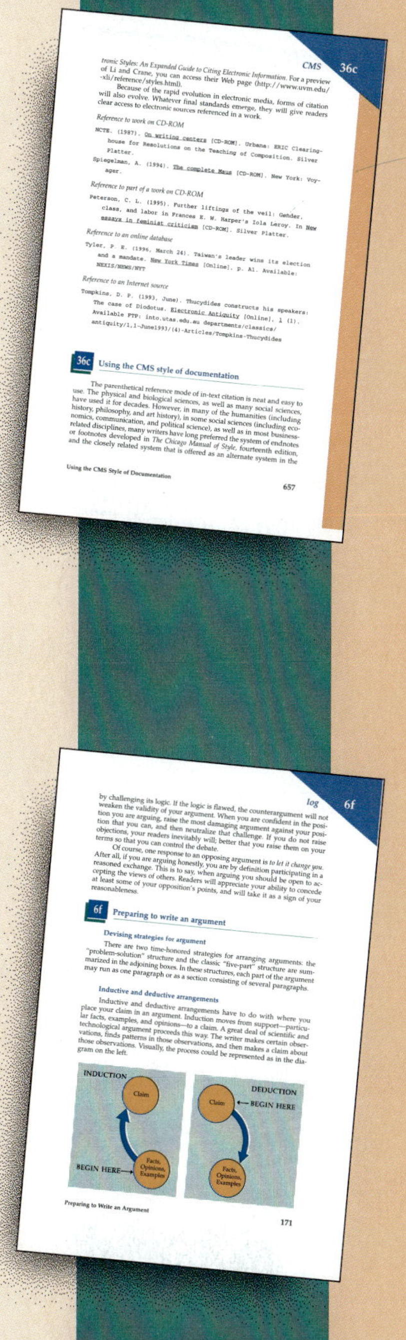

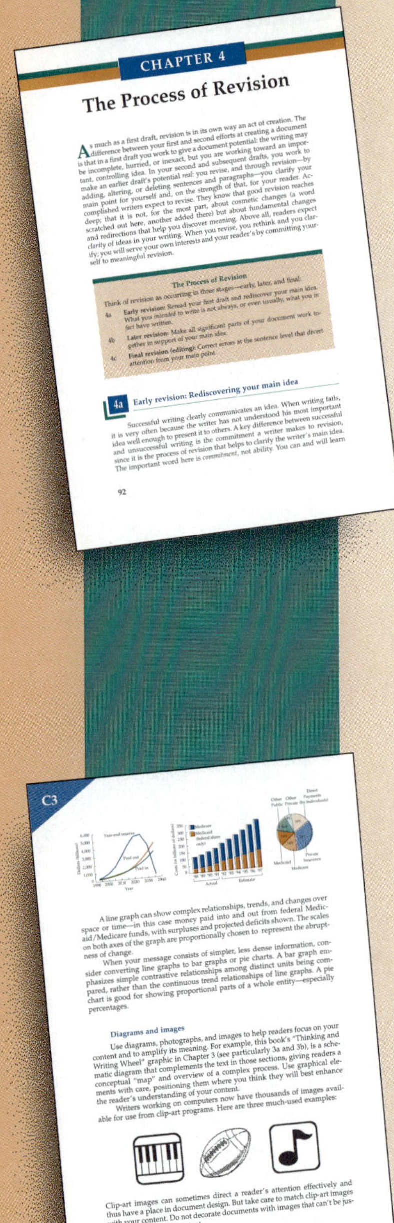

CHAPTER 4

The Process of Revision

As much as a first draft, revision is in its own way an act of creation. The
difference between your first and second efforts at creating a document
is that in a first draft you work to give a document potential: the writing may
be incomplete, hurried, or inexact, but you are working toward an important, controlling idea. In your second and subsequent drafts, you work to
make an earlier draft's potential *real*: you revise, and through revision—by
adding, altering, or deleting sentences and paragraphs—you clarify your
main point for yourself and, on the strength of that, for your reader. Accomplished writers expect to revise. They know that good revision reaches
deep; that it is not, for the most part, about cosmetic changes (a word
scratched out here, another added there) but about fundamental changes
and redirections that help you discover meaning. Above all, readers expect
clarity of ideas in your writing. When you revise, you rethink and you clarify; you will serve your own interests and your reader's by committing yourself to meaningful revision.

The Process of Revision

Think of revision as occurring in three stages—early, later, and final:

4a **Early revision:** Reread your first draft and rediscover your main idea.
What you *intended* to write is not always, or even usually, what you in
fact have written.

4b **Later revision:** Make all significant parts of your document work together in support of your main idea.

4c **Final revision (editing):** Correct errors at the sentence level that divert
attention from your main point.

4a Early revision: Rediscovering your main idea

Successful writing clearly communicates an idea. When writing fails,
it is very often because the writer has not understood his most important
idea well enough to present it to others. A key difference between successful
and unsuccessful writing is the commitment a writer makes to revision,
since it is the process of revision that helps to clarify the writer's main idea.
The important word here is *commitment*, not ability. You can and will learn

92

C3

A line graph can show complex relationships, trends, and changes over
space or time—in this case money paid into and out from federal Medic-
aid/Medicare funds, with surpluses and projected deficits shown. The scales
on both axes of the graph are proportionally chosen to represent the abruptness of change.

When your message consists of simpler, less dense information, consider converting line graphs to bar graphs or pie charts. A bar graph emphasizes simple contrastive relationships among distinct units being compared, rather than the continuous trend relationships of line graphs. A pie
chart is good for showing proportional parts of a whole entity—especially
percentages.

Diagrams and images

Use diagrams, photographs, and images to help readers focus on your
content and to amplify its meaning. For example, this book's "Thinking and
Writing Wheel" graphic in Chapter 3 (see particularly 3a and 3b), is a schematic diagram that complements the text in those sections, giving readers a
conceptual "map" and overview of a complex process. Use graphical elements with care, positioning them where you think they will best enhance
the reader's understanding of your content.

Writers working on computers now have thousands of images available for use from clip-art programs. Here are three much-used examples:

Clip-art images can sometimes direct a reader's attention effectively and
thus have a place in document design. But take care to match clip-art images
with your content. Do not decorate documents with images that can't be justified on the basis of content.

The Visual Design of Documents

812

The first handbook to consider writing as a skill used in all college disciplines

The Allyn & Bacon Handbook is based on the premise that the composition course is only the *first* college course in which writing will be a valuable and essential skill. One of the book's primary goals is to help students master the types of reading and writing assignments that are crucial to their college success.

- *NEW!* **A boxed feature, "Across the Curriculum,"** shows students how basic rhetorical skills in thinking, composing, and writing are distinctively applied by writers in disciplines across the curriculum.
- Coverage of grammar, punctuation, and mechanics offers real academic and student writing **drawn from several disciplines** as a basis for **examples and exercises.**
- Contains **four student research papers in the humanities, social sciences, and natural sciences** with models and guidelines for MLA, APA, CBE, and CMS documentation.
- Includes **unique individual chapters on the disciplines,** including writing and reading in the humanities (with full treatment on **writing about literature**), in the social sciences, and in the natural sciences. Each deals with making arguments and working with typical assignments in the discipline.
- Each chapter…
    - reviews patterns for writing to inform and for making arguments in the discipline area
    - reviews typical kinds of reading and audience situations
    - presents assignments typically found in the discipline
    - presents a complete student paper

Appendices have been revised and updated

- *NEW!* **Appendix A, "Writing with Computers,"** includes collaborative writing and peer editing techniques.
- *NEW!* **Appendix C, "The Visual Design of Documents,"** provides guidelines for using headings and graphics in report writing, and for using effective diagrams, charts, and graphs in research and technical documents, as well as in newsletters and Web pages.

Research chapters are redesigned to promote accessibility and focus on student issues

The research paper section of *The Allyn & Bacon Handbook* integrates critical thinking, the writing process, and writing across the curriculum, drawing heavily on critical thinking concepts from Chapters 1 and 2 in the use of sources, and incorporating phases of the writing process from Chapters 3 through 6. It also looks ahead to research assignments in the three major disciplines (Chapters 37 through 39).

- *NEW!* A new sample paper demonstrates how **research writing evolves from student interaction with sources.** Chapters offer exceptional depth in evaluating, quoting, summarizing, or paraphrasing sources to advance a student's original thinking in a source paper.
- *NEW!* Addresses **conventions for citing electronic sources,** including CD-ROMs and online materials.
- **Follows student papers in progress** from the prewriting to revising stages, with particular focus on evolving a successful thesis, and on the use of sources from across the disciplines.
- Documentation coverage includes **MLA, APA, CBE, and CMS formats.**

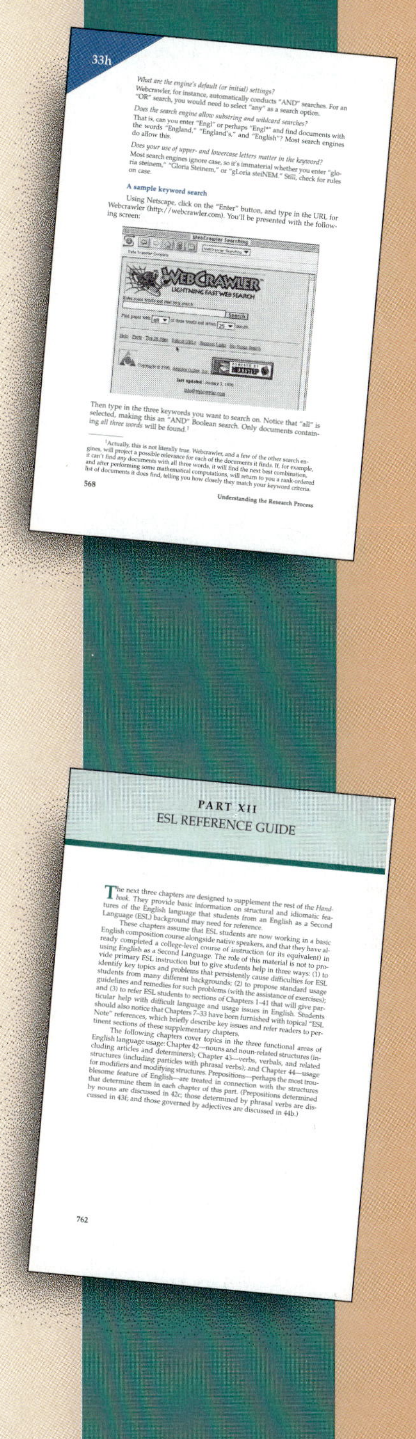

33h

What are the engine's default (or initial) settings?
Webcrawler, for instance, automatically conducts "AND" searches. For an "OR" search, you would need to select "any" as a search option.

Does the search engine allow substring and wildcard searches?
That is, can you enter "Engl" or perhaps "Engl*" and find documents with the words "England," "England's," and "English"? Most search engines do allow this.

Does your use of upper- and lowercase letters matter in the keyword?
Most search engines ignore case, so it's immaterial whether you enter "gloria steinem," "Gloria Steinem," or "gLoria steiNEM." Still, check for rules on case.

A sample keyword search

Using Netscape, click on the "Enter" button, and type in the URL for Webcrawler (http://webcrawler.com). You'll be presented with the following screen:

Then type in the three keywords you want to search on. Notice that "all" is selected, making this an "AND" Boolean search. Only documents containing *all three words* will be found.[1]

[1]Actually, this is not literally true. Webcrawler, and a few of the other search engines, will project a possible relevance for each of the documents it finds. If, for example, it can't find *any* documents with all three words, it will find the next best combination, and after performing some mathematical computations, will return to you a rank-ordered list of documents it does find, telling you how closely they match your keyword criteria.

568 **Understanding the Research Process**

PART XII
ESL REFERENCE GUIDE

The next three chapters are designed to supplement the rest of the *Handbook*. They provide basic information on structural and idiomatic features of the English language that students from an English as a Second Language (ESL) background may need for reference.

These chapters assume that ESL students are now working in a basic English composition course alongside native speakers, and that they have already completed a college-level course of instruction (or its equivalent) in using English as a Second Language. The role of this material is not to provide primary ESL instruction but to give students help in three ways: (1) to identify key topics and problems that persistently cause difficulties for ESL students from many different backgrounds; (2) to propose standard usage guidelines and remedies for such problems (with the assistance of exercises); and (3) to refer ESL students to sections of Chapters 1-41 that will give particular help with difficult language and usage issues in English. Students should also notice that Chapters 7–33 have been furnished with topical "ESL Note" references, which briefly describe key issues and refer readers to pertinent sections of these supplementary chapters.

The following chapters cover topics in the three functional areas of English language usage: Chapter 42—nouns and noun-related structures (including articles and determiners); Chapter 43—verbs, verbals, and related structures (including particles with phrasal verbs); and Chapter 44—usage for modifiers and modifying structures. Prepositions—perhaps the most troublesome feature of English—are treated in connection with the structures that determine them in each chapter of this part. (Prepositions determined by nouns are discussed in 42c; those determined by phrasal verbs are discussed in 43f; and those governed by adjectives are discussed in 44b.)

762

ESL coverage throughout addresses the particular needs of non-native speakers

- **Part XII, "ESL Reference Guide,"** includes three chapters, "Using English Nouns, Pronouns, and Articles," "Using English Verbs,"and "Using Modifiers and Connectors in English Sentences" that provide supplemental help for international students.
- Useful **"ESL Notes"** are included throughout the text to remind students of potential trouble spots.
- Help for instructors on ESL topics is strongly supported in the Instructor's Annotated Edition, particularly through **"ESL Cues."** Many "cues" contain unique information on how to address culture- and language-specific issues.

frag 12a

Spotlight on Common Errors—
SENTENCE CONSTRUCTION AND FRAGMENTS

and fragments. For full explanations and suggested revisions, follow the cross-references to chapter sections.

FRAGMENT ERRORS arise when writers incorrectly mark a group of words as a sentence. Apply a three-part test to confirm that a grouping of words can stand alone as a sentence (see 12a).

Test 1: Locate a verb: A sentence must have a verb.

Churchill *was* a leader. [Verb—*was*]

A leader of great distinction. [No verb—this grouping of words cannot be a sentence; it is a FRAGMENT.]

When he *became* Prime Minister. [Verb—*became*—BUT this word grouping fails Test 3 below, so it is still a FRAGMENT.]

REVISED Churchill was ***a leader of great distinction.***

NOTE: Be sure the word selected as a verb is not a verbal, which looks like a verb but actually serves as a subject, object, or modifier (see 7a-4).

After *serving* his country in the first World War.
[Verbal: *serving* looks like a verb but is actually an object in the prepositional phrase beginning with *after*. This grouping of words is therefore a FRAGMENT.]

REVISED **After serving his country in the first World War,** he became Prime Minister.

Test 2: Locate the verb's subject: A sentence must have a subject.

Churchill was a leader. [Subject—*Churchill*]

When he became Prime Minister. [Subject—*he*—BUT this word grouping fails Test 3 so it is still a FRAGMENT.]

Test 3: Be sure that words such as *when, while, because* or *who, which, that* do not prevent the word group from being a sentence (see subordinating conjunctions and relative pronouns, 19b-1–2).

SENTENCE Churchill *was* a leader.
[No words prevent the grouping from being a sentence.]

FRAGMENTS **When he became Prime Minister.** **Who became Prime Minister.**
[*When* (a subordinating conjunction) and *who* (a relative pronoun) prevent these word groups from standing alone as sentences.]

REVISED **He became Prime Minister.**

See 12b–12d for ways to correct fragments once you have identified them.

275

dev 3d

4 Devising a sketch of your paper, or developing a formal outline

Look to your working thesis for clues about the ideas you will need to develop in your essay. For an academic paper to succeed, you must develop all directly stated or implied ideas in the thesis. You may want to regard your thesis as a contract. In the final draft, the contract exists between you and your reader; the thesis promises the reader a discussion of certain material, and the paper delivers on that promise. As a tool used in writing a first draft, your working thesis is a provisional contract.

Identifying significant parts of your thesis

To create a sketch of your first draft, study your working thesis and identify all significant elements, stated directly or indirectly. In your paper, you are obliged to develop each of these elements and to explain how it is related to others. Write the working thesis at the top of a page and circle its significant words. You can then ask development questions of, or make comments about, each circled element. If you are thorough in quizzing your thesis, you will identify most of its significant parts. (You may not discover some parts until you write a first draft.) Having identified these significant parts, briefly sketch the paper you intend to write.

Question or Make Comments about Your Thesis in Order to Identify Major Sections of Your Paper

Questions
how does/will it happen?
how to describe?
what are some examples?
what are the reasons for?
what is my view?
compared to what?
what is the cause?
any stories to tell?
how?
when?
what has prevented/will prevent it from happening?
who is involved?
what are the key features?
what are the reasons against?
how often?
possible to classify types or parts?
what is the effect of this?
which ones?

Comments
define
review the facts
review the reasoning
explain the contrast or paradox

Option: Preparing a formal outline of your paper

Many writers feel that a rough sketch is sufficient for beginning the first draft of a paper. Others feel more comfortable with a formal plan of ac-

79

Writing a Thesis and Devising a Sketch of Your Paper

INNOVATIVE PEDAGOGY
Designed for success

Creating a text that offers students the most complete and current coverage of composition is only part of the story behind *The Allyn & Bacon Handbook*. Presenting this material in an efficient, highly accessible manner is another. The pedagogy has been designed to enhance the presentation of key concepts — **to make it easy for students to access information and easy for them to learn.**

The many innovative pedagogical aids integrated throughout *The Allyn & Bacon Handbook* include:

Clean, attractive design

A clean, uncluttered **four-color design** provides crisp guidelines in writing and language at every level — without confusing or idiosyncratic symbols.

"Spotlight on Common Errors"

Nine "Spotlight" boxes **help students identify and solve those errors that writers make most frequently.** Each "Spotlight" identifies the error and then states the rules that should be followed, giving examples of faulty and revised sentences with referrals to chapter sections for full explanations.

Highlight Boxes

Throughout each chapter, color-enhanced highlight boxes feature short, succinct entries that **summarize fundamental writing rules and troubleshooting techniques.**

"Critical Decision" Boxes

These boxes are designed to help students with **choices** that they will need to make in developing sentences, paragraphs, and essays.

"Across the Curriculum" Boxes

This new feature shows students the uses of basic writing and rhetorical skills in **cross-disciplinary situations.**

Expanded examples, illustrations, and exercises

Fifty percent of these are new to this edition and are taken from a **wide range of disciplines.**

SUPPLEMENTS FOR THE STUDENT
Greater resources for better learning

The Allyn & Bacon Workbook
Kathleen Shine Cain, Merrimack College

This student workbook contains unique critical thinking exercises as well as simplified versions of the explanations in the text. The workbook provides an abundance of additional exercise work on critical thinking, the writing process, and argumentation, as well as basic grammar, sentence faults, punctuation and mechanics, vocabulary usage, and ESL concerns.

Electronic Grammar Handbook

This electronic version of *The Allyn & Bacon Handbook* provides a pop-up window for easy access to information while writing with a word processor. Words or topics can be accessed three ways: through the Table of Contents, through the Index, or by a keyword or topic search. The program includes hypertext links to related areas, as well as bookmark and annotation features that allow students to "customize" their handbook.

Grammar Software

Ten interactive modules provide lessons for mastering the most common errors made in writing. Each lesson offers 100 separate exercise sentences, along with basic guidelines and "Help" frames with background information. The modules perform automatic scoring so students can track their progress.

CLAST and TASP Study Guides

Special workbooks are available to prepare students for writing and usage topics in English sections of the CLAST and TASP competency tests as given in Florida and Texas.

NEW! **CompSite**

Allyn & Bacon's new website is designed to provide additional resources and supplements for students and instructors. See page *IAE xii* for more information.

CHAPTER 4

The Process of Revision

KEY FEATURES

ESL CUE

GROUP ACTIVITY

The Process of Revision

4a Early revision: Rereading your first draft and rediscover your main idea.

4b Later revision: Make all significant parts of your document work together in support of your main idea.

4c Final revision (editing): Correct errors at the sentence level that divert attention from your main point.

4a Early revision: Rediscovering your main idea

92

8b ca

ESL CUE

REFERENCE

TEACHING IDEAS

2 Use the subjective case for pronouns with the linking verb *be*.

8b Using pronouns in the objective case

1 Use the objective forms for pronouns functioning as objects.

210

Case in Nouns and Pronouns

THE INSTRUCTOR'S ANNOTATED EDITION

Provides on-the-spot references and teaching aids

The Instructor's Annotated Edition (IAE) facilitates your teaching efforts. Carefully designed to support you throughout the course, the IAE augments the student text with succinct marginal annotations related to key topics in each chapter. Each type of annotation, identified by a headline, appears on a wide margin page in a gold panel.

The following annotations are found in the Instructor's Annotated Edition:

Key Features

Positioned at the beginning of each chapter, "Key Features" provides you with a quick overview of the chapter's coverage, giving you an at-a-glance preview of what students should learn from the chapter.

Looking Back and Looking Ahead

These references appear at different points throughout each chapter of the text. Each relates to a specific concept covered in the chapter and connects it with material covered earlier in the text or in an upcoming chapter. These annotations help you link important ideas and quickly integrate them among chapters.

ESL Cues

"ESL Cues" identify the areas in which international students may have trouble and provide suggestions on how to deal with them. Careful consideration has been given to addressing problems that students from a variety of language backgrounds might encounter.

Group Activities

Designed to assist you in encouraging collaborative learning in the classroom, "Group Activities" show how students can work together on a specific aspect of the writing process, helping to reinforce major concepts and sharpen skills.

Teaching Ideas

"Teaching Ideas" provide you with additional approaches to teaching specific chapter material, particularly in the areas of Critical Thinking, Writing Across the Curriculum, and Multicultural Differences. Each annotation offers suggestions for effectively presenting key concepts to students, as well as providing additional readings and highly focused assignments.

For Discussion

These annotations precede select "Exercise" and "Additional Exercise" annotations within most chapters. Each recommends topics and approaches for classroom discussions that help examine skills reinforced in both sets of exercises.

Exercises

Answers to the student exercises are provided wherever appropriate.

Additional Exercises

"Additional Exercises" are provided as supplements to exercises in the Student Edition. Ready for immediate assignment, these are designed to give students further practice honing their writing and grammatical skills.

Reference

"Reference" annotations support key points throughout the text, providing brief descriptions of and references for professional readings that can add new dimensions to your approach to teaching the subject matter.

Annotations appear only in the margins of the Instructor's Annotated Edition. They are not printed in the student edition.

3. Read and reread the opening and closing paragraphs of the text. Look for a sentence or two—the thesis—that seems to summarize the whole. "Interrogate" that sentence, following the advice in 3d-4. Link specific parts of the sentence to different parts (or sections) of the text. Understand what you can; identify what you cannot understand—and then take *specific* questions to a fellow student or your professor.

3 Applying techniques for writing summaries

The techniques for writing summaries can now be applied to an example passage found in Chapter 1: Bernadine Healy's article in *The Chronicle of Higher Education* (see 1e-1). You may want to reread the selection so that you understand the preparations for summary that follow.

Prepare: Make notes for a summary.

These preparatory notes are based on the above plan for writing summaries. The first note concerns Bernadine Healy's purpose; the second is a clear statement of the thesis—in the writer's own words, not Healy's. Finally, there is a one-sentence summary of each paragraph in the article.

PURPOSE to argue

THESIS Women must break stereotyped gender thinking, their own and that of others, if they are to take their rightful place in the sciences.

IDENTIFY SECTIONS

Section 1 (¶1): Opener: Identifies the problem

¶1: Surveys on the prevalence of women in the sciences show that fewer women than men major in the sciences in college and that more women than men drop their science major.

Section 2 (¶s 2–5): Reasons women drop science majors

¶2: According to another study, women drop their science majors because science faculty and fellow (male) students treat them poorly.

¶3: One example: an article from a respected journal that blames working women for current social ills.

¶4: Statistics show that male teachers in science (in four-year schools) outnumber female teachers by more than 4 to 1 and out-tenure women teachers by more than 8 to 1.

¶5: Healy reports that in her field, medicine, the statistics are equally unbalanced.

Section 3 (¶s 6–7): Record of women scientists in funding research

¶6: The record of women scientists and MD's in securing research funds from the National Institutes of Health is mixed: the success rate of

Writing a Summary

29

2a

REFERENCES

BUCKLER, PATRICIA PRODINI. "Reading, Writing, and Psycholinguistics: An Integrated Approach Using Joyce's 'Counterparts.'" *Teaching English in the Two-Year College* 12 (1985): 22–31. Assignments in a freshman course follow Rosenblatt's reading model and Moffett's writing model.

LAMBERT, JUDITH R. "Summaries: A Focus for Basic Writers." *Journal of Developmental Education* 8 (1984): 10–12, 32. Describes various advantages of teaching students to summarize.

SHERRARD, CAROL. "Summary Writing: A Topographical Study." *Written Communication* 3 (1986): 324–43. The longer the summary, the more likely an inexpert writer will use his or her own words instead of copying parts of the original.

LOOKING BACK

The use in this section of Bernadine Healy's piece from *The Chronicle of Higher Education* reinforces the interconnectedness of reading and writing. This section reminds students that what they are doing when writing a summary is a continuation of what they did in Chapter 1, as critical readers.

GROUP ACTIVITY

It can be extremely useful for students to compare summaries. Ask them to share their summaries in small groups, comparing them for *content*: length, main points, detail, and the like. When there are differences, each student should try to defend his or her choice. In articulating their reasons, students will come to a better understanding of what constitutes an effective summary.

ADDITIONAL EXERCISE A

ACROSS THE CURRICULUM Choose a brief section from a textbook in one of your other courses. (It would be doubly helpful if you chose something you're studying at the moment.) Using the guidelines here, write a summary of the section. Then think about how you understood the section before you actually summarized it and how you understand it afterward. Write a brief paragraph explaining what you learned through summarizing.

37a

LOOKING BACK

All of the chapters in this part of the handbook rely heavily on ideas discussed in Chapter 6 (Writing and Evaluating Arguments), especially the material on modes of inquiry in various disciplines. If you haven't yet covered Chapter 6 in class, it would be useful to do so now. Otherwise, students should review the chapter on their own in order to make better use of the information in this part of the handbook.

guing in that discipline. You can help yourself focus on the purpose of argumentation in your humanities classes by posing these questions:

- What sorts of questions will I investigate in this course?
- How do the texts I study help to focus my attention on these questions?
- How do students in this discipline make claims about a text? How do they support these claims?

Claims and evidence

In making a *claim* in the humanities, a writer usually interprets a text. That is, the writer attempts to explain how the text is meaningful—how, for instance, a poem's images direct the reader's attention to certain themes, how an essay confirms or contradicts our understanding of a particular problem, how the content of a letter or diary suggests a revised understanding of some historical event. One much-relied-on process for making and supporting claims in the humanities goes something like this: during the process of reading, you begin to see a pattern emerge—you notice certain details and forge a link between them. (See the discussion of "thesis" at 3d and of "argumentative thesis" at 6b.) At first the pattern may not be well defined; but as you read and reread, the pattern becomes increasingly clear until you can express it as a formal claim. Your claim becomes the basis of an argument that says, in effect: here is one way in which this text is meaningful. You then provide *evidence* for your claim by pointing readers to the same passages in the text that helped you to detect a pattern, explaining why these passages are significant and how they confirm the reasonableness of your claim. The process of claim and support, then, looks like this:

1. Read a text and discover in it certain patterns that help to make the text meaningful (see 37d for hints on detecting patterns in literary works).
2. Reread and confirm that the pattern exists, and then make a claim: a formal statement in which you interpret some element of the text, its relationship to the reader, or its relationship to the writer and the times in which it was written.
3. Refer to the text as evidence for your claim.
4. Comment on or discuss these references (optional).

Consider the following examples of how claims are made and supported in major areas of the humanities.

A literary study. In a paragraph from an essay entitled "The Greatness of *Huckleberry Finn*," the literary critic Lionel Trilling claims that Huck Finn is a character who sympathizes with the misfortunes of others. As you read the paragraph, you will be watching Trilling make his claim *after* he had discovered it for himself. Trilling is persuasive, and you might find yourself thinking "This isn't an interpretation; it's a fact." But Trilling *is* interpreting the novel, and he is trying to convince you that his interpretation is both accurate and useful:

670

Writing and Reading in the Humanities

INSTRUCTOR'S RESOURCE MANUAL FOR
THE
ALLYN & BACON
HANDBOOK
LEONARD J. ROSEN
LAURENCE BEHRENS
THIRD EDITION
PREPARED BY KATHLEEN SHINE CAIN

SUPPLEMENTS FOR THE INSTRUCTOR
Greater resources for more effective teaching

Instructor's Resource Manual

Designed to provide additional teaching suggestions, the IRM includes:

- detailed suggestions for integrating critical thinking, writing across the curriculum, and argument concepts into the composition course
- additional suggestions for teaching non-native speakers
- an expanded discussion of ways to use the text
- suggested syllabi and strategies for teaching critical thinking and writing across the curriculum
- background information on how to grade papers and conduct a peer classroom
- an annotated bibliography

Test Bank/Diagnostic Test Bank

Two 50-item grammar and mechanics diagnostics with error analysis, keyed to the Handbook, can be used to make placement decisions or measure a student's progress.

An exercise bank consists of 600 additional exercises in a variety of formats that provide extra practice for the grammar, mechanics, and punctuation sections of the Handbook.

Computerized Test Bank

This is a computerized version of the exercise bank described above, available in Windows and Macintosh formats.

Transparency Masters

This set of transparency masters includes diagrams, charts, and key concepts illustrated from the text.

Additional supplements are being developed.

Ask your Allyn & Bacon representative for details.

Teaching College Writing

Maggy Smith, University of Texas at El Paso

This book of teaching suggestions offers composition instructors many practical ideas to help organize and teach college writing. The text covers subjects such as the kinds of activities necessary in preparing a course, how to plan for the first few days of class, how to teach the elements of the writing process, and provides a summary of approaches to grading.

The Allyn & Bacon Sourcebook for College Writing Teachers

James C. McDonald, University of Southwestern Louisiana

This collection of readings by foremost scholars on theories and pedagogies in composition covers critical thinking and reading, collaborative learning, writing with computers, and other topics.

Answer Key for The Allyn & Bacon Workbook

NEW! **CompSite**

Allyn & Bacon's new website is designed to provide additional resources and supplements for students and instructors. **See page *IAE xii* for more information.**

Visit Allyn & Bacon online!

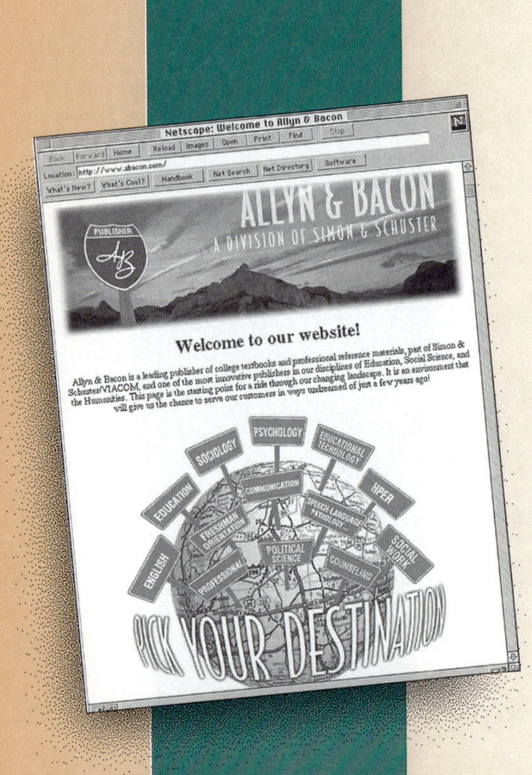

Allyn & Bacon Website

Get on the road to better educational resources! If you're already connected to the Internet, visit us on the World Wide Web. Browse our catalog, meet our editors, find in-depth information on our texts, keep up with the latest trends in the field, and more! Online textbook resources in English are constantly being developed at **http://www.abacon.com.**

CompSite

The future in English. Allyn & Bacon continues its tradition of innovation, making use of the latest technologies to bring you and your students up-to-the-minute, comprehensive information.

Look for *CompSite,* Allyn & Bacon's World Wide Web site devoted to composition. Instructors and students will be able to interact with peers, as well as find resources for planning classes and writing papers, links to other composition-related sites, and more!

America Online

If you are considering an Allyn & Bacon textbook for adoption, we'll waive the America Online membership fee for the first two months! Use this introduction to access a wide range of interactive services, the Internet, and *College Online,* the Simon & Schuster Higher Education area.

Call 1-800-827-6364 and mention #4314 to get started!

AMERICA Online

Information is accurate as of date of printing.
Some restrictions may apply on some items.
Ask your Allyn & Bacon representative for more information.

Instructor's Annotated Edition

THE Allyn & Bacon HANDBOOK

Third Edition

LEONARD J. ROSEN
Harvard University
Expository Writing Program

LAURENCE BEHRENS
University of California, Santa Barbara

Annotations Prepared by
Leonard J. Rosen
and
Kathleen Shine Cain
Merrimack College

Allyn & Bacon

Boston London Toronto Sydney Tokyo Singapore

Vice President and Editor-in-Chief, Humanities: Joseph Opiela
Developmental Editor: Allen Workman
Editorial Assistant: Kate Tolini
Marketing Manager: Lisa Kimball
Sr. Editorial Production Administrator: Susan McIntyre
Editorial Production Service: Kathy Smith
Interior Text Design: Deborah Schneck
Composition Buyer: Linda Cox
Manufacturing Buyer: Megan Cochran
Cover Administrator: Linda Knowles

A Viacom Company
160 Gould Street
Needham Heights, MA 02194
Internet: www.abacon.com
America Online: Keyword: College Online

ISBN 0-205-26109-4

Printed in the United States of America

10 9 8 7 6 5 4 3 2 1 02 01 00 99 98 97 96

CONTENTS

The Instructor's Annotated Edition

Annotations for the instructor appear in the wide margins of this Instructor's Edition. They include overviews of chapter topics; cross-reference comments linking closely interrelated topics; "Teaching Ideas," "Discussion," and "Group Activities" suggesting class or collaborative learning activities and "ESL Cue" comments about distinctive features of English usage that may have an impact on international students. The annotations also include "Additional Exercises" and answers (or suggested answers) to the Exercises in the text. In addition, the annotations furnish bibliographical "References" for professional articles related to handbook chapter topics, with a descriptive sentence or abstract for each publication.

The *Instructor's Resource Manual* by Leonard Rosen and Kathleen Shine Cain provides additional material for new and experienced instructors, including expanded suggestions for using the text and for teaching writing across the disciplines, suggested syllabi, grading procedures, and approaches to conducting a peer classroom. The manual also provides an extensive reference bibliography and a section on working with ESL students.

Brief Contents of the Allyn & Bacon Handbook

THE Allyn & Bacon HANDBOOK

Third Edition

LEONARD J. ROSEN
Harvard University
Expository Writing Program

LAURENCE BEHRENS
University of California, Santa Barbara

Allyn & Bacon

Boston London Toronto Sydney Tokyo Singapore

Vice President and Editor-in-Chief, Humanities: Joseph Opiela
Developmental Editor: Allen Workman
Editorial Assistant: Kate Tolini
Marketing Manager: Lisa Kimball
Sr. Editorial Production Administrator: Susan McIntyre
Editorial Production Service: Kathy Smith
Interior Text Designer: Deborah Schneck
Composition Buyer: Linda Cox
Manufacturing Buyer: Megan Cochran
Cover Administrator: Linda Knowles

Allyn & Bacon
A Viacom Company
160 Gould Street
Needham Heights, MA 02194
Internet: www.abacon.com
America Online: Keyword: collegeOnline

Library of Congress Cataloging-in-Publication Data

Rosen, Leonard J.
The Allyn & Bacon handbook / Leonard J. Rosen, Laurence Behrens. -- 3rd ed.
p. cm.
Includes bibliographical references and index.
ISBN 0-205-26107-8
1. English language—Rhetoric—Handbooks, manuals, etc. 2. English language—Grammar—Handbooks, manuals, etc. I. Behrens, Laurence. II. Title.
PE1408.R677 1997
808'.042—dc20 96-18638
CIP

Printed in the United States of America
10 9 8 7 6 5 4 3 2 1 02 01 00 99 98 97 96

The Allyn & Bacon Handbook — A Reference You'll Never Outgrow

As someone who's been out of college and working in marketing for two years, I don't find it easy to write an introduction for a book about grammar, mechanics, and other such imposing topics. Imagine the pressure of knowing your writing will precede 800 some pages of *dos* and *don'ts* about writing. Especially when you haven't taken an English class since freshman year.

On the other hand, I'm fortunate to have next to me on the couch a comprehensive, easy-to-understand handbook about writing on any subject, for any purpose and in any situation. In fact, it's the handbook you're holding right now.

Whether you're a college freshman or the president of a large corporation, writing is a skill you will use almost every day of your life. You'll be assigned essays in your freshman composition course. You'll be required to write a thesis to complete your graduate study in psychology. Your boss may ask you to write a marketing proposal for a prospective client. Your twelve-year-old son will ask for your help on his research paper about insects of the rainforest.

Sources such as an encyclopedia or the Internet will provide you with the facts, and a dictionary will give you the words and their definitions. But where do you look for help on putting your thoughts together? On how to write sentences that effectively communicate your ideas? On the right way to construct paragraphs that are clear and concise, and that have an impact on the reader?

Just as you need a dictionary and reference books as part of your permanent library, you also need a handbook. It's something to which you'll refer when you have a question about when to use a semicolon or how to document a source—you know, those pesky questions that you won't find answered in a dictionary.

The more you write, the more you'll learn, and your writing situations will always be changing. *The Allyn & Bacon Handbook* is designed for writers at all levels, so you'll never outgrow it.

The Allyn & Bacon Handbook

It's a grammar reference.

It's a reference on the writing process.

It's a reference on documentation.

It's a reference for all of your classes.

It's a reference for business writing.

How is *The Allyn & Bacon Handbook* specifically geared for use beyond your freshman composition course?

It's a grammar reference. There will be times when you'll want to make sure you're not splicing your commas or putting a quotation mark in the wrong place. Perhaps you can't remember when to use *lay* rather than *lie.* Through features such as "Spotlight on Common Errors," you'll be able to quickly and easily find the answers to your questions on grammar and usage. If you're a nonnative speaker, you'll find Part XII, the *ESL Reference Guide*, particularly useful.

It's a reference on the writing process. Having problems narrowing your topic for your ten-page sociology paper? Can't come up with an appropriate thesis sentence? Refresh your memory by reading Chapters 3 and 4 in Part II, *Writing as a Process.*

It's a reference on documentation. You'll probably have to write several research papers during your college career. Part IX, *Writing the Research Paper,* will help you whether you're taking notes from a book or gathering information on the World Wide Web. Most importantly, you'll have a handy reference that will remind you how to document a journal, a book with two authors, and even a movie or a CD-ROM.

It's a reference for all of your classes. Throughout the text, "Writing Across the Curriculum" boxes will show you writing strategies for a variety of courses, including science, psychology, and humanities. Turn also to Part X, *Writing and Reading in the Disciplines,* for more detailed, discipline-specific information.

It's a reference for business writing. How many résumés do you think get tossed because they are poorly written? Plenty! Before you send out that application, read Chapter 40, *Writing in a Business Environment,* to make sure your résumé ends up in the "interview" pile and not in the trash. Refer to this section throughout your career for reminders on how to write specific types of letters and memos, and to make sure your proposals and reports are on target, as well as error-free.

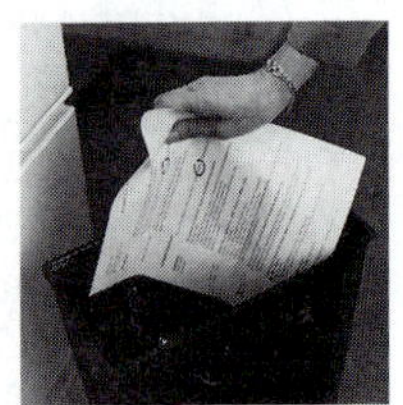

Take a look at the next two pages and get a feel for the organization of *The Allyn & Bacon Handbook.* It's inherently simple to use, with several ways to find what you need to know. Think of some questions and flip through to find the answers. Once you're familiar with the *The Allyn & Bacon Handbook,* you'll want to hang on to it beyond Freshman Composition. It's more than just a college handbook—it's a reference you'll never outgrow.

Lisa Linard
Ohio University, Class of 1994

To Spot-Check for Common Errors

1 **Check the back endpaper chart.** The nine sections in this chart cover over 90 percent of the most common sentence and punctuation errors you are likely to make. Look in these sections for sentence patterns and word forms close to what you have written. If any of the examples or explanations lead you to suspect an error in your work, follow the references to one of the text chapters.

SPOTLIGHT ON COMMON ERRORS

1. FORMS OF NOUNS AND PRONOUNS **See the SPOTLIGHT (page 208, Chapter 8).**

Apostrophes can show possession or contraction. Never use an apostrophe with a possessive pronoun.

Faulty Forms	Revised
The scarf is *Chris.* It is *her's.*	The scarf is *Chris's.* It is *hers.*
Give the dog *it's* collar.	Give the dog *its* collar.
Its a difficult thing.	*It's* [it is] a difficult thing.

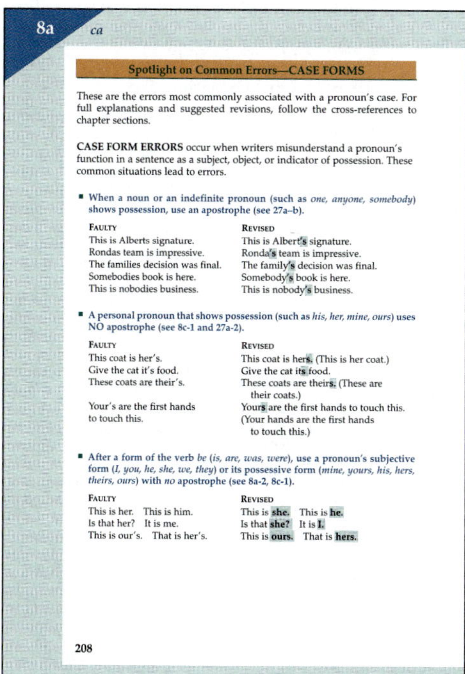

8a *ca*

Spotlight on Common Errors—CASE FORMS

These are the errors most commonly associated with a pronoun's case. For full explanations and suggested revisions, follow the cross-references to chapter sections.

CASE FORM ERRORS occur when writers misunderstand a pronoun's function in a sentence as a subject, object, or indicator of possession. These common situations lead to errors.

- **When a noun or an indefinite pronoun (such as *one, anyone, somebody*) shows possession, use an apostrophe (see 27a–b).**

Faulty	Revised
This is Alberts signature.	This is Albert's signature.
Rondas team is impressive.	Ronda's team is impressive.
The families decision was final.	The family's decision was final.
Somebodies book is here.	Somebody's book is here.
This is nobodies business.	This is nobody's business.

- **A personal pronoun that shows possession (such as *his, her, mine, ours*) uses NO apostrophe (see 8c-1 and 27a-2).**

Faulty	Revised
This coat is her's.	This coat is hers. (This is her coat.)
Give the cat it's food.	Give the cat its food.
These coats are their's.	These coats are theirs. (These are their coats.)
Your's are the first hands to touch this.	Yours are the first hands to touch this. (Your hands are the first hands to touch this.)

- **After a form of the verb *be* (*is, are, was, were*), use a pronoun's subjective form (*I, you, he, she, we, they*) or its possessive form (*mine, yours, his, hers, theirs, ours*) with *no* apostrophe (see 8a-2, 8c-1).**

Faulty	Revised
This is her. This is him.	This is **she.** This is **he.**
Is that her? It is me.	Is that **she?** It is **I.**
This is our's. That is her's.	This is **ours.** That is **hers.**

208

2 **Go to the green-tinted "spotlight" summary page that matches your situation.** Colored "spotlight" pages in nine chapters give basic recognition patterns and sentences that fit common error situations.

3 **Narrow the search. Find a sentence or situation** that more closely resembles a sentence you have written. *Note* the revision suggested. Do you suspect a possible error? If so, *note* the reference to the chapter section where this revision is explained.

4 **Go to the Handbook section; find a usage guideline and example** that describes the possible error in your work. Challenge your sentence: Does it meet the Handbook's usage guideline? Make a decision about revising your sentence.

To find key terms and topics

1 Use these information locators:

- *Front endpapers:* The compact contents chart provides an overview of the section and page numbers of the major topics.
- *Main contents:* This detailed listing shows sections and pages for all topics and usage guidelines.
- *Index:* This alphabetical listing shows the page numbers of every key term, word, or topic.
- *Revision symbols—inside back endpaper:* This guide to common instructor markings will help locate discussions of revision topics.
- *Useful checklists, summaries, and boxes—inside front endpaper:* Locates the special panels that provide rapid checklists of basic procedures.
- *"Spotlight on Common Errors":* See the facing page.

2 To narrow the search, look for these features on each page:

- *Tab* shows the section-number combination for every topic. A *symbol* next to the tab shows typical instructor markings used to call attention to the topic.
- *Section number* gives chapter and section letter accompanying the *heading* that states or identifies a usage guideline.
- *Subsection number* identifies subtopics.
- *Explanations* describe how or why processes or usage guidelines operate. *Cross-references* lead to related background or definitions found elsewhere in the Handbook. *Bold type* identifies key terms being defined on location or in a cross-reference.
- *Revision examples* are labeled to identify problems and the best revisions. In the nine chapters devoted to the most common errors, additional examples appear beneath the headings as an aid to spotting errors.
- *Boxed checklists,* summaries or "critical decisions" boxes are in shaded panels.
- *Footer* briefly identifies chapter section topics.

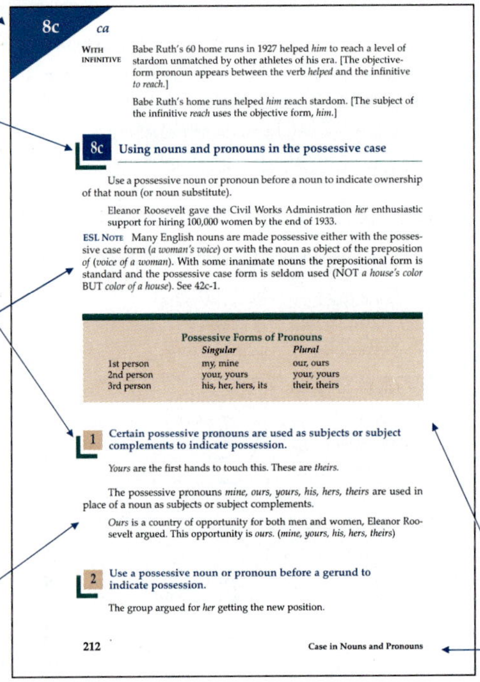

8c *ca*

WITH INFINITIVE Babe Ruth's 60 home runs in 1927 helped *him* to reach a level of stardom unmatched by other athletes of his era. [The objective-form pronoun appears between the verb *helped* and the infinitive *to reach.*]

Babe Ruth's home runs helped *him* reach stardom. [The subject of the infinitive *reach* uses the objective form, *him.*]

8c Using nouns and pronouns in the possessive case

Use a possessive noun or pronoun before a noun to indicate ownership of that noun (or noun substitute).

Eleanor Roosevelt gave the Civil Works Administration *her* enthusiastic support for hiring 100,000 women by the end of 1933.

ESL NOTE Many English nouns are made possessive either with the possessive case form (*a woman's voice*) or with the noun as object of the preposition *of* (*voice of a woman*). With some inanimate nouns the prepositional form is standard and the possessive case form is seldom used (NOT *a house's color* BUT *color of a house*). See 42c-1.

Possessive Forms of Pronouns

	Singular	*Plural*
1st person	my, mine	our, ours
2nd person	your, yours	your, yours
3rd person	his, her, hers, its	their, theirs

1 Certain possessive pronouns are used as subjects or subject complements to indicate possession.

Yours are the first hands to touch this. These are *theirs.*

The possessive pronouns *mine, ours, yours, his, hers, theirs* are used in place of a noun as subjects or subject complements.

Ours is a country of opportunity for both men and women, Eleanor Roosevelt argued. This opportunity is *ours.* (*mine, yours, his, hers, theirs*)

2 Use a possessive noun or pronoun before a gerund to indicate possession.

The group argued for *her* getting the new position.

212 Case in Nouns and Pronouns

CONTENTS

PREFACE TO THE INSTRUCTOR

The Allyn & Bacon Handbook in its first two editions was unique in offering students direct and accessible links among the skills of critical thinking, reading, and writing—in the composition classroom and throughout the curriculum. The success of this approach has encouraged us to build further on what has proved most useful. We now give added focus to the skills of critical thinking and their relation to writing processes, both for basic writing and for research writing. We emphasize how writers apply basic rhetorical and stylistic strategies in many disciplines, as highlighted in a new panel feature, "Across the Curriculum." Most important, we have created an exceptionally thorough handbook-based introduction to the Internet and to using Internet resources in research. The third edition, while it replaces half of its examples, papers, and exercises with fresh material throughout the book, retains its comprehensive ESL coverage and its distinctive alternate reference ("Spotlight") system designed to help students locate trouble spots in editing with minimal use of formal terms.

Critical thinking

With its opening chapters—"Critical Thinking and Reading" and "Critical Thinking and Writing"—*The Allyn & Bacon Handbook* continues to mark a departure in the world of handbooks. We open with specific strategies for developing critical thinking skills that students can apply immediately to their reading assignments and to the writing that follows from these assignments. This approach, based on a survey of current research in the field, follows our conviction that writing at the college level is most often based on reading. If students want to write well, they must also read well—a philosophy demonstrated in Chapters 1 and 2, where the reading materials that provide the basis for discussion and illustration become a key resource for the evolving paper in Chapters 3 and 4.

Writing as a process

Chapters 3 through 6 on writing processes are designed to serve both as a quick-reference tool and as a mini-rhetoric, with assignments that call on students to write and revise paragraphs and whole papers. *Revision,* here, is key: the process of writing, discovery, and rediscovery through revision yields an example student paper that undergoes fundamental changes in its thinking—changes that would have been impossible had the writer not worked recursively from invention to multiple drafts through to a final effort. Similarly, the student paper in the research chapters (Part IX, Chapters 33–36) demonstrates how a writer's thinking evolves through reading, writing, and rewriting. Throughout these sections of the text, and in the sections devoted to sentence construction and word choice, we emphasize the role of revision in clarifying meaning and achieving a clean, spare style.

Because we have found that writing improves significantly when students give careful and sustained attention to a paper's governing sentence, we have made our discussion of thesis far more extensive than is commonly found in handbooks. Colleagues have found especially evocative our comparison of theses with one-, two-, or three-story levels of intellect, as envisioned by Oliver Wendall Holmes.

Writing across the curriculum and argumentation

Our comprehensive cross-curricular chapters (37, 38, and 39) orient students to the kinds of thinking, reading, and writing they will be called on to do in their various courses. After a general introduction devoted to characteristic assumptions and questions, each cross-curricular chapter reviews patterns for writing to inform and for making arguments in its discipline area; it reviews typical kinds of reading and audience situations; and it presents types of assignments found in the discipline, a complete student paper, and a listing of specialized reference materials. Two of the student papers in these chapters explore the topic of alcohol (from differing disciplinary perspectives). The third paper is a literary analysis of Kate Chopin's "A Shameful Affair"; the story appears in its entirety in the chapter.

Writing about literature. A guiding assumption of this book is that college-level writing is based to a great extent on reading. Recognizing that for some composition classrooms reading involves literature as a context for writing, Chapter 37 includes material on writing about literature. The chapter retains its unique detail on making arguments throughout the humanities, but it also develops principles for writing about literature by providing specific guidelines and examples, including the story and student paper on Kate Chopin's "A Shameful Affair."

Argumentation in the disciplines. As an outgrowth of this book's pervasive attention to critical thinking and its emphasis on writing and evaluating arguments, Chapers 37–39 provide the only handbook treatment of foundations for making claims in each discipline across the curriculum. Chapter 6, the first in a handbook to offer a Toulmin-based model for constructing arguments, uses basic terminology that composition students can put to use in any discipline. Combined, these chapters offer more depth than any handbook available in constructing claims and arguments across the disciplines.

The research paper

The research paper section of this handbook integrates critical thinking, the writing process, and writing across the curriculum. It draws heavily on critical thinking concepts from Chapters 1 and 2 in the use of sources; it incorporates phases of the writing process from Chapters 3–6; it also looks ahead to research assignments in the three major discipline areas (Chapters 37 through 39). The result is a strong treatment on the use and evaluation of sources and their integration into students' writing. In addition, the documentation coverage in Chapter 36 treats four different conventions: the MLA system, the APA system, the footnote style (based on the *Chicago Manual of Style*), and the CBE systems used in the sciences. Also addressed are conventions for citing electronic sources: CD-ROMs and online materials. These sections, with their research paper samples from a variety of discipline areas, provide comprehensive coverage on research.

Guidelines and choices in sentence revision

Any experienced writer knows that there is often more than one solution to a common sentence error. Therefore, when appropriate, we discuss alternative solutions and encourage students in their role as writers to make decisions. When usage is a matter of strict convention, we offer firm, clear guidelines for eliminating common errors and understanding key concepts of grammar, usage, and style. We have used student and professional writing from the disciplines as the basis for more than 90 percent of the exercises *and* example sentences. Both exercises *and* examples almost always feature connected discourse from a variety of disciplines—on topics as varied as micro-breweries and Elizabethan stagecraft. To make the book easy to use as a reference tool and visually appealing, we have created numerous boxes that summarize important information, provide useful lists, or apply critical thinking to decisions and choices.

The "Spotlight" system: An alternative way to locate errors

To help students identify remedies for the most common trouble spots in grammar and usage, this handbook has developed the unique "Spotlight on Common Errors." This system offers an alternative for students who may be uncomfortable or unfamiliar with the formal terminology of grammar needed to chase errors in a traditional index. Students can find their way to remedies for common errors using the three parts of the "Spotlight" system:

1. The Spotlight chart on the back endpaper, with its broad view of error patterns, refers students to
2. The color-tinted "Spotlight" summary pages in selected chapters, which provide error recognition and brief remedies, in turn referring students to
3. Chapter sections with detailed explanations and revisions.

A few basic recognition examples are featured in all three elements of the "Spotlight" system. The use of the "Spotlight" system is described on the back endpaper, on the "Spotlight" summary pages, and in the "How to Use This Book" section following the title page.

Comprehensive ESL coverage

Students whose native language is not English have been entering mainstream composition courses in increasing numbers, with varying degrees of prior preparation from specialized English as a Second Language (ESL) courses. As a result, composition instructors have been called on to help international students cope with features of English that have not traditionally caused problems for native speakers. This handbook provides international students with unique help at three levels:

ESL notes in the text: These notes briefly identify troublesome English language features before referring readers to pertinent descriptive units in ESL Chapters 42–44.

Three ESL chapters: The chapters of the ESL section, developed with help from Will Van Dorp of Northern Essex Community College, summarize troublesome features of English language usage in three functional areas: nouns and related structures (Chapter 42); verbs and related structures (Chapter 43); and modifying structures (Chapter 44). Idioms and constructions with prepositions and particles—especially troublesome forms for international students—are treated in appropriate sections in all three chapters.

Notes to the instructor: The ESL Cues in the Annotated Instructor's Edition promote individualized help for international students, especially if their first language may encounter grammatical interference from linguistic features of English, or if their cultural conventions of writing, rhetoric, and research may differ from those prevailing in American colleges. The "ESL Cues" were developed by Andrew and Gina Macdonald of Loyola University in New Orleans, based on extensive practical experience in both composition and ESL programs.

New to This Edition

Critical thinking: Expanded coverage

We have expanded coverage of critical thinking and its relation to the writing process in two key places: in the rhetoric section (Chapters 1–4) and in the research section (Chapters 33–35). The evolving papers in both places show student writers changing their thinking, and their theses, as they work through a real writing process. While following the same topic sequence as in the second edition, Chapters 1 and 2 now use a refined group of fresh examples (focused on the topic of women and computers) to serve as continuous source readings for demonstrating student thinking and writing skills.

The new reading selections in Chapters 1 and 2 provide occasions for critical thinking, but also serve as background material for the essay developed in Chapters 3 and 4, where the student writer's emerging ideas are sparked by earlier reading.

Distinctive coverage for using Internet tools in research

In Chapter 33, "Understanding the Research Process," this edition presents an extremely thorough introduction to the Internet and to using Internet resources in research. Developed with help from Rick Branscomb of Salem State College (Massachusetts), this chapter is designed to help students think of the Internet as a resource as important as the school library. Students are introduced to resources on the World Wide Web, gopher, ftp (file transfer protocol), and WAIS as well as user groups, listservs, and e-mail. Each focused section provides definitions and then discusses access and reliability. Students will also learn about the logic of keyword searches (a sample search is provided with examples of web pages uncovered in each step of a typical search), strategies for conducting searches (which tools to use when), and storing online sources (specifically, the trade-offs in downloading large files versus notetaking). In Chapter 36, students learn the conventions for citing electronic sources. We have tried to infuse our discussion of Internet research through the more general discussion of the research process. Our goal is to make the third edition of this handbook an industry leader in the use of Internet resources in student writing.

Substantially revised chapters on research

We have largely rewritten the chapters on research, improving accessibility, interweaving a discussion of the Internet, and using as a new backbone a paper entitled "What Do We Want at the Mall?"—an examination of mall culture and the issue of community. In developing the example paper, student writer Jason Koman discovers that his source materials—some found in the library, some found on the Internet—did not "give" him the argument he was expecting to write. The sources require Jason to rethink initial premises, to adjust his research question, and to conduct additional research before completing his effort. These chapters on the research process clearly emphasize what we want our students to know: that the process of research is a process of challenging and clarifying one's thinking—through a judicious use of source materials.

Substantially new examples and exercises

We have replaced 50 percent of all examples, exercises, and student papers in an effort to keep the book timely and fresh. Of special note is the new literary analysis in Chapter 37. Student writer Brandy Brooks analyzes color imagery in Kate Chopin's "A Shameful Affair." Users of the handbook will be able to read the story, printed in full, in the chapter.

Writing across the curriculum: Expanded coverage

We have added a new "Across the Curriculum" box feature that highlights the ways in which writers beyond the composition classroom use strategies discussed in the handbook to advance their written work. Twelve such boxes examine an element of the writer's craft being put to use in a specific disciplinary context—for instance, the use of analogies by a physicist, or the use of subordination and coordination by an economist. To expand our already distinctive discussion of claims and evidence for writing in each of the disciplines, we wanted to demonstrate how the specific, writerly strategies we emphasize in the composition classroom are highly valued when students write in other courses.

New appendix material

The revised Appendix A on computer writing updates the discussion on basic techniques for word processing, adding two new subsections on using disks or networks for collaborative learning and peer editing.

A new Appendix C on document design provides guidelines for using headings and graphics in report writing, and guidelines for choosing and using effective diagrams, charts, and graphs in research and technical documents.

Supplements for the student

For students who need a self-help study workbook and for instructors who want to assign work that parallels the handbook, *The Allyn & Bacon Workbook,* 3rd Edition, by Kathleen Shine Cain of Merrimack College, continues to serve as a distinctive source for student supplementary work. With its abridged topical explanations keyed to handbook sections, it offers a new set of illustrative examples and an abundance of additional exercises. Most distinctively, these exercises include new readings and assignment materials suited to in-class or self-study work on critical thinking. Exercises also provide extensive supplementary work on the writing process, paragraph structure, sentence construction, punctuation and mechanics, and material on ESL features.

Two self-help supplements are available for students working on computers: first, a new *On-line Handbook*; and second, *Grammar Teacher,* a set of computer-based tutorial exercises. (These are described under "software" below.) For other software materials for students, consult your Allyn & Bacon representative.

Finally, special workbooks are available to prepare students for writing and usage topics in English sections of the CLAST competency tests as given in Florida.

Supplements for the instructor

The *Instructor's Annotated Edition* of the handbook features succinct annotations in the margins of each chapter to provide instructional help in a wide variety of areas, including ESL, the writing process, teaching with text examples, suggested assignments, and extensive professional references. This material has evolved over three editions with contributions from several individuals, notably Kathleen Shine Cain of Merrimack College.

The *Instructor's Resource Manual* provides background material for both new and experienced instructors. It contains suggested syllabi and exercise sequences, extensive sections on teaching for critical thinking and writing across the curriculum, and practical ideas and materials for teaching writing processes, research processes, writing about literature, and argumentation. The manual includes a separate section of "Notes on Teaching Composition to International Students" and also a complete bibliography of key topics in the composition curriculum.

Testing and exercise instruments in computerized form and in booklet form are also available to support the instructor's composition program. Two Diagnostic Tests are keyed to the text; a test analysis for every error item identifies a topic and handbook or workbook section to which students can be referred for specific help. Second, a computerized Exercise Bank contains hundreds of exercise examples keyed to grammar and usage topics in the handbook, providing extra material for students needing practice either independently or in a class or lab setting.

Software and audiovisual supplements

"The Allyn & Bacon On-Line Handbook" is available in Macintosh and IBM Windows formats for students to install on word-processing software. It provides an easy-access window on the word-processing screen in which abridged sections of the handbook appear on request.

To help students with basic grammar and usage lessons, *Grammar Teacher,* a set of computer-based tutorial disks, has been authored by Professor Eva Thury of Drexel University. These tutorials, available in Macintosh and IBM Windows formats, can serve as computer-based workbook lessons for use in the classroom or in a learning lab setting.

A package of twenty transparency masters presents key text diagrams and exhibits along with examples for lectures and demonstration pieces for use in focusing classroom discussions. A custom series of ten professionally produced video teaching lessons, forming *The Allyn & Bacon Video Grammar Library,* is also available free to adopters for use in classrooms or learning laboratories. These 10-minute lessons present separate topics in grammar, mechanics, sentence structure, and special topics such as sexist language and plagiarism.

From the smallest details to the broadest themes that motivated us to undertake this project, we have aimed to make *The Allyn & Bacon Handbook* a single, coherent text that both demonstrates and celebrates the rich variety of academic writing. We invite you to continue contacting us with your comments and suggestions. It is through such welcome conversations that we continue to refine our work.

Acknowledgments

A number of people have helped us with special contributions to key elements of the text and supplements of this edition. Special thanks go to Kathleen Shine Cain of Merrimack College for her fine work on the instructor's annotations, and to Professors Andrew and Gina Macdonald of Loyola University for their wisdom and experience in the "ESL Cue" notes based on work with both ESL and composition sections over many years. In the text we are most grateful to Richard Branscomb of Salem State College for contributions in Chapters 33 and 34 on electronic resources, and also to Will Van Dorp of Bradford College and Northern Essex Community College, for his apt examples and descriptions on ESL topics in Chapters 42–44.

To the many reviewers who took time to critique our work both in the earlier editions and in this revision we give warm thanks. The following reviewers were both generous and realistic in their comments; we are grateful for the force and insight of their arguments, which led us to rethink and improve on countless dimensions of this text. For their reviews of the first edition, many thanks go to Chris Anson, University of Minnesota; Phillip Arrington, Eastern Michigan University; Kathleen Shine Cain, Merrimack College; Barbara Carson, University of Georgia; Thomas Copeland, Youngstown State University; Sallyanne Fitzgerald, University of Missouri, Saint Louis; Dale Gleason, Hutchinson Community College; Stephen Goldman, The University of Kansas; Donna Gorrell, St. Cloud State University; Patricia Graves, Georgia State University; John Hanes, Duquesne University; Kristine Hansen, Brigham Young University; Bruce Herzberg, Bentley College; Vicki Hill, Southern Methodist University; Jeriel Howard, Northeastern Illinois State University; Clayton Hudnall, University of Hartford; David Joliffe, University of Illinois at Chicago; Kate Kiefer, Colorado State University; Nevin Laib, Franklin and Marshall University; Barry Maid, University of Arkansas at Little Rock; Thomas Martinez, Villanova University; Mary McGann, University of Indianapolis; Walter Minot, Gannon University; Jack Oruch, University of Kansas; Twyla Yates Papay, Rollins College; Richard Ramsey, Indiana/Purdue University at Fort Wayne; Annette Rottenberg, University of Massachusetts, Amherst; Mimi Schwartz, Stockton State College; Louise Smith, University of Massachusetts, Boston; Sally Spurgin, Southern Methodist University; Judith Stanford, Rivier College; Barbara Stout, Montgomery College; Ellen Strenski, University of California, Los Angeles; Christopher Thaiss, George Mason University; Michael Vivion, University of Missouri, Kansas City; and Barbara Weaver, Ball State University.

For their reviews of the second edition, thanks to Bruce Appleby, Southern Illinois University; Linda Bensel-Myers, University of Tennessee; Melody Brewer, University of Toledo; Therese Brychta, Truckee Meadow Community College; Christopher Burnham, New Mexico State University; Peter Carino, Indiana State University; Neil Daniel, Texas Christian University; Virginia Draper, Stevenson College; Ray Dumont, University of Massachusetts, Dartmouth; Kathy Evertz, University of Wyoming; Barbara Gaffney, University of New Orleans; Ruth Greenberg, Jefferson Community College; Stephen Hahn, William Paterson College; Kathleen Herndon, Weber State University; Maureen Hoag, Wichita State University; Ralph Jenkins, Temple University; Rodney Keller, Ricks College; Judith Kohl, Dutchess Community College; Douglas Krienke, Sam Houston State University; Wendell Mayo, Indiana University–Purdue University Fort Wayne; Charles Meyer, University of Massachusetts, Boston; Joan Mullin, University of Toledo; Patricia Murray, California State University, Northridge; Richard Nordquist, Armstrong State University; Jon Patton, University of Toledo; Randall Popken, Tarleton State University; Kirk Rasmussen, Utah Valley Community College; Sally Barr Reagan, University of Missouri; David Roberts, Samford University; John Shea, Loyola University; Margot Soven, La Salle University; Ann Taylor, Salem State College; Elizabeth Tentarelli, Merrimack College; and Richard Zbaracki, Iowa State University.

We owe special thanks to reviewers of the third edition, many of whom reminded us that a widely used handbook is always a candidate for more and better improvements. Especially helpful in holding us to high standards was John Clark, Bowling Green State University, as well as Patsy Callaghan, Central Washington University; Michel deBenedictis, Miami Dade Community College; Kathryn Fitzgerald, University of Utah; Nancy Jermark, Hutchinson Community College; Todd Lundberg, Cleveland State University; Kevin Morris, Greenville Technical College; Ruth Morris, Greenville Technical College; Donna Nelson, Bowling Green State University; Carol Scheidenhelm, Northern Illinois University; Nancy Schneider, University of Maine, Augusta; Margaret Shaw, Kent State University; Laura Yowell, Hutchinson Community College; and Trudy Zimmerman, Hutchinson Community College. Most of these people brought useful experience with the second edition to bear on many helpful comments that led directly to important revisions with this new edition.

Many others helped us along the way; their particular contributions are too numerous to list, but we gratefully acknowledge their assistance. From Bentley College, we thank Tim Anderson, Christy Bell, Lindsey Carpenter, Luigi Cassetta, Robert Crooks, Nancy Esposito, Barbara Gottfried, Sherman Hayes, Tom Heeney, Richard Kyte, Donald McIntyre, Kathy Meade, and George Radford. We thank other colleagues as well: John Clarke of the University of Vermont, whose work on critical thinking aided the formulating of our pedagogy for the book, and Carol Gibbens of the University of California, Santa Barbara, for suggestions on the reference unit. Thanks go to Burke Brown, University of Southern Alabama; Eric Godfrey, Ripon College; Clarence Ivie, University of Southern Alabama; John Laucus, University Librarian, Boston University; William Leap, The American University; Larry Renbaum, Georgetown University Law School; Carol G. Schneider, Association of American Colleges; Alison Tschopp, Boston University Law School; and Arthur White, Western Michigan University.

As writers we are indeed fortunate to work with an editorial, production, marketing, and sales staff as fine as the team at Allyn & Bacon. Joe Opiela, Vice President and Editor-in-Chief for Humanities, shared and helped to shape our vision for this book. Throughout the manuscript's writing and rewriting, Joe proved himself a tireless advocate and a steady source of helpful ideas. Allen Workman, with his more than twenty years of experience, again showed himself to be one of the industry's premier developmental editors. Susan McIntyre and Kathy Smith shepherded the manuscript through production with an unfailing eye for detail.

Major support for this handbook has come from the Allyn & Bacon marketing team: Lisa Kimball, Marketing Manager and John Gilman, Vice President for Sales. Bill Barke, President, and Sandi Kirshner, Senior Vice President and Editorial Director, of Allyn & Bacon have generously committed the editorial, production, and marketing resources needed to make this a project in which all concerned can take pride. To all we give hearty and warm thanks.

Leonard Rosen, Harvard University, Expository Writing Program
Laurence Behrens, University of California, Santa Barbara

PART I
THINKING CRITICALLY

CHAPTER 1

Critical Thinking and Reading

Especially in college, your success as a writer will require that you be an effective reader. This chapter, which begins a book that will serve your reference needs throughout college and beyond, has a twofold purpose: first, to suggest general habits of mind that will prepare you for thinking critically about college-level reading materials and, second, to provide you with *particular* strategies for understanding and beginning to write about sources.[1]

ACTIVE, CRITICAL HABITS OF MIND

Try to develop habits of mind that prompt you to think critically about what you read. "Critical" in this sense does not mean negative but, rather, *active* and *alert.* Critical habits include being alert to similarities and differences; posing questions; setting issues in broader contexts; and forming and supporting opinions. Developing the habits of a critical thinker will prepare you for working with the source materials on which you will base much of your writing.

1a Active, critical thinkers search for, and question, similarities and differences.

Two or more sources on a particular topic will nearly always present similarities and differences concerning facts, interpretations of facts, value judgments, or policies that the writers think you ought to pursue. With practice, you can approach similarities and differences with questions that will get you thinking critically. Freshman writer Lou Cassetta demonstrates how,

[1]We use the terms *source materials, sources,* and *texts* interchangeably to mean any reading selection.

KEY FEATURES

Taken together, this chapter and the next (Critical Thinking and Writing) form the foundation for the entire handbook. In this chapter students are reassured that they do indeed think critically all the time; here, that thinking is applied to academic circumstances. The strategy for critical thinking and reading can be broken down into three stages: pre-reading, reading, and post-reading. During all three stages students are encouraged to comprehend, to question, and to integrate the material with their own experience and with other ideas they've encountered. Although critical reading takes more time initially than casual reading, students are reassured that in the end, critical reading saves them from having to reread material later on. The chapter introduces concepts that will be applied throughout the handbook in the form of **Critical Decisions** boxes: being alert to differences, challenging and being challenged by sources, being alert to broader contexts, and forming and supporting opinions. These "critical habits of mind" lead to specific activities that students can apply to reading selections: reading to understand, to respond, to evaluate, and to synthesize. Throughout the chapter, the reader is presented as an active participant in communication with the writer, rather than as a passive receiver of information. To reinforce the concept of active reader, many examples and exercises focus on selected, brief readings that establish a context for discussing critical thinking and reading.

using two sources on gender differences in the fields of science education and technology. You will follow Lou, and this topic, through several chapters as he begins his thinking about an essay and works through the process of writing to arrive at a finished essay (see 4f). Watch closely how Lou's observation of similarities and differences leads to questions that deepen his investigation into the topic.

From "Women and Technology in American Life" (1979)

For the better part of its cultural life, the United States has been idealized as the land of practicality, the land of know-how, the land of Yankee ingenuity. No country on earth has been so much in the sway of the technological order or so proud of its involvement in it. Doctors and engineers are central to our culture; poets and artists live on the fringes.

If practicality and know-how and willingness to get your hands dirty down there with the least of them are signatures of the true American, then we have been systematically training slightly more than half of our population to be un-American. I speak, of course, of women. While we socialize our men to aspire to feats of mastery, we socialize our women to feats of submission. Men are hard; women are soft. Men are meant to conquer nature; women are meant to commune with it. Men are rational, women irrational; . . . We have trained our women to opt out of the technological order as much as we have trained our men to opt into it.

This is probably just as much true today as it was in the heyday of the archetypically passive, romantic Victorian female. An interesting survey of American college girls' attitudes toward science and technology in the 1960s revealed that the girls were planning careers, but that they could not assimilate the notion of becoming engineers—and this is equally revealing—that there was no single occupation

From "Men, Women, Computers" (1994)

Blame (a) culture (b) family (c) schools (d) all of the above. Little boys are expected to roll around in the dirt and explore. Perfect training for learning to use computers, which often requires hours in front of the screen trying to figure out the messy arcanum of a particular program. Girls get subtle messages—from society if not from their parents—that they should keep their hands clean and play with their dolls. Too often, they're discouraged from taking science and math—not just by their schools but by their parents as well.

. . .

In one intriguing study by the Center for Children and Technology, a New York think tank, men and women in technical fields were asked to dream up machines of the future. Men typically imagined devices that could help them "conquer the universe," says Jan Hawkins, director of the center. She says women wanted machines that met people's needs, "the perfect mother."

Someday, gender-blind education and socialization may render those differences obsolete. But in the meantime, researchers say both visions are useful. If everyone approached technology the way women do now, "we wouldn't be pushing envelopes," says Cornelia Bruner, associate director of the center. "Most women, even those who are technologically sophisticated, think of machines as a means to an end." Men think of machines as an ex-

TEACHING IDEAS

Given that much American education operates on what Paulo Freire calls the "banking concept" (instructors make "deposits" of knowledge into students' heads), critical thinking may be a foreign—and intimidating—notion to some students. A rather simple exercise can dispel some of their fears. Ask students to recall their favorite classes, especially those in which they feel they learned a great deal. As they discuss these classes, ask them to focus on how the class was conducted. Chances are, the most meaningful classes will be those in which teachers fostered a good deal of discussion and demanded thinking from the students. Simply reminding students that they've had positive experiences in the past with what these first two chapters call "critical thinking" should ease their minds about what lies ahead.

The material in this chapter relies on the following books:

BROWNE, NEIL M., and STUART M. KEELEY. *Asking the Right Questions.* 2nd ed. Englewood Cliffs, NJ: Prentice-Hall, 1986.

CLARKE, JOHN H. *Patterns of Thinking: Integrating Learning Skills in Content Teaching.* Boston: Allyn and Bacon, 1990.

JONES, BEAU FLY, et al., eds. *Strategic Teaching and Learning: Cognitive Instruction in the Content Areas.* Alexandria, VA: ASCD, 1987.

KUHN, THOMAS. *The Structure of Scientific Revolutions.* 2nd ed. Enlarged. Chicago: U Chicago P, 1970.

KURFISS, JOANNE G. *Critical Thinking: Theory, Research, and Possibilities.* ASHE-ERIC Higher Education Report No. 2. Washington, DC: Association for the Study of Higher Education, 1988.

MARZANO, ROBERT J., et al. *Dimensions of Thinking: A Framework for Curriculum and Instruction.* Alexandria, VA: ASCD, 1988.

RORTY, RICHARD. *Philosophy and the Mirror of Nature.* Princeton: Princeton UP, 1979.

TOULMIN, STEPHEN, RICHARD RIEKE, and ALLAN JANIK. *An Introduction to Reasoning.* New York: Macmillan, 1979.

"Women and Technology . . ." *(cont'd)*

that they thought their male contemporaries and their parents would be less pleased to have them pursue. . . . It is no wonder that women have played such minor roles in creating technological change; in fact, it is a wonder that there have been any female engineers and inventors at all.

—RUTH SCHWARTZ COWAN

"Men, Women, Computers" *(cont'd)*

tension of their own power, as a way to "transcend physical limitations." That may be why they are likely to come up with great leaps in technology, researchers say. Without that vision, the computer and its attendant industry would not exist.

—BARBARA KANTROWITZ

As a reader, prepare yourself to find similarities and differences in the articles you read. Here are Lou Cassetta's observations on the selections concerning gender and technology:

Similarities

Both Cowan (a historian of science) and Kantrowitz (a writer for *Newsweek*) agree that men and women are taught to adopt certain attitudes toward science and technology. Early on, boys learn to "get their hands dirty"—to discover how things work, to tinker. Early on, girls learn to stay clean and to concentrate on feelings and home life.

Differences

Ruth Cowan says that "women have played such minor roles in creating technological change" because they have been socialized that way—taught to steer clear of the sciences. With fewer women in the sciences, naturally fewer women will be leaders in these fields. Kantrowitz suggests that men and women already in the sciences view their activities quite differently: men view technology as an extension of their own power while women view technology as a means of getting things done.

- Kantrowitz reports on the usefulness of different outlooks between men and women scientists, even if these outlooks are learned. Cowan does not even imagine that differences can be useful.
- Cowan seems pretty much certain that men and women are entirely the same in their potential and that, given time and an even-handed education, men and women would perform equally in the sciences and technology. Kantrowitz leaves open the possibility that some differences might be inborn. (She says that education "may" erase differences.)

Spotting similarities or differences in your reading is one way to begin having a conversation with your sources and, more generally, with a given topic. (In fact, in the final draft of the student essay you will read in 4f, Lou Cassetta develops the differences he has observed between Kantrowitz and Cowan.) Based on your observations of differences, try posing questions. The more questions you pose and attempt to answer, and the greater the variety of your questions, the more deeply you will know a reading selection. The deeper your knowledge, the more convincingly you will write.

GROUP ACTIVITY

Working in groups of three, students can read the pieces by Cowan and Kantrowitz to determine similarities and differences. Next, ask students to *react* to each piece—first individually, and then in group discussion.

LOOKING AHEAD

The passages here by Cowan and Kantrowitz are referred to in the student paper that becomes the illustration piece in Chapters 2, 3, and 4. You might want to alert your students that the materials will eventually be synthesized into a paper. One of the points to make here is that a critical reading of sources helped student Lou Cassetta to discover ideas. One need not regard source materials only as potential support for ideas that are developed elsewhere. Sources themselves—and, most importantly, a student's response to them—can provide an excellent basis for generating ideas.

ADDITIONAL EXERCISE A

Ask students to analyze the structure of the first five paragraphs of any three front-page news accounts. Students could present their findings orally to the class. The assignment will help to develop in students an awareness that news stories have a structure, which can aid the students' general newspaper reading.

TEACHING IDEAS

ACROSS THE CURRICULUM In many disciplines, especially in the sciences, research projects begin with a researcher's noticing a difference or discrepancy: results of an experiment differ from what was expected. The difference leads naturally to a search for explanations. This search can be an important impetus to new experiments. Ask students to consult their textbooks in other disciplines for evidence that researchers are alert to and act on differences.

CRITICAL THINKING

Alverno College of Wisconsin has published a series of books on teaching critical thinking in the content areas. In their *Teaching Critical Thinking in Psychology* (1986), the editors present a theory that a discrepancy between observed events and the observer's "knowledge base" initiates critical thinking. Richard Kasschau of the University of Houston develops the model in Part I of the book. Parts II and III are devoted to a series of assignments in psychology that are designed to create for students discrepancies that launch critical thinking.

ESL CUE

ESL students (and native speakers) might confuse "critical" with "negative criticism," and might feel uncomfortable with the idea of being openly confrontational or argumentative. Emphasizing the idea of noticing key differences and actively raising questions would be a positive and productive way to present "critical" thinking.

GROUP ACTIVITY

You might create a group assignment in which students, working in groups of three, regard one another as "texts." Provide students with a single brief reading that raises a controversial issue. Ask one student to interview the other two in the group, soliciting reactions to the reading. The student who conducts the interview will take notes and then will synthesize, on the spot, by (1) presenting a summary of key points in the reading; and (2) selecting one or two criteria by which to compare and contrast the reactions of groupmates. When one student finishes, the next begins with a new brief reading, then an interview. The activity asks students to distinguish key pieces of information: the article, interview of Subject A, and interview of Subject B; then to selectively synthesize information. The articles used to launch discussion can be as brief as a paragraph. The goal is to get students thinking on their feet.

EXERCISE 1

Individual responses

Question similarities.

If two statements look alike, ask *why.* Are the facts the same? Are the interpretations of facts the same? Have facts been established in the same way? Examine opinions: If two or more authors share the same view, what does this suggest? Is the reasoning or value system underlying these views necessarily the same? Do you share this reasoning or value system? What social conditions might explain the similarities? Other questions are possible. The point is that your awareness of similarity marks a *beginning* point for your thinking. Here's how Lou Cassetta works with the similarities he's noticed:

> Cowan wrote in 1979, when women scientists and engineers were relatively scarce. Kantrowitz's work (1994) is much more recent, and she begins with the fact that there are successful women scientists and engineers. Both writers acknowledge gender-based attitudes regarding science and technology. But has anything changed in fifteen years? What's the current news on women who major in the sciences? Do they also drop out?

Questions such as these can prompt new inquiry—perhaps a search for new sources. On the pages that follow, Lou locates an article that answers his question about women students in the sciences today.

Question differences.

Differences also point to questions. When authors disagree about facts, you should ask *why.* Do methods of determining facts differ? Which presentation of facts seems more authoritative? Examine opinions: when they differ, investigate. What logic, what values, underlie differing opinions? If writers disagree over what policies we should follow, ask why. Do their analyses of problems differ? Are their assumptions about correct or ethical behaviors different? Many questions are possible based on differences. Your awareness of differences marks a beginning point for thinking. Here's how Lou Cassetta explores the differences he's noticed:

> Kantrowitz writes about differences among men and women scientists. Are these entirely learned? Are there any differences between male and female behavior that are inborn? How could I find out? If I believe Cowan, I'd probably say that male and female science would be identical in a world where science education was gender neutral. But Kantrowitz points to differences. These may or may not be learned.

Again, questions prompt new investigation. Lou Cassetta found an answer to these questions in one of his psychology texts. See the excerpt from that text on page 7.

EXERCISE 1

Every day, for a week, read three or more newspapers—your town's local paper(s) and one or more of the following: the *New York Times,* the *Wall Street Journal,* and *USA Today*. Pay special attention to each paper's coverage of a single news event. Read the accounts and observe differences—among the three or between what any of the pieces report and your own experience. Pose questions based on these differences. Finally, outline a plan for potential research based on your questions.

1b Active, critical thinkers challenge, and are challenged by, sources.

Beyond searching for similarities and differences, try to maintain a generally questioning attitude when you read. Some questions you can direct to a source; others, to yourself. In both cases, your goal is to begin exploring the source and the issues it raises. Many readers consider the following guidelines to be useful:

1 Challenge the author: Ask questions of the source.

Every reading invites specific questions, but the following basic questions can get you started in your effort to read any text critically:

- What central problem, issue, or subject does the text explore? What are the reasons for this problem? What are the effects of this problem?
- What is the most important, or the most striking, statement the author makes? Why is it important or striking?
- Who is the author, and what are the author's credentials for writing on this topic? What is the author's stake in writing this? What does the author have to gain?
- How can I use this selection? What can I learn from it?

2 Challenge yourself: Ask questions of yourself.

A critical reading points in two directions: to the text(s) you are reading, and to *you*. The questions you ask about what you read can prompt you to investigate your experience, values, and opinions. As part of any critical reading, allow the issues that are important to the text to *challenge* you. Question yourself and respond until you know your views about a topic. Pose the following questions to yourself:

- What can I learn from this text? Will this knowledge change me?
- What is my background on this topic? How will my experience affect my reading?
- What is the origin of my views on the topic?
- What new interest, or what new question or observation, does this text spark in me?
- If I turned the topic of this selection into a question on which people voted, how would I vote—and why?

ESL CUE

The Western academic practice of teaching critical thinking through student-teacher class discussion is far from universal, with the majority of students (especially from Asia and the Middle East) viewing their role as more passive than U.S. instructors may be accustomed to: receiving and memorizing truths passed down by authority figures—without questioning such information. This concept of role affects classroom behavior, with the Japanese, for instance, believing that "the nail that sticks up gets hammered down." Such students often consider volunteering to answer or participating in class discussion a violation of the rules. This difference in cultural attitudes must be dealt with early in the course with a discussion of what acceptable classroom behavior is; why Americans value critical commentary, particularly in give-and-take Socratic dialogue; how necessary it will be to success in an American college.

Hall, Edward T. *The Silent Language.* Garden City, NY: Anchor Press, 1973.

Harris, P. R., and R. T. Moran. *Managing Cultural Differences.* Houston, TX: Gulf Publishing Co., 1979.

Kohls, Robert. *Developing Intercultural Awareness.* Washington, DC: The Society for Intercultural Education, 1981.

BACKGROUND

See Section E, "Critical Thinking, Reading, and Writing," in James C. McDonald, *The Allyn & Bacon Sourcebook for College Writing Teachers* (Boston, MA: 1996). McDonald has gathered three sources that provide some context for the materials in Chapter 1: "A Relationship Between Reading and Writing: The Conversational Model," by Charles Bazerman; "Five Ways of Interpreting a Text," by John Peters; and "Helping Students Use Textual Sources Persuasively," by Margaret Kantz. Peters is particularly helpful when students get stuck, and provides a formal set of questions that students can pose when reading. Peters summarizes his five categories and associated questions as follows:

(continued)

The Social Perspective
What social concerns does the text reveal?
How does the text relate to the past?
How does the text relate to right now?
The Emotional Perspective
Does the text contain objects of emotion?
Are there emotional conflicts?
What is the tone of the text?
The Rhetorical Perspective
How can the form be described?
Which rhetorical modes do you find?
How would you describe the author's style?
What about ambiguity?
The Logical Perspective
What debatable issue is raised?
What conclusions are reached?
Is there sufficient evidence?
Does the text take opposing views into account?
The Ethical Perspective
What "highest good" does the text envision?
What ethical convictions are revealed?

BACKGROUND

The "Across the Curriculum" boxes highlight a defining feature of the *Allyn & Bacon Handbook:* the emphasis on writing and critical thinking across the curriculum. You might let students know that their handbook offers material in Chapters 37–39 that will help them pose questions and formulate arguments when they are writing in courses beyond freshman composition.

The premise of cross-curricular thinking in the book is that certain features of argumentation and critical thinking pertain to *all* academic work: thus, this example on being alert to differences. At the same time, disciplines have their own specific ways of arguing, which students should know about before venturing to write papers in their other courses. This text is meant to help students develop an awareness of the features of thinking and writing that generalize across disciplines, in addition to those that are discipline-specific.

EXERCISE 2

Individual responses

Here are Lou Cassetta's thoughts on his background with gender and technology:

> I've definitely seen differences in the ways men and women talk about technology. Last summer, when I interviewed for the data entry job, I scored points when I could talk shop about the boss's laptop computer. Today, a lot of guys talk about computer power the way they used to talk about cars: power and speed are key. How do women talk about computers?[2]

ACROSS THE CURRICULUM

Being Alert to Differences

Whatever the discipline you're studying, you'll find faculty and students alike searching for differences, or discrepancies—for information and explanations that are supposed to fit neatly together but do not. Differences lead to questions; questions, to investigations; and investigations (very often) to writing projects. In the opening paragraph of a paper on international relations, policy analyst Gerald Segal observes a contradiction that launches his essay on the cultural conflicts Asians can expect in the coming century.* Wherever you find differences in your studies, whether in your government class or your physics class, *use* them to think critically.

> The twenty-first century is supposed to be the "Pacific Century," but it is also supposed to be the age of information technology. Yet these two strands of the future do not fit together very well. As anyone who has tried to plug in a portable modem in Japan will know, the East Asians are not as technologically advanced as many ~~Americans and~~ Europeans think. Even more important, and despite all their confidence about their economic success, East Asians are becoming seriously worried about their ability to resist the challenges posed by the new technology to their core values and the authority of their states.

A contradiction in two views of the future

Discipline focus: international relations

A difference brings challenges

*Gerald Segal is a senior fellow at the International Institute for Strategic Studies. His article "Asians in Cyberia" appeared in *The Washington Quarterly* 18.3 (1995).

EXERCISE 2

Reread the three newspaper articles you selected for Exercise 1. Based on suggestions in the preceding section, pose questions that challenge the underlying assumptions in each piece. Also, use one or two of the pieces as a basis for posing questions that challenge *you.*

[2] Reflecting on this question helped Lou to formulate part of the thesis for his essay (4f).

1c Active, critical thinkers set issues in a broader context.

Whenever possible, identify the issues and questions that are important to a single reading selection and then think large: assume that every particular issue, concern, or problem that you read about exists in a larger context—a larger cluster of related issues, concerns, or problems. This larger context will not always be obvious. Often, you will have to work to discover it. Here is a set of techniques for doing so:

- Begin by identifying one or more issues that you feel are important to a text.
- Assume that each issue is an instance, or example, of something larger. Your job is to speculate on this larger something.
- Write the name of the issue at the top of a page, or on the computer screen. Below this, write a question: "What is this a part of?" Then write a one-paragraph response.
- Reread your response, and briefly state the broader context.
- Use this broader context to stimulate more thought on the reading selection and to generate questions about issues of interest.
- Option: Begin an investigation. Find new reading selections about the issues you've defined.

Lou Cassetta found a textbook from his psychology class that directly addressed several broader issues he had identified concerning gender roles. Here are Lou's notes on these issues:

> Women pursuing careers in the sciences, and dropping out, is part of a larger question about the ways women and men pursue jobs, generally, and the ways gender plays a role. The current thinking is that most intellectual abilities are the same between men and women. We see more men or women in certain jobs because of training, not inborn ability. Still, some differences between the sexes exist, and researchers haven't yet defined these completely. For now, differences in learning seem to explain the differences between the sexes.

Here is the paragraph from a psychology text that helped Lou Cassetta set issues in a broader context:

> There is no doubt that men and women are different—biological differences certainly exist—but researchers are still trying to sort out basic intellectual differences to determine if they exist and under what conditions. Biologically based mechanisms may account for some gender-based behaviors, but learning is far more potent in establishing and maintaining sex-role stereotypes and gender-specific attitudes. Our society continues to reinforce gender-based activities. This shapes the behavior of children and

CRITICAL THINKING

In *Cultivating Thinking in English and the Language Arts* (NCTE, 1991), Robert Marzano discusses four principles of learning and thinking, one of which is that "learning involves the construction of meaning." A key to this constructive process, says Marzano, is that "the learner acquires new knowledge by attaching what she already knows to what she is about to learn." Attempting to identify larger contexts can be an important part of the student's linking what is known to what is not. Larger contexts provide a cognitive frame in which students operate. Often, students need only remind themselves that these larger frames exist; then these frames help students to link new knowledge to old.

ADDITIONAL EXERCISE B

Ask students to examine Lester Lefton's *style* as a writer. The categories for analysis might be: sentence structure, sentence length, or use of contrasts. What conclusions do the students draw? Whether you work inductively or deductively on this brief assignment, this point can be made: Lefton is a stylist—ease of reading is important to him. This and other brief examples of discipline-specific writing in the book can be used to reinforce the point that good writing is welcomed across the curriculum—not just in composition class.

EXERCISE 3

Individual responses

LOOKING AHEAD

This section of Chapter 1 raises for students the importance of forming and supporting opinions, which at its root is a matter of making arguments. See Chapter 6 for an extensive discussion of argumentation, following the Toulmin model. See also the cross-curricular chapters, 37–39, in which the authors discuss the important elements of argument—including claims and standards of evidence—in the humanities, social sciences, and sciences.

EXTRA HELP

Some learning laboratories, study skill centers, or special education departments may have access to computer programs with lesson units on critical thinking, such as the following:

> *Critical Reading, Lesson Series A-H.* Eight disks published by Borg-Warner Educational Systems. Lesson units instruct secondary-level readers in critical thinking and reasoning patterns; four units focus on contrasts/alternatives, inclusive categories, conditional statements, and inductive reasoning. Reviewed by Wilson, J. "Critical Reading." *Learning Disability Quarterly* 8 (1985): 64–66.

adolescents into sex roles. But as our society's view changes, so will gender-based activities.

—Lester Lefton, *Psychology,* 4th ed. (Boston: Allyn and Bacon, 1991)

EXERCISE 3

Explore the larger context suggested by the differing news accounts of the three articles that you found for Exercise 1. Create a phrase that summarizes one issue, subject, or problem that you think is important to these accounts. Place that phrase at the top of a page and the question "What is this a part of?" below it. Then write an answer in order to identify a broader context. Based on this broader context, generate an action plan: identify some research activity that could follow from your writing.

1d Active, critical thinkers will form, and support, opinions.

Know what you think about what you see and read. Have an opinion and be able to support it. Opinions generally follow from responses to questions such as these:

- Has the author explained things clearly?
- In what ways does this topic confuse me?
- Has the author convinced me of his or her main argument?
- What is my view on this topic?
- Would I recommend this source to others?

Whatever your opinion, be prepared to support it with comments that are based on details about what you have seen or read. Later in this chapter (see 1g), you will learn techniques for reading to evaluate a source; and in Chapter 2 (see 2b), you will learn techniques for writing an evaluation—a type of writing in which you formally present your opinions and give reasons for holding them. It is not practical or necessary for you to develop a formal response (oral or written) to every source you read. Just the same, as a critical and active thinker, you should be able to offer reasons for believing as you do. Here's Lou Cassetta's opinion, based on the articles he's read thus far on the representation of women in the sciences and technology. This opinion becomes a fundamental part of his final essay (4f).

> Kantrowitz appeals to me. She makes the same argument that Cowan does—that a great deal of gender behavior is learned. She's probably right. But Kantrowitz goes a step further and suggests that gender differences can be useful. So much of what I read suggests that differences, all differences, are damaging. If differences are learned and not inborn, then education must be even-handed. But if there are inborn differences between the sexes, I believe we should define these and then use them to our advantage. I wouldn't let differences prevent women or men from pursuing whatever jobs interested them. But real differences should be valued.

You and your classmates may agree or disagree about particular ideas, as they are expressed in a source. In either case, you should be able to have an informed discussion about these ideas. For an extensive discussion on stating and supporting opinions, see Chapter 6 on argumentation.

EXERCISE 4

Use the suggestions in the preceding section to develop an opinion based on one or more of the articles you selected for Exercise 1. In writing, state your opinion in a sentence or two. Then, in a brief paragraph, support your opinion by pointing to particular paragraphs or sentences in the news accounts.

EXERCISE 4

Individual responses

COMPONENTS OF A CLOSE, CRITICAL READING

The habits of mind discussed in the first part of this chapter prepare you in a general way for thinking critically about what you see and hear. Noticing differences, challenging and being challenged by sources, setting issues in a broader context, and forming and supporting opinions—these habits of mind, so important to thinking critically, do not necessarily lead to formal statements on your part about the materials you encounter. When teachers and, later, employers ask that you read and use source materials as a basis for writing, you *will* need to formalize and systematize your critical thinking skills. A close, critical reading requires that you read to understand, respond, evaluate, and synthesize as appropriate to your task. These are the component parts of a close, critical reading that you will find discussed in this section. The forms of writing associated with close reading—summary, evaluation, analysis, and synthesis—are discussed in Chapter 2.

LOOKING AHEAD

ACROSS THE CURRICULUM The material covered in the following sections will be useful in Chapter 34 (Using Sources). Since students are sometimes assigned research papers in other courses before covering the topic in Composition, you may want to call attention to the chapter, as well as the chapters on writing in the disciplines (Part X, Chapters 37, 38, and 39).

Reading and *re*reading

To a greater or lesser extent, you will naturally mix into a single reading the tasks of reading to understand, to respond, to evaluate, and to synthesize. The goal of a close, critical reading is to make sure you perform these tasks well. To do so, even the most experienced readers find they must read a text two or more times. For instructional purposes, we discuss the four types of close, critical reading in four sections (1e–1h). We do *not* mean to suggest by this arrangement that you read your sources four times. This is not practical, nor is it usually warranted. Still, you should commit yourself to reading however much is necessary to understand, respond, evaluate, and synthesize. In the sections that follow, you will get a clearer idea of what each of these tasks entails.

1e Critical reading (1): Reading to understand

Every use to which you can put a source is based on your ability to understand it. Without understanding you can do nothing, and so understanding must be your very first goal as a critical reader.

1 Setting goals for reading to understand

The steps in reading to understand can be summarized as follows:

- *Identify the author's purpose.* This will likely be to inform or to argue.
- *Identify the author's intended audience.* The text will be written with particular readers in mind. Determine if you are the intended audience.
- *Locate the author's main point.* Every competently written text has a main point that you should be able to express in your own words.
- *Understand the structure of the text.* If the author is arguing, locate the main point and supporting points; if the author is presenting information, locate the main point and identify the stages into which the presentation has been divided.
- *Identify as carefully as possible what you do not understand.*

Read the following selection, which is typical of the reading you might encounter in one of your courses. (This happens to be a source that Lou Cassetta used in writing his essay on gender and technology.) Throughout this chapter, we will add layers of notes to this passage in order to demonstrate strategies for reading to understand, respond, evaluate, and synthesize. The notes you see on the passage here illustrate how you might read to understand. (Lou uses the symbols ♀ and ♂ to indicate women and men, respectively.) Techniques for annotating in this way follow the passage itself.

GROUP ACTIVITY

Sometimes it's difficult for individual students to use the strategies outlined in this section. If they work in small groups, however, dialogue can trigger observations, questions, and responses. If you are using a reading anthology in class, assign one of the essays for students to use as practice in reading to understand. (Or reproduce a short essay from one of your collections.) Having worked through a reading with the support of a group, students should be better able to handle subsequent readings on their own.

NOTE TO THE INSTRUCTOR

As presented here, part of the reader's effort to understand a text (under "goals of reading to understand") includes what some teachers would describe with the term *analysis;* in that use, the term denotes an effort to understand a text by studying its structure—where the main point is placed and exactly where that point is supported. Here that effort is incorporated into the activity of reading to understand. This text reserves the term *analysis* to denote what a writer generates (see 2c) when applying some theory or principle systematically to a text or to an experience.

From The Chronicle of Higher Education

BERNADINE HEALY,
DIRECTOR OF THE NATIONAL INSTITUTES OF HEALTH

Section 1 opener: Identifies the problem

Surveys: ♂ in science have advantage over ♀.

According to studies conducted by the Pew Charitable Trust Science Education Program and researchers at the University of Colorado at Boulder,
fewer women than men declare science as a major
in college, and a greater proportion of women
abandon science for other majors. As a graduate of
1 Vassar—then a single-sex school—I note that there
is an interesting exception to this trend: All wom-
en's colleges lose fewer of their science majors to
other fields. Based on my personal experience, I
believe that women's colleges can engender an
environment and a mindset in which there are no
barriers based on gender, an environment that
encourages women to pursue "nontraditional"
fields—like science and medicine.

Section 2: Reasons ♀ drop science

Treated poorly

Why do women drop out of science? A study
by the American Association for the Advancement
2 of Science found that women in science classes are
subject to more negative treatment than their male
colleagues—by both faculty and other students.

Perhaps one recent, glaring piece of evidence in
3 support of this AAAS study is the article by a dis-

tinguished professor at the University of Alberta —favorably peer-reviewed and published by the *Canadian Journal of Physics.* This "Scientific" observational study blames most of the ills of modern society, including corruption and cheating, on working mothers.

♂ teachers have the numbers and power. Fewer ♀ in science

Such attitudes are easier to understand—if not condone—when one considers the fact that most science faculty are men. A 1990 report by the National Science Foundation shows a total of 151,400
4 men teaching in science departments at four-year colleges and universities, compared with 34,900 women. While 104,400 (68.9 per cent) of the men were tenured, only 12,600 (36 per cent) of the women had received tenure.

Example: Medicine

My own field of medicine mirrors the trends found in science. Although women now make up 38 per cent of medical students and women's academic performance is virtually indistinguishable from men's, women rarely achieve leadership positions on medical-school faculties. With some 14,171 women now on medical-school faculties,
5 women represent 21.5 per cent of all faculty members. However, they occupy what might be called an academic ghetto: 49.8 per cent are clustered at the assistant-professor level, while only 9.8 per cent have achieved the rank of full professor. Today, no medical school is headed by a woman dean; in 1990, there were two.

Section 3: Record of ♀ and $, in science

Once they have survived the rigors of their education in the classroom, the laboratory, *and* the faculty lounge, how do women scientists and MD's fare in securing support for their research? The good news is that women's share of research grant
6 money from the National Institutes of Health has doubled since 1981, and in 1990–91, women's and men's success rates for competing research project grants became virtually equal. However, women submitted and received only 19 per cent of these awards.

Another difference is that women's research is a bargain: Women applicants request less mon-
7 ey than their male colleagues, on average about $30,000 less. Thus, in 1990–91, women received a mere 16 per cent of funds for research project grants. . . .

Section 4: Country needs women

In view of some negative treatment in the classroom and discouraging employment and funding
8 prospects, the astonishing thing is that young women pursue careers in science and medicine at all!

REFERENCES

BROOKFIELD, STEPHEN D. *Developing Critical Thinkers.* San Francisco: Jossey-Bass, 1987. Describes how critical thinking skills learned in school can be applied to everyday life.

GOLUB, JEFF, and the NCTE Committee on Classroom Practices, eds. *Activities to Promote Critical Thinking.* Urbana: NCTE, 1986. A collection of essays containing practical advice on teaching critical thinking.

NEWKIRK, THOMAS, ed. *Only Connect: Uniting Reading and Writing.* Upper Montclair, NJ: Boynton/Cook, 1986. A collection of essays emphasizing the role interpretation plays in reading and writing.

SCHLESINGER, MARK A. "The Road to Teaching Thinking." *JGE: The Journal of General Education* 36 (1984): 182–96. An evaluation of four current approaches to teaching thinking.

SCHOR, IRA. *Critical Thinking and Everyday Life.* 1980. Rpt. Chicago: U Chicago P, 1987. Based on Freirean principles, encourages critical thinking as part of a practical "liberatory pedagogy."

SEIGEL, MARJORIE, and ROBERT CAREY. *Critical Thinking: A Semiotic Perspective.* Urbana: ERIC/ RCE & NCTE, 1989. Critical thinking must be approached within the frame of reference provided by particular disciplines.

REFERENCES

BLACKMON, JO ANNE RAIFORD, and HOWARD I. BERRENT. "Open to Suggestion: OH RATS—A Note-taking Technique." *Journal of Reading* 27 (1984): 548–50. A system for note-taking during reading helps students understand material better.

BUCKLER, PATRICIA PRONDINI. "Reading, Writing, and Psycholinguistics: An Integrated Approach Using Joyce's 'Counterparts.'" *Teaching English in the Two-Year College* 12 (1985): 22–31. Assignments in a freshman course follow Rosenblatt's reading model and Moffett's writing model.

DILLON, GEORGE. *Constructing Texts.* Bloomington: Indiana UP, 1981. Readers do more than simply decode texts; they make meaning from the text.

MEYERS, CHET. *Teaching Students to Think Critically.* San Francisco: Jossey-Bass, 1986. Teachers can develop visual models to represent critical thinking in various disciplines.

EXTRA HELP

The steps developed here in 1e-2 share some features with traditional "SQ3R" techniques, which go back to the 1940s (Robinson, H. *Why Pupils Fail in Reading.* U Chicago P, 1946). Those methods place special emphasis on the student's effort in forming key "challenge" questions throughout the reading process, and then seeking the answers that will reinforce memory and comprehension. This stepwise questioning process has been repeatedly shown to be effective in helping students to improve comprehension at all levels from learning-

But it is fortunate—and important—for our country that they do. By the year 2000, women and minorities will account for 68 per cent of the new workers. Coupled with the fact that, if cur-
9 rent trends continue, the United States will face a shortage of scientists and physicians by the end of the century, it is safe to say that sustaining America's scientific and biomedical preeminence depends upon attracting—and retaining—talented women and minorities.

U.S. will need more ♀ scientists.

If we are to ensure our country's future competitiveness, we must change the prevailing culture—the rules of the game—in our classrooms,
10 boardrooms, laboratories, and faculty lounges. To do so, we must recognize that brains, not brawn, will dominate the next century, and that means more than ever we must tap into the brain power of women. . . .

Section 5: Break conventions

Eighty years ago, when British women were trying to win the right to vote, they played by men's rules: They broke windows in Parliament Square. Many of the women were treated brutally and arrested. Their leader, Emmeline Pankhurst, pointed out that every advance of men's rights has been marked by violence and the destruction of property. She defended the women's actions, saying, "Why should women go to Parliament Square
11 and be battered about and insulted, and most important of all, produce less effect than when they throw stones? We tried it long enough. We submitted for years patiently in insult and assault. Women had their health injured. Women lost their lives. . . . After all, is not a woman's life, is not her health, are not her limbs more valuable than panes of glass? There is no doubt of that, but most important of all, does not the breaking of glass produce more effect upon the Government?"

Parallel case: ♀ seeking right to vote: 1900s

While I am not advocating that American women in science resort to such behaviors—or even to
12 the breaking of test tubes—it is clear that all of us in the scientific community have a lot of breaking to do—especially old rules, self-defeating habits, and glass ceilings.

Change—without violence

2 Applying techniques for reading to understand

When you know that you must base later writing on a source you are reading, you should consciously adopt a system for reading to understand.

There are many systems you can follow, but each commonly entails reading in three stages.

Preview Skim the text, reading quickly both to identify the author's purpose and to recall what you know about the topic.

Read Read with pen in hand, making notes (on separate sheets or on photocopied pages) about the content and the structure of the text. Stop periodically to monitor your progress.

Review Skim the text a second time to consolidate your notes: jot down questions and highlight especially important passages.

What follows are techniques for taking notes on information important to understanding a source. These same techniques led to notes Lou Cassetta made on the passage by Bernadine Healy, above.

Preview the text.

- *Read titles, openings, and closings in full.* This preview will give you a sense of topic, audience, purpose, and main point. Read the title and guess the relationship between the title and text. If you are reading an article or a chapter of a book, read the opening and closing paragraphs in full. If you are reading a book, read the preface along with the first and last chapters.
- *Skim the rest of the text.* A brief look at the text will help you to understand the structure, or layout, of the source. When skimming an article, read all headings along with a few sentences from every second or third paragraph. When skimming a book, review the table of contents and then read the opening and closing paragraphs of each chapter.
- *Recall what you know about the topic.* A review of your previous exposure to a topic will prepare you to be interested and ready with questions as you begin reading. After skimming a text, think about the topic: reflect on your personal history with it.
- *Predict what you will learn from reading.* Based on your quick review of the text and your knowledge of the topic, predict what you will learn. Predictions form an important part of a close, critical reading by keeping you focused on the content and alert to potential difficulties.

Read the text.

Read with a pen or pencil in hand and make notes that will help you understand.

- *Identify the author's purpose.* The author's purpose will likely be to inform or to argue. Locate passages that illustrate this purpose.
- *Underline important phrases and sentences.* Your underlining or highlighting of important information should work with your notes (see below) so that you can return to the text and spot the author's main topic at a glance.
- *Write notes that summarize your underlining.* You can summarize important points of an explanation or an argument by writing brief phrases in the

deficient to near-proficiency. (Wong, B., and W. Jones, "Increasing metacomprehension in learning disabled and normally achieving students through self-questioning training." *Learning Disability Quarterly* 5.2 (1982): 228–38.) Idea-generating strategies such as "mapping" (3d-7) have also been shown to be effective as analytical tools to help in comprehension (Kameeni, E. J., and D. C. Simmons, *Designing Instructional Strategies: The Prevention of Academic Learning Disabilities.* Columbus, OH: Charles Merrill, 1990).

Students with a history of difficulty in reading comprehension can usually get extra help from various developmental reading textbooks in study skill centers. In addition, a variety of remedial computer programs have been designed to build up comprehension skills by degree. These programs often emphasize sentence-completion exercises at graduated levels, focusing on such basic functions as those identified in the adjoining text. Some learning laboratories, study skill centers, or special education departments may have access to programs such as the following (or other more recent products in this rapidly developing technology).

The first two programs feature paragraphs with structured omissions for readers to fill in.

Cloze Plus. Millikin Publishing Co. Six levels of exercises (from a basic 5th-grade reading level). Reviewed by Boygo, J., and P. M. Hardiman. "Cloze." *Journal of Learning Disabilities* 18 (1985): 364–65.

Comprehension Power Program. Millikin Publishing Co. Twelve levels of exercises featuring vocabulary words as well as structural reading skills, suited for secondary-level students. Reviewed by Lindemann, S. K. *Journal of Learning Disabilities* 18 (1985): 495–96.

Critical Reading, Lesson Series A–H. Eight disks published by Borg-Warner Educational Systems. Lesson units instruct secondary-level readers in critical thinking and reasoning patterns; four units focus on contrasts/alternatives, inclusive categories, conditional statements, and inductive reasoning. Reviewed by J. Wilson, "Critical Reading." *Learning Disability Quarterly* 8 (1985): 64–66.

margins; this will help you to understand as you read and to recall important information as you reread.

- *Identify sections.* A section of a text is a grouping of related paragraphs (see 5a). Sometimes, an author will provide section headings; at other times, you will need to write them. In either case, your awareness of sections will help you understand the structure of a text.
- *Identify difficult passages.* Use a question mark to identify passages that confuse you, and circle unfamiliar words. Unless a particular word is repeated often and seems central to the meaning of a text, postpone using a dictionary until you complete your reading. Frequent interruptions to check the meaning of words will fragment your reading and disrupt your understanding (see 22e).
- *Periodically ask: Am I understanding?* You should stop at least once during your reading to ask yourself this question. If you are having trouble, change your plan for reading. For especially difficult selections, try dividing the text into small sections and reading one section at a sitting. Read until you understand each section, or until you can identify what you do not understand.

Review the text.

After reading and making notes, spend a few minutes consolidating what you have learned. Focus on the content of the passage and its structure. Understand the pattern by which the author has presented ideas and information. The additional minutes of review that you devote now will crystallize what you have learned and be a real help later on, when you are asked to refer to and *use* the selection, perhaps for an exam or paper.

- *Consolidate information.* Skim the passage and reread your notes. Clarify them, if necessary, so that they accurately represent the selection. Reread and highlight (with boxes or stars) what you consider to be the author's significant sentences or paragraphs.
- *Organize your questions.* Review the various terms and concepts you have had trouble understanding. Organize your questions concerning vocabulary and content. Use dictionaries; seek out fellow students or a professor to clarify especially difficult points. Even if you do not pursue these questions immediately, you should clarify what you do not understand. Your questions, gathered into one place, such as a journal, will be an excellent place to begin reviewing for an exam.

EXERCISE 5

Individual responses

EXERCISE 5

Using the techniques discussed in the preceding section, read to understand (a) an editorial from a newspaper's OP-ED page or (b) any article in which a writer clearly expresses an opinion on a topic of interest to you. On a photocopy of the article, underline what you consider to be important sentences and phrases, and make notes that summarize important ideas and information. In addition, identify the different sections of the passage.

1f Critical reading (2): Reading to respond

Your personal response to a text is the second component of a critical, comprehensive reading. If your responses are to be informed, you must understand what you have read—which is why your first job is to understand. This done, focus on yourself. Explore your responses to the text.

1 Setting goals for reading to respond

The overall goal of reading to respond is to identify and explore *your* reactions to a text. More specifically, these goals are as follows:

- Reflect on your experience and associations with the topic of a text. Know what you feel about a text—know your emotional response.
- Let the text challenge you.
- Use the text to spark new, imaginative thinking.

Following is the passage by Bernadine Healy, which you read in 1e-1, along with Lou Cassetta's comments. Reread a portion of the same passage, this time observing the second layer of notes in blue, which represent freshman writer Lou Cassetta's response to the passage. Recommended techniques for highlighting in this way follow. You will have a chance to practice these techniques on the passage you chose for Exercise 5.

*From **The Chronicle of Higher Education***

Effective stats: I didn't know the numbers were so one-sided!

4 [M]ost science faculty are men. A 1990 report by the National Science Foundation shows a total of 151,400 men teaching in science departments at four-year colleges and universities, compared with 34,900 women. While 104,400 (68.9 per cent) of the men were tenured, only 12,600 (36 per cent) of the women had received tenure.

♂ teachers have the numbers and power. Fewer ♀ in science

. . .

Section 4: Country needs women

8 In view of some negative treatment in the classroom and discouraging employment and funding prospects, the astonishing thing is that young women pursue careers in science and medicine at all!

9 But it is fortunate—and important—for our country that they do. By the year 2000, women and minorities will account for 68 per cent of the new workers. Coupled with the fact that, if current trends continue, the United States will face a shortage of scientists and physicians by the end of the century, it is safe to say that sustaining America's scientific and biomedical preeminence de-

U.S. will need more ♀ scientists.

ADDITIONAL EXERCISE C

Following is a letter written by Major Sullivan Ballou to his wife, Sarah, one week before he was killed at the first Battle of Bull Run. This letter, read during the acclaimed documentary *The Civil War,* prompted thousands of calls to public television stations across the country. What is your response? Read and reflect on the letter; then write out your thoughts in a few paragraphs.

July 14, 1861

Camp Clark, Washington
My very dear Sarah:

The indications are very strong that we shall move in a few days—perhaps tomorrow. Lest I should not be able to write again, I feel impelled to write a few lines that may fall under your eye when I shall be no more.

I have no misgivings about, or lack of confidence in, the cause in which I am engaged, and my courage does not halt or falter. I know how strongly American Civilization now leans on the triumph of the Government, and how great a debt we owe to those who went before us through the blood and sufferings of the Revolution. And I am willing—perfectly willing—to lay down all my joys in this life, to help maintain this Government, and pay that debt . . .

Sarah, my love for you is deathless, it seems to bind me with mighty cables that nothing but Omnipotence could break; and yet my love of Country comes over me like a strong wind and bears me unresistibly on with all these chains to the battle field.

The memories of the blissful moments I have spent with you come creeping over me, and I feel most gratified to God and to you that I have enjoyed them so long. And hard it is for me to give them up and burn to ashes the hopes of future years, when, God willing, we might still have lived and loved together, and seen our sons grown up to honorable manhood around us. I have, I know, but few and small claims upon Divine Providence, but something whispers to me—perhaps it is the wafted prayer of my little Edgar, that I shall return to my loved ones. If I do not, my dear Sarah, never forget how much I love you,

(continued)

and when my last breath escapes me on the battle field, it will whisper your name. Forgive my many faults, and the many pains I have caused you. How thoughtless and foolish I have often times been! How gladly would I wash out with my tears every little spot upon your happiness . . .

But, O Sarah! If the dead can come back to this earth and the unseen around those they loved, I shall always be near you; in the gladdest days and in the darkest nights . . . always, always, and if there be a soft breeze upon your cheek, it shall be my breath, as the cool air fans your throbbing temple, it shall be my spirit passing by. Sarah, do not mourn me dead; think I am gone and wait for thee, for we shall meet again.

pends upon attracting—and retaining—talented women and minorities.

If we are to ensure our country's future competitiveness, we must change the prevailing culture—the rules of the game—in our classrooms,
10 boardrooms, laboratories, and faculty lounges. To
do so, we must recognize that brains, not brawn,
will dominate the next century, and that means
more than ever we must tap into the brain power
of women. . . .

Section 5: Break conventions

We'd be fools not to depend equally on ♂ and ♀.

♀ have been fighting for a long time.

Parallel case: ♀ seeking right to vote: 1900s

Eighty years ago, when British women were
trying to win the right to vote, they played by
men's rules: They broke windows in Parliament
Square. Many of the women were treated brutally
and arrested. Their leader, Emmeline Pankhurst,
pointed out that every advance of men's rights has
been marked by violence and the destruction of
property. She defended the women's actions, say-
11 ing, "Why should women go to Parliament Square
and be battered about and insulted, and most important of all, produce less effect than when they
throw stones? We tried it long enough. We submitted for years patiently in insult and assault.
Women had their health injured. Women lost their
lives. . . . After all, is not a woman's life, is not her
health, are not her limbs more valuable than panes
of glass? There is no doubt of that, but most important of all, does not the breaking of glass produce more effect upon the Government?"

She's too conservative. Why <u>not</u> break some windows!

Change—without violence

While I am not advocating that American wom-
en in science resort to such behaviors—or even to
the breaking of test tubes—it is clear that all of us
12 in the scientific community have a lot of breaking
to do—especially old rules, self-defeating habits,
and glass ceilings.

2 Applying techniques for reading to respond

You can achieve the goals of reading to respond when you approach a text with a set of questions that continually returns your focus to *you* and *your* reactions. Here is a sampling of such questions.

Questions that promote a personal response

- *Which one or two sentences did I respond to most strongly in this text? What was my response?* Usually, you will read one or two sentences that will prompt reactions. Name these reactions. Explore your reasons for being excited, angry, thoughtful, surprised, or threatened. Keep the focus on you.

- *What is the origin of my views on this topic? Who else shares my views?* If you are reading on a controversial topic, explore where and under what circumstances you learned about the topic. For the sake of developing a response, criticize the views of people who believe as you do. Apply this criticism to yourself. What do you discover?
- *If I turned the topic of this text into a question on which people voted, how would I vote—and why?* This question can help involve you with the text, since casting a vote requires some interest, if only self-interest, in a topic. Try getting involved with the text by locating a debate in the text and by taking sides.
- *What new interest, question, or observation does this text spark in me?* Use a text to spark your own thinking. Let the text help you pose new questions or make new observations. Use the text as a basis for speculation.

See 37d for a discussion on a special case of reading to respond: responding to literature.

Many of the techniques just discussed are illustrated in the passage by Bernadine Healy, in 1f-1. Observe the personal nature of Lou Cassetta's notes. Two of Lou's comments clearly represent a point of view: "Effective statistics" and "We'd be fools not to depend equally on men and women." These comments differ in kind from those that summarize, such as "Fewer women major in science." Responses, by definition, are personal. They will differ from one reader to the next, and you can expect a range of responses among your classmates to Healy's thesis (that women must break the habits of conventional gender thinking if they are to take their rightful place in the sciences).

EXERCISE 6

Reread the passage you selected for Exercise 5, this time to respond. Write notes and underline phrases and sentences, based on your response. Use a different color pen or pencil for your notes this time than you used while reading to understand, so that you can recreate your various layers of reading.

EXERCISE 6

Individual responses

1g Critical reading (3): Reading to evaluate

Evaluating a text is the third component of a close, critical reading. Having understood and responded to a text, you are in a position to investigate its strengths and weaknesses—that is, to evaluate it. You will not find every text to be of equal value: equally accurate, equally useful, equally convincing, equally well written. As a critical reader, you should determine the extent to which an author has succeeded or failed in presenting material; and you should be able to explain why you and the author agree or disagree.

ESL CUE

ESL students from Asian and Middle Eastern countries may be disturbed by the concept of evaluation of a source. They will not take for granted the necessity to do so, and Middle Eastern students especially may have attitudes toward journalistic sources which diverge dramatically from Western attitudes.

REFERENCE

AARONS, VICTORIA. "Ethical Issues: A Rhetorical Methodology." *The Writing Instructor* 4 (1985): 83–88. Using ethical issues for discussion in composition class encourages critical thinking.

1 Setting goals for reading to evaluate

You have four goals in reading to evaluate:

- Distinguish between an author's use of facts and opinions.
- Distinguish between an author's assumptions (fundamental beliefs about the world) and your own.
- Judge the effectiveness of an explanation.
- Judge the effectiveness of an argument.

Following is part of the passage by Bernadine Healy, which you read in 1e-1, where you saw summary notes, and again in 1f-1, where you saw response notes. Reread the passage, this time observing a third layer of notes in green, Lou Cassetta's evaluation of the passage. Recommended techniques for reading to evaluate follow.

From **The Chronicle of Higher Education**

Effective stats: I didn't know the numbers were so one-sided!

♂ teachers have the numbers and power. Fewer ♀ in science

[M]ost science faculty are men. A 1990 report
by the National Science Foundation shows a total
of 151,400 men teaching in science departments at
4 four-year colleges and universities, compared
with 34,900 women. While 104,400 (68.9 per cent)
of the men were tenured, only 12,600 (36 per cent)
of the women had received tenure.

Stats very useful

. . .

Section 4: Country needs women

But: does sexism account for all difference?

In view of some negative treatment in the classroom and discouraging employment and funding
8 prospects, the astonishing thing is that young
women pursue careers in science and medicine at
all!

U.S. will need more ♀ scientists.

But it is fortunate—and important—for our
country that they do. By the year 2000, women
and minorities will account for 68 per cent of the
new workers. Coupled with the fact that, if cur-
9 rent trends continue, the United States will face a
shortage of scientists and physicians by the end of
the century, it is safe to say that sustaining America's scientific and biomedical preeminence depends upon attracting—and retaining—talented
women and minorities.

If we are to ensure our country's future competitiveness, we must change the prevailing culture—the rules of the game—in our classrooms,
10 boardrooms, laboratories, and faculty lounges. To
do so, we must recognize that brains, not brawn,
will dominate the next century, and that means
more than ever we must tap into the brain power
of women. . . .

Section 5: Break conventions

We'd be fools not to depend equally on ♂ and ♀.

♀ have been fighting for a long time.

Parallel case: ♀ seeking right to vote: 1900s

Case not parallel—right to vote is basic human right; access to science depends on ability.

Eighty years ago, when British women were trying to win the right to vote, they played by men's rules: They broke windows in Parliament Square. Many of the women were treated brutally and arrested. Their leader, Emmeline Pankhurst, pointed out that every advance of men's rights has been marked by violence and the destruction of property. She defended the women's actions, saying, "Why should women go to Parliament Square
11 and be battered about and insulted, and most important of all, produce less effect than when they throw stones? We tried it long enough. We submitted for years patiently in insult and assault. Women had their health injured. Women lost their lives. . . . After all, is not a woman's life, is not her health, are not her limbs more valuable than panes of glass? There is no doubt of that, but most important of all, does not the breaking of glass produce more effect upon the Government?"

She's too conservative. Why <u>not</u> break some windows!

Change—without violence

While I am not advocating that American women in science resort to such behaviors—or even to the breaking of test tubes—it is clear that all of us
12 in the scientific community have a lot of breaking to do—especially old rules, self-defeating habits, and glass ceilings.

2 Applying techniques for reading to evaluate

When you are reading to evaluate, you want to be alert to an author's use of *facts, opinions,* and *definitions,* and his or her *assumed views of the world.* You will also want to know if an author's purpose is primarily to inform or to argue, so that you can pose specific questions accordingly.

Distinguish facts from opinions.

Before you can evaluate a statement, you should know whether it is being presented to you as a fact or an opinion. A **fact** is any statement that can be verified.

Nationwide, the cost of college tuition is rising.

New York lies at a more southerly latitude than Paris.

Andrew Johnson was the seventeenth President of the United States.

The construction of the Suez Canal was completed in 1869.

These statements, if challenged, can be established as true or false through appropriate research. As a reader evaluating a selection, you might question the accuracy of a fact or how the fact was shown to be true. You might doubt, for instance, that Paris is a more northerly city than New York. The argument

ADDITIONAL EXERCISE D

Label each of the following statements as *fact* or *opinion.* Be prepared to defend your choice.

1. Socialism died with the fall of the Eastern European governments.
2. Improperly dumped toxic waste presents environmental hazards.
3. Socrates was the greatest philosopher in ancient Greece.
4. Large corporations have a social responsibility to the communities in which they operate.
5. All humans are created equal.

ESL EXERCISE

List the assumptions that you made about the United States and about Americans before you came to this country. Which assumptions have proven true? Which assumptions have proven false? What caused you to change your mind?

ESL EXERCISE

List the assumptions that you made about American colleges and universities before you came to this country. Which assumptions have proven true? Which assumptions have proven false? What caused you to change your mind? (Note that Spanish speakers might confuse "college" with the Spanish false cognate term *colegio,* which means *high school.*)

is quickly settled by reference to agreed-upon sources—in the case of Paris, a map.

An **opinion** is a statement of interpretation and judgment. Opinions are not true or false in the way that statements of fact will be. Opinions are more or less well supported. If a friend says, "That movie was terrible," this is an opinion. If you ask why and your friend responds, "Because I didn't like it," you are faced with a statement that is unsupported and that makes no claim on you for a response. Someone who writes that the majority of U.S. space missions should not have human crews is stating an opinion. Someone who refers to the *Challenger* disaster is referring to a fact, a matter of historical record. Opinions are judgments. If an opinion is supported by an entire essay, then the author is, in effect, demanding a response from you.

Identify the strongly stated opinions in what you read, and then write a *comment note:* in the margin, jot down a brief note summarizing your response to the opinion. Agree or disagree. Later, your note will help you crystallize your reactions to the selection.

Distinguish your assumptions from those of an author.

An **assumption** is a fundamental belief that shapes people's views. If your friend says that a painting is "beautiful," she is basing that statement, which is an opinion, on another, more fundamental opinion—an assumed view of beauty. Whether or not your friend directly states what qualities make a painting beautiful, she is *assuming* these qualities and is basing her judgment on them. If the basis of her judgment is that the painting is "lifelike," this is an assumption. Perhaps she dislikes abstract paintings and you like them. If you challenged each other on the point or asked *why,* you both might answer: "I don't know why I think this way. I just do." Sometimes assumptions are based on clearly defined reasons, and other times (as in the painting example) they are based on ill-defined feelings. Either way, the opinions that people have (if they are not direct expressions of assumptions themselves) can be better understood by identifying the underlying assumptions.

Consider two sets of assumptions

When you read a source, two sets of assumed views about the world come into play: yours and the author's. The extent of your agreement with an author depends largely on the extent to which your assumptions coincide. Therefore, in evaluating a source, you want to understand the author's assumptions concerning the topic at hand, as well as your own. To do so, you must perform two related tasks: identify an author's opinions, and determine whether each opinion is based on some other opinion or assumed view.

Identify direct and indirect assumptions

Assumptions may be stated directly or indirectly. In either case, your job as a critical reader is to identify and determine the extent to which you agree with them.

TEACHING IDEAS

M. Neil Brown and Stuart M. Keeley, in *Asking the Right Questions,* 2nd ed. (Prentice-Hall, 1986) usefully distinguish among three types of assumptions:

> **Value assumptions** are core beliefs about the way the world *should* work. They are based on the intensity with which a person believes in certain fundamental values, such as the dignity of human life, the proper role of government, or the obligation to make moral decisions.
>
> **Descriptive assumptions** are accounts of how the world *in fact* works—how people interact, how things get done—accounts that an author assumes to be true.
>
> **Definitional assumptions** are, as the term implies, definitions that an author holds to be true.

TEACHING IDEAS

One of the most familiar documents in this country, the Declaration of Independence, provides a clear example of stated assumptions: "We hold these truths to be self-evident, that all men are created equal, that they are endowed by their Creator with certain unalienable Rights, that among these are Life, Liberty and the pursuit of Happiness. . . ." Any students having difficulty with the concept of assumptions can be asked to keep in mind the first words in these lines.

ADDITIONAL EXERCISE E

Reproduce the following paragraph, written by Anna Freud and Dorothy Burlingham, and ask students to identify the authors' assumptions.

> Work in the War Nurseries is based on the idea that the care and education of young children should not take second place in wartime and should not be reduced to wartime level. Adults can live under emergency conditions and, if necessary, on emergency rations. But the situation in the decisive years of bodily and mental development is entirely different. It has already been generally recognised, and provision has been made accordingly, that the lack of essential foods, vitamins, etc., in early childhood will cause lasting

Assumption stated directly

#1 A nation is justified in going to war only when hostile forces threaten its borders.

#2 A nation is justified in going to war when hostile forces threaten its interests anywhere in the world.

At times, an author hints at, but does not directly state, an assumed view—as in this example:

Assumption not stated

#3 A conflict 7,000 miles from our border does not in any way threaten this nation, and we are therefore not justified in fighting a war that far from home.

Sentence #3 is based on the assumption expressed in sentence #1. Suppose you were reading an editorial and came across sentence #3. In a close, critical reading you would see in this statement an unexpressed assumption about the reasons nations *should* go to war. If you can show that an author's assumed views (whether directly or indirectly expressed) are flawed, then you can argue that all opinions based on them are flawed and should be rejected, or at least challenged.

Distinguish your definitions of terms from those of an author.

Consider this statement: *Machines can explore space as well as and, in some cases, better than humans.* What do the words *as well as* and *better than* mean? If an author defines these words one way and you define them another, you and the author are sure to disagree. In evaluating a source, identify the words that are important to the author's presentation. If the author does not define these words directly, then state what you believe the author's definitions to be. At times you will need to make educated guesses based on your close reading of the source.

Question sources that explain and sources that argue.

Outside of the literature classroom, you will read sources that are written primarily to inform or to argue. As a critical reader engaged in evaluating a source, determine the author's primary purpose and pose questions accordingly.

Sources that explain

When a selection asks you to accept an explanation, a description, or a procedure as accurate, pose—and respond to—these questions:

- For whom has the author intended the explanation, description, or procedure? The general public—nonexperts? Someone involved in the same business or process? An observer, such as an evaluator or a supervisor?
- What does the text define and explain? How successful is the presentation, given its intended audience?

bodily malformation in later years, even if harmful consequences are not immediately apparent. It is not generally recognised that the same is true for the mental development of the child. Whenever certain essential needs are not fulfilled, lasting psychological malformations will be the consequence. These essential elements are: the need for personal attachment, for emotional stability, and for permanency of educational influence.

Working with Brown and Keeley's classification (see the Teaching Idea on the preceding page) we can observe that a value assumption and a descriptive assumption are explicitly made in this paragraph. On the basis of these directly stated assumptions, Freud and Burlingham, directors of three wartime nurseries in England during World War II, presented in their book several case studies on children and their reactions to war.

Value Assumption
(what an author wants the world to be like): "The care and education of young children should not take second place in wartime and should not be reduced to wartime level."

Descriptive Assumption
(how an author believes the world works): "Whenever certain needs are not fulfilled, lasting psychological malformations will be the consequence."

REFERENCE

DEANE, BARBARA. "Putting the Inferential Process to Work in the Classroom." *CCC* 27 (1976): 50–52. Classroom activities can assist students in developing the ability to make inferences.

ADDITIONAL EXERCISE F

Identify in the following statements value assumptions, descriptive assumptions, and definitional assumptions, and indicate whether the assumptions are explicitly stated or implied.

1. Only by experience can anyone realize how deep, and dark, and foul is that pit of abominations [slavery]. (Harriet A. Jacobs)

(continued)

2. It is easier for a camel to go through the eye of a needle, than for a rich man to enter into the kingdom of God. (The Gospel according to St. Matthew)
3. I consider the written word inferior to the spoken. (Gloria Naylor)
4. The world must be made safe for democracy. (Woodrow Wilson)

EXERCISE 7

Individual responses

GROUP ACTIVITY

To underscore the fact that different readers respond differently to the same text, have students share their responses to this exercise in small groups. Ask them to focus on the *evaluative* comments they've made, and to discuss differences with an eye toward clarifying their own responses rather than convincing others that their responses are "correct."

- How trustworthy is the author's information? How current is it? If it is not current, are the points being made still applicable, assuming more recent information could be obtained?
- If the author presents a procedure, what is its purpose or outcome? Who would carry out this procedure? When? For what reasons? Does the author present the stages of the procedure?

Sources that argue

When a selection asks you to accept an argument, pose—and respond to—these questions:

- What conclusion am I being asked to accept?
- What reasons and evidence has the author offered for me to accept this conclusion? Are the reasons logical? Is the evidence fair? Has the author acknowledged and responded to other points of view?
- To what extent is the author appealing to logic? to my emotions? to my respect for authorities?[3]

Many of the techniques just discussed are illustrated in the notes made for the sample passage by Bernadine Healy, in 1g-1. The third layer of comments that you see (in green) would prepare a reader for writing a formal evaluation of the passage.

EXERCISE 7

Reread the passage you selected for Exercise 5, this time to evaluate the success of the author's presentation. Write notes and underline phrases and sentences, based on the discussion in the preceding section. Use a different color pen or pencil for your notes than the ones you used while reading to understand and reading to respond, so that you can recreate your various layers of reading.

1h Critical reading (4): Reading to synthesize

Once you have understood, responded to, and evaluated a single source, you are in a position to link that source with others. By establishing links between one author and others (including yourself), you achieve a synthesis: an *integration* of sources. Synthesis is the fourth and in some ways the most complex component of a close, critical reading: it requires that you read and understand *all* your source materials and that you respond to and evaluate each one.

[3]See 6h for a full discussion of evaluating arguments.

1 Setting goals for reading to synthesize

You are the organizing force of a synthesis. Without your active involvement with source materials, without your creative and integrating ideas, synthesis is impossible. You have four goals in reading to synthesize:

- Read to understand, respond to, and evaluate multiple sources on a subject, problem, or issue.
- Understand your own views on the subject, problem, or issue. Be able to state these views in a sentence or two.
- Forge relationships among source materials, according to your purpose. In a synthesis, *your* views should predominate. Use the work of various authors to support what you think.
- Generally, try to create a conversation among sources. Be sure that yours is the major voice in the conversation.

2 Applying techniques for reading to synthesize

When you are reading to synthesize, you want to be alert to the ways in which various sources "talk to" each other concerning a particular topic. Seek out relationships among sources. Be sure to consider yourself as a source—and a valuable one.

Students find the following plan helpful when writing syntheses:

- *Read, respond to, and evaluate multiple sources on a topic.* It is very likely that the authors will have different observations to make. Because you are working with the different sources, you are in a unique position to draw relationships among them.
- *Subdivide the topic into parts and give each a brief title.* Call the topic that the several authors discuss *X*. What are all the parts, or the subdivisions, of *X* that the authors discuss? List the separate parts, giving each a brief title.
- *Write cross-references for each part.* For each subdivision of the topic, list *specific* page references to whichever sources discuss that part. This is called *cross-referencing.* Once you have cross-referenced each of the topic's parts, you will have created an index to your reading selections.
- *Summarize each author's information or ideas about each part.* Now that you have generated cross-references that show you which authors discuss which parts of topic *X,* take up one part at a time and reread all the passages you have cross-referenced. Summarize what each author has written on particular parts of the topic.
- *Forge relationships among reading selections.* Study your notes and try to link sources. Here are several relationships that you might establish:

  Comparison: One author *agrees* with another.

  Contrast: One author *disagrees* with another.

  Example: Material in one source *illustrates* a statement in another.

REFERENCE

Zeller, Robert. "Developing the Inferential Reasoning of Basic Writers." *CCC* 38 (1987): 343–45. Asking students to infer relationships between photographs and writing encourages critical thinking.

ADDITIONAL EXERCISE G

Find a current topic covered in several newspapers or weekly newsmagazines. (In addition to local and city newspapers, you might consider *Time, Newsweek, U.S. News, The Christian Science Monitor.*) Using the strategy outlined in 1a, analyze the relationships among the sources.

Definition: Material from several sources, considered together, may help you *define* or redefine a term.

Cause and effect: Material from one source may allow you to *explain directly* why certain events occur in other sources.

Personal response: You find yourself agreeing or disagreeing with points made in one or more sources. Ask yourself *why* and then develop an answer by referring to specific passages.

For ways to synthesize details you've observed in a work of literature, see 37d, 2–4.

Cross-reference each part and summarize.

In actual course work, your reading selections will come from different journals, newspapers, and books—and cross-referencing should prove useful. Assume that you have identified parts of your topic and have listed page numbers from your sources that relate to each part. Following the page references, you would write a brief note summarizing the author's information or ideas. In Exercise 8 you are asked to do just this.

Forge relationships among your sources.

Based on your close reading of each selection and on your cross-references and notes, you should be able to establish relationships among the readings. Five general questions should get you started.

1. Which authors agree?
2. Which authors disagree?
3. Are there examples in one source of statements or ideas expressed in another?
4. What definitions can you offer, based on the readings?
5. Do you detect a cause-and-effect relationship in any of the readings?

EXERCISE 8

Individual responses

EXERCISE 8

Lou Cassetta has gathered four sources on the topic of gender and technology (Cowan, 1a; Kantrowitz, 1a; Lefton, 1c; and Healy, 1e). If you reread them, you'll find that you can make several cross-references that link the facts and ideas presented by one author with those presented by others. In this exercise, consider yourself a source: what are *your* responses and evaluative comments on each selection? Based on the sources provided in this chapter, we identify four parts of the topic to get you started making connections across readings. Try to identify at least one other part. Note: do not expect each author to have something to say about each part.

1. *Broader, historical perspective: men/women in science and in larger society*

   Cowan:
   Kantrowitz:
   Lefton:

Healy:
You:

2. *Numbers of women in science and technology*

Cowan:
Kantrowitz:
Lefton:
Healy:
You:

3. *Causes of the wide differences in numbers*

Cowan:
Kantrowitz:
Lefton:
Healy:
You:

4. *Appreciation of differences between women and men*

Cowan:
Kantrowitz:
Lefton:
Healy:
You:

CHAPTER 2

Critical Thinking and Writing

KEY FEATURES

This chapter continues the discussion of critical thinking begun in Chapter 1, presenting critical writing as progressing naturally from critical reading. The emphasis on questioning remains as students are introduced to four patterns of academic writing: summary, evaluation, analysis, and synthesis. Each pattern is explained in terms of specific goals; for each pattern, techniques are offered to help students begin to write, based on reading. Additionally, each pattern is shown to involve elements of other patterns: for instance, analysis, evaluation, and synthesis all involve elements of summary. To demonstrate the connections between reading and writing, the authors use selections that students have read in Chapter 1 to illustrate summary, evaluation, and analysis. Several of the student exercises are also based on reading selections in Chapter 1. The synthesis section of the chapter likewise builds on several of the readings in Chapter 1. For each of the patterns of writing presented in the chapter, students are given models and are then invited to practice the strategies themselves. With the foundation provided by Chapters 1 and 2, students will be able to understand the links between reading and writing at the college level.

LOOKING AHEAD

ACROSS THE CURRICULUM While this section states that summary, evaluation, analysis, and synthesis are essentially the same regardless of the discipline, you may want to refer students to Part X for extensive treatment of writing, with particular emphasis on research in humanities, social sciences, and sciences. (See Chapters 37, 38, and 39.) Writing in a business environment is covered in Chapter 40.

You will often be asked to demonstrate your understanding of sources by writing summaries, evaluations, analyses, and syntheses—four forms of writing that are fundamental to college-level work. Each form emphasizes a particular way of thinking about texts,[1] and each is built on particular skills in critical reading.

Forms of writing that build on reading

- **Summary.** When you summarize, you briefly—and neutrally—restate the main points of a text. Summary draws on your skills of reading to understand (see 1e).
- **Evaluation.** When you evaluate, you judge the effectiveness of an author's presentation and explain your agreement or disagreement. Evaluation draws on your skills of reading to understand (1e), reading to respond (1f), and reading to evaluate (1g).
- **Analysis.** When you analyze, you use the clearly defined principles set out by one or more authors to investigate the work of other authors (or to investigate various situations in the world). Analysis draws on your skills of reading to understand (1e), reading to respond (1f), and reading to evaluate (1g).
- **Synthesis.** When you synthesize texts, you gather the work of various authors according to *your* purpose. Synthesis draws on your skills of reading to understand (1e), reading to respond (1f), reading to evaluate (1g), and reading to synthesize (1h).

The cumulative layers of writing

The forms of writing discussed in this chapter are interrelated. You will write summaries as part of writing evaluations, analyses, and syntheses. Before you evaluate an author's presentation, you are obligated to demonstrate through summary that you understand the text. When you gather and synthesize multiple texts for a research paper, you will summarize *and* evaluate the texts as you forge relationships among them. When you conduct an analysis, you must have thoroughly understood and evaluated the principles you apply; this calls for written summary and evaluation as part of your analysis.

[1]We use the term *text* interchangeably with *source* to mean any reading selection.

These forms of academic writing are cumulative: one builds on the next in much the same way that strategies for reading comprehensively do. For clarity of presentation, we discuss summary, evaluation, analysis, and synthesis in separate sections and as separate tasks. In practice—in the texts you read and in the papers you write—you will find that these forms of writing and thinking merge into one another.

2a Writing a summary

Fundamental to working with sources in any academic setting is the **summary**, a brief, neutral restatement of a text. You will read texts in every course, and before you can comment on them or otherwise put them to use, you must first demonstrate an ability to understand authors on their own terms. Like any piece of writing, summary calls for you to make decisions and to plan, draft, and revise. While sometimes called for on exams, a summary more typically appears as part of evaluations, analyses, and syntheses. The following three assignments require summaries.

Assignments that explicitly call for a summary

MATHEMATICS	Read the article "Structuring Mathematical Proofs," by Uri Leron [*The American Mathematical Monthly* 90 (March 1983): 174–185]. In two to four typed pages, summarize the concept of linear proof, giving one good example from the course.
FILM STUDIES	Summarize Harvey Greenberg's discussion of *The Wizard of Oz.*
SOCIAL PSYCHOLOGY	Write a summary of your textbook's discussion of the "realistic conflict theory." Make sure that you address the theory's explanation of prejudice as an intergroup conflict.

An assignment may not explicitly call for a summary but may require it just the same, as in the following example. In completing this assignment, a student would need to summarize the Mary Shea argument and then respond.

Assignment that implies the need for a summary

BUSINESS ETHICS	In "Good Riddance to Corporate America," Mary Shea argues that highly credentialed women MBAs are beginning to quit corporate America because of its "essential emptiness." How convinced are you by Shea's argument?

1 Setting goals for writing a summary

The focus of a summary is on a specific text, *not* on your reactions to it. Overall, your goal is to restate the text, as briefly as possible, in your own words. More specifically, you should aim to meet these goals:

- clearly state the author's purpose in writing (for instance, to inform, explain, argue, justify, defend, contrast, or illustrate);
- clearly state the author's thesis; and
- clearly state the author's main points in support of this thesis.

LOOKING AHEAD

The material covered in the following sections will be useful in Chapter 34 (Using Sources). Since students are sometimes assigned research papers in other courses before covering the topic in Composition, you may want to call attention to that chapter, as well as the chapters on writing in the disciplines (Chapters 37, 38, and 39).

The material in this chapter relies on the following books:

JONES, BEAU FLY, et al., eds. *Strategic Teaching and Learning: Cognitive Instruction in the Content Areas.* Alexandria, VA: ASCD, 1987.

KUHN, THOMAS. *The Structure of Scientific Revolutions.* 2nd ed. Enlarged. Chicago: U Chicago P, 1970.

KURFISS, JOANNE G. *Critical Thinking: Theory, Research, and Possibilities.* ASHE-ERIC Higher Education Report No. 2. Washington, DC: Association for the Study of Higher Education, 1988.

MARZANO, ROBERT J., et al. *Dimensions of Thinking: A Framework for Curriculum and Instruction.* Alexandria, VA: ASCD, 1988.

RORTY, RICHARD. *Philosophy and the Mirror of Nature.* Princeton: Princeton UP, 1979.

TOULMIN, STEPHEN, RICHARD RIEKE, and ALLAN JANIK. *An Introduction to Reasoning.* New York: Macmillan, 1979.

REFERENCES

LANGER, JUDITH A. "Learning through Writing: Study Skills in the Content Areas." *Journal of Reading* 29 (1986): 400–06. Composing full essays about a reading promotes more effective learning than simply taking notes and responding to questions.

MAIMON, ELAINE P., BARBARA F. NODINE, and FINBARR O'CONNOR. *Thinking, Reasoning, and Writing*. New York: Longman, 1989. Offers methods of teaching based on theories of reading and writing as social acts.

MORRIS, BARBARA S. *Disciplinary Perspectives on Thinking and Writing*. Ann Arbor: English Composition Board, 1989. A collection of essays illustrating different modes of inquiry and approaches to writing among various disciplines.

NEWKIRK, THOMAS, ed. *Only Connect: Uniting Reading and Writing*. Upper Montclair, NJ: Boynton/Cook, 1986. A collection of essays emphasizing the role interpretation plays in reading and writing.

2 Understanding techniques for writing a summary

Summary begins with an application of the skills discussed in 1e, reading to understand. There you were advised to make notes as you previewed, read, and reviewed a text. Before you attempt to follow the guidelines below and write a summary, read 1e and apply the skills discussed there to any text you are about to summarize.

Students find the following process helpful in preparing for and writing a summary:

- Determine the purpose of the source—for instance, to inform, explain, argue, justify, defend, compare, contrast, or illustrate.
- Summarize the thesis. Based on the notes you have made and the phrases or sentences you have highlighted while reading, restate the author's main point in your own words. In this statement, refer to the author by name; indicate the author's purpose (e.g., to argue or inform); and refer to the title.
- Summarize the body of the text.

  STRATEGY 1: Write a one- or two-sentence summary of every paragraph. Summarize points important to supporting the author's thesis. Omit minor points and omit illustrations. Avoid the temptation to translate phrase for phrase from sentences in the text.

  STRATEGY 2: Identify sections (groupings of related paragraphs) and write a two- or three-sentence summary of each section.
- Study your paragraph or section summaries. Determine the ways in which the paragraphs or sections work together to support the thesis.
- Write the summary. Join your paragraph or section summaries with your summary of the thesis, emphasizing the relationship between the parts of the text and the thesis.
- Revise for clarity and for style. Quote sparingly. Provide transitions where needed.

Techniques for summarizing an especially difficult text

When the topic of a text is completely new to you, or when you are reading a text intended for an audience that has more experience with a topic than you have, reading to understand—and writing a summary—will be especially difficult. In addition to the reading strategies discussed in 1e, try these reading strategies to help you understand and summarize a difficult text:

1. Identify every example in the text and ask: what point is being illustrated here? Make a list of these points. Considered together, they will reveal the author's thesis.
2. Look for repeated terms or phrases. Define them, consulting specialized dictionaries or encyclopedias, if necessary.

3. Read and reread the opening and closing paragraphs of the text. Look for a sentence or two—the thesis—that seems to summarize the whole. "Interrogate" that sentence, following the advice in 3d-4. Link specific parts of the sentence to different parts (or sections) of the text. Understand what you can; identify what you cannot understand—and then take *specific* questions to a fellow student or your professor.

3 Applying techniques for writing summaries

The techniques for writing summaries can now be applied to an example passage found in Chapter 1: Bernadine Healy's article in *The Chronicle of Higher Education* (see 1e-1). You may want to reread the selection so that you understand the preparations for summary that follow.

Prepare: Make notes for a summary.

These preparatory notes are based on the above plan for writing summaries. The first note concerns Bernadine Healy's purpose; the second is a clear statement of the thesis—in the writer's own words, not Healy's. Finally, there is a one-sentence summary of each paragraph in the article.

PURPOSE to argue

THESIS Women must break stereotyped gender thinking, their own and that of others, if they are to take their rightful place in the sciences.

IDENTIFY SECTIONS

Section 1 (¶1): Opener: Identifies the problem

¶1: Surveys on the prevalence of women in the sciences show that fewer women than men major in the sciences in college and that more women than men drop their science major.

Section 2 (¶s 2–5): Reasons women drop science majors

¶2: According to another study, women drop their science majors because science faculty and fellow (male) students treat them poorly.

¶3: One example: an article from a respected journal that blames working women for current social ills.

¶4: Statistics show that male teachers in science (in four-year schools) outnumber female teachers by more than 4 to 1 and out-tenure women teachers by more than 8 to 1.

¶5: Healy reports that in her field, medicine, the statistics are equally unbalanced.

Section 3 (¶s 6–7): Record of women scientists in funding research

¶6: The record of women scientists and MD's in securing research funds from the National Institutes of Health is mixed: the success rate of

REFERENCES

BUCKLER, PATRICIA PRONDINI. "Reading, Writing, and Psycholinguistics: An Integrated Approach Using Joyce's 'Counterparts.' " *Teaching English in the Two-Year College* 12 (1985): 22–31. Assignments in a freshman course follow Rosenblatt's reading model and Moffett's writing model.

LAMBERT, JUDITH R. "Summaries: A Focus for Basic Writers." *Journal of Developmental Education* 8 (1984): 10–12, 32. Describes various advantages of teaching students to summarize.

SHERRARD, CAROL. "Summary Writing: A Topographical Study." *Written Communication* 3 (1986): 324–43. The longer the summary, the more likely an inexpert writer will use his or her own words instead of copying parts of the original.

LOOKING BACK

The use in this section of Bernadine Healy's piece from *The Chronicle of Higher Education* reinforces the interconnectedness of reading and writing. This section reminds students that what they are doing when writing a summary is a continuation of what they did in Chapter 1, as critical readers.

GROUP ACTIVITY

It can be extremely useful for students to compare summaries. Ask them to share their summaries in small groups, comparing them for *content*: length, main points, detail, and the like. When there are differences, each student should try to defend his or her choice. In articulating their reasons, students will come to a better understanding of what constitutes an effective summary.

ADDITIONAL EXERCISE A

ACROSS THE CURRICULUM Choose a brief section from a textbook in one of your other courses. (It would be doubly helpful if you chose something you're studying at the moment.) Using the guidelines here, write a summary of the section. Then think about how you understood the section before you actually summarized it and how you understand it afterward. Write a brief paragraph explaining what you learned through summarizing.

women applicants is now equal to that of men; but far fewer women apply for grants.

¶7: Grants awarded to women scientists and MD's average $30,000 less than grants awarded to men.

Section 4 (¶s 8–10): The country's needs/women's contributions

¶8: Given the negative treatment, Healy is surprised "that young women pursue careers in science and medicine at all."

¶9: By the turn of the century, the United States will need more scientists and physicians.

¶10: The United States will need to depend on both women and minorities to fill the gap.

Section 5 (¶s 11–12): The need to break conventional thinking

¶11: Eighty years ago, British women seeking the right to vote broke windows at Parliament to get attention.

¶12: Healy does not endorse violent protest, but she believes that in their effort to gain an equal footing in the sciences women have "a lot of breaking to do—especially old rules, self-defeating habits, and glass ceilings."

Write the summary.

Join paragraph or section summaries to the thesis and emphasize the relationship of parts.

> Bernadine Healy, director of the National Institutes of Health, argues that women must break stereotyped gender thinking, their own and that of others, if they are to take their rightful place in the sciences. According to recent studies, women are being excluded and are excluding themselves from careers in the sciences. At the undergraduate level, fewer women than men major in the sciences in college, and more women than men drop their science majors. In faculty positions, men outnumber women by more than 4 to 1 and out-tenure them by more than 8 to 1. Women endure such severe negative pressure from classmates, teachers, and professional journals that Healy is surprised "that young women pursue careers in science and medicine at all." By the turn of the century, she observes, the United States will need more scientists and physicians. For the country to remain competitive, more women will need to pursue careers in the sciences. But to do so, they will need to break "old rules, self-defeating habits, and glass ceilings."

EXERCISE 1

Individual answers

EXERCISE 1

Working with the article you selected for Exercises 5–7 in Chapter 1, and with the notes you made while reading that selection, write a summary. For specific help in doing so, follow the advice given in this section.

2b Writing an evaluation

In an **evaluation** you judge the effectiveness and reliability of a text and discuss the extent to which you agree or disagree with its author. Consider the following assignments, which call for evaluation.

SOCIOLOGY Write a review of Christopher Lasch's *Culture of Narcissism.*

HISTORY In "Everyman His Own Historian," Carl L. Becker argues for a definition of history as "the memory of things said and done." Based on your reading in this course, evaluate Becker's definition.

PHYSICS Write a review of *Surely You're Joking, Mr. Feynman!*

Writing an evaluation formalizes the process of reading to evaluate, which, in turn, depends on reading to understand and to respond (see 1e,f). Evaluation will always entail summary writing (see 2a), since before you can reasonably agree or disagree with an author's work or determine its effectiveness, you must show that you understand and can restate it.

1 Setting goals for writing an evaluation

You have two primary goals when writing to evaluate, and both depend on a critical, comprehensive reading: (1) to judge the effectiveness of the author's presentation, focusing for the moment only on the *quality* of the presentation; then (2) to agree and/or disagree with the author and explain your responses.

2 Understanding techniques for writing an evaluation

The basic pattern of evaluation is as follows: (1) offer a judgment about the text; (2) refer to a specific passage—summarize, quote, or paraphrase; and (3) explain your judgment in light of the passage referred to. If you can remember these components of evaluation, you will help to establish your authority as someone whose insights a reader can trust.

Prepare: Make notes on the effectiveness of the presentation.

You will evaluate the effectiveness and reliability of a presentation according to the author's purpose for writing. If the author is arguing a position, you bring one set of criteria, or standards of judgment, to bear on the text; if the author is informing—providing explanations or presenting procedures or descriptions—you bring to bear another set of criteria. You can use certain criteria for evaluating any text.

TEACHING IDEAS

As students move from critical reading to critical writing, a journal can be most helpful. Anne Berthoff suggests (in the essay cited on page 33) that students keep a notebook in which they record initial observations, questions, and comments on one side, and then *respond* to those notes on the other side. The result is a conversation of sorts—the right side in dialogue with the left. Such a journal is the ideal place for students to make the transition between reading and writing. In fact, in addition to the dialogue described above, the journal can also include summaries and evaluative notes. Keeping these notes in a designated notebook rather than on any available scrap of paper lends them an air of permanence.

ESL CUE

ESL students from Asian and Middle Eastern countries may be disturbed by the concept of evaluation of a source. They will not take for granted the necessity to do so, and the latter, especially, may have attitudes toward journalistic sources that diverge dramatically from Western attitudes.

ADDITIONAL EXERCISE B

Sometimes it's difficult to separate the content of a selection from its presentation; if you don't like or agree with what an author is saying, often you don't give the author credit for a well-written piece. In order to force yourself to consider presentation, scan some brief opinion pieces in current newspapers and magazines and find a selection with which you disagree—strongly, if possible. Then analyze the author's presentation based on the guidelines in 2b-2.

Criteria for texts that inform or *persuade*

Use the following criteria to judge the effectiveness of any text. Remember to support your evaluation by referring to and discussing a specific passage.

Accuracy Are the author's facts accurate?

Definitions Have terms important to the discussion been clearly defined—and if not, has lack of definition confused matters?

Development Does each part of the presentation seem well developed, satisfying to you in the extent of its treatment? Is each main point adequately illustrated and supported with evidence?

Criteria for texts that inform

When an author writes to inform, you can evaluate the presentation based on any of the preceding criteria as well as on the ones discussed in this section. Remember to support your evaluation by referring to and discussing a specific passage.

Audience Is the author writing for a clearly defined audience who will know what to do with the information presented? Is the author consistent in presenting information to one audience?

Clarity How clear has the author been in defining and explaining? Is information presented in a way that is useful? Will readers be able to understand an explanation or follow a procedure?

Procedure Has the author presented the stages of a process? Is the reader clear about the purpose of the process, about who does it and why?

Criteria for texts that persuade

When an author writes to persuade, you can evaluate the presentation based on any of the preceding criteria as well as on the ones that follow. Remember to support your evaluation by referring to and discussing specific passages.

Fairness If the issue being discussed is controversial, has the author presented opposing points of view? Has the author seriously considered and responded to these points? (See 6e.)

Logic Has the author adhered to standards of logic? Has the author avoided, for instance, fallacies such as personal attacks and faulty generalization? (See 6h.)

Evidence Do facts and examples fairly represent the available data on the topic? Are the author's facts and examples current? Has the author included negative examples? (See 6h.)

Authority Are the experts that the author refers to qualified to speak on the topic? Are the experts neutral? (See 6d-3 and 6h.)[2]

---

[2]In 6h you will find an extended discussion of evaluating arguments.

Prepare: Make notes on your agreement and disagreement with the author.

By applying the criteria above, you may decide that a selection is well written. Just the same, you may disagree with the author in part or in whole, or you may agree. In either case, you should examine the reasons for your reactions. For instance, in Lou Cassetta's evaluation of Bernadine Healy's article on women in science (2b-3), he acknowledges the usefulness of the statistics that Healy cites, but he disagrees with the parallel Healy wants to draw between women who threw stones at Parliament, protesting for their right to vote, and women who wish to take a fully equal role in the scientific community.

Whatever your reaction to a text, you should (1) identify an author's views, pointing out particular passages in which these views are apparent; (2) identify your own views; and (3) examine the basis on which you and the author agree or disagree. For the most part, you can explain agreements and disagreements by examining both your assumptions and the author's. Recall from Chapter 1 that an assumption is a fundamental belief that shapes people's opinions. Here is a format for distinguishing your views from the author's. (For an example of note making that follows this format, see 2b-3.)

Author's view on topic *X:*

Author's assumption:

My view:

My assumption:

Prepare: Organize your notes and gain a general impression.

Once you have prepared for writing an evaluation by making notes, review your material and try to develop an overall impression of the reading. In writing an evaluation, you will have enough space to review at least two, but probably not more than four or five, aspects of an author's work. Therefore, be selective in the points you choose to evaluate. Review your notes concerning the quality of the presentation and the extent of your agreement with the author; select the points that will best support your overall impression of the reading. As with any piece of formal writing, plan your evaluation carefully. If you are going to discuss three points concerning a selection, do so in a particular order, for good reasons. Readers will expect a logical, well-developed discussion.

Students find these steps helpful in preparing evaluations:

- Introduce the topic and author: one paragraph. One sentence in the introduction should hint at your general impression of the piece.
- Summarize the author's work: one to three paragraphs. If brief, the summary can be joined to the introduction.
- Briefly review the key points in the author's work that you will evaluate: one paragraph.
- Identify key points in the author's presentation; discuss each in detail: three to six paragraphs. If you are evaluating the quality of the author's

ADDITIONAL EXERCISE C

Using the newspaper or magazine selection you analyzed for presentation in Additional Exercise B, list the author's assumptions and your reactions according to the guidelines in section 2b-2.

REFERENCES

BERTHOFF, ANNE E. "A Curious Triangle and the Double-Entry Notebook: Or, How Theory Can Help Us Teach Reading and Writing." *The Making of Meaning: Metaphors, Models, and Maxims for Writing Teachers.* Upper Montclair, NJ: Boynton/Cook, 1981. In a double-entry notebook, or dialogic journal, students respond to readings and then respond at length to their original responses.

CARELLA, MICHAEL J. "Philosophy as Literacy: Teaching College Students to Read Critically and Write Cogently." *CCC* 34 (1983): 57–61. An approach to evaluating philosophical arguments without merely summarizing them.

HAHN, STEPHEN. "Counter-Statement: Using Written Dialogue to Develop Critical Thinking and Writing." *CCC* 38 (1987): 97–100. Using debate can help students evaluate assumptions and opinions.

MCCORMICK, KATHLEEN. "Teaching Critical Thinking and Writing." *The Writing Instructor* 2 (1983): 137–44. Critiquing flawed essays can help students develop skills of analysis and evaluation.

presentation, state your criteria for evaluation explicitly; if you are agreeing or disagreeing with opinions, try to identify the underlying assumptions (yours and the author's).

- Conclude with your overall assessment of the author's work.

The order of parts in the written evaluation may not match the actual order of writing. You may be unable to write the third section of the evaluation without first having evaluated the author's key points—the next section. The evaluation will take shape over multiple drafts.

3 Applying techniques for writing evaluations

Bernadine Healy's argument on women in science (1e-1) provides an opportunity to demonstrate how you can evaluate a text. The first step of evaluation, neutrally presenting an author's views in a summary, was developed earlier in this chapter (2a-3). Beyond the summary, your evaluation will address one or both of these questions: How effective and reliable is the author's presentation? Do I agree with the author?

How effective and reliable is the author's presentation?

In 2b-2 you found ten criteria, or standards of judgment, one or more of which you can use to determine the effectiveness and reliability of a source: accuracy, definitions, development, audience, clarity, procedure, fairness, logic, evidence, and authority. Following is an example of how three of these standards—evidence, authority, and logic—become criteria for evaluating Healy's discussion. This particular evaluation assumes that the author is arguing: Healy is trying to convince us that women are unequal partners with men in the sciences because of gender stereotypes that must be broken.

EVIDENCE

> Healy uses statistics well. Numerically, men outnumber women in the sciences. Male researchers and teachers have higher rates of tenure and grant rewards; women drop out of science at a greater rate than do men. These statistics can be cited in any essay on the topic of gender and technology.

AUTHORITY

> In writing this piece, Healy drew on her own experience as a physician and as the director of the National Institutes of Health. On both counts, she comes across as authoritative. She also cites evidence from two national, well-respected organizations: The American Association for the Advancement of Science, and the Pew Charitable Trust Science Education Program. Healy seems to be a completely reliable source for statistics and authoritative opinions.

LOGIC

> At the end of her argument, Healy tries to set the current role of women in science in a larger, historical context. Referring to a protest by British women who threw stones at Parliament in an effort to gain voting rights, Healy points out that sometimes we need to break things in order to ad-

ACROSS THE CURRICULUM

What counts as acceptable evidence in an argument changes as one moves from one disciplinary context to the next. In the absence of a specific discipline setting, the criteria for evaluating evidence offered in this chapter are helpful. But students should be aware of differences, which they will find discussed in the "Claims and Evidence" discussions in Chapters 37–39: writing and reading in the humanities, social sciences, and sciences.

TEACHING IDEAS

You might ask students what, aside from Healy's position as director of the National Institutes of Health, establishes her authority in her article. Students might be concerned that unless they are similarly "high powered" they cannot possibly sound authoritative in their own essays—which is *not* true. Thus, it might be a good idea to examine the qualities of Healy's piece that characterize it as authoritative in its own right: her willingness to draw on personal experience, which she presents in a public, non-self-indulgent way; her references to source materials; her serious tone; her broad perspective.

LOOKING AHEAD

You might refer students to the discussion in 6h—"Evaluating arguments and avoiding common errors." This discussion, in addition to the discussion in this chapter, will provide ample criteria on which to evaluate the logic of a presentation.

vance. As a generalization, this point seems fair. But her example of women and voting rights does not exactly parallel the case of women in science. Eighty years ago, getting the vote involved women demanding moral and political rights that were theirs because they were human beings. Everyone can agree that women should have the same access to careers in science as men have; but success in science—the right to teach, do research, and hold senior positions—is not an issue of basic human rights (as voting is), but depends on knowledge and on success in both the laboratory and the classroom. Whether women have the same knowledge or research success in the sciences as men have is the issue here, not basic human rights. Healy's example of voting rights, while colorful, is not the best parallel for her argument.

Do I agree with the author?

One of your jobs as an alert reader is to respond (see 1f). When you do so, make notes: point out specific passages that illustrate the author's view, summarize that view, respond, and then explain the assumptions underlying both your view and the author's. In a thoroughly active reading, you would point to many such passages and make notes. When you write a formal evaluation, choose the passages that seem the most interesting to you and appear to involve the author's main point most directly. Here's an example response to a point made by Healy:

HEALY'S VIEW ¶s 3–4	Healy refers to a sexist statement in the *Canadian Journal of Physics:* working mothers cause many of society's ills. Healy explains that the overt sexism of this statement is "easier to understand . . . when one considers the fact that most science faculty are men."
HEALY'S ASSUMPTIONS	(a) Sexism thrives in cultures dominated by men. (b) Sexist attitudes are responsible for the unequal treatment of women in the sciences.
MY VIEW	Healy's explanation is too general.
MY ASSUMPTION	(a) The sexism of one particular writer does not explain the fact that there are many more men in the sciences than women, nor does it establish that all or even most male scientists are sexist. (b) Sexist attitudes undoubtedly cause some exclusion of women in the sciences; but other causes—such as differences in the intellectual styles of men and women—might also exist and should be explored.

TEACHING IDEAS

If you assign a collection of essays and/or articles for your students, you might point them to a single paragraph of one selection in which an author is stating a view based on an *implicit* assumption. Ask the students to do with that paragraph what the writer is doing here: agree or disagree with the stated view and then (the hard part) explain the basis of agreement or disagreement by examining assumptions. It is important to understand that students, every bit as much as the authors they read, base their views of the world on assumptions both stated and unstated. Students may find it some consolation to hear that ferreting out assumptions can be difficult work.

Evaluation of Bernadine Healy's Argument on Women in Science

The feminist revolution of the 1960s and 70s in many ways changed the way Americans thought about the roles of women and men: women

Introduction sets context for Healy

came to be seen as more than mothers and homemakers, and men as more than winners of the weekly paycheck. Gender roles became more varied. More women pursued careers in medicine, law, and business. More men stayed home to care for their children.

Yet after a quarter-century marked by considerable progress in gender awareness, we still see signs of sexism. In an article appearing in The Chronicle of Higher Education, Bernadine Healy, director of the National Institutes of Health, argues that sexism is alive and well in scientific research and education. According to the studies she cites, fewer college women than men major in the sciences, and more women than men drop their science majors. Moreover, faculties are predominantly male, providing relatively few role models for would-be women scientists. In general, women endure such severe negative pressure from classmates, teachers, and professional journals that Healy is surprised "that young women pursue careers in science and medicine at all." For the country to remain competitive, Healy asserts, more women will need to pursue careers in the sciences. But in order for them to do so, the scientific community must break sexist, stereotyped thinking.

Summary

Healy points to problems that should concern educators at all levels, members of government, and scientists themselves. If women are turning away from careers in science, not because they lack interest or ability but because they are subjected to intensive "negative treatment," we face a serious problem. As Healy makes clear, America's future competitiveness depends on its "scientific and biomedical preeminence"; and discounting women's contributions in these areas is not only unfair but self-defeating. As a nation, we must fight to give access to all women who seek careers in

Preview of key points in evaluation

ADDITIONAL EXERCISE D

Ask students to read the Op-Ed page of a local or national newspaper and to bring to class any articles in which the writer is evaluating the argument, and ultimately assumptions, of another writer. Have students come to class prepared to point out key elements of the evaluation. In class, ask students to take additional steps: to define and evaluate the assumptions of the evaluator; and then to state their own views and to define the assumptions underlying them.

the sciences. But in our efforts to do so, we should also acknowledge that sexism may not explain every statistic that shows women to be outnumbered by men in the sciences.

Hint of some criticism to come

Healy's argument that American science is sexist is, in fact, based largely on statistical evidence. Drawing on studies conducted by the Pew Charitable Trust Science Education Program, the National Science Foundation, and the American Association for the Advancement of Science, she paints a devastating picture of women in the sciences and their position of powerlessness relative to men. As of 1990, 151,400 men taught in the sciences as compared to 34,900 women; 68.9 percent of the men were tenured, compared to 36 percent of the women. As of 1992, none of the nation's medical schools were run by a woman.

Author's facts noted

Such one-sided statistics demand explanation, and Healy is quick to offer one: sexism. To illustrate her point, she cites an article in a refereed journal that claims working mothers are responsible for many of society's ills, "including corruption and cheating." Attitudes such as this deserve Healy's attack, but she skirts the edge of sexism herself when she argues that these "attitudes are easier to understand--if not condone--when one considers the fact that most science faculty are men."

Author's explanation noted

The sexism of one particular writer does not explain the fact that there are many more men in the sciences than women, nor does it establish that all or even most male scientists are sexist. Sexist attitudes undoubtedly explain some exclusion of women in the sciences; but Healy has not established that sexism is the only cause--and this is her underlying assumption. Further, she assumes that intellectually men are identical to women and that any disparity in their numbers within the scien-

Author's explanation is challenged

Author's assumptions noted

2b

LOOKING BACK

As the writer's reference to Kantrowitz suggests, an evaluation can involve more than the single source being evaluated. In this instance, the writer draws on information learned in another source and uses it as leverage in the evaluation at hand. Students have seen the Kantrowitz piece at the beginning of Chapter 1. You may want to ask students to reread the Kantrowitz excerpt and then ask: Has the writer, here, made appropriate use of that source?

tific community points to sexism. On this point she may be only partially right.

Writing in an article on gender and technology in Newsweek, Barbara Kantrowitz reports on a "study by the Center for Children and Technology . . . [where] men and women in technical fields were asked to dream up machines of the future. Men typically imagined devices that could help them 'conquer the universe,' . . . [while] women wanted machines that met people's needs" (55). Researchers at the center found that men tend to push the scientific frontier due to an interest in pushing physical limits. By contrast, women, "'even those who are technologically sophisticated, think of machines as a means to an end'" (55). Differences in intellectual styles or interests might very well lead women and men to different careers, or to different paths within a given career. This is not to say that men are more or less capable than women when it comes to science or any other field. The research does at least suggest, however, that men and women may not be identical intellectually. If this is so, we have another, if only partial, explanation for the statistics Healy cites. Sexism alone may not explain the numbers.

Evaluator introduces a second source to establish a competing assumption

If further research clarifies gender differences, we must never allow them to stand as excuses for sexist barriers in the sciences or other fields. Individual women and men must have the absolute right to pursue any profession, without hindrances. But we would be foolish to ignore real gender differences or, worse yet, to claim they do not exist in our rush to call institutions sexist. Ultimately, Healy is correct to argue that we "have a lot of breaking to do" of gender stereotypes we thought were buried long ago. But Healy and others in the scientific community would themselves be unscientific to conclude, before thorough

Consequences of new assumption, if proven

Conclusion: evaluator agrees, in part, with author

Evaluator also disagrees with author

study, that sexism is the only cause of women's current underrepresentation in the sciences.

Works Cited

Healy, Bernadine. "Quotable." The Chronicle of Higher Education 25 Mar. 1992: B5.

Kantrowitz, Barbara, et al. "Men, Women & Computers." Newsweek 16 May 1994: 48-55.

EXERCISE 2

Write an evaluation of the article you summarized in Exercise 1. In preparing for your evaluation, take notes both on the author's presentation—for instance, its fairness and use of evidence and logic—and on your response to the author's key points. In writing the evaluation, use the summary you have written, but be aware that you may need to alter it by dividing it into several parts—first presenting a one-paragraph overall summary and then more sharply focused summaries of individual points you wish to evaluate.

2c Writing an analysis

An **analysis** is an investigation that you conduct by applying a principle or definition to an activity or to an object in order to see how that activity or object works, what it might mean, or why it might be significant. Analysis enables you to make interpretations. You might analyze, for instance, an event, condition, behavior, painting, novel, play, or television show. As an illustration of the range of ways analysis can be used, read the following four assignments from different disciplines. Notice how each asks students to apply a principle or a definition.

Sociology Write an essay in which you place yourself in American society by locating both your absolute position and relative rank on each single criterion of social stratification used by Lenski & Lenski. For each criterion, state whether you have attained your social position by yourself or if you have "inherited" that status from your parents.

Literature Apply principles of Jungian psychology—that is, an archetypal approach to literature—to Hawthorne's "Young Goodman Brown." In your reading of the story, apply Jung's concepts of the *shadow, persona,* and *anima.*

Physics Use Newton's Second Law ($F = ma$) to analyze the acceleration of a fixed pulley, from which two weights hang: m_1 (.45 kg) and m_2 (.90 kg). Having worked the numbers, explain in a paragraph the principle of Newton's law and your method of

EXERCISE 2

Individual responses

NOTE TO THE INSTRUCTOR

This book reserves the term *analysis* to denote what a writer generates (as in 2c) when applying some theory or principle systematically to a text or to an experience. Some teachers may also use the term *analysis* to denote the reader's effort to understand a text by studying its structure and determining where the main point is placed and exactly where that point is supported. Here that effort is incorporated into the activity of reading to understand (see 1e).

FOR DISCUSSION

To help students understand analysis, use references to popular culture. Start with the theory that popular television programs reflect the conditions of mainstream society. Then ask students to choose programs from their childhood years and the present. (If you teach older adults, you'll have an even broader range to choose from.) This exercise will not be structured nearly as precisely as the written exercises students will encounter in their classes, but it should help them to realize that analysis is not something foreign to them.

applying it to solve a problem. Assume that your reader is not comfortable with mathematical explanations: do not use equations in your paragraph.

FINANCE Using Guilford C. Babcock's "Concept of Sustainable Growth" [*Financial Analysts Journal* 26 (May–June 1970): 108–114], analyze the stock price appreciation of the XYZ Corporation, figures for which are attached.

In these assignments, students are asked to analyze themselves (their place in society), a short story, the acceleration of a pulley, and the stock performance of a corporation. In every discipline, certain principles and definitions play a key role in helping researchers to pose questions from a particular point of view, in order to better understand the activities and objects under study. Teachers will assign analyses to determine the extent to which you have understood principles and definitions important to your coursework. A key test of understanding is *application:* can you apply what you have learned to new situations? By writing an analysis, you show that you can. Analysis builds on skills of reading to understand (1e) and writing summaries (2a).

1 Setting goals for writing an analysis

An analysis should show readers how an activity or object works, what it might mean, or why it is significant. The specific goals of analysis are to:

- Understand a principle or definition and demonstrate your understanding by using it to study an activity or an object.
- Thoroughly apply this principle or definition to all significant parts of the activity or object under study.
- Create for the reader a sense that your analysis makes the activity or object being studied understandable—if not for the first time, then at least in a new way.

Different analyses lead to different interpretations.

What you discover through analysis depends entirely on which principles you apply to the activity or object under study. One event or text, analyzed according to different principles, will yield different interpretations. For example, over the years many writers have analyzed the L. Frank Baum classic, *The Wizard of Oz,* and the movie based on it. These writers have arrived at different interpretations, according to the different principles or definitions they applied to the story. Consider three specific insights into *The Wizard of Oz,* based on an application of three different principles.

PSYCHOLOGICAL ANALYSIS At the dawn of adolescence, the very time she should start to distance herself from Aunt Em and Uncle Henry, the surrogate parents who raised her on their Kansas farm, Dorothy Gale experiences a hurtful reawakening of her

TEACHING IDEAS

If time permits, having students read the three full analyses of *The Wizard of Oz* cited on pages 40–41 can be a good stimulus for class discussion. Even as they write their own analyses, students need to appreciate that other analyses of identical material are possible, given other criteria. Competing analyses of the same text, in this case Dorothy's dream journey to Oz, make this point explicitly.

fear that these loved ones will be rudely ripped from her, especially her Aunt (Em—M for Mother!). [Harvey Greenberg, *The Movies on Your Mind* (New York: Dutton, 1975).]

POLITICAL ANALYSIS

[*The Wizard of Oz*] was originally written as a political allegory about grass-roots protest. It may seem harder to believe than Emerald City, but the Tin Woodsman is the industrial worker, the Scarecrow [is] the struggling farmer, and the Wizard is the president, who is powerful only as long as he succeeds in deceiving the people. [Peter Dreier, "Oz Was Almost Reality," *Cleveland Plain Dealer* 3 Sept. 1989.]

LITERARY ANALYSIS

The Kansas described by Frank Baum is a depressing place. Everything in it is gray as far as the eye can see: the prairie is gray, and so is the house in which Dorothy lives. As for Auntie Em, "The sun and wind . . . had taken the sparkle from her eyes and left them a sober gray; they had taken the red from her cheeks and lips, and they were gray also. She was thin and gaunt, and never smiled now." And "Uncle Henry never laughed. . . . He was gray also, from his long beard to his rough boots." The sky? It was "even grayer than usual." [Salman Rushdie, "Out of Kansas," *New Yorker* 11 May 1992.]

Different analytical approaches yield different insights, and no analysis can be ultimately correct. There will be as many different interpretations of *The Wizard of Oz*, for instance, as there are principles of analysis; and each, potentially, has something to teach us. Not every analysis will be equally useful, however. An analysis is useful or authoritative to the extent that a writer (1) clearly defines a principle or definition to be applied; (2) applies this principle or definition thoroughly and systematically; and in so doing (3) reveals new and convincing insights into the activity or object being analyzed.

2 Understanding the techniques for writing an analysis

Prepare: Turn the principle or definition you are using to guide your analysis into a question—and then *probe*.

When preparing to write an analysis, you must be satisfied that you thoroughly understand the definition or principle you will be using. Read and reread the material that will become your analytical tool, and think of this material as a lens through which you will see new elements of the object under analysis. Turn your material into a series of questions that you will direct at the object under analysis. Here's a section of an analysis from another student essay, "The Coming Apart of a Dorm Society," in which freshman writer Edward Peselman uses the insights of a sociologist to analyze life in his dormitory. In the actual essay, the analysis is quite extensive as Edward draws on a half-dozen of the sociologist's observations. He converts

ESL CUE

All allusions to literature, films, history, current events, and the like are by definition culturally biased. What is meant by cultural literacy is so variant that the instructor would be well advised to confirm that students have seen *The Wizard of Oz.*

TEACHING IDEAS

ACROSS THE CURRICULUM Ask students to investigate how analyses are conducted in a discipline they are studying. The point of the exercise is twofold: for students to discover that analysis is an activity fundamental to academic inquiry; and for students to see that material within any disciplinary setting can be analyzed in multiple ways. Depending on the method used, information generated by analyses will differ, not only in a writing classroom but in other classrooms as well. Students could report on their findings orally.

these to questions, which he then directs to dormitory life. First, Edward introduces a concept:

> According to sociologist Randall Collins, what a powerful person wishes to happen must be achieved by controlling others (61).

Next, Edward applies this concept. He turns it into a question (though the question never appears in the essay itself): How does Collins's observation about power help to explain what happened in my dorm? Edward's *answer* becomes part of the analysis:

> Collins's observation helps define who had how much power in our dormitory's social group. Marc and Eric clearly had the most power. Everyone feared them and agreed to do pretty much what they wanted. Through violent words or threats of violence, they got their way. I was next in line: I wouldn't dare to manipulate Marc or Eric, but the others I could manage through occasional sarcasm. To avoid my quips, Benjamin became very cooperative. Up and down the pecking order, we exercised power through macho taunts, challenges, and biting language.

Before writing your analysis, direct as many questions as possible to the object under study and make many notes. In your final written piece, you will not draw on every note, but only on those that prove most revealing—and you won't be able to tell which these are until you actually begin posing questions. Many students find the following guide for writing analyses helpful. The third entry assumes you've made a preliminary analysis and are choosing to incorporate the most revealing insights into your essay.

- Introduce and summarize the activity or object to be analyzed. Whatever parts of this activity or object you intend to analyze should be mentioned here.
- Introduce and summarize the key definition or principle that will form the basis of your analysis.
- Analyze. Systematically apply elements of this definition or principle to parts of the activity or object under study. Part by part, discuss what you find.
- Conclude by reviewing all the parts you have analyzed. To what extent has your application of the definition or principle helped you to explain how the object works, what it might mean, or why it is significant?

3 Applying techniques for writing analyses

The most common error in writing analyses is to present your readers with a summary only. Summary is naturally a *part* of analysis: you will need to summarize the object or activity you are examining and the principle or definition with which you are working, if this is not known to your readers. You must then take the next step and *apply* the principle or definition, using it as an investigative tool.

ACROSS THE CURRICULUM

Writing an Analysis

Faculty and students across the curriculum write analyses. Consider the opening paragraphs of an article by political scientist Sharon D. Wright.* Observe how Wright (1) provides background information on the topic to be analyzed (voter support for a presidential candidate) and (2) introduces a principle ("the rational voter model") that will guide her analysis. You will follow similar organizational steps in writing analyses for courses across the curriculum.

Background information on topic to be analyzed

In 1988 and 1992, Lenora Branch Fulani, a developmental psychologist and political activist, cast historic bids for the presidency. In 1988, she became the first African American and the first woman candidate to be placed on the ballot in all 50 states and in the District of Columbia. She was also the first Black woman to qualify for over $1 million in federal primary matching funds. Unlike prior African American presidential candidates, Shirley Chisolm and Jesse Jackson, Fulani had no affiliation with the Democratic party. Her candidacy was sponsored by the New Alliance Party, an independent political organization. In 1988, one major purpose of her presidential bid was to challenge the legal barriers to independent candidates, who were excluded from presidential debates and had to collect a substantial number of petition signatures in order to be placed on state ballots. In addition, she wanted to point out the necessity of voting for independent contenders, even if they were unlikely to be victorious, as a way to end the Democratic party's exploitation of the Black vote. In 1992, she only received approximately 75,000 votes, but actively favored the independent candidacy of Ross Perot. Fulani asked citizens to vote independent, either for herself or for Perot, whom she pledges to endorse in the 1996 presidential election.

Discipline focus: political science

This research will first describe the philosophy of Lenora Fulani and the New Alliance Party. It will then apply the rational voter model developed by Barzel and Silberberg (1973), in order to examine the research question, What factors influenced voter support for Lenora Fulani in the 1988 presidential election? The data used in this study were collected from 1988 and 1992 issues of the *Congressional Quarterly Almanac.* According to Barzel and Silberberg, . . .

Principle to guide the analysis

*Sharon D. Wright is an assistant professor of Pan African Studies at the University of Louisville. Her article "Outside Corporate America and Inside the Real Mainstream: The Presidential Bids of Lenora Fulani," appeared in the *Western Journal of Black Studies* 19.1 (1995).

EXERCISE 3

Individual responses

LOOKING AHEAD

You may want to remind students that whenever they write a research paper, which will be often, they will need to synthesize source materials. Synthesis is a key element of research. Students can anticipate the research papers they will write later in the semester or in another semester by turning to Chapters 33–36.

TEACHING IDEAS

You can help demystify synthesis by introducing the topic with this activity. Ask students to list all the factors they considered when deciding on a college. Students should be as thorough as possible in their list making. They should then study their lists and write a paragraph that recreates their decision making. Which factors weighed more or less heavily in the decision? How did students blend competing factors? Next, discuss with students how they synthesized often disparate information to reach an informed decision. In nonacademic contexts, students synthesize information all the time. In an analogous way, synthesis of academic print sources involves a blending of information. Students will learn to take intuitive skills that they already possess and apply them in new ways.

EXERCISE 3

Choose one of the three lines of analysis presented at the start of 2c-1—approaches to analyzing the classic film *The Wizard of Oz* from a psychological, political, or literary view. Apply one of these analytic schemes to the movie, identifying key elements of the movie that can be explained in terms of the analytic principles offered.

2d Writing a synthesis

A **synthesis** is a written discussion in which you gather and present source materials according to a well-defined purpose. In the process of writing a synthesis you answer these questions: (1) Which authors have written on my topic? (2) In what ways can I link the work of these authors to one another and to my own thinking? (3) How can I best use the material I've gathered to create a discussion that supports *my* views? The following assignment calls for synthesis:

SOCIOLOGY This semester we have read a number of books, articles, and essays on the general topic of marriage: its legal, religious, economic, and social aspects. In a 5-page paper, reflect on these materials and discuss the extent to which they have helped to clarify, or confuse, your understanding of this "sacred institution."

The word *synthesis* does not appear in this assignment; nonetheless, the professor is asking students to gather and discuss sources. Note the importance of the writer here. Given multiple sources, a dozen students working on this sociology assignment would produce a dozen different papers; what would distinguish one paper from the next and make each uniquely valuable is the *particular* insights of each student. You are the most important source in any synthesis. However much material you gather into a discussion, your voice should predominate.

No synthesis is possible without a critical, comprehensive reading of sources. The quality of a synthesis is tied directly to the quality of prior reading. You have the best possible chance of producing a meaningful synthesis when you have read sources to understand (1e), respond (1f), evaluate (1g), and synthesize (1h). At one point or another, a synthesis will draw on all your skills of critical reading and writing; synthesis therefore represents some of the most sophisticated and challenging writing you will do in college.

Ensuring that your voice is heard

When writing a synthesis, avoid letting sources dominate a discussion unless you are being asked to write a literature review (see 39c-2—though even in this case your point of view dominates in that you select the articles to be discussed and determine the principles that organize discussion). In its most extreme form, the error of allowing sources to dominate leads to a series of summaries in which the writer, making no attempt at merging sources, disappears. The problem can be avoided if you remember that a synthesis should draw on your insights first, and only then on the insights of others. *A paper organized as a series of summaries of separate sources, introduced by a statement such as "Many authors have discussed topic X," is* not *a synthesis because it makes no attempt to merge ideas.*

Do Not Become Invisible in Your Papers

The DANGER signs:

1. Your paragraphs are devoted wholly to the work of the authors you are synthesizing.
2. Virtually every sentence introduces someone else's ideas.
3. The impulse to use the first-person *I* never arises.

Instead of writing a string of paragraphs organized around the work of others, write paragraphs organized around your own statements. In the context of a paper on advertising, a discussion organized as summaries of separate sources would leave you invisible. Generally, a statement such as the one that follows indicates that the writer will never appear.

> Several authors have discussed the topic of advertising.

This statement, and the paper likely to be built on it, is *source* based and exhibits all the danger signals mentioned in the preceding box. By contrast, a paper in which the author is present will show an active, interested mind engaged with the reading material and headed in some clear direction, with a purpose:

> The topic of advertising is guaranteed to generate debate whenever it is discussed. It is rare to find a person who does not have strong, specific opinions about advertising and its effects on our culture.

This statement is *writer* based. The writer's purpose and direction are made known, and we sense the reading material will not overshadow the writer. If you find source materials monopolizing your work, reexamine your thesis and make it into a writer-based statement.

1 Setting goals for writing a synthesis

Your goal in writing a synthesis is to create and participate in a discussion, joining your views on a topic to the views of others. Specifically, you want to do the following:

- Understand your purpose for writing.
- Define your topic and your thesis (see 3d).

ADDITIONAL EXERCISE E

ACROSS THE CURRICULUM Assume that you are writing papers about the topics that underlie the statements below. The statements are tentative opening lines, but the writer is invisible. Rewrite each statement so that the writer's voice can be heard. (Don't worry about whether or not you'd be able to follow through on the statement; the exercise is designed only to give you practice in making your voice heard among all the sources.)

1. Some corporate executives advocate a hierarchical model, with decisions being made at the top; others espouse a model in which decisions are made collaboratively.
2. Four top analysts have four different opinions on how long the current recession will last.
3. While one group of researchers believes that obesity is the result of specific eating disorders, another group cites studies indicating that heredity is responsible for obesity.
4. Critical opinion is divided on who was the best filmmaker of the eighties: Woody Allen, Francis Ford Coppola, or Bruce Beresford.

TEACHING IDEAS

ACROSS THE CURRICULUM Good writing in any discipline shows the writer's commitment to a topic. You might ask students to turn to the student papers in the cross-curricular chapters of the handbook (37–39). Alternately, students could bring to class a journal article or essay that they are reading for another class. The assignment could be: How does the author show his or her commitment to the topic in this selection? Where do you see evidence of the writer's commitment? In an effective synthesis, sources are drawn together for a purpose that is important to the writer. Students can benefit from seeing that writers across the curriculum are committed to their ideas.

- Locate the work of others who have written on this topic and read to understand, respond, and evaluate.
- Forge relationships among sources; link the thinking of others to your own thinking.
- Create a discussion governed by your views; draw on sources as contributors to a discussion that you design and control.

TEACHING IDEAS

To illustrate how a researcher forges relationships among sources, you might bring to class notes you have gathered for one of your own research projects. Photocopy five or eight note cards and distribute them to the class. (You would bring the same, individual cards to class.) By distributing a paragraph you had written on this material, you could show students how you inferred relationships among notes drawn from different sources. You might then show students how this one paragraph fits into the larger scheme of a paper.

2 Understanding techniques for writing a synthesis

In writing a synthesis, you will at some point write partial summaries, evaluations, and analyses. Synthesis draws on these forms and is larger and more ambitious than any one of them: summary and evaluation treat single sources; analysis is limited to an application of one source (or set of ideas) to a second source; but synthesis merges sources and looks for larger patterns of relation.

Cross-referencing ideas

A synthesis organized by *ideas* shows that you are intellectually present and involved with the material you have gathered. To organize a paper by ideas, you must first divide the topic into the component parts that the various authors take up in their discussions. These component parts then become the key ideas around which you organize your paper. You can follow this method when your writing is based on library research. Cross-referencing is a necessary step in the process (see 1h-2); once you have identified a component part of a topic and cross-referenced authors' discussions, you are nearly ready to write. In response to Exercise 8 in Chapter 1, you worked on completing a note sheet. If you have not completed this assignment, do so now.

LOOKING AHEAD

See the student research paper in Chapter 35. There, students will see notecards from different sources juxtaposed and, on the facing page, a paragraph in the example research paper in which the writer synthesizes the information on those cards. The point to make here is that student writers will use their synthesis skills frequently; it's not an obscure skill they're learning, but a central one. In Chapter 35, they get to see this skill in operation.

Clarifying relationships among authors

Your cross-referenced notes enable you to lay out and examine what several authors have written about *particular* parts of a topic, in this case gender and technology. Working with what your sources say on a particular point, you can now forge relationships. Sources can be related in a variety of ways, but you will find that patterns emerge, which can be identified by asking several questions.

Which authors agree?
Which authors disagree?
Are there any examples in one source of statements made in another?
Can you offer any definitions?
Are any readings related by cause and effect?

Pose these questions (and others that occur to you) to get a conversation started among the particular parts of the topic you've identified. Ask: If these authors could talk to one another, what would they say—based on what they've written? What would *you* say to each of them? With whom do you agree? Why? Who seems right, or more authoritative? Take notes in response to these questions. When the time comes for writing, you may not use all your notes, but you will be prepared to launch a discussion in which you and your sources participate.

Many students find the following guidelines helpful when synthesizing source materials:

- Read sources on the topic; subdivide the topic into parts and infer relationships among parts, cross-referencing sources when possible.
- Clarify relationships among authors by posing questions (e.g., Which authors agree? Which authors disagree? etc.)
- Write a thesis (see 3d) that ensures your voice is heard and that allows you to develop sections of the paper in which you refer to sources.
- Sketch an outline of your paper (3d-4), organizing your discussion by *idea*, not by summary. Enter the names of authors into your outline along with notes indicating how these authors will contribute to your discussion.
- Write a draft of your paper and revise, following strategies discussed in Chapter 4.

3 Applying techniques for writing a synthesis

Since the writer's own views should predominate in a synthesis, no two syntheses, even if based on the same source materials, will be the same. Below is an example of how Lou Cassetta generated a conversation among his sources. In an early stage of note-taking, Lou listed his authors and cross-referenced the passages in which the authors commented on a particular point that interested him: the causes of number disparities between women and men in the sciences. Here, Lou summarizes each author's position on the point; he states what each would say to at least one other author; and then he responds personally to each author. (Lou is working with source materials from Chapter 1. See page numbers to locate the sources.)

What causes wide differences in numbers between women and men in the sciences?

COWAN (2): Cowan believes that social training explains the number differences between women and men in the sciences. She writes that "We have trained our women to opt out of the technological order as much as we have trained our men to opt into it."

KANTROWITZ (2): Kantrowitz opens with three explanations for the difference: culture, family, and schools—all social groups that teach gender roles. On this much Kantrowitz and Cowan agree. But Kantrowitz refers to a study suggesting that men and women exhibit different scientific imaginations (acquired via learned behavior or innate difference—Kantrowitz doesn't say which). Kantrowitz says differences may be useful. Cowan and Healy see differences as proof of sexism.

LEFTON (7): Lefton reports that differences exist between men and women, though research hasn't identified these; but he also views learning as "far more potent in establishing and maintaining sex-role stereotypes." Lefton and Kantrowitz leave room for some explanation of numbers in the sciences besides social training—which I think makes sense.

HEALY (10): Healy agrees entirely with Cowan that training accounts for the sex-role differences we see in the sciences. She and Cowan share the assumption that men and women are identical, intellectually, and that sexism alone explains the different numbers in the workplace.

LOU CASSETTA: I'm not looking for reasons to justify the one-sided numbers in the sciences. Sexism *is* a problem. But it seems only logical to suggest that biology plays some role in shaping a man's or a woman's intellect—and can have some influence on the type of science (*not* the quality of science) that each does. Lefton and Kantrowitz at least allow for the possibility. Cowan and Healy do not. I think that recognizing differences can lead to more productive use of our human resources.

Once you have narrowed a topic, identified its parts, and assembled sources that discuss these parts, you are in a position (as Lou Cassetta has demonstrated) to get a conversation started among your sources. The next step is to write your synthesis, which will require you to think critically not only about what other writers say on a topic but about what *you* have to say. Your voice, and your insights, are crucial elements in a synthesis; they are the elements that distinguish your efforts from those of others writing on the same topic. In Chapter 3, you will follow Lou Cassetta's progress as he draws relationships among sources and, just as importantly, draws on his own experience to create an effective essay.

EXERCISE 4

Individual answers

EXERCISE 4

You have seen Lou Cassetta's efforts to forge relationships among the selections on gender you've read in Chapters 1 and 2: Ruth Schwartz Cowan (2), Barbara Kantrowitz (2), Lester Lefton (7), and Bernadine Healy (10). Given that no two readers respond to a passage in quite the same way, take your turn in forging relationships among these sources. Identify two or three parts of the larger topic of gender-role socialization, which these authors discuss. Then follow Lou Cassetta's lead and generate a conversation among your sources.

PART II
WRITING AS A PROCESS

CHAPTER 3

Planning, Developing, and Writing a Draft

There may be as many strategies for planning, developing, and writing a draft as there are writers. Just the same, one principle holds true for all: a writer's thoughts take shape through the very act of writing and rewriting. That is, when you write you are also thinking; and when you revise you are thinking again about your topic and clarifying ideas for yourself—and, in the process, for your readers. Experienced writers produce a first draft and then revise at least once.

The three stages of writing are, broadly speaking, distinct. Different activities take place in each stage and the stages unfold more or less in this order: preparing to write, writing, and revising. But the stages also blend into each other. In the middle of a first draft, you may pause to revise an important sentence or paragraph, deciding to make one part of your document nearly finished while other parts remain rough or not yet written. In a first draft, you may discover new approaches to your topic and stop to write new lists and make new outlines, activities associated with preparing to write. Typically, writers loop backward and forward through the three stages of writing—several times for any one document. The process of writing is ***recursive***: it bends and it circles, and it is illustrated well with a wheel. (See the illustration on page 51.)

3a Discovering your topic, purpose, and audience

1 Understanding your topic

In both college and business, you can expect to be assigned topics for writing and to define topics for yourself. In either case, you will write most efficiently, and with greatest impact, when you write about what you know (or what you can learn in a reasonably brief time); when you find some way

KEY FEATURES

This chapter introduces students to the practical applications of critical thinking and reading with respect to the writing process. Students will come to understand that it is only through trying out various ideas in drafts that they can develop a clear understanding of just what they want to say in a paper. Both the recursive nature of the writing process and the notion that ideas develop and change during the course of that process are emphasized in this chapter. Particularly helpful is the metaphor of the "writing wheel," which allows students to visualize the essential unity of the entire writing process. The more traditional prewriting concepts of purpose, audience, idea generation, organization, drafting, revising, and the like are covered with a fresh perspective provided by the writing wheel metaphor. In addition, strategies for analyzing audience, generating ideas, narrowing theses, organizing material, and providing unity and coherence are introduced. The development of a student paper on gender and technology from general ideas through rough draft is provided to illustrate the various stages in the writing process. Lou Cassetta's paper—an analysis of gender equity in the computer field and its possible causes—progresses from journal entries, idea-generating strategies, outlines, and thesis development drafts, offering students

(continued)

clear, relevant examples of precisely the processes they will find themselves going through as they work on their own papers. Reinforcing this focus on students' own writing, exercises throughout the chapter encourage students to work through the writing process using *their own ideas* rather than simply responding to material generated by others.

ESL CUE

Writing as a process will be an unfamiliar concept to most international students, although teachers in some cultures do in fact "intervene" with help in the stages of composition. Many students, however, may expect instructors to be uninterested in the process, focusing only on the final product. It may be worth explaining clearly what a "draft" is supposed to be; what the responsibilities of teacher and student are in the improvement of early drafts; and what degree of dependency on the instructor (or tutors, peer editors, other readers) is proper. This last point is crucial if later plagiarism problems are to be forestalled.

REFERENCES

BERLIN, JAMES A. "Contemporary Composition: The Major Pedagogical Theories." *CE* 44 (1982): 765–77. Instructors should pay close attention to the particular process approach they employ in the classroom.

GEBHARDT, RICHARD. "Initial Plans and Spontaneous Composition: Toward a Comprehensive Theory of the Writing Process." *CE* 44 (1982): 620–27. Whether a linear or recursive composing model is used, all writers discover as they write.

HILLOCKS, GEORGE, JR. *Research on Written Composition.* Urbana: ERIC, 1986. 1–62. A survey of studies on the writing process since 1963.

LINDEMANN, ERIKA. *A Rhetoric for Writing Teachers.* 2nd ed. New York: Oxford UP, 1987. 11–30. A thorough overview of the complexities involved in the writing process (includes bibliography).

MACKENZIE, NANCY. "Teaching the Composing Process: A Three-Part Project." *The Writing Instructor* 1 (1982): 103–11. Practical classroom

An Overview of the Writing Process

Preparing to write

3a **Discovering your topic, purpose, and audience.** Know your topic and, if necessary, research it. Know your purpose for writing and use this to generate and organize ideas. Keep specific readers in mind as you write.

3b **Generating ideas and information.** Use strategies such as free-writing or reading to generate the ideas and information on the basis of which you will write your draft.

3c **Reviewing and categorizing ideas and information.** Review the material you have generated and group like ideas and information into categories.

3d **Writing a thesis and devising a sketch of your paper.** Study the material you have assembled and write a working thesis, a statement that will give your draft a single, controlling idea. Based on your thesis, sketch your draft.

Writing

3e **Writing a draft.** Prepare a draft of your document by adopting a strategy suited to your temperament. As you write, expect to depart from your sketch.

Revising

4a **Early revision: Rediscovering your main idea.** Refine your thesis; use it to revise for unity, coherence, and development. Be sure that the broad sections of your document and the sentences within your paragraphs are coherent and lead logically from one to the next.

4b **Later revision: Bringing your main idea into focus.** Read and clarify individual sentences. Correct problems with grammar, usage, punctuation, and spelling.

to own your topic; and when you sufficiently narrow your topic so that you can write on it fully within an allotted number of pages.

Know your topic.

Readers respect, and demand, authority in a writer. Since college writing and business writing are usually based on information or on the ideas of others, knowing your topic will usually require some investigation on your part. Students find the following sequence helpful as they investigate and refine their topics:

> **Read:** If you do not know a topic well, read sources and gather information: letters, photographs, articles, lecture notes—whatever is pertinent. Read until you understand all the aspects of your topic that you will be writing about.

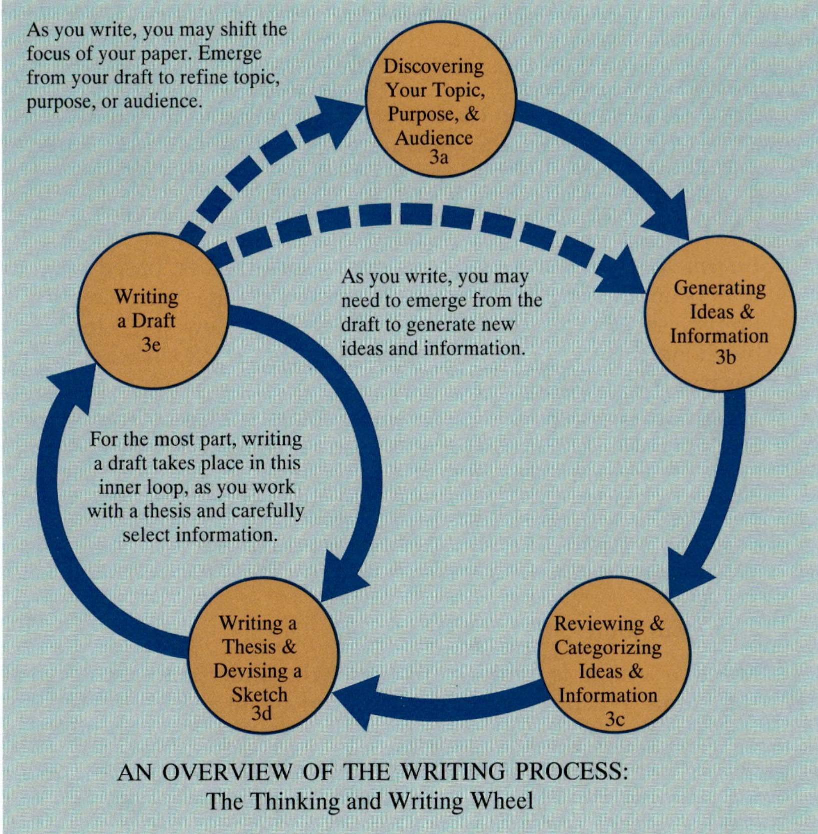
As you write, you may shift the focus of your paper. Emerge from your draft to refine topic, purpose, or audience.
Discovering Your Topic, Purpose, & Audience 3a
Generating Ideas & Information 3b
Reviewing & Categorizing Ideas & Information 3c
Writing a Thesis & Devising a Sketch 3d
Writing a Draft 3e
As you write, you may need to emerge from the draft to generate new ideas and information.
For the most part, writing a draft takes place in this inner loop, as you work with a thesis and carefully select information.
AN OVERVIEW OF THE WRITING PROCESS:
The Thinking and Writing Wheel

Interview: Locate people who are knowledgeable about your topic and interview them. Read sufficiently before the interview so that you do not pose questions that can be answered with basic research. Develop pointed questions that yield information and ideas unique to this source. (See 33g-3 for help on generating good questions.)

Reflect: Investigate your personal commitment to the topic. What experiences have you had that influence your thinking? How has your point of view been shaped by these experiences? Issues on which you might write may require that you take a stand. Know your position. (See 1b for strategies that can aid reflection.)

Illustration: Knowing Your Topic

Assignment: The Board of Trustees at your school has just voted to ban overnight guests in campus dormitory rooms. Write an essay responding to

strategies to make students aware of the writing process.

PERL, SONDRA. "Understanding Composing." *CCC* 31 (1980): 363–69. Emphasizes the recursive nature of composing.

SELZER, JACK. "Exploring Options in Composing." *CCC* 35 (1984): 276–84. Encourages experimentation to discover composing styles appropriate to individual students.

STOTSKY, SANDRA. "On Planning and Writing Plans—Or Beware of Borrowed Theories!" *CCC* 41 (1990): 57. Cautions that ambiguity with regard to key terms in research on planning can have serious implications for the teaching of writing.

TEDLOCK, DAVID. "The Case Approach to Composition." *CCC* 32 (1981): 253–62. Argues that cases provide useful assignments in writing courses.

TEACHING IDEAS

It's worth spending some time acquainting students with the writing wheel; the metaphor will recur throughout this chapter and Chapter 4, and it will be tremendously helpful to students as they develop their own writing processes. Simply asking students to comment on their perceptions of the several points on the wheel will get them thinking about what terms like "organize" and "thesis" really mean. It's also useful to ask them how their concept of the writing process would change if the metaphor were a writing *line* instead of a wheel.

TEACHING IDEAS

You might ask students to bring in a photocopy of one source article they are working with in a different discipline. Have students review the critical thinking categories in Chapter 1—being alert to differences, broadening contexts, challenging and being challenged, and forming and supporting opinions. Then ask students to read their articles to identify where and why authors make these "critical moves." Variation: you could supply the article for the entire class, in which follow-up discussions would be possible.

FOR DISCUSSION

Readers need to be secure about a writer's command of a subject, or the writer's authority is undermined. To reinforce this point, discuss with students occasions in which they were aware that someone did not know what he or she was talking about. After several students have volunteered stories, ask: "What were the signals that the speaker did not know his or her topic?" List these signals on the board. Then pose a second question: "What were your reactions to these speakers?" You can similarly list responses.

Examining the two lists, you and the class can discuss the ways a writer's not knowing his or her topic can sabotage an essay and prompt in readers a negative reaction.

REFERENCE

FLOWER, LINDA, and JOHN R. HAYES. "A Cognitive Process Theory of Writing." CCC 32 (1981): 365–87. Composing defined in terms of goal-oriented thinking processes.

the decision. Assume that you will submit your work to the college newspaper for publication.

Before writing:

Read: (1) Read the minutes of the trustees' meeting to determine exactly who supported the measure, who opposed it, and on what grounds. (2) In the library, locate as many college bulletins as you can to determine which other schools in the country have such a ban in place.

Interview: (1) Interview administrators and trustees, based on your understanding of their positions (from the minutes you have read). Prepare specific questions for each trustee interviewed. (2) Interview by phone directors of dormitories and students at schools where a similar ban is in effect.

Reflect: Recall experiences of entertaining guests in your dormitory room. Can you classify guests in any way: as family? friends from home? boyfriend/girlfriend? Does the category of guest affect how you, your friends, your parents, or the administration might feel about overnight visits?

Own your topic.

Effective writing is produced by those who understand *and* are committed to a topic. When you are committed, you are interested, and your interest will help to engage your readers. If you are assigned a topic that does not, at first, stimulate you, try these strategies:

- *Stretch the topic to fit your interests.* Redefine the assignment in such a way that it touches on your experience and at the same time is acceptable to your professor.
- *Identify a debate concerning the topic and choose sides.* Try to understand why the topic is debatable (if it is) and whom the topic affects, as well as the merits and limitations of each side of the debate. To stimulate interest, personalize the debate. Imagine yourself affected by it and take a position.
- *Talk with friends.* Sometimes informal conversations will help you to identify elements of a topic that interest you. Get a conversation going, listen, and participate. What aspects of the topic interest other people? Become engaged yourself.

Illustration: Owning Your Topic

Assignment: Select three advertisements that describe similar products. Which ad is most effective? Why?

Stretch the topic to fit your interests: (1) Compare ads for a product that you or someone you know buys or would like to buy. (2) Choose ads to study based on the product you would promote if given a large budget. (3) Choose a product category based on how you or someone you know has been *influenced* by a certain ad.

Identify a debate concerning the topic: Identify ads that have stirred public controversy or comment, such as ads that use children to sell products to other children. Begin with the debate and then find examples of multiple ads for a common product.

Talk with friends: Gather three ads for a product and show them to a small group of friends. Ask for their response. Get a discussion going by asking which ad is most effective—and why. Listen closely for comments that you might build on in an essay.

ACROSS THE CURRICULUM

Broadening the Context

Across the curriculum, both faculty and students create occasions to think critically by asking: *How are the details of what I'm studying an instance, or an example, of something larger?* Read the opening sentences of an article by media researcher Shelley Stamp Lindsey.* Observe how she takes a particular event, "the fight for female enfranchisement"—or the right to vote—and identifies it as a particular, interesting example of a larger issue: the changing images of womanhood as expressed in visual media such as posters and films. Whatever the discipline area, you can gain new, critical insight on your topic and possibly identify a new focus for writing and research by broadening the context.

Initial topic is women's suffrage

Much more than the vote was at stake in the campaign for women's suffrage. As the fight for female enfranchisement escalated in America during the early teens, the debate grew to encompass issues far beyond the ballot, or even the larger question of gender equality. Competing claims furnished a landscape where new ideals of feminine behavior could be tested—*and contested*—against women's increasing prominence in civic affairs. Indeed, female voting rights engaged a struggle over the very definition of modern womanhood.

Writer broadens topic to "modern womanhood"

With the image of femininity at stake, much of the debate was waged in *visual* terms, in posters, cartoons, pageants, marches, and ultimately on movie screens where conservatives and activists fought over appropriate manifestations of "womanliness." In fact a significant body of films on women's suffrage emerged as the debate escalated in the early teens, nearly a full decade before the passage of the Nineteenth amendment in 1920.

Discipline focus: study will be in visual arts

*Shelley Stamp Lindsey is an assistant professor of Film Studies at the University of California, Santa Cruz. Her article "*Eighty Million Women Want*—? Women's Suffrage, Female Viewers, and the Body Politic" appeared in *Quarterly Review of Film and Video* 16.1 (1995).

ADDITIONAL EXERCISE A

Beyond demonstrating command of a topic, a writer must also demonstrate a commitment to it, or risk losing the reader's interest. Invariably, the best writing in any field is done by those who for one reason or another "own" their topics; that is, the writers show a compelling interest in their work. Such commitment helps readers to become interested as well.

Ask students to bring to class a section of a book or an article from a journal or magazine. Students should be prepared to discuss the ways in which the author demonstrates a commitment to the subject. You might analyze either of two sample papers—by Lou Cassetta (4f) or Alison Tschopp (6g).

REFERENCE

ROHMAN, D. GORDON. "Pre-writing: The State of Discovery in the Writing Process." *CCC* 16 (1965): 106–12. Approaches invention from the perspective of meditation techniques.

ESL EXERCISE

Perceptions of time vary not just from person to person but from culture to culture. Address the following issues as a class exercise.

1. Discuss how late you can be for a serious appointment (a job interview, a visit to an academic counselor) before you are "too late" (you need the excuse of a major accident to get yourself back in good graces).
2. Make up a chart indicating how people from different cultures define "permissible lateness time." Your chart might need to allow for individual differences and for people who are early or late no matter what the rules of their culture.
3. Write up the results of your chart as a report.

ADDITIONAL EXERCISE B

Ask students to work with *any* writing assignment in your class or in another that they will be obliged to complete during the course of the semester. Working with that assignment, ask students to plan a strategy for knowing the topic, owning the topic, and narrowing the topic. Each student could present his or her plan in small groups. Presentations would turn into brainstorming sessions in which groupmates would make suggestions for knowing, owning, and narrowing a topic. You might advise students that group brainstorming sessions are commonplace in industry, where workers frequently turn to colleagues in an effort to generate and refine ideas.

ADDITIONAL EXERCISE C

Use the strategies outlined in this section to produce two appropriately narrow topics for each of the broad topics listed below:

1. popular music
2. environmentalism
3. women in business
4. parent-child relationships

REFERENCE

COE, RICHARD M. "If Not to Narrow, Then How to Focus: Two Techniques for Focusing." CCC 32 (1981): 272–77. Discusses value of techniques that emphasize focusing rather than simply narrowing a topic.

EXERCISE 1

Individual responses

EXERCISE 2

Individual responses

ESL EXERCISE

The "polite distance" we maintain with others is often described as a "bubble of space" used to keep strangers at a safe distance from us. Except in elevators and subways, people in North America keep a "nose-to-nose" distance of at least one foot (30.5 centimeters), and as much as two feet (61 centimeters). Address the following issues as a class exercise:

Restrict and define your topic.

Know how long your document is expected to be, and limit your writing accordingly. Avoid the frustration of choosing a broad topic (for example, the controversy over affirmative action) for a brief paper or report—a mistake that will guarantee a superficial product. The briefer your document is expected to be, the more narrowly directed your topic should be. Students find the following guidelines helpful as they work to restrict their topics:

- *Divide the topic into constituent parts.* Ask yourself: What are the component parts of this topic? What parts (or subtopics) do I know the most about? Can I link subtopics together in meaningful ways? In which subtopic am I most interested?
- *Ask a journalist's questions.* To restrict a topic and focus on a subtopic that interests you, pose questions, as appropriate: *who, what, where, when, why, how?* Often, a response to one or more of these questions can become the focus of a paper.

Illustration: Restricting and Defining Your Topic

Assignment: Choose a broad topic about which you know a great deal and subdivide it, in preparation for beginning work on an essay.

Broad topic: Gender roles in the computer field

Topic divided into parts:

More men than women choose to work with computers
Men treat computers like high-priced toys
Women use computers as a tool, not as a diversion
Men like to talk about technology
Women are underrepresented in the field of computers

Focused topic (a combination of the last two items above): The significance of "guy talk" about technology and how it excludes women

EXERCISE 1

List three topics with which you are intimately familiar and about which you can write for *public* view. Subdivide each topic into as many parts as you can. Eventually, you will select from these parts a focus for your paper.

EXERCISE 2

Of the topics you have narrowed in Exercise 1, which do you care most about? Write a brief paragraph in which you explain to yourself the *reasons* you are interested in one of these narrowed topics.

2 Identifying your purpose

Think of an object, an idea, an emotion, a relationship, or an institution: think of anything at all and you can probably explain it, argue about it, reflect on its significance, or make it the subject of an artistic work. There are four basic purposes or aims for writing: to *inform,* to *persuade,* to *express,* and to *entertain.* Since you will generally be asked to produce informative and persuasive pieces in college, this book is devoted primarily to these types of writing.

Informative writing

When writing to *inform,* your job is to present a topic and to explain, define, or describe it so that the reader understands its component parts, its method of operation, its uses, and so on. The following assignments call for informative writing.

LITERATURE Cite three examples of metaphor in *Great Expectations* and explain how each works.

CHEMISTRY Explain the chemical process by which water, when boiled, becomes steam.

PSYCHOLOGY What is "cognitive dissonance" and in what ways does it contribute to the development of personality?

What the reader already knows about the topic will in large part determine the level of language you use and the difficulty of the information that you present. A professor of aeronautical engineering discussing the flight of planes would use one vocabulary with engineering students and another vocabulary with an audience that had no technical background. (See 3a-3.)

Persuasive writing

When you write to *persuade,* your job is to change a reader's views about a topic. As with informative writing, the persuasive writer must carefully consider the reader's prior knowledge in order to provide the background information necessary for understanding. If you lacked a background in international business, for instance, you might not be persuaded about the need to master a foreign language in college. The person urging you to learn Spanish or Japanese would need to inform you, first, of certain facts and trends. As a persuasive writer, you will provide information both to establish understanding and to provide a base for building an argument. (See Chapter 6, which is devoted entirely to argumentation.) The following assignments call for persuasive writing.

ASTRONOMY Given limited government money available for the construction and updating of astronomical observatories, which of the projects discussed this semester deserve continued funding? Argue for your choices based on the types of discoveries you expect the various projects to make in the next five years.

SOCIOLOGY You have read two theories on emotions: the Cannon-Bard theory and the James-Lange theory. Which seems the more convincing to you? Why?

1. Discuss how many inches/centimeters your culture "recommends" as a polite distance to keep from others (you may have to experiment and measure this distance). What do people do when this rule is violated and the distance becomes either too close or too far?
2. Make up a chart indicating how people from different cultures define "politeness distance."
3. Write up the results of your chart as a report.

TEACHING IDEAS

Since students are often unaware of their own writing processes, much less the reasons for their choices, it's a good idea to ask them to keep a writer's log focusing on the details of their progress in composing a paper. If responses to the exercises dealing with their own writing can be kept separate from other exercises, they can trace the process they used to produce a final draft. While early log entries tend to be superficial (e.g., "I chose this topic because I know a lot about it"), gradually students begin to show more awareness of the reasons for their choices.

REFERENCES

KINNEAVY, JAMES L. *A Theory of Discourse.* Englewood Cliffs: Prentice, 1971. A classification of discourse based on purpose and emphasis.

KNOBLAUCH, C. H. "Intentionality in the Writing Process: A Case Study." *CCC* 331 (1980): 153–59. Argues that a writer's purpose shifts during the course of the writing process.

TEACHING IDEAS

The distinctions between informative and persuasive writing on the one hand and expressive writing on the other are in some sense arbitrarily drawn. Expressive writing can become an excellent means for a writer's understanding his or her personal commitment to a topic. The expressive writing may remain private, but some echo of it will often be found in an accomplished writer's public utterances. For this reason many teachers begin a writing sequence with a personal, expressive exercise. Students are encouraged to explore an idea

(continued)

privately. A second assignment might ask students to take a view articulated in an expressive, personal piece and to convert it to a public utterance—into an essay that informs or persuades.

EXERCISE 3

Individual responses

ESL EXERCISE

Different cultures have different rules for touching: who can touch whom, under what social circumstances, and what parts of the body are considered "private" or taboo for touching. Address the following issues as a class exercise.

1. Discuss how sex, age, authority, and family relationship figure in the rules about touching. Draw two stick figures on the board, label them "male" and "female," and indicate permissible touching areas.
2. Make up a chart indicating how people from different cultures define "permissible touching areas."
3. Write up the results of your chart as a report.

ADDITIONAL EXERCISE D

In order to get a better sense of the importance of audience awareness, it's sometimes helpful to analyze the audience for something that's already been written. Choose a magazine with which you're familiar, and after perusing several issues, write an analysis of the magazine's intended audience. For assistance, refer to the questions listed in 3a-3.

ADDITIONAL EXERCISE E

Ask students to consider three different occasions for writing about a single topic—waste disposal, and the need for recycling. First, students should assume that they are writing for housekeepers and are arguing for recycling. Second, students should assume that they are writing for factory managers and again are arguing for recycling. Third, students should assume that they are writing an Op-Ed piece for taxpayers and are arguing for recycling. How might the content of what is written, along with the rhetorical strategy, change as the audience changes?

MARKETING Select three ads that describe similar products. Which ad is most effective? Why?

Expressive writing and writing to entertain

Expressive writing—sometimes private and recorded as journal entries, sometimes written for public view—focuses on an exploration of your own ideas and emotions. When it is private, expressive writing can lead you to be more experimental, less guarded, perhaps even more honest than in a paper meant for others. When it is public, expressive writing will not be a journal entry, but rather an essay in which you reflect on your impressions. In many composition courses, the first part of a semester or an entire semester will be devoted to expressive writing. The least frequent purpose of academic writing is to *entertain.* Possibly you will write a poem, story, or play in your college career; and certainly you will read forms of writing that are intended to entertain readers. What makes a piece of writing entertaining is itself a subject for debate. It suffices to say here that writing to entertain need not be writing that evokes smiles.

Purposes for writing may overlap: in a single essay, you may inform, persuade, and entertain a reader. But if an essay is to succeed, you should identify a *single,* primary purpose for writing. Otherwise, you risk having a document that tries to do all things but does none well.

EXERCISE 3

Return to the writing you produced for Exercises 1 and 2, in which you divided broad topics into subtopics and then selected one narrowed topic as particularly interesting. This (or the topic suggested below) will become your topic for a five-page paper. Write a brief paragraph explaining your purpose for this paper. Although purposes may overlap to some extent, decide on one of two primary purposes for this paper: to inform *or* persuade your reader. If the topics in Exercises 1 and 2 left you uninspired, you may want to try this one:

The Board of Trustees at your school has just voted to ban overnight guests in campus dormitory rooms. Write an essay responding to the decision. Assume that you will submit your work to the college newspaper for publication. (For help getting started on this topic, see the illustration panel on page 51: "Knowing Your Topic.")

3 Defining your audience

Unless you are making a journal entry, you will write in order to communicate *with* someone: whether your intent is primarily to inform or persuade, you must know your audience since what you write will depend greatly on who will read it. With readers who understand your topic, you can assume a common base of knowledge. For instance, if you were preparing a paper on gene splicing for an audience of nonbiologists, you would be obliged to cover rudimentary concepts in language that nonspecialists would understand. In preparing a paper on the same topic for fellow biology majors, you would be free to use technical terms and to discuss higher-level material. Questions that you ask about an audience *before you write a first draft* can help you make decisions concerning your paper's content and level of language.

Writing for an unspecified audience

If your audience is not clearly specified, then regard your professor as the main reader. Do not think that because he or she is an expert on the topic of your paper you are relieved of developing points thoroughly. Many writing assignments are developed expressly to gauge what you know about a topic; in these instances, to omit information intentionally will prove disastrous.

Audience Needs Analysis

Pose these general questions, regardless of your purpose:

- Who is the reader? What is the reader's age, sex, religious background, educational background, and ethnic heritage?
- What is my relationship with the reader?
- What impact on my presentation—on choice of words, level of complexity, and choice of examples—will the reader have?
- Why will the reader be interested in my paper? How can I best spark the reader's interest?

If you are writing to inform, pose these questions as well:

- What does the reader know about the topic's history?
- How well does the reader understand the topic's technical details?
- What does the reader need to know? want to know?
- What level of language and content will I use in discussing the topic, given the reader's understanding?

If you are writing to persuade, pose both sets of questions above as well as the following:

- What are the reader's views on the topic? Given what I know about the reader (from the preceding questions), is the reader likely to agree with my view on the topic? to disagree? to be neutral?
- What factors are likely to affect the reader's beliefs about the topic? What special circumstances (work, religious conviction, political views, etc.) should I be aware of that will affect the reader's views?
- How can I shape my argument to encourage the reader's support, given his or her present level of interest, level of understanding, and beliefs?

REFERENCES

EDE, LISA, and ANDREA LUNSFORD. "Audience Addressed/Audience Invoked: The Role of Audience in Composition Theory and Pedagogy." *CCC* 35 (1984): 155–71. Suggests a theory of audience that balances a writer's power with effective communication of ideas to an audience.

FLOWER, LINDA. "Writer-Based Prose: A Cognitive Basis for Problems in Writing." *CE* 41 (1979): 19–37. Suggests that early drafts are written for the writer; only in later drafts do readers' needs become significant.

KROLL, BARRY. "Writing for Readers: Three Perspectives on Audience." *CCC* 35 (1984): 172–85. Overemphasis on audience can lead to neglect of a writer's voice, subject, or purpose.

LONG, RUSSELL C. "Writer-Audience Relationships: Analysis or Invention?" *CCC* 31 (1980): 221–26. Suggests strategies for creating audiences.

ONG, WALTER J., S. J. "The Writer's Audience Is Always a Fiction." *PMLA* 90 (1975): 9–21. Readers should be aware that writers invent their own audiences.

PARK, DOUGLAS. "Analyzing Audiences." *CCC* 37 (1986): 478–88. In order to invent an audience, writers must define the social context in which they are writing.

PFISTER, FRED R., and JOAN PETRICK. "A Heuristic Model for Creating a Writer's Audience." *CCC* 31 (1980): 213–20. The right questions can be helpful in creating audience.

ROTH, ROBERT G. "The Evolving Audience: Alternatives to Audience Accommodation." *CCC* 38 (1987): 47–55. Student writers, rather than focusing on the attributes of an audience, should concentrate instead on how to claim an audience's attention.

TEACHING IDEAS

Uninitiated as they are in academic discourse, students have a difficult time understanding why some of their writing (e.g., "Shakespeare, a famous writer of plays . . .") strikes their teachers as comically inappropriate. To help students understand the teacher's view, ask students to think about some nonacademic

(continued)

subject on which they are experts. Have them imagine a group of similarly experienced experts, and then ask them to write a paragraph that vastly underestimates the degree of knowledge shared by the expert audience. Then the students should analyze what is wrong with their paragraph, specifying the errors that signaled to the audience that the writer was inexperienced.

Make the jump, now, to academic expertise. As freshmen and sophomores, students will be inexperienced in their various subjects of study. Invariably, they will make the errors they constructed in their example paragraphs. The best beginning students can do is to be aware of the question: What sorts of things do writers say or not say in this discipline? Student writers may be unable to answer the question, but it will help to keep them sensitive to the conventions of various disciplines. Entering a course with this sensitivity should prove a useful stance for any student.

GROUP ACTIVITY

Questions about how much to tell the audience should be particularly relevant to students taking introductory courses in areas other than composition. Dividing students into small groups, ask them to choose one introductory course and answer the following questions about it: What key terms, concepts, and names did you learn for the first time in this course? As the course continued, what terms, concepts, and names became so familiar that you no longer needed explanation? How are those terms, concepts, and names treated in the text as they become more familiar? In the instructor's lectures? In what situations do you find it necessary to explain or identify those terms, concepts, and names? Why do you have to explain them sometimes?

EXERCISE 4

Individual responses

ESL EXERCISE

Interview at least four American students about teacher expectations and classroom behavior. Write a short paper contrasting their attitudes of what is proper and improper with

When Does Your Audience Need to Know More?

Consider these points when deciding whether your audience needs to know more about a key term or person.

- Major personalities referred to in textbooks or in lectures will help constitute the general, shared knowledge of a discipline. In all cases, *refer to people in your papers either by their* last *names or by their first* and *last names.* Do not identify "giants of a field" with explanatory tags like *who was an important inventor in the early part of the twentieth century.*
- Terms that have been defined at length in a textbook or lecture also constitute the general, shared knowledge of a discipline. Once you have understood these terms, use them in your papers—but do not define them. Demonstrate your understanding by using the terms accurately.
- The same people and terms not requiring definition in an academic context may well need to be defined in a nonacademic one. Base decisions about what information to include in a paper on a careful audience analysis.

Assume that the professor functions as an expert editor who will review your paper before passing it on to another reader. This second reader is *not* an expert on your topic and must therefore rely fully on your explanation. Assume that this reader is skeptical and neutral regarding your topic. The reader will hear you out, but will probe with questions and will require that you develop general statements with specific illustrations and that you defend any assertions needing support.

EXERCISE 4

Return to the topic you selected in Exercise 3, where you wrote a paragraph explaining your purpose for a proposed five-page paper. Working with your topic and your purpose (to inform or persuade), answer the questions in the Audience Needs Analysis box three times, once for each of three different audiences: a friend at another school, your parents, and some other audience of your choosing. Select one of these audiences as the one to whom you will direct your paper.

4 Analyzing topic, purpose, audience—and the writing occasion

Each new writing project constitutes a distinct *occasion for writing* and requires that you understand anew the relationship of topic, purpose, and audience. As a writer, you will analyze each occasion and decide on the tone and the register you will adopt.

Tone is a writer's general attitude toward the reader and the subject. Through an accumulation of signals, some subtle and others not, readers can tell whether you are interested in your topic and whether you are committed, engaged, humble, proud, irritable, irreverent, or defensive. Appreciate that a paper *will* have, and cannot help but have, a characteristic tone. English offers numerous ways of saying the same thing. For example, the most simple request can be worded to reflect a variety of tones.

May I have the salt?	Give me that salt!	Salt!
Pass the salt.	Pass the salt, please.	

For every writing occasion, choose a tone that you think is appropriate to your topic or that, in your judgment, your readers will think appropriate. Mismatching tone and topic can create problems. Imagine a writer's discussing some grim event with a lighthearted, devil-may-care tone. Readers would surely turn away, and thus the purpose of communication would be defeated.

Register is the degree of formality in your writing. In adopting a **formal register,** you adhere to all the rules and conventions of writing expected in the professional and academic worlds. Formal writing is precise and concise; it avoids colloquial expressions, and it is thorough in content and tightly structured. The **informal register** is common in personal correspondence and journals, and tends to be conversational. Word choice is freely colloquial and structure need not be as tightly reasoned as in a formal paper. Occasional lapses in grammar, usage, spelling, or punctuation matter little in personal correspondence and not at all in personal journal writing. The **popular register** is typical of most general interest magazines. It adheres to all conventions of grammar, usage, spelling, and punctuation; it is also carefully organized. The language, however, is more conversational than that found in formal writing. Heavy emphasis is placed on engaging readers and maintaining their interest. For suggestions on matching tone and register to the writing occasion, see 21e on the use of formal English.

Versatile writers can shift register and tone as the writing occasion requires. You can inform or persuade a reader in *any* register or tone, but once

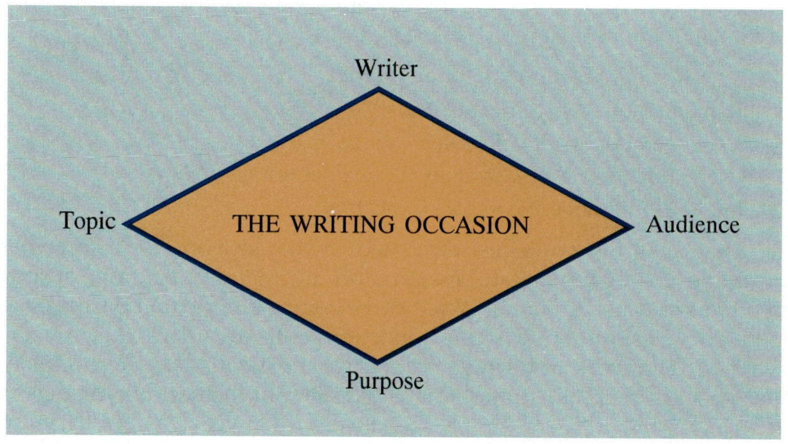

the attitudes of students from your culture. Speculate about the reasons for such differences.

FOR DISCUSSION

Since it's usually helpful to use examples relevant to students' own experiences, consider discussing tone in the following way. Ask students to think about situations in which they consciously altered their tone because of purpose or audience. To stimulate discussion, you might suggest the tone adopted by the student asking an instructor for an extension on a paper, or the different tone used in relating the story of a dangerous white-water rafting expedition to a concerned parent and to an interested friend. As students become aware of how often they adopt a particular tone in their everyday lives, it should become easier for them to consider tone in their academic writing.

ADDITIONAL EXERCISE F

Ask students to use the illustration on this page to diagram the changing writing occasion in Exercise 5. Students should be able to see that topic, writer, and audience remain the same. The writer's purpose changes from one letter to the next.

LOOKING AHEAD

See 34e-2 on paraphrasing sources. One motive for paraphrase is to retain the content ideas of a source piece but to alter the tone, which a writer might find inappropriate for his or her paper. Note that the example selection that is paraphrased is later used in the student research paper. See the paper in Chapter 35, paragraph E (along with facing page discussion of the paraphrase).

BACKGROUND

See *Teaching College Writing,* by Maggy Smith (Boston: Allyn & Bacon, 1995): "Prewriting: Preparing Students to Write," 65–102. The discussion is thorough and filled with practical advice for shaping in-class discussions about the early stages of the writing process. Smith specifically addresses the writing occasion on 67–73.

chosen, register and tone should be used consistently (21e). The diagram on page 59 suggests the need for a balanced, four-way relationship among the basic elements of the writing occasion.

EXERCISE 5

Write a series of three brief letters to a mail-order business. Ask why you have not received the computer software you ordered and paid for. The letters should show a change in tone, moving from a neutral inquiry in the first letter to annoyed concern in the second to controlled anger in the third. In each case, maintain a formal tone. Avoid using colloquial expressions.

EXERCISE 6

Given the audience and the purpose you have chosen for the paper you are planning (see your answers to Exercises 3 and 4), decide on the tone and register you should adopt.

3b Generating ideas and information

It is not easy to generate ideas about a topic. In most academic writing, a combination of efforts is usually needed: you will reflect on your own experience and think a topic through to get ideas for writing; and you will conduct research in a library, in a lab, or in the field. At times you may stare at your topic, a word on a blank page, and feel as though there is *nothing* to write about. However, there are proven strategies for generating ideas and information.

When you are generating material, try to put the critic in you to sleep and give yourself the freedom to have ideas—bad ones as well as good ones. As a writer, you will need to be both creator and critic. At this early stage in the process, avoid being too hard on yourself lest you dampen the creative impulses you will need to write a good paper. Create—and then *later* evaluate and choose. As you review the various strategies for generating ideas and information, bear in mind this "User's Manual":

- No one method will work for all topics.
- Some methods may not suit your style of discovery.
- Some methods work well when combined.
- Move quickly to a new strategy if one does not work.
- Tell your internal critic to take a vacation.

The invention strategies discussed in this section can complement each other; you will generate one type of information using one strategy and other types using others. When you examine *all* the material you have generated, you should find ample opportunities to advance to the next stage of writing. The work of a single student, Lou Cassetta (whose completed paper appears in 4f), illustrates how you might put the various strategies to use.

EXERCISE 5

Individual responses

EXERCISE 6

Individual responses

REFERENCES

CORBETT, EDWARD P. J. *Classical Rhetoric for the Modern Student.* New York: Oxford UP, 1965. 94–174. Discussion of classical schemes for invention.

FLOWER, LINDA S., and JOHN R. HAYES. "Problem-Solving Strategies and the Writing Process." *CE* 39 (1977): 442–48. Techniques to assist in development of ideas.

LAUER, JANICE. "Issues in Rhetorical Invention." *Essays on Classical Rhetoric and Modern Discourse.* Eds. Robert J. Connors, Lisa S. Ede, and Andrea A. Lunsford. Carbondale: Southern Illinois UP, 1984. 127–39. Assumptions writers make about the composing process inform the strategies used for prewriting.

YOUNG, RICHARD. "Recent Developments in Rhetorical Invention." *Teaching Composition: 12 Bibliographic Essays.* Ed. Gary Tate. Fort Worth: Texas Christian UP, 1987. 1–38. A survey of research on invention since 1973.

LOOKING BACK—AND AHEAD

The student essay, which is in the process of being developed in this chapter, actually began to take shape with the reading selections presented and discussed in Chapters 1 and 2—specifically, with the pieces by Cowan, Kantrowitz, and Healy. Lou Cassetta's responses to these pieces helped to generate ideas for his essay, the first draft of which is located at the end of Chapter 3 and the second and final drafts of which you will find in Chapter 4.

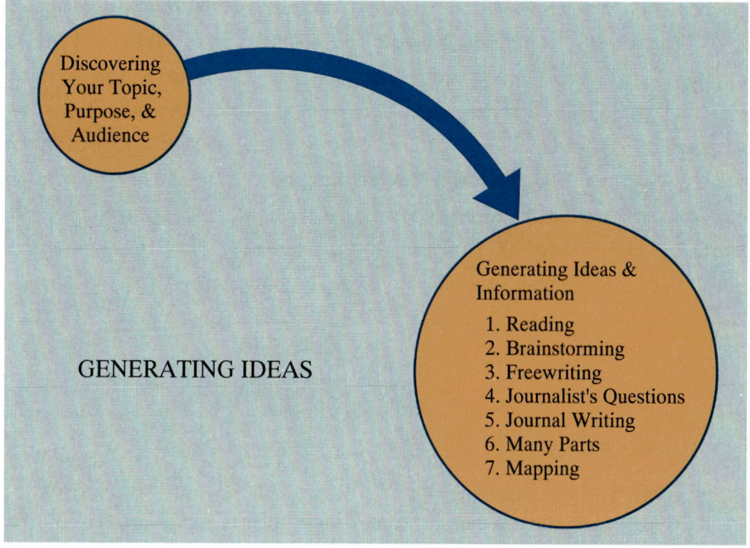

1 Reading

Most academic writing is based on reading. Early in the writing process, when you are still not precisely sure what your topic will be, reading can be an excellent stimulus. Even if you do not plan to depend heavily on sources in a paper, reading about your tentative topic will help you to generate ideas. Source materials may present compelling facts or strongly worded opinions with which to agree or disagree. Above all, read to *respond.* Be alert to your responses and jot them down; they may later become important to your paper. (See Chapter 1 and the discussion of strategies for reading effectively.) If you are writing a paper that will not draw heavily on sources, use your reading mainly as a stimulus. If you are writing a research report, read to generate the information you will then use to write the paper. In this case, realize that you will need to cite sources (see Chapter 36).

At the time Lou Cassetta was preparing to write, he was enrolled in an introductory psychology course. He browsed through the textbook and found that material on gender roles sparked his interest. Lou's tentative topic was Gender Roles and Technology. Lou made the following notes, based on readings from his textbook and other sources.

Illustration: Lou Cassetta's Paper

READING

According to my textbook, society creates most of the behavioral differences between men and women. Nevertheless, research

TEACHING IDEAS

ACROSS THE CURRICULUM One of the most difficult things to get students to understand about higher education (especially liberal arts education) is the interrelatedness of their courses. Occasionally students have been known to apologize for introducing irrelevant material when they make a connection between what's being covered in one course and an issue that arises in another course. A brief discussion of the relevance of their courses to topics they've chosen to write about will help them shed that misconception.

REFERENCES

See two reprinted articles on the composing process in James C. McDonald, *The Allyn & Bacon Sourcebook for College Writing Teachers.* Boston: Allyn & Bacon, 1996: Patricia Bizzell, "Composing Processes: An Overview"; and W. Ross Winterowd, "Rhetorical Invention."

```
still has not been able to pinpoint any gender-specific intellec-
tual differences. Many women tend to avoid computers, while a
great number of men treat computers as an enjoyable and exciting
diversion. In my opinion, women do not avoid computers because of
any inherent genetic instruction, but it is society that tells
them to pay little attention to technology. Women who do choose
to explore technology do not treat machines the way men do. Their
insight in the field of computers may prove to be very helpful,
if they are given the chance to express themselves.
```

2 Brainstorming

The object of **brainstorming** is to write quickly and, once finished, to return to your work with a critical eye. Place your topic at the top of a page, and then list any related phrase or word that comes to mind. Set a time limit of five or ten minutes, and list items as quickly as you can. All items are legitimate for your list, since even an allegedly bad idea can spark a good one. To brainstorm in a small group, a technique that allows the ideas of one person to build on those of another, write your topic on a board or sheet of easel paper. (If you have no topic, see "Freewriting," 3b-3.) Sit in a circle and ask each member of the group to offer two or three words or phrases for your list. Work around the circle a second time, asking each member to add another one or two ideas, based on an item already mentioned. Finally, open the floor to anyone who can add more ideas. As a ground rule, urge each group member to understand that all ideas are equally useful.

After you have generated your list, group related items and set aside items that do not fit into a grouping. Groupings with the greatest number of items indicate areas that should prove fertile in developing your paper. Save the results of your brainstorming session for your next step in the planning process: selecting, organizing, and expanding information.

Illustration: Lou Cassetta's Paper

BRAINSTORMING

```
                Men discussing computers
need for speed--men want the newest and fastest machines
jargon--men like to know the buzzwords
knowledge--men like to impress each other with facts and figures
learning--find out about the latest information by word of mouth
exclusion--only the well versed can "talk shop"
```

ADDITIONAL EXERCISE G

To emphasize just what it is a writer does and how a writer works, you might ask students to interview someone else who writes, either for work or for personal reasons, and ask how that person gets her/his ideas. They might speak with a professor, a parent or other relative, a professional with whom they are in contact (health care providers, employers, etc.), or someone else that they can identify and phone with relative ease. They should then write two to three pages that describe the person's writing, and also how that person generates ideas that are indeed "worth committing oneself to" and worth "a reader's attention." Results of these interviews should be shared in class discussion.

```
advice--everybody has some to give
bonding--men create close friendships through these
    conversations
opinions--opinions about products often overshadow facts
excess--some men go too far and spend or do too much
women--are not invited to (are not interested in?) these
    conversations
future--high hopes for future machines
sharing--helping friends with their own computers
```

Lou grouped his list as follows. The question mark denotes the "left-over" category, which includes items Lou did not know how to group.

Men discussing computers

Negatives	Positives	?
exclusion	knowledge	need for speed
opinions	learning	jargon
excess	advice	future
women	bonding	
	sharing	

3 Freewriting and focused freewriting

Freewriting is a technique to try when you are asked to write but have no topic. Think for a moment about the subject area in which you have been asked to write. Recall lectures or chapters read in textbooks. Choose a broad area of interest and then start writing for some predetermined amount of time—say, five or ten minutes. Alternately, you can write until you have filled a certain number of pages (typically one or two). As you write, do not stop to puzzle over word choice or punctuation. Do not stop to cross words out because they do not capture your meaning. Push on to the next sentence. Freely change thoughts from one sentence to the next, if this is where your thinking takes you. Once you have reached your time limit or page allotment, read over what you have done. Circle ideas that could become paper topics. To generate ideas about these specific topics, you may then try a more focused strategy for invention: brainstorming, focused freewriting, or any of the other strategies that will be discussed in later sections.

Focused freewriting gives you the benefits of freewriting, but on a *specific* topic. The end result of this strategy is the same as brainstorming, and so the choice of invention strategies is one of style: do you prefer making lists or writing sentences? Begin with a definite topic. Write for five or ten minutes; reread your work; and circle any words, phrases, or sentences

REFERENCES

Elbow, Peter. *Writing with Power: Techniques for Mastering the Writing Process.* New York: Oxford UP, 1981. Thorough description of the uses of freewriting.

—. *Writing without Teachers.* New York: Oxford UP, 1973. One of the earliest discussions of the value of freewriting.

Reynolds, Mark. "Make Free Writing More Productive." *CCC* 39 (1988): 81–82. Provides guidelines for generating useful freewriting.

Southwell, Michael G. "Free Writing in Composition Classes." *CE* 38 (1977): 676–81. Freewriting can be used to strengthen skills and to develop formal papers.

that look potentially useful. Draw lines that link circled words, and make notes to explain the linkage. Then clarify these linkages on a separate sheet of paper. The result will be a grouping of items, some in sentence form, that looks like the result of brainstorming. Save your work for the next step in planning: selecting, organizing, and expanding information.

Following is a portion of Lou's focused freewrite on the topic "talking shop."

TEACHING IDEAS

Discuss with students how Lou Cassetta's focused freewriting helped him develop a sense of coherence about his own ideas. Point out for students the three stages of thinking in evidence on this page: first, Cassetta freewrites; second, he circles what he thinks are related thoughts; third, he takes a large step and actually relates these thoughts, organizing them into a pattern that he can use to begin thinking in a more focused way about his topic. Urge students to be aware of similar processes taking place in themselves as they freewrite and attempt to identify specific ideas that can turn into the subject of a paper.

Illustration: Lou Cassetta's Paper

FOCUSED FREEWRITING

I have always talked shop. I have had many conversations about machines and technology. It started with automobiles. I tried to learn as much as I could about cars, and used my knowledge to impress and to bond. Men definitely bond when talking about machines. I often talked to the same people about both cars and computers. It's <u>all the same</u> really. The need for speed--I've got it. Although I've never had the latest or best computer, I always knew the latest developments in the industry. Some people went to the other extreme. They not only knew about the latest developments in the industry, they went out and bought them. I'm glad I'm not rich, or I'd have a lot of outdated computers lying around by now. The industry changes so quickly. That's what makes it so exciting. Exciting for men, at least. Women never chimed in about computers and cars. That's guy talk. It may not be "locker room" profanity, but women count themselves out of it just the same. Computers and cars are "toys for the boys" and women count themselves out at a very early age. It really shouldn't be that way, but men have dominated the computer world so much, that women are not even given a chance to offer their opinions.

Lou organized his freewriting into these categories:

<u>Talking Shop</u>
-male bonding
-cars and computers same
-need for speed

<u>Exciting for Men</u>
-"toys for the boys"
-men have dominated
-women aren't given chance (or aren't interested)

ESL EXERCISE

Select a classmate from a different language, cultural, or national group. Write down a series of questions to help you find out what your classmate's career goals are and what past experiences led to those goals. Ask your classmate the questions. Then write a short biography focused on those past events which brought your classmate to where she or he is today. Your audience will be a third classmate to whom you are introducing your new friend.

4 The journalist's questions

You have read or heard of the journalist's questions: *who, what, when, where, why,* and *how.* In answering the questions, you can define, compare, contrast, or investigate cause and effect. Again, the assumption is that by thinking about parts you will have more to write about than if you focused on a topic as a whole. The journalist's questions can help you to restrict and define a topic (see 3a-1), giving you the option to concentrate, say, on any three parts of the whole: perhaps the *who, what,* and *why* of the topic. Under the topic of mapping (3b-7), you will find Lou Cassetta's notes made in response to three of the journalist's questions.

5 Journal writing

You might keep a journal in conjunction with your writing course. A *journal* is a set of private, reflective notes that you keep, in which you describe your reactions to lectures, readings, discussions, films, current events —any topic touching on your course work. A journal borrows from both diary writing and course notebooks.

- As in a diary, your journal entries are private, reflective, and "safe" in the sense that you know no one is looking over your shoulder; thus, you are free to experiment with ideas and to express your thoughts honestly without fear of consequences.
- Unlike a diary, a journal focuses on matters relating to your course work and not on matters of your private life, unless such observations tie in with your course work.

Journal writing gives you an opportunity to converse with yourself in your own language about what you have been studying. You pose questions, develop ideas, reflect on readings, speculate and explore, and try to pinpoint confusions. The more you write, the more you clarify what you know and, equally important, what you do not know. The language of your journal entries should reflect your voice: use the words, expressions, and rhythms of vocabulary that you use when you chat with friends.

Punctuation is not important as long as you can reread your journal entries. Periodically review your journal entries, looking for ideas in which you seemed particularly interested. As with freewriting, use these ideas as the basis for a more focused strategy of invention.[1]

---

[1]Discussion of journal writing here is based on Toby Fulwiler, ed., *The Journal Book* (Portsmouth, NH: Boynton/Cook-Heinemann, 1987) 1–7.

REFERENCE

WASHINGTON, EUGENE. "WH-Questions in Teaching Composition." *CCC* 28 (1977): 54–56. Techniques for generating information using journalist's questions.

TEACHING IDEAS

Students who have never used journals before are often at a loss as to what to write; the result is often either a series of mini-essays clearly aimed at a professorial audience or a tedious, unproductive diary. It's a good idea to check journal entries periodically in the first few weeks of class to let students know if they're making good use of the journal as a writer's tool. Asking students with particularly good journals for permission to reproduce sample entries can help those who haven't yet "got the hang of it." (Privacy is a problem here, but it can be dealt with. Always ask permission; always maintain student anonymity; if possible, distribute sample entries to students in a different class; and ideally, build a collection of sample entries to be used in subsequent years.)

REFERENCES

BERTHOFF, ANNE E. *Forming/Thinking/Writing: The Composing Imagination.* Rochelle Park, NJ: Hayden, 1978. Invaluable information on the role of journals in the composing process.

BLAU, SHERIDAN. "Invisible Writing: Investigating Cognitive Processes in Composition." *CCC* 34 (1983): 297–312. Suggests freewriting with an empty pen, removing temptation to review what's already written.

FULWILER, TOBY. "The Personal Connection: Journal Writing across the Curriculum." *Language Connections.* Urbana: NCTE, 1982. Emphasizes use of journals as "writing to learn" in all content courses.

—, ed. *The Journal Book.* Portsmouth, NH: Boynton/Cook-Heinemann, 1987. A collection of essays on journal use across the curriculum.

HUFF, ROLAND, and CHARLES R. KLINE, JR. *A Contemporary Writing Curriculum: Rehearsing,*

(continued)

Composing, and Valuing. New York: Columbia UP, 1987. 1–51. Describes a course with journal writing at its core.

WHITEHILL, SHARON. "Using the Journal for Discovery: Two Devices." CCC 38 (1987): 472–74. Presents practical strategies for using journals to generate ideas.

TEACHING IDEAS

Both the "many parts" strategy and mapping attempt to get writers thinking about parts of a topic, as opposed to a monolithic and undifferentiated whole. Once students begin to see parts, they can begin to see relations; and it is the relationships that students create that sustain a paper. To help students appreciate the advantages of thinking about parts, begin class one day with the abrupt assignment: "Write on *X*—15 minutes. Begin." Students will be lost and disgruntled—with reason! *X* might be ozone depletion, government bureaucracy, consumer electronics—any very broad, undifferentiated topic will do. After a minute or so (time enough to let students appreciate the futility of the assignment), tell them to stop, and ask them why they found making a beginning difficult. There might be several answers to this question: Who are we writing to? What is our purpose? What specifically about this topic are we supposed to address?

The writing occasion entails all three questions, and each must be answered precisely if writing is to succeed. For the moment, focus on the need for a writer to work with a carefully defined topic. That is, focus on the last question: What specifically about this topic are we supposed to address? Using the "many parts" strategy or mapping on the chalkboard, show students how they can take a broad, ill-defined topic and illuminate it for themselves by examining parts. Students will readily see that it is more profitable to talk about parts of a broad topic and the relation of parts than it is to talk in generalities about the whole.

ESL EXERCISE

The use of living space varies from culture to culture, with some groups valuing open space

6 The "many parts" strategy[2]

Another method for generating ideas about a topic is to list its parts. Number the items on your list. Then ask: "What are the uses of Number 1? Number 2? Number 3?" and so on. If *uses of* does not seem to work for the parts in question, try *consequences of*: "What are the consequences of Number 1?" The *many parts* strategy lets you be far more specific and imaginative in thinking about the topic as a whole than you might be ordinarily. Once you have responded to your questions about the uses or consequences of some part, you might pursue the one or two most promising responses in a focused freewrite.

Illustration: Lou Cassetta's Paper

THE "MANY PARTS" STRATEGY

```
I.    What are the parts of gender roles in computing?
      1. Women are discouraged from using computers.
      2. Men treat computers as an enjoyable hobby.
      3. Women treat computers like tools.
One part, explored:
II.   What are the consequences of discouraging women from
      using computers?
      -computers become the domain of men and only men
      -women avoid technology in general
      -women cannot relate to men through discourse on
       technology
      -it is difficult for women to work in the computer
       industry
      -computer industry loses women's insights
```

7 Mapping

If you enjoy thinking visually, try **mapping** your ideas. Begin by writing your topic as briefly as possible (a single word is best). Circle the topic and draw three, four, or five short spokes from the circle. At the end of each spoke place one of the journalist's questions, making a major branch off the spoke for every answer to a question. Now, working with each answer indi-

[2]This strategy is adapted from John C. Bean and John D. Ramage, *Form and Surprise in Composition: Writing and Thinking Across the Curriculum* (New York: Macmillan, 1986) 170–71.

Illustration: Lou Cassetta's Paper

MAPPING THE JOURNALIST'S QUESTIONS

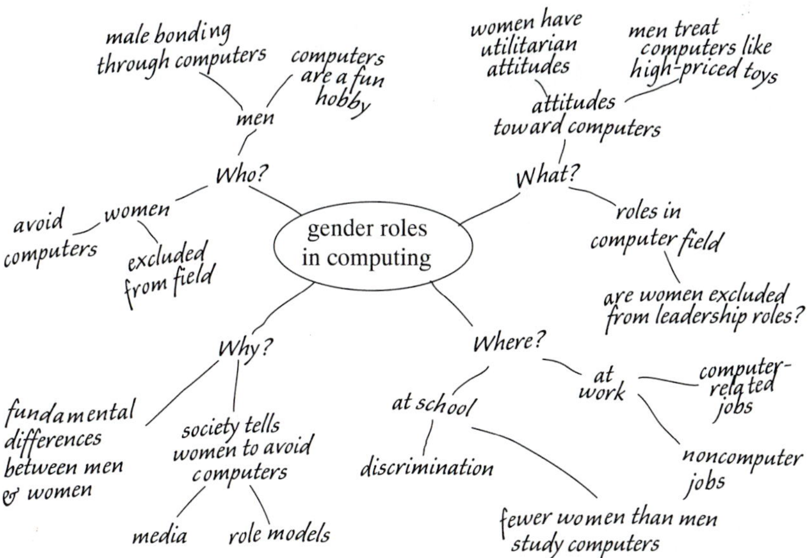

vidually, pose one of the six journalist's questions once again. After you have completed the exercise, you will have a page that places ideas in relation to one another. Notice how the "map" distinguishes between major points and supporting information.

EXERCISE 7

Generate ideas about three of the following topics, using *two* of the previously mentioned methods of invention for each idea. The results of this exercise will provide the basis for your answer to Exercise 10.

river rafting	the symphony	dorm life
a cousin	compulsory draft	space flight

EXERCISE 8

If you are preparing a paper as you read this chapter, use any *three* methods of invention to generate ideas about your topic. The end result of your work should be several categories of grouped ideas.

3c Reviewing and categorizing ideas and information

Not all of the information you have generated will be equally useful. Therefore, your next task in the writing process is to select those ideas that

and "emptiness" and others preferring closeness and "filled" areas. For example, British fashion of a hundred years ago was to fill every possible area of a room with furniture and decoration, in marked contrast with modern Japanese or Scandinavian fashions. Address the following issues as a class exercise.

1. Discuss preferences for large living space as opposed to a small living space. OR discuss preferences for few furnishings and uncluttered space as opposed to much furniture and filled space.
2. Draw a diagram of a single room, labeling the kind of furniture you would typically expect to find in your culture.
3. Compare your diagram with those of other students and then make conclusions about how your culture regards the use of space. Write your observations up as a short report.

ESL CUE

The concept of mapping and outlining may be new to some ESL students, who will need practice seeking unifying categories. Vocabulary limitations sometimes make brainstorming activities extremely difficult for ESL students.

TEACHING IDEAS

Students should be encouraged during this and similar exercises to try to distinguish between strategies that they find productive and those that don't yield satisfactory results. Since people process information differently, it's extremely helpful to understand early on the types of strategies that work best for the individual writer.

EXERCISE 7

Individual responses

EXERCISE 8

Individual responses

TEACHING IDEAS

For students who begin the writing process *without* a clear governing idea, the creation of categories is a crucially important step in the development of a working thesis. The creation of categories is a prethesis intellectual development; categories articulate for the writer what he or she considers to be the emergent "big ideas" in the material. The creation of categories is a time for students to be alert and active, for the categories they derive will create the possibilities for the thesis to follow.

GROUP ACTIVITY

If students are in fact working on their own papers as they study this chapter, a group activity can be helpful at this stage. Since novice writers tend to lose objectivity rather early in the writing process, and since they often have little confidence in their control over the material, trying to develop categories for their own paper can be a daunting task. Analyzing another student's material, however, can be less intimidating. In groups of three, have each student pass his or her prewriting ideas to the student to the left. Each member of the group will then try to develop categories for another student's material. After the first round, the material is again passed to the left. When students are finished developing categories, they can discuss in turn each student's material. As readers justify the categories they've chosen, the writer gets two fresh perspectives on his or her material. (Exercises like this early in the writing process can also make peer evaluation of drafts much more comfortable for students.)

look most promising. *Promising* in this context is an inexact term, and at this stage of the writing process there is no way to be exact. Until you have completed a first draft, you cannot know for certain the content of your paper. Despite the plans you make when preparing to write, your actual writing is where you will discover much of your content. For this reason, the choices you make about which ideas and information to include in a paper must be based on hunches: informed guesses about what will work.

1 Reviewing ideas and making meaningful categories

Make sense of the information you have generated by creating categories. A category is akin to a file drawer into which you place related materials. Your job is to consolidate: take all the ideas and information you have generated; spread your notes out before you; and then take a clean sheet of paper and group ideas. Give each new grouping a general category name. Beneath each category name, list subordinate, or supporting, information.

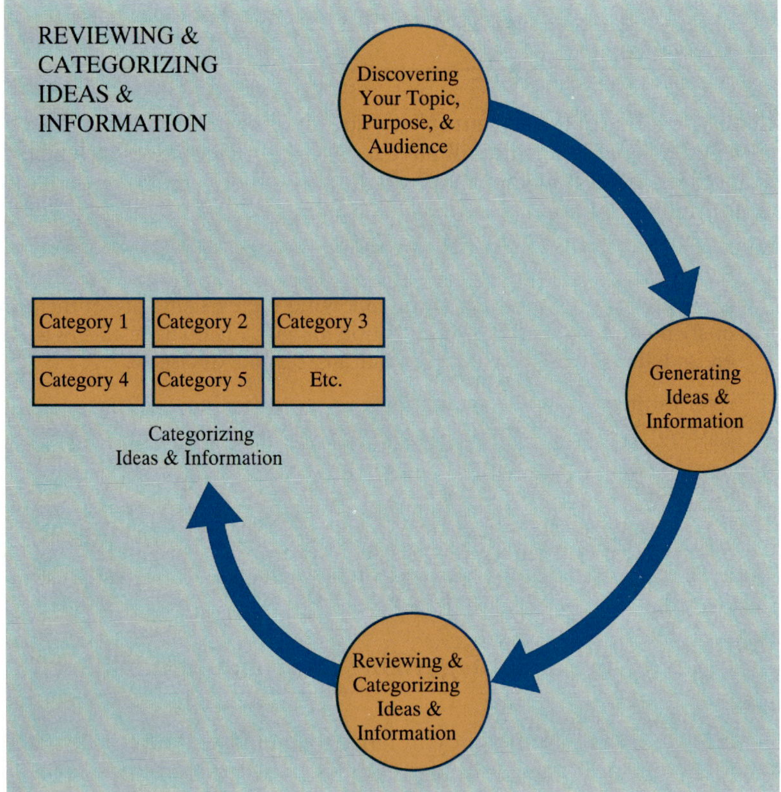

Lou Cassetta generated five categories of information on which he could base a paper. Following is one of these categories, with information consolidated from the results of four different methods for generating information.

Illustration: Lou Cassetta's Paper

SELECTING INFORMATION INTO CATEGORIES

<u>Conflicting attitudes between men and women about computers</u>
-men like to talk about computers--and experience "male bonding"
-women show less interest in talking about computers
-computers represent the traditional technical domain of men
-women excluded from high-level positions in computer field
-fewer women than men study computers
-computer field losing women's contributions and insights

2 Organizing information *within* categories

Organize information within categories to clarify your ideas and their relation to each other. First, you will need to identify main, or *general,* points within each category and the subordinate, or *specific,* points supporting them, which is exactly what you will do when writing a paper. Use an informal outline or a tree diagram to organize major and supporting points within a category.

Illustration: Lou Cassetta's Paper

ORGANIZING INFORMATION WITHIN CATEGORIES

Organization by informal outline

<u>Conflicting attitudes between men and women about computers</u>

<u>Major point:</u> Men like to talk about computers--and experience "male bonding"

<u>Supporting points:</u> (1) Men like to talk about many kinds of technology; (2) I often had long talks about computer hardware with friends

<u>Major point:</u> Many women seem less interested than men in talking about computers

<u>Supporting points:</u> (1) I rarely have conversations about technology with women; (2) Some women say that computers are a "guy thing"--like cars.

ADDITIONAL EXERCISE H

THINKING CRITICALLY In order to practice distinguishing between major and supporting points, choose a brief article from the magazine you used for Additional Exercise A. Working backward from finished product to informal outline, list the major points and supporting points found in the article.

Major point: Women choose not to use computers

Supporting point: Some computer classes have fewer women than men

Organization by tree diagram

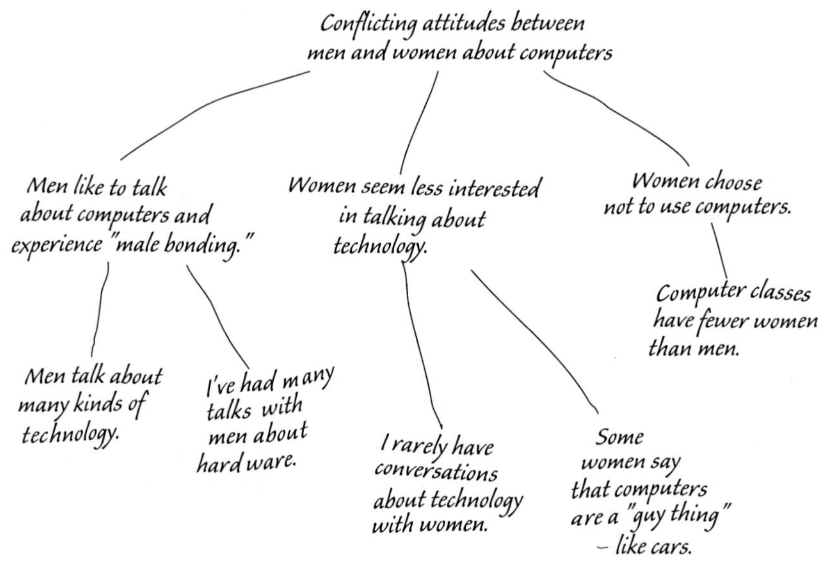

3 Expanding information: Filling in gaps

Organizing material within a category is an excellent technique for revealing which of your main points will need further development once you begin writing a first draft. When Lou Cassetta organized his category on the conflicting attitudes between men and women about computers, he realized that he had neglected to generate enough supporting materials for his point about women who choose *not* to use computers. When Lou asked, "What other examples of women not using computers can I point to?" answers came quickly. An asterisk marks the two additions to the category.

Major point: Some women choose not to use computers

Supporting points: (1) Some computer classes have fewer women than men

*Few women I know would call computers a hobby

*The Internet is dominated by men and by male "flaming"

TEACHING IDEAS

Full development depends on a writer's level of content knowledge, level of rhetorical knowledge (i.e., awareness of when a statement needs support), and motivation for exploring an idea. Lacking any of these, a writer will not have the tools to develop an idea. To impress this point on students, have them play teacher/reader to their peers. A paired activity can be set up in the following way:

> Each student chooses a topic on which he or she is expert and can be a teacher. As teacher, the student gathers three brief readings on the topic and presents it to a partner. The partner reads the materials and writes a one-page reaction paper, responding to any single aspect of the topic. The student/teacher's job will be to read for the clarity and development of the partner's main idea.
>
> After partners complete the assignment and discuss their recommendations, elicit from the class observations on what features of a paper constitute "full" development. Having taken their turns as teachers, your students should have something to say.

Look to each of your main points to see how you might add supporting points. You may need to read additional sources to fill in gaps. Developing categories fully at this stage will maximize the information you will have to work with when devising a thesis.

EXERCISE 9

Select the most promising information from your efforts to generate ideas about your topic, as defined in Exercise 8. *Form categories:* consolidate information from all three invention strategies. Write a brief sentence or phrase of definition for each category. *Organize each category* into a main point and supporting points. Finally, *expand information:* fill in gaps and if you are interested (or if your professor requires it) seek out source material that you can use in your paper. At the conclusion of this exercise, each category should have a main point supported by at least two specific, subordinate points.

3d Writing a thesis and devising a sketch of your paper

A **thesis** is a general statement that you make about your topic, usually in the form of a single sentence, that summarizes the controlling idea of your paper. You cannot produce a fully accurate **final thesis** until you have written a complete draft. When sitting down to a first draft, you will at best have a **working thesis**: a statement that, based on everything you know about your topic, should prove to be a reasonably accurate summary of what you will write.

Like any sentence, a thesis consists of a subject and a predicate—that is, a verb and its associated words (see 7a-1). The *subject* of a thesis statement identifies the *subject* of your paper. The *predicate* represents the claim or assertion you will make about that subject.

Realize that your ideas for a paper and, consequently, for your thesis develop and change as your paper develops. Don't be bound by a single sentence at the beginning of your draft. Your working thesis *will* change. Nonetheless, you must depend on it to get you started.

1 Focusing on the subject of your thesis

As much as possible, you want the subject of your thesis statement to name something that is relatively specific and well defined; you want to name something you can discuss thoroughly within the allotted number of pages. How will you focus your subject?

Build on the fact that you have organized your information into categories. To settle on a subject for your thesis, review your categories and select from among them your most promising and interesting material. Most likely, you will focus on only a fraction of this material in your actual paper.

EXERCISE 9

Individual responses

ADDITIONAL EXERCISE I

If you prefer to have students work inductively to understand how a thesis works, ask them to read any or all of the seven example student papers in this book located in Chapters 4, 6, 35, and 36–39. For each paper, the thesis sentence is highlighted. In preparation for class discussion or possibly individual or group presentations, ask students to explain the relation between the highlighted thesis and the paper that follows from it.

TEACHING IDEAS

The creation of a thesis is an act of thinking, a point sometimes lost on students who believe that theses somehow reside in the material they are studying, not in the writer. You might want to emphasize the student's activity: the thesis should clarify a relationship that the student discovers in the material being used. Students can find a diagrammatic explanation of the process in the writing wheel. Without a thoughtful, creative writer to forge connections among categories, no mature thesis and no mature paper is possible.

TEACHING IDEAS

Students sometimes mistake a *topic* for a *thesis.* A little practice in distinguishing between the two can help tremendously when it comes time to develop their own thesis statements. The sentence analogy is a good one, since most students understand the basic parts of a sentence. You might ask students to peruse a brief article (perhaps a selection in the reading anthology, if the class is using one) and list several sentences that make clear statements. As they distinguish between the *subjects* of the sentences and the *statements* themselves, they should come to a clearer understanding of what constitutes a thesis statement.

ADDITIONAL EXERCISE J

To clarify the notion of "ambition" as it pertains to theses, you might give students the opportunity to generate sets of theses with varying levels of ambition. Have students choose a topic they know especially well: a topic about which they consider themselves expert. Next, have students generate three theses for this topic—of low, middle, and high ambition. Students could then present these statements to the class (following a brief introduction to the topic), with accounts of why one thesis is more ambitious than others.

Focusing the Subject of a Thesis with Questions

One useful way to limit and focus the subject of your thesis is to pose a journalist's questions: *who, what, when, where,* and *which aspects.*

Subject (too broad): wilderness
Limiting questions: which aspects?
Focused subject: wilderness camping

2 Basing your thesis on a relationship you want to clarify

Once you have focused your subject, you must make an assertion about it; that is, you must complete the predicate part of your thesis. If you have ever written a paper before, you recognize this as the moment of chaos coalescing into order. If you have generated ideas on your own, you have several pages of notes; if you have conducted research, you have filled out perhaps fifty file cards. You cannot write until you have begun to forge relationships among the ideas and information that you have generated. It is only *in the process* of forging relationships—trying to make logical connections one way, seeing that a certain tactic does not work, trying other tactics, and constantly making adjustments—that sense emerges and you come to know what you think about your material.

In examining the notes you have generated and organized into categories, ask yourself: What new statement can I make that helps to explain this material (if I am writing an informative paper) or to explain my reactions to this material (if I am writing a persuasive paper)? Think of a relationship that ties all—or part—of your material together. You will express this relationship in the predicate part of your thesis.

3 The thesis and your ambitions for a paper

Whether you intend to inform or persuade, the relationship that you assert in your thesis can be more or less ambitious: when the assertion is ambitious, your thesis and the paper that you build from it will be, too. The legal scholar and Supreme Court justice Oliver Wendell Holmes (1841–1935) once characterized intellectual ambition in terms of the number of levels, or stories, in a building. His description captures the qualities that distinguish barely adequate theses from competent and more challenging ones:

> There are one-story intellects, two-story intellects, and three-story intellects with skylights. All fact collectors who have no aim beyond their facts are one-story men. Two-story men compare, reason, generalize, using the

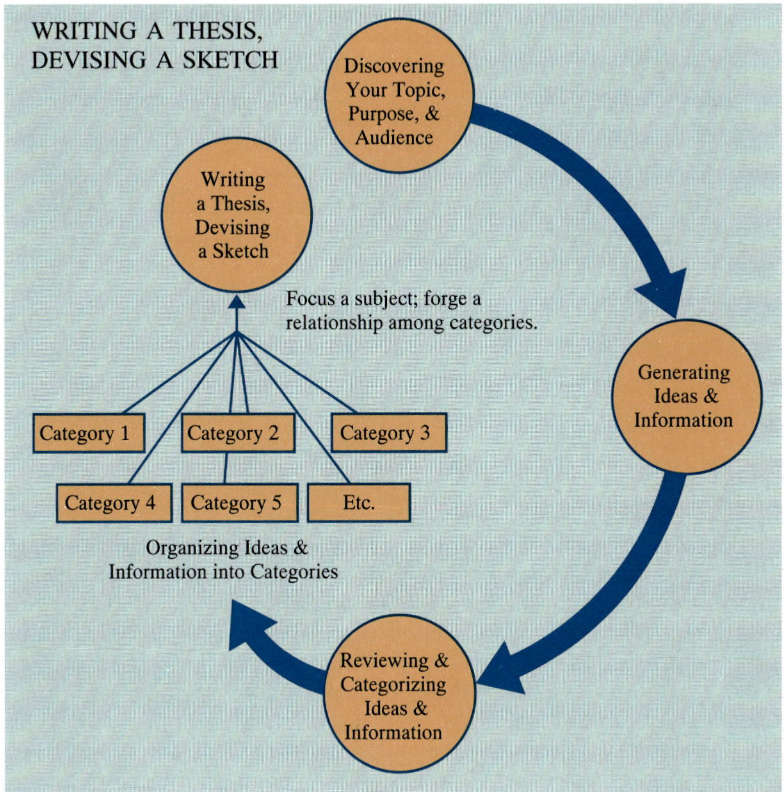

labor of fact collectors as their own. Three-story men idealize, imagine, predict—their best illumination comes from above the skylight.[3]

One-story thesis

A one-story thesis leads to informative writing and demonstrates that you can gather and report facts. Any paper that follows from such a thesis requires little more than a stitching together of summaries. Strong papers do not use one-story theses. Only on some essay exams will a paper developed in support of a one-story thesis be appropriate in college writing.

---

[3]Oliver Wendell Holmes, cited in Esther Fusco, "Cognitive Levels Matching and Curriculum Analysis," *Developing Minds: A Resource Book for Teaching Thinking,* ed. Arthur L. Costa (Alexandria, VA: ASCD, 1985) 81.

Illustration: Examples of a One-Story Thesis

(1) Wilderness camping poses many challenges.
—Challenge #1
—Challenge #2, etc.

(2) Lou Cassetta's one-story thesis:
Women are not entering the field of computers in large numbers.
—Society tells them that computers are the domain of men
—Men are discriminating against them

Each one-story thesis requires little more than a summary of the topic's component elements. The writers make no attempt to forge relationships among these elements.

LOOKING AHEAD

The discussion in Chapter 5 of patterns of development refers specifically to the varieties of inference covered here. To further reinforce the interconnectedness of all phases of the writing process, you might inform students that this material will come in handy when they begin to revise paragraphs in their first drafts.

Two-story thesis

Holmes suggests that a thinker is someone who compares facts, generalizes from them, or reasons with them: that is, a thinker *argues* or *informs* with some degree of sophistication. Someone who reasons will define, order, classify, delineate a process, or establish cause and effect—all types of thinking and writing discussed in this book. When you can reason with facts, you are working with a two-story thesis because you are seeing facts *in relation to one another*; you are making inferences and seeing implications. By contrast, the writer of a one-story thesis sees and can write about only one set of facts at a time. A two-story thesis shows an engaged mind at work, *making connections* where none existed previously.

Illustration: Examples of a Two-Story Thesis

(1) Like holding a mirror to your personality, wilderness camping shows you to yourself—for better *and* worse.
—Wilderness camping described
—The camper in the wilderness, described
—Ways in which the wilderness elicits personal response, positive and negative

(2) Lou Cassetta's thesis:
Computers have become the domain of men, who have developed a language about computers that excludes women.
—Society has long defined computing as an activity for men only.
—Some men have patterned their lives and language around computers.
—The development of computing as a male activity has caused women to avoid the field of computing.

Each two-story thesis forges a relationship between two previously unrelated elements: between wilderness camping and self-reflection and between the domains of men and the language of computers.

CRITICAL DECISIONS

Devise an action plan: A thesis is an action plan for the paper you intend to write. The predicate part of a thesis establishes a relationship that you believe brings meaning to the material that you are working with. Once you determine this relationship, your goal is to demonstrate it in your paper.

Theses that lead to *informative* papers

In the examples that follow, the key, informational relationship of each thesis is italicized.

Sequential order: You place your information and ideas in a logical order, or sequence—a pattern of first, second, third. . . .

> A creative thinker *will study a problem, arrive at a solution, and then delay accepting that solution until she has explored alternatives.*

Definition: Your information, considered as a whole, allows you to define a term.

> Creativity *is the act of recognizing problems and finding solutions.*

Classification: You find enough examples of something that you can recognize varieties.

> The four types of creativity *are visual, verbal, musical, and mathematical.*

Comparison or contrast: After studying two or more people, places, things, or ideas, you are able to demonstrate differences.

> Of the four types of creativity, visual and verbal *differ the most.*

Theses that lead to *argumentative* papers

In the examples that follow, the key argumentative relationship of each thesis is italicized.

Generalization: Representative examples of a group allow you to infer a general principle that is true for all members of that group.

> Creative students *are essential to the success of any classroom.*

Causation: You can show that certain actions lead to certain effects or that certain effects follow from certain actions or conditions.

> The causes of creativity *are complex and involve a rich mixture of inheritance and learning.*

Sign: You can establish that one thing tends to occur in the presence of (and therefore is a sign of) another.

> Risk taking *is a sign of creativity.*

REFERENCE

D'Angelo, Frank. *A Conceptual Theory of Rhetoric.* Cambridge: Winthrop, 1975. Patterns of development are also patterns of thought.

LOOKING BACK

In 3c, students were reviewing and categorizing ideas and information. The connection between that activity and formulating a thesis becomes clear with the two- and three-story theses, in which the student must forge a relationship between two previously unrelated elements. Again, the student's obligation as writer is to be *active.* In a three-story thesis, the writer must not only forge a relationship but show a willingness to go beyond the material in some original way.

Three-story thesis

In addition to making connections where none existed previously, a three-story thesis shows a writer willing to take intellectual risks: that is, the writer is willing to expand the scope of the paper, widening its context in order to take up a broader, more complex, and (if executed well) more important discussion. A three-story thesis will create a paradox, a tension among its parts, by setting opposites against each other.[4] In a thesis with tension, you often find the conjunctions *although* and *even if.* The writer's job is to navigate between paradoxical opposites. The reader, sensing tension, wants to know what happens and why.

The three-story thesis, the most ambitious of the three types, can be enormously satisfying as you set out to "idealize, imagine, [or] predict." Holmes remarks that illumination for such a thinker comes "from above the skylight." The metaphor does not suggest someone waiting to be inspired by mysterious agents; rather, the skylight metaphor suggests a mind that is open to a world outside itself and is ready to question. The very best papers are built on three-story theses. These papers tend to be argumentative.

Illustration: Examples of a Three-Story Thesis

Wilderness camping teaches that we must preserve what is brutal in Nature, even at the expense of public safety.

—Rigors of wilderness camping

—Potential danger to public

—Paradox: dangers notwithstanding, wilderness must be maintained

Lou Cassetta's three-story thesis:

Since women are as capable as men in technology-related fields, they need to participate in discussing computer technology on the same level as men do to succeed in the field.

—There are some significant differences in attitude between men and women about computers.

—Men have often related to each other through talking about computers, while women have not.

—In dealing with men who now dominate the computer field, women should learn the men's subtleties of language about technology.

—Paradox: If women are as capable as men, why can't they use whatever language suits them?

Each three-story thesis broadens the scope of the paper and creates interest through paradoxical opposites. Each thesis promises a paper that will be argumentative. Lou Cassetta develops his three-story thesis in his second draft. However, he ultimately discovers that he cannot support such a thesis

---

[4]The term *tension,* as it relates to the thesis statement, is borrowed from John C. Bean and John D. Ramage, *Form and Surprise in Composition: Writing and Thinking Across the Curriculum* (New York: Macmillan, 1986) 168–69.

adequately, and he revises it in the final draft. Lou's first draft appears in 3f; his problems with the thesis in revision appears in 4a and 4e; and his final draft appears in 4f.

What sort of paper are you writing?

As you create a working thesis, consider whether you are writing a one-, two-, or three-story thesis. You should not feel compelled to write a three-story thesis (and a three-story paper) for every assignment. Many writing tasks are one-story jobs: summaries, for instance, and responses to certain essay questions do not call for imaginative engagement on your part. Then again, you may not have enough time to develop a three-story thesis, or you may not know enough about the material to write ambitiously on it. When you have the opportunity, though, try for at least a two-story thesis.

Sometimes you will understand the ambition of your paper before you set out to write it; at other times you will not have a clear sense of how "large" a paper you are writing until you get midway or most of the way through a draft and discover or challenge your ideas. In any event, the point of the Holmes metaphor is for you to appreciate what sort of paper you are writing as you sit down to *revise* your first draft. Reread the draft; see what you have; and determine how ambitious your final draft should be. You will choose your final thesis, and shape your final paper, accordingly.

Generating a Working Thesis

1. Focus and restrict your subject so that you will be able to write specifically on it in the number of pages allotted.
2. Assemble the notes—arranged in categories—that you have generated for your paper.
3. Forge a relationship that clarifies the material you have assembled.
4. Devise a sentence—a working thesis—that links the relationship you have forged with your focused subject.
5. Determine how ambitious you will be with your thesis—and your paper.
6. Let your thesis evolve as you develop and challenge your thoughts on your topic.

EXERCISE 10

Refer to your results from Exercise 9. Given the ideas you generated write one-, two-, and three-story theses for this topic.

EXERCISE 10

Individual responses

GROUP ACTIVITY

A simple group activity can generate healthy discussion of the thesis statements students have written so far. Have students formulate questions for each other's thesis statements. Not only will writers have more productive questions to use toward an outline, but they'll also begin to appreciate that each reader looks at a thesis (or an entire essay) from a unique perspective.

REFERENCES

The following articles offer advice on specific patterns of development:

BERMAN, NEIL. "Language, Process, and Tinkertoys." *CCC* 26 (1975): 390–92.

DEAN, TERRY. "Causal, Not Casual: An Advance Organizer for Cause-and-Effect Compositions." *Structuring for Success in the English Classroom.* Ed. Candy Carter. Urbana: NCTE, 1982. 92–97.

HAICH, GEORGE D. "If the Reader Never Saw One, How Would You Describe It?" *CCC* 26 (1975): 298–300.

WILCOX, LANCE. "Time Lines in the Composing of Narratives: A Graphic Aid to Organization." *The Writing Instructor* 6 (1987): 162–73.

LOOKING AHEAD

The quizzing technique discussed here is also a technique used to help students revise their work. See 4b-1–2 for a discussion on testing a paper or sections of a paper for unity and coherence.

CRITICAL DECISIONS

Challenge and be challenged: Quizzing your working thesis to determine major sections of your paper.

In writing a thesis, you compress a great deal of information into a single sentence; in writing a paper based on this thesis, you will need to "unpack" and discuss this information. Use the following technique as an aid to unpacking: challenge, or quiz, your thesis with questions (see box on page 79). The technique will lead to a sketch of your paper.

Thesis

define (capable) — *which fields?* (technology-related fields)

Since women are as capable as men in technology-related fields, they need to participate in discussing computer technology on the same level as men do to succeed in the field.

Are they not succeeding now? Why not, if women are as capable? (to succeed in the field)

How do each talk about computers? (participate in discussing computer technology on the same level as men do)

Sketching the paper

—Define which technology-related fields. Define *capability.*

—Examine why women are not prospering in technology-related fields.

—Discuss how men, as opposed to women, talk about computers.

—Discuss men's outlook on computers and contrast it with women's.

—Explain the paradox: the political reality of the hi-tech workplace is that men dominate; even though women are as technically capable as men, they do not advance through corporate management. If the problem is social (and related to the way men talk), the solution should be social as well.

Thesis

review the reasoning (By instituting a curfew and acting on what it believed was the students' behalf) — *define "students' behalf" from students' and administration's point of view*

By instituting a curfew and acting on what it believed was the students' behalf, the administration undermined the moral and educational principles it wanted to uphold.

how? (undermined) — *define both* (moral and educational principles)

Sketching the paper

—Review the reasoning: in setting a curfew, the administration said it was acting in the best interest of students

—Define "students' behalf" from student and administrative perspectives

—Define moral issues and educational principles at issue

—Explain the paradox: in mandating morality through a curfew, the administration denied students a chance to grapple with moral issues and reach mature decisions on their own. The administration undermined its own educational aims.

Devise an action plan: A sketch based on your thesis is an action plan, a paper to be written. Depending on your preference, you can fill in the sketch, converting it to a detailed outline, or you can work with it as a sketch. In either case, this plan—closely connected to your thesis—sets an agenda for the paper to follow.

4 Devising a sketch of your paper, or developing a formal outline

Look to your working thesis for clues about the ideas you will need to develop in your essay. For an academic paper to succeed, you must develop all directly stated or implied ideas in the thesis. You may want to regard your thesis as a contract. In the final draft, the contract exists between you and your reader; the thesis promises the reader a discussion of certain material, and the paper delivers on that promise. As a tool used in writing a first draft, your working thesis is a provisional contract.

Identifying significant parts of your thesis

To create a sketch of your first draft, study your working thesis and identify all significant elements, stated directly or indirectly. In your paper, you are obliged to develop each of these elements and to explain how it is related to others. Write the working thesis at the top of a page and circle its significant words. You can then ask development questions of, or make comments about, each circled element. If you are thorough in quizzing your thesis, you will identify most of its significant parts. (You may not discover some parts until you write a first draft.) Having identified these significant parts, briefly sketch the paper you intend to write.

Question or Make Comments about Your Thesis in Order to Identify Major Sections of Your Paper

Questions

how does/will it happen?
how to describe?
what are some examples?
what are the reasons for?
what is my view?
compared to what?
what is the cause?
any stories to tell?
how?
when?
what has prevented/will prevent it from happening?
who is involved?
what are the key features?
what are the reasons against?
how often?
possible to classify types or parts?
what is the effect of this?
which ones?

Comments

define
review the facts
review the reasoning
explain the contrast or paradox

Option: Preparing a formal outline of your paper

Many writers feel that a rough sketch is sufficient for beginning the first draft of a paper. Others feel more comfortable with a formal plan of ac-

FOR DISCUSSION

A little extra time spent on these concepts now can make the job of evaluating drafts and final papers much easier on instructor and student alike: If students truly understand the meanings of *unity* and *coherence,* they'll understand instructors' comments that refer to the terms. A discussion of what students understand by the terms, with particular reference to paragraphs or essays they consider unified and coherent (see 5c and 5d), can serve to make paper evaluation a good deal more meaningful.

REFERENCES

PODIS, JOANNE M., and LEONARD A. PODIS. "Identifying and Teaching Rhetorical Plans for Arrangement." *CCC* 41 (1990): 430–42. Offers an alternative taxonomy to assist writers in arrangement of material in essays.

PODIS, LEONARD A. "Teaching Arrangement: Defining a More Practical Approach." *CCC* 31 (1980): 197–204. Suggests strategies for teaching students to shape essays.

FOR DISCUSSION

Probably one of the most despised terms in student-dom is *outline:* some students may recall horror stories of being required to produce formal outlines prior to drafting a paper, while others may simply recall frustration with the whole concept. (Instructors have their share of stories as well.) During the course of a discussion of these stories, students might be asked to speculate on why the formal-outline-prior-to-draft assignment is so awful. If they read the section carefully, they should appreciate the purpose of an outline—and perhaps understand why the best outlines are produced only *after* at least one draft has been completed.

tion—an outline with clearly delineated major and minor points. In collaborative writing situations, with different writers responsible for various sections of the project, a formal outline is probably the only way to reach agreement on what each writer will contribute.

Whatever your choice, be aware that before the first draft is written, any form of plan is, at best, *provisional* and subject to change. Outlines are sketches for getting started; they help you to unify your paper and to avoid discussing any topic not closely related to your thesis. They also help you to develop all significant points of your thesis, and they help you to achieve coherence—to ensure that all parts of the plan will lead logically from one to the next. Typically, the parts of an outline are arranged in a logical order: the topic is divided into at least two constituent parts and each part is discussed separately. The order can be *spatial,* in terms of the location of the parts, or *chronological,* in terms of time sequence, or it can be based on some other criterion such as priority of importance to the issue at hand.

Useful as an outline can be, you will still need to discover the important elements of your paper during the process of writing and, necessarily, your outline or sketch will change as the writing takes shape.

Illustration: Formal Outline

What are the key features? *What are the reasons for?* *How will it happen?*

Thesis: Establishing colonies on the moon will be possible by the early 21st century.

Who's involved? *What will prevent it from happening?*

I. Colonizing the moon
  A. Base
  B. Missions
    1. Science
      a. Astronomy
      b. Geology
    2. Industry
      a. Mining
      b. Crystal growth
  C. Inhabitants
    1. Specialists
    2. Nonspecialists

II. Designing and building the base
  A. Designers
    1. Architects
    2. Psychologists
    3. Engineers
  B. Construction
    1. Materials
    2. Methods
    3. Crews
    4. Dangers

A formal outline establishes the major sections and subsections of your paper. The outline shows how each section is supported by points you plan to discuss (see 18e). It also shows how these points are themselves supported. The goal of a formal outline is to make visible the material you plan to use in the paper. Standard outline form is as follows: uppercase roman numerals indicate the most general level of heading in the outline; these headings correspond with major sections of your paper. Uppercase letters mark the major points you will use in developing each heading. Arabic numbers mark the supporting points you will use in developing main points. Lowercase letters mark further subordination—support of supporting points. Note that the entries at each level of heading are grammatically parallel (see 18e); that each level of heading has at least two entries; and that only the first letter of an entry is capitalized. A formal outline need not show plans for your introduction or conclusion.

Illustration: Formal Outline with Sentences

Each item of a formal outline can also be written as a sentence, which you may prefer in your efforts to begin writing. The following is one section of the preceding outline, written in sentence form.

B. There will be two broad missions for a Moon Base.
   1. The first mission will be scientific.
      a. By setting up telescopes on the far side of the moon, astronomers will have an unparalleled view of the universe.
      b. Geologists studying samples of lunar soil will be able to learn both about earth's origin and about the origin of the solar system.
   2. The second mission will be industrial.
      a. Mining companies will be able to begin commercial operations almost immediately.
      b. In the light moon gravity, technicians will be able to grow superior crystals.

EXERCISE 11

Turn to the two- and three-story theses you wrote in Exercise 10. Circle significant words or phrases, pose development questions, and prepare an informal or a formal outline of your paper. Then expand your outline into a first draft of your paper (3e).

3e Writing a draft

Your working thesis and your sketch or outline are essential for giving you the confidence to begin a first **draft.** Realize, however, that your final paper will *not* be identical to your original plans, even if they were carefully prepared. Once begun, writing will lead you to discard and revise your original ideas and will lead to new ideas as well. Through writing you will *explore* your subject. As you do, obstacles and opportunities will present themselves: by keeping your eyes open, you will be ready to avoid one and seize the other.

REFERENCE

Holloway, Karla F. C. "Teaching Composition Through Outlining." *Teaching the Basics—Really!* Ed. Ouida Clapp. Urbana: NCTE, 1977. 36–39. Outlines can be a useful strategy in teaching the composing process.

EXERCISE 11

Individual responses

TEACHING IDEAS

This section will reinforce the notion that the "perfect" outline comes only *after* an essay has been written. Those students who rely too heavily on outlines may find the ideas put forth in this section daunting; rigid outlines have always provided a safety net for them. (Of course, slavish adherence to outlines has probably resulted in a string of mediocre papers as well.) If it is emphasized here that the drafting stage is where mistakes are okay, indeed where they're *supposed* to occur, the entire process of producing drafts might be made less painful for insecure students.

The object of a first draft is to get ideas down on paper, to explore them, and to establish the shape of your paper. The object is *not* to produce anything that is readable to anyone other than yourself. Finished, readable documents come through revision. When sitting down to write a draft, successful writers know they will be revising. They understand, in advance, that they will review *every* sentence and paragraph they produce and will rewrite many of them. This understanding can help you: If you can adopt the expert's attitude with regard to first and subsequent drafts, you will free yourself to write quickly—and imperfectly. You will give yourself permission to write in ways that you know will be imperfect but that will nonetheless be an essential step in achieving a final product.

ADDITIONAL EXERCISE K

To get a sense of how different writers adopt different strategies for drafting, interview several people who write, either for a living or for their own enjoyment. (Professors are ideal candidates for such interviews; many write for both reasons. Writing Center staff are also accustomed to talking about their writing process.) Ask your subjects how they move from outline to draft. As you record their responses, note the differences between writers. Which of the processes most closely resembles yours? In what ways? Do the various responses offer any advice to you on your own movement from outline to draft? If so, what specific changes do you plan to make?

Strategies for Drafting

Working yourself through the draft

1. Write *one* section of the paper at a time: write a general statement that supports some part of your thesis, then provide details about the supporting statement. Once you have finished a section, take a break. Then return to write another section, working incrementally in this fashion until you have completed the draft.
   - Alternately, write one section of the paper and take a break. Then reread and revise that one section before moving to the next. Continue to work in this fashion, one section at a time, until you complete the draft.
2. Accept *two* drafts, minimum, as the standard for writing any formal paper. In this way, you give yourself permission to write a first draft that is not perfect.
3. If you have prepared adequately for writing, then trust that you will discover what to write *as* you write.
4. Save substantial revisions concerning grammar, punctuation, usage, and spelling for later. In your first draft(s), focus on content.

ESL CUE

Writer's block is not the same for ESL students as for native speakers. ESL students might be unable to generate information because of a total lack of experience with the topic or understanding of its significance. For instance, an assignment asking ESL students to write on the cigarette smoking controversy may produce limited or poor papers because for much of the world cigarette smoking is an unquestioned way of life; in other words, our controversy is not an understandable controversy for them. Papers on topics like the military draft or AIDS may also produce skewed results. What we take for granted as being of universal concern is not necessarily so.

1 Beating writer's block

Journalists, novelists, beginning writers, writing teachers, graduate students, business people, students in freshmen composition: *everybody* avoids writing at some point or another. Odd as it may seem, this information can be of comfort: if you avoid writing, be assured that avoidance does *not* mean you have done things poorly or that you do not "have what it takes" to be a competent writer. Avoidance and the anxiety that causes it are natural parts of the writing process. By no means are they ever-present parts, and if you devote sufficient time to preparing yourself to write, you minimize the danger of writer's block. Still, preparing is not the same as writing a draft, and you inevitably face a moment in which you decide to take a step—or not. Think about the feelings you get when you do not want to write. When you are stuck as a writer, what might you be telling yourself? And how might you get unstuck?

STUCK *I cannot get started.* I am afraid of the blank page—or its electronic equivalent, the empty screen: However fully formed ideas for writing may come to me, I can only write one word after the next. And as I do, what I *have not* written seems so vast that I cannot make a beginning.

UNSTUCK *Prepare yourself mentally to write one section of the paper, not the entire paper.* Three-page papers, just like 500-page books, get written one section at a time. When you sit down to write a draft, identify a *section:* a grouping of related paragraphs that you can write in a single sitting.

STUCK *I want my writing to be perfect.* My early attempts to express anything are messy. I get a sinking feeling when I reread my work and see how much revision is needed. Whenever I cannot think of the right word, I freeze up.

UNSTUCK *Accept* two *drafts, minimum, as the standard for writing any formal paper.* When you understand that you will rewrite the first draft of all formal papers or letters, you can give yourself permission to write a first draft quickly and at times imprecisely.

STUCK *Why advertise my problems?* I worry about grammar, punctuation, and spelling, and I do not want to embarrass myself.

UNSTUCK *Use a writer's reference tools.* Many people are nervous about these errors. The fear is real. As long as you know how to use standard desk references—a dictionary and a handbook—there is no need to memorize rules of grammar, punctuation, and spelling. Of course, knowing the rules *does* save you time.

2 Working with your sketch or outline

Following are three strategies for using your sketch or outline as a basis for writing. None of these strategies is *correct* in the sense that one produces a better draft than the others. All will get you a first draft, and all have advantages and disadvantages. How you choose to use a sketch or outline is a matter of your temperament as a writer.

Adhering closely to your outline

One strategy for writing a draft is to follow closely the sketch or outline you made prior to actual drafting. To make full and frequent use of the detailed outline you have assembled makes a great deal of sense, as long as you are aware that your paper *will* deviate from the outline.

BACKGROUND

See Maggy Smith, *Teaching College Writing.* Boston: Allyn & Bacon, 1995. Chapter 7: "Drafting: The Essay's 'Outer Shape' and 'Inner Parts,' " 103–21.

REFERENCES

BLOOM, LYNN Z. "Research on Writing Blocks, Writing Anxiety, and Writing Apprehension." *Research in Composition and Rhetoric.* Eds. Michael G. Moran and Ronald F. Lunsford. Westport: Greenwood, 1984. 71–91. An examination of strategies for overcoming writer's block (includes research).

BRANNON, LIL, MELINDA KNIGHT, and VERA NEVEROW-TURK. *Writers Writing.* Upper Montclair, NJ: Boynton/Cook, 1983. Writing and revising are not discrete stages in the writing process.

ELBOW, PETER. "Quick Revising," "Thorough Revising," "Revising with Feedback," and "Cut and Paste Revising and the Collage." *Writing with Power: Techniques for Mastering the Writing Process.* New York: Oxford UP, 1981. Practical advice on all areas of revising.

HARRIS, MURIEL. "Composing Behaviors of One- and Multi-Draft Writers." *CE* 51 (1989): 174–91. A look at revising practices of student writers, emphasizing differences between those who do and those who do not write multiple drafts.

HILLOCKS, GEORGE, JR. *Research on Written Composition.* Urbana, ERIC, 1986. 39–49. A review of current research on revising, with emphasis on strategies.

LINDEMANN, ERIKA. *A Rhetoric for Writing Teachers.* 2nd ed. New York: Oxford UP, 1987. 171–88. A discussion of several revising strategies (includes bibliography).

MURRAY, DONALD. "Teaching the Motivating Force of Revision." *Learning by Teaching.* Upper Montclair, NJ: Boynton/Cook, 1982. The act of revising can itself motivate writers.

ROSE, MIKE. "Rigid Rules, Inflexible Plans, and the Stifling of Language: A Cognitivist Analysis of Writer's Block." CCC 31 (1980): 389–401.

(continued)

Writers who use guidelines rather than rigid rules seldom experience blocking.

SCHWARTZ, MIMI. "Revision Profiles: Patterns and Implications." *CE* 45 (1983): 549–58. Writers revise according to the category into which they fit.

TEACHING IDEAS

As students begin to write their first drafts and encounter problems with writer's block, remind them that their goals are actually different at each stage of the writing process: the first draft is primarily aimed to clarify the controlling idea and the sections of the paper needed to support that idea; the second draft should work on the full development of each part and each paragraph; grammar and mechanical considerations can be largely ignored until the paper is nearly finished, as attention to them early on can be wasted as the text is rewritten or deleted.

TEACHING IDEAS

It can be helpful for students to spend some time reacquainting themselves with the writing wheel at this point. Many student writers tend to consider a first draft a finished product; the wheel illustrates the occasions for revising that present themselves as writers encounter difficulty with the draft. Understanding that it's okay to move back to an earlier stage in the writing process will help students feel confident even when the draft doesn't seem to be progressing as it should. Many student writers need constant reassurance that their frustrations don't stem from their inadequacies, but rather provide evidence that they are indeed writers. The visual image of the wheel offers some of that reassurance.

ADDITIONAL EXERCISE L

Having recorded observations on your writing process in your writer's log, try to "plug in" your own process on the writing wheel. Using the labels provided in the diagram, offer more specific descriptions of what you do at each of the "loops" on the wheel. Compare your diagram to those of a few of your classmates. What similarities can you find? Differences?

Advantages

By regularly consulting your outline, you will feel that you are making progress toward the completion of your paper.

Disadvantages

A comprehensive outline can so focus your vision that you will not allow yourself to stray and discover the true territory of your paper. The paper planned will be the paper written, for better or worse.

Adhering loosely to your outline

Some writers prefer to use a sketch or outline exclusively as a strategy for preparing; in the actual drafting of the paper, they abandon their plan in favor of one that they generate *while* writing the draft. Examine your outline, studying its first section carefully, and then begin writing. The outline is set aside and, once writing is under way, a new outline for each section of the paper you are about to write is created, based on the material you have just written. As you complete each section, update and adjust your outline.

Advantages

This strategy gives you the best chance of discovering material, since each new section of the paper is based on the writing you have just completed and not on an outline prepared in advance.

Disadvantages

The same freedom that gives you room to be creative can result in paragraphs that do not lead logically from one to the next and whole groupings of paragraphs that drift away from the working thesis.

Combining strategies

Some writers like to give themselves more freedom than close adherence to a predraft outline allows, but at the same time they prefer more structure than the outline-as-you-go approach provides. These writers borrow from both methods. First, they carefully review their predraft outline for each section of the paper before writing it; then they write the section *without* further reference to the outline. At the end of each section, they compare their work against the outline and plan to add or delete material as needed. They also look ahead to the next section and revise the outline, if necessary.

3 Writing one section of your paper at a sitting

Unless you are writing an introduction, conclusion, or transition, every paragraph that you write will be situated in a grouping of paragraphs, or a **section** that constitutes part of the larger document. Think of the draft you are writing as a series of sections: typically groupings of three, four, or five related paragraphs. Plan to write *one* section of your paper at a sitting. Then take a break. Sooner than you realize, the pages will add up and you will have finished the draft.

As your draft develops, you will probably find yourself devoting a section to each major point you wish to develop. (Recall that you were able to identify these points, at least most of them, by "quizzing" your working thesis—see page 78.) Every section of your paper should have a dominant, controlling focus—a **section thesis** that explicitly announces the major point you will address in the grouping of paragraphs to follow. The section thesis will help you to write your draft and, eventually, will help your readers to follow your discussion.

4 Recalling the key relationship in your thesis

Once you express a relationship in the predicate part of your thesis, you will want to develop that relationship by giving examples and providing support. *The types of paragraphs you write in a paper are tied directly to the relationships that you express in your thesis.* For instance, if your thesis states that you have inferred a sequence concerning your subject, then surely at least several of the paragraphs that you write will be introduced with *first, second, third,* and so on. If your thesis suggests a comparison, then surely you will organize a certain number of paragraphs in one of the two ways discussed under "comparison/contrast" in 5e-6. Your papers will consist of many paragraphs, of course; and only certain ones will directly develop the relationship in the predicate part of your thesis, but these will be the key paragraphs in your paper. Others will lead up to or away from these key paragraphs. Therefore, at some point in the writing of your draft, explicitly recall the key relationship of your thesis.

How to Write One Section of a Paper

1. **Prepare to write.** Identify purpose and define audience; generate and organize ideas and information; and devise a working thesis.
2. **Identify sections of the paper.** Ask of your thesis: What parts must I develop in order to deliver on the promise of this statement? Your answer of perhaps three or four points will identify the sections you need to write to complete that statement.
3. **Plan to write one section of your paper at a sitting.** If a section is long, divide it into manageable parts and write one part at a sitting.
4. **Write individual paragraphs.** Each paragraph will be related to others in the section. As you begin a second paragraph, clearly relate it to the first; relate the third paragraph to the second, and so on until you finish writing the section. Then take a break.
5. **Write other sections, one at a time.** Continue writing, building one section incrementally on the next, until you complete your first draft.

TEACHING IDEAS

The suggested technique of writing at least three related paragraphs at a sitting can help to free students of writer's block. Students should first understand that their first-draft paragraphs *will* be revised; with this knowledge, students should be more free to investigate and experiment with their writing, secure in knowing that no other readers need see their preliminary work. By helping students to focus on producing *sections,* you simultaneously help them to think of their drafts structurally and to beat the often demoralizing habit of stopping after each sentence to labor over the next. The fine-tuning of sentences is a matter for second- and third-draft attention.

5 Identifying and resolving problems in mid-draft

It is likely that at some point in the writing process you will find yourself unable to steam ahead, one section after the next. You will encounter obstacles, which you can recognize as follows: You are aware that your work in one section of the paper is not as good as it is elsewhere, or you make several attempts at writing a section and find that you simply cannot do it. When you are feeling especially frustrated, stop. Step back from your work and decide how you will get past this obstacle. Ask: Why am I having trouble? Here are several possibilities:

1. You do not have enough information to write. You have not gathered enough information or, if you have, you may not thoroughly understand it.
2. You do not understand the point you planned to make or its relation to the rest of your paper.
3. The point you planned to make no longer seems relevant or correct, given what you have discovered about your subject while writing.
4. You recognize a gap in the structure of your paper, and you suddenly see the need to expand an existing section or to write an entirely new section.
5. The material in the section seems inappropriate for your audience.
6. You have said everything you need to in a page, but the assignment calls for six to ten pages.
7. At the moment, you do not have the attention span to write.

Each of these obstacles can frustrate your attempts at writing, and only you can know what is for you a normal or abnormal level of frustration. Whatever your tolerance, develop sensors to let you know when things are not going well. Frustration usually occurs for a good reason, so you should trust the reaction and then act on it. You will come of age as a writer the moment you can realize you are having trouble and can then step away to name your problem and find a solution.

6 Working collaboratively

In assigning a writing project, your professor may ask you to work collaboratively—that is, in a group. The great advantage of creating and writing a document collaboratively is that you can put the power of several minds to work on a task that might prove overwhelming for one person. Both in content and in presentation, however, your group's work should read as though *one* person had written it even if several people have been involved in the actual writing.

- To minimize rewriting, meet with group members before any writing takes place. Agree on a structure for the overall document and then assign parts to individual group members. Agree on a consistent point of view for the paper.

- At a second meeting after writing has just begun, ask each group member to outline his or her section and to discuss its structure. As a group, think specifically of the ways in which one section will build from and lead to another. Also raise and address any problems encountered thus far in the writing.
- At the completion of a first draft, distribute the assembled document to the entire group and have each member revise for content and consistency of perspective.
- Incorporate all revisions in a single version of the document. *One* member of the group should then take responsibility for rewriting the paper so as to ensure continuity of style and voice.

3f Student paper: Rough draft

Here is Lou Cassetta's rough draft, preparations for which you have followed throughout Chapters 1–3. His instructor's comments appear in the margins and at the end of the draft. You'll see this draft revised a second and third time in Chapter 4. Lou's thesis is highlighted.

Rough Draft

Fantasizing about computers, cars, and new technology is "guy talk." I've done my share, and being able to talk the talk enabled me to get a job last summer in data entry at one of the world's largest consulting firms. There are many reasons that men, mostly, bond with machines. Many studies show that boys are encouraged to do, while girls are encouraged to watch. In our culture, girls are systematically taught not to care about machines. Only those who fight can rise above the antitechnology lessons they learned as children. Then they can enter the computer field. But when they do, they find only men.

You'll need to support these claims. Otherwise, you've already lost half your readers.

The labelling of computers as a masculine technology has created a fundamental difference between the ways that most women and most men perceive computer hardware. Many men treat their computers in the same way that muscle

Please reexamine cause and effect, here. What's the effect? What's the cause?

TEACHING IDEAS

The position the student writer takes in this essay can justifiably be called sexist. You might ask students to read and comment—and then write a note to Lou Cassetta about a plan for revision. Students in your class should be alerted to the fact that in the process of revising, Lou altered his position—but he had to do a great deal of work to get to that point. See the note immediately following.

LOOKING AHEAD

Lou Cassetta revised his essay twice, and both revisions are shown in Chapter 4. In the first revision, Lou clarified the nascent positions taken in this rough draft—in such a way that the teacher commenting on the draft was able to directly address Lou's assumptions about gender. Lou responded with a memo that outlined his plans for a second revision. The memo was approved, and he produced his final draft.

One of the points to make with your students regarding this example essay is that it illustrates how—and why—thinking about one's topic can change during, and as a consequence of, the writing process. This same point is illustrated once again in the student research paper, where the writer significantly alters his thesis during the research stages of his project.

The writing process, then, is a *thinking* process. Students have a chance to observe these mutually interdependent processes at work in the evolution of Lou Cassetta's paper.

car enthusiasts treat their hot rods. Both want the fastest, most powerful machines that money can buy. Although I am writing this paper on one of the most antiquated PCs imaginable, it is money--not desire--that prevents me from purchasing a fast computer. I can't imagine keeping this dinosaur for much longer, despite the fact that it has served me well for many years.

In contrast, Esther Dyson the editor of an influential software-industry newsletter, said that she doesn't "really care about [her computer's] innards, [she] just want[s] it to work" (qtd. in Kantrowitz 50). Oliver Strimpel, executive director of The Computer Museum in Boston, finds this pattern very common among male and female computer owners. "Men tend to be seduced by the technology itself. . . . [Females] seem to think that machines were meant to be used like the microwave oven or the dishwasher" (qtd. in Kantrowitz 50).

"seem to think"? Strimpel is sounding a bit sexist, here.

What explains the difference? Clearly social conditioning matters. Biology may mix with social training to account for gender differences. Perhaps women and men in fact differ in intellectual styles and interests. But as psychologist Lester Lefton says, "learning is far more potent in establishing and maintaining sex-role stereotypes and gender-specific attitudes" (347).

There should be no doubt that the stereotypes have very real consequences. In the classroom, the mere presence of men is enough to deter women from studying computers. Research has shown that in schools attended by both sexes, women tend to abandon a major in science more often than they do in women's colleges (Healy).

Whatever the source of women's attitudes toward technology, the results are clear. Little

TEACHING IDEAS

You might ask students to read the teacher's comments on the draft—and then to agree or disagree with the view that Lou's source, Oliver Strimpel, is "sounding a bit sexist." One point worth making is that the teacher does not assume Strimpel is sacred. Sources are to be argued with, and challenged—which is the explicit message of Chapters 1 and 2. You might ask students if Lou Cassetta is accepting Strimpel's testimony here as accurate. Do students themselves accept Strimpel's views? If some do and some don't, what does this say, then, about the use of sources?

TEACHING IDEAS

The paragraphs in this first draft are quite sketchy. Ideas are not developed. You might ask students how they would go about developing any one of Lou Cassetta's paragraphs.

Careful with statistics. Compared to what?

more than one third of bachelor's degrees in computer science are awarded to women. Fewer women than men pursue this education further: women earn about 27 percent of master's degrees in computer science, and a mere 13 percent of Ph.D.'s (Wylie 3+).

How pertinent is this ¶ to developing your main pt.?

I have seen an extreme case of a man's obsession with the newest technology conflict with his wife's utilitarian view of technology. I know a man who purchased a 486 computer in 1990 for $5000, a sum that was far beyond his budget. He did not need the machine to earn his living--it was just an expensive toy. Although one can now buy an even more powerful machine for $1600, Mr. G's computer was the best available at that time. This ridiculous act helped to break the bonds of a twenty-year marriage. Mrs. G had no desire to keep up with the expanding computer market.

Lou- why should women have to play by men's rules? Your assumptions may be sexist!

Must?! On what grounds do you say must?

If the minority of women in the world of computers wish to prove themselves as capable as men, the path is clear: women must be able to speak the language of their male counterparts. It is not unfair to expect someone, male or female, to learn the language of the computer industry when their job involves computers. People use many different types of speech depending on the occasion. For instance, the tone of this essay is much different than the tone I use when talking with my friends at home in the Bronx. As a student, I adopt the language of academic writing because I want to do well on my term papers. In the same way, women must choose to speak the language of computers developed by a male-dominated computer industry.

I had a job last summer in data entry and beginning-level programming. That job was certainly male dominated, with no female employees. Had a woman with my same skills applied for the data entry job, she may not have been

TEACHING IDEAS

Students rightfully feel some sense of triumph when they complete a draft. They've taken ideas and cast them into a document that, in at least preliminary form, have a beginning, middle, and end. This said, students then have to contend with the consequences of what they write. In this case, Lou Cassetta is being challenged. The teacher notes that his statements may be sexist. Call attention to this challenge. You might make this an opportunity to discuss with students how a draft—even though it represents progress over a sketch or outline—represents a point for *beginning* discussion. The discussion ends when the writer produces a final draft. In the meantime, the process is one of revision, of reassessing the work and rebuilding it to a point where arguments made can be considered valid, even if they don't convince all readers.

TEACHING IDEAS

Here and with the letter to Lou Cassetta, students might want to argue with the teacher. Is Lou, indeed, sounding condescending? If you put this question to the entire class, disagreement will likely follow. You might productively use this disagreement to discuss the extent to which absolute agreement will ever be reached over an essay such as Lou's. (It won't.) And given the inevitability of disagreements, what, then, becomes the guiding purpose of revision? You'll want to intercept and correct the easy cynicism of some students who conclude that since everyone will disagree in the end, anyway, one draft of a paper is as good as another. Not so! Given a single, main idea, a draft can be more or less compelling, can be argued well or argued poorly. In the humanities, at least, agreement among all readers is not the goal. Clarity of exposition is—and this is what Lou is aiming for in the various drafts of his essay.

I see you want to be fair-minded, here; but you sound condescending.

hired unless she was able to impress my boss through a simple conversation about computers. I am sure that there are many women who have lost jobs to men who were better able to impress other males with a knowledge of technology. Very likely the women were just as qualified as the men but the men, talking shop, appeared to know more about technology.

Qualified women losing jobs to men, and women stalling out in middle-management or lower-rung faculty positions is a sad state of affairs for many reasons. It is disheartening to think that despite the many strides toward equality that women have made over the years, the field of computers is vastly dominated by men. Nevertheless, the field of computers needs women. Women's perspectives about computers would help the computer field if women were given more of a chance to make executive decisions.

How would they help?

Until young women learn to ignore the messages that men, not women, use technology, and until we as a society start generating positive images of women in technology, the computer field will miss out on the innovative perspectives women in high-level positions would bring.

Again: what kinds of innovations?

Where is your "Works Cited" list?

General comments: You're exploring a complex issue, here. Realize that your claim has consequences: it's easy to read this draft and conclude that you're sexist (which, from conversations with you, I don't think is true).

You seem to be writing a problem-solution essay. In Part I, your definition of the problem, you could be clearer. What is your background in the area on which you're writing? I think you'll want to establish your credibility here. Also, you can be clearer about cause and effect. What causes the problem you've defined? Once you are clear on this, solutions follow. (You may want to consider that effects—women being underrepresented in the sciences, for instance—can sometimes themselves be causes.) See my requests for expansion and details. As for your solution, you need to expand (it's only 1¶ at present).

Be aware of your own assumptions about gender. Your advice to women about using male language will strike many readers as outrageously, unacceptably sexist—unless you explain your solution more clearly and show that you've considered other solutions, none of which work.

If you continue to locate your thesis (your solution) deep into the essay, be sure to prepare your reader for it earlier on—possibly even in the title. Try using a single phrase throughout that focuses the reader's attention. Essays can be very effective when they go against the grain of current opinion. Certainly this essay cuts against the grain: all the more reason for you to be clearer. I look forward to reading the second draft.

CHAPTER 4

The Process of Revision

KEY FEATURES

This chapter continues the discussion of the writing process begun in Chapter 3 and culminates with the final draft of Lou Cassetta's essay on gender in the computer industry. In the revising process, students are advised to consider both unity and coherence, first from the perspective of the entire paper, then individual sections or paragraphs, and then sentences. In discussing the use of instructors' and peer editors' comments, the chapter acknowledges the need for honesty, respect, and thoughtfulness on the part of both writer and reviewer. As in Chapter 3, exercises are designed primarily to guide students through the process of drafting and revising their own papers. Of special note is the extent to which Lou Cassetta revised his essay. For this student writer, the process of writing became a process of rethinking—and thus reflects what students do in most composition courses.

ESL CUE

ESL students will have learned to follow teacher instructions on the correction of "errors," but will probably not understand the process of writing/revising to improve, on their own, the structure and development of an argument. Some might be revising for the first time ever.

GROUP ACTIVITY

Sometimes students have difficulty getting distance from their writing, even when they've left it alone for a day or so. Other readers, on the other hand, can offer a fresh reading of the paper. Arrange students in groups according to the directions outlined in the Group Activity in 3c-1. Readers then answer simple, nonjudgmental questions about each draft:

1. What is the working thesis of this paper? Where does it appear?

As much as a first draft, revision is in its own way an act of creation. The difference between your first and second efforts at creating a document is that in a first draft you work to give a document potential: the writing may be incomplete, hurried, or inexact, but you are working toward an important, controlling idea. In your second and subsequent drafts, you work to make an earlier draft's potential *real*: you revise, and through revision—by adding, altering, or deleting sentences and paragraphs—you clarify your main point for yourself and, on the strength of that, for your reader. Accomplished writers expect to revise. They know that good revision reaches deep; that it is not, for the most part, about cosmetic changes (a word scratched out here, another added there) but about fundamental changes and redirections that help you discover meaning. Above all, readers expect *clarity* of ideas in your writing. When you revise, you rethink and you clarify; you will serve your own interests and your reader's by committing yourself to meaningful revision.

The Process of Revision

Think of revision as occurring in three stages—early, later, and final:

4a **Early revision:** Reread your first draft and rediscover your main idea. What you *intended* to write is not always, or even usually, what you *in fact* have written.

4b **Later revision:** Make all significant parts of your document work together in support of your main idea.

4c **Final revision (editing):** Correct errors at the sentence level that divert attention from your main point.

4a Early revision: Rediscovering your main idea

Successful writing clearly communicates an idea. When writing fails, it is very often because the writer has not understood his most important idea well enough to present it to others. A key difference between successful and unsuccessful writing is the commitment a writer makes to revision, since it is the process of revision that helps to clarify the writer's main idea. The important word here is *commitment,* not ability. You can and will learn techniques of revision. What you alone can provide is the commitment to rework drafts until they express your meaning *exactly*. Early revision involves adding, altering, or deleting entire paragraphs with the sole purpose of clarifying your main idea. Commit yourself to real and meaningful revision, and your writing will be good consistently; back away from this commitment, and your writing will fail to the degree that you back away.

Strategies for Early Revision

Pose three questions to get started on early revision. Your goal is to rediscover and clarify what you have written in a first draft. Here are some tactics to help you discover your main idea:

- What I *intended* to write in my first draft may not be what I have *in fact* written. What is the main idea of this first draft?

  Underline one sentence in your draft in answer to this question; if you cannot find such a sentence, write one.

  Choose a title for your second draft. The title will help you to clarify your main idea.

- Does what I have written in this draft satisfy my original purpose for writing?

  Review the assignment or set of instructions that began your writing project. Restate the purpose of that assignment. Reread your draft to determine the extent to which you have met this purpose. To the degree that you have not, plan to revise.

- Does my writing communicate clearly to my audience?

  Think of your audience and reread your draft with this audience clearly in mind. If need be, revise your level of language, your choice of illustrations, and your general treatment of the topic in order to help your audience understand.

1 Choosing a revision strategy that suits you

There are as many different strategies for revising a paper as there are for writing one, and the strategy you choose will depend on your temperament. Some first-draft writers work on individual paragraphs, revising continually until they achieve their idea for that paragraph before they move on. Others write and revise one section of their paper at a time, revising a grouping of related paragraphs continually until that grouping functions as a single, seamless unit. Still other writers complete an entire first draft and then revise. The approach to revision advocated here is that a writer make several "passes" over a draft and on each pass revise with a different focus. First, revise the largest elements (the sections); on the next pass, revise paragraphs within sections; and on the final pass (or passes), revise individual sentences within paragraphs. Choose a revision strategy that suits your temperament.

2. Is there evidence of any competing thesis? If so, where does it appear?
3. Which thesis seems more consistent with the body of the paper? Why?

In addition to helping writers hone their theses, this activity provides nonthreatening practice for later peer editing sessions in which students make judgments on each other's papers.

TEACHING IDEAS

Bring to class multiple drafts of a paper or essay you have recently finished. Or bring multiple drafts of a single paragraph. Students are often fascinated to learn that their composition teachers practice the very principles they teach. With various drafts of a page before you and the students, discuss how your early revisions of a paragraph or page differ from later revisions. Recreate for students your thinking as you moved closer to the final form of a passage. Then make the link to student writing and to your expectations for early and later revisions in their work.

ADDITIONAL EXERCISE A

Ask students to prepare a lesson on revision, to be presented in a small group. Students should make and distribute photocopies of their various rewrites of one page, or a particular set of paragraphs, beginning with the final draft. After students have reported in their groups on the process of revision, have the group summarize the various strategies for revision just presented. Groups could write major points on sheets of easel paper that would be taped on the walls of the room, and you could lead the class in examining similarities and differences in revision technique. Doubtless, the class will observe more than one strategy at work, which is just the point of the discussion in 4a-1.

TEACHING IDEAS

Students sometimes have difficulty appreciating the change of perspective needed when making the transition from first draft to second and subsequent drafts. In a first draft, the writer is primarily a creative force directed *partially* by a critical awareness of how a draft should develop. In a second draft, the writer shifts intellectual modes and becomes a creative *critic* whose main purpose is to evaluate the large-scale content and structural elements of the first draft. Criticism must be creative in the sense that it is never enough for the writer to find a problem; the writer must also be alert to multiple solutions, several of which might be explored until the right fix is found for the draft. Moving to later drafts, the writer focuses on smaller units—the section, the paragraph, and the sentence. With each draft comes a corresponding narrowing of critical focus, from large elements to smaller. Student writers may not appreciate how they can help themselves through the process of revision by explicitly acknowledging these changing perspectives.

BACKGROUND

See Maggy Smith, *Teaching College Writing* (Boston: Allyn & Bacon, 1995). Chapter 8: "Rewriting—Revising." 122–39. Smith's discussion is applied and quite helpful in planning, setting the agenda for, and working through conferences with students. Smith also discusses peer discussion groups.

ADDITIONAL EXERCISE B

ACROSS THE CURRICULUM In order to understand more fully the notion of a thesis as a contract, explain what you would expect the writer to address given the following thesis statements:

1. The fall of communist governments in Eastern Europe has made it necessary for capitalist economies to reassess their values.
2. In bringing Alice Walker's *The Color Purple* to the screen, Steven Spielberg abandoned the essence of Celie's conversations with God.

2 Strategies for clarifying and developing your main idea

The overall objective of your first revision of a draft, which will be your major revision, is to rediscover your main idea. You began your first draft with a main idea that you wanted to develop. But what you intended to write may not be what you have in fact written. Now is the time to check. On the basis of your evaluation, you will plan a second draft.

Reread your first draft with care, looking for some sentence other than your working thesis that more accurately describes what you have written. Often, such a "competing" thesis appears near the end of the draft, the place where you force yourself to summarize. If you can find no competing thesis and are sure that your original working thesis does not fit the paper you have written, modify the existing working thesis or write a new one. Be prepared to quiz the new thesis as you did before. See the box in 3d-4 to review techniques for doing this.

Illustration: Lou Cassetta's Paper

REVISING THE THESIS

As Lou reread his first draft and reacted to challenges from his instructor, he still did not find a competing thesis. He felt that he'd written a first draft on more or less the topic he intended. His goal in revision was to refine, rather than to reinvent, his essay. In doing this, Lou clarified the thesis enough to reveal a need to reinvent his essay. For now, though, observe how he extends and slightly modifies the thesis so that it might meet with fewer objections from readers. Changes in the revised thesis are set in boldface:

First-draft thesis:

If the minority of women in the world of computers wish to prove themselves as capable as men, the path is clear: women must be able to speak the language of their male counterparts.

Second-draft thesis:

If the minority of women in the world of computers wish to prove themselves as capable as men, the path is clear **and, very likely, painful: women should learn** to speak the language of their male counterparts.

Note two changes in the revision. Lou now writes that women *should* (as opposed to *must*) learn the language, suggesting a less absolute view and more concern—though he is still clearly making a value judgment. In adding that the solution will "very likely" be painful for women who follow his advice, he suggests a growing awareness that these social issues are complex and have consequences. Still, Lou has not yet seriously challenged some of his assumptions, and he has lots of reevaluating and revising work ahead of him.

Outline the sections of a revised paper.

Recall that a *section* of your paper is a group of related paragraphs (see 3e-3 and 5a-1). Based on your revised thesis and on your development questions and comments about that thesis, outline the sections of a revised paper.

Illustration: Lou Cassetta's paper

REVISING THE OUTLINE

Once Lou revised his thesis, he created an obligation to revise the body of his essay so that sections would develop every element of the new thesis. Compare the outline of the draft Lou has completed with the outline of the draft he intends to write. Sections added to the second-draft outline are boldfaced:

Draft 1	*Draft 2*
Introduction (¶1)	Introduction (¶1)
Problem	Problem
Problem defined (¶2)	**Differences, men/women**
Effects of problems: differences (¶3)	**re: computers (¶s 2–3)**
Explanation of differences (¶4)	Explanation of differences (¶4)
Consequences of problem (¶s 5–6)	Problem defined (¶5)
Example—Mr. G. (¶7)	Solution
Solution	Solution proposed (¶6)
Solution proposed (¶8)	**Other solutions explored (¶7)**
Conclusion (¶s 9–11)	**Psychological costs of solution (¶8)**
	Conclusion (¶9)

Lou's revised thesis sets a new agenda for him to pursue in the revised essay. Primarily, Lou plans to expand discussion of his proposed solution. Whereas he previously allotted seven paragraphs to a statement of the problem and only one paragraph to the proposed solution in draft 1, Lou now plans to even the treatment in draft 2.

Incorporate sections of your first draft into your revised outline.

Study your new outline. Reexamine your first draft to determine how much of it will fit, with or without changes, into your plans for the final paper. Then, retrieve your first draft and cut and paste usable sections of this draft onto your final outline. Be sure to reread each sentence of first-draft writing that you move into the second draft. Every sentence must contribute toward developing the meaning of your newly conceived thesis.

LOOKING AHEAD

Working with a computer can be enormously helpful in relieving students of the tedium of revision. Those sentences and paragraphs that remain largely unchanged from one draft to the next can be block copied, if a word-processing program permits, between two documents that the student shuttles between on the same screen. Ask students to see Appendix A, Writing with a Computer, as they begin the process of revision.

BACKGROUND

See two reprinted articles in James C. McDonald, *The Allyn & Bacon Sourcebook for College Writing Teachers* (Needham: Allyn & Bacon, 1996): Lester Faigley and Stephen Witte, "Analyzing Revision"; and Ann E. Berthoff, "Recognition, Representation, and Revision."

ADDITIONAL EXERCISE C

ACROSS THE CURRICULUM Sometimes it's helpful to look at paragraphs written by professionals in order to better understand the concepts of unity and coherence. Find a brief (two- to four-page) self-contained section in one of your textbooks, and analyze it for unity and coherence. Use strategies such as the following: find the thesis; outline the selection; relate sections or paragraphs to the thesis; identify the logic that underlies the arrangement of paragraphs; identify transitional words, phrases, sentences, and paragraphs.

LOOKING BACK

In revision, writers adopt something of an adversarial response to their own work. To perfect their work, they need to think critically about it, which entails challenging their assertions and their defenses of those assertions. The habit of challenging oneself promotes critical thinking at all stages of the writing process, particularly in revision. See the discussion at 1b, where many of the questions suggested for challenging source materials can be directed toward the student's own work.

CRITICAL DECISIONS

Use the Thinking and Writing Wheel adapted from Chapter 3 to guide you through the revision process:

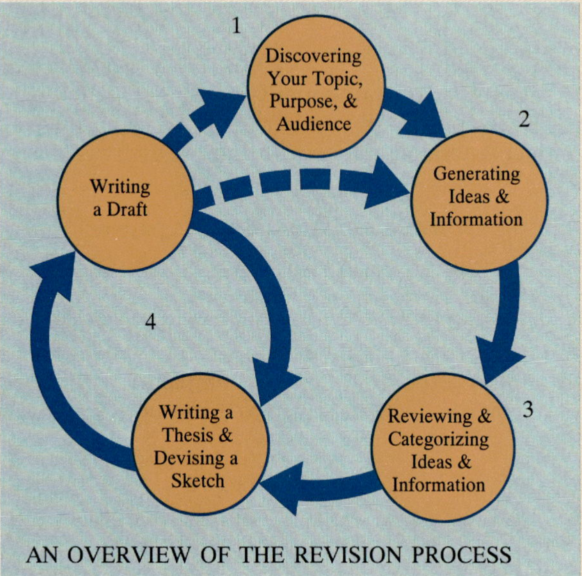

AN OVERVIEW OF THE REVISION PROCESS

1. While revising, you may need to leave the draft to reconsider your topic, purpose, or audience. Ask: If this is an explanation, is the topic clear? Are the audience's needs well defined? If this is an argument, will this draft convince readers? Can the claim be further supported? Have objections been raised—and answered?
2. While revising, you may need to leave the draft and return to your source materials, searching for information and quotations that will help develop key points. You may also need to leave the draft to pursue and develop new ideas.
3. Once generated, fresh materials need to be integrated into the essay. Your revised essay must be coherent and unified. How will you achieve these goals?
4. (a) **Early Revision:** Revise, incorporating new elements into your draft. Emerge from this inner loop as often as necessary to clarify your topic, purpose, and audience; to generate new materials; and to incorporate new elements into the revision. At the end of early revision, you will probably not need to leave this inner loop for new materials.

   (b) **Later Revision:** Revise, concentrating on the ways in which sections —groupings of related paragraphs—work together to support the essay's main idea.

   (c) **Final Revision:** Revise, refining your essay's tone, sentence structure, and word choice. The essay should be error-free.

Write new sections of the final outline, as needed.

The preceding step will leave you with a partial paper: a detailed outline, some of the sections of which (imported from your first draft) are close to complete, other sections of which are indicated in the sketchiest possible terms by a phrase in your outline. You will need to write these sections from scratch. Before beginning a new section of your paper, write a section thesis to help focus your efforts (see 3e-3 and 5a-2).

3 Reconsidering purpose and audience

Purpose

At some point in the process of revision you will want to reconsider your earliest reasons for writing. You may have been asked to explain, describe, argue, compare, analyze, summarize, define, discuss, illustrate, evaluate, or prove. (See explanations of these and other important word meanings in assignments in 41b.) With your purpose firmly in mind, evaluate your first draft to determine the extent to which you have met that purpose. Alter your revision plans, if necessary, to satisfy your reason for writing.

- Identify the key verb in the assignment and define that verb with reference to your topic. (See 41b.)
- If you have trouble understanding the purpose, seek out your professor or your professor's assistant. Bring your draft to a conference and explain the direction you've taken.
- Once you identify the parts of a paper that will achieve a stated purpose, incorporate those parts into your plans for a revised draft.

Audience

Revisit your initial audience analysis (see 3a-3); will your audience be classmates, fellow majors, or a professor? Take whatever conclusions you reached in your analysis and use them as a tool for evaluating your first draft. You may find it useful to pose these questions:

- How will this subject appeal to my readers?
- Is the level of difficulty with which I have treated this subject appropriate for my readers?
- Is my choice of language, in both its tone (see 3a-4) and its level of difficulty, appropriate for my readers?
- Are my examples appropriate in interest and complexity for my readers?

Make changes to your revision plans according to your analysis of the first draft.

4 Choosing and using a title

Before rewriting your paper, use your revised thesis to devise a title. A title creates a context for your readers; a title alerts readers to your topic and

LOOKING AHEAD

Ask students to respond to the change of titles in the drafts of Lou Cassetta's paper. The title changes from first to second to third draft—and these changes represent the evolution in Lou's thinking. The first draft, titled "Rough Draft," was ill-focused. Once Lou focused in the second draft, "The Value of Shop Talk," he articulated assumptions that proved to be problematic. Lou revised a final time and produced "Gender Differences in the Computer Industry." You might want to discuss the ways in which a title reflects or suggests content. As content shifts, so will (must) the title.

your intentions for treating it. Forcing yourself to devise a title before beginning your major revision will help you to clarify your main idea. A *descriptive* title directly announces the content of a paper and is appropriate for reports and write-ups of experiments: occasions when you are expected to be direct. An *evocative* title is a playful, intriguing, or otherwise indirect attempt to pique a reader's interest. Both descriptive and evocative titles should be brief (no longer than ten words).

EXERCISE 1

Individual responses

EXERCISE 1

Following advice offered in this section, revise the first draft of the paper you wrote in response to Exercise 11, in Chapter 3. Your early revision may be a major one, requiring you to rework your thesis and to redefine major sections of the paper.

TEACHING IDEAS

One concern of balance and development can be underscored by class discussion of information from other classes. Have students choose an introductory course they've taken recently and answer the following questions (collect answers on the blackboard or an overhead transparency): What key terms, concepts, and names did you learn for the first time in this course? As the course continued, what terms, concepts, and names became so familiar that you no longer needed explanation? How are those terms, concepts, and names treated in the text as they become more familiar? In the instructor's lectures? In what situations do you find it necessary to explain or identify those terms, concepts, and names? Why do you have to explain them sometimes? Now ask them to keep these questions in mind as they consider their present text. Have they provided enough information? Have they begun to use shortened references too soon (or too late)?

To underscore ideas of unity and topic sentence placement before students work on their own drafts, choose another essay from the text and ask students (1) to identify main thesis, section theses, and topic sentences in each paragraph; (2) to evaluate the unity on each level; and (3) to consider how effectively the topic sentence in each paragraph has been positioned or how it might be revised.

4b Later revision: Bringing your main idea into focus

Your first major revision of a draft (the revision you achieved if you completed Exercise 1) requires the courage to look deep into your paper and make fundamental changes in order to present a single idea clearly. Later revisions will not be dramatic or far-reaching, and will require for the most part that you understand and are able to systematically apply certain principles of organization. Three principles of organization important to a later revision are unity, coherence, and balance.

1 Focusing the paper through unity

A paper is unified when the writer discusses only those elements of the subject implied by its thesis. Unity is a principle of logic that applies equally to the whole paper, to sections, and to individual paragraphs. In a unified paper, you discuss only those topics that can be anticipated by someone who reads your thesis.

A unified discussion will not stray from the sentence that organizes and focuses any one of these principal parts of a paper. Recall that a *thesis* announces and controls the content of an entire essay, and that a *section thesis* announces and controls the content of a section. Just so, a *topic sentence* announces and controls the content of a single paragraph. Think of the topic sentence as a paragraph-level *thesis,* and you will see the principle of unity at work at *all* levels of the paper. At each level of the essay, a general statement is used to guide you in assembling specific, supporting parts.

ESSAY-LEVEL UNITY	The thesis (the most general statement in the essay) governs your choice of sections in a paper.
SECTION-LEVEL UNITY	Section theses (the second-most general statements in the essay) govern your choice of paragraphs in a section.

Paragraph-level unity Topic sentences (the third-most general statements in the essay) govern your choice of sentences in a paragraph.

A unified section of a paper is a discussion of those topics implied by your section thesis (see 3e-3 and 5a-2). Every topic generated by quizzing the thesis will become a *section* of your final paper. You will devote at least one paragraph, and maybe more, to developing each section, or subtopic, of the thesis. In a unified paragraph, you discuss only one topic, the one implied by your topic sentence (see 5c).

2 Focusing the paper through coherence

Coherence describes the clarity of the relationship between one unit of meaning and another: between sections of a paper, between paragraphs within sections, and between sentences within paragraphs. Like unity, coherence is a principle of logic that applies equally to the whole paper, to sections, and to individual paragraphs. A *whole paper* is coherent when its sections (groupings of related paragraphs) follow one another in a sensible order. A *section* of the paper is coherent when the individual paragraphs that constitute it follow one another in a sensible order. And a *paragraph* is coherent when individual sentences that comprise it follow one another in a sensible order. At every level of a paper, you establish coherence by building logical bridges, or transitions, between thoughts. A **transition** may be a word, a sentence, or a paragraph devoted to building a smooth, logical relationship. In all cases, a transition has a double function: to remind readers of what they have just read and then to forecast for them what they are about to read. Transitional expressions include *additionally, likewise, first, second (and so on), afterward, for example, of course, accordingly, however, in conclusion,* and *on the whole.* (See 5d-3 for a detailed discussion of transitions and a more complete list.)

Transitions serve to highlight relationships that already exist between sections, paragraphs, or sentences that you have placed in a particular order. If you have trouble finding a word or sentence to serve as an effective transition, reexamine the sentences, paragraphs, or sections that you are trying to link. You may not have arranged them coherently in the first place and may need to rearrange them.

As you revise your paper, pause to analyze its sections *in relation* to each other. Rearrange sections, if need be, in order to improve the logical flow of ideas among the largest units of meaning, the paper's sections.

3 Focusing the paper through balance

Balance is a principle of development that guides you in expanding, condensing, and cutting material as you revise. First drafts are typically uneven in the amount of attention given to each section of a paper. In revision,

GROUP ACTIVITY

Have students work on each other's drafts in small groups. Ask them to work on the unity of the essay at each level: overall, by section, by paragraph. Ask them to identify the main thesis. Does every section of the essay relate directly (and solely) to the thesis of the paper? Ask them to identify each section thesis. Does each paragraph in the section relate directly (and solely) to the section thesis? Ask them to identify each topic sentence. Does each sentence in a paragraph relate directly (and solely) to the topic sentence? Have students write a short report (1–2 pages) of how effectively the writer has achieved unity at this stage of her/his writing, or what else would be necessary to create a more unified final draft.

TEACHING IDEAS

Students sometimes will need the idea reinforced that the *principles* of unity and coherence remain the same, whether they are applied at the level of the essay, the section, or the paragraph. Unity deals with the treatment of like ideas; coherence, with the smooth linkage of ideas. The relative size of the parts being grouped and linked will change as one's focus changes. In unifying or making coherent a paper, one looks to the paper's sections; in unifying or making coherent a section, one looks to paragraphs; in unifying or making coherent a paragraph, one looks to sentences. Students need to learn the principles only once and then apply them in slightly differing ways.

ACROSS THE CURRICULUM

Sentence-Level Revision

Writers in all disciplines revise their sentences, trying to make them more precise, concise, and readable. Whatever the discipline in which you work, you can expect reading materials to be the product of multiple revisions. As a writer across the disciplines, you will be expected to revise your sentences until they precisely and concisely express your meaning. In this example, computer scientist Linda Cohen revises a brief paragraph on the automation of semiconductor (computer-chip) manufacturing.

First draft: Because technicians introduce particulate matter into the environment, automated equipment and robots are used in the manufacture of semiconductor chips. Oil from the skin, dust, hairs from eyelashes, and even residue smoke from the lungs can contaminate the chips, rendering them worthless. Robot arms handle the delicate semiconductor wafers, using vacuum suction, transferring them from one process to the next, while automated equipment sends information on the process to a host computer without involving a technician.

Revisions: ~~Because~~ *Human* technicians introduce ~~particulate matter~~ *dirt* into the *cleanroom* environment ~~automated equipment and robots are used in the manufacture~~ of semiconductor ~~chips~~ *manufacturing.* Oil from the skin, dust, hairs from eyelashes, and even residue smoke from the lungs can contaminate the chips, rendering them worthless. *For this reason, the process is now automated.* Robot arms *with suction devices* handle the delicate semiconductor wafers, ~~using vacuum suction, transferring them from one process to the next, while automated equipment sends information on the process to a host computer without involving a technician.~~ *eliminating humans and their contaminants from the process.*

Final draft: Human technicians introduce dirt into the cleanroom environment of semiconductor manufacturing. Oil from the skin, dust, hairs from eyelashes, and even residue smoke from the lungs can contaminate the chips, rendering them worthless. For this reason, the process is now automated. Robot arms with suction devices handle the delicate semiconductor wafers, eliminating humans and their contaminants from the process.

one of your jobs is to review the weight (the extent of development) you have given each of the topics you have discussed and to determine how appropriate that weight is to the importance of that particular point. At times, you will need to *expand:* to add material, in which case you will need to return to the notes you made in preparing to write. You may need to generate new information by reflecting on your subject, by conducting additional library research, or both. At times, you will need to *condense:* to take a lengthy paragraph, for example, and reduce it to two sentences. At other times you will need to *cut:* to delete sentences because they are off the point or because they give too much attention to a subordinate point.

EXERCISE 2

Revise your first draft for unity, coherence, and balance following the guidelines discussed in this chapter.

EXERCISE 2

Individual responses

4c Final revision

1 Editing

Editing is revision at the sentence level: the level at which you attend to style, grammar, punctuation, and word choice. Depending on their preferences, writers will edit (just as they revise) throughout the writing process, from the first draft through to the last. It would be misleading to state flatly that the process of sentence-level rewriting should wait until all issues of unity and coherence are resolved. Still, to the extent that you *can* hold off, save editing until the later drafts, once you are relatively confident that your paper has a final thesis and that the major sections of the paper are in order. In any event, don't allow sentence-level concerns to block your writing process early on—especially since the sentence you are fretting over may not even make it to the final draft.

Matters of precision are not so easily held off, however. Precise wording means precise thinking, and your ability to think clearly at any point in the draft will affect your subsequent writing. Use your judgment. If you find yourself struggling with the wording of an especially important sentence, take the time to edit and get it right. But if you are groping for a word in a sentence that is not central to your thinking, hold off on editing. Later in the writing process you will have time enough to settle questions of style, grammar, punctuation, usage, and spelling. You need not memorize rules concerning these matters as long as you can recognize problems and seek help in a handbook or a dictionary.

A suggestion made in the preface is worth repeating here: take an hour to read the introductions to each of the chapters in the handbook. If such a review is not realistic, then read the introductions to the chapters on sentence errors (see 12–16), effective sentences (see 17–20), and punctuation (see 24–29). Your review will give you a sense of the types of errors to watch for when editing. In addition, you can use the "Spotlight on Common Errors" device in the endpapers and in key chapters of this book. Use the "Spotlight" pages as checklists for uncovering and revising the most common sentence and punctuation errors.

REFERENCES

LAIB, NEVIN. "Conciseness and Amplification." CCC 41 (1990): 443–58. Uses a historical approach to argue for balance between brevity and elaboration in prose.

WILLIAMS, JOSEPH. *Style: Ten Lessons in Clarity and Grace.* 2nd ed. Glenview: Scott Foresman, 1985. Practical advice on how to correct errors in style, covering words, sentences, and paragraphs.

2 Proofreading

Before you call a paper finished, check for minor errors that may annoy readers and embarrass you. Reread your paper to identify and correct misspelled words; words (often prepositions) omitted from sentences; words that have been doubled; punctuation that you tend to forget; and homonyms (writing *there* instead of *their*). If you have trouble spotting these minor errors in your writing, find a way to disrupt your usual pattern of reading so that the errors will become visible to you. One technique is to photocopy your work and have a friend read it aloud. You read along and make corrections. Another technique is to read each line of your paper in reverse order, from the last word on the line to the first. This approach forces you to focus on one word at a time. Besides checking for minor errors, review your occasion for writing one last time to make sure you have prepared your manuscript in an appropriate form. (See Appendix B on Manuscript Form and Preparation.)

3 Determining when a final draft is *final*

At some point you must determine that your paper is finished. In the age of word processing, this is not always an easy decision since you can make that one last correction and have the computer print a new page with relative ease. If you work with a typewriter and not a computer, then the decision about your final draft is more clear-cut. At some point you will refuse to retype another page if the change you are making does not seem worth the effort.

When changes seem not to improve the product, then you have reached an end to revision and editing. To consider a draft final, you should be satisfied that your paper has met these standards:

- The paper has a clearly stated main point to communicate.
- It has met all requirements of unity and coherence at the levels of the paper, section, and paragraph.
- It is punctuated correctly and is free of errors in grammar and usage.

Stylistically, you could edit your papers *ad infinitum.* For especially important papers, take extra time to ensure that your writing is crisp and direct and that your sentence rhythms are pleasing. But once you have met your obligations in the final draft, any changes you make will amount to refinements of an already competent work. To be sure, stylistic editing can mean the difference between a good work and an excellent one. Eventually, however, you will reach a point at which changes do not improve the quality of your paper. When you reach this point, stop.

EXERCISE 3

Edit the draft of the paper you have revised for purpose, coherence, and balance. Realize that you may need to make several passes at your draft to put it into final form. Now proofread your final draft.

TEACHING IDEAS

While most instructors are experienced in responding to student drafts, many still fight the tendency to "bleed all over the paper." From the instructor's perspective, of course, a detailed response is an indication of the care the instructor has given the paper. From the student writer's perspective, unfortunately, an excessively annotated paper can be devastating: where does she even *begin* to revise? Many of us have heard the lament, "This is so terrible; I might as well toss it out and start over!" A few guidelines might be helpful in considering where and how to comment on drafts:

Look at the big picture—as the student makes global revisions, many of the problem areas in the present draft will be revised extensively.

Respond as a reader, not a teacher—students need to understand that teachers are simply audiences with a gradebook.

Don't think in terms of grades—none of these comments are designed to justify a grade; they're designed exclusively with revision in mind.

In fact, some instructors choose to write only an end comment on drafts, focusing on the primary considerations that need to be addressed.

EXERCISE 3

Individual responses

4d Responding to editorial advice from peers or professors

One of your jobs as a writer is to learn how to give and receive editorial advice. All writers can benefit from an editor, a person whose fresh perspective can identify trouble spots that escaped the writer's view. If you are working collaboratively with your peers you will discover this quickly. There are two basic ground rules for giving and receiving editorial advice: the first concerns ego and the second, honesty.

1 Receiving advice

Without question, it is difficult and sometimes painful to be told by an instructor or fellow student that your paper needs a major revision. As the writer of a paper that does not yet succeed, you should be aware that critical comments, provided they come from a responsible source, are being directed at your work and not at you. To the extent possible, disengage your ego from the editorial review and respond not according to your hurt feelings but to the substance of the comments directed at your paper.

As a writer, you have the absolute prerogative to accept, to accept partially, or to reject editorial advice. If you truly disagree with your editor, even one who will at some point be grading you, then you should hold your ground and thoughtfully explain what you were trying to do in the paper, what you would like to do, and why you cannot accept a particular suggestion for revision. *Thoughtfully* is the key word here. First, give your editor the benefit of any doubt and assume that the advice offered is well founded. If the advice seems wrong, say: "I don't understand . . . Could you explain again. . . ." If you understand the editor's advice and continue to disagree, say so—and give your reasons. But remember that if the editor is responsible, he or she has the interests of your paper in mind and is making suggestions to improve your effort. These suggestions deserve an honest hearing.

2 Giving advice

As an editor, you will want to be similarly mindful of ego and honesty. First, you must allow the writer his or her topic and interest in it. Do not criticize because a topic does not interest you. Next, realize that this is not your paper that you are commenting on. Disinvest your ego from the job so that you do not attempt in your comments to make the paper yours. Realize as well the power of your criticism. Many people feel fragile about their writing, and when you must criticize, be respectful. Most writing has something good in it. Start there and be specific with your praise. State "I like this sentence," and say why. Then compare passages that don't work to those that do, and explain the differences you see. Be honest with your criticism.

TEACHING IDEAS

One of the most rewarding—and most difficult—activities that student writers engage in is peer editing. It's rewarding because students become adept at revising by looking closely at the work of others; they also develop a greater sense of being real writers when their audience is expanded beyond the instructor. But it's difficult for students to offer honest criticism; it's so much easier and more pleasant to praise whatever drafts come their way. Perhaps the most effective way to counter the tendency to "be nice and not hurt anyone's feelings" is to expose that attitude for the myth it is: It's not "nice" to remain silent about an obvious problem when the writer faces grading by a demanding instructor. Students need to understand that refusing to be honest when evaluating each other's drafts is a selfish behavior. That being said, they also need to know how to phrase their comments so as not to "hurt anyone's feelings." One way instructors may facilitate tactful comments is to design an evaluation sheet that calls for responses to be phrased in nonjudgmental ways. The "group activities" guidelines throughout this chapter allow students to offer meaningful feedback in nonthreatening ways.

GROUP ACTIVITY

Sometimes it's easier for students to offer criticism of drafts when they don't have to face the writer. Before asking students to evaluate each other's drafts, you may wish to distribute anonymous drafts for students to practice on. These drafts may be from your files or drafts you've composed for the occasion. (Using genuine student drafts shouldn't be a problem if you've received permission and if you preserve anonymity by not using material that's less than three years old.) In groups, students can evaluate the sample drafts and discuss their responses.

Guidelines for Peer Editing

1. Understand your role as an editor. Disinvest your ego and work to improve the paper according to the author's needs, not your own.
2. Ask the writer to identify elements of the paper to which you should pay special attention.
3. Questions you might consider as you are reading:

   Is the writer helping me to become interested in this topic?

   Do all the parts of this paper seem to be present? Are general points backed up with specific examples?

   Is the writing at the sentence level sharp?

   How much help does the writer need with the nuts and bolts of grammar and punctuation?
4. Begin with the positive. Whether you are writing your editorial comments or are delivering them in conference, begin with the parts of the paper that you liked. If at all possible, find *something* that is worthy of a compliment.
5. Be specific with criticism. When you see room for improvement, identify specific words, sentences, or paragraphs, and state specifically what you think needs changing and why. If possible, build your constructive criticisms on earlier strengths:

   Avoid statements such as "This is vague."

   Strive for statements such as "Your sentences in this section don't have the same vivid detail as your earlier sentences."
6. End your editorial advice with a summary of what you have observed. Then suggest a point-by-point action plan for the writer. That is, advise the writer on specific steps to take that will lead to an improved paper.

The better you edit other people's work, the more proficient you will become at editing your own. Whatever your editorial skills, you can benefit from the editorial advice of others precisely because they are not you and can therefore offer a fresh perspective. In developing your own guidelines for giving editorial advice, you may want to build on the notes in the box above.

4e Revising a first draft

Here is Lou's second draft, followed by his instructor's comments and a note on Lou's conference with his instructor. As it turned out, writing a second draft brought to light several of Lou's unchallenged assumptions about women and men in the computer industry. As a result, Lou revised his essay far more substantially in a third (and final) draft, for which he developed an entirely new thesis. Lou's thesis is highlighted.

REFERENCES

BECK, JAMES P. "Asking Students to Annotate Their Own Papers." CCC 38 (1982): 322–23. Discusses effectiveness of students' evaluating the strategies used in their own papers.

GERE, ANN RUGGLES. *Writing Groups: History, Theory, and Implications.* Carbondale: Southern Illinois UP, 1987. A review of writing groups, including theory and practice. Includes annotated bibliography.

GRIMM, NANCY. "Improving Students' Responses to Their Peers' Essays." CCC 37 (1986): 91–94. Practical advice on using response groups in the classroom.

HARRIS, JEANNETTE. "Proofreading: A Reading/Writing Skill." CCC 38 (1987): 464–66. Highlights strategies students can use to proofread without getting caught up in content of a paper.

HERRINGTON, ANNE J., and DEBORAH CADMAN. "Peer Review and Revising in an Anthropology Course: Lessons for Learning." CCC 42 (1991): 184–99. Argues that a collaborative approach to writing is valuable in "content" courses as well as in writing classes.

TRIMBUR, JOHN. "Collaborative Learning and Teaching Writing." *Perspectives on Research and Scholarship in Composition.* Eds. Ben W. McLelland and Timothy R. Donovan. New York: MLA, 1985. 87–109. Analysis of collaborative learning, emphasizing implications for classrooms.

REFERENCES

BUTTURF, DOUGLAS R., and NANCY I. SOMMERS. "Placing Revision in a Reinvented Rhetorical Tradition." *Reinventing the Rhetorical Tradition.* Eds. Aviva Freedman and Ian Pringle. Conway: L & S Books, 1980. 99–104. Instructors' comments should focus on revision.

The Value of Shop Talk

(Second Draft)

When I applied for a job in computer data entry last summer at one of the world's largest management consulting firms, I never thought that my experience as a grease monkey would help. Although knowing how to work a gas pump did not make me a better typist, I learned important communication skills at the gas station that I used to get the office job. At the gas station, my co-workers and I always talked about the fastest and most sophisticated automobiles and how much we would like to own them. When I applied for the data entry position, I impressed my boss by engaging in a conversation about his laptop computer. Many men are fascinated by the newest and fastest machines and love to talk about them. I have always taken part in conversations about these machines, and for once it paid off.

Many men treat their computers in the same way that muscle car enthusiasts treat their hot rods. Both want the fastest, most powerful machines that money can buy. Although I am writing this paper on one of the most antiquated PCs imaginable, it is money--not desire--that prevents me from purchasing a fast computer. I can't imagine keeping this dinosaur for much longer, despite the fact that it has served me well for many years. In contrast, Esther Dyson, editor of an influential software-industry newsletter, said that she doesn't "really care about [her computer's] innards, [she] just want[s] it to work" (qtd. in Kantrowitz 50). Oliver Strimpel, executive director of The Computer Museum in Boston, finds this pattern very common among male and female computer owners. "Men tend to be seduced by the technology itself. . . . [Females] seem to think that machines were meant to be used like the microwave

HARRIS, MURIEL. *Teaching One-to-One.* Urbana, IL: NCTE, 1986. A practical discussion of the conference method of teaching writing.

HELLER, DANA A. "Silencing the Soundtrack: An Alternative to Marginal Comments." *CCC* 40 (1989): 210–15. Demonstrates an alternative method, based on post-structuralist theory, of responding to student papers.

LINDEMANN, ERIKA. *A Rhetoric for Writing Teachers.* 2nd. ed. New York: Oxford UP, 1987. 207–33. A discussion of meaningful comments on student texts (includes bibliography).

ROBERTSON, MICHAEL. "Is Anybody Listening?" *CCC* 37 (1986): 87–91. Instructors should focus comments on text's content rather than its style or technique.

SHAW, MARGARET L. "What Students Don't Say: An Approach to the Student Text." *CCC* 41 (1991): 45–54. Uses recent critical and literary theory to help instructors make responses that encourage students to think critically about their content and their writing/reading process.

SIEMINSKI, GREG C. "Couching Our Cutting the Compassion." *CCC* 42 (1991): 211–17. Using the analogy of surgery, argues that instructors must "cultivate a bedside manner" in student conferences.

SOMMERS, NANCY. "Responding to Student Writing." *CCC* 33 (1982): 148–56. An analysis of the problems involved in teachers' responses to students' texts.

LOOKING AHEAD

You might ask students to compare Lou Cassetta's use of the Esther Dyson quotation at this point in his second draft with his use near the end of his third draft.

LOOKING BACK

If students have worked through Chapter 3, they will have seen illustrations of Lou Cassetta's preparing to write this draft. Before they read it, you might ask your students to review Cassetta's various notes, his working thesis, and his sketch. See the various illustration panels in Chapter 3, which present a realistic view of the effort entailed in preparing to write a first draft.

TEACHING IDEAS

You may want to point out to students that the teacher's comments on Cassetta's first draft are restricted to matters of content. Cassetta has made various sentence-level errors, and students can assume the teacher has noted these. The teacher wants Cassetta to reconsider *content,* primarily, and *structure* when thinking about a first major revision. At the appropriate point, late in the writing process, Cassetta devotes time to revising sentences. Early on, he focused on larger concerns.

TEACHING IDEAS

You might ask students to summarize Lou's key positions in this draft. Likely, students will concentrate on the claim made in paragraph 6. How objectionable is the claim? How reasonable a job has Lou done in defending it? Lou's teacher did not believe the claim was well supported or that assumptions underlying it were examined with care. As with the first draft, you might invite students to respond not only to the paper itself but to the teacher's response to the paper.

oven or the dishwasher" (qtd. in Kantrowitz 50).

Even among women who are technologically sophisticated, we find differences in fundamental attitudes about technology and its uses. Newsweek writer Barbara Kantrowitz reports the following:

> In one intriguing study by the Center for Children and Technology, a New York think tank, men and women in technical fields were asked to dream up machines of the future. Men typically imagined devices that could help them "conquer the universe," says Jan Hawkins, director of the center. She says women wanted machines that met people's needs, "the perfect mother." . . . If everyone approached technology the way women do now, "we wouldn't be pushing envelopes," says Cornelia Bruner, associate director of the center. "Most women, even those who are technologically sophisticated, think of machines as a means to an end." Men think of machines as an extension of their own power. (55)

What explains the difference? Clearly social conditioning matters. Biology may mix with social training to account for gender differences we see in the sciences and technology. Perhaps women and men in fact differ in intellectual styles and interests. But as psychologist Lester Lefton says, "learning is far more potent in establishing and maintaining sex-role stereotypes and gender-specific attitudes" (347).

There can be no doubt that the stereotypes have very real consequences. In the classroom, the presence of men--both as teachers and as fellow students--is enough to deter women from studying computers. Research has shown that in schools attended by both sexes, women tend to abandon a major in science more often than they do in women's colleges (Healy). Little more than one third of bachelor's degrees in computer science are awarded to women. Fewer women than men pursue this education further: women earn about 27 percent of master's degrees in computer science, and a mere 13 percent of Ph.D.'s (Wylie 3). These effects of gender stereotyping, in turn, become causes. Each new generation of women that abandons science and technology sets an unhappy precedent for the next generation. The cycle continues.

Lou: Challenge your assumptions! See note 1 at the end of your paper.

If the minority of women in the world of computers wish to prove themselves as capable as men, the path is clear and, very likely, painful: women should learn to speak the language of their male counterparts. That women can do the technical work of engineers and scientists is beyond question--millions have demonstrated their skills. If ability is not the issue, then social interaction must be. Relatively few women advance beyond middle management in computer hardware and software companies (Kantrowitz 52). To advance in the computer industry, women will need to address the social problem. One sure way of doing this is to show an interest in talking about computers--that is, in learning the value of "shop talk."

Lou: Consider alternatives? See note 2 at the end of your paper.

Ironically, for one who advocates more fairness for women in the computer field, I find myself offering what some might call sexist advice: I'm suggesting that women become more like men, at least in their speech. But the need to speak the language of the dominant group is a political reality. Women could try to revolutionize the computer industry and higher education from the outside--with their own language, spoken in their own corporations and schools. But this approach is not realistic. The problems women face in the computer industry are part of a much larger, society-wide problem of gender

FOR DISCUSSION

In this paragraph, Lou Cassetta is trying to fend off criticism of his position, which he has anticipated. You might ask students (1) whether or not Lou has characterized the criticism fairly and (2) whether or not he has responded to the criticism (that he's offering sexist advice) successfully.

discrimination. Fundamental assumptions about the roles men and women play in society change slowly. The quickest way for women to advance in the computer industry will be for women to integrate themselves into existing companies, rise to the top, and then change the rules. They can best do this through channels of communication already present.

Lou: Another assumption? See note 3 at the end of your paper.

Success may come with a high psychological cost, as women talk in ways that, perhaps, don't interest them. But it is not unfair to expect people, male or female, to learn the language of the computer industry when their jobs involve computers. People use many different types of speech depending on the occasion. On the job, women can speak the language of computers developed by a male-dominated computer industry. Even as their on-the-job language helps them to break social barriers and advance through corporations, women can drop that language the moment they leave the office each afternoon.

My job last summer was certainly male dominated, with no female programmers. Had a woman with my same skills applied for the data entry job, she may not have been hired unless she was able to impress my boss through a simple conversation about computers. I am sure that there are many women who have lost jobs to men who were better able to impress other males with a knowledge of technology. Very likely the women were just as qualified as the men but the men, talking shop, appeared to know more about technology. Women can correct this unfair situation. They can begin talking shop.

Works Cited

Healy, Bernadine. "Quotable: The Astonishing Thing Is That Young Women Pursue Careers in Science and Medicine at All." The Chronicle of Higher Education 25 Mar. 1992: B5.

Kantrowitz, Barbara. "Men, Women and Computers." Newsweek 16 May 1994: 48-55.

Lefton, Lester. Psychology. 4th ed. Boston: Allyn and Bacon, 1991.

Wylie, Margie. "No Place for Women: Internet Is Flawed Model for the Infobahn." Digital Media 4.8 (1995): 3+. Digital Media Online. Online. Nexis. 19 Nov. 1995.

Lou:

You've revised in earnest; now your writing is clear enough for me to identify and challenge three unexamined assumptions, the first two of which cause problems for your proposed solution.

(1) In asking women to talk like men you are assuming, through a process you've not yet defined, that "talking shop" will somehow make women equal in the workplace. Why? How? Unless you carefully explain this process and give readers a chance to evaluate, your proposed solution cannot stand.

(2) Does a person's being competent obligate him or her to talk shop? You assume so; and what follows is a belief that those who talk shop will be perceived as competent and will rise in an organization. Have you considered an alternate assumption? I know people (some, computer scientists!) who don't feel compelled to talk shop in order to demonstrate knowledge. This they demonstrate through work well done. Here's a competing view of competence that creates a problem for you. I'm not sure that even men must talk shop in order to succeed.

(3) Please examine your assumption that being able to talk shop—that is, having a technical vocabulary—is the same as being competent in a field. Is it? I could learn buzzwords and "talk shop" with the guys; but surely a high-tech vocabulary, alone, would not make me computer literate. For example, you talk shop but are not, yet, a computer scientist. Your data entry job, after all, required typing (not computer) skills.

Still, you're onto something useful in this essay. If we begin with the view that there might well be differences between men and women, aside from the physical, then exploring the ways these differences manifest themselves in the computer field seems quite interesting. Please hold to your proposed solution if you believe in it; but you'll need to address my criticisms. You might, on the other hand, want to revise your solution. Or perhaps you'll want to shift away from a problem-solution format altogether and concentrate, instead, on perceived or real gender differences in the computer field. Whatever your decision, let's consider your next draft final.

A Conference with Lou Cassetta

Lou was not pleased with this response to his second draft. In conference with his instructor over the draft, his first remark was: "I'm going to have to start over!" Point by point, Lou addressed the challenges to his assumptions. He said that he wasn't prepared to explain, in any authoritative

FOR DISCUSSION

You might use the opportunity of Lou Cassetta's conference with his teacher as an occasion to discuss conference protocol, agendas, and expectations with your students. It may be worth noting Lou's exasperation here. He has responded to the teacher's request for clarifications; why, then, is his essay not acceptable? True, the clarifications were made in draft 2—but just enough to allow the teacher to identify and challenge Lou's key assumptions. Many students need to be disabused of the notion that revision is a cosmetic affair, concerning sentences, only. In Lou's case, revision fundamentally changed the thinking in the essay, as students will see in the final draft.

way, the process of how successful shop talk leads to advancement in a job. It was his "instinct" that this process was effective, but he had nothing more concrete to offer (no corroborating sources, for instance) and so he abandoned the point. Lou also admitted that he hadn't considered that successful people might *not* want to talk shop. And he agreed that using buzzwords is not equivalent to having knowledge of a subject. "Is there anything to salvage?" he asked.

Indeed, there was. Lou decided to back away from the problem-solution structure of his essay, because it was the solution—the importance of women's talking shop—that exposed his flawed assumptions. Lou reported that he was still interested in the computer industry and in exploring why the industry was so weighted in favor of men. Here's an excerpt from a memo to his instructor on his planned revision:

FOR DISCUSSION

After their conference, the teacher invited Lou to submit a memo suggesting plans for a revision. Lou responded with the memo, presented here, which you might discuss with students. Perhaps they would find memos of use in communicating quickly with their teacher. Such an exchange can easily take place via e-mail.

> I'm going to drop my solution about talking shop; it's getting me in trouble and making me out to be a sexist pig, which I'm not. I'm honestly committed to breaking down barriers.
>
> I'd like to revise by exploring two types of mistakes I see being made in the computer industry. The first mistake has to do with sexism: there are many more men than women in the industry, and there's this general belief that women aren't good with math and science. The second mistake is the belief that there are <u>no</u> differences between the sexes. I'm not talking about intellect--but something else: maybe the way men and women use machines. It seems to me that real differences could be put to advantage. I could use most of my same sources--and even my same introduction, which could illustrate the problem of sexism.
>
> My new working thesis:
>
> > Two errors have prevented us from making greater strides in the computer industry: the error of ignorance--the belief that women are not equal to the complexity of computers, and the error of fearfulness--the belief that women and men must be exactly alike.

4f Sample paper: Final draft

The process of writing two drafts and responding to criticism clarified for Lou Cassetta several problems with his thinking about women and men in the computer industry. In the process of writing, he discovered a *new* thesis—the basis of which you can find in his earliest responses to the sources he read on his topic. For instance, on page 8, see Lou's note on the article by Barbara Kantrowitz, in which he states that we should acknowledge differences between the sexes when it comes to computers. That response influenced the writing of his new thesis and gave his final draft a fresh direction.

As you will see, Lou Cassetta spent time refining his sentences so that they would read effortlessly. You will find in his essay the paradox evident in all good writing: when sentences are clear and easy to read, they mask the considerable effort that went into making them. Good writing looks to readers as if it took no work at all; the writer knows otherwise.

Gender Differences in the Computer Industry
(Final Draft)

When I applied for a job in computer data entry last summer at one of the world's largest management consulting firms, I never thought that my experience as a grease monkey would help. Although knowing how to work a gas pump did not make me a better typist, I learned important communication skills at the gas station that I used to get the office job. At the gas station, my co-workers and I always talked about the fastest and most sophisticated automobiles and how much we would like to own them. When I applied for the data entry position, I impressed my boss by engaging in a conversation about his laptop computer. Many men are fascinated by the newest and fastest machines and love to talk about them. I have always taken part in conversations about these machines, and for once it paid off.

My being able to talk shop did not mean that I had any particular expertise regarding computers; in fact, I didn't need a great deal of expertise, at least at first, for a data entry job that largely involved typing. Still, my ability to talk shop helped me to get that job--which is exactly the problem.

FOR DISCUSSION

This paragraph represents an immediate departure from the second draft, which opened with the same scenario of Lou's interviewing for a job in the computer industry. Instead of launching into a direct (and flawed) comparison of what men know as opposed to women, as Lou does in draft 1, he reflects on his experience and claims that it suggests a problem. As an opening to the essay, the strategy works well. The problem invites the reader to follow Lou into the essay, as he reflects and, perhaps, points the way to a solution.

The signs are everywhere that gender stereotyping has followed women and men from our general culture into computer culture. Most industry executives are men, and relatively few women advance beyond middle management in computer hardware and software companies (Kantrowitz 52). The glass ceiling that has blocked advancement of women in other settings throughout corporate America has blocked their advancement in the computer industry as well. When promoting sexism in the corporation, industry executives don't openly endorse the more neanderthal characterizations of women as natural-born homemakers. A more subtle sexism exists, which begins with the patronizing view that while women are of course as smart as men, it is men, not women, who are more naturally inclined to technology. And thus we should expect to find more men in technologically intensive fields.

It's an old story, the view that men are good at math and logical thinking and, therefore, naturally excel at computers. In fact, numerous studies have failed to find any such "natural" superiority among boys. When differences are observed, they can be traced to social settings--for instance, to the differing interactions of teachers with their male and female students (American Association 74). Historian of science Ruth Schwartz Cowan believes that America has systematically trained its women to avoid technology:

> No country on earth has been so much in the sway of the technological order or so proud of its involvement in it. Doctors and engineers are central to [American] culture; poets and artists live on the fringes.
>
> If practicality and know-how and willingness to get your hands dirty down there with the least of them are signatures of the true American, then we have been systematically training slightly more than half of our population to be un-American. I speak, of course, of women. . . . We have trained our women to opt out of the technological order as much as we have trained our men to opt into it. (62)

In the seventeen years since Cowan made these observations, more women have entered the computer field. Still, problems persist. Writing in The Chronicle of Higher Education about America's training of women for careers in science, Bernadine Healy, Director of the National Institutes of Health, cites a "study by the American Association for the Advancement of Science [that] found that women in science classes are subject to more negative treatment than their male colleagues--by both faculty and other students." Healy further reports that women are underrepresented in the sciences. For instance, during the 1992-93 academic year (the most recent year for which figures are available), women earned little more than one-third of bachelor's degrees in computer science, compared to their earning 54 percent of all bachelor's degrees awarded. Fewer

LOOKING BACK

Students have seen the source of this quotation, and others in this essay, in Chapters 1 and 2. It is worth noting for students that the process of reading critically helped Lou to formulate thoughts that eventually found their way into the final draft. Lou did not use source materials merely as support, late in the process, in his attempt to persuade readers; Lou used sources early in the process of writing, before he had any clear idea of the thesis he would be pursuing.

women than men pursued this education: women earned about 27 percent of master's degrees in computer science, as opposed to earning 54 percent of the master's degrees overall. And a mere 13 percent of Ph.D.'s in computer science went to women, as opposed to 38 percent of all doctorates awarded (Wylie 3; United States 174). Women achieve their share of degrees, but disproportionately few seek careers in computer science.

The number of women in this field is up over the past twenty years; but almost certainly, gender stereotyping continues to affect women's career choices. Each new generation of women that embraces a field such as computer science sets a good precedent for the next generation. Over time, gender inequalities can be corrected. The evidence is clear, however, that sexism continues to infect both academics and, as measured by the lack of senior executive positions for women, the computer industry. In continuing the fight against sexism, we must hunt down and discredit false claims of differences between women and men regarding technology. The more we do so, the more girls will regard the sciences as simply another career choice for which they are as qualified as boys.

Yet what will we do if we find there are <u>real</u> differences between the sexes regarding technology? It is almost impossible to believe that men and women are alike in every way, aside from the physical. Differences are bound to exist, and we would be as foolish to avoid pursuing them, for fear of being politically incorrect, as we have been in insisting that women aren't any good at math and science. We should use real differences positively, as a source of advancement. One fruitful area for research might be the ways in which women and men use computers.

Generalizations never apply to all individuals; but impressionistic evidence suggests that men tend to treat their computers in the same way that muscle car enthusiasts treat their hot rods. Both want the fastest, most powerful machines that money can buy. The relationship that women enjoy with computers seems to differ. Esther Dyson, editor of an influential software-industry newsletter, characterizes the relationship this way: I don't "really care about its innards, I just want it to work" (qtd. in Kantrowitz 50). Oliver Strimpel, executive director of The Computer Museum in Boston, finds this pattern very common among male and female computer owners.

LOOKING BACK

You might ask students: How effective is Lou's use of statistics here, as opposed to his use in his first draft? There are differences, which students might discuss. For instance, Lou offers a fuller comparison in this draft. The one-third of women pursuing degrees in computer science (cited in draft 1) meant little until the reader could compare the statistic with the total number of women seeking degrees (information provided here).

FOR DISCUSSION

Lou wants to make a statement here that he allows may be politically incorrect: that there may exist real differences between men and women and that we should, he asserts, take advantage of these. You might ask students if they find this position any less (or more) offensive than Lou's original position, that women must learn shop talk.

GROUP ACTIVITY

Ask students to work in groups of three or four and to plot the changes in Lou Cassetta's thinking. (The goal, here, is to have students understand clearly that fundamental thinking in the draft changed, not "merely" the writing. The writing *is* the thinking.) Next, ask students to monitor their own changing responses to Lou's essay, as the essay evolved. After these discussions, which may take 20 or 30 minutes, you might hold a class-wide discussion.

"Men tend to be seduced by the technology itself," he says, while women are more inclined to look past the technology and judge a machine's efficiency and overall usefulness (qtd. in Kantrowitz 50).

These impressions, although unproved, are provocative. If sociologists or anthropologists confirm them (and, again, we're not discussing intellectual ability but, rather, style of interacting with computers), we must be brave enough to admit that, at least in some measures, women and men do differ. Differences are neutral: they do not suggest better or worse, equal or unequal. Well understood differences between the sexes could provide information with which to better design machines and software. We might look for less "muscular" machines and more intuitive operating systems; we might expect more variety among video games and see, perhaps, fewer slice-em-up, kung-fu warriors.

My job last summer was completely dominated by men. Had a woman with my same skills applied for the data entry job, she may not have been hired unless she was able to impress my boss through a conversation about his laptop. Too bad. In a smarter, not to mention more equitable, world, my boss would have interviewed women candidates along with men and found plenty (of both) who were qualified. By asking intelligent questions, he might have discovered that women and men could bring different, equally valid perspectives to bear on the work done in his office. He could have used these perspectives to his company's advantage, improving his product.

While advances in the computer industry have been rapid, two errors have prevented us from making even greater strides: the error of ignorance--the belief that women are not equal to the complexity of computers, and the error of fearfulness--the insistence, due to pressures of political correctness, that women and men must be exactly alike. These errors diminish our potential; and not until we eliminate them will America be putting its full human resources to work in an industry that demands our very best.

FOR DISCUSSION

Ask students to reread the final draft of the essay with this question in mind: To what extent is the essay improved by Lou Cassetta's use of source materials? Specifically, how has the use of sources affected the essay? Would the essay have succeeded without reference to any sources? From this discussion, you might make the transition to the use students will be making of source materials in your own class and in others.

Works Cited

American Association of University Women. The AAUW Report: How Schools Shortchange Girls. Washington: AAUW, 1992.

Cowan, Ruth Schwartz. "From Virginia Dare to Virginia Slims: Women and Technology in American Life." Technology and Society 20.1 (1979): 51-63.

Healy, Bernadine. "Quotable: The Astonishing Thing Is That Young Women Pursue Careers in Science and Medicine at All." The Chronicle of Higher Education 25 Mar. 1992: B5.

Kantrowitz, Barbara. "Men, Women and Computers." Newsweek 16 May 1994: 48-55.

United States Dept. of Education. Digest of Educational Statistics. Washington: GPO, 1995.

Wylie, Margie. "No Place for Women: Internet Is Flawed Model for the Infobahn." Digital Media 4.8 (1995): 3+. Digital Media Online. Online. Nexis. 19 Nov. 1995.

CHAPTER 5

The Paragraph and the Paper

KEY FEATURES

In keeping with current scholarship, this chapter treats paragraphs as units in a larger text. Emphasis throughout is on paragraphs not only as individual units, but as parts of a *section,* which is itself part of a whole essay. Interspersed between examples of individual paragraphs, then, are examples of larger sections. This attention to context reinforces the advice given to students to work on their papers one section at a time. As the traditional features of topic sentence, unity, coherence, and development are covered, the student's attention is always focused on the "big picture," i.e., how the paragraph works both internally and within its context. Topic sentences, for example, are discussed with regard to the paragraph and to the thesis of the section in which the paragraph is found. The same is true for treatment of other essential features. Throughout the chapter, decisions on paragraphing are considered in light of the purpose of the paper, of the section, and of the paragraph itself. Coverage of introductions, conclusions, and paragraph length takes into consideration both purpose and audience: students are advised to consider the needs of readers when framing their papers and when dividing paragraphs. As in previous chapters, several exercises are designed for use with students' own writing. The use of one set of paragraphs for several exercises gives students the opportunity to analyze the same section with respect to several essential features. Using the chapter to revise their own essays and to analyze the work of others should help students understand paragraphs from both the writer's and the reader's perspectives.

A **paragraph** is a group of related sentences organized by a single, controlling idea. Marked with an indented first word (typically five spaces from the left margin), a paragraph can be as brief as a sentence or longer than a page. Paragraphs rarely stand alone: they are extended units of thought that, carefully pieced together, build the content of a paper. In this chapter you will learn about the characteristics of a well-written paragraph and the relationship of individual paragraphs to larger units of thought.[1]

5a The relationship of single paragraphs to a whole paper

At times, you may feel that generating a paragraph is easy enough, but that writing an entire essay, paper, or report is beyond your abilities. (How will I *ever* write twenty pages?) In these moments, you need to remember that whole documents are written one paragraph at a time and whole paragraphs, one sentence at a time.

1 The relationship of paragraphs to sections

Just as sentences are the units that comprise individual paragraphs, paragraphs are the units that comprise whole letters, essays, and reports. Aside from specialized occasions for writing such as summaries and short-answer essay exams, you will seldom write a single, isolated paragraph. Usually, any paragraph will be situated in a grouping—a **section**—that constitutes part of the larger document. Except for the beginning of a paper and the end (see 5f), any one paragraph will be involved directly with at least two others: the one immediately preceding and the one that follows. If you can write a group of three related paragraphs in a single sitting, you will be able to piece together an entire paper.

[1]Example paragraphs from various sources are consecutively numbered throughout the chapter for ease of reference.

The following paragraphs form a section—one part of a chapter—of Helen Keller's autobiography. At the age of nineteen months, Keller was stricken by a disease that left her deaf and blind. Not until she was seven, with the arrival of her teacher Anne Sullivan, did Keller discover language. The moment described in these famous paragraphs is one of extraordinary awakening: the realization that things in the world have names. These paragraphs are related; they read as a carefully written section, as if they appeared from the pen of the author all at the same instant. Be assured, however, that Keller wrote this section of her autobiography one paragraph at a time, one sentence at a time. She was twenty-two and a sophomore at Radcliffe College when *My Life Story* was published.

> The morning after my teacher came she led me into her room and gave
> me a doll. The little blind children at the Perkins Institution had sent it and
> Laura Bridgman had dressed it; but I did not know this until afterward.
> When I had played with it a little while, Miss Sullivan slowly spelled into
> my hand the word "d-o-l-l." I was at once interested in this finger play and
> tried to imitate it. When I finally succeeded in making the letters correctly
> 1 I was flushed with childish pleasure and pride. Running downstairs to my
> mother I held up my hand and made the letters for doll. I did not know
> that I was spelling a word or even that words existed; I was simply mak-
> ing my fingers go in monkey-like imitation. In the days that followed I
> learned to spell in this uncomprehending way a great many words, among
> them *pin, hat, cup* and a few verbs like *sit, stand* and *walk.* But my teacher
> had been with me several weeks before I understood that everything has
> a name.
>
> One day, while I was playing with my new doll, Miss Sullivan put my
> big rag doll into my lap also, spelled "d-o-l-l" and tried to make me un-
> derstand that "d-o-l-l" applied to both. Earlier in the day we had had a tus-
> sle over the words "m-u-g" and "w-a-t-e-r." Miss Sullivan had tried to
> impress it upon me that "m-u-g" is *mug* and that "w-a-t-e-r" is *water,* but I
> persisted in confounding the two. In despair she had dropped the subject
> for the time, only to renew it at the first opportunity. I became impatient at
> 2 her repeated attempts and, seizing the new doll, I dashed it upon the floor.
> I was keenly delighted when I felt the fragments of the broken doll at my
> feet. Neither sorrow nor regret followed my passionate outburst. I had not
> loved the doll. In the still, dark world in which I lived there was no strong
> sentiment or tenderness. I felt my teacher sweep the fragments to one side
> of the hearth, and I had a sense of satisfaction that the cause of my dis-
> comfort was removed. She brought me my hat, and I knew I was going out
> into the warm sunshine. This thought, if a wordless sensation may be
> called a thought, made me hop and skip with pleasure.
>
> We walked down the path to the well-house, attracted by the fragrance
> of the honeysuckle with which it was covered. Someone was drawing
> water and my teacher placed my hand under the spout. As the cool stream
> gushed over one hand she spelled into the other the word *water,* first
> slowly, then rapidly. I stood still, my whole attention fixed upon the mo-
> 3 tions of her fingers. Suddenly I felt a misty consciousness as of something
> forgotten—a thrill of returning thought; and somehow the mystery of
> language was revealed to me. I knew then that "w-a-t-e-r" meant the won-

LOOKING BACK

Students will be able to make ample use of revision strategies covered in Chapter 4 as they work through Chapter 5. Throughout this chapter, paragraphs are treated as units in a larger whole, and decisions on composing and revising are always considered in context. Some linear-minded students may consider material in this chapter repetitive; use such observations as an opportunity to reinforce both the recursive nature of the writing process and the interrelatedness of all segments of a text.

REFERENCES

BAMBURG, BETTY. "What Makes a Text Coherent?" CCC 34 (1983): 417–29. Paragraph coherence has as much to do with the entire essay as it does with the paragraph itself.

BRADDOCK, RICHARD. "The Frequency and Placement of Topic Sentences in Expository Prose." *Research in Teaching Writing* 8 (1974): 287–304. The topic-sentence-first paragraph is not commonly used by professional writers.

D'ANGELO, FRANK. "The Topic Sentence Revisited." CCC 37 (1986): 431–41. Topic sentences increase readability of prose.

LINDEMANN, ERIKA. *A Rhetoric for Writing Teachers.* 2nd ed. New York: Oxford UP, 1987. 141–57. Advocates approach using various theories of teaching paragraphs.

MORAN, MICHAEL G. "The English Paragraph." *Research in Rhetoric and Composition: A Bibliographic Sourcebook.* Eds. Michael G. Moran and Ronald F. Lunsford. Westport: Greenwood, 1984. 425–50. Discusses definitions of paragraphs that focus on the individual unit and on the relationship of the unit to the whole text.

POPKEN, RANDELL L. "A Study of Topic Sentence Use in Academic Writing." *Written Communication* 4 (1987): 209–28. Study reveals that topic sentences are common in professional prose.

ROGERS, PAUL, JR. "A Discourse-Centered Rhetoric of the Paragraph." CCC 17 (1966): 2–11. Paragraphs can be understood fully only in terms of the purposes of the larger text.

derful cool something that was flowing over my hand. That living word awakened my soul, gave it light, hope, joy, set it free! There were barriers still, it is true, but barriers that could in time be swept away.

I left the well-house eager to learn. Everything had a name, and each name gave birth to a new thought. As we returned to the house every object which I touched seemed to quiver with life. That was because I saw everything with the strange, new sight that had come to me. On entering
4 the door I remembered the doll I had broken. I felt my way to the hearth and picked up the pieces. I tried vainly to put them together. Then my eyes filled with tears; for I realized what I had done, and for the first time I felt repentance and sorrow.

I learned a great many new words that day. I do not remember what they all were; but I do know that *mother, father, sister, teacher* were among them—words that were to make the world blossom for me, "like Aaron's
5 rod, with flowers." It would have been difficult to find a happier child than I was as I lay in my crib at the close of that eventful day and lived over the joys it had brought me, and for the first time longed for a new day to come.

—HELEN KELLER, *My Life Story*

2 The relationship of sections to the whole paper

A **thesis** explicitly states the topic you will address in a paper and either directly or indirectly suggests the points you will make about that topic (see 3d). You will probably devote one section of your paper to discussing each point you wish to develop. For each section of your paper you will write a **section thesis,** a statement that explicitly announces the point you will address in the section and either directly or indirectly suggests what you will discuss relating to this point. You will organize your discussion in paragraphs.

The section thesis organizing the paragraphs by Helen Keller appears at the end of ¶1: *"But my teacher had been with me several weeks before I understood that everything has a name."* The next four paragraphs focus on and develop various aspects of this statement.

¶2 Events leading to the moment of discovery: an account of Sullivan's frustrated attempts to teach Keller.

¶3 The moment of discovery: clearly the most famous in the autobiography, Keller realizing the mystery of language.

¶4 Consequence 1 of the discovery: objects quivering with life and Keller knowing repentance and sorrow for the first time.

¶5 Consequence 2 of the discovery: joy in having learned that everything has a name.

These five paragraphs form a distinct section of one chapter in Keller's autobiography. The section as a whole is *unified* and *well developed* in that all paragraphs focus on and amply discuss a single controlling idea: the section thesis highlighted previously. Each paragraph is unified and well developed; each focuses on and amply discusses its own more narrowly defined

ADDITIONAL EXERCISE A

Students may find the following paragraphs of interest. They were written by Anne Sullivan and concern the same event that Keller describes.

April 5, 1887

I must write you a line this morning because something very important has happened. Helen has taken the second great step in her education. She has learned that *everything has a name, and that the manual alphabet is the key to everything she wants to know.*

In a previous letter I think I wrote you that "mug" and "milk" had given Helen more trouble than all the rest. She confused the nouns with the verb "drink." She didn't know the word for "drink," but went through the pantomime of drinking whenever she spelled "mug" or "milk." This morning, while she was washing, she wanted to know the name for "water." When she wants to know the name of anything, she points to it and pats my hand. I spelled "w-a-t-e-r" and thought no more about it until after breakfast. Then it occurred to me that with the help of this new word I might succeed in straightening out the "mug-milk" difficulty. We went out to the pump-house, and I made Helen hold her mug under the spout while I pumped. As the cold water gushed forth, filling the mug, I spelled "w-a-t-e-r" in Helen's free hand. The word coming so close upon the sensation of cold water rushing over her hand seemed to startle her. She dropped the mug and stood as one transfixed. A new light came into her face. She spelled "water" several times. Then she dropped on the ground and asked for its name and pointed to the pump and the trellis, and suddenly turning round she asked for my name. I spelled "Teacher." Just then the nurse brought Helen's little sister into the pump-house, and Helen spelled "baby" and pointed to the nurse. All the way back to the house she was highly excited, and learned the name of every object she touched, so that in a few hours she had added thirty new words to her vocabulary. Here are some of them: *Door, open, shut, give, go, come,* and a great many more.

P.S.—I didn't finish my letter in time to get it posted last night; so I shall add a line. Helen got up this morning like a radiant

Unity, Coherence, and Development

- Each *paragraph* of a paper consists of *sentences* that are

  Unified: The sentences are all concerned with a central, controlling idea.

  Coherent: The sentences are arranged in a clear order, according to a definite plan.

  Well developed: The sentences provide details that explain and illustrate the paragraph's controlling idea.

- Each *section* of a paper consists of *paragraphs* that are

  Unified: The groups of paragraphs are devoted to one controlling idea, a section thesis that develops some part of the thesis.

  Coherent: The groups of paragraphs within a section are arranged in a clear order, according to a definite plan.

  Well developed: The groups of paragraphs provide details that explain and illustrate the section's controlling idea.

- Every *paper* consists of *sections* (groups of related paragraphs) that are

  Unified: Each section is devoted to developing one part of the thesis, the central organizing idea of the paper.

  Coherent: The sections are arranged in a clear order, according to a definite plan.

  Well developed: Each section of the paper provides details important for developing the thesis.

controlling idea. And because each paragraph builds on the one that precedes it and is positioned according to a clear plan, the whole section is *coherent.* In the same way, every paragraph in the section is itself coherent since the sentences of each lead from one to the next and establish a clear pattern of relation.

EXERCISE 1

Read the following section of a paper on school violence, written by student Jim Walker. Analyze Jim's paragraphs as follows: (1) identify his controlling idea, or section thesis; (2) explain how the section is unified, developed, and coherent.

Student Example: Jim Walker

The problem of aggressive acts is real and can be lethal as more
students bring weapons to school. We know that aggression is a
fact of life. Social psychologists have several theories about what
causes it, including aggression-as-instinct, frustration that leads to
6 aggression, and aggression learned from the social environment.

fairy. She has flitted from object to object, asking the name of everything and kissing me for very gladness. Last night when I got in bed, she stole into my arms of her own accord and kissed me for the first time, and I thought my heart would burst, so full was it of joy.

—Anne Sullivan

Students may be asked to analyze Sullivan's paragraphs as follows: (1) Identify the controlling idea (the section thesis). (2) Explain how the entire section is unified, developed, and coherent. Here are suggested responses:

1. Controlling idea: Sentences 2 and 3, ¶6.
2. Unity: ¶7 opens with reference to Helen's ability to distinguish between related concepts, then moves to the word for "water" for a breakthrough. Naming "water" leads to naming other things. ¶8 reveals that the naming continues into the next day.
   Development: Section is developed primarily through example—use of "mug," "milk," "drink," and "water" keeps section focused on names for things related to drinking. When this concept is established, words focus on people—"Teacher," "baby."
   Coherence: The section coheres through the use of chronological order.

EXERCISE 1

These three paragraphs are devoted to the problem of aggressive acts at school—and a possible solution to this problem. Jim Walker's section thesis is located in the final two sentences of paragraph 6: "school is the place where a lot of different people come together and, more times than we like, turn aggressive. School is also the place where students can learn to get along and resolve conflicts without resorting to violence." The section is unified. All paragraphs address the topic of aggression (school-based) and its possible solution. Walker first defines aggression briefly and locates it, for the purposes of this discussion, at school (paragraph 6). Paragraph 7 identifies aggressive behavior among a school's "bad apples," and suggests that school authorities, while able to respond, "can't be everywhere." Thus, students need tools to cope with aggression—a point developed in paragraph 8. The logic within paragraphs, and from one paragraph to the next, is clear; the section is coherent as well as unified.

EXERCISE 2

Individual responses

ADDITIONAL EXERCISE B

CRITICAL THINKING Find two interesting paragraphs from textbooks, magazines, or other collections. Using the analysis of the Curtis paragraph as a model, evaluate the unity, development, and coherence of these paragraphs. Then compare the two: Is one a better paragraph than the other? If so, why? How do the two differ in development and coherence?

Whatever the causes, school is the place where a lot of different people come together and, more times than we like, turn aggressive. School is also the place where students can learn to get along and resolve conflicts without resorting to violence.

There is a small part of every group in a big, multicultural high school that is aggressive. These are the bad apples who are always talking trash, trying to be bad, walking around with that mad-dog stare. These are the aggressive ones who threaten other students by calling them names like sissy or punk, by pushing them to fight so
7 the toughs can add to their reputation as the baddest. Fortunately, schools can respond. Vice-principals love to mix it up with students who have an aggressive attitude. But vice-principals and plainclothes police can't be everywhere. Students need some tools of their own to help reduce levels of aggression, to protect themselves, and to decide to stop feeding the cycle of violence by arming themselves.

Better communication and social skills can help. All students need to be aware of what some students know by instinct: that you can divert or reduce aggression with a quick apology or with humor. This is what social psychologists call reducing levels of arousal by introducing an incompatible response. Also, the school can implement Peer Mediation where if students feel a physical or emotional threat, they can report it and discuss it with other students.
8 Students talk through the issues with each other—and talking, it turns out, is the important thing: getting two sides together to talk rather than using weapons or fists to solve differences. Talking can also show students that disagreements are not worth a trip to the emergency room or the legal problems or medical bills—the consequences of violence that movies and rap videos don't usually show. If more students would have used these simple measures at my high school, I'm convinced that at least several fights could have been avoided.

EXERCISE 2

Choose *one* section of a textbook chapter to study in depth. (Define a *section* as a group of related paragraphs preceded by a subheading.) Closely read each paragraph in this section, and prepare an analysis by responding to three points: (1) Identify the controlling idea (the section thesis) of the section. (2) Explain how the entire section is unified, developed, and coherent. (3) Discuss how the section fits into the overall structure of the chapter.

5b The paragraph: Essential features

In important ways, a paragraph and an essay are essentially alike. Both must be *unified* if they are to be comprehensible: all sentences of a paragraph must refer to one organizing idea, just as all paragraphs of an essay must concern one organizing idea. Both an essay as a whole and its individual paragraphs must be *well developed:* sentences in a paragraph must explain or defend well the main point of a paragraph, just as paragraphs of an essay must explain or defend a thesis. In addition, both a paragraph and an essay must be *coherent:* sentences of a paragraph must be arranged in some order, just as paragraphs in an essay must follow from one to the next according to some clear progression of ideas. If you can master the techniques necessary for making a single paragraph unified, well developed, and coherent, then by adapting these same techniques and by expanding your focus, you will be able to write and organize an entire essay.

The following is an example of a well-written paragraph from a biology text.

> Life on this planet began in water, and today, almost wherever water is found, life is also present. There are one-celled organisms that eke out their entire existence in no more water than that which can cling to a grain of sand. Some species of algae are found only on the melting undersurfaces of polar ice floes. Certain species of bacteria and certain blue-green algae can tolerate the near-boiling water of hot springs. In the desert, plants race
> 9 through an entire life cycle—seed to flower to seed—following a single rainfall. In the jungle, the water cupped in the leaves of a tropical plant forms a microcosm in which a myriad of small organisms are born, spawn, and die. We are interested in whether the soil of Mars and the dense atmosphere surrounding Venus contain water principally because we want to know whether life is there. On our planet, and probably on others where life exists, life and water have been companions since life first began.
>
> —HELENA CURTIS, "Water"

Examine the qualities that make this grouping of sentences a paragraph, a unit of thought. First, each of the six sentences constituting the body of Curtis's paragraph is narrowly focused by a single, controlling idea: *water* and its relation to life. Given this focus, the grouping of sentences is unified. Observe as well that Curtis develops her central idea with six sentences arranged according to a clear plan. In the first five, she associates water with life on earth. Notice how she moves from an extreme presented in one sentence to an opposite extreme presented in the next.

Curtis's next-to-last sentence about water on Mars or Venus extends observations made concerning water and life on earth to other planets, and once again she drives home her point, which she repeats by way of summary in the paragraph's last sentence. She has taken care to present eight *unified* sentences that *develop* a central idea and that are arranged in a meaningful, *coherent* order. Thus, Curtis has written a paragraph: a well-developed unit of thought organized around a single idea and arranged according to some definite plan.

EXERCISE 3

Read the following group of sentences and explain why it can justifiably be called a paragraph. In your explanation (1) identify the central, organizing idea that unifies the sentences; (2) identify the parts of the paragraph that

ESL CUE

Problems with paragraphing often reflect a difference in accepted patterns of representing thought rather than simple language difficulties. The concept of the paragraph differs greatly between cultures, with romance languages accepting and even encouraging what we would term "digression" as a way to create variety and interest, a sense of "fullness." Farsi speakers, for example, value such subtlety that the central idea may not become clear until the very end, with the development following a circular or looping pattern constructed of high-level abstractions. The straightforward, linear paragraph movement considered the norm in U.S. schools is actually typical only of English, and may even be valued less highly in British prose. See Robert B. Kaplan's discussion of paragraph differences in "Cultural Thought Patterns in Inter-Cultural Education," *Language Learning* 16 (1966): 1–20.

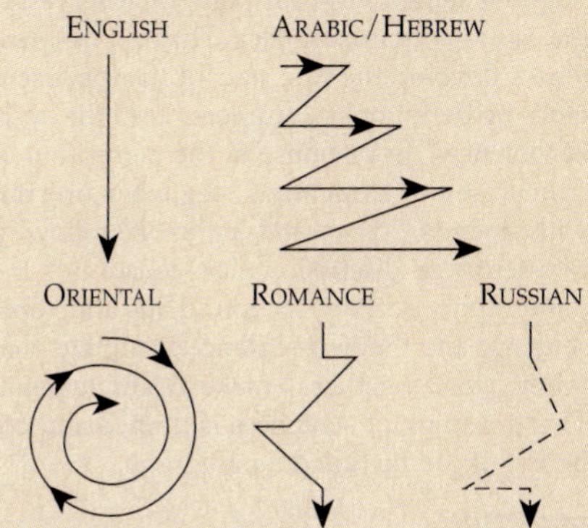

Paragraph conventions in different languages also vary greatly in their tolerance of digression. While frequent digression in the English paragraph is a decided fault, the practice may be viewed as a sign of fluency, knowledgeability, and confidence even in languages not greatly distant from English, such as Spanish and Russian.

The concept of paragraph development by patterns, for example from most common to least common or from general to particular, by consistent space or time order or degree, might seem obvious to English speakers, but is not so obvious in other languages where im-

(continued)

peratives of content may be more important than sequences of order. Consequently, a clear explanation of differences between methods of paragraph development will be needed to supplement this handbook. ESL students will see the models, but may not understand them or believe their currency.

ESL CUE

Spanish speakers may not have the concept of indentation and might use initial dashes instead:"—Another key concern is . . . "

Depending on the conventions of the country of origin, the paragraphs of Spanish speakers may be short, like newspaper paragraphs, or there may be no paragraphing at all. The idea of indentation and paragraph division might be lacking in ESL students from a number of different language groups.

EXERCISE 3

The first sentence of this paragraph serves as the central, organizing idea. The next five sentences develop the first part of the topic sentence by defining how rumors "feed the cycle of violence." In response to the perception of danger, some "students . . . begin hanging out with friends." Fear and paranoia follow, a two-sentence discussion that constitutes the paragraph's second section. Thus the topic sentence and the two-sentence groupings that follow work together to make a definite point. This grouping of sentences is unified and coherent. It can be called a paragraph.

ESL CUE

Vietnamese tends not to distinguish between oral and written structures, so Vietnamese students writing in English may be highly informal with the lengthy rambling style of oral discourse.

ESL EXERCISE

Print up a selection without paragraphs and have students mark where they think paragraph divisions should fall and why. The resulting discussion might make very clear why students have difficulty writing unified, focused paragraphs.

explain or defend this central idea; and (3) explain how the sentences are organized according to a definite, coherent plan.

Student Example: Jim Walker

Rumors can feed the cycle of violence in high schools by increasing the levels of fear and anger among students. Big city high schools are busy places in which there are extensive, and effective, rumor grapevines. A rumor about somebody disrespecting somebody else may buzz through the school and get everyone talking. Word-of-mouth chatter, friends talking casually to other friends and passing along news, can add layers of anger on top of the original response to the rumor—which may be completely unfounded. No one knows, after all, since no one has bothered to check the rumor's basis in fact. True or not, the rumor makes students afraid to pass each other in the halls, uncertain of what may happen. Some students who feel threatened may become afraid of getting jumped, so they begin hanging out with friends for protection. Fear slides into paranoia when others, responding to the original rumor and the second- and third-layer rumors, bring knives, or worse, to school. Rumors can be insidious.

5c Writing and revising to achieve paragraph unity

A unified paragraph will focus on, will develop, and will not stray from a paragraph's central, controlling idea or **topic sentence.** Recall that a *thesis* announces and controls the content of an entire essay, and that a *section thesis* announces and controls the content of a section. Just so, a *topic sentence* announces and controls the content of sentences in a single paragraph. Think of the topic sentence as a paragraph-level *thesis,* and you will see the principle of unity at work at *all* levels of the paper. At each level of the essay, a general statement is used to guide you in assembling specific, supporting parts.

ESSAY-LEVEL UNITY	The thesis (the most general statement in the essay) governs your choice of sections in a paper.
SECTION-LEVEL UNITY	Section theses (the second-most general statements in the essay) govern your choice of paragraphs in a section.
PARAGRAPH-LEVEL UNITY	Topic sentences (the third-most general statements in the essay) govern your choice of sentences in a paragraph.

Within a paragraph, a topic sentence can appear anywhere, provided that you recognize it and can lead up to and away from it with some method in mind. If you have read the example paragraphs in this chapter thus far, you have seen topic sentences placed at virtually all locations in a paragraph: at the beginning, one sentence after the beginning, the middle, the end, and both the beginning *and* end. The basic positions of a paragraph's topic sentence are discussed below.

Placing the topic sentence at the beginning of a paragraph

Very often, a topic sentence is placed first in a paragraph. You will want to open your paragraphs this way when your purpose is to inform or persuade a reader and you wish to be as direct as possible, as in the following example.

> 11 The college town is an American institution. Throughout the 19th century, it was common practice to locate private colleges in small towns like Amherst in Massachusetts, Middlebury in Vermont and Pomona in California. The idea was that bucolic surroundings would provide the appropriate atmosphere for the pursuit of learning and (not incidentally) remove students from the distractions and temptations of the big city. The influence of the small college on its town was minimal, however, beyond providing a few local residents with service jobs.
>
> —Witold Rybcynski, "Big City Amenities"

Witold Rybcynski begins the paragraph with a direct statement: *The college town is an American institution.* Every subsequent sentence focuses on and develops this topic sentence.

2 Placing the topic sentence in the middle of a paragraph

When you want to present material on two sides of an issue in your paragraph, consider placing the topic sentence in the middle of the paragraph. Lead up to the topic sentence with supporting material concerning its first part; lead away from the topic sentence with material concerning its second part, as in the following example:

> 12 A host of simple-minded cliches about Moslems and Islam exists. When the hostage crisis in Iran occurred, most Westerners began to view all Moslems, the followers of Islam, as Arab or Iranian militants seeking to return the world to the 14th century. There is, however, great diversity in Islam, a religion that covers one-seventh of the earth's inhabitable area and includes a sixth of its population. To judge all Moslems as the same is as futile as judging all Christians and Jews in the same way. Most of the world's 800 million Moslems are not fatalistic radicals. Like most Christians and Jews, they, too, devoutly believe in and respect God and seek to live a good life in peace with others.
>
> —Jack Shaheen, "In Search of the Arab"

Jack Shaheen's topic sentence is the pivot on which this paragraph turns: *There is, however, great diversity in Islam, a religion that covers one-seventh of the earth's inhabitable area and includes a sixth of its population.* Two sentences lead up to this topic sentence, preparing for it; three sentences follow and develop this topic sentence.

TEACHING IDEAS

If you're using an anthology in this course, find appropriate sections of essays for students to examine for placement of topic sentences. Students may choose for themselves the essays they wish to examine, but if you want to provide examples of various placements for topic sentences, you'll want to make the selections yourself. (If you're not using an anthology in the course, you can reproduce several sections from books on your own bookshelves.) As students see the ideas discussed in this chapter illustrated in essays found in other sources, they'll have an easier time relating the material to their own writing.

TEACHING IDEAS

Few writers calculate, while producing a first draft, where exactly they will place a paragraph's topic sentence or whether they will write such a sentence. Explicit concern with this matter is best saved for revision, when the writer does not need to disrupt the creation of ideas in order to attend to the structural elements of paragraph design. The search for topic sentences should not be a mechanical one to satisfy an injunction that "every paragraph must have a topic sentence." Rather, urge students to check for topic sentences as a technique for ensuring paragraph unity. After all, a paragraph succeeds when it is based on a well-focused idea. Paragraphs that lack a unifying idea are in danger of flying apart and losing the reader. In revision, writers can work to keep the reader's focus by identifying topic sentences and checking to see whether other sentences in a paragraph concern the same, narrowly focused idea.

ESL EXERCISE

Choose a grammatical interference problem between your first language and English. "Grammatical interference" means that the mental habit involved in the grammatical form in the first language causes mistakes or confusion in the second language, English. In one well-organized paragraph, explain the gram-

(continued)

matical interference problem, providing numerous examples to make it clear to your audience, which is teachers who do not speak your language and who do not understand why you make so many mistakes.

The order of your paragraph should be as follows: a clear topic sentence at the beginning expressing the problem and the reason for the problem; at least two supporting examples with explanations of each; and a concluding sentence or two clearly aimed at the teacher who is your audience.

Remember that your strategy is to make your mistake part of a general pattern, not a personal or private problem that other speakers of your language do not share.

ADDITIONAL EXERCISE C

Ask students to read any of the sample student papers in Chapters 4, 6, 35, and 37–39. For any paper, have the students identify section theses and topic sentences as a check to ensure that the paragraphs and sections of the paper are unified. Groups of students could read the same paper and discuss their findings among themselves. Students could discuss placement of topic sentences and the degree to which variety (or lack of variety) contributes to (or detracts from) the paper.

TEACHING IDEAS

Students who have been carefully trained to include a topic sentence for every paragraph might try this experiment with one of their completed papers. Find one or two paragraphs from which the topic sentence could be removed without negatively affecting the reader's understanding of the material. Students may need to add transitional phrases. Have students, in groups, read over competing versions of the same paragraph, with and without a topic sentence, in the context of two or three neighboring paragraphs from the original paper. Students can discuss the extent to which the paragraph improves or is harmed by the omitted topic sentence.

3 Placing the topic sentence at the end of a paragraph

When writing an informative or argumentative paper, in specific paragraphs you may want to postpone the topic sentence until the end. You would do this to ensure that readers would consider all the sentences in a paragraph before coming to your main point. The strategy works especially well when you are arguing, as in the following example.

> It is a fact that many children today are watching a great deal of televised fare that is inappropriate for their age and sophistication level. This concern raises two possible courses of action. If we take the position of technology determinist Neil Postman that "it is pointless to spend time or energy deploring television or even making proposals to improve it," then
> 13 the only response is to lock the television set up, or do whatever is necessary to keep it away from the innocent eyes of children. But if we believe that television can offer the potential to complement and enliven children's literacy experiences, it is imperative that greater efforts be made to improve both the quality of programming, and children's viewing habits.
>
> —SUSAN B. NEUMAN, "The Myth of the TV Effect"

If you place the last sentence of this paragraph first, you see that subsequent sentences support and develop the idea that *greater efforts be made to improve both the quality of programming, and children's viewing habits.* This statement is debatable, a fact that Susan Neuman implicitly acknowledges by presenting two solutions to the opening problem (that children are watching television inappropriate for their age and level of sophistication). She follows with the first solution, which she rejects, and then offers a competing solution, which she endorses. By delaying her paragraph's main idea, Neuman ensures that her audience will have some background on the problem and reason enough to agree with her position.

4 Omitting the topic sentence from the paragraph

In narrative and descriptive papers, and much less frequently in informative and persuasive papers, writers will occasionally omit the topic sentence from a paragraph. In a narrative paragraph in which you are telling a story, including the topic sentence may be too heavy handed and may ruin an otherwise subtle effect. The subject of descriptive writing may be so obvious that including a topic sentence seems redundant. When you decide to omit a topic sentence from a paragraph, take care to write the paragraph as though a topic sentence were present. With respect to unity, this means that you should focus each sentence on the implied topic and should not include any sentence that strays from that implied topic. Helen Keller does exactly this in ¶2 (page 117). Had she written a topic sentence for this paragraph, it might have read as follows: *The events immediately leading up to my discovery of language showed how thoroughly difficult and insensitive a child I was.*

ACROSS THE CURRICULUM

Effective Paragraphs: Using Analogies

Analogies are especially effective in presenting difficult concepts to an audience that is not likely to grasp these concepts intuitively. In *A Brief History of Time,* theoretical physicist Stephen Hawking describes the birth of a star.* Addressing fellow physicists, Hawking would dispense with analogies; he'd likely present equations and use specialized terms. But in his hugely popular book, written for nonspecialists, he aids the reader's understanding by explaining difficult theoretical concepts in terms of events and phenomena more easily grasped by his readers.

> A star is formed when a large amount of gas (mostly hydrogen) starts to collapse in on itself due to its gravitational attraction. As it contracts the atoms of the gas collide with each other more and more frequently and at greater and greater speeds—the gas heats up. Eventually, the gas will be so hot that when the hydrogen atoms collide they no longer bounce off each other, but instead coalesce to form helium. The heat released in this reaction, which is like a controlled hydrogen bomb explosion, is what makes the star shine. This additional heat also increases the pressure of the gas until it is sufficient to balance the gravitational attraction, and then the gas stops contracting. It is a bit like a balloon—there is a balance between the pressure of the air inside, which is trying to make the balloon expand, and the tension on the rubber, which is trying to make the balloon smaller. Stars will remain stable like this for a long time, with heat from the nuclear reactions balancing the gravitational attraction.

Analogy

The nuclear reaction of a star is analogous to a controlled hydrogen bomb explosion.

Analogy

The counterbalancing forces—gravitation and expansion—created by the nuclear reactions in a star are analogous to the counterbalancing forces operating in a balloon.

*The passage is excerpted from Stephen Hawking, *A Brief History of Time* (New York: Bantam, 1988) 82–83.

The following is an example of an informative paragraph with an implied topic sentence.

> Glossy brochures [from colleges to prospective high-school applicants]
> tend to portray a diverse group of beaming students frolicking happily
> and thinking deep thoughts on every page. "They're all the same," recalled
> one college freshman, happy to be finished with the process. Each bro-
> 14 chure speaks of "rich diversity" and "academic rigor" and dozens of other
> high-minded ideals that are often in reality nothing more than hollow
> catch-phrases. Likewise, any campus can look beautiful through the lens
> of an admissions office photographer. Just remember, the building that

looks so picturesque in the fading twilight could be part of the law school, miles from where the undergraduates study.

—*Yale Daily News* Staff, "The Insider's Guide to the Colleges"

The sentence that comes closest to being a topic sentence is the paragraph's final one. Yet even this sentence implies, rather than states directly, the following main idea: *When reviewing glossy college brochures, high-school students should not assume that they are being presented with a fully accurate portrayal of undergraduate life.* Placed at the head of this paragraph, this sentence would function adequately as a topic sentence. The existence and placement of every sentence in the paragraph is governed by this implied sentence, just as if it had been stated directly.

EXERCISE 4

Individual responses

EXERCISE 4

Reread several paragraphs that you have recently written for one of your classes. Choose one paragraph to revise for unity: add, delete, or modify sentences as needed.

EXERCISE 5

See suggested answers to Exercises 1 and 3.

EXERCISE 5

Locate the topic sentence in paragraphs 6, 7, 8, and 10 of Jim Walker's paper on school violence. Analyze each paragraph and be prepared to discuss how every sentence contributes to the paragraph's unity.

TEACHING IDEAS

ACROSS THE CURRICULUM Arrangement is a concept that can be illustrated by an analogy to film. Virtually all students are familiar with movies, so a discussion of arrangement in those terms can be useful. Ask students to think of the camera sweeping across a room or a landscape in a given scene in order to understand arrangement by space—after all, this kind of arrangement is more visual than literal. For arrangement by time they can think of scene sequences in films, parts of the film when the action seems most important. Arrangement by importance presents more of a challenge. But with a little prodding, some students should be able to recall movies in which the action is general and dispersed in certain scenes, only to move to specific, focused action in later scenes. As they realize that the filmmaker uses these techniques according to the needs of the plot, purpose, and audience, they'll come to understand the similar reasons for making arrangement decisions when writing paragraphs.

5d Writing and revising to achieve paragraph coherence

Your job in ensuring the overall coherence of a paragraph is to make clear the logic by which you position sentences in the paragraph. When your paragraphs are coherent, readers will understand the logic by which you move from one sentence to the next, toward or away from your topic sentence. When writing the first draft of a paper, you may not have a plan to ensure paragraph coherence; you may not even have a clear idea of every paragraph's main point. Revision is the time when you sort these matters out, when you can make certain that each paragraph has a clear purpose and a clear, coherent plan for achieving that purpose.

1 Arranging sentences to achieve coherence

There are standard patterns for arranging paragraphs. The most common are arrangements by space, by time, and by importance. If it occurs to you as you are writing a first draft that one of these patterns lends itself to the particular point you are discussing, then by all means write your paragraph with that pattern in mind. It is not necessary, though, that you map out patterns of coherence ahead of time.

Arrangement by space

You can help readers visualize what you are describing by arranging a paragraph spatially. Start the reader at a well-defined position with respect to the object being described, and then move him or her from that position to subsequent ones by taking systematic steps, one at a time, until your description is complete. In planning the paragraph, you might divide the object into the parts that you will describe; next, devise a definite plan for arranging these parts. Your description could proceed from front to back, right to left, top to bottom, outside to inside, and so on: the choice is yours. Once you choose a plan for organizing details, stick to the plan and you will help your readers to visualize your topic, as in this paragraph on the streets of Edinburgh.

> By the 17th and 18th centuries, Edinburgh was already overbuilt. Gray stone buildings filled every nook and cranny along the city's maze of roads and alleys. Space was so scarce inside the city walls that doctors, merchants and other professionals conducted their business in the pubs that lined the streets. . . . When Edinburgh needed more room to pack in
> 15 people, the resourceful Scots had to expand upward. It was not uncommon . . . for some buildings to go up 12 to 14 stories. The higher floors were reserved for the upper crust of Scottish society. The richer you were, the farther away you lived from the dark, wet and always filthy Edinburgh streets.
>
> —George Homsy, "From Kings to Caddies in Edinburgh"

The spatial organization in this paragraph rests on a principle of upward movement, the need for which was created by overcrowding at the base. The lower stories of buildings are associated with squalor. The upper stories are literally the realm of the upper class.

Arrangement by time

You can arrange a paragraph according to a sequence of events. Start the paragraph with a particular event, and move forward or backward in time in some definite order. Give your readers signals in each sentence that emphasize the forward or backward movement. In these example paragraphs on the rise of homelessness in the 1980s, the writer moves the reader forward in time with a series of phrases and single words, which are highlighted.

> If the large numbers of the homeless lived in hospitals before they reappeared in subway stations and in public shelters, we need to ask
> 16 where they were and what they had been doing from 1972 to 1980. Were they living under bridges? Were they waiting out the decade in the basements of deserted buildings?
>
> No. The bulk of those who had been psychiatric patients and were released from hospitals during the 1960s and early 1970s had been living in the meantime in low-income housing, many in skid-row hotels or board-

REFERENCES

Becker, A. L. "A Tagmemic Approach to Paragraph Analysis." *CCC* 16 (1965): 237–42. Paragraphs are usually arranged according to a TRI (topic-restriction-illustration) pattern or a PS (problem-solution) pattern.

Brostoff, Anita. "Coherence: 'Next to' Is Not 'Connected To.' " *CCC* 32 (1981): 278–94. Teaching coherence should emphasize logical connections, sequencing, and clear relationships within paragraphs and larger texts.

Christensen, Francis. "A Generative Rhetoric of the Paragraph." *CCC* 16 (1965): 144–56. Paragraphs can be understood by considering them in terms of sentence types (coordinate, subordinate, or a combination of the two).

Halliday, M. A. K., and Rugaiya Hasan. *Cohesion in English.* London: Longman, 1976. An extensive discussion of cohesion at the paragraph and essay level.

Markels, Robin Bell. *A New Perspective on Cohesion in Expository Paragraphs.* Carbondale: Southern Illinois UP, 1984. Cohesion should not be explained exclusively in syntactic terms; it involves semantics as well.

Sloan, Gary. "The Frequency of Transitional Markers in Discursive Prose." *CE* 46 (1984): 158–79. Transitional markers are not used frequently by college writers or professionals.

Smith, Rochelle. "Paragraphing for Coherence: Writing as Implied Dialogue." *CE* 46 (1984): 8–21. Applies reader response theory to understanding paragraph coherence as implied dialogue between writer and reader.

Stotsky, Sandra. "Types of Lexical Cohesion in Expository Academic Discourse." *CCC* 34 (1983): 430–46.

Winterowd, W. Ross. "The Grammar of Coherence." *CE* 31 (1971): 828–35. Discusses linkages between sentences and between paragraphs.

Witte, Stephen P., and Lester Faigley. "Coherence, Cohesion, and Writing Quality." *CCC* 32 (1981): 189–204. Questions classroom emphasis on cohesion over coherence.

TEACHING IDEAS

Just as with examinations of a paragraph's unity, a writer is more likely to profit by examining a paragraph's coherence *in revision.* While producing a first draft, the writer is concerned foremost with generating ideas. The finely tuned progression of those ideas in a first draft is less important than getting ideas down on paper. It is in revision, typically, that a writer will craft a paragraph, attending to matters of unity by deleting sentences if they are off the topic or adding sentences in the interest of topic development. And it is in revision when the writer brings specific strategies for paragraph coherence to the draft. The movement of ideas from specific to general or vice versa depends on the strategic effects the writer wants to create. You can illustrate the crafting of paragraphs in revision by bringing a few of your own to class, in various draft forms. Especially useful would be a demonstration of how you altered the organization of a paragraph in order to achieve some rhetorical purpose, or in order to present specific material more efficiently.

> ing houses. Such housing—commonly known as SRO (single-room occupancy) units—was drastically diminished by the gentrification of our cities that began in 1970. Almost 50 percent of SRO housing was replaced by luxury apartments or by office buildings between 1970 and 1980, and the remaining units have been disappearing at even faster rates. As recently as 1986, after New York City had issued a prohibition against conversion of
> 17 such housing, a well-known developer hired a demolition team to destroy a building in Times Square that had previously been home to indigent people. The demolition took place in the middle of the night. In order to avoid imprisonment, the developer was allowed to make a philanthropic gift to homeless people as a token of atonement. This incident, bizarre as it appears, reminds us that the profit motive for displacement of the poor is very great in every major city. It also indicates a more realistic explanation for the growth of homelessness during the 1980s.
>
> —JONATHAN KOZOL, "Distancing the Homeless"

Arrangement by importance

Just as you discuss different parts of a thesis at different locations in a paper, you will discuss different parts of a topic sentence at different locations in a paragraph. When revising, be aware of a paragraph's component parts so that you can arrange these parts in the most logical, accessible order. Arrangement is largely determined by where you position the topic sentence. How will your sentences lead up to and away from the topic sentence? You should be aware of two basic patterns: general to specific and specific to general.

General to specific: When the topic sentence begins the paragraph

By far the most common method for arranging sentences in a paragraph is to begin with your topic sentence and follow with specific, supporting details. When beginning a paragraph this way, decide how to order the information that will follow. You might ask: What does this paragraph's topic sentence obligate me to discuss? What are the *parts* of this paragraph and in what order will I discuss them? In this paragraph, Jerry Dennis explains how birds increase the chances that their fledglings will survive.

> There is a simple reason so many birds remain with one mate: the kids. The demands of raising young often take the full attention of two adults. Biologists like to discuss the behavior in economic terms, speaking of parental "investment," and pointing out that it is more profitable for a male bird intent on propagating his own genes to stick with one mate and
> 18 ensure the survival of a brood than to impregnate many females haphazardly. Once committed to monogamy, a male bird takes the job seriously. He may help build nests, take turns brooding the eggs, gather food, and stand watch. In studies where the male has been removed, the percentages of eggs that hatch and fledglings that survive decline dramatically.
>
> —JERRY DENNIS, "Mates for Life"

Specific to general: When the topic sentence ends the paragraph

When you are writing a description or narration or arguing a point, you may want to delay your topic sentence until the final sentence of a paragraph. Here you reverse the standard arrangement of a paragraph and move from specific details to a general, concluding statement. The goal is to build one sentence on the next so securely that the final sentence strikes the reader as inevitable.

> Einstein . . . wrote: "The most beautiful experience we can have is the mysterious. It is the fundamental emotion which stands at the cradle of all true art and true science." At first, this might seem a strange thought. We are frequently asked to believe that science is the antithesis of mystery.
> 19 Nothing could be further from the truth. Mystery invites the attention of the curious mind. Unless we perceive the world as mysterious—queer and wonderful—we will never be curious about what makes it tick.
>
> —CHET RAYMO, "To Light the Fire of Science, Start with Some Fantasy and Wonder"

In this example, Raymo begins with a specific quotation from Albert Einstein. Raymo develops the paragraph by exploring Einstein's use of the word *mysterious.* In so doing, he moves from the specific (the quotation) to the general, his larger point, which he locates in the paragraph's final sentence: our sense of the world's mystery is what prompts our investigations.

2 Achieving coherence with cues

When sentences are arranged with care, you need only highlight this arrangement to ensure that readers will move easily through a paragraph. To highlight paragraph coherence, use **cues:** words and phrases that remind readers as they move from sentence to sentence (1) that they continue to read about the same topic, and (2) that ideas are unfolding logically. Four types of cues help to highlight sentence-to-sentence connections: pronouns, repetition, parallel structures, and transitions (5d-3). Accomplished writers usually combine techniques in order to highlight paragraph coherence. Often, they wait until the revision stage to add cues to a paragraph, when they are better able to discern the paragraph's shape.

LOOKING AHEAD

Concepts covered in this section will be covered in greater depth in Chapters 14 (Pronoun Reference), 18 (Maintaining Sentence Parallelism), and 19 (Building Emphasis—repetition section). Students having difficulty understanding any of these concepts can be referred to the appropriate chapters later in the book.

Pronouns

The most direct way to remind readers that they continue to examine a certain topic as they move from sentence to sentence is to repeat the most important noun, or the subject, of your topic sentence. To prevent repetition from becoming tiresome, use a pronoun to take the place of this important noun. Every time a pronoun is used, the reader is *cued,* or reminded, about the paragraph's main topic. In the following example, *he* and *his* take the place of the name *Peter Hall.* These pronouns are repeated five times, tying the paragraph together without dulling the reader with repetition.

Illustration: Pronoun Substitution

The choice of Peter Hall to supply vigorous entrepreneurial leadership
was logical. Only twenty-nine, he was already an eminent director. He had
earned his credentials with the theatre work he began at Cambridge and
continued with the Elizabethan Theatre Company, formed by Oxford and
20 Cambridge students to tour Shakespeare plays. More impressive and at-
tention-getting was his direction of the 1955 premiere at the London Arts
Theatre of Samuel Beckett's *Waiting for Godot,* an event that alone would
have entered Hall's name into theatre history.

—ROGER CORNISH AND VIOLET KETELS, *Landmarks of Modern British Drama*

Repetition

While unintentional repetition can make sentences awkward, planned repetition can contribute significantly to a paragraph's coherence. The strategy is to repeat identically or to use a substitute phrase to repeat an important word or words in a paragraph. As with pronoun use, repetition cues readers, reminding them of the paragraph's important information. In the example concerning the word *performance,* combinations of the following four words are repeated eight times: *performance/performer, minstrels, scops, and gleemen.* Skillful use of repetition ties sentences together without boring the reader. Repetition helps to make this paragraph coherent.

Illustration: Word Repetition

Although the performance practices of the Church held considerable
power and influence, the medieval audience was familiar with other types
of performance events. The jongleurs and the troubadours of southern
France were professional performers who glorified heroic life and courtly
love in verse, often singing of love in rather earthy terms. In Anglo-Saxon
21 England, such performers were called scops and gleemen; later, they were
known as minstrels. Usually accompanying themselves with a harp, minstrels probably composed such literary texts as *Widsith, Doer's Lament,* and

Beowulf. Just as important, each of these texts offers a picture of the minstrels' performance work.

—RONALD J. PELIAS, *Performance Studies*

Parallelism

Chapter 18 is devoted entirely to a discussion of **parallelism:** the use of grammatically equivalent words, phrases, and sentences to achieve coherence and balance in your writing. A sentence whose structure parallels that of an earlier sentence has an echo-like effect, linking the content of the second sentence to the content of the first. As with pronoun use and skillful repetition, parallel structures cue readers by highlighting the paragraph's important information.

Illustration: Parallelism

STUDENT EXAMPLE: JIM WALKER

22 All students need to be aware of what some students know by instinct: that you can divert or reduce aggression with a quick apology or with humor. This is what social psychologists call reducing levels of arousal by introducing an incompatible response. Also, the school can implement Peer Mediation where if students feel a physical or emotional threat they can report it and discuss it with other students. Students talk through the issues with each other—and talking, it turns out, is the important thing: getting two sides together to talk rather than using weapons or fists to solve differences. Talking can also show students that disagreements are not worth a trip to the emergency room or worth the legal problems or medical bills—the consequences of violence that movies and rap videos don't usually show. If more students would have used these simple measures at my high school, I'm convinced that at least several fights could have been avoided.

Parallel structures found *within* sentences are:

you can divert or reduce
with a quick apology or with humor

TEACHING IDEAS

ACROSS THE CURRICULUM A concerted effort has been made in this book to include examples of writing from across the curriculum because they illustrate to students that the principles of good writing discussed in the composition classroom generalize. In paragraph 21 we see repetition used to ensure paragraph coherence. In paragraph 22, student Jim Walker, writing on school violence, demonstrates the use of parallelism.

As an exercise, ask students to photocopy a page from an article or a book being read for another course. Have them study one paragraph and point out the author's use of various techniques to ensure coherence. Students should watch for pronouns, repetition, parallel structures, and transitions.

what social psychologists call reducing levels of arousal by introducing . . .
if students feel a physical or emotional threat
they can report it and discuss it
disagreements are not worth a trip to the emergency room or the legal problems . . .

LOOKING AHEAD

Students may want to peruse Chapter 19 (Coordination and Subordination) as they study this section. Considering the later chapter here could help students when they reach the editing stage of their own papers: they'll understand coordination and subordination in the context of paragraph coherence rather than in the context of rules for sentence structure.

3 Highlighting coherence with transitions

Transitions establish logical relationships between sentences, between paragraphs, and between whole sections of an essay. A transition can be a single word, a phrase, a sentence, or an entire paragraph. In each case it functions the same way: first, it either directly summarizes the content of a preceding sentence (or paragraph) or it implies that summary. Having established a summary, transitions then move forward into a new sentence (or paragraph), helping the reader anticipate what is to come. For example, when you read the word *however,* you are immediately aware that the material you are about to read will contrast with the material you have just read. In so brief a transition, the summary of the preceding material is implied—but present. As the reader, *you* do the summarizing.

LOOKING BACK

This chapter emphasizes the point that paragraphs do not stand in isolation but, rather, exist in a broader context of related paragraphs. See 5a and, more generally, for a discussion of how awareness of a broader context contributes to critical thinking, see 1c.

CRITICAL DECISIONS

Set issues in a broader context: Revising paragraphs for coherence

As a writer, you probably have too much to do in a first draft to monitor the relationship among sentences and paragraphs or to develop coherence: the smooth flow of ideas. In a second or third draft, however, once you are settled on your final thesis and on the structure of your paper, you should evaluate your sentences in the broader context of paragraphs, and paragraphs in the broader context of sections (groupings of related paragraphs).

- **Revise every paragraph within its section.** To revise an individual paragraph, examine it in relation to the ones that come before and after. Develop the habit of including transitional words at the beginning or end of paragraphs to help readers move from one paragraph to the next. If you have difficulty writing a particular transition, rethink the logical connection between paragraphs. Transitions highlight a logic already present. A rough transition, always a disruption to the smooth flow of ideas, is a sign of faulty logic.
- **Revise every sentence within its paragraph.** Once you are sure of a paragraph's place in your paper, revise its component sentences to ensure coherence. Evaluate each sentence in relation to the sentences that come before and after. Use cues—pronouns, parallelism, repetition and transitions—to help move the reader from one sentence to the next through a paragraph.

Transitions *within* paragraphs

Transitions act as cues by helping readers to anticipate what is coming *before* they read it. Within a paragraph, transitions tend to be single words or short phrases.

Illustration: Transitions

When we think about addiction to drugs or alcohol we frequently focus on negative aspects, ignoring the pleasures that accompany drinking or drug-taking. And yet the essence of any serious addiction is a pursuit of pleasure, a search for a "high" that normal life does not supply. It is only
23 the inability to function without the addictive substance that is dismaying, the dependence of the organism upon a certain experience and an increasing inability to function normally without it. Thus people will take two or three drinks at the end of the day not merely for the pleasure drinking provides, but also because they "don't feel normal" without them.

—Marie Winn, "The Plug-in Drug"

Transitions *between* paragraphs

Transitions placed between paragraphs help readers move through sections of your paper. If you have done a good job of arranging paragraphs so that the content of one leads logically to the next, the transition will highlight a relationship that already exists by summarizing the previous paragraph and telegraphing something of the content of the paragraph that follows. A transition between paragraphs can be a word or two—*however, for example, similarly*—a phrase, or a sentence.

Student Example: Mike Bergom

Machines today are being integrated with all aspects of life, music included. For instance, we have seen the development of the synthesizer, the electric bass, and the electronic wind instrument (a flute-like instrument
24 connected to a computer). These new instruments have slowly begun to infiltrate jazz clubs around the world. Recording techniques have also progressed to technologies such as multitrack digital recording and digital tone modulation and amplification. Jazz has definitely not gone untouched by the pervasive force of technology.

And yet several young jazz musicians are saying "No!" to technology and are pursuing, with acoustic instruments, what might be called the "roots" of jazz. Trumpeter and jazz historian Wynton Marsalis, sax-

ophonist and former *Tonight Show* band leader Branford Marsalis, and
acoustic guitarist Mark Whitfield—these musicians, all under 35 years old,
refuse to use the latest technologies in their music. They instead employ
25 traditional instrumentation and jazz formats. On the face of it, this rejection is odd: as a culture, we are quick to demand and accept new technologies. We scramble for faster computers, we insist on cars with dual
airbags, we debate which electric toothbrush will keep our smiles brightest. Why, then, do these young musicians, who have grown up in a technological age, refuse what has been designed to help them?

The first part of this transitional sentence recalls the preceding paragraph with the words *musician* and *technology,* and then sets a strong contrast with the words *and yet* and *"No!"* The second part of this transitional sentence points to the content in the remainder of the paragraph: the jazz musicians who are using acoustic instruments.

Transitions *between* sections

At times, you may want to write a paragraph-length transition between sections of a paper, as in ¶27 of this example:

The electronic age has given us an almost magical ability to store, retrieve, and analyze data. Whether you're making travel plans, checking the
status of an insurance policy, or changing an assumption in a five-year
26 plan, the computer can provide almost instantaneous answers to questions
that only a decade ago might have remained unanswered for a day, a week,
or even a month.

But the electronic age has not given us a paperless office. In fact, in a
single year computers are said to churn out some 1200 pages of print for
27 every man, woman, and child in the United States. Although they help us
manage individual pieces of data, computers have increased our information overload.

In the midst of this overload, at a time when multimedia commands so
much attention, it's useful to remember the fundamental power of print.
28 Print is tangible; it has a life of its own. You can read it when you want, at
your own pace, and keep it for future reference. And with desktop technology, you can produce more pages faster and cheaper than ever before.

—Ronnie Shushan and Don Wright, *Desktop Publishing by Design*

Whatever its length, a transition will establish a clear relationship between sentences, parts of sentences, paragraphs, or entire sections of an essay. Transitions serve to highlight relationships already present by virtue of a writer's having positioned sentences or paragraphs next to one another. Whenever you have trouble finding a word or sentence to serve as an effective transition, reexamine the sentences or paragraphs you are trying to link: it may well be that they are not arranged coherently, and thus are in need of revision. The following box lists the most common transitions, arranged by type of relationship.

Transitional Expressions

To show addition	additionally, again, also, and, as well, besides, equally important, further, furthermore, in addition, moreover, then
To show similarity	also, in the same way, just as . . . so too, likewise, similarly
To show an exception	but, however, in spite of, on the one hand . . . on the other hand, nevertheless, nonetheless, notwithstanding, in contrast, on the contrary, still, yet
To indicate sequence	first, second, third, . . . next, then, finally
To show time	after, afterwards, at last, before, currently, during, earlier, immediately, later, meanwhile, now, recently, simultaneously, subsequently, then
To provide an example	for example, for instance, namely, specifically, to illustrate
To emphasize a point	even, indeed, in fact, of course, truly
To indicate place	above, adjacent, below, beyond, here, in front, in back, nearby, there
To show cause and effect	accordingly, consequently, hence, so, therefore, thus
To conclude or repeat	finally, in a word, in brief, in conclusion, in the end, on the whole, thus, to conclude, to summarize

ADDITIONAL EXERCISE D

This list does not exhaust the possibilities of transitional expressions. Ask students to read any ten pages of text of any article in an effort to add items to this list of general transitional expressions. Students should be prepared to explain the twofold function of the transition: to recall to the reader's mind what has come before, and to enable the reader to anticipate what is to follow.

4 Combining techniques to achieve coherence

Experienced writers will often combine the four techniques just discussed to establish coherence within a paragraph. A skillful mix of pronouns, repeated words and phrases, parallel structures, and transitions will help to maintain the focus of a paragraph and will provide multiple cues, or signposts, that help readers find their way from one sentence to the next.

Illustration: Achieving Coherence

For many people the years after age sixty are filled with excitement. Financially, two-thirds of American workers are covered by pension plans provided by their employers. Socially, most maintain close friendships and stay in touch with family members. Some, however, experience financial

29 problems, while others experience loneliness and isolation because many of their friends and relatives have died or they have lost touch with their families. In the United States, there are now as many people over the age of sixty as there are under the age of seven, yet funding for programs involving the health and psychological well-being of older people is relatively limited.

—LESTER LEFTON, *Psychology*

In this paragraph, Lefton combines techniques for achieving coherence. He sets up parallel sentences with the words *Financially* and *Socially.* He also uses parallelism within sentences, for instance: *as many people over the age of sixty as there are under the age of seven.* As pronoun substitutes for the word *people,* Lefton uses *most, some, others, their,* and *they.* He uses the transitional words *however* and *yet.* And he keeps the paragraph focused by repeating the word *people,* using several logical subsets of that general term: *workers, family members, friends, relatives,* and *older people.*

EXERCISE 6

Individual responses

EXERCISE 6

Choose any four example paragraphs in this chapter. For each paragraph, identify the techniques that the author uses to establish coherence. Show the use of pronouns, repetition, parallel structures, and transitions. In addition, identify the use of transitions between paragraphs.

EXERCISE 7

Individual responses

EXERCISE 7

Reread a paragraph you have recently written, and circle all words that help to establish coherence. If few words suggest themselves to you for circling, this may be a sign that your paragraph lacks coherence. Photocopy your paragraph and then revise it for coherence, using the techniques discussed previously: arrange sentences according to a pattern and then highlight that arrangement with pronouns, repeated words, parallel structures, and transitions. When you are done revising, write a clean copy of the paragraph and make photocopies of both the original and the revision for classmates in a small-group discussion. Prepare a brief presentation in which you discuss the changes you have made.

5e Writing and revising to achieve well-developed paragraphs

One important element of effective writing is the level of detail you can offer in support of a paragraph's topic sentence. To *develop* a paragraph means to devote a block of sentences to a discussion of its core idea. Sentences that develop will explain or illustrate, and will support with reasons or facts. The various strategies presented here will help you to develop paragraphs that inform and persuade.

Developing Paragraphs: Essential Features

In determining whether a paragraph is well or even adequately developed, you should be able to answer three questions without hesitation:

- **What is the main point of the paragraph?**
- **Why should readers accept this main point?** (That is, what reasons or information have you provided that would convince a reader that your main point is accurate or reasonable?)
- **Why should readers care about the main point of this paragraph?**

When writing the first draft of a paper, you may not stop to think about how you are developing the central idea of every paragraph. There is no need to be this deliberate in first-draft writing. By the second draft, however, you will want to be conscious of developing your paragraphs. The most common technique is **topical development,** that is, announcing your topic in the opening sentence; dividing that topic into two or three parts (in the case of chronological arrangement, into various *times*); and then developing each part within the paragraph.

The patterns of paragraph development that follow mirror the varieties of relationship that can underlie a paper's thesis. You forge relationships among materials you have gathered in planning a paper, and these relationships become a key component of your working thesis (see 3d). The key paragraphs of any paper will be the ones that express and develop the patterns of relation that lie at the core of either the working thesis or a section thesis. These same patterns of relation (shown in 3d-3) can be used to develop ideas in individual paragraphs.

1 Narratives and description

Stories that you tell (*narrative*) and events or scenes that you describe (*description*) are two strategies for development that can give a paper vivid detail.

Narratives

Narratives usually involve descriptions; a narrative's main purpose is to recount for readers a story that has a point pertinent to the larger essay. Brief stories are often used as examples. Most often, narratives are se-

ADDITIONAL EXERCISE E

Choose one set of general statements from the following list, and develop a paragraph by providing specific details related to the core idea. As you develop the paragraph, keep in mind the guidelines in the box.

1. Trying to hold down a job while caring for a family (*or* while pursuing a college degree) can pose many problems. Frequently, the individual trying to balance the two ends up shortchanging both.
2. The perfect vacation should offer equal amounts of relaxation, excitement, and enlightenment.
3. The kind of music played on radio stations in a given city can reveal a good deal about the inhabitants' ages, interests, and socioeconomic status.

REFERENCE

COHAN, CAROL. "Writing Effective Paragraphs." *CCC* 27 (1976): 363–65. Development can be taught by considering topic sentences to be questions requiring answers.

GROUP ACTIVITY

CRITICAL THINKING Actually covering each of the patterns of development in succession during class time can become tedious, no matter how interesting the model paragraphs may be. A group activity can make this section far more interesting to discuss, as well as help students understand the patterns better. Divide the class into groups (the number will depend on the class size and your own thoughts on whether to include topical development, whether to split classification and division, and other such considerations). Each group will be responsible for finding, reproducing, and analyzing one paragraph that illustrates a specific pattern of development. (If you're using an anthology that includes a rhetorical table of contents, you may want to simply refer students to that—although much of the challenge will be eliminated.) Groups will then present their paragraphs to the entire class. This activity encourages critical reading for style, invites evaluation of written material, and provides students the opportunity to teach themselves through their discussions.

TEACHING IDEAS

ACROSS THE CURRICULUM Students should not assume that narration is "merely" for personal (journal or letter) writing or for fiction. In the social sciences, particularly in reports on field studies, narration is an important skill.

Descriptions are also used widely across the curriculum. For an example of description in a qualitative field study, see "The Story of Edward," by Paul Rollinson, at 38b-1. Like any effective description, Rollinson's prose gives the reader a clear sense of a character and a place. For another example in the social sciences, see "Factors Influencing the Willingness to Taste Unusual Foods," by Laura P. Otis, at 38b-1. For an example of description in the sciences, see the "methods" section in the student paper on the fermentation of wine, at 39d. You might ask students how the descriptive qualities of these three pieces differ.

LOOKING BACK—LOOKING AHEAD

An example by definition stands in relation to a larger point the writer wishes to make. On this point, see 1c, the discussion of larger contexts as it relates, generally, to critical thinking. In that discussion, students are urged to ask of particular cases: "What's this a part of?" In the present discussion, students are being urged to ask: "How can I support my general point by directing the reader to a particular instance?" The questions are inversions of one another, and students will do well to develop a facility in moving in their thinking from the general to the specific and from the specific to the general. Later, in 6d-1, students will see that the argument from generalization draws on this same relationship: generalizations are made possible when one has studied a number of representative examples. The writer who makes a generalization is obliged to prove it by citing examples.

quenced chronologically and occur in an essay either as a single paragraph or as a grouping of paragraphs. The challenge in writing a narrative is to keep readers involved both in the events you are relating and in the people involved in those events. In the example that follows, *Time* magazine reporter David Van Biema's narration of a deliberately perpetrated Amtrak derailment in Arizona adds vivid and chilling detail to his extended discussion of "diabolically elegant" criminals who model their crimes on those of the past:

> It was a chilly, 60 degree night in southern Arizona last Monday. The moon was full, and Amtrak's 12-car Sunset Limited, bearing 248 passengers and 20 crew members, was doing between 50 and 55 m.p.h. as it approached a gentle curve not too far from the tiny town of Hyder. It was 1:20 A.M., and most of the passengers on the train, which is especially popular among retirees traveling from Los Angeles to Miami and back, were in bed. Suddenly, they were not so much awakened as catapulted from
> 30 sleep. Those who kept their wits about them remember a terrible, prolonged shriek of metal against metal. For others, their waking sensation was pain, as they smashed into a wall or a chair or a sink. The Limited's two diesel locomotives had safely crossed a 30-ft.-high trestle over a desert gulch. But the next five cars—a dormitory car for crew members, two sleeping cars for passengers and a dining car—had jumped the rails. One hit the ground below; the other three hung down from the trestle like beads in a giant's necklace.
>
> —DAVID VAN BIEMA, "Murder on the Sunset Limited"

Description

All writers must make observations and describe what they see. What counts as an accurate and worthwhile description will vary according to circumstance, but generally it can be said that a writer who can evoke in us a clear sense of sight, feeling, smell, hearing, or taste earns our admiration. The following paragraph is a brief but poignant portrait of the homeless population of New York City:

> There are more-visible people in need. There are the legions of homeless, lying on the benches in Grand Central Terminal, huddled in doorways against the cold, carrying their lives on their backs, trading subsistence for
> 31 life. In soup kitchens they lean over their meals as though in prayer and use the broth to warm as well as feed them, and use their dinnertime to stoke their beaten souls as well as their empty stomachs.
>
> —ANNA QUINDLEN, "A City's Needy"

2 Example

An example is a particular case of a more general point. After topical development, development by example is probably the most common method of supporting the core idea of a paragraph. Examples *show* readers what you mean; if an example is vivid, readers will have a better chance of remembering your general point. The topic sentence of a paragraph may be developed with one extended example or several briefer ones. It is common for writers to include an example along with other strategies for developing a paragraph. Several transitions are commonly used to introduce examples: *for example, for instance, a case in point, to illustrate.* In this paragraph, a counselor who advises high-school students on the college admissions process uses a funny story to illustrate a point about nervousness.

> Nervousness [in a college interview] . . . is absolutely and entirely nor-
> mal. The best way to handle it is to admit it, out loud, to the interviewer.
> Miles Uhrig, director of admission at Tufts University, sometimes relates
> this true story to his apprehensive applicants: One extremely agitated
> young applicant sat opposite him for her interview with her legs crossed,
> wearing loafers on her feet. She swung her top leg back and forth to
> 32 some inaudible rhythm. The loafer on her top foot flew off her foot, hit
> him in the head, ricocheted to the desk lamp and broke it. She looked at
> him in terror, but when their glances met, they both dissolved in laughter.
> The moral of the story—the person on the other side of the desk is also a
> human being and wants to put you at ease. So admit to your anxiety and
> don't swing your foot if you're wearing loafers! (By the way, she was
> admitted.)
>
> —ANTHONY F. CAPRARO, III, "The Interview"

3 Sequential order/process

If you have ever cooked a meal by following a recipe, you have read paragraphs patterned as a sequence of steps, as a process. Such a paragraph will not explain the causes of a particular outcome—it will not, for instance, explain the chemical reactions that cake batter undergoes when placed in an oven. A paragraph that presents a process will show carefully sequenced events. The range of possibilities is endless: what is the process by which people fall in love? by which children learn? by which a computer chip is manufactured? Each of these cases, different as they are, requires a clear delineation of steps. In paragraphs organized as a process, you may want to use transitions that show sequence in time: *first, second, after, before, once, next, then,* and *finally.*

> The first and simplest type of iron furnace was called a bloomery, in
> which wrought iron was produced directly from the ore. The ore was
> heated with charcoal in a small open furnace, usually made of stone and
> blown upon with bellows. Most of the impurities would burn out, leaving
> a spongy mass of iron mixed with siliceous slag (iron silicate). This spongy
> mass was then refined by hammering, reheating, and hammering some
> more, until it reached the desired fibrous consistency. During the ham-
> 33 mering, the glasslike slag would be evenly distributed throughout the iron
> mass. This hammered slab of wrought iron, or "bloom," was then ready to
> forge into some usable object. There were many furnaces of this type in

TEACHING IDEAS

ACROSS THE CURRICULUM For three examples of how a sequential order, or process, is presented differently in different curricular contexts, see the following examples in this book: Lou Cassetta's paper (gender differences in the computer industry), 4f; the "methods" section of the article by Laura P. Otis, 38b-1; the "materials and methods" section of the paper by Clarence Ivie, 39d.

FOR DISCUSSION

Often definitions can be stated simply, and writers can assume that readers will share their understanding of a term. But definitions will, at times, become an occasion for arguments. You may want to discuss with students Carl Becker's argument in defining the term "history."

> [History is a word] that I wish to reduce to its lowest terms. In order to do that I need a very simple definition. I once read that "history is the knowledge of events that have occurred in the past." That is a simple definition, but not simple enough. It contains three words that require examination. The first is knowledge. Knowledge is a formidable word. I always think of knowledge as something that is stored up in the *Encyclopaedia Britannica* or the *Summa Theologica:* something difficult to acquire, something at all events that I have not. Resenting a definition that denies me the title of historian, I therefore ask what is most essential to knowledge. Well, memory, I should think (and I mean memory in the broad sense, the memory of events inferred as well as the memory of events observed); other things are necessary too, but memory is fundamental: without memory no knowledge. So our definition becomes, "History is the memory of events that have occurred in the past." But events—the word carries an implication of something grand, like the taking of the Bastille or the Spanish-American War. An occurrence need not be spectacular to be an event. If I drive a motor car down the crooked streets of Ithaca, that is an event—something done; if the traffic cop bawls me out, that is an event—something said; if I have evil thoughts of him for so doing, that is an

(continued)

event—something thought. In truth anything done, said, or thought is an event, important or not as may turn out. But since we do not ordinarily speak without thinking, at least in some rudimentary way, and since the psychologists tell us that we cannot think without speaking, or at least not without having anticipatory vibrations in the larynx, we may well combine thought events and speech events under one term; and so our definition becomes, "History is the memory of things said and done in the past." But the past—the word is both misleading and unnecessary: misleading, because the past, used in connection with history, seems to imply the distant past, as if history ceased before we were born; unnecessary, because after all everything said or done is already in the past as soon as it is said or done. Therefore I will omit that word, and our definition becomes, "History is the memory of things said and done." This is a definition that reduces history to its lowest terms, and yet includes everything that is essential to understanding what it really is.

—CARL BECKER, "Everyman His Own Historian"

LOOKING AHEAD

Defining terms is an important part of argumentation. See 6b-2 for more on defining terms in an argument. See also Ludwig Wittgenstein's *definition of family resemblances* (37a-2), a term he defines by asking what is common to "the proceedings that we call 'games.' "

Colonial America, but they were later almost entirely replaced by cold-blast furnaces. The main drawback of this direct method of making wrought iron was its limited production. On the other hand, a bloomery required a much smaller investment of money and labor to set up and operate than did a blast furnace.

—ELIOT WIGGINTON, "Furnaces"

Definition

Paragraphs of definition are always important. In informative writing, readers can learn the meaning of terms needed for understanding difficult concepts. In essays intended to persuade, writers define terms in order to establish a common language with the reader, an important first step toward gaining the reader's agreement. Once a term is defined, it can be clarified with examples, comparisons, or descriptions. The paragraph that follows is informative in character—more or less announcing its definition.

> Alzheimer's disease is a slow death of the brain in which the first disturbing symptom is increasing forgetfulness. People with AD can no longer recall recent events or assimilate new information and ideas. They constantly misplace objects and repeat questions that have just been answered. Eventually they develop aphasia (loss of language), agnosia (inability to recognize people and objects), and apraxia (inability to perform everyday actions). They search their minds for words they have always
> 34 known. They have increasing difficulty in following a conversation; their own talk becomes disjointed and empty, their vocabulary impoverished and their language simplified. Their judgment declines, and they lose the capacity to generalize and classify. They start a routine action and no longer know how to finish it. They cannot find their way even in familiar places, or recall the day of the week or time of year. Cooking, driving, and using tools become too complicated for them. Toward the end they have difficulty in dressing and even using the bathroom and eating.
>
> —HARVARD MEDICAL SCHOOL, "Mental Health Letter"

Division and classification

Division (also called *analysis*) and classification are closely related operations. A writer who divides a topic into parts to see what it is made of performs an analysis. Analysis is an act of critical thinking that can be put to several ends. A careful study of parts can be instrumental in comparing and contrasting, in understanding a process, and in inferring cause and effect. While a paragraph may emphasize a definition, comparison, process, or cause, in each case this emphasis is made meaningful at least in part through analysis.

A *classification* is a grouping of like items. The writer begins with what may appear at first to be bits of unrelated information. Gradually, patterns of similarity emerge and the writer is able to establish categories by which to group like items. In the example that follows, Brian Fagan considers the various locations at which archaeological digs are made and then classifies or groups the digs according to common features. Because establishing categories is a matter of judgment, another writer might well classify archaeological sites differently. Fagan's paragraph begins with his topic sentence. Notice that once he defines various classes, he devotes a sentence or two to developing each.

> Archaeological sites are most commonly classified according to the activities that occurred there. Thus, cemeteries and other sepulchers like Tutankhamun's tomb are referred to as **burial sites.** A 20,000-year-old Stone Age site in the Dnieper Valley of the Ukraine, with mammoth-bone houses, hearths, and other signs of domestic activity, is a **habitation site.** So too are many other sites, such as caves and rockshelters, early Mesoamerican farming villages, and Mesopotamian cities—in all, people lived and carried out greatly diverse activities. **Kill sites** consist of bones of slaughtered game animals and the weapons that killed them. They are found in East Africa and on the North American Great Plains. **Quarry sites** are another type of specialist site, where people mined stone or metals to make specific tools. Prized raw materials, such as obsidian, a volcanic glass used for fine knives, were widely traded in prehistoric times and profoundly interest the archaeologist. Then there are such spectacular **religious sites** as the stone circles of Stonehenge in southern England, the Temple of Amun at Karnak, Egypt, and the great ceremonial precincts of lowland Maya centers in Central America at *Tikal,* Copán, and Palenque. **Art sites** are common in southwestern France, southern Africa, and parts of North America, where prehistoric people painted or engraved magnificent displays of art.
>
> —BRIAN FAGAN, *Archaeology*

6 Comparison/contrast

To *compare* is to discuss the similarities between people, places, objects, events, or ideas. To *contrast* is to discuss differences. The writer developing such a paragraph conducts an analysis of two or more subjects, studying the parts of each and then discussing the subjects in relation to each other. Specific points of comparison and contrast make the discussion possible. Suppose you are comparing and contrasting a computer and the human brain. Two points you might use to make the discussion meaningful are the density with which information is packed and the speed with which information is processed. You could analyze a computer and a human brain in light of these two points, and presumably your analysis would yield similarities *and* differences.

Paragraphs of comparison and contrast should be put to some definite use in a paper. It is not enough to point out similarities and differences; you must *do* something with this information: three possibilities would be to classify, evaluate, or interpret. When writing your paragraph, consider two common methods of arrangement: by subject or point-by-point.

FOR DISCUSSION

Aside from being a technique for organizing paragraphs, comparison and contrast has long been used to organize entire essays. If you assign a book of readings in your class, most likely it will contain at least one example of a comparison-contrast essay.

Organizing a Paragraph of Comparison and Contrast

Comparison and contrast is a type of analysis in which parts of two (or more) subjects are studied and then discussed in terms of one another. Particular points of comparison and contrast provide the means by which to observe similarities and differences between subjects. A comparative analysis is usually arranged in one of two ways.

Arrangement by subject

Topic sentence (may be shifted to other positions in the paragraph)
Introduce Subject A
  Discuss Subject A in terms of the first point
  Discuss Subject A in terms of the second point
Introduce Subject B
  Discuss Subject B in terms of the first point
  Discuss Subject B in terms of the second point
Conclude with a summary of similarities and differences.

Arrangement, point-by-point

Topic sentence (may be shifted to other positions in the paragraph)
Introduce the first point to be compared and contrasted
  Discuss Subject A in terms of this point
  Discuss Subject B in terms of this point
Introduce the second point to be compared and contrasted
  Discuss Subject A in terms of this point
  Discuss Subject B in terms of this point

When the comparisons you want to make are relatively brief, arrangement by subject works well. Readers are able to hold in mind the first part of the discussion as they read the second. When comparisons are longer and more complex, a point-by-point discussion helps the reader to focus on specific elements of your comparative analysis. Paragraphs developed by comparison and contrast use transition words such as *similarly, also, as well, just so, by contrast, conversely, but, however, on the one hand/on the other,* and *yet.*

In the following paragraph, Stephen Jay Gould organizes his comparative discussion by subject. First, he discusses his Subject A: the "testable proposals" of science. Then Gould discusses his Subject B: "useless speculation." At the end of this second discussion, Gould contrasts A and B, observing that speculation "turns in on itself" while "good science . . . reaches out." Note that when a comparative discussion becomes relatively long, you have the option of splitting it into two paragraphs, as Gould does in this example.

> Science works with testable proposals. If, after much compilation and scrutiny of data, new information continues to affirm a hypothesis, we may accept it provisionally and gain confidence as further evidence mounts. We can never be completely sure that a hypothesis is right, though we

36 may be able to show with confidence that it is wrong. The best scientific hypotheses are also generous and expansive: they suggest extensions and implications that enlighten related, and even far distant, subjects. Simply consider how the idea of evolution has influenced virtually every intellectual field.

Useless speculation, on the other hand, is restrictive. It generates no testable hypothesis, and offers no way to obtain potentially refuting evidence. Please note that I am not speaking of truth or falsity. The speculation may well be true; still, if it provides, in principle, no material for
37 affirmation or rejection, we can make nothing of it. It must simply stand forever as an intriguing idea. Useless speculation turns in on itself and leads nowhere; good science, containing both seeds for its potential refutation and implications for more and different testable knowledge, reaches out.

—STEPHEN JAY GOULD, "Sex, Drugs, Disasters"

In the next paragraph, Michele Pelletier uses a point-by-point arrangement to compare and contrast two types of armies of the fifteenth and sixteenth centuries: militias and mercenary forces. She first defines each type of army, and then contrasts their motives for and proficiency in fighting. Notice that the writer uses her comparisons to make a point: both the mercenary and militia experiences "have found their way into American military history of the past thirty years."

Student Example: Michele Pelletier

Armies of volunteers and conscripts are today's versions of the militias and mercenary forces that existed in the 15th and 16th centuries. Militias were armies made up of citizens who were fighting for their home country. Mercenaries were professional soldiers who, better trained than militia men (they were always men), were hired by foreign countries to fight
38 wars. Mercenaries had no cause other than a paycheck: if the country that hired them did not pay, they would quit the battlefield. Mercenaries may have been fickle, but technically they were good fighters. Militia men may not have been as technically proficient as mercenaries, but they had the will to fight. Both of these traditions—fighting for a cause and fighting for money—have found their way into American military history of the past thirty years.

7 Analogy

An **analogy** is a comparison of two topics that, on first appearance, seem unrelated. An analogy gains force by surprising a reader, by demonstrating that an unlikely comparison is not only likely but in fact is illuminating. Well-chosen analogies can clarify difficult concepts. In the following example, the unacceptable (to the author) failure rate of condoms as protection against contracting AIDS is compared to a hypothetical failure rate in cars. The author is arguing that 100 percent safety and dependability must be demanded in both cases. The words *like* and *analogous to* often signal the

FOR DISCUSSION

Creative analogies can be helpful to an argument. You might share with students the following excerpt from Amitai Etzioni's "Children of the Universe" (Rpt. in *Utne Reader* May/June 1993, 53):

> Consider for a moment parenting as an industry. As farming declined, most fathers left to work away from home generations ago. Over the past 20 years, millions of American mothers have sharply curtailed their work in the "parenting industry" by moving to work outside the home. By 1991 two-thirds (66.7 percent) of all mothers with children under 18 were in the labor force, and more than half (55.4 percent) of women with children under the age of 3 were. At the same time, a much smaller number of child-care personnel moved into the parenting industry.
>
> If this were any other business, say, shoemaking, and more than half of the labor force had been lost and replaced with fewer, less-qualified hands and still we asked the shoemakers to produce the same number of shoes of the same quality, we would be considered crazy. But this is what happened to parenting. . . .

See 6d-1 to see the ways in which analogy can be used in an argument (as above). Note that there is a point at which any analogy breaks down. For instance, Etzioni's assumption that parenting is an industry, comparable to shoemaking, must be accepted for the analogy to work. If the assumption is questioned, the analogy loses force. The well-chosen analogy, however, can advance an argument.

beginning of an analogy. After describing the first of the two topics in the comparison, the writer may follow with an expression such as *just so* or *similarly* and then continue with the second part of the comparison.

> AIDS is a killer disease and any measures taken to prevent its trans-
> mission must be 100 percent effective. For condoms to be the answer to
> 39 AIDS, they must be used every time and can never break or leak. Neither
> criterion is ever likely to be met. Condoms may mean "safer" sex, but is
> "safer" acceptable for this deadly epidemic?
> Suppose that, for unknown reasons, automobiles suddenly began to ex-
> plode every time someone turned the ignition. Motorists were getting
> blown up all over the country. Finally, the government comes out with a
> 40 solution. Just put this additive in the fuel, they say, and the risk of explo-
> sion will go down 90 percent. Would you consider the problem solved?
> Would you still keep driving your car? I doubt it. Then why do we accept
> condoms as the solution for AIDS?
>
> —STEVEN SAINSBURY, "Condoms: Safer, But Not 'Safe' Sex"

LOOKING AHEAD

See 6d-1 for a discussion of cause-and-effect reasoning and its place in argumentation. For examples of how paragraphs arranged by cause and effect are used in actual papers, see the student essay in 6g, in which Alison Tschopp argues that the real cause of children's problems with advertisements is not advertising but lack of parental supervision. See also 38d, paragraph 2, in which Kristy Bell argues that one reason women alcoholics are invisible is that they are well protected by family and friends. The larger point to make in these examples is that the cause-and-effect paragraph forms *one* part of a larger argument. For an example of extended cause-and-effect thinking common to science writing, see the lab report in 39d. The report, in effect, is an argument in which Clarence Ivie proves that using a certain strain of yeast produces (i.e., *causes* the formation of) a superior wine.

8 Cause and effect

Development by cause and effect shows how an event or condition has come to occur. Inferring a causal relationship between events requires careful analysis. As discussed elsewhere (see 6d-1), causes are usually complex, and a writer must avoid the temptation to oversimplify. Frequently, therefore, cause-and-effect reasoning is developed over several paragraphs. When you are developing a causal connection, avoid the mistake of suggesting that because one event precedes another in time, the first event causes the second. A causal relationship is not always so clear-cut, a point that James Watts and Alan Davis acknowledge in the following paragraph on the Depression of the 1930s. Paragraphs developed by cause and effect frequently use these transition words: *therefore, thus,* and *consequently.*

> The depression was precipitated by the stock market crash in October
> 1929, but the actual cause of the collapse was an unhealthy economy. While
> the ability of the manufacturing industry to produce consumer goods had
> increased rapidly, mass purchasing power had remained relatively static.
> 41 Most laborers, farmers, and white-collar workers, therefore, could not af-
> ford to buy the automobiles and refrigerators turned out by factories in the
> 1920s, because their incomes were too low. At the same time, the federal
> government increased the problem through economic policies that tended
> to encourage the very rich to over-save.
>
> —JAMES WATTS AND ALAN F. DAVIS, *Your Family in Modern American History*

Writers may combine methods of developing a paragraph's core idea, as needed. The same paragraph that shows an example may also show a comparison or contrast. No firm rules constrain you in developing a paragraph. Let your common sense and an interest in helping your reader understand your subject be your guides.

EXERCISE 8

Return to Exercise 2 (page 120) in which you selected one section of a textbook chapter to study in depth. If you have not done so, complete that exercise, and then for that same block of paragraphs analyze each paragraph and identify its pattern of development.

EXERCISE 8

Individual responses

EXERCISE 9

In one paragraph compare and contrast your first day as a student at your present school with your first day in any other circumstance. Take care to choose two or three points on the basis of which you will generate your comparison and contrast. Be sure your comparison and contrast is put to some purpose (perhaps you will classify, interpret, or evaluate). Express this purpose in your paragraph's topic sentence. See ¶s 36, 37, and 38 for possible models.

EXERCISE 9

Individual responses

EXERCISE 10

Reread a paper you have recently written and select a paragraph to revise so that its topic sentence is thoroughly developed. Use any of the patterns of development presented here so that you are able, without hesitation, to answer the three questions in the box on page 137. Make photocopies of your original paragraph and your revision; plan to address a small group of classmates and explain the choices you have made in revision.

EXERCISE 10

Individual responses

5f Writing and revising paragraphs of introduction and conclusion

The introduction and conclusion to a paper can be understood as a type of transition. Transitions provide logical bridges in a paper: they help readers to move from one sentence to another, one paragraph to another, and one section to another (see 5d-3). At the beginning of a paper, the introduction serves as a transition by moving the reader from the world outside of your paper to the world within. At the end of the paper, the conclusion works in the opposite direction by moving readers from the world of your paper back to their own world—with, you hope, something useful gained by their effort.

1 Introductions

Writing an introduction is often easier once you know what you are introducing; for this reason many writers choose not to work seriously on an introduction until they have finished a draft and can see the overall shape and content of a paper. Other writers need to begin with a carefully written introduction. If this is your preference, remember not to demand perfection of a first draft, especially since the material you will be introducing has yet to be written. Once it is written, your introduction may need to change.

FOR DISCUSSION

Reproduce several introductions that provide a frame of reference (these can be gathered from anthologies or student papers). Ask students to discuss what signals they pick up from the paragraphs—what they learn about the writer, the approach, the language, the type of evidence or detail that will be used, and the like.

TEACHING IDEAS

While it's always a bit dangerous to focus on negative examples, many students do need to be made aware of some taboos with regard to introductions. If you can frame your discussion in terms of the approach in this chapter, you can address the problem of the hesitant introduction—the "I don't really know much about this but here goes anyway" variety. If the introduction provides readers with their first impression of the writer, then certainly the writer doesn't want to sound ignorant or insecure. Similarly, if you focus on the differences between introductions from various disciplines, you can steer students away from using inappropriate introductions such as the "In this paper I will" for humanities or the introductory anecdote for sciences.

ADDITIONAL EXERCISE F

Assignment: Ask students to read any one of the sample student papers in Chapters 4, 6, 35, and 37 through 39. In each case, students should study the writer's strategy used in the introduction. Students should then prepare themselves to argue that the introduction is or is not effective. One variation on the assignment would be to ask that students also prepare an alternate introduction to the paper. (See also Additional Exercise H, in which students are asked to do the same with the paper's conclusion.)

The introduction as a frame of reference

Introductions establish frames of reference. On completing an introduction, readers know the general topic of your paper; they know the disciplinary perspective from which you will discuss this topic; and they know the standards they will use in evaluating your work. Readers quickly learn from an introduction if you are a laboratory researcher, a field researcher, a theorist, an essayist, a reporter, a student with a general interest, and so on. Each of these possible identities implies for readers different standards of evidence and reasoning by which they will evaluate your work. Consider the paragraph that follows. The introduction, explicitly in the thesis and implicitly in the writer's choice of vocabulary, establishes a frame of reference that alerts readers to the type of language, evidence, and logic that will be used in the subsequent paper. Thus situated, readers are better able to anticipate and evaluate what they will read.

Illustration: Writing in the Humanities

STUDENT EXAMPLE: SARIKA CHONDRA

James Joyce's "Counterparts" tells the story of a
man, Farrington, who is abused by his boss for not
doing his job right. Farrington spends a long time
42 drinking after work; and when he finally arrives home,
he in turn abuses—he beats—his son Tom. In eleven
pages, Joyce tells much more than a story of yet another alcoholic venting failures and frustrations on
family members. *In "Counterparts," Farrington turns to drink in order to gain power—in much the same way his wife and children turn to the Church.*

Language of literary analysis

Evidence: based on close reading of a story

Logic: generalization

Drinking and church going related to a need for power

Also comparison/contrast

By comparison, read the following introduction to a paper written from a sociological perspective. This paragraph introduces a paper you will find in Chapter 38, Writing and Reading in the Social Sciences.

Illustration: Writing in the Social Sciences

STUDENT EXAMPLE: KRISTY BELL

Currently, in the United States, there are at least two million women alcoholics (Unterberger, 1989, p. 1150).

Language of sociology

43 Americans are largely unaware of the extent of this debilitating disease among women and the problems it presents. Numerous women dependent on alcohol remain invisible largely because friends, family, co-workers, and the women themselves refuse to acknowledge the problem. *This denial amounts to a virtual conspiracy of silence and greatly complicates the process of diagnosis and treatment.*

Language of sociology

Evidence: based on review of sociological literature

Logic: cause and effect. Will show how denial complicates diagnosis and treatment.

The introduction as an invitation to continue reading

Aside from establishing a frame of reference and set of expectations about language, evidence, and logic, an introduction also does—or does not—establish in your reader a desire to *continue* reading. A complete introduction provides background information needed to understand a paper. An especially effective introduction gains the reader's attention and gradually turns that attention toward the writer's thesis and the rest of the paper. Writers typically adopt specialized strategies for introducing their work. In the discussion that follows you will learn several of these strategies, all of which can be developed in one or two paragraphs, at the end of which you will place your thesis. These examples by no means exhaust the possible strategies available to you for opening your papers.

Student Example: Daniel Burke, "Defense of Fraternities"

44 A revolutionary event took place at Raleigh Tavern in 1776, an event that has added an important dimension to my life at college. In fact, nearly all American undergraduates are affected in some way by the actions of several students from the College of William and Mary on December 5, 1776. The formation of the first Greek-letter fraternity, Phi Beta Kappa, started the American college fraternity-sorority tradition that today can be an important addition to your undergraduate education.

In this example, student writer Daniel Burke provides pertinent historical information that sets a context for the paper. By linking a "revolutionary event" in 1776 to his own life over two hundred years later, Burke captures the reader's interest.

The following example begins with a question, the response to which leads to the author's thesis. (The reference to "Valenti" is to Jack Valenti, who was head of the Motion Picture Production Association when Stephen Farber wrote his book.)

How are [movie] ratings actually determined? Official brochures on the rating system provide only very brief general definitions of the four categories, and I do not believe the categories can or should be defined much more specifically. It is impossible to set hard-and-fast rules; every film is different from every other film, and no precise definition could possibly cover all films made. Valenti has frequently toyed with the idea of more detailed definitions, though any rigid demarcations between the categories inevitably seem hopelessly arbitrary.

—STEPHEN FARBER, *The Movie Rating Game*

See 5f-3 for two additional strategies for opening a paper: using a quotation and telling a story.

Strategies for Writing Introductions

1. Announce your topic, using vocabulary that hints at the perspective from which you will be writing. On completing your introduction, readers should be able to anticipate the type of language, evidence, and logic you will use in your paper.
2. If readers lack the background needed to understand your paper, then provide this background. In a paragraph or two, choose and develop a strategy that will both orient readers to your subject and interest them in it: define terms, present a brief history, or review a controversy.
3. If readers know something of your subject, then devote less (or no) time to developing background information and more time to stimulating interest. In a paragraph or two, choose and develop a strategy that will gain the reader's attention: raise a question, quote a source familiar to the reader, tell a story, or begin directly with a statement of the thesis.
4. Once you have provided background information and gained the reader's attention with an opening strategy, gradually turn that attention toward your thesis, which you will position as the last sentence of the introductory paragraph(s).

2 Conclusions

One important job in writing a paper is to explain to readers what you have accomplished and why your ideas are significant. Minimally, a conclusion will summarize your work, but often you will want to do more than write a summary. Provided you have written carefully and believe in what you have written, you have earned the right to expand on your paper's thesis in a conclusion: to point the reader back to the larger world and to suggest the significance of your ideas in that world. This is exactly what Jim Walker does in the conclusion of his paper, several paragraphs of which you've seen as illustrations in this chapter.

ADDITIONAL EXERCISE G

ACROSS THE CURRICULUM Find representative introductions (of chapters, sections, essays) from the reading you're doing for courses in two different disciplines. Consider all science courses to be one discipline, all economics/sociology/psychology/political science/business courses to be another, and all literature/language/history/philosophy/fine arts to be another. Using what you've learned about introductions in this chapter, compare the two samples and explain how they reflect different frames of reference for readers.

ESL EXERCISE

Choose the two or three grammatical problems with English that have been most difficult for you to solve. Preferably, these would be grammatical problems different from the grammatical interference problem you wrote about earlier, although there might be some overlap. In one well-organized paragraph, explain the problems, giving numerous examples to make them clear to your audience.

The order of your paragraph should be as follows: a clear topic sentence at the beginning expressing the problems and the reason for them; at least three supporting examples with explanations of each; and a conclusion.

Your conclusion should explain what steps you plan to take to remember and/or correct the problems in the future. Be specific about this; don't just say you plan to try harder.

Student Example: Jim Walker

It will be in schools that students learn effective social and communication skills that will help reduce the levels of aggression and divert the
damage that rumors, confrontations, and fights cause. Talking about differences, talking through differences, and deflecting aggressive acts by
46 apologizing and by our sense of humor will show by example that we have
the heart to live together and have the courage and good sense to get
along. We can break the cycle of violence by seeing weapons as part of the
problem, not as the solution to the lethal levels of violence in our society.

A conclusion gives you an opportunity to answer a challenge that all readers raise—*So what? Why should this paper matter to me? What actions should I take?* A well-written conclusion will answer these questions and will leave readers with a trace of your thinking as they turn away from your paper and back to their own business.

The example conclusions that follow do not exhaust the strategies for closing your papers; these examples should, however, give you a taste of the variety of techniques available. Here is a paragraph that presents the simplest possible conclusion: a summary—in this case, of an argument that colleges must cut costs and rethink their educational missions if they are to avoid going bankrupt. This concluding paragraph summarizes the author's key points:

> Already most colleges are looking carefully at ways to cut costs. But this
> cost-cutting is not examining basic questions about how a college is orga-
> nized to provide for the advancement of knowledge and student learning.
> It is time to ask basic questions, to conceptualize fundamentally different
> 47 ways—less costly ways—of providing education. Higher education will
> have to make hard choices. It will not be able to satisfy every need or re-
> spond to every constituent. The colleges that ask, and answer, basic ques-
> tions about how to educate students in less expensive ways will be the
> colleges that survive.
>
> —Daniel S. Cheever, Jr., "Higher and Higher Ed"

A more ambitious conclusion will move beyond a summary and call for involvement on the reader's part. For instance, you might ask the reader to address a puzzling or troubling question, to speculate on the future, or to reflect on the past. In this next example, the reader is given a challenge. (The complete essay appears in 6g.)

Student Example: Alison Tschopp

The task of shaping children's values, like their diets, is better addressed through ongoing discussions between parents and children than
through limiting the right of free speech. There is no need to silence advertisers in order to teach values or protect the innocent and unskeptical.
The right to free speech is protected by the Constitution because as a nation we believe that no one person is capable of determining which ideas
are true and rational. Like media critic Jean Kilbourne, we may disagree
48 with some of the messages being conveyed through advertising—say, the

FOR DISCUSSION

Reproduce several conclusions that provide a summary of and comment on the whole essay (these can be gathered from anthologies or student papers). Ask students to discuss how the conclusions signal that the essay is finished, how they avoid simply repeating material from the paper, and how they build on the summary.

message that women are attractive only when they are young and thin (44). Like Peggy Charren, we can agree that advertisements can create stresses in a family's life (15). Nevertheless, we must allow all ideas a place in the market place. As Charles O'Neil, an advertiser and a defender of the medium, suggests, "[a]dvertising is only a reflection of society; slaying the messenger will not alter the fact" that potentially damaging or offensive ideas exist (196). If we disagree with the message sent in an ad, it is our responsibility to send children a different message.

Strategies for Writing Conclusions

1. **Summary.** The simplest conclusion is a summary, a brief restatement of your paper's main points. Avoid conclusions that repeat exactly material presented elsewhere in the paper.
2. **Summary and Comment.** More emphatic conclusions build on a summary in one of several ways. These conclusions will:

   set ideas in the paper in a larger context
   call for action (or research)
   speculate or warn
   purposefully confuse or trouble the reader
   raise a question
   quote a familiar or authoritative source
   tell a story

3 The opening and closing frame

You might consider creating an introductory and concluding frame for your papers. The strategy is to use the same story, quotation, question—any device that comes to mind—as an occasion both to introduce your subject and, when the time is right, to conclude emphatically. Provided the body of a paper is unified, coherent, and well developed, an opening and closing frame will give the paper a pleasing symmetry. In the following example, Rachel L. Jones works with a quotation.

Introduction

William Labov, a noted linguist, once said about the use of black English, "It is the goal of most black Americans to acquire full control of the standard language without giving up their own culture." He also suggested that there are certain advantages to having two ways to express
49 one's feelings. I wonder if the good doctor might also consider the goals of
those black Americans who have full control of standard English but who are every now and then troubled by that colorful, grammar-to-the-winds patois that is black English. Case in point—me.

TEACHING IDEAS

As with introductions, conclusions can also pose problems for students. Again framing your discussion in terms of the approach in this chapter, you can address the problem of the repetitive conclusion—the "In conclusion I have said" variety. By clarifying what's meant by "comment" you can steer students away from the conclusion that introduces an entirely new idea. Finally, again by focusing on the differences between disciplines, you can help students avoid producing conclusions inappropriate to the discipline in which they're writing.

ADDITIONAL EXERCISE H

Ask students to read any one of the sample student papers in Chapters 4, 6, 35, and 37 through 39. In each case, students should study the writer's strategy used in the conclusion. Students should then prepare themselves to argue that the conclusion is or is not effective. One variation on the assignment would be to ask that students also prepare an alternate conclusion to the paper. (See also Additional Exercise F, in which students are asked to do the same with the paper's introduction.)

ADDITIONAL EXERCISE I

ACROSS THE CURRICULUM Find representative conclusions (of chapters, sections, essays) from the reading you're doing for courses in two different disciplines, using the categories found in Additional Exercise G. Using what you've learned about conclusions in this chapter, compare the two samples and explain the methods they use to signal that the paper is finished, as well as the message they leave with the reader.

Conclusion

I would have to disagree with Labov in one respect. My goal is not so much to acquire full control of both standard and black English, but to one day see more black people less dependent on a dialect that excludes them from full participation in the world we live in. I don't think I talk white; I think I talk right.

—RACHEL L. JONES, "What's Wrong with Black English"

EXERCISE 11

Locate a collection of essays and/or articles: any textbook that is an edited collection of readings will work. Read three articles and examine the strategies the authors use to introduce and conclude their work. Choose one article to analyze more closely. Examine the strategies for beginning and ending the selection and relate these strategies to the selection itself. Why has the writer chosen these *particular* strategies? Be prepared to discuss your findings in a small group.

EXERCISE 12

In connection with a paper you are writing, draft *two* opening and *two* closing paragraphs, using different strategies. Set your work aside for a day or two and then choose which paragraphs appeal to you the most. Be prepared to discuss your choices in a small group.

5g Determining paragraph length

Paragraphs vary greatly in length. As long as the governing idea of a paragraph remains clear, all sentences are unified, and the paragraph is coherent, then in theory a paragraph can be one sentence, five sentences, or twenty. This said, you should realize that readers will tire of a paper whose paragraphs are consistently one typewritten page or longer. If for no other reason than to give readers visual relief, keep paragraphs moderate in length. *Moderate* is a variable and personal term. Perhaps you decide that visually your paragraphs should average one-third to two-thirds of a typewritten page. If your sentences tend to be brief, your average number of sentences per paragraph may be ten or twelve; if your sentences tend to be long, the average number of sentences per paragraph may drop to six.

Devote your energies to the content of your paragraphs first. Turn to paragraph length in the later stages of revision when you are relatively satisfied with your work. Then think of your reader and the way your paragraphs appear on the page. Visually, does the length of your paragraphs invite the reader into your paper? Consistently short paragraphs may send the signal that your ideas are not well developed. Consistently long paragraphs may give the impression that your writing is dense or that your ideas are not well differentiated. You should freely divide a long paragraph for

EXERCISE 11

Individual responses

EXERCISE 12

Individual responses

GROUP ACTIVITY

The following activity can be done more easily if students compose their essays on computers: Since paragraph length has a great deal to do with the needs of the reader, ask students to make two copies of a brief paper *without any paragraph divisions.* In groups of three, each student will mark the other two papers for paragraph divisions. The ensuing discussion of differences between each reader (and the writer's original divisions) will encourage students to analyze the relative demands that content, purpose, and audience place on a writer in determining paragraph length.

REFERENCES

EDEN, RICK, and RUTH MITCHELL. "Paragraphing for the Reader." *CCC* 37 (1986): 416–30. Various choices in paragraphing should be made with audience expectations in mind.

STERN, ARTHUR A. "When Is a Paragraph?" *CCC* 27 (1976): 253–57. Calls into question descriptions of paragraphs as logical units.

ADDITIONAL EXERCISE J

See the "For Discussion" annotation on page 139. Ask students to read the paragraph in which Carl Becker defines "history." Then have students mark the places that, for reasons of length, they would begin new paragraphs.

Suggested response:

> Break between . . . *three words that require examination.* and *The first is knowledge.*
>
> Break between . . . *events that have occurred in the past.* and *But events. . . .*
>
> Break between . . . *things said and done in the past.* and *But the past. . . .*

reasons of length alone. A new paragraph created because of length does not need its own topic sentence, provided this paragraph is a clear continuation of the one preceding it.

Brief paragraphs of one, two, or three sentences can be useful for establishing transitions between sections of a paper (see ¶27) and, as illustrated in this next example, for creating emphasis.

> In a nation with 40 million handguns—where anyone who wants one can
> get one—it's time to face a chilling fact. We're way past the point where
> registration, licensing, safety training, waiting periods, or mandatory sen-
> 51 tencing are going to have much effect. Each of these measures may save
> some lives or help catch a few criminals, but none—by itself or taken to-
> gether—will stop the vast majority of handgun suicides or murders. A
> "controlled" handgun kills just as effectively as an "uncontrolled" one.
>
> Most control recommendations merely perpetuate the myth that with
> 52 proper care a handgun can be as safe a tool as any other. Nothing could be
> further from the truth. A handgun is not a blender.
>
> Those advocating a step-by-step process insist that a ban would be too
> radical and therefore unacceptable to Congress and the public. A hardcore
> 40 percent of the American public has always endorsed banning hand-
> 53 guns. Many will also undoutedly argue that any control measure—no mat-
> ter how ill-conceived or ineffective—would be a good first step. But after
> more than a decade, the other foot hasn't followed.
>
> —Josh Sugarmann, "The NRA Is Right"

If in revising a first draft you find that your paragraphs are consistently two or three sentences long, consider ways in which you can further develop each paragraph's topic sentence. Unless you are writing in a journalism class or in some other context where consistently brief paragraphs are valued, once again the advice is to maintain a moderate length and only rarely—for clear reasons—use very brief or very long paragraphs.

CHAPTER 6

Writing and Evaluating Arguments

Arguments provide a way of knowing about and participating in the world. Through argumentation, you exchange views with parents, friends, and associates; when differences arise, you try to influence others so that they will agree with you. In academic circles, researchers construct their views of the world through arguments. They experiment, read critically, and administer surveys; and then, observing patterns, they make statements—the truth, probability, or desirability of which they try to demonstrate through arguments. In this chapter you will learn the elements essential to arguing in *any* context. Later, in Chapters 37–39, you will learn how these elements change according to the discipline in which you are writing.[1]

6a An overview of argument

An *argument* is a process of influencing others, of changing minds through reasoned discussion. Arguments consist of three parts: claim, support, and reasoning. The relationships among these parts give an argument its force. No argument is possible unless claim, support, and reasoning pull together to make a persuasive whole.

CLAIM — A claim is an argument's thesis, a statement about which people will disagree. There are three types of claims (see 6b); whichever one you use, you need to define terms with care.

- Claims about facts
- Claims about what is valuable
- Claims about policy

SUPPORT — Support consists of facts, opinions, and examples that you present to readers so that they will accept your claim. Usually, you will present several types of support for a claim (6c).

REASONING — Reasoning is the pattern of thought that connects support to a claim. Each type of support involves a corresponding form of reasoning. Reasoning will be based on appeals to a reader's logic, respect for authority, or emotion.

[1]The approach to argument taken here is based on the work of Stephen Toulmin, as developed in *The Uses of Argument* (Cambridge: The University Press, 1958).

KEY FEATURES

The material in this chapter is based primarily on the Toulmin model of argument. In keeping with the critical thinking coverage in Chapters 1 and 2, the process of constructing an argument is approached not as a presentation of conclusions but as a *way of knowing* through active inquiry about the world. Since modes of inquiry differ among the disciplines, the chapter emphasizes throughout that the form an argument takes, as well as the type of evidence provided, depends on the discipline. Making note of these differences early on in the handbook prepares students for the in-depth coverage of writing in the disciplines to follow in Chapters 37, 38, and 39. The discussion of argument focuses on developing a claim and marshaling evidence; appealing to logic, authority, and emotion; rebutting opposing arguments; and devising an overall strategy for presenting the argument. In exercises students move between development of their own arguments and analysis of material presented to them; both types of exercises pay particular attention to the needs of audience. The final section of the chapter deals with evaluating existing arguments, emphasizing what are often referred to as logical fallacies, covered here as flaws in making inferences. Approaching these fallacies from the perspective of inference rather than logic is consistent with the Toulmin approach.

ESL CUE

Argumentation is a concept European students will understand and relate to with ease. For example, Polish students in particular will revel in argumentation and French students or students trained in a French system will prob-

(continued)

ably have very systematic ways of setting up and controlling argumentation. Greek students, predictably, will probably have had some training in classical rhetorical strategies. However, the concept of argumentation will be alien to many Asian students for whom confrontation is an anathema. They will try to provide a balanced discussion on both sides of an issue, with a focus on compromise and conciliation. Indonesians in particular will find the concept of argumentation at odds with their culture's whole philosophy of behavior and human relationships, in which confrontation suggests chaos and hence must be avoided.

LOOKING AHEAD

ACROSS THE CURRICULUM The Toulmin model of argumentation, adopted here, suggests that certain features of argument, including claim, support, and reasoning, remain constant regardless of the discipline or "field" in which one happens to be arguing. What changes from one discipline to the next, says Toulmin, is the notion of what counts as a legitimate claim; what counts as acceptable support; and what counts as valid reasoning. This chapter introduces the overarching elements of argumentation: claim, support, and reasoning. The cross-curricular chapters on writing and reading in the humanities, the social sciences, and the sciences (Chapters 37–39) address *directly* the defining features of argumentation in these discipline areas. Thus, Chapter 6 and the cross-curricular chapters work in tandem. Students need not read them together; all chapters in this book are independent. But reading Chapter 6 will provide useful background to the cross-curricular chapters.

GROUP ACTIVITY

In order to help students become aware of the various considerations necessary for an effective argument, you might ask them to work in small groups to construct an argument for a position that's relevant to them: convincing a teacher to make a final exam a take-home exam, for example, or getting parents' permission to spend a semester abroad. As they discuss what will and will not be effective, one

- Appeals to logic (6d-1)
- Appeals to authority (6d-2)
- Appeals to emotion (6d-3)

Sample argument

The arguments you write will usually be longer than the one that follows, but the principles involved will be the same. Note how three kinds of support are offered for the claim that a college education can help you to think critically. Each statement of support is connected to the claim by a specific type of reasoning. As in any argument, claim, support, and reasoning pull together to make a persuasive case.

Illustration: Argument

1st statement of support (Appeal to logic) Do not expect your undergraduate college education to prepare you for a *specific* job. Seventy percent of college graduates take jobs unrelated to their majors, and what is true of them is likely to be true of you. What, then, is the value of college? No single answer could satisfy everyone, but most would accept this *partial* answer: **Claim** a college education can help you to think critically. **2nd statement of support (Appeal to authority)** The importance of thinking critically cannot be overstated. Robert Ornstein of the Institute for the Study of Human Knowledge put it this way: "Solutions to the significant problems facing modern society demand a widespread, qualitative improvement in thinking and understanding. . . . We need a breakthrough in the *quality* of thinking employed both by decision-makers at all levels of society and by each of us in our daily affairs." **3rd statement of support (Appeal to emotion)** Effective, strategic thinkers are needed urgently and are appreciated everywhere, and you will do well to make clear thinking an explicit goal of your studies. **Key term defined** Specifically, you should learn to identify and solve problems; to plan strategically; to challenge others and yourself; and to generate new ideas and information.

Analysis: The example paragraph consists of three sets of statements that support the claim. Each is based on a corresponding type of reasoning. Claim, support, and reasoning function as one persuasive whole:

(1) **Support:** Fact (most students take jobs unrelated to their major)
Reasoning: Appeal to logic (a generalization—what's true of most will be true of you)

Claim: (about value): A college education can help you to think critically, and thinking critically is a good thing.

(2) **Support:** Opinion (statement by Robert Ornstein)
Reasoning: Appeal to authority (Ornstein is an expert on thinking and learning; his testimony is valuable)

(3) **Support:** Opinion (you will do well to make clear thinking a goal of college)
Reasoning: Appeal to emotion (self-interest will lead you to agree)

Key term defined: Critical thinking is the ability to identify and solve problems, to plan strategically, to challenge, and to generate.

While writing an argument, you should aim to pull claim, support, and reasoning together so that you construct a persuasive whole. If you discover that the parts are not fitting together as expected, let your difficulty be a signal that you may need to modify your claim. Never alter your facts to fit the thesis.

EXERCISE 1

In a paragraph, recall an argument that you had recently in which some issue of importance to you was debated. With whom did you argue? What positions did you and the other person (people) argue? What was the outcome? To what extent did your powers of persuasion affect the argument's outcome?

6b Making a claim (an argumentative thesis)

Any paper that you write in college will have a claim, a single statement that crystallizes your purpose for writing and governs the logic and development of the paper. The claim, also called an *argumentative thesis,* will express your view on a subject. Your goal in the argument is to defend your claim as being true, probable, or desirable. Because the claim thesis is a specialized case of thesis statements for all varieties of writing, the discussion here assumes that you have read the material in 3d.

1 Answering questions with your claim

Arguments provide answers to one of three types of questions: questions of *fact, value,* or *policy.*

student in the group records the reasons for acceptance and rejection of specific approaches. When the groups analyze these reasons, they'll become aware of such considerations as audience, understanding of the issue, and dealing with opposing views.

EXTRA HELP

Students who find it difficult to follow arguments or reasoning patterns can get extra help through a remedial computer program designed to build critical thinking skills through graded lessons in reading.

Critical Reading, Lesson Series A-H. Eight disks published by Borg-Warner Educational Systems. Lesson units instruct secondary-level readers in critical thinking and reasoning patterns; four units focus on contrasts/alternatives, inclusive categories, conditional statements, and inductive reasoning. Reviewed by Wilson, J. "Critical Reading." *Learning Disability Quarterly* 8 (1985): 64–66.

FOR DISCUSSION

The terms *claim, support,* and *reasoning* will be used throughout the chapter. This example is designed as a miniature version of arguments that students will make, and it illustrates the features of claim and three kinds of support, each of which is connected to the claim with a specific kind of reasoning. Urge students to read this paragraph and then to skim the chapter, where they will learn about varieties of claim, support, and reasoning and how a writer must pull them together in a single argument to persuade readers. Students should realize that, typically, distinct strategies of support and reasoning form distinct sections of an argument. Instead of producing an argument of one paragraph, as in this example, students will be writing multi-paragraph (indeed, multipage) arguments. To better appreciate this point, students should read the example argumentative essay by Alison Tschopp at 6g.

EXERCISE 1

Individual responses

REFERENCES

TOULMIN, STEPHEN. *The Uses of Argument.* New York: Cambridge UP, 1964. Characterizes effective arguments as consisting of "claim," or argument itself; "data," or evidence in support of argument; and "warrant," or general principles linking the two.

The Toulmin model used in this chapter is developed in the following works:

BRENT, DOUG. "Young, Becker and Pike's 'Rogerian' Rhetoric: A Twenty-Year Reassessment." *CE* 53 (1991): 452–65. While Young, Becker, and Pike's rhetoric has begun to "show its age," the Rogerian principle of consensus on which their rhetoric is based is still powerful.

BROCKRIEDE, WAYNE, and DOUGLAS EHNINGER. "Toulmin on Argument: An Interpretation and Application." *Quarterly Journal of Speech* 46 (1960): 44–53.

FAHNESTOCK, JEANNE, and MARIE SECOR. "Teaching Argument: A Theory of Types." *CCC* 34 (1983): 20–30. A rhetorical/generative approach to argument is preferable to other approaches because of its applicability to various situations.

FRISCH, ADAM. "The Proposal to a Small Group: Learning to 'See Otherwise.' " ERIC, 1989. ED 303 796. Students should address arguments to small groups with clearly defined values.

MCCLEARY, WILLIAM J. "A Case Approach for Teaching Academic Writing." *CCC* 36 (1985): 203–12. Describes course in which students are asked to construct arguments based on a collection of legal evidence.

PERELMAN, CHAIM. "The Premises of Argumentation." *The Realm of Rhetoric.* Notre Dame: U of Notre Dame P, 1982. 21–32. Emphasizes common ground as the basis for all discourse, including argument.

RIEKE, RICHARD, and MALCOLM SILLARS. *Argumentation and the Decision Making Process.* 2nd ed. Glenview: Scott, 1984.

ROTTENBERG, ANNETTE. *Elements of Argument.* 2nd ed. Boston: Bedford, 1988.

TOULMIN, STEPHEN, RICHARD RIEKE, and ALLAN JANIK. *An Introduction to Reasoning.* New York: Macmillan, 1979.

Claims that answer questions of fact

A *question of fact* can take the following forms:

Does X exist?
Does X lead to Y?
How can we define X?

The first question can be answered with a *yes* or *no.* The second question leads to an argument about cause and effect. If one thing leads to or causes another, the writer must show how this happens. The third question is an argument about definitions. At times, definitions can be presented without debate; at other times, writers will argue to define a term in a particular way and then will build an entire presentation based on that definition.

Once established as true, a statement of fact can be used as evidence in other arguments. For instance, in a problem-solution argument (see the box at 6f) the writer must establish that a problem exists; once this fact is established, the writer can make a second argument in support of a particular solution.

Example theses

Extrasensory perception does not exist.

Chronic fatigue syndrome *is* real, though its causes are not entirely understood.

Stories describing near-death experiences have not withstood scientific scrutiny.

Claims that answer a question of value

A *question of value* takes the form: *What is X worth?* You make an argument about value when at the conclusion of a hearty meal you pat your belly and smile. In more academic circumstances, scholars argue about value when they review and comment on one another's work—for instance, calling a theory *powerful* or *elegant.* Determinations of value are based on standards called *criteria* that are explicitly stated and then used to judge the worth of the object under review. (See 2b, "Writing an evaluation.")

Example theses

So-called "cold fusion," if it proves practical, will have tremendous economic and humanitarian value.

Though it raises useful questions, Eric Smith's research linking intelligence and birth order is flawed.

Nabokov's *Lolita* is a great novel.

Claims that answer a question of policy

A *question of policy* takes the form: *What action should we take?* Politics is a major arena for arguments of policy. In this arena, arguments help to de-

ACROSS THE CURRICULUM

Claims and Evidence

As you move from one academic discipline to another, you will observe that arguments—the way in which writers attempt to convince others—change. Arguments in *all* disciplines consist of claims, evidence, and logic; in this chapter, you are learning about these fundamentals. What writers and readers accept as a legitimate claim, and as legitimate evidence and logic, changes from one discipline to the next. Each discipline area has its own conventions, and to argue successfully requires learning these conventions—which you will find discussed in some detail in Chapters 37, 38, and 39. Each chapter presents a full research paper that illustrates successful arguments being made. Compare, for instance, how the claims a writer will make change from one discipline area to the next. In Chapter 37 (Writing and Reading in the Humanities), you learn the following:

> To make a claim about literature, find a pattern of meaning in a literary text. Confirm and refine that pattern; state it in a sentence and you will have your claim. (See 37a-2.)

In Chapter 38 (Writing and Reading in the Social Sciences), you learn this:

> Claims in the social sciences will often commit you to observing the actions of individuals or groups and to stating how these actions are significant, both for certain individuals and for the people responding to them. (See 38a-2.)

And in Chapter 39 (Writing and Reading in the Sciences), you learn this:

> Scientific arguments often involve two sorts of claims. The first takes the form *X is a problem* or *X is somehow puzzling.* This claim establishes some issue as worthy of investigation, and it is on the basis of this claim that experiments are designed. . . . The process continues when you make a second claim that attempts to explain the anomaly. Such a claim takes this form: *X can be explained as follows.* (See 39a-2.)

termine which legislative actions are taken and how huge sums of money are spent. *Should the legislature raise taxes? Should the United States support totalitarian regimes?* These questions about what *ought* to be done prompt arguments based on claims of policy.

Example theses

Instead of reducing the budget of the National Endowment for the Arts and the National Endowment for the Humanities, the legislature ought to consider protecting and restoring these budgets.

Students who do not meet the curriculum criteria set forth by their school districts should not be permitted to advance to the next grade level.

Academic professionals should receive salaries commensurate with the salaries of professionals employed in private industry.

FOR DISCUSSION

ACROSS THE CURRICULUM The examples provided here are from science and literature. Since many freshman composition courses are made up of students from different majors, a class discussion of examples of arguments found in different disciplines can be useful. Ask students to recall one argument from a course in their major, and list the topics on the board. After the topics are listed, the class can choose one and develop a claim, list sources for data, describe the logic, and speculate on a conclusion for that topic. Not only will this activity reinforce the treatment of basic academic argument in the text, but it will also allow students to practice argumentation in a relatively nonthreatening way.

LOOKING AHEAD

ACROSS THE CURRICULUM Following Toulmin, students should anticipate that as they move from one disciplinary area to another, what counts as a claim will differ.

One of the underlying assumptions of this handbook is that as they move from one discipline to the next, students need to appreciate that patterns of claim, support, and reasoning change. Following the boxed statements about claims, Chapters 37–39 each demonstrate through multiple examples and a full research paper the uses of claim, support, and reasoning across the disciplines.

EXERCISE 2

Individual responses

REFERENCES

GAGE, JOHN T. "Teaching the Enthymeme: Invention and Arrangement." *Rhetoric Review* 2 (1983): 38–50. The importance of audience to the construction of an effective argument can best be taught by using the enthymeme.

PORTER, JEFFREY. "The Reasonable Reader: Knowledge and Inquiry in Freshman English." *CE* 49 (1987): 332–44. A reader's "participation" in a text is organized by the enthymeme.

EXERCISE 3

Terms that might be circled:

"pervaded"—examples of contempt that pervade society might be given.

"rules and ethics"—specific rules or ethical principles might be defined.

"standards . . . he once believed in"—which standards, particularly? Could Tuchman assume that we could agree on these?

"worst enemies"—what constitutes "worst" in this sense?

"security"—Tuchman seems to use the word in a particular way—peace of mind, perhaps.

"lesson, . . . wisdom"—she's operating with lessons in mind. These have been so thoroughly violated that her cynicism and despair are obvious.

EXERCISE 2

Choose two subjects and pose questions of fact, value, and policy about them. Of each topic, ask: Does X exist? (or Does X lead to Y? or How can we define X?) What is the value of X? and What should we do with regard to X? Answer these questions with statements that could serve as claims for later arguments. Possible topics: artificial intelligence, post–traumatic stress disorder, ozone holes, gene splicing.

2 Defining terms in the argumentative thesis

In order to provide the basis for a sound argument, all words of a claim must be carefully defined so that people are debating the same topic. Consider this claim, which answers a question of policy: *The United States should not support totalitarian regimes.* Unless the term *totalitarian regimes* is clearly defined (and distinguished, say, from authoritarian regimes), the argument could not succeed. The writer, the reader, and various experts referred to in the argument might define and use the word *totalitarian* differently. If this happened, a reader could not be sure about what was being argued and no meaningful exchange of ideas would take place. Take care to examine your claims and, if one term or another requires it, actually write a paragraph of definition into your argument. If you suspect that your audience will not accept your definition, then you will need to argue for it. Entire arguments are sometimes needed to define complex terms, such as *honor.* If a key term in your claim is not complicated, then a paragraph or even a sentence of definition will suffice. With terms well defined, argumentation can begin.

EXERCISE 3

Circle any terms needing definitions in the following claims. Choose any two of the terms you have circled and explain why they need to be defined.

Example: [The (sins) of the United States] in the twentieth century—greed, violence, inhumanity—have been profound, with the result that the pride and the (self-confidence of the nineteenth century) have turned to (dismay and self-disgust.)

The writer (historian Barbara Tuchman) assumes that readers have a well-developed historical sense—that they can cite specific examples of this country's "greed, violence, [and] inhumanity" and that they understand the basis of the United States' "self-confidence" in the nineteenth century. If her audience had a less developed understanding of history, Tuchman would need to define these sins and the country's earlier self-confidence. Only then would readers be able to understand her references to "dismay and self-disgust."

1. In the United States we have a society pervaded from top to bottom by contempt for the law.

2. Government—including the agencies of law enforcement—business, labor, students, the military, the poor no less than the rich, outdo each other in breaking the rules and violating the ethics that society has established for its protection.
3. The average citizen, trying to hold a footing in standards of morality and conduct he once believed in, is daily knocked over by incoming waves of venality, vulgarity, irresponsibility, ignorance, ugliness, and trash in all senses of the word.
4. Our government collaborates abroad with the worst enemies of humanity and liberty.
5. It wastes our substance on useless proliferation of military hardware that can never buy security no matter how high the pile.
6. It learns no lesson, employs no wisdom, and corrupts all who succumb to Potomac fever.

6c Offering three types of support for a claim

You can offer facts, opinions, and examples as support for your claims. A *fact* is a statement that can be verified, proven true or false. As a writer you should be able to verify facts on demand, and most often you will do this by referring to an authoritative source. (This is one of the reasons for documenting your papers.) For the most part, once facts are presented and accepted by experts in a given field, the rest of us can be content to accept them as well. Facts are constantly being updated and revised as a consequence of research. It is therefore essential that you refer to the most recent sources possible.

An *opinion* is a statement of interpretation and judgment. Opinions are themselves arguments and should be based on evidence in order to be convincing. Opinions are not true or false in the way that statements of fact are. Rather, opinions are more or less well supported. You can stengthen your own argument by referring to the opinions of experts who agree with you. An *example* is a particular instance of a statement you are trying to prove. The statement is a generalization, and by offering an example you are trying to demonstrate that the generalization is correct.

EXERCISE 4

Provide paragraph-length examples for two of the following general statements. If you feel that the statement is inaccurate, revise it to your liking. Then provide an example based on your own experience.

1. During the first weeks of a semester, freshmen are unsure of themselves socially.
2. Assignments at the college level are much more demanding than those in high school.
3. My friend ____________ (you provide the name) usually offers sound advice.

EXERCISE 4

Individual responses

ESL EXERCISE

On the basis of talks with Americans, past readings about the United States, and discussions with classmates, non-native students might list some of the cultural assumptions of Americans. What concepts or values do Americans hold important?

Teachers might guide students to discover such values as individualism, competition, informality, directness, cause/effect logic, self-help, personal choice, a short-term view of the future, trouble-shooting/problem solving, and practicality.

TEACHING IDEAS

ACROSS THE CURRICULUM The notion that different disciplines require different kinds of evidence will probably be new to most students. Ask each student to interview a faculty member from a specific discipline, asking two questions: (1) What sort of evidence is usually required to support an argument in the discipline? (2) What sort of evidence does the instructor him- or herself find most convincing? When students report to the class, a picture should emerge illustrating the need to understand the requirements of different disciplines and different audiences within those disciplines.

EXERCISE 5

Individual responses

GROUP ACTIVITY

Many students place too much weight on facts and opinions. Since facts are indisputable, some students fail to realize that they can be interpreted in different ways. And since "we're all entitled to our own opinions," some students don't understand the relative merits of well and poorly supported opinions. Ask small groups of students to find two opposing

CRITICAL DECISIONS

Form, and support, opinions: Finding support for your arguments

Once you have decided on a claim, turn your attention to gathering support. Question your claim vigorously: What will readers need to see in order to accept your view as true, probable, or desirable? Assemble support from the various categories available to you:

- **Facts:** Find sources on your topic. Take notes on any facts that you think are pertinent. Remember that the facts you gather should accurately represent the available data.
- **Statistics:** Again, find sources on your topic. Begin with the U.S. Government Printing Office, which publishes volumes of statistics on life in the United States. Locate other publications, particularly statistical studies.
- **Expert opinions:** Locate experts by reviewing source materials and checking for people whose work is referred to repeatedly. Also compare bibliographies and look for names in common. Within a week or so of moderately intensive research, you will identify acknowledged experts on a topic. Quote experts when their language is particularly powerful or succinct; otherwise, summarize or paraphrase.
- **Emotions:** Do not underestimate the power of emotions in swaying readers to your position. If you are arguing honestly and believe in your claim, then you can in good conscience appeal to the emotions of your readers. Discover their needs and explain, perhaps through an example, how the issues important to you affect them.

Devise an action plan: Take advantage of the various kinds of support available to you when arguing. To the extent it is appropriate for the context in which you are arguing, make appeals to logic, authority, *and* emotion. Think strategically about how best to position your facts, statistics, expert opinions, and appeals to emotion.

EXERCISE 5

With pen in hand, reread the paragraphs you wrote in answer to Exercise 4. Circle your statements of opinion. Underline your statements of fact. Do any patterns emerge? (Instead of working with your own paragraphs, you might switch papers with a classmate.)

6d Reasoning and lines of argument

Reasoning in an argument is the pattern of thinking you use to connect statements of support to your claim. Formally, types of reasoning are referred to as *lines of argument.* There are three lines of argument available to you in presenting claims of fact, value, and policy. You can appeal to the reader's sense of logic, respect for authority, and emotion. The following chart summarizes the main lines of argument you can use when connecting supporting statements to a claim. To support a claim of fact, for instance, you would look to the chart and see that you could argue in any of six ways. There are five ways to argue for claims of value and five for claims of policy. In presenting a claim, you will typically offer several statements of support and, correspondingly, several lines of argument.

Matching lines of argument with types of claims

	Claims of Fact	*Claims of Value*	*Claims of Policy*
Appeals to Reason			
generalization	x	x	
causation	x		x
sign	x		
analogy	x	x	x
parallel case	x	x	x
Appeals to Authority	x	x	x
Appeals to Emotion		x	x

Adapted from Wayne Brockriede and Douglas Ehninger, "Toulmin on Argument: An Interpretation and Application," *Quarterly Journal of Speech* 46 (1960): 53.

1 Appealing to logic

An appeal to reason is by far the most common basis for arguing in the academic world. This section demonstrates five of the most common appeals to logic. You can argue from generalization, from causation, from sign, from analogy, or from parallel case.

Argument from generalization

Given several representative examples of a group (of people, animals, paintings, trees, washing machines, whatever), you can infer a general principle or *generalization*—a statement that applies to other examples of that group. In order for a generalization to be fair, you must select an adequate number of examples that are typical of the entire group; you must also acknowledge the presence of examples that apparently disprove the generalization. Arguments from generalization allow you to support claims that answer questions of fact and value.

Sample argument

As litter, plastic is unsightly and deadly. Birds and small animals die after getting stuck in plastic, six-pack beverage rings. Pelicans accidentally hang themselves with discarded plastic fishing line. Turtles choke on plastic bags or starve when their stomachs become clogged with hard-to-excrete, crumbled plastic. Sea lions poke their heads into plastic rings and have their jaws locked permanently shut. Authorities estimate that plastic refuse annually kills up to 2 million birds and at least 100,000 mammals.

—Gary Turbak, "60 Billion Pounds of Trouble"

opinion pieces on the same topic. They might look at *The Nation* and *The National Review,* or they might look at two newspapers with opposing editorial viewpoints. Once the group has decided on the selections, they can list the facts that are used to support opposing views, and the opinions that are supported by those facts.

TEACHING IDEAS

ACROSS THE CURRICULUM Writers support arguments according to the conventions of a discipline. In the sciences, for instance, relatively little credence is given to expert opinions, while in the humanities writers are taught to call on authorities in support of a claim. Students can learn something of the uses of evidence across the curriculum by turning to the sample papers in 37e, 38d, and 39d. Ask students to read these papers and make their observations concerning the use of evidence.

FOR DISCUSSION

In thinking about making arguments, students should know that this table summarizes potential strategies. Arguments cannot be assembled "cookbook fashion." The student writer must know his or her material and, above all, know the audience in order to understand whether appeals to logic, authority, or emotion are likely to be successful. Part of any preparation for argument should be a thorough audience analysis (see 3a-3). Having made some strategic decisions about the type of appeal that will be made, the writer is still faced with a question of how to position particular appeals within the argument. Perhaps as an overview to reasoning in argumentation, students should read the example essay later in this chapter, in which two appeals to logic are made and one appeal to authority. Some students do not understand that multiple appeals can be made within a single argument; the art of argumentation lies in making the appeals work in unison.

CLAIM	Plastic litter kills animals.
SUPPORT	Birds, turtles, sea lions, and various mammals have died from plastic litter.
REASONING	Generalization. Danger to the animals cited can be generalized to other animals that come into contact with plastic litter.

Argument from causation

In an argument from causation, you begin with a fact or facts about some person, object, or condition. (If readers are likely to contest these facts, then you must make an argument to establish them before pushing on with an argument from causation.) An argument from *causation* enables you to claim that an action created by that person, object, or condition leads to a specific result or effect: Sunspots cause the aurora borealis. Dieting causes weight loss. Smoking causes lung cancer. Working in the opposite direction, you can begin with what you presume to be an effect of some prior cause: the swing of a pendulum, inattention among school children, tornadoes. Of this presumed effect, you ask: "What causes this?" If you are a scientist or social scientist, you might perform an experiment. Establishing a direct causal link is seldom easy, for usually multiple causes will lead to a single condition (think of the inattentive child at school). In arguing causation, therefore, you need to be sensitive to complexity. Arguments of causation allow you to support a claim that answers a question of fact or of policy. Cause-and-effect reasoning also allows you to use a problem-solution structure in your arguments. (See the box at 6f.)

Sample argument

Under primitive agricultural conditions the farmer had few insect problems. Those arose with the intensification of agriculture—the devotion of immense acreages to a single crop. Such a system set the stage for explosive increases in specific insect populations. Single-crop farming does not take advantage of the principles by which nature works; it is agriculture as an engineer might conceive it to be. Nature has introduced great variety into the landscape, but man has displayed a passion for simplifying it. Thus he undoes the built-in checks and balances by which nature holds the species within bounds. One important natural check is a limit on the amount of suitable habitat for each species. Obviously then, an insect that lives on wheat can build up its population to much higher levels on a farm devoted to wheat than on one in which wheat is intermingled with other crops to which the insect is not adapted.

—RACHEL CARSON, *Silent Spring*

CLAIM	Insect problems arose with the practice of intensive, single-crop farming.
SUPPORT	The variety of vegetation in natural habitats discourages infestation; natural habitats have "checks and balances."

REFERENCES

DEANE, BARBARA. "Putting the Inferential Process to Work in the Classroom." *CE* 27 (1976): 50–52. Classroom activities can assist students in making accurate inferences.

EDE, LISA S., and ANDREA LUNSFORD. "On Distinctions between Classical and Modern Rhetoric." *Essays on Classical Rhetoric and Modern Discourse.* Ed. Robert J. Connors, Lisa S. Ede, and Andrea A. Lunsford. Carbondale, IL: Southern Illinois P, 1984. 37–49. Self-explanatory title.

FULKERSON, RICHARD. "Technical Logic, Comp-Logic, and the Teaching of Writing." *CCC* 39 (1988): 436–52. Modern informal logic is preferable to technical or comp-logic.

KAUFER, DAVID S., and CHRISTINE M. NEUWIRTH. "Integrating Formal Logic and the New Rhetoric: A Four Stage Heuristic." *CE* 45 (1983): 380–89. The heuristic begins with a summary and ends with a final essay based on principles of formal logic.

KNEUPPER, CHARLES W. "Teaching Argument: An Introduction to the Toulmin Model." *CCC* 29 (1978): 237–41. Students can improve their ability to write arguments by applying Toulmin's simplified model.

LEVIN, GERALD. "On Freshman Composition and Logical Thinking." *CCC* 28 (1977): 359–64. Controversial essays can enhance the teaching of patterns of argument.

RAPKINS, ANGELA A. "The Uses of Logic in the College Freshman English Classroom." *Activities to Promote Critical Thinking: Classroom Practices in Teaching English.* Urbana: NCTE, 1986. Even when teaching argument toward the end of a semester, instructors should introduce students to logic early on.

TRENT, JIMMIE D. "Toulmin's Model of an Argument: An Examination and Extension." *QJS* 54 (1968): 252–59. The Toulmin model should be considered a supplement to syllogism, not a substitute.

Reasoning Cause and effect. By creating one-crop farms and eliminating the checks and balances of natural habitats, farmers caused their own insect problems.

Argument from sign

A sore throat and fever are signs of flu. Black smoke billowing from a window is a sign of fire. Risk taking is a sign of creativity. In an argument from *sign,* two things are correlated; that is, they tend to occur in the presence of one another. When you see one thing, you tend to see the other. A sign is *not* a cause, however. If your big toe aches at the approach of thunderstorms, your aching toe may be a sign of approaching storms, but it surely does not cause them. Economists routinely look to certain indexes (housing starts, for instance) as indicators, or signs, of the economy's health. Housing starts are *correlated with* economic health, often by means of a statistical comparison. If a sign has proven a particularly reliable indicator, then you can use it to support a claim that answers a question of fact.

Sample argument

Anxiety over the body as a kind of wasteland is implicit in appeals in advertisements about retaining and restoring moisture. . . . Dry skin . . . [is] a sign of a woman who is all dried up and is not sexually responsive—and who may also be sterile. This is because water is connected, in our psyches, with birth. It is also tied to purity, as in baptismal rites when sin is cleansed from a person. All of this suggests that words and images that picture a body of a woman as being dehydrated and losing water have great resonance.

—Arthur Asa Berger, "Sex as Symbol in Fashion Advertising"

Claim In advertisements, words and images of dehydration resonate for readers and viewers.

Support Readers have profound psychological associations with dryness.

Reasoning Sign. Dry skin is a sign of sterility and infertility, deeply resonant themes for men and women.

Argument from analogy

An argument from *analogy* sets up a comparison between the topic you are arguing and another topic that initially appears unrelated. While suggestive and at times persuasive, an analogy actually proves nothing. There is always a point at which an analogy will break down, and it is usually a mistake to build an argument on analogy alone. Use analogies as you would seasonings in cooking. As one of several attempts to persuade your reader, an analogy spices your argument and makes it memorable. You can use analogies in support of claims that answer questions of fact, value, or policy.

LOOKING AHEAD

ACROSS THE CURRICULUM Have students compare the markedly different ways in which cause and effect is argued in the sciences (see the student paper at 39d) and in the humanities (see the student paper in 6g).

ADDITIONAL EXERCISE A

A great many advertisements are based on implicit claims of sign and claims of cause and effect. Ask students to examine print ads and television ads, select one for close study, and prepare an analysis of the advertiser's claims. Students should be able to make explicit the claim based on sign or on cause and effect. Students should also be prepared to state whether or not the claim is supported by evidence in the ad.

LOOKING BACK

In Chapter 5, page 143, see another example of argument from analogy. In that passage, the author uses an analogy of the shoemaking industry to illustrate a point he is making about the "parenting industry."

Sample argument

In closing, we might describe learning with an analogy to a well-orchestrated symphony, aimed to blend both familiar and new sounds. A symphony is the complex interplay of composer, conductor, the repertoire of instruments, and the various dimensions of music. Each instrument is used strategically to interact with other instruments toward a rich construction of themes progressing in phases, with some themes recurring and others driving the movement forward toward a conclusion or resolution. Finally, each symphony stands alone in its meaning, yet has a relationship to the symphonies that came before and those that will come later. Similarly, learning is a complex interaction of the learner, the instructional materials, the repertoire of available learning strategies, and the context, including the teacher. The skilled learner approaches each task strategically toward the goal of constructing meaning. Some strategies focus on understanding the incoming information, others strive to relate the meaning to earlier predictions, and still others work to integrate the new information with prior knowledge.

—Beau Fly Jones, et al., "Learning and Thinking"

Claim Learning involves a complex blend of learner, materials, and context.

Support In a symphony orchestra, meaning (sound) is created through interaction of musicians, conductor, composer, and history.

Reasoning Analogy. The complex interactions needed to create symphonic music are analogous to the interaction needed to create meaning for a learner.

LOOKING AHEAD

See the student essay in this chapter (second paragraph from the end, page 178) for an example of how an argument from parallel case can be used. Alison Tschopp is careful to cite a case that raises First Amendment issues similar to the ones raised in her paper about the legality and wisdom of limiting television advertisements directed at children. Note that Tschopp uses argument from cause and an appeal to authority as well.

Argument from parallel case

While an analogy argues a relationship between two apparently unrelated people, objects, conditions, or events, an argument from **parallel case** argues a relationship between directly related people, objects, events, or conditions. The implicit logic is this: the way a situation turned out in a closely related case is the way it will (or should) turn out in this one. Lawyers argue from parallel case whenever they cite a prior criminal or civil case in which the legal question involved is similar to the question involved in a current case. Because the earlier case ended a certain way (with the conviction or acquittal of a defendant, or with a particular monetary award), so too should the present case have this outcome. An argument from parallel case requires that situations presented as parallel be alike in essential ways; if this requirement is not met, the argument loses force. The argument would also be weakened if someone could present a more nearly perfect parallel case than yours. You can use a parallel case in support of claims that answer questions of fact, value, or policy.

Sample argument

By the year 2000, women and minorities will account for 68 per cent of the new workers. Coupled with the fact that, if current trends continue, the

United States will face a shortage of scientists and physicians by the end of the century, it is safe to say that sustaining America's scientific and biomedical preeminence depends upon attracting—and retaining—talented women and minorities.

If we are to ensure our country's future competitiveness, we must change the prevailing [male-dominated] culture [of science and technology]—the rules of the game—in our classrooms, boardrooms, laboratories, and faculty lounges. To do so, we must recognize that brains, not brawn, will dominate the next century, and that means more than ever we must tap into the brain power of women. . . .

Eighty years ago, when British women were trying to win the right to vote, they played by men's rules: They broke windows in Parliament Square. Many of the women were treated brutally and arrested. Their leader, Emmeline Pankhurst, pointed out that every advance of men's rights has been marked by violence and the destruction of property. She defended the women's actions, saying, "Why should women go to Parliament Square and be battered about and insulted, and most important of all, produce less effect than when they throw stones? We tried it long enough. We submitted for years patiently in insult and assault. Women had their health injured. Women lost their lives. . . . After all, is not a woman's life, is not her health, are not her limbs more valuable than panes of glass? There is no doubt of that, but most important of all, does not the breaking of glass produce more effect upon the Government?"

While I am not advocating that American women in science resort to such behaviors—or even to the breaking of test tubes—it is clear that all of us in the scientific community have a lot of breaking to do—especially old rules, self-defeating habits, and glass ceilings.

—BERNADINE HEALY, director of the National Institutes of Health, *The Chronicle of Higher Education*

CLAIM To take their rightful place in the scientific community, women must first challenge the male-dominated culture of science.

SUPPORT In the early twentieth century, British women who fought to gain entry into the political community (by winning the right to vote) first had to challenge the male-dominated culture of British politics. Women protested at Parliament Square and broke windows.

REASONING Parallel case. Just as during the early twentieth century women needed to fight to enter British politics, women today need to fight to enter into and advance in scientific fields.

2 Appealing to authority

Two types of authority are important in arguments: the authority you bring as a writer and the authority of those who have expert knowledge on the topic that concerns you. Of the two types, *you* are the essential one, since you are present in every argument you make. From one argument to the next, you may or may not call on expert sources (according to your purpose and the needs of your audience).

Establishing yourself as an authority

Intangible elements such as trustworthiness, decency, thoroughness, and engagement are quite different from, but just as important as, the logical force you bring to an argument. An argument impinges on the will of your readers. It asks them to change their minds, and such a request will, to some extent, make anyone feel vulnerable. After all, you are asking the reader to admit: "I was wrong on that issue, or my thinking was unclear. I'll accept what *you* have to say." To make such a change requires something of an emotional submission ("I'll follow you on this point") as well as an intellectual one ("Your reasons are better than mine"). Before readers will agree, they need to trust the person who asks for their agreement; as a maker of arguments, you must therefore work to establish your trustworthiness—your authority to speak and make a claim. *Authority* in this sense is not the same as having expert knowledge; it has to do, rather, with establishing a presence that readers can yield to in a self-respecting way.

How do you establish this trust? Be honest, first of all. The point is so obvious it hardly seems worth making; but readers generally have a good nose for dishonesty. One whiff and they will turn away—for good. Beyond honesty, which is the main thing, strike a reasonable tone (see 21e) and choose a level of language appropriate for the occasion (see 3a-4). Read thoroughly enough on your topic to establish that, although you are not an expert, you do know the important issues and are knowledgeable enough to have an opinion worth considering.

TEACHING IDEAS

CRITICAL THINKING Advertising is the most visible example of appeals to authority and emotion in our society. Ask students to peruse magazines and newspapers, as well as television commercials, for ads that illustrate these appeals. (If you have access to a VCR, students can tape commercials at home and replay them for the class.) Using the most appropriate student examples, ask students to analyze and evaluate the appeals in the ads—not only for the type of appeal but also for intended audience and effectiveness of argument.

Referring readers to experts

As a writer, you greatly help your cause when you can quote experts on a subject who support your point of view. You should realize, though, that experts are likely to disagree. For instance, in court cases both prosecution and defense present expert witnesses, sworn to tell the truth. One expert says a defendant is sane and competent to stand trial; a second expert says the opposite. No doubt, the experts *are* telling the truth. But expert *opinions* are just that: interpretations of facts. Facts usually lend themselves to multiple interpretations, and you should not be discouraged when authorities seem to contradict one another.

Whether you find contradictions or not, sources of authority must be authoritative. If they are not, any argument built on an appeal to authority will falter. One of your important challenges, then, both as a writer of arguments and as a critical reader, is to evaluate the worthiness of sources that you and others use. Is the expert testimony that you or others are drawing on truly expert? If you are not an expert in the field, how can you tell? A number of general guidelines should help you make this determination.

Once you have determined to the best of your ability that an expert whom you wish to quote is indeed expert, you must then identify those points in your discussion where appeals to authority will serve you well. You may want to mix appeals to authority with appeals to reason and, perhaps, to emotion. Appeals to authority can be used to support claims that answer questions of fact, value, and policy.

Use *Authoritative* Sources

1. Prefer acknowledged authorities to self-proclaimed ones.
2. Prefer an authority working within his or her field of expertise to one who is reporting conclusions about another subject.
3. Prefer first-hand accounts over those from sources who were separated by time or space from the events reported.
4. Prefer unbiased and disinterested sources over those who can reasonably be suspected of having a motive for influencing the way others see the subject under investigation.
5. Prefer public records to private documents in questionable cases.
6. Prefer accounts that are specific and complete to those that are vague and evasive.
7. Prefer evidence that is credible on its own terms to that which is internally inconsistent or demonstrably false to any known facts.
8. In general, prefer a recently published report to an older one.
9. In general, prefer works by standard publishers to those of unknown or "vanity" presses.
10. In general, prefer authors who themselves follow [standard] report-writing conventions. . . .
11. When possible, prefer an authority known to your audience to one they have never heard of. . . .

Source: Thomas E. Gaston and Bret H. Smith, *The Research Paper: A Common-Sense Approach* (Englewood Cliffs: Prentice Hall, 1988) 31–33.

Sample argument

Leo Marx claims that Melville's "Bartleby the Scrivener" is autobiographical.

Claim Herman Melville's "Bartleby the Scrivener" is a story about Melville.

Support Leo Marx says so.

Reasoning Authority. Leo Marx is a respected literary critic who has taught at leading universities; his insights are valuable and are worth examining.

3 Appealing to emotion

Appeals to reason are based on the force of logic; appeals to authority are based on the reader's respect for the opinions of experts. By contrast, appeals to *emotion* are designed to tap the audience's needs and values. Argu-

TEACHING IDEAS

Appeals to emotion are too often considered ineffective or underhanded. In order to illustrate a legitimate appeal to emotion, use a piece with which most students are already familiar: Martin Luther King Jr.'s "I Have a Dream" speech. Students who have studied the history of the civil rights movement will be aware of the impact of the speech; others will recognize the inherent decency and dignity in King's words. (And of course, the fact that the speech is so heavily anthologized is evidence of its effectiveness.) If you can find copies of both the speech and King's "Letter from Birmingham Jail," you could contrast the appeals to authority in the latter with the emotional appeals in the former.

ments based on appeals to reason and authority may well turn out to be valid; but validity does not guarantee that readers will *endorse* your position. For instance, you might establish with impeccable logic that the physical condition of your community's public schools has deteriorated badly, to the point of affecting the performance of students. While true, your claim may not carry force enough to persuade the Town Council to vote on a bond issue or to raise taxes—two actions that would generate the requisite money to renovate several buildings. To succeed in your effort or in any appeal to emotion, you must make your readers feel the same urgency to act that you do. The following paragraphs were written as part of a holiday charity drive by a writer and editor for the *New York Times.* Anna Quindlen's purpose in writing was to prompt readers to make a donation. Her argumentative claim was *People should give what they can afford to the needy.* Observe how she engages her readers' emotions.

> *Sample argument*
>
> There are . . . [children] who come into the world with heroin or cocaine in their frail bodies, who flail in their cribs with the poison in their veins. There are the ones who are born with acquired immune deficiency syndrome, born to die because their parents used dirty needles. There are the ones who are left in hospitals to lie in the metal cribs, their only stimulation the occasional visit from a nurse. There are those who are freezing, and starving, and those who are beaten and bruised.
>
> A doctor in the neonatal intensive care unit at one city hospital looked around at the incubators one afternoon and wondered aloud about the tubes, the medicines needed to make the premature thrive and the sickly ones bloom. It was not at all uncommon, she said, to find that an infant who had been coaxed from near death to life in the confines of that overly warm room, in one of those little plastic wombs, had turned up two or three years later in the emergency room with cigarette burns, broken bones, or malnutrition.
>
> —ANNA QUINDLEN, "A City's Needy"

CLAIM People should give what they can to the needy.

SUPPORT There are children in New York suffering terribly, through no fault of their own.

REASONING Emotion. The plight of these blameless, helpless children touches the reader, who almost certainly lives in better circumstances. Quindlen moves the reader to pity, and pity may prompt a contribution.

On the basis of an audience analysis (see 3a-3), you can sketch a profile of your readers and consider strategies suited to win their emotional support. Plan your emotional appeal by beginning with a claim that has already been supported by an appeal to reason. In your efforts to raise taxes for school renovation, you could show photographs, produce a list of items in need of repair, and quote expert witnesses who believe that children's learning suffers in deteriorating environments. Having argued by an appeal to reason, you can then plan an emotional appeal.

Making an Emotional Appeal

1. List the needs of your audience with respect to your subject: these needs might be physical, psychological, humanitarian, environmental, or financial.
2. Select the category of needs best suited to your audience and identify emotional appeals that you think will be persuasive.
3. Place the issue you are arguing in your reader's lap. Get the reader to respond to the issue emotionally.
4. Call on the reader to agree with you on a course of action.

The limits of argument

In the real world, even the best argument may fail to achieve its objective. Some subjects—for example, abortion or capital punishment—are so controversial or so tied to preexisting religious or moral beliefs that many people have long since made up their minds one way or the other and will never change them. Such subjects are so fraught with emotion that logical arguments are ineffective in persuading people to rethink their positions. Sometimes, also, your audience has a vested interest in *not* being persuaded by your arguments. (Perhaps your audience has a financial stake in holding to an opposing position.) When your audience feels significantly threatened by the prospect of your victory, it is futile to insist on the validity of your argument.

EXERCISE 6

Write the sketch of an argument, your claim for which should be based on the following scenario:

> Imagine yourself a student at a college or university where the Board of Trustees has voted to institute a curfew on dormitory visitors. After 11 P.M. on weekdays and 1 A.M. on weekends, no student may have a guest in his or her dormitory room. The rule simply put: no overnight guests.

Decide on a claim, and determine whether it answers a question of fact, value, or policy. Consult the chart on "Matching Lines of Argument with Types of Claims" on page 161 and plan a discussion in which you argue three ways in support of your claim. (Make sure these arguments are consistent with the type of claim you are making—see the chart.)

6e Making rebuttals

By definition, arguments are subject to challenge, or to counterarguments. Because reasonable people will disagree, you must be prepared when arguing to acknowledge differences of opinion and to address them—for two reasons. First, by raising a challenge to your own position you force yourself to see an issue from someone else's perspective. This can be a valuable lesson in that challenges can prompt you to reevaluate and refine your

EXERCISE 6

Individual responses

TEACHING IDEAS

Uncertain of their own powers of persuasion, students sometimes try to ignore opposing arguments in hopes that those arguments will never arise. In order to provide students with practice in acknowledging the opposition, ask them to write out their positions on several controversial issues (preferably issues you've assigned as paper topics). Once they've articulated their positions, their task will be to argue for the *opposing* position. Thus before they've even begun to construct their own arguments, they're playing devil's advocate. When they do develop their own positions, they'll be well aware of the objections they might encounter.

LOOKING AHEAD

See the sample student paper in this chapter for an example of how an argument can open by posing a problem and rebutting unacceptable solutions. Following the rebuttal, the writer introduces another solution. The tactic is often referred to as "strawman."

REFERENCE

WINDER, BARBARA E. "The Delineation of Values in Persuasive Writing." *CCC* 29 (1978): 55–58. Students should articulate their opponent's position as well as their own in order to understand differences in values.

CRITICAL DECISIONS

Be alert to differences: Responding to opposing points of view

Expect opposition. When you have located opposing points of view, use the occasion to extend your thinking. Let disagreement enhance the quality of your argument.

- **The facts are in dispute.** When the facts you are relying on in an argument are disputed—a potentially serious challenge—you must investigate both the validity of your facts and the opposition's.

  Check the credibility of sources. Be sure that your sources are reliable; if you discover some dispute about reliability, you must meet this challenge head on: raise it in your argument and, if you can, establish the trustworthiness of your information. If you have trouble doing so, abandon questionable sources and be grateful to your opposition.

  If both sources (yours and the opposition's) are equally reliable, ask: Through what process of investigation were these facts established? Different methods of investigation can lead to different perceptions of the facts. Acknowledge these methods in your argument and state clearly which methods you (or your sources) have relied on.

- **Expert opinions are in dispute.** Experts *will* disagree, and most writers can find experts, real or so-called, to support or attack an argument. Respond to differences of expert opinion by checking qualifications. Lacking expertise in a subject, you may have some trouble doing this. Try these strategies, both of which can help you to reaffirm, or discount, the usefulness of expert opinion:

  Strategy 1: To validate expertise, be sure that an author is referred to in several sources. If the author were a fringe personality, you would not find repeated, serious references to his or her work.

  Strategy 2: To validate expertise, locate a book written by the person in question. Locate two reviews, which will be written by someone at least familiar with the topic. From the reviews you will get a sense of a book's strengths and weaknesses, and you will learn something of the author's reputation.

  If the experts holding opposing views are reliable, you will need to acknowledge the disagreement in your argument. Determine its basis. If you find a conflict of assumptions, investigate and discuss these. If you find your assumptions still worth supporting, then support them—with reasons.

Devise an action plan: Use the differences you find to clarify your own thinking on a topic. When your opposition has a valid point, acknowledge it openly and adjust. Show that you expect differences and can incorporate them into your thinking.

views. In addition, challenges pique a reader's interest. Research shows that when tension (that is, disagreement) exists in an argument, readers maintain interest: they want to know what happens or how the argument is resolved.

Once you acknowledge opposing views, respond with a *rebuttal,* an argument of opposition. One type of response is to reject the counterargument by challenging its logic. If the logic is flawed, the counterargument will not weaken the validity of your argument. When you are confident in the position you are arguing, raise the most damaging argument against your position that you can, and then neutralize that challenge. If you do not raise objections, your readers inevitably will; better that you raise them on your terms so that you can control the debate.

Of course, one response to an opposing argument is *to let it change you.* After all, if you are arguing honestly, you are by definition participating in a reasoned exchange. This is to say, when arguing you should be open to accepting the views of others. Readers will appreciate your ability to concede at least some of your opposition's points, and will take it as a sign of your reasonableness.

6f Preparing to write an argument

Devising strategies for argument

There are two time-honored strategies for arranging arguments: the "problem-solution" structure and the classic "five-part" structure are summarized in the adjoining boxes. In these structures, each part of the argument may run as one paragraph or as a section consisting of several paragraphs.

Inductive and deductive arrangements

Inductive and deductive arrangements have to do with where you place your claim in an argument. Induction moves from support—particular facts, examples, and opinions—to a claim. A great deal of scientific and technological argument proceeds this way. The writer makes certain observations, finds patterns in those observations, and then makes a claim about those observations. Visually, the process could be represented as in the diagram on the left.

LOOKING AHEAD

For a clear example of the inductive arrangement, see the student research paper in Chapter 35. For a clear example of deductive arrangement, see the student paper in Chapter 37—a literary analysis.

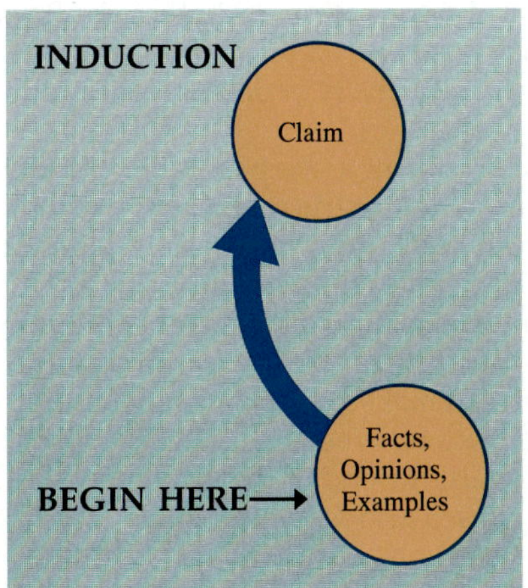

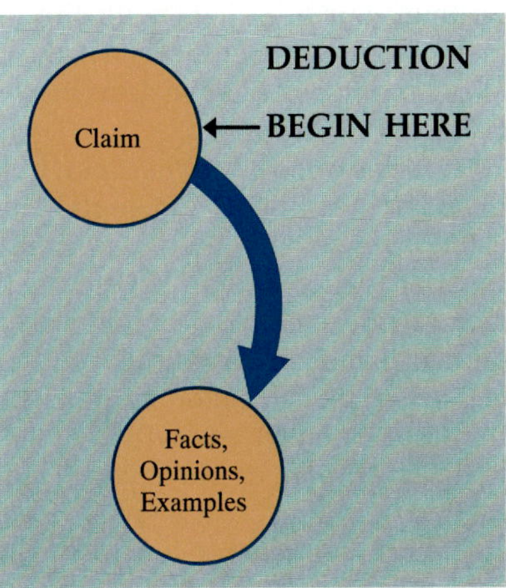

Deduction, which is shown in the diagram on the right, moves from a claim to support—to particular facts, opinions, and examples. A good deal of writing in the humanities, in politics, and in law proceeds this way. The writer begins with a general principle or claim, the truth, likelihood, or desirability of which is then proven.

REFERENCE

KATULA, RICHARD A., and RICHARD W. ROTH. "A Stock Issues Approach to Writing Arguments." CCC 31 (1980): 183–96. Emphasizes the problem-solution approach to argument.

Writing an Argument: The Problem–Solution Structure

I. There is a serious problem.
   A. The problem exists and is growing.
      (Provide support for this statement.)
   B. The problem is serious.
      (Provide support.)
   C. Current methods cannot cope with the problem.
      (Provide support.)

II. There is a solution to the problem. (Your claim goes here.)
   A. The solution is practical.
      (Provide support.)
   B. The solution is desirable.
      (Provide support.)
   C. We can implement the solution.
      (Provide support.)
   D. Alternate solutions are not as strong as the proposed solution.
      (Review—and reject—competing solutions.)

Source: Adapted from Richard D. Rieke and Malcolm O. Sillars, *Argumentation and the Decision Making Process* (Glenview: Scott, Foresman, 1984) 163.

What determines whether you will use an inductive or deductive arrangement for your argument? First, realize that in either approach you *begin* writing your argument with the identical information: in both cases, you know before you begin writing the draft what your claim, support, and lines of reasoning will be. The decision to move inductively or deductively is a decision about strategy.

You can position the claim in your argument at the beginning, middle, or end of the presentation. In the problem–solution structure, you see that the claim is made only after the writer introduces a problem. Working with the five-part structure, you have more flexibility in positioning your claim. One factor that can help determine placement is considering the members of your audience and the likelihood of their agreeing with you. When an audience is likely to be neutral or supportive, you can make your claim early on with the assurance that you will not alienate readers. When an audience is likely to disagree, plan to move your claim toward the end of the presentation, in that way giving yourself space to build consensus with your readers, step by step, until you reach a conclusion.

Writing an Argument: The Classic Five-Part Structure

1. Introduce the topic to be argued. Establish its importance.
2. Provide background information so that readers will be able to follow your discussion.
3. State your claim (your argumentative thesis) and develop your argument by making a logical appeal based on the following factors (discussed in 6d-1, 6d-2, and 6d-3): generalization, causation, sign, analogy, parallel case, or authority. Support your claims with facts, opinions, and examples. If appropriate, mix an emotional appeal or an appeal to authority with your logical appeals.
4. Acknowledge counterarguments and treat them with respect. Rebut these arguments. Reject their evidence or their logic or concede some validity and modify your claim accordingly. Be flexible: you might split the counterarguments and rebut them one at a time at different locations in the paper; or you might begin the paper with a counterargument, rebut it, and then move on to your own claim.
5. Conclude by summarizing the main points of your argument. Then remind readers of what you want them to believe or do.

Readers tend to remember most clearly what they read last. Thus, you may want to present your reasons in support of your claim in the order of least to most emphatic. Conversely, you may want to offer your most emphatic reasons in support of a claim at the very beginning of the argument. In one strong move you might gain the reader's agreement and then cement that agreement with reasons of secondary importance. Any argument can be arranged in a variety of ways. Decisions you make about placing your claim and arranging your points of support will depend on your assessment of the members of your audience and their probable reactions to your views.

EXERCISE 7

In light of the discussion in this section, return to the argument you outlined in Exercise 6 and introduce at some point in the outline an argument counter to your own. In a paragraph, discuss how you would rebut the counterargument or accept it in part so as to neutralize any damage it could do to your own claim.

EXERCISE 7

Individual responses

Gathering materials for argument

Writing an argument is more a re-creation of thinking than an exploration. Exploration—through writing or through talking with friends—comes prior to writing a first draft. Consider writing a *pre*draft: a brief paper, intended for your eyes only, in which you explore the position you want to take in your argument. Whatever your method for doing so, arrive at your views on a topic—your claim—*before* you sit down to write the draft. As you begin, you should understand the support you will present and the lines of reasoning you will use to link that support to your claim. You will flesh out the discussion as you write; but the backbone of your argument should be carefully thought out ahead of time.

Gathering Materials for Your Argument

1. Gather material on your subject. Generate information on your own—see 3b; if necessary, conduct research. See Part IX on library research.
2. Review the material you have gathered. Decide what you think about the topic, and in a single sentence answer a question of fact, value, or policy. Your one-sentence answer to the question will be the claim of your argument.
3. Understand your audience: What do they know about the topic? What do they need to know? To what sorts of appeals will they respond?
4. Plan out the lines of argument you will present in support of your claim.
5. Identify strong counterarguments and plan to rebut and neutralize them. Possibly concede some of your opposition's points.
6. Sketch your argument, deciding on placement of your claim and arrangement of your lines of argument.
7. Write a draft of your argument, realizing that you will need to backtrack on occasion to get new information or to rethink your strategy. As with the writing of any paper, writing an argument will be a messy, backward-looping activity that often requires mid-course corrections. See Chapter 3 on the necessary uncertainties in preparing for and writing a first draft.
8. Revise two or three times. See Chapter 4 for advice.

EXERCISE 8

Individual responses

EXERCISE 8

Based on your outline in Exercise 7, write the draft of a five-page argument.

6g A sample argument

The following argument, "Advertising to Children Should Not Be Banned," utilizes (with some modification) the classic five-part structure for writing arguments presented on page 173. Alison Tschopp, a student at Boston University, begins her argument by introducing her topic (the problem of television advertising directed at children) and then provides pertinent background information. But before stating her claim and developing an argument, she summarizes and rejects one proposed solution to the problem she has identified. Alison reverses steps #3 and #4 in the five-part structure, a strategy sometimes referred to as "strawman": the idea is to present one argument for the purpose of tearing it down, as a prelude to presenting your own reasonable alternative. When Alison introduces her own claim, a solution to the problem of advertising directed at children, she argues primarily from cause and from parallel case.

Advertising to Children Should Not Be Banned

Are television commercials rotting the minds and bodies of our children? Some people think so, especially when it comes to advertisements for expensive toys and foods of questionable nutritional value. Impressionable children are easy prey for marketers, say the critics (Charren 14). And advertisements can perpetuate attitudes and myths that are harmful to children's development, such as the myth that girls are not as aggressive as boys or that boys are not sensitive enough to care for a baby-doll (Kilbourne 45).

Introduction: statement of the problem

We know that advertisers are persuasive, and we know that the power of advertisements over children is directly related to the amount of television that children watch. According to a survey cited in a recent article by American Federation of Teachers President Albert Shanker, one-quarter of nine year olds in this country watch 42 hours of television each week--approximately eight hours of which is devoted to advertisements. The most obvious way to eliminate the exposure to so much advertising is to limit television viewing. Still, we are not about to eliminate television from the American household. In a best-case scenario, we might reduce viewing time by half. If we could return our children to viewing a modest 25 hours of weekly television (the 1977 level), they would still be seeing nearly 260 hours of advertisements each year. Is this acceptable?

Background information

Peggy Charren, president of Action for Children's Television (ACT), a national con-

FOR DISCUSSION

You might ask students to note the places in the first few paragraphs where Alison Tschopp signals that a hard-driving argument is coming. How does Tschopp set up the argument? How effective is she in defining a problem? Where does her neutral presentation of the problem (to the extent students can agree that anything about the piece is neutral) give way to argument? At what point in the presentation do student readers feel themselves responding to the argument—either agreeing or disagreeing? Ask students to study what's happening in the essay at this point. Generally, the goal would be to have students reading with increased alertness to the point that the author is trying to shape their thinking. By the end of their reading, students should have a clear sense of how successful this "shaping" has been.

FOR DISCUSSION

You might locate a copy of Charren's article and distribute it to students. Having read the piece that Tschopp critiques, students might respond to Tschopp's treatment of Charren. Is it fair? Balanced?

sumer's group, says no and recommends banning television ads directed at children. Charren argues that our constitution's First Amendment, which protects freedom of speech, should be suspended to allow such a ban. She maintains that television ads directed at children do not deserve First Amendment protection on the grounds that, since children cannot fully appreciate the persuasive nature of advertisements, TV commercials are inherently unfair and deceptive (15).

A proposed solution to the problem

Charren begins her argument by discussing the child consumer. She criticizes companies that advertise to children for asking children to "make complex and reasoned consumer judgments" (13). She explains that, since children do not comprehend advertisers' motives, they are not armed with the reasonable skepticism with which adults evaluate advertisements--and that, therefore, the advertisers' right to free speech, at least with respect to children, should be limited. The right of free speech in our society is so important that anyone who proposes that we limit it bears a heavy burden of presenting a compelling argument. But Charren does not. First, she assumes that the skepticism portrayed by adult viewers of advertisements protects them (and could likewise protect children) from advertisers' power of persuasion. But realistically, few people are immune to the advertiser's art. In his article "The Language of Advertising Claims," Jeffrey Schrank asserts that skepticism does not protect consumers because advertising works "below the level of conscious awareness and it works even on those who claim immunity to its message" (156).

Proposed solution rejected—1st reason

Most adult viewers in this country watch advertisements and believe that "no attack is taking place" (Schrank 156), which is precisely the condition under which Charren claims that children watch televised advertising. Yet we hear no one arguing that because adults are being manipulated we should therefore ban television advertising. What we do hear--from the Supreme Court--is that when ads are blatantly deceptive or unfair, they are not protected by the First Amendment. Basically, the Court has said that it is never legal for an advertiser to lie--either to children or to adults.

But such protection is not enough for Charren, who believes that children make, and should be protected in making, important consumer decisions. She argues that advertisements aimed at affecting these decisions are unfair, and that children are being persuaded improperly. To illustrate, she claims that ads, specifically for sugared cereals, are deceptive and teach children to make unreasonable food choices. She feels that advertisers' reminders that cereal is "part of a balanced breakfast" do not give children information sufficient for judging the issues. In support of her argument, she cites a study where two-thirds of the preschoolers tested believed that a bowl of cereal alone constituted a balanced meal (15).

Proposed solution rejected—2nd reason

Most parents know that preschoolers and children in grades 1 through 4 (through age 11) cannot be depended upon to choose for themselves, for instance, a well-balanced diet or to understand the principles of comparison shopping for price and quality. We do not expect that children make these decisions alone; parents are responsible for guiding their children's decisions. Young children do not have the resources to do the shopping. Parents do. Preschoolers do not make their own meals. Parents do. If children are not getting all their nutritional needs fulfilled, this is not caused by advertisers but by families that

FOR DISCUSSION

You might discuss with students the writer's use of sources in this essay. To what extent is the quality of the argument dependent on the use of sources? More generally, you might focus student attention on the *way* Alison Tschopp integrates quotations into her own sentences.

lack resources for making balanced choices. If children are duped into choosing poorly made or overpriced but cleverly advertised products, this is not the fault of advertisers but of a family situation that permits children to influence important consumer decisions without a counterbalancing influence from parents.

Parents play a key role in a child's development, nutritional and otherwise. A parent's close involvement with children, not limiting the First Amendment, is the appropriate countermeasure to the power of advertisers. Let parents interact with their children and begin their own persuasive campaign! Perhaps children are being confused when messages seen on television advertisements conflict with messages heard at home. But conflict in itself is not "bad." Parents must guide their children towards appropriate conclusions in making most decisions: what clothes to wear; what cereal to eat; what toys are worthwhile. As children mature they must learn to evaluate and resolve such questions for themselves. Keeping the world, with its sometimes harmful and often confusing messages, from children does not offer protection. If that were the case, how high would we need to build walls to block out the everyday assaults on the lives of our children? Do we ban the evening news because of its frequently upsetting content? Do we stop talking about the threat of drugs? No. What we do is acknowledge to our children that dangers exist, and then we exercise parental judgment: we teach children and hope they learn well enough to one day manage on their own.

Claim (Argumentative thesis)

Argument from cause (the real problem is lack of parental involvement, not advertisements)

Children receive conflicting messages from a variety of sources which cannot be silenced: teachers, books, friends, and television programs. We have, from time to time, experimented in this country with limiting access to

Argument from parallel case (other attempts made to limit materials)

FOR DISCUSSION

Tschopp's key transition in the argument comes here, as she turns the responsibility for making decisions from children to their parents. Tschopp shifts the blame for poor decision making from advertisers to parents—or to parents in conjunction with their children. Readers of the argument need to accept this shifting of blame in order to accept Tschopp's later argument, that advertisers should not be constrained. You might survey students to determine how successfully they think Tschopp is arguing here.

potentially damaging or offensive materials, such as books and movies. But these experiments have not withstood legal challenges. The courts have decided that Americans have the right to choose what they see or hear and that writers and others have the right to create what they wish. Certain extreme instances, like child pornography, are so offensive and damaging to the children being filmed that as a society we <u>have</u> said that such products are repugnant and should not be supported by viewers who argue it is their right to see such material. And, in part, this is the argument that Charren is making about advertisements directed at children. But as a society we have agreed to limit speech only in the most extreme cases. There is nothing in the making of advertisements that is as purposefully vulgar or hurtful as there is in child pornography. If anything, advertising more closely resembles the language of our everyday speech: we live, after all, in a consumer society and advertising is the language of consumerism. In this sense, Charren's real argument is with America's values, and on this point she may be right. But values cannot be legislated. They must be taught.

Potential objection to proposed solution

Objection rebutted

The task of shaping children's values, like their diets, is better addressed through ongoing discussions between parents and children than through limiting the right of free speech. There is no need to silence advertisers in order to teach values or protect the innocent and unskeptical. The right to free speech is protected by the Constitution because as a nation we believe that no one person is capable of determining which ideas are true and rational. Like media critic Jean Kilbourne, we may disagree with some of the messages being conveyed through advertising--say, the message that women are attractive only

Conclusion

TEACHING IDEA

Once Tschopp makes her claim, she begins to argue, using the tools laid out in this chapter—particularly the "lines of reasoning" from Toulmin. Have students consult the chapter to review the strategies that Tschopp employs: argument from cause, argument from parallel case, rebuttal, and appeal to authority.

when they are young and thin (44). Like Peggy Charren, we can agree that advertisements can create stresses in a family's life (15). Nevertheless, we must allow all ideas a place in the market place. As Charles O'Neil, an advertiser and a defender of the medium, suggests, "[a]dvertising is only a reflection of society; slaying the messenger will not alter the fact" that potentially damaging or offensive ideas exist (196). If we disagree with the message sent in an ad, it is our responsibility to send children a different message.

Appeal to an authority

Works Cited

Charren, Peggy. "Should We Ban TV Advertising to Children? YES." National Forum: The Phi Kappa Phi Journal 59.4 (1979): 13–16.

Kilbourne, Jean. "The Child as Sex Object: Images of Children in the Media." The Educator's Guide to Preventing Child Abuse. Ed. Mary Nelson and Kay Clark. Santa Cruz: Network Publications, 1986. 40–46.

O'Neil, Charles A. "The Language of Advertising." Exploring Language. 6th ed. Ed. Gary Goshgarian. New York: HarperCollins, 1992. 186–97.

Schrank, Jeffrey. "The Language of Advertising Claims." Teaching About Doublespeak. Urbana, IL: National Council of Teachers of English, 1976. 156–62.

Shanker, Albert. "Where We Stand: TV Chastity Belt." New York Times 7 Mar. 1993, sec. 4: 7.

GROUP ACTIVITY

As students respond to each other's drafts, you may want to ask peer reviewers to pay specific attention to opposing views. Requiring each reviewer to provide one opposing point not already found in the paper will help the writer evaluate his or her acknowledgment of the opposition.

6h Evaluating arguments and avoiding common errors

Whether you are evaluating your own arguments or someone else's, there are several common errors to watch for. Correct these errors in your own writing, and raise a challenge when you find them in the writing of others.

1 Defining terms

Your evaluation of an argument should begin with its claim. Locate the claim and be sure that all terms are well defined. If they are not, determine whether the lack of definition creates ambiguities in the argument itself. For example, the term *generosity* might appear, without definition, in a claim. If that term and the claim itself were later illustrated with the example of a mall developer's "generously offering the main corridors of the mall for exhibitions, during the Christmas Season, of waste recycling demonstrations by Scouting troops," you might justifiably question the validity of the argument. If you define *generosity* as the giving of oneself freely and without any expectation of return, then you might wonder how generous the mall developer is really being. Certainly the increased traffic flow through the mall would boost business, and the supposed generosity might be an advertising ploy. As the reader of this argument, you would be entitled to raise a challenge; if you were the writer, you could by carefully defining terms avoid later challenges to your implied view of the word *generosity.* For instance, you could define the word as "any action, regardless of its motive, that results in the greatest good for the greatest number of people." This one sentence (specifically, the phrase *regardless of its motive*) lets you fend off the challenge, which you could rebut by saying: "Sure, the mall developer is increasing traffic to the mall, and probably profits as well; the developer is also educating an entire community about the importance of recycling. Here is a situation in which everyone wins. To be generous, you don't need to be a martyr."

2 Examining lines of reasoning

As you have seen, the lines of reasoning that a writer develops—generalization, causation, and so on—establish logical support for a claim. If you as the reader feel that the argument's reasoning is not valid, then you are entitled to raise a challenge because if this is flawed, the validity of the claim may be in doubt. Any of the following seven types of fallacies, or flaws, will undermine an argument's logic. The first four flaws specifically address the lines of reasoning you will use to make arguments from generalization, causation, sign, and analogy.

1. *Faulty generalization.* Generalizations may be flawed if they are offered on the basis of insufficient data. It would not be valid, for instance, to make the generalization that left-handed people are clumsy because all three lefties of your acquaintance are clumsy. A more academic example: Assume you had administered a survey to students in your dorm. In studying the results you discovered that attitudes toward joining fraternities and sororities were evenly split. Slightly more than 50 percent wanted to join, a bit less than 50 percent did not. It would be a

LOOKING BACK

CRITICAL THINKING If students have not already read Chapter 1, Critical Thinking and Reading, now would be a good time to direct their attention to 1g, "Critical reading: Reading to evaluate." Even if Chapter 1 has already been covered, a quick review would be helpful.

LOOKING BACK

See 1g and 2b for extended discussions of reading to evaluate and writing an evaluation. Students can use the information in 6h to evaluate definitions, logic, and evidence.

ADDITIONAL EXERCISE B

Look through a couple of weeks' worth of editorial pages from your local newspaper, and choose two or three editorials and letters to the editor that seem to offer "shaky" arguments. Evaluate the arguments based on the material in this section: Has the writer defined terms? Are the inferences valid? If not, what flaws in making inferences are apparent? Is the evidence flawed? If so, what flaws in evidence are apparent?

REFERENCE

DYRUD, MARILYN A. "Teaching Logic." ERIC, 1984. ED 284 311. Letters to the editor can teach students the importance of avoiding logical fallacies.

ADDITIONAL EXERCISE C

Read the following scenarios and evaluate the statements associated with each for logical fallacies. Name the fallacy and briefly explain how the statement illustrates it.

1. Sam's acquaintance writes all her papers the evening (and early morning) before they are due, and she is forever getting good grades. Sam concludes: "For my next paper, I won't start writing until twenty-four hours before it's due."
2. Louise flies to a distant city to visit a friend who attends school there. The taxi driver who takes her from the airport to a bus depot is surly. At the depot, the ticket agent seems more intent on reading the paper than on helping Louise find her way to the suburban campus. When she finally arrives at her friend's school, Louise remarks, "The people in this town aren't very friendly."
3. As part of your research on a paper you are writing, you watch a State House debate on universal health care. One state representative makes this remark: "We will adopt the universal health care bill as written and give everyone in this state equal access to medical facilities, or we will say to the poor among us that their good health is less important than ours. Distinguished members of this governing body, the choice is yours."

Suggested responses:

1. *faulty cause and effect*—Sam incorrectly assumes that the sole cause for his acquaintance's good grades is the time factor. *Or confusing correlation with causation*—Sam mistakes the coincidences of his acquaintance's good grades and her timing for a cause-and-effect situation.
2. *faulty generalization*—Louise bases a judgment of an entire city's population on the behavior of two workers in the city.
3. *either/or reasoning*—The representative doesn't take into account that there are more than two choices involved here.

faulty generalization to claim on the basis of this one survey that students on your campus are evenly split on joining fraternities and sororities. In order for your generalization to be accurate, the survey would need to have been administered campus-wide, if not to every student, then at least to a representative cross-section.

2. *Faulty cause and effect.* Two fallacies can lead a writer to infer incorrectly that one event causes another. The first concerns the ordering of events in time. The fact that one event occurs before another does *not* prove that the first event caused the second. (In Latin, this fallacy is known as *post hoc,* a brief form of *post hoc, ergo propter hoc*—after this, therefore because of this.) If the planets Venus and Jupiter were in rare alignment on the morning of the Mt. St. Helens eruption, it would not be logical to argue that an alignment of two planets caused the volcano to erupt. The second flaw in thinking that leads to a faulty claim of causation is the belief that events must have *single* causes. Proving causation is often complicated, for many factors usually contribute to the occurrence of an event. What caused the layoff of production-line workers at the General Motors plant in Framingham, Massachusetts? An answer to this question would involve several issues, including increased competition from foreign auto manufacturers, a downturn in the economy, the cost of modernizing the Framingham assembly line, a need to show stockholders that there were fewer employees on the payroll, and a decision to build more cars out of the country. To claim that *one* of these is the sole cause of the plant shutdown would be to ignore the complexity of the event.

3. *Confusing correlation with causation.* There is a well-known saying among researchers that *correlation does not imply causation.* In one study on creativity, researchers correlated *risk taking* and *a preference for the unconventional* with groups of people classified as creative. It would not be logical to infer from this correlation that creativity *causes* risk taking or a preference for the unconventional or that these traits *cause* creativity. The most that can be said is that the traits are associated or correlated with—they tend to appear in the presence of—creative people. Arguments made with statistical evidence are usually subject to this limitation.

4. *Faulty analogy.* The key components of an analogy must very nearly parallel the issues central to the argument you are making. The wrong analogy not only will *not* clarify, but also will positively confuse. For instance, an attempt to liken the process of writing to climbing a flight of stairs would create some confusion. The analogy suggests that the writing process occurs in clearly delineated steps, when progress in actual writing is seldom so neat. The stages of writing do not progress "step by step" until a final draft is achieved. It is more accurate to say that the process of writing loops back on itself and that the process of revision takes place not just at the end of writing (the last step) but throughout. So the stairs analogy might confuse writers who, reflecting on their own practices, do not see neat linear progress and therefore assume they must be doing something wrong. Analogies should enhance, not obscure, understanding.

5. *Either/or reasoning.* Assume that someone is trying to persuade you that the United States ought to intervene militarily in a certain conflict many thousands of miles from U.S. territory. At one point in the argument you hear this: "Either we demonstrate through force that the United States continues to be a world power or we take a backseat, passive role in world affairs. The choice is clear." Actually, the choice is not at all clear. The person arguing has presented two options and has argued for one. But many possibilities for conducting U.S. foreign policy exist besides going to war or becoming passive. An argument will be flawed when its author preselects two possibilities from among many and then attempts to force a choice.
6. *Personal attacks.* Personal attacks, known in Latin as *ad hominem* arguments, challenge the person presenting a view rather than the view itself. You are entitled to object when you read or hear this type of attack: "The child psychologist on that talk show has no kids, so how can he recommend anything useful to me concerning my children?" Notice that the challenge is directed at the person who is presenting ideas, not at the ideas themselves. The psychologist's advice may well be excellent, but the *ad hominem* attack sidesteps the issues and focuses instead on personality. Here is a variant on the *ad hominem* argument: "The speaker is giving what sounds like good advice on child rearing, but she is neither a psychologist nor an educator, so we really shouldn't base our actions on her views." In this case, the critic is dismissing a statement because the speaker is not an acknowledged expert. This kind of criticism can be legitimate if an argument is being directly based on the authority of that speaker's expertise, and you *should* give preference to sources that are authoritative. Nonetheless, it is sidestepping the other issues in an argument to dismiss an apparently useful observation by dismissing the person who offers it. At the very least, statements should be evaluated on their merits.
7. *The begged question.* Writers who assume the validity of a point that they should be proving by argument are guilty of begging the question. For instance, the statement "All patriotic Americans should support the President" begs a question of definition: what *is* a patriotic American? The person making this statement assumes a definition that he should in fact be arguing. By making this assumption, the writer sidesteps the issue of definition altogether. The point you want to make must be addressed directly through careful argument.

3 Examining evidence

Arguments also can falter when they are not adequately or legitimately supported by facts, examples, statistics, or opinions. Refer to the following guidelines when using evidence.

Facts and examples

1. *Facts and examples should fairly represent the available data.* An example cannot be forced. If you find yourself needing to sift through a great deal of evidence *against* a point you wish to make in order to find one confirming fact or example, take your difficulty as a sign and rethink your point.
2. *Facts and examples should be current.* Facts and examples need to be current, especially when you are arguing about recent events or are drawing information from a field in which information is changing rapidly. If, for example, you are arguing a claim about the likelihood of incumbent politicians being reelected, you should find sources that report on the most recent elections. If you are trying to show a trend, your facts and examples should also be drawn from sources going back several years, if not decades.
3. *Facts and examples should be sufficient to establish validity.* A generalization must be based on an adequate number of examples and on representative examples. To establish the existence of a problem concerning college sports, for instance, it would not do to claim that because transcripts were forged for a handful of student-athletes at two schools a problem exists nationwide.
4. *Negative instances of facts and examples should be acknowledged.* If an argument is to be honest, you should identify facts and examples that constitute evidence *against* your position. Tactically, you are better off being the one to raise the inconvenient example than having someone else do this for you in the context of a challenge. For example, an argument might conclude that a particular advertising company has consistently misrepresented facts about its products. The arguer would be less than ethical to omit from the discussion several advertisements that were entirely legitimate in their treatment of facts. The wiser strategy would be for the arguer to address these negative examples (negative in the sense that they apparently disprove the claim), either turning them to advantage or at the very least neutralizing them.

Statistics

5. *Statistics from reliable and current sources should be used.* Statistics are a numerical compression of information. Assuming that you do not have the expertise to evaluate the procedures by which statistics are generated, you should take certain commonsense precautions when selecting statistical evidence. First, cite statistics from reliable sources. If you have no other way of checking reliability, you can assume that the same source cited in several places is reliable. The U.S. government publishes volumes of statistical information and is considered a reliable source. Just as with facts and examples, statistics should be current when you are arguing about a topic of current interest.

6. *Comparative statistics should compare items of the same logical class.* If you found statistical information on housing starts in New England in one source and in a second source found information on housing starts in the Southwest, you would naturally want to compare the numbers. The comparison would be valid only if the term "housing starts" was defined clearly in both sources. Lacking a definition, you might plunge ahead and cite the statistics in a paper, not realizing that one figure included apartment buildings in its definition of "housing" while the other included only single-family homes. Such a comparison would be faulty.

Expert opinions

7. *"Experts" who give opinions should be qualified to do so.* Anyone can speak on a topic, but experts speak with authority by virtue of their experience. Cite the opinions of experts in order to support your claims. Of course you will want to be sure that your experts are, in fact, expert; and evaluating the quality of what they say can be troublesome when you do not know a great deal about a topic. You can trust a so-called expert as being an authority if you see that person cited as such in several sources. For experts who are not likely to be cited in academic articles or books, use your common sense. If you were arguing that birchbark canoes track better in the water than aluminum canoes, you would want to seek out a person who has considerable experience with both. (See the box in 6d-2 for more on evaluating expert opinions and choosing authoritative sources.)
8. *Experts should be neutral.* You can disqualify an expert's testimony for possible use in your argument if you find that the expert will profit somehow from the opinions or interpretations offered. Returning to the example of the birchbark canoe: you would want to cite as an authority in your paper the person who has paddled hundreds of miles in both aluminum and birchbark canoes, not the one who earns a living making birchbark canoes.

PART III

UNDERSTANDING GRAMMAR

CHAPTER 7

Constructing Sentences

KEY FEATURES

Opening on a note reassuring to students, this chapter emphasizes the difference between *implicit* and *explicit* knowledge of sentence structure. The chapter continues the movement from larger units of discourse (essays) through smaller units (paragraphs) to yet smaller units (sentences). While understanding sentence structure is discussed in the context of writing and revising, the initial discussion uses traditional grammatical terminology. It makes sense to use such terms as "subject" and "predicate," since most students are familiar with them. As students gain confidence in identifying not only the major parts of sentences but also the parts of speech that constitute those sentence parts, they are ready to move on to a study of sentence types. In keeping with the approach used in the previous section, the sections covering sentence types focus on meaning rather than rules. And as in the treatment of the rudiments of sentence structure, coverage of sentence types begins with basic types and moves on, using what students have learned in the first part of the chapter to discuss expanding sentences by modifying them with increasingly complex phrases and clauses. All of the standard sentence patterns are covered in fairly traditional terms, but the emphasis remains on meaning, not rules. Even a brief discussion of punctuation is explained in terms of the meaning of the entire sentence. The last part of the chapter offers both functional and structural defi-

If you are a lifelong speaker of English, then you are an expert in the language—in its grammar, its vocabulary, its sentence structures, and the proper relationships among its words. When you speak, people understand. You *know* English, but in all likelihood your knowledge is *implicit.* That is to say, you can do just fine communicating verbally, and yet you may not know the textbook definition of *participle,* for instance—even though you use participles correctly every day. Although you will seldom need to talk of participles, you will gain confidence as a writer by making your implicit knowledge *explicit.*

7a Understanding sentence parts

The sentence is our basic unit of communication. Sentences, of course, are composed of words, each of which can be classified as a part of speech. As you review definitions of nouns, verbs, and the other parts of speech, remember that these are parts of a whole: meaning in language is built on the *relationship* among words.

1 The basics: Recognizing subjects and predicates

The fundamental relationship in a sentence is the one between a subject and its predicate. Every sentence has a **subject:** a noun or noun-like word group that engages in the main action of the sentence or is described by the sentence. In addition, every sentence has a **predicate:** a verb, and other words associated with it, that state the action undertaken by a subject or the condition in which the subject exists.

A **simple subject** is the single noun or pronoun that identifies what the sentence is about or produces the action of the sentence. The **simple predicate** is the main sentence verb. You can gain a great deal of confidence from your ability to divide a sentence into its subject and predicate parts; you will improve your ability to avoid fragments and to write sentences with varied, interesting structures. Again, recall that subjects and predicates consist of nouns, verbs, and other parts of speech. Learning these parts of speech and their functions will help you understand how sentences operate. In the sentences that follow, the simple subject is marked "ss" and the simple predicate, "sp."

Subject	Predicate
In small doses, alcohol (ss: alcohol)	acts as a stimulant. (sp: acts)
Large doses (ss: doses)	act as a depressant. (sp: act)
Individuals under the influence (ss: Individuals)	often become more aggressive. (sp: become)
Alcohol consumption (ss: consumption)	interferes with one's ability to foresee negative consequences. (sp: interferes)
A person's actions (ss: actions)	can grow extreme in the presence of this drug. (sp: can grow)

2 Nouns

A **noun** (from the Latin *nomen,* or name) is the part of speech that names a person, place, thing, or idea.[1] Only nouns can be introduced by an **article** or a **determiner,** the words *a, an,* and *the*: a rock; an animal; the truth. The **indefinite article,** *a* or *an,* introduces a generalized noun: *a* person can be any person. The indefinite article *a* appears before nouns beginning with a consonant; *an* is placed before nouns beginning with a vowel or unpronounced *h*—as in *hour*: *a* book, *an* hour. The **definite article,** *the,* denotes a specific noun: *the* book. Nouns can also be accompanied by certain classes of words that limit what they refer to. The most common limiting words (and their categories) are: *this, that, these, those* (demonstrative); *any, each, some* (indefinite); *one, two, first, second,* etc. (numerical); *which, that, whose,* etc. (relative).

ESL NOTE The use of articles or of various limiting, quantifying, or determining words indicates whether an English noun names a person or thing that is specific or definite. Nouns that name something generic, nonspecific, or abstract are used without these words or with indefinite limiting words like *some* or *any* (see 42a-2 and 42-b).

[1]We owe our discussions of the parts of speech to Hulon Willis, *Modern Descriptive English Grammar* (San Francisco: Chandler, 1972).

nitions of sentences. Exercises provide students with ample practice in identifying and composing various types of sentences.

TEACHING IDEAS

CRITICAL THINKING Some students with sentence-level writing problems have become so fearful of the specter of grammar and sentences that they're convinced they'll simply "never get it." For that reason, it's probably worth a few minutes of class time to ask them to write out any definition of a sentence they can recall learning. Then ask them how meaningful the definition is: Can they use it to identify a sentence? to identify something that isn't a sentence? How *do* they determine whether or not a group of words is a sentence? Most students, after some initial hesitation, will be able to provide some parameters for sentences. This chapter will reinforce the basic knowledge these students have. If they can begin the chapter with confidence, then they're far more likely to make use of the material in it.

ADDITIONAL EXERCISE A

This exercise is designed to show you just how much you really do know about sentences. In the following paragraph, mark off places where you'd end a sentence. (You can also supply commas where you think they're needed, but that's not necessary for the purposes of this exercise.) Then compare your response to other students' responses. As you discuss differences, try to explain why you divided the paragraph as you did. (There are several different ways of dividing the paragraph.)

> The Supreme Court hears about 125 to 130 cases during the seven months each year that it is in session these cases are chosen from over 5,000 petitions most of which are prepared by highly specialized law firms but every year 200 to 300 petitions are submitted by individuals on their own behalf these cases are called *pro se* the Latin words for "for himself" in most years no more than one or two *pro se* cases are heard and fewer result in a positive decision many of these petitions are prepared by prisoners who have given up on lawyers one of the

(continued)

most famous of these cases was that of Clarence Gideon a poor man who was convicted without having been represented by a lawyer Gideon's petition which he wrote out by hand was accepted by the Court and resulted in a landmark ruling that people who can't afford lawyers must be given the opportunity to be represented by a court-appointed lawyer.

Possible response:

The Supreme Court hears about 125 to 130 cases during the seven months each year that it is in session. These cases are chosen from over 5,000 petitions, most of which are prepared by highly specialized law firms. But every year 200 to 300 petitions are submitted by individuals on their own behalf. These cases are called *pro se,* the Latin words for "for himself." In most years no more than one or two *pro se* cases are heard, and fewer result in a positive decision. Many of these petitions are prepared by prisoners who have given up on lawyers. One of the most famous of these cases was that of Clarence Gideon, a poor man who was convicted without having been represented by a lawyer. Gideon's petition, which he wrote out by hand, was accepted by the Court and resulted in a landmark ruling that people who can't afford lawyers must be given the opportunity to be represented by a court-appointed lawyer.

ESL CUE

The following texts are useful references for ESL students having problems with English grammar:

AZAR, BETTY. *Understanding and Using English Grammar.* 2 vols. Englewood Cliffs, NJ: Prentice-Hall.

COOK, MARY JANE. *Trouble Spots of English Grammar, a Test-Workbook for ESL.* 2 vols. New York: Harcourt Brace Jovanovich.

FRANK, MARCELLA. *Modern English.* 2 vols. Englewood Cliffs, NJ: Prentice-Hall.

GRAHAM, SHEILA, and WYNN CURTIS. *Harbrace ESL Workbook.* New York: Harcourt Brace Jovanovich.

HOLSCHUH, LOUIS. *The Elements of English Grammar.* 2 vols. New York: St. Martin's Press.

The use of a plural form or a numerical limiting word often indicates whether an English noun names a person or thing that can be counted—that is, a count noun (versus a mass or noncount noun that names uncountable quantities or abstractions). See the box on this page and 42a-1.

Nouns change their form to show **number;** they can be made singular or plural: *boy/boys, child/children, herd/herds.* They also undergo limited change in form to show **possession,** but, unlike pronouns (see 7a-6), they do this only with the addition of an apostrophe and usually an *s: girl's, children's, herd's.* Finally, nouns can be classified according to categories of meaning that affect the way they are used, as shown in the following box.

Classification of Nouns

Proper nouns, which are capitalized, name particular persons, places, or things:

Sandra Day O'Connor, Chevrolet, "To His Coy Mistress"

Common nouns refer to general persons, places, or things and are not capitalized:

judge, automobile, poem

Count nouns can be counted:

cubes, cups, forks, rocks

Mass nouns cannot be counted:

sugar, water, air, dirt

Concrete nouns name tangible objects:

lips, clock, dollar

Abstract nouns name an intangible idea, emotion, or quality:

love, eternity, ambition

Animate versus **inanimate nouns** differ according to whether they name something alive:

fox and *weeds* versus *wall* and *honesty*

Collective nouns are singular in form but plural in sense:

crowd, family, group, herd

Specific uses of nouns are addressed in several places in this handbook.

Nouns: as modifiers 11g
Nouns: agreement with verbs 10a
Nouns: as complements 7b
Nouns: as clauses 7e-3
Nouns with articles and determiners 42b
Nouns: as objects 7b
Nouns: phrases 7d-2 and 3
Nouns: showing possession 27a, 8c
Nouns: as subjects 7b

3 Verbs

A **verb,** the main word in the predicate of a sentence, expresses an action, describes an occurrence, or establishes a state of being.

ACTION	Eleanor *kicked* the ball.
OCCURRENCE	A hush *descended* on the crowd.
STATE OF BEING	Thomas *was* pious.

Verbs change form on the basis of their **principal parts.** Building from the **infinitive** or **base form** (often accompanied by **to**), these parts are the **past tense,** the **present participle,** and the **past participle.**

Base form	*Past tense*	*Present participle*	*Past participle*
to escape	escaped	am escaping	escaped
to ring	rang	am ringing	rung

The principal parts of a verb have a major role in how the verb shows **tense,** the change in form that expresses the verb's action in time relative to a present statement.

There are four varieties of verbs in English; each establishes a different relationship among sentence parts, as shown in the following box.

Classification of Verbs

Transitive verbs transfer action from an actor—the subject of the sentence—to a person, place, or thing receiving that action (see 9d-1).

buy, build, kick, kiss, write
Wanda *built* a snowman.

Intransitive verbs show action; yet no person, place, or thing is acted on (see 9d-1).

fall, laugh, sing, smile
Stock prices *fell.*

Linking verbs allow the word or words following the verb to complete the meaning of a subject (see 11d).

be (am, is, are, was, were, has/have been), look, remain, sound, seem, taste
Harold *seems* happy.

Helping or **auxiliary verbs** help to show the tense and mood of a verb (see 9c and 43d).

be (am, is, are, was, were), has, have, had, do, did, will
I *am* going. I *will* go. I *have* gone. I *did* go.

Modal auxiliaries such as *might, would, could,* and *must* help a verb to express urgency, obligation, and likelihood (see 9c-1 and 43d).

I *should* go. I *might* go. I *could* go.

ESL CUE

Some languages, such as Russian, Korean, and Japanese, have no articles, so the concept of the article, not just our distinction between definite and indefinite articles, will need explanation. Some languages that do have articles do not make the general/specific distinction English speakers make. Because of the way Spanish and Italian pronounce "i," speakers of those languages will easily confuse "this" and "these."

LOOKING AHEAD

Coverage of major parts of speech in this chapter is rudimentary and geared toward understanding the function of parts of speech in individual sentences. For more extensive discussion of these parts of speech, see Chapters 8 (Case in Nouns and Pronouns), 9 (Verbs), and 11 (Adjectives and Adverbs).

LOOKING BACK

You may want to remind students that they've dealt with the idea of subject and predicate in a larger context when discussing developing a working thesis for their papers (base your thesis on a relationship you have forged). Understanding the relationship between the entire essay and the individual sentence will help students understand sentences in terms of units of discourse.

TEACHING IDEAS

Sometimes students continue to resist learning this material even though they've seen its relevance, offering the common excuse "When will I ever use this stuff?" You might counter that they can indeed "use this stuff" right now, and throughout their lives, to help them understand what they read. Ask students to recall difficult passages they've encountered in their course. Sometimes it's hard to figure out what the passage means. A reader who knows enough about sentence structure to identify the simple subject and simple predicate, however, can isolate the kernel of meaning and work from there, making the process of understanding the passage that much easier.

ESL NOTE To determine whether a word in a sentence is a verb, apply the test sequence described in 12a (on sentence fragments).

See Chapter 9 for a detailed discussion of verbs. The following list provides a brief index to more information on verb use.

Verbals

A **verbal** is a verb form that functions in a sentence as an adjective, an adverb, or a noun. There are three types of verbals: gerunds, participles, and infinitives. A **gerund**, the *-ing* form of a verb without its helping verbs, functions as a noun.

> *Editing* is both a skill and an art. [The gerund is the subject of the sentence.]
>
> I am tired of *editing.* [The gerund is an object of a preposition.]

A **participle** is a verb form that modifies nouns and pronouns. Its present and past forms make up two of the verb's principal parts, as shown previously.

> The *edited* manuscript was 700 pages. [The past participle modifies the noun *manuscript.*]
>
> The man *editing* your manuscript is Max Perkins. [The present participle modifies the noun *man.*]

An **infinitive,** often preceded by *to,* is the base form of the verb (often called its *dictionary form*). An infinitive can function as a noun, adjective, or adverb.

> *To edit* well requires patience. [The infinitive functions as the noun subject of the sentence.]
>
> The person *to edit* your work is Max Perkins. [The infinitive functions as an adjective.]
>
> He waited *to edit* the manuscript. [The infinitive functions as an adverb.]

TEACHING IDEAS

The concept of a verbal can be confusing to some students; they have difficulty understanding why a verbal cannot function as a verb in a sentence. It may be helpful to ask students to construct sentences using forms of *edit* in the predicate position. Or you may want to present them with the following sentences, asking them to distinguish between the use of *edit* as a verb in these sentences and as a verbal in the sample sentences in the text:

> She *is editing* the book with skill and art.
> I *am editing* the essay even though I am tired.
> Max Perkins *edited* that manuscript.
> Max Perkins *was editing* the manuscript when I called.
> Max Perkins *will edit* the manuscript.

ESL CUE

Students should be reminded that because gerunds serve the function of nouns and may appear wherever a noun appears, one gerund equals one noun and therefore takes a singular verb. Gerunds often, though not always, refer to action in the past or action from the past to the present (in contrast to infinitives, which refer to the future). When gerunds are placed as objects of the verb, this distinction is vital to clear communication, as in the following.

The following list is a brief index to other information on verbals.

Important Relationships between a Subject and Verb

A complete sentence must have both a subject and a verb. A word grouping that lacks a subject, a verb, or both is considered a fragment. See Chapter 12 on fragments and Chapter 16 for a special class of fragments—grammatically "mixed" constructions.

INCOMPLETE At the beginning of the meeting. [There is no verb.]

REVISED At the beginning of the meeting, the treasurer reported on recent news.

INCOMPLETE The fact that this is an emergency meeting. [The use of *that* leaves the statement incomplete, without a verb.]

REVISED This is an emergency meeting of the board.

A sentence must have a *logically compatible* subject and verb. A sentence in which a subject is paired with a logically incompatible verb is sure to confuse readers, as you will see in Chapter 16.

INCOMPATIBLE The meeting room is sweating. [A room does not normally sweat.]

REVISED Those gathered in the meeting room are sweating.

A sentence must have a subject and verb that *agree in number.* A subject and verb must both be singular or plural. The conventions for ensuring consistency are found in Chapter 10.

INCONSISTENT The treasurer are a dynamic speaker. [The plural verb does not match the singular subject.]

REVISED The treasurer is a dynamic speaker.

A sentence must have a subject close enough to the verb to ensure clarity. Meaning in a sentence can be confused if the subject/verb pairing is interrupted with a lengthy modifier. See Chapter 15 for a discussion of misplaced modifiers.

INTERRUPTED We because of our dire financial situation and our interests in maintaining employee welfare have called this meeting.

REVISED We have called this meeting because of our dire financial situation and our interests in maintaining employee welfare.

5 Adjectives

By modifying or describing a noun or pronoun, an **adjective** provides crucial defining and limiting information in a sentence. It can also provide

He stopped seeing her./He stopped to see her.
He remembered going there./He must remember to go there.

Also, gerunds take the possessive pronoun.

his book/his having done that.

Another helpful rule is that two- and three-part verbs always take a gerund instead of an infinitive object: "look forward to going" not "look forward to go."

Recognizing gerund and infinitive subjects may be difficult for ESL students, who might benefit from practice underlining subjects, as in "*Getting to know you* will be fun" and "*To be or not to be* was Hamlet's question."

REFERENCES

CHRISTENSEN, FRANCIS. "A Generative Rhetoric of the Sentence." *CCC* 14 (1963): 155–61. Adding to the basic sentence can help students become more fluent writers of cumulative sentences.

GORRELL, DONNA. "Controlled Composition for Basic Writers." *CCC* 32 (1981): 308–16. Students who practice manipulating the writing of others can become skilled in producing their own sentences.

KOLLN, MARTHA. "Closing the Books on Alchemy." *CCC* 32 (1981): 139–51. Understanding grammatical terminology provides students with a means of controlling their own writing.

TRAUGOTT, ELIZABETH CLOSS. *A History of English Syntax: A Transformational Approach to the History of English Sentence Structure.* New York: Holt, 1972. Transformational grammar provides a meaningful perspective from which to study sentence structure.

WILLIAMS, JOSEPH M. "The Phenomenology of Error." *CCC* 32 (1981): 152–68. Instructors should look at sentence errors in terms of writing behavior that can be altered if given sufficient attention.

FOR DISCUSSION

In order to familiarize students with the function of adjectives and adverbs in a sentence, ask them to identify and discuss the role played by the various modifiers in the following passage.

> Female slaves seldom escaped harassment from owners. Nearly all young slave women—some of them only girls—regularly encountered the terrifying prospect of rape or attempted rape. The young slave Harriet Jacobs unwillingly endured the sexual attentions of her unscrupulous master, who continually pressured her to fulfill his desires. She refused adamantly. Consequently, she was occasionally subjected to severely painful beatings.

nonessential but compelling information to help readers see, hear, feel, taste, or smell something named. Adjectives include the present and past participle forms of verbs, such as *fighting* Irish, *flying* wing, *baked* potato, and *written* remarks. The single-word adjectives in the following sentences are italicized.

> Climate plays an *important* part in determining the *average* numbers of a species, and *periodical* seasons of *extreme* cold or drought I believe to be the most *effective* of *all* checks.
>
> —CHARLES DARWIN, *On the Origin of Species*

6 Adverbs

An **adverb** can modify a verb, an adjective, an adverb, or an entire sentence. Adverbs describe, define, or otherwise limit, generally answering these questions: *when, how, where, how often, to what extent,* and *to what degree.* Although many adverbs in English are formed by adding the suffix *-ly* to an adjective, some are not: *after, ahead, already, always, back, behind, here, there, up, down, inside, outside.* **Descriptive adverbs** describe individual words within a sentence.

> The poor *unwittingly* subsidize the rich. [The adverb modifies the verb *subsidize.*]
>
> Poverty *almost* always can be eliminated at a higher cost to the rich. [The adverb modifies the adverb *always.*]
>
> Widespread poverty imposes an *increasingly* severe strain on our social fabric. [The adverb modifies the adjective *severe.*]

Conjunctive adverbs establish adverb-like relationships between whole sentences. These words—*moreover, however, consequently, thus, therefore, furthermore,* and so on—play a special role in linking ideas and sentences. (See 7a-9 and 19a-3.) Chapter 11 provides a detailed discussion of adjectives and adverbs. The following is a brief index to more information on adjectives and adverbs.

7 Pronouns

Pronouns substitute for nouns. The word that a pronoun refers to and renames is called its **antecedent.** Like a noun, a pronoun shows **number**—it can be singular or plural. Depending on its function in a sentence, a pronoun will change form—that is, its **case:** it will change from **subjective,** to **objec-**

tive, to **possessive.** The following examples show this change in case for the pronoun *he,* which in each instance is a substitute for the noun *Jake.*

> **antecedent** … **pronoun (subjective)**
> Jake reads a magazine. *He* reads a magazine.

> **antecedent** … **pronoun (objective)**
> The magazine was given to Jake. The magazine was given to *him.*

> **antecedent** … **pronoun (possessive)**
> Jake's subscription is running out. *His* subscription is running out.

There are eight classes of pronouns.

Personal pronouns (*I, me, you, us, his, hers,* etc.) refer to people and things.

> When sugar dissolves in water, the sugar molecules break *their* close connection within the sugar crystal.

Relative pronouns (*who, whose, which, that,* etc.) begin dependent clauses (see 7e) and refer to people and things.

> The presence of the sugar, *which* is now in solution, changes many of the properties of the water.

Demonstrative pronouns (*this, these, that, those*) point to the nouns they replace.

> *These* changes involve the water's density, boiling point, and more.

Interrogative pronouns (*who, which, what, whose,* etc.) form questions.

> *What* does boiling sugar water have to do with coating caramel apples?

Intensive pronouns (*herself, themselves,* and other compounds formed with *-self* or *-selves*) repeat and emphasize a noun or pronoun.

> The sugar *itself* can be recovered from the water by the simple act of boiling.

Reflexive pronouns (*herself, themselves,* and other compounds formed with *-self* or *-selves*) rename—reflect back to—a preceding noun or pronoun.

> The ease of recovery demonstrates that sugar molecules do not bind *themselves* strongly to water molecules.

Indefinite pronouns (*one, anyone, somebody, nobody, everybody,* etc.) refer to general, or nonspecific, persons or things.

> *Anyone* who has stained a shirt with salad dressing knows that water will not dissolve oil.

ADDITIONAL EXERCISE B

Compose a paragraph in which you use at least five of the classes of pronouns. Identify each pronoun you use by class, and where appropriate, by case and number.

Reciprocal pronouns (*one another, each other*) refer to the separate parts of a plural noun.

The many solvents available to chemists complement *one another.*

The following is a brief index to more information on pronouns.

- Pronouns: agreement in person and number 10a, b
- Pronouns: reference to antecedent 14a–e
- Pronouns: case—subjective, objective, possessive 8a–d
- Pronouns: relative pronouns 8f, 14e

8 Prepositions

A **preposition** links a noun (or word group substituting for a noun) to other words in a sentence—to nouns, pronouns, verbs, or adjectives. *In, at, of, for, on, by,* are all prepositions. Many common prepositions are shown in the following box. Along with the words that follow them, prepositions form **prepositional phrases,** which function as adjectives or adverbs. In the following sentence, an arrow leads from the (three) prepositional phrases to the (three) words modified. Note that the middle prepositional phrase modifies *evolution* in the first prepositional phrase.

The theory *of evolution by natural selection* was proposed *in the 1850s.*

ESL Note Prepositions occur in a very wide variety of English constructions that are often highly idiomatic. They are often followed by a noun or pronoun in the objective form or case (see 8b-1 and 42c), thus forming a modifying prepositional phrase (see 7d-1).

When used with certain verbs, prepositions (as well as certain adverbs like *down, out,* and *away*) are called *particles,* combining with the simple form of the verb into a *phrasal verb* that has a distinct new meaning (see 43f). These phrasal-verb meanings with their particles are listed in standard English dictionaries.

When used with an adjective and the verb *be* followed by an object, a preposition forms a distinctive idiomatic construction (see 44b). In this form, many adjectives must be used with very specific prepositions. (See also 16g-3 and 18a-1 for this usage in parallel constructions.) Such idiomatic usages are hard to find in standard English dictionaries.

The following is a brief index to more information on prepositions.

- Prepositions: and fragments 12c-2
- Prepositions: and mixed constructions 16g-3, 18a
- Prepositions: using objective-case pronouns 8b-1
- Prepositions: punctuating introductory phrases 25a
- Prepositions: punctuating nonessential phrases 25d
- Prepositions: with nouns 42c
- Prepositions: with verbs 43f
- Prepositions: with adjectives 44b

ESL CUE

Because their languages may not depend on word order to the degree that English does, many ESL students will be confused by English words that retain the same spelling even though they serve different grammatical functions, as exemplified by the Groucho Marx saying: "Time *flies like* an arrow; fruit *flies like* a banana."

Marking out prepositional phrases before determining subject and verb is a good rule of thumb to help students distinguish subjects and verbs: "~~In the back of the room behind the huge desk~~ stood an antique clock ~~of the type~~ revered ~~by his grandparents~~."

In Japanese the object precedes the verb.

The following literal translation from Chinese makes clear the word order interference problems possible:

> "he in/on/at here that daughter also to be very good looking"

The student speaking or writing in English must recast such statements in terms of their content and intent, finding English equivalents instead of translating literally; yet even students highly fluent in English who "think in" their new language will sooner or later stumble over localized word order interference problems. Sympathy and tolerance are appropriate.

ESL CUE

There is little logic to English speakers' use of prepositions, and such use differs in British and American English. In fact, American usage can vary as well ("stand on line"—East Coast; "stand in line"—other regions). ESL students may *never* master English prepositions com-

Common Prepositions

Single-word prepositions

about	beyond	off
above	by	on
across	concerning	onto
after	despite	out
against	down	outside
along	during	over
among	except	through
around	for	to
as	from	toward
before	in	under
behind	into	until
below	like	up
beneath	near	with
between	of	

Multiword prepositions

according to	contrary to	on account of
along with	except for	on top of
apart from	in addition to	outside of
as for	in back of	owing to
because of	in case of	with regard to
by means of	in spite of	with respect to

9 Conjunctions

Conjunctions join sentence elements or entire sentences in one of two ways: either by establishing a coordinate or *equal* relationship among joined parts or by establishing a subordinate or *unequal* relationship. (Subordinating conjunctions are discussed in detail in 7e. Coordinating and correlative conjunctions are discussed in Chapter 19.) Briefly, conjunctions are classified in four ways: as coordinating conjunctions, conjunctive adverbs, correlative conjunctions, or subordinating conjunctions.

Coordinating conjunctions join parallel elements from two or more sentences into a single sentence: *and, but, or, nor, for, so, yet.* (For uses of coordinating conjunctions see 10a-2, 3, 19a-1, and 25b.)

> Infants only cry at birth, *but* within a few short years they speak in complete sentences.

Conjunctive adverbs create special logical relationships between the clauses or sentences joined: *however, therefore, thus, consequently,* etc. (For uses of conjunctive adverbs see 13b-4, 19a-3, and 26b.)

pletely and *should not be expected to.* They can learn usage of some of the most common prepositions through rote memory, and there are some rules to help with prepositions of location, but even a seemingly bilingual student can be recognized as a non-native speaker by occasional preposition abuse.

Sometimes a helpful rule can be invented; for instance, most English words beginning with "co-," "col-," "com-," "con-," or "cor-," take the preposition "with," as in "cooperate with," "collaborate with," "communicate with," "connect with," "correspond with," because this prefix carries the idea of "together." "On" used for location frequently refers to the surface and "in" to the interior as in "on the desk" as opposed to "in the desk," but the difference between "on" the sofa and "in" the chair relates to the construction of those furnishings: the sofa without arms, the chair enclosing and enveloping. You use "on" if you must step up to board ("get on a bus," "get on a train," "get on a large ship") but "in" if you must step down ("get in a small boat," "get in a car"). Contrast "*in* a canoe" with "*on* a raft." The best rule for "on" and "in" contrasts "touching" (visual correlative: *O*) and "enclosed" (**O**): "Those who ride *on the back of a tiger are in danger of ending up* in the tiger" (with apologies to J. F. Kennedy).

Multiword prepositions will be the hardest ones for non-native speakers to recognize as prepositions, and prepositions used in two- and three-part verbs will confuse everyone.

GROUP ACTIVITY

Students can help each other identify conjunctions, interjections, and expletives by working together on a selected passage. Divide students into groups of three or four, and ask each group to choose a passage from a work of fiction for this activity. (Fiction, especially children's fiction, is preferable here because it is more likely than nonfiction to include interjections.) As students work together to identify conjunctions, interjections, and expletives, they should find themselves discussing the function of these words in the sentences. Arguments over whether or not "it" in a given sentence is more appropriately labeled a pronoun rather than an expletive will help students learn to distinguish between parts of a sentence.

ESL CUE

ESL students may need help distinguishing between "since," which takes a specific initial time (since 3 P.M.; since July 3) and "for," which takes a length or period of time (for two hours; for 10 days).

ESL CUE

Some romance language speakers (Spanish, Italian, Portuguese) will have difficulty with the concept of the expletive since it does not exist in their language. Their tendency will be to leave out the "there" or "it" and to simply begin with a "be" verb as they would in their language: "Is hot." "Is over there." Calling attention to the problem often helps the student self-correct.

> Infants can only cry at birth. Within a few short years, *however,* they can speak in complete sentences.

Correlative conjunctions are pairs of coordinating conjunctions that place extra emphasis on the relationship between the parts of the coordinated construction: *both/and, neither/nor, not only/but also,* etc. (For uses of correlative conjunctions see 10a-3.)

> Three-year-olds *not only* speak in complete sentences, *but* they *also* possess vocabularies of hundreds or even thousands of words.

Subordinating conjunctions connect subordinate clauses to main clauses: *when, while, although, because, if, since, whereas,* etc. (For uses of subordinating conjunctions see 7e-1 and 19b-1.)

> *When* children reach the age of three, they can usually carry on complete conversations with their peers and with adults.

10 Interjections

An **interjection** is an emphatic word or phrase. When it stands alone, it is frequently followed by an exclamation point. As part of a sentence, the interjection is usually set off by commas.

> Oh, they're here. Never!

11 Expletives

An **expletive** is a word that fills a slot left in a sentence that has been rearranged. *It* and *there* function as expletives—as filler words without meanings of their own—in the following examples.

BASIC SENTENCE A sad fact is that too few Americans vote.

WITH EXPLETIVE It is a sad fact that too few Americans vote.

BASIC SENTENCE Millions of people are not voting.

WITH EXPLETIVE There are millions of people not voting.

Expletives are used with the verb *be* in sentences with a delayed subject. Sentences with expletives can usually be rearranged back to their basic form. Try to delete expletives from your writing to achieve a spare, concise style (see Chapter 17).

EXERCISE 1

Place a slash (/) between the subject and predicate parts of the following sentences. Identify the simple subject and simple predicate of each sentence with the abbreviations "ss" and "sp." Circle prepositions.

ss sp

Example: The physics (of) particle behavior / is important (for) designing safe and efficient processing plants.

1. Vega, the hapless hit man of *Pulp Fiction,* brought new life to John Travolta's career.
2. The actor earned his second Oscar nomination for playing Vega.
3. The first, of course, came in 1977 for his breakthrough in *Saturday Night Fever.*
4. Between the poles of these two pictures, Travolta had gone from household name to all-but-employable.
5. But now Travolta is once again at the top of his game.

7b Understanding basic sentence patterns

There are five basic sentence patterns in English, from which virtually all of the sentences you read in this and other books are built. Each of the five sentence patterns consists of a subject and predicate. Depending on the sentence's structure, the predicate may contain a **direct object**, an **indirect object,** or a (subject or object) **complement.** The basic pattern diagrams that follow include definitions of these key terms and concepts.

		Predicate
Pattern 1:	Subject	verb
	We	*look.*

Subject: a noun or noun-like word group that produces the main action of the sentence or is described by the sentence.

Predicate: a verb, and other words associated with it, that state the action undertaken by the subject or the condition in which the subject exists.

		Predicate	
Pattern 2:	Subject	verb (tr.)	direct object
	Stories	*excite*	*the imagination.*

Direct object: a noun, or group of words substituting for a noun, that receives the action of a transitive verb (tr.). A direct object answers the question *What or who is acted upon?*

		Predicate		
Pattern 3:	Subject	verb (tr.)	indirect object	direct object
	Stories	*offer*	*us*	*relief.*

Indirect object: a noun, or group of words substituting for a noun, that is indirectly affected by the action of a verb. Indirect objects typically follow transitive verbs such as *buy, bring, do, give, offer, teach, tell, play,* or *write.* The indirect object answers the question *To whom or for whom has the main action of this sentence occurred?*

EXERCISE 1

Prepositions are underscored here instead of circled.

1. Vega, the hapless hit man <u>of</u> *Pulp Fiction,* / brought new life <u>to</u> John Travolta's career. (ss: Vega; sp: brought)
2. The actor / earned his second Oscar nomination <u>for</u> playing Vega. (ss: actor; sp: earned)
3. The first, of course, / came <u>in</u> 1977 <u>for</u> his breakthrough <u>in</u> *Saturday Night Fever.* (ss: first; sp: came)
4. <u>Between</u> the poles <u>of</u> these two pictures, Travolta / had gone <u>from</u> household name <u>to</u> all-but-employable. (ss: Travolta; sp: had gone)
5. But now Travolta / is once again <u>at</u> the top <u>of</u> his game. (ss: Travolta; sp: is)

ADDITIONAL EXERCISE C

ACROSS THE CURRICULUM Make a photocopy of a brief passage from a textbook in one of your other courses. In order to practice identifying sentence parts and parts of speech, mark off the simple subjects and simple predicates according to the instructions for Exercise 1, and then, using abbreviations (n-noun, v-verb, adj-adjective, adv-adverb, pro-pronoun, prep-preposition, con-conjunction, and—if there are any—int-interjection), try to identify as many parts of speech as you can.

REFERENCES

HERRINGTON, ANNE J. "Grammar Recharted: Sentence Analysis for Writing." *Writing Exercises from "Exercise Exchange."* Vol. 2. Urbana: NCTE, 1984. 276–87. Using a simplified chart, students can become more adept at recognizing sentence patterns.

LUNSFORD, ANDREA. "Cognitive Development and the Basic Writer." *CE* 41 (1979): 38–48. With appropriate assignments, basic writing students can develop skills in sentence development.

STERNGLASS, MARILYN. "Composition Teacher as Reading Teacher." *CCC* 27 (1976): 378–82. Students who read analytically can develop an understanding of sentence structure.

EXERCISE 2

Individual responses

FOR DISCUSSION

After students have completed Exercise 2, ask for volunteers to have their paragraphs analyzed by the class. Reproduce sample paragraphs on the board or on an overhead projector, and ask the class to identify the sentence patterns within the paragraph. When there is disagreement over certain sentences, students should explain the reasons for their decisions. The ensuing discussion will reinforce students' understanding of the five basic sentence patterns.

		Predicate		
Pattern 4:	Subject	verb (tr.)	direct object	object complement
	They	*make*	*us*	*tense.*

OBJECT COMPLEMENT: an adjective or noun that completes the meaning of a direct object by renaming or describing it. Typically, object complements follow verbs such as *appoint, call, choose, consider, declare, elect, find, make, select,* or *show.*

		Predicate	
Pattern 5:	Subject	verb (linking)	subject complement
	We	*are*	*readers.*

SUBJECT COMPLEMENT: a noun or adjective that completes the meaning of a subject by renaming or by describing it. Subject complements follow linking verbs such as *appear, feel, seem, remain,* as well as all forms of *be.*

EXERCISE 2

Working with a topic of your choice, write a paragraph in which you use each of the five basic sentence patterns.

Example: The curtain finally rose. [Sentence Pattern 1] The set was lavish. [Sentence Pattern 5] The actors wore period costumes. [Sentence Pattern 2] The set design gave the audience a feast for the eyes. [Sentence Pattern 3] The critics declared it an absolute smash. [Sentence Pattern 4]

7c Expanding sentences with single-word modifiers

Principles of sentence expansion can be found at work in virtually any paragraph you read. The first technique for expanding sentences is to add modifiers—descriptive, modifying information. The nouns and verbs in the five basic sentence patterns can be modified by adjectives and adverbs.

1 Modifying nouns and verbs with adjectives and adverbs

VERB MODIFIED BY ADVERB I read *thoroughly.*

NOUN MODIFIED BY ADJECTIVE A novel will engage an *active* imagination.

2 Positioning modifiers

The position of an adverb can be shifted in a sentence from beginning to middle to end. Depending on its location, an adverb will change the meaning of a sentence or the rhythm. When placing an adverb, take care that it modifies the word you intend it to modify.

SHIFTED MEANING I am *only* moving my bed (that is, doing nothing more important than moving).

I am moving *only* my bed (that is, no other furniture).

SHIFTED RHYTHM *Sometimes,* stories can provide emotional relief.

Stories *sometimes* can provide emotional relief.

Stories can provide emotional relief *sometimes.*

A single-word adjective is often positioned directly before the noun it modifies, although writers make many variations on this pattern. When more than one noun in the sentence could be described by the adjective, take particular care to place the adjective closest to the noun it modifies. See Chapter 15 on editing to correct misplaced modifiers and 44b for the sequence of adjective modifiers in a typical English sentence.

A *good* story will excite a reader. [*Story* is the word modified.]

A story will excite a *good* reader. [*Reader* is the word modified.]

EXERCISE 3

Use single-word adjectives or adverbs to modify the nouns and verbs in the following sentences.

Example: A man walked down a street.
An *old* man walked *slowly* down a *tree-lined* street.

1. College tuition rises. [Sentence Pattern 1]
2. Students hold jobs. [Sentence Pattern 2]
3. The jobs give them wages. [Sentence Pattern 3]
4. Joblessness makes the students tense. [Sentence Pattern 4]
5. The wages are vital. [Sentence Pattern 5]

EXERCISE 4

Take the paragraph you wrote for Exercise 2 and modify its nouns and verbs as you have done in Exercise 3.

7d Modifying and expanding sentences with phrases

A **phrase** does not express a complete thought, nor can it stand alone as a sentence. Phrases consist of nouns and the words associated with them, or verb forms not functioning as verbs (called *verbals*) and the words associated with them. Phrases function in a sentence as modifiers and as objects, subjects, or complements. As such, they can be integrated into any of the five sentence patterns (see 7b) to add detail.

EXERCISE 3

1. College tuition rises sharply. [Sentence Pattern 1]
2. Most students hold part-time jobs. [Sentence Pattern 2]
3. The work-study jobs give them additional wages. [Sentence Pattern 3]
4. Joblessness always makes the students tense. [Sentence Pattern 4]
5. The combined wages are absolutely vital. [Sentence Pattern 5]

GROUP ACTIVITY

Exercise 4 adapts well to group work. Ask students to meet in groups of three or four and share responses. The group will then decide, for each sentence, which is the best response and offer reasons for their decision. Since a primary purpose for studying sentence structure is to expand the writer's ability to compose, sharing responses to this exercise and weighing the relative merits of the chosen modifiers can offer students some initial insight into style.

EXERCISE 4

Individual responses

LOOKING AHEAD

Many of the types of phrases covered in this section, when punctuated as if they were sentences, become sentence fragments. Common culprits are infinitive phrases, participles, and absolutes. Paying careful attention to their role as modifiers here may make it easier for students to understand their treatment in Chapter 12 (Sentence Fragments).

FOR DISCUSSION

To begin this section on a lighter note, you might ask students to think of humorous examples of misplaced phrases. You might begin with a few favorites of your own—many visitors to certain midwestern cities are treated to stories like the one about the babysitter who took literally the mother's order to "Throw the baby down the stairs a cookie." Students can either think up their own examples or use examples they've heard or read. Why not have some fun with the language while studying it?

ADDITIONAL EXERCISE D

In groups of three or four, take the following basic sentences and add modifiers and modifiers within modifiers, making sure to keep the sentence coherent. (The point at which one more modifier would make the sentence "topple" is the point at which to stop adding.)

1. Arturo sang.
2. Keisha taught Mary Ellen the dance.
3. The members welcomed the nonmembers.
4. Ben, Alicia, and Samantha were the stars.
5. The performers made their parents proud.

Adding prepositional phrases

A preposition links nouns and pronouns to other words in a sentence. (See 7a-8 for a list of commonly used prepositions.) Together with its noun, called an *object,* a preposition forms a **prepositional phrase,** which functions in a sentence as a modifier—such as an adjective or an adverb.

Adjective Stories can excite the imaginations *of young people.*

Adverb Paul reads *in the evening.*

Adding verbals: Infinitive phrases

A verbal is a verb form functioning not as a verb but instead as a noun, adjective, or adverb. An infinitive—the base form or dictionary form of a verb—often is preceded by the word *to.* Infinitives function as adjectives, adverbs, or nouns, but behave as verbs in that they can be modified with adverbs and can be followed with direct and indirect objects. Infinitives and the various words associated with them form **infinitive phrases.**

Noun subject *To read in the evening* is a great pleasure.

Noun object Some children start *to read at an early age.*

Adjective Stories offer us a chance *to escape dull routines.*

Adverb We read *to gain knowledge.*

Adding verbals: Gerund and participial phrases

When appearing without its helping verbs, the *-ing* form of the verb functions as a noun and is called a **gerund.** Without its helping verb, the present or past participle can function as an adjective. Like infinitives, both gerunds and participles form phrases by taking objects and modifiers. A noun or pronoun appearing before a gerund is often called the subject of the gerund; this pronoun or noun must be written in its possessive form. In the following sentences, the gerund phrase functions as the object of the preposition *of.*

Gerund We did not approve of *Paul's* reading all night. [The gerund phrase functions as the object of the preposition *of.* A noun in the possessive case is used before the gerund.]

Faulty We did not approve of *him* reading all night. [The pronoun before the gerund does not use the possessive case.]

Revised We did not approve of *his* reading all night.

Adding noun phrases

A **noun phrase** consists of a noun accompanied by all of its modifying words. A noun phrase can be quite lengthy, but it always functions as a single noun—as the subject of a sentence, as the object of a verb or preposition, or as a complement.

SUBJECT	*Even horror stories with their gruesome endings* can delight readers.
DIRECT OBJECT	A tale of horror will affect *anyone who is at all suggestible.*
COMPLEMENT	Paul is *someone who likes to read horror stories.* [The phrase is a subject complement.]

5 Adding absolute phrases

Unlike other phrases, **absolute phrases** consist of both a subject and a predicate—although an incomplete predicate. Absolute phrases modify entire sentences, not individual words. When you use an absolute phrase, set it off from your sentence with a comma or pair of commas (see Chapter 25). An absolute phrase is formed by deleting the linking verb *be* from a sentence.

SENTENCE	His hands were weak with exhaustion.
ABSOLUTE PHRASE	his hands weak with exhaustion
NEW SENTENCE	His hands weak with exhaustion, Paul lifted the book off its shelf. [The phrase modifies the basic sentence, *Paul lifted. . . .*]

An absolute phrase may also be formed by changing the main verb of a sentence to its *-ing* form, without using an auxiliary.

SENTENCE	His hands trembled with exhaustion.
ABSOLUTE PHRASE	his hands trembling with exhaustion
NEW SENTENCE	His hands trembling with exhaustion, Paul lifted the book off its shelf.

6 Adding appositive phrases

Appositive phrases rename nouns. The word *appositive* describes the positioning of the phrase *in apposition to,* or beside, the noun. Appositives are actually "clipped" sentences—the predicate part (minus the verb) of Sentence Pattern 5.

		Predicate	
Pattern 5:	Subject	verb (linking)	subject complement
	Paul	*is*	*an old college friend.*

APPOSITIVE PHRASE	an old college friend
NEW SENTENCE	Paul, an old college friend, is an avid reader.

EXERCISE 5

In the sentences that follow, circle all single-word modifiers and underline all modifying phrases.

ESL CUE

Most ESL students will never have been introduced to absolutes, will find them most puzzling, and will tend to equate them with comma splice problems, especially when the central verb is a passive form so it looks more complete than it is: "Their work completed, they went home." Marcella Frank's *Modern English, Part II* has a clear explanation of how and when to use absolutes.

EXERCISE 5

1. *On a clear, moonless night,* he says, the *brightest* objects *in the sky* are the planets *nearest Earth.* The prepositional phrase *On a clear, moonless night* functions as an adverb modifying *are.* (Within this phrase *clear* and *moonless* are adjectives and modify the noun *night.*)
   Brightest is an adjective and modifies the noun *objects.*
   The prepositional phrase *in the sky* functions as an adjective by modifying the noun *objects.*
   The phrase *nearest Earth* functions as an adjective by modifying the noun *planets.*
2. *Looking more closely,* we can see *that the stars near Earth appear to be fixed,* but they are not.
   The participial phrase *looking more closely* functions as an adjective modifying *we.* (Within this phrase *more closely* functions as an adverb modifying the verbal *looking.*)
   The noun clause *that the stars near Earth appear to be fixed* functions as direct object of the verb *see.* (Within this phrase *near Earth* functions as an adjective modifying the noun *stars,* and the infinitive phrase *to be fixed* functions as a subject complement to *stars.*)
3. *To measure the distance of a star from Earth,* scientists calculate the number *of years* it takes the star's light *to reach us.*
   The infinitive phrase *To measure the distance of a star from Earth* functions as an adverb modifying the verb *calculate.* (Within this phrase *of a star* functions as an adjective modifying the noun *distance.*)
   The prepositional phrase *of years* functions as an adjective by modifying the noun *numbers.*
   The infinitive phrase *to reach us* functions as an adverb modifying *takes.*
4. *His calculations having proved it,* Sir William Herschel confirmed *that our galaxy (the Milky Way) forms a spiral.*
   The absolute phrase *His calculations having proved it* modifies the entire sentence.
   The noun clause *that our galaxy (the Milky Way) forms a spiral* functions as the direct object of the verb *confirmed.* (Within this

Example: (Recently,) Stephen W. Hawking published a (popularized) version of his ideas about space and time.

- *Recently* is an adverb and modifies the verb *published.*
- *Popularized* is an adjective and modifies the noun *version.*
- Two prepositional phrases—*of his ideas about space and time*—function as an adjective by modifying the noun *version.*
- The second prepositional phrase, *about space and time,* functions as an adjective by modifying the object of the preceding phrase, *ideas.*

1. On a clear, moonless night, he says, the brightest objects in the sky are the planets nearest Earth.
2. Looking more closely, we can see that the stars near Earth appear to be fixed, but they are not.
3. To measure the distance of a star from Earth, scientists calculate the number of years it takes the star's light to reach us.
4. His calculations having proved it, Sir William Herschel confirmed that our galaxy (the Milky Way) forms a spiral.
5. We now know that our galaxy is only one of some hundred thousand million galaxies.
6. Each of those hundred thousand million galaxies contains a hundred thousand million stars.

7e Modifying and expanding sentences with dependent clauses

A **clause** is any grouping of words that has both a subject and a predicate. There are two types of clauses. An **independent** (or **main**) **clause** can stand alone as a sentence. Any sentence fitting one of the five structural patterns reviewed in 7b is an independent clause. A **dependent** (or **subordinate**) **clause** cannot stand alone as a sentence because it is usually introduced either with a subordinating conjunction (e.g., *while*) or with a relative pronoun (e.g., *who*). There are four types of dependent clauses: adverb, adjective, noun, and elliptical clauses.

Adding dependent adverb clauses

Dependent **adverb clauses** that modify verbs, adjectives, and other adverbs begin with subordinating conjunctions and answer the question *when, how, where, how often, to what extent,* or *to what degree.* Subordinating conjunctions establish a distinct logical relationship between the clauses joined.

Placed at the head of a clause, a subordinating conjunction makes one sentence grammatically dependent on another. When the subordinating conjunction *if,* for example, is placed at the head of a sentence, it renders that sentence grammatically dependent, unable to stand alone.

Subordinating Conjunctions and the Logical Relationships They Establish

To show condition: *if, even if, unless,* and *provided that*
To show contrast: *though, although, even though,* and *as if*
To show cause: *because* and *since*
To show time: *when, whenever, while, as, before, after, since, once,* and *until*
To show place: *where* and *wherever*
To show purpose: *so that, in order that,* and *that*

See 7a-9 for a discussion of conjunctions.

MAIN CLAUSE PLUS SUBORDINATING CONJUNCTION	*if* + Food is repeatedly frozen and thawed.
DEPENDENT CLAUSE	if food is repeatedly frozen and thawed

Although it consists of a subject and predicate, this last grouping of words is no longer a sentence. To make sense, this clause must be set in a dependent relationship with an independent clause.

If food is repeatedly frozen and thawed, it will spoil.

For guidance on punctuating sentences with dependent clauses, see 25a-1.

2 Adding dependent adjective clauses

Like adjectives, **adjective clauses** modify nouns. The clauses usually begin with the relative pronoun *which, that, who, whom,* or *whose.* The following examples show an adjective clause modifying the subject of a sentence.

People *who lived through the Depression of the 1930s* remember it well.

A country *that had prospered in the first two decades of the century* now saw massive unemployment and hardship.

For a discussion of when to use which relative pronoun, see 8f.

3 Adding dependent noun clauses

Noun clauses function exactly as single-word nouns do in a sentence: as subjects, objects, complements, and appositives. Noun clauses are introduced with the pronoun *which, whichever, that, who, whoever, whom, whomever,* or *whose* or with the word *how, when, why, where, whether,* or *whatever.*

phrase the phrase *the Milky Way* functions as an appositive to the noun *galaxy.*)

5. We *now* know that *our galaxy is only one of some hundred thousand million galaxies.*
   Now is an adverb and modifies the verb *know.*
   The noun clause *that our galaxy is only one of some hundred thousand million galaxies* functions as the direct object of the verb *know.* (Within this phrase the prepositional phrase *of some hundred thousand million galaxies* functions as an adverb by modifying the adjective *one,* and *some hundred thousand million* functions as an adjective by modifying the noun *galaxies.*)
6. Each *of those hundred thousand million galaxies* contains *a hundred thousand million* stars.
   The prepositional phrase *of those hundred thousand million galaxies* functions as an adjective by modifying the pronoun *each.* (Within this phrase *hundred thousand million* functions as an adjective by modifying the noun *galaxies.*)
   A hundred thousand million functions as an adjective by modifying the noun *stars.*

LOOKING AHEAD

Just as phrases and subordinate clauses sometimes transform themselves into fragments, sentences beginning with conjunctive adverbs sometimes latch onto adjoining sentences to become comma splices or fused sentences. As with phrases and subordinate clauses, paying careful attention to dependent clauses as modifiers here may make it easier for students to understand their treatment in Chapter 13 (Comma Splices and Fused Sentences).

LOOKING AHEAD

Dependent clauses, like some of the phrases in 7d, sometimes end up as sentence fragments. As with phrases, paying careful attention to dependent clauses as modifiers here may make it easier for students to understand their treatment in Chapter 12 (Sentence Fragments).

REFERENCES

CROWHURST, MARION. "Sentence Combining: Maintaining Realistic Expectations." *CCC* 34 (1983): 62–72. The claims made by advocates of sentence combining need to be examined with scrutiny.

DAIKER, DONALD, ANDREW KEREK, and MAX MORENBERG. "Sentence Combining and Syntactic Maturity in Freshman English." *CCC* 29 (1978): 36–41. A report on the results of a successful experiment in sentence combining.

———. *Sentence Combining: A Rhetorical Perspective.* Carbondale: Southern Illinois UP, 1985. A collection of essays on sentence combining techniques and classroom use.

O'HARE, FRANK. *Sentence-Combining: Improving Student Writing without Formal Grammar Instruction.* Urbana: NCTE, 1973. Through sentence combining, students can develop mature style even without grammar instruction.

SOLOMON, MARTHA. "Teaching the Nominative Absolute." *CCC* 26 (1975): 356–61. A practical discussion of teaching students to recognize and use the nominative absolute.

STRONG, WILLIAM. "Creative Approaches to Sentence Combining." Urbana: ERIC Clearinghouse on Reading and Communication Skills, 1986. ERIC ED 274 985. A discussion of the history of sentence combining, with suggestions for classroom use.

EXERCISE 6

1. Job seekers tend to deemphasize interpersonal skills even though this is a poor strategy in a business climate that seeks those who can communicate effectively and work as team members.
2. Since even in a high-tech world people still have to eat, many people are studying the culinary arts.
3. Because parents are entering the work force in increasing numbers, the need for child-care workers and preschool workers expands.
4. If you should find a job that fulfills you personally, that love will eventually help your career in terms of dollars and cents.
5. Since a shortage of labor in entry-level construction jobs seems likely in the near future, the construction industry is offering training and making outreach efforts.

SUBJECT — *That ozone holes have already caused blindness and skin cancer in grazing animals* suggests the need for immediate legislative action.

OBJECT — Apparently, few inhabitants of populous northern cities are aware of *how the depletion of ozone in the upper atmosphere can harm living organisms—humans included.*

COMPLEMENT — The looming danger that ozone depletion poses is *why researchers have sounded an alarm.*

4 Working with elliptical clauses

An **elliptical clause** has an omitted word or words, but the sense of the clause remains clear. Often, the words omitted are relative pronouns and the logically parallel second parts of comparisons. An elliptical clause functions exactly as a clause would, were all its words restored. In the following example, the words in parentheses are usually omitted.

> English speakers, with their verb tenses and numerous words for divisions of years, weeks, and days, have a far different concept of time than the Hopis do (have a concept of time).

EXERCISE 6

Combine each of the sentence pairs that follow by using a subordinating conjunction.

Example: Competition in the job market is intense. Job seekers need to approach their task strategically.

Because competition in the job market is intense, job seekers need to approach their task strategically.

1. Job seekers tend to deemphasize interpersonal skills. This is a poor strategy in a business climate that seeks those who can communicate effectively and work as team members.
2. Even in a high-tech world, people still have to eat. Many people are studying the culinary arts.
3. Parents are entering the work force in increasing numbers. The need for child-care workers and preschool workers expands.
4. You should find a job that fulfills you personally. That love will eventually help your career in terms of dollars and cents.
5. A shortage of labor in entry-level construction jobs seems likely in the near future. The construction industry is offering training and making outreach efforts.

7f Classifying sentences

1 Functional definitions

Sentences are classified by structure and by function. There are four functional types: statements, questions, exclamations, and commands. Statements, called **declarative** sentences, are by far the most common of the four types and make direct assertions about a subject. A question, or **interrogative** sentence, is formed either by inverting a sentence's usual word order (*She did sing./Did she sing?*) or by preceding the sentence with a word such as *who, whom, which, when, where, why,* or *how.* An exclamation, or **exclamatory** sentence, used rarely in academic writing, serves as a direct expression of a speaker's or writer's strong emotion. Commands, or **imperative** sentences, are an expression of an order or urgent wish addressed to a second person.

DECLARATIVE	The driver turned on the ignition.
INTERROGATIVE	Was the engine flooded?
EXCLAMATORY	What an awful fire! How terrible!
IMPERATIVE	Get back! Don't you go near that!

2 Structural definitions

As you expand sentences by adding phrase- and clause-length modifiers, or by combining two or more sentences, you change the structural relationships within sentences. There are four structural classes of sentences in English: simple, compound, complex, and compound-complex. Good stylistic sense dictates that you vary sentence types and lengths. See the discussion in Chapter 20.

Each of the five basic sentence patterns discussed in 7b qualifies as a **simple sentence:** each has a single subject and a single predicate. The designation "simple" refers to a sentence's structure, not its content. A simple sentence, with all its modifying words and phrases, can be long.

> Vampirism figures prominently in two major works of literary criticism from the first half of this century—Mario Praz's *The Romantic Agony* and D. H. Lawrence's *Studies in Classical American Literature.* [This sentence consists of one subject, *vampirism,* and one simple predicate, *figures.*]

Then again, a simple sentence can be relatively brief.

> Vampirism figures prominently in two major works of literary criticism.

Compound sentences have two subjects and two predicates. They are created when two independent clauses are joined with a coordinating or correlative conjunction or with a conjunctive adverb. Coordinating conjunctions express specific logical relations between the elements they join. *Or* and *nor* suggest choice, one positive and the other negative. *And* joins elements by addition. *But* and *yet* join elements by establishing a contrast. *For* and *so* are the only coordinating conjunctions that must join entire sentences. The others may join sentence elements and entire sentences. *For* suggests a cause of an occurrence. *So* suggests a result of some action. Correlative conjunctions such as *either/or* and conjunctive adverbs such as *however* can also be used to create compound sentences. For details on how coordination can be used to create sentence emphasis, see 19a.

TEACHING IDEAS

Exercise 6 offers students the opportunity to engage in *sentence combining,* a method that some scholars consider more powerful than traditional grammatical approaches in teaching sentence structure. Among the references on page 204 you'll find a number of useful works on sentence combining. If you aren't familiar with the method, you may want to brush up on it and devise a few sentence combining exercises for your own students. If you do this, try to start with discrete sentences (as in Exercise 6) and only after students have completed some of these exercises move on to continuous discourse (as in Exercise 7).

ADDITIONAL EXERCISE E

Compose a paragraph in which you use at least one of each functional type of sentence (declarative, interrogative, exclamatory, imperative). Identify each sentence type with an abbreviation (dec-declarative, int-interrogative, exc-exclamatory, imp-imperative). [NOTE: This exercise is an ideal candidate for a group activity. Students enjoy composing paragraphs collaboratively, and their discussion as they compose will help reinforce their understanding of the sentence types.]

ESL EXERCISE

Choose a grammatical interference problem between your first language and English. "Grammatical interference" means that the mental habit involved in the grammatical form in the first language causes mistakes or confusion in the second language, English. In one well-organized paragraph, explain the grammatical interference problem, providing numerous examples to make it clear to your audience, which is teachers who do not speak your language and who do not understand why you make so many mistakes.

The order of your paragraph should be as follows: a clear topic sentence at the beginning expressing the problem and the reason for the problem; at least two supporting examples with explanations of each; and a concluding sentence or two clearly aimed at the teacher who is your audience.

Remember that your strategy is to make your mistakes part of a general pattern, not a personal or private problem that other speakers of your language do not share.

FOR DISCUSSION

A discussion of the various ways in which sentences can be combined may make students more aware of style. Collect students' responses to this exercise, and (with permission, of course) distribute several successful versions. Ask students to discuss not only why these versions represent good writing, but also the effects of the different stylistic choices the students made. (You could also make this a small group activity along the lines of the group activity outlined for Exercise 4.)

EXERCISE 7

1. A common thread connects Fugard's work: the respect for humanity, the search for dignity, and the struggle to cultivate trust and hope in a demeaning world.
2. Fugard's tenacious, weathered looks reflect his struggles.
3. In this computer age, Fugard uses a tortoise-shell Parker pen to write his plays, which include *A Lesson from Aloes, The Road to Mecca, "Master Harold" . . . and the Boys,* and *My Children, My Africa,* all successfully produced in America.
4. For Fugard, there are signs that South Africa is changing: the freeing of Nelson Mandela, the lifting of the ban on the African National Congress, and the government's willingness to negotiate.
5. During the mid-1960s, Fugard continued writing and staged classic plays with the Serpent players, the country's first nonwhite theater troupe.

ADDITIONAL EXERCISE F

Expand the paragraph you composed for Additional Exercise E to include at least one example of each structural type of sentence (simple, compound, complex, compound-complex). You may use existing sentences in the paragraph to represent a structural type. Identify each sentence type with an abbreviation (s-simple, cd-compound, cx-complex, cd-cx-compound-complex). [NOTE: This exercise would also work well as a group activity.]

As the Undead, the vampire casts no shadow and has no reflection, but he (or she) manifests prominent canine teeth. [The conjunction *but* joins two independent clauses.]

Complex sentences consist of an independent clause and one or more dependent clauses. As shown in 7e, the four kinds of dependent clauses can be introduced with subordinating conjunctions (see 7a-9) or relative pronouns (see 7a-7). For details on how complex sentences help to create sentence emphasis, see 19b.

Stoker's *Dracula* is dignified and still *until* he explodes into ravenous action. [The subordinating conjunction *until* signals a dependent adverb clause.]

The vampire myth has been attributed to a renegade sect of Christians *who* claimed to have solved the mystery of Christ's resurrection. [The relative pronoun *who* signals a dependent clause that modifies *Christians.*]

Compound-complex sentences consist of at least two independent clauses and one subordinate, dependent clause.

Ann Rice's vampires seem to regard vampirism amorally, *and* whatever scruples they feel about their predatory nature gradually subside *as* they become increasingly inhuman. [The coordinating conjunction *and* signals a compound sentence, and the subordinating conjunction *as* signals a dependent clause in a complex sentence.]

EXERCISE 7

Use the clauses and phrases provided to build up the core sentence. Add conjunctions when they are necessary to the logic of your expanded sentence.

Example: Athol Fugard is a South African playwright. (a) plays confront difficulties (b) interracial relations (c) his troubled country

Athol Fugard is a South African playwright whose plays confront the difficulties of interracial relations in his troubled country.

1. A common thread connects Fugard's work. (a) respect for humanity (b) search for human dignity (c) struggle to cultivate trust and hope in a demeaning world.
2. Fugard's looks reflect his struggles. (a) tenacious (b) weathered
3. Fugard handwrites his plays. (a) in this computer age (b) with a tortoise-shell Parker pen (c) which include *A Lesson from Aloes, The Road to Mecca, "Master Harold" . . . and the Boys,* and *My Children, My Africa,* all successfully produced in America
4. South Africa is changing. (a) for Fugard there are signs (b) the freeing of Nelson Mandela (c) the lifting of the ban on the African National Congress (d) the government's willingness to negotiate
5. Fugard continued writing. (a) during the mid-1960s (b) he staged classic plays with the Serpent players (c) the country's first nonwhite theater troupe

CHAPTER 8

Case in Nouns and Pronouns

The term **case** refers to a noun or pronoun's change in form, depending on its function in a sentence. Nouns do not change their form when their function changes from subject to object. Especially when revising, you may change a pronoun's function—say, from object to subject. By understanding how a pronoun's function changes, you will be prepared to make a corresponding change to the pronoun's form. There are eight classes of pronouns. Most troublesome are the **personal pronouns,** which refer to people and things, and these will be the focus of discussion.

8a Using pronouns in the subjective case

1 Use the subjective case when a pronoun functions as a subject, as a subject complement, or as an appositive that renames a subject.

She speaks forcefully. The speaker is *she.*
The executive officers—and only *they*—can meet here.

SUBJECT OF AN INDEPENDENT CLAUSE	In September 1908, Orville Wright began demonstration flights of the Wright Brothers' "Signal Corps Flyer" at Fort Meyer, Virginia; *he* invited a young Signal Corps officer, Lieutenant Thomas Selfridge, to be a passenger.
SUBJECT OF A DEPENDENT CLAUSE	When *they* attempted a fourth circuit of the parade grounds, the Flyer's right propeller hit a bracing wire and cracked.
SUBJECT COMPLEMENT	The Flyer slammed into the ground, pinning Selfridge and Wright beneath the wreckage; so severely injured were *they* that medics could not revive the unconscious Selfridge. Orville's injuries kept him hospitalized for seven weeks.
APPOSITIVE THAT RENAMES A SUBJECT	Thomas Selfridge—*he* alone—bears the grim distinction of being the first person to be killed in the crash of a powered airplane.

Pronouns Used as Subjects

	Singular	*Plural*
1st person	I	we
2nd person	you	you
3rd person	he, she, it	they

KEY FEATURES

Case is approached in this chapter from the perspective of clarity in written discourse rather than rules of grammar. Case of nouns and pronouns is important to the *meaning* of the sentence; it is for this reason that students should study case. Because in most instances student writers have little problem with case, the chapter opens with a focus on the most troublesome pronouns, i.e., personal pronouns. Nonstandard usage is acknowledged, particularly with respect to the stuffy-sounding "It is I," but the chapter bows to standard usage (as it should) where formal academic discourse is concerned, offering alternatives to the reversed linking verb construction. The various situations in which a choice must be made are presented in a straightforward, traditional manner, and wherever it is possible to explain choices through meaning rather than rules, that is the approach taken. Exercises provide ample practice for students who need to master the concept of case.

LOOKING AHEAD

If you're already aware of students who have difficulty signaling the possessive noun by apostrophe *s,* you may want to refer them now to 27a.

FOR DISCUSSION

Since most students have problems with only a few of these common errors, you might want to initiate a class discussion of errors most relevant to your students. Ask students to identify from the Spotlight on Common Errors examples of usage familiar to them and to make their own list of common errors. Students can then discuss the function of the pronouns in the examples, thereby reinforcing their understanding of case forms. (In large classes, this activity might begin with small groups. The groups will identify their common errors, and then the class as a whole will discuss the list of errors compiled from each group's report.)

Spotlight on Common Errors—CASE FORMS

These are the errors most commonly associated with a pronoun's case. For full explanations and suggested revisions, follow the cross-references to chapter sections.

CASE FORM ERRORS occur when writers misunderstand a pronoun's function in a sentence as a subject, object, or indicator of possession. These common situations lead to errors.

- **When a noun or an indefinite pronoun (such as *one, anyone, somebody*) shows possession, use an apostrophe (see 27a–b).**

FAULTY	REVISED
This is Alberts signature.	This is Albert**'s** signature.
Rondas team is impressive.	Ronda**'s** team is impressive.
The families decision was final.	The family**'s** decision was final.
Somebodies book is here.	Somebody**'s** book is here.
This is nobodies business.	This is nobody**'s** business.

- **A personal pronoun that shows possession (such as *his, her, mine, ours*) uses NO apostrophe (see 8c-1 and 27a-2).**

FAULTY	REVISED
This coat is her's.	This coat is her**s.** (This is her coat.)
Give the cat it's food.	Give the cat it**s** food.
These coats are their's.	These coats are their**s.** (These are their coats.)
Your's are the first hands to touch this.	Your**s** are the first hands to touch this. (Your hands are the first hands to touch this.)

- **After a form of the verb *be* (*is, are, was, were*), use a pronoun's subjective form (*I, you, he, she, we, they*) or its possessive form (*mine, yours, his, hers, theirs, ours*) with *no* apostrophe (see 8a-2, 8c-1).**

FAULTY	REVISED
This is her. This is him.	This is **she.** This is **he.**
Is that her? It is me.	Is that **she?** It is **I.**
This is our's. That is her's.	This is **ours.** That is **hers.**

- **When a personal pronoun (such as *I, me, you, he, she, it*) follows the word *and,* choose the pronoun's form as if the pronoun were alone in the sentence (see 8d and 8b-1).**

FAULTY	REVISED
Sally and me went to the movies.	Sally and **I** went to the movies. [TEST: I went to the movies alone.]
She and me went. Her and me went.	She and **I** went. [TEST: She went. I went.]
Tom went with Sally and I.	Tom went with Sally and **me.** [TEST: Tom went with me.]
It's a secret between you and I.	It's a secret between you and **me.** [TEST: It's a secret between me and a friend.]
That's between he and Sally.	That's between **him** and Sally. [TEST: That's between him and a friend.]

- **Use *its* to show possession; use *it's* ONLY for a contraction of *it is* (see 27a-2).**

FAULTY	REVISED
A dog hates it's fleas.	A dog hates **its** fleas.
Its raining.	**It's** raining. (It is raining.)

- **For a contraction with the verb *be* (*is, are*), use an apostrophe (see 27a-2).**

FAULTY	REVISED
Its a difficult position.	It**'s** a difficult position. (It is a difficult position.)
Their coming home.	They**'re** coming home. (They are coming home.)
There coming home.	They**'re** coming home. (They are coming home.)
Shes home.	She**'s** home. (She is home.)
Your home.	You**'re** home. (You are home.)
Whos there?	Who**'s** there? (Who is there?)

ESL CUE

Vietnamese students might have major problems with pronouns, commonly confusing "he" and "she," which sound almost identical to their ears. Part of the problem is that pronouns of person (*he, she, we, they, you*) are mainly reserved for "rude" street slang and are replaced in polite Vietnamese with special nouns to identify personal relationships precisely.

Speakers of Spanish and other gender-based languages will tend to use "he" or "she" where English speakers would say "it."

Because in many languages the verb form differs according to subject, ESL students might insert unnecessary pronouns equal to the sentence subject, especially when a lengthy series of modifiers separates subject from verb:

"The room that they had just finished remodeling ~~it~~ was lovely."

REFERENCE

Shaughnessy, Mina P. *Errors and Expectations: A Guide for the Teacher of Basic Writing.* New York: Oxford UP, 1977. Chapter 4. Some students have difficulty with plural and possessive nouns regardless of their use of the forms in speech.

TEACHING IDEAS

MULTICULTURAL DIFFERENCES This handbook stresses the importance of writers' choices with regard to style and meaning. The first of those choices with respect to pronoun use is whether to use standard English. This issue is particularly relevant to speakers of certain dialects, especially black English vernacular, where the apostrophe *s* possessive is not used. If appropriate for your classroom, you might want to call attention to some of the differences between standard edited English and other dialects, as well as the difference between formal academic prose and what is known as "imaginative literature." A case in point is Alice Walker, whose frequently anthologized essay "In Search of Our Mothers' Gardens" is written in standard edited English, but whose highly respected novel *The Color Purple* is written primarily in black English vernacular, complete with apostrophe-*s*-less

2 Use the subjective case for pronouns with the linking verb *be.*

The speaker is *she.* These are *they.* It is *I.*

The linking verb *be* in a sentence serves as a grammatical "equals" sign (see 11d); it links the subject of the sentence to a completing or "complement" word that is made identical to the subject. When pronouns are involved in this equation, they too are made identical to the subject and are also used in the subjective form.

Clinton *was* President. It was *he,* the President, who spoke.

The use of subjective pronoun forms is quite clear in sentences with normal word order (subject + *be* + complement), but writers need to remember that subjective forms are used in the same equation when sentence order is reversed.

In nonstandard or informal usage it is fairly common to hear a linking-verb construction using an objective form: as in "It's me" or "This is her." But in academic English these constructions should be revised using a subjective pronoun that maintains sentence logic and consistency: "It's I" and "This is she."

Informal or nonstandard It isn't *me* in the White House; the decision makers are never *us* ordinary folks.

Revised It isn't *I* in the White House; the decision makers are never *we* ordinary folks. [These linking-verb constructions require the same subjective form they would have required in a sentence with normal word order.]

To some writers, the word order in this revised sentence sounds stilted. If this is your view, the best remedy is to reorder the sentence in question.

Reordered *I* am not in the White House; *we* ordinary folks are never the decision makers. [Use normal order and subjective-case pronouns.]

The decision makers don't consult *us.* [Use normal word order and an objective-case pronoun.]

8b Using pronouns in the objective case

1 Use the objective forms for pronouns functioning as objects.

The governor handed *her* the report. The job appealed to *me.* We enjoyed taking *them* to dinner.

Pronouns functioning as the object of a preposition, as the object or indirect object of a verb, or as the object of a verbal take the objective form.

Pronouns Used as Objects

	Singular	*Plural*
1st person	me	us
2nd person	you	you
3rd person	him, her, it	them

Object or indirect object of verb (see 7b)

President Clinton used the word "funk" to describe his perception of the mood of 1990s America; immediately a reporter asked *him* what he meant. [*Him* is the indirect object of *asked.*]

Object of preposition (see 7d-1)

Hastening to reverse the impression that he perceived America as plunging into a downward spiral, Clinton invoked the terms "malaise" and "funk," insisting that there was a world of difference between *them.* [*Them* is the object of the preposition *between.*]

Appositive that renames the object (see 7d-6)

Unfortunately, the President's attempt to explain this distinction, even with the coaching of his advisors, muddied the waters even more; it became apparent to both parties—*him and the reporters*—that the verbal mistake would become news. [The appositive phrase *him and the reporters* renames and clarifies *both parties,* which is the object of the preposition *to.* The pronoun in the appositive must also be in the objective case: *him.*]

Object of verbal (see 7a-4)

One reporter, pressing *him* to define his terms, had succeeded only in revealing Clinton's Humpty-Dumpty-like eagerness to make words mean whatever he happened to want them to mean. [The participial phrase beginning with *pressing* modifies the noun *reporter. Him* is the object of the present participle—or verbal—*pressing.*]

2 Use the objective form for pronouns functioning as the subject of an infinitive.

Study enabled *us* to reach the goal.

When a pronoun appears between a verb and an infinitive, the pronoun takes the objective form. In this position, the pronoun is called the subject of the infinitive.

possessives. The relative demands of the two forms of prose, and the reasons for acknowledging the place of standard and nonstandard English, could provoke a meaningful discussion.

GROUP ACTIVITY

Ask students to form groups of three or four and compose a paragraph in which they use pronouns serving the following functions:

object of verb
indirect object of verb
object of preposition
appositive that renames object
object of verbal
subject of infinitive

Then ask groups to exchange paragraphs. The second task of each group will be to identify and explain the function of each of the objective case pronouns in the other group's paragraph.

TEACHING IDEAS

This advice is sure to confuse weaker writers: Why should the *objective case* be used for a pronoun that's a *subject?* Of course, it's a good question. If students think of the pronoun as doing double duty as the subject of the infinitive phrase but as the object of the verb in the main clause, then they can justify using the objective case.

ESL CUE

Expect confusion about noun-noun formations like "table top" and "car engine" as opposed to "table's top" and "car's engine." The students may have learned the rule that people and animals appear in the possessive form ("John's car"; "her dog's bone") but that inanimate objects take the "of" formation ("the center of the room"; "top of the desk"). They might ask why we can say "desk top" but not "room center."

WITH INFINITIVE Babe Ruth's 60 home runs in 1927 helped *him* to reach a level of stardom unmatched by other athletes of his era. [The objective-form pronoun appears between the verb *helped* and the infinitive *to reach.*]

Babe Ruth's home runs helped *him* reach stardom. [The subject of the infinitive *reach* uses the objective form, *him.*]

8c Using nouns and pronouns in the possessive case

Use a possessive noun or pronoun before a noun to indicate ownership of that noun (or noun substitute).

Eleanor Roosevelt gave the Civil Works Administration *her* enthusiastic support for hiring 100,000 women by the end of 1933.

ESL NOTE Many English nouns are made possessive either with the possessive case form (*a woman's voice*) or with the noun as object of the preposition *of* (*voice of a woman*). With some inanimate nouns the prepositional form is standard and the possessive case form is seldom used (NOT *a house's color* BUT *color of a house*). See 42c-1.

Possessive Forms of Pronouns

	Singular	*Plural*
1st person	my, mine	our, ours
2nd person	your, yours	your, yours
3rd person	his, her, hers, its	their, theirs

1 Certain possessive pronouns are used as subjects or subject complements to indicate possession.

Yours are the first hands to touch this. These are *theirs.*

The possessive pronouns *mine, ours, yours, his, hers, theirs* are used in place of a noun as subjects or subject complements.

Ours is a country of opportunity for both men and women, Eleanor Roosevelt argued. This opportunity is *ours.* (*mine, yours, his, hers, theirs*)

2 Use a possessive noun or pronoun before a gerund to indicate possession.

The group argued for *her* getting the new position.

When appearing before a gerund, an *-ing* word that functions as a noun, a pronoun should use the possessive form.

GERUND *Her* lobbying helped to legitimize the role of women in government. [The pronoun before the gerund specifies whose *lobbying*.]

Problems with pronouns before gerunds occur when the *-ing* word is confused with a participle, which has the same *-ing* form but functions as an adjective. A participle is often preceded by an objective pronoun.

OBJECT PLUS PARTICIPLE After he had used the word "funk" to describe America's mood, President Clinton quickly tried to do damage control. One account describes *him* circling the room, "schmoozing with various reporters," trying to extricate himself from his linguistic gaffe. [*Him,* a direct object of *describes,* is modified by the participle *circling,* which functions as an adjective.]

In a similar construction, *circling the room . . .* can be preceded by the possessive *his.*

POSSESSIVE WITH GERUND One account describes *his circling the room* in an attempt to do damage control as the quick, instinctive move of a professional politician.

The focus in this last sentence is no longer on *him* (on Clinton) but on *his circling*—a difference in meaning. Since gerunds and participles both have distinctive uses in sentences, be sure to choose the correct pronoun form to help convey your meaning. Confusion between an *-ing* word's function—as a gerund or as a participle—can lead to errors.

FAULTY Hard work resulted in *them* getting government jobs. [*Getting* is mistakenly treated as a participle and is incorrectly preceded by an objective pronoun.]

REVISED Hard work resulted in *their* getting government jobs. [*Their* indicates possession of the gerund *getting . . . jobs.*]

EXERCISE 1

Based on your analysis of each of the following sentences, fill in the blanks with an appropriate subjective, objective, or possessive pronoun: *I/we, you, he/she/it/they; me/us, you, him/her/it/them; my/mine/our/ours, your/yours, his/her/hers/its/their/theirs.*

Example: ____________ changing costumes, mid-performance, amused the audience.

Changing costumes is a gerund phrase and takes a possessive pronoun. *His* (or *her*) changing costumes, mid-performance, amused the audience.

1. Delegates to the convention watched ____________ changing positions on important issues and deserted the candidacy.
2. Delegates wanted ____________ to remain steadier under challenges from contenders.

LOOKING BACK

The use of the possessive before a gerund is often confusing to students—even experienced writers sometimes find it one of the more difficult conventions of English to follow. It might be worthwhile to spend some time discussing the difference between a gerund and a participle, referring students to coverage of these forms in 7a-4.

ESL CUE

"Whose" is a difficult form for speakers of romance languages, who often say instead "who his." Reminding Spanish speakers that "whose" corresponds to *"de quién"* makes it easier for them to remember to use "whose." However, the form is a trouble spot for speakers of many languages.

ESL CUE

Similar sounds promote confusion: "who's/whose," "he's/his."

ESL students may confuse the object form after a verb of perception with the possessive form needed to accompany a gerund object.

"I saw him playing the guitar."
versus
"She enjoys his playing the guitar."
but not
"She enjoyed him playing the guitar."

EXERCISE 1

1. her/his (if meaning is focused on "positions") OR her/him (if meaning is focused on the person who was changing)
2. her/him
3. they
4. them
5. Ours

GROUP ACTIVITY

Students often listen to their peers more readily than to their teachers. With this in mind, form groups with at least one skilled student in each group to discuss responses to these exercises. As students defend their choices, the skilled students will be able to "teach" the less skilled, and will learn how to communicate their knowledge.

EXERCISE 2

1. they
2. she/he
3. I/you/we/they
4. her/his/their/our/my
5. he

ADDITIONAL EXERCISE A

ACROSS THE CURRICULUM Photocopy from one of your textbooks a brief passage that contains a number of pronouns. Circle all of the pronouns, and then list them. Using what you've learned about case and function so far, identify the pronouns by case and explain their function in the sentence.

3. After ____________ left the convention, the delegates searched for a restaurant.
4. The newly elected president arrived and said the delegates had worked so effectively that she wanted to give ____________ a banquet.
5. "____________ is an organization that recognizes honest effort," the president said.

EXERCISE 2

Complete the sentences that follow by filling in the blanks with pronouns or nouns of the appropriate form.

1. Presenting the newly discovered evidence—the intruder's gloves—to the district attorney, the chief inspector said: "These are ____________."
2. It is ____________ who has won.
3. It is ____________ who have won.
4. This is ____________ contest.
5. Mark answered the phone and, listening to a person asking for him, said: "Yes, this is ____________."

8d In a compound construction, use pronouns in the objective or subjective form according to their function in the sentence.

Sally and *I* went to the movies. Tom went with Sally and *me.*

The coordinating conjunction *and* can create a compound construction—a doubled subject or object. These can sometimes mask how a pronoun functions in a sentence. When you have difficulty choosing between a subjective or objective pronoun in a compound construction, try this test: *Create a simplified sentence by dropping out the compound;* then *try choosing the pronoun.* With the compound gone in the simpler construction, you should be able to tell whether the pronoun operates as a subject or an object.

Compound subject

Pierre and Marie Curie worked collaboratively; together Marie and *he* discovered polonium and radium. [The subjective pronoun forms the second part of a compound subject.]

CONFUSED Marie and *him* received the Nobel Prize in physics in 1903. [The pronoun subject is mistakenly put in the objective form.]

SIMPLIFIED Marie received the Nobel Prize; *he* also received it. [In the simplified construction the need for the subjective pronoun is clear.]

REVISED Marie and *he* received the Nobel Prize in 1903.

Compound object

The 1903 Nobel Prize in physics was awarded to Pierre and *her* for their work on radioactivity. [The objective pronoun is the object of a preposition in a compound construction.]

Confused An award was presented to Pierre and *she* in 1903, for their work on radioactivity. [In this construction, the pronoun functions as part of the preposition's compound object. Mistakenly, the pronoun is made subjective.]

Simplified The award was presented to Pierre; it was also presented to *her.*

Revised An award was presented to Pierre and *her* in 1903.

8e Pronouns paired with a noun take the same case as the noun.

1 For first-person plural pronouns (*we, us*) paired with a noun, use the same case as the noun.

We first-year students face important challenges.
Transitions can be challenging for *us* first-year students.

The first-person plural pronoun *we* or *us* is sometimes placed before a plural noun to help establish the identity of the noun. Use the subjective-case *we* when the pronoun is paired with a noun subject and the objective-case *us* when the pronoun is paired with an object of a verb, verbal, or preposition. To test for the correct pronoun, simplify the sentence and *drop out* the paired noun. In the simpler sentence, you should be able to determine which pronoun case is required.

Nonstandard *Us* strikers demand compensation. [*Strikers* is the subject of the sentence, and the pronoun paired with it should be the subjective-case *we.*]

Simplified *We* . . . demand compensation. [The need for subjective-case *we* is now clear.]

Revised *We* strikers demand compensation.

Nonstandard Give *we* strikers a fair share. [*Strikers* in this sentence is the indirect object of the verb *give,* and the pronoun paired with it should be the objective-case *us.*]

Simplified Give *us* . . . a fair share. [The need for objective-case *us* is now clear.]

Revised Give *us* strikers a fair share.

2 In an appositive, a pronoun's case should match the case of the noun it renames.

The executive officers—and only *they*—can attend.
Give this report to Linda—*her* and no one else.

Pronouns may occur in an **appositive—**a word or phrase that describes, identifies, or renames a noun in a sentence. If so, the pronoun must

ADDITIONAL EXERCISE B

For each of the following sentences, use the *drop out* rule to determine the case of each underlined pronoun. Cross out and replace each incorrect pronoun.

1. Jane Addams was influenced by her father's staunch abolitionist tendencies; both Jane and <u>him</u> were devout Quakers.
2. When faced with pressures to marry and raise families, Addams and her college friends said, "Give <u>we</u> women a chance to forge our own destiny."
3. When considering Addams's legacy, some consider the tremendous success of settlement houses for immigrants the legacy of one woman—<u>her</u>.
4. Addams was assisted in her efforts to establish Hull House by her friend Miss Starr; the city's immigrant population revered both women—Addams and <u>she</u>.
5. One resident of Hull House remarked, "Miss Addams has provided all of <u>us</u> poor folks with a life of the mind as well as of the body."

Answers:

1. Jane Addams was influenced by her father's staunch abolitionist tendencies; both Jane and ~~him~~ he were devout Quakers.
2. When faced with pressures to marry and raise families, Addams and her college friends said, "Give ~~we~~ us women a chance to forge our own destiny."
3. Correct
4. Addams was assisted in her efforts to establish Hull House by her friend Miss Starr; the city's immigrant population revered both women—Addams and ~~she~~ her.
5. Correct

take the same case as the noun being renamed. Once again you can test for pronoun choice by simplifying the sentence: *Drop the noun being renamed out of the sentence.* The simpler sentence that remains will usually reveal what pronoun case is required.

Renamed subject	Clinton's attempt to explain the difference between "malaise" and "funk," even with the coaching of his advisors, only served to show that both parties—*he* and the reporters—had failed to do their homework.
Confused	Both parties—*him* and the reporters—had failed to do their homework.
Simplified	*He* and the reporters failed to do their homework.

8f Choose the appropriate form of the pronouns *whose, who, whom, whoever,* and *whomever* depending on the pronoun's function.

The basic forms of the relative pronouns *whose, who, whom, whoever,* and *whomever* are shown in the following table. A relative pronoun's form depends on its function within its own clause.

Forms of the Relative Pronoun "Who(m)/Who(m)ever"

Subjective	*Objective*	*Possessive*
who	whom	whose
whoever	whomever	—

FOR DISCUSSION

Whom is one of those words that's come to be associated with "cultured" language; people frequently misuse it, apparently thinking *whom* is "proper" English while *who* is not. To set the record straight, ask students to come up with sentences in which *who* or *whom* appears. (You may want to begin with a couple of your own.) After writing the sentences on the board, have the class decide which of the two forms is appropriate in each sentence, and explain why. This exercise should help dispel the notion that *whom* is a sign of "culture."

1 In a question, choose a subjective, objective, or possessive form of *who(m)* or *who(m)ever* according to the pronoun's function.

Who is going? To *whom* are you writing? *Whose* birthday is it?

To test the correct choice for these pronouns at the beginning of a question, mentally *answer* the question, substituting the personal pronouns *I/me, we/us, he/him,* or *she/her* for *the relative pronoun.* Your choice of the subjective or objective form in the answer sentence will likely be quite clear, and it will be the same choice to make for the form of *who(m)* or *who(m)ever.*

Question	(Who/whom) are you addressing?
Answer	You are addressing (he/*him*). [The choice of the objective form is clear.]
Revised	*Whom* are you addressing? [The objective form is correct.]

Question For (who/whom) are you writing?

Answer You are writing for (she/*her*). [The choice of the objective form is clear.]

Revised For *whom* are you writing? [The objective form is correct.]

The possessive form *whose* can begin a question if the pronoun shows possession of the noun that immediately follows. To determine whether a possessive pronoun is correct for a sentence, replace the initial pronoun in the question with *what* and then mentally answer that question: If the answer requires that you use *his, her, their,* or *its* in place of the relative pronoun, then choose the possessive form, *whose.*

Question What name goes on the envelope? [Is a pronoun in the possessive case—his/her/their/its—needed?]

Possessive *Whose* name goes on the envelope?

2 In a dependent clause, choose the subjective, objective, or possessive form of *who(m)* or *who(m)ever* according to the pronoun's function within the clause.

Henry Taylor, *who* writes poems, lives in Virginia. Taylor, *whom* critics have praised, has a new book. The poet, *whose* book won a prize, lives quietly.

To choose the correct case for a relative pronoun in a dependent clause, eliminate the main clause temporarily; consider the pronoun's function *only* in the dependent clause. When deciding between the subjective or objective forms, apply the following tests.

Determine whether the relative pronoun functions as the subject of a dependent clause.

If the relative pronoun is followed immediately by a verb, you should probably use the subjective-case *who* or *whoever.* To be sure that the choice of pronouns is correct, substitute the word *I, we, you, he,* or *she* for *who* or *whoever.* Does this yield a legitimate sentence? If so, the choice of the subjective case is correct.

Subjective Your request will be of concern to (whoever/whomever) gets it.

Simplified (Whoever/whomever) gets it. [The pronoun is followed by a verb, *gets,* so the likely choice of pronouns will be *whoever.*]

Revised Your request will be of concern to *whoever* gets it.

Determine whether the relative pronoun functions as an object in the dependent clause.

If the relative pronoun is followed immediately by a noun or by the pronoun *I, we, you, he, she, few, some, many, most, it,* or *they,* you should prob-

GROUP ACTIVITY

Ask students, in groups of three or four, to compose a paragraph about a prominent figure (from politics, the arts, entertainment, sports, or some other public sphere) in which they use the pronouns *whose, who, whom, whoever,* and *whomever.* As they negotiate with one another on the function of the pronouns within sentences, they should gain a clearer understanding of relative pronoun use.

ably use the objective-case *whom* or *whomever.* To be sure of the choice, consider the dependent clause as if it were a sentence by itself (without the main clause). Rearrange the clause into normal word order and then substitute the word *him, her,* or *them* for the relative pronoun. If one of these newly substituted pronouns fits into the sentence as an object of a verb, verbal, or preposition, then the choice of the objective-case *whom* or *whomever* is correct.

OBJECTIVE Please send this to *whomever* it might interest. [The relative pronoun is followed by the pronoun *it,* so the choice of pronoun will likely be objective form. A second test: The objective-case *them,* substituted for *whomever,* yields a rearranged sentence, "It might interest *them.*"]

Determine whether the relative pronoun needs to show possession.

If the relative pronoun beginning a dependent clause needs to show possession, then you should use the possessive-case *whose.* Confirm the choice by substituting the word *his, her, their,* or *its* for the relative pronoun. A sentence should result when the dependent clause is considered by itself.

POSSESSIVE Daly, *whose* theories on urban wildlife have generated heated discussion, believes that we can profit by finding nature in our cities. [The possessive-case *his* yields a sentence: "*His* theories on urban wildlife . . ."]

8g Choose the case of a pronoun in the second part of a comparison depending on the meaning intended.

I studied Keats more than *him* (more than I studied Arnold—him).
I studied Keats more than *she* (more than Margo—she—studied Keats).

The words *than* and *as* create a comparison.

Calcutta is more densely populated *than* New York.

The new magneto engines are as efficient *as* traditional combustion engines.

For brevity's sake, writers and speakers often omit the second part of a comparison. Written in their complete form, the preceding examples would read as follows.

Calcutta is more densely populated than New York is densely populated.

The new magneto engines are as efficient as traditional combustion engines are efficient.

A comparison links two complete clauses. The brief form of a comparison is its "clipped" form; the fully expressed comparison, its "complete" form. When you compare people and use pronouns in the second part of your

CRITICAL DECISIONS

Challenge your sentences: Apply a test for *who* and *whom*

In a clause the relative pronouns *who* and *whom* take the place of nouns (or pronouns) that function as subjects or objects. Choosing the correct relative pronoun requires that you see that pronoun in relation to the words immediately following. You must examine the broader context of the clause in which the pronoun is located. Two questions should help you to choose between *who* and *whom* correctly.

- **Is the relative pronoun followed by a verb?**

  —"Yes": choose the subjective-case *who* or *whoever.*

  A relative pronoun followed by a verb indicates the pronoun occupies the subject position of the clause. To confirm this choice, substitute *I, we, you, he,* or *she* for the pronoun.

  Clinton, *who* won by a landslide in the electoral college, did not win as convincingly in the popular vote. [*Who* is followed by a verb, and when it is converted to *he* it yields a sentence: "*He* won by a landslide. . . ."]

  —"No": choose the objective-case *whom* or *whomever.* See the next test.

- **Is the relative pronoun followed by a noun or by any of these pronouns: *I, we, you, he, she, few, some, many, most, it, they*?**

  —"Yes": choose the objective-case *whom* or *whomever.*

  A relative pronoun followed by a noun or one of the listed pronouns indicates that the normal order of the clause (subject-verb-object) has been rearranged, suggesting the need for a pronoun in its objective form. To confirm your choice of *whom* or *whomever,* consider the pronoun and the words immediately following. Rearrange these words and substitute *him, her,* or *them* for the relative pronoun.

  Clinton, *whom* most analysts counted out of the presidential race, surprised supporters and detractors alike. [*Whom* is followed by *most,* and when it is converted to *him* it yields a sentence: "Most analysts counted *him* out."]

comparison, be sure to express your exact meaning. At times, the pronoun in the second part of a comparison will take the place of a noun functioning as a subject, in which case use the subjective form: *he, she, we.*

COMPLETE Some think that Prospero is a more perplexing figure than Hamlet is perplexing. [*Hamlet* functions as a subject in the second part of the comparison. A pronoun replacement for *Hamlet* would take the subjective form.]

COMPLETE Some think that Prospero is a more perplexing figure than *he* is perplexing.

CLIPPED Some think that Prospero is a more perplexing figure than *he.*

At times, the pronoun in the second part of a comparison will take the place of a noun functioning as an object, in which case use the objective form: *him, her, us.*

ADDITIONAL EXERCISE C

Compose ten sentences, each of which includes either *who* or *whom.* Then review each sentence, applying the test for proper use of the pronouns. In which cases did you use the correct form? If you made an error, how can you make sure that you use the correct form in the future?

Complete Many critics are more intrigued by Prospero than they are intrigued by Hamlet. [*Hamlet* functions as the object of the preposition *by* in the second part of the comparison. A pronoun replacement for *Hamlet* would take the objective form.]

Complete Many critics are more intrigued by Prospero than they are intrigued by *him.*

Clipped Many critics are more intrigued by Prospero than by *him.*

Avoid "clipping" the second part of a comparison unless all its parts are obvious. If you do clip the comparison, mentally recreate the full comparison to determine the function of the noun your pronoun is replacing. When that noun functions as a subject, use pronouns in the subjective form; when that noun functions as an object, use pronouns in the objective form.

EXERCISE 3

1. she
2. Correct
3. Whom
4. Correct
5. you, him
6. Correct
7. we
8. Correct
9. Correct
10. Correct
11. Her, us

EXERCISE 3

In the following sentences, correct the usage of the italicized pronouns. If a pronoun choice is correct, circle the pronoun.

Example: Anne told me it was Simon's fault; but between you and *I,* she's as much to blame as *him.*

Anne told me it was Simon's fault; but between you and *me,* she's as much to blame as *he.* [Pronouns that follow a preposition must be objective case: thus, between you and me. The second part of the comparison requires a subjective-case pronoun: She is to blame as much as *he is to blame.*]

1. It was *her* who wanted to leave early.
2. *She* is a better manager than *he.*
3. "*Who* do you want to reach?" asked the operator.
4. *He* is an employee in *whom* the firm has placed great trust.
5. Eric prepared a meal for both *you* and *he.*
6. *You* and *he* have been out of town for two months.
7. Maintaining discipline in the classroom is a problem *us* teachers face.
8. Maintaining discipline in the classroom is a problem facing *us* teachers.
9. *Whoever* drew the shortest straw would be the one to take our complaints to the Principal.
10. Beth, *who* drew the shortest straw, cheerfully accepted her unpleasant task.
11. *She* being so willing and pleasant was an inspiration to *us* all.

CHAPTER 9

Verbs

The verb forms you select will convey three important messages that are the focus of this chapter: *tense*—an indication of when an action or state of being occurs; *mood*—your judgment as to whether a statement is a fact, a command, or an unreal or hypothetical condition contrary to fact; and *voice*—your emphasis on the actor of a sentence or on the object acted on.

KEY FEATURES

This chapter takes a practical approach to verbs, opening with a discussion of the principal parts of regular verbs. As in Chapter 8 (Case in Nouns and Pronouns), the question of nonstandard forms is addressed in terms of accepted use in formal academic prose. In fact, early in the chapter the point is made that even among speakers of standard English, rapid conversation eliminates the *-s* and *-ed* endings. This approach is consistent with Part II (Writing as a Process), placing the writer's choices in the context of the purpose of the discourse and the needs of the audience: in everyday speech, endings are eliminated without consequence, while in formal discourse the appropriate use of endings is essential. A list of irregular verbs is provided for quick reference in case of confusion over appropriate forms. In discussing auxiliaries and modals, the chapter provides only as much information as students need to make appropriate choices. The section on intransitive verbs contains a brief discussion of three of the more troublesome pairs of words in the language: *sit/set, lie/lay,* and *rise/raise.* All of the above topics are covered in such a way that the chapter can be used as an easy reference tool; the student will not become bogged down with extensive linguistic analysis. Tense, voice, and mood are dealt with similarly, paying particular attention to sequencing tenses within a sentence, a problem many students face in written discourse. Exercises provide practice in choosing, identifying, and correcting verb forms, as well as in commenting on the meaning of a passage with respect to the tense used by the writer.

VERB FORMS

9a Using the principal parts of regular verbs consistently

All verbs other than *be* have two basic forms and three principal parts; these five forms and parts are the foundation for all the varied uses of verbs. A full dictionary entry may present these forms and parts: base form, *-s* form, past tense, past participle, and present participle.

The Principal Parts of Regular Verbs

Base form	*Present tense (-s form)*	*Past tense*	*Past participle*	*Present participle*
share	shares	shared	shared	sharing
start	starts	started	started	starting
climb	climbs	climbed	climbed	climbing

Most verbs in the dictionary are **regular** in that they follow the simple, predictable pattern shown in the box, in which the past tense and past participle are identical. (For regular verbs, only base forms appear in most dictionaries.)

1 Recognizing the forms of regular verbs

Alison *walks* to the theater. Yesterday, she *walked* there.
She *has walked* often. She *is walking* there now.

FOR DISCUSSION

Since most students have problems with only a few of these common errors, you might want to initiate a class discussion of errors most relevant to your students. Ask students to identify from the Spotlight on Common Errors examples of usage familiar to them and to make their own list of common errors. Students can then discuss the function of verb tense and form in sentences, thereby reinforcing their understanding of verb use. (In large classes, this activity might begin with small groups. The groups will identify their common errors, and then the class as a whole will discuss the list of errors compiled from each group's report.)

Spotlight on Common Errors—VERBS

These are errors most commonly associated with verb use. For full explanations and suggested revisions, follow the cross-references to chapter sections.

TENSE ERRORS: Keep clear the time relationships among two or more verbs in closely linked clauses or sentences.

- **If you refer to *past events occurring at roughly the same time,* use past-tense verbs (see 9f):**

FAULTY

Tom *had traveled* where jobs *presented* themselves. [past perfect/past]
Tom *traveled* where jobs *had presented* themselves. [past/past perfect]
[The different tenses wrongly suggest that the events happened at different times.]

REVISED

past event ... past event
Tom *traveled* where jobs *presented* themselves. [past/past]
[The sentence refers to events that occurred at the same time.]

- **If you refer to *past events occurring one before the other,* use the past tense for the more recent event and the past perfect for the earlier event.**

FAULTY

I *remembered* Mrs. Smith, who *showed* me kindness. [past/past]
[The tenses wrongly suggest that actions occurred at the same time.]

REVISED

later event ... earlier event
I *remembered* Mrs. Smith, who *had shown* me kindness. [past/past perfect]
[Mrs. Smith's "showing" occurred before the remembering.]

BUT if a key word (such as *before* or *after*) establishes a clear time relation, then the past perfect form of the verb is not used.

earlier event ... later event
I *was* unable to follow current events, *before* Mrs. Smith *showed* me how to read. [past/past]

- **Avoid abrupt tense shifts between closely linked sentences (see 16b).**

FAULTY TENSE SHIFT

The problem started when Fred *forgot* his appointment. Today he *comes* in late again. [past/present]

Revised

The problem started when Fred *forgot* his appointment. Today he *came* in late again.
[All action is in the past tense.]

ERRORS OF VERB FORM occur when writers confuse regular verbs with irregular verbs, the moods of verbs, and transitive verbs such as *lay* with intransitive verbs such as *lie.*

- **Regular/irregular: Know whether a verb is regular or irregular (see 9b).**

Faulty	Revised
I begun the story.	I *began* the story.
I had drank three full glasses.	I *had drunk* three full glasses.

- **Mood: When writing about an event that is unreal or hypothetical, use a verb's subjunctive forms. Expressions such as *recommend, suggest,* and *it is important* signal an unreal or hypothetical event (see 9h).**

Faulty	Revised
I recommend that Sarah builds a playhouse.	I recommend that Sarah *build* a playhouse.

In sentences expressing unreal conditions and beginning with *if,* use *were* in the first part of the sentence and *would* as a helping verb in the second part (see 9h).

Faulty	Revised
If it was any colder, the pipes will freeze.	*If it were* any colder, the pipes *would freeze.*

- **Transitive/intransitive: Use a transitive verb (*set, lay, raise*) to show an action transferred from an actor to an object. Use an intransitive verb (*sit, lie, rise*) to limit action to the subject (see 9d).**

Faulty	Revised
Sit the books on the table.	*Set* the books on the table. [Transitive]
It hurts only when I set.	It hurts only when I *sit.* [Intransitive]
I think I'll lay down.	I think I'll *lie* down. [Intransitive]
Lie the blanket in the corner.	*Lay* the blanket . . . [Transitive]

The forms of *lie* and *lay* are particularly tricky. (See page 232.)

Faulty	Revised
Yesterday, I laid down to rest.	Yesterday, I *lay* down to rest.
I had lain the book on the table.	I had *laid* the book on the table.

TEACHING IDEAS

In order to acquaint students with using the dictionary, ask them to look up and list the principal parts of five regular verbs. In addition to revealing one of the features of a dictionary, this activity will also reinforce the distinctions between the principal parts.

Base form + the *-s form* = *present tense*

The **base** (or infinitive) **form** of a verb—often called its **dictionary form**—is the base from which all changes are made. Use the base form of a verb with *no* ending for occasions when the action of a verb is present for plural nouns or for the personal pronouns *I, we, you,* or *they.*

> Alaska's Pacific mountains *create* a region of high peaks, broad valleys, and numerous island fjords.

The ***-s form*** of a verb (creates, tries, loves) occurs with third-person, singular subjects when an action is in the present. A verb's *-s* form (add *-s* or *-es* to a verb) is used in three instances: with the personal pronouns *he, she,* or *it;* with any noun that can be replaced by these pronouns; and with a number of indefinite pronouns (such as *something* or *no one*), which are often considered singular.

> Alaska's north slope *consists* of the plateaus and coastal regions north of the Brooks mountain range.

Difficulties with subject–verb agreement occur when a writer is unsure whether to use a verb's base form or *-s* form in a sentence. For a discussion of subject–verb agreement, see Chapter 10.

Past-tense form

The **past tense** of a verb indicates that an action has been completed in the past. The regular verbs follow a predictable pattern in forming the past tense by taking the suffix *-ed* or *-d.*

> Secretary of State William H. Seward *arranged* for the purchase of Alaska from Russia in 1867.

Irregular verbs follow no such pattern: their base forms change their root spelling to show the past tense (see 9b).

Two participle forms

For regular verbs, the form of the **past participle** is identical to that of the past tense. A verb's past participle is used in three ways: paired with *have,* the past participle functions as a main verb; paired with *be,* the past participle forms a passive construction; and, paired with a noun or pronoun, the past participle functions as an adjective.

> With the Russian treasury *depleted* [adjective] after the Crimean War, the Tsar *had decided* [main verb] to sell the western-most part of his empire, which *was colonized* [passive construction] very sparsely by Russians.

ESL NOTE Both past and present participles have uses as adjective modifiers, usually placed before the nouns or pronouns modified—as in *a confused speaker* or *a confusing speaker.* Note that while the past and present participles from this verb are related in meaning, they work in opposite directions on the word modified (see 44a-1).

The **present participle,** the *-ing* form of the verb, has three uses: it functions as a main verb of a sentence and shows continuing action when paired with a form of *be* (*am, are, is, was, were*); it functions as an adjective when paired with a noun or pronoun; or it functions as a noun, in which case it is called a *gerund* (see 7a).

> The *decimating* [gerund] of seal herds *was proceeding* [main verb] at an *alarming* [adjective] rate.

ESL NOTE The role of a gerund in a sentence is determined by the verb being used. Certain verbs pair idiomatically with gerunds, as in *go swimming* or *enjoy swimming* (see 43e-2). Gerunds can be objects of certain prepositions that are idiomatically determined by the preceding verb: *I have reasons for coming* versus *I decided on walking.* Certain other verbs are paired idiomatically with the other verbal noun form, the infinitive (see 43e-2).

2 Revising nonstandard verb forms by using standard *-s* and *-ed* forms

NONSTANDARD He walk home.
REVISED He walked home.

In rapid conversation, many people skip over *-s* and *-ed* endings. In some dialects the base (or infinitive) form of the verb is used in place of verbs with *-s* and *-ed* endings. Writers of standard academic English, however, need to observe the regular forms.

NONSTANDARD She was *ask* to read this assignment. She *like* to stay up late and she *be* still wide awake.

REVISED She was *asked* to read it. She *likes* to stay up late and she *is* still wide awake. [Base forms have been replaced by standard verb forms with *-s* and *-ed* endings.]

9b Learning the forms of irregular verbs

Most verbs are regular in that they form the past tense and past participle with the suffix *-ed* or *-d.* An irregular verb will form its past tense and past participle by altering the spelling of the base verb, as in *build/built* or *bring/brought.* A dictionary entry for an irregular verb shows the principal parts and basic forms of a verb as the first information in the entry. This will show you when a verb is irregular—when it does not take an *-ed* ending in its past tense and past participle forms. Because irregular verbs are some of the most commonly used words in the language, most speakers and readers

ESL CUE

Students should be reminded that because gerunds serve the function of nouns and may appear wherever a noun appears, one gerund equals one noun and therefore takes a singular verb. Gerunds often, though not always, refer to action in the past or action from the past to the present (in contrast to infinitives, which refer to the future). When gerunds are placed as objects of the verb, this distinction is vital to clear communication, as in the following.

> He stopped seeing her./He stopped to see her.
>
> He remembered going there./He must remember to go there.

Also gerunds take the possessive pronoun.

> his book/his having done that.

Another helpful rule is that two- and three-part verbs always take a gerund instead of an infinitive object: "look forward to going," not "look forward to go."

Recognizing gerund and infinitive subjects may be difficult for ESL students, who might benefit from practice underlining subjects, as in "*Getting to know you* will be fun" and "*To be or not to be* was Hamlet's question."

TEACHING IDEAS

MULTICULTURAL DIFFERENCES Like the introduction to Chapter 8 (Case in Nouns and Pronouns), this section stresses the importance of writers' choices with regard to style and meaning. The first of those choices in academic writing is whether to use standard English. This issue is particularly relevant to speakers of certain dialects, particularly black English vernacular, where the *-s* and *-ed* endings are not used as they are in standard English. If appropriate for your classroom, you might want to call attention to some of the differences between standard edited English and other dialects, as well as the difference between formal academic prose and what is known as "imaginative literature." A case in point is Alice Walker, whose frequently anthologized essay "In Search of Our Mothers'

(continued)

Gardens" is written in standard edited English, but whose highly respected novel *The Color Purple* is written primarily in black English vernacular, using verbs without *-s* and *-ed* endings. The relative demands of the two forms of prose, and the reasons for acknowledging the place of standard and nonstandard English, could provoke a meaningful discussion.

ESL CUE

A common ESL mistake is to omit the *-s* in the third-person singular, present tense. Be sure to warn that verbs of perception ("see," "hear") and verbs of stasis or state of being ("be," "appear," "seem," "remember," "forget," "love") require the simple present or simple past and cannot be progressive. Discussing the difference between "I think he should be president" (an intellectual position) as opposed to "I am thinking about what to do this summer" (a temporary thought) should help clarify the problem. Also compare "I drink coffee" (a consistent preference) and "I am drinking coffee" (a current action).

ESL CUE

Certain English verbs are troublesome for ESL students because English has several verbs where the student's native language has only one. For example, Japanese, Spanish, Italian, and French have only one word for the English "do" and "make." It helps to note that "do" often, though not always, involves mechanical activity, whereas "make" is creative: The teacher *makes* up the exercise, but the student *does* the exercise. There are also a number of confusing idiomatic "do" and "make" expressions, such as "do the right thing," "do someone a favor," "do good," "do away with," as opposed to "make a speech," "make mistakes," "make a living," "make arrangements," "make an impression," "make progress," "make up one's mind," and so forth. "Make" can be confused with "create" as well: We "make (or create) a mess" but "create (but never "make") disorder," with "make" having more physical and conventional applications than its more formal equivalent. We create poetry, confusion, progeny, and discord. In general, students

are accustomed to, and expect, them. You should take care to use correct irregular forms. Memorize troublesome forms or look them up as necessary.

Be

The most frequently used verb in our language, *be,* is also the only verb with more than five forms. It functions both as the main verb in a sentence and as a frequently used auxiliary verb (see 9c and 7a-3). The eight forms of *be* are shown in the box.

The Principal Parts of *be*

Base form	*Present tense*	*Past tense*
(to) be	he, she, it *is*	he, she, it *was*
	I *am*	I *was*
	we, you, they *are*	we, you, they *were*
	Past participle	***Present participle***
	been	*being*

The following box contains the principal parts for a partial list of irregular verbs. Remember that the past participle is the form of the verb used with the auxiliary *have.* Without the auxiliary, it functions as an adjective.

Some Irregular Verb Forms

Base form	*Past tense*	*Past participle*
bear	bore	borne, born
beat	beat	beaten
become	became	become
begin	began	begun
bend	bent	bent
bind	bound	bound
bite	bit	bit, bitten
bleed	bled	bled
blow	blew	blown
break	broke	broken
bring	brought	brought
build	built	built
burn	burned, burnt	burned, burnt
burst	burst	burst

(continued)

Base form	Past tense	Past participle
buy	bought	bought
catch	caught	caught
choose	chose	chosen
cling	clung	clung
come	came	come
cost	cost	cost
cut	cut	cut
dig	dug	dug
dive	dove, dived	dived
do (does)	did	done
draw	drew	drawn
drink	drank	drunk
drive	drove	driven
eat	ate	eaten
fall	fell	fallen
feed	fed	fed
feel	felt	felt
fight	fought	fought
find	found	found
flee	fled	fled
fling	flung	flung
fly	flew	flown
forbid	forbade, forbad	forbidden *or* forbid
forget	forgot	forgot *or* forgotten
freeze	froze	frozen
get	got	got, gotten
give	gave	given
go	went	gone
grow	grew	grown
hang[1]	hung	hung
have (has)	had	had
hear	heard	heard
hide	hid	hidden
hit	hit	hit
keep	kept	kept
know	knew	known
lead	led	led
leave	left	left
lend	lent	lent
lose	lost	lost
make	made	made
mean	meant	meant
pay	paid	paid
prove	proved	proved *or* proven
read	read	read

(continued)

[1]*Hang* as an irregular verb means to *suspend.* When *hang* means to *execute,* it is regular: *hang, hanged, hanged.*

whose languages have "all purpose" verbs (a word like "make" used for many activities) should be advised to choose a specific English verb if a familiar "make" construction does not come to mind: not "make" but "cook a meal," "write a paper," "build a house."

"Say" and "tell" cause similar confusion for the same reason. It might help to give a series of examples of usage: tell time, tell a story or joke, tell me, tell the difference, but say hello, say grace, say that we should go, say "Let's go!," but never "say me" or "explain me." ESL students also tend to confuse verbs of perception with verbs of action, as in "hear" and "listen to," "see" and "watch," a distinction that may be made differently in other languages.

Both Japanese and Spanish speakers tend to use the past tense inappropriately, not for the historical past, but for regular, repeated behavior.

The present perfect tense does not exist in many Asian languages, so the idea of a verb that connects the past with the present, either because of action started in the past and continuing to the present ("I have lived here for many years") or because of action completed in the past but affecting a present course of action ("I have already eaten"), needs special attention.

Greeks will tend to overuse the present progressive, treating it as equivalent to a simple present tense. Indians and Pakistanis will tend to use the present progressive tense for all situations: present, future, and maybe even past. Slavic language speakers will use the simple present in the same way.

ADDITIONAL EXERCISE A

Choose five of the irregular verbs (other than *be*) from the list provided and construct three sentences with each: one using the base form, one using the past tense form, and one using the past participle form. (If you have difficulty using the past participle form, consult the sections on tense and voice below.)

REFERENCES

EPES, MARY. "Tracing Errors to the Sources: A Study of the Encoding Processes of Adult Basic Writers." *Journal of Basic Writing* 41 (1985): 4–33. Speakers of nonstandard English can benefit from traditional grammar instruction.

FARR, MARCIA, and HARVEY DANIELS. *Language Diversity and Writing Instruction.* New York: ERIC Clearinghouse on Urban Education and Urbana: NCTE, 1986. Nonstandard dialects present specific challenges to educators; appropriate teaching strategies can help students master standard forms.

SHAUGHNESSY, MINA P. *Errors and Expectations: A Guide for the Teacher of Basic Writing.* New York: Oxford UP, 1977. Chapter 4. Some students have difficulty with inflections because of the absence of inflection in their own speech.

SMITHERMAN, GENEVA. *Talkin and Testifyin.* Boston: Houghton, 1977. Speakers of Black English use an abbreviated inflection system, and sometimes transfer that use to their writing.

WOLFRAM, WALT, and RALPH W. FASOLD. *The Study of Social Dialects in American English.* Englewood Cliffs, NJ: Prentice-Hall, 1974. This text contains an extensive analysis of verb forms in Black English, including a discussion of problems related to education.

TEACHING IDEAS

Most students will recognize in this list several verbs that pose problems for them. It might be useful to ask students to cull from these pages a personal list of problem irregular verbs. For each verb, have students write out the base, past, and past participle forms of the verb, followed by three sentences using each form. This list can be used both for study and for reference as students edit their papers.

ESL CUE

ESL students will need to be encouraged to simply memorize a list like the one in 9b in order to master irregular verbs. Spanish speakers frequently confuse "fall/fell" with "feel/felt." "Lie/lay/lain" versus "lay/laid/ laid" versus "lie/lied/lied" confuse all. The fact that "lie," "sit," and "rise" do not take objects, while "lay," "set," and "raise" do helps facilitate use, as in "She lay in the sun" (location) versus "She laid *her books* on the floor" (first

Some Irregular Verb Forms (continued)

Base form	*Past tense*	*Past participle*
ride	rode	ridden
ring	rang	rung
run	ran	run
say	said	said
see	saw	seen
seek	sought	sought
send	sent	sent
shake	shook	shaken
shine[2]	shone	shone
sing	sang	sung
sink	sank	sunk
sleep	slept	slept
speak	spoke	spoken
spend	spent	spent
spring	sprang, sprung	sprung
stand	stood	stood
steal	stole	stolen
stick	stuck	stuck
strive	strove	striven
swear	swore	sworn
swim	swam	swum
swing	swung	swung
take	took	taken
teach	taught	taught
tear	tore	torn
tell	told	told
think	thought	thought
throw	threw	thrown
wake	woke, waked	waked, woken
wear	wore	worn
wind	wound	wound
wring	wrung	wrung
write	wrote	written

[2]*Shine* as an irregular verb means to *emit light.* When *shine* means to *polish,* it is regular: *shine, shined, shined.*

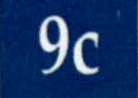

9c Using auxiliary verbs

An **auxiliary** (or helping) **verb** is combined with the base form of a verb or the present or past participle form to establish tense, mood, and voice in a sentence. This combination of verbs creates a **verb phrase.** The most frequently used auxiliaries are *be, have,* and *do. Be* functions as an auxiliary when it combines with the *-ing* form of a verb to create the progressive tenses (as in I *am going*). *Have* functions as an auxiliary when it combines with the past participle form of a verb to create the perfect tenses (as in I *have gone*). *Do* functions as an auxiliary when it combines with the base form of a verb to form questions, to show emphasis, and to show negation. (*Do* you care? I *do* care. I *don't* care.)

ESL NOTE For illustrations of the varied uses for auxiliary verbs in English, see 43c–d.

1 Use modal auxiliaries to refine meaning.

The producers *should* agree to this. They *must* agree.
They *might* agree to these terms.

When paired with the base form of a verb, a **modal auxiliary** expresses urgency, obligation, likelihood, possibility, and so on: *can/could, may, might, must, ought to, should, would.* Unlike the auxiliaries *be, have,* and *do,* most of these modal auxiliaries do not change form. They follow singular or plural subjects in the first, second, or third person. Modal auxiliaries can follow the pronouns *I, we, you, he, she, one, it, they.* Observe how meaning in a sentence changes depending on the choice of modal auxiliary.

I must resign.	I ought to resign.	I would resign.
I could resign.	I can resign.	I might resign.

Modal auxiliaries can combine with other auxiliaries to create complex verbal phrases that require careful use.

I ought to have resigned. I might have been resigning.

The auxiliaries *will* and *shall* establish the future tense.

When shall I resign? She will resign then.

ESL NOTE For illustrations of how modal auxiliaries affect word order and verb constructions, see 43d.

2 Revise nonstandard auxiliaries by using standard forms of *be*.

FAULTY She going to class. REVISED She is going to class.

Some dialects form present-tense auxiliary constructions with variations on the base form of *be*. For written academic English, these forms must be revised.

NONSTANDARD She *be* singing beautifully. [The base form of *be* is a nonstandard usage here. The *-s* form of the verb is needed.]

NONSTANDARD She singing a beautiful melody. [The *be* form has been dropped.]

REVISED She *is* singing a beautiful melody. [The base form of *be* in the auxiliary has been replaced by the standard *-s* form.]

object, then location); "She sat in the chair" (location) versus "She set *the table* for four" (object) or "His words set *her mind* at rest" (object); "The sun rises every morning" (time) versus "They raised *the flag*" (object) or "They raised *chickens*" (object).

ESL CUE

There is little logic to English speakers' use of prepositions, and such use differs in British and American English. In fact, American usage can vary as well ("stand on line"—East Coast; "stand in line"—other regions). ESL students may *never* master English prepositions completely and *should not be expected to.* There are some rules to help with prepositions of location, but even a seemingly bilingual student can be recognized as a non-native speaker by occasional preposition abuse.

Multiword prepositions will be the hardest ones for non-native speakers to recognize as prepositions, and prepositions used in two- and three-part verbs—called *particles* (see 43f) —will confuse every non-native speaker of English.

ESL EXERCISE

Write down as many two- and three-part verbs as you can using (1) get (2) check (3) look. Go over these in class, discussing the way the preposition or particle changes the meaning.

ESL students can *never* get enough practice with these forms, and not knowing them or misusing them can create confusion and misunderstanding.

ADDITIONAL EXERCISE B

When is an auxiliary not an auxiliary? In the following sentences, identify the verbs *be, have,* and *do* as auxiliary verbs or main verbs.

1. Melinda *has* gone to school already.
2. She *did* not complete her homework last night.
3. Christine *is* a senior in high school this year.
4. Both girls *have* regularly scheduled study hours each evening.
5. Melinda *was* planning to finish her homework in the morning.

Answers:

1. auxiliary; 2. auxiliary; 3. main; 4. main; 5. auxiliary

EXERCISE 1

Identify the main verb and any auxiliary verb associated with it in the sentences that follow.

Example: Peru presents many contrasts to a traveler. (The verb is *presents.*)

1. Peru has both modern cities such as Lima and ancient ones such as Cuzco.
2. Anthropologists believe Cuzco to be the oldest continuously inhabited city in the western hemisphere.
3. In fact, the city's population is actually growing.
4. Travelers have long admired the city's massive walls.
5. Craftsmen began work on the cathedral in 1659 and finished nearly one hundred years later.
6. The Pizzeria Giorgio Gourmet exemplifies the old and the new.
7. The restaurant serves a thoroughly modern food—pizza; yet the restaurant incorporates into its architecture an Inca-built wall.

EXERCISE 2

In the sentences that follow, use the appropriate form of the irregular verb.

Example: Over the past five years, nearly every woman in our therapy groups [confess] to a negative body image. [confessed]

Most of the women we interviewed had negative body images, not because they [have] ____1____ homely bodies but because they [see] ____2____ themselves incorrectly. Their images of their bodies [be] ____3____ distorted. In the cases of some women, this distortion was so extreme that their bodies [become] ____4____ caricatures. Many of the women also [feel] ____5____ to some extent alienated from their own bodies. This estrangement is probably inevitable, given the fact that women have been [teach] ____6____ to perceive the mind as divorced from the body.

9d Using transitive and intransitive verbs

Action verbs are classified as *transitive* and *intransitive.* A **transitive verb** (marked with the abbreviation **tr.** in the dictionary) transfers an action from a subject to an object; the action of an **intransitive verb** is limited to the subject of a sentence.

1 Distinguish between verbs that take direct objects and those that do not.

Sharon studied. Sharon studied her lecture notes.

A large number of verbs regularly take a direct object and are always transitive; others never take an object and are always intransitive.

ESL CUE

Spanish speakers tend to misuse "should" as an equivalent of "expect to" in sentences where native speakers would mean obligation, saying, for example, "I should see him," when they mean "I expect to see him" rather than "I have an obligation or need to see him." However, they may not use "should" properly for expectation, saying "He would be here any minute" instead of "He should be here any minute."

Students trained in British English might tend to avoid "do have" formations, particularly in questions: "Have you any potatoes?"

Most ESL students find the distinction between "have" as a verb and "have" as an auxiliary difficult to make, especially in the perfect forms ("has had"/"had had"), and the use of "could" for ability, possibility, and politeness confusing:

"He could play the piano well."
"You could be right about that."
"Could you please help me with this?"

There may be some confusion of contractions, especially the use of "*-s*" inappropriately: "She's some eggs" for "She has some eggs."

EXERCISE 1

1. has
2. believe
3. is growing
4. have admired
5. began, finished
6. exemplifies
7. serves, incorporates

EXERCISE 2

1. have
2. saw
3. were
4. became
5. felt
6. taught

GROUP ACTIVITY

The different meanings achieved through the use of auxiliaries and modal auxiliaries make for an interesting group activity. Assign each

Transitive The politician kissed the baby. [The transitive verb *kissed* transfers action from *politician* to *baby.*]

Intransitive The politician smiled. [An action is performed, but no object is acted on.]

Many verbs can have both a transitive and an intransitive sense. Such "two-way" verbs will take a direct object or not depending on their use.

Intransitive She runs every day. [The verb takes no object.]

Transitive She runs a big business. [The verb has changed meaning and now takes an object.]

ESL Note Note that a transitive verb is the *only* type that can be made passive (see 9g); neither intransitive nor most linking verbs can take a passive form in modern English. For specifics on transitive verbs and passive constructions, see 43a-1.

2 Avoid confusion between the verbs *sit/set, lie/lay, rise/raise.*

Set the books on the table.
It hurts only when I *sit.*
I think I'll *lie* down for a rest.
Lay the blanket in the corner.

Difficulties in distinguishing between transitive and intransitive verbs lead to misuse of *sit/set, lie/lay,* and *rise/raise.* The forms of these verbs are shown in the box on page 232. Because the meaning of the verbs in each pairing is somewhat similar, the verbs are sometimes used interchangeably in speech. In formal writing, however, careful distinctions should be maintained: the first verb in each pair is intransitive—it takes no object—while the second verb is transitive.

Sit is normally an intransitive verb; its action is limited to the subject.

adverb
You sit *on the bench.*

Set is a transitive verb. It transfers action to an object, which must be present in the sentence.

object adverb
You set <u>*the papers*</u> *on the bench.*

Lie is an intransitive verb; its action is limited to the subject.

adverb
I lie *on the couch.*

Lay is a transitive verb. It transfers action to an object, which must be present in the sentence.

group a main verb, and ask them first to compose a sentence using that verb in its base form. Then have groups alter the sentence by pairing the verb with as many modal auxiliaries as possible and then combining the modals with other auxiliaries, creating a new sentence each time. For each sentence, ask students to explain the shifts in meaning as they use different modals and auxiliaries.

ESL CUE

List the request forms in English from the least polite (the command form) to the most polite.

This activity should allow teachers to discuss the differences between such forms as "Might I help you?" and "Would you be so kind as to . . . ?" Note in particular how the choice of form relates not simply to the degree of formality and of politeness but to the type of relation between the people involved. Would it be correct to ask a roommate with whom one is very close, "Might I help you?" Would it be correct to tell a university president to whom one wishes to show respect, "Come help me!"?

ESL EXERCISE

Write two letters to a friend.

1. The first should use hypothetical forms such as "if," "unless," and "suppose" as well as advice forms like "should," "had better," and "have to" to give suggestions to a friend who is coming from your country to visit you at your school.
2. The second should follow the same pattern as the first, but should explain that your friend did not have a good time because of a failure to follow your advice and suggestions. Use past tense advice forms such as "should have" and unreal conditionals such as "if you had."

REFERENCE

Halliday, M. A. K. *System and Function in Language.* Ed. Gunther Kress. London: Oxford UP, 1976. Chapter 11. Traditional definitions of transitive verbs are incomplete.

ADDITIONAL EXERCISE C

Compose six sentences, one each for the verbs *sit/set, lie/lay,* and *rise/raise.* If you need help in distinguishing between any of the pairs, consult the explanations provided in the text.

EXERCISE 3

1. set
2. sat
3. lay
4. raised
5. rose

EXERCISE 4

1. hoped left
2. was
3. fought be
4. transferred bartering were
5. had expanded

object **adverb**
I lay *the pillow on the couch.*

Rise is an intransitive verb; its action is limited to the subject.

adverb
I rise *in the morning.*

Raise is a transitive verb. It transfers action to an object, which must be present in the sentence.

object **adverb**
I raise *the flag each morning.*

The Principal Parts of *sit/set, lie/lay,* and *rise/raise*

Base form	*Present tense*	*Past tense*	*Past participle*	*Present participle*
sit	sits	sat	sat	sitting
set	sets	set	set	setting
lie	lies	lay	lain	lying
lay	lays	laid	laid	laying
rise	rises	rose	risen	rising
raise	raises	raised	raised	raising

EXERCISE 3

Choose the appropriate form of *sit/set, lie/lay,* or *rise/raise* in these sentences.

Example: A squirrel was (*sit/set*) ___________ on a picnic table.

A squirrel was *sitting* on a picnic table.

1. A man walked by and (*sit/set*) ___________ a newspaper on a nearby table.
2. He then (*sit/set*) ___________ down and unfolded the paper.
3. From one pocket he produced a tomato, which he (*lie/lay*) ___________ on the paper.
4. From another pocket came a salt shaker, which he (*rise/raise*) ___________ ceremoniously.
5. The squirrel (*rise/raise*) ___________ at the scent of food.

EXERCISE 4

In the following sentences, fill in the blanks with the appropriate form of the verb indicated in parentheses.

Example: The First World War _________ (begin) as an Old World War.

The First World War *began* as an Old World War.

1. Everything about the war expressed the world that Americans ___________ (hope) they had ___________ (leave) behind.

2. That Old World __________ (be) a battlefield of national ambitions, religious persecutions, and language barriers.
3. European armies had __________ (fight) over whether a nation's boundary should __________ (be) on one side or the other of a narrow river.
4. Old World monarchs had __________ (transfer) land from one flag to another, __________ (barter) people as if they __________ (be) mere real estate.
5. In the 1800s, the English, French, and German empires __________ (expand) across the globe.

TENSE

9e Understanding the uses of verb tenses

A verb's **tense** indicates when an action has occurred or when a subject exists in a given state. There are three basic tenses in English: *past, present,* and *future.* Each has a **perfect** form, which indicates a completed action; each has a **progressive** form, which indicates ongoing action; and each has a **perfect progressive** form, which indicates ongoing action that will be completed at some definite time.

1 The varied uses of the present tense

Present: I start the engine.
Present perfect: I have started the engine.
Present progressive: I am starting the engine.
Present perfect progressive: I have been starting the engine.

The simple present

A verb's base form is the present-tense form for first- and second-person subjects, singular or plural (*I, we, you* play), as well as plural third-person subjects (*they* play). A present-tense verb for a third-person, singular noun or pronoun ends with the suffix *-s* (*he* plays). The **simple present tense** indicates an action taking place in the writer's present time: *You see these words.* But the present tense in combination with other time-specific expressions (such as *after, before, when,* or *next week*) indicates other time references, such as ongoing action or future action (see 9f-1).

After I arrive, I will *call.*

Before I arrive, I will *call.*

When I arrive, *pretend* you don't know me.

Next week, Nelson *dances* at the White House.

FOR DISCUSSION

Many students have difficulty with the perfect progressive tenses—the two-auxiliaries-plus-participle seems a bit unwieldy at times. You may want to give students a little practice with it as you begin your discussion of tense. Ask students to suggest four or five main verbs. After you've written them on the board, the entire class will construct a base sentence, changing it first to present perfect, then to present progressive, and so on through the past tenses. If students can see how the perfect progressive is *built* from the simple progressive, they may have an easier time using it in their own writing.

ESL CUE

Speakers of Asian languages (including Thai, Korean, Chinese, and Vietnamese) will have difficulty with tenses because these languages use a single verb symbol for all tenses and then vary meaning by appending a time indicator. The symbol for "I am," "I was," and "I will be" is the same in these languages, and there is a single symbol for "has," "have," and "had."

Speakers of romance languages, in turn, will have tense difficulties because their verb systems are more complex than those in English.

TEACHING IDEAS

The concept of the historical present is one worth spending a little time on—especially if students are studying literature in this class. You may simply want to emphasize the appropriate use of historical present, or you may want to remind students that they frequently use it when they're telling stories ("So then I go, and then she goes. . . ."). You may even want to open the issue for discussion, asking students to explain in their own words why the historical present is appropriate for literature.

The historical present

The so-called **historical present tense** is used when referring to actions in an already existing work: a book, a report, an essay, a movie, a television show, an article, and so on. Action in an existing work is always present to a reader or viewer.

> In *The Songlines,* Bruce Chatwin *explores* the origins and meanings of Aboriginal "walkabouts" in Australia.

The historical present tense is also used when referring to movies.

> In *Blade Runner,* Harrison Ford *plays* a world-weary detective whose job it *is* to disable renegade, human-like robots.

Additionally, the present tense is used to express information that, according to current scientific knowledge or accepted wisdom, is true or likely to be true.

> Evidence *indicates* that Alzheimer's patients *show* a decrease in an important brain transmitter substance.
>
> Absence *makes* the heart grow fonder.
>
> She *is* an excellent dentist.

The present tense is also used to indicate a generalized time or a customary, repeated action.

> Time *flies.*
>
> Each Tuesday I *walk* to the bakery.

The present perfect tense

The **present perfect tense** is formed with the auxiliary *have* or *has* and the verb's past participle. This tense indicates an action completed at an indefinite past time.

> I *have returned* and she *has left.*

The present perfect tense also indicates an action that, although begun at some past time, continues to have an impact in the present.

> He *has* recently *given* support to museums.

ESL Note Expressions for duration of time, such as *since* and *for*, require the use of the perfect tense.

Faulty I *was* here *since* four o'clock and *waited* here *for* many hours. [The simple past is not used with these expressions showing duration of time.]

Revised I *have been* here *since* four o'clock and *have waited* here for many hours. [The present perfect is used.]

In constructions that indicate a specific past time using phrases or clauses (with *when, after, before, while*), the simple past is required.

Faulty I *have met* him at eight o'clock and I *have left* after he arrived. [These expressions for a specific past time or event do not use the perfect.]

Revised I *met* him at eight o'clock and I *left* after he arrived.

For more information on the use of tenses with time expressions, see 43b-2.

The present progressive tense

The **present progressive tense** is formed with the auxiliary *is, am,* or *are* and the verb's present participle. This tense indicates a present, ongoing action that may continue into the future.

She *is considering* a move to Alaska.

ESL Note Certain verbs such as *have* are generally not used in a progressive tense, except with some idioms: *having a good time; having a baby* (see 43b-1).

The present perfect progressive tense

The **present perfect progressive tense** is formed with the auxiliary *has been* or *have been* and the verb's present participle. This tense indicates an action that began in the past, is continuing in the present, and may continue into the future.

She *has been studying* English for a year.

2 The past and future tenses

PAST TENSES

Past: I started the engine.
Past perfect: I had started the engine.
Past progressive: I was starting the engine.
Past perfect progressive: I had been starting the engine.

The simple past tense

Regular verbs form the **simple past tense** by adding *-d* or *-ed* to the infinitive of the verb; irregular verbs form the past tense in less predictable ways and are best memorized or verified in a dictionary. The simple past tense indicates an action completed at a definite time in the past.

Mothers *found* themselves unable to give their daughters accurate and positive perceptions about their bodies since they themselves *were* preoccupied with faulty body images of their own.

ESL CUE

There may be some confusion of progressives that depend on shifts in verb meaning. For example, the word "think" in "He is thinking about what to do next" emphasizes mental activity, while "think" in "He thinks she spoke the truth" emphasizes a conclusion or opinion reached through past processes. In general, verbs expressing a completed mental process (believe, consider, forget, know, remember, think, understand) or states of being (am, appear, have, seem) or perceptions (feel, hear, see, taste) do not take progressive forms. A few of these verbs may be made progressive, but doing so changes their meaning.

"I am considering buying a car [a decision-making process]

versus

"I consider my choice the best" [an already completed decision]

ESL CUE

The past perfect tense does not exist in some languages and, even when it does, ESL students often have trouble distinguishing between use of the simple past and the past progressive. It is important to communicate that the "had" of the past progressive form can be used *only* when there are two actions in the past and when one of those past actions occurs *before* the other. It is always the earlier action which takes the "had": "After he had stolen the car, he discovered it belonged to a policeman."

Help students distinguish between "Just as he was turning the corner, a car hit him" and "Just as he had turned the corner, a car hit him."

(continued)

It helps to explain that the past perfect and the past perfect progressive differ only in degree of emphasis, while the past and the past progressive differ in both use and meaning, with the past progressive emphasizing action in progress, usually interrupted by a limited, nonprogressive action: "While she was talking on the phone, her toast burned."

There may be some confusion about present tense forms used as future forms: "I leave/am leaving tomorrow" versus "I am writing a letter." The "is to" future formation may cause difficulties, and teaching students that the form is equivalent to "is going to" or "is supposed to" may help, as in "She is to take her test tomorrow."

FOR DISCUSSION

Of all the past tenses, the past perfect seems to be the most misunderstood among students. Often students will use it in place of simple past, sometimes to indicate an event that happened long ago, and sometimes for no easily discernible reason. If you have noticed problems associated with past perfect tense, you may want to ask students to explain the concept in their own words, perhaps providing their own examples of appropriate use of past perfect. Students who have misused it in their own writing might be asked to edit their papers for proper use of the tense.

The past perfect tense

The **past perfect tense** is formed with the auxiliary *had* and the verb's past participle. This tense indicates a past action that has occurred prior to another action.

> By the time a girl reached puberty, she *had* already *developed* a negative body image.

The past progressive tense

The **past progressive tense** is formed with the auxiliary *was* or *were* and the verb's present participle. This tense indicates an ongoing action conducted—and completed—in the past.

> In the 70s women *were striving* for a thin boyish figure.

The past perfect progressive tense

The **past perfect progressive tense** is formed with the auxiliary *had been* and the verb's present participle. This tense indicates a past, ongoing action completed prior to some other past action.

> During the three decades preceding the 70s, however, women *had been trying* to project a more full-figured look.

FUTURE TENSES

Future: I will start the engine.
Future perfect: I will have started the engine.
Future progressive: I will be starting the engine.
Future perfect progressive: I will have been starting the engine.

The future tense

The **future tense** consists of the base form of the verb along with the auxiliary *will* for all nouns and pronouns. This tense indicates an action or state of being that will begin in the future. In very formal writing, the first person *I* and *we* have traditionally taken the auxiliary *shall;* increasingly, this word is reserved for opening (first-person) questions implying obligation: "Shall I?"

> Even if a woman does match the current ideal body image, she still must realize that she *will* not *fit* the mold forever.

ESL NOTE English has no simple future tense but expresses future events with a variety of constructions, including some uses of the present tense (described above), as well as auxiliaries and such expressions as *going to* or *about to* (see 43b-3).

The future perfect tense

The **future perfect tense** is formed with the verb's past participle and the auxiliary *will have.* This tense indicates an action occurring in the future, prior to some other action.

> By the time many girls reach the age of 16, they *will have spent* hundreds of dollars on such products as reducing aids, diet foods, fitness equipment, self-help manuals.

The future progressive tense

The **future progressive tense** is formed with the auxiliary *will be* (or *shall be*) and the verb's present participle. This tense indicates an ongoing action in the future.

> Many young women believe that if they do not maintain a standard of physical loveliness, they *will be enduring* loneliness, ostracism, and the contempt of others for the rest of their lives.

The future perfect progressive tense

The **future perfect progressive tense** is formed with the auxiliary *will have been* and the verb's present participle. This tense indicates an ongoing action in the future that will occur before some specified future time.

> By the year 2000, many women born in the early 1960s *will have been dieting* for as long as 30 years.

9f Sequencing verb tenses

Although a sentence will always have a main verb located in its independent clause, it may have other verbs as well: a complex sentence will have a second verb in its dependent clause, and a sentence with an infinitive or participle (verb forms that function as adjectives, adverbs, and nouns) will also have at least two verbs or verb forms. Since every verb shows tense, any sentence with more than one verb may indicate actions that occur at different times. Unless the sequence of these actions is precisely set, confusion will result.

UNCLEAR Before I *leave,* I *reported* on my plans. [The logic of this sentence suggests that two events (one in each clause) are related, but the time sequencing of the events—one future, the other past—makes the relationship impossible.]

CLEAR Before I *leave,* I *will report* on my trip. [The two actions take place in the future, one action earlier than the other.]

CLEAR Before I *left,* I *reported* on my plans. [The two actions take place in the past, one action earlier than the other.]

ESL CUE

The concept of the future perfect puzzles many non-English speakers and the tense is nonexistent in languages as diverse as Arabic and Cambodian. Confident, assertive predictions about the future might even be deemed blasphemous or simply impossible in some cultures.

FOR DISCUSSION

Among future tenses, the most problematic seems to be future perfect progressive—perhaps simply because of the number of auxiliaries required to produce it correctly. But students also may need to discuss specific situations in which it should be used. Ask students to generate sentences using future perfect progressive, and then ask them to explain why that tense is appropriate in those sentences. If students can explain the use of future perfect progressive in terms of a time line, they should come to understand more clearly the role played by the auxiliaries. It is the existence of the specific future time reference that necessitates the use of *have* as an auxiliary. Without *have,* the future action's relationship to that time reference would be unclear.

ESL EXERCISE

Describe what you plan to be doing exactly ten years from today in the future. Be specific about your location, your career, your family status, and your financial situation.

ESL CUE

ESL students will need a lot of practice with sequencing verb tenses. Their grammar classes will have taught them the tenses as separate entities, and so they will have had little practice with the mix of tenses common in most writing.

Common tense sequence mistakes include using the future instead of the present or present perfect tense in a subordinate clause whose main clause is future ("After I will finish the dishes, I will go to the movies"); failing to use the past perfect to indicate time earlier than another past tense time ("The thief took

(continued)

everything the students brought home from school"); forgetting that wishes and unreal conditionals take a tense one step further into the past than the time they refer to ("I wish I took that course last year"); or using the past perfect with a present, a present perfect, or a future ("After I had finished the work, I will go to Caracas").

ADDITIONAL EXERCISE D

In the following sentences, write out the verb in parentheses in a tense appropriate to the meaning of the sentence:

1. For years before the girls in Salem Village (begin) accusing local people of witchcraft, disputes over land boundaries (plague) the town.
2. In 1691 the village (be) without a minister for years, but when Samuel Parris (arrive), he (proclaim), "Before the year (be) out, I (sweep) the devil from your midst!"
3. In the winter of that year, while his daughter and his niece (study) Scripture, they (begin) to shake and scream.
4. By the time the doctor (arrive), the girls (behave) strangely for days.
5. His conclusion (be) chilling: "The girls (be) bewitched."
6. Thus an episode (begin) that (baffle) us now and (baffle) others in years to come.

Answers:

1. For years before the girls in Salem Village began accusing local people of witchcraft, disputes over land boundaries had plagued the town.
2. In 1691 the village had been without a minister for years, but when Samuel Parris arrived, he proclaimed, "Before the year is out, I will have swept the devil from your midst!"
3. In the winter of that year, while his daughter and his niece were studying Scripture, they began to shake and scream.
4. By the time the doctor arrived, the girls had been behaving strangely for days.
5. His conclusion was chilling: "The girls are bewitched."
6. Thus an episode began that baffles us now and will baffle others in years to come.

Sequence the events in complex sentences with care.

Jones *attacked* Representative Kaye, who *had proposed* the amendment.
Jones *has spent* months preparing for the trial that *will begin* next week.

A complex sentence joins an independent clause with a dependent clause. Generally, look to the logical relationship between events in the two clauses and choose verb tenses that clarify that relationship.

Establishing a relationship between two events, both of which occur in the past

Use the simple past for one past event—and any of the four past tenses for the other event.

If the two past events happened at the same time, use the simple past tense for both or combine the simple past with the past progressive tense.

The settlers *lived* where the land *supported* them. [A simple past tense is followed by another simple past.]

Shelley *wrote* her letters while she *was traveling* to Moscow. [A simple past is followed by a past progressive.]

If the two past events happened one before the other, use the simple past (or past progressive) for the more recent event, and use the past perfect (or past perfect progressive) to establish the earlier event.

We *understood* that she *had been working* on the solution for years. [The past perfect progressive establishes that her work occurred earlier than our understanding.]

Frank *called* the doctor who *had operated* on him. [The past perfect established that the operation came before the call.]

Frank *had called* the doctor who *operated* on him yesterday. [The past perfect established that the call came before the operation.]

If key expressions establish that one past event happened before the other, the simple past tense is used for both events.

Last Wednesday Frank *called* the doctor who *operated* on him. [The key expression *last Wednesday* establishes that the call came before the operation.]

ESL Note Indirect quotation or reported speech is a common case of tense sequence involving two verbs. A main verb, such as *says,* makes the report while another makes the indirect quotation in a *that . . .* clause—often occurring at a different time from the report: *She says that she will go.* When one event occurs before another, the verb sequence requires careful attention (see 43b-4).

Establishing a relationship between a past event and a future event

Use the simple past tense for the past event and the simple future or the future progressive for the future event.

We *reserved* tickets for the play that *will open* on Saturday. [The reservations were made in the past for a play that opens in the future.]

We *reserved* tickets for the play that *will be opening* on Saturday. [The reservations were made in the past for a play that opens in the future.]

Establishing a relationship between a past event and an acknowledged fact or condition

Use the simple past tense for the past event and the simple present tense for the acknowledged fact or condition.

The study *concluded* that few people *trust* strangers. [The study has been completed and has reached a conclusion about human nature.]

Helen *contacted* the lawyer who *has* the best reputation. [The contact was made in the past with someone who has an ongoing reputation.]

We *found* evidence that the theory *is* correct. [The finding in the past is that the theory was and continues to be correct.]

Use the past perfect tenses for the past event and the simple present tense for the acknowledged fact or condition.

Smith *had argued* that everyone *needs* basic services. [The argument occurred in the past concerning an ongoing need.]

GROUP ACTIVITY

Students will better understand how to sequence verb tenses if they practice with their own sentences. Divide students into groups of three or four and ask each group to generate additional sentences that exemplify the relationships outlined in this section. When finished, each group will report to the class as a whole, reading their sentences and explaining the reasons why they have sequenced tenses as they have. (If it's possible for groups to write their sentences on transparencies, all the better. Then the class can see as well as hear the sentences.) As students explain their choices, they will gain a firmer grasp of the concept of sequencing verb tenses.

2 Choose verb tense in an infinitive phrase based on your choice of verb in the main clause.

Ellen hoped to get rich. To have voted was critical.

An **infinitive phrase** begins with the word *to* placed before a verb such as *see, want, watch, wish, need, go, like,* and *hope.* A present infinitive shows an action that occurs at the same time as or later than the action of the main verb. In the following sentences, the main verb is underlined.

Many critics rejected Roland Jaffe's film adaptation of *The Scarlet Letter.* After much pre-release publicity, critics <u>arrived</u> *to see* a screen version that took many liberties with Hawthorne's original story. [*To see* shows an action at the same time as *arrived.*]

Purists anticipating the movie evidently <u>expected</u> *to see* a more faithful adaptation. [*To see* shows a possible action in the future, later than *expected.*]

A perfect infinitive is formed by placing the auxiliary *have* between the word *to* and the past participle of the verb. A perfect infinitive phrase shows an action that occurs before the action of the main verb.

> *To have played* the role of Hester Prynne presented actress Demi Moore with an opportunity to portray the wrongness of censoring women who have something powerful to communicate. [The opportunity *presented* to Demi Moore is past; her having *played* the role of Hester occurred earlier than, and created, the opportunity.]

ESL Note Certain transitive verbs take an infinitive or infinitive phrase as their object (as in the examples above), while other verbs (such as *enjoy*) take a gerund as object (see 43e-2).

3 Choose the verb tense of a participle based on your choice of verb in the main clause.

> *Arriving* early, the speaker had time to relax.
> *Having* thoroughly *studied* the matter, the judge made her decision.
> *Impressed* with the novel, Marie recommended it to friends.

Participles, past and present, function as adjectives in a sentence. A participle in its present (*-ing*) form indicates an action that occurs at the same time as the action of the sentence's main verb. The main verb in each of the following examples is underlined once, and the participial phrase is underlined twice.

> *Starting with a few unmemorable roles in a few forgettable films,* Moore worked in relative obscurity for several years. She quickly built momentum, however, with her work in *Blame It on Rio* and *St. Elmo's Fire.* [Moore's efforts at the beginning of her career occurred at the same time as her working in obscurity. Both actions occur in the past.]

A participle's present perfect form (the past participle preceded by the auxiliary *having*) shows an action that occurs before that of the main verb.

> *Having proven her versatility in such films as Ghost, A Few Good Men, and Disclosure,* Moore turned to the role of Hester because she admired that character's courage. [Moore played roles in these earlier movies before she took on the role of Hester in *The Scarlet Letter.*]

A participle in its past form (the base form + *-ed* for regular verbs) shows an action that occurs at the same time as or earlier than the action of the main verb.

> *Hauled from place to place during a childhood that saw her family move 48 times in 13 years,* Moore formed strong, clear, and steady goals for her career and her personal life. [The memory of moving existed for Moore both before and during her efforts to form goals for her career and personal life.]

EXERCISE 5

In each sentence that follows, identify the tense of the italicized verb. Then choose the appropriate tense for subsequent verbs in each sentence.

Example: Personality *is* the unique but stable set of characteristics and behavior that ___________ (set) each individual apart from all others.

is present tense *sets* present tense

1. Most people *have accepted* the view that human beings ___________ (possess) specific traits that ___________ (be) fairly constant over time.
2. You *may be* surprised ___________ (learn) that until recently a heated debate ___________ (exist) in the behavioral sciences over the definition's accuracy.
3. On one side of this debate *were* scientists who ___________ (contend) that people ___________ (do) not ___________ (possess) lasting traits.
4. According to these researchers (whom we *will term* the "anti-personality" camp), behavior ___________ (be) shaped largely by external factors.
5. On the other side of the controversy *were* scientists who ___________ (hold), equally strongly, that stable traits ___________ (do) exist.

VOICE

9g Using the active and passive voices

Voice refers to the emphasis a writer gives to the actor in a sentence or to the object acted upon. Because only transitive verbs (see 9d) transfer action from an actor to an object, these verbs exhibit the active and passive voices. The **active voice** emphasizes the actor of a sentence.

Brenda scored the winning goal.

Thomas played the violin.

In each case, an actor, or agent, is *doing* something. In a **passive-voice** sentence, the object acted on is emphasized.

The winning goal was scored by Brenda.

The violin was played by Thomas.

The emphasis on the object of a passive-voice sentence is made possible by a rearrangement of words—the movement of the object, which normally follows a verb, to the first position in a sentence. A passive-voice construction also requires use of the verb *be (is, are, was, were, has been, have been)* and the preposition *by*.

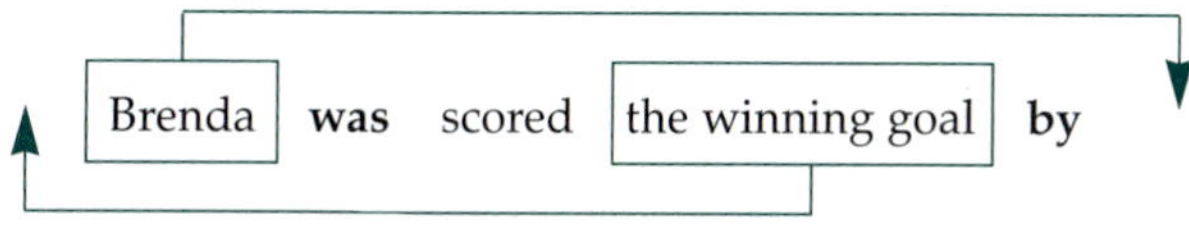

The winning goal was scored by Brenda.

EXERCISE 5

1. *have accepted* present perfect; *possess* present; *are* present
2. *may be* modal present; *to learn* infinitive; *existed* past
3. *were* past; *contended* past; *do* present; *possess* present
4. *will term* future; *is* present
5. *were* past; *held* past; *do* present

ESL CUE

Intransitive verb forms that never take the passive will confuse most ESL students. Giving them a list (die, fall, happen, occur, sleep) of such terms will help.

ESL students will have trouble distinguishing between active and passive adjectives, and will write "I am a boring student" instead of "I am a bored student." Thus, the concept of "performing" versus "receiving the action" needs emphasis.

Students will have learned to distinguish active forms from passive forms, but will probably have little or no experience judging which form is best for which circumstances. Exercises reinforcing such judgment are beneficial.

"My car was stolen" versus "That man stole my car"

or

"The transaction was carried out without a problem"

versus

"Her associate carried out the transaction without a problem."

ESL EXERCISE

Write an invitation to a banquet, a dinner party, a cocktail party, or some other formal event. You must use the passive voice for all directions. Specify time, location, suitable dress, activity, guests, and so forth. You might use verbs such as: invite, request, require, prefer, and serve.

REFERENCE

WILLIAMS, JOSEPH M. *Style: Ten Lessons in Clarity and Grace.* Glenview: Scott, 1981. 8–32. Discusses voice from the perspective of style.

GROUP ACTIVITY

Students often have difficulty with the passive voice; many of them seem to think it's always taboo, while others use it far too often. In order to put the issue into perspective, ask groups to compose a brief story written entirely in passive voice. When they've finished, they can edit out any passives that seem inappropriate, keeping those that seem to work. When they write the story in the passive voice, they should get a sense of how wordy and awkward it can be, and when they justify their revisions, they should begin to understand the appropriate place of the passive voice in written discourse.

In a further transformation of the active-voice sentence, you can make the original actor/subject disappear altogether by deleting the prepositional phrase.

The winning goal was scored.

1 Use a strong active voice for clear, direct assertions.

STRONGER A guidance counselor recommended the book.
WEAKER A book was recommended.

In active-voice sentences, people or other agents *do* things. Active-voice sentences attach ownership to actions and help create a direct, lively attitude between the subject and the reader. By contrast, passive-voice sentences are inherently wordy and reliant on the weak verb *be*. Unintended overuse of the passive voice makes prose dull. Unless you have a specific reason for choosing the passive voice (see the following discussion), use the active voice.

You can make a passive-voice sentence active by restoring a subject/verb sequence. Rewording will eliminate both the preposition *by* and the form of *be*. Note that if an actor of a passive-voice sentence is not named, you will need to provide a name.

PASSIVE (WEAK)	In 1858, Stephen Douglas was challenged to a series of historic debates. [The "challenger" is not named.]
ACTIVE (STRONGER)	In 1858, Abraham Lincoln challenged Stephen Douglas to a series of historic debates.
PASSIVE (WEAK)	The senate race was won by Douglas, but a national reputation was established by Lincoln.
ACTIVE (STRONGER)	Douglas won the senate race, but Lincoln established a national reputation.

2 Use the passive voice to emphasize an object or to deemphasize an unknown subject.

OBJECT EMPHASIZED	The funding goal was reached earlier than expected.
ACTOR(S) EMPHASIZED	We reached the funding goal earlier than expected.

While you should generally prefer the active voice for making direct statements, you will find the passive voice indispensable on two occasions: to emphasize an object and to deemphasize an unknown subject/actor.

Emphasize an object with a passive construction.

When the subject/actor of a sentence is relatively unimportant compared to what is acted on, use the passive voice both to deemphasize the subject/actor and to emphasize the object. The passive voice will shift the subject/actor to a prepositional phrase at a later position in the clause. You may then delete the phrase.

ACTIVE	We require twelve molecules of water to provide twelve atoms of oxygen.
PASSIVE (ACTOR RETAINED)	Twelve molecules of water are required by us to provide twelve atoms of oxygen.
PASSIVE (ACTOR DELETED)	Twelve molecules of water are required to provide twelve atoms of oxygen.

Deemphasize an unknown subject with the passive voice.

You may deemphasize or delete an *unknown* subject/actor by using the passive voice. Instead of writing an indefinite subject/actor (such as *someone* or *people*) into a sentence, use the passive voice to shift the subject/actor to a prepositional phrase. You may then delete the phrase.

ACTIVE	People mastered the use of fire some 400,000 years ago.
PASSIVE (ACTOR RETAINED)	The use of fire was mastered by people some 400,000 years ago.
PASSIVE (ACTOR DELETED)	The use of fire was mastered some 400,000 years ago.

EXERCISE 6

Change the passive-voice sentences that follow to the active voice and change active-voice sentences to passive. Invent a subject if need be for the active-voice sentences.

Example: A trillion dollars will be claimed by retirement plans in the next few years. [The passive voice involves the verb *will be claimed.*]

Retirement plans will claim a trillion dollars in the next few years. [The verb *will claim* is expressed in the active voice.]

1. Nearly 18.5 million Americans maintain 401(k) retirement plans.
2. The 401(k) plan is recommended by economists, politicians, and investment advisers as a key to a comfortable retirement.
3. In practice, however, the 401(k) is often mismanaged by the plan holder's employer.
4. Some workers have voiced their concerns about the structuring and funds allocation of their 401(k)s.

EXERCISE 6

1. Retirement plans of the 401(k) type are maintained by nearly 18.5 million Americans.
2. Economists, politicians, and investment advisers have recommended the 401(k) plan as a key to a comfortable retirement.
3. In practice, however, the plan holder's employer often mismanages the 401(k).
4. Concerns about the structuring and funds allocation of their 401(k)s have been voiced by some workers.
5. As it turns out, alternative, possibly better, plans are not investigated by the company executives who choose 401(k) plans for their employees.

5. As it turns out, the company executives who choose 401(k) plans for their employees do not investigate alternative, possibly better, plans.

MOOD

9h Understanding the uses of mood

The **mood** of a verb indicates the writer's judgment as to whether a statement is a fact, a command, or an unreal or hypothetical condition contrary to fact. In the **indicative mood,** a writer states a fact, opinion, or question. Most of our writing and speech is in the indicative mood.

The mayor has held office for eight years. [fact]

The mayor is not especially responsive. [opinion]

Did you vote for the mayor? [question]

In the **imperative mood,** a writer gives a command, the subject of which is "you," the person being addressed. In this book, for example, the imperative addresses readers with specific guidelines for writing or making revisions. An imperative uses the verb in its base form. Often, the subject of a command is omitted, but occasionally it is expressed directly.

Follow me!

Do not touch that switch.

Don't you touch that switch!

By using the **subjunctive mood,** a writer shows that he or she believes an action or situation is unreal or hypothetical. With a subjunctive verb, a writer can also make a recommendation or express a wish or requirement, usually preceded by such a verb construction as *recommend, suggest, insist, it is necessary,* or *it is important.* The **present subjunctive** uses the base form (infinitive) of the verb for all subjects.

I recommend that he *develop* his math skills before applying.

I recommend that they *develop* their skills.

The **past subjunctive** uses the past-tense form of the verb—or, in the case of *be*—the form *were.*

If management *assumed* traveling costs, the team would be happier.

He wished he *were* four inches taller.

ESL NOTE *If* constructions require a subjunctive verb form only when they express a condition that is considered unreal or hypothetical. Section 43b-5 demonstrates differences between real and unreal conditions with *if* constructions.

ESL CUE

All of the discussion on mood will be confusing for ESL students, whose language texts do not use the word "subjunctive." For *if* forms and "wishes," ESL texts use terms like "real" versus "unreal," "conditionals," and "*if*-clauses contrary to fact" to help distinguish when to use past tense forms. ESL practice with *urge, recommend, suggest, command,* and so forth focuses on these terms' being equivalents of *must* or *should* and therefore on taking the short forms of the verb common with use of *should* and *must* to avoid redundancy, as in "I suggest that he ~~should~~ see a doctor." The *if* formation will be familiar, but the use of *as though* or *as if* to express the hypothetical will probably be new territory.

To avoid confusion, remind ESL students that the *would* form cannot be used with *I* because if the *I* wishes to do something, the question is not one of *will* but of *ability*: "I would if I could" not "I would if I would." The sentence "I would if I could but I can't" is a socially useful mantra to practice.

TEACHING IDEAS

To help students understand the use of subjunctive mood with *if* constructions, you may want to offer the following quotations:

Subjunctive:
If it were in my power to forgive you for your reckless cruelty, I would do so. (Joseph Nye Welch)

I truly wish there were some sort of badge of dishonor that a non-voter would have to wear. (India Edwards)

Indicative:
If the human race wants to go to hell in a basket, technology can help it get there by jet. (Charles M. Allen)

If you rest, you rust. (Helen Hayes)

Ask students to explain the distinction between the two pairs of quotations. Their responses should help them understand the idea that subjunctive mood is used to indicate conditions contrary to fact.

1 Use the subjunctive mood with certain *if* constructions.

If I owned a dog, I would walk it every day.

When an *if* clause expresses an unreal or hypothetical condition, use the subjunctive mood. In a subjunctive *if* construction, the modal auxiliary *would, could, might,* or *should* is used in the main clause. (See 9c-1 for a discussion of modals.)

FAULTY If Tom was more considerate, he would have called. [Clearly, Tom was not considerate (he did not call), and so the indicative or "factual" mood is at odds with the meaning of the sentence.]

SUBJUNCTIVE If Tom *were* more considerate, he would have called.

SUBJUNCTIVE If I *were* elected, I might raise taxes.

NOTE: When an *if* construction is used to establish a cause-and-effect relationship, the writer assumes that the facts presented in a sentence either are true or could very possibly be true; therefore the writer uses an indicative ("factual") mood with normal subject–verb agreement.

FAULTY If I were late, start without me.

REVISED If I am late, start without me. [The lateness is assumed to be a likely or possible fact.]

2 Use the subjunctive mood with *as if* and *as though* constructions.

He dances as though he were weightless.

When an *as if* or *as though* construction sets up a purely hypothetical comparison that attempts to explain or characterize, use the subjunctive mood.

FAULTY She swims as if she *was* part fish. [But since the speaker knows she is not, the indicative ("factual") mood is inconsistent.]

REVISED She swims as if she *were* part fish.

SUBJUNCTIVE He writes quickly, as though he *were* running out of time. [The sentence assumes that he is not running out of time.]

3 Revise to eliminate auxiliary *would* or *could* in subjunctive clauses with *if, as if,* or *as though.*

CLEAR If I had listened, I would have avoided the problem.
CONFUSING If I would have listened, I would have avoided the problem.

In subjunctive constructions like those shown previously, the modal auxiliary verbs *would, could,* or *should* may appear in the main clause to help

TEACHING IDEAS

Students who frequently misuse *would* and *could* in subjunctive clauses might be advised to use the following strategy to edit their papers: After identifying subjunctive structures in the paper, check to see if the auxiliaries are used twice in the same sentence. If they are, then the sentence probably needs to be revised.

Example: If I *would* have known that the storm was coming, I *would* have stocked up on supplies.

The appearance of the auxiliary twice in the same sentence should alert the writer to the error.

indicate that its action is unreal or is conditional. The auxiliaries *would* and *could* cannot appear in the *if* clause, however, since this creates a kind of "double conditional"; these auxiliaries must be replaced with the appropriate subjunctive form.

Faulty If the mate at the wheel *would have* been alerted, the oil spill would have been avoided.

Revised If the mate at the wheel *had* been alerted, the oil spill would have been avoided.

Faulty He could have acted as though he *could have* seen the reef.

Revised He could have acted as though he *had* seen it.

4 Use the subjunctive mood with a *that* construction.

I think it is important that he arrive early.

Use the subjunctive mood with subordinate *that* constructions expressing a requirement, request, urging, belief, wish, recommendation, or doubt. In each of these constructions, the word *that* may be omitted.

The rules require that we *be* present.

I wish that I *were* a painter.

We recommend that he *accept* the transfer.

ESL Note *That* clauses can occur in a variety of sentences not requiring a subjunctive form. See 43b-6 for rules in constructions involving *wish that*.

EXERCISE 7

Use the subjunctive mood, as appropriate, in revising the sentences that follow.

Example: Some experts claim that unmarried couples living together would be happier if they would make finances and spending an explicit topic of discussion and negotiation.

Some experts claim that unmarried couples living together would be happier if they made finances and spending an explicit topic of discussion and negotiation.

1. The couples often wish that there are more precedents to help them decide who pays for what.
2. If each partner communicated his or her expectations to the other, there are fewer squabbles over "your crackers" and "my paper towels."
3. Some experts recommend that each partner keeps a separate bank account but also open a joint checking account to cover household expenses.
4. Experts suggest that each party should be fully informed about the discretionary spending of the other.
5. One specialist in her book *Financial Planning for Couples* recommends that the partner with the higher income pays a proportionately higher share of joint household expenses.

EXERCISE 7

1. The couples often wish that there were more precedents to help them decide who pays for what.
2. If each partner were to communicate his or her expectations to the other, there would be fewer squabbles over "your crackers" and "my paper towels."
3. Some experts recommend that each partner keep a separate bank account but also open a joint checking account to cover household expenses.
4. Experts suggest that each party be fully informed about the discretionary spending of the other.
5. One specialist, in her book *Financial Planning for Couples,* recommends that the partner with the higher income pay a proportionately higher share of joint household expenses.

CHAPTER 10

Agreement

Agreement is a term that describes two significant relationships in a sentence: between a subject and a verb and between a pronoun and an antecedent. These elements occur in pairs. The subject of a sentence must be paired with a verb to make a complete statement. A subject and its verb are either *both* singular or *both* plural.

A pronoun derives meaning from its relation to the noun, or antecedent, that it renames. A pronoun and its antecedent are also either *both* singular or *both* plural.

KEY FEATURES

In this chapter the practical explanation of sentence components continues. Both subject–verb agreement and pronoun–antecedent agreement are covered thoroughly. There are a number of helpful hints for students to use when questions of agreement arise, such as the "tradeoff" technique for subject–verb agreement in the third person. There is also ample warning about problems in subject–verb agreement, such as intervening words and phrases and compound subjects. Indefinite pronouns and collective nouns, as well as plural nouns with singular meaning, receive extensive coverage because of the unique difficulties they pose. The approach to these topics and to others in the chapter, as in previous chapters, is straightforward and relatively traditional. In coverage of pronoun–antecedent agreement, particular attention is paid to alternatives to the use of the generic masculine. In this section the term "gender-appropriate" pronoun is used, and the subject of sexist language is handled firmly but tactfully. The alternatives provide writers with several ways to avoid using the generic masculine inappropriately. Extensive exercises give students the opportunity to practice their skills in agreement.

SUBJECT–VERB AGREEMENT

Subjects and verbs must agree in both number and person. The term **number** indicates whether a noun is singular (denoting one person, place, or thing) or plural (denoting more than one). The term **person** identifies the subject of a sentence as the same person who is speaking (the first person), someone who is spoken to (the second person), or someone or something being spoken about (the third person). Pronouns differ according to person.

	First-person subject	*Second-person subject*	*Third-person subject*
Singular	I	you	he, she, it
Plural	we	you	they

Agreement between a verb and first- or second-person pronoun subject does not vary. The pronouns *I, we,* and *you* take verbs *without* the letter *s.*

I walk. We walk. You walk.

I scream, you scream, we scream—for ice cream.

Problems of confusion sometimes occur, however, in the forms of agreement for third-person subjects and verbs.

10a Make a third-person subject agree in number with its verb.

The suffix *-s* or *-es,* affixed to a present-tense verb, indicates an assertion about a singular third-person subject (A frog do*es* this.); the suffix *-s* or *-es,* affixed to most nouns or third-person pronouns, indicates a plural (Frogs do this.).

FOR DISCUSSION

Since most students have problems with only a few of these common errors, you might want to initiate a class discussion of errors most relevant to your students. Ask students to identify from the Spotlight on Common Errors examples of usage familiar to them and to make their own list of common errors. Students can then discuss the function of agreement in sentences, thereby reinforcing their understanding of the concept. (In large classes, this activity might begin with small groups. The groups will identify their common errors, and then the class as a whole will discuss the list of errors compiled from each group's report.)

Spotlight on Common Errors—AGREEMENT

These are the errors most commonly associated with agreement between subject and verb or pronoun and antecedent. For full explanations and suggested revisions, follow the cross-references to chapter sections.

AGREEMENT ERRORS occur when the writer loses sight of the close link between the paired subjects and verbs, or between pronouns and the words they refer to (antecedents). Paired items should both be singular (referring to *one* person, place, or thing) or both be plural (referring to *more than one* person, place, or thing).

- **A subject and its verb should both be singular or both be plural (they should agree), whether or not they are interrupted by a word or word group (see 10a-1). Match subject and verb. Disregard interrupting words.**

FAULTY	REVISED
Some people, when not paying attention, easily *forgets* names.	Some **people,** when not paying attention, easily ***forget*** names.

- **A sentence with a singular subject needs a singular form of the verb *be* (*am, is, was*); a sentence with a plural subject needs a plural form of the verb *be* (*are, were*) (see 10a-7). To ensure agreement in sentences beginning with the subject, ignore words following the verb *be.***

FAULTY	REVISED
The reason for her success *are* her friends.	The **reason** for her success ***is*** her friends.

When the subject comes after the verb in sentences beginning with *it* or *there,* verb and subject must still agree. Ignore the word *it* or *there.*

FAULTY	REVISED
There *is* seven hills in Rome.	There ***are* seven hills** in Rome. [The subject, *hills,* needs a plural verb.]

- **When *and* joins words to create a two-part subject or a two-part pronoun referent, the sense is usually plural and so the matching verb or pronoun is plural (see 10a-2–3). When *or/nor* creates a two-part subject or pronoun referent, the nearer word determines whether the matching verb or pronoun is singular or plural (see 10b-1–2).**

FAULTY	REVISED
A cat and a dog often *shares* **its** food.	A cat and a dog often ***share* their** food. [Here, *cat and dog* serve as a two-part subject and as a two-part referent.]

FAULTY	REVISED
Neither the rats nor the dog *chase* **their** tail.	Neither the rats nor the dog ***chases* its** tail. [The verb and pronoun match the nearer singular subject, *dog*.]

The "tradeoff" technique

To remember the basic forms of third-person agreement for most verbs in the present tense, you may find it helpful to visualize something like a balanced tradeoff of *-s* endings between most noun subjects and their verbs: if one ends with an *-s*, then the other does not. Thus if the noun subject is singular and lacks an *-s* or *-es* ending, then the singular verb takes the *-s* ending. If the subject is a plural noun with an *-s* ending, then it takes the *-s* and the plural verb does not.

SINGULAR A boy__ hikes. A girl__ swims. A kid__ does it.

PLURAL The boys hike__. The girls swim__. Kids do__ it.

If a noun or pronoun has a plural sense, even if it does not end with an *-s* (e.g., children, oxen, geese, they, these), then the tradeoff technique still applies. Since the noun or pronoun is plural (just as it would be if it were a word made plural with an *-s* ending), the verb is also plural—that is, the verb now lacks its *-s* ending.

SINGULAR A child plays. He plays. He does it.

PLURAL Children play __. They play __. They do__ it.

NOTE: The "tradeoff" technique does not apply when a verb is paired with an auxiliary (or helping) verb (see 9c). Verbs so paired do *not* use *-s*.

A child will play.	He may play.	He might do it.
Children should play.	They could play.	They must do it.

Revising nonstandard verb and noun forms to observe *-s* and *-es* endings

In rapid conversation people sometimes skip over the *-s* or *-es* endings of verbs that are paired with singular nouns. In some English dialects, the base (or infinitive) form of the verb is used for singular nouns. Standard academic English, however, requires that writers observe subject–verb agreement.

NONSTANDARD	He read the book.	NONSTANDARD	She do it.
STANDARD	He read*s* the book.	STANDARD	She do*es* it.

1 A subject agrees with its verb regardless of whether any phrase or clause separates them.

The *purpose* of practicing daily for several hours is to excel.

Often a subject may be followed by a lengthy phrase or clause that comes between it and the verb, confusing the basic pattern of agreement. To

ESL CUE

Common ESL agreement problems include the following: a plural "a number" versus a singular "the number"; a singular form for "everyone/everybody/every man, woman, and child/each of them/none of them"; a singular form for quantities such as "five dollars/ two quarts/four pounds/twenty minutes"; words that end in "s" but take a singular such as "mathematics/news/mumps/billiards/athletics"; words that are one item but take a plural such as "scissors/jeans/pants/eyeglasses"; words that may be singular or plural depending on meaning such as "ethics/acoustics/ barracks/chicken/fish"; indefinite pronouns that depend on an "of" phrase, as in "half of the class" versus "half of the students"; and plural group nouns formed from adjectives such as "the poor/the good/the bad/the ugly/the inconsiderate."

Discussing the difference between count and mass (noncount) nouns ("cars" versus "sugar"; "luggage/baggage" versus "suitcases/bags") is a must, as is a focus on verb agreement with whatever comes after the "or" or "nor" in an "either/or" or "neither/nor" sequence. Marking out prepositional phrases helps ESL students decide on agreement.

ESL students need a great deal of practice with consistency of pronoun reference since it will be a new concept for many of them.

ESL CUE

Chinese and Vietnamese nouns have no singular or plural forms, so the concept of agreement is difficult for speakers of these languages to understand.

LOOKING BACK

MULTICULTURAL DIFFERENCES If a discussion of the -s ending and nonstandard dialects is relevant to your classroom, refer also to 9a-2 and 9c-2.

TEACHING IDEAS

MULTICULTURAL DIFFERENCES If you find that students have difficulty with plurals not formed by adding -*s*, you can ask the class to generate a list of such words, writing them on the board and having students write them in their notebooks. Then they'll have a list handy whenever they're in doubt. This activity is especially useful for non-native speakers.

ADDITIONAL EXERCISE A

ACROSS THE CURRICULUM Peruse the books you're reading for your classes to find three examples of sentences in which subject and verb are separated by lengthy clauses or phrases. Copy the sentences, and then rewrite them so that subject and verb are closer together. (You'll probably need more than one sentence to replace each original.) In comparing the two versions, answer the following questions: Which seems clearer, the original or your rewrite? Why? Which *sounds* better? Why? Which seems more effective overall? Why?

clarify the matching of the subject with the verb, mentally strike out or ignore phrases or clauses separating them. Verbs in the following examples are underlined; subjects are italicized.

> *Downward mobility*—a swift plunge down America's social and economic ladders—poses an immediate and pressing problem. [The verb *poses* agrees with its singular subject, *downward mobility,* not with the plural *ladders* in the interrupting phrase.]
>
> *One* of my friends in a nearby town has heard this. [The prepositional phrases must be ignored to make the singular *one* agree with *has.*]

The words *each* and *every* have a singular sense. When either of these words precedes a compound subject joined by *and,* use a singular verb.

> *Every* city and county in Massachusetts has struggled with the problem of downward mobility.

EXCEPTION: When *each* follows a compound subject, the sense is plural and the plural verb is used.

> Boston and New York *each* are launching programs to reeducate workers.

NOTE: Phrases beginning with "in addition to," "along with," "as well as," "together with," or "accompanied by" may come between a subject and its verb. Although they add material, these phrases do *not* create a plural subject; they must be mentally stricken out to determine the correct number of the verb.

FAULTY *The anthropologist,* as well as social researchers such as statisticians and demographers, are always looking for indicators of change in status. [The interrupting phrase before the verb gives a false impression of a plural subject.]

REVISED *The anthropologist,* as well as social researchers such as statisticians and demographers, is always looking for indicators of change in status. [The singular subject *anthropologist* agrees with the singular verb.]

2 A compound subject linked by the conjunction *and* is in most cases plural.

> *UPS and Federal Express* compete with the U.S. postal system.

When a compound subject linked by *and* refers to two or more people, places, or things, it is usually considered plural.

PLURAL *Statistical information* and *the analysis based upon it* allow an anthropologist to piece together significant cultural patterns. [The compound subject has a plural sense. Thus the verb, *allow,* is plural.]

EXCEPTION: When a compound subject refers to a single person, place, or thing, it is considered singular.

Singular Whatever culture she studies, *this anthropologist* and *researcher* concerns herself with the relations among husbands, wives, children, kin, and friends. [The compound subject has a singular sense—it refers to one person and can be replaced by the singular pronoun *she.* Thus the verb, *concerns,* is singular.]

3 When parts of a compound subject are linked by the conjunction *or* or *nor,* the verb should agree in number with the nearer part of the subject.

Neither the crew members nor the *captain* speaks Arabic.

When all parts of the compound subject are the same number, agreement with the verb is fairly straightforward.

Either John or *Maria* sings today.

Either the Smiths or the *Taylors* sing today.

When one part of the compound subject is singular and another plural there can be confusion; the subject nearer the verb determines the number of the verb. If the nearer subject is singular, the verb is singular.

Singular According to popular wisdom, either poor habits or *ineptitude* is responsible when an individual fails to succeed in American culture. [The singular subject, *ineptitude,* is nearer to the verb; therefore the verb, *is,* is singular.]

When the subject nearer the verb is plural, the verb is plural.

Plural Neither the downwardly mobile individual nor the *people* surrounding him realize that losing a job is often due to impersonal economic factors. [The plural subject, *people,* is nearer to the verb; therefore the verb, *realize,* is plural.]

Note: Subject–verb agreement in this situation may appear to be mismatched unless the plural part of the compound subject is placed closest to the verb. Avoid such awkwardness by revising to place the plural part closest to the verb.

4 Most indefinite pronouns have a singular sense and take a singular verb.

Virtually *everybody* in developed countries travels by bus.
Many who live elsewhere have no choice but to walk.

Indefinite pronouns (such as *any* and *each*) do not have specific antecedents—they rename no particular person, place, or thing and thus raise questions about subject–verb agreement.

GROUP ACTIVITY

Ask groups to generate five sentences, some of which follow this model: "The rules for the annual fly-fishing competition (*was/were*) revised last year." When finished, each group passes its sentences on to another group, which chooses between the singular and plural verbs. As students generate sentences, decide on the number of the verb, and discuss their responses, they'll come to a fuller understanding of how to determine the number of an ambiguous third-person subject.

REFERENCE

Shaughnessy, Mina P. *Errors and Expectations: A Guide for the Teacher of Basic Writing.* New York: Oxford UP, 1977. 16–43. Speakers of nonstandard dialects need special attention when trying to master standard verb forms.

TEACHING IDEAS

One of the most common "errors" in English usage is the *"everyone . . . their"* construction. You may want to discuss the idea of *convention* with students, letting them know that while many people use this construction, the conventions of formal academic discourse dictate that pronouns replacing *everyone* be singular. You may also want to read for yourself the Kolln article listed in the references in this chapter. She is not alone in her opposition to labeling this usage an error.

ESL CUE

Remind ESL students that "each," "every," "everybody," "everything," "one," and "none" will *always* take a singular verb, even when used to encompass a group and when followed by a list, as in "Every man, woman, and child in the group *is* here."

ADDITIONAL EXERCISE B

In the following sentences, determine whether the collective noun has a singular or a plural meaning, and choose the verb accordingly.

1. After the loss, the team bickered among (itself, themselves).
2. The crowd booed heartily, expressing (its, their) disapproval.
3. A Brownie troop could have forged (its, their) way around the field more effectively than this team.
4. The press corps shook (its, their) heads in disbelief.
5. A couple who had both bet against the team happily collected (its, their) winnings.

Answers:

1. plural—themselves
2. singular—its
3. singular—its
4. plural—their
5. plural—their

The following indefinite pronouns have a singular sense:

another	each one	more	one
any	either	much	other
anybody	every	neither	somebody
anyone	everybody	nobody	someone
anything	everyone	none, no one	something
each	everything	nothing	

SINGULAR *Much* of the law concerning the admissibility or exclusion of evidence involves standards of truth and fairness.

SINGULAR Although there was some evidence indicating the guilt of O. J. Simpson, *nothing* was sufficient to prove beyond a reasonable doubt that the accused was guilty.

The indefinite pronouns *both, ones,* and *others* have a plural sense and take a plural verb.

PLURAL Some critics of the trial believe that the verdict damaged the American jurisprudence system; *others* argue that the system worked splendidly and proved that tainted evidence has no place in a court of law.

The indefinite pronouns *all, any, more, many, enough, none, some, few,* and *most* have a singular or plural sense, depending on the meaning of a sentence.

Try substituting *he, she, it, we,* or *they* for the indefinite pronoun. The context of a sentence will give you clues about the number of its subject.

PLURAL Millions of Americans watched the trial. *Most* were tuned in as if to a soap opera. [*Most* (Americans) has a plural sense. It can be replaced by the pronoun *they,* and thus it takes a plural verb, *were.*]

SINGULAR Some of the public interest in the trial was sparked by the legal maneuverings of well-paid lawyers. But *most* of the interest was rooted in voyeurism. [*Most* (of the interest) can be replaced by the pronoun *it.* The singular sense, here, creates the need for a singular verb, *was.*]

5 Collective nouns have a plural or a singular sense, depending on the meaning of a sentence.

At this school, the *faculty* meets as a group with the President.

When a collective noun, such as *audience, band, bunch, crew, crowd, faculty, family, group, staff, team,* and *tribe,* refers to a single unit, the sense of the noun is singular and the noun takes a singular verb. The context of a sentence will give you clues about the number of its subject.

SINGULAR The *jury* hears all the evidence presented by both the prosecution and the defense. [The *jury* is referred to as a single unit; it has a singular sense and takes a singular verb, *hears.*]

When the collective noun refers to individuals and their separate actions within a group, the sense of the noun is plural and the noun takes a plural verb.

Plural The *jury* often have diverse reactions to the evidence they hear. [*Jury* in this case emphasizes the actions of individual members; thus it has a plural sense and takes a plural verb, *have.*]

6 Nouns plural in form but singular in sense take singular verbs.

Economics depends heavily on mathematics.

The nouns *athletics, economics, mathematics, news, physics,* and *politics* all end with the letter *-s,* but they nonetheless denote a single activity.

Note: *Politics* can be considered plural, depending on the sense of a sentence.

News of a layoff causes some people to feel alone and blame themselves.

Politics often comes into play. [*Politics* has a singular sense and takes a singular verb.]

7 A linking verb agrees in number with its subject, not with the subject complement.

One *reason* for his success is his friends.

His *friends* are one reason for his success.

In a sentence with a linking verb, identify the singular or plural subject when deciding the number of the verb. Disregard any distracting phrase or clause that interrupts the subject and verb; also disregard the subject complement *following* the linking verb.

Singular The *reason* for Simpson's acquittal was the many mistakes made by the police in gathering evidence. [The singular verb *was* agrees in number with the singular subject, *reason,* not with the plural subject complement, *mistakes.*]

Plural *The many mistakes made by the police in gathering evidence* were the reason for Simpson's acquittal. [The plural verb, *were,* agrees in number with the plural subject, *mistakes,* not with the singular subject complement, *reason.*]

8 In sentences with inverted word order, a verb should agree in number with its subject.

Here *is* Michael. Here *are* Janice and Michael. There *is* a strategy.

The subject of an English sentence is normally placed before a verb. When this order is rearranged, the subject and verb continue to agree in number. Most errors with rearranged sentences occur with the verb *be.*

GROUP ACTIVITY

If students are able to come up with their own collective and plural-form / singular-sense nouns, they are more likely to remember the conventions regarding agreement. Ask groups to generate two lists, one of collective nouns and one of plural-form nouns taking singular verbs. Once the groups have listed five or six words in each category, the lists can be exchanged and new groups will generate sentences using the words. This activity should heighten students' awareness of the choices they must make with regard to subject-verb agreement.

TEACHING IDEAS

If your students' writing problems warrant it, provide them with practice in dealing with the various kinds of subjects in this section by asking them to generate sentences that follow the patterns illustrated. This activity can be especially helpful both to students who make errors in these areas and to students who tend to avoid complex constructions that might produce errors. When students see that they can indeed produce appropriate constructions, they're likely to apply what they've learned in their papers.

ADDITIONAL EXERCISE C

Rearrange the following sentences to eliminate *here* or *there*, expletives, and questions, choosing the verb that agrees with the subject.

1. There (is, are) a property tax cut planned for next year.
2. (Do, Does) the mayor support it?
3. It (is, are) the city council members who don't want the cut.
4. The reporter stated, "Here (is, are) the woman who proposed the cut."
5. There (is, are) several strong arguments against tax cuts.

Answers:

1. A property tax cut *is* planned for next year.
2. The mayor *does* support it.
3. It *is* the city council members who don't want the cut.
4. The reporter stated, "Here *is* the woman who proposed the cut."
5. There *are* several strong arguments against tax cuts.

ESL CUE

Some romance language speakers (Spanish, Italian, Portuguese) will have difficulty with the concept of the expletive since it does not exist in their language. Their tendency will be to leave out the "there" or "it" and to simply begin with a "be" verb as they would in their language: "Is hot." "Is over there." Calling attention to the problem often helps the student self-correct.

ESL CUE

A general distinction between the expletive "there" and the expletive "it" is that "there" is normally followed by a noun while an "it" is normally followed by an adjective, except in cases of identification, time, and distance.

ESL CUE

Students should be reminded that, because gerunds serve the functions of nouns and may appear wherever a noun appears, one gerund equals one noun and therefore takes a singular verb.

Here and *there* as adverbs

When inverted sentences begin with *here* and *there* as adverbs, the verb will agree in number with the subject (which follows the verb), not with the adverb.

NORMAL The adviser said, "The Pattersons are here." [The plural subject, *Pattersons,* needs a plural verb.]

REARRANGED The adviser said, "Here *are* the Pattersons."

SINGULAR The adviser said, "Here *is* David Patterson."

Expletives

The words *it* and *there* often function as **expletives,** words that fill gaps in a sentence when normal word order is reversed (see 7a-11). *There* can never serve as the subject of a sentence. Disregard it when determining whether the sentence has a singular or plural subject.

PLURAL There were several *factors* that influenced the outcome of the Simpson trial. [*There* is disregarded; the plural subject, *factors,* needs to agree with a plural verb, *were.*]

SINGULAR There was a single *factor,* however, that was most significant—the lack of high quality evidence. [*There* is disregarded; the singular subject, *factor,* needs to agree with a singular verb, *was.*]

Notice that the expletive *it* is always followed by a singular verb.

SINGULAR It is a very good *idea* to help them.

ESL NOTE Some languages do not use *expletives.* In this very common form, a "dummy subject" or filler word *it* or *there* occupies a position normally filled by the subject, followed by the verb *be* or any linking verb: *There were children inside.* The real subject, *children,* is on the other side of the linking verb "equation" (see 11d). See 43a-2 and 7a-11 for ways to use this construction; see 14e and 17a for ways to avoid wasting words with expletives.

Questions

Inverting a sentence's word order is one method of forming a question. The relocated verb must still agree in number with the subject.

STATEMENT He really *wants* to hold on to that idea.

QUESTION Does *he* really want to hold on to that idea? [The verb *does want* agrees with the subject *he.*]

Many questions are formed with *wh* words (*what, where, when, why*), with a verb following the *wh* word and a noun following that. The verb and noun should agree in number.

SINGULAR What is *the cost* to him of abandoning it?

PLURAL What are *the costs* aside from that?

9 The verb of a dependent clause introduced by the pronoun *which, that, who,* or *whom* should agree in number with the pronoun's antecedent.

The *books, which* are old, are falling apart. *Which book* is mine?

In such a dependent clause, both the pronoun subject (*which, that,* etc.) and verb are dependent for their number on an antecedent in the main clause.

PLURAL The judicial *systems* of other nations, *which* are not necessarily based on the premise that the accused is innocent until proven guilty, might have dealt quite differently with the Simpson case. [The relative pronoun, *which,* renames the plural antecedent, *systems;* the relative pronoun has a plural sense and the verb following must be plural.]

SINGULAR The *price* we pay, *which* is that sometimes our judicial system allows the guilty to go free, is worth the saving of one innocent life. [The relative pronoun, *which,* renames the singular antecedent, *price;* the relative pronoun has a singular sense and the verb following must be singular.]

10 Phrases and clauses that function as subjects are treated as singular and take singular verbs.

To swim well is the first prerequisite for scuba diving.
That the child is able to cough is a good sign.

Often a noun clause, or a phrase with a gerund or infinitive, will act as the subject of a sentence. Such a construction is always regarded as a singular element in the sentence.

SINGULAR *That a guilty man or woman might "get away with murder"* strikes many as too high a price to pay for American-style justice, which obligates the prosecution to prove its case beyond a reasonable doubt. [The noun clause introduced by *that* functions as the subject of this sentence and has a singular sense. It therefore takes a singular verb, *strikes.*]

SINGULAR *To believe that the inflammatory arguments of the Simpson defense team were the reason for his acquittal* is to miss a key point: it was a lack of definitive evidence that truly undermined the prosecution's case. [The long infinitive phrase functions as the subject of this sentence and takes a singular verb, *is.*]

ADDITIONAL EXERCISE D

ACROSS THE CURRICULUM Photocopy a passage from a textbook in one of your other courses. Underline clauses introduced by the pronouns *which, that, who,* and *whom,* and circle the verbs in these clauses. Then underline phrases and clauses functioning as subjects and circle the main verbs in those sentences. This activity should help you better understand subject-verb agreement.

11 Titled works, key words used as terms, and companies are treated as singular in number and take singular verbs.

Classics is an overused word. "The Killers" is a Hemingway story.

Titles of works, names of companies or corporations, underlined or italicized words referred to as words, numbers, and units of money are regarded as singular entities in a sentence and take singular verbs.

SINGULAR *"So You Think O. J. Got Away with Murder"* is the title of one reporter's article on the outcome of and response to the Simpson acquittal.

SINGULAR *Probably guilty* is a finding many in the public wished the jury could have reached, but it's a verdict not allowed in American law.

SINGULAR *The 1990s* is a decade that will be inextricably linked to the O. J. Simpson trial.

EXERCISE 1

1. is
2. is assures seem
3. is
4. has
5. work

EXERCISE 1

In the following sentences, determine whether a subject is singular or plural. Choose the correct form in parentheses and be able to explain your choice.

Example: How (do/does) we get other people to agree with us?

How *do* we get other people to agree with us? [The subject of the sentence is the plural pronoun, *we.* Even though the auxiliary part of the verb, *do,* is placed before the subject to form a question, the full verb (including the auxiliary) and the subject must agree in number.]

1. One reason for making a purchase (is/are) a buyer's emotional needs.
2. There (is/are) no single method that (assure/assures) success in persuading others; still, several methods (seem/seems) helpful.
3. One effective way of getting a "yes" from other people (is/are) to get them to like us.
4. Flattery, an extremely common tactic for gaining compliance, (has/have) a long history.
5. Both flattering people and getting them to talk about themselves (work/works) in surprisingly consistent ways.

PRONOUN–ANTECEDENT AGREEMENT

An **antecedent** is a word—usually a noun, sometimes a pronoun—that is renamed by a pronoun. Pronouns in the following examples are underlined and antecedents are italicized.

antecedent pronoun

Van Leeuwenhoek called the microorganisms that he found everywhere in vast numbers "little animals."

A pronoun's antecedent must be clearly identified in order for the pronoun itself to have a meaningful reference (see Chapter 14 on pronoun reference). A pronoun and antecedent must agree in *number, person,* and *gender.* **Gender** refers to whether a noun or pronoun is feminine, masculine, or neuter.

Mary flies planes. She flies planes. (feminine)

Bob rides trolleys. He rides trolleys. (masculine)

A trolley runs on tracks. It runs on tracks. (neuter)

In most cases, as in the preceding examples, a pronoun is easily matched to its antecedent in terms of person (first, second, or third), number (singular or plural), and gender (masculine or feminine). At times, however, the choice of the right pronoun requires careful attention.

10b Pronouns and their antecedents should agree in number.

Of the three components that determine pronoun selection, agreement in number causes the most difficulty—for the same reason that subject–verb agreement is sometimes difficult: the *number* of a noun (either as subject or antecedent) is not always clear. The following conventions will help you to determine whether an antecedent is singular or plural.

1 A compound antecedent linked by the conjunction *and* is usually plural.

Watson and Crick were awarded a Nobel prize for their achievement.

Plural In all early attempts at classification, living things were separated into two major groups—*the plant kingdom* and *the animal kingdom.* These were then subdivided in various ways. [The compound antecedent has a plural sense; therefore the pronoun renaming it is plural in form.]

Plural In the 4th century B.C., *Aristotle* made a study of the animal kingdom and *Theophrastus* studied the plant kingdom; their systems for classifying animals and plants began the scientific effort of classifying all living things. [The compound antecedent has a plural sense; therefore the pronoun renaming it is plural in form.]

Exceptions: When a compound antecedent with parts joined by the conjunction *and* has a singular sense, use a singular pronoun.

Singular *An English naturalist* and *writer,* Thomas Blythe, used his classification scheme to identify more than 18,000 different types of plants. [The compound antecedent refers to one person—Thomas Blythe; therefore the pronoun renaming it is singular.]

The words *each* and *every* have a singular sense. When either of these words precedes an antecedent joined by *and,* use a singular pronoun.

FOR DISCUSSION

Students probably have a good deal more experience with pronoun–antecedent problems than we realize. As they read texts on complex subjects and write complicated papers for their various courses, they often find themselves mired in structures that are beyond their control. It might be useful to situate a discussion of agreement in the student's own academic lives. Ask students about the difficulty they have reading complex material and suggest that they bring in examples of troublesome passages. Ask them also to talk about the problems they encounter when they write about complicated issues; again, they can be encouraged to bring in samples of their own writing. A discussion of these problems can lead to an appreciation of how understanding pronoun-antecedent agreement can help students comprehend some of their more difficult reading and sort out meaning in their own writing.

REFERENCES

KOLLN, MARTHA. "Everyone's Right to Their Own Language." *CCC* 37 (1986): 100–02. Argues from a common usage standpoint that constructions such as "everyone . . . their" should not be called errors.

SKLAR, ELIZABETH S. "The Tribunal of Use: Agreement in the Indefinite Constructions." *CCC* 39 (1988): 410–22. Indefinite pronouns sometimes take on singular, sometimes plural, meanings.

SINGULAR Every *visible organism* and *microscopic organism* has its own distinctive, two-word Latin name according to the system designed by Carolus Linnaeus in the early eighteenth century.

EXCEPTION: When *each* follows an antecedent joined by *and,* the sense is plural and the plural pronoun is used.

PLURAL Daly and Blythe have *each* made their contribution to our understanding of classification systems.

2 When parts of a compound antecedent are linked by the conjunction *or* or *nor,* a pronoun should agree in number with the nearer part of the antecedent.

Neither the captain nor the *crew members* understood *their* predicament.

This pattern of agreement with *or* or *nor* follows the same convention as does subject–verb agreement (10a-3).

SINGULAR Neither the traditional two-kingdom systems nor the recent five-kingdom *system* is complete in its classification of organisms. [The pronoun is nearer to the singular "system" and so agrees in the singular.]

NOTE: Avoid awkward pronoun use by revising to place the plural part of the compound antecedent nearer to the pronoun.

REVISED Neither the five-kingdom system nor the traditional two-kingdom *systems* are complete in their classifications. [The plural part of the antecedent is revised to fall nearer to the pronoun; the sentence is no longer awkward in its agreement.]

Make pronouns agree in number with indefinite pronoun antecedents.

Each one has her own job. *Both* have begun their research.

Indefinite pronouns (such as *each, anyone,* and *everyone*) do not refer to particular persons, places, or things. Most often, an indefinite pronoun used as an antecedent will have a singular sense. When it does, rename it with a singular pronoun.

SINGULAR *Each* of the millions of organisms now living has its own defining features.

When an indefinite pronoun (such as *both* or *others*) functions as an antecedent and has a plural sense, rename it with a plural pronoun.

PLURAL Some organisms are readily classified as animal or plant; *others,* most often the simplest single-cell organisms, find themselves classified in different ways, depending on the classification system used.

A few indefinite pronouns (such as *some, more,* or *most*) can have a singular or a plural sense, depending on the context of a sentence. Determine the number of an indefinite pronoun antecedent before selecting a pronoun replacement.

PLURAL *Some* of the simplest living organisms defy classification, by virtue of their diversity. [*Some* has a plural sense.]

SINGULAR *Some* of the recent research made possible by microscopes is startling in its findings that certain unicellular organisms like the euglena have both plant-like and animal-like characteristics. [*Some* has a singular sense.]

4 Make pronouns agree in number with collective noun antecedents.

A well-informed group, the *faculty* is outspoken in its opinions.
The *faculty* at the gathering shared their thoughts on the issue.

Collective nouns will be singular or plural depending on the meaning of a sentence. When a collective noun such as *audience, band, group,* or *team* refers to a *single unit,* the sense of the noun as an antecedent is singular and takes a singular pronoun.

SINGULAR A *group* of similar organisms that interbreed in nature is called a species and is given its own distinct Latin name. [*Group* has a singular sense.]

When a collective noun refers to individuals and their *separate actions* within a group, the sense of the noun as an antecedent is plural and takes a plural pronoun.

PLURAL Human beings are the only *group* of primates who walk on two legs, without the aid of their hands. [*Group* has a plural sense.]

10c Rename indefinite antecedents with gender-appropriate pronouns.

A lawyer serves *his or her* clients. Lawyers serve *their* clients.

Indefinite pronouns that have a singular sense and refer to people (as opposed to places or things) will likely refer to both males *and* females. Traditionally, the generic *he* or *his* was used to rename an indefinite antecedent,

FOR DISCUSSION

SEXIST LANGUAGE While the generic masculine has been out of favor in academe for quite some time, it's alive and kicking elsewhere in society. Thus many students may consider this section much ado about nothing. It might be useful to ask students to discuss their feelings about the subject, particularly the traditional explanation that the masculine pronoun was inclusive of females. Of course, if this were completely true, then why the need to preface professional titles for women ("woman doctor," "woman lawyer") or to change suffixes of generic terms to accommodate females ("actress," "heroine")? If no student offers this line of argument, you may want to offer it yourself to see what kind of response it receives.

CRITICAL DECISIONS

Set issues in a broader context: Understand the gender messages implied by your pronouns

Gender-specific pronoun use can be inaccurate and offensive. Be aware, when choosing a pronoun, of the larger social setting in which you work. To avoid unintentional sexism, use five techniques, either alone or in combination. For more discussion on gender reference, see 21g.

1. **Use the constructions *he or she, his or her,* and *him or her* in referring to an indefinite pronoun or noun.** Choose this option when the antecedent of a pronoun must have a singular sense. Realize, however, that some readers object to the *he or she* device as cumbersome. The variants *(s)he* and *he/she* are considered equally cumbersome. The *he or she* device can work, provided it is not overused.

   AWKWARD To some extent, *a biologist* must decide for him- or herself which system of classification he or she will use.

   REVISED To some extent, *a biologist* must decide which system of classification he or she will use.

   REVISED To some extent, *a biologist* must decide which system of classification to use. [The infinitive *to use* avoids the *he or she* difficulty.]

2. **Make a pronoun's antecedent plural.** If the accuracy of a sentence will permit a plural antecedent, use this device to avoid unintentional sexism in pronoun selection.

   PLURAL To some extent, *biologists* must decide for themselves which system of classification *they* will use. [Note the possible shift in meaning: *biologists* may imply a group discussion.]

3. **Use the passive voice to avoid gender-specific pronouns—but only if it is appropriate to deemphasize a subject.** Note, however, that using the passive voice creates its own problems of vague reference. (See 9g-2 and 17b-1.)

   NEUTRAL It is every biologist's responsibility to specify which system of classification *is being used.*

4. **Reconstruct the entire statement so as to avoid the problem.** Often it is easier to rewrite sentences to avoid pronouns altogether.

   NEUTRAL When choosing among competing systems of classification, the biologist makes a choice that greatly affects later work both in the field and in the lab. [*Later work* is left without a limiting, gender-specific modifier.]

5. **Link gender assignments to specific indefinite antecedents.** Some writers will arbitrarily assign a masculine identity to one indefinite antecedent and a feminine identity to another. The gender assignments are then maintained throughout a document.

   ALTERNATE GENDER ASSIGNMENTS A *biologist* must decide which system of classification she will use. An *anthropologist* must also choose when selecting the formal, stylistic, and technological attributes he will use in distinguishing ancient objects from one another.

such as *each* or various nouns without specific gender identity. Today, many find this generic use offensive.

Offensive To some extent, *a biologist* must decide for himself which system of classification he will use.

The use of *himself* and *he* in this sentence would exclude female biologists, of whom there are many. In addition to being inaccurate, this exclusion will offend anyone sensitive to the ways in which language can inflict harm. Be aware of the gender content of your pronoun choice.

REFERENCE

Bryony, Shannon. "Pronouns: Male, Female, and Undesignated." *ETC.: A Review of General Semantics* 45 (Winter 1988): 334–36. To avoid using the generic masculine, a plural pronoun should be acceptable.

EXERCISE 2

Revise the following sentences to ensure agreement between pronouns and antecedents. Eliminate the generic *he.* Place a check before the sentences in which a pronoun agrees in number with its antecedent.

Example: The characters, plots, and settings of Stephen King's stories have haunted readers with its believable eeriness.

The characters, plots, and settings of Stephen King's stories have haunted readers with *their* believable eeriness.

1. In one of these novels, a 1958 Plymouth Fury is a jealous monster who seeks out and destroys the enemies of her male owner.
2. Anyone who considers himself a horror connoisseur has read at least some of the novels of Stephen King.
3. Whenever King's novels are turned into motion pictures, it grosses millions of dollars.
4. In their adaptation of King's short novel "The Body" into the full-length feature film *Stand by Me,* artist and director Rob Reiner created a tenderhearted crowd pleaser, quite unlike other movies made from King's novels.

EXERCISE 2

1. In one of the novels, a 1958 Plymouth Fury is a jealous monster who seeks out and destroys the enemies of her male owner.
2. Those who consider themselves horror connoisseurs have read at least some of the novels of Stephen King.
3. Whenever King's novels are turned into motion pictures, they gross millions of dollars.
4. In his adaptation of King's short novel "The Body" into the full-length feature film *Stand by Me,* artist and director Rob Reiner created a tenderhearted crowd pleaser, quite unlike other movies made from King's novels.

EXERCISE 3

Revise the following gender-biased sentences so that they do not stereotype males or females or restrict references to males. When you make singular nouns plural, other words in the sentence will change.

Example: The behaviorist theory in psychology assumes that man's response to his environment is similar to the response of other animals.

The behaviorist theory in psychology assumes that humans respond to their environment in the same ways that other animals do.

1. Each operator answers her phone.
2. As part of her job, a nurse prepares injections for her patients.
3. A miner would take a canary below ground to make sure the air was safe for him to breathe.
4. A pilot, today, takes much of his training in flight simulators.
5. Recent research has suggested a relationship between the amount of time a child watches television and his later performance in school.

EXERCISE 3

Suggested revisions:

1. Each operator answers his or her phone.
2. As part of their job, nurses prepare injections for their patients.
3. Miners would take a canary below ground to make sure the air was safe for them to breathe.
4. A pilot, today, takes much of his or her training in flight simulators.
5. Recent research has suggested a relationship between the amount of time children watch television and their later performance in school.

EXERCISE 4

Suggested revisions:

The haunted house *looms* large in American literature and film. Some of the most famous *have been* Poe's castle in "The Masque of the Red Death," his "house" of Usher, Shirley Jackson's Hill House, the Bates mansion in Hitchcock's *Psycho,* and the suburban home in *The Amityville Horror.* A relatively recent haunted house story, a genre piece in the tradition of horror classics, *was* King's *The Shining.* Readers of the book or viewers of the movie *were* sure to satisfy their need for chills and thrills. As is the case in so many stories of the haunted house, the characters are never entirely sure where they fit into the house's scheme of things.

EXERCISE 4

Revise the following paragraph to ensure agreement between subject and verb and between pronoun and antecedent. Also, revise any sentence in which the generic *he* is used.

> The haunted house loom large in American literature and film. Some of the most famous has been Poe's castle in "The Masque of the Red Death," his "house" of Usher, Shirley Jackson's Hill House, the Bates mansion in Hitchcock's *Psycho,* and the suburban home in *The Amityville Horror.* A relatively recent haunted house story, a genre piece in the tradition of horror classics, were King's *The Shining.* Any reader of the book or viewer of the movie was sure to satisfy his need for chills and thrills. As is the case in so many stories of the haunted house, none of the characters are ever entirely sure where he fits into the house's scheme of things.

CHAPTER 11

Adjectives and Adverbs

Adjectives and adverbs are **modifiers**—*descriptive* words, phrases, or clauses that enliven sentences with vivid detail. In Chapter 7 you learned how phrases and clauses function as modifiers. But even when dealing with single-word modifiers, as in this chapter, you can see that the effectiveness of modifiers depends on keeping straight the two main types: adjectives and adverbs.

KEY FEATURES

The first example presented here illustrates the focus of the entire chapter: the function of adjectives and adverbs is to make sentences clearer and more vivid. As in other chapters on sentence elements, the approach is straightforward and relatively traditional. A chart shows the distinctive functions of the two parts of speech, and the forms are clearly described. Nonstandard usage is treated with tact. The treatment of problem words such as *good/well* and *bad/badly* includes a number of examples to guide students, and a chart lists irregular forms of comparison for easy reference. Exercises focus on editing sentences.

11a Distinguishing between adjectives and adverbs

Some basic distinctions between the use of adjectives and adverbs are summarized in the following box.

Distinguishing Adjectives from Adverbs

An **adjective** modifies a noun or pronoun and answers these questions:

Which: The *latest* news arrived.

What kind: An *insignificant* difference remained.

How many: The *two* sides would resolve their differences.

An **adverb** modifies a verb and answers these questions:

When: *Tomorrow,* the temperature will drop.

How: The temperature will drop *sharply.*

How often: Weather patterns change *frequently.*

Where: The weather patterns *here* change frequently.

An **adverb** also modifies adjectives, adverbs, and entire clauses:

Modifying an adjective: An *especially* large group enrolled.

Modifying a clause: *Consequently,* the registrar closed the course.

Modifying an adverb: Courses at this school *almost* never get closed.

When choosing between an adjective and adverb form for a sentence, identify the word being modified and determine its part of speech. Then follow the conventions presented in this chapter.

Identifying and using adjectives

An **adjective** modifies a noun or pronoun by answering these questions: **which?** the *tall* child; **what kind?** the *artistic* child; **how many?** *five* children. Pure adjectives are not derived from other words: *large, small, simple, difficult, thick, thin, cold, hot.* Many adjectives, however, are derived from nouns.

Base noun	*Suffix*	*Adjective*
science	-ic	scientific
region	-al	regional
book	-ish	bookish

Adjectives are also derived from verbs.

Base verb	*Suffix*	*Adjective*
respect	-ful	respectful
respect	-ed	respected (past participle)
respect	-ing	respecting (present participle)
demonstrate	-ive	demonstrative
hesitate	-ant	hesitant

Writers frequently build up their desired meanings by taking a word and adapting its base form, thereby converting the word into the part of speech needed for a new sentence.

The audience maintained a (respect + ful) silence.

The (region + al) conference was about to begin.

ESL Note The past and present participles formed from the same basic verb are related in meaning. Consider, though, how two forms derived from a transitive verb (such as *confuse*) may work in opposite directions on the word modified: *a confused speaker* experiences confusion, while *a confusing speaker* gives others this experience (see 44a-1).

Placement

A single-word adjective is usually placed before the word it modifies. Occasionally an adjective will appear after a noun or pronoun—usually when the adjective is formed by a phrase or clause.

The speaker was received with *enthusiastic* applause.

The speaker, *bookish* and *hesitant,* approached the podium.

ESL Note In most English sentences, two or more adjectives that accumulate as modifiers before a noun or pronoun are typically given a standard order or sequence. For example, adjectives describing nationality and color are typically placed nearer than others to the noun or pronoun.

Confusing *a blue Japanese cheerful flower*

Typical *a cheerful blue Japanese flower*

ESL CUE

ESL trouble spots will be distinguishing between "hard" and "hardly," "a few" and "few," "a little" and "little," "some" and "any," and using "well" and "good" correctly. The distinction between "I have *a* little time/money" and "I have little time/money" is *not* self-evident, even to many fluent second-language speakers, and may have damaging social consequences.

ESL CUE

Spanish speakers tend to have difficulty with "too," using it as an equivalent of "very" instead of as a negative form involving an explanation: "He is too tall to enter without bending over" or "She is too tired to work any longer." Try to have students articulate what it means to have "too much money" or "too much love." Also contrast the following:

"She is very hungry."
"She is too hungry to wait for us."
"She is hungry enough to eat a horse."

ESL CUE

Marcella Frank's *Modern English, Part I* has a complete chapter on adverbs, and the final section of the chapter practices distinguishing between adverbs and adjectives, as in "He felt bad" as opposed to "He did that badly."

ADDITIONAL EXERCISE A

GROUP ACTIVITY In groups of three or four, modify the following sentences by adding single-word adjectives and adverbs. Then compare your responses to those of other groups. How does the meaning of each sentence change as a result of the modifiers used?

1. A skier sped down the slope.
2. The boxer danced around his opponent.
3. The colonel inspected her office.
4. The child cried.
5. An artist contemplated the scene.

LOOKING BACK

If any students need to refresh their memories with regard to the role of parts of speech in a sentence, refer them to Chapter 7 (Constructing Sentences).

Section 44f-1–2 describes typical patterns for placement of English adjective modifiers.

Identifying and using adverbs

An **adverb** modifies a verb by answering several questions: **When?** *Yesterday,* the child sang. **How?** The child sang *beautifully.* **How often?** The child sings *regularly.* **Where?** The child sang *here.* Adverbs modify adjectives: The child sang an *extremely* intricate melody. Adverbs can modify other adverbs: The child sings *almost* continuously. Certain adverbs can modify entire sentences: *Consequently,* the child's voice has improved.

Pure adverbs are not derived from other words: *again, almost, always, never, here, there, now, often, seldom, well.* Many adverbs, however, are formed from adjectives. These adverbs may be formed simply by adding the suffix *-ly* to adjectives.

Adjective	*Add -ly*	*Adverb*
beautiful		beautifully
strange		strangely
clever		cleverly
respectful		respectfully

However, an *-ly* ending alone is not sufficient to establish a word as an adverb, since certain adjectives show this ending: a friend*ly* conversation, a love*ly* afternoon. In any standard dictionary look for the abbreviations **adj.** and **adv.,** which will distinguish between the forms of a word.

Thousands of words in our language have both adjective and adverb forms. Consider the noun *grace,* defined by the *American Heritage Dictionary* as "seemingly effortless beauty or charm of movement, form, or proportion." *Graceful* and *gracious* are adjectives, and *graciously, gracefully,* and *gracelessly* are adverbs.

Placement

The location of an adverb may be shifted in a sentence, depending on the rhythm and emphasis a writer wants to achieve. An adverb (as a word, phrase, or clause) can appear in the sentence's beginning, middle, or end.

Formerly, Zimbabwe was known as Rhodesia.

Zimbabwe was *formerly* known as Rhodesia.

Zimbabwe was known as Rhodesia, *formerly.*

A note of caution: Lengthy adverb phrases and clauses should not split sentence elements that occur in pairs, such as a subject and verb or a verb and its object (see 15d). Also, limiting modifiers such as *only, almost,* or *nearly* must be carefully placed close to the word they modify (see 15b).

ESL Note While the placement of most English adverbs is flexible, limiting adverbs and others require specific positions in the sentence, as described in 44c-1–2.

ADDITIONAL EXERCISE B

ACROSS THE CURRICULUM Make a photocopy of a brief passage from one of your textbooks. Circle the adjectives and adverbs and draw arrows to the words they modify. Then, for each sentence in the passage, explain how the adjectives enhance meaning.

REFERENCES

Christensen, Francis. "A Generative Rhetoric of the Sentence." CCC 14 (1963): 155–61. Use of modifiers improves students' prose style.

Shaughnessy, Mina P. *Errors and Expectations: A Guide for the Teacher of Basic Writing.* New York: Oxford UP, 1977. Chapter 6. Building vocabulary can help students break away from standard, overused modifiers.

ESL CUE

Initial emphatic negative adverbial phrases requiring reversed word order will prove difficult and confusing for most ESL students: "Never in a million years will I marry you" or "Not once did she try to help." Confusing also are the rules for word order with initial adverbial phrases of place: "In the center of the room was an ornate table" or "Near the fireplace stood an antique lamp." Many ESL students will tend to put the subject before the verb with these patterns.

ESL CUE

Adverb placement is not treated clearly in most ESL texts. Such texts do not explain well the shifts in meaning and emphasis possible through shifts in placement, so the examples in this section require close attention. Students will have trouble with placement of adverbs in three-part verbs: frequency/time between the first two parts, manner/degree between the last two, as in "She had *rarely* been so *completely* enchanted" or "*Yesterday* she had *nearly* been *completely* convinced." This is because native speakers have an instinctual sense of when a variation of this standard pattern is necessary, as in "She has *recently* been advancing *more slowly,*" but cannot always articulate clearly why this variation must occur. (In this

(continued)

case the extra word makes the final two words a phrase of manner, and phrases of manner follow the verb just as phrases of frequency follow phrases of manner: "I understand him more and more fully each time I see him.")

EXERCISE 1

adj adj adj
1. Our culture prefers the assertive, flexible,
adj
and extroverted individual over the
adj adj adj
introverted, cautious, and inhibited
individual.
adj
2. The popular perception is that the
adj adj adv
introverted personality is uptight, socially
adj adj
isolated, unable to achieve goals, and
adj
prone to melancholy.
3. One could argue, however, that since
adj
introverted behavior is not rewarded by
adj adv
our culture, introverts should naturally feel
adj
underappreciated.
adv adj
4. Some theorists correctly observe that such
adj
individuals have been responsible for
adj adj adj
much of the artistic, scientific, scholarly
adj
achievement of the human race.
adj adv
5. Social scientists theorize that in earlier
adj
historical epochs, introverts contributed
adv adj
subtly to social stability.

EXERCISE 2

(Individual responses for sentence portion):

1. substance (noun) substantive (adj) substantively (adv)
2. reason (noun) reasonable (adj) reasonably (adv)

EXERCISE 1

Identify the single-word adjectives and adverbs in the following sentences; also identify the words being modified.

Example: Every personality has its introverted (adj) and extroverted (adj) parts.

American culture greatly (adv) exaggerates the virtues of extroversion.

1. Our culture prefers the assertive, flexible, and extroverted individual over the introverted, cautious, and inhibited individual.
2. The popular perception is that the introverted personality is uptight, socially isolated, unable to achieve goals, and prone to melancholy.
3. One could argue, however, that since introverted behavior is not rewarded by our culture, introverts should naturally feel underappreciated.
4. Some theorists correctly observe that such individuals have been responsible for much of the artistic, scientific, and scholarly achievement of the human race.
5. Social scientists theorize that in earlier historical epochs, introverts contributed subtly to social stability.

EXERCISE 2

Convert the following nouns and verbs to adjectives and adverbs; convert the adjectives to adverbs. (Use a dictionary for help, if necessary.) Then use each newly converted word in a sentence.

Example: courtesy (noun)	courteous (adjective)	courteously (adverb)

A courteous driver will signal before turning.

substance
reason
argue
wonderful
colossal

11b Use an adverb (not an adjective) to modify verbs as well as verbals.

Adverbs are used to modify verbs even when a direct object stands between the verb and its modifier.

FAULTY If you measure an object in Denver *precise,* it will weigh somewhat less than the same object measured in Washington. [The adjective *precise*—following a direct object—is used incorrectly to modify the verb *measured.*]

REVISED If you measure an object in Denver *precisely,* it will weigh somewhat less than the same object measured in Washington.

Faulty A *precise* measured object in Denver will weigh somewhat less than the same object measured in Washington. [The adjective *precise* incorrectly modifies the participle *measured.*]

Revised A *precisely* measured object in Denver will weigh somewhat less than the same object measured in Washington.

Faulty An object's weight can be determined by measuring it *careful* against a known weight. [The adjective *careful* incorrectly modifies the gerund *measuring.*]

Revised An object's weight can be determined by measuring it *carefully* against a known weight.

11c Use an adverb (not an adjective) to modify another adverb or an adjective.

Although informal or nonstandard usage occasionally finds adjectives like *real* or *sure* functioning as adverbs ("a real bad time," "it sure was good"), standard academic usage requires that adverbs modify adjectives and other adverbs.

Nonstandard A *reasonable* accurate scale can measure hundredths of a gram. [The adjective *reasonable* incorrectly modifies the adjective *accurate.*]

Revised A *reasonably* accurate scale can measure hundredths of a gram.

Faulty An object on the Moon weighs *significant* less than it does on Earth. [The adjective *significant* incorrectly modifies the adverb *less.*]

Revised An object on the Moon weighs *significantly* less than it does on Earth.

11d Use an adjective (not an adverb) after a linking verb to describe a subject.

The following verbs are linking verbs: forms of *be* (*is, are, was, were, has been, have been*), *look, smell, taste, sound, feel, appear, become, grow, remain, seem, turn,* and *stay.* A sentence with a linking verb establishes, in effect, an equation between the first part of the sentence and the second:

A LINKING VERB *B*, or *A* = *B*.

In this construction, the predicate part, *B,* is called the *subject complement.* The function of a **subject complement** is to rename or modify the subject of a sentence, which is a noun. The subject complement may be a noun, pronoun, or adjective—but *not* an adverb. In these examples, the linking verbs are followed by adjectives that describe a subject.

3. argue (noun) arguable (adj) arguably (adv)
4. wonderful (adj) wonderfully (adv)
5. colossal (adj) colossally (adv)

FOR DISCUSSION

This section provides an ideal opportunity to discuss the differences between formal written English and informal usage. Ask students to name various adjectives and adverbs found in informal, nonstandard usage. Responses will probably include teenage slang such as *wicked* and *majorly* as adverbs, as well as the more common *super* as both adjective and an adverb. Encourage students to identify situations in which such language is appropriate and those in which it is out of place. The ensuing discussion should help students appreciate the advice on formal written English provided in this section.

ESL CUE

The term *linking verb* might be new for ESL students, but the concept will not be.

LINKING The dessert looks *delicious.*

The crowd turned *violent.*

The pilots were *thirsty.*

IMPORTANT EXCEPTIONS: Several linking verbs, especially those associated with the five senses, can also express action. When they do, they are considered *action* (not linking) *verbs* and are modified by adverbs.

ACTION Palmer looked *menacingly* at the batter. [*Looked* is an action verb with an adverb modifier.]

LINKING Palmer looked angry and *menacing.* [*Looked* is a linking verb, with the adjective *menacing* describing the subject's apparent attitude.]

ACTION The storm turned *violently* toward land. [*Turned* is an action verb with an adverb modifier.]

LINKING The storm turned *violent.* [*Turned* is now a linking verb meaning "became." The adjective *violent* is linked as a modifier to *storm.*]

Good, well, bad, badly

The words *good* and *well, bad* and *badly* are not interchangeable in formal writing (though they tend to be in conversation). The common linking verbs associated with well-being, appearance, or feeling—*looks, seems, appears, feels*—can cause special problems. The rules of usage follow.

1 Good and well

Good is an adjective, used either before a noun or after a linking verb to describe the condition of a subject.

ACCEPTABLE Kyle looks good. [After a linking verb, *good* describes the subject's appearance.]

Kyle is a good dancer. [*Good* modifies the noun *dancer.*]

NONSTANDARD Susan drives good. [*Drives* is an action verb and requires an adverb as modifier.]

REVISED Susan drives well.

The word *well* can be used as either an adjective or an adverb. It has limited use as an adjective only after certain linking verbs (*looks, seems, be/am/is/are*) that describe the subject's good health.

ACCEPTABLE Robert looks well. [*Looks* is a linking verb. The sense of this sentence is that Robert seems to be healthy.]

Well functions as an adverb whenever it follows an action verb.

NONSTANDARD Janet sings good. [*Sings* is an action verb and requires an adverb as modifier.]

REVISED Janet sings well.

TEACHING IDEAS

Like the pronoun *whom* and the phrase *you and I, well* and *badly* are often mistakenly identified as signals of "cultured" speech; people frequently use these adverbs inappropriately, assuming that *well* and *badly* are "proper" English while *good* and *bad* are not. You might want to remind students that although "He looks *well*" is appropriate, a statement such as "That tie looks *well* on him" is actually incorrect, and should be revised to read "That tie looks *good* on him."

2 Bad and badly

Bad is an adjective, used before a noun and after a linking verb to describe a subject. Again, the linking verbs that involve appearance or feeling —*looks, seems, appears, feels*—can cause special problems.

FAULTY Marie feels badly. [*Feels* is a linking verb and must tie the subject, *Marie,* to an adjective.]

REVISED Marie feels bad. [As an adjective, *bad* is linked to the subject to describe *Marie* and her mental state.]

EXCEPTION: The verb *feels* could possibly be an action verb indicating a sense of touch rather than a linking verb indicating well-being: "The blind reader feels braille letters carefully and well." Only in this limited meaning would the phrases "feels badly" or "feels well" be used properly to show how that sense is operating.

Badly is an adverb, used after an action verb or used to modify an adjective or adverb.

NONSTANDARD John cooks bad. [*Cooks* is an action verb and must be modified by an adverb.]

REVISED John cooks badly.

EXERCISE 3

Browse through a dictionary and locate five words that have both adjective and adverb forms. Write a sentence for the two uses of each word—ten sentences in all. Draw an arrow from each adjective or adverb to the word modified.

Example: *patient* The people in the waiting room were patient.

patiently The people waited patiently.

EXERCISE 4

Fill in the blank in each sentence with *good, well, bad,* or *badly* and draw an arrow from the word chosen to the word modified.

Example: The team's prospects are ____________ .

The team's prospects are *good.*

1. Tom has been looking ____________ .
2. If he were under a doctor's supervision, he might look ____________ .
3. He certainly sleeps ____________ .
4. A ____________ sleeper can put in eight hours a night.
5. Sleeping ____________ can make one feel old in a hurry.

EXERCISE 3

Individual responses

EXERCISE 4

1. Tom has been looking bad.
2. If he were under a doctor's supervision, he might look well.
3. He certainly sleeps well.
4. A good sleeper can put in eight hours a night.
5. Sleeping badly can make one feel old in a hurry.

ADDITIONAL EXERCISE C

Add adjectives and adverbs to the sentences below to make them clearer and more lively. (Remember that adjectives and adverbs can be phrases and clauses as well as single words.)

1. Martin planted a garden.
2. The plants grew.
3. Martin took a vacation.
4. Sherry looked after the garden.
5. Everything in the garden died.

ADDITIONAL EXERCISE D

Rewrite all of the incorrect sentences below, revising for accuracy, completeness, and logic of adjective forms.

1. Suellen and Marc ran a race to see who was the fastest.
2. Our chocolate chip cookies are chewier.
3. Of all the children, the youngest is more favored by the parents.
4. We saw the most unique necklace at the flea market.

Answers:

1. Suellen and Marc ran a race to see who was faster.
2. Our chocolate chip cookies are chewier *than yours.* (suggested revision)
3. Of all the children, the youngest is *most* favored by the parents.
4. We saw *a nearly* unique necklace at the flea market. (suggested revision)

GROUP ACTIVITY

Ideally this activity should make use of a draft that students are currently working on, but they can use a past paper if necessary. In groups of three or four, have students pass their drafts to the left. Then ask students to analyze each other's papers for the effective use of adjectives and adverbs. (The emphasis should be on effectiveness rather than correctness.) The analysis can include identifying all modifiers and explaining their role, commenting on what the modifiers contribute to the paper, asking questions about the paper that would lead to inclusion of more modifiers, and the like. This activity will offer students more practice in peer review, and will help them see how modifiers contribute to the effectiveness of written discourse.

11e Using comparative and superlative forms of adjectives and adverbs

Both adjectives and adverbs change form to express comparative relationships. The base form of an adjective or adverb is called its **positive** form. The **comparative** form is used to express a relationship between two elements, and the **superlative** form is used to express a relationship among three or more elements. Most single-syllable adverbs and adjectives, and many two-syllable adjectives, show comparisons with the suffix *-er* and superlatives with *-est.*

	Positive	*Comparative*	*Superlative*
Adjective	crazy	crazier	craziest
	crafty	craftier	craftiest
Adverb	near	nearer	nearest
	far	farther	farthest

Adverbs of two or more syllables and adjectives of three or more syllables change to the comparative and superlative forms with the words *more* and *most.* Adjectives and adverbs show downward (or negative) comparisons with the words *less* and *least* placed before the positive form. If you are uncertain of an adjective's or adverb's form, refer to a dictionary.

	Positive	*Comparative*	*Superlative*
Adjective	elegant	more/less elegant	most/least elegant
	logical	more/less logical	most/least logical
Adverb	beautifully	more/less beautifully	most/least beautifully
	strangely	more/less strangely	most/least strangely

Use irregular adjectives and adverbs with care.

A number of adjectives and adverbs are irregular in forming comparatives and superlatives, and they must be memorized. Consult the following box for these basic forms.

Irregular Forms of Comparison

	Positive	***Comparative***	***Superlative***
Adjective	good	better	best
	bad	worse	worst
	little	less	least
	many	more	most
	much	more	most
	some	more	most
Adverb	well (also adj.)	better	best
	badly	worse	worst

2 Express comparative and superlative relationships accurately, completely, and logically.

Accuracy

Use the comparative form of adverbs and adjectives to show a relationship between two items; use the superlative form when relating three or more items.

Two items In the winter months, New York is colder than Miami.

Two items First-year students are often more conscientious about their studies than second-year students.

Multiples America Online was voted by *PC Magazine* as the "Best Choice" of all online servers.

Completeness

If the elements of a two- or three-way comparison are not being mentioned explicitly in a sentence, be sure to provide enough context so that the comparison makes sense.

Incomplete Jason is more efficient. [More efficient than whom? More efficient at what?]

Revised Jason is the more efficient runner. [Two runners are being compared.]
or
Jason is a more efficient runner than Dylan.

Logic

Certain adjectives have an absolute meaning—they cannot be logically compared. It makes no sense, for instance, to discuss greater or lesser degrees of *perfect* (although in advertising and in conversation, people often try). *Perfect* represents a logical endpoint of comparison, as do the words *unique, first, final, last, absolute, infinite,* and *dead.* Note, though, that a concert performance might be *nearly* perfect or a patient on an operating table *almost* dead. Once *perfection* or *death* is reached, comparisons literally make no sense.

Illogical The story was submitted in its most final form.

Revised The story was submitted in its final form.
or
The story was submitted in nearly final form.

11f Avoid double comparisons, double superlatives, and double negatives.

Double comparisons/superlatives

Adjectives and adverbs show comparative and superlative relationships either with a suffix (*-er*/*-est*) *or* with the words *more, most, less, least.* It

ESL CUE

The double comparison and double superlative are common ESL mistakes because students have learned the "more/most" pattern and will use it in all situations.

TEACHING IDEAS

"Less Calories!" is a claim seen all too frequently in product advertising today. Since the claim is so familiar, you may want to call particular attention to it in order to acquaint students with the appropriate use of adjectives with count nouns and with mass nouns.

CRITICAL DECISIONS

Be alert to differences: Apply a test for choosing comparative forms—few / fewer / fewest, little / less / least, many, much

When making comparisons, note the differences between elements that can be counted and those that cannot (see 7a-2 and 42a-1). Then choose the appropriate form for your comparison.

- **For nouns that can be counted, downward comparisons must be made with *few, fewer,* or *fewest.***

  FAULTY Frozen yogurt has *less* calories than ice cream. [Since *calories* can be counted, *less* is the wrong comparative term.]

  REVISED Frozen yogurt has *fewer* calories than ice cream.

- **For mass nouns, which cannot be counted (see 7a-2), downward comparisons must be made with *little, less,* or *least.***

  FAULTY "Drinker's Delight" coffee has *fewer* caffeine than regular coffee. [Since *caffeine* is a mass noun and cannot be counted, *fewer* is the wrong comparative term.]

  REVISED "Drinker's Delight" coffee has *less* caffeine than regular coffee.

- **For nouns that can be counted, use the adjective *many,* not *much.***

  FAULTY Ice cream has *much* calories. [Since *calories* can be counted, *much* is the incorrect adjective form.]

  REVISED Ice cream has *many* calories.

TEACHING IDEAS

Students may be interested to know that there is a form of double negative that is acceptable in standard English, although the doubling involves a negative modifier and a prefix rather than two negative modifiers. For emphasis, it is appropriate to say "He was *not un*accustomed to failure." Such usage, however, is normally restricted to situations in which the writer or speaker wishes to call attention to the double negative.

ESL CUE

Romance languages, along with a number of others, rely on the double negative as a common and acceptable formation, so patterns such as "I don't have no money" sound natural to speakers of these languages.

Vietnamese and Cambodian students, in particular, will find positive and negative patterns in English confusing. Where English speakers will say "No, I can't," Vietnamese speakers might say "Yes, I can't" and Cambodian speakers will say "Yes, I can" if they perceive the expectation of a positive reply and "Yes, I can't" if they perceive the expectation of a negative reply.

is redundant and awkward to use the *-er/-est* suffix with *more/most* or *less/least.*

FAULTY The World Trade Center is more taller than the Chrysler Building.

REVISED The World Trade Center is taller than the Chrysler Building.

FAULTY That is the least likeliest conclusion to the story.

REVISED That is the least likely conclusion to the story.

Double negatives

Double negatives—the presence of two modifiers that say "no" in the same sentence—are redundant and sometimes confusing, though fairly common in nonstandard usage. A clear negation in a sentence should be expressed only once. Combine the negatives *not, never, neither/nor, hardly,* or *scarcely* with *any, anything,* or *anyone.* Do not combine these negatives with the negatives *no, none, nothing,* or *no one.*

NONSTANDARD I didn't have none.
I didn't have no cash. [These double negatives risk the implication that the speaker in fact has cash.]

REVISED I had none.
I didn't have any cash.

NONSTANDARD I hardly had none.

REVISED I hardly had any.

NONSTANDARD I never had nothing.

REVISED I never had anything.
I had nothing.

11g Avoid overusing nouns as modifiers.

A noun can modify another noun and thus function as an adjective. A few examples include *gate* keeper, *toll* booth, *cell* block, *beauty* parlor, *parlor* game, *finger* puppet, and *tax* collector. Noun modifiers provide handy shortcuts, but when two or more nouns are stacked before a third noun to function as adjectives, the result is logically and stylistically disastrous.

UNCLEAR The textbook Civil War chapter review questions are due tomorrow.

The sentence falters because we are given five seemingly unrelated nouns from which to choose a subject: *textbook, Civil War, chapter, review,* and *questions.* Unstack noun modifiers by moving the subject to the beginning of the sentence and arranging modifying nouns into phrases.

REVISED The *review questions* [subject] *from the textbook's chapter* [prep. phrase with possessive] *on the Civil War* [prep. phrase] are due tomorrow.

ESL NOTE With noun modifiers, sequence and placement are more critical than with adjectives or adverbs (see 44a-2 on noun modifiers). Some of the conventions for ordering cumulative adjective modifiers may also apply to nouns (see 44f).

EXERCISE 5

Correct the problems with comparative and superlative forms in the following sentences.

Example: Of the three Brontë sisters, Emily was the taller.

Of the three Brontë sisters, Emily was the tallest. [The superlative is needed to differentiate among three or more people.]

1. Anne Brontë, the younger sister, wrote *Agnes Grey* and *The Tenant of Windfell Hall.*
2. Charlotte is better known for *Jane Eyre.*
3. Charlotte was the longest-lived of the three sisters.
4. Emily was the stubbornest: though seriously ill, she refused to see a doctor and insisted on performing her usual chores.
5. Emily was the more private of the three authors; she remained an enigma even to her family.

ESL CUE

Speakers of languages with a Germanic base are more likely to overuse nouns and modifiers than speakers of non-Germanic languages.

EXERCISE 5

1. *Youngest* is correct only if the reader knows that there were three sisters (suggestion—add in "three"): Anne Brontë, the youngest of the ^three sisters, wrote *Agnes Grey* and *The Tenant of Windfell Hall.*
2. Charlotte is best known for *Jane Eyre.*
3. Correct
4. Correct
5. Emily was the most private.

PART IV
WRITING CORRECT SENTENCES

CHAPTER 12

Sentence Fragments

KEY FEATURES

Since many students really aren't sure what a fragment is, this chapter begins with a brief, clear definition of the error, followed by a detailed strategy to check for completeness of sentences. The examples of each type of fragment focus on the major culprits, especially verbals, subordinate conjunctions, and relative pronouns. With a wealth of examples to study, students should be able to recognize the type(s) of fragments they produce, thereby simplifying the editing of their papers. After categorizing fragments, the chapter moves immediately to strategies for eliminating them. Methods of editing for fragments are clearly delineated; again, if students are aware of the specific types of fragments they produce, they can make use of the chart to correct their errors. The chapter also acknowledges the intentional fragment, with the warning that the effectiveness of this construction hinges on the fact that it is indeed a breach of the rules, and thus should be used rarely. As in preceding chapters, the material here is presented in a straightforward, traditional manner, with an emphasis on clear, effective communication rather than rules and errors. Exercises require identification and correction of fragments, as well as identification of types of fragments. The latter exercises should help students classify their own errors.

One important goal of writing is to keep readers focused on clearly stated ideas. Few errors are more disruptive of this goal than the **sentence fragment,** a partial sentence punctuated as if it were a complete sentence. Because it is only a partial sentence, a fragment leaves readers confused, trying to guess at what claims or statements are being made. To be a sentence, a group of words must first have a subject and a predicate (see 7a-1). A sentence fragment may lack either a subject or a predicate—and sometimes both. A fragment may also be a dependent clause (see 7e) that has not been joined to an independent (or main) clause.

FRAGMENT Like scratching an itch [The clause lacks both a subject and a verb, since *scratching* is a verbal. (See 12c.)]

REVISED Using profanity can be like scratching an itch in that both tend to relieve tension. [A subject and a verb are added to create a sentence.]

FRAGMENT Although excessive use of profanity is boorish and can indicate a personality disorder. [This unit is a dependent clause.]

REVISED Although excessive use of profanity is boorish and can indicate a personality disorder, a modest amount of profanity is common in virtually everyone's speech. [The clause is joined to an independent clause.]

12a Check for completeness of sentences.

Avoid writing fragments by checking your sentences for grammatical completeness. There are three tests you can conduct:

1. Locate a verb.
2. Locate the verb's subject.
3. Check for subordinating conjunctions or relative pronouns.

Spotlight on Common Errors— SENTENCE CONSTRUCTION AND FRAGMENTS

These are the errors most commonly associated with sentence construction and fragments. For full explanations and suggested revisions, follow the cross-references to chapter sections.

FRAGMENT ERRORS arise when writers incorrectly mark a group of words as a sentence. Apply a three-part test to confirm that a grouping of words can stand alone as a sentence (see 12a).

Test 1: Locate a verb: A sentence must have a verb.

Churchill *was* a leader.	**A leader of great distinction.**	**When he *became* Prime Minister.**
[Verb—*was*]	[No verb—this grouping of words cannot be a sentence; it is a FRAGMENT.]	[Verb—*became*—BUT this word grouping fails Test 3 below, so it is still a FRAGMENT.]

REVISED Churchill was ***a leader of great distinction.***

NOTE: Be sure the word selected as a verb is not a verbal, which looks like a verb but actually serves as a subject, object, or modifier (see 7a-4).

After *serving* his country in the first World War.

[Verbal: *serving* looks like a verb but is actually an object in the prepositional phrase beginning with *after.* This grouping of words is therefore a FRAGMENT.]

REVISED **After serving his country in the first World War,** he became Prime Minister.

Test 2: Locate the verb's subject: A sentence must have a subject.

Churchill was a leader.	***When he became Prime Minister.***
[Subject—*Churchill*]	[Subject—*he*—BUT this word grouping fails Test 3 so it is still a FRAGMENT.]

Test 3: Be sure that words such as *when, while, because* or *who, which, that* do not prevent the word group from being a sentence (see subordinating conjunctions and relative pronouns, 19b-1–2).

SENTENCE Churchill *was* a leader.
[No words prevent the grouping from being a sentence.]

FRAGMENTS ***When* he became Prime Minister.** ***Who* became Prime Minister.**

[*When* (a subordinating conjunction) and *who* (a relative pronoun) prevent these word groups from standing alone as sentences.]

REVISED **He became Prime Minister.**

See 12b–12d for ways to correct fragments once you have identified them.

FOR DISCUSSION

Since most students have problems with only certain types of fragments, you might want to initiate a class discussion of errors most relevant to your students. Ask students to identify from the Spotlight on Common Errors examples of fragments familiar to them and to make a personal list of common types of fragments. Students can then discuss how fragment errors arise, thereby reinforcing their understanding of sentence completeness. (In large classes, this activity might begin with small groups. The groups will identify their common types of fragments, and then the class as a whole will discuss the list of types compiled from each group's report.)

ESL CUE

Most ESL students will have difficulty recognizing as fragments phrases containing a passive participle, confusing, for example, the past tense, as in "His style bored her," with the passive participle, as in "His work finished more rapidly than he expected."

LOOKING BACK

References to Chapter 7 (Constructing Sentences) appear throughout this chapter. Section 7b (Understanding basic sentence patterns) could be especially helpful to students with a need for more basic instruction. If Chapter 7 has not been covered yet, or if some time has passed since it was covered, you may want to spend a little time on that material now.

First test: Locate a verb.

Every sentence has a verb. To be sure you've written a sentence, find the verb. Be sure that the word you settle on as the verb of the sentence is not a verbal (see 7a-4). There are three types of verbals you should disqualify when looking for sentence verbs: verb forms ending in *-ing,* verb forms ending in *-ed* (when not paired with a subject), and verb forms introduced with the infinitive *to.*

Verb forms ending in *-ing* must be preceded by a form of *be* (e.g., *is, are, were, was, has been,* etc.) in order to function as sentence verbs.

FRAGMENT His arguing a long and tiresome case without any sensitivity to his readers. [*Arguing* is a verbal since it is not preceded by a form of *be.*]

REVISED *He was* arguing a long and tiresome case without any sensitivity to his readers. [*Was arguing* is a verb. The subject of the revised sentence is *he.*]

Verb forms ending in *-ed* may be called *participles* and function as adjectives, not as verbs, when they are preceded by an article (*a, an,* or *the* [see 7a-2]), by a noun or pronoun in its possessive form (e.g., *Paul's, his*), or by a preposition (*of, by, for,* etc.). To function as a verb, such a form must be paired with a subject.

FRAGMENT The calculated, high risk. [*Calculated* functions as a participle describing *risk.*]

REVISED *Susan calculated* the high risk. [*Calculated* is paired with a subject, *Susan,* to become a verb.]

REVISED Susan's *calculated risk* paid off. [*Calculated* is a participle describing the subject *risk.* A verb, *paid,* has been added.]

FRAGMENT A series of legislated revolutionary reforms. [*Legislated* is a participle describing reforms.]

REVISED *Congress legislated* revolutionary reforms. [*Legislated* is a verb with a subject, *Congress.*]

Verb forms introduced with the infinitive marker *to* never function as sentence verbs; another verb must be added to make a sentence.

FRAGMENT To appreciate the alternative.

REVISED *Frank failed* to appreciate the alternative. [The verb *failed* has been added along with the subject *Frank.*]

Second test: Locate the verb's subject.

Once you have located a verb, ask *who* or *what* makes its assertion or action and you will find the subject.

FRAGMENT Separated visible light into a spectrum of colors.

Revised *Isaac Newton* separated visible light into a spectrum of colors. [The subject, *Isaac Newton,* is needed to answer the question *Who separated?*]

Fragment First attempted an analysis of the short story.

Revised *Edgar Allan Poe* first attempted an analysis of the short story. [A subject, *Edgar Allan Poe,* is added to answer the question *Who first attempted an analysis?*]

Imperative sentences—commands—often lack a subject; still, they are considered sentences since the implied subject is understood to be *you.*

Imperative sentence	Understood as
Open the door!	You open the door.
Come here, please.	You come here, please.

ESL Note The subject of a sentence in English, unlike that in many other languages, is expressed directly as a separate word in one location only. Because the subject is not implied in the form of a verb (other than the imperative) or other sentence part, identifying the subject with a specific word is critical to the structure of an English sentence (see 7a-1 and 7b).

Third test: Check for subordinating conjunctions or relative pronouns.

Be certain that a subject and verb are not preceded by a subordinating conjunction or that a relative pronoun taking the place of a subject does not make the clause dependent. If a word grouping consists of a subject and predicate, it is a sentence *unless* it contains a subordinating word, either an opening subordinating conjunction or a relative pronoun taking the place of its subject.

Subordinating conjunctions

after	although	as if	assuming that
because	before	how	if
provided that	since	though	unless
until	whenever	where	while

A subordinating conjunction placed at the beginning of an independent clause renders the clause dependent, so that it cannot stand alone as a complete sentence. If the conjunction is eliminated, the clause will stand as a sentence. If the clause is combined with another sentence, the new dependent clause will function as if it were an adverb.

Fragment Though people may have a personality disorder. [The conjunction *though* makes the clause dependent on another assertion.]

Revised ~~Though~~ People may have a personality disorder. [Dropping the conjunction makes a simple sentence.]

Revised Though people may have a personality disorder, *they may see their behavior as normal.* [The dependent clause now functions as an adverb.]

ESL CUE

Because their languages may not depend on word order to the degree that English does, many ESL students will be confused by English words that retain the same spelling even though they serve different grammatical functions, as exemplified by the Groucho Marx saying: "Time *flies like* an arrow; fruit *flies like* a banana."

Marking out prepositional phrases before determining subject and verb is a good rule of thumb to help students distinguish subjects and verbs: "~~In the back of the room behind the huge desk~~ stood an antique clock ~~of the type~~ revered ~~by his grandparents.~~"

In Japanese the object precedes the verb.

The following literal translation from Chinese makes clear the word order interference problems possible:

> "he in/on/at here that daughter also to be very good looking"

The student speaking or writing in English must recast such statements in terms of their content and intent, finding English equivalents instead of translating literally; yet even students highly fluent in English who "think in" their new language will sooner or later stumble over localized word order interference problems. Sympathy and tolerance are appropriate.

TEACHING IDEAS

Advertising is notorious for sentence fragments. To give students practice in identifying fragments, ask them to collect examples from various advertisements in magazines and newspapers. Then ask them to identify the cause of the fragments.

EXERCISE 1

1. Correct
2. Fragment—fails Tests 1 and 2 (no subject and no verb)
3. Fragment—fails Tests 1 and 3 (no verb, dependent clause)
4. Correct
5. Correct

REFERENCE

HARRIS, MURIEL. "Mending the Fragmented Free Modifier." CCC 32 (1981): 175–82. Free modifiers, although they risk producing sentence fragments, should not be discouraged in student writing.

RELATIVE PRONOUNS

that	which	whichever	who
whoever	whom	whomever	

A relative pronoun taking the place of a subject in a clause signals that the clause is dependent and cannot stand alone as a complete thought. If the pronoun is eliminated, the clause will stand as a sentence. If it is combined with another sentence, the dependent clause will function as if it were an adjective.

FRAGMENT People who have a personality disorder. [*Who* takes the place of the subject *people,* creating a dependent clause.]

REVISED People ~~who~~ have a personality disorder. [Eliminating *who* leaves a simple sentence.]

REVISED People who have a personality disorder *see their behavior as acceptable.* [*People* is the subject of a verb, *see,* with a *who* clause as adjective modifier.]

EXCEPTION: When one of the above-listed relative pronouns introduces a question, it becomes an interrogative (questioning) pronoun. The resulting construction is not considered to be a fragment: *Who has a personality disorder?*

EXERCISE 1

Use the three-part test to identify fragments and to explain the cause of each fragment. Place a check before complete sentences, and circle the numbers of items that are fragments.

Example: When the author of one study claims that groups moving in unison tend to think alike.

Fragment—fails test 3 (The word *when* prevents the clause from standing alone as a sentence.)

1. Rhythmic movements help to establish a group bond.
2. Giving the group a certain advantage over the other groups.
3. One reason why armies put so much emphasis on drilling new recruits.
4. Possibly movement in unison represents or fosters identical, in-group thinking.
5. The Nazi parade is a striking example of the connection between lockstep movement and lockstep thinking.

12b Eliminate fragments: Revise dependent clauses set off as sentences.

A dependent clause functions as a modifier—either as an adverb (see 19b-1) or as an adjective (see 19b-2). A dependent clause that has been set off incorrectly as a sentence can be corrected in one of two ways: by converting the clause to an independent clause or by joining the clause to a new sentence.

1 Convert the dependent clause to an independent clause.

FRAGMENT Even though the president attended the meeting.
CLEAR The president attended the meeting.

If the dependent clause begins with a subordinating conjunction, delete the conjunction and you will have an independent clause—a sentence.

FRAGMENT While Americans keep recycling the same old clichés.

REVISED ~~While~~ Americans keep recycling the same old clichés.

If a dependent clause uses a relative pronoun, eliminate the relative pronoun, replacing it with a noun or personal pronoun, and you will have an independent clause.

FRAGMENT Many students, who might read more often.

REVISED Many students ~~who~~ might read more often. [The eliminated relative pronoun leaves the noun, *students,* as the subject.]

REVISED ~~Many students~~ *They* might read more often. [The eliminated relative pronoun is replaced by the pronoun, *they.*]

2 Join the dependent clause to a new sentence.

FRAGMENT Though the president attended.
CLEAR Though the president attended, she did not speak.

The dependent clause introduced by a subordinating conjunction can be made to function as an adverb by joining it to an independent clause. When the dependent clause introduces a sentence, set it off with a comma (see 25a-1). When the clause ends a sentence, do not use a comma (but see 25a-3).

FRAGMENT If our culture did not perceive and portray reading as an almost antisocial activity.

REVISED *Many students might read more often* if our culture did not portray reading as an almost antisocial activity.

A dependent clause fragment that uses a relative pronoun can be made to function as an adjective (a relative clause) by attaching it to an independent clause. If the new relative clause is not essential to defining the noun it modifies, set the clause off with a *pair* of commas. If the new relative clause *is* essential to the definition, do not use commas (see 25d-1).

FRAGMENT Verdenal Johnson, a president of the Association for the Encouragement of Correct Pronunciation, Spelling and Usage in Public Communications, who has with a felt-tipped marker corrected errors on public signs. [The noun and modifying clause have no verb.]

ESL CUE

Many Japanese students have been trained to believe that beginning an English sentence with "and" or "but" or "so" is a way to make their writing seem more natural and will have difficulty giving up this practice, while European students might feel that fragments make their writing seem more creative. Vietnamese writing style and punctuation precludes the idea of fragments, comma splices, or fused sentences: they simply do not exist. Instead, the sentences flow much like conversation, with few formal regulations.

Revised Verdenal Johnson, who has with a felt-tipped marker corrected errors on public signs, served as president of the Association for the Encouragement of Correct Pronunciation, Spelling and Usage in Public Communications. [The *who* clause functions as an adjective in a sentence with a new verb *served*.]

Fragment A society that prefers to watch sequels and reruns rather than something stimulating, even if difficult. [The noun and its modifying clause have no verb.]

Revised Johnson claims that a thoughtful, provocative use of language generally goes unnoticed in a society that prefers to watch sequels and reruns rather than something stimulating, even if difficult. [The noun and its modifying clause become part of a new sentence (as the object of the preposition *in*).]

EXERCISE 2

Identify fragments in the following pairs. Combine pairs to make complete sentences.

Example: Even though Anheuser-Busch, Miller, G. Heileman, Coors, and Pabst brew 95 percent of the 200 million barrels of beer produced annually in the United States. These companies are not the only producers of American beer.

Even though Anheuser-Busch, Miller, G. Heileman, Coors, and Pabst brew 95 percent of the 200 million barrels of beer produced annually in the United States, these companies are not the only producers of American beer.

1. While only eight microbreweries existed in the United States a decade ago. Today seventy microbreweries are brewing more than 65,000 barrels of specialty beers a year.
2. Microbreweries are winning awards for the tastiness of their products. Which has caused the large producers to alter their production and advertising techniques.
3. Because microbrewery beer is often free of additives. It must be sold locally.
4. Local production, distribution, and advertising has become a key to microbrewery success. Which depends on creating the perception among buyers of a freshness and healthfulness not available in mass-market beers.
5. Even though image is important. Quality of the product is what has convinced an increasing number of American beer drinkers to buy from local, smaller breweries.

12c Eliminate fragments: Revise phrases set off as sentences.

Phrases consist of nouns and the words associated with them or verb forms not functioning as verbs (called *verbals*) and the words associated with them. Phrases function as sentence parts—as modifiers, subjects, objects,

EXERCISE 2

1. While only eight microbreweries existed in the United States a decade ago, today seventy microbreweries are brewing more than 65,000 barrels of specialty beers a year.
2. Microbreweries are winning awards for the tastiness of their products, which has caused the large producers to alter their production and advertising techniques.
3. Because microbrewery beer is often free of additives, it must be sold locally.
4. Local production, distribution, and advertising has become a key to microbrewery success, which depends on creating the perception among buyers of a freshness and healthfulness not available in mass-market beers.
5. Even though image is important, quality of the product is what has convinced an increasing number of American beer drinkers to buy from local, smaller breweries.

GROUP ACTIVITY

Once students have completed this exercise, have them discuss their responses in groups. The inevitable differences between various correct responses will help students understand the number of possible ways to construct sentences without falling into error. The discussion should also help students who have yet to master the concept of the fragment. (This activity can be used for all subsequent exercises in the chapter.)

Eliminating Fragments from Your Writing

1. **Revise dependent clauses set off as sentences.**
   Convert the dependent clause to an independent clause.

   FRAGMENT Although computers may be revolutionizing the world.

   REVISED ~~Although~~ Computers may be revolutionizing the world.

   Join the dependent clause to a new sentence.

   FRAGMENT Although computers may be revolutionizing the world.

   REVISED Although computers may be revolutionizing the world, *relatively few people understand how they function.*

2. **Revise phrases set off as sentences.**
   There are various kinds of phrases: verbal, prepositional, absolute, and appositive (see 7d). None can stand alone as a sentence.

   FRAGMENT After years of drought.

   REVISED ~~After~~ Years of drought *can devastate a national economy.*

   REVISED After years of drought, *a nation's economy can be devastated.*

3. **Revise repeating structures or compound predicates set off as sentences.**
   Repeating elements and compound predicates cannot stand alone. Incorporate such structures into an existing sentence or add words to construct a new sentence.

   FRAGMENT College sports has long been conducted as a business. A profitable business. [The repeating element is a fragment.]

   REVISED College sports has long been conducted as a business—*a* profitable business. [The repeating element has been incorporated into an existing sentence.]

   FRAGMENT Some coaches achieve legendary status on campus. And are paid legendary salaries. [The second element is part of a compound verb.]

   REVISED Some coaches achieve legendary status on campus *and* are paid legendary salaries. [The second verb and its associated words are incorporated into an existing sentence.]

and complements—but never as sentences. The various kinds of phrases are defined in 7d. As with dependent clauses that form fragments, you may either convert phrases to complete sentences by adding words, or you may join phrases to independent clauses.

1 Revising verbal phrases

Participial and gerund phrases (functioning as modifiers or nouns)

FRAGMENT Crossing out the word *very.*

REVISED Verdenal Johnson ~~crossing~~ crosses out the word *very.* [The phrase is rewritten as a sentence.]

TEACHING IDEAS

You may want to use this box to reinforce in students a sense of responsibility for correcting their own mistakes. Ask students to check their personal lists of fragment types (from the Spotlight on Common Errors note, page 275) against the types enumerated in the box. If they can find that they frequently produce fragments similar to those listed here, they can make a checklist for use when revising and editing their papers.

GROUP ACTIVITY

Clearly the most profitable way to teach students how to avoid fragments is to work with their own writing. Ask students to bring in several papers in order to take part in this activity. When you divide students into groups, try to mix strong and weak writers. Then have each group work together on one student's writing at a time, identifying fragments caused by phrases set off as sentences and revising according to the guidelines in the handbook. The group's attempts to determine what constitute fragments and how to revise them should generate healthy discussion. This discussion will help strong writers articulate their implicit understanding of grammatical rules and weak writers gain an understanding of such rules.

Revised Crossing out the word *very,* the copyeditor Verdenal Johnson encourages writers to use more specific words—for example, *crimson* for *very red.* [The participial phrase, functioning as an adjective, is joined to an independent clause.]

Revised Crossing out the word *very* is one of the first actions that Verdenal Johnson takes as a copyeditor. [The phrase is used as a gerund, functioning as a noun, to become the subject of an independent clause.]

Infinitive phrases (functioning as nouns)

Fragment To delete the word *very.*

Revised Johnson prefers to delete the word *very* when she works as a copyeditor. [The phrase is rewritten as a sentence.]

2 Revising prepositional phrases (functioning as modifiers)

Fragment With its ready-made expressions and terse, imprecise phrases.

Revised With its ready-made expressions and terse, imprecise phrases, American English is truly the language of people in a hurry. [The phrase is joined to an independent clause.]

3 Revising absolute phrases (modifying an entire sentence)

Fragment Our shorthand style of speech mirroring our fast-paced existence.

Revised Our shorthand style of speech mirrors our fast-paced existence. [The phrase is rewritten as a sentence.]

Revised Our shorthand style of speech mirroring our fast-paced existence, we Americans tend to use filler words such as "you know" or "I mean," according to Norman Cousins. [The phrase is joined as a modifier to an independent clause.]

4 Revising appositive phrases (renaming or describing other nouns)

Fragment A mix of words and pictures characterized by immediacy and by dynamism.

Revised "Electronic Literacy" is a mix of words and pictures characterized by immediacy and dynamism. [The phrase is rewritten as a sentence.]

Revised Many deplore the loss of print literacy and decry the rise of "electronic literacy," a mix of words and pictures characterized by immediacy and dynamism. [The phrase renames the final noun in the independent clause.]

EXERCISE 3

Identify the numbered units that are fragments, and correct them by joining them to independent clauses. Then specify what type of phrase the fragment has become in the new sentence. Place a check before any sentence needing no revision.

Example: (1) In order to comprehend the nature of stress, we must consider three related issues. (2) *Physiology, the nature of stressors, and personality.*

(1) In order to comprehend the nature of stress, we must consider three related issues: physiology, the nature of stressors, and personality. [The fragment is joined with the independent clause to become an appositive renaming *issues.*]

(1) Physiologically, the body prepares itself for stress. (2) By eliciting an immediate and vigorous alarm reaction. (3) Alarm is soon replaced by resistance. (4) A state in which activation remains relatively high but at levels a person can sustain over a long period of time. (5) If stress persists, the body's resources may become depleted. (6) Exhaustion occurs. (7) The ability to cope decreasing sharply over time. (8) A person risks severe biological damage by remaining exhausted for too long. (9) *Stressors* can be defined as those elements in the environment that produce an urge in the individual to approach a stressful activity. (10) To flee from it as well.

EXERCISE 3

1. and 2. Join fragment (2) with (1) as a prepositional phrase.
3. and 4. Join fragment (4) with (3) as an appositive.
5. A correct sentence.
6. A correct sentence.
7. and 8. Join fragment (7) with (8) as an absolute phrase.
9. and 10. Join fragment (10) with (9) as an infinitive phrase.

12d Eliminate fragments: Revise repeating structures or compound predicates set off as sentences.

FRAGMENT As large as the capitol's rotunda

CLEAR The foyer was large, as large as the capitol's rotunda.

Repetition can be an effective stylistic tool (see 19c-2). Repeated elements, however, are not sentences but sentence parts and should not be punctuated as sentences. Use a comma or dashes to set off repeated elements.

FRAGMENT Children begin for the first time to differentiate themselves from others as they enter adolescence. *As they begin to develop a personal identity.* [The subordinate *as* clause cannot stand alone.]

REVISED Children begin for the first time to differentiate themselves from others as they enter adolescence, as they begin to develop a personal identity. [The clause is subordinated.]

FRAGMENT Adolescents want to know they belong in the social order. An order shaped by forces they barely understand. [The phrase and clause need a connection.]

REVISED Adolescents want to know they belong in the social order—an order shaped by forces they barely understand. [The structure repeats and expands the term *social order.*]

EXERCISE 4

1. Specialists suggest that setting up a workable system to organize yourself is only a small, first step.
2. The most significant organizing principle in life is a wastebasket in every room and a willingness to use them.
3. A common myth is that highly creative people are "naturally" messier and more chaotic than those who are relatively uncreative, and that being organized and artistic are incompatible.
4. A *Wall Street Journal* article reported that people spend an average of six weeks a year looking for things in their offices. That is unbelievable!

FOR DISCUSSION

Reproduce several brief passages with intentional fragments, including one or two that aren't particularly effective. (These can be from published prose or from your own pen.) Ask students to edit the passages to eliminate the fragments, and decide which version is more effective. In class discussion, students can defend their positions, thereby clarifying for them the function of the intentional fragment.

REFERENCES

ELBOW, PETER. *Writing without Teachers.* New York: Oxford UP, 1973. 30–31. Fragments should not be viewed as errors but rather as specific stylistic devices.

Compound predicates consist of two sentence verbs (and their associated words) joined with a coordinating conjunction, such as *and* or *but.* The two predicates share the same subject and are part of the same sentence. When one half of the compound predicate is punctuated as a sentence, it becomes a fragment. To correct the fragment, join it to a sentence that contains an appropriate subject or provide the fragment with its own subject.

FRAGMENT The process of maturation is lifelong. *But is most critical during the adolescent years.* [The last unit has no subject.]

REVISED The process of maturation is lifelong. But *the process* is most critical during the adolescent years. [The unit is given its own subject.]

REVISED The process of maturation is lifelong but is most critical during the adolescent years. [The phrase is joined to the preceding sentence as a compound predicate.]

EXERCISE 4

Identify which of the following units are fragments. Correct each by writing a new sentence or by joining the fragment to an independent clause.

Example: Messiness in the workplace. How does it affect your productivity? [The first unit lacks a verb.]

How does messiness in the workplace affect your productivity? [The fragment replaces the pronoun *it* and becomes the subject of the question.]

1. Specialists suggest that setting up a workable system to organize yourself is only a first step. A small one.
2. The most significant organizing principle in life is a wastebasket in every room. And a willingness to use them.
3. A common myth is that highly creative people are "naturally" messier and more chaotic than those who are relatively uncreative. That being organized and artistic are incompatible.
4. A *Wall Street Journal* article reported that people spend an average of six weeks a year looking for things in their offices. Unbelievable!

12e Use fragments intentionally on rare occasions.

Whose business was it? No one's.
The speaker made his point. Barely.

Experienced writers will occasionally use sentence fragments by design. These intentional uses are always carefully fitted to the context of a neighboring sentence, sometimes answering an implied question or completing a parallel structure that has been separated for emphasis. Such intentional uses occur mainly in personal or expressive essay writing or in fiction, when writers want to alter the rhythm of paragraphs and thereby call attention to fragments or to reproduce the staccato rhythms of speech or thought. A fragment should be used rarely if at all in academic prose, where it will probably be regarded as a lapse, not as a stylistic flourish.

INTENTIONAL USE OF FRAGMENTS

There are fewer and fewer students, I find, who have playful imaginations. Please understand that I am not asking for profound creativity. *Or resourceful inventiveness.* Rather, I should like to see more students whose minds sparkle.

—ARLEN J. HANSEN, "The Imagination Gap"

Democrats favored bureaucratic delivery of education and other services because bureaucracies serve everyone equally. Badly, perhaps, but equally.

—GEORGE F. WILL

We are lucky in that the central fact of our country is both inspiring and true: America is the place formed of the institutionalization of miracles. Which made it something new in the history of man, something—better.

—PEGGY NOONAN

EXERCISE 5

Correct each sentence fragment either by joining it with an independent clause or by rewriting it as an independent clause.

Example: When the influential scholar Ulrich B. Phillips declared in 1918 that slavery in the Old South had impressed upon African savages the glorious stamp of civilization. He set the stage for a long and passionate debate. [The first unit is a dependent clause.]

When the influential scholar Ulrich B. Phillips declared in 1918 that slavery in the Old South had impressed upon African savages the glorious stamp of civilization, he set the stage for a long and passionate debate. [The dependent clause is connected to the sentence that follows it.]

1. As the decades passed and the debate raged on. One historian after another confidently professed to have deciphered the real meaning of slavery. That "peculiar institution."
2. The special situation of the female slave remained unexamined. Amidst all this scholarly activity.
3. Because the ceaseless arguments about her "sexual promiscuity" or her "matriarchal" proclivities obscured the condition of Black women during slavery.
4. If and when a historian sets the record straight on the experiences of enslaved Black women. She (or he) will have performed an inestimable service.
5. It is not for the sake of historical accuracy alone that such a study should be conducted. For lessons can be gleaned from the slave era. That will shed light on Black women's and all women's current battle for emancipation.
6. The enormous space that work occupies in Black women's lives today. Follows a pattern established during the very earliest days of slavery.
7. Compulsory labor overshadowed every other aspect of women's existence. The slave system defined Black people. As chattel. Since women, no less than men, were viewed as profitable labor units. They might as well have been genderless as far as the slaveholders were concerned.

KLINE, CHARLES R., JR., and W. DEAN MEMERING. "Formal Fragments: The English Minor Sentence." *Research in the Teaching of English* 11 (1977): 97–110. In certain circumstances, fragments are not only acceptable but effective.

EXERCISE 5

1. As the decades passed and the debate raged on, one historian after another confidently professed to have deciphered the real meaning of slavery, that "peculiar institution."
2. The special situation of the female slave remained unexamined amidst all this scholarly activity.
3. The ceaseless arguments about her "sexual promiscuity" or her "matriarchal" proclivities obscured the condition of Black women during slavery.
4. If and when a historian sets the record straight on the experiences of enslaved Black women, she (or he) will have performed an inestimable service.
5. It is not for the sake of historical accuracy alone that such a study should be conducted, for lessons can be gleaned from the slave era that will shed light on Black women's and all women's current battle for emancipation.
6. The enormous space that work occupies in Black women's lives today follows a pattern established during the very earliest days of slavery.
7. Compulsory labor overshadowed every other aspect of women's existence. The slave system defined Black people as chattel. Since women, no less than men, were viewed as profitable labor units, they might as well have been genderless as far as the slaveholders were concerned.

ADDITIONAL EXERCISE A

Look through your graded papers to find instructor's comments regarding fragments. Reread the papers, identifying the fragments as you read by using the three-part test. Then identify the cause of the fragment and correct it. (If you don't have any graded papers handy, look through any body of writing you've done recently.)

CHAPTER 13

Comma Splices and Fused Sentences

KEY FEATURES

The emphasis in this chapter, as in previous revising and editing chapters, is on producing clear, lively prose. Approached from this standpoint, correcting comma splices and fused sentences becomes not an exercise in following rules but rather a courtesy extended from the writer to the reader. In fact, few comma splices and fused sentences render an essay incoherent; they do, however, distract the reader from the content of the essay. Learning to identify and correct these errors, then, becomes one more way to refine a piece of written discourse. In dealing with the topic, this chapter remains consistent with previous chapters in its straightforward approach. Beginning on a positive note, the chapter identifies five acceptable ways to mark sentence boundaries, and then explains the two ways in which those boundaries can be blurred. The chapter acknowledges that a comma splice indicates that the writer recognizes the need for some sort of break, but chooses punctuation that isn't up to the job. Errors are dealt with by looking at the common reasons why writers make them (e.g., fusing or splicing sentences of explanation to sentences being explained, confusing conjunctive adverbs and conjunctions). Strategies for correcting comma splices and fused sentences are explained with clear examples. Exercises, using sentences and paragraphs, provide students with practice in identifying and correcting errors.

Sentence grammar is built on the fundamental rule that independent clauses—complete sentences—are the basic units for making a statement. Sentences must be kept distinct from one another. When sentence boundaries are blurred, statements become confused; readers must turn away from the content of a paper and struggle to decipher which combinations of words might form meaningful units.

To keep your statements distinct and clear, remember: independent clauses must be separated with a period, a semicolon, or a colon, or they must be carefully linked with a conjunction and appropriate punctuation.

Five Ways to Mark the Boundary between Sentences

Mark a sentence boundary with punctuation.

1. Use a period: He laughed. He danced. He sang.
2. Use a semicolon: He laughed; he danced and sang.

Mark a sentence boundary with a conjunction and punctuation.

3. Use a coordinating conjunction: He laughed, and he danced.
4. Use a subordinating conjunction: While he laughed, he danced.
5. Use a conjunctive adverb: He laughed; moreover, he danced.

Sentence boundaries can become blurred in two ways: with comma splices or with fused (run-on) sentences. In the **fused** (or **run-on**) **sentence**, the writer fails to recognize the end of one independent clause and the beginning of the next.

FUSED SENTENCE — The blurring of sentence boundaries can create a comprehension problem readers must often stop to decipher which combinations of words form meaningful units. [*Readers* is a new subject of a new independent clause; a period or semicolon should precede it.]

The writer of a **comma splice** recognizes the end of one independent clause and the beginning of the next, but marks the boundary between the two incorrectly—with a comma.

Spotlight on Common Errors—SENTENCE CONSTRUCTION AND SENTENCE BOUNDARIES

These are the errors most commonly associated with sentence construction and sentence boundaries. For full explanations and suggested revisions, follow the cross-references to chapter sections.

RECOGNIZING SENTENCE BOUNDARIES: The end of a sentence is usually marked with a period. Not marking the end clearly will result in a FRAGMENT (see 12a), a FUSED SENTENCE (see 13b-1), or a COMMA SPLICE (see 13b-1).

> CORRECT: Winston Churchill became a leader. He served his country in the first World War. Churchill was a leader of distinction.
>
> FUSED SENTENCES: Winston Churchill became a leader he served his country in the first World War Churchill was a leader of distinction.
>
> COMMA SPLICES: Winston Churchill became a leader, he served his country in the first World War, Churchill was a leader of distinction.

REVISING ERRORS OF SENTENCE CONSTRUCTION: Learn to recognize sentence boundaries (see 12a). Link sentences with these strategies:

- **Link by combining parts of two sentences into one (see 12c).**

  Winston Churchill became a leader. Churchill was a leader **of distinction.**

  ↓

  Winston Churchill became a leader of distinction.

- **Link by using a comma plus one of these conjunctions—*and, but, or, nor* (see coordinating conjunctions, 13b-2, 19a-1).**

  Winston Churchill served his country in the first World War***, and*** he became a leader of distinction.

- **Link by using a semicolon (see 13b-3, 26a–c).**

  Winston Churchill served his country in the first World War; he became a leader of distinction.

- **Link by using a semicolon (or period) and a word like *however, consequently,* or *therefore* (see conjunctive adverbs, 13b-4, 19a-3).**

  Winston Churchill served his country in the first World War***; subsequently,*** he became a leader of distinction.

- **Link by using a word such as *when, while,* or *because* (see subordinating conjunctions, 13b-5, 19b).**

  After he served his country in the first World War, Winston Churchill became a leader of distinction.

FOR DISCUSSION

Since many students have problems with either fused sentences or comma splices, but not both, you might want to initiate a class discussion of errors most relevant to your students. Ask students to identify from the Spotlight on Common Errors examples of sentence errors familiar to them and to characterize their own errors accordingly. Students can then discuss how fused sentences and comma splices arise, thereby reinforcing their understanding of sentence boundaries. (In large classes, this activity might begin with small groups. The groups will identify their errors, and then the class as a whole will discuss the types compiled from each group's report.)

LOOKING BACK

References to Chapter 7 (Constructing Sentences) appear throughout this chapter. If Chapter 7 has not been covered yet, or if some time has passed since it was covered, you may want to spend a little time on that material now.

ESL CUE

Romance-language speakers (especially of Spanish) will persist in making comma faults because of a very different conception of comma use. The Spanish sentence can easily run to eighty or more words, with clauses joined snugly by commas; there is no "fault" or "splice" involving commas, but rather a comfortable sense of fullness and continuity, a sense missing in the seemingly (to Spanish speakers) attenuated English version. Thus native Spanish speakers will require reminders to keep sentences short and tightly connected, and perhaps, some confidence building that their English prose is not "too simple." Vietnamese experience some of the same difficulty.

TEACHING IDEAS

Comma splices are more common than fused sentences, and they often reflect punctuation problems rather than problems understanding sentences. Therefore, you may want to ask students who produce comma splices to actually memorize the five ways of marking sentence boundaries.

TEACHING IDEAS

Some students have trouble understanding what the terms "comma splice" and "fused sentence" mean. Some may have to unlearn the term "run-on" and learn "fused." You can explain that "run-on" was often misused to characterize overly long sentences that were in fact grammatically correct. "Fused" is a more accurate term, relying on the image of joining two separate things together. "Comma splice" is more easily understood if students think of splicing film—also creating an image of joining two pieces together.

13a Identify fused sentences and comma splices.

FUSED Winston Churchill served in World War I he became a leader of great distinction.

COMMA SPLICE Winston Churchill served in World War I, he became a leader of great distinction.

CLEAR Winston Churchill served in World War I. He became a leader of great distinction.

Before submitting a draft of your work to be read or reviewed by others, read your sentences aloud. When you listen to your writing, you can often catch errors that go undetected when you read silently. Look for long sentences that seem to consist of two or more separate statements, or those that seem so long they force you to stop midway to take a breath. Be on the alert, especially, for the following three circumstances in which fused sentences and comma splices are found.

1. **A sentence of explanation, expansion, or example** is frequently fused to or spliced together with another sentence that is being explained, expanded on, or illustrated. Even if the topics of the two sentences are closely related, the sentences themselves must remain distinct.

   FUSED The Pre-Raphaelite Brotherhood was a group of young, enthusiastic painters, poets, and painter-poets their artistic aims varied widely.

   COMMA SPLICE The Pre-Raphaelite Brotherhood was a group of young, enthusiastic painters, poets, and painter-poets, their artistic aims varied widely.

   REVISED The Pre-Raphaelite Brotherhood was a group of young, enthusiastic painters, poets, and painter-poets. Their artistic aims varied widely.

2. **The pronouns** ***he, she, they, it, this,*** **and** ***that,*** when renaming the subject of a sentence, can signal a comma splice or a fused sentence. Even when the subject named or renamed in adjacent sentences is identical, the sentences themselves must be kept distinct.

   FUSED Dante Gabriel Rossetti was a poet he was also a painter.

   COMMA SPLICE Dante Gabriel Rossetti was a poet, he was also a painter.

   REVISED Dante Gabriel Rossetti was a poet, and he was a painter.

3. **Conjunctive adverbs** (words such as *however, furthermore, thus, therefore,* and *consequently*) **and transitional expressions** (phrases such as *for example* and *on the other hand*) are commonly found in fused or spliced clauses. Conjunctive adverbs and transitions always link complete sentences. Writers must reflect this linkage with appropriate punctuation: a period or semicolon. (For a complete list of conjunctive adverbs, see 19a and 19a-3.)

FUSED SENTENCE Ninety percent of the Hispanic vote is concentrated in nine states that cast seventy-one percent of all electoral ballots consequently Hispanics have emerged as a nationally influential group of voters in presidential politics.

COMMA SPLICE Ninety percent of the Hispanic vote is concentrated in nine states that cast seventy-one percent of all electoral ballots, consequently, Hispanics have emerged as a nationally influential group of voters in presidential politics.

REVISED Ninety percent of the Hispanic vote is concentrated in nine states that cast seventy-one percent of all electoral ballots. Consequently, Hispanics have emerged as a nationally influential group of voters in presidential politics. [*Consequently* starts a new main clause.]

EXERCISE 1

Use a slash mark (/) to identify the points at which the following sentences are fused or spliced together.

Example: Designers of advertisements for professional medical journals use multiple strategies for convincing their readers sometimes they use shocking visual images.

Designers of advertisements for professional medical journals use multiple strategies for convincing readers / sometimes they use shocking visual images.

1. Advertisements for aspirin and other pain relievers are incredibly dull, they are so like one another, so unmemorable that we remember them only because of their sheer frequency.
2. Unlike most other advertising, pain reliever commercials are very modest in their claims, in other words, they promise only partial relief from minor aches and only relatively quickly.
3. One would expect that such commercials would press harder to represent both the intensity of the pain as well as the joy of relief however these advertisements never suggest that the sufferer was ever in acute pain or that the sufferer's relief is now total.
4. Oddly enough, ads for pain relievers claim very little, they are undramatic, uninteresting.
5. The advertisements that physicians and surgeons see in their professional journals do attempt to represent acute pain, the difference may be attributable to the fact that the audience in this case (doctors) is not experiencing pain itself, but rather is treating pain.

13b Correct fused sentences and comma splices in one of five ways.

1 Separate independent clauses with a period (and sometimes a colon).

COMMA SPLICE Cotton was once the lead farm product in Alabama, today poultry has replaced it.

TEACHING IDEAS

Conjunctive adverbs and transitional expressions account for a significant percentage of comma splices in student writing; many students treat these words as if they were conjunctions. Put two columns on the board, one labeled "conjunctive adverbs/transitional expressions," the other "coordinating/subordinating conjunctions." Ask students to name all the words they can to fill in the lists (refer to Chapter 7 [Constructing Sentences] if necessary). They can copy the lists for easy reference.

EXERCISE 1

1. Advertisements for aspirin and other pain relievers are incredibly dull, / they are so like one another, so unmemorable that we remember them only because of their sheer frequency.
2. Unlike most other advertising, pain reliever commercials are very modest in their claims, / in other words, they promise only partial relief from minor aches and only relatively quickly.
3. One would expect that such commercials would press harder to represent both the intensity of the pain as well as the joy of relief / however these advertisements never suggest that the sufferer was ever in acute pain or that the sufferer's relief is now total.
4. Oddly enough, ads for pain relievers claim very little, / they are undramatic, uninteresting.
5. The advertisements that physicians and surgeons see in their professional journals do attempt to represent acute pain, / the difference may be attributable to the fact that the audience in this case (doctors) is not experiencing pain itself, but rather is treating pain.

GROUP ACTIVITY

Exercise 1 and subsequent exercises are ideal for group work. Have students either complete the exercises in groups or compare their responses after completing the exercises individually. Either way, as they negotiate responses or defend their choices, they'll understand more clearly the appropriate punctuation of sentences.

CLEAR Cotton was once the lead farm product in Alabama. Today, poultry has replaced it.

Using a period is the most obvious way to repair a fused or spliced construction, especially when the first independent clause is not very closely related in content to its neighbor, and when you do not want to link the two with a conjunction. But when using a period to repair faulty constructions, take care that your paragraphs do not become choppy. See the discussion on sentence variety in Chapter 20.

Occasionally, writers use a colon between independent clauses when the first sentence is a formal and emphatic introduction to an explanation, example, or appositive in the second sentence.

FUSED SENTENCE Logging is often the first step in deforestation it may be followed by complete clearing of trees and a deliberate shift to unsound land uses.

COMMA SPLICE Logging is often the first step in deforestation, it may be followed by complete clearing of trees and a deliberate shift to unsound land uses.

REVISED Logging is often the first step in deforestation. It may be followed by complete clearing of trees and a deliberate shift to unsound land uses.

REVISED Logging is often the first step in deforestation: it may be followed by complete clearing of trees and a deliberate shift to unsound land uses. [The colon gives the opening clause an emphatic introductory function.]

2 Link clauses with a comma and a coordinating conjunction.

FUSED January may be the coldest month it is a month of great productivity.

CLEAR January may be the coldest month**, but** it is a month of great productivity.

Use a comma placed *before* a coordinating conjunction—*and, but, or, nor, for, so,* and *yet*—to link sentences that are closely related in content and that are equally important. Like all conjunctions, coordinating conjunctions establish clear and definite logical relationships between the elements joined, so choose conjunctions with care. (See 19a for a detailed discussion of coordinating conjunctions.)

FUSED SENTENCE Deforestation has a severe environmental impact on soil in heavy tropical rains soil erodes quickly.

COMMA SPLICE Deforestation has a severe environmental impact on soil, in heavy tropical rains soil erodes quickly.

REVISED Deforestation has a severe environmental impact on soil, for in heavy tropical rains soil erodes quickly.

ESL CUE

Most ESL students will never have been introduced to absolutes, will find them most puzzling, and will tend to equate them with comma splice problems, especially when the central verb is a passive form so it looks more complete than it is: "Their work completed, they went home." Marcella Frank's *Modern English, Part II* has a clear explanation of how and when to use absolutes.

REFERENCES

BAMBERG, BETTY. "Periods Are Basic: A Strategy for Eliminating Comma Faults and Run-on Sentences." *Teaching the Basics—Really!* Ed. Ouida Clapp. Urbana: NCTE, 1977. 97–99. Teaching punctuation as an integral part of sentence structure helps students avoid problems with comma splices and fused sentences.

MEYER, EMILY, and LOUISE Z. SMITH. *The Practical Tutor.* New York: Oxford UP, 1987. 177–201. A thorough analysis of the causes of sentence errors, with guidelines for helping students overcome them.

SHAUGHNESSY, MINA P. *Errors and Expectations: A Guide for the Teacher of Basic Writing.* New York: Oxford UP, 1977. 16–43. Comma splices reflect larger problems with written discourse, and should be addressed accordingly.

CRITICAL DECISIONS

Challenge and be challenged: Choosing a method to link independent clauses

Sentence boundaries clearly marked with a period help readers focus on, and understand, one thought at a time. When you want to show the relationship *between* sentences and get readers to consider one thought in light of another, then you should link clauses. You have various options for doing so; which option you choose depends on the relationship you want to establish between independent clauses.

- **Do you want one independent clause to announce another?** If so, use a colon to make the announcement (see 13b-1).

  SEPARATED The race was postponed for one reason. The sponsors withdrew their support.

  LINKED The race was postponed for one reason**:** the sponsors withdrew their support.

- **Do you want to relate but maintain equal emphasis between two independent clauses?** If so, use a coordinating conjunction with a comma, a conjunctive adverb with a semicolon or period, or a semicolon to link the clauses (see 13b-2–4 and 19a).

Coordinating conjunction with a comma

SEPARATED Runners had already arrived. They were angry with the postponement.

LINKED Runners had already arrived**, and** they were angry with the postponement.

Conjunctive adverb with a semicolon or a period

SEPARATED The sponsors cited financial worries. They had political concerns as well.

LINKED The sponsors cited financial worries**; however,** they had political concerns as well.

Semicolon

SEPARATED One faction of runners wanted to boycott all future races in that city. Another faction wanted to stage a protest march.

LINKED One faction of runners wanted to boycott all future races in that city**;** another faction wanted to stage a protest march.

- **Do you want to link two independent clauses but emphasize one more than the other?** If so, use a subordinating conjunction to link the clauses (see 13b-5 and 19b).

  SEPARATED The press was embarrassing. The sponsors canceled the race permanently.

  LINKED **Because** the press was embarrassing**,** the sponsors canceled the race permanently.

TEACHING IDEAS

Many comma splices (and a few fused sentences) are actually the result of sound thinking on the part of student writers. For example, the student who joins two sentences with a comma often recognizes that the sentences are linked; the problem arises when the student doesn't understand the options open to him or her. Careful attention in class to the Critical Decisions box may help those who know that two sentences should be closely linked but don't know how to link them. You may want to ask students to compare their papers to the box and identify types of errors they make frequently. The box will provide them with the strategies they need to follow through on their hunches about relationships between sentences.

3 Link clauses with a semicolon.

Fused Wind is one cause of erosion water is another cause.

Comma splice Wind is one cause of erosion, water is another cause.

Clear Wind is one cause of erosion; water is another cause.

Use a semicolon in place of a comma and a coordinating conjunction to link sentences that are closely related and equally important. The semicolon links independent clauses without making the relationship between them explicit. You might choose a semicolon to repair a fused or spliced construction either when the relationship between clauses is crystal clear and a conjunction would be redundant or when you wish to create anticipation—leaving your readers to discover the exact relationship between clauses.

Fused sentence Experience reinforces the argument that deforestation has not been a path to economic development in most tropical countries it has instead been a costly drain on resources.

Comma splice Experience reinforces the argument that deforestation has not been a path to economic development, in most tropical countries it has instead been a costly drain on resources.

Revised Experience reinforces the argument that deforestation has not been a path to economic development; in most tropical countries it has instead been a costly drain on resources.

4 Link clauses with a semicolon (or period) and a conjunctive adverb.

Comma splice Joyce Carol Oates is a novelist, essayist, playwright, and poet, she is a distinguished scholar.

Clear Joyce Carol Oates is a novelist, essayist, playwright, and poet; moreover, she is a distinguished scholar.

Use conjunctive adverbs—words such as *however, furthermore, thus, therefore,* and *consequently*—to link closely related, equally important clauses. (See 19a and 19a-3 for a complete list of conjunctive adverbs.) Conjunctive adverbs establish the same relationships, such as addition, contrast, and cause, as do coordinating conjunctions. The conjunctive adverbs, however, are more formal and a little stiffer, but also more rigorous and forceful than coordinating conjunctions. As well, conjunctive adverbs and coordinating conjunctions create different rhythms in the sentences you are linking. Choose conjunctions based on the relationships you wish to establish in your paragraphs.

Place a period between clauses when you want a full separation of ideas. Place a semicolon between clauses when you want to emphasize the

ADDITIONAL EXERCISE A

Identify the following examples as either *fused sentences (fs)* or *comma splices (cs),* and then correctly punctuate the sentences according to the guidelines in 13b.

1. Hortense Powdermaker's family business success was sometimes uncertain, she grew up acutely conscious of money and class.
2. Powdermaker worked in a clothing factory while in college after graduation she became a union organizer.
3. Many of the men's clothing shops in Cleveland were unionized, however, the largest remained unorganized.
4. Many of the young girls in the Cleveland factory were Bohemian and Italian therefore, communication with them was a problem.
5. The first union meeting in Cleveland was a failure, immediately preceding the meeting, many union sympathizers were fired.

Answers:

1. cs/ Because Hortense Powdermaker's family business success was sometimes uncertain, she grew up acutely conscious of money and class.
2. fs/ Powdermaker worked in a clothing factory while in college. After graduation she became a union organizer.
3. cs/ Many of the men's clothing shops in Cleveland were unionized; however, the largest remained unorganized.
4. fs/ Many of the young girls in the Cleveland factory were Bohemian and Italian; therefore, communication with them was a problem.
5. cs/ The first union meeting in Cleveland was a failure; immediately preceding the meeting, many union sympathizers were fired.

link between ideas. As with most adverbs, a conjunctive adverb can shift its location in a sentence. If placed at the beginning, the conjunctive adverb is followed (usually) by a comma. If placed in the middle, it is usually set off by a pair of commas. And if placed at the end, it is preceded by a comma. Wherever you place the adverb, be sure to use a period or a semicolon between the two clauses you have linked.

FUSED SENTENCE Deforestation is not irreversible once a forest is cleared regeneration takes a lifetime.

COMMA SPLICE Deforestation is not irreversible, once a forest is cleared regeneration takes a lifetime.

REVISED Deforestation is not irreversible; however, once a forest is cleared, regeneration takes a lifetime. [The semicolon emphasizes the link between ideas.]

REVISED Deforestation is not irreversible. However, once a forest is cleared, regeneration takes a lifetime. [The period makes a full separation.]

REVISED Deforestation is not irreversible. Once a forest is cleared, however, regeneration takes a lifetime.

5 Link clauses with a subordinating conjunction or construction.

COMMA SPLICE Hannibal crossed the Alps, he defeated the Romans in the Po Valley.

CLEAR **After** Hannibal crossed the Alps, he defeated the Romans in the Po Valley.

Use a subordinating conjunction or construction to join fused or spliced independent clauses. By placing a subordinating conjunction at the beginning of an independent clause, or by using a relative pronoun such as *who, whom, which,* or *that,* you render that clause dependent, unable to stand alone as a complete thought. The new dependent clause will function as a modifier. Be aware of comma use with these constructions: when the clause begins a sentence, a comma often follows it to signal the reader that the main point of the sentence, the independent clause, is being delayed. By the same logic, when an independent clause begins a sentence, the dependent clause that follows very often does not use a comma. (See 19b for a discussion of subordination.)

FUSED SENTENCE International development-assistance agencies have begun to lend help a number of governments are now strengthening their forest-management programs.

COMMA SPLICE International development-assistance agencies have begun to lend help, a number of governments are now strengthening their forest-management programs.

REVISED Because international development-assistance agencies have begun to lend help, a number of governments are now strengthening their forest-management programs. [A dependent clause begins the sentence.]

REVISED A number of governments are now strengthening their forest-management programs because international development-assistance agencies have begun to lend help. [A dependent clause ends the sentence.]

REVISED A number of governments are now strengthening the forest-management programs that have begun to get help from international development-assistance agencies. [A dependent relative clause ends the sentence, creating a different meaning.]

Conjunctions and Punctuation

Coordinating Conjunctions

and but so or for nor yet

Use coordinating conjunctions with punctuation in this pattern:

Independent clause , CONJUNCTION independent clause

FUSED SENTENCE Newton developed calculus he discovered laws of gravity.

COMMA SPLICE Newton developed calculus, he discovered laws of gravity.

REVISED Newton developed calculus, and he discovered laws of gravity.

Conjunctive Adverbs

however furthermore thus therefore consequently

Use conjunctive adverbs with punctuation in these patterns:

Independent clause ; CONJUNCTION , independent clause

Independent clause . CONJUNCTION , independent clause

REVISED Newton developed calculus; moreover, he discovered laws of gravity.

REVISED Newton developed calculus. Moreover, he discovered laws of gravity.

Subordinating Conjunctions

after although because once since though while

Use subordinating conjunctions with punctuation in these patterns:

CONJUNCTION clause , independent clause

Independent clause CONJUNCTION clause

REVISED After Newton developed calculus, he discovered laws of gravity.

REVISED Newton discovered laws of gravity after he developed calculus.

ADDITIONAL EXERCISE B

Look through your graded papers to find instructors' comments regarding fused sentences and/or comma splices. Reread the papers, identifying the errors as you read by using the three guidelines in 13a. Then revise the errors. (If you don't have any graded papers handy, look through any body of writing you've done recently.)

EXERCISE 2

1. Fused sentence, comma splice
   Genetic engineering is the technique by which scientists alter or combine hereditary materials. Genes are part of all living material: they carry chemical information that determines every organism's characteristics.
2. Fused sentence
   The movement of creating genetically engineered organisms began in the early 1900s based on the earlier experiments of the Austrian monk Gregory Mendel. He laid the foundation for future experiments with his work on cross-breeding in plants.

EXERCISE 2

Using any of the strategies discussed in this chapter, correctly punctuate the following word groupings in which you find fused sentences or comma splices. In each case, name the error (or errors) you are correcting.

Example: Genetic engineering has been called the great scientific breakthrough of the century there are still many doubts concerning its potential effects on our environment.

Fused sentence. Genetic engineering has been called the great scientific breakthrough of the century**. However,** there are still many doubts concerning its potential effects on our environment.

1. Genetic engineering is the technique by which scientists alter or combine hereditary materials, genes are part of all living material they carry chemical information that determines every organism's characteristics.
2. The movement of creating genetically engineered organisms began in the early 1900s based on the earlier experiments of the Austrian monk Gregory Mendel he laid the foundation for future experiments with his work on cross-breeding in plants.
3. Scientists have discovered the benefits and uses of genetically engineered organisms in agriculture one of the first examples is the ice-minus bacterium created by Steve Lindow and Nicholas Panopoulos.
4. Lindow and Panopoulos realized that a bacterium commonly found in plants produces a protein that helps ice to form causing damaging frost, they removed this unfavorable gene, they prevented ice from forming on greenhouse plants.
5. Researchers hope in 20 to 30 years to create corn and wheat plants that can fix their own nitrogen in this way the plants would not need to be fertilized, this would save anywhere from $3 to $14 billion annually.
6. Geneticists have found beneficial uses of engineered organisms in agriculture, they have also found ways to use these organisms to clean up environmental hazards for instance, Dr. Anandra M. Chakrabarty has engineered an organism that breaks up oil spills.

EXERCISE 3

Correct the fused sentences and comma splices in the following paragraph, making use of all five strategies discussed in this chapter. One consideration governing your choice of corrections should be sentence variety. Vary methods for correcting fused and spliced clauses to avoid repeating sentence structures in consecutive sentences.

Whatever they may believe about what happens to the soul after death most cultures bury their dead. Given the grim fact of history that corpses can sometimes pile up at an alarming rate, it has not always been easy for managers of cemeteries, in a way cemetery planning is much like urban planning. Streets have to be mapped out and plots need to be sold, often, above-ground structures—mausoleums—have to be designed and executed. A chapel of some sort is usually called for—decorated Gothic or vertical Gothic, above all the cemetery must be landscaped in such a way as to afford comfort to the mourners.

3. Fused sentence
   Scientists have discovered the benefits and uses of genetically engineered organisms in agriculture. One of the first examples is the ice-minus bacterium created by Steve Lindow and Nicholas Panopoulos.
4. Comma splice
   Lindow and Panopoulos realized that a bacterium commonly found in plants produces a protein that helps ice to form causing damaging frost. They removed this unfavorable gene, and they prevented ice from forming on greenhouse plants.
5. Fused sentence, comma splice
   Researchers hope in 20 to 30 years to create corn and wheat plants that can fix their own nitrogen. In this way the plants would not need to be fertilized, and this would save anywhere from $3 to $14 billion annually.
6. Fused sentence, comma splice
   Geneticists have found beneficial uses of engineered organisms in agriculture. They have also found ways to use these organisms to clean up environmental hazards: for instance, Dr. Anandra M. Chakrabarty has engineered an organism that breaks up oil spills.

EXERCISE 3

Suggested revisions:

Whatever they may believe about what happens to the soul after death, most cultures bury their dead. Given the grim fact of history that corpses can sometimes pile up at an alarming rate, it has not always been easy for managers of cemeteries. In a way, cemetery planning is much like urban planning. Streets have to be mapped out, plots need to be sold, and often, above-ground structures—mausoleums—have to be designed and executed. A chapel of some sort is usually called for—decorated Gothic or vertical Gothic. Above all, the cemetery must be landscaped in such a way as to afford comfort to the mourners.

CHAPTER 14

Pronoun Reference

KEY FEATURES

Unclear pronoun reference, a common error among student writers, is treated extensively. Rather than emphasize errors, however, the chapter sections approach the topic from a positive perspective, classifying the various strategies a writer can use to assure clear pronoun reference. Among these strategies are keeping pronouns close to their antecedents, making certain that the antecedent is stated in the sentence, and avoiding indefinite antecedents. The use of the latter in casual, everyday speech is acknowledged, but as in previous chapters, the need for more clarity in formal written discourse is emphasized. Specific pronouns that often cause problems are dealt with in separate sections: *it* as an expletive and pronoun, as well as the inappropriate use of *who, which,* and *that.* As in previous chapters, exercises provide ample practice in identifying and correcting errors.

LOOKING BACK

References to Chapter 7 (Constructing Sentences) appear throughout this chapter. If Chapter 7 has not been covered yet, or if some time has passed since it was covered, you may want to spend a little time on that material now.

TEACHING IDEAS

If students have difficulty remembering the meaning of *antecedent,* you can explain that the prefix *ante* means "before." Students who have taken American history may recall that *antebellum* means *before* the Civil War. Otherwise, give students the literal meaning of *antecedent:* "that which goes before."

A **pronoun** substitutes for a noun, allowing you to talk about someone or something without having to repeat its name (see 7a-7). To serve this function, a pronoun must take on meaning from a specific noun; the pronoun must make a clear and unmistakable reference to the noun for which it substitutes—called its **antecedent.** When the reference is not clearly made to a specific noun, the meaning of the whole sentence can become vague or confused.

UNCLEAR Michelangelo had a complex personality, as did Raphael, though *his* was the more complex. *His* art was not nearly so typical of the High Renaissance, and *he* was frequently irascible—as impatient with the shortcomings of others as with *his* own.

To whom do the pronouns *he* and *his* refer in these sentences? No one can tell. The sentences need to be revised, and the pronouns and antecedents must be placed with care to keep readers moving forward.

REVISED Michelangelo had a complex personality, as did Raphael, though *Michelangelo's* was the more complex. *His* art was not nearly so typical of the High Renaissance, and *he* was frequently irascible—as impatient with the shortcomings of others as with *his* own. [The proper noun replaces an unclear pronoun, providing a reference point for all the pronouns that follow.]

14a Make pronouns refer clearly to their antecedents.

CONFUSING When Mark and Jay return home, *he* will call.
CLEAR When Mark and Jay return home, *Mark* will call.

Revise a sentence whenever a pronoun can refer to more than one antecedent. Use a noun in place of a pronoun, if needed for clarity; or reposition a pronoun so that its antecedent is unmistakable.

CONFUSING In 1949, astronomer Gerard Kuiper proposed the existence of a comet-strewn belt girting our solar system, although the same theory had been advanced by British astronomer K. E. Edgewater two years earlier. Astronomer Hal Levin comments that there is much uncertainty as to whether Kuiper knew about him. [Does the pronoun *him* refer to Levin or Edgewater?]

REVISED In 1949, astronomer Gerard Kuiper proposed the existence of a comet-strewn belt girting our solar system, although the same theory had been advanced by British astronomer K. E. Edgewater two years earlier. Astronomer Hal Levin comments that there is much uncertainty as to whether Kuiper knew about Edgewater.

Describing a person's speech indirectly can lead to unclear pronoun reference. Occasionally, if you can document what was said, you can convert indirect quotations to direct ones in order to clarify a pronoun's reference. Otherwise, you can restate the sentence carefully to avoid confusion among the nouns.

CONFUSING One of the astronomers, showing telescopic photos of the belt to the reporter, said that *he* didn't know whether *he* had discovered the home base of the comets or whether *he* was simply seeing the effects of cosmic rays hitting the lens of the telescope's camera. [Do any of these *he*s refer to the reporter?]

DIRECT STATEMENT One of the astronomers, showing telescopic photos of the belt to the reporter, said: "I didn't know whether I had discovered the home base of the comets or whether I was simply seeing the effects of cosmic rays hitting the lens of the telescope's camera."

RESTATEMENT One of the astronomers told the reporter that the photos could have been pictures of the home base of our comets or simply an optical effect produced by cosmic rays hitting the lens of the telescope's camera.

ESL NOTE In a standard English sentence, the subject is not repeated elsewhere in the sentence with an unnecessary pronoun. Pronouns are also involved when the subject is renamed in a dependent clause (see 7e-2). Repeated subjects must be avoided in sentences with long dependent clauses separating subjects from verbs (see 14e-1 and 44d-1).

14b Keep pronouns close to their antecedents.

CONFUSING The *statement* that Dr. Parker made and that she issued as a formal warning infuriated the mayor, who knew *it* would alarm the public.

CLEAR Issued as a formal warning, Dr. Parker's *statement* alarmed the public, and *it* infuriated the mayor.

Even when pronoun choice is correct, too many words between a pronoun and its antecedent can confuse readers. If in a long sentence or in adjacent sentences several nouns appear between a pronoun and its proper antecedent, these nouns will incorrectly claim the reader's attention as the word renamed by the pronoun.

CONFUSING *Prehistoric peoples* used many organic substances, which survive at relatively few archaeological sites. Bone and antler were commonly used, especially in Europe some fifteen thousand years ago. *They* relied heavily on plant fibers and baskets for their material culture. [The pronoun *they* must refer to *prehistoric peoples,* since only people can *rely,* but the intervening nouns distract from this reference.]

FOR DISCUSSION

Since most students have problems with only certain types of pronoun reference errors, you might want to initiate a class discussion of errors most relevant to your students. Ask students to identify from the Spotlight on Common Errors examples of reference errors familiar to them and to characterize their own errors accordingly. Students can then discuss how pronoun reference errors can occur, thereby reinforcing their understanding of the need for clarity in pronoun use. (In large classes, this activity might begin with small groups. The groups will identify their errors, and then the class as a whole will discuss the types compiled from each group's report.)

Spotlight on Common Errors—PRONOUN REFERENCE

These are the errors most commonly associated with pronoun reference. For full explanations and suggested revisions, follow the cross-references to chapter sections.

PRONOUN REFERENCE ERRORS arise when a sentence leaves readers unable to link a pronoun with an *antecedent*—a specific noun that the pronoun refers to and renames (see 7a-7). If the identity of this antecedent is unclear, readers may miss the reference and become confused. Four error patterns lead to problems with pronoun reference.

- **A pronoun should refer clearly to a single noun. When the pronoun can refer to either of two (or more) nouns within a sentence or between sentences, revise sentences for clarity (see 14a).**

Within a sentence

FAULTY	REVISED
When Mark and Jay return home, *he* will call. [To whom does *he* refer?]	When Mark and Jay return home, *Mark* will call.

Between sentences

FAULTY	REVISED
The conversation between Clara and Nancy lasted two hours. At the end, *she* was exhausted. [Which one is *she*?]	The conversation between Clara and Nancy lasted two hours. At the end, *Clara* was exhausted.

- **A pronoun should be located close to the noun it renames. When a pronoun is too far from its antecedent, revise the sentence to narrow the distance and clarify meaning (see 14b).**

Within a sentence

FAULTY	REVISED
The statement that Dr. Parker made about a city water fountain and that she issued as a formal warning infuriated the mayor, who knew *it* would alarm the public. [Does *it* clearly refer to the faraway *statement* and not to something else?]	Issued as a formal warning, Dr. Parker's *statement* about a city water fountain alarmed the public, and *it* infuriated the mayor. [Less distance between the pronoun and antecedent makes the reference clear.]

Between sentences

FAULTY
Major oil spills have fouled coastlines in Alaska, France, and England and have caused severe ecological damage. *Some* could almost certainly be avoided. [Does *some* refer to faraway *spills* or to *coastlines*?]

REVISED
Major oil spills have fouled coastlines in Alaska, France, and England and have caused severe ecological damage. *Some spills* could almost certainly be avoided. [*Spills* is added to clear up the reference.]

- **The pronouns *this* and *that* should refer to specific words. When either is used as a one-word summary of a preceding sentence, revise to clarify the reference between sentences by adding an additional word or phrase of summary (see 14c-3).**

FAULTY
The purpose of the conference was to explore the links between lung cancer and secondhand smoke. *This* was firmly established. [What was established?]

REVISED
The purpose of the conference was to explore the links between lung cancer and secondhand smoke. *This connection* was firmly established. [A summary word added makes the reference clear.]

- **Once you establish a pattern of first-person *(I/we)*, second-person *(you)*, or third-person pronouns *(he/she/it/they)* in a sentence or paragraph (see 8a, 8b), keep references to your subject consistent. Prevent confusion by avoiding shifts and revising sentences for consistency (see 16a-1).**

Within a sentence

FAULTY
Students generally fare better when *you* are given instruction on taking lecture notes. [Confusion arises between third-person *students* and second-person *you*. Who is the subject?]

REVISED
Students generally fare better when they are given instruction on taking lecture notes.[Consistent third person]
OR
As a student *you* will generally fare better when you are given instruction on taking lecture notes.

Between sentences

FAULTY
Students fare better when given instruction on basic skills. *You* can improve *your* notetaking after getting help with the techniques. [Have *students* suddenly become *you*?]

REVISED
Students fare better when given instruction on basic skills. *They* can improve *their* notetaking after getting help with the techniques.

EXERCISE 1

1. The ritual of greeting varies from culture to culture. Americans ask "How are you?" whereas Filipinos ask "Where are you going?"—a question that seems prying to Americans.
2. Professor Deborah Tannen claims that while conducting research in a corporate environment, she found many women who rightly perceived themselves as highly successful; these women felt that their coworkers, but not necessarily high-level management, shared this perception.
3. The men whom Tannen interviewed often told her that if a woman hadn't been promoted, it was because the woman didn't deserve it.

GROUP ACTIVITY

This and subsequent exercises are ideal for group work. Have students either complete the exercises in groups or compare their responses after completing the exercises individually. Either way, as they negotiate responses or defend their choices, they'll understand more clearly the appropriate punctuation of sentences.

CLOSER ANTECEDENT *Prehistoric peoples* used many organic substances, which survive at relatively few archaeological sites. *They commonly used* bone and antler, especially in Europe some fifteen thousand years ago. *They* also relied heavily on plant fibers and baskets for their material culture. [The pronoun subject, *they,* is added to the second sentence in order to maintain a clear antecedent. The pronoun subject of the third sentence is thereby made clear.]

PRONOUN REPLACED *Prehistoric peoples* used many organic substances, which survive at relatively few archaeological sites. Bone and antler were commonly used, especially in Europe some fifteen thousand years ago. *The desert peoples of western North America* relied heavily on plant fibers and baskets for their material culture. [A new subject replaces the confusing pronoun.]

The relative pronouns *who, which,* and *that,* when introducing a modifying adjective clause, should be placed close to the nouns they modify (see 19b-2).

CONFUSING Prehistoric peoples used many organic substances difficult to find at archaeological sites, which included bone and antler. [Does *which* refer to *sites* or *substances*?]

CLOSER ANTECEDENT Prehistoric peoples used many organic substances, including bone and antler, which survive at relatively few archaeological sites.

EXERCISE 1

Rewrite the sentences that follow so that pronouns are replaced or are close to and refer clearly to the nouns they rename. Place a check beside the sentences that need no revision.

Example: When Bob talks with Joe by phone, he can hardly get a word in edgewise because he expects a more delayed response from him.

When Bob talks with Joe by phone, Bob can hardly get a word in edgewise because he expects a more delayed response from Joe. [The pronouns are replaced with nouns.]

1. The ritual of greeting varies from one culture to another; for example, Americans ask: "How are you?" whereas Filipinos ask "Where are you going?"—a question that seems prying to them.
2. Professor Deborah Tannen claims that while conducting research in a corporate environment, she found many women who rightly perceived themselves as highly successful; these women felt that their coworkers shared this perception but that higher-level management did not recognize it.
3. The men whom Tannen interviewed often told her that if she hadn't been promoted, it was because she didn't deserve it.

14c State a pronoun's antecedent clearly.

To be clear, a pronoun's antecedent should be stated directly, either in the sentence in which the pronoun appears or in an immediately preceding sentence. If the antecedent is merely implied, the pronoun's meaning will be weak or imprecise and the reader will probably be confused.

1 Make a pronoun refer to a specific noun antecedent, not to a modifier that may imply the antecedent.

CONFUSING From films such as *Fantasia* in 1940 to *Aladdin* in 1992, Disney studios have raised *it* to an art form.

CLEAR From films such as *Fantasia* in 1940 to *Aladdin* in 1992, Disney studios have raised *animation* to an art form.

Although an adjective may imply the antecedent of a pronoun, an adjective is not identical to and thus cannot serve as that antecedent. Revise sentences so that a *noun* provides the reference for a pronoun.

CONFUSING Two glass rods will repel each other when they are electrified. *It* is created from a buildup of positive and negative charges in the rods. [What does *it* refer to?]

NOUN ANTECEDENT Two glass rods will repel each other when they carry *electricity. It* is created from a buildup of positive and negative charges in the rods.

NOUN ANTECEDENT Two glass rods will repel each other when they carry *electricity, which* is created from a buildup of positive and negative charges in the rods.

PRONOUN REPLACED Two *electrified* glass rods will repel each other. *Electricity* arises from the buildup of positive and negative charges in the rods.

2 Make a pronoun refer to a noun, not the possessive form of a noun.

CONFUSING *Sally's* case is in trouble. Does *she* know that?

CLEAR *Sally* is in trouble with this case. Does *she* know that?

Although the possessive form of a noun may imply the noun as the intended antecedent of a pronoun, this form is not identical to, and thus is not clear enough to serve as, that antecedent. Revise sentences so that a *noun* provides the reference for a pronoun. Alternately, change the pronoun so that it, too, is in the possessive form.

ADDITIONAL EXERCISE A

ACROSS THE CURRICULUM Photocopy several paragraphs from one of your textbooks. Try to find a passage that narrates an event: a scientist's discovery, a historical figure's accomplishments, or a section of a short story or novel. Circle all of the pronouns in the selection, and draw arrows to their antecedents. How frequently does the writer keep pronouns close to their antecedents? If there are cases in which the two are separated by long phrases or clauses, is the pronoun reference still clear? If you answer "no" for any parts of the passage, rewrite those parts to make the reference clearer.

TEACHING IDEAS

The topics covered in this section, especially 3 and 4, reflect frequent errors in student papers. If you can determine which errors are more common in your class, you can ask students to revise a passage that includes those errors. The passage can be either one you've copied from a text and "doctored" to introduce errors or one you've designed yourself to closely approximate your students' more common errors.

ESL CUE

ESL students find sentences in which the relative clause pronoun has been omitted most confusing and have trouble separating subordinate clauses from main clauses in such situations. With adjective clauses in which the verb takes a preposition, ESL students might add an extraneous "it"; they do so most frequently if the relative clause pronoun is omitted.

"He soon caught up with the car which his girlfriend was riding in ~~it.~~"

"He soon caught up with the car his girlfriend was riding in ~~it.~~"

Confusing The *Greeks'* knowledge of magnetic forces was evident before 600 B.C. *They* observed how certain minerals, such as loadstone, have the ability to attract pieces of iron.

Noun antecedent The *Greeks* had knowledge of magnetic forces before 600 B.C. *They* observed how certain minerals, such as loadstone, have the ability to attract iron. [The possessive form—*Greeks'*—is eliminated to provide an antecedent for the pronoun *they.*]

Pronoun replaced The *Greeks'* knowledge of magnetic forces was evident before 600 B.C. *Their scientists* observed how certain minerals, such as loadstone, have the ability to attract pieces of iron.

3 Give the pronouns *that, this, which,* and *it* precise reference.

Confusing The paper proposed to link cancer and secondary smoke. *This* was established.

Clear The paper proposed to link cancer and secondary smoke. *This connection* was established.

The pronouns *that, this, which,* and *it* should refer to specific nouns. Avoid having them make vague reference to the overall sense of a preceding sentence.

Confusing Magnets have two poles—called north and south poles—and these poles obey the same kind of rule as electric charges: like poles repel each other and unlike poles attract each other. *This* was not well understood until the twentieth century. [What, exactly, does *this* refer to?]

Antecedent provided Magnets have two poles—called north and south poles—and these poles obey the same kind of rule as electric charges: like poles repel each other and unlike poles attract each other. *This phenomenon* was not well understood until the twentieth century.

Confusing Knowledge of atomic structure was advanced in the late nineteenth century by British scientist J. J. Thomson, *which* established that one component of the atom, electrons, are negatively charged. [The pronoun *which* does not refer to a particular noun.]

Antecedent provided Knowledge of atomic structure was advanced in the late nineteenth century by British scientist J. J. Thomson, *who* established that one component of the atom, electrons, are negatively charged.

Confusing Thomson believed atoms of matter contain two kinds of particles, intermingled: negatively charged electrons and positively charged protons. *That* was the impetus other physicists needed to refine even further the structural model of the atom. [No single word serves as the antecedent of *that.*]

Pronoun replaced Thomson believed atoms of matter contain two kinds of particles, intermingled: negatively charged electrons and positively charged protons. *Thomson's theory* was the impetus other physicists needed to refine even further the structural model of the atom.

REFERENCES

LAKOFF, GEORGE. "Pronouns and Reference." *Notes from the Linguistic Underground.* Ed. James D. McCawley. New York: Academic Press, 1976. 275–335. A thorough discussion of various issues involved in pronoun reference.

MOSKOVIT, LEONARD. "When Is Broad Reference Clear?" CCC 34 (1983): 454–69. At times, broad pronouns without specific antecedents are indeed clear.

SLOAN, GARY. "Relational Ambiguity Between Sentences." CCC 39 (1988): 154–65. Comparing written and spoken discourse can be beneficial when studying pronoun reference.

GROUP ACTIVITY

Because students are more likely to learn rules when working with their own writing, analysis of pronoun reference errors in their papers can be beneficial. Ask students to bring in several papers in order to take part in this activity. When you divide students into groups, try to mix strong writers with weak ones. Then have each group work together on one student's writing at a time, identifying unclear pronoun references, particularly those involving *that, this, which, it, they,* and *you.* The group's attempts to determine which references are unclear and how to revise them should generate healthy discussion. This discussion will help strong writers to articulate their implicit understanding of grammatical rules and weak writers to gain an understanding of such rules.

4 Avoid indefinite antecedents for the pronouns *it, they,* and *you.*

NONSTANDARD *It* will rain tomorrow.

STANDARD *We* are expecting rain tomorrow.

Expressions such as "you know," "they say," and "it figures" are common in speech and informal writing. The pronouns in these expressions do not refer to particular people—or, in the case of *it,* to a particular object. These pronouns are said to have *indefinite* reference. In academic writing, pronouns should refer to specific antecedents. *You* should be used either to address the reader directly or for a direct quotation; *it* and *they* should refer to particular things, ideas, or people.

NONSTANDARD Today, *they say* that an atom has a nucleus with neutrons and protons.

STANDARD Today, *physicists believe* that an atom has a nucleus with neutrons and protons.

NONSTANDARD Because physicists work with abstract models and mathematical languages, *you* must almost take what physicists say as an item of faith.

STANDARD Because physicists work with abstract models and mathematical languages, *nonscientists* must almost take what physicists say as an item of faith.

How to Revise Unclear Pronoun Reference

1. Provide a clear, nearby antecedent.
2. Replace the pronoun with a noun and thereby eliminate the problem of ambiguous reference.
3. Totally recast the sentence to avoid the problem of ambiguous reference.

5 Avoid using a pronoun to refer to the title of a paper in the paper's first sentence.

A pronoun should have a reference in the sentence in which it appears or in an immediately preceding sentence. A title, while directly related to a paper or essay, does not occur *within* the paper or essay and thus cannot function appropriately as an antecedent.

A TITLE "Eliot's Desert Images in *The Waste Land*"

A FIRST SENTENCE They are plentiful, and their cumulative effect is to leave readers thirsty—in both body and soul.

FIRST SENTENCE REVISED Desert images in T. S. Eliot's *The Waste Land* are plentiful, and their cumulative effect is to leave readers thirsty—in both body and soul.

TEACHING IDEAS

If you're aware of students whose writing lacks clarity because of overuse of *it,* then you may find the following exercise useful. Ask those students to gather three or four of their papers and circle every use of *it,* labeling the word as either an expletive or a pronoun. Above each pronoun use of *it* (or in the margin) they are to name the pronoun's antecedent. An inability to determine the antecedent and/or an overabundance of expletives should alert the student that there is a problem with clarity in his or her writing. Such students might be advised to use this exercise with every future draft until the problem is alleviated.

ESL CUE

Some romance-language (Spanish, Italian, Portuguese) speakers will have difficulty with the concept of the expletive since it does not exist in their language. Their tendency will be to leave out the "there" or "it" and to simply begin with a *be* verb as they would in their language: "Is hot." "Is over there." Calling attention to the problem often helps the student self-correct.

14d Avoid mixing uses of the pronoun *it.*

CONFUSING *It* will be a successful experiment if the computer doesn't overload *its* memory.

CLEAR The experiment will succeed if the computer doesn't overload *its* memory.

The word *it* functions both as a pronoun and as an expletive (see 7a-11)—that is, as a space filler in a rearranged sentence.

AS AN EXPLETIVE *It* is clear that the committee is resisting the initiative. [The entire "that . . . " clause is the subject.]

AS A PRONOUN Although the committee voted, *it* [i.e., the committee] showed no leadership.

Avoid using the word *it* both as an expletive and as a pronoun in the same sentence.

CONFUSING *It* is clear that *it* is shirking *its* responsibilities.

WEAK *It* is clear that the committee is shirking *its* responsibilities.

CLEAR Clearly, the committee is shirking *its* responsibilities.

14e Use the relative pronouns *who, which,* and *that* appropriately.

1 Selecting relative pronouns

Relative pronouns (see 7e-2) introduce dependent clauses that usually function as adjectives. The pronouns *who, which,* and *that* rename and refer to the nouns they follow. The pronoun *who* can refer to people or to divinities or personified animals.

> The most highly respected baseball player in the year 1911 was Ty Cobb, *who* had joined the Detroit Tigers in 1905.

That refers to animals, things, or people (when not referring to a *specific* person, in which case the pronoun *who* is used).

> For decades, Cobb held a record *that* remained unbreakable—until Pete Rose stroked his 4192nd career hit in 1985.

Which refers to animals and things.

> His career, *which* lasted 24 years, was marked by extraordinary statistics—for example, a batting average of .367, 2244 runs, and 892 stolen bases.

CRITICAL DECISIONS

Be alert to differences: Apply a test for choosing *who, which,* or *that*—with or without commas.

Writers can be unsure of themselves when choosing relative pronouns (*who, which,* and *that*) and when using commas with relative clauses. Relative pronouns begin relative clauses, and these function in a sentence as if they were adjectives: they modify nouns. You can apply three tests for deciding which pronoun to use and whether or not to use commas.

Identify the noun being modified.

- **Is this a proper noun—the name of a *specific* person (George), place (Baltimore), or thing (Levis)?** If yes, then use the pronoun *who, whom,* or *whose* (for a person) or *which* (for a place or thing) *with* commas. The noun does not need the modifying clause to specify its meaning. This clause is *nonessential* (see 25d).

  My friend George, *who* is constantly angry, has developed a stress disorder.

  The harbor area in Baltimore, *which* is the largest city in Maryland but not the capital, has changed significantly in the last twenty years.

  The Levis, which fit me well, were on sale.

- **Is the noun being modified a common noun—an unspecified person (people), place (city), or thing (pants)?** If yes, then it is quite likely that the modifying information of the clause is essential for specifying the noun's identity. Use *who, whom,* or *whose* (for a person) and *which* or *that* (for a place or thing) *without* commas. The modifying clause is *essential* (see 25d).

  People *who* are constantly angry often develop stress disorders.

  The cities *that* are of greatest interest to me are all accessible by train. The cities *which* are of greatest interest to me are all accessible by train.

  The pants *that* fit me best were on sale.

- **Is the identity of the common noun being modified made clear and specific to the reader in the context of the paragraph?** If yes, then treat the common noun in the same way that you would a proper noun: use a relative clause, with commas.

  Over a year ago, I met the woman *who* is seated at that table in the corner. The woman, *whose* name I can't remember, is a friend of Joan's.

  [In the first sentence, the relative clause *who is seated . . .* is needed to identify which woman, presumably in a roomful of people. In the second sentence, the reader knows who is being referred to, so the relative clause in that sentence (*whose name . . .*) is nonessential and takes commas.]

ESL NOTE Avoid repeating the subject of a sentence with an unnecessary pronoun, especially when a long dependent clause separates a subject from its verb (see 44d-1).

ADDITIONAL EXERCISE B

ACROSS THE CURRICULUM This exercise should reinforce your understanding of the use of relative pronouns in essential and nonessential clauses. Photocopy a long passage from a textbook used in one of your other classes, and underline all of the relative clauses. Based on the guidelines in this box, identify each of the clauses as essential or nonessential. Then, for each clause, explain why the author chose to use the relative pronoun he or she did.

TEACHING IDEAS

The concept of essential and nonessential is often difficult for students to grasp. Thus, although the focus of this section is on pronouns rather than on punctuation, it may be useful to clarify the distinction between essential and nonessential for students at this point.

Write on the board a sentence that has two distinct meanings depending on whether or not the subordinate clause is essential. Write the sentence first with the comma, and then erase the comma. Ask students how the meaning changes when the comma is removed. A sentence like "Professor Shannon failed all her students, who had missed the exam" is a good example. Did all of Professor Shannon's students miss the exam? Did she fail only that group of students who missed the exam? As they work with sentences like this, students will gain a clearer understanding of how important it is to be able to distinguish essential from nonessential items.

NOTE

Many writers reserve the use of *that* for essential modifiers. These writers would therefore consider the first, but not the second, sentence about Márquez as correct. The authors take the position that the essential use of *which* is a stylistic choice best left to the writer.

EXERCISE 2

1. Though storm experts generally understand the preconditions of severe storms, they are unsure of specific details—an uncertainty

AVOID The taller *man,* who ran away quickly, *he* recognized me. [An unnecessary pronoun repeats the subject.]

REVISED The taller man, who ran away quickly, recognized me.

2 Using relative pronouns in essential and nonessential clauses

ESSENTIAL People who are constantly angry become stressed.

NONESSENTIAL Jim, who is constantly angry, has become stressed.

Use either *that* or *which* depending on whether a clause begun by one of these words is essential or nonessential to the meaning of the noun being modified. Use *that* or *which* (with *no* commas around the dependent clause) to denote an **essential** (or restrictive) **modifier**—a word, phrase, or clause that provides information crucial for identifying a noun.

> As a young man, Gabriel García Márquez advocated many left-wing proposals for reform *that* were not in the end accepted.
>
> As a young man, Márquez advocated many left-wing proposals for reform *which* were not in the end accepted.

As the noun being modified becomes more specific (when it becomes a proper noun, for instance, that identifies a *particular* person, place, or thing), then a modifying clause is no longer essential since the core information of the noun is already established. Use *which* (*with* commas around the dependent clause) to denote a **nonessential** (or nonrestrictive) **modifier.**

> Norman, Oklahoma, *which* has been dubbed the "Storm-chasing capital of the U.S.," is the home of the National Severe Storm Laboratory. [Since the location is specifically identified, any modifying information is nonessential.]

Use *who* to denote either an essential or a nonessential modifier.

ESSENTIAL As recently as the 1970s, meteorologists *who* conducted storm chases were viewed as irresponsible by many of their colleagues. [Since there are many meteorologists and none is named, the information in the modifying clause is essential.]

NONESSENTIAL Eric Rasmussen, who is a meteorologist on staff at the Laboratory, makes the decision whether or not to send his "storm-chasing troopers" on a mission to study, measure, and photograph emergent twisters. [Since a *particular* meteorologist is named, the modifying clause is nonessential.]

See 25d for a full discussion of essential and nonessential modifiers with commas.

EXERCISE 2

Revise the following sentences so that pronouns refer clearly to their antecedents. Place a check beside the sentences that need no revision.

Example: "Tornado Alley" gets its name from what is essentially an atmospheric slugfest that occurs seasonally over the midwest. This is due to the collision of a cold current of air from the Rockies with warm, moist air drifting north from the Gulf of Mexico.

"Tornado Alley" gets its name from what is essentially an atmospheric slugfest that occurs seasonally over the midwest. *This seasonal fight* is due to the collision of a cold current of air from the Rockies with warm, moist air drifting north from the Gulf of Mexico.

1. Though storm experts generally understand the preconditions of severe storms, they are unsure of specific details—which is a problem for the millions who reside in Tornado Alley.
2. These have killed about 18,000 people over the course of the past 200 years.
3. It can contain winds of 200 miles per hour, or even higher.
4. The updraft of a tornado generally narrows, causing it to spin even faster. This can cause severe damage during the peak of the storm.
5. Vorticity is a quality of the air itself which can interact with the updraft of a thunderstorm; it can spawn a tornado.

EXERCISE 3

The pronouns *this, that, these, which,* and *it* are often used ambiguously, especially when they refer to ideas, situations, or circumstances not previously identified or clearly explained. In the following sequence of sentences, avoid vagueness by rewriting sentences to provide clear references. Use information from adjoining sentences to provide references.

Example: Archaeology offers a unique approach to studying long-term change in human societies. This has characterized the study of humankind in North America.

Archaeology offers a unique approach to studying long-term change in human societies. *This approach* has characterized the study of humankind in North America.

1. Unfortunately, archaeologists have only recently undertaken it in the context of the European Contact Period.
2. In the past they somewhat rigidly saw it as the ending point of prehistory, when Native Americans came into the orbit of Western civilization.
3. This was apparent especially because archaeologists tended to be preoccupied with the classification of discrete periods in the past, rather than with the processes of cultural change.
4. These were given names such as Paleo-Indian, Archaic, Woodland, and so on.
5. In short, these narrowly constrained the interests of archaeologists.
6. Now they are taking a closer look at the phenomenon of European Contact as a part of long-term developments in that society.

that poses problems for millions who live in Tornado Alley.

2. These storms have killed about 18,000 people over the course of the past 200 years.
3. These storms can contain winds of 200 miles per hour, or even higher.
4. The updraft generally narrows, causing the tornado to spin even faster. This narrowing updraft can cause severe damage during the peak of the storm.
5. Vorticity is a quality of the air itself. When interacting with the updraft of a thunderstorm, vorticity can spawn a tornado.

EXERCISE 3

1. Unfortunately, archaeologists have only recently undertaken this approach [*or* such studies] in the context of the European Contact Period.
2. In the past archaeologists somewhat rigidly saw the European Contact Period as the ending point of prehistory, when Native Americans came into the orbit of Western civilization.
3. This rigidity was apparent especially because archaeologists tended to be preoccupied with the classification of discrete periods in the past, rather than with the process of cultural change.
4. These periods were given names such as Paleo-Indian, Archaic, Woodland, and so on.
5. In short, these categories narrowly constrained the interests of archaeologists.
6. Now archaeologists are taking a closer look at the phenomenon of European Contact as a part of long-term developments in that society.

ADDITIONAL EXERCISE C

Look through your graded papers to find instructors' comments regarding unclear pronoun reference. Reread the papers, identifying the errors as you read by using the strategies outlined in this chapter. Then revise the errors. (If you don't have any graded papers handy, look through any body of writing you've done recently.)

CHAPTER 15

Misplaced and Dangling Modifiers

KEY FEATURES

As in previous chapters, the approach of this chapter is positive, with each section covering one strategy for assuring proper placement of modifiers. Limiting modifiers, squinting modifiers, lengthy modifiers between subject and verb, split infinitives, and the like are explained in clear, simple terms with extensive examples. In covering dangling modifiers, the chapter pays special attention to the role of passive voice in such constructions. Exercises provide extensive practice in identifying and correcting problems.

LOOKING BACK

References to Chapter 7 (Constructing Sentences) appear throughout this chapter. If Chapter 7 has not been covered yet, or if some time has passed since it was covered, you may want to spend a little time on that material now.

A modifier can be a single word: a *sporty* car; a phrase: Joanne drove *a car with racing stripes*; or a dependent clause: *After she gained confidence driving a sporty car,* Joanne took up racing. In order to function most effectively, a modifier should be placed directly next to the word it modifies. If this placement disrupts meaning, then the modifier should be placed *as close as possible* to the word it modifies. These two principles inform the discussion that follows.

MISPLACED MODIFIERS

15a Position modifiers so that they refer clearly to the words they should modify.

CONFUSING	A truck rumbled down the street, gray with dirt.
CLEAR	A dirty, gray truck rumbled down the street. A truck rumbled down the gray, dirty street.

Readers expect a modifier to be linked clearly with the word the writer intended it to modify. When this link is broken, readers become confused or frustrated.

CONFUSING This chair was designed for weekend athletes with extra padding.

REVISED This chair with extra padding was designed for weekend athletes.

Here is a more complicated example of a sentence made confusing by a misplaced modifier.

CONFUSING The behavior of a chemical compound in the laboratory that is put together is similar to the behavior of an identical compound obtained from plants and animals growing in nature.

The example frustrates readers because key elements in the sentence do not seem to fit: Does *in a laboratory* modify *compound* or *behavior*? Is it the *laboratory* that is *put together*? The writer has misplaced the modifier *in the laboratory.* When the prepositional phrase is repositioned, the sentence becomes clear.

Spotlight on Common Errors—MODIFIERS

Four errors are most commonly associated with modifiers. For full explanations and suggested revisions, follow the cross-references to chapter sections.

MODIFIER ERRORS arise under two conditions: when the word being modified is too far from the modifier (a misplaced modifier); and when the word being modified is implied but does not appear in the sentence (a dangling modifier). Both errors will confuse readers.

- **Position a modifier near the word it modifies (see 15a).**

Faulty	Revised
A truck rumbled down the street, gray with dirt. [What is gray and dirty?]	A **dirty, gray** truck rumbled down the street. A truck rumbled down the **gray, dirty** street.

- **Make a modifier refer clearly to one word (see 15c).**

Faulty	Revised
The supervisor who was conducting the interview thoughtfully posed a final question. [Was this a thoughtful interview or thoughtful question?]	The supervisor who was conducting the interview posed a final, **thoughtful question.** The supervisor, who was conducting a **thoughtful interview,** posed a final question.

- **Reposition a modifier that splits sentence elements (see 15d–15g).**

Faulty	Revised
Vigorous exercise—complemented by a varied diet that includes nuts, grains, vegetables, and fruits—is one key to fitness. [The "key to fitness" is unclear.]	Vigorous exercise, **one key to fitness,** should be complemented by a varied diet that includes nuts, grains, vegetables, and fruits.
The agent signed, with her client seated beside her, the contract. [What is "signed" is unclear.]	With her client seated beside her, the agent **signed the contract.**

- **Make introductory phrases refer clearly to a *specific* word in the independent clause (see 15h-1–2).**

Faulty	Revised
After considering his difficulty in the interview, the application was withdrawn. [Who withdrew the application?]	After considering his difficulty in the interview, **the candidate withdrew** his application.

FOR DISCUSSION

Since most students have problems with only certain types of common modifier errors, you might want to initiate a class discussion of errors most relevant to your students. Ask students to identify from the Spotlight on Common Errors examples of modifier errors familiar to them and to characterize their own errors accordingly. Students can then discuss how such errors occur, thereby reinforcing their understanding of the need for clarity in placement of modifiers. (In large classes, this activity might begin with small groups. The groups will identify their errors, and then the class as a whole will discuss the types compiled from each group's report.)

ACROSS THE CURRICULUM

Using Modifiers

Modifiers are fundamental sentence elements, and writers use them in every discipline area. *Placement* is the key to effective use. Single words, phrases, and clauses are placed close to the word modified, either before or after it. Given this link, the modifier can do its job of bringing descriptive, specific detail to a sentence. In the following example, historian Simon Schama uses modifiers of varying length and positionings to create rich detail in his discussion of Henry David Thoreau.* Whatever the discipline, you can always observe modifiers at work in what you read, and you can use them in your writing.

> Returning to the cabin in the woods by Walden Pond, a catch of fish tied to his pole, Henry David Thoreau was seized with an overwhelming urge to eat raw woodchuck. It was not that he was particularly hungry. And he already knew the taste of woodchuck, at least cooked woodchuck, for he had killed and eaten an animal that had been complacently dining off his bean field. It was simply the force of wildness he suddenly felt possessing his body like an ancient rage.

Modifying clause

the force of wildness <u>he suddenly felt possessing his body</u>

Modifying phrases

<u>Returning to the cabin in the woods by Walden Pond, a catch of fish tied to his pole</u>, Henry David Thoreau

he already knew the taste of woodchuck, <u>at least cooked woodchuck</u>,

possessing his body <u>like an ancient rage</u>

Modifying words

<u>overwhelming</u> urge <u>raw</u> woodchuck <u>particularly</u> hungry <u>already</u> knew

<u>complacently</u> dining his <u>bean</u> field <u>suddenly</u> felt an <u>ancient</u> rage

*The passage is excerpted from Simon Schama, *Landscape and Memory* (New York: Knopf, 1995) 571.

Revised The behavior of a chemical compound that is put together *in the laboratory* is similar to the behavior of an identical compound obtained from plants and animals growing in nature.

If a phrase or clause beginning a sentence functions as an adjective modifier, then the first words after the modifier—that is, the first words of the independent clause—should include the noun being modified.

Confusing A small, Green Mountain town, Calvin Coolidge was born in Plymouth, Vermont. [Who or what is a *Green Mountain town?*]

Revised Calvin Coolidge was born in Plymouth, Vermont, a small, Green Mountain town. [*Green Mountain town* is now positioned next to what it modifies: *Plymouth, Vermont.*]

ESL Note In most English sentences, two or more adjectives that accumulate as modifiers before a noun or pronoun are typically given a standard order or sequence. Section 44f-1–2 describes typical patterns for placement of English adjective modifiers.

EXERCISE 1

Reorganize or rewrite the following sentences so that the misplaced modifier is correctly placed. (You may need to add a word or two in some sentences and provide something specific for the modifier to describe.) Place a check mark beside any sentence in which modifiers are used clearly.

Example: Turning to black subculture as an alternative to homogenized mainstream culture, black slang and music became increasingly common among American teenagers after 1950.

Turning to black subculture as an alternative to homogenized mainstream culture, American teenagers after 1950 began using black slang and listening to black music. [The sentence is given a new subject, *American teenagers,* that can be modified by the introductory phrase.]

1. Black rhythm and blues with its typical twelve-bar structure among white teenagers became rock 'n' roll's most common format.
2. Organized by a disc jockey in Cleveland, Ohio, two-thirds of the audience for a stage show featuring black rhythm and blues acts in 1953 were white.
3. Strung down the center of the theater, black and white members of the audience were separated by a rope that was often gone by the end of the performance.
4. Combining elements of black rhythm and blues and white country western music, American teenagers found rock 'n' roll attractive.

15b Position limiting modifiers with care.

The children trusted only him.
Only the children trusted him.

In conversation, **limiting modifiers**—words such as *only, almost, just, nearly, even,* and *simply*—are often shifted within a sentence with little concern for their effect on meaning. When written, however, a limiting modifier is taken literally to restrict the meaning of the word placed directly after it. Observe how meaning changes as the position of a limiting modifier changes.

Nearly 90 percent of the 200 people who served in Presidential cabinets from 1897 to 1973 belonged to the social or business elite.

Ninety percent of the *nearly* 200 people who served in Presidential cabinets from 1897 to 1973 belonged to the social or business elite.

Placement of the limiting modifier *nearly* fundamentally alters the meaning of these sentences. To establish meaning clearly, position limiting modifiers with care.

EXERCISE 1

1. Black rhythm and blues with its typical twelve-bar structure became rock 'n' roll's most common format among white teenagers.
2. Organized in 1953 by a disc jockey in Cleveland, Ohio, a stage show featuring black rhythm and blues acts was seen by an audience that was two-thirds white.
3. Black and white members of the audience were separated by a rope that was strung down the center of the theater and that was often gone by the end of the performance.
4. Because rock 'n' roll combined elements of black rhythm and blues and white country western music, American teenagers found it attractive.

GROUP ACTIVITY

This and subsequent exercises are ideal for group work. Either have students complete the exercises in groups or compare their responses after completing the exercises individually. As students negotiate responses or defend their choices, they'll understand more clearly the appropriate placement of modifiers.

GROUP ACTIVITY

Only is one of those words that can change the meaning of a sentence drastically, simply by being moved around. Ask groups to place the word in as many different positions as they can in a sentence similar to this: Charles kissed Diana on her cheek. After they've exhausted the possibilities, they can discuss the extent to which each placement alters the meaning of the sentence. This activity should reinforce the importance of placing modifiers carefully.

EXERCISE 2

1. Only one study indicated that one-quarter to one-third of patient health records contain errors.
   One study indicated that only one-quarter to one-third of patient health records contain errors.
2. For many years even the Medical Information Bureau was known for being uncooperative with patients who desperately needed access to their records.
   For many years the Medical Information Bureau was known for being uncooperative even with patients who desperately needed access to their records.
3. Massachusetts patients have a right to see any medical document retained even by a hospital supported or licensed by the state.
   Massachusetts patients even have a right to see any medical document retained by a hospital supported or licensed by the state.
4. Through the "patient advocate" of his or her hospital, any patient can obtain almost any personal health information.
   Through the "patient advocate" of his or her hospital, almost any patient can obtain any personal health information.

GROUP ACTIVITY

Squinting modifiers are harder than other misplaced modifiers to catch when revising; the writer already knows the meaning of his or her sentences, and this type of error doesn't stand out the way some others do. To give students practice in recognizing these problems, have groups compose four or five sentences including squinting modifiers, and then pass the sentences on to another group for correction. This activity will give students practice in reading sentences closely for such errors.

EXERCISE 2

Use the limiting modifier in parentheses to rewrite each sentence two ways, giving each version a different meaning.

Example: Acquiring a copy of one's own medical records is very difficult since medical records are the property of physicians and health-care facilities. (usually)

Acquiring a copy of one's own medical records is *usually* very difficult since medical records are the property of physicians and health-care facilities.

Acquiring a copy of one's own medical records is very difficult since medical records are *usually* the property of physicians and health-care facilities.

1. One study indicated that one-quarter to one-third of patient health records contain errors. (only)
2. For many years the Medical Information Bureau was known for being uncooperative with patients who desperately needed access to their records. (even)
3. Massachusetts patients have a right to see any medical document retained by a hospital supported or licensed by the state. (even)
4. Through the "patient advocate" of his or her hospital, any patient can obtain any personal health information. (almost)

15c Reposition modifiers that describe two elements simultaneously.

CONFUSING The supervisor conducting the interview thoughtfully posed a final question.

CLEAR The supervisor conducting the interview posed a final, thoughtful question.

A **squinting modifier** appears to modify two words in the sentence—the word preceding it and the word following it. To convey a clear meaning, the modifier must be repositioned so it can describe only a *single* word.

CONFUSING The official being questioned aggressively shut the door. [What does *aggressively* describe—how the official was being questioned or how the official shut the door?]

REVISED The official, who was being questioned aggressively, shut the door. [A clause is set off to become a nonessential modifier of *official*.]

REVISED The official who was being questioned shut the door aggressively. [*Aggressively* is moved to an unambiguous position and modifies *shut*.]

CRITICAL DECISIONS

Challenge sentences: Question your placement of modifiers
Modifiers provide much of the interest in a sentence; but when misused, they undermine communication by forcing readers to stop and figure out your meaning. In every case, you should know precisely *which* word in a sentence you are modifying. Posing three questions should help you to be clear.

- **What modifiers am I using in this sentence?** To use modifiers effectively and correctly, you should be able to recognize modifiers when you write them. Single words, phrases, and clauses can function as modifiers.

Modifying word (see 7c)

ADJECTIVE The artist made a *deliberate* effort.

ADVERB The artist succeeded *brilliantly.*

Modifying phrase (see 7d)

ADJECTIVE The painting, *displayed on a dark wall,* glowed.

ADVERB Patrons responded *with an unusual mix of excitement and nervousness.*

Modifying clause (see 7e)

ADJECTIVE Many attended the opening, *which had become a much anticipated event.*

ADVERB *After the gallery closed that evening,* the staff celebrated.

- **What word is being modified? (See 15a–c.)**

The artist made a *deliberate* effort. [The noun *effort* is being modified.]

The artist succeeded *brilliantly.* [The verb *succeeded* is being modified.]

Several patrons who returned repeatedly called the young artist "a wonder."

[Confusing: The single-word modifier *repeatedly* seems to modify two words, *returned* and *called.*]

Having made a commitment of time and money, it was gratifying to see a successful show.

[Confusing: The phrase *having made a commitment of time and money* does not modify any specific word.]

- **Does the modifying word, phrase, or clause clearly refer to this word? (See 15a–c, 15h.)**

On returning, several patrons repeatedly *called* the young artist "a wonder."

[The modifier *repeatedly* now clearly modifies the verb *called.*]

Having made a commitment of time and money, *the manager* was gratified to see a successful show.

[The modifying phrase now clearly modifies the noun *manager.*]

ESL CUE

Remind ESL students that single or phrasal participles may be placed before or after the noun they describe, but that adjective clauses are less versatile and must always go directly after the noun and preferably immediately adjacent to the noun. Note the contrast:

"Seeing the problem, the women agreed to . . . " and

"The women, seeing the problem, agreed to . . . "

in contrast to

"The women, who saw the problem, agreed to . . . "

but never

"Who saw the problem, the women agreed . . . "

nor

"The women, standing near us, who saw the problem, agreed . . . "

EXERCISE 3

1. Sometimes going to the movies makes me wish I were an actress.
   Going to the movies makes me sometimes wish I were an actress.
2. The equation that Steven thought he had thoroughly analyzed confused him on the exam.
   The equation that Steven thought he had analyzed confused him thoroughly on the exam.
3. Reprimanding his son, the father angrily pushed the shopping cart down the supermarket aisle.
   Reprimanding his son angrily, the father pushed the shopping cart down the supermarket aisle.
4. Under questioning, the suspect thoroughly believed his constitutional rights were being violated.
   The suspect being questioned believed his constitutional rights were being violated thoroughly.
5. Frequent long walks help me to relax.
   Frequently, taking long walks helps me to relax.

GROUP ACTIVITY

Exercise 3 not only helps students understand the importance of avoiding lengthy modifiers that split subjects and verbs, but it also injects a bit of humor into the class. Provide students with three or four basic sentences, and ask groups to expand each sentence by placing a lengthy modifier between the subject and the verb. On completion of the task, groups can compete for the honor of having come up with the lengthiest, most obstructive modifiers. Possible sentences:

> The *Enterprise* intercepted the Klingon vessel.
>
> The Navajo Tribal Police awarded Jim Chee their highest honor.
>
> The manager pulled Ice T's "Cop Killer" off the shelves.
>
> Nelson Mandela was released from prison.

EXERCISE 3

The following sentences are made awkward by squinting modifiers. Revise each sentence twice so that the modifier describes a different word in each revision.

Example: Sitting in the hot summer sun often accelerates the skin's aging process.

Sitting *often* in the hot summer sun accelerates the skin's aging process. [*Often* modifies *sitting*—the sense being that one must sit in the sun many times to accelerate the skin's aging.]

Often, sitting in the hot summer sun accelerates the skin's aging process. [The sense here is that sitting in the sun even once or a few times can accelerate the aging of the skin.]

1. Going to the movies sometimes makes me wish I were an actress.
2. The equation that Steven thought he had analyzed thoroughly confused him on the exam.
3. The father reprimanding his son angrily pushed the shopping cart down the supermarket aisle.
4. The suspect being questioned thoroughly believed his constitutional rights were being violated.
5. Taking long walks frequently helps me to relax.

15d Reposition a lengthy modifier that splits a subject and its verb.

CONFUSING One key to fitness—which should be complemented by a varied diet that includes nuts, grains, vegetables, and fruit—is exercise.

CLEAR One key to fitness is vigorous exercise; another is a varied diet that includes nuts, grains, vegetables, and fruit.

Meaning in a sentence depends on the link a writer establishes between a subject and its verb. We commonly interrupt or split these elements with adjective phrases and clauses; and provided these modifiers make a distinct modifying unit and do not suspend the link between subject and verb for too long, they need not confuse readers.

> Union labor, *demoralized by downsizing and by union-busting ploys,* has shrunk from representing 35 percent of the workforce to barely 15 percent in 1995.

It is also common to find a one- or two-word adverb between a subject and verb.

> Today's unions, *apparently,* have been unable to improve the lot of the average worker.

Lengthy modifiers, however, disrupt the link between subject and verb and should be repositioned to keep that link clear.

CONFUSING Stagnant blue-collar wages, *which (after adjusting for inflation) have not risen for 20 years, despite the fact that corporate profits have skyrocketed,* is one reason why workers are angry and increasingly pro-union.

REVISED *Despite the fact that corporate profits have skyrocketed,* blue-collar wages have remained stagnant over the past 20 years *(after adjusting for inflation)—which is one reason for increasing anger and pro-union sympathies among workers.* [Modifying elements have been shifted to the beginning and the end of the sentence; the core sentence is no longer interrupted.]

REVISED *Despite the fact that corporate profits have skyrocketed,* blue-collar wages have remained stagnant over the past 20 years (after adjusting for inflation). This lack of progress is one reason for increasing anger and pro-union sympathies among workers. [The final modifying element has been revised and is now a separate sentence.]

Avoid Splitting Paired Sentence Elements with Lengthy Modifiers

Each of the five basic sentence patterns (see 7b) presents paired parts of speech that function together to create meaning. Avoid splitting the following elements with lengthy modifiers that disrupt meaning.

		Predicate		
Pattern 1:	Subject	verb		
	Sarah	*arrived.*		
Pattern 2:	Subject	verb (tr.)	direct object	
	Sarah	*embraced*	*her family.*	
Pattern 3:	Subject	verb (tr.)	indirect object	direct object
	Sarah	*brought*	*them*	*presents.*
Pattern 4:	Subject	verb (tr.)	direct object	object complement
	Sarah	*considered*	*her family*	*a blessed sight.*
Pattern 5:	Subject	verb (linking)	subject complement	
	She	*was*	*relieved.*	

(In each pattern, everything after the Subject is bracketed as *Predicate*.)

EXERCISE 4

Reposition modifiers in rearranged, rephrased, or divided sentences to establish clear links between subjects and verbs. Try rewriting sentences in more than one way.

ESL CUE

For Americans correct adjective order is intuitive; for ESL students it must be learned consciously. Both Marcella Frank's *Modern English, Part I* and Betty Azar's *Understanding and Using English Grammar* have excellent charts detailing the logic behind our adjective order system.

Spanish, Korean, and Vietnamese, as well as a number of other languages, place the adjective after the noun: the house red. This accounts for what may seem peculiar constructions, even in highly fluent students who occasionally "forget" and revert to the deep structure of the mother tongue. The surface error rarely causes confusion except in one of the few cases of English reversible adjectives and nouns: house cat / cat house, ice free / free ice, etc.

Another troubling adjective problem concerns number: many languages make nouns and adjectives agree in number while English adjectives take only the singular or non-numbered form. Thus Spanish speakers writing in English have the fairly common habit of adding a number inflection to adjectives: the reds houses.

TEACHING IDEAS

Because of the importance of modifiers in breathing life into an essay, students would do well to understand their use thoroughly. To that end, ask students to gather three or four of their papers and identify the modifiers. Single-word modifiers can be circled, and phrases and clauses underlined and labeled *p* or *c*. Then ask students to draw an arrow from the modifier to the word modified. This exercise should help students understand why some of their modifiers work so well; it will also alert them to problems involving misplaced, squinting, or dangling modifiers.

TEACHING IDEAS

Not many elements of grammar and usage can be considered fun to study. Misplaced and dangling modifiers, however, are the exception. You might want to loosen things up a bit in class by writing a couple of humorous ex-

(continued)

amples on the board—"After asking Eileen to the prom, the dog chewed up my tuxedo pants," for example. Students can then try to compose a few of their own. The student examples will represent a number of the possible errors covered in the chapter, and some may not even be dangling or misplaced modifiers. Rather than discussing those issues at the moment, however, have students keep a copy of the sentences generated; after completing the chapter they can try to match up the sentences with the types of errors represented here.

EXERCISE 4

1. Hyperinstruments perform the chores of playing a musical instrument with the virtuosity of the most accomplished musician. Such instruments allow the player to control the tempo and volume of the performance.
2. Machover, the child of a musician and computer graphics specialist, had been exposed to both music and computers from his childhood. He eventually abandoned traditional instruments for electronic ones.
3. Machover insists that the average music lover is neglected while an elite corps of musicians receives all the serious attention. Machover sees this as a system that deprives the average player of the joy of performance. He favors democratizing music.

Example: "Hypermusic," a product of both musical instrument and computer, which blends the sounds produced by traditional instruments with simple-to-operate computer interfaces, thus allowing the player, whether musically trained or not, to sound like a virtuoso, is the brainchild of Tod Machover of MIT.

"Hypermusic," a product of both musical instrument and computer, blends the sounds produced by traditional instruments with simple-to-operate computer interfaces. The brainchild of Tod Machover of MIT, this new technology allows the player, whether musically trained or not, to sound like a virtuoso.

1. Hyperinstruments, which perform the chores of playing a musical instrument with the virtuosity of the most accomplished musician, allow the player to control the tempo and volume of the performance.
2. Machover, the child of a musician and a computer graphics specialist, who had thus been exposed to music and computers from childhood, eventually abandoned traditional instruments for electronic ones.
3. Machover, insisting that the average music lover is neglected while an elite corps of musicians receives all the serious attention, a system that deprives the average player of the joy of performance, favors democratizing music.

15e Reposition a modifier that splits a verb and its object or a verb and its complement.

Confusing The agent signed, with her client seated beside her, the contract.

Clear With her client seated beside her, the agent signed the contract.

A lengthy adverb phrase or clause can create an awkward sentence if it splits a verb and its object or a verb and its complement. Reposition these adverbs by placing them at the beginning or the end of a sentence.

Awkward A number of presidents have emphasized *in foreign disputes* nonintervention. [The verb and object are split.]

Revised A number of presidents have emphasized nonintervention *in foreign disputes.*

Awkward Millard Fillmore became, *after serving eight years as a U.S. representative from New York,* the elected vice president in 1848. [The verb and complement are split.]

Revised *After serving eight years as a U.S. representative from New York,* Millard Fillmore was elected vice president in 1848.

Note that one- or two-word adverbial modifiers commonly appear before a direct object or complement.

CLEAR Zachary Taylor became *in 1848* the twelfth President.

However, when a modifier (or a combination of them) places too great a distance between a verb and its object or complement, the modifier should be repositioned.

AWKWARD Millard Fillmore became, *on the death of Taylor in 1850,* the thirteenth President of the United States.

REVISED Millard Fillmore became the thirteenth President of the United States *on the death of Taylor in 1850.*

EXERCISE 5

Reposition modifiers in order to restore clear links between verbs and objects or complements in these sentences.

Example: One of Machover's strangest inventions, the "hypercello," seamlessly blends, by programming the computer to "sense" the cellist's tiniest arm movements, musician and instrument.

One of Machover's strangest inventions, the "hypercello," seamlessly blends musician and instrument by programming the computer to "sense" the cellist's tiniest arm movements.

1. The experience of listening to a hypercello performance is, since one can't tell where the player leaves off and the computer takes over, a strange one.
2. Machover is planning, given his emphasis on making musical performance available to the nonprofessional, an interactive event called *Brain Opera.*
3. Attendees at *Brain Opera* will learn to play, even though they may never have picked up a musical instrument in their lives, hyperinstruments.
4. The audience of *Brain Opera* will perform, after they have learned to play the easier types of hyperinstruments, followed by taking part in sessions involving increasingly complex music games, their very own opera.
5. One wonders what standards critics will use to judge *Brain Opera,* which is eccentric, visionary, and radical, a success.

EXERCISE 5

1. The experience of listening to the hypercello in performance is strange since one can't tell where the player leaves off and the computer takes over.
2. Given his emphasis on making musical performance available to the nonprofessional, Machover is planning an interactive event called *Brain Opera.*
3. Attendees at *Brain Opera* will learn to play hyperinstruments even though they may never have picked up a musical instrument in their lives.
4. The audience of *Brain Opera* will perform their very own opera after they have learned to play the easier types of hyperinstruments and have taken part in sessions involving increasingly complex music games.
5. One wonders what standards of success critics will use to judge *Brain Opera,* which is eccentric, visionary, and radical.

15f Reposition a modifier that splits the parts of an infinitive.

CONFUSING Her wish to boldly and decisively break the record won many supporters.

CLEAR Her wish to break the record, boldly and decisively, won many supporters.

An **infinitive** is the dictionary or **base** form of a verb: *go, walk, see.* In a sentence, the infinitive form is often immediately preceded by the word *to: to go, to walk, to see.* Because the base word of the infinitive is a verb, the words that modify infinitives are adverbs. In conversation, emphasis on a

TEACHING IDEAS

Gone (thank goodness) are the days when splitting an infinitive was the grammatical equivalent of fratricide. However, it's worth calling students' attention to the admonition to (closely) follow a safe course by eliminating the infinitive entirely. Unless they know their audience, they should assume that a split infinitive is unacceptable.

short adverbial modifier sometimes interrupts the two parts of an infinitive: *"Please try to quickly move up."* Such an interruption in long or complex written sentences can be disruptive to the intended meaning.

Move an adverb to a position before or after an infinitive, or rewrite the sentence and eliminate the infinitive.

SPLIT Many managers are unable *to* with difficult employees *establish* a moderate and reasonable tone.

REVISED Many managers are unable *to establish* a moderate and reasonable tone with difficult employees.

SPLIT One of a manager's responsibilities is *to* successfully *manage* conflict.

REVISED One of a manager's responsibilities is *to manage* conflict successfully.

Occasionally, a sentence with a split infinitive will sound more natural than a sentence rewritten to avoid the split. This will be the case when the object of the infinitive is a long phrase or clause and the adverbial modifier is short.

SPLIT Some managers like to *regularly* interview a variety of workers from different departments so that potential problems can be identified and averted.

Avoiding the split may become somewhat awkward.

NO SPLIT Some managers like to interview *regularly* a variety of workers from different departments so that potential problems can be identified and averted.

NO SPLIT Some managers like *regularly* to interview a variety of workers from different departments so that potential problems can be identified and averted.

Some readers do not accept split infinitives, no matter what the circumstances of a sentence. Others feel that the issue is one of style. The safe course for a writer is to avoid the split by eliminating the infinitive or changing the modifier.

MODIFIER CHANGED *On a regular basis,* some managers like to interview a variety of workers from different departments so that potential problems can be identified and averted.

15g Reposition a lengthy modifier that splits a verb phrase.

CONFUSING The search for fairy tale origins has for over two centuries fascinated scholars.

CLEAR The search for fairy tale origins has fascinated scholars for over two centuries.

A *verb phrase* consists of a main verb and its auxiliary or helping verb. Like an infinitive, a verb phrase is a grammatical unit. Unlike infinitives, verb phrases are commonly split with brief modifiers.

In developed countries, the commitment to children as a natural resource *has* long *been linked* to huge investments in education and health care.

The sense of a verb phrase is disrupted when it is split by a lengthy modifying phrase or clause. Repair the split by relocating the modifier.

Confusing Despite severe economic limitations, many third-world countries *have* in efforts to improve the health, well-being, and education of children *invested* large sums.

Revised Despite severe economic limitations, many third-world countries *have invested* large sums in efforts to improve the health, well-being, and education of children.

EXERCISE 6

In the following sentences, reposition modifiers in order to repair split infinitives and restore clear links between auxiliary and main verbs.

Example: In one of Machover's music games, "Sonic Simon Says," players must try to, whatever their initial reservations, imitate simple melody patterns invented by the computer.

In one of Machover's music games, "Sonic Simon Says," players must try to imitate simple melody patterns invented by the computer, whatever their initial reservations.

1. To effectively play a musical instrument in most cases requires years of patient practice, but Machover's hyperinstruments may change all of that.
2. In another one of Machover's music games, "wild orchestration," players can, as music is being performed by the hyperorchestra, change the instrumentation of a given musical piece.
3. Enormous speakers will, as audience members come and go, blast the continuously evolving *Brain Opera* throughout the auditorium.
4. Machover's hyperinstruments make it possible for anyone to, musically creative or not, conduct an orchestra or play like a musical prodigy.
5. There are already some instruments on the market that allow players to, whether they are interested in composing or simply jamming with a favorite artist, live out the fantasy of playing like a pro.

EXERCISE 6

1. To play a musical instrument effectively in most cases requires years of patient practice, but Machover's hyperinstruments may change all that.
2. In another one of Machover's music games, "wild orchestration," players can change the instrumentation of a given musical piece as it is being performed by the hyperorchestra.
3. As audience members come and go, enormous speakers will blast the continuously evolving *Brain Opera* throughout the auditorium.
4. Machover's hyperinstruments make it possible for anyone, musically creative or not, to conduct an orchestra or play like a musical prodigy.
5. There are already some instruments on the market that allow players, whether they are interested in composing or simply jamming with a favorite artist, to live out the fantasy of playing like or with the very best.

DANGLING MODIFIERS

15h Identify and revise dangling modifiers.

Confusing After considering these issues, the decision was postponed.

Clear After considering these issues, the candidate postponed his decision.

A modifier is said to "dangle" when the word it modifies is not clearly visible in the same sentence. Correct the error by rewriting the sentence, making sure to include the word modified.

1 Give introductory clauses or phrases a specific word to modify.

An introductory phrase or clause will modify a specific word in a sentence, most often a subject or verb. First-draft sentences beginning with long introductory phrases or clauses often contain dangling modifiers, perhaps because complex openings lead a writer to assume that the word being modified is obvious. The modified word will *not* be obvious to a reader unless it appears in the sentence that follows the introductory remark. Revision involves asking what the opening clause or phrase modifies and rewriting the sentence to provide an answer.

DANGLING Dominated though they are by a few artists who repeatedly get the best roles, millions of people flock to the cinemas. [Who or what are dominated? If the *millions* are not, the main clause lacks a visible word to be modified.]

REVISED Dominated though they are by a few artists who repeatedly get the best roles, *movies* continue to attract millions of people. [With a rewritten main clause, the opening clause is immediately followed by a noun it can modify.]

DANGLING After appearing in *The Maltese Falcon,* it was clear that Warner Brothers had a box-office star. [Who appeared in the film?]

REVISED After appearing in *The Maltese Falcon,* Humphrey Bogart became Warner Brothers' box-office star.

2 Rewrite passive constructions to provide active subjects.

Often a modifying phrase that begins a sentence will dangle because the independent clause is written in the passive voice (see 9g). Missing from this passive-voice sentence is the original subject, which would have been modified by the introductory phrase or clause. Correct the dangling modifier by rewriting the independent clause in the active voice.

DANGLING With his weary, sardonic style and his cigarettes lipped loosely, the persona of the private detective was etched into the American psyche. [The persona of the private detective was etched *by whom*?]

REVISED WITH ACTIVE VOICE With his weary, sardonic style and his cigarettes lipped loosely, Bogart etched the persona of the private detective into the American psyche.

FOR DISCUSSION

The dangling modifier is one of those errors that students find very hard to understand. The word modified is usually *implied* in the sentence, so the error is sometimes difficult to spot. It's probably worthwhile to spend some time making sure that students understand what the problem is. One way to do this is to reproduce a passage with several dangling modifiers, and have the class as a whole identify and correct the errors. The discussion that ensues should clarify the problem for most students.

REFERENCES

CHAIKA, ELAINE. "Grammars and Teaching." *CE* 39 (1978): 770–83. Dangling modifiers can be explained from a linguistic standpoint.

KOLNN, MARTHA. *Understanding English Grammar.* 2nd ed. New York: Macmillan, 1986. Chapter 2. Dangling participles often result from opening main clauses with *it* or *there.*

PIXTON, WILLIAM H. "The Dangling Gerund: A Working Definition." *CCC* 24 (1973): 193–99. The dangling gerund can be defined separately from other dangling modifiers.

WILLIAMS, JOSEPH. *Style: Ten Lessons in Clarity and Grace.* 2nd ed. Glenview: Scott, 1985. 145–48. Dangling modifiers are one of many problems encountered when students begin working with longer sentences.

EXERCISE 7

Repair the dangling modifiers that follow by restoring the word modified to each sentence. (You will find this word in parentheses.) Place a check in front of any sentence in which modifiers are used correctly.

Example: Having conquered an area stretching from the southern border of Colombia to central Chile, civilian and military rule was maintained for two hundred years before the Spanish discovery of America. (the Incas)

Having conquered an area stretching from the southern border of Colombia to central Chile, *the Incas* maintained civilian and military rule for two hundred years before the Spanish discovery of America.

1. Centering on the city of Cuzco in the Peruvian Andes, the coastal and mountain regions of Ecuador, Peru, and Bolivia were included. (the empire)
2. As the only true empire existing in the New World at the time of Columbus, wealth both in precious metals and in astronomical information had been assembled. (the Inca empire)
3. Knitting together the two disparate areas of Peru, mountain and desert, an economic and social synthesis was achieved. (the Incas)
4. Growing and weaving cotton and planting such domesticated crops as corn, squash, and beans, Peru had been settled dating from before 3000 B.C. (the Incas)

EXERCISE 7

1. Centering on the city of Cuzco in the Peruvian Andes, the empire included the coastal and mountain regions of Ecuador, Peru, and Bolivia.
2. As the only true empire existing in the New World at the time of Columbus, the Inca empire had assembled wealth both in precious metals and in astronomical information.
3. Knitting together the two disparate areas of Peru, mountain and desert, the Incas achieved an economic and social synthesis.
4. Growing and weaving cotton and planting such domesticated crops as corn, squash, and beans, the Incas had settled Peru dating from before 3000 B.C.

ADDITIONAL EXERCISE A

Look through your graded papers to find instructors' comments regarding misplaced or dangling modifiers. Reread the papers, identifying the errors as you read by using the strategies outlined in this chapter. Then revise the errors. (If you don't have any graded papers handy, look through any body of writing you've done recently.)

CHAPTER 16

Shifts and Mixed Constructions

KEY FEATURES

This final chapter in Part IV maintains the focus on the relationship between writer and audience. Shifts and mixed constructions are treated as flaws in *consistency*, flaws that make it more difficult for the reader to follow the writer's line of reasoning. With frequent cross-references to other relevant chapters, this chapter takes students step by step through the various obstacles to consistency in sentence structure. The emphasis, as in previous chapters, is primarily on how to construct and revise appropriate sentences rather than on how to avoid breaking rules. All of the significant issues are covered, including consistency in person, tense, tone, comparison, and the like. The arrangement moves students within each major division from subject to predicate to entire sentence. The approach is straightforward and practical, acknowledging throughout the specific demands of formal written discourse. Examples and exercises are plentiful, providing students ample practice in revising problem structures.

Consistency is an essential quality of language, allowing us to learn and master vocabulary and sentence structure. When we open a book, we expect to read words from left to right; different, or suddenly shifting, positioning of sentences on the page would disorient us. Just so, we expect that within sentences writers will adhere to certain patterns or conventions. When these patterns are violated, clear communication suffers.

SHIFTS

Aside from the content it communicates, a sentence expresses other important information: whether a singular or plural subject is speaking or being spoken to; whether action takes place in the present, future, or past; whether a subject is acting or being acted on; whether the occasion for writing is formal or informal; and whether a subject is speaking directly or indirectly. Once a writer makes a decision about these matters, that decision should be followed conscientiously within any one sentence. To do otherwise will confuse readers.

16a Revise shifts in person and number.

The term **person** identifies whether the speaker of a sentence is the person speaking (the first person), the person spoken to (the second person), or the person spoken about (the third person). **Number** denotes whether a person or thing is singular or plural (see 7a-2 and 7a-7).

Pronoun Forms (Subjective Case)

	Singular	*Plural*
First Person	I	we
Second Person	you	you
Third Person	he, she, it, one, a person	they, people

1 Revise shifts in person by keeping all references to a subject consistent.

A shift from one person form to another obscures a subject's identity, changing the reference by which the subject is known. Shifts in person often occur when a writer switches from the second person (you) to the first person (I, we) or to the third person (he, she, it). You can avoid this difficulty by recognizing the first-, second-, or third-person orientation of your sentences and by maintaining consistency.

INCONSISTENT A person who is a nonsmoker can develop lung troubles when you live with smokers.

THIRD PERSON A person who is a nonsmoker can develop lung troubles when he or she lives with smokers.

SECOND PERSON If you are a nonsmoker, you can develop lung troubles if you live with smokers.

2 Revise shifts in number by maintaining consistent singular or plural forms.

Shifts in number can occur when a writer uses pronouns (see 10b and 14a). Pronouns should agree in number with the nouns they replace. You can avoid shifting number and confusing readers by maintaining a clear plural or singular sense throughout a sentence.

INCONSISTENT At the turn of the century, it was common for a man to come to the United States alone and work to raise money so that family members could later join them.

REVISED At the turn of the century, it was common for a man to come to the United States alone and work to raise money so that family members could later join him.

Any significant words related to a subject or object should match its number.

INCONSISTENT The seven candidates for the judgeship have a liberal record.

REVISED The seven candidates for the judgeship have liberal records.

When, in an effort to avoid sexist language, you change the number of a subject from singular to plural, be sure to change the number of subsequent pronouns that refer to the subject (see 10c).

SEXIST REFERENCE Any candidate should file his papers by noon on December 1.

REVISED BUT INCONSISTENT Any candidate should file their papers by noon on December 1.

REVISED Any candidates should file their papers by noon on December 1.

LOOKING BACK

This would be an opportune time to review the material on pronoun–antecedent agreement, especially with regard to number. If you haven't covered Chapter 10 (Agreement) yet, you may want to refer students to 10a on number agreement. Reviewing the cross-referenced material will reinforce students' understanding of the importance of consistency in number.

EXERCISE 1

1. A typical monastic community would usually confine its dramatic activities to Christmas, Easter, and perhaps one or two saints' days.
2. Although we can locate a number of saints' plays in the early drama of Western Europe, we can't find them all collected in one place.
3. Until the nineteenth century, comedy was inappropriate to serious religious dramas; audiences saw it as almost blasphemous.
4. The villainous characters in medieval drama are usually comic but not lovable; they are insensitive, even cruel.

LOOKING BACK

If you haven't covered Chapter 9 (Verbs) in class, this would be a good time to refer students to the relevant sections, especially 9f on sequencing tenses. Even if they have studied the chapter, some students may need to refresh their memories.

EXERCISE 1

Correct shifts in person and number in the following sentences.

Example: During the ninth and tenth centuries, some members in the Catholic Church's hierarchy suggested that by using elements of stage drama, we could enhance the appeal of public worship.

During the ninth and tenth centuries, some members in the Catholic Church's hierarchy suggested that by using elements of stage drama, *the Church* could enhance the appeal of public worship.

1. A typical monastic community would usually confine their dramatic activities to Christmas, Easter, and perhaps one or two saints' days.
2. Although we can locate a number of saints' plays in the early drama of Western Europe, you can't find them all collected in one place.
3. Until the nineteenth century, comedy was inappropriate to serious religious dramas; they saw it as almost blasphemous.
4. The villainous characters in medieval drama are usually comic but not lovable; he is insensitive, even cruel.

16b Revise shifts in tense, mood, and voice.

Tense, mood, and *voice* denote important characteristics of main sentence verbs: when the action of the verb occurs, what a writer's attitude toward that action is, and whether the *doer* or *receiver* of the action is emphasized. When these characteristics are treated inconsistently, readers can be confused.

1 Revise shifts in tense by observing the appropriate sequence of verb tenses.

A verb's **tense** shows when an action has occurred or when a subject exists in a certain state of being (see 9e and 9f). The tenses are marked by verb endings and auxiliary verbs.

He walk*ed* home.	He *was* walk*ing* home.
He walk*s* home.	He *is* walk*ing* home.
He *will* walk home.	He *will be* walk*ing* home.

Tenses are often changed within sentences in regular and consistent patterns. Shifts in tense that disrupt these patterns strike readers as illogical, especially when the shifts alter the logic or time sequencing within or between sentences.

INCONSISTENT The road climbed from the Montezuma Castle National Monument, and the vegetation changes from desert scrub to scrub pines and finally to thick forests of Ponderosa Pine.

CONSISTENT The road climbed from the Montezuma Castle National Monument, and the vegetation *changed* from desert scrub to scrub pines and finally to thick forests of Ponderosa Pine. [The past tense is used consistently.]

The "historical present tense" is often used in academic writing to refer to material in books or articles or to action in a film (see 9e-1).

INCONSISTENT In her article, Karen Wright referred to Marshall McLuhan's global village and asks rhetorically, "Who today would quarrel with McLuhan's prophecy?" [The reference to Wright's work should either be past or "historically" present, but not both.]

CONSISTENT In her article, Karen Wright refers to Marshall McLuhan's global village and asks rhetorically, "Who today would quarrel with McLuhan's prophecy?"

Occasionally, a shift of tense in one sentence will be needed to establish a proper sequence of events.

ACCEPTABLE After he *had read* of experiments in electricity, Nathaniel Hawthorne *observed* that the world *was becoming* "a great nerve." [The tenses change from past perfect to past to past progressive. See Chapter 9 for a full discussion of tenses.]

2 Revise for shifts in mood.

A verb's **mood** indicates whether a writer judges a statement to be a fact, a command, or an occurrence contrary to fact (see 9h). Sentences in the **indicative mood,** by far the most common, are presented as fact. In the **imperative mood,** writers express commands—addressing them usually to an implicitly understood "you." In the **subjunctive mood,** writers express doubt or a condition contrary to fact (see 9h-1–4). When mood shifts in a sentence, readers cannot be sure of a writer's intended judgment about the information presented. You can avoid confusion by choosing a mood (most often the indicative) and using it consistently.

INCONSISTENT If the writing process were easy, students will not need to take classes in composition. [The sentence shifts from the "doubtful" subjunctive to the "factual" indicative, leaving readers unsure about what is intended.]

CONSISTENT If the writing process were easy, students would not need to take classes in composition. [Consistent use of the subjunctive makes the writer's judgment clear.]

3 Revise for shifts in voice.

A **transitive verb**—one that transfers action from a subject to an object—can be expressed in the active or passive voice. The natural state of a

GROUP ACTIVITY

Many students, even otherwise sophisticated writers, have difficulty with the historical present. If students are writing about literature in this or another class, the following exercise may help them grasp the concept of the historical present. Ask students to bring in one or two literary analyses in order to take part in this activity. When you arrange students in groups, try to include in each group one student who uses the historical present appropriately. Then have each group work together on one student's writing at a time, checking for consistent use of the historical present. As the groups attempt to determine when this tense is appropriate, they will become more comfortable with one of the conventions of academic writing.

verb is the active voice. In the sentence *Mary kicked the ball,* the verb (*kicked*) transfers action from the subject (*Mary*) to the direct object (*the ball*). An **active-voice sentence** emphasizes the *doer* of an action. A rearrangement of words yields a **passive-voice sentence,** which emphasizes the *receiver* of an action: *The ball was kicked by Mary.*

Both the active and passive voices have their uses (see 9g-1–2). However, if writers shift from one voice to the other in a single sentence, both emphasizing and deemphasizing a subject (or *doer* of an action), then readers will be confused. Avoid the difficulty by choosing an active *or* a passive voice in any one sentence.

INCONSISTENT Columbus arrived in the New World and it was believed he had found the coast of Asia. [The shift from active voice to passive leaves doubt about who believed this.]

CONSISTENT Columbus arrived in the New World and believed he had found the coast of Asia.

EXERCISE 2

1. Business has always been attracted by the language of football, for example, and it often invokes terms such as "team player," "game plan," and "optioned out."
2. The connection is far from accidental in that both areas celebrate aggression.
3. If there were any doubt left about this close association, just look at the extravagant sums that companies pay in order to rent private viewing suites at sports complexes.
4. Politicians routinely use sports talk to curry favor with sports-minded voters.
5. By using sports analogies, politicians and businesspeople often transform complex ethical issues into simple matters of strategy.

ADDITIONAL EXERCISE A

ACROSS THE CURRICULUM Photocopy a brief passage from one of your textbooks, and pay close attention to the sequencing of tenses, consistency of mood, and use of voice. How does the writer's use of verbs help the reader understand the passage? Are there any apparent inconsistencies (in voice, for example)? If so, can you explain why the writer may have chosen to shift voice?

EXERCISE 2

Correct the shifts in tense, voice, and mood in the following sentences.

Example: Sports metaphors are popular in modern speech; they appeared most often in the language of advertising, business, and politics.

Sports metaphors are popular in modern speech; they *appear* most often in the language of advertising, business, and politics.

1. Business has always been attracted by the language of football, for example, and it often will have invoked terms such as "team player," "game plan," and "optioned out."
2. The connection is far from accidental in that both areas celebrated aggression.
3. If there were any doubt left about the connection between sports and business, recent surveys show that companies pay extravagant sums in order to rent private viewing suites at sports complexes.
4. Politicians will routinely use sports talk, and they use these figures of speech to curry favor with sports-minded voters.
5. Politicians and businesspeople use sports analogies, and complex ethical issues are often transformed into simple matters of strategy.

16c Revise for shifts in tone.

Tone refers to the writer's attitude toward the subject or the audience and is signaled by the qualities that make writing formal or informal, learned or breezy, measured or hysterical. Without doubt, tone is a difficult element to revise since so much determines it: choice and quality of description, verb selection, sentence structure, and sentence mood and voice. Tone changes depending on a writer's audience: you will adopt one tone in a letter to a friend and an altogether different tone when writing a paper for your art history professor. The level of diction used in a writer's choice of words is a major factor affecting tone. See 3a-4 and the box in 21e for more on matching the tone of a paper to your occasion for writing.

In papers that you prepare for your courses, your tone should be characterized by writing that is precise, logical, and formal, though not stuffy nor filled with jargon (see 21e). Abrupt shifts from any established basic tone in a paper will be disconcerting to readers.

DISCONCERTING In his famous painting *Persistence of Memory,* Salvador Dalí creates his most haunting allegory of empty space in which time is deader than a doornail. [The final slang expression creates an informal tone inconsistent with a formal analysis.]

CONSISTENT In his famous painting *Persistence of Memory,* Salvador Dalí creates his most haunting allegory of empty space in which time is at an end. [A more formal expression is consistent with the analysis.]

EXERCISE 3

Correct any shifts in tone in the following sentences so that the sentences are consistent.

Example: Can you name a person who is always in a hurry, is extremely competitive, and blows his stack frequently?

Can you name a person who is always in a hurry, is extremely competitive, and is often angry?

1. In contrast, can you think of someone who is so low-key that he's a couch potato, not very competitive, and easygoing in relations with others?
2. You now have in mind two *homo sapiens* who could be described as showing Type A and Type B behavior patterns.
3. Type A individuals get frazzled by stress more easily and tend to suffer more coronary problems than Type Bs.
4. Type Bs have the patience of the blessed saints and perform well under high levels of stress and on tasks involving complex judgments and accuracy.
5. Who would make the better executive, the better spouse, the better party animal?

16d Maintain consistent use of direct or indirect discourse.

Direct discourse reproduces exactly, with quotation marks, spoken or written language. **Indirect discourse** approximately reproduces the language of others, capturing its sense, though not its precise expression (see 28a-1).

DIRECT Lawrence asked, "Is that the telephone ringing?"

INDIRECT Lawrence asked whether the telephone was ringing.

GROUP ACTIVITY

Exercise 3 is ideal for group work. Identifying inappropriate words and phrases, as well as negotiating appropriate replacements, will provide students with useful practice in revising for consistent tone.

EXERCISE 3

Suggested responses:

1. Replace "couch potato" with "sedentary."
2. Replace "*homo sapiens*" with "people."
3. Replace "get frazzled" with "become agitated."
4. Replace "the patience of the blessed saints" with "great patience."
5. Replace "party animal" with "better social companion."

ADDITIONAL EXERCISE B

This exercise should help you understand the differences between indirect and direct discourse, making it easier for you to be consistent in your own writing. In the following sentences, change indirect discourse to direct discourse, and vice versa.

1. In the *New York Times,* David Low wrote, "I have never met anybody who wasn't against war."
2. When faced with disclosures about the Watergate scandal, Richard Nixon told his aides, "I want you to stonewall it."
3. Martin Luther King Jr., in his most famous speech, said that he had a dream.
4. Elizabeth Ray told the House Ethics Committee that she couldn't type. She couldn't file. She couldn't even answer the phone.
5. In a speech to her fellow senators, Margaret Chase Smith said that she thought it was high time that they remembered that they had sworn to uphold and defend the Constitution.

Answers:

1. In the *New York Times,* David Low wrote that he had never met anybody who wasn't against war.
2. When faced with disclosures about the Watergate scandal, Richard Nixon told his aides that he wanted them to stonewall it.

(continued)

3. Martin Luther King Jr., in his most famous speech, said, "I have a dream."
4. Elizabeth Ray told the House Ethics Committee, "I can't type. I can't file. I can't even answer the phone."
5. In a speech to her fellow senators, Margaret Chase Smith said, "I think it is high time that we remember that we have sworn to uphold and defend the Constitution."

EXERCISE 4

1. The great physicist Niels Bohr nailed a horseshoe on a wall in his cottage because he understood that it brought luck whether one believed or not.
2. The mystery writer Agatha Christie believed that being married to an archaeologist, a man whose business it was to excavate antiquities, was a stroke of great good luck, because as she got older he showed more interest in her.
3. In a feverish letter from a battlefield in Italy, Napoleon wrote Josephine that he had received her letters and asked if she had any idea of what they were doing to him.

LOOKING BACK

A careful reading (or rereading) of Chapter 7 (Constructing Sentences) can be helpful to students as they work through this material. Since a paper filled with mixed constructions reflects the writer's failure to control specific sentence patterns, a clear understanding of those patterns can assist the writer in revising.

Mixing discourse in one sentence can disorient a reader by raising doubts about what a speaker has actually said. You can avoid the problem by making a conscious choice to refer to another's speech either directly or indirectly.

INCONSISTENT In his inaugural speech, John F. Kennedy exhorted Americans to ask what they could do for their country, not "what your country can do for you." [The direct quotation following the indirect discourse raises unnecessary questions about what Kennedy actually said.]

CONSISTENT In his inaugural speech, John F. Kennedy exhorted Americans to ask what they could do for their country, not what their country could do for them.

CONSISTENT In his inaugural speech, John F. Kennedy exhorted Americans, "Ask not what your country can do for you, ask what you can do for your country."

EXERCISE 4

Correct the shifts in discourse in the following sentences by making direct quotations indirect.

Example: As a boy in his teens, Albert Einstein asked how our view of the world would change if "I rode on a beam of light."

As a boy in his teens, Albert Einstein asked how our view of the world would change if we rode on beams of light.

1. The great physicist Niels Bohr nailed a horseshoe on a wall in his cottage because "I understand it brings you luck whether you believe or not."
2. The mystery writer Agatha Christie believed that being married to an archaeologist, a man whose business it was to excavate antiquities, was a stroke of great good luck, because as she got older "he shows more interest in me."
3. In a feverish letter from a battlefield in Italy, Napoleon wrote Josephine that he had received her letters and that "do you have any idea, darling, what you are doing, writing to me in those terms?"

MIXED CONSTRUCTIONS

A **mixed construction** occurs when a sentence takes a reader in one direction by beginning with a certain grammatical pattern and then concludes as if the sentence had begun differently. The resulting mix of incompatible sentence parts invariably confuses readers.

16e Establish clear, grammatical relations between sentence parts.

Mixed constructions are common in speech. We can compensate for grammatically inconsistent thoughts in speech with gestures or intonation, and listeners usually understand. But readers work at a disadvantage, for they cannot see or hear our attempts to correct jumbled expressions. More so than listeners, readers are likely to be sensitive to and confused by mixed constructions.

MIXED If a stage set is poorly designed is when a set looks and "feels" absolutely complete even without the presence of the actors because a good set design needs the presence of actors to be complete.

This construction is a fragment (see 12a). The construction begins with a dependent clause—an *if* clause that readers expect to see followed by an independent *then* clause, which never appears. Instead, the *if* construction is followed by the verb *is* and by a second dependent clause, beginning with *when*. Revise mixed constructions by rearranging words until you create an independent clause.

REVISED If a stage set is poorly designed, then it will look and "feel" absolutely complete even without the presence of the actors. [An independent clause beginning with *then* now completes the introductory *if* construction.]

REVISED A stage set that looks and "feels" absolutely complete is probably poorly designed because a good design needs actors to be complete. [The mixed construction is avoided by eliminating the *if* construction.]

Proofread carefully to identify and correct mixed constructions, which tend to occur in predictable patterns.

"The fact that"

The expression "the fact that" and words immediately associated with it result in a mixed construction when writers forget that the expression begins a noun clause that functions as a subject or object. Writers see the subject and verb of the clause and mistakenly conclude that they have written a sentence.

MIXED The fact that design elements are as important to a play's success as actors. [Even though *are* is a verb and *design elements* functions as a noun, this string of words is not a sentence. It is a noun clause that could take the place of a noun in another sentence, as below.]

REVISED The fact that design elements are as important to a play's success as actors is often overlooked by beginning students of theater. [The noun clause *The fact that . . . actors* functions as the subject of the sentence.]

REVISED Design elements are as important to a play's success as actors. [Deleting the words *the fact that* converts the dependent noun clause to an independent clause. The main verb is *are.*]

An adverb clause

Adverb clauses begin with subordinating conjunctions—words such as *when, because,* and *although* (see the box in 19a). A mixed construction oc-

REFERENCES

CARKEET, DAVID. "Understanding Syntactic Errors in Remedial Writing." *CE* 38 (1977): 682–86, 695. Mixed constructions occur when students lose track of how they began a sentence, and should be treated accordingly.

D'ELOIA, SARAH. "The Uses—and Limits—of Grammar." Rpt. in *The Writing Teacher's Sourcebook.* Eds. Gary Tate and Edward P. J. Corbett. New York: Oxford UP, 1981. 225–43. Tangled syntax results from inexperienced writers trying to put complex ideas into acceptable prose form.

FREEMAN, DONALD C. "Linguistics and Error Analysis: On Agency." *The Territory of Language.* Ed. Donald A. McQuade. Carbondale: Southern Illinois UP, 1986. 165–73. Applying the concept of "agency" to an analysis of sentence structure can help students correct problems such as mixed constructions.

KRISHNA, VALERIE. "The Syntax of Error." *Journal of Basic Writing* 1 (1975): 43–49. Mixed constructions are a result of weakness in the core sentence.

SHAUGHNESSY, MINA P. *Errors and Expectations: A Guide for the Teacher of Basic Writing.* New York: Oxford UP, 1977. 44–89. A lengthy discussion of underlying causes of and strategies for overcoming mixed constructions.

curs when the final word of an introductory adverb clause also serves as the subject (or a word modifying the subject) of an independent clause.

Mixed When a set is successful design pleases actors and theatergoers alike. [The last word of the adverb clause, *successful,* is also used to modify the subject, *design.*]

Revised When a set is successful, the design pleases actors and theatergoers alike. [The adverb clause ends with *successful;* the independent clause begins with *the.*]

Revised A successfully designed set pleases actors and theatergoers alike.

A prepositional phrase

A prepositional phrase consists of a preposition (*by, of, in,* etc.) and a noun—the object of the preposition (see 7d-1). A noun functioning as the object of a prepositional phrase cannot simultaneously function as the subject of an independent clause.

Mixed By creating a functional set design can help the audience believe the "place" on the stage is real. [The words *creating a functional set design* operate as part of the prepositional phrase beginning with *by* and as the subject of the independent clause.]

Revised Creating a functional set design can help the audience view the stage as a believable other world. [*Creating . . . design* now functions only as the subject of the independent clause. The preposition *by* has been cut.]

Revised By creating a functional set design, a designer can help the audience view the stage as a believable other world. [The prepositional phrase remains, and a new subject, *a designer,* is added.]

16f Establish consistent relations between subjects and predicates.

A second type of mixed construction occurs when the predicate part of a sentence does not logically complete its subject. The error is known as **faulty predication** and most often involves a form of the verb *be,* a linking verb that connects the subject complement in the predicate part of the sentence with the subject. You are familiar with the sentence pattern _A_ is _B_ : *The child is happy* (see 7b, Pattern 5). In this sentence the verb functions as an equals sign. If the subject complement, *B,* is logically inconsistent with the subject, *A,* then the predicate is faulty and the sentence will confuse readers.

Inconsistent The power of an electron microscope is keenly aware of life invisible to the human eye. [Can a microscope's power be keenly aware?]

Revised The resolving power of an electron microscope helps us to be keenly aware of life invisible to the human eye. [Now it is people (*us*) who have been made aware.]

REVISED Aided by the resolving power of the electron microscope, we have grown keenly aware of life invisible to the human eye.

Faulty predication occurs in three other constructions involving the verb *be* and sentence pattern _A_ is _B_ or _A_ = _B_ . If in writing a definition you begin the subject complement (*B*) with the word *when* or *where,* or if in giving a reason you begin the subject complement with *because,* you may create a mixed construction.

FAULTY Electron illumination is when beams of electrons instead of light are used in a microscope. [In this sentence pattern, the subject (*electron illumination*) must be renamed by a noun or described by an adjective.]

FAULTY The reason electron microscopes have become essential to research is because their resolving power is roughly 500,000 times greater than the power of the human eye. [In this sentence pattern, the subject (*reason*) must be renamed by a noun or described by an adjective.]

The sentence pattern of *subject / linking verb / subject complement* requires an adjective or a noun to serve as subject complement. The words *when, where,* and *because* begin adverb clauses and, thus, do not fit grammatically into the pattern. Revise a faulty predicate by changing the adverb clause to a noun clause or by changing the verb and reordering the sentence. Usually a revision requires adding and deleting words.

REVISED Electron microscopes have become essential because their resolving power is roughly 500,000 times greater than the power of the human eye.

Verbs other than *be* can assert actions or states that are not logically consistent with a subject. Wherever you find faulty predication, correct it.

FAULTY The rate of Native American enrollment in institutions of higher learning sees an improvement in the last ten years. [A *rate* cannot see.]

REVISED The rate of Native American enrollment in institutions of higher learning has increased in the last ten years.

REVISED Over the last ten years, educators have seen an increase in the rate of Native American enrollment in institutions of higher learning.

EXERCISE 5

Revise the sentences that follow in two ways, making each consistent in grammar or meaning. Place a check beside any sentence that needs no revision.

Example: By implanting cats with microchip bar codes could resolve Novato, California's problem with strays.

Implanting cats with microchip bar codes could resolve Novato, California's problem with strays.

By implanting cats with microchip bar codes, the town of Novato, California tried to resolve its problem with strays.

EXERCISE 5

Suggested responses:

1. Strays were overrunning the town and creating both a health problem and a nuisance. The fact was that strays were overrunning the town and creating both a health problem and a nuisance.
2. With the development of minute, pellet-sized bar codes, animal control officers had a radical alternative to neutering or destroying strays.

(continued)

The development of minute, pellet-sized bar codes gave animal control officers a radical alternative to neutering or destroying strays.

3. Correct
4. One sign of trouble surfaced when animal rights groups protested the "indignity" of the solution and when comedians asked: "Are we next?"

   The first sign of trouble appeared when animal rights groups protested the "indignity" of the solution. The second sign appeared when comedians asked: "Are we next?"
5. Those who vigilantly protect against invasions of privacy fear advanced, miniaturized technology used for instant identification.

   Advanced, miniature technology used for instant identification scares those who vigilantly protect against invasions of privacy.

GROUP ACTIVITY

Because of the options available in Exercise 5, it presents an ideal opportunity for group work. If students compare their individual responses, they may find that there are more than two ways to revise many of the sentences.

TEACHING IDEAS

Perhaps more than any other issue in this chapter, the incomplete sentence reflects problems with translating from spoken to written discourse. This translation can be confusing to students. Sometimes it's difficult for students to integrate what seem to be mixed messages about writing: on one hand they're admonished to write in their own voices, while on the other they're warned about the dangers of importing spoken constructions into written discourse. This may be a good time to remind students that listeners can rely on any number of cues, from inflection to rhythm, in making sense of what a speaker says. In writing, however, those cues are missing, so consistency in construction becomes all the more important. The *voice* in written discourse can be identical to that in speech; it's the *conventions* that differ.

1. The fact that strays were overrunning the town and creating a health problem and a nuisance.
2. When minute, pellet-sized bar codes became available and created a radical alternative to neutering or destroying strays.
3. With the bar code implants, runaway cats could be identified and quickly returned to pet owners instead of being destroyed.
4. One sign of trouble was when animal rights groups protested the "indignity" of the solution and when comedians asked: "Are people next?"
5. Advanced, miniaturized technology used for instant identification breathes fear into those who vigilantly protect against invasions of privacy.

INCOMPLETE SENTENCES

An **incomplete sentence,** as its name implies, is one that lacks certain important elements. A fragment (see Chapter 12), the most extreme case of an incomplete sentence, has no subject or predicate. In less extreme cases, a sentence may lack a word or two, which you can identify and correct with careful proofreading.

16g Edit elliptical constructions to avoid confusion.

Both in speech and in writing, we omit certain words in order to streamline communication. These "clipped" or shortened sentences are called **elliptical constructions,** and, when used with care, they can be concise and economical. But elliptical constructions may confuse readers if a writer omits words that are vital to sentence structure.

1 Use *that* when necessary to signal sentence relationships.

You can omit *that* and create an elliptical construction if the omission does not confuse readers.

> The problem (that) town planners of Novato, California tried to correct by mandating microchip implants for cats paled by comparison to the bad press they received for mandating a Brave New World for pets.

If the omission of *that* alters the relationship among words in a sentence, then restore *that* to the sentence.

UNCLEAR Thoughtful people honestly fear an implant of miniature ID tags in cats is a precursor to implants in humans. [The wording incorrectly points to *an implant* as the object of *fear.*]

CLEAR Thoughtful people honestly fear *that* an implant of miniature ID tags in cats is a precursor to implants in humans. [The word *that* now indicates that an entire noun clause will serve as the object of *fear.*]

ESL Note *That* clauses can occur in a variety of sentences. Notice that the noun clauses retain their structure even when the specific word *that* is omitted. For special rules in constructions involving *wish that . . .*, see 43b-6.

Indirect quotation or reported speech is a very common special case of tense sequence involving two verbs in a *that* clause (see 43b-4).

2 Provide all the words needed for parallel constructions.

Elliptical constructions are found in sentences where words, phrases, or clauses are joined by the conjunction *and* or are otherwise made parallel. Grammatically, an omission is legitimate when a word or words are repeated *exactly* in all compound parts of the sentence, as in the following examples. Words that could be omitted are placed in parentheses. (See the discussion of parallelism at 18a–b.)

Parallel According to one widely accepted theory, humans possess sensory (memory), short-term (memory), and long-term memory. [A word is omitted.]

Parallel Information moves from short- (term memory) to long-term memory when we think about its meaning or (when we think) about its relationship to other information already in long-term memory. [A clause is omitted.]

An incomplete sentence results when words omitted in one part of an elliptical construction do not match identically the words appearing in another part.

Not parallel Sensory and short-term memory *last* seconds or minutes, while long-term memory years or decades.

Parallel Sensory and short-term memory *last* seconds or minutes, while long-term memory *lasts* years or decades.

The omitted word, *lasts,* is not identical to the word in the first part of the parallel structure, *last.* One verb completes a singular subject and the other a plural subject, as in the following example.

Not parallel One long-term memory *is triggered* by fleeting sight or smell and others by sounds.

Parallel One long-term memory *is triggered* by fleeting sight or smell and others *are triggered* by sounds.

Parallel One long-term memory *may be triggered* by fleeting sight or smell and others by sounds.

3 Use the necessary prepositions with verbs in parallel constructions.

Elliptical constructions also result from the omission of a preposition that functions idiomatically as part of a complete verb phrase: believe *in,*

ADDITIONAL EXERCISE C

ACROSS THE CURRICULUM Photocopy a long passage from one of your textbooks, and underline all of the parallel constructions that you can find. Examine the writer's use of parallelism, paying particular attention to completeness and use of appropriate prepositions. How does the effective use of parallelism help the reader understand the material? How does it contribute stylistically to the passage?

check *in,* handed *in,* hope *in,* hope *for,* looked *up,* tried *on,* turned *on.* When these expressions are doubled by the conjunction *and,* and you wish to omit the second preposition, be sure this preposition is identical to the one remaining in the sentence. (See 18a-2 and 18a-3 on parallel constructions.) In the following example, the doubled preposition is *on*: relied *on* and ultimately thrived *on.*

> In 1914, Henry Ford opened an auto manufacturing plant that relied and ultimately thrived on principles of assembly-line production.

To be omitted from a parallel construction, a preposition must be identical to the one left remaining in the sentence. If the prepositions are not identical, then *both* must appear in the sentence so that the full sense of each idiomatic expression is retained.

Faulty Henry Ford believed and relied *on* the assembly line as a means to revolutionize American industry.

Revised Henry Ford believed *in* and relied *on* the assembly line as a means to revolutionize American industry.

16h Make comparisons consistent, complete, and clear.

Writers have many occasions to devote sentences, paragraphs, and even entire essays to writing comparisons and contrasts. To make comparisons effective, you should compare logically consistent elements and state comparisons completely and clearly. (In Chapter 11 you will find more on comparative forms of adjectives and adverbs.)

1 Keep the elements of a comparison logically related.

The elements you compare in a sentence must in fact be comparable—of the same logical class.

Illogical Modern atomic theory provides for fewer types of atoms than Democritus, the ancient Greek philosopher who conceived the idea of atoms. [Atoms are being compared with Democritus, a person. The comparison must be made logical.]

Logical Modern atomic theory provides for fewer types of atoms than did Democritus, the ancient Greek philosopher who conceived the idea of atoms.

2 Complete all elements of a comparison.

Comparisons must be made fully, so that readers understand which elements in a sentence are being compared.

INCOMPLETE Democritus believed there existed an infinite variety of atoms each of which possessed unique characteristics—so that, for instance, atoms of water were smoother. [Smoother than what?]

COMPLETE Democritus believed there existed an infinite variety of atoms each of which possessed unique characteristics—so that, for instance, atoms of water were smoother than atoms of fire.

INCOMPLETE The ideas of Democritus were based more on speculation. [More on speculation than on what?]

COMPLETE The ideas of Democritus were based more on speculation than on the hard evidence of experimentation.

3 Make sure comparisons are clear and unambiguous.

Comparisons that invite alternate interpretations must be revised so that only one interpretation is possible.

UNCLEAR Scientists today express more respect for Democritus than his contemporaries. [Two interpretations: (1) Democritus's contemporaries had little respect for him; (2) scientists respect the work of Democritus more than they respect the work of his contemporaries.]

CLEAR Scientists today express more respect for Democritus than they do for his contemporaries.

CLEAR Scientists today express more respect for Democritus than his contemporaries did.

EXERCISE 6

Revise the sentences that follow to eliminate problems with mixed constructions. Place a check beside any sentence that needs no revision.

Example: We have a special reverence and fascination *with* fire.

We have a special reverence *for* and fascination *with* fire.

1. Since ancient times, fire has been regarded more as a transforming element than sheer destructive power.
2. Medieval alchemists believed in fire resided magical properties.
3. In legend, Prometheus's gift of fire made humans better, and for this Prometheus was punished.
4. Although humans have used fire for about 400,000 years, not all people have known how to *make* fire.

FOR DISCUSSION

Advertising is notorious for its use of incomplete comparative elements. Ask students to come up with examples of slogans including such incomplete comparisons as "creamier," "lighter," or "more robust." After writing the slogans on the board, ask students to speculate on the reasons advertisers might have for leaving comparisons incomplete. The ensuing discussion should alert students to the purpose of complete comparisons.

EXERCISE 6

1. Since ancient times, fire has been regarded more as a transforming element than as a sheer destructive power.
2. Medieval alchemists believed that in fire resided magical properties.
3. In legend, Prometheus's gift of fire made humans better than animals, and for this Prometheus was punished.
4. Correct

PART V
WRITING EFFECTIVE SENTENCES

CHAPTER 17

Being Clear, Concise, and Direct

KEY FEATURES

This part of the handbook shifts emphasis on revision from grammatical correctness to clarity and style. Students revising at this level will need to exercise good judgment. This chapter fosters the development of judgment by returning to the theme of earlier chapters, namely, that writers must make choices reflecting both the purpose of the paper and the obligation to the reader. In dealing with the major topics of conciseness and use of strong verbs, the chapter provides a number of strategies for revision. Students are reminded, however, that wordiness and weak verbs in early drafts are not indicative of poor writing skills. On the contrary, the chapter reiterates the notion that in the draft stage the writer concentrates on establishing the paper's purpose, organization, and development. Focusing on sentence-level revisions in early drafts tends to slow a writer's momentum. Thus the material covered in this chapter is presented as a stage of revision, not a correction of errors. Exercises reinforce this presentation; the sentences are not *wrong,* they're just *long*—and rather unclear in the bargain.

I have made this letter longer than usual, only because
I have not had time to make it shorter.

—Blaise Pascal

Over three hundred years ago, the French mathematician and philosopher Pascal knew what writers know today: writing concisely is a challenge that takes time. Just like Pascal, you face a decision when rereading your first draft sentences: Should you revise? What will you get in return for your efforts at making sentences briefer? The answer is *clarity* and directness.

Revising sentences for clarity and directness means more than making a correct, complete expression. Revision at this level means making choices about wording that will help your audience to clearly understand your ideas. Your knowledge of an audience's readiness and level of understanding will strongly influence your choices.

17a Revise to eliminate wordiness.

There are many kinds of wordiness, including the use of empty words and phrases (see 21b-3, 21e-4, 21h-2); passive-voice constructions (see 9g); and buzzwords, redundancy, and unnecessary repetition. When you are revising a first draft, search out wordiness and eliminate it. Try to avoid saying things two different ways or with two words when one will do. Eliminating extra words is a reliable way to give your message direct impact; padded wording never makes writing sound more authoritative. If used as filler to meet the length requirement of an assignment, padded writing will backfire by obscuring your message to readers, causing them to be confused and annoyed.

1 Combine sentences that repeat material.

When writing a first-draft paragraph you are apt to string together sentences that repeat material. When revising your work, combine sentences to eliminate wordiness and to sharpen focus.

WORDY The high *cost* of multimedia presentations is due to the combined *cost* of studio shoots and *expensive* video compression. The *costs* of graphic design and programmers are also high. [The word *cost* and its equivalents appear four times.]

COMBINED Studio shoots, video compression, graphic design, and programmers' work all contribute to the high cost of multimedia presentations.

2 Eliminate wordiness from clauses and phrases.

Eliminate wordiness by eliminating relative pronouns and by reducing adjective clauses to phrases or single words.

COMPLEX Josephine Baker, *who was* the first black woman to become an international star, was born poor in St. Louis in 1906. [The clause creates some interruption in this complex sentence.]

CONCISE Josephine Baker, the first black woman to become an international star, was born poor in St. Louis in 1906.

COMPLEX Many were drawn by her vitality, *which was* infectious.

CONCISE Many were drawn by her infectious vitality. [A simple sentence is created.]

OPTION Her vitality was infectious; many were drawn by it. [Simple independent clauses are created.]

Wordiness can also be eliminated by shortening phrases. When possible, reduce a phrase to a one-word modifier (see 7c).

WORDY *Recent revivals of* Baker's French films have included *rereleases of subtitled versions of* "Zou-Zou" and "Princess Tam-Tam."

CONCISE *Recently* Baker's French films "Zou-Zou" and "Princess Tam-Tam" have been *rereleased with subtitles.* [The phrases are reduced to simpler modifiers.]

3 Revise sentences that begin with expletives.

Expletive constructions (*it is, there is, there are, there were*) fill blanks in a sentence when a writer inverts normal word order (see 7a-11, 14d). Expletives are almost always unnecessary, and should be replaced with direct, active verbs, whenever possible.

ESL CUE

English is far more compact than many languages. Consequently, the concept of eliminating wordiness is vital for most non-native speakers, but difficult. They will confuse eliminating unnecessary words with eliminating discussion and detail, mainly because the acceptable writing style of many languages (like Spanish, Portuguese, and Italian) is far more discursive and abstract than that of English. Another difficulty in the move toward compact language is the student's paucity of synonyms to replace longer, explanatory phrases.

FOR DISCUSSION

The Pascal quotation at the beginning of the chapter provides an excellent opportunity to talk about length. The words probably sound strange to students accustomed to spending their time trying to make something long enough to satisfy an assignment. Ask students which takes longer to write, a five-page paper or a two-page paper? Chances are, most students will consider the two-page paper easier. Then ask them to speculate on why they often find themselves spending time lengthening their papers rather than shortening them. The responses to this question will probably have something to do with not having enough to say about a subject. If you can remind students of what they've learned in Part II (Writing as a Process), you can steer the discussion toward the responsibility of the writer to the audience—and to purpose. If a writer finds that she only has enough information to fill two pages of a five-page paper, then rather than hauling out the padding, she ought to be hauling herself to the library. If students can understand that the purpose is not to fill the pages but to make what's in the pages meaningful and clear, then they'll be in an appropriate frame of mind to approach this chapter.

REFERENCES

LANHAM, RICHARD. *Analyzing Prose.* New York: Scribner's, 1983. Extensive advice on revising for style.

WILLIAMS, JOSEPH. *Style: Ten Lessons in Clarity and Grace.* 2nd ed. Glenview: Scott, 1989. Provides guidelines for writers seeking to improve sentence style.

ESL CUE

Some romance-language (Spanish, Italian, Portuguese) speakers will have difficulty with the concept of the expletive since it does not exist in their language. Their tendency will be to leave out the "there" or "it" and to simply begin with a "be" verb as they would in their language: "Is hot." "Is over there." Calling attention to the problem often helps the student self-correct.

WORDY *There were many reasons why* Josephine Baker was more successful in Europe than in America. [The expletive is unnecessary here.]

DIRECT Josephine Baker was more successful in Europe than in America for several reasons.

WORDY *It is* because Europeans in the 1920s were interested in anything African *that* they so readily responded to Baker's outrageous style. [The expletive is indirect; it also sets up an unnecessary *that* clause.]

DIRECT Because Europeans in the 1920s were interested in anything African, they readily responded to Baker's outrageous style.

4 Eliminate buzzwords.

Buzzwords are vague, often abstract expressions that sound as if they mean something but are only "buzzing" or adding noise to your sentence, without contributing anything of substance (see 21c–d). Buzzwords can be nouns: *area, aspect, case, character, element, factor, field, kind, sort, type, thing, nature, scope, situation, quality.* Buzzwords can be adjectives, especially those with broad meanings: *nice, good, interesting, bad, important, fine, weird, significant, central, major.* Buzzwords can be adverbs: *basically, really, quite, very, definitely, actually, completely, literally, absolutely.* Eliminate buzzwords. When appropriate, replace them with more precise expressions.

WORDY *Those types of major* disciplinary problems are *really quite* difficult to solve. [None of these buzzwords has any meaning.]

CONCISE Disciplinary problems are difficult to solve.

WORDY *Basically,* she was *definitely* a *nice* person.

CONCISE She was friendly. [*Kind, thoughtful, sweet, outgoing,* or any other more precise adjective could replace the vague *nice.*]

5 Eliminate redundant writing.

Occasional, intentional repetition can be a powerful technique for achieving emphasis (see 19c-2). Writers may not realize they are repeating themselves, and the result for readers is usually a tedious sentence. When you spot unintended repetition in your own writing, eliminate it.

REDUNDANT James English believes that a lottery, *jackpot* mentality has undermined the will of Americans to succeed through hard work.

REVISED James English believes that a lottery mentality has undermined the will of Americans to succeed through hard work.

REDUNDANT Historically, immigrants *who came to this country* arrived in America expecting to work long hours; even if they did not benefit directly *from their 70-hour weeks,* they believed their children would.

Revised	Historically, immigrants arrived in America expecting to work long hours; even if they did not benefit directly from their efforts, they believed their children would.

Redundant phrases

A **redundant phrase** repeats a message unnecessarily. Redundant phrases include *small in size, few in number, continue to remain, green in color, free gift, extra gratuity, repeat again, combine together, add to each other, final end.* Make your sentences concise by omitting one part of a redundant phrase.

Redundant	Today, the earlier belief in the value of hard work seems like naive *innocence.*
Concise	Today, the earlier belief in the value of hard work seems naive.
Redundant	The quickest route to expendable *extra* income in the 90s is to hit the lottery.
Concise	The quickest route to expendable income in the 90s is to hit the lottery.

6 Eliminate long-winded phrases.

Long-winded phrases such as *at this point in time* do not enhance the meaning or elegance of a sentence. Such expressions are tempting because they come to mind ready-made and seem to add formality, sophistication, and authority to your writing. But do not be fooled. Using such phrases muddies your sentences, making them sound either pretentious or like the

Avoiding Wordy Expressions

Wordy	Direct
at this moment (point) in time	now, today
at the present time	now, today
due to the fact that	because
in order to utilize	to use
in view of the fact that	because
for the purpose of	for
in the event that	if
until such time as	until
is an example of	is
would seem to be	is
the point I am trying to make*	——
in a very real sense*	——
in fact, as a matter of fact*	——

* These expressions are fillers and should be eliminated.

ESL CUE

Some language interference may result from direct translations of common expressions, such as "make groceries" instead of "buy groceries" in Spanish, Italian, and French. Sometimes a specific and a general meaning combine into one word which makes translation a peculiar kind of metaphorical synaesthesia, as in such common Ibo expressions as:

English	Ibo English
I smell it.	I hear the smell of it.
The soup tastes good.	The soup is sweet. (whether sour or salty)

Problems with reflexives may produce similar confusions:

The dress doesn't fit. (English)	The dress cannot enter me. (Ibo)

GROUP ACTIVITY

Playing with wordy passages can be both educational and enjoyable. Ask each group to compose an overly wordy paragraph, using the expressions listed here. (Of course, they can also add any of their own.) Then the paragraphs can be passed to another group, whose task it is to eliminate the excess. In composing the wordy passages students will be parodying what they do if they tend to pad their essays, and in revising they'll practice a skill that will come in handy when they start cutting the excess out of those essays.

work of an inexperienced writer. Eliminate these phrases and strive for simple, clear, direct expression.

WORDY *In the final analysis,* hard work is hard and *in a very real sense* explains why some people would rather bet on the lottery than work a 60-hour week.

REVISED The demands of working hard may explain why some people would rather bet on the lottery than work a 60-hour week.

EXERCISE 1

Revise these sentences to eliminate wordiness by combining repeated material, reducing phrases and adjective clauses, and avoiding expletives.

Example: What type of consumer do you want to advertise to? Specifying the target or consumer that you want to reach with your product is the main step in advertising.

Effective advertising targets specific consumers.

1. When defining the purpose of advertising some experts admit that it is a manipulation of the public while others insist that advertising promotes the general well-being of its audience.
2. Advertising is one of the most eye-catching methods of selling a product. This is because advertising is a medium of information.
3. There are many consumers who are drawn to a product because the advertising campaign has been effectively utilized.
4. There are many qualities which an advertisement must have to lure the public to buy its product. The advertisement must be believable, convincing, informative, and persuasive. With these qualities in the ads, they will be the first ones to sell.
5. Like I mentioned before, it is not only women who are being portrayed sexually. Men are used in many advertisements also.
6. There exists a built-in sexual overtone in almost every commercial and advertisement around.
7. Advertising is one of several communications forces which performs its role when it moves the consumer through successive levels. These levels include unawareness, awareness, comprehension, conviction, and action.

EXERCISE 2

Revise the following sentences to eliminate wordiness.

Example: Early forms of advertisements were messages to inform the consumers of the benefits and the availability of a product.

Originally, advertisements informed consumers of a product's benefits and availability.

1. The producer must communicate with the product's possible customers in a way that is quite personal and quite appealing to the customer.
2. By identifying the product you start to narrow down the range of people you want to buy the product.
3. Advertising is a complex, but not mysterious, business.

EXERCISE 1

Suggested responses:

1. Some experts admit that advertising manipulates the public; others insist that it benefits its audience.
2. Advertising is one of the most eye-catching sales methods because it imparts information.
3. Many consumers are drawn to a product by an effective advertising campaign.
4. To lure the public, the advertisement must be believable, informative, and persuasive.
5. Men as well as women are portrayed sexually.
6. Most commercials have built-in sexual overtones.
7. Advertising moves the consumer from unawareness, through comprehension and conviction, to action.

GROUP ACTIVITY

This and subsequent exercises are ideal for group work. Have students either complete the exercises in groups or compare their responses after completing the exercises individually. Either way, as they negotiate responses or defend their choices, they'll understand more clearly the value of clarity, conciseness, and directness.

EXERCISE 2

1. The producer's communication must be personally appealing to the possible customer.
2. Identifying the product narrows the range of possible customers.
3. Although advertising is complex, it is not mysterious.
4. Today's successful advertiser is opportunistic.

4. To summarize a successful advertiser in today's world in one word, it would have to be opportunistic.
5. From campaign to campaign there are many different objectives and goals ads are trying to accomplish.
6. It used to be that women were mainly portrayed in the kitchen or in other places in the home.
7. We find advertising on television, on the radio, in newspapers and magazines, and in the phone book, just to name a few places.

17b Use strong verbs.

A verb is like an engine. Strong verbs move sentences forward and precisely inform readers about the action a subject is taking or the condition or state in which the subject exists. One way to improve a draft is to circle all your verbs, revising as needed to ensure that each verb makes a crisp, direct statement.

Give preference to verbs in the active voice.

Sentences with verbs in the active voice emphasize the actor of a sentence rather than the object that is acted on (see 9g).

ACTIVE A cancer patient using the Internet can access volumes of cyberspace-stored medical information about the nature and prognosis of his or her disease.

PASSIVE Volumes of cyberspace-stored medical information about the nature and prognosis of his or her disease can be accessed by a cancer patient.

PASSIVE Volumes of cyberspace-stored medical information about the nature and prognosis of one's disease can be accessed. [The actor is not named.]

Unless a writer intends to focus on the object of the action, leaving the actor secondary or unnamed, the active voice is the strongest way to make a direct statement. When the actor needs to be named, a passive-voice sentence is wordier and thus weaker than an active-voice sentence.

PASSIVE This widespread availability of medical information is not viewed favorably in all quarters. [The passive voice obscures the identity of those who hold negative views.]

ACTIVE Some doctors view the widespread availability of medical information unfavorably.

PASSIVE It is feared that the sheer volume combined with the uncensored nature of Internet material will mislead and/or confuse patients. [The passive voice conceals the identity of those who are in doubt.]

5. Advertising campaigns strive for many different goals.
6. In the past women were portrayed in the kitchen or in other home settings.
7. Advertising appears in all print and on all electronic media.

ADDITIONAL EXERCISE A

Photocopy an essay from a popular magazine such as *Time* or *Newsweek* (essays usually appear on the last page of those two magazines). First, circle all of the verbs. How many are passive? Why do you suppose the writer made those verbs passive? Would any have been more effective in the active voice? How many instances can you find of *be* or *have* as main verbs? Are those verbs necessary, or could any of them have been replaced by more active verbs? Next, underline all of the nouns derived from verbs. Could any of these have been recast as verbs? Why do you suppose the writer chose to keep them as nouns? Finally, how do strong verbs contribute to the effect of the passage?

REFERENCE

TUFTE, VIRGINIA. *Grammar as Style.* New York: Holt, 1971. Grammatical choices such as use of passive or active voice are stylistic choices as well.

ACROSS THE CURRICULUM

Using Strong Verbs

Writers in all disciplines have good reason to use strong verbs, which heighten a reader's interest by establishing clear and vigorous relationships between the actors of a sentence and what is acted on. Unless you have good reason to deemphasize this relationship (see 9g-2), choose strong verbs when writing, regardless of discipline area. Observe, for instance, the use of verbs in this introduction to a scientific article on the analysis of DNA fragments from mummified humans.* (We have boldfaced the verbs.)

> Using sensitive techniques of molecular biology, we **have investigated** the possibility of recovering and analyzing genetic materials (deoxyribonucleic acid, DNA) from mummified human tissue and bone from selected archaeological sites in Greenland. Simple extraction procedures of both skin and bone samples **yielded** DNA material in purified form. Using human specific probes, we **demonstrated** that a minor, but distinct, portion of the purified DNA material was of human origin. Further analysis **showed** the remaining portion of the isolated DNA to consist mainly of DNA of fungal origin. The finding of DNA of human origin in mummified skin and bone samples, in particular, **opens up** the possibility for detailed anthropological genetic studies.

In each of the five sentences excerpted here, the authors use a strong verb in the main clause. Cumulatively, these verb choices send a message to the reader: that the authors feel excitement for their work and think it significant. Readers may not register this message directly; still, the verb choices communicate enthusiasm and confidence, a message readers are certain to receive. Whatever the discipline area in which you find yourself writing, prefer strong, active verbs.

*The passage is excerpted from Ingolf Thuesen and Jan Engberg, "Recovery and Analysis of Human Genetic Material from Mummified Tissue and Bone," *Journal of Archaeological Science* 17 (1990): 679. A longer excerpt of this article appears in Chapter 39.

ACTIVE Some physicians fear that the sheer volume combined with the uncensored nature of Internet material will mislead or confuse patients.

2 Use forms of *be* and *have* as main verbs only when no alternatives exist.

The verb *be* is essential in forming certain tenses, as in a progressive tense.

> The ability to retrieve medical information so readily *is fostering* in many patients an urge to question the kind of care they are receiving.

In a sentence of definition, *be* functions as an equal sign.

> The National Cancer Institute, the National Institutes of Health, and the University of Pennsylvania Medical Center *are* three Web sites on the Internet that patients can consult to answer the most common questions.

REFERENCES

DAIKER, DONALD, ANDREW KEREK, and MAX MORENBERG. "Sentence Combining and Syntactic Maturity in Freshman English." CCC 29 (1978): 36–41. A report on the results of a successful experiment in sentence combining.

———. *Sentence Combining: A Rhetorical Perspective.* Carbondale: Southern Illinois UP, 1985. A collection of essays on sentence combining techniques and classroom use.

O'HARE, FRANK. *Sentence-Combining: Improving Student Writing without Formal Grammar In-*

Beyond these uses, *be* is a weak verb. When possible, replace it with a strong, active-voice verb.

WEAK — Many health care professionals *are of the opinion* that health information on the Internet is not the appropriate vehicle by which to teach people about serious health issues.

STRONGER — Many health care professionals *claim* that health information on the Internet is not the appropriate vehicle by which to teach people about serious health issues. [The stronger verb makes a more active sentence.]

The verb *have* functions as an auxiliary in forming the perfect tenses. This verb tends to make a weak and indirect statement when used alone as the main verb of a sentence. Replace forms of *have* with strong, active-voice verbs.

WEAK — The easy accessibility of medical information *has* the effect of getting patients more involved in planning their treatment programs. [The verb produces a vague statement.]

STRONGER — The easy accessibility of medical information *enables* patients to become more involved in planning their treatment programs. [The new verb is more direct and has a specific meaning.]

3 Revise nouns derived from verbs.

A noun can be formed from a verb by adding a suffix: dismiss/dismiss*al*, repent/repent*ance*, devote/devot*ion*, develop/develop*ment*. Often these constructions result in a weak, wordy sentence, since the noun form replaces what was originally an active verb and requires the presence of a second verb. When possible, restore the original verb form of a noun derived from a verb.

WORDY — Many patients *made the discovery* that communication with other patients via the Internet *was helpful* in providing emotional support to everyone. [The writer could replace *discovery* and *helpful* with stronger forms of the verbs.]

DIRECT — Many patients *discovered* that communicating with other patients via the Internet *helped* everyone emotionally. [The verbs are more direct and so, too, is the sentence.]

WORDY — The Internet is capable of acting as a tool for the dissemination of health information.

DIRECT — The Internet can disseminate health information.

EXERCISE 3

Revise these sentences for clarity and directness by changing passive verbs to active verbs, replacing weak verbs with strong verbs, and converting nouns made from verbs back into verbs.

Example: Both positive and negative reactions to a product should be expected.

struction. Urbana: NCTE, 1973. Through sentence combining, students can develop mature style even without grammar instruction.

STRONG, WILLIAM. "Creative Approaches to Sentence Combining." Urbana: ERIC Clearinghouse on Reading and Communication Skills, 1986. ERIC ED 274 985. A discussion of the history of sentence combining, with suggestions for classroom use.

EXERCISE 3

Suggested responses:

1. People understand that advertising is communication between the buyer and the seller.

(continued)

2. Advertising aims to expose a certain product to a targeted audience.
3. Without catalogue viewership, consumers forget the product because they can't view it again.
4. Thomas R. Forrest's "Such a Handsome Face: Advertising Male Cosmetics" discusses effective marketing.
5. Today a man's appearance contributes to his success.
6. Several aspects of advertising are essential to successfully marketing a product.
7. Advertisers should ask five questions before implementing a successful advertising campaign.
8. Associating a product with something desirable increases its visibility.

EXERCISE 4

Suggested revisions:

Although advertisers use many approaches, sexism appears in the majority of ads lately. And the problem appears to be getting worse.

Twenty years after the feminist movement, sexist ads still exploit females. Recently Miller Beer's insert in campus newspapers attempted to lure college kids on spring break with guidelines for picking up bikini-clad women. Outraged college females threatened to boycott the product. However, the protests failed because the National Advertising Review Board hasn't issued guidelines on using women in ads since 1978. In addition, few agencies enforce regulations on sexism in ads—probably because top management is male dominated.

Many advertising executives say that sexism in ads is unavoidable, stating that advertisers must appeal to such huge audiences that they can't keep everyone happy. Apparently sexism in advertising will remain a problem.

ADDITIONAL EXERCISE B

As you revise your drafts of any papers you're working on at present, concentrate on conciseness, clarity, and directness. Try to identify the specific kinds of problems you have in this area so that you can look out for them in future drafts. Compare your revision to the original: How much shorter is the revision? How much clearer?

Consumers should expect both positive and negative reactions to products.

1. Advertising has always been generally understood as a form of communication between the buyer and the seller.
2. The aim of advertising is to give exposure of a certain product to a targeted audience.
3. Without catalogue viewership the product may be forgotten because the consumer will not have the ability to view it again.
4. There is a discussion of effective marketing in Thomas R. Forrest's article which is entitled "Such a Handsome Face: Advertising Male Cosmetics."
5. It has been noticed that in today's society a man's appearance is thought to be an important factor in his success.
6. There are several aspects of advertising that are seen to be essential to the successful marketing of a product.
7. Five questions should be asked before the implementation of a successful advertising campaign.
8. The association of a product with something that is desirable increases its visibility.

EXERCISE 4

Revise the following first draft of a student paper. Use all the techniques described in this and related chapters to achieve conciseness, clarity, and directness.

> Advertising can be displayed in many different ways. One major way that advertisers try to sell their products is through the use of sexism. Sexism is portrayed in the majority of ads lately and it appears to be only getting worse.
>
> It is now over twenty years after the feminist movement and sexism is as big of a problem as ever. Usually in the advertising industry it is the female that is used in the ad that portrays sexism: however, male sexism is found also. The latest problem occurred when Miller Beer tried to hook spring-break college bound kids with an ad insert for campus newspapers about annual trips to Florida that are often taken by college students. The ad included sketches of women in bikinis with hints of ways for these college kids to "pick up women." This ad insert drew a lot of attention from college students, mainly females that were outraged over it. There were even threats to boycott the product. However there were no results because the National Advertising Review Board has not issued guidelines on the use of women in ads since 1978. Also, there are very few agencies that have particular rules or regulations on sexism in ads. This could be due to the fact that the top managements are mostly male.
>
> Everyone knows that sexism is used in advertisements all over the place but the question is, are they avoidable? Many advertising executives say no because they feel that advertisers have to address themselves to such a huge chunk of people that they are never going to be able to make everyone happy. This is why sexism and stereotyping in advertising is such a big problem today.

CHAPTER 18

Maintaining Sentence Parallelism

In writing, **parallelism** involves matching a sentence's structure to its content. When two or more ideas are parallel (that is, closely related or comparable), a writer can emphasize similarities as well as differences by creating parallel grammatical forms.

Parallel structures help sentences to cohere by establishing clear relationships among sentence parts. Through their closely matched word elements, parallel structures present ideas in a logical comparison or contrast. Parallelism in writing thus draws on your skills in creating a logical analogy, a comparison, or a parallel argument (see 6d-1). To use parallelism effectively, you must become consciously logical and systematic about how you present parallel ideas.

18a Use parallel words, phrases, and clauses with coordinating conjunctions.

Whenever you use a coordinating conjunction (*and, but, for, or, nor, so, yet*), the words, phrases, or clauses joined form a *pair* or a *series* (a list of three or more related items) and become *compound* elements: compound subjects, objects, verbs, modifiers, and clauses. For sentence parts to be parallel in structure, the compound elements must share an equivalent, but not necessarily identical, grammatical form. If in one part of a parallel structure a verb is modified by a prepositional phrase, then a corresponding verb in the second part of the sentence should also be modified by a prepositional phrase—*but* that phrase need not begin with the same preposition.

Using parallel words

NOT PARALLEL The candidate was a visionary but insisting on realism.

PARALLEL The candidate was visionary *but* realistic.

Words that appear in a pair or a series are related in content and should be parallel in form.

NOT PARALLEL At the center of his "multiple intelligence" theory, psychologist Howard Gardner identifies specific and a variety of types of intelligence, rather than one monolithic "IQ" score.

KEY FEATURES

Like the previous chapter, this chapter emphasizes stylistic revisions that make the reader's job more pleasant and profitable. In the initial analysis, the chapter takes students step by step through a sample structure, showing every point at which the two parts of the structure parallel each other. Illustration of parallelism in words, phrases, and clauses follows, with clear examples and simple strategies for achieving parallel structures at the sentence level. Throughout this section the underlying purpose of most parallelism—comparing or contrasting elements—is implied. When the chapter moves on to parallel sentences and paragraphs, the focus on comparison/contrast becomes more apparent, as parallelism is seen in light of a paragraph's controlling idea. Lists and outlines are also covered, providing students with a comprehensive look at the various uses of parallel structures. As in other chapters, exercises offer extensive practice in revising.

TEACHING IDEAS

Parallelism is a topic in which form and content seem to converge; both the structure and the idea establish a comparison or a contrast. It's worth pointing this out to students, whose view of the relevance of grammatical structures is often obscured by rule-based understanding. Presenting a few additional parallel sentences at the beginning of the chapter can help students see that form really does follow function—in the case of parallelism, at least.

GROUP ACTIVITY

This activity can help students understand the need to recognize both correct and faulty parallel structures. Ask each group to generate five to ten sentences, using a variety of parallel structures. Completed sentences will then be passed on to another group for correction. As students compose the sentences, they will find themselves discussing the nature of parallel structures, and as they correct sentences, they will engage in a discussion of how to recognize problems in parallelism.

Determine the parallel elements.

Gardner identifies Slot 1 and Slot 2 types of intelligence, rather than one monolithic "IQ" score.

Gardner identifies *specific* and Slot 2 types of intelligence, rather than one monolithic "IQ" score.

In this sentence the adjective *specific* completes Slot 1 and the noun *variety* completes Slot 2. In order for the sentence to be parallel, both slots must show the same part of speech. In this case, the words should be adjectives, since both are being used to modify the noun *types.*

Revise so that parallel elements have equivalent grammatical form.

PARALLEL At the center of his "multiple intelligence" theory, psychologist Howard Gardner identifies *specific* and *varied* types of intelligence, rather than one monolithic "IQ" score. [Two adjectives are now comparable in grammatical structure.]

If the elements that should be logically parallel shift their function in a sentence, they may well shift their part of speech. In the following sentence, the parallel words are nouns—acting as a subject.

PARALLEL *Mathematics* and *art* are two of Gardner's seven types of intelligence. [The parallel terms are nouns.]

If these parallel words needed to modify the word *intelligence* in a second sentence, then the nouns would be changed to their adjective form:

PARALLEL *Mathematical* and *artistic* intelligence are two of Gardner's seven types. [The parallel terms are adjectives.]

In parallel constructions, idiomatic terms must be expressed completely (see also 16g-3).

NOT PARALLEL White people were called "Flop Ears" by some Indians who were both aghast and entertained *by* the way white parents grabbed their children by the ears to discipline them.

Determine the parallel elements.

who were both Slot 1 and Slot 2 the way white parents grabbed their children by the ears to discipline them.

The preposition *at* is necessary for completing the first verb phrase, since the idiom is *aghast at,* not *aghast by.*

Revise so that parallel elements have equivalent grammatical form.

PARALLEL White people were called "Flop Ears" by some Indians who were both aghast *at* and entertained *by* the way white parents grabbed their children by the ears to discipline them. [Each parallel item now has its proper idiomatic preposition.]

CRITICAL DECISIONS

Be alert to differences *and* similarities: Match parallel content with parallel phrasing

Words and word groups that refer to comparable content should show comparisons with parallel phrasing. The only indication of *faulty parallelism* may be that a sentence sounds "off" or illogical. Learn to recognize situations that call for parallel structures and to correct sentences with faulty parallelism.

Recognize situations that call for parallel structures.

Any time you use a coordinating conjunction (*and, but, or,* or *nor*), you are combining elements from two or more sentences into a single sentence.

The children are fond of ice cream. The children are fond of salty pretzels.

Combined elements are logically comparable, and they should share a single grammatical form; otherwise, they are not parallel.

PARALLEL The children are fond of ice cream and salty pretzels.

The children are fond of eating ice cream and salty pretzels.

NOT PARALLEL The children are fond of ice cream and eating salty pretzels.

Correct faulty parallelism.

1. *Recognize a sentence that is not parallel.*

NOT PARALLEL Before they had horses, Indians hunted buffalo by chasing them over blind cliffs, up box canyons, or *when they went* into steep-sided sand dunes.

To revise a sentence with faulty parallelism, *determine which elements should be parallel* (that is, logically comparable), and then *revise the sentence so that these elements share an equivalent grammatical form.* Think of parallel elements as word groupings that complete slots in a sentence. The same grammatical form that you use to complete any one slot in a parallel structure must be used to complete all remaining slots.

2. *Determine the parallel elements.*

by chasing them __*Slot 1*__, __*Slot 2*__, and __*Slot 3*__.

by chasing them *over blind cliffs,* __*Slot 2*__, and __*Slot 3*__.

Because Slot 1 is completed with a prepositional phrase (*over blind cliffs*), Slots 2 and 3 should be filled with prepositional phrases. The series *over blind cliffs, up box canyons, or* when they went *into steep-sided sand dunes* lacks parallel structure because the third element in the series introduces a *when* clause, which is not consistent with the grammatical form of Slot 1.

3. *Revise so that parallel elements have equivalent grammatical form.*

PARALLEL Before they had horses, Indians hunted buffalo by chasing them *over blind cliffs, up box canyons,* or *into steep-sided sand dunes.*

GROUP ACTIVITY

There is perhaps no stronger evidence of the staying power of parallel structures than children's fairy tales and nursery rhymes. Children remember the rhymes and lines from the fairy tales not only because of rhyming words but because of the parallel structures used. Offer students one or two examples ("All the king's horses and all the king's men," "I'll huff and I'll puff and I'll blow your house down," "Over the river and through the woods," etc.), and ask groups to come up with several more examples on their own. Then have them rewrite the lines without parallel structure ("All the king's horses and a full complement of the king's men," "I'll huff and by puffing I'll blow your house down," "Over the river and walking down the path in the woods," etc.). It won't take much discussion for students to recognize how powerful the parallel structure can be.

FOR DISCUSSION

Since most students have problems with only a few of these common errors, you might want to initiate a class discussion of errors most relevant to your students. Ask students to identify from the Spotlight on Common Errors examples of usage familiar to them and to make their own list of common errors. Students can then discuss the function of effective parallel structures in good writing, thereby reinforcing their understanding of the relationship between style and content. (In large classes, this activity might begin with small groups. The groups will identify their common errors, and then the class as a whole will discuss the list of errors compiled from each group's report.)

Spotlight on Common Errors—PARALLELISM

These are the errors most commonly associated with parallelism. For full explanations and suggested revisions, follow the cross-references to chapter sections.

FAULTY PARALLELISM occurs when writers compare or contrast sentence parts without using similarly constructed wordings. In the examples that follow, parallel structures are highlighted.

- **Conjunctions suggest comparisons and require parallel structures.**

Conjunctions such as *and* and *but* require parallel structures (see coordinating conjunctions, 18a).

FAULTY	REVISED
The candidate was a visionary but insisting on realism. [The verb forms *was a visionary* and *insisting* are not parallel.]	The candidate was **visionary** but **realistic.** [Similarly worded adjectives are linked by the conjunction *but.*]
The candidate attended meetings, spoke at rallies, and she shook thousands of hands. [The candidate's three activities are not parallel.]	The candidate **attended meetings, spoke at rallies,** and **shook thousands of hands.** [The candidate's three activities are similarly worded.]

Paired conjunctions such as *either/or* and *both/and* require parallel structures (see correlative conjunctions, 18b).

FAULTY	REVISED
Depending on your tolerance for adventure, traveling without a map can either be exciting or you can be frustrated. [The words that describe traveling—*exciting* and *you can be* frustrated—are not parallel.]	Depending on your tolerance for adventure, traveling without a map can either be **exciting** or **frustrating.** [Similarly worded adjectives are joined by the conjunction *either/or.*]
Explorers can be both afraid of the unknown and, when they encounter something new, they want to understand it. [The verb forms *can be afraid* and *want to understand* are not parallel.]	Explorers can be both **afraid of the unknown** and **curious about it.** [Similarly worded adjectives and phrases are joined by the conjunction *both/and.*]

- **Direct comparisons and contrasts require parallel structures (see 18c).**

FAULTY
The staff approved the first request for funding, not the second presenter requesting funds. [The objects *request* and *presenter* are not parallel.]

REVISED
The staff approved **the first request for funding,** not **the second.** [The requests being contrasted share similar wording.]

FAULTY
The old American frontier was frequently lawless, and so too anyone who surfs the Internet must grow accustomed to life without a central, regulating authority. [The compared items are not parallel.]

REVISED
The Internet, no less than **the old American frontier,** is a lawless place that lacks a central, regulating authority. [Compared items, the *Internet* and the *frontier,* are similarly worded; both are now completed with the second part of the sentence: *is a lawless place. . . .*]

- **Lists require parallel structures (see 18e).**

FAULTY
Make sure you pack the following in your kit:
—an alcohol solution that will cleanse wounds
—bandages
—Remove splinters with a tweezers.
—matches
[Items in the list are not parallel.]

REVISED
Make sure you pack the following in your kit:
—**alcohol**
—**bandages**
—**tweezers**
—**matches**
[Items in the list are similarly worded.]

2 Using parallel phrases

Not parallel The judge had an ability to listen to conflicting testimony and deciding on probable guilt.

Parallel The judge had an ability to listen to conflicting testimony *and* to decide on probable guilt.

To echo the idea expressed in a phrase in one part of a sentence, use a phrase with the same grammatical structure in another part.

Not parallel The theater world did not always welcome women on the English stage: in the thirteenth and fourteenth centuries, they were permitted to perform, but in Shakespeare's day they were relegated to the audience; when the theaters reopened in 1660, women became once more a visible presence.

Determine the parallel elements.

they __Slot 1__, __Slot 2__, and __Slot 3__

they *were permitted*, *were relegated*, and __Slot 3__

Slots 1 and 2 are completed with a verb in the past tense and passive voice. Slot 3 is not parallel because the verb appears in the active voice.

Revise so the elements have equivalent grammatical form.

Parallel The theater world did not always welcome women on the English stage: in the thirteenth and fourteenth centuries, they were permitted to perform, but in Shakespeare's day they were relegated to the audience; when the theaters reopened in 1660, women *were* once more *allowed* a visible presence.

You always have the choice to make passive-voice verbs active, in which case the verbs in the sentence still need to be parallel.

Parallel The theater world did not always welcome women on the English stage: in the thirteenth and fourteenth centuries, they *performed* regularly, but in Shakespeare's day they *could not perform;* when the theaters reopened in 1660, women once more *became* a visible presence. [In this revision, all verbs appear in their active-voice form and, thus, are parallel.]

3 Using parallel clauses

Not parallel Before the storm's end but after the worst was over, the captain radioed the Coast Guard.

Parallel Before the storm had ended *but* after the worst was over, the captain radioed the Coast Guard.

A *clause* is a grouping of words that has a complete subject and predicate. Both independent clauses (that is, sentences) and dependent clauses

REFERENCES

Corbett, Edward P. J. *Classical Rhetoric for the Modern Student.* New York: Oxford UP, 1965. 402–08, 429. Emphasizes the significance of parallelism in sentence style.

Graves, Richard L. "Symmetrical Form and the Rhetoric of the Sentence." *Rhetoric and Composition: A Sourcebook for Teachers and Writers.* Ed. Richard L. Graves. Upper Montclair, NJ: Boynton/Cook, 1984. 119–27. Parallelism in writing reflects a human way of looking at the world.

Lindemann, Erika. *A Rhetoric for Writing Teachers.* 2nd ed. New York: Oxford UP, 1987. Chapter 9. Discussion of sentence combining includes treatment of parallelism.

Walker, Robert L. "The Common Writer: A Case for Parallel Structure." CCC 21 (1970): 373–79. Argues that professional writers employ parallelism more than they do free modifiers.

Williams, Joseph M. "The Phenomenology of Error." CCC (1981): 152–68. When dealing with errors in parallelism, instructors must consider the student's stylistic choices.

ADDITIONAL EXERCISE A

Complete the following sentences with your own words, filling in the slots with words, phrases, and clauses parallel to the italicized structures.

1. Colette *drove the children to school,*_____, and _____.
2. Colette drove *the children to school,*_____, and _____.
3. Colette drove the children *to school,*_____, and _____.
4. Colette drove the children to *school,*_____, and _____.
5. *Colette drove the children to school,* _____, and _____.

[Note: While the content of responses will vary, all students should recognize that in each sentence, the italicized structure is the one with which the responses should be parallel.]

can be set in parallel, provided they are parallel in content. At times, brief sentences can be used to form items in a series. When choosing such a structure, make sure each sentence is parallel in form.

NOT PARALLEL (INDEPENDENT CLAUSES) During those historical periods when women did not appear on the stage, boys played female roles; thus, a young actor first uttered Juliet's tender words to Romeo, with a well-trained male performer first revealing Lady Macbeth's evil schemes.

Determine the parallel elements.

During those historical periods when women did not appear on the stage, boys played female roles; thus, Slot 1 and Slot 2 .

During those historical periods when women did not appear on the stage, boys played female roles; thus, *a young actor first uttered Juliet's tender words to Romeo* and Slot 2 .

Slot 1 is completed with a clause that has a subject, a verb in the past tense, an object, and a modifying phrase. The words in Slot 2 of this sentence, *with a well-trained male performer . . .* , are a prepositional phrase. Not being a clause, Slot 2 is not parallel with Slot 1.

Revise so that parallel elements have equivalent grammatical form.

PARALLEL During those historical periods when women did not appear on the stage, boys played female roles; thus, *a young actor first uttered Juliet's tender words to Romeo,* and *a well-trained male performer first revealed Lady Macbeth's evil scheming.* [The parallel elements are independent clauses.]

OPTION During those historical periods when women did not appear on the stage, boys played female roles; thus, young actors *first uttered Juliet's tender words to Romeo* and *first revealed Lady Macbeth's evil schemes.* [The sentence now has a compound, parallel predicate.]

In order to maintain parallel structure in sentences that have a pair or series of dependent relative clauses, you will need to repeat the relative pronouns *who, whom, which,* and *what.*

NOT PARALLEL (DEPENDENT CLAUSES) Archimedes was the celebrated mathematician of antiquity *who* invented the Archimedean screw, *who* explained the theory of the lever, and *he* defended his native Syracuse against the Romans with great mechanical skill.

Determine the parallel elements.

Archimedes was the celebrated mathematician of antiquity Slot 1 , Slot 2, and Slot 3 .

Archimedes was the celebrated mathematician of antiquity *who invented the Archimedean screw,* Slot 2 , and Slot 3 .

Slot 1 is completed with a relative clause beginning with the relative pronoun *who*. Slots 2 and 3 must have the same structure: each slot must be completed with a clause that begins with the word *who* (but see the variation immediately following).

Revise so that parallel elements have equivalent grammatical form.

PARALLEL Archimedes was the celebrated mathematician of antiquity *who* invented the Archimedean screw, *who* explained the theory of the lever, and *who* defended his native Syracuse against the Romans with great mechanical skill.

VARIATION: Brief words that begin a series (for example, a relative pronoun such as *who,* a preposition such as *by* or *in,* and the infinitive *to*) may be written once at the beginning of the first item in the series and then omitted from all remaining items.

PARALLEL Archimedes was the celebrated mathematician of antiquity *who* invented the Archimedean screw, explained the theory of the lever, and defended his native Syracuse against the Romans with great mechanical skill.

A CAUTION: If one of these introductory words appears in more than one part of the series but not in *all* parts, the use of parallelism will be faulty.

ACROSS THE CURRICULUM

Parallelism

Making sentence elements parallel is, perhaps, the single most successful strategy you can adopt for giving your sentences a professional polish. You will find writers in all disciplines using parallel structures to make their presentations concise, rhythmically balanced, and logical—as author Harold Livesay demonstrates in this excerpt from his biography of Andrew Carnegie. In three sentences, Livesay employs three sets of parallel structures.* Whatever the subject area, expect to encounter numerous examples of parallelism in your reading; and attempt, when possible, to employ parallelism in your writing.

> Carnegie's twelve years' experience on the Pennsylvania Railroad shaped his subsequent career. On the railroad he assimilated the managerial skills, grasped the economic principles, and cemented the personal relationships that enabled him to become successively manager, capitalist, and entrepreneur. His most spectacular achievement—building Carnegie Steel into the world's largest steel producer—rested primarily on his successful transfer of the railroads' managerial methods to the manufacturing sector of the economy.

Parallel structure: On the railroad he A, B, and C.

On the railroad he *assimilated* the managerial skills, *grasped* the economic principles, and *cemented* the personal relationships . . .

Parallel structure: that enabled him to become successively A, B, and C.

. . . that enabled him to become successively manager, capitalist, and entrepreneur.

Parallel structure: rested primarily on his successful transfer of A to B.

rested primarily on his successful transfer of the railroads' managerial methods to the manufacturing sector of the economy.

*This passage is excerpted from Harold Livesay, *Andrew Carnegie and the Rise of Big Business* (Boston: Little, Brown, 1975) 29.

Not parallel I want *to* go home, wash up, and *to* eat.

Parallel I want *to* go home, *to* wash up, and *to* eat.
I want *to* go home, wash up, and eat.

18b Use parallelism with correlative conjunctions.

Not parallel Explorers can be both afraid of the unknown and, when they encounter something new, they want to understand it.

Parallel Explorers can be *both* afraid of the unknown *and* curious about it.

Whenever you join parts of a sentence with pairs of words called *correlative conjunctions* (*either/or, neither/nor, both/and, not only/but also*), you must use the same grammatical form in both parts. Once again, think of the conjunction as creating parallel slots in the sentence. Whatever grammatical structure is used to complete the first slot must be used to complete the second.

Not parallel After defeating Custer at Little Bighorn, Crazy Horse managed both to stay ahead of the Army and *escape.*

Determine the parallel elements.

managed both Slot 1 and Slot 2 .

managed both *to stay ahead of the army* and Slot 2 .

Slot 2 must take the same form as Slot 1. Each must be a verb in its infinitive form: *to* ______.

Revise so that parallel elements have equivalent grammatical form.

Parallel After defeating Custer at Little Bighorn, Crazy Horse managed both *to stay* ahead of the Army and *to escape.*

Variation: By slightly modifying the sentence—by moving the word *to* outside of the parallel structure created by the correlative conjunction—you can eliminate the word *to* in both of the sentence's parallel slots.

managed *to* both Slot 1 and Slot 2 .

managed *to* both *stay ahead of the army* and Slot 2 .

Parallel After defeating Custer at Little Bighorn, Crazy Horse managed *to* both *stay ahead of the Army* and *escape.*

18c Use parallelism in sentences with compared and contrasted elements.

Not parallel The staff approved the first request for funding, not the second presenter who requested funds.

TEACHING IDEAS

To help students understand the use of parallel constructions with correlative conjunctions, you may want to engage in the following class exercise: In succession, write on the board the pairs of correlative conjunctions (*either/or, neither/nor, both/and, not only/but also*). Then ask students to volunteer sentences using each of the constructions. After writing several sentences on the board, stop and ask for an evaluation of their effectiveness. Some students will be able to point out errors; others will need to have the errors explained to them. (In larger classes, you may start this activity with groups. Each group will generate sentences according to the selected patterns, and the entire class will evaluate the sentences' effectiveness.)

ADDITIONAL EXERCISE B

ACROSS THE CURRICULUM Photocopy a page or two from one of your textbooks, and underline all parallel words, phrases, and clauses. Rewrite a couple of the sentences, eliminating the parallel structure. Compare the two: How does the use of parallelism contribute to the *meaning* of the passage? How does it affect the *style* of the passage?

EXERCISE 1

Suggested responses:

1. Designating Asian Americans as the "model minority" is problematic not only because the term obscures the diversity of the group but also because it distorts their small representation in top-ranking positions in the United States.
2. Some sociologists say that racism is rooted in a preference for one's "own kind" rather than in social causes.
3. Conflict theorists feel that racism results from competition for scarce resources, unequal distribution of power, and increased racial tension during periods of economic decline.
4. Neither corporate managers nor the workers whom they supervise tend to wield the

PARALLEL The staff approved the first request for funding, *not* the second request.

When words, phrases, or clauses are compared or contrasted in a single sentence, their logical and grammatical structures must be parallel (see 16h). Expressions that set up comparisons and contrasts include *rather than, as opposed to, on the other hand, not, like, unlike,* and *just as/so too.*

NOT PARALLEL The word "mensch," derived from Yiddish, describes an assertive, affectionate man, while a "schnook" (also derived from Yiddish) is forever being spineless and sneaky. [The adjectives *spineless* and *sneaky* are not in parallel with the noun *man;* the verb *is being* is not in parallel with the verb *describes.*]

Determine the parallel elements.

The word "mensch," derived from Yiddish, Slot 1, while a "schnook" (also derived from Yiddish) Slot 2.

The word "mensch," derived from Yiddish, *describes an assertive, affectionate man,* while a "schnook" (also derived from Yiddish) Slot 2.

Slot 1 consists of a present-tense verb and a noun that is modified by two adjectives; Slot 2 begins with a verb in the present progressive tense (*is being*), which is followed by two adjectives. Slot 2 should take the same basic form as Slot 1.

Revise so that parallel elements have equivalent grammatical form.

PARALLEL The word "mensch," derived from Yiddish, *describes an assertive, affectionate man,* while a "schnook" (also derived from Yiddish) *describes someone who is spineless and sneaky.* [The adjectives in Slot 2, *spineless and sneaky,* appear in a relative clause and modify the noun *someone.*]

EXERCISE 1

The following sentences contain coordinating or correlative conjunctions, or elements of comparison and contrast. Revise each to correct the faulty parallel structure.

Example: Native Americans have one of the highest unemployment rates in the nation, the lowest educational attainment of any U.S. minority group, and they fare worst in the area of health.

Native Americans have one of the highest unemployment rates in the nation, the lowest educational attainment of any U.S. minority group, and *the worst record of health care.* [Each slot in the series now begins with an adjective in its superlative form: *highest, lowest, worst.* Each adjective is followed by a noun and each noun by a prepositional phrase.]

1. Designating Asian Americans as the "model minority" is problematic not only because the term obscures the diversity of the group but they are represented in only a small percentage of top-ranking positions in the United States.

2. Some sociologists say that racism is rooted in a preference for one's "own kind" rather than social causes.
3. Conflict theorists feel that racism results from competition for scarce resources and an unequal distribution of power and racial tension increases during periods of economic decline.
4. Corporate managers do not tend to wield the political power of professionals such as lawyers and doctors, nor workers whom they supervise.
5. Either the percentage of the elderly living below the poverty line has decreased or to underestimate the number of elderly living in poverty is prevalent.

political power of professionals such as lawyers and doctors.

5. Either the percentage of the elderly living below the poverty line has decreased or the number of elderly living in poverty has been underestimated.

18d Use parallelism among sentences to enhance paragraph coherence.

Like many other towns on the Great Plains, Nicodemus, Kansas *was founded* in the 1870s. *Unlike any other* that still survives, *it was founded* by black homesteaders.

Because parallel grammatical structures highlight parallel ideas among sentence parts, parallelism is an excellent device for organizing sentence content. But parallelism can also help to relate the parts of an *entire paragraph* by highlighting the logic by which a writer moves from one sentence to the next. Parallel structures bind a paragraph's sentences into a coherent unit.

PARALLEL SENTENCES WITHIN A PARAGRAPH

> A house divided against itself cannot stand. I believe this government cannot endure, permanently half slave and half free. I do not expect the Union to be dissolved. I do not expect the house to fall. But I do expect it will cease to be divided. It will become all one thing, or all the other.
>
> —ABRAHAM LINCOLN, 1858

In this famous passage, Lincoln uses parallel structures to show relationships not only among single words or phrases, but also among whole sentences. Elements of the first sentence (*house, divided*) are repeated near the end of the paragraph. Lincoln repeats the phrase *I do not expect* twice and then produces a parallel contrast with *But I do expect* in a third repetition. The final two sentences repeat *it will* with different verbs. The last sentence sets up a parallel opposition governed by *all.* These parallel repetitions of words, phrases, and structures help to make the paragraph coherent by highlighting relationships among sentences. Such relationships could be mapped in parallel "slot" diagrams similar to those used for sentences. Parallel structures also give the paragraph an emphatic, memorable rhythm.

LOOKING BACK

It might be helpful for students to review Chapter 5 (The Paragraph and the Paper) when they read this section. The use of parallelism can enhance a paragraph's unity, coherence, and development.

ADDITIONAL EXERCISE C

In order to practice building a paragraph around parallel structure, write an imitation of Lincoln's paragraph on the house divided. Begin with one of the following sentences (or choose your own):

A teenage marriage cannot last.
A great concert can revitalize the soul.
A child born in the ghetto will never be free.

18e Use parallel entries when writing lists or outlines.

A list or outline divides a single large subject into equal or coordinate elements. A grocery list is the simplest example: *grocery* is the subject, and all

ADDITIONAL EXERCISE D

As you revise drafts of any papers you're working on at present, look for places where parallel structure would make the paper more effective. A potential revision might be a series of words, or two phrases or clauses, or even a pair of sentences. Occasionally a paragraph can be arranged around parallel structures (as you have seen in this section).

ADDITIONAL EXERCISE E

Using the information in the following paragraph, develop a list of parallel items.

> The Playground Committee has identified three major phases of the program. First, we'll have to raise funds by holding bake sales and doing things like raffling off prizes. Some other communities have had success with selling cookbooks too. Then we have to interview architects to find one who can do what we want in the space we have. He or she will also have to be affordable, and, of course, the plans that the architect comes up with will have to be attractive and imaginative. The last stage will involve mobilizing the townspeople to build the playground. We have to get volunteers to sign up to work. We'll also need people to donate and cook food for the volunteers. And there won't be enough tools, so people will have to lend us those.

Suggested responses:

Playground planning involves three major phases:

> raising funds (bake sales, raffles, cookbook sales)
>
> finding an architect (space, affordability, attractiveness)
>
> building the playground (construction help, food, tools)

the subdivisions appear as nouns (*steak, cheese, turnips, ketchup*). However, lists or outlines may also be written in phrases or clauses. When preparing a paper or taking notes from a book, keep the elements of lists and outlines in equivalent grammatical form. As with parallel elements in a sentence, parallel elements in a list or outline will highlight the logical similarities that underlie parallel content.

1 Making lists

A *list* is a displayed series of items that are logically similar or comparable and are expressed in grammatically parallel form. A list that is not parallel can be very confusing.

Not parallel

Those attending should be prepared to address these issues:

- morale of workers
- Why do we need so much overtime?
- getting more efficient
- We need better sales tools.

A list or outline can be a helpful way to organize your thoughts. To keep the logic of similar or comparable ideas in line, all items of a list should be expressed in equivalent grammatical form. The preceding example shows a list with four forms: a noun phrase, a question, a verb in its *-ing* form, and a sentence. Choosing any one of these forms as a standard for the list would make the list parallel.

Parallel

Those attending should be prepared to address these issues:

- morale of workers
- necessity of overtime
- need for efficiency
- need for better sales tools

Parallel

Those attending should be prepared to address these issues:

- improving worker morale
- reducing the need for overtime
- improving efficiency
- reevaluating sales tools

2 Making outlines

An **outline** is essentially a logically parallel list with further subdivisions and subsections under individual items in the list. To make an outline that will help you write a paper or take summarizing notes from a book, follow the guidelines shown in 3d-4. You should keep elements at the same level of generality in the outline parallel in form.

Not parallel

Chapter Title: Jefferson Takes Power [clause]

A. The man and his policies [compound nouns]

B. Buying Louisiana [-*ing* form of a verb]

C. Jefferson, Marshall, and the courts [compound nouns]

D. There's trouble on the seas [clause]

In this outline, the subdivisions within the chapter are written three different ways: as an independent clause, as a noun or noun phrase, and as a verb in its -*ing* form. You need to choose *one* of these grammatical structures to make a logically parallel outline. Any choice can be correct, but one may be preferable for your purposes. Often a compromise choice is to outline entries as nouns or noun phrases.

Parallel, with a subdivision

Chapter Title: Jefferson in Power

A. The man and his policies

B. The Louisiana Purchase

C. Jefferson, Marshall, and the courts

D. Trouble on the seas

1. The benefits of neutrality
2. The dangers of neutrality

As you expand the outline in greater detail, once again present each entry of the subdivision in parallel form. Within each subdivision, list all parallel items at the same level of generality. If you wanted to subdivide items in the outline to a still more particular level of detail, you would once again make the listed elements of the next subdivision parallel in form.

EXERCISE 2

Outline the major sections of any chapter in one of your textbooks, using the author's subheadings or your own. Then choose one section to outline in detail. Make parallel entries in your outline for every paragraph in that section, maintaining a consistent grammatical form.

EXERCISE 3

Repeat Exercise 2, using a paper you have recently written. Once you have outlined your paper, use the outline as a tool for evaluating the coherence of your work. Based on your outline, what observations can you make about the structure of your paper?

EXERCISE 2

Individual responses

EXERCISE 3

Individual responses

CHAPTER 19

Building Emphasis with Coordination and Subordination

KEY FEATURES

This chapter incorporates material found in several other chapters to offer students guidelines for achieving a desired *effect* in their writing. As in Chapter 18, form is closely tied to content. In exploring various techniques for building emphasis, the chapter asks students to consider the nature of the ideas in the paper before deciding what and how to emphasize. The chapter treats techniques such as coordinate structures for equal ideas, conjunctive adverbs for balance, and subordinate structures to emphasize relationships between ideas, as well as specialized techniques such as punctuation, repetition, and specialized sentences. The chapter also presents the problems and tradeoffs associated with certain techniques. Examples and exercises are plentiful; exercises offer practice with individual sentences and paragraphs. Throughout the chapter, students are provided with straightforward, practical advice for carrying revision beyond the stage of editing out errors.

LOOKING BACK—LOOKING AHEAD

As indicated in the introduction, this chapter makes use of material found in several other chapters. Students may want to reread the preceding Chapters 17 and 18, and take a look at Chapters 20 (Controlling Length and Rhythm) and 21 (Choosing the Right Word).

To emphasize a thought, a writer assigns special weight or importance to particular words in a sentence and to particular sentences in a paragraph. You are in the best position to make decisions about emphasis once you have written a draft and have your main points clearly in mind. Then you can manipulate words, phrases, and clauses to create the effects that will make your writing memorable.

Sentence emphasis does not exist independently of content. While your readers may admire the elegance and force of your writing, they must also be convinced that the content of your sentences and paragraphs is clear and logical as well as grammatical. As they consider what your sentences say, readers will appreciate any efforts you make to convert adequate, unemphatic writing into memorable prose.

Emphatic writing uses specific, concrete images (21c, d); is concise and direct (Chapter 17); employs parallelism (Chapter 18); and is varied (Chapter 20). Your writing can improve immensely if you apply the techniques discussed here; but remember that no amount of emphasis can salvage sentences that are seriously flawed in content, grammar, usage, or punctuation.

COORDINATION

19a Use coordinate structures to emphasize equal ideas.

As a unit of thought, a sentence is naturally emphatic. Like a story, it has a beginning, middle, and end. One important and very common technique for both creating emphasis and eliminating wordiness is **coordination,** combining sentence elements by the use of coordinating and correlative conjunctions and conjunctive adverbs. Elements in a coordinate relationship share equal grammatical status and equal emphasis.

CRITICAL DECISIONS

Challenge sentences: Know when to coordinate or subordinate sentence elements

Coordination and subordination are methods of linking sentences and sentence parts. The following sentences can be joined in various ways to establish coordinate or subordinate relationships. Presently, each sentence—*because* it is a sentence—receives equal emphasis.

> (1) A complete suit of armor consisted of some 200 metal plates. (2) The armor of the fifteenth century offered protection from cross bows. (3) Armor offered protection from swords. (4) Armor offered protection from early muskets. (5) A suit of armor weighed 60 pounds. (6) A suit of armor would quickly exhaust the soldier it was meant to protect.

Choosing when to link sentences with coordination or subordination requires that you be clear about (1) the level of emphasis you want to give particular information and (2) the specific logical relationships you want to establish.

Why choose coordinate relationships?

Coordinating Conjunctions and the Relationships They Establish

To show addition: *and*
To show contrast: *but, yet*
To show choice: *or, nor*
To show cause: *for*
To show consequences: *so*

Use coordinating conjunctions to link sentences by giving equal emphasis to specific words (in this case, words from sentences 2, 3, and 4).

> The armor of the fifteenth century offered protection from cross bows, swords, *and* early muskets.

Use coordinating conjunctions to link sentences by giving equal emphasis to specific phrases (in this case, verb phrases from sentences 1 and 5).

> A complete suit of armor consisted of some 200 metal plates *and* weighed 60 pounds.

Use coordinating conjunctions to link and give equal emphasis to whole sentences, in this case sentence 6 and the combination of sentences 2, 3, and 4.

> The armor of the fifteenth century offered protection from cross bows, swords, and early muskets; *but* the armor would quickly exhaust the soldier it was meant to protect.

Conjunctive Adverbs and the Relationships They Establish

To show contrast: *however, nevertheless, nonetheless,* and *still*
To show cause and effect: *accordingly, consequently, thus,* and *therefore*
To show addition: *also, besides, furthermore,* and *moreover*
To show time: *afterward, subsequently,* and *then*
To show emphasis: *indeed*
To show condition: *otherwise*

Use conjunctive adverbs to link and give equal emphasis to two sentences. Conjunctive adverbs can be shifted from the beginning to the middle or to the end of the second sentence (which is not possible with coordinating conjunctions—see 19a-3).

(continued)

GROUP ACTIVITY

This activity can help students appreciate the distinction between and within coordinate and subordinate sentence elements. Ask each group to link two or more of the six sentences presented in the box to form a variety of coordinate and subordinate structures. (They can use the linked sentences in the box as guides.) Each group should produce five or six different sentences, which they will then present to the class. In general discussion, students can comment on the different effects of linking sentences through coordination and subordination.

GROUP ACTIVITY

Because the exercises in this chapter allow for a number of different responses, all but Exercise 5 would make ideal group activities. Whether students negotiate responses in groups or compare individual responses, they'll get a good sense of the various choices open to writers as they revise for emphasis.

ESL CUE

Spanish speakers frequently confuse "after" with "afterwards" (as in, "After, they went home") because of translation models in Spanish-English pocket dictionaries.

Japanese students might consistently treat subordinate clauses as main clauses.

ADDITIONAL EXERCISE A

ACROSS THE CURRICULUM Make three photocopies of several consecutive paragraphs from one of your textbooks. (You'll use the other two copies in subsequent exercises.) Underline all coordinate structures, and identify the words indicating equal ideas as coordinating conjunctions, correlative conjunctions, or conjunctive adverbs. How many times does the writer use coordination? How often are words joined? Phrases? Clauses? How does the use of coordination help the writer achieve emphasis in the passage?

ESL CUE

ESL students will probably find coordination far easier than subordination, where the specialized connective words might confuse them. For example, they might understand that "despite/in spite of/although/even though/however/nevertheless" are all used for a contrast that is concessive, but they might also use such terms interchangeably. They might need help distinguishing which subordinators go with clauses ("although/even though/in spite of the fact that") and which words connect between sentences rather than subordinate ("however/nevertheless/nonetheless"). "Otherwise," "even if," and "unless" are particularly troublesome. Many ESL students cannot distinguish between "in addition" and "besides" because their grammar texts did not do so. Distinguishing between the coordinator "so" and the subordinator "so that" and the use of "so" or "such" in adverbial clauses of result is also confusing.

"He was tired so he went home."
"He went home so that he could get some rest."
"He was so tired that he went home."
"He was such a tired man that he went home."

CRITICAL DECISIONS (continued)

The armor of the fifteenth century offered protection from cross bows, swords, *and* early muskets; *however,* the armor would quickly exhaust the soldier it was meant to protect.

Conjunctive adverbs vs. coordinating conjunctions: Both conjunctive adverbs and coordinating conjunctions give equal emphasis to and establish similar logical relations between the sentences they join. Why choose one over the other? Differences are subtle and, if the sentences are punctuated correctly (see Critical Decisions box, page 461), both choices are correct. Because a conjunctive adverb's *only* function is to join whole sentences, it is the more emphatic choice. Use a conjunctive adverb when the sentences being joined are long or complicated (when the content requires a strong logical connection) or when you otherwise want to emphasize the relationship between sentences.

Why choose subordinate relationships?

Subordinating Conjunctions and the Relationships They Establish

To show condition: *if, even if, unless,* and *provided that*
To show contrast: *though, although, even though,* and *as if*
To show cause: *because* and *since*
To show time: *when, whenever, while, as, before, after, since, once,* and *until*
To show place: *where* and *wherever*
To show purpose: *so that, in order that,* and *that*

Subordinating conjunctions link whole clauses but, in the process, give one clause greater emphasis. Use a subordinating conjunction when you want one of the two sentences you are linking to modify (that is, to describe or to comment on) the other.

Because it weighed 60 pounds, a suit of armor would quickly exhaust the soldier it was meant to protect.

Designate one sentence as subordinate by placing a conjunction at its head; thereafter, the sentence is referred to as a *dependent clause* (in this example, *Because it weighed 60 pounds*). Emphasis in a sentence linked with subordination is given to the *independent clause* (in this example, to *a suit of armor . . . protect*). See the discussion on relative pronouns (14e, 19b-2, 25d-1–2), which also begin dependent clauses.

1 Give equal emphasis to elements with coordinating conjunctions.

The **coordinating conjunctions** *and, but, or, nor, so, for, yet* offer an efficient way of joining parallel elements from two or more sentences into a single sentence. The following sentences are parallel in content.

A market allows sellers of goods to interact with buyers.

A market allows sellers of services to interact with buyers.

By using the coordinating conjunction *or,* you can create a compound sentence in which each independent clause has equal grammatical status.

A market allows sellers of goods to interact with buyers, *or* a market allows sellers of services to interact with buyers.

If words are repeated in coordinate clauses, you can economize by coordinating sentence *parts,* in this case the objects of two prepositional phrases. In the following sentence, *goods* and *services* receive equal emphasis.

COMBINED A market allows sellers of goods *or* services to interact with buyers. [The object of the preposition has been doubled with a coordinating conjunction.]

Coordinating conjunctions express specific logical relations between the elements they join. *Or* and *nor* suggest choice, one positive and the other negative. *And* joins elements by addition. *But* and *yet* join elements by contrast. *For* suggests a cause of an occurrence. *So* suggests a result of some action. *For* and *so,* when used as coordinating conjunctions, join entire independent clauses. All other coordinating conjunctions may join sentence elements and entire sentences. Coordinating conjunctions must be used with appropriate punctuation to show that two ideas share the same emphasis.

TO ESTABLISH EQUALITY BETWEEN WORDS

Darwin was a pioneer in biology *and* a thinker with an exceptionally fertile mind. [The coordinating conjunction *and* allows the writer to explain two aspects of Darwin in the same sentence.]

TO ESTABLISH EQUALITY BETWEEN PHRASES

Darwin theorized that evolutionary changes proceed not in jumps *but* in leaps. [*But* contrasts prepositional phrases of equal weight.]

TO ESTABLISH EQUALITY BETWEEN CLAUSES

Darwin's theory of natural selection was his most daring, *for* it dealt with the mechanism of evolutionary change. [The independent clause after *for* permits the writer to give an explanation or reason for the first clause.]

Evolutionists from Darwin on have always emphasized the continuity of populational evolution, *yet* they have ignored the fact that even continuous evolution is mildly discontinuous. [The independent clause after *yet* permits the writer to establish an exception to the first clause.]

2 Give equal emphasis to elements by using correlative conjunctions.

Correlative conjunctions are pairs of coordinating conjunctions that emphasize the relationship between the parts of the coordinated construction. The following are the common correlative conjunctions:

either/or	*both/and*	*not only/but*
neither/nor	*whether/or*	*not only/but also*

The first word of the correlative is placed before the first element to be joined, and the second word of the correlative before the second element.

Both supply *and* demand are theoretical constructs, not fixed laws.

FOR DISCUSSION

To give students an idea of the stylistic capacity of coordinating conjunctions, present them with quotations such as the following and ask them to comment on how the structures serve to emphasize the content.

"He had the air of a man who did not believe what he heard or what he himself was saying. He was the first cynic I had met." (Maya Angelou)

"I believe by this time both of us began to realize we were leading two separate lives that no longer fitted together. . . . I was relieved when it was all over and glad we parted with a mutual affection and respect which still endures." (Margaret Bourke-White)

"We stopped at the driving range. . . . I reared back and swung with all my might. I caught that ball square, but I came around so hard that the club hit the light post on the follow through and broke in two." (Babe Didrikson Zaharias)

"I believe that I was the only one of my class of 150 who graduated without a definite plan for earning her living. . . . I did not want to teach school, nor had I taken the courses necessary for this occupation." (Margaret Morse Nice)

"No one means all he says, and yet very few say all they mean, for words are slippery and thought is viscous." (Henry Adams)

ADDITIONAL EXERCISE B

ACROSS THE CURRICULUM Choose a topic from one of your courses, and compose a paragraph in which you use at least three pairs of different correlative conjunctions. (Make sure the topic is specific: e.g., the relationship between interest rates and economic growth, the role of sibling rivalry in family relationships, or the influence of Zora Neale Hurston on Alice Walker.) When you review your paragraph, try to determine how the correlative conjunctions contribute to its meaning.

ACROSS THE CURRICULUM

Emphasis through Coordination and Subordination

Coordination and subordination are fundamental tools of sentence construction that give writers in all discipline areas a means of controlling emphasis. Observe how economist Milton Friedman uses coordination and subordination, giving some elements equal weight and others, unequal.* Whether you are studying economics or biology, you will find writers using these fundamental tools.

> In a free-enterprise, private property system, a corporate executive is an employee of the owners of the business. He has direct responsibility to his employers. That responsibility is to conduct the business in accordance with their desires, which generally will be to make as much money as possible while conforming to the basic rules of the society, both those embodied in law and those embodied in ethical custom. Of course, in some cases his employers may have a different objective. A group of persons might establish a corporation for . . . [another] purpose—for example, a hospital or a school. The manager of such a corporation will not have money profit as his objective but the rendering of certain services.

Coordinate words

A, *B* system

free-enterprise, private property system (comma replaces *and*)

for example, *A* **or** *B*

for example, a hospital **or** a school

Coordinate phrases

both those in *A* **and** those in *B*

both those embodied in law **and** those embodied in ethical custom

will not have *A* **but** *B*

will not have money profit as his objective **but** the rendering of . . . services

Subordinate clause (clause modifies *desires*)

That responsibility is to conduct the business in accordance with their desires, **which** generally will be to make as much money as possible. . .

*The passage is excerpted from Milton Friedman, "The Social Responsibility of Business Is to Increase Its Profits," *New York Times Magazine* 13 Sept. 1970.

3 Use conjunctive adverbs to give balanced emphasis to sentence elements.

Conjunctive adverbs, also called *adverbial conjunctions,* create compound sentences in which the independent clauses that are joined share a logically balanced emphasis. The following conjunctions (as well as others—

see the Critical Decisions box on page 359) provide logical linkages between sentences: *however, otherwise, indeed, nevertheless, afterward,* and *still.* (See 7a-9 and especially 13b-4 for uses of conjunctive adverbs.)

> *Linked sentences*
>
> As the price of a good or service increases, the quantity of the good or service demanded is expected to decrease. *Moreover,* as the price of a good or service decreases, the quantity of the good or service demanded is expected to increase.

Conjunctive adverbs, like most adverbs, can be moved around in a sentence.

> We almost take for granted that rain will replenish whatever amount of water we may use up. Water, *however,* is no longer the infinitely renewable resource that we once thought it was.

In the second sentence, the conjunctive adverb may be moved.

> *However,* water is no longer the infinitely renewable resource that we once thought it was.

Note: Because conjunctive adverbs have the force of transitional elements, they are usually set off in a sentence with commas. It is virtually automatic that with the use of a conjunctive adverb one of the joined independent clauses will contain a comma, as in all the preceding examples. (See 13b-4 for avoiding comma splices when using conjunctive adverbs.)

4 Revise sentences that use illogical or excessive coordination.

Problems with coordination arise when writers use conjunctions aimlessly, stringing unrelated elements together without regard for an equal or balanced relationship of ideas in the joined elements.

Faulty coordination

Two elements linked by a conjunction show faulty coordination when they are not logically related. Revise or reorganize sentences to establish groupings that make sense, using coordination for elements of closely related importance.

Faulty As a species, spiders can be found in all sorts of habitats, such as the tundra environment of mountain peaks, the deepest crevices of caves, bog-like environments or even the most scorching deserts, and spiders are not particularly adaptable to new habitats. [The writer coordinates these sentences improperly: clearly, the writer intends a contrast.]

Revised As a species, spiders can be found in all sorts of habitats, such as the tundra environment of mountain peaks, the deepest crevices of

TEACHING IDEAS

Students, particularly those preparing for a career in elementary education, will be interested to know that when young children begin to write, they frequently produce narratives full of faulty and excessive coordination. You may want to gather samples of children's writing either from your own education department or from students themselves. Ask students to bring in their own examples of writing from their children, their brothers and sisters, or their nieces and nephews, or samples from their own grade-school days. As students examine such writing, they may want to speculate on the relationship between stylistic sophistication and cognitive abilities.

caves, bog-like environments or even the most scorching deserts; but a given spider will not be particularly adaptable to a new habitat.

Excessive coordination

Readers look to a writer for signals about logical relationships among ideas, as well as for what is important in a paragraph. If a writer has aimlessly used coordinating conjunctions to join every statement to the next, readers will see no real connections among the ideas; no single idea will stand out. In reviewing first-draft writing, study your use of coordinating and correlative conjunctions and of conjunctive adverbs. Coordinate structures should be retained only when you have deliberately equated main ideas.

FAULTY Because the young princess Marie Antoinette of Austria was to be handed over by the Austrian government to the care of the French monarchy, she had to cross the national boundary line all alone and she had to remove all her articles of Viennese clothing and replace them with French-made ones, and she could retain no trinket or jewelry, no matter what its sentimental value might have been.

REVISED Because the young princess Marie Antoinette of Austria was to be handed over by the Austrian government to the care of the French monarchy, she had to cross the national boundary line all alone. Next, she had to remove all her articles of Viennese clothing and replace them with French-made ones. She could retain no trinket or jewelry, no matter what its sentimental value might have been.

EXERCISE 1

Combine the following sets of sentences so that whole sentences or parts of sentences show equal emphasis. Use coordinating conjunctions, correlative conjunctions, or conjunctive adverbs.

Example: Ostriches grow from egg to 150-pound bird in nine months. A young python of five pounds requires ten to twenty years to reach 120 pounds.

Ostriches grow from egg to 150-pound bird in nine months, but a young python of five pounds requires ten to twenty years to reach 120 pounds.

1. Why living things evolve is only partly understood. How living things evolve is only partly understood.
2. Monkeys, apes, and man are all good manipulators of hand-eye coordination. No mammal can rival the chameleon for eye-tongue coordination.
3. Snake anatomy contains the most clever feeding apparatus. Snake anatomy also contains the most intricately efficient feeding apparatus.
4. The snake opens its jaws. It begins to engulf the monkey. It is not hurried. It is deliberate. It is precise.
5. The Nunamiu Eskimo believe that wolves know where they are going when they set out to hunt caribou. They believe that wolves learn from

EXERCISE 1

Suggested responses:

1. How and why living things evolve are only partly understood.
2. Monkeys, apes, and man are all good manipulators of hand-eye coordination. No mammal, however, can rival the chameleon for eye-tongue coordination.
3. Snake anatomy contains the most clever and intricately efficient feeding apparatus.
4. The snake opens its jaws and begins to engulf the monkey. It is not hurried, but deliberate and precise.
5. The Nunamiu Eskimo believe not only that wolves know where they are going when they set out to hunt caribou, but also that wolves learn from ravens where caribou might be. Moreover, they believe certain wolves in a pack never kill, and others specialize in killing small game.
6. When the wolves come together, they make squeaking noises and encircle each other.

ravens where caribou might be. They believe certain wolves in a pack never kill. Others, they believe, specialize in killing small game.

6. When the wolves come together, they make squeaking noises. They encircle each other. They rub and push one another. They poke their noses into each other's neck fur. They back away to stretch. They chase each other. They stand quietly together. Then they are gone down a vague trail.
7. Mexico still has a small population of wolves. Large populations remain in Alaska and Canada.

EXERCISE 2

Rewrite the sentences in the following paragraph by using coordinating conjunctions, correlative conjunctions, or conjunctive adverbs along with appropriate punctuation. Remember that you want to show equality between ideas or parts of ideas. Be sure that the revised paragraph is cohesive and coherent.

The smallest living creatures known are viroids. Each is composed of fewer than 10,000 atoms. They can cause several different diseases in plants. They have probably most recently developed from more complex organisms rather than less complicated ones. They are so simple in structure. One wonders how they could be alive at all. They survive because they are parasites. They commandeer much larger cells and force that cell to begin making more viroids like themselves.

EXERCISE 3

Rewrite the following sets of sentences to correct problems of faulty coordination.

1. Plants adapted to cold climates can conduct photosynthesis at temperatures far below those of their warmer weather compatriots, and some evergreens still maintain the process at 0°C, and some algae that inhabit hot water springs can do likewise at 75°C, and yet most plants photosynthesize best between 10° and 35°C.
2. Many arthropods are definitely "dressed to kill." The scorpion sports sharp jaws, strong pincers, and it packs a nasty sting, but it is outclassed by the black widow spider, and her bite can be lethal if untreated, and yet centipedes will attack and paralyze prey twice their size with a bite.

SUBORDINATION

19b Use subordinate structures to emphasize a main idea.

Writers use **subordination** within sentences to give more emphasis to one idea than to another. The basic idea always appears in an **independent clause,** a core statement that can stand alone as a sentence in itself. To state another idea closely linked to that core statement writers add a **dependent clause,** which cannot stand by itself. A dependent clause begins with a sub-

They also rub and push one another. They poke their noses into each other's fur, and back away to stretch. They not only chase each other but also stand quietly together. Then they are gone down a vague trail.

7. Mexico still has a small population of wolves, but large populations remain in Alaska and Canada.

EXERCISE 2

The smallest living creatures known are viroids. Each is composed of fewer than 10,000 atoms and can cause several different diseases in plants. They have probably most recently developed from more complex organisms rather than from less complicated ones; yet they are so simple in structure that one wonders how they could be alive at all. They survive because they are parasites; thus, they commandeer much larger cells and force those cells to begin making more viroids like themselves.

EXERCISE 3

1. Plants adapted to cold climates can conduct photosynthesis at temperatures far below those of their warmer weather compatriots; in fact, some evergreens still maintain the process at 0° C. Some algae that inhabit hot water springs can do likewise at 75° C; however, most plants photosynthesize best between 10° and 35° C.
2. Many arthropods are definitely "dressed to kill"; for example, the scorpion sports sharp jaws and strong pincers, and packs a nasty sting. Nonetheless, it is outclassed by the black widow spider. Her bite can be lethal if untreated; similarly, centipedes will attack and paralyze prey twice their size.

LOOKING BACK

Some students may need to refresh their memories regarding subordinate clauses. Encourage them to take the advice offered here and review the appropriate sections of Chapter 7 (Constructing Sentences).

ordinating conjunction, such as *if, although,* or *because* (see the Critical Decisions box in 19a for a complete list), or with a relative pronoun: *who, which,* or *that.* A sentence with both dependent and independent clauses is known as a **complex sentence.** (For more information on dependent clauses, see 7e.)

GROUP ACTIVITY

Using subordinate structures can be intimidating for students who fall prey to fragments, comma splices, and fused sentences. A simple group activity can provide these students with practice and confidence. Making sure that the skill level of each group is mixed, ask groups to compose six sentences using the subordinating conjunctions from the Critical Decisions box in 19a. As the groups generate their sentences, weaker students will benefit from listening to the strategies of the stronger students, and the stronger students will benefit from having to articulate those strategies.

1 Use subordinating conjunctions to form dependent adverb clauses.

A subordinating conjunction placed at the beginning of an independent clause (a complete sentence) renders that clause *dependent.* Once dependent, this clause can be joined to an independent clause and will function like an adverb. In this new complex sentence, the independent clause will receive the primary emphasis, with the dependent clause closely linked to it in a subordinate relationship. To create a dependent adverb clause, begin with two sentences that you think could be combined.

> Married women could not leave the home for the twelve-hour work days required in the mills.
>
> Married women lost their ability to earn income.

When you place a subordinating conjunction at the head of the dependent clause, the clause will function like an adverb in the new complex sentence.

> Because married women could not leave the home for the twelve-hour work days required in the mills,

Join the now dependent clause to the independent clause.

> Because married women could not leave the home for the twelve-hour work days required in the mills, they lost their ability to earn income.

Emphasis and logical sequence determine the placement of a dependent adverb clause.

AT THE BEGINNING

> When the Triangle Shirtwaist Factory fire broke out in a rag bin on a quiet Saturday afternoon in 1911, it spread extraordinarily quickly due to the mass of tissue paper and bits of material that littered the workroom floor. [The writer wants to set a context immediately; the dependent clause at the beginning of the sentence creates tension: readers finish the clause wanting to know more information—which is provided in the main clause.]

IN THE MIDDLE

> The fire, though it claimed 146 lives, did result in the addition of 30 new ordinances to the New York City fire code. [The dependent clause sets a contrast mid-sentence; again, tension is created and readers have a motivation to continue with the main clause.]

AT THE END

> The terrorized, virtually all-female workforce was hampered in its efforts to leave because management had purposefully designed narrow escape passages in an effort to spot and catch pilferers. [Here, the information in

the dependent clause qualifies in a shocking way the information in the main clause.]

2 Use *that, which,* and *who* to form dependent adjective clauses.

A dependent **adjective clause** modifies a noun in an independent clause. Adjective clauses are introduced by relative pronouns that rename and refer to the nouns they follow. The pronoun *who* can refer to people or to personified divinities or animals. *That* refers to people, animals, or things. *Which* refers to animals and things. To create a dependent adjective clause, begin with two sentences that you think could be combined.

> Transylvania qualifies as one of the most fought-over regions in all of Europe.
>
> Transylvania witnessed the bloody clashes of Bulgarians, Magyars, Huns, and other eastern tribes between the fourth and twelfth centuries.

Substitute a relative pronoun for the subject of the dependent clause, the clause that will function like an adjective in the new complex sentence.

> which witnessed the bloody clashes of Bulgarians, Magyars, Huns, and other eastern tribes between the fourth and twelfth centuries,

Join the now dependent clause to the independent clause.

> Transylvania, which witnessed the bloody clashes of Bulgarians, Magyars, Huns, and other eastern tribes between the fourth and twelfth centuries, qualifies as one of the most fought-over regions in all of Europe.

3 Use subordination accurately to avoid confusion.

Three errors are commonly associated with subordination: inappropriate and ambiguous use of subordinating conjunctions, illogical subordination, and excessive subordination.

Inappropriate and ambiguous use of subordinating conjunctions

The subordinating conjunction *as* is used to denote both time and comparison.

> As human beings became more advanced technologically, they learned to domesticate animals and plants rather than to forage and hunt.

As is occasionally used to indicate cause: *Mary didn't arrive this morning,* as *she missed her plane.* This usage is apt to confuse readers, who may expect *as* to indicate time or comparison. When you wish to establish cause and effect, use the subordinating conjunction *because.*

ADDITIONAL EXERCISE C

Combine the following pairs of sentences, forming adjective clauses introduced by *that, which,* and *who.*

1. Muslims were adversely affected by the breakup of the Soviet Union.
   Muslims have been persecuted for centuries.
2. Bosnia fell victim to the "ethnic cleansing" perpetrated by Serbia.
   Bosnia was once a part of Yugoslavia.
3. Anti-Muslim violence also erupted in the former Burma.
   Anti-Muslim violence plagued Bosnia.
4. Islam was under siege in other parts of the world.
   Islam has enjoyed continued growth in Europe and North America.
5. One U.S. group is the African American community.
   The African American community has seen a significant conversion to Islam.

Suggested responses:

1. Muslims, who have been persecuted for centuries, were adversely affected by the breakup of the Soviet Union.
2. Bosnia, which was once a part of Yugoslavia, fell victim to the "ethnic cleansing" perpetrated by Serbia.
3. The anti-Muslim violence that plagued Bosnia also erupted in the former Burma.
4. Islam, which has enjoyed continued growth in Europe and North America, was under siege in other parts of the world.
5. One U.S. group that has seen a significant conversion to Islam is the African American community.

TEACHING IDEAS

If you are aware of students whose writing exhibits problems with inappropriate, ambiguous, illogical, or excessive subordination, you may want to suggest to them the following activity: After reading 19b-3, review several of your papers for evidence of this problem. Underline the offending sentences and on a separate sheet of paper, rewrite them to eliminate

(continued)

the problems. Now read the entire paper with the revised sentences. How do your revisions make your meaning clearer? How do they improve your writing stylistically?

ADDITIONAL EXERCISE D

Using the second photocopy you made for Exercise A, underline all subordinate structures and circle each subordinating conjunction. What kind of relationship does each subordinating conjunction establish? (Refer to the Critical Decisions box in 19a.) How many times does the writer use subordination? How often are subordinate clauses placed at the beginning of the sentence? In the middle? At the end? How does the use of subordination help the writer achieve emphasis in the passage?

CONFUSING *As* the plough is used as a wedge to divide the soil, it is the most powerful invention in all agriculture.

REVISED *Because* the plough is used as a wedge to divide the soil, it is the most powerful invention in all agriculture. [The reason for the plough's being a powerful invention is given in the adverbial clause, requiring a conjunction that indicates *cause.*]

The preposition *like* is used as a subordinating conjunction in informal speech. In formal writing, use the subordinating conjunction *as* in place of *like* when a conjunction is needed.

NONSTANDARD American agriculture did not have the plough and the wheel *like* Middle Eastern agriculture did.

REVISED American agriculture did not have the plough and the wheel *as* Middle Eastern agriculture did.

Illogical subordination

The problem of illogical subordination arises when a dependent clause does not establish a clear, logical relationship with an independent clause. To correct the problem, reexamine the clauses in question and select a more accurate subordinating conjunction or, if the sentences warrant, a coordinating conjunction.

FAULTY *Although* she was agitated at being shut up in a matchbox for so long, the female scorpion seized the first opportunity to escape.

The subordinating conjunction *although* fails to establish a clear, logical relationship between the dependent and independent clauses. The content of the dependent clause gives no reason for the scorpion's wanting to escape.

REVISED *Because* she was agitated at being shut up in a matchbox for so long, the female scorpion seized the first opportunity to escape. [The dependent clause explains the reason for the scorpion's escape and requires a subordinating conjunction denoting *cause.*]

Excessive subordination

As with coordination, a writer may overuse subordination. When all or most parts of a long sentence are subordinate in structure, readers may have trouble identifying points of particular importance. In your review of a first draft, study your use of subordinating conjunctions and relative pronouns. Retain subordinate structures when you have deliberately made the ideas of one clause dependent on another. Choose some other sentence structure when the clauses you are relating do not exist in a dependent/independent relationship.

FAULTY The manatee, which is a very tame beast but extremely unattractive with its dull gray skin, has a hippopotamus-like head and virtually no neck, so that one wonders how the creature could ever have been mistaken for the lovely creature that is supposed to be the mermaid, although there are those who claim that if the animal is seen from sufficiently far away as it sits on the rocks, the lines of its head could convey the impression of flowing hair.

REVISED The manatee, which is a very tame beast but extremely unattractive with its dull gray skin, has a hippopotamus-like head and virtually no neck. One wonders how the creature could ever have been mistaken for the lovely creature that is supposed to be the mermaid. There are those who claim that if the animal is seen from sufficiently far away as it sits on the rocks, the lines of its head could convey the impression of flowing hair.

EXERCISE 4

Revise each pair of sentences that follow by creating a complex sentence with one dependent clause and one independent clause. Place the dependent clause in whatever position you think will best demonstrate the relationship of that clause to the main idea.

Example: The Viennese naturalist Konrad Lorenz took a degree in medicine. Later, Konrad Lorenz became director of the Max Planck Institute for behavioral physiology.

After he took a degree in medicine, the Viennese naturalist Konrad Lorenz became director of the Max Planck Institute for behavioral physiology. [A dependent adverb clause is joined to an independent clause to form a complex sentence.]

1. Social animals such as crows will attack or "mob" a nocturnal predator. The nocturnal predator sometimes appears during the day.
2. A fox is followed through the woods by a loudly screaming jay. The fox's hunting is spoiled.
3. Poisonous or foul-tasting animals have chosen the "warning" colors of red, white, and black. Predators associate these with unpleasant experiences.
4. Scent marks of cats act like railway signals. The scent marks prevent collision between two cats.
5. The surroundings become stranger and more intimidating to the animal. The readiness to fight decreases proportionately.

OTHER DEVICES FOR ACHIEVING EMPHASIS

19c Use special techniques to achieve emphasis.

Coordination and subordination are fundamental to the structure of so many sentences that often they go unnoticed as devices for directing a reader's attention. Not so subtle are special stylistic techniques like repetition and contrast, which writers use to achieve highly visible and at times dramatic prose. Precisely because they are so visible, you should mix these techniques both with subordination and coordination and with less emphatic simple sentences in a paragraph.

EXERCISE 4

Suggested responses:

1. Social animals such as crows will attack or "mob" a nocturnal predator that sometimes appears during the day.
2. The fox's hunting is spoiled when it is followed through the woods by a loudly screaming jay.
3. Because poisonous or foul-tasting animals have chosen the "warning" colors of red, white, and black, predators associate these colors with unpleasant experiences.
4. Scent marks, which act like railway signals, prevent collision between two cats.
5. As the surroundings become stranger and more intimidating to the animal, the readiness to fight decreases proportionately.

FOR DISCUSSION

The techniques outlined here are found frequently in advertising, especially for plays and movies. Ask students to collect copies of ads that include one or more of these techniques. Choose the most representative ads to use as examples for a class discussion identifying and evaluating the effectiveness of the techniques.

Punctuate, capitalize, and highlight to emphasize words.

Punctuation, capitalization, and highlighting work *with* sentence content to create emphasis. *Capitalizing* a word, especially if it is not a proper name and hence is usually not begun with an uppercase letter, is one sure way to create emphasis. Capitalizing all the letters of a word, as in FIRE, will attract even more attention. So, of course, will **boldfacing** a word. In academic writing, strictly limit your use of these techniques and depend, instead, on the wording of your sentences to create emphasis. Occasionally, however, you might use uppercase letters for effect.

> There does not seem to be any point in my knowing for the rest of my life that, during 1964, 720 tons of soot fell on every square mile of New York City, yet there it is in my notebook, labeled "FACT."

Used sparingly, an exclamation point adds emphasis and will help a reader to share a writer's amazement, enthusiasm—or, in some cases, contempt (see 24c). Ending a sentence with a *colon* sets for your reader an expectation that important, closely related information will follow. The words after a colon are emphasized (see 29a). A *dash,* which you will show on a typewriter or computer as a double hyphen (- -), creates a pause in a sentence and the expectation that some significant comment will follow. Used sparingly, a dash is an excellent tool for emphasis. Overused, it creates a choppy effect and will annoy readers (see 29b).

Information set within *parentheses* will be viewed by readers as an aside—interesting, useful, but ultimately nonessential information. Parentheses give material special attention, but of a curious sort: parenthetical material limits its own emphasis and says in effect, pay attention, but not *too much.* Thus, material set off in parentheses is simultaneously emphasized and deemphasized (see 29c).

2 Repeat words, phrases, and clauses to emphasize ideas.

Intentional repetition is a powerful technique for creating emphasis. With repetition, words echo for a reader. Whatever is repeated, if it is repeated well, will be remembered. When using repetition, maintain parallel structure (see Chapter 18) and avoid overuse. Our language and certain others seem naturally "tuned" to two and three repetitions in any one sentence. Words, phrases, and clauses doubled by coordinating conjunctions create by far the most typical instances of repetition. It is both more emphatic and less wordy to write

> A market allows sellers of goods or services to interact with buyers.

instead of

> A market allows sellers of goods to interact with buyers. A market allows sellers of services to interact with buyers.

TEACHING IDEAS

In order to give students a sense of the power of repetition, you may want to add to the brief list of memorable lines printed here, and ask students to offer some examples from their own reading.

> "To the American people, it is inconceivable that military security can rest upon injustice, upon power, upon the ill-gotten fruits of imperialism and oppression." (Frank Tannenbaum)

> "We don't eliminate the problems that people have simply by eliminating the people." (right-to-life pamphlet)

> "I see one-third of a nation ill-housed, ill-clad, ill-nourished." (Franklin Delano Roosevelt)

> "Death? Why this fuss about death? Use your imagination, try to visualize a world *without* death! . . . Death is the essential condition of life, not an evil." (Charlotte Perkins Gilman)

> "Blues are the songs of despair, but gospel songs are the songs of hope." (Mahalia Jackson)

REFERENCES

CHRISTENSEN, FRANCIS. "A Generative Rhetoric of the Sentence." *Notes Toward a New Rhetoric: Essays for Teachers.* 2nd ed. Eds. Francis Christensen and Bonniejean Christensen. New York: Harper, 1978. The cumulative sentence can be effective in achieving emphasis of ideas in sentences.

CORBETT, EDWARD P. J. "Approaches to the Study of Style." *Teaching Composition: 12 Bibliographical Essays.* 2nd ed. Ed. Gary Tate. Fort Worth: Texas Christian UP, 1987. 83–130. A survey of recent scholarship on style.

———. *Classical Rhetoric for the Modern Student.* New York: Oxford UP, 1965. 410–16. Analyzes characteristics of sentence style.

Using repetition to triple sentence elements is more dramatic than doubling and will give a sentence an arresting, memorable rhythm. Think of Caesar's "I came, I saw, I conquered"; or the phrasing in the Declaration of Independence: "Life, Liberty and the pursuit of Happiness"; or Lincoln's lines at Gettysburg: "government of the people, by the people, for the people." (In each case, note the parallel structures.) One repetition too many can ruin a sentence, however, transforming a dramatic rhythm into a boring catalogue: *On arriving home, I folded the laundry, cooked dinner, read the paper, bathed my kids, finished the taxes, and went to sleep.*

To summarize, doubled sentence elements are commonplace and slightly emphatic; tripled elements are clearly emphatic; and quadrupled elements can tax a reader's patience, unless the sentence is carefully crafted. Generally, try not to follow one sentence that has a repeated structure with a second sentence of a similar structure. Too much repetition within either a sentence or a paragraph will create an unpleasant, overly balanced effect.

One special case of repetition concerns the *appositive phrase,* used to rename a noun. Although an appositive does not exactly repeat a word, in content the appositive is a technique based on repetition. In the following example, the phrase *a symbolic embodiment of its territorial status* renames (that is, repeats) the noun *flag.*

> Today each nation flies its own flag, a symbolic embodiment of its territorial status.

3 Use contrasts to emphasize ideas.

Contrast, otherwise known as *antithesis* or *opposition,* creates emphasis by setting one element in a sentence off against another, in the process emphasizing both. When using this technique, be sure that the elements you set in contrast have parallel structures.

> Requiring more skill to use and initially more unwieldy to master than the dictionary, *Roget's College Thesaurus* is, nonetheless, a valuable and timesaving aid for the struggling writer.

> If you apply to a college that won't promise to lock in its tuition rates, make sure to check the terms of your financial aid package; if you don't, you may find that after the freshman year your grants have been transformed into loans.

4 Use specialized sentences to create emphasis.

Sentence length is variable and depends both on a writer's preferences and on an audience's needs; still, readers do not expect a steady diet of four- or five-word sentences. Nor do they expect one-sentence paragraphs. Purposefully violating these (and other) expectations regarding the sentence can create emphasis (see 20a and 20b).

LANHAM, RICHARD. *Analyzing Prose.* New York: Scribner's, 1983. Extensive advice on revising for style.

WILLIAMS, JOSEPH. *Style: Ten Lessons in Clarity and Grace.* 2nd ed. Glenview: Scott, 1989. Provides guidelines for writers in pursuit of stylistic emphasis in their writing.

The brief sentence

An especially brief sentence located anywhere in a paragraph will call attention to itself. The following paragraph concludes emphatically with a four-word sentence.

> If you apply to a college that won't promise to lock in its tuition rates, make sure to check the terms of your financial aid package; if you don't, you may find that after the freshman year your grants have been transformed into loans. That can be disastrous.

The one-sentence paragraph

Because it is so rare, a one-sentence paragraph calls attention to itself. Often these emphatic paragraphs begin or conclude an essay. In the following example, the one-sentence paragraph appears mid-essay and is both preceded and followed by long paragraphs.

> . . . Not only are fruit seeds dispersed in the coyote's scat, the seeds' pericarp dissolves in his digestive tract, increasing the chance of germination by 85 percent.
>
> A coyote's breath is rumored to be so rank that he can stun his prey with it.
>
> Most people may never see a coyote—especially if they go looking for one—but everyone can hear them at night. They're most vocal from December to February, during the mating season. . . .

The periodic sentence

Most sentences can be classified as *cumulative.* They begin with a subject and gather both force and detail as one reads, beginning to end. The advantage of a cumulative sentence is that it directly and emphatically announces its business by beginning with its subject.

CUMULATIVE SENTENCE Most people may never see a coyote—especially if they go looking for one—but everyone can hear them at night.

A *periodic* sentence delays the subject and verb in an effort to pique the reader's interest. Information placed at the head of the sentence draws readers in, creating a desire to find out what happens. Emphasis is given to the final part of the sentence, where the readers' need to know is satisfied.

PERIODIC SENTENCE Washing machines, garbage disposals, lawn mowers, furnaces, TV sets, tape recorders, slide projectors—all are in league with the automobile to take their turn at breaking down whenever life threatens to flow smoothly for their enemies.

EXERCISE 5

Read the sets of sentences that follow and underline the emphatic elements in each. Label the specific techniques each writer uses: coordination, subordination, punctuation, capitalization, repetition, contrast, or sentence length. Choose one set of sentences to analyze closely. Write your analysis in paragraph form.

> Birth is a hideous thing in *Frankenstein* even before there is a monster. . . . It is in her journal and her letters that Mary Shelley reveals the workshop of her own creation, where she pieced together the materials for a new species of romantic mythology. They record a horror story of maternity of the kind that literary biography does not provide again until Sylvia Plath. . . . [S]he was pregnant, barely pregnant but aware of the fact, when at the age of sixteen she ran off with Shelley in July 1814. . . . In February 1815 Mary gave birth to a daughter, illegitimate, premature, and sickly. . . . Mary notes that she breast-fed the baby; that Fanny, her half-sister, came to call; that Claire Claremont, her stepsister, who had run off with Mary, kept Shelley amused. Bonaparte invaded France, the journal tells us, and Mary took up her incessant reading program. . . . [T]he baby died in March. "Find my baby dead," Mary wrote. "A miserable day."
>
> —Ellen Moers

> In books I've read since I was young I've searched for heroines who could serve as ideals, as models, as possibilities—some reflecting the secret self that dwelled inside me, others pointing to whole new ways that a woman (if only she dared!) might try to be. The person that I am today was shaped by Nancy Drew; by Jo March, Jane Eyre and Heathcliff's soul mate Cathy; and by other fictional females whose attractiveness or character or audacity for a time were the standards by which I measured myself.
>
> I return to some of these books to see if I still understand the powerful hold that these heroines once had on me. I still understand.
>
> —Judith Viorst

EXERCISE 6

Use the various techniques you have learned in this chapter to combine the short, choppy sentences that follow, rewording them to make an engaging paragraph.

> There are self-regulated devices in the body. One of these can provide long-term immunity from diseases such as mumps or measles. This same device somehow also causes the AIDS virus, if present, to infect the immune cells. This discovery was made by researchers. They work at Virginia Commonwealth University in Richmond. They found that the HIV virus can get coated with antibodies. Even so, the virus will attack the surrounding T-cells (immune cells).

EXERCISE 5

Repetition:
Mary notes that . . . that Fanny . . . that Claire Claremont
[S]he was pregnant, barely pregnant . . . illegitimate, premature, and sickly

Brief Sentence:
Find my baby dead . . .

Subordination:
where she pieced . . .
When at the age of sixteen . . .

Coordination:
in her journal and her letters
barely pregnant but aware of the fact
and Mary took up her incessant reading program

Representative responses: Analyses will vary.

ADDITIONAL EXERCISE E

Using the third photocopy you made for Exercise A, underline and identify all special techniques for achieving emphasis. How many times does the writer use special techniques? How many different techniques does the author use? How does the use of special techniques help the writer achieve emphasis in the passage?

ADDITIONAL EXERCISE F

As you revise drafts of any papers you're working on at present, use the techniques covered in this chapter to achieve emphasis. Remember that the ideas you want to communicate will determine the specific technique you use. Compare the revision to the original. How has adding emphasis improved the effectiveness of your paper?

EXERCISE 6

Suggested revision:

Of the self-regulated devices in the body, there is one that can provide long-term immunity from diseases like mumps and measles; yet this same device somehow also causes the AIDS virus, if present, to infect immune cells. This discovery was made by researchers at Virginia Commonwealth University in Richmond who found that the HIV virus, though coated with antibodies, will nonetheless attack the surrounding T-cells (immune cells).

CHAPTER 20

Controlling Length and Rhythm

KEY FEATURES

This final chapter on revising sentences focuses almost exclusively on style. At this stage of revision a paper should be grammatically correct and the ideas clearly presented; now is the time to consider how it sounds. The strategies presented in the chapter bear out the promise of the introduction: creating effective sentences *can* be learned. Students are reminded that content and commitment precede stylistic concerns; the pretty package doesn't matter if there's nothing of consequence in it, or if the giver doesn't care about it. If students do have significant content, and if they are committed to the paper, then they're ready to learn strategies for controlling sentence length and rhythm. The strategies presented follow a logical progression, with initial focus on monitoring length, then on varying length, and finally on controlling rhythm. In addition to extensive sample paragraphs, a paragraph from a student paper is analyzed for length and rhythm. Exercises also provide students with practice in revising and analyzing model paragraphs, along with ample opportunity to apply the material in the chapter to their own papers.

There is less art than you might think in creating effective sentences. A writer's intuition is built on very specific skills, which are used so often and are so familiar that they become automatic or intuitive. A writer's intuition has first to do with content and commitment. Effective sentences are always the work of someone who has something to say, who believes in that content, and who therefore will take time to revise so that the sentences are not only accurate and correct but also inviting.

Beyond content and commitment, good writing has much to do with timing: how long a sentence takes to read and what rhythmic effects are encountered along the way. Considerations of length and rhythm alone will not make a sentence memorable. But any significant content, once established, can be expressed with a more or less effective style, and effective style has a great deal to do with sentence length and rhythm (as well as conciseness, parallelism, and emphasis—see Chapters 17, 18, and 19).

20a Monitoring sentence length

1 Track the length of your sentences.

Often, without realizing it, writers will work with favorite sentence patterns. For reasons of personal preference and audience analysis, the average length of each writer's sentences will differ. Common sense dictates that when a sentence gets so long that readers forget important sentence parts (for instance, the subject), sentence length should be revised.

Track the length of your sentences. Especially in the late stages of revision, once you are certain of a paper's content, you are in a good position to monitor the length of sentences, which is the first step in varying length and rhythm. *Variety* means variation from an average. If you want to vary sentence length, you must be aware of the average length of your sentences. The information in the box on the next page will help you make that determination.

As you begin tracking sentence length, following a technique like the one suggested here will not be necessary for long. Soon you will develop a writer's intuition about sentence length; you will begin to vary the number of words from sentence to sentence because you *feel* the need. This *feeling* will be based on an analysis similar to the one shown here.

Tracking Sentence Length

Any given sentence in a paragraph is long or short in relation to the *average* number of words per sentence in that paragraph. A simple process of counting and dividing will reveal your average sentence length.

1. Number the sentences in a paragraph and write those numbers in a column on a piece of paper.
2. Count and record the number of words in each sentence.
3. Add the word counts for step 2 to obtain the total number of words in the paragraph.
4. Divide the number of words in the paragraph (step 3) by the number of sentences in the paragraph (step 1): this number is your average sentence length for the paragraph.

Consider a sentence to be *average* in length if it has *five words more or less* than your average. Consider a sentence *long* if it has six or more words more than your average and *short* if it has six or fewer words less than your average.

5. Return to the listing you made in step 2, and designate each sentence of your paragraph as *average* length, *short,* or *long.* These designations apply to your writing only. They are relative terms, representing different sentence lengths for different writers.

2 Vary sentence length and alternate the length of consecutive sentences.

Regardless of average sentence length, good writers will (1) write sentences in a paragraph that vary from their average and (2) avoid placing two or more very short or very long sentences consecutively (see 19c-4).

The paragraph below was written by a student, Jenafer Trahar. At twenty words, Trahar's average sentence length is slightly less than that of other stylistically strong writers. She is careful both to vary length and to alternate lengths in consecutive sentences.

> (1) One major problem with the commercialization of college sports is the exploitation of student-athletes, many of whom come to school on athletic scholarships. (2) Frequently, student-athletes don't deserve to be admitted to a school. (3) Many colleges routinely lower admissions requirements for their ball players, and some schools will even waive requirements for that exceptional athlete, who without his sports abilities might not have had a place on a college campus. (4) Most kids not interested in academics would normally shun a college education. (5) But for gifted athletes, college appears to be a road that leads to the pros. (6) Or so they think. (7) According to Richard Lapchick of the Center for the Study of Sport in Society, twelve thousand high school athletes participate in sports in any one year, but only one will subsequently play for a professional team.
>
> —JENAFER TRAHAR

REFERENCES

CHRISTENSEN, FRANCIS. "A Generative Rhetoric of the Sentence." *Notes Toward a New Rhetoric: Essays for Teachers.* 2nd ed. Eds. Francis Christensen and Bonniejean Christensen. New York: Harper, 1978. The cumulative sentence can be effective in achieving emphasis of ideas in sentences.

CORBETT, EDWARD P. J. "Approaches to the Study of Style." *Teaching Composition: 12 Bibliographical Essays.* 2nd ed. Ed. Gary Tate. Fort Worth: Texas Christian UP, 1987. 83–130. A survey of recent scholarship on style.

———. *Classical Rhetoric for the Modern Student.* New York: Oxford UP, 1965. 410–16. Analyzes characteristics of sentence style and structure.

LANHAM, RICHARD. *Analyzing Prose.* New York: Scribner's, 1983. Extensive advice on revising for style.

WALPOLE, JANE R. "The Vigorous Pursuit of Grace and Style." *The Writing Instructor* 1 (1982): 163–69. An analysis of revision for style.

WILLIAMS, JAMES D. *Preparing to Teach Writing.* Belmont, CA: Wadsworth, 1989. 301–02, 306. A discussion of sentence style, including length.

WILLIAMS, JOSEPH. *Style: Ten Lessons in Clarity and Grace.* 2nd ed. Glenview: Scott, 1989. Provides guidelines for writers in pursuit of stylistic emphasis in their writing.

FOR DISCUSSION

To ease students into monitoring sentence length, you may want to have the class practice together on the paragraph below.

> Because my mother was thrifty and talented, I had always worn handmade Heidi dresses or high-style outfits bought at Filene's Basement. When I wasn't dressing up, I was stripping down to bare bottom and marching down the neighbor's driveway. By comparison, the Academie clothing was boring and restrictive, two no-nos in my view. Every day we wore the same black uniform with a white stiff collar and clip-on black leatherette bow tie. Black serge bloomers covered white cotton panties, and a vest with attached garters held up long black cotton stockings. We even

(continued)

had black serge aprons to keep us clean. This unnatural attire cost twelve dollars for two complete sets, with the apron extra at a dollar twenty-five. My attempts at distinctive trim were always thwarted. The Sisters confiscated my dandelion chains and buttercup bracelets and made me scrub clean the crayon embroidery on my celluloid cuffs. (Gretchen Sentry)

1. 21	148 words + 9 sentences = 16.4 –
2. 18	word average sentence length
3. 14	*Paragraph has two long sen-
4. 19	tences, one short, two long, one
5. 19	short, one long, one short, one long.
6. 10	*No short sentences are placed
7. 18	consecutively.
8. 8	*Twice two long sentences are
9. 21	placed consecutively, each preceded by or followed by short sentences.

TEACHING IDEAS

One of the most successful pedagogical techniques in composition is for the instructor to share his or her writing with the class. Analysis of sentence length provides an ideal opportunity for you to take this step. Find several paragraphs with which you are comfortable, and ask the class to perform an analysis on them, noting the variety of lengths as well as the placement of sentences of different lengths within the paragraphs. (In large classes, you may want to begin this exercise with small groups. When groups report their findings to the class, a general discussion can follow.)

EXERCISE 1

Individual responses

GROUP ACTIVITY

Ask students to do this exercise in groups—students who understand the concept can help out those who aren't sure of what they're doing. Then they can compare average sentence lengths, proving for themselves that average length is indeed different for different writers. They can also compare the variety of sentence lengths used by different writers in a single paragraph.

Analysis of sentence length

(20 word avg.)
1. 24 words (average)
2. 11 words (short)
3. 36 words (long)
4. 12 words (short)
5. 15 words (average)
6. 4 words (short)
7. 36 words (long)

$138 \div 7 \approx 20$

Trahar's sentence lengths are varied: three short, two long, two average.

- No short sentences are placed consecutively.
- No long sentences are placed consecutively.
- No sentences of average length are placed consecutively.

Notice that Trahar varies sentence lengths in the paragraph, and at no point does she write consecutive sentences of the same length. Trahar regularly alternates short sentences with long or average-length ones.

Varying Sentence Length and Alternating the Length of Consecutive Sentences

While no precise formula exists for determining how many long or short sentences should be used in a paragraph, you may find these general principles helpful:

- Determine the average length of sentences in a paragraph.
- Plan to vary from that average by using short and long sentences.
- Use short sentences to break up strings of longer ones.
- Avoid placing short sentences consecutively unless you are doing so for specific stylistic effect.
- Avoid placing more than two or three long sentences consecutively.
- Avoid placing more than three or four sentences of average length consecutively.

EXERCISE 1

Choose three paragraphs you have written recently (not necessarily from the same paper) and analyze them for sentence length. Follow the steps laid out in the preceding box. On finishing your analysis, you should have figured your average sentence length for each paragraph and designated each sentence in the paragraph as *short, average,* or *long.* Write a brief paragraph in which you summarize your findings.

20b Strategies for varying sentence length

Once you have determined the average length of your sentences and the extent to which you vary from that average, you should become familiar with techniques for manipulating sentence length. The techniques discussed here will be helpful *only* if you are working with sentences that are already concise and direct. Sentence length can always be reduced by eliminating wordiness, and revising for conciseness should be your first strategy in managing sentence length. See Chapter 17 for advice.

1 Control the use of coordination.

Coordination—the use of coordinating and correlative conjunctions and of conjunctive adverbs to compound sentence elements—is the principal means by which parts of two or more sentences are joined into a single sentence (see 19a). In its favor, coordination reduces the overall length of a paragraph by allowing a writer to combine sentence parts (or entire sentences) and eliminate redundancy. The following is a partial paragraph.

> Between 12,000 and 10,000 B.C., the massive icecap began to recede. The sea level rose as the enormous quantities of ice melted. At the same time, huge land masses such as Britain and Scandinavia, once ice-covered, began to reappear.

The cost of combining sentences with coordination is that the length of the revised sentence will increase. The first sentence in the preceding paragraph has eleven words, and the set of sentences, thirty-nine. In revision, three sentences are combined into one, but that one sentence now has thirty-five words:

> Between 12,000 and 10,000 B.C., the massive icecap which had covered huge land masses such as Britain and Scandinavia began to recede, and the enormous quantities of melting ice caused the sea level to rise.

If you decided that the combined sentence made possible by coordination was too long (and you would only know this in relation to the sentences preceding and following it in an actual paragraph), you could break the combined sentence in two:

> Between 12,000 and 10,000 B.C., the massive icecap which had covered huge land masses such as Britain and Scandinavia began to recede. The enormous quantities of melting ice caused the sea level to rise.

In this second revision, the first sentence has twenty-two words, and the set of sentences, thirty-four—still a reduction in length from the original.

2 Control the use of modifying phrases and clauses.

One way of controlling sentence length is to control the extent to which you use modifying phrases and clauses (see 7d, e). Two types of clauses and four types of phrases can function in sentences as adjectives or adverbs.

Infinitive phrases can function as adjectives or adverbs.

LOOKING BACK

This section refers students to several chapters in the handbook. If you can determine which students could benefit from reviewing a specific area, assign that chapter to the students.

TEACHING IDEAS

If you are aware of students whose uncertainty about their writing results in excessive coordination, you may want to spend some extra time with them on this section. Ask these students to review several of their papers for problems with excessive coordination. After underlining relevant sentences, they can revise by breaking up overly long sentences. As they read the entire paper with their revisions, they should comment on the effect of eliminating excessive coordination.

ADDITIONAL EXERCISE A

Reduce the length of each of the following sentences by converting modifying clauses to phrases and converting clauses or phrases to single words.

1. Many children who belong to the working class do not derive benefits from education.
2. In elite schools, children develop their powers of analysis and intellect.
3. Because they feel overwhelmed by difficult material, some students withdraw.
4. Children whose parents have a good deal of money attend the best schools.
5. When parents become involved, schools often prosper.

Suggested responses:

1. Many working-class children do not derive benefits from education.
2. In elite schools, children develop their analytical and intellectual powers.
3. Feeling overwhelmed by difficult material, some students withdraw.
4. Children of wealthy parents attend the best schools.
5. With parental involvement, schools often prosper.

ADJECTIVE Water is not a resource *to squander.*

ADVERB Ranchers draw water from the Ogallala aquifer *in order to feed livestock.*

Prepositional phrases can function as adjectives or adverbs.

ADJECTIVE We assume incorrectly that rain will replenish whatever amount *of water* we may use up.

ADVERB Ranchers and farmers have begun arguing *over water rights.*

Participial phrases function as adjectives.

ADJECTIVE *Alarmed by the diminishing supply of water,* rural and municipal leaders have begun serious attempts to find new sources.

Appositive phrases function as adjectives.

ADJECTIVE In Los Angeles, *a city that has suffered through severe droughts,* engineers have considered building desalination plants.

Clauses with subordinating conjunctions function as adverbs.

ADVERB *When a city is threatened with water shortages,* rationing often becomes necessary.

Clauses with relative pronouns function as adjectives.

ADJECTIVE The melting of ice, *which would be towed south from the Arctic Ocean,* is one solution that would supply millions of gallons of fresh water.

Convert modifying clauses to phrases.

If you determine that a sentence is too long in relation to its neighbors, you can reduce sentence length by converting a modifying clause into a phrase.

> *When a city is threatened with water shortages,* drastic actions become necessary.
>
> *In times of drought,* drastic actions become necessary. [The dependent clause is shortened to two prepositional phrases.]

Move modifying phrases from one sentence to another.

If you determine that a sentence is too long in relation to its neighbors, you may be able to strip a sentence of a modifier, which you can then move to an adjacent sentence (where it may have a new function).

> In Los Angeles, *a city that has suffered through severe droughts,* engineers have considered building desalination plants.
>
> In Los Angeles, engineers have considered building desalination plants. Recently, *that city has suffered through severe droughts,* and municipal leaders are now ready to consider long-term solutions to a persistent problem. [The appositive phrase is converted to a subject and predicate in the new sentence.]

Substitute a single-word modifier for a phrase- or clause-length modifier.

If you determine that a sentence is too long in relation to its neighbors, you may be able to convert phrases or clauses to single-word adjectives or adverbs. In the following example an important detail (about towing icebergs) is lost in the conversion and would need to be added to some other sentence; still, the desired result, a briefer sentence, is achieved.

> The melting of ice, *which would be towed south from the Arctic Ocean,* is one solution that would supply millions of gallons of fresh water.
>
> The melting of *arctic* ice is one solution that would supply millions of gallons of fresh water.

3 Control the use of phrases and clauses used as nouns.

Sentences can be combined by converting the key words of one sentence into a phrase or clause that then functions as a noun (as a subject, object, or complement) in a second sentence. The disadvantage of the revision is that the newly combined sentence tends to be long.

Infinitive phrases can function as nouns:

> The English during the Tudor period drank ale in place of water.
> It was a widespread custom.

Combined *To drink ale with one's breakfast,* rather than water, was a widespread custom in Tudor England. [The infinitive phrase functions as the subject.]

Gerund phrases can function as nouns:

> As methods of *preserving meat,* they resorted to "dry-salting" or to soaking (or dipping) the meat in vinegar. [The gerund phrase functions as object of the preposition *of.*]

Noun phrases and clauses can function as nouns:

> Since *poison by intent and poison by spoiled food* result in the same miserable end, monarchs *would* routinely keep food samplers nearby. [The noun phrase functions as the subject of the dependent clause.]
>
> The kitchen is *where the tasting began,* and the test was repeated just before the food was served. [The noun clause functions as a subject complement.]

If you determine that a sentence is too long in relation to its neighbors, try to identify a phrase or clause functioning as a noun. Revise the sentence, possibly moving the noun phrase or clause into its own sentence.

Sentence with a noun clause *The fact that much of the water was polluted* was one main reason the Tudor English substituted ale for water.

Revision Much of the water in Tudor England was polluted. This condition prompted many to substitute ale for water.

GROUP ACTIVITY

This activity will provide students with the opportunity to use clauses and phrases as nouns and to judge the effectiveness of such use within paragraphs. Ask each group to compose a paragraph of five or six sentences, in which several sentences use a clause or a phrase as a noun. Upon completing this task, each group will pass their paragraphs on to another group. The second group will determine which sentences in the paragraph seem too long and which seem to be a comfortable length. Students should discover that in a paragraph the appropriate length of a sentence will be determined not only by the sound of the sentence itself but also by its positioning in the paragraph. Some sentences that seem fine out of context may seem too long in relation to the surrounding sentences in the paragraph.

EXERCISE 2

Exercise 2 is a rewrite of a paragraph by Northrop Frye, from *The Educated Imagination.* Frye's original paragraph appears at the end of the chapter as the example to be analyzed in Exercise 5.

EXERCISE 3

Individual responses

GROUP ACTIVITY

This exercise, as well as Exercise 4, will work well with groups. Have students compare responses in small groups. After hearing all of the responses, the group can decide which is the most appealing, and explain why.

ADDITIONAL EXERCISE B

Rewrite each of the following sentences by moving the modifiers and transitions to as many different positions as possible in each sentence. Then read all of the sentences aloud to get a sense of the different rhythms.

1. Although it seems to be a simple word, *territory* can mean many different things.
2. For example, one's personal territory is the immediate area surrounding one's body.
3. Among nations, territory means the land governed by a particular state.
4. In cities, certain territories belong to different gangs.

ESL NOTE Noun clauses in English have several uses. Notice the special rules in constructions involving *wish that* . . . (see 43b-6). Indirect quotation or reported speech is a very common special use involving *that* clauses. Section 43b-6 describes the tense sequences encountered in reported speech.

EXERCISE 2

Use any of the strategies discussed thus far in the chapter to combine the following sentences. Vary sentence length and alternate the length of consecutive sentences. Following is a brief listing of conjunctions you may want to use (see 19a, b). *Coordinating conjunctions:* and, but, or, nor, for, so, yet. *Correlative conjunctions:* not only/but also, either/or, both/and. *Conjunctive adverbs:* however, moreover, furthermore, therefore, consequently. *Subordinating conjunctions:* when, although, while, since, because, before. *Relative pronouns:* who, which, that.

> I have been teaching English literature in a university. I have also been studying literature. I have been doing these things for twenty-five years. Certain questions stick in one's mind in this job; actually, they do in any job. They persist not only because people keep asking them. Such questions stick in one's mind because they are inspired by the very fact of being in a university. First one might ask what is the benefit of studying literature. Then one might ask whether literature helps us think more clearly, or whether it helps us feel more sensitively, or whether literature helps us live a better life than we could if we did not have it.

EXERCISE 3

Follow the instructions in Exercise 2 and revise the three paragraphs that you analyzed for sentence length in Exercise 1. Revise to vary sentence length and to alternate the length of consecutive sentences.

20c Strategies for controlling sentence rhythm

1 Use modifying phrases and clauses to alter sentence rhythm.

Varying sentence openings is the most direct way of varying the rhythm of a sentence or the cadence with which the sentence is read. Sentences consist of a subject, followed by a verb and then an object (if the verb is transitive) or a complement (if the verb is linking). Any of these important elements can be modified, and it is primarily through placement of modifiers that sentences change rhythm. When you want to alter sentence rhythm, revise sentence structure by changing the extent and location of your modifiers.

MODIFIERS CONCENTRATED AT THE *BEGINNING* OF A SENTENCE:

> *Providing a sense of solidarity for the community,* the National Puerto Rican Forum voiced the concerns of its members and lobbied for new laws.

ACROSS THE CURRICULUM

Controlling Sentence Length and Rhythm

You will find writers in all discipline areas who vary sentence length and rhythm to achieve an effective style. Varied sentences—short with long, simple patterns interspersed with compound and complex ones—help to maintain a reader's interest. Regardless of disciplinary background, the writer's constant goal is to interest readers. In the following passage, psychologist David Shapiro attempts to define, in part, "rigid thinking." Observe how Shapiro varies sentence length, controls sentence rhythm with phrases and clauses, and uses different sentence types.*

> What exactly is meant by rigidity of thinking? Consider as a commonplace example the sort of thinking one encounters in a discussion with a compulsive, rigid person, the kind of person we also call "dogmatic" or "opinionated." Even casual conversation with such a person is often very frustrating, and it is so for a particular reason. It is not simply that one meets with unexpected opposition. On the contrary, such discussion is typically frustrating just because one experiences neither real disagreement nor agreement. Instead, there is no meeting of minds at all, and the impression is simply of not being heard, of not receiving any but perfunctory attention.

Sentence types: question, command, direct statement

Sentence structures: simple, compound, complex

Sentence length (based on an average length of 18 words): short, long, average, short, average, long

Purposeful repetition:

"a compulsive, rigid person, the kind of person we also call . . . "
"the impression is simply of not being heard, of not receiving . . . "

*The passage is excerpted from David Shapiro, *Neurotic Styles* (New York: Basic, 1965) 24.

5. For people living in the suburbs, territory might be the neighborhood.

Answers:

1. *Territory,* although it seems to be a simple word, can mean many different things.
   Territory can mean many different things, although it seems to be a simple word.
2. One's personal territory, for example, is the immediate area surrounding one's body.
   One's personal territory is the immediate area surrounding one's body, for example.
3. Territory among nations means the land governed by a particular state.
4. Certain territories in cities belong to different gangs.
   Certain territories belong to different gangs in cities.
5. Territory for people living in the suburbs might be the neighborhood.
   Territory might be the neighborhood for people living in the suburbs.

MODIFIERS CONCENTRATED IN THE *MIDDLE* OF A SENTENCE:

> The Forum, *the first such organization on the mainland USA,* was established by members of the Puerto Rican community in New York City.

MODIFIERS CONCENTRATED AT THE *END* OF A SENTENCE:

> The Forum and similar organizations have lobbied for laws *that outlaw discriminatory practices against Puerto Ricans in such matters as housing, employment, voting rights, and education.*

Sentence rhythm is also related to length. A brief sentence with relatively few modifiers offers a strong rhythmical contrast to longer, heavily modified sentences.

> The Commonwealth of Puerto Rico was created in 1952.

Vary the position of phrases.

Phrases that function as adverbs (see 20b-2) may, like adverbs, be moved around in a sentence. Because such movement can change meaning

ADDITIONAL EXERCISE C

Revise the following sentences to smooth out the rhythm. If necessary, divide a sentence into two sentences.

1. Job dissatisfaction, a problem that affects workers at any point in their careers, because of its pervasiveness, costs American business billions.
2. In the past, when much of the workforce was blue collar, and white-collar jobs seemed meaningful, job dissatisfaction seemed confined to factory workers.
3. One cost to business, according to a study at the University of Louisville, is found in absenteeism, which results in lost productivity and high replacement expenses.
4. Inept managers, who often mistreat employees, or authoritarian bosses, who don't allow workers a say in how a business is run, can be a cause of negative employee attitudes, which result in absenteeism and poor performance.
5. Some companies, eager to change employee attitudes, now that they understand the problem better, have begun programs which seem successful.

Suggested responses:

1. Job dissatisfaction can affect workers at any point in their careers. Because of its pervasiveness, such dissatisfaction costs American business billions.
2. Job dissatisfaction seemed confined to factory workers in the past, when much of the workforce was blue collar and white-collar jobs seemed meaningful.
3. According to a University of Louisville study, absenteeism is one cost to business, resulting in lost productivity and high replacement expenses.
4. Negative employee attitudes resulting in absenteeism and poor performance can be caused by inept managers, who often mistreat employees, or by authoritarian bosses, who don't allow workers a say in how a business is run.
5. Some companies, now that they understand the problem better, are eager to change employee attitudes. They have begun programs which seem successful.

as well as sentence rhythm, beware of altering the meaning of your sentences when revising for style.

> I reached our new home *on Monday,* wondering whether the movers would arrive.

SHIFTED RHYTHM *On Monday,* I reached our new home, wondering whether the movers would arrive.

SHIFTED MEANING I reached our new home, wondering whether the movers would arrive *on Monday.* [The timing of the movers' arrival has now become the issue.]

A phrase that functions as an adjective (see 20b-2) should be placed as close as possible to the noun it modifies to avoid confusion and faulty reference.

FAULTY Zebulon Pike ventured west to the Rockies, *an explorer of the Mississippi.*

REVISED Zebulon Pike, *an explorer of the Mississippi,* ventured west to the Rockies.

SHIFTED RHYTHM *An explorer of the Mississippi,* Zebulon Pike ventured west to the Rockies.

Vary the position of clauses.

Like single-word adverbs and phrases functioning as adverbs, adverb clauses can be moved around in a sentence. An adverb clause that begins a sentence can be shifted to the interior or to the end of the sentence. The placement of the clause determines its punctuation.

> *After so many white settlers had come from England,* it was not surprising that the English language, English customs, and English ways of government dominated America.
>
> It was not surprising, *after so many white settlers had come from England,* that the English language, English customs, and English ways of government dominated America.
>
> It was not surprising that the English language, English customs, and English ways of government dominated America *after so many white settlers had come from England.*

Place a dependent clause that functions as an adjective next to the word it modifies. Neglecting to do so may confuse readers. (See Chapter 15 on revising to correct misplaced modifiers.)

FAULTY The Great Pyramid at Giza has a base area of 13 acres which was built in the fourth dynasty for the pharaoh Khufu.

REVISED The Great Pyramid at Giza, which was built in the fourth dynasty for the pharaoh Khufu, has a base area of 13 acres.

SHIFTED RHYTHM Built in the fourth dynasty for the pharaoh Khufu, the Great Pyramid at Giza has a base area of 13 acres.

Vary the position of transitions.

Experienced writers make frequent use of **transitions,** words that like logical bridges help readers move from one idea to another within a sentence, between sentences, or between paragraphs (see 5d-3). Brief transitions include *for instance, for example, on the one hand, on the other hand, in addition,* and *additionally.* Conjunctive adverbs also serve as transitions: *however, moreover, consequently,* and *therefore.* Transitions like these can be moved around in a sentence; when their position changes, sentence rhythm changes.

> Advertising is an ancient art. *For example,* some early advertisements appear about three thousand B.C. as stenciled inscriptions on bricks made by the Babylonians.

> Advertising is an ancient art. Some early advertisements, *for example,* appear about three thousand B.C. as stenciled inscriptions on bricks made by the Babylonians.

2 Revise individual sentences with a disruptive rhythm.

As with the length of a sentence, the rhythm of a sentence should be evaluated both on its own terms and in relation to neighboring sentences. A sentence that starts and stops a reader repeatedly has a disruptive rhythm and should be revised.

DISRUPTIVE RHYTHM Francisco Goya's *Los Caprichos,* a series of eighty etchings, published in 1799, described by the author as a criticism of "human errors and vices," and now considered as one of his finest works, was a commercial failure.

Because its erratic, bumpy rhythm interferes with understanding, this sentence needs revision. Revision in this case might lead to two sentences:

REVISED Francisco Goya's *Los Caprichos,* a series of eighty etchings, was published in 1799. Described by the author as a criticism of "human errors and vices," it is now considered as one of his finest works even though, with only 27 sets having been sold, it was a commercial failure.

3 Revise groups of sentences to avoid a repetitive rhythm.

The rhythm of a sentence in isolation might be perfectly acceptable. Set in a paragraph, however, this same sentence may have a rhythm that too closely resembles the rhythm of other sentences. Unintentional repetition of sentence structures and rhythms usually results in a stylistically weak paragraph. Revise by restructuring one or more sentences.

UNINTENTIONALLY REPEATING RHYTHM

> A series of eighty etchings, Francisco Goya's *Los Caprichos* was published in 1799. Described by the author as a criticism of "human errors and vices," it is now considered as one of his finest works. With only 27 sets having been sold, it was considered a commercial failure.

The sentence structures and rhythms in this paragraph too closely resemble each other: every sentence begins with a modifying phrase or clause. For stylistic reasons, the structure of one or more sentences should be changed.

REVISED A series of eighty etchings, Francisco Goya's *Los Caprichos* was published in 1799. The series was described by the author as a criticism of "human errors and vices." Now considered as one of his finest works, it was a commercial failure, with only 27 sets having been sold.

4 Vary sentence types.

Sentences are classified by structure and function. There are four functional types of sentences (7f-1). The direct statement is a *declarative* sentence: *The driver turned the ignition key.* The question is an *interrogative* sentence: *Was the engine flooded?* The exclamation, or *exclamatory* sentence, expresses emotion: *What an awful fire! How terrible!* The command, or *imperative* sentence, expresses an order or strong desire: *Get back! Don't go near that!*

Use occasional questions for variety and focus.

For the most part, academic writing is restricted to declarative and interrogative sentences. Researchers and writers pose questions, conduct investigations, and write responses. The occasional question posed in a paragraph will be important to the content, but a question also introduces a unique rhythm.

Vary the structure of sentences.

Varying sentence structure, as you have seen in 20c, will vary sentence rhythm. There are four structural types (see 7f-2). Writing that is strong stylistically tends to mix all four types of structure. A **simple sentence** has a single subject and a single verb or predicate. (In the examples that follow, simple subjects will be underlined once and simple predicates, twice.)

> Before the rise of the railroad, most business people based decisions on experience, instinct, and information that was often guesswork.

A **compound sentence,** which has two subjects and two predicates, is created when a writer joins two independent clauses with a conjunction (see 7f-2 and 19a).

> Textile mills used fairly complex methods of planning, but they still relied on preindustrial operations.

TEACHING IDEAS

Ask students to analyze one or two of their papers, identifying each sentence type within the paper. While most academic papers will consist primarily of declarative sentences, you can advise students of the option to insert an occasional interrogative sentence to vary the rhythm. Ask students to find places in their papers where a question might be appropriate, and to attempt to use occasional questions in future papers.

GROUP ACTIVITY

This activity can help both accomplished and weaker writers alike to appreciate the role of sentence structures in a paragraph. Ask students to bring in one or two of their papers. (Papers used for the preceding "Teaching Ideas" exercise would be fine.) Then divide the class into groups with mixed abilities, and ask students within groups to exchange papers. Students will then identify the structure of each sentence within the papers, trying to determine whether more variety is needed. The discussion that follows within groups should help students develop the ability to make informed stylistic decisions about their writing.

A **complex sentence** has one independent clause and one or more dependent clauses (see 7e and 19b). The dependent clause in this example is italicized.

> The system of train control developed by American railroads accomplished a managerial revolution *that brought more change in business decision-making and operational methods in twenty-five years than had occurred in the preceding five centuries.*

A **compound-complex sentence** has at least two independent clauses and one dependent clause. The dependent clause in this example is italicized.

> *When an employee performed badly in a well-managed shop,* the shop lost only that employee's output; no great harm resulted.

Varying Sentence Rhythm

Variety in sentence structures and rhythms is the mark of stylistically strong writing. While no rules govern exactly how a writer should vary rhythm from sentence to sentence, you may find the following general principles helpful.

- Use phrases, clauses, and transitional expressions to vary sentence beginnings.
- Consciously shift the location of phrase- and clause-length modifiers in a paragraph: locate modifiers at the beginning of some sentences, in the middle of others, and at the end of others.
- Use short sentences to break up strings of long, heavily modified sentences.
- Limit your concentration of phrase- and clause-length modifiers to one and possibly two locations in a sentence. Heavily modifying a sentence at the beginning, middle, *and* end will create a burden stylistically.
- Vary sentence types.

Analyze sentence rhythm.

As an illustration of a student's effective use of sentence variety, consider again the paragraph by Jenafer Trahar in 20a-2. Here are the types of sentences she used:

(Structural) type of sentence	*Sentence opens with*
1. complex	noun phrase functioning as the subject
2. simple	single-word modifier
3. compound-complex	subject
4. simple	subject
5. simple	coordinating conjunction and modifying phrase
6. simple	coordinating conjunction
7. compound	modifying phrase

The preceding analysis may look technical, but peel away the numbers and structural descriptions and you have a paragraph that succeeds in both content and style. While her sentences are declarative (typical of academic writing), Trahar makes use of all four structural sentence types: simple, compound, complex, and compound-complex. What is more, she nicely varies the openings of her sentences, beginning twice with simple subjects, once with a long phrase that functions as a subject, and the remainder of the time with a modifier or a conjunction.

Jenafer Trahar's paragraph is stylistically sophisticated. Every technique she has used to gain that sophistication has been discussed in this chapter, and you can apply these same techniques to your own writing. Like Trahar, you will need to begin with a subject you care about. When revising for style, you may want to consult other chapters in this section on matters of conciseness (17), parallelism (18), and emphasis (19).

EXERCISE 4

Revise the following paragraph to eliminate the choppiness created by too many short sentences. In your revision, use all the techniques you have learned in this chapter for varying sentence length and rhythm.

> The term "derelicts" in naval usage refers to abandoned ships. Derelicts are rarely seen anymore. They were more frequently sighted in the days of the tall-masted sailing ships. At one time they were considered dangerous. In the days before radar, a passing ship could encounter a derelict with absolutely no warning. For example, in 1906, the *St. Louis* had a near-collision with the derelict *Dunmore.* Some derelicts managed to remain afloat for several months. The *Fanny Wolston* stayed afloat for at least 1408 days. Derelicts are to the sea what ghost towns are to the Old West. They become ghostly entities. They were floating haunted houses. The wreck inspires pity. The derelict evokes awe.

EXERCISE 5

Read the paragraph that follows, and analyze the component sentences for length and rhythm. Structure your analysis like the analysis of Jenafer Trahar's paragraph in 20a-2. Be sure to include a paragraph that summarizes your observations.

> For the past twenty-five years I have been teaching and studying English literature in a university. As in any other job, certain questions stick in one's mind, not because people keep asking them but because they're the questions inspired by the very fact of being in such a place. What good is the study of literature? Does it help us think more clearly, or feel more sensitively, or live a better life than we could without it?
>
> —NORTHROP FRYE

EXERCISE 6

Reexamine the three paragraphs that you revised for sentence length in Exercise 3. Revise these paragraphs a final time for sentence rhythm, using the techniques you have learned in this chapter.

EXERCISE 4

Suggested revision:

The term "derelicts" in naval usage refers to abandoned ships. Derelicts, more frequently sighted in the days of the tall-masted sailing ships, are rarely seen anymore. At one time they were considered dangerous because, in the days before radar, a passing ship could encounter a derelict with absolutely no warning; for example, in 1906, the *St. Louis* had a near collision with the derelict *Dunmore.* Some derelicts managed to remain afloat for several months, like the *Fanny Wolston,* which stayed afloat for at least 1408 days. Derelicts are to the sea what ghost towns are to the Old West in that they become ghostly entities, floating haunted houses. While the wreck inspires pity, the derelict evokes awe.

EXERCISE 5

This paragraph is the original version of the paragraph for analysis in Exercise 2. Frye's sentences average twenty words. The first and last sentence of the paragraph are of average length; the second sentence is long; the third sentence is short. No sentences of the same length are placed consecutively.

Sentence length	Sentence opens with	Sentence type
1. average	Modifying phrase	simple
2. long	Modifying phrase	complex
3. short	Interrogative marker—*what*	simple
4. average	Interrogative marker—verb	simple (implied compound)

EXERCISE 6

Individual responses

PART VI
USING EFFECTIVE WORDS

CHAPTER 21

Choosing the Right Word

Your purpose as a writer and your intended audience profoundly affect your **diction**—your choice of words. Like the overall tone of a document, diction can be high or low, formal or informal, or any register between (see 3a-4). The English language usually gives you options in selecting words. Readers have a certain attention span and a certain radar; they know when writers are invested in their work—when, for instance, writers have taken time to state a thought precisely or to render a description vividly. A document that shows little concern for word choice will quickly lose its readers.

21a Learning denotation and connotation

Your first concern in selecting a word is to be sure that its **denotation,** or dictionary meaning, is appropriate for the sentence at hand. A careless writer might, for instance, state that in performing their jobs diplomats should know when to *precede.* Is this the intended meaning (when to go first), or did the writer mean that diplomats should know when to *proceed* (when to go forward)? Although these words look similar and sound nearly the same, their denotations are very different. Once you are satisfied that you are using a word correctly according to its denotation, consider its **connotations**—its implications, associations, and nuances of meaning. Consider these sentences:

His speech was *brief.*

His speech was *concise.*

His speech was *curt.*

His speech was *abbreviated.*

Brief, concise, curt, and *abbreviated:* These adjectives suggest brevity—but only the word "brief" has this single meaning, with no other associations. The word "brief" suggests nothing about the content of what is said, aside from its duration. Of the four adjectives, "curt" suggests a brief remark, but one made with a degree of rudeness. "Abbreviated" suggests that

KEY FEATURES

Beginning the section on effective word choice, this chapter calls attention to the fact that using appropriate diction reveals a writer's commitment to the subject and to the reader. The chapter begins with a discussion of denotation and connotation. In order to emphasize the importance of connotation, a particularly imaginative exercise asks students to choose from a group of synonyms the words they'd like to see describing themselves. A discussion of diction problems follows, focusing on common difficulties faced by student writers. As in previous chapters, the emphasis is on the positive. Rather than being warned away from certain usage, students are presented with strategies that will help them avoid problems. Standard topics such as idiom, general and specific words, figures of speech, and jargon are covered thoroughly. A refreshingly frank discussion of formal standard English acknowledges the political implications of standardization and the internal consistency of dialects, while at the same time conceding the need for a norm. Sexist language receives equally frank treatment, emphasizing the exclusion implicit in generic masculine terms. Examples are plentiful, and exercises allow students to create as well as to revise model passages.

ESL CUE

Students from the language groups that English has frequently borrowed from will have a problem with "false friends," words in English that look or sound very similar to words

(continued)

in their own language but that mean something different. (The formal term for these is *false cognates.*) For example, Spanish speakers will automatically misuse words like "molest," "sympathize," "reunion," "actual," "real," "college," "contradictory," and "frontier." French, Greek, and Russian speakers will have similar translation difficulties. In fact, the modern Greek use of many words is totally different from the meanings of English words derived from ancient Greek. See C.W.E. Kirk-Greene, *French False Friends* (Boston: Routledge & Kegan Paul, 1981) for a helpful discussion of this type of problem.

Unlike English speakers, second-language students will *not* have a wide range of synonyms in their own languages. English has an estimated 500,000 total words, while Spanish and French have only 200,000 and Russian has only 100,000. Such languages depend more on context, innuendo, and multiple meanings than does English, whose multiple vocabularies derived from the Anglo-Saxon, French, and Greek/Latin are notoriously troublesome for second-language learners. What we gain in number of words, however, we perhaps lose in shades of connotation. Even the very best language-to-language dictionaries are 50 percent shorter than an equivalently bulky though pedestrian English-to-English dictionary, and thus stint connotation and subtlety. For home use, every ESL student should own a respectable English-to-English dictionary of at least 40,000 words.

Students who rely on dictionaries that translate from their language to English should be warned that such dictionaries may be dated or erroneous.

EXERCISE 1

Individual responses

GROUP ACTIVITY

To accustom students to differentiating between shades of meaning, provide groups with three or four common words for which there are several synonyms with different connotations (e.g., *crowd, angry, thin*). Ask groups to come up with as many synonyms as they can, and discuss the differences in connotations.

the speaker has more to say, but is being purposely brief. And "concise" suggests mental rigor and discipline, directed at making one's statements as brief and accurate as possible. Your choice among these words with their different connotations will make a difference in how readers react to your writing.

EXERCISE 1

Given the following set of words, state which word in each set you would prefer someone to use in describing you. Why? Choose one set of words and, in a paragraph, discuss what you understand to be the differences in connotation among the words. Use a dictionary, if necessary.

1. thrifty, economical, provident, frugal
2. reserved, inhibited, restrained, aloof
3. strange, bizarre, eccentric, peculiar, weird
4. lively, alert, enthusiastic, pert, spirited, sprightly
5. sentimental, emotional, maudlin, mushy

21b Revising awkward diction

At times you may find the abbreviation *"AWK"* in the margins of your papers, with a line leading to a phrase or to a particular word. *Awkward diction,* or word choice, interrupts the process of communication. It momentarily stops an audience from reading by calling attention to a word that is somehow not quite right for a sentence. How can you avoid this difficulty? Until you have more experience with the ways of words, you will not be able to avoid it entirely. However, you can minimize awkward writing by guarding against four common errors: inappropriate connotation, inappropriate idiom, straining to sound learned, and unintentional euphony (rhyming, etc.).

1 Choosing words with an appropriate connotation

Frequently, *awkward diction* means that a word's connotation is inappropriate. The sentence in which the word appears is grammatical; the word in question is the right part of speech; but the word's meaning seems only partially correct for the sentence.

AWKWARD The professor urged *abstinence* in times of emotional stress. [Does the writer mean to suggest the avoidance of alcohol only? The sentence seems to suggest something else.]

If you look at a dictionary's usage entry for abstinence, you will see that there are synonyms for this word with nearly the same denotation but which might have a less awkward and limited connotation.

REVISED The professor urged *sobriety* in times of emotional stress.

REVISED The professor urged emotional *restraint.* [The revisions do not limit the advice to avoiding alcohol.]

2 Following standard English idioms

An **idiom** is a grouping of words, one of which is usually a preposition, whose meaning may or may not be apparent based solely on simple dictionary definitions. Moreover, the grammar of idioms—particularly the choice of prepositions used with them—is a matter of customary usage and is often difficult, if not impossible, to explain. Native speakers of English know intuitively that "running *across* an old letter" is a legitimate phrase (often listed in the dictionary), while "running *in* an old letter" is not. The difference is very difficult to explain, even for native speakers. Often, our attempts at using idioms result in awkwardness.

NOT IDIOMATIC When the intruder left, the manager *got the courage* to call the police. [Idiomatically, we do not normally *get* courage; we either have it or we do not.]

IDIOMATIC When the intruder left, the manager *got up the courage* to call the police. [The standard idiom implies that courage is summoned from within when needed.]

To avoid awkwardness, memorize idioms or do not use them at all. You can refer to the detailed listings in a dictionary to find some idioms; for others, you must listen carefully to the patterns of common usage. The box on the following page shows some common idiomatic expressions in English.

3 Writing directly rather than straining to sound learned

When you are new to an area of study, or for that matter new to a social group, it is natural to want to fit in and sound as if you know what you are talking or writing about. In academics, this desire shows when students strain to take on the learned diction of professors. Some students try so hard they will use words that do not exist in any dialect of English.

AWKWARD The character's grief and *upsetion* were extreme. [The word does not exist.]

AWKWARD *Disconcern* is common among the employees at that factory. [*Disinterest, indifference,* or *unconcern* could be used.]

At times, students straining at sophistication will choose lengthy, complicated phrasings when simpler ones will do; they will favor pretentious language because they believe this is the way learned people express themselves. The following sentence is *not* erudite.

AWKWARD The eccentricities of the characters could not fail to endear them to this reader.

REVISED I found the eccentric characters endearing.

REFERENCE

ALTICK, RICHARD D., and ANDREA A. LUNSFORD. *Preface to Critical Reading.* 6th ed. New York: Holt, 1984. Chapter 1. Connotation is put to many uses in advertising, politics, and literature.

TEACHING IDEAS

Many college students rely heavily on the thesaurus when writing their papers. Of course, while the thesaurus can be an invaluable tool for the writer, it also can lead inexperienced writers into lexical trouble. You may want to advise students now (as well as at other times) that they should never use from a thesaurus a word with which they are unfamiliar. You may also want to introduce them to another, more useful tool for writers, the dictionary of usage. One of the more popular ones is *The Merriam Webster Dictionary of English Usage* (1989), available in paperback.

TEACHING IDEAS

Students, like the rest of us, rarely think about idioms. To help them become more aware of the many idioms in the language, use the list as a starting point and ask for additional idioms. If you have any nonnative speakers in the class, you'll probably get quite a response from them. You may want to offer a few idioms of your own, such as *take in a show, stand up to someone, think it over,* to "prime the pump."

FOR DISCUSSION

Since you're probably covering this chapter after having covered the writing process and many of the revision chapters, students should be ready to discuss why some of them try to sound scholarly when they write. Now that they have more confidence in their writing, they may be able to recognize strategies—including trying to sound learned—that an insecure writer uses to cover up perceived failings.

GROUP ACTIVITY

In addition to illustrating the problems associated with unintentional euphony, this exercise can also inject a bit of humor into the class. Ask groups to come up with five or six sentences with too many rhyming words and/or too much alliteration. When groups report to the class, the class as a whole can determine which group has come up with the most outrageous examples. Such an exercise will help students recognize unintentional euphony in their own papers, but will spare them the embarrassment of public scrutiny of their work.

ESL CUE

Idiomatic combinations with prepositions are treated in three categories in the ESL chapters; see 42c, 43f, and 44b. Other idiomatic combinations are also treated; see especially 43e-2 on idioms with gerunds and infinitives.

ESL CUE

English places greater emphasis on specificity than do most languages; in fact, in some cultures the abstract is preferred to the concrete. As a consequence, the degree of specificity re-

Some Common Idioms in American English

We *arrived at* a conclusion.
We *arrived in* time.
We *arrived on* time.
We *brought in* the cake.
We *brought up* the rear of the parade.
Except for my close friends, no one knows of my plan.
Don't call, *except in* emergencies.
I often *get into* jams.
Get up the courage to raise your hand.
I *got in* just under the deadline.
Good friends will *make up* after they argue.
How did you *make out* in your interview?
We'll *take out* the trash later.
Next week, the Red Sox *take on* the Orioles.
The senate will *take up* the issue tomorrow.
A large crowd *turned out.*
At midnight, we will *turn in.*
The request was *turned down.*

4 Listening for unintentional euphony

In a poem, **euphony**—the pleasing sound produced by certain word combinations—is put to literary ends, and the effect can be memorable. A sentence in an essay or report, however, can be awkward when a writer unintentionally creates rhymes or alliterations (words that begin with the same consonant sound) that distract the reader from a sentence's meaning.

AWKWARD Particularly in poetry, euphony is put to literary ends. [The rhymes and alliterations distract from the meaning.]

SIMPLIFIED In a poem, euphony is used for literary ends.

The surest way to avoid unintentional rhymes or alliterations is to listen for them as you read your work aloud. Reading aloud forces you to slow down and hear what you have written. It can also help you to become aware of sentence rhythms. Finally, reading aloud can be an aid to proofreading—catching misspelled words, inadvertently misused homonyms (writing *affect* instead of *effect*), omitted words (often a preposition), and doubled words.

21c Using general and specific language

Specific details, illustrations, and observations are more vivid and more memorable than *general* remarks. To comment that a book about fourteenth-century Europe was *interesting* is so general as to be meaningless. By contrast, to state that you were perplexed by your morbid fascination with Barbara Tuchman's description of bubonic plague in fourteenth-century Europe—*that* is a specific comment.

Successful writers shuttle back and forth between the general and specific, since to dwell at either end of this spectrum for too long will tax a reader's patience. The writer who concentrates on details and will not generalize gives the impression of being unable to see "the big picture." Conversely, the writer who makes nothing but general claims will leave readers restless for specific details that would support these claims. Read the following sets of sentences. One is specific, the other general. Consider the differences.

> Genetically engineered organisms can be of great benefit to agriculture. Scientists have discovered or are working on organisms that can make plants frost and herbicide resistant and can help plants produce their own nitrogen.

> Scientists have discovered the benefits and uses of genetically engineered organisms in agriculture. One important example is the ice-minus bacterium created by Steve Lindow and Nicholas Panopoulos. Realizing a bacterium commonly found in plants produces a protein that helps ice to form, these scientists removed the unfavorable gene and thereby prevented ice from forming on greenhouse plants. Others have manipulated genetic materials to create tobacco that kills attacking insects and to produce plants that resist herbicides. Geneticists hope in 20 to 40 years to produce plants such as corn and other grains that "fix" their own nitrogen—that will be able to extract nitrogen from the atmosphere without relying on nitrifying bacteria. If such a plant could be created, U.S. farmers would save $3 to $4 billion annually in fertilizer costs and could save one third of all crops lost each year to pests.

In the first example, the writer makes a claim and supports it with three general examples, each of which is named quickly and left undeveloped. In the second example, the writer makes the same claim; but this time, details are provided that give readers specific information about genetically engineered organisms. Details such as these help to establish the writer's authority and give readers reasons to accept the writer's claim as true or probable. To produce effective, academic writing, writers shuttle between general claims and specific, supporting details.

EXERCISE 2

Create three lists, the first item of each being a very general word, the next item somewhat less general, the next still less general, and so on. The completed list, top to bottom, will proceed from general to specific.

Example: nation, state, county, city, neighborhood, street, house

EXERCISE 3

Choose a topic that you know well (sports, music, art, etc.) and write a general sentence about it. Then, in support of that sentence, write two additional sentences rich in specific detail.

quired in a given writing assignment will need to be illustrated with examples, and most ESL students will need particular instructions about how to generate such detail. In Farsi, for example, the broader and more encompassing your topic and your early treatment of it, the better; specifics are saved for endings.

Spanish speakers in particular will tend to use a high level of abstraction to sound sophisticated and serious. Furthermore, a Spanish locution such as "*la gente,*" or "the people," might have deep, almost mystical, associations for Spanish speakers, or it might change meaning in context, in one situation meaning "villagers," in another "the public," in still another "the downtrodden masses," but it sounds too general ("the people"—which people?) for English speakers. This use of a single abstraction for a series of different, more specialized meanings results in writing that in English sounds far too abstract.

Spanish, Italian, Russian, Greek, and French speakers have been taught to use overarching abstractions to write properly about literature and the arts, and will be surprised and disturbed by the degree of specificity asked of them by American teachers.

TEACHING IDEAS

Ask students to analyze several of their own papers for general and specific language. They can underline all of the general words, and circle all of the specific words. Have students ask themselves some questions about their writing as a result of their analyses: What is the ratio of general to specific words in their papers? Does one or the other seem to predominate? Does the topic influence the ratio? How might a better balance improve a given paper?

EXERCISE 2

Individual responses

EXERCISE 3

Individual responses

GROUP ACTIVITY

These exercises will work well with groups. It's almost always easier to generate ideas with others rather than individually, and students can challenge one another to come up with the most appropriate responses to Exercise 3. For Exercise 4, students can either generate the sentences together or share responses.

ADDITIONAL EXERCISE A

ACROSS THE CURRICULUM Photocopy a brief passage from one of your textbooks. Underline all of the general words, and circle all of the specific words. What is the proportion of general to specific words? How do the words relate to one another? How does the combination of both contribute to the effectiveness of the passage?

REFERENCE

OHMANN, RICHARD. "Use Definite, Specific, Concrete Language." *CE* 41 (1979): 390–97. Encouraging students to be specific is fine, but instructors should remember that abstract words are appropriate when identifying abstract ideas.

Example: Topic—Cooking an omelette

General sentence:

Making omelettes is a delicate operation.

Specific sentences:

Use a well-seasoned omelette pan—cast iron, well greased, clean but never thoroughly scrubbed.

Scramble the eggs with a splash of water (not milk), blending lightly so as not to toughen the cooked eggs.

21d Using abstract and specific language

Like general words, **abstract** words are broad. They name categories or ideas, such as *patriotism, evil,* and *friendship.* **Concrete** expressions (a *throbbing* headache, a *lemon-scented* perfume) provide details that give readers a chance to see, hear, and touch—and in this way to understand how an idea or category is made real. Just as with general and specific language, you should seek a balance between the abstract and concrete. Writers who dwell on the concrete give readers the impression of literal mindedness, perhaps even denseness. Writers who dwell on the abstract give the impression of being vague or aloof.

As with the general and specific, balance is the key—and not just in literary writing or autobiography but in all disciplines where writers labor to give concrete meaning to their ideas. See, for example, the balanced use of abstract and concrete terms in the following paragraph on biological inheritance.

> Among all the symbols in biology, perhaps the most widely used and most ancient are the hand mirror of Venus (♀) and the shield and spear of Mars (♂), the biologists' shorthand for male and female. Ideas about the nature of biological inheritance—the role of male and female—are even older than these famous symbols. Very early, men must have noticed that certain characteristics—hair color, for example, a large nose, or a small chin—were passed from parent to offspring. And throughout history, the concept of biological inheritance has been an important factor in the social organizations of men, determining the distribution of wealth, power, land, and royal privileges.
>
> —HELENA CURTIS

Notice that the abstract term *symbol* is given two more concrete examples: the hand mirror of Venus and the shield and spear of Mars. The abstract term *characteristics* is given concrete examples: *hair color, a large nose, a small chin.* And the abstract phrasing *social organizations of men* is given more concrete examples: *power, wealth, land, social privileges.* Of these last examples, though, one can imagine more concrete cases (*what kinds of privileges?*); but Curtis does not provide these, and in any event the paragraph does not call for them. The important point is that Curtis *does* weave the abstract with the concrete (even if some of these examples could be made more concrete).

EXERCISE 4

Take an abstract word such as *honesty, truth, friendship,* or *chaos,* and, in two or three sentences, link that word with a specific person, place, or event. Then provide concrete, descriptive details that help give meaning to the abstraction.

21e Using formal English as an academic standard

Academic writing is expected to conform to standards of **formal English**—that is, the English described in this handbook. There are many standards, or dialects, of English in this country, all of which are rich with expressive possibilities. Why formal English should be the acknowledged standard is, by some accounts, a purely political tactic orchestrated by the powerful to keep the less powerful disenfranchised. Those who grow up speaking formal English are born (so goes the argument) into an upper-range socioeconomic class that has a vested interest in maintaining its privileges. People who are privileged will admit into their circle only those who speak as they speak and who, presumably, share the same values because they share the same language.

In any case, it is clear that business, government, and academic communication would suffer if there were no accepted norm for language in a society. Some standard of communication is necessary, if only for the sake of efficiency. That the standard happens to be formal English has alienated some, and from a descriptive linguist's perspective it is certainly true that formal English is inherently no more *correct* than any other dialect of English. Linguists teach us that dialects—for instance, ones using the nonstandard *ain't*—are rule governed, just as formal English is rule governed. The diction of formal English is not better; it *is,* however, the only widely accepted standard for communicating among the many groups of English speakers. As a college student, you are learning communication skills that will enable you to reach the widest possible audience, and for that purpose you need to develop skill in formal English.

Academic writing avoids language that by virtue of its private references limits a reader's understanding or limits the audience. Slang, jargon, and regional or ethnic dialect language are examples of writing specific to particular groups. When you write to members of the *same* social group, profession, or region, there are two clear advantages to using in-group language: first, it is efficient, and second, it can help to cement a group's identity. When you address an audience *beyond* the group, slang, jargon, dialect, and regionalisms restrict what that audience can understand.

1 Revise most slang expressions into standard English.

Slang is the comfortable, in-group language of neighborhood friends, coworkers, teammates, or of any group to which we feel we belong. Assume for the moment you do not windsurf, and you happen to overhear a con-

EXERCISE 4

Individual responses

FOR DISCUSSION

Most students have probably been taught that there's such a thing as "proper" English, and all other variations—including dialects—are "improper." This attitude, of course, is being reinforced at present by some state and federal efforts to make English an official language. While proponents of these movements don't specify standard edited English, their rhetoric makes clear that regional, racial, or ethnic dialects are not what they mean by English. Students need to be able to discuss this issue. For many of them, self-image is inextricably tied to their ability to produce standard academic prose. If there are racial or ethnic minorities in your class, or nonnative speakers, that's all the more reason to discuss the concept of a standard. It's not necessary to "buy" the argument that language is a political weapon to discover that the ability to use standard English indeed separates the powerful from the less powerful.

ESL CUE

Nonnative English speakers will have no basis for judging between formal diction and slang and may use the two interchangeably; how formal or informal their usage is will depend on whether they learned English in a classroom setting or from daily use. If they learned from daily use, their English will include much slang and their instructor will have to call attention to its use regularly and consistently if they are to learn to hear the difference.

Vietnamese are used to distinguishing between formal and informal language mainly in terms of increased patterns of politeness for older generations.

FOR DISCUSSION

Students may not be aware that they are surrounded by examples of formal, popular, and informal writing. Ask them to inspect the written material they come in contact with every day—textbooks, resource material, novels, periodicals, newspapers, pamphlets, advertising copy, and the like—and to bring in examples of each type of writing. In class discussion, ask students to describe the samples they've brought, explaining the ways in which the samples represent formal, popular, or informal writing. You may also want to ask students to identify situations in which they are called on to produce each type of writing. This classroom exercise should reinforce the material in the Critical Decisions box.

CRITICAL DECISIONS

Set issues in a broader context: Choosing the right tone and register for your papers

Every sentence of every paper you write has a characteristic tone which, intended or not, communicates information about you: about your assumptions concerning the reader and about your knowledge of and attitude toward your topic. Choose a tone that helps you to meet the expectations of readers while satisfying your purpose as a writer. You will choose a formal, informal, or popular tone and register (3a-4).

Choosing an appropriate tone requires that you carefully analyze the writing occasion (see 3a-4)—the topic, your purpose, and your audience—and that you then make decisions about your document's level of content, language, and style.

- **Match the tone and register of your writing to the writing occasion—to your topic, your purpose, and the needs of your audience.**

FORMAL *Likely audience*—specialists or knowledgeable nonspecialists. *Content*—choose content that goes beyond introductory material. *Language*—to the extent that you understand and are comfortable with technical language, use it whenever needed for precision. *Style*—adhere to all the rules and conventions expected of writing in the subject area. Complicated and, if necessary, long sentences are acceptable if needed for precision. For guidance on format, see pieces similar to the one you are writing or consult a discipline-appropriate style guide (see 37e, 38d, 39d).

POPULAR *Likely audience*—nonspecialists willing to follow a detailed presentation. *Content*—choose content similar to that of a formal presentation, but avoid any examples or explanations that require specialized understanding. Emphasize (but do not necessarily limit yourself to) content that intersects with the readers' experiences and will keep them engaged. *Language*—avoid specialized terms whenever possible, though if you must use them for precision, carefully prepare for and define them. *Style*—adhere to all conventions of grammar, usage, spelling, etc. Some slang or colloquial language is acceptable, but keep it to a minimum. Avoid specialized formats, but organize content in a sensible, orderly way. Closely monitor your sentences, alternating length and rhythm for best effect (see Chapter 20).

INFORMAL *Likely audience*—nonspecialists looking for general information. *Content*—choose content that closely intersects your readers' experiences; otherwise, readers will lose interest. Coverage of topic should be introductory. Draw only on the most accessible examples and cases. *Language*—do not use specialized terms. Generally, keep sentences brief. *Style*—adhere to conventions of grammar, usage, spelling, etc. Slang or colloquial language is accepted, especially when you are familiar with the local or in-group speech of your readers. A narrative, first-person format may be useful.

versation between windsurfers in which someone says that she was *dialed in* or *completely powered.* What do these words mean? To someone not involved with the sport, nothing specific. Slang can be descriptive and precise for those who understand; it can just as readily be confusing and annoying to those who do not. In some cases, slang may mislead: the same expression can have different meanings for different groups. For example, *turbo charged* has distinctly different meanings for computer aficionados and for race-car enthusiasts and is likely to be vague and confusing when used outside of those settings. In the interest of writing accessibly to as many people as possible, avoid slang expressions in academic papers.

2 Replace regionalisms and dialect expressions with standard academic English.

Regionalisms are expressions specific to certain areas of the country. Depending on where you were born, you will use the word *tonic, soda, cola,* or *pop* to describe what you drink with your *sub, hoagie, grinder,* or *hero.* In a few states, when you are driving fast and a *smokey* catches up with you, your insurance rates will skyrocket. Words that have a clear and vivid reference in some areas of the country may lack meaning in others or have an unrelated meaning. For instance, *muss* means "to make messy" in some places and "to fight" in others. *Bad* means "good" in some places and "bad" in others.

Dialect expressions are specific to certain social or ethnic groups, as well as regional groups, within a country. Like regionalisms, dialects can use a specialized vocabulary and sometimes a distinctive grammatical system. Especially with respect to verbs (see Chapter 9), regional and ethnic dialect usage may regularly differ from standard English in omitting auxiliary verb forms. ("I done everything I can" or "It taken him all day" omit the standard auxiliary *have, had,* or *has.* "They be doing all right" replaces the standard *are* with the infinitive or base form *be.*) These are grammatically consistent and correct usages within the dialects they represent, but they address their language to a specific and restricted group rather than to a general audience. Like slang, regionalisms and dialect usages are appropriate for the audience that understands them; however, for general audiences in academic writing, they should be avoided.

3 Reduce colloquial language to maintain clarity and a consistent level of academic discourse.

Colloquial language is informal, conversational language. Colloquialisms do not pose barriers to understanding in the same way that slang, jargon, and regionalisms do; virtually all long-time speakers of English will understand expressions like *tough break, nitty-gritty,* and *it's a cinch.* In formal English, however, colloquialisms are rewritten or "translated" to maintain precision and to keep the overall tone of a document consistent. A few translations follow.

REFERENCES

BOLINGER, DWIGHT. "Stigma, Status, and Standard." *Language, the Loaded Weapon: The Use and Abuse of Language Today.* New York: Longman, 1980. 44–57. There is no objective justification for considering one dialect preferable to another.

GIANNASI, JENEFER M. "Language Varieties and Composition." *Teaching Composition: Twelve Bibliographic Essays.* Rev. ed. Ed. Gary Tate. Fort Worth: Texas Christian UP, 1987. A review of sociolinguistic studies of language varieties, with particular emphasis on classroom implications.

LABOV, WILLIAM. *Language in the Inner City: Studies in Black English Vernacular.* Philadelphia: U of Pennsylvania P, 1972. Black English is a dialect governed by its own rules, consistent with the culture in which it is spoken.

ACROSS THE CURRICULUM

Word Choice and Audience

In discussing a specialized topic, writers in any discipline should understand their audience's comfort with specialized language. An audience of experts will understand technical terms; an audience of nonexperts will not. And so you will find writers across the curriculum carefully controlling their word choice depending on an audience's needs. Observe, below, how paleontologist and evolutionary biologist Stephen Jay Gould shifts his vocabulary from technical to nontechnical.* To readers of the specialized journal *Evolution,* Gould (and co-author David Woodruff) use technical language to report on the shell of the snail *Cerion:*

> *Cerion* possesses an ideal shell for biometrical work. . . . It reaches a definitive adult size with a change in direction of coiling and secretion of a thickened apertural lip; hence, ontogenic and static variation are not confounded. (1026)

To readers of his *Hen's Teeth and Horse's Toes: Further Reflections in Natural History,* written for the general public, Gould avoids technical terms:

> In personal research on the West Indian land snail *Cerion,* my colleague David Woodruff and I find the same two morphologies again and again in all the northern islands of the Bahamas. Ribby, white, or solid-colored, thick and roughly rectangular shells inhabit rocky coasts at the edges of banks where islands drop abruptly into deep seas. Smooth, mottled, thinner, and barrel-shaped shells inhabit calmer and lower coasts at the interior edges of banks, where islands cede to miles of shallow water. (143)

In both cases, Gould's word choice is precise and concise. He chooses the *level* of his language, however, based on the needs of his audience, just as you should. The observation holds for all discipline areas: know your audience; choose your language accordingly.

*The first passage is from Stephen Jay Gould and David Woodruff, "Fifty Years of Interspecific Hybridization: Genetics and Morphometrics of a Controlled Experiment on the Land Snail *Cerion* in the Florida Keys," *Evolution* 41 (1987): 1026. The second passage is from Stephen Jay Gould, *Hen's Teeth and Horse's Toes* (New York: Norton, 1983), 143.

Colloquial	*Formal*
it's a cinch	it is certain
tough break	unfortunate
got licked	was beaten

Some colloquial expressions are also worn-out figures of speech whose meanings have become vague or obscure (see 21f-3).

4 Revise to restrict the use of jargon.

Jargon is the in-group language of professionals, who may use acronyms (abbreviations of lengthy terms) and other linguistic devices to take shortcuts when speaking with colleagues. When writers in an engineering environment refer to RISC architecture, they mean machines designed to allow for **R**educed **I**nstruction **S**et **C**omputing. RISC is an easy-to-use acronym, and it is efficient—as long as one engineer is writing or speaking to another. (If the in-group that uses these expressions is a prestigious one, the use of jargon can become a form of false or pretentious writing—see 21h-2.) The moment communication is directed outside the professional group, a writer must take care to define terms. The following sentences illustrate highly technical, in-group language among biologists. The writers are addressing upper-division biology majors with language that nonbiologists will find difficult to follow.

> *Writing directed to an in-group audience*
> Clostridia are ubiquitous, versatile, anaerobic flagellated microorganisms that generally form spores. As a group, they will ferment almost anything organic except plastics—sugars, amino acids and proteins, polyalcohols, organic acids, purines, collagen, and cellulose.
>
> —LYNN MARGULIS and KATHLENE V. SCHWARTZ

By contrast, in this next passage biologists are addressing a general student population, only a fraction of whom are biology majors.

> *Writing directed to a general audience*
> Historically, biology has been considered a "soft" science whose subject was more complex and "laws" less rigorous than disciplines such as chemistry and physics. This soft status, however, has been rapidly changing since the medical discovery of the role of microorganisms in disease, Darwin's theory of evolution by natural selection, Mendel's description of the rules by which traits are inherited, and the understanding of the way DNA both duplicates itself and determines the details for the manufacture of proteins that comprise all living things.
>
> —DORIAN SAGAN and LYNN MARGULIS

Language that is specialized by a particular group, for a particular purpose, is universal. Literary critics will speak of *deconstruction,* philosophers of *positivism,* sociologists of *dyads,* and mathematicians of *sigma functions.* When you become part of a group, academic or otherwise, you will be expected and will find it convenient to use in-group language. You will need to interpret that language for outsiders, of course; but even within the group, if you can communicate precisely without using jargon, do so.

EXERCISE 5

Think of a group—social, geographic, or professional—to which you belong and which you know well. Write a paragraph on some subject using in-group language: slang, jargon, or regionalisms. When you are finished, translate your paragraph into formal English, rewriting in-group expressions so that the paragraph can be read and understood by a general audience.

REFERENCES

BARZUN, JACQUES. *Simple and Direct.* New York: Harper, 1976. Chapter 3. To avoid slipping into jargon, avoid nouns ending in *-tion* and verbs ending in *-ize.*

BOLINGER, DWIGHT. "Another Case in Point: The Jargonauts and the Not-So-Golden Fleece." *Language, the Loaded Weapon: The Use and Abuse of Language Today.* New York: Longman, 1980. 125–37. An extensive analysis of the generation and perpetuation of jargon in contemporary English.

EXERCISE 5

Individual responses

REFERENCES

CORBETT, EDWARD P. J. *Classical Rhetoric for the Modern Student.* New York: Oxford UP, 1965. Recognizing figures of speech in their reading opens up for students the possibility of using them.

DEVET, BONNIE. "Bringing Back More Figures of Speech into Composition." *Journal of Teaching Writing* 6 (1987): 293–304. Current theories of composition lend credence to the notion that figures of speech should be taught.

LAKOFF, GEORGE, and MARK JOHNSON. *Metaphors We Live By.* Chicago: U of Chicago P, 1980. Metaphors influence both the expressive and conceptual components of language.

PERRINE, LAURENCE. "Four Forms of Metaphor." *CE* 33 (1971): 125–38. Metaphors can be classified into four distinct forms, each of which has a variety of uses.

ESL CUE

Most ESL students receive little or no instruction in the use of similes, analogies, and metaphors, except to memorize cliché expressions for recognition purposes. Furthermore, many languages either do not use such language extensively or they use it in an entirely different way from English. Russian, Polish, and Greek come closest to English in their heavy reliance on metaphorical diction. Spanish and Italian seem to rely on proverbs more than on metaphors, and Chinese and Japanese have the metaphorical connection built into the graphic character itself as well as into the word, confusing the issue. Whatever the original language, there is no guarantee students will find metaphors such as "the nose of the airplane" or "the foot of the mountain" self-explanatory. Metaphors such as "tooth of the saw," "eye of the needle," "neck of the bottle," and the like offer good beginning points for engaging discussions of "how metaphorical" different languages are.

21f Using figures of speech with care

Similes, analogies, and *metaphors* are **figures of speech,** carefully controlled comparisons that clarify or intensify meaning. Perhaps your spirit *soars* when you read this line of poetry: "Come live with me and be my love." The figurative use of *soar* creates an image of birds in flight, of elevation and clear vision. Literally speaking, birds and planes soar; spirits do not. English allows for the pairing of unlikely, even totally opposite images to help readers feel and see as writers do. In academic writing, figurative language is used across disciplines, though in some disciplines more freely than in others.

Figurative language in the sciences

The author of one well-respected book on scientific writing advises caution in using figures of speech in the life sciences and physical sciences. "Use [them] rarely in scientific writing. If you use them, use them carefully."[1] Following the logic of this advice, a biologist who is writing to fellow biologists would not report that in the course of an experiment water turned *ice* cold. This figurative language, however suggestive to nonscientists, lacks precision (ice cold water *is* ice). Biologists reading the article will want to know the precise temperature of the water, and they expect that temperature to be given in degrees. However, scientists in control of their writing *do* use figurative language at times, when addressing colleagues but more often when attempting to convey to the general public complicated, specialized knowledge. Thus (as illustrated later) you will find physicists and physicians as well as philosophers and poets using figures of speech, all to the same end: to communicate in ways that literal language, alone, fails to do.

There are many techniques for using language figuratively. As you read in the disciplines, you will encounter three figures most often: *simile, analogy,* and *metaphor.*

1 Use similes, analogies, and metaphors.

A **simile** is a figure of speech in which two different things—one usually familiar, the other not—are explicitly compared. The properties of the thing known help to define what is unknown. Similes make comparison very explicit, often using the word *like* or *as* to set up the comparison.

> Plastic is the new protector; we wrap the already plastic tumblers of hotels in more plastic, and seal the toilet seats *like* state secrets after irradiating them with ultraviolet light.
>
> —LEWIS THOMAS
> Physician, researcher

[1]Robert A. Day, *How to Write and Publish a Scientific Paper,* 3rd ed. (Phoenix: Oryx Press, 1988) 155.

The wind whistled in the street and the music ghosted from the piano *as* leaves over a headstone and you could imagine you were in the presence of genius.

—BRUCE CHATWIN
Traveler, writer

A particle of spin 2 is *like* a double-headed arrow: it looks the same if one turns it round half a revolution (180 degrees).

—STEPHEN HAWKING
Physicist

As with a simile, the purpose of an **analogy** is to make an explicit comparison that explains an unknown in terms of something known. Analogies most often use direct comparison to clarify a process or a difficult concept. An analogy can be developed in a single sentence; extended analogies can be developed over a paragraph or several paragraphs. The primary purpose of an analogy is to clarify.

Just as a trained mechanic can listen to a ping in a car's engine and then diagnose and correct a problem, so too an experienced writer can reread an awkward sentence and know exactly where it goes wrong and what must be done to correct it.

Extended analogies usually begin and end with certain *cues,* or words that signal a reader that an analogy is about to be offered or concluded. Words that mark a transition to an analogy are *consider, by analogy,* and *just as.* The transition from analogy back to a main discussion is achieved with expressions like *similarly, just so, so too,* and *in the same way.* (See 6d-1 for use of analogies in building an argument.)

Just as with a simile and an analogy, a **metaphor** illustrates or intensifies something relatively unknown by comparison with something familiar. In the case of metaphor, however, the comparison is implicit: the thing or idea that is relatively unknown is spoken of in terms closely associated with a significant feature of the thing that is known. The key features of the "known" are attributed directly to the "unknown." In the expression *hand of time,* for instance, the abstract term *time* is given a physical attribute. *Like* and *as* or other signals of explicit comparison are not used in metaphors.

In the mirror of his own death, each man would discover his individuality.

—PHILIPPE ARIÈS
Historian

The metaphor suggests that contemplating death allows people to see themselves in revealing ways.

Metaphors are not restricted to poetry or academic writing; they are used everywhere in our daily speech when an abstract or unknown idea, thing, or activity is spoken of in terms associated with something else. When we say "round up everybody," we implicitly compare the activity to a cattle roundup. When we say "Walk the thin line between good and bad," we compare a moral dilemma to a tightrope act. By speaking of people who have been "jerked around" or "left hanging," we compare their general situation to those physical activities. At times, such metaphorical comparisons, if not

ADDITIONAL EXERCISE B

Locate a selection in a literature anthology—it can be a poem, a story, a play, or an essay—and read through several pages looking for similes, analogies, and metaphors. Write down several that you find strong and apt, and explain why they impress you.

TEACHING IDEAS

Ask students to offer examples of similes, analogies, and metaphors from their own reading. You may want to start off by offering a few examples of your own. Here are several possibilities:

Loneliness is the most terrible poverty. (Mother Teresa)

Life in the twentieth century is like a parachute jump: you have to get it right the first time. (Margaret Mead)

Psychiatry's chief contribution to philosophy is the discovery that the toilet is the seat of the soul. (Alexander Chase)

It is wise to apply the refined oil of politeness to the mechanism of friendship. (Colette)

You cannot walk the middle of the road holding hands with tradition on one side and modernism on the other. You have to make a choice. (Alvin E. Rolland)

ESL EXERCISE

1. Keep a record of metaphors you notice in your reading, both popular (magazines, newspapers) and academic (textbooks, journals). Why do they seem to be used? What do they add to the text? Are they universal or are they culturally determined? Explain with examples.
2. Write a well-organized paragraph about the problems of foreign students. Use a metaphor or metaphors to make these problems visual.

well matched to the situation, can create more confusion for the reader than clarity.

2 Revise mixed metaphors.

Like all comparisons, metaphors need to match elements that can be compared logically (even if not explicitly). The metaphorical comparison must be consistent. Keep your language focused on a single metaphorical image throughout a sentence. Otherwise, you risk a **mixed metaphor,** which will stop your readers for a hearty laugh—at your expense. You would not, for instance, want to be the author of this.

MIXED METAPHOR — This story weaves a web that herds characters and readers into the same camp. [The comparison mixes spiderwebs with cattle roundups.]

CONSISTENT — This story weaves a web that tangles characters and readers alike.

3 Replace worn-out metaphors (clichés) with fresh figures.

In a famous essay, "Politics and the English Language," writer George Orwell warns against the *worn-out metaphor.*

> A newly invented metaphor assists thought by evoking a visual image, while on the other hand a metaphor which is technically "dead" (e.g., *iron resolution*) has in effect reverted to being an ordinary word and can generally be used without loss of vividness. But in between these two classes there is a huge dump of worn-out metaphors which have lost all evocative power and are merely used because they save people the trouble of inventing phrases for themselves.

Orwell proceeds to offer his list of worn-out metaphors, also called **clichés.** These include *play into the hands of, no axe to grind, swan song,* and *hotbed.* These trite expressions, current when Orwell's essay was written in 1945, are with us still. Modern-day expressions that can be added to this list of clichés include *the game of life, counting chickens before they hatch, water over the dam* or *under the bridge,* and *burning bridges.* Work to create your own metaphors; keep them vivid; and keep them consistent.

EXERCISE 6

In a few sentences, use figurative language to describe the approach of a thunderstorm, the effect of a sunny morning on your mood, or the feeling of just having finished the last exam of a long and difficult semester.

REFERENCE

NILSEN, DON L. F. "Clichés, Trite Sayings, Dead Metaphors, and Stale Figures of Speech in Composition Instruction." *CCC* 27 (1976): 278–82. An exercise using clichés and dead metaphors can heighten students' appreciation of fresh figures of speech.

EXERCISE 6

Individual responses

21g Eliminating biased, dehumanizing language

Language is a tool; just as tools can be used for building, they can also be used to dismantle. You have heard and seen the words that insensitive people use to denigrate whole groups. Equally repugnant is language used to stereotype. Any language that explicitly or subtly characterizes an individual in terms of a group is potentially offensive. Writers must take care to avoid stereotyping.

Sexism in diction

Sexism in English is a particular problem when value judgments are linked with male or female reference. The issue can become a sensitive one in almost any sentence, since English has no gender-neutral pronoun in the third-person singular. Consider this sentence: *A doctor should wash ______ hands before examining a patient.* English demands that we choose the possessive pronoun *his* or *her* to complete this thought. Until recently, the designated "neutral" pronoun was usually masculine (*his*), but changing times have made this usage potentially offensive. It is obvious that women, along with men, are physicians, engineers, attorneys, construction workers, accountants, realtors, etc. Men, along with women, are elementary school teachers, nurses, cooks, tailors, receptionists, and secretaries. Given these circumstances, it is both offensive and inaccurate to imply by one's choice of a single pronoun that men or women, exclusively, inhabit one or another profession. (See 10c on gender pronouns.) Gender-offensive language can also be found in such expressions as chair*man*, *man*kind, *man*power, *mother*ing, etc. Reread late drafts of your writing to identify potentially gender-offensive language. Unless the context of a paragraph clearly calls for a gender-specific reference, follow the suggestions given in the box to avoid offending your readers.

Some Potentially Offensive Gender-Specific Nouns

Avoid: stewardess (and generally nouns ending with *-ess*)
Use: flight attendant

Avoid: chairman
Use: chair or chairperson

Avoid: woman driver; male nurse
Use: woman who was driving; driver; nurse; man on the nursing station

Avoid: mankind
Use: people; humanity; humankind

Avoid: workmen; manpower
Use: workers; work force; personnel

Avoid: the girl in the office
Use: the woman; the manager; the typist

Avoid: mothering
Use: parenting, nurturing

FOR DISCUSSION

Few students should have trouble understanding why racial or ethnic slurs are offensive, but many still think the attention paid to sexist language is an overreaction. You may want to ask students if they've ever been in social or family situations where they've felt left out—perhaps they recall a family gathering at which conversation excluded the children, or they've felt ostracized at a party by the "in group." If they can make the analogy between these situations and the linguistic ostracism of women, they may be able to appreciate the move toward inclusive language. You also may want to ask what it means when you add a suffix or a qualifier to a word (*stewardess, woman doctor*)—the base word is the norm and the qualifier or suffix indicates an exception to the norm.

REFERENCES

BOLINGER, DWIGHT. "A Case in Point: Sexism." *Language, the Loaded Weapon: The Use and Abuse of Language Today.* New York: Longman, 1980. 89–104. Evidence of the debasement of women in the English language abounds.

CAMERON, DEBORAH. *Feminism and Linguistic Theory.* London: Macmillan, 1985. An extensive linguistic analysis of sexism in language, both explicit and implicit.

MILLER, CASREY, and KATE SWIFT. *The Handbook of Non-Sexist Writing.* 2nd ed. New York: Harper, 1988. Sexism is inherent in the English language, but there are strategies for overcoming linguistic bias.

VARDELL, SYLVIA M. " 'I'm No Lady Astronaut': Nonsexist Language for Tomorrow." Urbana: ERIC Clearinghouse on Reading and Communication Skills, 1985. ERIC ED 266 472. An extensive analysis of sexism in English, with suggestions for eliminating it.

Rewrite gender-stereotyping nouns as neutral nouns.

SEXIST A cover letter, along with a résumé, should be sent to the *chairman* of the department. [The male suffix may be taken to imply that the writer expects this person to be male.]

NEUTRAL A cover letter, along with a résumé, should be sent to the department *chair.*

SEXIST *Man's* need to compete may be instinctive. [A generic male noun or pronoun referring to all of humanity is unacceptable.]

NEUTRAL *The human* need to compete may be instinctive.

Balance references to the sexes.

SEXIST The *men* and *girls* in the office contributed generously to the Christmas Fund. [A reference singling out females as children in an adult setting is demeaning.]

NEUTRAL The *men* and *women* in the office contributed generously to the Christmas Fund. [In a school setting the reference might be to *boys* and *girls.*]

Make balanced use of plural and gender-specific pronouns.

See the Critical Decisions box in 10c for five strategies that will help you to correct gender problems with pronoun use.

SEXIST A doctor should wash *his* hands before examining a patient. [Here the generic male pronoun implies that the writer expects most doctors to be male.]

NEUTRAL *Doctors* should wash *their* hands before examining patients. [The plural strategy is used; see 10c.]

EXERCISE 7

Identify gender-offensive language in the following paragraph. Rewrite sentences in whatever way you feel is needed to make the gender references neutral.

The elementary school teacher, especially at the early grades, has her hands full with helping children adjust to a formal learning environment. Not all of the girls and young men in her class will understand that school is not, primarily, a place for play. Learning, of course, should be fun; but the elementary school teacher must be sure that her students appreciate the distinctions between playground play and intellectual play. By the later grades, a teacher will want his students to understand that serious intellectual play is the business of school. Women and boys in high school must appreciate that ideas should be celebrated with, not hidden from, classmates.

EXERCISE 7

Suggested revision:

Elementary school teachers, especially at the early grades, have their hands full with helping children adjust to a formal learning environment. Not all of the girls and boys in class will understand that school is not, primarily, a place for play. Learning, of course, should be fun; but elementary school teachers must be sure that their students appreciate the distinctions between playground play and intellectual play. By the later grades, teachers will want their students to understand that serious intellectual play is the business of school. Women and men in high school must appreciate that ideas should be celebrated with, not hidden from, classmates.

21h Avoiding euphemistic and pretentious language

Sometimes writers betray an anxious, condescending, or self-inflated attitude through their word choices. These attitudes may arise from a variety of motives, but the result is almost always a loss of clear expression.

1 Restrict the use of euphemisms.

The **euphemism** is a polite rewording of a term that the writer feels will offend readers. Invariably, euphemisms are longer than the words they replace and by definition are less direct: instead of *dead* or *died,* you will find *passed on, passed away, mortally wounded.* You may also find these clichés: *kicked the bucket, bit the dust, didn't make it, met his/her Maker, caught the Last Train, went to the Great Beyond,* and so on. If you are concerned about using expressions that might offend readers, create a context within a sentence or paragraph that may soften a potentially harsh word choice.

EUPHEMISM No one wanted to tell the child that his dog had gone to the Great Beyond.

REVISED Breaking the news to the child that his dog had died was very painful.

In nonacademic writing, use discretion in selecting a euphemism. Debate with yourself your use of language and then make your choice.

2 Eliminate pretentious language.

Pretentious language is unnecessarily ornate and puffed-up with its own self-importance; it suggests a writer is concerned more with image than with clear communication. See 17a-2, 4, and 6 on eliminating wordiness. Pretentious writers will often choose the windy version of everyday expressions that seem too common.

Pretentious	*Direct*
It appears to me that	I believe
In the final analysis	In conclusion
The individual who . . .	The person who . . .
utilize	use
demonstrate	show
functionality	function

Because many topics you will study are complex and technical, you should expect to encounter new and difficult vocabularies in your college career. In specialized areas of study, you will find that writers need technical terms to communicate precisely. Writing that requires specialized terms is very different from pretentious writing that is calculated to bolster a writer's ego. In your own work, you can distinguish between a legitimate technical term and a pretentious one by being both a concise and a precise writer.

GROUP ACTIVITY

Ask groups to compose a paragraph filled with euphemism and pretentious language. Not only will students have a good time doing it, but they'll also recognize how silly such language sounds. After the groups have completed the task, you may even want to have a contest to see which is the most outrageous paragraph.

REFERENCES

COE, RICHARD M. "Public Doublespeak—Let's Stop It." *English Quarterly* 19 (1986): 236–38. The variety of euphemism called "doublespeak" presents a danger that English teachers should address.

ENRIGHT, D. J., ed. *Fair of Speech: The Uses of Euphemism.* Oxford: Oxford UP, 1985. A collection of essays on the history, variety, and uses of euphemisms in the language.

ADDITIONAL EXERCISE C

Revise the following passage by eliminating pretentious language.

> In point of fact, if any given individual of the male gender is to be in possession of respect for his essential self, then that individual, it would seem apparent, must hold knowledge of his talents or capabilities. Thus, one might be in agreement with the contention that of primary importance to the individual desirous of a self that can be the object of respect would be a full-fledged assessment of areas in which the individual exhibits strengths as well as those in which the individual reveals weaknesses. The individual in question is, by and large, in an exceedingly unlikely position to fall prey to confusion with regard to an overdeveloped sense of ego as opposed to a more genuine and valid appreciation for the true nature of the self if, in fact, that individual is in a state of comprehension regarding the essence of his being.

(continued)

Suggested response:

If a man is to respect himself, he must know his talents and capabilities. An assessment of his strengths and weaknesses, then, should be a primary goal of the man seeking self-respect. A man is far less likely to confuse egotism with self-respect if he knows who he is.

EXERCISE 8

Representative responses:

Pretentious: In the final analysis, the one unending truth that we must as a nation uphold is mutual respect.

Direct: As citizens of this nation, we must respect one another.

Pretentious: Mutual respect, a tolerance for difference, is premised on the notion that we ought to expect from others the same considerations that we believe we ourselves are due.

Direct: Mutual respect is based on the principle that people should do to others as they expect others to do to them.

Pretentious: Setting aside, for the moment, high-minded rationales for respecting one another—the Judeo-Christian tradition, for instance, that we ought to love one another—we can observe that for very practical reasons mutual respect serves our own ends.

Direct: For very practical reasons, mutual respect serves our own ends.

Adhering to these two principles—the one helping you to cut wordiness and the other helping you to maintain precision—should make you aware of pretentious language, which can *always* be cut from a sentence.

PRETENTIOUS LANGUAGE	Cross-cultural treatises give every indication that all cultures establish relatively distinct gender differentiation.
DIRECT LANGUAGE	Studies from around the world show that all cultures establish clear roles for men and women.
SPECIALIZED LANGUAGE (NO REVISION NEEDED)	Index futures differ from other futures contracts in that they are not based on any underlying commodity or financial instrument that can be delivered; therefore, there is no cash market associated with them.

This passage on "index futures" comes from a book on investing. Students of finance would understand, or would be expected to understand, the terms *index futures, futures contracts, commodity, financial instrument,* and *cash market.* None of the words in this legitimately technical passage is calculated to bolster the writer's ego, as was the case in the preceding example.

Distinguishing Pretentious Language from Legitimate Technical Language

Bear in mind two principles when attempting to eliminate pretentious language:

- **Be concise:** Use as few words as possible to communicate clearly. Delete whole sentences or reduce them to phrases that you incorporate into other sentences; reduce phrases to single words; choose briefer words over longer ones. (See 17a for a full discussion of conciseness.)
- **Be precise:** Make sure your sentences communicate your *exact* meaning. If you need to add clarifying words, add as few words as possible. Use technical language for precision only when no other language will do.

EXERCISE 8

In the sentences that follow, identify and revise what you feel are examples of pretentious writing. Find other samples of writing, perhaps from a current newspaper, and conduct a similar analysis.

> In the final analysis, the one unending truth that we must as a nation uphold is mutual respect. Mutual respect, a tolerance for difference, is premised on the notion that we ought to expect from others the same considerations that we believe we ourselves are due. Setting aside, for the moment, high-minded rationales for respecting one another—the Judeo-Christian tradition, for instance, that we ought to love one another—we can observe that for very practical reasons mutual respect serves our own ends.

CHAPTER 22

Dictionaries and Vocabulary

A living language is continually evolving; it is always shifting and changing; it is flexible and yet precise. English is just such a language. Two thousand years ago nobody spoke English; it did not exist. Today, in the last decade of the twentieth century, it is the first truly global language, more widely spoken and written than any language has ever been. English originally spread through British imperialism to such countries as the United States, Canada, Australia, New Zealand, India, and various African and Caribbean nations. But the demise of the British Empire in no way signaled the demise of English as an international language. Rather, as the novelist Salman Rushdie notes, "English, no longer an *English* language, now grows from many roots; and those whom it once colonized are carving out large territories within the language for themselves. The Empire is striking back." At the same time, the cultural dominance of American English, the international language of multinational corporations, science and technology, rock music, Hollywood films, television, and mass consumerism continues to further the dissemination of English worldwide.[1]

USING DICTIONARIES

The emergence of English as a constantly changing global language raises the question of what constitutes "English" and/or the various Englishes. It is the job, indeed often the life work, of the editors and compilers of dictionaries to help readers understand the most current usages of words in the language. The dictionary will tell you what forms and meanings have become widely used or are in restricted use. On the basis of this information, you must decide which forms and meanings are most precisely suited to your purpose. In the next sections you will find descriptions of what is included in a typical dictionary entry, followed by descriptions of the abridged and unabridged dictionaries which have best met the dual challenge of currency and comprehensiveness.

22a Exploring dictionaries of the English language

Dictionaries give us far more than a list of words and their meanings. They not only define a given word, but also provide a brief description of its

[1]This introduction is based on Robert McCrum, William Cran, and Robert MacNeil, *The Story of English* (New York: Elisabeth Sifton Books/Viking, 1986) 19–48.

KEY FEATURES

This chapter takes the historical approach to vocabulary, noting that language is a living, growing entity in a constant state of flux. Thus the contribution of dictionaries is established: they provide us not only with spellings and definitions for words, but also with roots, usage labels, and etymology, among other things. The introduction to dictionary use is thorough, drawing a clear distinction between the functions of abridged and unabridged dictionaries, and acquainting students with other types of dictionaries as well, such as specialized dictionaries, dictionaries of synonyms, and discipline-specific dictionaries. Throughout these sections examples are abundant and clearly explained. Exercises provide students with the opportunity to familiarize themselves with several kinds of dictionaries. The chapter addresses vocabulary in the context of language learning in general, admonishing students against rote vocabulary learning in favor of developing a vocabulary through encounters with new words. The advice in this section is practical: students learn how to make educated guesses about word meanings on the basis of roots, prefixes, suffixes, and context. Exercises provide practice in using strategies for making educated guesses and for consulting dictionaries. The chapter ends with guidelines for building a personal vocabulary file.

ESL CUE

Look up the word *foreign* and make a list of synonyms. Discuss with your classmates how these words differ in connotations from each other and from the corresponding words in other languages. Then contrast the connotations of the most positive synonym with the connotations of the most negative synonym to illustrate the differences between them.

etymology, spelling, division, as well as pronunciation, and related words and forms. Here is a typical set of entries:

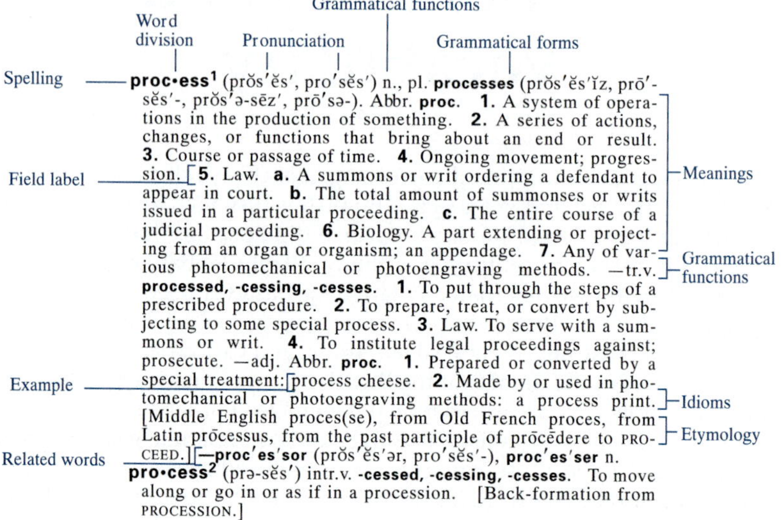
proc•ess¹ (prŏs′ĕs′, prō′sĕs′) n., pl. **processes** (prŏs′ĕs′ĭz, prō′sĕs′-, prŏs′ə-sēz′, prō′sə-). Abbr. **proc.** **1.** A system of operations in the production of something. **2.** A series of actions, changes, or functions that bring about an end or result. **3.** Course or passage of time. **4.** Ongoing movement; progression. **5.** Law. **a.** A summons or writ ordering a defendant to appear in court. **b.** The total amount of summonses or writs issued in a particular proceeding. **c.** The entire course of a judicial proceeding. **6.** Biology. A part extending or projecting from an organ or organism; an appendage. **7.** Any of various photomechanical or photoengraving methods. —tr.v. **processed, -cessing, -cesses.** **1.** To put through the steps of a prescribed procedure. **2.** To prepare, treat, or convert by subjecting to some special process. **3.** Law. To serve with a summons or writ. **4.** To institute legal proceedings against; prosecute. —adj. Abbr. **proc.** **1.** Prepared or converted by a special treatment: process cheese. **2.** Made by or used in photomechanical or photoengraving methods: a process print. [Middle English proces(se), from Old French proces, from Latin prōcessus, from the past participle of prōcēdere to PROCEED.] —**proc′es′sor** (prŏs′ĕs′ər, prō′sĕs′-), **proc′es′ser** n.
pro•cess² (prə-sĕs′) intr.v. **-cessed, -cessing, -cesses.** To move along or go in or as if in a procession. [Back-formation from PROCESSION.]

1 Understanding standard entry information in dictionaries

Most dictionary entries include more information on words than many people expect. In a typical entry you can find:

- *Spelling* (including variations, especially British versus American spellings—see Chapter 23 for more on rules of spelling)
- *Word division* indicating syllabication and where a word should be divided, if necessary
- *Pronunciation* (including variations)
- *Grammatical functions* (parts of speech)
- *Grammatical forms* (plurals, principal parts of irregular verbs, other irregular forms)
- *Etymology* (a given word's history/derivation)
- *Meanings* (arranged according to either currency or frequency of use, or earliest to most recent use)
- *Examples* of the word in context
- *Related words, synonyms* and *antonyms*
- *Usage labels* (see 22a-2)
- *Field labels* (for words that have discipline-specific meanings)
- *Idioms* that include the word

ADDITIONAL EXERCISE A

In order to get a rudimentary sense of the history of modern English, find an English "family tree" in an unabridged dictionary, and trace modern English back to its origins. In reverse order, list all of the other languages that evolved into modern English. List also the other modern languages that are "cousins" of English.

Answers:

Modern English, Middle English, Old English, West Germanic, Germanic, Indo-European. "Cousins" are Dutch, Afrikaans, Low German, German Yiddish, and Frisian.

REFERENCE

MARKWARDT, ALBERT H. "Dictionaries and the English Language." Rpt. in *Introductory Readings on Language.* Ed. Wallace L. Anderson and Norman Stageberg. New York: Holt, 1970. 114–28. A discussion of the two forms of dictionaries, the prescriptive and descriptive.

2 Usage labels

Usage refers to how, where, and when a word has been used in speech and writing. When preparing papers in an academic or business setting, use formal English as a standard (see 21e). That is, use words not otherwise labeled as nonstandard. There are several such nonstandard labels to be aware of. When you see the label *slang* assigned to the entry *prof,* for instance, the dictionary is indicating that in standard, formal English usage that word is not accepted. Aware of this *restriction* on the word, you would probably decide not to use it in formal writing. There are other categories of restricted usage, and these are generally listed and explained in the front matter of most dictionaries:

- *Colloquial:* used conversationally and in informal writing
- *Slang:* in-group, informal language; not standard
- *Obsolete:* not currently used (but may be found in earlier writing)
- *Archaic:* not commonly used; more common in earlier writing
- *Dialect:* restricted geographically or to social or ethnic groups; used only in certain places with certain groups
- *Poetic, literary:* used in literature rather than everyday speech

EXERCISE 1

Consult your dictionary to answer the following questions about grammatical function.

1. Which of the following nouns can be used as verbs: *process, counsel, dialogue, hamper, instance*?
2. How do you make these nouns plural: *annals, humanity, armor, accountancy, deer, analysis, medium, sister-in-law, knife*?
3. What are the principal parts of these verbs: *hang, begin, break, forbid, rise, set*?
4. What are the comparative and superlative forms of these adverbs and adjectives: *unique, bad, mere, initial, playful*?

EXERCISE 2

Using two different dictionaries, list and comment on the usage restrictions that are recorded for the following words:

1. get-up
2. whither
3. hipster
4. maverick
5. hit
6. max

Example: ain't

Webster's New Collegiate Dictionary (Springfield, MA: G. & C. Merriam, 1974)

though disapproved by many and more common in less educated speech, used orally in most parts of the U.S. by many educated speakers esp. in the phrase *ain't I*

The American Heritage Dictionary, 2nd College Edition (Boston: Houghton Mifflin, 1982)

EXERCISE 1

1. process, counsel, hamper
2. annals, humanities, armors, accountancies, deer, analyses, media, sisters-in-law, knives
3. hang, hung, hung, hanging, hangs, *or* hang, hanged, hanged, hanging, hangs;
   begin, began, begun, beginning, begins;
   break, broke, broken, breaking, breaks;
   forbid, forbade, forbidden, forbidding, forbids;
   rise, rose, risen, rising, rises;
   set, set, set, setting, sets
4. ______ (*unique* is an absolute term)
   bad, worse, worst
   ______ , merest
   ______ (*initial* is an absolute term)
   playful, more playful, most playful

EXERCISE 2

Responses depend on dictionary being used.

Ain't has acquired such a stigma over the years that it is beyond rehabilitation, even though it would serve a useful function as a contraction for *am not* and even though its use as an alternate form for *isn't, hasn't, aren't,* and *haven't* has a good historical justification. In questions, the variant *aren't I* is acceptable in speech to a majority of the Usage Panel, but in writing there is no generally acceptable substitute for the stilted *am I not.*

COMMENT: *The American Heritage Dictionary* is clearly sympathetic to the word but seems resigned (even disappointed!) that *ain't* will never be acceptable as a standard word in the language. *Webster's* makes a class distinction between the "educated" and "less educated" and seems elitist about the word's usage.

TEACHING IDEAS

For two reasons it would be worthwhile for you to choose an abridged dictionary for the entire class to use: (1) It ensures consistency as students do these exercises and consult the dictionary for other reasons, and (2) it ensures that students have a dictionary *to* consult.

22b Choosing a dictionary

Because the English language is constantly changing and is used in so many environments around the world, no dictionary can ever claim to be the final authority on every possible current meaning or correct usage for the words it lists. A dictionary's authority rests mainly on its attempt to be reasonably comprehensive and linguistically accurate in recording the most frequently used meanings of a word. Dictionaries further try to be as balanced as possible in recording the kind of usage and the restrictions on usage that have been observed for each meaning. In addition, dictionaries record a time dimension for changes in meaning: some list the earliest meanings on record first, moving on to the more recent; others reverse the sequence to start with contemporary meanings. All dictionaries record the basic categories of information shown in the previous section.

1 Comparing abridged dictionaries

The most convenient and commonly used dictionaries in households, businesses, and schools are called "abridged"—or shortened. They do not try to be as exhaustive or complete as the "unabridged" dictionaries (described in 22b-2). An abridged dictionary tries to give as much information as possible in one portable volume. You will find that several dictionaries claim the name *Webster's,* after the early American lexicographer Noah Webster. Since his name is in the public domain and is not copyrighted, it appears in the titles of a number of dictionaries with varying characteristics. The following list includes only some of the more widely used abridged dictionaries.[2]

[2] The descriptions of abridged, unabridged, and discipline-specific dictionaries that follow are adapted from entries in Eugene Sheehy, *Guide to Reference Books,* 10th ed. (Chicago: American Library Association, 1986); Diane Wheeler Strauss, *Handbook of Business Information: A Guide for Librarians, Students and Researchers* (Englewood, CO: Libraries Unlimited, Inc., 1988); and Bohdan Wynar, *ARBA Guide to Subject Encyclopedias and Dictionaries* (Littleton, CO: Libraries Unlimited, 1986).

The American Heritage Dictionary, 3rd ed. (Houghton Mifflin, 1992) includes about 200,000 entries. It differs from most other dictionaries in that it presents the most contemporary meaning of a word first, rather than proceeding historically. Guidance to good usage is provided by extensive usage-context indicators and "Usage Notes" which reflect the opinions of a panel of usage experts. The dictionary contains many photographs, illustrations, and maps. Foreign words and the names of mythological and legendary figures appear in the regular listings, while biographical and geographical entries and abbreviations are listed in the back.

The Concise Oxford Dictionary of Current English, 8th ed. (Oxford University Press, 1990) is the briefest of the abridged dictionaries listed here. It is based on the work for the unabridged *Oxford English Dictionary* (see 22b-2) and includes current usage and illustrative quotations, scientific and technical terms, many colloquial and slang expressions, and both British and American spellings. There are no illustrations, and little front or back matter.

The Random House College Dictionary (Random House, 1975) is based on the unabridged *Random House Dictionary of the English Language* (see 22b-2). The dictionary contains about 155,000 entries, and it lists the most common usage of a word first. It indicates informal and slang usage and synonyms and antonyms, and lists recent technical words along with biographical and geographical names as part of its main entries. A manual of style is included as part of its back matter.

Webster's Tenth New Collegiate Dictionary (G. & C. Merriam, 1993) is based on *Webster's Third New International Dictionary of the English Language* (see 22b-2) and includes some 160,000 entries emphasizing "standard language." Labels indicating usage occur less frequently than in other desk dictionaries. Entries give full etymologies followed by definitions in chronological order, with the most recent meaning listed last. It includes extensive notes on synonyms and illustrative quotations. Foreign words and phrases, biographical and geographical names, and a manual of style are listed separately as back matter.

Webster's New World Dictionary of the American Language, Third Edition (Simon & Schuster, 1988) has a contemporary American emphasis and uses a star to indicate Americanisms—words that first became part of the language in the United States. Definitions are listed in chronological order, with the earliest first, and extensive etymologies, synonyms, and usages are provided. Proper names, place names, abbreviations, and foreign phrases are included in the main listings.

EXERCISE 3

Look up the following words in one of the abridged dictionaries listed above. How many different meanings does each word have? From observing older meanings versus the more current meanings, how would

TEACHING IDEAS

If your library is equipped with a variety of abridged dictionaries, you may want to use the following activity to acquaint students with their use. Ask students, in teams perhaps, to examine two abridged dictionaries (not on the list here) in the library. They can then report to the class on the features of the dictionaries, offering advice on which is preferable. This exercise may even be used in order to decide on a dictionary for the class to use.

EXERCISE 3

Responses depend on dictionary being used.

you describe the overall shifts in meaning that some words have undergone over time?

1. double
2. foul
3. conductor
4. weird
5. cross
6. funky

GROUP ACTIVITY

Unabridged dictionaries are fascinating places to visit. Assign each group a specific unabridged dictionary that's in your library. (Depending on the size of your class and the number of dictionaries in the library, some dictionaries will be investigated by more than one group.) The group's task is simply to find out how many kinds of information—aside from the standard syllabication, pronunciation, and definition—can be found in the dictionary. Remind students to look not only at sample entries, but at front and rear appendices as well. Groups can then report to the class on what can be found in these dictionaries.

2 Comparing unabridged dictionaries

The compilers of unabridged dictionaries attempt to be exhaustive both in recounting the history of a word and in describing its various usages. For quick reference—to check spelling, meaning, or commonplace usage, an abridged dictionary will serve you well. But when you are puzzled by or otherwise curious about a word and its history (for instance, if you want to know the route by which the word *farm* has made its way into the language), you will want to consult an unabridged dictionary where the principle for compiling an entry is *thoroughness*.

The second edition of *The Oxford English Dictionary* (Oxford: Clarendon Press), prepared by J. A. Simpson and E. S. C. Weiner, was published in 1989 and includes the text of the first edition (1933), the *Supplement* (1972–1986), and almost 5,000 new entries for a total of more than 500,000 words. It is the great dictionary of the English language, arranged chronologically to show the history of every word from the date of its entry into the language to its most recent usage, supported by almost two million quotations from the works of more than 5,000 authors since 1150. The *O.E.D.* is an invaluable source for scholars.

The Random House Dictionary of the English Language (Random House, 1987) is considerably briefer than the other unabridged dictionaries listed here, though it is particularly current, and includes extensive usage notes. The back matter includes several foreign word lists and an atlas with colored maps.

Webster's Third New International Dictionary of the English Language (G. & C. Merriam, 1986) includes about 450,000 entries, with special attention to new scientific and technical terms. The third edition of 1986 emphasizes the language as currently used (though entries are arranged chronologically, with the earliest uses first), with a descriptive approach to usage, construction, and punctuation. Many obsolete and rare words have been dropped. Although the third edition is widely used as a descriptive standard, some scholars prefer the more prescriptive approach of the second edition of 1959. Most college students will find that the third edition meets their needs and is convenient to use.

EXERCISE 4

Individual responses

EXERCISE 4

Choose two of the words you looked up in Exercise 3 and compare what you found with the entry for the same word in an unabridged dictionary, preferably *The Oxford English Dictionary.* Briefly characterize the history of each word, explaining how its meaning has shifted over time.

22c Using specialized dictionaries of English

Abridged and unabridged dictionaries of the English language can provide you with a wealth of general information about language. However, there will be times when you will need to consult a specialized dictionary which focuses on a specific kind of word or language information, such as slang, etymologies, synonyms, antonyms, and accepted usage. The following are some particularly useful specialized dictionaries.

1 Dictionaries of usage

When your questions regarding the usage of a word are not adequately addressed in a standard dictionary, consult one of the following dictionaries of usage:

A Dictionary of Contemporary American Usage, ed. Bergen Evans and Cornelia Evans

Dictionary of Modern English Usage, ed. H. W. Fowler

Dictionary of American-English Usage, ed. Margaret Nicholson

Modern American Usage, ed. Jacques Barzun

2 Dictionaries of synonyms

Dictionaries that present synonyms of words can be a great help for writers wanting to expand vocabulary. A caution, though: while synonyms have approximately the same denotation, their connotations (or nuances of meaning) differ. Before using a synonym, be sure that you thoroughly understand its connotation (see also 22e-3).

Webster's Dictionary of Synonyms

The New Roget's Thesaurus of the English Language in Dictionary Form

3 Other specialized dictionaries

The dictionaries listed here are specialized sources for the historical and social dimensions of word use.

Dictionaries of origins/etymologies

The information on word origins in basic dictionaries can be pursued in more detail in the following specialized references.

Dictionary of Word and Phrase Origins, ed. William Morris and Mary Morris

REFERENCES

SCHWEIK, ROBERT, and DIETER RIESNER. *Reference Sources in English and American Literature: An Annotated Bibliography.* New York: Norton, 1977. Section XXII. "Dictionaries." A comprehensive list of specialized dictionaries.

SLEDD, JAMES, and WILMA R. EBBITT. *Dictionaries and That Dictionary.* Chicago: Scott, 1962. The usage policy of *Webster's Third New International Dictionary of the English Language* spurred controversy, much of it covered here.

EXERCISE 5

Suggested responses:

1. Standard American English or as current slang among young people.
2. Standard British English or for specialists referring to caged birds.
3. Standard American English or referring to a religious ceremony.
4. Sixties slang.
5. Formal, pretentious, or poetic language.
6. Current slang among young people.

The Oxford Dictionary of English Etymology, ed. C. T. Onions
Origins: A Short Etymological Dictionary of Modern English, ed. Eric Partridge

Dictionaries of slang and idioms

Many terms omitted or given only brief notice in basic dictionaries are described in great detail in slang dictionaries.

The New Dictionary of American Slang, ed. Robert Chapman
Dictionary of Slang and Unconventional English, ed. Eric Partridge
Dictionary of American Slang, ed. Harold Wentworth and Stuart Berg Flexner

Dictionaries of regionalism or foreign terms

The *Dictionary of American Regional English,* compiled by linguist Frederic Cassidy, is the standard work on regional and dialect expressions in America.

Dictionary of American Regional English, ed. Frederic Cassidy
Dictionary of Foreign Phrases and Abbreviations, ed. Kevin Guinagh. 3rd ed.
Dictionary of Foreign Terms, ed. Mario Pei and Savatore Ramondino
Harper Dictionary of Foreign Terms, ed. C. O. Sylvester Mawson and Charles Berlitz. 3rd ed.

EXERCISE 5

Look up the following words in a dictionary of usage and a dictionary of origins. Based on information you find out about the meanings, origins, and uses of each word from these specialized sources, characterize the kind of writing or the kind of audience for which each term seems most appropriate.

1. awesome
2. mews
3. celebrate
4. groovy
5. ere
6. flunk

BUILDING VOCABULARY

You will need a good vocabulary to understand discussions in texts and to follow lectures. As you move from discipline to discipline, vocabularies will change: you will, in effect, learn new languages. As a writer, you will need a good vocabulary to help you write precisely. This said, you should realize that *vocabulary power* alone, notwithstanding the promises of correspondence courses, does not a writer make. A modest but precise vocabulary will suffice in most cases, so long as you use it in sentences that are structured well, in paragraphs that are coherent, and in essays and reports that show a careful development of ideas. Vocabulary does not exist independently from any of these elements.

22d Learning root words, prefixes, and suffixes

Where applicable, the editors of college dictionaries will place in square brackets [ ] abbreviations of languages from which words are derived. Some of the abbreviations (and their spelled out versions) include: *F,* French; *Gk,* Greek; *LL,* Late Latin; *L,* Latin; *Heb,* Hebrew; *ME,* Middle English; *Dan,* Danish; *D,* Dutch; *G,* German; *LG,* Low German; *Flem,* Flemish; *Ital,* Italian; *OW,* Old Welsh; *Span,* Spanish; *Skt,* Sanskrit; and *OPer,* Old Persian. There are more than 100 languages from which the half-million words of English are derived. Modern words are often variants of earlier forms that have snaked their way through history, changing outward appearances for different peoples at different times—though retaining a recognizable core or root. The study of the history of words is called **etymology.** In the square brackets of dictionary entries you will usually find either the abbreviation **fr.** or the symbol <, meaning *derived from.*

Once a word enters the language, its core or *root* is often used as the basis of other words that are formed with *prefixes* and *suffixes*—letters coming before, or after, the root. When you can recognize root words, prefixes, and suffixes, often you will be able to understand the meaning of a new word without checking a dictionary.

EXERCISE 6

Using two unabridged dictionaries, research the etymology of a word. In four or five sentences, trace the word's use over time.

1 Becoming familiar with root words

A root anchors a plant or tree in the ground and provides a structural and nutritional base from which it can grow. The **root** of a word anchors it in language, providing a base from which meaning is built. When you encounter an unfamiliar word, try identifying its root; with help from the context of the surrounding sentence, you can often infer an appropriate definition. Consider the following sentence:

Beautiful and *beauteous* are paronymous words.

You have come upon an unfamiliar word, *paronymous.* You might say: "This reminds me of another word—*anonymous.*" Immediately, you sense that the similar sounding words share a root: *nymous.* You know that *anonymous* means "having an unknown name." It is not so tremendous a leap to conclude that the root *nymous* means *name.* Now you examine the sentence once more and make an educated guess, or inference. What do the words *beautiful* and *beauteous* have to do with *names*? The words themselves tell you—that they are built on a single name: *beauty.* If you guessed that *paronymous* means "derived from the same word (or root)," you would be correct.

TEACHING IDEAS

This activity is especially profitable in multiethnic or multilingual classes: Ask students to think of words in languages other than English that sound like English words. (Students whose first language is not English will be adept at this.) After generating a list of words, ask students to choose several and look them up in an unabridged dictionary. They can then discover whether the similarity between words in different languages results from common derivation, from one modern language's having borrowed the word from another, or from mere coincidence (as unlikely as that may seem).

EXERCISE 6

Responses depend on dictionary being used.

ADDITIONAL EXERCISE B

ACROSS THE CURRICULUM Make three photocopies each of passages from one of your textbooks. (The additional photocopies will be used for subsequent exercises.) Underline all words with roots recognizable from the box on the next page, and identify the language of the root. From which language do most of the roots seem to be taken? Based on your understanding of the discipline, why do you think this is so? Compare your findings to those of other students using textbooks from different disciplines. What are the similarities between disciplines? the differences?

Whether you know a root word or make an educated guess about its meaning, your analysis will aid reading comprehension and, in the process, will improve your vocabulary. Many of the root words in English come from Latin and Greek. The following box contains a small sample of root words.

Common Root Words

Root	Definition	Example
acus [Latin]	needle	acute, acumen
basis [Greek]	step, base	base, basis, basement, basic
bio- [Greek]	life	biography, biology, bionic
cognoscere [Latin]	to know	recognize, cognizant, cognition
ego [Latin]	I	ego, egocentric, egotistical
fleure [Latin]	flow	flow, fluid, effluence
grandis [Latin]	large	grandiose, aggrandize
graphein [Greek]	to write	graph, graphic
hydro [Greek]	water	hydraulic, dehydrate
hypnos [Greek]	sleep	hypnosis, hypnotic
jur, jus [Latin]	law	jury, justice
lumen [Latin]	light	illuminate, luminary
manu- [Latin]	hand	manage, management, manual, manipulate
mare [Latin]	sea	marine, marinate, marina, marinara
matr- [Latin]	mother	maternal, matrilineal
pathos [Greek]	suffering	empathy, sympathy
patr- [Latin]	father	paternal, patriarch
polis [Greek]	city	metropolis, police
primus [Latin]	first	primitive, prime, primary
psych [Greek]	soul	psychological, psyche
scrib, script [Latin]	to write	describe, manuscript
sentire [Latin]	to feel	sentiment, sentimental, sentient, sense, sensitive
sol [Latin]	sun	solstice, solar, solarium
solvere [Latin]	to release	solve, resolve, solution, dissolve, solvent
tele [Greek]	distant	telegraph, telemetry
therm [Greek]	heat	thermal, thermos
truncus [Latin]	trunk	trunk, trench, trenchant
veritas [Latin]	truth	verity, verify, veritable
vocare [Latin]	to call	vocal, vocation, avocation

2 Recognizing prefixes

A **prefix**—letters joined to the beginning of a root word to qualify or add to its meaning—illustrates its own definition: the root *fix* comes from the Latin *fixus,* meaning "to fasten"; *pre* is a prefix, also from Latin, meaning "before." The prefix joined to a root creates a new word, the meaning of which is "to place before." Recognizing prefixes can help you isolate root words. The prefix and the root, considered together, will allow you to infer a meaning. Prefixes can indicate number, size, status, negation, and relations in time and space. The following are some frequently used prefixes.

Prefixes indicating number

Prefix	*Meaning*	*Example*
uni-	one	unison, unicellular
bi-	two	bimonthly, bicentennial, bifocal
tri-	three	triangle, triumvirate
multi-	many, multiple	multiply, multifaceted
omni-	all, universally	omnivorous, omniscient
poly-	many, several	polytechnic, polygon

Prefixes indicating size

Prefix	*Meaning*	*Example*
micro-	very small	microscopic, microcosm
macro-	very large	macroeconomics
mega-	great	megalomania, megalith

Prefixes indicating status or condition

Prefix	*Meaning*	*Example*
hyper-	beyond, super	hyperactive, hypercritical
neo-	new	neonate, neophyte
para-	akin to	parachute, paramilitary
pseudo-	false	pseudoscience, pseudonym
quasi-	in some sense	quasi-official, quasi-public

Prefixes indicating negation

Prefix	*Meaning*	*Example*
anti-	against	antibiotic, antidote, anticlimax
counter-	contrary	counterintuitive, counterfeit
dis-	to do the opposite	disable, dislodge, disagree
mal-	bad, abnormal, inadequate	maladjusted, malformed, malcontent, malapropism
mis-	bad, wrong	misinform, mislead, misnomer
non-	not, reverse of	noncompliance, nonalcoholic, nonconformist, nonessential

Prefixes indicating spatial relations

Prefix	*Meaning*	*Example*
circum-	around	circumspect, circumscribe
inter-	between	intercede, intercept
intra-	within	intravenous, intramural
intro-	inside	introvert, intrude

ADDITIONAL EXERCISE C

Using the second photocopy from Additional Exercise B, circle all of the prefixes. How dependent is the text on words with prefixes? What prefixes, if any, seem to predominate? Compare your findings to those of other students using textbooks from different disciplines. What are the similarities between disciplines? the differences?

ADDITIONAL EXERCISE D

Using the third photocopy from Additional Exercise B, circle all of the suffixes. How dependent is the text on words with suffixes? What suffixes, if any, seem to predominate? Compare your findings to those of other students using textbooks from different disciplines. What are the similarities between disciplines? the differences?

Prefixes indicating relations of time

Prefix	*Meaning*	*Example*
ante-	before	antecedent, anterior
paleo-	ancient	Paleolithic, paleography
post-	after	postdate, postwar, posterior
proto-	first	protohuman, prototype

3 Analyzing suffixes

A **suffix**—letters joined to the end of a word or a root—will change a word's grammatical function. Observe how with suffixes a writer can give a verb the forms of a noun, adjective, and adverb.

VERB	impress
NOUN	impression
ADJECTIVE	impressive
ADVERB	impressively

The following are some frequently used suffixes.

Noun-forming suffixes

Verb	+	*Suffix*	*(Meaning)*	=	*Noun*
betray		-al	(process of)		betrayal
participate		-ant	(one who)		participant
play		-er	(one who)		player
construct		-ion	(process of)		construction
conduct		-or	(one who)		conductor
Noun	+	*Suffix*	*(Meaning)*	=	*Noun*
parson		-age	(house of)		parsonage
king		-dom	(office, realm)		kingdom
sister		-hood	(state, condition of)		sisterhood
strategy		-ist	(one who)		strategist
Armenia		-n	(belonging to)		Armenian
master		-y	(quality)		mastery
Adjective	+	*Suffix*	*(Meaning)*	=	*Noun*
pure		-ity	(state, quality of)		purity
gentle		-ness	(quality of, degree)		gentleness
active		-ism	(act, practice of)		activism

Verb-forming suffixes

Noun	+	*Suffix*	*(Meaning)*	=	*Verb*
substance		-ate	(cause to become)		substantiate
code		-ify	(cause to become)		codify
serial		-ize	(cause to become)		serialize

Adjective	+	*Suffix*	*(Meaning)*	=	*Verb*
sharp		-en	(cause to become)		sharpen

Adjective-forming suffixes

Noun	+	*Suffix*	*(Meaning)*	=	*Adjective*
region		-al	(of, relating to)		regional
claim		-ant	(performing, being)		claimant
substance		-ial	(of, relating to)		substantial
response		-ible	(capable of, fit for)		responsible
history		-ic	(form of, being)		historic
Kurd		-ish	(of, relating to)		Kurdish
response		-ive	(tends toward)		responsive
Verb	+	*Suffix*	*(Meaning)*	=	*Adjective*
credit		-able	(capable of)		creditable
abort		-ive	(tends toward)		abortive

EXERCISE 7

Identify and initially define, without using a dictionary, the roots, prefixes, and suffixes of the following sets of words. Then check your definitions against dictionary entries.

1. photometry, photogenic, photograph, photoelectric
2. excise, concise, precise, incisive
3. conduce, reduce, deduce, produce
4. optometrist, optician, ophthalmologist, optical
5. discourse, recourse
6. diverge, converge
7. convert, pervert, revert
8. tenable, tenacious, retain
9. memoir, remember
10. remorse, morsel

22e Strategies for building a vocabulary

1 Use contextual clues and dictionaries.

In college, you will spend a great deal of your time reading, and reading provides the best opportunities for expanding your vocabulary. When a new word resists your analysis of root and affix (prefix or suffix), reach for a dictionary or let the context of a sentence provide clues to meaning. Contextual clues will often let you read a passage and infer fairly accurate definitions of new words—accurate enough to give you the sense of a passage. Indeed, using a dictionary to look up *every* new word in the name of thor-

EXERCISE 7

To be checked in the dictionary

ADDITIONAL EXERCISE E

Add a prefix and/or a suffix to each of the following words, and then write each new word in a sentence:

1. comfort
2. attend
3. impose
4. direct
5. lone

Possible new words:

1. comforting, comfortable, discomfort
2. attendance, attendant, attention
3. superimpose, imposing
4. direction, misdirected, directory
5. lonely, alone

REFERENCES

Journal of Basic Writing 2 (1979). Special issue on teaching vocabulary.

PYLES, THOMAS. *Words and Ways of American English.* New York: Random, 1952. Chapters 1, 2, 7, 8. Many words in American speech are borrowed from other languages, or adapted from them.

oughness can so fragment a reading that you will frustrate—not aid—your attempts to understand. Focus first on the ideas of an entire passage; circle or otherwise highlight new words, especially repeated words. Then, if the context has not revealed the meaning, reach for your dictionary.

In the passage that follows, possibly unfamiliar vocabulary is set in italics. Do not stop at these words. Note them, but then complete your reading of these paragraphs from an astronomy text by George O. Abell:

> Let us once again compare the *propagation* of light to the propagation of ocean waves. While an ocean wave travels forward, the water itself is *displaced* only in a *vertical* direction. A stick of wood floating in the water merely bobs up and down as the waves move along the surface of the water. Waves that propagate with this kind of motion are called *transverse* waves.
>
> Light also *propagates* with a transverse wave motion, and travels with its highest possible speed through a *perfect vacuum.* In this respect light differs markedly from sound, which is a physical vibration of matter. Sound does not travel at all through a vacuum. The *displacements* of the matter that carry a sound *impulse* are in a *longitudinal* direction, that is, in the direction of the propagation, rather than at right angles to it.

EXERCISE 8

Individual responses

ADDITIONAL EXERCISE F

ACROSS THE CURRICULUM Locate in one of your textbooks a passage that includes several words that are new to you. Before looking them up in the dictionary, try to determine their meaning based on the context. Write out your tentative definition, and then check it with the dictionary definition. If the meanings are close, you've done a good job of making an educated guess.

LOOKING BACK

Students who tend to use a thesaurus in hopes of sounding more educated should follow the advice given in this section and take another look at Chapter 21 (Choosing the Right Word).

EXERCISE 8

Based on context alone, make an educated guess about the italicized words in the paragraphs on light and sound waves. Write down the definition you would give each word. Then look up each word in an unabridged dictionary. How do your definitions compare?

2 Collect words—and use them.

If a word is mentioned more than twice, you should know its formal definition since its repeated use indicates that the word is important. Look the word up if you are not sure of its meaning. When attempting to *increase* your vocabulary, proceed slowly when putting newly discovered words to use in your own writing and speech. As an aid to vocabulary building, you may want to create a file of new words, as described in the box on the next page.

3 Use the thesaurus with care.

A thesaurus (literally from the Greek word meaning "treasure") is a reference tool that lists the synonyms of words and, frequently, their antonyms. Because the thesaurus is found in many computerized word processing programs, its use has become dangerously easy. If you find yourself turning to a thesaurus merely to dress up your writing with significant-sounding language, spare yourself the trouble. Unfortunately, sentences like the one that follows are too often written in a transparent effort to impress—and the effect can be unintentionally comical.

Pretentious The *penultimate* chapter of this novel left me *rhapsodic.*

This sentence shares many of the problems associated with pretentious diction (see 21h-2). It also suggests how the *diction* (the level) of the two italicized words chosen from the thesaurus is likely to contrast sharply with the diction that characterizes the rest of a paper. Often, the sense of the word (its denotation or connotation) may be slightly off the mark—not precisely what the meaning of the sentence requires (see 21a). In either case, a sentence with such "treasures" usually stands out as awkward (see 21b). A more restrained choice of words would produce a better sentence.

Revised I was overwhelmed by the next to last chapter of this novel.

By no means should you ignore the thesaurus; it is, in fact, a treasury of language. But when you find a word, make sure you are comfortable with it—that it is *your* word—before appropriating it for use in a paper.

A Personal Vocabulary File

- Make a set of flash cards with a new word and the sentence in which it appears on one side of each card; place the definition on the other side.
- Review the cards regularly. Categorize them by discipline or by part of speech. Practice changing the vocabulary word's part of speech with suffixes.
- Expand entries in your file when you find a previously filed word used in a new context.
- Consciously work one or two new words into each paper that you write, especially when the new words allow you to be precise in ways you could not otherwise be.

4 Build discipline-appropriate vocabularies.

Each discipline has a vocabulary that insiders, or professionals, use when addressing one another; one of your jobs as you move from class to class will be to recognize important words and add them to discipline-specific vocabularies that you will develop. The longer you study in a discipline, and especially if you should major in it, the larger and more versatile your specific vocabulary will be. Discipline-specific vocabularies consist of two types of words: those that are unique to the discipline and those that are found elsewhere, though with different meanings. For example, the word *gravity* occurs in contexts outside of the physics classroom. In a newspaper article or essay you might find *gravity* used to suggest great seriousness: *The gravity of the accusations caused Mr. Jones to hire a famous attorney.* Present-day physicists use the word *gravity* in an altogether different sense.

Discipline-specific vocabularies also consist of words unique to a particular field of study. The sheer volume of these words makes it impossible

EXERCISE 9

Individual responses

EXERCISE 10

Individual responses

to review them here; suffice it to say that as you see new terms repeated in texts or hear them recurring in the speech of your professors, you should note these words and learn their definitions. As you move from introductory courses in a subject to upper-level courses, the new terms will become more familiar.

EXERCISE 9

Take an informal survey to see if you can identify five words or phrases unique to a particular group of people. Listen to fraternity or sorority members on campus addressing members of their own houses; listen closely in a locker room to members of a team with which you have practiced; or sit in on a campus club meeting or a session of the student government. List the five words or phrases; then define each expression and illustrate its community-specific use in a sentence.

EXERCISE 10

Review your notes and text for one course and identify five words or phrases particular to that subject. The words or phrases might well occur in contexts beyond the course but will, as well, have a course-specific meaning. List the words or phrases; then define each expression and illustrate its discipline-specific use in a sentence.

CHAPTER 23

Spelling

English is an eclectic language derived from several different sources, including Old German, Scandinavian, and Norman French, as well as Latin and Greek. With such a mixed vocabulary, it is remarkable how closely most English spellings are associated with the sounds of words. Nevertheless, many words that look or sound alike may in fact derive from different sources, and thus be spelled or pronounced differently. With practice in writing and reading, certain basic patterns emerge that connect spelling to word sounds. Spelling can be mastered by learning a few rules and the exceptions to those rules. Spelling "demons" can be overcome by recognizing the words you most commonly misspell and remembering devices for memorizing their correct spelling.

23a Overcoming spelling/pronunciation misconnections

Long-time speakers and readers of English have learned basic connections between sounds and letter combinations that help them spell a large number of words. However, for historical reasons certain combinations of letters are not always pronounced in the same way (for example: th*ough*t, b*ough*, thr*ough*, dr*ough*t, etc.). In addition, regional and dialect variations in pronunciation may drop or vary the pronunciation of certain endings of auxiliary verbs. It is safer to try to keep a visual image of a word in your mind, rather than to rely on what you hear to help you to spell a word correctly.

Recognizing homonyms and commonly confused words

One of the most common causes of spelling confusion is **homonyms**—words that sound alike, or are pronounced almost alike, but that have different spellings and meanings. The following box lists the most commonly confused homonyms and near homonyms.

Commonly Confused Homonyms and Near Homonyms

accept [to receive]
except [to leave out]
advice [recommendation]
advise [to recommend]
affect [to have an influence on]
effect [result; to make happen]

all ready [prepared]
already [by this time]
bare [naked]
bear [to carry, endure; an animal]
board [piece of wood]
bored [uninterested]

(continued)

KEY FEATURES

Spelling is rarely a pleasant subject to discuss, especially with students. But what we have to say is often judged by how well or poorly we spell the words. Regardless of how arbitrary the spelling rules for English words may be, and irrespective of the fact that some of the world's best writers can't spell, people still tend to judge a piece of writing by its spelling. The chapter begins on a historical note, explaining why English seems to have so many different spelling rules. After establishing the need to master spelling rules, the chapter goes on to discuss those rules clearly and thoroughly. All of the standard rules are covered, from "*i* before *e*" to irregular plurals. In addition, the final section of the chapter proposes a few strategies for developing spelling skills. Throughout the chapter, exercises provide students with valuable practice in learning and applying the rules.

FOR DISCUSSION

It's no secret that many students believe that when they "go out into the world" they won't need to know how to spell. It would be useful to question them about this belief at the beginning of the chapter. Among the reasons you're likely to hear is the availability of the computer spell-checker. Of course, spell-checkers don't spell the word for you. They also miss some of the most common misspellings, homonyms—only the most sophisticated programs are context-sensitive. Another argument is that the secretary will take care of the spelling. But who checks the secretary's spelling? How will you know that he or she is a capable speller if you're not? And what if the secretary gets mad at you on the day you're sending a letter to your most influential client and types exactly what you've written? A brief discussion of the importance of learning spelling rules should help students understand the need to study this chapter.

ESL CUE

Spanish speakers might persist in spelling "which" as "wich" since the "wh" sound does not exist for them, just as Japanese students frequently reverse the letters "*l*" and "*r*," as in "She lan down the rane" for "She ran down the lane" because Japanese does not distinguish between these two sounds. Arabic speakers might tend to leave out or confuse vowels because their lettering system focuses on consonants. Russians might use "*z*'s" in place of "*s*'s" because of their alphabet system, while Spanish speakers will add an initial "*e*" to words beginning with "*s*": estudy, estupid.

Students whose languages spell relatively phonetically, such as Spanish students, will have more trouble spelling correctly than, say, French students who are accustomed to more eccentric rules for spelling.

Spellings such as "differes" may derive from first language rules for syllabification requiring more vowels than English uses.

ADDITIONAL EXERCISE A

Choose six sets of words from the list of homonyms and near homonyms. If possible, choose sets that you have difficulty with. For each set, write one sentence incorporating all words in the set.

REFERENCES

BROWN, ALAN S. "Encountering Misspellings and Spelling Performance: Why Wrong Isn't Right." *Journal of Educational Psychology* 80 (1988): 488–94. An empirical study reveals that teaching or testing spelling by using incorrectly spelled words can be counterproductive; students retain the misspelling as well as the correct spelling.

CHOMSKY, CAROL. "Reading, Writing, and Phonology." *Harvard Education Review* 40 (1970): 287–309. English spelling derives more from underlying lexical meaning than from pronunciation.

CUMMINGS, D. W. *American English Spelling: An Informal Description*. Baltimore: Johns Hopkins UP, 1988. Chapters 1 & 11. A thorough and sometimes whimsical account of the development of English spelling rules, with particular attention to the hazards of phonetic spelling.

Commonly Confused Homonyms and Near Homonyms *(continued)*

brake [stop, device for stopping]
break [to smash, destroy]
buy [purchase]
by [next to, through]
capital [city seat of government]
capitol [legislative or government building]
cite [quote, refer to]
sight [vision, something seen]
site [place, locale]
complement [something that completes]
compliment [praise]
conscience [moral sense, sense of right/wrong]
conscious [aware]
discreet [respectfully reserved]
discrete [distinct, separate]
dominant [controlling, powerful]
dominate [to control]
elicit [to draw out]
illicit [illegal]
eminent [distinguished]
immanent [inborn, inherent]
imminent [expected momentarily]
fair [just; light-complexioned; lovely]
fare [fee for transportation; meal]
gorilla [ape]
guerilla [unconventional soldier]
heard [past tense of *to hear*]
herd [group of animals]
hole [opening]
whole [entire, complete]
its [possessive form of *it*]
it's [contraction of *it is*]
lead [guide; heavy metal]
led [past tense of *to lead*]
lessen [decrease]
lesson [something learned]
loose [not tight, unfastened]
lose [misplace, fail to win]
moral [object-lesson, knowing right from wrong]
morale [outlook, attitude]
passed [past tense of *to pass*]
past [after; beyond; a time gone by]
patience [forbearance]
patients [those under medical care]
peace [absence of war]
piece [part or portion of something]
personal [private, pertaining to an individual]
personnel [employees]
plain [simple, clear, unadorned; flat land]
plane [carpenter's tool, flat surface, airplane]
presence [attendance, being at hand]
presents [gifts; gives]
principal [most important; school administrator]
principle [fundamental truth, law, conviction]
scene [setting, play segment]
seen [past participle of *to see*]
shore [coastline]
sure [certain]
stationary [standing still]
stationery [writing paper]
straight [unbending]
strait [narrow waterway]
than [besides; as compared with]
then [at that time; therefore]
their [possessive form of *they*]
there [opposite of *here*]
they're [contraction of *they are*]
threw [past tense of *to throw*]
through [by means of, finished]
thorough [complete]
to [toward]
too [also, in addition to]
two [number following *one*]
weak [feeble]
week [seven days]
weather [climatic conditions]
whether [which of two]
whose [possessive form of *who*]
who's [contraction of *who is*]
your [possessive form of *you*]
you're [contraction of *you are*]
yore [the far past]

EXERCISE 1

From each pair or trio of words in parentheses, circle the correct homonym. Then make up sentences using each of the other word[s] correctly.

1. Funeral etiquette in some cultures dictates that you should pay (your/you're) respects to the deceased by making (sure/shore) to spend a few quiet moments at the (beer/bier).
2. (There/they're/their) child (threw/through) a rock at (hour/our) child.
3. With the release of the (imminent/eminent) physicist's groundbreaking discovery, the presentation of the Nobel prize seemed (immanent/imminent).
4. If (your/you're) harboring any (illusion/allusion) about becoming a concert pianist someday, (your/you're) bound to be disappointed.
5. The technical staff is devising a method by which the (devise/device) can be installed by even nontechnical personnel.

2 Recognizing words with more than one form

A subgroup of homonyms that many people find particularly troublesome consists of words that sometimes appear as one word and other times appear as two words.

> We *always* work hard, in *all ways.*
>
> By the time everyone was *all ready* to go, it was *already* too late to catch the early show.
>
> It *may be* a question of etiquette, but *maybe* it's not.
>
> *Everyday* attitudes are not always appropriate *every day.*
>
> Walking *in to* the theater, he accidentally bumped *into* the usher.
>
> Once we were *all together,* we were *altogether* convinced the reunion had been a wonderful idea.

Unlike *always/all ways* and *already/all ready, all right* and *a lot* do not vary: they can be written only as two words.

FAULTY It's *alright* with me if Sally comes along.

REVISED It's *all right* with me if Sally comes along.

FAULTY James has *alot* of homework to do tonight.

REVISED James has *a lot* of homework to do tonight.

3 Memorizing words with silent letters or syllables

Many words contain silent letters, such as the *k* and the *w* in *know* or the *b* in dum*b*, or letters that are not pronounced in everyday speech, such as the first *r* in February. The simplest way to remember the spelling of these words is to commit them to memory, mentally pronouncing the silent letters

EXERCISE 1

1. Funeral etiquette in some cultures dictates that you should pay (<u>your</u>/you're) respects to the deceased by making (<u>sure</u>/shore) to spend a few quiet moments at the (beer/<u>bier</u>).
2. (There/they're/<u>their</u>) child (<u>threw</u>/through) a rock at (hour/<u>our</u>) child.
3. With the release of the (imminent/<u>eminent</u>) physicist's groundbreaking discovery, the presentation of the Nobel prize seemed (immanent/<u>imminent</u>).
4. If (your/<u>you're</u>) harboring any (<u>illusion</u>/allusion) about becoming a concert pianist someday, (your/<u>you're</u>) bound to be disappointed.
5. The technical staff is devising a method by which the (devise/<u>device</u>) can be installed by even nontechnical personnel.

as you do so. Following is a list of frequently used words whose mispronunciation in everyday speech often leads to misspelling.

ai*s*le	Feb*r*uary	paradi*g*m
can*d*idate	forei*g*n	*p*neumonia
clim*b*	gover*n*ment	priv*i*lege
condem*n*	int*e*rest	prob*a*bly

4 Distinguishing between noun and verb forms of the same word

Many spelling problems occur when noun and verb forms of a word have different spellings.

Verb	*Noun*
advise	advice
describe	description
enter	entrance
marry	marriage

5 Distinguishing American from British and Canadian spellings

The endings of various words differ depending on whether the American version or the British version of the word is being used. Though each is correct, when in America, do as the Americans do. Above all, you should be consistent. If you are not sure what the correct version of the word is, consult your dictionary, making sure you know whether the dictionary "prefers" British or American variations.

American	*British*
-or (humor, color)	-our (humour, colour)
-ment (judgment)	-ement (judgement)
-tion (connection)	-xion (connexion)
-ize (criticize, realize)	-ise (criticise, realise)
-er (center, theater)	-re (centre, theatre)
-led (traveled)	-lled (travelled)

Other American/British variations include gray/grey and check/cheque.

TEACHING IDEAS

Regardless of who won the Revolutionary War, many Americans still hold the belief that "British is better," and if not better, certainly classier. Thus we go to *theatres* in cultural *centres.* Students should be made aware that regardless of whether it's better, British spelling is *not* acceptable in American English writing.

23b Learn basic spelling rules for *ie/ei.*

Despite the troublesome aspects of English spelling detailed previously, there are a number of general rules that greatly simplify the task of spelling words correctly.

The *i* before *e* rule you learned in grammar school still holds true: "*i* before *e* except after *c,* or when pronounced *ay,* as in n*ei*ghbor."

i before *e*

achieve	experience
belief/believe	field
brief	fiend/friend

Except after *c*

ceiling	receipt/receive
conceit	deceit/deceive
conceive	perceive

ei pronounced *ay*

beige	neighbor
eight(h)	heinous
freight	vein

Exceptions

ancient	foreign
height	seize
either	weird

Finally, if the *ie* is not pronounced as a unit, the rule does not apply: science, conscientious, atheist.

EXERCISE 2

Insert *ie* or *ei* in the following words. If necessary, use a dictionary to confirm your choice.

forf ___ t	s ___ zure	p ___ rce
financ ___ r	f ___ nt	pat ___ nce
consc ___ nce	h ___ ress	counterf ___ t
defic ___ nt	sl ___ ght	r ___ fy

23c Learn rules for using prefixes.

Prefixes are placed at the beginnings of words to qualify or add to their meaning. The addition of a prefix never affects the spelling of the root word: do not drop a letter from or add a letter to the original word.

un	+	usual	=	unusual
mis	+	statement	=	misstatement
under	+	rate	=	underrate
dis	+	service	=	disservice
anti	+	thesis	=	antithesis
de	+	emphasize	=	deemphasize

The following are also used as prefixes: *en, in, ante, inter, pre, per, pro,* and *over.*

FOR DISCUSSION

Since *ie/ei* words are among the most troublesome for students to spell correctly, you may want to ask students in class which of the words on these lists cause them problems. (They may also come up with words not on the list.) After writing a few of the words on the board, ask if other students have developed strategies for spelling the words correctly. In this way students can help each other out as they try to master spelling rules.

EXERCISE 2

forfeit	seizure	pierce
financier	feint	patience
conscience	heiress	counterfeit
deficient	sleight	reify

23d Learn rules for using suffixes.

A **suffix** is an ending added to a word in order to change the word's function. For example, suffixes can change a present tense verb to a past tense verb (help, help*ed*); make an adjective an adverb (silent, silent*ly*); make a verb a noun (excite, excite*ment*); or change a noun to an adjective (force, forc*ible*). Spelling difficulties often arise when the root word must be changed before the suffix is added.

1 Learn rules for keeping or dropping a final *e*.

Many words end with a silent *e* (hav*e*, mat*e*, rais*e*, confin*e*, procur*e*). When adding a suffix to these words, you can use the following rules.

The basic rule: If the suffix begins with a vowel, drop the final silent *e*.

accuse	+	ation	=	accusation	sedate	+	ive	=	sedative
inquire	+	ing	=	inquiring	cube	+	ism	=	cubism
debate	+	able	=	debatable	pore	+	ous	=	porous

Exceptions

The silent *e* is sometimes retained before a suffix that begins with a vowel in order to distinguish homonyms (dyeing/dying); to prevent mispronunciation (*mileage,* not milage); and especially, to keep the sound of *c* or *g* soft.

courage	+	ous	=	courageous	embrace	+	able	=	embraceable
outrage	+	ous	=	outrageous	notice	+	able	=	noticeable

Rule: If the suffix begins with a consonant, keep the final silent *e*.

manage	+	ment	=	management	acute	+	ness	=	acuteness
sedate	+	ly	=	sedately	force	+	ful	=	forceful
blame	+	less	=	blameless					

Exceptions

When the final silent *e* is preceded by another vowel, the *e* is dropped (*argument,* not arguement; *truly,* not truely).

Other exceptions include:

judge	+	ment	=	judgment	awe	+	ful	=	awful
acknowledge	+	ment	=	acknowledgment	whole	+	ly	=	wholly

EXERCISE 3

Combine the following words and suffixes, retaining or dropping the final *e* as needed. Check your choices in the dictionary to make sure they are correct.

1. investigate + ive
2. malice + ious
3. due + ly
4. trace + able
5. singe + ing
6. service + able
7. complete + ly
8. mistake + en
9. grieve + ance
10. binge + ing

2 Learn rules for keeping or dropping a final *y*.

When suffixes are added to words that end in a final *y*, use the following rules.

Rule: When the letter immediately before the *y* is a consonant, change the *y* to *i* and then add the suffix.

beauty + ful = beautiful
breezy + er = breezier
worry + some = worrisome

comply + ant = compliant
busy + ness = business
study + ous = studious

Exceptions

Keep the final *y* when the suffix to be added is *-ing*.

study + ing = studying   comply + ing = complying

Keep the final *y* for some one-syllable root words.

shy + er = shyer   wry + ly = wryly

Keep the final *y* when the *y* is the ending of a proper name.

Janey/Janeys   Bobby/Bobbylike

Keep the final *y* when it is preceded by a vowel, and then add the suffix.

journey + ing = journeying
deploy + ment = deployment
spray + ed = sprayed

buoy + ant = buoyant
play + ful = playful
coy + ly = coyly

EXERCISE 4

Combine the following root words and suffixes, changing the *y* to *i* when necessary.

1. supply + er
2. stultify + ing
3. testy + er
4. rarefy + ed
5. joy + ousness
6. convey + ance
7. cry + er
8. Kennedy + s
9. plenty + ful
10. day + ly

Learn rules for adding *-ally*.

Rule: Add *-ally* to make an adverb out of an adjective that ends with *ic*.

terrific + ally = terrifically
caustic + ally = caustically

EXERCISE 3

1. investigative
2. malicious
3. duly
4. traceable
5. singeing
6. serviceable
7. completely
8. mistaken
9. grievance
10. binging

EXERCISE 4

1. supplier
2. stultifying
3. testier
4. rarefied
5. joyousness
6. conveyance
7. crier
8. Kennedys
9. plentiful
10. daily

GROUP ACTIVITY

In order to help students become more comfortable with checking their spelling of suffixes, you may want to use the following activity. After dividing the class into groups of three or four, assign a list of words to which various suffixes can be added. As groups try to add one or more suffixes to the words, they can help each other determine which rules apply and where to look in the handbook for help. Possible words include:

happy	energetic
passive	love
bitter	contempt
sense	oppose
announce	justify

fantastic + ally = fantastically
emphatic + ally = emphatically
music + ally = musically

Exception

public + ly = publicly

4 Learn the rule for adding *-ly.*

Rule: Add *-ly* to make an adverb out of an adjective that does not end with *ic.*

hesitant + ly = hesitantly
helpful + ly = helpfully
fortunate + ly = fortunately
fastidious + ly = fastidiously
conscientious + ly = conscientiously

5 Learn the rule for adding *-cede, -ceed,* and *-sede.*

Words that sound like *seed* are almost always spelled *-cede.*

intercede	concede	precede
accede	recede	secede

Exceptions

Only supersede uses *-sede.*

Only exceed, proceed, and succeed use *-ceed.*

6 Learn rules for adding *-able* or *-ible.*

These endings sound the same, but there is an easy way to remember which to use.

Rule: If the root word is an independent word, use the suffix *-able.* If the root is not an independent word, use the suffix *-ible.*

comfort + able = comfortable	audible
advise + able = advisable	plausible
agree + able = agreeable	compatible

Exceptions

culpable, probable, resistible

7 Learn rules for doubling the final consonant.

A word that ends in a consonant sometimes doubles the final consonant when a suffix is added.

Rule: Double the final consonant when a one-syllable word ends in a consonant preceded by a single vowel.

flip + ant = flip*p*ant   slip + er = slip*p*er
flat + en = flat*t*en   split + ing = split*t*ing

Rule: Double the final consonant when adding a suffix to a two-syllable word if a single vowel precedes the final consonant and if the final syllable is accented once the suffix is added.

control + er = control*l*er
concur + ence = concur*r*ence
commit + ing = commit*t*ing

Rule: Do not double the final consonant when it is preceded by two or more vowels, or by another consonant.

sustain + ing = sustaining
comport + ed = comported
insist + ent = insistent

Rule: Do not double the final consonant if the suffix begins with a consonant.

commit + ment = commitment
fat + ness = fatness

Rule: Do not double the final consonant if the word is *not* accented on the last syllable, or if the accent shifts from the last to the first syllable when the suffix is added.

beckon + ing = beckoning
prefer + ence = preference

EXERCISE 5

Add the correct suffix to the following roots, changing the roots as necessary. Consult a dictionary as needed.

1. benefit + ed
2. realistic + (-ly or -ally?)
3. contempt + (-able or -ible?)
4. parallel + ing
5. proceed + ure
6. reverse + (-able or -ible?)
7. allot + ment
8. occur + ence
9. room + mate
10. control + (-able or -ible?)

EXERCISE 5

1. benefited
2. realistically
3. contemptible
4. paralleling
5. procedure
6. reversible
7. allotment
8. occurrence
9. roommate
10. controllable

23e Learn rules for forming plurals.

There are several standard rules for making words plural.

LOOKING AHEAD

The practice of forming plurals with an apostrophe is becoming more prevalent among students (perhaps, in part, because it is becoming more prevalent in the public). You may want to refer your students now to 27d-3 for the admonition that the apostrophe is never used to form the plural of a regular noun.

1 Learn the basic rule for adding *-s/-es.*

Adding *-s*

For most words, simply add *-s.*

gum/gums
season/seasons
automobile/automobiles
investment/investments

Adding *-es*

For words ending in *-s, -sh, -ss, -ch, -x,* or *-z,* add *-es.*

bus/buses
bush/bushes
mistress/mistresses
watch/watches
tax/taxes
buzz/buzzes

For words ending in *-o,* add *-es* if the *o* is preceded by a consonant.

tomato/tomatoes
potato/potatoes
hero/heroes
veto/vetoes

Exceptions

pro/pros, piano/pianos, solo/solos
soprano/sopranos

Add *-s* if the final *o* is preceded by a vowel.

patio/patios
zoo/zoos

2 Learn the rule for plurals of words ending in *-f* or *-fe.*

To form the plural of some nouns ending in *-f* or *-fe,* change the ending to *-ve* before adding the *-s.*

half/halves
elf/elves
leaf/leaves
yourself/yourselves

Exceptions

scarf/scarfs/scarves
belief/beliefs
hoof/hoofs/hooves
proof/proofs
motif/motifs

3 Learn the rule for plurals of words ending in *-y.*

For words that end in a consonant followed by *-y,* change the *y* to *i* before adding *-es* to form the plural.

amenity/amenities
raspberry/raspberries
enemy/enemies
mystery/mysteries

Exceptions

proper names such as McGinty/McGintys; Mary/Marys
For words ending in a vowel followed by *-y,* add *-s.*

monkey/monkeys delay/delays
alloy/alloys buy/buys

4 Learn the rule for plurals of compound words.

When compound nouns are written as one word, add an *-s* ending as you would to make any other plural.

snowball/snowballs mailbox/mailboxes
breakthrough/breakthroughs

When compound nouns are hyphenated or written as two words, the most important part of the compound word (usually a noun that is modified) is made plural.

sister-in-law/sisters-in-law head of state/heads of state
nurse-midwife/nurse-midwives city planner/city planners

5 Learn the irregular plurals.

Some words change internally to form plurals.

woman/women goose/geese
mouse/mice tooth/teeth

Some Latin and Greek words form plurals by changing their final *-um,* *-on,* or *-us* to *-a* or *-i.*

curricul*um*/curricul*a* criteri*on*/criteri*a*
syllab*us*/syllab*i* medi*um*/medi*a*
dat*um*/dat*a* stimul*us*/stimul*i*
alumn*us*/alumn*i*

For some words, the singular and the plural forms are the same.

deer/deer sheep/sheep fish/fish
species/species moose/moose
elk/elk rice/rice

EXERCISE 6

Make the following words plural. Check your answers in the dictionary.

1. calf
2. memorandum
3. torch
4. chief
5. kilowatt-hour
6. knife
7. editor-in-chief
8. heresy
9. gas
10. ego

ADDITIONAL EXERCISE B

Begin your personal spelling list now. Go over papers that have been handed back to you recently and list all the words that were misspelled. Make two columns next to that list. In the first, write the words correctly, and in the second, write the reason for the misspelling. When you scan the reasons, you'll probably find out that your problem lies with one or two rules. Maintain the list, and you'll soon know which rules to memorize.

Example: acceptible acceptable
-ible/-able endings

EXERCISE 6

1. calves
2. memorandums or memoranda
3. torches
4. chiefs
5. kilowatt-hours
6. knives
7. editors-in-chief
8. heresies
9. gases
10. egos

REFERENCES

Clapp, Ouida, Ed. *Teaching the Basics—Really!* Urbana: NCTE, 1977. Includes articles by Muriel Harris and Ann Ruggles Gere on improving spelling skills.

Clark, Roger, and I. Y. Hashimoto. "A Spelling Program for College Students." *Teaching English in the Two-Year College* 11 (1984): 34–38. Students can improve their spelling through a program that involves keeping a personal spelling dictionary.

Dobie, Ann R. "Orthographical Theory and Practice, or How to Teach Spelling." *Journal of Basic Writing* 5 (1986): 41–48. Various methods for helping students improve their spelling are presented here.

Shaughnessy, Mina P. *Errors and Expectations: A Guide for the Teacher of Basic Writing.* New York: Oxford UP, 1977. 160–86. If students can learn the causes of their spelling problems, they can take steps to improve.

23f Developing spelling skills

In addition to learning the spelling rules detailed earlier, there are several ways to improve your spelling skills.

- Memorize commonly misspelled words.
- Keep track of the words that give you trouble. See if you can discern a pattern, and memorize the relevant rule.
- Use the dictionary. Check words whose spelling you are not sure of, and add them to your personal list of difficult-to-spell words. If you are not sure of the first few letters of a word, look up a synonym of that word to see if the word you need is listed as part of the definition.
- Pay attention when you read: your mind will retain a visual impression of a word that will help you remember how it is spelled.
- You may also develop mnemonic devices—techniques to improve memory—for particularly troublesome words. For instance, you might use the *-er* at the end of pap*er* and lett*er* as a reminder that station*ery* means writing pap*er*, while station*ary* means st*a*nding still.
- Edit and proofread carefully, paying particular attention to how the words look on the page. You will find as you train yourself that you will begin to recognize spelling errors, and that you actually know the correct spelling but have made an old mistake in haste or carelessness.
- On word processors, use a spell-checker, but realize that this computer aid will only identify misspelled words: if you have used an incorrect homonym, but have spelled it correctly, the spell-checker will not highlight the word.

PART VII
USING PUNCTUATION

CHAPTER 24

End Punctuation

The ending of one sentence and the beginning of the next is a crucial boundary for readers. Sentences provide the primary medium for delivering isolatable, comprehensible chunks of information, and readers are highly sensitive to signals that show when they come to a full stop. When sentence boundaries are blurred, readers have trouble grouping a writer's words into meaningful segments. The end-of-sentence boundary in English is marked in three ways: with a period, a question mark, or an exclamation point.

THE PERIOD

24a Using the period

The **period** is our workhorse mark of punctuation, the one used most often for noting a full stop—the end of a sentence.

1 Placing a period to mark the end of a statement or a mild command

It is conventional to end statements or mild commands with a period.

For quite some time after the *Titanic*'s collision with the iceberg, the people on board did not believe themselves to be in danger.

After all, the *Titanic* was supposed to be unsinkable.

"Women and children must get into the lifeboats."

A restatement of a question asked by someone else is called an **indirect question.** Since it is really a statement, it does not take a question mark.

DIRECT QUESTION — Many of the women who were being urged to board the life rafts asked, "Is this truly necessary?"

STATEMENT — Many of the women who were being urged to board the life rafts asked whether this measure was truly necessary.

KEY FEATURES

This first chapter on punctuation discusses, appropriately, marks that signal the end of a sentence. The role of the sentence in providing individual "chunks of meaning" is emphasized, as is the need for the reader to get the proper signals to indicate the boundaries of that unit. The three ways of marking these boundaries—periods, question marks, and exclamation points—are explained thoroughly. Examples are plentiful, and exercises provide students with practice in punctuating individual sentences and entire paragraphs.

REFERENCES

LANHAM, RICHARD A. *Style: An Anti-Textbook.* New York: Yale UP, 1974. Chapter 6. Punctuation is a method of providing in written discourse the signals that we hear in spoken discourse.

SHAUGHNESSY, MINA P. *Errors and Expectations: A Guide for the Teacher of Basic Writing.* New York: Oxford UP, 1977. Chapter 2. A practical discussion of students' difficulties with end punctuation.

TEACHING IDEAS

Few students have difficulty using the period appropriately in ordinary sentences. However, the complications that arise with quotations, parentheses, and abbreviations make it more difficult to determine the exact placement of the period. Students should try to memorize the rules in these two sections; barring that, simply remind them that they now know where to look when they have questions.

Students who are familiar with British conventions may have questions about the period after abbreviations such as *Mr.* and *Mrs.* In British English those abbreviations do not call for a period.

LOOKING AHEAD

For more information on abbreviations, see Chapter 31 a–e (Abbreviations and Numbers).

2 Placing periods in relation to end quotation marks and parentheses

A period is always placed inside a quotation mark that ends a sentence.

> The rule was, at least on the port side of the ship, "Women and children only."

When a parenthesis ends a sentence, place a period outside the end parenthesis if the parenthetical remark is not a complete sentence (see 29c). If the parenthetical remark is a separate complete sentence, enclose it entirely in parentheses and punctuate it as a sentence—with its own period.

FAULTY There was, in fact, enough room on the life rafts for first and second-class women and children, but no allowance had been made for steerage passengers (that is, economy class—the cheapest fare.).

REVISED There was, in fact, enough room on the life rafts for first and second-class women and children, but no allowance had been made for steerage passengers (that is, economy class—the cheapest fare).

REVISED There was, in fact, enough room on the life rafts for first and second-class women and children, but no allowance had been made for steerage passengers. (Steerage was defined as economy class, the cheapest fare.)

3 Using a period with abbreviations

The following are considered abbreviations that conventionally end with a period:

> Mr. Mrs. Ms. (even though this is not an abbreviation)
> apt. Ave. St. Dr. Eccles. mgr.

When an abbreviation ends a sentence, use a single period.

FAULTY The lawyers addressed their questions to Susan Turner, Esq..

REVISED The lawyers addressed their questions to Susan Turner, Esq.

When an abbreviation falls in the middle of a sentence, punctuate as if the word abbreviated were spelled out.

FAULTY The award envelope was presented to Susan Turner, Esq. who opened it calmly.

REVISED The award envelope was presented to Susan Turner, Esq., who opened it calmly.

See 31a–e for a full discussion of abbreviations.

Use no periods with acronyms or certain long abbreviations.

A number of abbreviations do not take periods—most often *acronyms* (NATO for *N*orth *A*tlantic *T*reaty *O*rganization), the names of large organizations (IBM for *I*nternational *B*usiness *M*achines), or government agencies (FTC for *F*ederal *T*rade *C*ommission). To be sure about the proper abbreviation of a word or organizational name, see the box at 31c and consult a standard dictionary for general purposes or specialized dictionaries when you are writing in a particular discipline. The following are some typical abbreviations:

ABC CNN AT&T USA ABM FAA

EXERCISE 1

Add, delete, or reposition periods in these sentences as needed.

Example: Organ transplants have increased since the development of immunosuppressive drugs such as cyclosporin

Organ transplants have increased since the development of immunosuppressive drugs such as cyclosporin.

1. According to one expert, "roughly 5,000 patients are waiting at any given moment for replacement livers. Ten thousand wait for kidneys." (Thomas)
2. Modern transplant techniques have created a rush for human organs and have given rise to what is ghoulishly called the "meat market"
3. "The ethical dilemmas raised by organ transplants are enormous," says Dr. Philip Wier (an ethicist at the Longwood Institute.)
4. Some poor people, faced with the prospect of starving, sell off their kidneys (This practice is the subject of intense debate in some state legislatures)

EXERCISE 1

1. According to one expert, "roughly 5,000 patients are waiting at any given moment for replacement livers. Ten thousand wait for kidneys" (Thomas).
2. Modern transplant techniques have created a rush for human organs and have given rise to what is ghoulishly called the "meat market."
3. "The ethical dilemmas raised by organ transplants are enormous," says Dr. Philip Wier (an ethicist at the Longwood Institute).
4. Some poor people, faced with the prospect of starving, sell off their kidneys. (This practice is the subject of intense debate in some state legislatures.)

THE QUESTION MARK

24b Using the question mark

1 Using a question mark after a direct question

Why do children develop so little when they are isolated from others?

Why is the crime rate higher in the city than the country, in impoverished areas more than other areas? Why do more males than females, more young people than older people, commit crimes?

Note: An indirect question restates a question put by someone else. The indirect question does not take a question mark.

Sociologists Eshleman and Cashion have asked why children develop so little when they are isolated from others.

Requests, worded as questions, are often followed by periods.

Would you pour another glass of wine.

Questions in a series inside a sentence will take question marks if each denotes a separate question.

When an automobile manufacturer knowingly sells a car that meets government safety standards but is defective, what are the manufacturer's legal responsibilities? moral responsibilities? financial responsibilities? [Note that these three "clipped" questions—these incomplete sentences—do not require capitalization.]

When the sense of the questions in a series is not completed until the final question, use one question mark—at the end of the sentence.

Will the agent be submitting the manuscript to one publishing house, two houses, or more?

TEACHING IDEAS

Unlike some other rules of English punctuation, the rule governing the order of question mark and end punctuation is simple and logical. You can call students' attention to the fact that this is a common-sense rule. You may want to emphasize the rule prohibiting the combination of question marks and other marks of punctuation. Especially tricky is the quoted question that doesn't end a sentence. Remind students that no comma is necessary in this situation. (This advice also applies to 24c, on exclamation points.)

2 Using a question mark after a quoted question within a statement

Placing the question mark *inside* the end quotation mark

When the question mark applies directly to the quoted material, place it inside the quotation mark.

In a dream, Abraham Lincoln remembered a stranger asking, "Why are you so common looking?"

Place the question mark inside the end quotation mark when the mark applies to *both* the quoted material *and* the sentence as a whole.

Don't you find it insulting that a person would comment directly to a president, "Why are you so common looking?"

See 28a-7 for more on quotations with questions.

Placing the question mark *outside* the end quotation mark

When the sentence as a whole forms a question but the quoted material does not, place the question mark outside the quotation.

Was it Lincoln who observed, "The Lord prefers common-looking people; that's the reason he makes so many of them"?

Note: Do *not* combine a question mark with a period, a comma, or an exclamation point.

Faulty "Are you going with him?!" asked Joan.

Revised "Are you going with him?" asked Joan.

Revised "Are you going with him!" shouted Joan.

3 Using a question mark within parentheses to indicate that the accuracy of information is in doubt even after extensive research

The question mark can be used to indicate dates or numerical references known to be inexact. The following are equivalent in meaning:

Geoffrey Chaucer was born in 1340 **(?).**

Chaucer was born about 1340.

Chaucer was born c. 1340. (The c. is an abbreviation for *circa,* meaning "around.")

Note: Do *not* use the question mark in parentheses to make wry comments in your sentences.

Faulty We found the play a stimulating **(?)** experience.

Revised Martin fell asleep in the play's first act, and I persuaded him to leave at intermission.

See 29c for more on parentheses.

EXERCISE 2

Add or delete question marks as needed. If necessary, reword sentences.

Example: The candidates' forum provided an illuminating **(?)** hour of political debate.

The candidates' forum failed to provide an illuminating debate.

1. Many people are quick to complain about the quality of political discourse in American politics, so why is it that more thoughtful people aren't running for elected office.
2. When we find that it is polling information, not philosophical conviction, that shapes the public remarks of political figures, is it any wonder that Americans turn cynical, refuse to vote, bemoan the absence of leadership.
3. Political scientists ask why Americans have one of the lowest voter turnouts among democratic nations?
4. Was it Marie Thompson who asked, "Why do we have so much difficulty rising to the challenge of our democratic traditions"?
5. Thompson reaches no firm answers when she concludes, "If the framers of the Constitution assumed an educated, caring citizenry, then we must wonder aloud—have we failed to meet the challenges laid down 200 years ago"?

EXERCISE 2

1. Many people are quick to complain about the quality of political discourse in American politics, so why is it that more thoughtful people aren't running for elected office?
2. When we find that it is polling information, not philosophical conviction, that shapes the public remarks of political figures, is it any wonder that Americans turn cynical? refuse to vote? bemoan the absence of leadership?
3. Political scientists ask why Americans have one of the lowest voter turnouts among democratic nations.
4. Was it Marie Thompson who asked, "Why do we have so much difficulty rising to the challenge of our democratic traditions?"
5. Thompson reaches no firm answers when she concludes, "If the framers of the Constitution assumed an educated, caring citizenry, then we must wonder aloud—have we failed to meet the challenges laid down 200 years ago?"

TEACHING IDEAS

A useful way to warn students against overusing the exclamation point is to remind them that if they feel the need to use an exclamation point to emphasize a sentence, then they probably haven't composed a sufficiently effective sentence to begin with. They should redirect their energies toward revising the sentence.

THE EXCLAMATION POINT

24c Using the exclamation point

In spoken conversation, exclamations are used freely, especially in moments of high passion. For some informal occasions, writers may be tempted to create with exclamation points what their tone of voice cannot show on paper. In academic writing, however, it is far more convincing to create emphasis by the force of your words, as opposed to the force of your punctuation.

1 Using the exclamation point—sparingly—to mark an emphatic statement or command

Overused exclamation points create a none-too-flattering portrait of a "breathy" or "flaky" writer who is highly excitable and not too credible. Save the exclamation point to call special attention to a unique, memorable sentence, the content of which creates its own emphasis. The exclamation point will highlight the emphasis already present.

> Enterprising archaeologists visit their dentists regularly, if only to obtain supplies of worn-out dental instruments, which make first-rate fine digging tools!
>
> Please! Let me do it myself! [The use of exclamation points with this emphatic exclamation and command is appropriate for duplicating spoken dialogue.]

Marking mild exclamations with periods or commas

> Please, let me do it myself.

Note: Do not combine an exclamation point with a period, comma, or question mark.

Faulty "Leave this room!," demanded the judge.

Revised "Leave this room!" demanded the judge.

Faulty "Can't you give us some privacy?!" he snarled.

Revised "Can't you give us some privacy!" he snarled.

EXERCISE 3

Read the following paragraphs on the subject of getting fired from a job and provide periods, question marks, and exclamation points as needed.

Many people who have lost their jobs report that the loss profoundly undermines their self-esteem They blame themselves They ask themselves "How can I be lovable, worthy, and competent if I have lost my job" Having to file an unemployment claim only serves to deepen their sense of shame

Even well-intentioned former coworkers are no source of comfort The newly unemployed often find that even the most sympathetic colleagues tend to abandon them These coworkers are terrified that the same thing might happen to them (in a climate of downsizing this fear is certainly justified) Others tell the victim that this loss is "the best thing that could ever happen to you" From the fired person's point of view, such people are merely trying to alleviate their own discomfort "They say that so that they won't have to worry about me" one woman commented The loss of one's job can cause a person to become cynical and suspicious

EXERCISE 3

Many people who have lost their jobs report that the loss profoundly undermines their self-esteem. They blame themselves. They ask themselves, "How can I be lovable, worthy, and competent if I have lost my job?" Having to file an unemployment claim only serves to deepen their sense of shame.

Even well-intentioned former coworkers are no source of comfort. The newly unemployed often find that even the most sympathetic colleagues tend to abandon them. These coworkers are terrified that the same thing might happen to them. (In a climate of downsizing this fear is certainly justified.) Others tell the victim that this loss is "the best thing that could ever happen to you." From the fired person's point of view, such people are merely trying to alleviate their own discomfort. "They say that so that they won't have to worry about me," one woman commented. The loss of one's job can cause a person to become cynical and suspicious.

CHAPTER 25

Commas

One important purpose of punctuation is to help readers identify clusters of related words, both between and within sentences. By far the most common mark used to distinguish one sentence from another is the period. *Within* sentences, the most common mark is the **comma,** and it is used primarily as a signal that some element, some word or cluster of related words, is being set off from a main sentence for a reason. Readers see the comma as a direct instruction from the writer on how to read and understand. Clear instructions will keep readers focused on the words in exactly the way the writer deems necessary. A well-used comma helps to move readers from the beginning of a sentence through to the end, effortlessly and with understanding. Poorly used, a comma will scatter meaning and create confusion. There is much to gain, therefore, in using commas precisely.

In this chapter you will find rules and guidelines for using the comma. Much of the logic of punctuating with commas is tied to the logic of a sentence's structure. See especially Chapters 13, 15, and 19, as well as Chapter 7.

25a Using commas with introductory and concluding expressions

1 Place a comma after a modifying phrase or clause that begins a sentence.

Yesterday, the faucet stopped working.
Once the weather turned cold, the faucet stopped working.

A sentence may begin with an opening phrase or clause that is neither the subject nor a simple modifier of the subject. If such an introductory element is longer than a few words, set it off from the main part of the sentence with a comma. The comma will signal the reader that the sentence's subject is being delayed.

According to landscape architect Robert Gibbs, urban shopping centers could learn a lot from suburban malls.

Because Gibbs possesses a commercial shrewdness, he is able to spot the flaws (from a commercial standpoint) in the most elegant street designs.

OPTION: The comma after an introductory word or brief phrase is optional.

KEY FEATURES

The comma might aptly be called the ubiquitous punctuation mark; commas seem to be everywhere. Because of the variety of uses this mark can be put to, many student writers have difficulty mastering its use. This chapter presents in exhaustive, clear detail all of the major uses of the comma in written English—from setting off introductory phrases to preventing misreading of long sections within a sentence. The underlying purpose of the comma, as stated in the introduction, is to help readers understand the writing on the page. Thus the treatment of comma use is always approached from the perspective of the logic of the sentence itself. Examples illustrate the appropriate use of commas in various situations, and exercises provide extensive practice in making decisions regarding comma use.

ESL CUE

Punctuation is an alien concept to students whose scripts differ from the English alphabet, and, even in languages that do use our alphabet, the rules for punctuation differ totally from ours. Spanish, for example, uses commas with greater frequency and for more purposes than does English, with commas between long series of main clauses being perfectly acceptable. For this reason, Spanish speakers will predictably have great difficulty understanding the concept of the comma splice. Vietnamese, in turn, has no standard rules for punctuation and, in fact, no requisite punctuation except signs to mark a stop. Vietnamese students influenced by French or English will put in punctuation to mark pauses, but they may do so haphazardly.

REFERENCES

LANHAM, RICHARD A. *Style: An Anti-Textbook.* New York: Yale UP, 1974. Chapter 6. Punctuation is a method of providing in written discourse the signals we hear in spoken discourse.

LINDEMANN, ERIKA. *A Rhetoric for Writing Teachers.* 2nd ed. New York: Oxford UP, 1987. Chapter 9. In discussing sentences, Lindemann refers to problems students encounter with internal punctuation.

MEYER, CHARLES F. "Teaching Punctuation to Advanced Writers." *Journal of Advanced Composition* 6 (1985–86): 117–29. More accomplished student writers can be taught to use punctuation for rhetorical effect.

MEYER, EMILY, and LOUISE Z. SMITH. *The Practical Tutor.* New York: Oxford UP, 1987. Chapter 9. Useful advice for helping students overcome punctuation problems.

SHAUGHNESSY, MINA P. *Errors and Expectations: A Guide for the Teacher of Basic Writing.* New York: Oxford UP, 1977. 14–43. A practical discussion of students' difficulties with commas.

THOMAS, LEWIS. "Notes on Punctuation." *The Medusa and the Snail: More Notes of a Biology Watcher.* New York: Viking, 1979. An imaginative and creative rumination on the joys and frustrations of punctuation.

> In fact a great many considerations are involved in the overlap of the physical and psychological environments for shopping.

When an introductory element consists of two or more phrases, a comma is required.

> As a commercial space with a retailing bias, the mall should have a design that does not let the shopper become distracted from buying.

NOTE: An opening verbal phrase or clause is set off with a comma if it is used as a modifier; an opening verbal used as a subject is *not* set off.

MODIFIER In creating a shopping environment that is too beautiful, commercial designers are failing to serve the needs of the merchants.

SUBJECT Creating a shopping environment that is too beautiful fails to serve the needs of the merchants.

2 Place a comma after a transitional word, phrase, or clause that begins a sentence.

> Actually, we've had this problem for years.

A transition is a logical bridge between sentences or paragraphs. As an introductory element, it is set off with a comma.

> Once division of labor by sex arose, it must have produced several immediate benefits for the early hominids. *First of all,* nutrition would have improved owing to a balanced diet of meat and plant foods. *Second,* each male or female would have become expert in only part of the skills needed for subsistence and would have increased his or her efficiency accordingly.

When a transitional element is moved to the interior of a sentence, set it off with a *pair* of commas. At the end of a sentence, the transitional element is set off with a single comma.

> Lipid molecules, *of course,* and molecules that dissolve easily in lipids can pass through cell membranes with ease.
>
> Lipid molecules and molecules that dissolve easily in lipids can pass through cell membranes with ease, *to cite two examples.*

3 Use a comma (or commas) to set off a modifying element that ends or interrupts a sentence *if* the modifier establishes a qualification, contrast, or exception.

> The ships return to port at all hours, often at night.
> The storm warning was broadcast on the A channel, not the B channel.

A QUALIFICATION

> The literary form *short story* is usually defined as a brief fictional prose narrative, *often involving one connected episode.*

A CONTRAST

The U.S. government located a lucrative project for an atomic accelerator in Texas, *not Massachusetts.*

AN EXCEPTION

The children of the rich are the group most likely to go to private preparatory schools and elite colleges, *regardless of their grades.*

When phrases or clauses of contrast, qualification, and exception occur in the middle of a sentence, set them off with a *pair* of commas.

The government chose Texas, *not Massachusetts,* as the site of a lucrative project for an atomic accelerator.

All seas, *except in the areas of circumpolar ice,* are navigable.

If a phrase or clause does *not* establish a qualification, contrast, or exception, do *not* use a comma to separate it from the sentence.

The faucet stopped working once the weather turned cold.

EXERCISE 1

The following sentences contain transitional expressions and modifying words or phrases. Rewrite each sentence so that the transition or modifier will come at the *beginning* of the sentence **or** at the *end.* Use commas as needed.

Example: Some of the Balkan nations of southeastern and south central Europe declared war on the waning Ottoman Empire in 1912.

In 1912, some of the Balkan nations of southeastern and south central Europe declared war on the waning Ottoman Empire.

1. Bulgaria attacked Serbia and Greece in 1913 in a second war over boundaries.
2. Bulgaria was carved up as a result of the 1913 war by its former Balkan allies and Turkey.
3. The assassination of the Archduke Ferdinand of Austria the following year brought on the First World War.
4. A sprawling new nation, Yugoslavia, was formed after the Austro-Hungarian Empire collapsed.
5. The aspirations of Croats and other minorities in Yugoslavia were suppressed under the tenuous domination of the Serbs.
6. The collapse of the Ottoman Empire at the same time left many ethnic Turks subject to their longtime foes the Bulgarians.
7. A million Armenians were slaughtered at the same time as a result of attempts at forging a new Turkish state in Anatolia.
8. Undermined by corrupt and meddling monarchs and by ethnic passions, parliamentary governments of southeastern Europe rose and fell.
9. The fall of Communist regimes in eastern Europe today has led to a resurgence of ethnic fighting.
10. "Ethnic cleansing" reminiscent of Nazi atrocities has annihilated whole villages.

GROUP ACTIVITY

All of the exercises in this chapter lend themselves to group activity. Have students respond to exercises individually, and then compare their responses with those of other group members. When the inevitable disagreement occurs, students will have to consult the handbook. Once they become accustomed to using the chapter, they'll likely continue to refer to it as they edit their papers.

EXERCISE 1

1. In a second war over boundaries, Bulgaria attacked Serbia and Greece in 1913.
2. As a result of the 1913 war, Bulgaria was carved up by its former Balkan allies and Turkey.
3. The following year, the assassination of the Archduke Ferdinand of Austria brought on the First World War.
4. After the Austro-Hungarian Empire collapsed, a sprawling new nation, Yugoslavia, was formed.
5. Under the tenuous domination of the Serbs, the aspirations of Croats and other minorities in Yugoslavia were suppressed.
6. At the same time, the collapse of the Ottoman Empire left many ethnic Turks subject to their longtime foes the Bulgarians.
7. As a result of attempts at forging a new Turkish state in Anatolia, a million Armenians were slaughtered at the same time.
8. Parliamentary governments of southeastern Europe rose and fell, undermined by corrupt and meddling monarchs and by ethnic passions.
9. Today, the fall of Communist regimes in eastern Europe has led to a resurgence of ethnic fighting.
10. Reminiscent of Nazi atrocities, "ethnic cleansing" has annihilated whole villages.

TEACHING IDEAS

It's worthwhile to ask students to keep in mind the guidelines presented in the Spotlight on Common Errors when they edit their papers. This outline can serve as a quick, easy reference for appropriate comma use.

FOR DISCUSSION

Since most students have problems with only a few of these common errors, you might want to initiate a class discussion of errors most relevant to your students. Ask students to identify from the list examples of usage familiar to them, and to make their own list of common errors. Students can then discuss the function of commas in sentences, thereby reinforcing their understanding of internal sentence punctuation. (In large classes, this activity might begin with small groups. The groups will identify their common errors, and then the class as a whole will discuss the list of errors compiled from each group's report.)

Spotlight on Common Errors—COMMA USE

These are clues to the errors most commonly associated with comma use. For full explanations and suggested revisions, follow the cross-references to chapter sections.

COMMA ERRORS arise when the use—or absence—of commas leaves readers unable to differentiate between a main sentence and the parts being set off. Five error patterns account for most of the difficulty with comma use.

- **Use a comma to set off introductory words or word groupings from the main part of the sentence (see 25a).**

Faulty	Revised
Yesterday the faucet stopped working.	Yesterday, the faucet stopped working.
Once the weather turned cold the faucet stopped working.	Once the weather turned cold, the faucet stopped working.

- **Do *not* use a comma to set off concluding words or word groupings from a main sentence (but see 25a-3 for exceptions).**

Faulty	Revised
The faucet stopped working, yesterday.	The faucet stopped working yesterday.
The faucet stopped working, once the weather turned cold.	The faucet stopped working once the weather turned cold.

- **Place a comma before the word *and, but, or, for,* or *so* when it joins two sentences (see 25b).**

Faulty	Revised
The faucet stopped working *and* the sink leaks.	The faucet stopped working, *and* the sink leaks.
I'll fix them myself *and* I'll save money.	I'll fix them myself, *and* I'll save money.

BUT use no comma if one key word, usually the subject, keeps the second grouping of words from being considered a sentence.

FAULTY	REVISED
I'll fix them myself, and save money.	I'll fix them myself and save money.

- **Use a comma to separate three or more items in a series (see 25c-1).**

FAULTY	REVISED
I'll need a washer a valve and a wrench.	I'll need a washer, a valve, and a wrench. *or* I'll need a washer, a valve and a wrench.

- **Use a *pair* of commas to set off from a sentence any word or word group that adds nonessential information (see 25d).**

FAULTY	REVISED
Ahorn Hardware which is just around the corner will have the materials I need.	Ahorn Hardware, which is just around the corner, will have the materials I need. [Since a specific hardware store is named and its identity is clear, the added information is nonessential and is set off with a pair of commas.]

BUT use *no* commas if a word or word group adds essential information needed for identifying some other word in the sentence.

FAULTY	REVISED
The hardware store, which is just around the corner, will have the materials I need.	The hardware store which is just around the corner will have the materials I need. [Since the added information is essential for identifying *which* hardware store (perhaps there is more than one store in the area), no commas are used. Note that in the case of essential information, many writers insist on using *that* to introduce the information.] The hardware store **that** is just around the corner will have the materials I need.

TEACHING IDEAS

Some students have developed a habit of placing the comma *after* the coordinating conjunction. You may want to place particular emphasis on the precise placement of the comma in these structures.

25b Using a comma before a coordinating conjunction to join two independent clauses

The faucet stopped working, and the sink leaks.
We can fix the problems ourselves, or we can call a plumber.

One of the principal ways to join two independent clauses is to link them with a comma and a coordinating conjunction: *and, but, or, nor* (see 19a-1).

> The changes in *Homo erectus* are substantial over a million years, *but* they seem gradual by comparison with those that went before.
>
> A computer's data and addressing information are stored in flip-flops within the various memory registers, *or* they take the form of an electrical signal that is moving through wires from one register to another.

Options: You have several options for linking independent clauses: (1) you can separate the clauses and form two distinct sentences—see 24a; (2) you can use a semicolon to link the clauses within one sentence—see 26a–b (and the Critical Decisions box there); (3) you can make one clause subordinate to another—see 19b (and the Critical Decisions box in 19a).

Note: When a coordinating conjunction joins two independent clauses, and when one or both of these clauses has internal punctuation, to prevent misreading change the comma appearing before the conjunction to a semicolon.

> Several thousand years ago, probably some lines of Neanderthal man and woman died out; but it seems likely that a line in the Middle East went directly to us, *Homo sapiens.*

25c Using commas between items in a series

One major function of the comma is to signal a brief pause that separates items in a series—a string of related elements.

1 Place a comma between items in a series.

We'll need a washer, a valve, and a wrench.

Items joined in a series should be parallel (see Chapter 18). Items can be single words, phrases, or clauses.

Words A Central Processing Unit contains a large number of special-purpose registers for storing *instructions, addresses,* and *data.*

Phrases Booms and busts have plagued economic activity since the onset of industrialization, *sporadically ejecting many workers from their jobs, pushing many businesses into bankruptcy,* and *leaving many politicians out in the cold.*

Option: Some writers prefer to omit the final comma in a series—the comma placed before the coordinating conjunction *and.* The choice is yours. Whatever your preference, be consistent.

Option Exercise appears *to reduce the desire to smoke, to lessen any tendency toward obesity* and *to help in managing stress.*

Note: When at least one item in a series contains a comma, use a semicolon to separate items and prevent misreading (see Chapter 26). For the same reason, use semicolons to separate long independent clauses in a series.

> I believe that the sun is about ninety-three million miles from the earth; that it is a hot globe many times bigger than the earth; and that, owing to the earth's rotation, it rises every morning and will continue to do so for an indefinite time in the future.

2 Place a comma between two or more coordinate adjectives in a series, if no coordinating conjunction joins them.

> Getting under the sink can be a tricky, messy job.

A series of adjectives will often appear as a parallel sequence: the *playful, amusing* poet; an *intelligent, engaging* speaker. When the order of the adjectives can be reversed without affecting the meaning of the noun being modified, the adjectives are called **coordinate adjectives.** Coordinate adjectives can be linked by a comma or by a coordinating conjunction.

Series with commas

> The stomach is a thick-walled, muscular sac that can expand to hold more than 2 liters of food or liquid.

Series with *and*

> The stomach is a thick-walled *and* muscular sac that can expand to hold more than 2 liters of food or liquid.

Series with commas

> The left hemisphere of the brain thinks sequential, analytical thoughts and is also the center of language.

Series with *and*

> The left hemisphere thinks sequential *and* analytical thoughts and is also the center of language.

Note: The presence of two adjectives beside one another does not necessarily mean that they are coordinate. In the phrase "the wise old lady," the adjectives could not be reversed in sequence or joined by *and;* the adjective *wise* describes *old lady,* not *lady* alone. The same analysis holds for the phrase "the ugly green car." *Green car* is the element being modified by *ugly.* Only coordinate adjectives modifying the same noun are separated by commas.

EXERCISE 2

Combine the following sentences with the conjunction indicated in brackets, and decide whether you need to use a comma. Recall that unless a conjunction joins independent clauses, no comma is needed.

EXERCISE 2

1. Proto-humans did not walk as well on two feet as we do, but they were better than we are at climbing trees and suspending themselves from branches.
2. Ancestors of present-day leopards were contemporary with early hominids and shared the same habitats.
3. Leopards cannot defend their kills from scavenging by lions, so they store their kills in trees.
4. Archaeologist John Cavallo thinks that early tree-climbing hominids may have fed off leopard kills stashed in trees, since leopards don't guard the carcasses of their kills.

EXERCISE 3

(In all sentences, the final comma in the series is optional.)

1. They possessed complex religious beliefs, symbolic world views radically different from those of Europeans, and cultural values Europeans did not understand.
2. Like other native populations "discovered" after them, Native Americans were exploited, decimated by exotic diseases, robbed of their lands, and ultimately stripped of their traditional cultures.
3. Survivors became serfs, slaves, or subordinate and often tangential elements in the new social order.
4. Therefore, for centuries Native Americans continued to resist Catholic missionaries, explorers, and settlers from all over Europe.

Example: Anthropologists are currently investigating whether early hominids (proto-humans) ate meat. [and] Did they obtain meat by hunting or scavenging?

Anthropologists are currently investigating whether early hominids (proto-humans) ate meat and whether they obtained it by hunting or scavenging.

1. Proto-humans did not walk as well on two feet as we do. [but] They were better than we are at climbing trees and suspending themselves from branches.
2. Ancestors of present-day leopards were contemporary with early hominids. [and] Ancestors of present-day leopards shared the same habitats as early hominids.
3. Leopards cannot defend their kills from scavenging by lions. [so] They store their kills in trees.
4. Archaeologist John Cavallo thinks that early tree-climbing hominids may have fed off leopard kills stashed in trees. [since] Leopards don't guard the carcasses of their kills.

EXERCISE 3

In each sentence, place a comma as needed between items in a series.

Example: Native American societies were based on notions of community mutual obligations and reciprocity and on close ties of kin.

Native American societies were based on notions of community, mutual obligation, and reciprocity and on close ties of kin.

1. They possessed complex religious beliefs symbolic world views radically different from those of Europeans and cultural values Europeans did not understand.
2. Like other native populations "discovered" after them, Native Americans were exploited decimated by exotic diseases robbed of their lands and ultimately stripped of their traditional cultures.
3. Survivors became serfs slaves or subordinate and often tangential elements in the new social order.
4. Therefore, for centuries Native Americans continued to resist Catholic missionaries explorers and settlers from all over Europe.

25d Using commas to set off nonessential elements

1 Identify essential (restrictive) elements that need no commas.

The hardware store which is just around the corner will have the materials I need.

When a modifier provides information that is necessary for identifying a word, then the modifier is said to be **essential** (or **restrictive**), and it appears in its sentence *without* commas.

> The world-renowned architect *commissioned to design a synagogue for the Beth Shalom congregation in Elkins Park, Pennsylvania* produced an architectural masterpiece.

There have been many famous architects. This sentence refers to the *one* architect hired by this congregation. Without the modifying phrase *commissioned to design a synagogue for the Beth Shalom congregation in Elkins Park, Pennsylvania,* the subject of this sentence, *the world-renowned architect,* could not be conclusively identified. Therefore, the modifying expression is essential, and no commas are used to set apart the phrase from the sentence in which it appears.

An essential modifier can also be a single word (or single name).

> The world-renowned architect *Frank Lloyd Wright* was born in 1869.

Without the name *Frank Lloyd Wright,* we would not know which world-renowned architect was born in 1869. By contrast, consider the following sentence.

> The designer of the Beth Shalom synagogue in Elkins Park, Pennsylvania, *Frank Lloyd Wright,* died the same year in which the synagogue was built.

In this sentence, the modifying information is no longer necessary because there was only one architect responsible for the design of this structure. Thus, *Frank Lloyd Wright* is considered nonessential information and is set off by a pair of commas.

An essential modifier can also be a clause.

> The cyclotron is an instrument *that accelerates charged particles to very high speeds.*

The noun modified—*instrument*—could be *any* instrument, and the clause that follows provides information essential to the definition of *which* or *what kind* of instrument.

2 Use a pair of commas to set off nonessential (nonrestrictive) elements.

> Ahorn Hardware, which is just around the corner, will have the materials I need.

If a word being modified is clearly defined (as, for instance, a person with a specific name is clearly defined), then the modifying element—though it might add interesting and useful information—is nonessential. When the modifier is not essential for defining a word, use commas to set the modifier apart from the sentence in which it appears.

TEACHING IDEAS

To reinforce the importance of distinguishing between essential and nonessential elements, you can write on the board a sentence that has two distinct meanings depending on whether or not the subordinate clause is essential. Write the sentence first with the comma, and then erase the comma. Ask students how the meaning changes when the comma is removed. A sentence like "Professor Shannon failed all of her students, who had missed the exam" is a good example. Did all of Professor Shannon's students miss the exam? Did she fail only that group of students who missed the exam? As they work with sentences like this, students will gain a clearer understanding of how important it is to be able to distinguish essential from nonessential elements.

REFERENCE

CHRISTENSEN, FRANCIS. "Restrictive and Nonrestrictive Modifiers Again." *Notes Toward a New Rhetoric: Nine Essays for Teachers.* 2nd ed. Ed. Francis Christensen and Bonniejean Christensen. New York: Harper, 1978. A discussion of the comma's role in constructing sentences with certain modifiers.

ADDITIONAL EXERCISE A

ACROSS THE CURRICULUM Photocopy a long passage from one of your textbooks, and underline all parenthetical and repeating elements set off by commas. How often does the author use such constructions? What is the effect of these constructions—how do they help the reader understand the material, and how do they make the reading itself easier and more pleasurable?

LOOKING BACK

Students may find it helpful to review the discussion of relative pronouns in essential and nonessential clauses as they cover this material. If you believe that they may benefit from such a review, refer them to 14e.

NONESSENTIAL Frank Lloyd Wright, *possibly the finest American architect of the twentieth century,* died in 1959.

The subject of the sentence has already been defined adequately by his name, *Frank Lloyd Wright.* The writer uses the modifying phrase not as a matter of definition but as an occasion to add nonessential information. The meaning of a sentence will change according to whether modifying elements are punctuated as essential or nonessential. The two pairs of sentences that follow are worded identically. Punctuation gives them different meanings.

ESSENTIAL The students *who have band practice after school* cannot attend the game.

NONESSENTIAL The students, *who have band practice after school,* cannot attend the game.

The essential modifier precisely defines *which* students will not be able to attend the game—only those who have band practice. The meaning of this first sentence, then, is that some students *will* be able to attend—those who do *not* have band practice. The nonessential modifier communicates that *all* of the students have band practice and that none can attend.

Punctuating Modifying Clauses with *Who, Which,* and *That*

The relative pronouns *who, which,* and *that* begin modifying clauses that can interrupt or end sentences.

WHO

Who can begin a clause that is essential to defining the word modified.

> Formal organizations designate managers *who help administrative units meet their specific goals.*

Who can also begin a nonessential clause. Note the presence of commas in this sentence.

> Frank Smith, *who is an administrative manager,* helps his administrative unit meet its goals.

WHICH

Similarly, *which* can begin an essential or a nonessential modifying clause.

> Two sites *which flourished in the dim yet documented past* are Saxon London and medieval Winchester. [essential]

> Some historical archaeologists excavate sites like Saxon London or medieval Winchester, *which flourished in the dim yet documented past.* [nonessential]

THAT

That always denotes an essential clause. Do not use commas to set off a modifying clause beginning with *that.*

> Two sites *that flourished in the dim yet documented past* are Saxon London and medieval Winchester. [essential]

3 Use commas to set off parenthetical or repeating elements.

The reasons she gave, all three of them, were convincing.

By definition, a parenthetical remark is not essential to the meaning of a sentence. The remark sometimes illuminates the sentence but by no means provides crucial information. Set off parenthetical expressions as you would any nonessential element.

> Lizzie Borden, *despite the weight of evidence against her,* was acquitted of the murder of her father and her stepmother.

Options: You have the choice of setting off parenthetical elements by using commas, parentheses, or dashes. Any of these options is correct, so base your decision on the level of emphasis you wish to give the parenthetical element. Dashes call the most attention to the element and parentheses the least attention.

Repeating elements

Repetition can both add useful information to a sentence and create pleasing sentence rhythms. By definition, a repeating element is nonessential, so the logic of setting off nonessential elements with commas applies. Set off a repeating element with a *pair* of commas if the element appears in the middle of a sentence. (You may also use a pair of dashes.) Use a comma or a dash and a period if the element concludes the sentence.

> The police investigation, *a bungled affair from start to finish,* overlooked crucial evidence and even managed to lose notes taken at the scene of the crime.

> Archaeologists working underwater have exactly the same intellectual goals as their dry-land colleagues—*to recover, reconstruct, and interpret the past.*

> These bare facts have become so familiar, *so essential in the conduct of an interlocking world society,* that they are usually taken for granted.

Appositives

One class of repeating element is called an **appositive phrase,** the function of which is to rename a noun. The phrase is called *appositive* because it is placed in *apposition* to—that is, *side by side* with—the noun it repeats. In the first example, the appositive *a bungled affair from start to finish* renames the subject of the sentence, *investigation.* The sentence could be rewritten and repunctuated as follows:

> *A bungled affair from start to finish,* the police investigation of the Borden case overlooked crucial evidence and even managed to lose notes taken at the scene of the crime.

Exception: When a nonessential appositive phrase consists of a series of items separated by commas, set it off from a sentence with a pair of dashes—not commas—to prevent misreading.

ESL CUE

ESL students need to focus on the difficult issue of deciding whether an appositive identifies and therefore needs no commas or whether it is extra information and therefore needs commas. A good way to demonstrate is with "my sister, Barbara," which indicates that there is only one sister and that that one sister is named "Barbara," as opposed to "my sister Barbara," the usage if there is more than one sister and if the name is necessary to identify which one of two or more sisters is being discussed.

A second problem is that of distinguishing the key noun from the appositive which modifies it. Reminding students that appositives add more detail and will therefore usually be the more specific noun will help clarify this.

CRITICAL DECISIONS

Form, and support, opinions: Within a sentence, distinguish essential from nonessential information

Comma placement regularly depends on a decision you make about whether certain qualifying (or additional) information is or is not essential to the meaning of a particular word. Your decision about this content determines how you punctuate your sentence.

A Test to Determine Whether Qualifying Information Is Essential or Nonessential

1. Identify the single word in the sentence being qualified by a word group.
2. Identify the qualifying word group.
3. Drop the qualifying word group from the sentence.
4. Ask of the single word from #1, above: Do I understand which one or who?
   a. If you can give a single answer to this question, the qualifying information is nonessential. Set the information off from the sentence with a *pair* of commas.
   b. If you cannot give a specific answer to the question, the qualifying information *is* essential. Include the information in the main sentence with *no* commas.

Example Sentences

Example 1: The bill which placed a fifty-cent tax on every pack of cigarettes was defeated.

1. Word being qualified: *bill*
2. Qualifying word group: *which placed a fifty-cent tax on every pack of cigarettes*
3. New sentence: *The bill was defeated.*
4. Do I understand which one? *No.*

Therefore, the qualifying information is essential; include it in the sentence *without* commas.

> The bill which placed a fifty-cent tax on every pack of cigarettes was defeated.

Example 2: Bill 307 which placed a fifty-cent tax on every pack of cigarettes was defeated.

1. Word being qualified: *Bill 307*
2. Qualifying word group: *which placed a fifty-cent tax on every pack of cigarettes*
3. New sentence: *Bill 307 was defeated.*
4. Do I understand which one? *Yes.*

Therefore, the qualifying information is nonessential; set it off from the sentence with a *pair* of commas.

> Bill 307, which placed a fifty-cent tax on every pack of cigarettes, was defeated.

CONFUSING Motion sickness, nausea, dizziness, and sleepiness, is a dangerous and common malady among astronauts.

REVISED Motion sickness—nausea, dizziness, and sleepiness—is a dangerous and common malady among astronauts.

EXERCISE 4

Combine the following pairs of sentences. Use commas to set off nonessential modifiers and omit commas when modifiers are essential.

Example: A number of Hollywood films have depicted historical events. Such films were often painstakingly researched.

A number of Hollywood films that have depicted historical events were often painstakingly researched.

1. Film by its very nature is better able than prose to present the event in all its intensity.
   Even the most sober historians are willing to admit that fact.
2. In some instances the film has turned out to be more historically accurate than the original historical account.
   Vivien Leigh's portrayal of a spirited Scarlett O'Hara is now considered to be a fairly accurate interpretation of the not-so-helpless Southern belle.
3. Of course there have been plenty of instances of mistakes in historical representation.
   A film might carefully reproduce the material culture of an era but skew the facts of the event.
4. Viewers are more comfortable if the film ratifies their personal biases.
   Hollywood history films tend to reflect the biases of their viewers, especially in political matters.
5. *Bonnie and Clyde* transformed a vapid Bonnie Parker into an aggressive moll. *Anne of the Thousand Days* transformed an ambitious and strong-willed Anne Boleyn into a lovesick, awestruck girl.
6. *A Man for all Seasons* presented a gentle, principled man.
   The historical Thomas More wrote that the execution of heretics was "lawful, necessary and well done."
7. *Bonnie and Clyde* and *Anne of the Thousand Days* were made only two years apart.
   These two films illustrate the rise of the generation gap of the 1960s.

25e Using commas to acknowledge conventions of quoting, naming, and various forms of separation

1 Use a comma to introduce or to complete a quotation.

Tom said, "I'll be back in two hours."

Commas set a quotation apart from the words that introduce or conclude the quotation. Commas (and periods) are placed *inside* end quotation marks.

EXERCISE 4

Suggested responses:

1. Even the most sober historians are willing to admit that film by its very nature is better able than prose to present an event in all its intensity.
2. In some instances, the film has turned out to be more historically accurate than the original historical account, as in *Gone with the Wind*'s spirited Scarlett O'Hara, now considered to be a fairly accurate interpretation of the not-so-helpless Southern belle.
3. A film that carefully reproduces the material culture of an era but skews the facts of the event is an instance of the many films that have made mistakes in historical representation.
4. Viewers, who are more comfortable if a film ratifies their personal biases, are often catered to by Hollywood history films that reflect those biases, especially in political matters.
5. *Bonnie and Clyde* transformed a vapid Bonnie Parker into an aggressive moll while *Anne of the Thousand Days,* which portrayed the fate of Anne Boleyn, reduced an ambitious and strong-willed woman into a lovesick, awestruck girl.
6. The historical Thomas More, who wrote that the execution of heretics was "lawful, necessary and well done," was presented by *A Man for all Seasons* as a gentle, principled man.
7. *Bonnie and Clyde* and *Anne of the Thousand Days,* made only two years apart, illustrate the rise of the generation gap of the 1960s.

GROUP ACTIVITY

CRITICAL THINKING Essential and nonessential elements pose problems for all writers, even on occasion for sophisticated writers. Thus it's worth the extra time it takes to give students practice in identifying and correctly punctuating these elements. Try to mix group membership to include both stronger and weaker students, and ask each group to compose five sentences without internal punctuation. Some of the sentences are to include essential information, some nonessential. Then the sentences will be passed on to another group for correct punctuation. The discussion in groups as students compose and punctuate the sentences should help them understand the concept more clearly.

TEACHING IDEAS

You may be aware of students who have problems with one or more of the specific uses for commas outlined here. If so, you can ask those students to evaluate past essays for evidence of comma problems. Have the students insert commas where necessary in these papers, and then reread them to appreciate how punctuation can contribute to clarity.

> The prizefighter Rocky Graziano once said, "I had to leave fourth grade because of pneumonia—not because I had it but because I couldn't spell it."

> Early in his career, Winston Churchill sported a mustache. At a fancy dinner, he argued with a woman who snapped, "Young man—I care for neither your politics nor your mustache."

> "Madam," responded Churchill, "you are unlikely to come into contact with either."

> (For more on using commas with quotations, see Chapter 28.)

Use a comma to set off expressions of direct address. If the expression interrupts a sentence, set the word off with a *pair* of commas.

> "Ed, did you bring your computer?"
> "Our business, Ed, is to sell shoes."

You will most often encounter expressions of direct address when writing dialogue or when quoting speakers addressing their audiences.

> "You, Sir, have the sense of a baboon."

> "Paul, run to the exit."

> "Run to the exit, Paul."

> "My fellow citizens, I come before you with a heavy heart."

> "I come before you, my fellow citizens, with a heavy heart."

Use a comma to mark the omission of words in a balanced sentence.

> The first train will arrive at 2 o'clock; the second, at 3 o'clock.

Sentences are balanced when identical clause constructions are doubled or tripled in a series. So that repeating words in the clauses do not become tedious to a reader, omit these words and note the omission with a comma.

> Some southern novelists attribute the character of their fiction to the South's losing the Civil War; others, to the region's special blending of climate and race; and still others, to the salubrious powers of mint juleps.

In this example, the comma and the word *others* substitute for *some southern novelists attribute the character of their fiction.*

Place a comma between paired "more/less" constructions.

> The less you smoke, the longer you'll live.

Some constructions involve a paired comparison of "more" of one element contrasted against "more" or "less" of another. Separate these elements with a comma to maintain a clear relationship between them.

The more wires a data base contains, the greater the number of bits it can move at a time.

The more some people get, the less they are willing to give.

5 Use a comma to set off tag questions that conclude a sentence.

This is the right house, isn't it?

A **tag question**, a brief question "tagged on" to a statement addressed to someone, should be set off from that statement. Tags are used for a variety of purposes, at times to suggest indecision or hesitancy.

You slipped into the office and read that letter, didn't you?

I have reached the only possible conclusion, haven't I?

6 Use a comma to set off yes/no remarks and mild exclamations.

"Yes, I'll call him right away."

"Oh well, I can put it off for another day."

7 Use commas according to convention in names, titles, dates, numbers, and addresses.

Commas with names and titles

Place a comma directly after a name if it is followed by a title.

Mr. Joe Smith, Executive Editor

Ms. Ann Jacobs, Senior Vice President

Lucy Turner, Ph.D.

Mr. Frank Reynolds, Esq.

Set off a title in commas when writing a sentence.

Mr. Joe Smith, Executive Editor, signed for the package.

Lucy Turner, Ph.D., delivered the commencement address.

Mr. Robert Jones, Sr., attended the ceremony.

Commas with dates

Place a comma between the day of the month and year. If your reference is to a particular month in a year and no date is mentioned, do not use a comma.

TEACHING IDEAS

As students apply for jobs, scholarships, special programs, and the like, they'll need to be aware of the conventions outlined in this section. You may want to remind them that this material will be useful throughout their college careers and beyond; thus they should keep reference books such as this on hand for consultation.

January 7, 1998   but   January 1998

When a date is written out, as in an invitation, use the following convention:

the seventh of January, 1998

No commas are used in the military convention for writing dates.

7 January 1998

If you include a day of the week when writing a date, use the following convention:

The package will be delivered on Wednesday, January 7, 1998.

Commas with numbers

Place a comma to denote thousands, millions, and so forth.

543   5,430   54,300   543,000   5,430,000   5,430,000,000

Some writers place no comma in four-digit numbers that are multiples of fifty.

2550   1600   but   1,625

Do *not* use commas when writing phone numbers, addresses, page numbers, or years.

Commas with addresses

When writing an address, place a comma between a city (or county) and state.

Baltimore, Maryland   Baltimore County, Maryland

Place no comma between a state and zip code.

Baltimore, Maryland 21215

When writing an address into a sentence, use commas to set off elements that would otherwise be placed on separate lines of the address.

Mr. Abe Stein, Senior Engineer
Stein Engineering
1243 Slade Avenue
Bedford, Massachusetts 01730

The control boards were shipped to Mr. Abe Stein, Senior Engineer, Stein Engineering, 1243 Slade Avenue, Bedford, Massachusetts 01730.

8 Use commas to prevent misreading.

CONFUSING   To get through a tunnel will need to be dug.

REVISED   To get through, a tunnel will need to be dug.

Although no rule calls for it, a comma may be needed to prevent misreading. Misreading can occur when numbers are placed together.

Confusing Down by twenty six members of the squad suddenly woke up.

Revised Down by twenty, six members of the squad suddenly woke up.

Misreading can occur when words that are often used as auxiliary verbs (e.g., *will, should,* forms of *be, do*) function as main verbs and occur before other verbs.

Confusing Those who do know exactly what must be done.

Revised Those who do, know exactly what must be done.

Misreading can occur when a word that functions both as a preposition and as a modifier (e.g., *after, before, along, around, beneath, through*) is used as a modifier and is followed by a noun.

Confusing Moments after the room began to tilt.

Revised Moments after, the room began to tilt.

Misreading can occur when identical words are placed together.

Confusing To speak speak into the microphone and press the button.

Revised To speak, speak into the microphone and press the button.

GROUP ACTIVITY

Students can come to understand the need for commas to prevent misreading, and have some fun, through the following activity. Ask groups to compose four or five sentences in which a comma is necessary to prevent a misreading. (They can use the sentences in the text as models.) The sentences will then be passed to another group whose task it will be to determine whether or not the commas are actually necessary.

EXERCISE 5

Decide whether commas are needed to clarify meaning in these sentences. Then make up three sentences of your own in which adding a comma will prevent misreading.

1. If you can come join us.
2. The doctor dressed and performed an emergency appendectomy.
3. The doctor dressed and sutured the wound.
4. From beneath the supports began to weaken.
5. By *twos* twenty children walked down the aisle.

EXERCISE 5

1. If you can come, join us.
2. The doctor dressed, and performed an emergency appendectomy.
3. no comma
4. From beneath, the supports began to weaken.
5. By *twos,* twenty children walked down the aisle.

Sentences—individual responses.

25f Editing to avoid misuse or overuse of commas

1 Eliminate the comma splice.

Confusing She climbed the ladder, she slid down the slide.

Revised She climbed the ladder. She slid down the slide.
She climbed the ladder, **and** she slid down the slide.

The most frequent comma blunder, the **comma splice,** occurs when a writer joins independent clauses with a comma.

FAULTY Christopher Columbus is considered a master navigator today, he died in neglect.

To revise a comma splice, see the following box and Chapter 13.

Four Ways to Avoid Comma Splices

1. Separate the two clauses with a period.

   Christopher Columbus is considered a master navigator today. He died in neglect.

2. Join the two clauses with a coordinating conjunction and a comma.

   Christopher Columbus is considered a master navigator today, but he died in neglect.

3. Join the two clauses with a conjunctive adverb and the appropriate punctuation.

   Christopher Columbus is considered a master navigator today; nevertheless, he died in neglect.

4. Join the two clauses by making one subordinate to the other.

   Although Christopher Columbus is considered a master navigator today, he died in neglect.

2 Eliminate commas misused to set off essential (restrictive) elements.

CONFUSING Athletes, who use steroids, invite disaster. [The sense is that *all* athletes use steroids, which is not true.]

REVISED Athletes who use steroids invite disaster. [Only those athletes who use steroids invite disaster.]

As noted in 25d-1, commas are not used with essential elements. The presence of commas can alter the meaning of otherwise identical sentences. Therefore, be sure of your meaning as you decide to punctuate (or not) a modifying element.

ESSENTIAL The students who signed the petition are eligible. [The *who* clause is essential and restricts the meaning of students to those who signed the petition.]

NONESSENTIAL The students, who signed the petition, are eligible. [The presence of commas signals that the *who* clause is nonessential. The sense of the sentence is that *all* the students signed the petition and are eligible.]

3 Eliminate commas that are misused in a series.

CONFUSING For tomorrow, memorize the poem, and the song.

Revised For tomorrow, memorize the poem and the song.

A comma is not placed before a coordinating conjunction if it connects only two elements in a series.

Faulty You cannot learn much about prices, and the amounts of goods traded from demand curves alone.

Revised You cannot learn much about prices and the amount of goods traded from demand curves alone.

A comma is *not* used after a second coordinate adjective.

Faulty One reason individuals engage in various efforts at self-improvement is that they can imagine alternate, improved, selves.

Revised One reason individuals engage in various efforts at self-improvement is that they can imagine alternate, improved selves.

A comma is not placed before the first item in a series or after the last item, unless the comma is required because of a specific rule.

Faulty A Central Processing Unit (CPU) is designed with a fixed repertoire of instructions for carrying out a range of tests involving, data manipulation, logical decision making, and control of the computer. [The comma should be eliminated before the first item in this series.]

Revised A Central Processing Unit (CPU) is designed with a fixed repertoire of instructions for carrying out a range of tests involving data manipulation, logical decision making, and control of the computer.

4 Eliminate commas that split paired sentence elements.

Confusing The police assisted, the emergency crew.

Revised The police assisted the emergency crew.

A comma is not placed between a subject and verb—even if the subject is lengthy.

Faulty What has sometimes been dramatically termed "the clash of civilizations," is merely the difference in the interpretation given by different societies to the same acts. [The noun clause subject should not be split from its verb *is.*]

Revised What has sometimes been dramatically termed "the clash of civilizations" is merely the difference in the interpretation given by different societies to the same acts.

A comma is not placed between a verb and its object or complement, nor between a preposition and its object.

Faulty One culture may organize, its social relations around rites of physical initiation. [The comma should not come between the verb and its object.]

GROUP ACTIVITY

Clearly the most profitable way to teach students how to use commas appropriately is to work with their own writing. Ask students to bring in several papers in order to take part in this activity. When you divide students into groups, try to mix strong and weak writers. Then have each group work together on one student's writing at a time, identifying comma errors and revising according to the guidelines in the handbook. The groups' attempts to determine when commas are appropriate and when not should generate healthy discussion. This discussion will help strong writers articulate their implicit understanding of punctuation rules and weak writers gain an understanding of such rules.

Revised One culture may organize its social relations around rites of physical initiation.

Faulty The principle of mutual respect among, neighboring peoples requires flexibility and tolerance. [The comma should not come between the preposition and its object.]

Revised The principle of mutual respect among neighboring peoples requires flexibility and tolerance.

5 Eliminate misuse of commas with quotations.

Confusing "Is anyone home?," he asked.
Revised "Is anyone home?" he asked.

A comma is not used after a quotation that ends with a question mark or an exclamation point.

Faulty "Get out!," cried the shopkeeper.

Revised "Get out!" cried the shopkeeper.

Faulty "Is this the way home?," asked Arthur.

Revised "Is this the way home?" asked Arthur.

A comma is not used to set apart words quoted (or italicized) for emphasis.

Faulty The list of, "exemplary," citizens the Governor referred to includes two convicted felons.

Revised The list of "exemplary" citizens the Governor referred to includes two convicted felons.

EXERCISE 6

Supply the commas for this dialogue between a young child and her nurse, adapted from Amy Tan's *The Joy Luck Club*.

I tugged Amah's sleeve and asked "Who is the Moon Lady?"

"Chang-o" replied Amah "who lives on the moon and today is the only day you can see her and have a secret wish fulfilled."

"What is a secret wish?" I asked her.

"It is what you want but cannot ask" said Amah.

"Then how will the Moon Lady know my wish?" I wanted to know.

"Because she is not an ordinary person" Amah explained.

EXERCISE 7

Correct the misuse of commas in the sentences that follow (from a parody of an anthropological study). Place a check before the sentences in which commas are used correctly.

EXERCISE 6

I tugged Amah's sleeve and asked, "Who is the Moon Lady?"

"Chang-o," replied Amah, "who lives on the moon, and today is the only day you can see her and have a secret wish fulfilled."

"What is a secret wish?" I asked her.

"It is what you want but cannot ask," said Amah.

"Then how will the Moon Lady know my wish?" I wanted to know.

"Because she is not an ordinary person," Amah explained.

Example: The daily body ritual, performed by the Nacirema people includes a mouth-rite.

The daily body ritual performed by the Nacirema people includes a mouth-rite.

1. Despite the fact that these people are so punctilious about the care of the mouth, this rite involves, a practice which strikes the uninitiated stranger as revolting.
2. It was reported to me that the ritual consists of inserting a small bundle of hog hairs into the mouth, along with certain magical powders, and then moving the bundle in a highly formalized series of gestures.
3. In addition to the private mouth-rite, the people seek out a holy-mouth-man once, or twice a year.
4. These practitioners have an impressive set of paraphernalia, consisting of a variety of, augers, awls, probes, and prods.
5. The use of these objects in the exorcism of the evils of the mouth involves, almost unbelievable ritual torture of the client.
6. The holy-mouth-man opens the client's mouth and using the above-mentioned tools enlarges any holes which decay may have created in the teeth.
7. Magical materials are put into, these holes.
8. If there are no naturally occurring holes in the teeth, large sections of one or more teeth are gouged out so that the supernatural substance, can be applied.
9. In the client's view, the purpose of these ministrations is to arrest decay, and to draw friends.
10. The extremely sacred and traditional character of the rite is evident in the fact that the natives return to the holy-mouth-men year after year, despite the fact that their teeth continue to decay.

EXERCISE 8

Correct the misuse of commas in the following paragraph. In making your corrections, you may need to add or delete words. You should feel free to combine sentences.

Example: The humidity level which was extremely high made the air feel as if it were 117 degrees.

The humidity level, which was extremely high, made the air feel as if it were 117 degrees.

It's no illusion that the earth has been getting hotter lately. For example the 1980s witnessed the hottest years since meteorological records began to be kept in the nineteenth century, in fact, the 1990s which so far have been a continuation of the same trend promise to remain just as warm and maybe even warmer. As one scientific observer put it "Planet Earth is running a fever." The killer heat wave, that claimed 566 lives in Chicago in July 1995, could have been a freak event but climatologists don't think so. They fear that the big heat wave of 1995 is actually a harbinger of more serious weather disturbances to come.

EXERCISE 7

1. Despite the fact that these people are so punctilious about the care of the mouth, this rite involves a practice which strikes the uninitiated stranger as revolting.
2. Correct
3. In addition to the private mouth-rite, the people seek out a holy-mouth-man once or twice a year.
4. These practitioners have an impressive set of paraphernalia, consisting of a variety of augers, awls, probes, and prods. (final comma is optional)
5. The use of these objects in the exorcism of the evils of the mouth involves almost unbelievable ritual torture of the client.
6. The holy-mouth-man opens the client's mouth and, using the above-mentioned tools, enlarges any holes which decay may have created in the teeth.
7. Magical materials are put into these holes.
8. If there are no naturally occurring holes in the teeth, large sections of one or more teeth are gouged out so that the supernatural substance can be applied.
9. In the client's view, the purpose of these ministrations is to arrest decay and to draw friends.
10. Correct

EXERCISE 8

Suggested response:

It's no illusion that the earth has been getting hotter lately. For example, the 1980s witnessed the hottest years since meteorological records began to be kept in the nineteenth century; in fact, the 1990s, which so far have been a continuation of the same trend, promise to remain just as warm and maybe even warmer. As one scientific observer put it, "Planet Earth is running a fever." The killer heat wave that claimed 566 lives in Chicago in July 1995 could have been a freak event, but climatologists don't think so. They fear that the big heat wave of 1995 is actually a harbinger of more serious weather disturbances to come.

CHAPTER 26

Semicolons

KEY FEATURES

The semicolon may well be the most troublesome punctuation mark for students to master. Its hybrid nature—functioning partly as a comma and partly as a period—makes the semicolon difficult for students to understand. This chapter opens with an explanation of its function as a "semi" stop that should help clear up the uncertainty many students feel when considering its use. The various uses of the semicolon are covered in a straightforward manner, and the distinction between it and other punctuation marks is clearly drawn. Rules for the primary use of semicolons, joining independent clauses, are followed by rules for using semicolons to prevent misreading and guidelines for avoiding errors. Exercises not only ask students to use the semicolon, but also to explain their reasons for punctuating sentences in specific ways.

TEACHING IDEAS

Students, like the rest of us, have an easier time making the right choice when they know *why.* Semicolons are probably misunderstood in part because students don't fully grasp the concept of related sentences. If you stress the thrust of the introduction, that the sentence's *meaning* as well as its structure determines whether a semicolon should be used, students should be more receptive to learning the rules.

ESL CUE

French uses the semicolon much as we do. However, in Spain the semicolon is used only to break up items in a list; in other Spanish cultures it may not even be used.

The main function of a **semicolon** is to separate elements. But as its name suggests, the semicolon serves to make only a "semi" or partial separation that maintains a relationship between independent elements. In its primary use, a semicolon can mark the end of one complete statement and the beginning of another. So can a period or a comma with a coordinating conjunction, of course. But whereas a period is chosen to make a full stop, a semicolon denotes a writer's decision to make a partial break. This chapter shows you the situations in which such a partial break is appropriate and gives you the tools for making such decisions as you write or revise your sentences.

26a Use a semicolon, not a comma, to join independent clauses that are intended to be closely related.

Secretariat won the race; Lucky Stars finished second.

Joining independent clauses with a semicolon is one of four basic ways to establish a relationship between clauses, ranging from full separation to subordination of one clause to another. (See the Critical Decisions box.) A comma should never be used to join independent clauses. (See Chapter 13 on comma splices.)

FAULTY In 1852 Mt. Everest was definitively identified as the highest mountain in the world, shortly thereafter it was named in honor of Sir George Everest, an early British Survey General of India.

REVISED In 1852 Mt. Everest was definitively identified as the highest mountain in the world; shortly thereafter it was named in honor of Sir George Everest, an early British Survey General of India.

Use semicolons to join closely related independent clauses, not to string unconnected statements together.

Semicolons can be overused. By themselves, they are not enough to make close connections from a series of statements that are simply added together.

OVERUSED In 1852 Mt. Everest was definitively identified as the highest mountain in the world; at the time it was believed to be 29,002 feet; we now know that its actual altitude is 29,028 feet.

Revised Mt. Everest, definitively identified in 1852 as the highest mountain in the world, was believed at the time to be 29,002 feet; we now know that its actual altitude is 29,028 feet.

CRITICAL DECISIONS

Challenge and be challenged: Using a period to separate sentences versus a semicolon or comma (with a conjunction) to link sentences

As a writer, you have options for separating or linking sentences by using coordination or subordination. (See Chapter 19.) This discussion focuses on using punctuation to communicate degrees of linkage between sentences and suggests varieties of coordinate, or equal, relationships.

Why separate sentences with a period?

Use a period to show a full separation between sentences.

Dante Alighieri was banished from Florence in 1302. He wrote the *Divine Comedy* in exile.

Why link sentences with a semicolon?

Use a semicolon, alone, to join sentences balanced in content and structure. Also use a semicolon to suggest that the second sentence completes the content of the first. The semicolon suggests a link but leaves it to the reader to infer how sentences are related.

Balanced sentence Agriculture is one part of the biological revolution; the domestication of animals is the other.

Suggested link Five major books and many articles have been written on the Bayeux tapestry; each shows just how much the trained observer can draw from pictorial evidence.

Why link sentences with a conjunctive adverb and a semicolon or period?

Use a semicolon with a conjunctive adverb (*however, therefore,* etc.) to emphasize one of the following relationships: addition, consequence, contrast, cause and effect, time, emphasis, or condition. With the semicolon and conjunctive adverb, linkage between sentences is closer than with a semicolon alone. The relationship between sentences is made clear by the conjunctive adverb.

Patients in need of organs have begun advertising for them**; however,** the American Medical Association discourages the practice.

Use a period between sentences to force a pause and then to stress the conjunctive adverb.

Patients in need of organs have begun advertising for them**. However,** the American Medical Association discourages the practice.

(continued)

REFERENCES

Lindemann, Erika. *A Rhetoric for Writing Teachers.* 2nd ed. New York: Oxford UP, 1987. Chapter 9. In discussing sentences, Lindemann refers to problems students encounter with internal punctuation.

Shaughnessy, Mina P. *Errors and Expectations: A Guide for the Teacher of Basic Writing.* New York: Oxford UP, 1977. A practical discussion of students' difficulties with semicolons.

Thomas, Lewis. "Notes on Punctuation." *The Medusa and the Snail: More Notes of a Biology Watcher.* New York: Viking, 1979. A whimsical but accurate description of the semicolon's function.

TEACHING IDEAS

This chart will help students understand the relationship between meaning and punctuation with regard to semicolon use. You may want to call their attention to the Critical Decisions box as a handy reference as they make decisions about appropriate use of semicolons in their own papers.

TEACHING IDEAS

It may enhance students' understanding of the uses of semicolons if they see more examples of the constructions described here. You may want to ask students to find examples of their own, providing the following as additional guidelines:

> With Jack Kennedy murdered, they had no hero to bind them; yet in memories of an idealized Camelot they had an image of a recent Golden Age to vivify the promise of liberalism. (Todd Gitlin)

> There must be, not a balance of power, but a community of power; not organized rivalries, but an organized common peace. (Woodrow Wilson)

> Perhaps our greatest responsibility is to re-pledge our continuing devotion to perpetuating a legacy of language in an age when the spoken word is suspected as "a glib and oily art," manipulative doublespeak; when the written word—badly written, of course—is unread; and when "vibrations" are alleged to be, not inarticulate throbbings, but true communication where every sentence begins with "I feel" and ends with "you know." (Paul Cubeta)

CRITICAL DECISIONS (continued)

Why link sentences with a comma and a coordinating conjunction?

Use a comma and a coordinating conjunction to join sentences in a coordinate relationship that shows addition, choice, consequence, contrast, or cause (see 19a-1). Since two sentences are fully merged into one following this strategy, linkage is complete. At the same time, this method offers the *least* emphasis in showing a coordinate relationship.

> Robotics has increased efficiency in the automobile industry**, but** it has put thousands of assembly-line employees out of work.

26b Use a semicolon, not a comma, to join two independent clauses that are closely linked by a conjunctive adverb.

> I had planned to call London**;** however, the circuits were busy.
> Eric arrived late the first day**;** thereafter, he was on time.

A conjunctive adverb is often used to establish a close connection between independent clauses. (See 19a and the Critical Decisions box in 26a.) With conjunctive adverbs, use a semicolon (or a period) between the clauses, never a comma. (Refer to Chapter 13.)

FAULTY Historical researchers cannot control the events they want to recreate, indeed, they often cannot find enough documentation to learn all the facts of an occurrence. [The comma after *recreate* makes a comma splice; a comma cannot be used to join independent clauses.]

REVISED Historical researchers cannot control the events they want to recreate**;** indeed, they often cannot find enough documentation to learn all the facts of an occurrence. [Here the conjunctive adverb creates a very close link between clauses.]

NOTE: When independent clauses are closely connected with a conjunctive adverb, the semicolon always falls between the clauses, no matter where the conjunctive adverb is located.

OPTION If chlorophyll is extracted from plant cells and exposed to light, it does momentarily absorb light energy**;** *however,* this energy is almost immediately reradiated as light.

OPTION If chlorophyll is extracted from plant cells and exposed to light, it does momentarily absorb light energy**;** this energy is almost immediately reradiated as light, *however.* [The semicolon falls between the independent clauses, even if the adverb is moved to the end of the sentence.]

NOTE: The use of a conjunctive adverb does not necessarily mean that there must be a semicolon between clauses. If you feel that the business of the first clause is finished, or that you do not need a sense of anticipation for the next clause, you can always make a full break between clauses with a period.

Option If chlorophyll is extracted from plant cells and exposed to light, it does momentarily absorb light energy. This energy, however, is almost immediately reradiated as light, usually of a different wavelength. [Here the writer intends for the period to mark a sharp boundary between clauses.]

26c Join independent clauses with a semicolon before a coordinating conjunction when one or both clauses contain a comma or other internal punctuation.

After the Shuttle landed, Perkins tried calling the President; but he didn't get through.

Short or uncomplicated independent clauses joined by coordinating conjunctions do not normally use a semicolon. However, internal commas or complicated subordinations within one of the independent clauses can create confusion and misreading; in such cases the clauses need stronger separation with a semicolon before the coordinating conjunction.

Agnosognosia, a normally temporary condition that often afflicts right-hemisphere stroke victims, manifests itself as the patient's denial of the physical existence of the paralyzed limb; and it is for this reason that neuroscientists are studying agnosognosia for clues about how the brain constructs reality.

26d Use a semicolon to separate items in a series when each item is long or when one or more items contain a comma.

I sent the letters to Baltimore, Maryland; Portland, Oregon; and Dallas, Texas.

Short or uncomplicated items in a series are normally separated only by commas (see Chapter 25). However, when the units to be separated are further subdivided with internal punctuation or are made up of complex clauses, it is necessary to provide stronger separation with a semicolon.

One neuroscientist, Vilayanur Ramachandran, is particularly interested in the functions and malfunctions of the brain and has investigated the neural wiring of vision; the riddle of agnosognosia; and, through research into the "phantom limb" phenomenon experienced by amputees, the ways in which the brain reconfigures itself during learning.

GROUP ACTIVITY

All three of the exercises in this chapter lend themselves to group activity. Have students respond to exercises individually, and then compare their responses with those of other group members. When the inevitable disagreement occurs, students will have to consult the handbook. Once they become accustomed to using the chapter, they'll likely continue to refer to it as they edit their papers.

ADDITIONAL EXERCISE A

Now that you have a good understanding of the various uses of the semicolon, apply that knowledge when revising your papers. Reread the drafts of any papers you're working on at present, and decide where semicolons might be appropriate—perhaps you've written two sentences that are very closely linked, or you have a list including lengthy items. Check also for instances when you may have misused or overused semicolons.

EXERCISE 1

Suggested revisions:

1. During the early years of the twentieth century, leisure assumed an increasingly important role in everyday life; amusement parks, professional baseball games, nickelodeons, and dance halls attracted a wide array of people anxious to spend their hard-earned cash. [The second sentence elaborates on the first, so a semicolon is more appropriate than a period. No conjunctive adverb is needed to show the relationship between the two sentences.]
2. Of all these new cultural endeavors, films were the most important; even the poorest worker could afford to take his family to the local movie theater. [The two sentences are closely related, but there isn't a logical connection between them requiring a conjunctive adverb.]
3. Cinemas took root in urban working class and immigrant neighborhoods; thereafter, they spread to middle-class districts of cities and into small communities throughout the country. [The conjunctive adverb is necessary to show the time sequence of the

26e Place semicolons *outside* of end quotation marks.

We read "Ode to the West Wind"; we then discussed the poem in detail.

A semicolon that separates independent clauses and other major elements is not part of a direct quotation.

One neurologist remarks that "we are used to thinking of our bodies as our selves"; in other words, unlike agnosogniacs, we "own" our body parts and have no trouble with expressing that ownership.

26f Edit to avoid common errors.

Use a comma, not a semicolon, after an introductory subordinate clause.

Use semicolons to link independent clauses; never use them to link subordinate to independent clauses (see Chapter 19).

FAULTY When a writer begins a new project; the blank page can present a barrier.

REVISED When a writer begins a new project, the blank page can present a barrier.

Use a colon, not a semicolon, to introduce a list.

FAULTY The writing process consists of three stages; planning, drafting, and revision.

REVISED The writing process consists of three stages: planning, drafting, and revision.

EXERCISE 1

Join the following pairs of sentences with a semicolon, with a semicolon and conjunctive adverb, or with a period and conjunctive adverb. Explain your decision.

Example: Politics and social realism have not been the hallmarks of the film industry in Hollywood.

Yet there was a time when liberal, conservative, and radical organizations made films for a mass audience aimed at politicizing millions of viewers.

Politics and social realism have not been the hallmarks of the film industry in Hollywood; yet there was a time when liberal, conservative, and radical organizations made films for a mass audience aimed at politicizing millions of viewers.

The sentences are closely enough related in meaning to warrant their being joined into a single, compound sentence. For this reason, the semicolon is appropriate. The conjunction *yet* is kept to establish the contrasting relationship between clauses. Without the conjunction this relationship might not be obvious to a reader.

1. During the early years of the twentieth century, leisure assumed an increasingly important role in everyday life.
   Amusement parks, professional baseball games, nickelodeons, and dance halls attracted a wide array of people anxious to spend their hard-earned cash.
2. Of all these new cultural endeavors, films were the most important. Even the poorest worker could afford to take his family to the local movie theater.
3. Cinemas took root in urban working-class and immigrant neighborhoods. They then spread to middle-class districts of cities and into small communities throughout the country.
4. As early as 1910 the appeal of movies was so great that nearly one-third of the nation flocked to the cinema each week.
   Ten years later, weekly attendance equaled fifty percent of the nation's population.
5. As is true today, early films were primarily aimed at entertaining audiences.
   But then, entertainment did not always come in the form of escapist fantasies.
6. Many of the issues that dominated Progressive-era politics were portrayed on the screen.
   While most of these films were produced by studios and independent companies, a significant number were made by what we might call today "special-interest groups."
7. The modest cost of making one- or two-reel films allowed many organizations to make movies to advance their causes.
   Moreover, exhibitors' need to fill their daily bills with new films meant these films would be seen by millions.

EXERCISE 2

In very long sentences semicolons are used in place of commas to prevent misreading. Combine, repunctuate, or otherwise revise the following sentences by using semicolons.

Example: The traditional view of the diffusion of Indo-European languages over wide areas holds that as nomadic mounted warriors conquered indigenous peoples, they imposed their own proto-Indo-European language, *which,* in turn, evolved in local areas into the various languages we know today.

But many scholars have become dissatisfied with this explanation.

The traditional view of the diffusion of Indo-European languages over wide areas holds that as nomadic mounted warriors conquered indigenous peoples, they imposed their own

two sentences, and their meanings are related closely enough to warrant a semicolon.]

4. As early as 1910 the appeal of movies was so great that nearly one-third of the nation flocked to the cinema each week; moreover, ten years later, weekly attendance equaled fifty percent of the nation's population. [The sentences are closely related, so a semicolon is preferable to a period. The conjunctive adverb emphasizes the importance of the second sentence.]
5. As is true today, early films were primarily aimed at entertaining audiences. Entertainment, however, did not always come in the form of escapist fantasies. [Separating the two sentences increases the drama of the second sentence. The conjunctive adverb is necessary to show the relationship between the two sentences.]
6. Many of the issues that dominated Progressive-era politics were portrayed on the screen; indeed, while most of these films were produced by studios and independent companies, a significant number were made by what we might call today "special-interest groups." [The second sentence fulfills part of the promise of the first, so a semicolon is appropriate. The conjunctive adverb emphasizes the relationship between the two sentences.]
7. The modest cost of making one- or two-reel films allowed many organizations to make movies to advance their causes. Moreover, exhibitors' need to fill their daily bills with new films meant these films would be seen by millions. [The two reasons given here are quite different, so a period is appropriate. The conjunctive adverb shows the relationship between the two sentences.]

EXERCISE 2

Suggested responses:

1. Linguists divide the languages of Europe into families: the Romance languages include French, Italian, Spanish, Portuguese, and Romanian; the Slavonic languages include Russian, Polish, Czech, Slovak, Serbo-Croat, and Bulgarian; the Germanic

(continued)

languages include German, Norwegian, Danish, and Swedish.

2. Many archaeologists accept a theory of "Kurgan invasions" as an explanation of the spread of Indo-European languages, but others dispute it because the archaeological evidence is not convincing. The core words, which resemble each other from place to place, may have changed meaning over time; moreover, the hordes of mounted warriors would have had no obvious reason for moving west at the end of the Neolithic period.
3. There are four models of how language change might occur according to a process-based view: initial colonization, by which an uninhabited territory becomes populated; linguistic divergence arising from separation or isolation, which some think explains the development of the Romance languages in Europe; linguistic convergence, whereby languages initially quite different become increasingly similar to each other; and, finally, linguistic replacement, whereby indigenous languages are gradually replaced by the language of people coming from the outside.

EXERCISE 3

Suggested responses:

1. Some sociologists have argued that belief in a literal devil is a matter of social class; a Princeton professor explains: "If you see Cadillacs in the church parking lot, you won't hear Satan preached inside"; but "if you see a lot of pickup trucks, you will."
2. Late twentieth-century American culture, however, is by and large devoid of a sense of an actual Devil.
3. Our preference is to explain the existence of evil in scientific or pseudoscientific terms; **thus** serial murderers, terrorists, and bloodthirsty dictators are explained as psychopaths or sociopaths. Evil is not perceived as punishment for our sins but rather as arbitrary and meaningless.
4. One cultural critic regards this loss of a sense of pure, radical evil as regrettable; he sees the disappearance of Satan as a "tragedy of the imagination."

proto-Indo-European language; *this language,* in turn, evolved in local areas into the various languages we know today. But many scholars have become dissatisfied with this explanation.

1. Linguists divide the languages of Europe into families: the Romance languages include French, Italian, Spanish, Portuguese, and Romanian. The Slavonic languages include Russian, Polish, Czech, Slovak, Serbo-Croat, and Bulgarian. The Germanic languages include German, Norwegian, Danish, and Swedish.
2. Many archaeologists accept a theory of "Kurgan invasions" as an explanation of the spread of Indo-European languages.

   But others dispute it because the archaeological evidence is not convincing, the core words, which resemble each other from place to place, may have changed meaning over time, and the hordes of mounted warriors would have had no obvious reason for moving west at the end of the Neolithic period.
3. There are four models of how language change might occur according to a process-based view: initial colonization, by which an uninhabited territory becomes populated, linguistic divergence arising from separation or isolation, which some think explains the development of the Romance languages in Europe, linguistic convergence, whereby languages initially quite different become increasingly similar to each other, and, finally, linguistic replacement, whereby indigenous languages are gradually replaced by the language of people coming from the outside.

EXERCISE 3

Correct the misuse of semicolons and, if necessary, the wording in the following sentences. Place a check by any sentence in which a semicolon is used correctly.

Example: Until the period of the Enlightenment, most Christians believed that an entity called the Devil existed; that he was not just a metaphor for evil but rather was evil incarnate.

Until the period of the Enlightenment, most Christians believed that an entity called the Devil existed and that he was not just a metaphor for evil but rather was evil incarnate.

1. Some sociologists have argued that belief in a literal devil is a matter of social class; a Princeton professor explains: "If you see Cadillacs in the church parking lot, you won't hear Satan preached inside;" but "if you see a lot of pickup trucks, you will."
2. Late twentieth-century American culture; however, is by and large devoid of a sense of an actual Devil.
3. Our preference is to explain the existence of evil in scientific or pseudoscientific terms; serial murderers, terrorists, and bloodthirsty dictators are explained as psychopaths or sociopaths; evil is not perceived as punishment for our sins but rather as arbitrary and meaningless.
4. One cultural critic regards this loss of a sense of pure, radical evil as regrettable, he sees the disappearance of Satan as a "tragedy of the imagination."

CHAPTER 27

Apostrophes

The **apostrophe** (') is used to show possession, mark the omission of letters or numbers, and mark plural forms. In speech, keeping these matters straight poses no problem. In writing, however, the three uses of the apostrophe very nearly overlap with certain words, creating confusion for the reader. Therefore, try to distinguish carefully among the uses of the apostrophe.

27a Using apostrophes to show possession with single nouns

1 For most nouns and for indefinite pronouns, add an apostrophe and the letter *s* to indicate possession.

Bill**'s** braces	the government**'s** solution
history**'s** verdict	somebody**'s** cat
Susan**'s** basketball	everyone**'s** business

For singular nouns ending with the letter *s, show possession by adding an apostrophe and* s if this new construction is not difficult to pronounce.

Ellis**'s** Diner   hostess**'s** menu   Orson Welles**'s** movie

NOTE: The possessive construction formed with *'s* may be difficult to read if it is followed by a word beginning with an *s* or *z* sound. If this is the case, you have the option of dropping the *s* after the apostrophe.

ACCEPTABLE Ellis**'** zipper   or   Ellis**'s** zipper

Whichever convention you adopt, be consistent.

2 Eliminate apostrophes that are misused or confused with possessive pronouns.

Personal pronouns have their own possessive case forms (see Chapter 8); they *never* use apostrophes to show possession.

Possession with Personal Pronouns

its	the book's binding	*its* binding
whose	Who owns the book?	*Whose* book is this?
your	the book owned by you	*your* book
yours	the book owned by you	The book is *yours.*

KEY FEATURES

Since this chapter is more likely to be used as a source of reference than as a classroom text, the focus is on rules governing apostrophes, with relatively little commentary. Use of apostrophes for possession, contractions, and plurals is covered extensively; in addition, extensive examples and lists of representative words are presented. Exercises provide students with ample practice in using apostrophes appropriately.

REFERENCE

WIENER, HARVEY S. *The Writing Room: A Resource Book for Teachers of English.* New York: Oxford UP, 1981. Practical advice on teaching possessive forms.

TEACHING IDEAS

Students may need to spend some time on this section in order to sort out their perceptions of when to use apostrophes and when not to. The following hint may be helpful: if students are uncertain about using apostrophes with personal pronouns such as *it's, who's, they're,* and the like, suggest that they try eliminating the contraction by spelling out the words: *it is, who is, they are,* etc. If they can spell out the words, then an apostrophe is appropriate; if they can't, then no apostrophe should appear. (Example: *It's* a good thing that the dog found *its* way home. *It is* a good thing that the dog found *its* way home.)

their	a book owned by Bob and Sue	*their* book
theirs	a book owned by Bob and Sue	The book is *theirs.*
her	a book owned by Sue	*her* book
hers	a book owned by Sue	The book is *hers.*
our	a book owned by us	*our* book
ours	a book owned by us	The book is *ours.*
his	a book owned by Bob	*his* book
his	a book owned by Bob	The book is *his.*

Distinguish personal pronouns in their possessive form from personal pronouns that are contractions.

For readers, the most annoying possible mixup with apostrophes occurs when personal pronouns meant to show possession are confused with personal pronouns that are contractions formed with the verb *be,* as shown here. (See the guidelines for making contractions in 27c.)

Personal Pronouns: Contractions Formed with Be

it's	*It is* doubtful he'll arrive.	*It's* doubtful he'll arrive.
who's	*Who is* planning to attend?	*Who's* planning to attend?
you're	*You are* mistaken.	*You're* mistaken.
there's	*There is* little to do.	*There's* little to do.
they're	*They are* home.	*They're* home.

Edit to eliminate apostrophes from personal pronouns that are meant to show possession, not contraction.

FAULTY You're order has arrived.

REVISED Your order has arrived.

For a plural noun ending with *s,* add only an apostrophe to indicate possession. For a plural noun not ending with *s,* add an apostrophe and the letter *s.*

bricklayer**s’** union	teacher**s’** strike
dancer**s’** rehearsal	me**n’s** locker
childre**n’s** games	cattl**e’s** watering hole

EXERCISE 1

Read the following sentences. As needed, use an apostrophe or an apostrophe and the letter *s* to make possessive each noun or pronoun in parentheses.

Example: With Windows 95, even the simple task of switching your computer off is serious business—you have to follow the (System) commands for shutdown.

EXERCISE 1

1. it's
2. your
3. Welcome window's
4. file name's
5. systems'
6. files'

With Windows 95, even the simple task of switching your computer off is serious business—you have to follow the System's commands for shutdown.

1. In fact, you can't hit that off switch until Windows 95 tells you that (its) safe to do so.
2. If you make it a habit to close each window once you've finished with it, you'll find that (you're) work space is maximized.
3. The (Welcome window) function is to provide you with a new Windows 95 tip each time you start a new session.
4. In Windows 95, a (file name) length can be as long as you want to make it.
5. Older (systems) file names had to be kept to an 8-character length (with a 3-character extension).
6. That long file name option sounds like a real advantage until you realize that if the particular program you are using still follows the 8-character rule, your (files) names are not going to be any longer; Windows 95 can't override your program.
7. On the other hand, the 8-character parameter challenges the (user) creativity—how else would you end up with a file name like "taxoops," a file that is actually a letter to the Internal Revenue Service.
8. Software developers, canny souls that they are, know that Windows 95 is not the cure-all for all computer ills and that awful things—like crashes—are still going to happen; (CyberMedia) software package, *First Aid for Windows,* promises to doctor your ailing system.
9. *(First Aid for Windows)* packaging even features the familiar Red Cross logo.
10. With PC healthcare systems readily available, the "DUMMIES" user need worry no more about a (device-driver) incompatibility.
11. The user doesn't have to wait for what seems like hours, waiting for the technical support (staff) advice.

7. user's
8. CyberMedia's
9. First Aid for Windows's
10. device-driver's
11. staff's

GROUP ACTIVITY

All of the exercises in this chapter lend themselves to group activity. Have students respond to exercises individually, and then compare their responses with those of other group members. When the inevitable disagreement occurs, students will have to consult the handbook. Once they become accustomed to using the chapter, they'll likely continue to refer to it as they edit their papers.

27b Using apostrophes to show possession with multiple nouns

Multiple nouns showing possession can be tricky to punctuate, since the apostrophe and the letter *s* will indicate who—and how many people—own what, either separately or together. Because establishing possession is so important (especially in our culture), take care when using the apostrophe with multiple nouns. Punctuate so that your sentences express your exact meaning.

1 To indicate possession when a cluster of words functions as a single noun, add an apostrophe and the letter *s* to the last word.

Executive Vice President**'s** role	Chief Executive Officer**'s** salary
brother-in-law**'s** car	First Deck Officer**'s** watch

GROUP ACTIVITY

It may take some time for students to comprehend fully the intricacies of apostrophe use, so the following activity might be helpful: ask groups to generate examples of phrases including nouns and indefinite pronouns, some of which require apostrophes and some of which do not. (They can use the examples in the Critical Decisions box as a guide.) However, no apostrophes should appear in any of the phrases. The completed phrases will then be passed on to other groups, whose task will be to determine which phrases require apostrophes and which do not. Discussion of where to use apostrophes should help students understand their use more clearly.

CRITICAL DECISIONS

Be alert to differences: Test your placement of apostrophes with nouns and with indefinite pronouns.

The personal pronouns *his, hers, ours, its, yours,* and *theirs* **never** use apostrophes. By contrast, nouns and indefinite pronouns (such as *somebody, other,* and *no one*) do use apostrophes to show possession. Nouns and indefinite pronouns also form plurals with the suffix *-s*. Apply the following tests to determine whether or not you should be using an apostrophe and *s* (*'s*) or the suffix *-s*, with no apostrophe.

Is the noun or indefinite pronoun followed by a noun? If so, then you probably intend to show possession. Use the possessive form *'s*.

noun — government*'s* policy

noun — hospital*'s* program

noun — family*'s* holiday

noun — other*'s* comment

Is a noun or indefinite pronoun followed by a verb or a modifying phrase? If so, then you probably intend to make the noun or indefinite pronoun plural. Use the suffix *-s,* with *no* apostrophe.

modifying phrase — government*s* in that part of the world

modifying phrase — famil*ies* having two or more children

modifying clause — hospital*s* that have large staffs

verb — other*s* believe

But if an omitted word is involved, you may need a possessive form.

Eric's friends attend Central High. Frank*'s* attend Northern.

[In the second sentence, the omitted noun *friends* is clearly intended as the subject of the sentence. The *'s* is needed to show whose friends—*Frank's.*]

2 **To indicate possession of an object owned jointly, add an apostrophe and the letter *s* to the last noun (or pronoun) named.**

Smith and Thompson**'s** interview notes are meticulous. [The notes belong jointly to, they were gathered jointly by, Smith and Thompson.]

Mary and Bill**'s** car needs a muffler. [The car belongs jointly to Mary and Bill.]

3 **To indicate individual possession by two or more people, add an apostrophe and the letter *s* to each person named.**

Judy**'s** and Rob**'s** interview notes are meticulous. [The reference is to two sets of notes, one belonging to Judy and the other to Rob.]

27c Using apostrophes in contractions to mark the omission of letters and numbers

When you join or compress words into a contraction, you omit letters to indicate a more rapid, informal pace of pronunciation. The omission *must* be marked in writing with an apostrophe. Similarly, when you omit numbers in a date, use an apostrophe. Because many readers consider contractions an informality, you may want to avoid using them in academic writing. When in doubt about the appropriateness of contractions and the register they indicate in a particular document, check with the professor who will be reading your work.

1 Use an apostrophe to indicate the omission of letters in a contraction.

can**’t** = can not won**’t** = will not you**’v**e = you have

2 Use an apostrophe to indicate the omission of numbers in a date.

the ’60s the ’80s the ’90s

3 Eliminate apostrophes from verbs in their -*s* form.

The -*s* ending used in regular verb formation does *not* involve the omission of any letters (see 9a). Any apostrophe that creeps into such verb endings should be eliminated.

FAULTY	He walk’s with a limp.	A cat eat’s mice.
REVISED	He wal**ks** with a limp.	A cat ea**ts** mice.

REFERENCE

FLESCH, RUDOLF. *The ABC of Style: A Guide to Plain English.* New York: Harper, 1964. 29–30. “Plain English” should include, not shun, contractions.

EXERCISE 2

Correct the use of apostrophes in the following sentences by adding or deleting apostrophes as needed. Place a check by the sentences in which apostrophes are used correctly.

Example: Rough weather sailing can be exciting, but only if you’re crew is well prepared for it.

Rough weather sailing can be exciting, but only if your crew is well prepared for it.

1. Bad weather inevitably puts you’re crew’s lives in danger.
2. Obviously their likely to be wetter and colder; foul weather gear should be available and distributed *before* the first splash lands in the cockpit.
3. Its equally important to take precautions to prevent risk of injury to limbs and body.

EXERCISE 2

1. your (crew’s is correct)
2. they’re
3. It’s
4. correct
5. your
6. your
7. who’s
8. correct
9. who’s
10. who’s

4. Those who normally lead a sedentary life are much more liable to injuries than those whose muscles are well exercised to withstand rubs, bumps, and twists.
5. Inadequate footwear, or none at all if you're feet are not hardened to such treatment, can lead to real pain if a toe is stubbed against a deck bolt or stanchion.
6. Make sure you have a working man-overboard pole—you're attention to safety could save someone's life.
7. Bad weather is particularly tiring and can result in seasickness; keep a watch to see whose becoming sick.
8. Seasickness and exhaustion combined can lead to a state of not caring what happens next to your boat and crew.
9. An exhausted sailor huddled in a wave- and windswept cockpit, peering into the murk, can easily come to see Poseidon, whose lashing the waves to fury out of spite.
10. Perhaps the easiest precaution to avoid problems in raw weather is to bring a crew whose not afraid of the tense environment faced while sailing in rough seas.

27d Using apostrophes to mark plural forms

As readers, we expect the letter *s* or letters *es* placed at the end of a word to show that the word is plural. Yet if we were to follow that convention with letters or symbols, we would quickly create a puzzle of pronunciation: *How many les in Lilliputian?* We avoid the confusion by adopting a different convention to form the plurals of letters, symbols, and so on.

1 Use an apostrophe and the letter *s* to indicate the plural of a letter, number, or word referred to as a word.

The letter, number, or word made plural should be underlined if typewritten or set in italics if typeset. Do *not* underline or italicize the apostrophe or the letter *s*.

Standard for Typewriter Usage

```
Mind your p's and q's.
How many 5's in sixty?
The frequent in's and with's reduced the effectiveness of
his presentation.
```

Standard for Typeset Usage

Mind your *p*'s and *q*'s.

How many *5*'s in sixty?

The frequent *in*'s and *with*'s reduced the effectiveness of his presentation.

TEACHING IDEAS

The situations covered here are rarely found in students' academic writing, but students will nevertheless encounter situations in which they'll need to know these rules. You may want to encourage them to keep handbooks such as this available for easy reference later in their careers.

EXCEPTION: When forming the plural of a proper noun (e.g., someone's name), omit the apostrophe but retain the letter *s*.

Standard for Typewriter Usage

`At the convention I met three Franks and two Maudes.`

Standard for Typeset Usage

At the convention I met three *Franks* and two *Maudes*.

Using an apostrophe in this case would mistakenly suggest possession and thus confuse a reader.

2 Use an apostrophe and the letter *s* to indicate the plural of a symbol, an abbreviation with periods, and years expressed in decades.

Do *not* underline or italicize the symbol, the abbreviation, or the decade.

Joel is too fond of using &'s in his writing.
With all the M.D.'s at this conference, I feel safe.
Computer-assisted software engineering will be important in the 1990's.

OPTION: Some writers omit the apostrophe before the letter *s* when forming the plural of decades, abbreviations without periods, and symbols.

1900s or 1900's
IBMs or IBM's
%s or %'s

Whichever convention you adopt, be consistent.

3 Eliminate any apostrophes misused to form regular plurals of nouns.

For a regular noun, an apostrophe is never used to create a plural form; rather, the apostrophe indicates possession (see 7a-2).

POSSESSIVE	the cat's meow	that idea's beginning
FAULTY PLURAL	Cat's eat meat.	Idea's begin in thought.
REVISED PLURAL	Cats eat.	Ideas begin.

EXERCISE 3

Follow the instructions in parentheses after each sentence to clarify possession.

Example: The *governor office personnel* have formed some close friendships. (Use apostrophes to indicate that the people who have become friends work in the office of the governor.)

EXERCISE 3

1. governor's
2. Mrs. Locke and her husband Ted's
3. Governor's
4. Isabelle Locke's and the governor's
5. Isabelle's and the governor's

The governor's office personnel have formed some close friendships.

1. Isabelle Locke works at the State House as the *governor Press Secretary.* (Use apostrophes to indicate that the Press Secretary for the governor is Isabelle Locke.)
2. *Mrs. Locke and her husband Ted house* is replete with pictures of government officials posing with the Locke family. (Use apostrophes to indicate that Mrs. Locke and Ted own their house together.)
3. The governor lives around the corner, in the *Governor Mansion.* (Use apostrophes to indicate that the governor lives in the mansion.)
4. *Isabelle Locke and the governor homes* are decorated similarly, both in a colonial style. (Use apostrophes to indicate that two different homes are being referred to.)
5. Often they'll have dinner together, cooked by *Isabelle and the governor husbands.* (Use apostrophes to indicate that the two husbands cook together.)

EXERCISE 4

Decide whether an apostrophe is needed to form plurals for the following letters, numbers, or words.

Example: b

b's (or *b*'s if typeset)

1. & 2. 42 3. 7 4. j 5. d 6. Karen

EXERCISE 5

Read the following paragraph on Donald Duck. Provide apostrophes and rewrite words as needed.

Theirs one basic product never stocked in Disneys store: parents. Disneys is a universe of uncles and grand-uncles, nephews and cousins. The male-female relationships existence is found only in eternal fiancés. Donald Duck and Daisy relationship, like Mickey Mouse and Minnie relationship, is never consummated or even legitimized through the all-American institution of marriage. More troubling, though, is the origin of all of the nephews and uncles in the Disney Comics worlds. Huey, Dewey, and Louie Uncle Donald is never known to have a sister or sister-in-law. In fact, most of Donald relatives are unmarried and unattached males, like Scrooge McDuck. Donalds own parents are never mentioned, although Grandma Duck purports to be the widowed ancestor of the Duck family (again no husband-wife relationship). Donald and Mickey girlfriends, Daisy and Minnie, are often accompanied by nieces of their own. Since these women are not very susceptible to men or matrimonial bonds, Disneys "families" are necessarily and perpetually composed of bachelors accompanied by nephews, who come and go. A quick look at Walt Disneys own biography demonstrates a possible reason for his comics anti-love, anti-marriage sentiments: Disneys mother is rarely mentioned, and his wifes role in his life was minimal at best. As for the future of the Magic Kingdoms demographic increases, it is predictable that they will be the result of extrasexual factors.

EXERCISE 4

1. &'s	4. *j*'s
2. 42's	5. *d*'s
3. 7's	6. *Karens*

EXERCISE 5

There's one basic product never stocked in Disney's store: parents. Disney's is a universe of uncles and grand-uncles, nephews and cousins. The male-female relationship's existence is found only in eternal fiancés. Donald Duck and Daisy's relationship, like Mickey Mouse and Minnie's relationship, is never consummated or even legitimized through the all-American institution of marriage. More troubling, though, is the origin of all of the nephews and uncles in the Disney Comics' worlds. Huey, Dewey, and Louie's Uncle Donald is never known to have a sister or sister-in-law. In fact, most of Donald's relatives are unmarried and unattached males, like Scrooge McDuck. Donald's own parents are never mentioned, although Grandma Duck purports to be the widowed ancestor of the Duck family (again no husband-wife relationship). Donald's and Mickey's girlfriends, Daisy and Minnie, are often accompanied by nieces of their own. Since these women are not very susceptible to men or matrimonial bonds, Disney's "families" are necessarily and perpetually composed of bachelors accompanied by nephews, who come and go. A quick look at Walt Disney's own biography demonstrates a possible reason for his comics' anti-love, anti-marriage sentiments: Disney's mother is rarely mentioned, and his wife's role in his life was minimal at best. As for the future of the Magic Kingdom's demographic increases, it is predictable that they will be the result of extrasexual factors.

CHAPTER 28

Quotation Marks

Quoting the words of others is a necessary, essential fact of academic life, both for professors and for students. As a writer you will make claims, cite the words and work of others, and then respond to those words. For the sake of both accuracy and fairness, your quotations must be managed precisely. (See 34f on quoting sources in research.) If you quote to help make a point, you must do so accurately since readers count on you for a faithful transcription of what another has written. (See Chapter 36 for conventions on citing sources in various disciplines.) This chapter will discuss the conventions for quoting as well as the stylistic tricks for smoothly incorporating quoted language into your work.

28a Quoting prose

1 Use double quotation marks (" ") to set off a short direct quotation from the rest of a sentence.

Short quotations—those that span four or fewer lines of your manuscript—may be incorporated into your writing by running them in with your sentences as part of your normal paragraphing. When quoting a source, reproduce exactly the wording and punctuation of the quoted material. For the most part, when you enclose the material in quotation marks, you will do so to indicate **direct discourse**, the exact re-creation of words spoken or written by another person. Direct discourse places another person's language directly before readers as if you (the writer) were not present.

DIRECT According to Bernadine Healy, Director of the National Institutes of Health, "By the year 2000, women and minorities will account for 68 per cent of the new workers."

Eric asked, "Can I borrow the car?"

Indirect discourse occurs when you quote the words of someone inexactly, and from a distance.

INDIRECT Eric asked if he could borrow the car.

Indirect discourse inserts your voice into the quotation. You mediate the quotation, or create the frame through which your readers perceive it.

ALTERING A QUOTATION: **Quotation marks** denote the *exact* reproduction of words written or spoken by someone else. Changes that you make to quoted

KEY FEATURES

This chapter will be a valuable reference tool for students who have trouble figuring out what to do with quotation marks. Use of quotation marks for direct quotations, dialogue, titles of short works, and emphasizing words, as well as other uses, is covered thoroughly. In addition, advice regarding quoted material within a quotation, placement of other punctuation with respect to quotation marks, and inappropriate use of quotation marks are all discussed. This material is especially pertinent to the proper uses of sources in the research paper, as discussed in 34f on quoting sources. Exercises allow students to use quotation marks in a number of ways, both in sentences and paragraphs.

TEACHING IDEAS

ACROSS THE CURRICULUM The introduction refers students to chapters that deal specifically with writing in various disciplines. Students should understand, however, that while *documentation* may vary by discipline, the rules for *punctuating a quotation* are the same in all disciplines.

ESL CUE

Indirect discourse will be a problem area. ESL students might query why something that remains true must take a past tense form to agree: "He said that his name was John." ("Isn't it still John?" they will ask.) The rule is: only unchanging facts of nature retain the present tense with an introductory past tense form.

"He said that the sun rises in the east and sets in the west."

but

"He said that the sun rose at six yesterday morning."

See 43b-4 on using verbs with reported speech.

material (such as words omitted or added) must be announced as such—either with brackets or ellipses (see 29d and e).

REFERENCES

SUMMEY, GEORGE, JR. *American Punctuation.* New York: Ronald, 1949. Chapter 9. An extensive discussion on quotation marks that is still relevant today.

The following style sheets provide advice on using quotation marks:

The Chicago Manual of Style. 14th ed. Chicago: U of Chicago P, 1993.

GIBALDI, JOSEPH. *MLA Handbook for Writers of Research Papers.* 4th ed. New York: MLA, 1995.

2 Use single quotation marks (‘ ’) to set off quoted material or the titles of short works within a quotation enclosed by double (“ ”) marks.

The use of single quotation marks can be shown by a comparison of original passages with quotations.

ORIGINAL PASSAGES

> The "business" of school for first-grade students is to learn the distinction between intellectual play and playground play.
>
> In preparation for class next week, read the first two chapters of our "In Flight" manual.

QUOTATIONS

> As educator Monica Landau says, "The 'business' of school for first-grade students is to learn the distinction between intellectual play and playground play."
>
> The class coordinator said that for next week we should "read the first two chapters of our 'In Flight' manual."

If you find it necessary to quote material within single quotation marks, use double marks once again.

> Historian Beth Bailey cites popular magazines as one source of information. "In *Mademoiselle*'s 1938 college issue," writes Bailey, "a Smith college senior advised incoming freshmen to 'cultivate an image of popularity' if they wanted dates. 'During your first term,' the senior wrote, 'get "home talent" to ply you with letters, invitations, and telegrams.' "

3 Use commas to enclose explanatory remarks that lie outside the quotation.

A comma is placed after an explanatory remark that introduces a quotation.

> According to Bailey, "Competition was the key term in the formula—remove it and there was no rating, dating, or popularity."

When a remark interrupts a quotation, a pair of commas or a comma and a period should be used. The conventions for punctuation are as follows: the first comma enclosing an explanatory remark notes the (temporary) ending of the quoted material and is placed inside the quotation. If the sentence continues past the explanatory comment, a second comma is placed before the quotation is reintroduced. If the sentence ends with an explanatory remark, a period is placed after that remark. In this case, when the quotation is resumed in a new sentence, the first letter of the quotation is capitalized.

"Rating, dating, popularity, competition," writes Bailey, "were catchwords hammered home, reinforced from all sides until they seemed a natural vocabulary."

"You had to rate in order to date, to date in order to rate," she adds. "By successfully maintaining the cycle, you became popular."

Note: When the word *that* introduces a direct quotation, or when an introductory remark has the sense of a "that" construction but the word itself is omitted, do not use a comma to separate the introduction from the quoted material. In addition, do not capitalize the first letter of the quotation.

Faulty Bailey discovered that, "The Massachusetts *Collegian* (the Massachusetts State College student newspaper) ran an editorial against using the library for 'datemaking.' "

Revised Bailey discovered that "the Massachusetts *Collegian* (the Massachusetts State College student newspaper) ran an editorial against using the library for 'datemaking.' "

See the Critical Decisions box later in 28a for more information on incorporating quotations into your sentences.

4 Display—that is, set off from text—lengthy quotations. Quotation marks are *not* used to enclose a displayed quotation.

Quotations of five or more lines are too long to run in with sentences in a paragraph. Instead they are displayed in a block format in a narrower indentation, without being enclosed by quotation marks.

> In his remarks, Bill Bradley spoke on the impressive economic growth of East Asia:
>
> > East Asia is quickly becoming the richest, most populous, most dynamic area on earth. Over the last quarter century, the East Asian economies grew at an average real growth rate of 6 percent annually while the economies of the United States and the countries of the European Community grew at 3 percent. East Asia's share of gross world product has more than doubled during the last twenty years, rising from 8 percent to 20 percent.

Manuscript form

Double space the displayed quotation and indent ten spaces from the left margin. Punctuate material as in the original text. Quotation marks inside a displayed quotation remain double (" ") marks. If one paragraph is being displayed, do not indent the first word of the paragraph. If multiple paragraphs are being displayed, indent the first word of each paragraph three additional spaces (that is, thirteen spaces from the left). However, if you are quoting multiple paragraphs and the first sentence quoted does not begin a paragraph in the original source, then do not indent the first paragraph in your paper.

TEACHING IDEAS

ACROSS THE CURRICULUM You may want to ask students to find examples of indented quotations from their textbooks in other disciplines. Here is one example from Roger Coleman's *The Art of Work: An Epitaph to Skill:*

> The crafts, as highly skilled work, encompass some of the most amazing of human achievements—the medieval cathedrals, the Bayeux Tapestry—and some of the most alienating forms of work imaginable, as Adam Smith described in this famous passage from *The Wealth of Nations:*
>
> > One man draws out the wire, another straightens it, a third cuts it, a fourth points it, a fifth grinds it at the top for receiving the head; to make the head requires two to three distinct operations; to put it on is a peculiar business; to whiten the pins is another; it is even a trade by itself to put them into the paper; and the important business of making a pin is, in this manner, divided into about eighteen distinct operations.

A displayed quotation is best introduced with a full sentence, ending with a colon. The colon provides a visual cue to the reader that a long quotation follows.

GROUP ACTIVITY

If students are working on research papers for this or another class, they can help each other with editing through this exercise: ask students to bring in samples of research papers. When in groups, they can exchange papers and edit each other's work for proper placement of quotation marks with regard to punctuation. Any disputes that arise will lead students to consult the handbook.

5 Place periods and commas inside the end quotation mark.

> "The big question is whether this kind of growth is sustainable," says Bradley.
>
> He adds, "Because American trade deficits must shrink in the years ahead, Asian nations can no longer count as heavily on expanding exports to the United States to fuel their growth."

EXCEPTION: When a pair of parentheses enclosing some comment or page reference appears between the end of the quotation and the end of the sentence, use quotation marks to note the end of the quoted text, place the parentheses, and then close with a period.

CONFUSING He adds, "Because American trade deficits must shrink in the years ahead, Asian nations can no longer count as heavily on expanding exports to the United States to fuel their growth. (1)"

REVISED He adds, "Because American trade deficits must shrink in the years ahead, Asian nations can no longer count as heavily on expanding exports to the United States to fuel their growth" (1).

6 Place colons, semicolons, and footnotes outside end quotation marks.

COLON Bradley directly asserts that "the futures of Asia and the United States are inextricably intertwined": Asian countries profited by U.S. growth in the 1980s, and the U.S. must profit by Asian growth in the '90s and beyond.

SEMICOLON Bradley believes that the United States must look to the East with the intention of forming a "strong, lasting partnership"; moreover, he states that we must do so without the condescension that has for so long characterized our relations with countries like Japan and South Korea.

FOOTNOTE Bradley believes that the United States must look to the East with the intention of forming a "strong, lasting partnership."[4]

7 Place question marks and exclamation points inside or outside end quotation marks, depending on meaning.

Place a question mark or exclamation point *inside* the end quotation marks when it applies to the quoted material only or when it applies to both the quoted material and the sentence as a whole. Place the mark *outside* the end quotation mark when the sentence as a whole forms a question or exclamatory remark but the quoted material does not.

MARK APPLIES TO QUOTED MATERIAL ONLY

Naturalist José Márcio Ayres began his field work on the ukaris monkey of the upper Amazon with this question: "How do these primates survive almost exclusively on the pulp and seeds of fruit, when the forests in which they live are flooded much of the year?"

MARK APPLIES BOTH TO QUOTED MATERIAL AND TO SENTENCE AS WHOLE

How can we, sitting comfortably in living rooms and libraries, appreciate the rigors of field research when even Ayres remarks, "Is the relative protection of the ukaris habitat at all surprising in light of the enormous swarms of mosquitoes one encounters in all seasons and at all hours of the day?"

MARK APPLIES TO SENTENCE AS A WHOLE BUT NOT TO QUOTATION

Bachelor ukaris looking for mates behave as badly as hooligans at a soccer match. Ayres reports that fights are frequent and that "after all this trouble, copulation may last less than two minutes"!

8 Place dashes inside quotations only when they are part of the quoted material.

PART OF QUOTED MATERIAL

Would-be competitors like "brocket deer, peccaries, agoutis, armadillos, and pacas—mammals common in upland habitats—"do not inhabit the ukaris forest, most likely because of the Amazon's annual flooding. This is one reason the ukaris has survived.

SEPARATE FROM QUOTED MATERIAL

Once the flood waters recede, each afternoon the ukaris descend from the upper canopy of trees—"where the temperature is uncomfortably high"—to forage for seedlings, which they dig up and eat.

EXERCISE 1

Use double quotation marks (" ") and single quotation marks (' ') to punctuate the sentences that follow. Words to be quoted are underlined.

Example: According to Carla Fernandez, One third of all offenders are in prison because of property offenses such as larceny, car theft, and burglary.

According to Carla Fernandez, "One third of all offenders are in prison because of property offenses such as larceny, car theft, and burglary."

1. Half of the prison population has been incarcerated for violent crimes such as assault, homicide, and rape.

GROUP ACTIVITY

All of the exercises in this chapter lend themselves to group activity. Have students respond to exercises individually, and then compare their responses with those of other group members. When the inevitable disagreement occurs, students will have to consult the handbook. Once they become accustomed to using the chapter, they'll likely continue to refer to it as they edit their papers.

EXERCISE 1

1. Half of the prison population has been incarcerated for "violent crimes such as assault, homicide, and rape."
2. The remaining 20 percent of offenders have been convicted of "offenses against public order" such as drug dealing.
3. In a speech on March 2, 1992, New York corrections official Stuart Koman voiced a widely held view: "Overcrowded prisons not only do not rehabilitate offenders, they teach offenders to reject the law-abiding life.

(continued)

One individual who has spent 13 of his 25 years behind bars said to me that 'I learned my techniques in jail. You know, the tools of my trade.' "

4. As sociologist Lauren Rose concludes, "Efforts to reform prisons and to make them real *penitentiaries*—institutions of penitence—have failed" (Jacobs 341).
5. "One dilemma that we now face," according to Rolf Hanson, "is to understand whether we want incarceration to correct criminal behavior or to punish it."

FOR DISCUSSION

No discussion of how to quote is complete without a focus on when to quote. Encourage students at this point to talk about their decisions to use quotations:

Have any of them ever chosen to quote on their own rather than in response to a teacher's instructions? If so, what contributed to the decision?

When assigned papers requiring quotations, how do students decide what and when to quote?

How often do students think the quotations they use really fit into their text?

What do they see as the relationship between the quotations and the text?

These and other similar questions should help students articulate their understanding of quotations as they ponder the advice found in the Critical Decisions box.

2. The remaining 20 percent of offenders have been convicted of offenses against public order, such as drug dealing.
3. In a speech on March 2, 1992, New York corrections official Stuart Koman voiced a widely held view: Overcrowded prisons not only do not rehabilitate offenders, they teach offenders to reject the law-abiding life. One individual who has spent 13 of his 25 years behind bars said to me that "I learned my techniques in jail. You know, the tools of my trade."
4. As sociologist Lauren Rose concludes, Efforts to reform prisons and to make them real *penitentiaries*—institutions of penitence—have failed (Jacobs 341).
5. One dilemma that we now face, according to Rolf Hanson, is to understand whether we want incarceration to correct criminal behavior or to punish it.

CRITICAL DECISIONS

Set issues in a broader context: Incorporating quotations into your writing

Knowing when to quote is something of an art, and you should see 34f for guidance on this matter. This discussion assumes you have decided to quote. The focus here is on determining *how much* to quote and on how to *incorporate* quoted materials into the logic and rhythm of your sentences.

The following examples draw on the following passage about shopping malls by the noted anthropologist Richard Stein (*The New American Bazaar*).

> When they are successful, shopping malls in American cities fulfill the same function as *bazaars* did in the cities of antiquity. The bazaars of the ancient and medieval worlds were social organisms—if we mean by this term self-contained, self-regulating systems in which individual human lives are less important (and less interesting) than the interaction of hundreds, and sometimes thousands, of lives.

How much to quote

Quote other writers when you find their discussions to be particularly lively, dramatic, or incisive or especially helpful in bolstering your credibility (see 34f). In general, quote as little as possible so that you keep readers focused on *your* discussion.

- **Quote a word or a phrase, if this will do.**

  Anthropologist Richard Stein refers to the American shopping mall as a "social organism."

- **Quote a sentence, if needed.**

  Stein sees in shopping malls a modern spin on an ancient institution: "When they are successful, shopping malls in American cities fulfill the same function as *bazaars* did in the cities of antiquity."

(continued)

CRITICAL DECISIONS *(continued)*

■ **Infrequently quote a long passage as a "block."**

Long quotations of five or more lines are set off as a block (see 28a-4). Limit your use of block quotations, which tempt writers to avoid the hard work of selecting for quotation *only* the words or sentences especially pertinent to the discussion at hand. If you decide that a long quotation is needed, introduce the quotation with a full sentence and a colon. The following might introduce the passage previously quoted from *The New American Bazaar.*

> Various commentators have claimed that shopping malls serve a social function. Anthropologist Richard Stein compares the mall to the bazaar in cities of old:
>
> > When they are successful, shopping malls . . .

Using attributive phrases

■ **Use attributive phrases.**

By using an attributive phrase like *Jones argues, Smith says,* or *according to Stein,* you alert readers to the fact that you are about to present someone else's words. (See the box in 34f-4 for a list of attributive verbs.) Tie these attributive phrases into the logic of your own sentences, linking the quotation with the content of your paper.

> Every American city now has its shopping malls. According to anthropologist Richard Stein, successful malls "fulfill the same function as *bazaars* did in the cities of antiquity."

■ **Interrupt a quotation with an attributive phrase.**

Place your attributive comment between a quotation's subject and verb or after an introductory phrase or clause in order to emphasize a key word. The word emphasized will come just before or after the interruption.

> "When they are successful," says Richard Stein, "shopping malls in American cities fulfill the same function as *bazaars* did in the cities of antiquity." [The interruption focuses attention on *shopping malls.*]

Split a quotation with an attributive remark to maintain the rhythm or continuity of your own paragraph. Compare these two versions of a quoted sentence.

ACCEPTABLE Every American city has its shopping malls, its equivalents of the ancient bazaar. As anthropologist Richard Stein points out, "The bazaars of the ancient and medieval worlds were social organisms . . . ."

PREFERRED Every American city has its shopping malls, its equivalents of the ancient bazaar. "The bazaars of the ancient and medieval worlds," says anthropologist Richard Stein, "were social organisms . . . ." [This version maintains paragraph coherence by keeping the reader's focus on the word *bazaar.*]

TEACHING IDEAS

You may want to provide students with further examples of the use of quotation marks in dialogue. If the course includes a component in imaginative literature, you'll have a wealth of examples at your disposal. Here is one further example:

> "Will you forgive me?"
>
> She doesn't answer right away, which is fine, because I have to get used to the fact that I said it.
>
> "Maybe," she says at last, "but I'm not the same girl."
>
> I'm about to say she hasn't changed, and then I realize how much she has changed. She has gotten smarter than I am by a long shot, to understand she is different.
>
> "I'm different now, too," I am able to admit. (Louise Erdrich)

(This example illustrates all of the issues regarding quotation in dialogue covered in this section.)

28b Quoting poetry, dialogue, and other material

1 Run-in brief quotations of poetry with your sentences. Indicate line breaks in the poem with a slash (/). Quote longer passages in displayed form.

A full quotation of or a lengthy quotation from a poem is normally made in displayed form (see 28a-4).

> The Black Riders
>
> 42
>
> I walked in a desert.
> and I cried:
> "Ah, God, take me from this place!"
> A voice said: "It is no desert."
> I cried, "Well, but—
> The sand, the heat, the vacant horizon."
> A voice said: "It is no desert."
>
> —STEPHEN CRANE

When quoting a brief extract—four lines or fewer—you can run the lines into the sentences of a paragraph, using the guidelines for quoting prose (see 28a); however, line divisions are shown with a slash (/) with one space before and one space after.

> Stephen Crane's bleak view of the human condition is expressed in lyric 42 of his series "The Black Riders." Walking in a desert, his narrator cries: " 'Ah, God, take me from this place!' / A voice said: 'It is no desert.' "

2 Use quotation marks to quote or write dialogue.

When quoting or writing dialogue, change paragraphs to note each change of speaker. Explanatory comments between parts of the quotation are enclosed with two commas. The first, signaling the (temporary) ending of the quoted material, is placed *inside* the end quotation mark. The second comma, signaling the end of the explanatory remark, is placed before the quotation mark that opens the next part of the quotation. When the quotation resumes, its first letter may be capitalized only if a new sentence has been started (in which case the comma concluding the explanatory material is changed to a period).

> "Nobody sees you any more, Helen," Nat began. "Where've you disappeared to?"
>
> "Oh, I've been around," she said, trying to hide a slight tremble in her voice. "And you?"
>
> "Is somebody there where you're talking that you sound so restrained?"
>
> "That's right."

"I thought so. So let me make it quick and clean. Helen, it's been a long time. I want to see you. What do you say if we take in a play this Saturday night? I can stop off for tickets on my way uptown tomorrow."

—BERNARD MALAMUD, *The Assistant*

In a speech of two or more paragraphs, begin each new paragraph with opening quotation marks to signal your reader that the speech continues. Use closing quotation marks *only* at the end of the final paragraph to signal that the speech has concluded.

3

Indicate the titles of brief works with quotation marks: chapters of books, short stories, poems, songs, sections from newspapers, essays, etc.[1]

I read the "Focus Section" of the *Boston Sunday Globe* every week.

"The Dead" is, perhaps, Joyce's most famous short story.

"Coulomb's law" is the first chapter in volume two of Gartenhaus's text, *Physics: Basic Principles.*

Manuscript form

When placed on the title page of a paper you are submitting to an instructor or peers, the title of your work should *not* be put in quotation marks. Only when you are quoting a title (yours or anyone else's) *in* a paper do you use quotation marks. However, if a title itself contains a title—a reference to some other work, you must quote appropriately. If the title of your own paper included a reference to a poem, the title would look like this:

Loneliness in Stephen Crane's "The Black Riders"

This same title, referred to *in* a sentence:

In his essay "Loneliness in Stephen Crane's 'The Black Riders,' " Marcus Trudeau argues that Crane's universe is unknowable and indifferent—but not, necessarily, hostile.

When a title is included in any other quoted material, double quotation marks (" ") change to single marks (' ').

4

Use quotation marks occasionally to emphasize words or to note invented words.

An uncommon usage of a standard term or a new term that has been invented for a special circumstance can be highlighted with quotation marks. Once you have emphasized a word with quotation marks, you need not use the marks again with that word.

LOOKING BACK

Students should be told that use of quotation marks for the purpose of emphasis should be confined to rare occasions. You may want to remind them that it is far better to use precise diction than to resort to punctuation in order to achieve emphasis (see Chapter 21).

[1]The titles of longer works—books, newspapers, magazines, long poems—are underlined in typewritten text and italicized in typeset text. (See Chapter 36.)

> We can designate as "low interactive" any software title that does not challenge learners to think. Low-interactive titles may be gorgeous to look at, but looking—not thinking—is what they invite learners to do.

Words that will be defined in a sentence, or words that are referred to as words, are usually italicized, though they are sometimes set in quotations. Definitions themselves, especially if they provide a translation of a word or phrase in another language, are placed in quotation marks.

> The meaning of the Latin injunction *carpe diem* is "seize the day."
>
> The name of the Greek Titan Prometheus means "forethought."

28c Eliminating misused or overused quotation marks

1 Eliminate phrases using quotation marks to note slang or colloquial expressions.

If your use of slang is appropriate for and important (as slang) in your paper, then no quotation marks are needed. If, on the other hand, you are uncomfortable with slang or colloquial expressions and choose to show your discomfort by using quotation marks, then find another, more formal way to express the same thoughts.

OVERUSED Kate promised she would "walk that extra mile" for Mark. [The quotation marks do not excuse the use of a cliché here.]

REVISED Kate promised to help Mark in any way she could.

2 Eliminate phrases using quotation marks to make ironic comments.

Express your thoughts as directly as possible through word choice.

MISUSED Dean Langley called to express his "appreciation" for all I had done.

REVISED Dean Langley called to complain about the accusations of bias I raised with reporters.

3 Eliminate quotation marks used to emphasize technical terms.

Assume your readers will note technical terms as such and will refer to a dictionary if needed.

MISUSED "Electromagnetism" is a branch of physics.

REVISED Electromagnetism is a branch of physics.

4 Eliminate quotation marks that are overused to note commonly accepted nicknames.

OVERUSED "Ted" Kennedy is a powerful senator.
REVISED Ted Kennedy is a powerful senator.

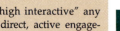

EXERCISE 2

Suggested response:
We can designate as "high interactive" any software that requires direct, active engagement on the part of the learner. High-interactive titles must not only look good, they must present learners with real puzzles to solve.

Reserve your use of quotation marks for unusual nicknames, which often appear in parentheses after a first name. Once you have emphasized a name with quotation marks, you need not use the marks again with that name.

> Ralph ("The Hammer") Schwartz worked forty years as a longshoreman in San Francisco and was fond of saying, "Don't end your life face down at the bottom of a bird cage."

EXERCISE 2

Correct the use of quotation marks to emphasize specific words in the following paragraph. Two of the eight expressions in quotation marks are emphasized correctly.

> We can designate as "high interactive" any software that requires direct, active engagement on the part of the learner. "High-interactive" titles must not only look good, they must present learners with real "puzzles" to solve. "Real" in this sense means "thinking" problems that are not solved by mere computation (which on-screen calculators can manage) or by quick reference to a passage of text (which basic "search" engines can easily do); "real" problems are ones that invite unique, learner-specific answers to problems that at first may seem unsolvable. The computer screen will not "give away" the answers. No: for a problem to be real, the learner, not the teacher, must solve it.

EXERCISE 3

Following is a passage on Columbus by naval historian J.H. Parry. Quote from the paragraph, as instructed here.

1. Introduce a quotation with the word *that.*
2. Introduce a quotation with a phrase and a comma. End the quotation with a page reference (which you will invent), noted in parentheses.
3. Introduce a quotation with a sentence and a colon.
4. Interrupt a quotation with the phrase "Parry states."
5. Follow a quotation with an explanatory remark.

> Columbus was not concerned with theory for its own sake, but with promoting a practical proposal. He did not study the available authorities in order to draw conclusions; he began with the conviction—how formed, we cannot tell—that an expedition to Asia by a westward route was practicable and that he was the man destined to lead it. He then combed the authorities known to him, and selected from them any assertion which supported his case. The practicability of the voyage—assuming that no major land mass barred the way—depended partly on the pattern of winds and currents likely to be encountered, but mainly on the distance to be covered. Columbus had to show that the westward distance from Europe to Asia was within the operating range of the available ships. We can trace, from what is known of his reading, from his own later writings, and from biography written by his son Hernando, how he set about it.

"Real" in this sense means thinking problems that are not solved by mere computation (which on-screen calculators can manage) or by quick reference to a passage of text (which basic search engines can easily do); real problems are ones that invite unique, learner-specific answers to problems that at first may seem unsolvable. The computer screen will not give away the answers. No: for a problem to be real, the learner, not the teacher, must solve it.

EXERCISE 3

This paragraph appears in J.H. Parry, *The Discovery of the Sea* (Berkeley: University of California Press, 1981), 188. Answers will vary. We provide here one possible response to each item in the exercise.

1. Introduce a quotation with the word *that.*

   Naval historian J.H. Parry suggests that "Columbus was not concerned with theory for its own sake, but with promoting a practical proposal."

2. Introduce a quotation with a phrase and a comma. End the quotation with a page reference (which you will invent), noted in parentheses.

   According to J.H. Parry, "Columbus had to show that the westward distance from Europe to Asia was within the operating range of the available ships" (188).

3. Introduce a quotation with a sentence and a colon.

   In making his case to financial backers, Columbus faced one major task: "[He] had to show that the westward distance from Europe to Asia was within the operating range of the available ships" (188).

4. Interrupt a quotation with the phrase "Parry states."

   "Columbus was not concerned with theory for its own sake," Parry states, "but with promoting a practical proposal."

5. Follow a quotation with an explanatory remark.

   Parry believes that Columbus "combed the authorities known to him, and selected from them any assertion which supported his case," which suggests the confidence, and even arrogance, of the Great Navigator.

CHAPTER 29

Other Marks

KEY FEATURES

Another chapter designed primarily for reference, this chapter covers the remaining marks of punctuation in English: the colon, the dash, parentheses, brackets, ellipses, and slashes. Each of these punctuation marks is covered in careful detail, providing clear examples of virtually every possible use for them. Since the colon and the dash are more common than the others, their treatment is more extensive—especially with regard to stylistic choices. Throughout the chapter, exercises allow students to punctuate sample sentences and to create their own sentences, using the various marks discussed in the chapter.

REFERENCES

The following style sheets provide advice on using these marks:

The Chicago Manual of Style. 14th ed. Chicago: U of Chicago P, 1993.

GIBALDI, JOSEPH. *MLA Handbook for Writers of Research Papers.* 4th ed. New York: MLA, 1995.

This chapter reviews the conventions for using colons, dashes, parentheses, brackets, ellipses, and slashes. Of these marks, the first three are the most frequently used. The colon, the dash, and parentheses are important marks for the writer concerned with style. They significantly alter and thereby vary the rhythm of sentence structures. Brackets and ellipses are marks you will need to know when incorporating quotations into your papers.

THE COLON

29a Using the colon

The **colon** is the mark of punctuation generally used to make an announcement. In formal writing, the colon follows only a *complete* independent clause and introduces a word, phrase, sentence, or group of sentences (as in a quotation). For readers, the colon gives an important cue about the relationship of one part of your text to another: the sentence before the colon leads directly to the word or words after, in the fashion of an announcement.

1 Edit to eliminate colons misused within independent clauses.

In formal writing, a colon must always follow a complete statement or independent clause. The mark must never be used as a break inside an independent clause.

FAULTY For someone who is depressed, the best two things in life are: eating and sleeping.

REVISED For someone who is depressed, the best two things in life are eating and sleeping.

REVISED For someone who is depressed, only two things in life matter: eating and sleeping.

2 Use a colon to announce an important statement or question.

You create emphasis in a paragraph when you write one sentence to introduce another. Greater emphasis is created when you conclude that introduction with a colon.

> How can it be that 25 years of feminist social change have made so little impression on preschool culture? Molly, now 6 and well aware that women can be doctors, has one theory: children's entertainment is made mostly by men.
>
> —KATHA POLLITT

3 Use a colon to introduce a list or a quotation.

If at the conclusion of an independent clause you want to introduce a list or a quotation, do so with a colon.

A LIST

> According to Cooley, the looking-glass self has three components: how we think our behavior appears to others, how we think others judge our behavior, and how we feel about their judgments.

A QUOTATION

> A New England soldier wrote to his wife on the eve of the First Battle of Bull Run: "I know how great a debt we owe to those who went before us through the Revolution. And I am willing, perfectly willing, to lay down all my joys in this life, to help maintain this government, and to pay that debt."

A colon can introduce either a list or a quotation that is set off and indented.

> A New England soldier wrote to his wife on the eve of the First Battle of Bull Run:
>
> > I know how great a debt we owe to those who went before us through the Revolution. And I am willing, perfectly willing, to lay down all my joys in this life, to help maintain this government, and to pay that debt.

> Chip designers use increased packing density of transistors in one of two ways:
>
> 1. They increase the complexity of the computers they can fabricate.
> 2. They keep the complexity of the computer at the same level and pack the whole computer into fewer chips.

NOTE: Both when lists and quotations are run in with sentences and when they are set off, the expression *as follows* or some variant often precedes the colon. If this expression is tagged onto a complete sentence, it is preceded by a comma.

> There are three reasons to reject the theory of spontaneous generation, as follows:

4 Use a colon to set off an appositive phrase, summary, or explanation.

Appositive

> Food sharing, in which individuals provision other members of a group, is extremely rare in mammals. In addition to bats, only a few species are

TEACHING IDEAS

Occasionally students use colons to introduce quotations when a comma or no punctuation is called for. Remind them that the example here shows a quotation preceded by a *complete sentence.* Only in situations such as this can a colon be used to introduce a quotation.

known to display such behavior: wild dogs, hyenas, chimpanzees, and human beings.

Summary

A number of recent studies reveal that female vampire bats cluster together during the day but at night reassort themselves, creating a fluid social organization that is maintained for many years: vampire bats are remarkably social.

Explanation

When Calais surrendered, King Edward (of England) threatened to put the city to the sword, then offered the people a bargain: he would spare the city if six of the chief burghers would give themselves up unconditionally.

5 Use a colon to distinguish chapter from verse in Biblical citations, hours from minutes, and titles from subtitles or subsidiary material.

Biblical citation

It is an irony that almost none of the literature of the people who gave us the alphabet has been preserved. Fragments of Phoenician poetry have survived in the Psalms, where the mountains are described as "a fountain that makes the gardens fertile, a well of living water" (Song of Songs 4:15).

Hours from minutes

8:15 A.M. 12:01 P.M.

Titles from subtitles or subsidiary material

The New American Bazaar: Shopping Malls and the Anthropology of Urban Life

6 Use a colon after the salutation in a formal letter, and in bibliographic citations.

Dear Ms. King:
Dear Dr. Hart:
Bikai, Patricia. "The Phoenicians." *Archaeology* Mar./Apr. 1990: 30.

EXERCISE 1

Correct the use of colons in these sentences. Add or delete colons as needed.

Example: Increasingly, grade-school Little League coaches of baseball, soccer, and football are confronting an uncomfortable problem rabid parents.

ADDITIONAL EXERCISE A

In the following sentences, replace the inappropriate punctuation marks introducing quotations. Place a check mark beside any correctly punctuated sentence.

1. The defense attorney addressed the jury in a solemn tone, "My client's life is in your hands."
2. The prosecuting attorney whispered to her assistant that the accused was: "guilty as sin."
3. Whereupon the judge growled "Ms. Mahoney, that remark was unprofessional."
4. The jury foreman asked the judge for clarification: "Are we free to consider lesser charges?"

Answers:

1. The defense attorney addressed the jury in a solemn tone: "My client's life is in your hands."
2. The prosecuting attorney whispered to her assistant that the accused was "guilty as sin."
3. Whereupon the judge growled, "Ms. Mahoney, that remark was unprofessional."
4. Correct

Increasingly, grade-school Little League coaches of baseball, soccer, and football are confronting an uncomfortable problem: rabid parents.

1. Youth soccer games provide an illustration: teenagers serving as referees: have been confronted in the most obnoxious way by parents snarling their disapproval at missed calls.
2. Adult coaches are used to parents whose egos interfere with their ability to watch a game: Young referees can be taught strategies to neutralize obnoxious parents. But no amount of preparation can avert the most serious damage caused by rabid parents the crushed ego of an 8-year-old whose father screams, "You're such a wimp!"
3. Communities around the country have begun to print pamphlets with titles like this "Helping Your Child to Enjoy Recreational Sports A Guide."

EXERCISE 2

Write brief sentences, as instructed.

1. Write a sentence with a colon that introduces a list.
2. Write a sentence with a colon that announces an emphatic statement.
3. Write a sentence with a colon that sets off an appositive phrase, summary, or explanation.

THE DASH

29b Using dashes for emphasis

On the typewritten page, the dash is written as two hyphens (--). The space between these hyphens closes when the dash is typeset (—).

1 Use dashes to set off nonessential elements.

Use dashes to set off brief modifiers, lengthy modifiers, and appositives. In contrast to pairs of commas and parentheses, dashes emphasize the nonessential element set off in a sentence (see 25d). If dashes are the most emphatic interrupting marks and parentheses the least emphatic, commas offer a third, middling choice—neither emphatic nor fully parenthetical.

Brief modifiers in mid-sentence

Seven to thirty percent of vampire bats in a cluster fail to obtain a sufficient blood meal on any given night. By soliciting regurgitated blood from a roostmate, a bat can fend off starvation—at least for one more night—and so have another chance to find a meal. [The phrase acts as an adverb, modifying *fend off*.]

EXERCISE 1

1. Youth soccer games provide an illustration: teenagers serving as referees have been confronted in the most obnoxious way by parents snarling their disapproval at missed calls.
2. Adult coaches are used to parents whose egos interfere with their ability to watch a game. Young referees can be taught strategies to neutralize obnoxious parents. But no amount of preparation can avert the most serious damage caused by rabid parents: the crushed ego of an 8-year-old whose father screams, "You're such a wimp!"
3. Communities around the country have begun to print pamphlets with titles such as "Helping Your Child to Enjoy Recreational Sports: A Guide."

GROUP ACTIVITY

This exercise and Exercises 3, 5, and 6 all lend themselves to group activity. Have students respond to exercises individually, and then compare their responses with those of other group members. When the inevitable disagreement occurs, students will have to consult the handbook. Once they become accustomed to using the chapter, they'll likely continue to refer to it as they edit their papers.

EXERCISE 2

Individual responses

GROUP ACTIVITY

This exercise and Exercise 4 can be completed in groups. As they compose the sentences together, students will learn to articulate their perceptions of the appropriate use of the colon.

TEACHING IDEAS

Some students see the dash as a type of "free agent" that can be used anywhere in a sentence. You may need to remind these students that dashes have specific functions. They're not a substitute for careful punctuation, nor are they to be used when the writer isn't sure of what other punctuation to use.

GROUP ACTIVITY

Practice in specific appropriate uses of the dash can help students appreciate its function. Ask groups to generate one sentence for each of the uses described in 29b, 1–4. Sentences will then be passed to another group, whose task it will be to comment on the sentences' effectiveness. The discussion that takes place as students compose and evaluate the sentences should help students understand how the dash is used.

When Do Writers Need Dashes?

Sentence constructions rarely *require* the use of dashes. The dash is a stylist's tool, an elective mark. It halts the reader within a sentence by creating a cha-cha, dance-like syncopation. On seeing the dash, readers pause; then they speed up to read the words you have emphasized. Then they pause once more before returning to the main part of your sentence:

EFFECTIVE Zoologist Uwe Schmidt discovered that shortly after birth, vampire bat pups are given regurgitated blood—in addition to milk—by their mothers.

Use the single dash to set off elements at the beginning or end of a sentence and a pair of dashes to set off elements in the middle. When elements are set off at the end of a sentence or in the middle, you have the choice of using commas or parentheses instead of dashes. Whatever punctuation you use, take care to word the element you set off so that it fits smoothly into the structure of your sentence. For instance, in the following sentence the nonessential element would be awkward.

AWKWARD Zoologist Uwe Schmidt discovered that shortly after birth, vampire bat pups are given regurgitated blood—they drink milk too—by their mothers.

BETTER Bat pups are given regurgitated blood—in addition to milk—by their mothers.

Lengthy modifiers

Within the past ten years, a new generation of investigators—armed with fresh insights from sociobiology and behavioral ecology—have learned much about social organization in the birds of paradise. [The phrase acts as an adjective, modifying *investigators.*]

Appositives

We study history to understand the present. Yet sometimes the present can help us to clarify the past. So it is with a San-speaking people known as the !Kung—a group of what were once called African Bushmen. [The appositive phrase renames the noun *!Kung.*]

NOTE: Use dashes to set off appositives that contain commas. Recall that a nonessential appositive phrase can also be set off from a sentence by a pair of commas (see 25d-3). When the appositive is formed by a series, the items of which are already separated by commas, dashes prevent misreading.

CONFUSING Since the turn of the century, the percentage of information workers, bankers, insurance agents, lawyers, science journalists, has gone from a trickle to a flood.

REVISED Since the turn of the century, the percentage of information workers—bankers, insurance agents, lawyers, science journalists—has gone from a trickle to a flood.

2 Use dashes to set off a significant repeating structure or an emphatic concluding element.

Repeating structure

To me the vitality of the bird of paradise's mating display was—and continues to be—one of nature's most thrilling sights. [The verb is repeated.]

Emphatic concluding remark

Once disposed of in the landfill, garbage is supposed to remain buried for eternity. So it was in Collier County, Florida—until we found several good reasons to dig it up again. [The dash sets off a sharply contrasting element, in this case a subordinate clause that functions as an adverb.]

Use dashes—with care. [This brief qualifying tag, a prepositional phrase, functions as an adverb.]

3 Use a dash to set off an introductory series from a summary or explanatory remark.

Strategic spots on the Boston Common are occupied by regiments of lunch-hour workers, and the Common is still the preferred site for political rallies. Pocket change, ball-point pens, campaign buttons—humanity's imprint continues to be recorded on the grassy slopes of the Boston Common. [This sentence structure, which begins with a series, is relatively rare.]

4 Use a dash to express an interruption in dialogue.

A dash used in dialogue shows interruption—speakers interrupting themselves or being interrupted by others. The dash used in dialogue also shows a change of thought or an uncompleted thought, a change in tone, or a pause.

> Adam studied his brother's face until Charles looked away. "Are you mad at something?" Adam asked.
>
> "What should I be mad at?"
>
> "It just sounded— "
>
> "I've got nothing to be mad at. Come on, I'll get you something to eat."
>
> —JOHN STEINBECK

5 Use a dash to set off an attribution (by name), following an epigram.

At blows that never fall you falter,
And what you never lose, you must forever mourn.

—GOETHE

Dashes used in this fashion often follow epigrams—succinct, provocative quotations placed at the beginning of a paper as a vehicle for the introduction. Typically, the writer opens such a paper with a direct reference to the epigram and its author: "In these lines from *Faust,* the main character laments his limited human powers. . . ."

EXERCISE 3

Add a dash or a pair of dashes to the following sentences.

Example: Many innovations the Chinese slipper, the Perrault godmother with her midnight injunction and her ability to change pumpkin into coach became incorporated in later versions of "Cinderella."

Many innovations—the Chinese slipper, the Perrault godmother with her midnight injunction and her ability to change pumpkin into coach—became incorporated in later versions of "Cinderella."

1. The chapbooks of the eighteenth century and nineteenth century, crudely printed tiny paperbacks, were the source of most children's reading in the early days of our country. Originally, these were books imported from Europe. But slowly American publishing grew. In the latter part of the nineteenth century one firm stood out McLoughlin Brothers.
2. Golden Press's *Walt Disney's Cinderella* set the new pattern for America's Cinderella. This book's text is coy and condescending. (Sample: "And her best friends of all were guess who the mice!")
3. There is also an easy-reading version published by Random House, *Walt Disney's Cinderella.* This Cinderella commits the further heresy of cursing her luck. "How I did wish to go to the ball," she says. "But it is no use. Wishes never come true."

   But in fairy tales wishes have a habit of happening *wishes accompanied by the proper action,* bad wishes as well as good.

EXERCISE 4

Write brief sentences, as instructed.

1. Write a sentence with a nonessential series placed mid-sentence, set off by a pair of dashes.
2. Write a sentence in which a nonessential element is set off at the end by a dash.
3. Write a sentence in which a dash or pair of dashes sets off a significant repeating structure or emphatic statement.

EXERCISE 3

1. The chapbooks of the eighteenth century and nineteenth century, crudely printed tiny paperbacks, were the source of most children's reading in the early days of our country. Originally, these were books imported from Europe. But slowly American publishing grew. In the latter part of the nineteenth century one firm stood out—McLoughlin Brothers.
2. Golden Press's *Walt Disney's Cinderella* set the new pattern for America's Cinderella. This book's text is coy and condescending. (Sample: "And her best friends of all were—guess who—the mice!")
3. There is also an easy-reading version published by Random House, *Walt Disney's Cinderella.* This Cinderella commits the further heresy of cursing her luck. "How I did wish to go to the ball," she says. "But it is no use. Wishes never come true."

   But in fairy tales wishes have a habit of happening—*wishes accompanied by the proper action,* bad wishes as well as good.

—Jane Yolen

EXERCISE 4

Individual responses

PARENTHESES

29c Using parentheses to set off nonessential information

Parentheses ( ) are used to enclose and set off nonessential dates, words, phrases, or whole sentences that provide examples, comments, and other supporting information. The remark enclosed by parentheses is the ultimate nonessential modifier; it presents the reader with an aside, an interesting but by no means crucial bit of information. To give nonessential remarks more emphasis, use commas or dashes. (See also the Critical Decisions box in 25d-3.)

1 Use parentheses to set off nonessential information: examples, comments, appositives.

Examples

The ground beetle *Pterostichus pinguedineus* vanished from Iowa 15,300 years ago, but today it survives in Alaska, in the Yukon, and in a series of isolated alpine refuges in the northern Appalachians (for example, the peak of Mt. Washington in New Hampshire).

Comments—explanatory or editorial

Beetles (especially those species that scavenge or that prey on other arthropods) are rapid colonizers and are among the first organisms to invade terrain opened up to them by changing climates.

Appositives

The information content of a slice of pizza (advertising, legal expenses, and so on) accounts for a larger percentage of its cost than the edible content does, according to Henry Kelley and Andrew W. Wyckoff of the Congressional Office of Technology Assessment.

2 Use parentheses to set off dates, translations of non-English words, and acronyms.

Dates

Thomas Aquinas (b. 1225 or 1226, d. 1274) is regarded as the greatest of scholastic philosophers.

Translations

The look on the faces of the Efe tribesmen made it clear that they could think of nothing worse than to have a *muzungu* (foreigner) living with them for even a day.

ADDITIONAL EXERCISE B

ACROSS THE CURRICULUM Academic writers make liberal use of parentheses. Look through your textbooks for other courses and try to identify examples of each of the uses of parentheses found in this section of the handbook. Copy the sentences to use as additional examples to refer to when you write academic papers.

TEACHING IDEAS

Students may need to be reminded that although acronyms are acceptable in academic writing, it is almost always necessary to identify the full name or title represented by the acronym. The first time the name or title is used, the acronym can be placed beside it in parentheses and used by itself thereafter.

Acronyms

Lucy Suchman, staff anthropologist of Xerox's Palo Alto Research Center (better known as PARC), watches workers in an airline operations room at San Jose International Airport to learn how they extract particular information from a chaotic assortment of radio, telephone, text, and video feeds. [Typically, an acronym is placed in parentheses directly after the first mention of a term or title subsequently referred to by its acronym.]

3 Use parentheses to set off numbers or letters that mark items in a series, when the series is run in with a sentence.

Interactive learning is student-centered two ways: **(1)** students set the pace of their own learning, calling on hypertext help to clarify concepts and information; and **(2)** students set the depth of their own learning, exploring those materials that particularly engage their interest.

When the series appears in list form, omit the parentheses:

Interactive learning is student-centered two ways:

1. Students set the pace of their own learning, calling on hypertext help to clarify concepts and information.
2. Students set the depth of their own learning, exploring those materials that particularly engage their interest.

4 Punctuate parentheses according to convention.

Words enclosed by parentheses should be punctuated according to standard practice. When a parenthetical remark forms a sentence, the remark should begin with an uppercase letter and end with an appropriate mark (period, question mark, or exclamation point) placed *inside* the end parenthesis. In all other cases, end punctuation should be placed outside the end parenthesis, and punctuation that would normally be placed directly after a word should be placed directly after the parenthetical remark.

FAULTY Like other nomads, the Bakhtiari think of themselves as a family, the sons of a single founding-father. (as did the ancient Jews)

REVISED Like other nomads, the Bakhtiari think of themselves as a family, the sons of a single founding-father (as did the ancient Jews).

FAULTY According to J. Bronowski, the Bakhtiari "think of themselves as a family, the sons of a single founding-father." (60)

REVISED According to J. Bronowski, the Bakhtiari "think of themselves as a family, the sons of a single founding-father" (60).

EXERCISE 5

Add parentheses to the following sentences to enclose nonessential information.

Example: Nearly all twin-lens reflex cameras and a few single-lens reflex SLR cameras are designed to accommodate roll film somewhat wider than 35 millimeters.

Nearly all twin-lens reflex cameras and a few single-lens reflex (SLR) cameras are designed to accommodate roll film somewhat wider than 35 millimeters.

1. Because of their size and the "look-down" viewing systems, twin-lens reflexes are not good for quick action candid shooting. An SLR is best in these situations.
2. The look-down viewing system is better for carefully composed photographs in a studio or home, for example when time is not of the essence.
3. For my money, the Canon AE-1 originally designed in 1971 remains one of the best and most flexible workhorse cameras that an amateur photographer could want.
4. I still cannot understand why any amateur photographer would want anything besides a good, reliable, single-lens reflex camera usually referred to as an SLR.

EXERCISE 5

1. Because of their size and the "look-down" viewing systems, twin-lens reflexes are not good for quick action candid shooting. (An SLR is best in these situations.)
2. The look-down viewing system is better for carefully composed photographs (in a studio or home, for example) when time is not of the essence.
3. For my money, the Canon AE-1 (originally designed in 1971) remains one of the best and most flexible workhorse cameras that an amateur photographer could want.
4. I still cannot understand why any amateur photographer would want anything besides a good, reliable, single-lens reflex camera (usually referred to as an SLR).

LOOKING AHEAD

Both this section and the next section on ellipses will come in handy when students work on research papers. You may want to refer them to the extensive discussion about using quotations in Chapter 34 (Using Sources).

BRACKETS

29d Using brackets for editorial clarification

Use brackets [ ] to clarify or insert comments into quoted material. Throughout this section the following passage will be altered to demonstrate the various uses of brackets. For an extended discussion of using quotations in a research paper, see 34f. Specifically, see 34f-3 for more on using brackets.

> Elephant sounds include barks, snorts, trumpets, roars, growls, and rumbles. The rumbles are the key to our story, for although elephants can hear them well, human beings cannot. Many are below our range of hearing, in what is known as infrasound.
>
> The universe is full of infrasound: It is generated by earthquakes, wind, thunder, volcanoes, and ocean storms—massive movements of earth, air, fire, and water. But very low frequency sound has not been thought to play much of a role in animals' lives. Intense infrasonic calls have been recorded from finback whales, but whether the calls are used in communication is not known.
>
> Why would elephants use infrasound? It turns out that sound at the lowest frequency of elephant rumbles (14 to 35 hertz) has remarkable properties—it is little affected by passage through forests and grasslands. Does infrasound, then, let elephants communicate over long distances?

1 Use brackets to insert your own words into quoted material.

Recall that quotation marks denote an *exact* reproduction of someone else's writing or speech. When you alter the wording of a quotation either

TEACHING IDEAS

Some students, especially those with a rudimentary knowledge of typewriter or word processor keyboards, have trouble distinguishing between parentheses and brackets when inserting material into quotations. You may want to help them remember the function of brackets by describing it this way: while parentheses can serve many functions, within quotations brackets serve one—they signal the reader that the material within is not a part of the original quotation.

by adding or deleting words, you must indicate as much to your reader with appropriate use of punctuation.

Brackets to clarify a reference

When quoting a sentence with a pronoun that refers to a word in another, nonquoted sentence, use brackets to insert a clarifying reference into the quotation. Delete the pronoun and add bracketed information; or, if wording permits (as in this example), simply add the bracketed reference.

> According to Katherine Payne, "Many [elephant rumbles] are below our range of hearing, in what is known as infrasound."

Brackets to weave quoted language into your sentences

The stylistic goal of quoting material in your papers is to make the fit between quoted language and your language seamless. To do this, you will sometimes need to alter a quotation if its structure, point of view, pronoun choices, or verb forms differ from those of the sentence into which you are incorporating the quotation. Show any changes to quoted text in brackets.

> The human ear can discern a wide band of sounds, but there are animals we can't hear without special equipment. Elephants emit inaudible (that is, to humans), very low-frequency rumbles called infrasound. At frequencies of 14 to 35 hertz, elephant rumbles have "remarkable properties—[they are] little affected by passage through forests and grasslands" (Payne 67).

The bracketed verb and pronoun have been changed from their original singular form to plural in order to agree in number with the plural *elephant rumbles.* The original subject of the quoted sentence was singular (*sound*). Quoting without brackets would have resulted in an awkward construction: *Elephant rumbles have "remarkable properties—it is. . . ."*

Brackets to show your awareness of an error in the quoted passage

When you quote a sentence that contains an obvious error, you are still obliged to reproduce exactly the wording of the original source. To show your awareness of the error and to show readers that the error is the quoted author's, not yours, place the bracketed word *sic* (Latin, meaning "thus") after the error.

> "Intense infrasonic calls have been recorded from finback whales, but weather [sic] the calls are used in communication is not known."

Brackets to note emphasis

You may wish to underline or italicize quoted words. To show readers that the emphasis is yours and not the quoted author's, add the bracketed expression *emphasis added, italics added,* or *italics mine.*

"The universe is *full* of infrasound: It is generated by earthquakes, wind, thunder, volcanoes, and ocean storms—massive movements of earth, air, fire, and water [italics mine]."

2 Use brackets to distinguish parentheses inserted within parentheses.

Katherine Payne reports that "sound at the lowest frequency of elephant rumbles (14 to 35 hertz [cycles per second]) has remarkable properties—it is little affected by passage through forests and grasslands."

ELLIPSES

29e Using an ellipsis to indicate a break in continuity

Just as you will need to add words in order to incorporate quotations into your sentences, so too you will need to delete words. An **ellipsis,** noted as three spaced periods (. . .), shows that you have deleted either words or entire sentences from a passage you are quoting. Throughout this section the following passage will be altered to demonstrate the various uses of ellipses. For an extended discussion of using quotations in a research paper, see 34f. Specifically, see 34f-3 for more on using ellipses.

> First, for Americans, the human cost of the Civil War was by far the most devastating in our history. The 620,000 Union and Confederate soldiers who lost their lives almost equaled the 680,000 American soldiers who died in all the other wars this country has fought combined. When we add the unknown but probably substantial number of civilian deaths—from disease, malnutrition, exposure, or injury—among the hundreds of thousands of refugees in the Confederacy, the toll of the Civil War may exceed war deaths in all the rest of American history.
>
> The ghastly toll gives the Civil War a kind of horrifying but hypnotic fascination. As Thomas Hardy once put it, "War makes rattling good history; but Peace is poor reading." The sound of drum and trumpet, the call to arms, the clashing of armies have stirred the blood of nations throughout history. As the horrors and the seamy side of a war recede into the misty past, the romance and honor and glory forge into the foreground.

1 Know when *not* to use an ellipsis.

Do *not* use an ellipsis to note words omitted from the beginning of a sentence. In the following example, three words are deleted.

FAULTY James McPherson observes that " . . . the human cost of the Civil War was by far the most devastating in our history."

TEACHING IDEAS

Although brackets within parentheses are acceptable, students should be warned that excessive layering of parenthetical material can be confusing to readers. Most of us have seen such layering carried to an absurd degree on occasion—with parentheses within brackets within parentheses—and can attest to the frustrations suffered by readers subjected to such a practice. Although few students will encounter the opportunity to layer parenthetical elements, it's still probably wise to warn them of their obligations to the reader.

GROUP ACTIVITY

In this activity, students will gain practice in using ellipses effectively and in altering quotations without distorting their meaning. Ask groups to use ellipses to eliminate material from the middle and the end of several sentences in the following passage. The altered passages can then be passed on to other groups for evaluation and comparison.

> Before industrialization, men frequently took responsibility for training boys as young as six years of age. If a boy did not work with his father, he was apprenticed to another man to learn a trade. Accordingly, most child-rearing manuals in colonial America were written for mothers *and* fathers. Because fathers were nearby, working in a family farm or shop, they played a large role in the rearing of their children, particularly their sons. After industrialization, when men went away to a job, their sons could not follow, and child-rearing advice more often was directed to women only. Boys were still expected to be men, of course, but they spent the first decade of their lives in a world in which they rarely saw grown men at work. (Mark Gerzon)

Revised James McPherson observes that "the human cost of the Civil War was by far the most devastating in our history."

Do *not* use an ellipsis if the passage you quote ends with a period and ends your sentence as well.

Faulty James McPherson believes that "the toll of the Civil War may exceed war deaths in all the rest of American history. . . ."

Revised James McPherson believes that "the toll of the Civil War may exceed war deaths in all the rest of American history."

2 Use an ellipsis to indicate words deleted from the middle of a sentence.

If you have deleted words mid-sentence from an original passage, indicate the deletion with an ellipsis. If the words omitted directly follow an internal mark of punctuation (comma, dash, colon, semicolon), retain that mark and then add the ellipsis.

> "[T]he human cost of the Civil War was . . . the most devastating in our history," writes James McPherson.
>
> "The sound of drum and trumpet, . . . [has] stirred the blood of nations throughout history."

3 Use an ellipsis to indicate words deleted from the end of a sentence.

You may delete the end of a sentence from a quoted passage while your own sentence continues. If so, retain any internal mark of punctuation (comma, dash, colon, semicolon) that directly follows the last quoted word. Then add the ellipsis.

> Though the "6,500 men killed and mortally wounded in one day near Sharpsburg were nearly double the number of Americans killed and mortally wounded in combat in all the rest of the country's nineteenth-century wars combined— . . ." (McPherson 42), many in the twentieth century continue to view the Civil War as a romance.

You may want to end your sentence with a quotation that does not end a sentence in the original. If so, whatever mark of punctuation (if any) follows the last quoted word in the original should be deleted. Then add a period and an ellipsis, following one of two conventions. If you *do not* conclude your sentence with a citation, place the sentence period after the final letter of the quotation; place the ellipsis; and conclude with the end quotation mark.

> Official mortality figures for the Civil War do not include the "probably substantial number of civilian deaths—from disease, malnutrition, exposure, or injury. . . ."

If you *do* conclude your sentence with a citation, skip one space after the final letter of the quotation; place the ellipsis and follow with an end quotation mark; skip one space and place the citation; and then place the sentence period.

> Official mortality figures for the Civil War do not include the "probably substantial number of civilian deaths—from disease, malnutrition, exposure, or injury . . ." (McPherson 42).

4 Use an ellipsis to show a pause or interruption.

In dialogue

> "No," I said. I wanted to leave. "I . . . I need to get some air."

In prose

> When I left the seminary, I walked long and thought hard about what a former student of divinity might do. . . . My shoes wore out, my brain wore thin. I was stumped and not a little nervous about the course my life would take.

THE SLASH

29f Using the slash

1 Use slashes to separate the lines of poetry run in with the text of a sentence.

Retain all punctuation when quoting poetry. Leave a space before and after the slash when indicating line breaks.

> The "hermit" of Robert Bly's poem of the same name "is a man whose body is perfectly whole. / He stands, the storm behind him, / And the grass blades are leaping in the wind. / Darkness is gathered in folds / About his feet. / He is no one."

2 Use slashes to show choice.

Use slashes, occasionally, to show alternatives, as with the expressions *and/or* and *either/or.* With this use, do not leave spaces before or after the slash.

> *Either/Or* is the title of a philosophical work by Kierkegaard.
>
> As a prank, friends entered the Joneses as a husband/wife alternate entry in the local demolition derby.

If your meaning is not compromised, avoid using the slash; instead, write out alternatives in your sentence.

LOOKING BACK

You may want to remind students at this point that lengthy passages from poetry are normally set off from the text rather than incorporated into it with slashes. See 28b-1.

Send a telegram and/or call to let us know you're well.

The sense, here, is that there are three options: send a telegram, call, *or* send a telegram *and* call. If two options are intended, then the sentence should be rewritten one of two ways.

Send a telegram and call to let us know you're well.

Send a telegram or call to let us know you're well.

3 Use a slash in writing fractions or formulas to note division.

The February 1988 index of job opportunities (as measured by the number of help wanted advertisements) would be as follows:

(47,230/38,510) × 100 = 122.6

1/2 5/8 20 1/4

EXERCISE 6

Construct sentences, as directed, in which you quote from the following passage by Sigmund Freud.

> (1) As to the origin of the sense of guilt, the analyst has different views from other psychologists; but even he does not find it easy to give an account of it. (2) To begin with, if we ask how a person comes to have a sense of guilt, we arrive at an answer which cannot be disputed: a person feels guilty (devout people would say "sinful") when he has done something which he knows to be "bad." (3) But then we notice how little this answer tells us. (4) Perhaps, after some hesitation, we shall add that even when a person has not actually *done* the bad thing but has only recognized in himself an *intention* to do it, he may regard himself as guilty; and the question then arises of why the intention is regarded as equal to the deed. (5) Both cases, however, presupose that one had already recognized that what is bad is reprehensible, is something that must not be carried out. (6) How is this judgement arrived at?

Example: Quote sentence 1, but delete the phrase "As to the origin of the sense of guilt. . . ."

According to Sigmund Freud, "the analyst has different views from other psychologists; but even he does not find it easy to give an account of it."

1. Quote sentence 2, beginning with "a person feels. . . ." Delete the parenthetical note.
2. Quote sentence 4 but delete the end of the sentence, beginning with "and the question. . . ."
3. Quote sentence 1 and use a bracketed reference to clarify the second use of the pronoun *it*.
4. Quote sentence 5 and show your awareness of the spelling error.

EXERCISE 6

1. Freud believes that "a person feels guilty. . . when he has done something which he knows to be 'bad.' "
2. "Perhaps, after some hesitation, we shall add that even when a person has not actually *done* the bad thing but has only recognized in himself an *intention* to do it, he may regard himself as guilty. . . ."
3. "As to the origin of the sense of guilt, the analyst has different views from other psychologists; but even he does not find it easy to give an account of [the origin of the sense of guilt]."
4. "Both cases, however, presupose [sic] that one had already recognized that what is bad is reprehensible, is something that must not be carried out."

PART VIII
USING MECHANICS

CHAPTER 30

Capitals and Italics

Capitals and italics are primarily graphic devices that give readers cues on how to read: where to look for the beginning of a new thought, which words in a sentence are emphasized, which words form titles or proper names, and so on. Capitals and italics are also very useful for special designations that can only be shown in writing.

CAPITALS

Before the late nineteenth century, printers manually composed words by placing molded letters in type holders, taking letters from individual compartments, or type cases, set on a nearby wall. Letters used most often (vowels, for instance) were kept on the wall's lower cases, within easy reach. Letters used less often (capital letters, for instance) were kept in a slightly less convenient location in upper cases. In spite of innovations that have made manual typesetting obsolete, we still retain the printer's original designations, upper and lower case, when referring to the appearance of type on a page. Readers depend on capital (uppercase) letters, in contrast to lowercase letters, as cues to help recognize when sentences begin and when a noun refers to a particular person, place, or thing.

30a Capitalize the first letter of the first word in every sentence.

The most basic use of capitals is to signal the start of sentences.

When a box of mixed-grain-and-nut cereal is shaken, large particles always rise to the top—for the same reason that, over time, stones will rise to the top of a garden lot or field.

1 Reproduce capitalization in a quoted passage.

Capitalize the first word of quoted material when you introduce a quotation with a brief explanatory phrase.

KEY FEATURES

This chapter covers thoroughly the numerous uses of capitals and italics. Students will need to understand many of these uses as they write papers for various classes; the chapter can answer virtually any question they may have. Coverage of capitals includes everything from capitalizing the first word of a sentence to capitals in abbreviations, with clear examples of each specific use. The same extensive treatment is accorded italics, with particular attention to the restraint that writers must exercise in using italics for emphasis. The exercises provide students with ample practice in both areas.

TEACHING IDEAS

Although this chapter will probably be used for reference rather than for classwork, you may want to encourage students to read through it once. Students may not even be aware of some uses for capitals. You can also call attention to the many options in capitalization, encouraging students to be consistent once they've chosen an option.

ESL CUE

Capitalization may be an alien concept to students whose script is not based on the English alphabet (Arabic, Chinese, Japanese, Korean, and so forth). They simply may not see the differences in size as meaningful and will tend to capitalize in odd places and rarely where they should. Greek capitalizes what are called "main nouns" and hence capitalization

(continued)

depends on a judgment about importance. Spanish and Italian use lowercase forms far more than does English.

REFERENCES

The following style sheets provide advice on using capitalization and italics:

The Chicago Manual of Style. 14th ed. Chicago: U of Chicago P, 1993.

Gibaldi, Joseph. *MLA Handbook for Writers of Research Papers.* 4th ed. New York: MLA, 1995.

> According to archaeologist Douglas Wilson, "Most of what archaeologists have to work with is ancient trash."

> "Most of what archaeologists have to work with is ancient trash," according to archaeologist Douglas Wilson.

Do not capitalize the first word of a quotation run into the structure of your sentence. When you change capitalization in a quoted text, indicate the change with brackets.

> Wilson says that archaeologists who dig through modern trash must come "[e]quipped with rubber gloves, masks, and booster shots."

2 Capitalize the first word in a parenthetical statement if the remark is a sentence.

> Once a sleepy suburban town whose workers commuted to Chicago every morning, Naperville, Illinois has acquired its own employment base. (It has become an "urban village," a "technoburb.")

If the parenthetical remark forms a sentence but is placed inside another sentence (this is a relatively rare occurrence), *do not* capitalize the first word after the parenthesis and *do not* use a period. However, do use a question mark or exclamation point if the parenthetical remark requires it.

> Naperville grew robustly (the population nearly quadrupled!), as Amoco and companies large and small erected what Governor James R. Thompson would later term "The Illinois Research and Development Corridor."

3 In a series of complete statements or questions, capitalize the first word of each item.

When a series is formed by phrases or incomplete questions, capitalization of the first word is optional.

Capitals — What causes air sickness? Is it inner-ear disturbance? Is it brain waves?

Optional — Air Force scientists want to know what causes motion sickness. Is it inner-ear disturbance? brain wave anomalies? disorienting visual signals?

Optional — Air Force scientists want to know what causes motion sickness. Is it inner-ear disturbance? Brain wave anomalies? Disorienting visual signals?

In a series of phrases run in with a sentence, the phrases are *not* capitalized.

> The program for low-input sustainable agriculture that has emerged from a recent federal study has three objectives: (1) to reduce reliance on fertilizer, pesticide, and other purchased resources to farms; (2) to increase farm profits and agricultural productivity; and (3) to conserve energy and natural resources.

In a displayed series, capitalization of the first word is optional.

OPTIONAL The program for low-input sustainable agriculture that has emerged from a recent federal study has three objectives:

1. To reduce reliance on fertilizer, pesticide, and other purchased resources to farms.
2. To increase farm profits and agricultural productivity.
3. To conserve energy and natural resources.

The word *to* could also be in lowercase letters in each number of the displayed series.

4 Capitalizing the first word of a sentence following a colon is optional.

OPTIONAL The program has two aims: The first is to conserve energy.
OPTIONAL The program has two aims: the first is to conserve energy.

30b Capitalize words of significance in a title.

Capitalize all words of significance in the titles of books, journals, magazines, articles, and art works. *Do not* capitalize articles (*a, an, the*) or conjunctions and prepositions that have four or fewer letters, except at the title's beginning. *Do* capitalize the first and last words of the title (even if they are articles, conjunctions, or prepositions), along with any word following a colon or semicolon.

Pride and Prejudice *Great Expectations*
The Sound and the Fury *The Joy Luck Club*
Much Ado About Nothing *West with the Night*
"The Phoenicians: Rich and Glorious Traders of the Levant"

Do not capitalize the word *the* if it is not part of a title or proper name.

the Eiffel Tower *The Economist*
the Mediterranean Sea *The Brothers Karamazov*

The first word of a hyphenated word in a title is capitalized. The second word is also capitalized, unless it is very short.

"The Selling of an Ex-President" *Engine Tune-ups Made Simple*
"Belly-down in a Cave: A Spelunker's Weekend"

30c Capitalize the first word in every line of poetry.

Lines of poetry are conventionally marked by initial capitals. The interjection *O*, restricted for the most part to poetry, is always capitalized. The word *oh* is capitalized only when it begins a sentence.

Break, break, break,
  On thy cold gray stones, O Sea!

TEACHING IDEAS

Whenever students are presented with an option, as in the case of capitalizing the first word of a sentence following a colon, they should be reminded that whatever option they choose, they must remain consistent throughout their text.

ADDITIONAL EXERCISE A

Look through an anthology of poetry or a general literature anthology for examples of poetry that defies conventional use of capitals. You may have to confine your search to contemporary poetry, since it is far more likely to deviate from convention. Why do you think certain poets deliberately break from the traditional rules of capitalization for poetry?

And I would that my tongue could utter
  The thoughts that arise in me.

—TENNYSON, from *"Break, Break, Break"*

NOTE: Some poets begin lines with lowercase letters—e. e. cummings, for instance. Others write verse that deliberately shifts some standard conventions. When quoting such poets, retain the capitalization of the original.

30d Capitalize proper nouns—people, places, objects; proper adjectives; and ranks of distinction.

Capitalizing the first letter of a noun helps to establish its identity. In general, capitalize any noun that refers to a *particular* person, place, object, or being that has been given an individual, or proper, name.

1 Capitalize names of people or groups of people.

Names of people are capitalized, as are titles showing family relationships *if* the title is part of the person's name.

Tom Hanks Martha Washington
Aunt Millie Uncle Ralph

Names of family relations—brother, aunt, grandmother—are not capitalized if not used as part of a particular person's proper name.

He phoned his grandmother, Bess Truman.
I saw my favorite aunt, Janet, on a trip to Chicago.

Names of political groups and of formal organizations are capitalized.

Democrats the Left
Republicans the Right
Communists Socialists

TEACHING IDEAS

Even the briefest perusal of contemporary popular writing and journalism indicates that there is no consensus regarding capitalization of *black* and *white.* Students should be advised to consider the writing context when deciding for themselves which option to choose. If, for example, a student is writing a paper on Brent Staples, then he or she should probably use lowercase in keeping with the author's choice. On the other hand, if the audience for a paper clearly prefers uppercase, then perhaps the writer should defer to the reader.

2 Capitalize religions, religious titles and names, and nationalities.

Religions, their followers, and their sacred beings and sacred documents are capitalized.

Judaism Jew the Bible
Catholicism Catholic the New Testament
Islam Muslim the Koran
God Allah Buddha

Nations and nationalities are capitalized.

America Americans Native Americans
Liberia Liberians Hispanic Americans
Czechoslovakia Czechs

NOTE: The terms *black* and *white,* when designating race, are usually written in lowercase, though some writers prefer to capitalize them (by analogy with other formal racial designations such as Mongolian and Polynesian).

3 Capitalize places, regions designated by points on the compass, and languages.

Places and addresses

Cascades	Asia
Idaho	England
Joe's Diner	Philadelphia
Main Street	Elm Boulevard

NOTE: Capitalize common nouns such as *main* or *center* when they are part of an address.

Names of regions and compass points designating the names of regions

Appalachia	the frozen Northwest
the Great Lakes	the Sun Belt
the sunny South	Mid-Atlantic

NOTE: A compass point is capitalized only when it functions as a noun and serves as the name of a particular area of the country. As a direction, a compass point is not capitalized.

NO CAPITALS I'll be driving northeast for the first part of the trip. [The word *northeast* in this sentence is a modifier and indicates a direction, not a region.]

We made a course to the northeast, but soon turned to the north. [These are compass points, not the names of regions.]

CAPITALS I'll be vacationing in the Northeast this year. [The word *Northeast* is the name of an area of the country.]

Names of languages

English	Arabic	Swahili
Spanish	Greek	Italian

4 Capitalize adjectives formed from proper nouns, and titles of distinction that are part of proper names.

Proper adjectives formed from proper nouns

English tea	French perfume
Cartesian coordinates	Balinese dancer

NOTE: Both *Oriental* and *oriental* are considered correct, though the capitalized form is more common. Both *Biblical* and *biblical* are considered correct.

TEACHING IDEAS

For a thorough discussion of capitalization, see Tom McArthur, *The Oxford Companion to the English Language* (Oxford: Oxford UP, 1992). McArthur calls attention to such trends as "internal" capitalization (WordPerfect, VisiCalc) and what he calls "letter-play" (VisiOn, CoR-TeXT) in the computer and trade worlds.

ESL CUE

Romance languages do not capitalize names of languages, religions, nationalities, or days of the week or month. Students from these language groups will regularly follow the capitalization rules of their language rather than those of English.

TEACHING IDEAS

Occasionally students will need to be reminded that "Day" is capitalized only when it is part of the holiday's name. While "I took my mother to dinner on Mother's Day" is correct, "I had to work on Easter Day" is not.

Titles of distinction

Capitalize a title of distinction when no words separate it from a proper noun. Do not capitalize most title designations if they are followed by the preposition *of.*

Governor Weld	William Weld, governor of Massachusetts
Mayor Edward G. Rendell	Edward G. Rendell, mayor of Philadelphia

Note: When titles of the highest distinction are proper names for a specific office—President, Prime Minister—they often remain capitalized, even if followed by a preposition and even if not paired with a specific name.

Jacques Chirac, President of France
Alisa Billings, Vice-President of Citizens Bank

The President arrived at 2 o'clock.
The Secretary of State flew to Geneva.

The Prime Minister's role is to lead both party and government.
A prime minister may do as she pleases. [A specific office is not being named.]

Capitalize titles and abbreviations of titles when they follow a comma—as in an address or closing to a letter.

Martha Brand, Ph.D.	Fred Barnes, Sr.
Sally Roth, M.D.	David Burns, Executive Vice-President

5 Capitalize the names of days, months, holidays, and historical events or periods.

Monday	New Year's Day
Saturday	Columbus Day
December	Revolutionary War
January	Paleozoic Era
Christmas	Middle Ages

Note: When written out, centuries and decades are not capitalized.

the nineteenth century   the fifties   the twenty-third century

Seasons are capitalized only when they are personified.

spring semester	Spring's gentle breath [The season is personified.]

6 Capitalize particular objects and name-brand products.

Mount Washington	USS *Hornet*
Jefferson Memorial	Sam Rayburn Building
Aswan Dam	
Bic pen	Ford Taurus
Whopper	Apple computer
Sony television	

Use capitals with certain abbreviations, prefixes, or compound nouns.

Capitalize abbreviations only when the words abbreviated are themselves capitalized.

Mister James Wolf	Mr. James Wolf
Apartment 6	Apt. 6
1234 Rockwood Avenue	1234 Rockwood Ave.
Silver Spring, Maryland	Silver Spring, Md.

Capitalize acronyms and abbreviations of companies, agencies, and treaties.

FAA (Federal Aviation Administration)
ABM Treaty (Anti-Ballistic Missile Treaty)
DEC (Digital Equipment Corporation)

The prefixes *ex, un,* and *post* are capitalized only when they begin a sentence or are part of a proper name or title.

a post-Vietnam event	the Post-Vietnam Syndrome
an un-American attitude	the Un-American Activities Committee

Capitalize a number or the first word in a compound number that is part of a name or title.

Third Avenue
the Seventy-second Preakness

EXERCISE 1

Correct the capitalization in these sentences. As needed, change lowercase letters to uppercase and change uppercase to lowercase.

New orleans, the louisiana city associated with the pre-lenten celebration of mardi gras, has also been the site of an even more unusual quasi-Religious festival. This one takes place on november 1, which in the church's calendar is the feast of all saints, otherwise known as all saints' day. The custom of this day in new orleans is the Washing of the Tombs. Since the city was built on the Bayou, the land is quite swampy. Thus most of the City's dead have, over the years, been buried in above-ground vaults. On all saints' day these vaults are cleaned, whitewashed, and decorated with flowers and wreaths. The favored flower is the Chrysanthemum. Despite all of the work going on, the atmosphere has been described as quite festive. Vendors do quite well peddling food, balloons, and even miniature skeletons.

ITALICS

A word set in italics calls attention to itself. On the typewritten (or handwritten) page, words that you would italicize are underlined. Italics have three principal uses: they give emphasis; they mark the plural forms of letters and numbers; and they denote titles of long works and certain names.

EXERCISE 1

New **O**rleans, the **L**ouisiana city associated with the pre-**L**enten celebration of **M**ardi **G**ras, has also been the site of an even more unusual quasi-**r**eligious festival. This one takes place on **N**ovember 1, which in the **C**hurch's calendar is the **F**east of **A**ll **S**aints, otherwise known as **A**ll **S**aints' **D**ay. The custom of this day in **N**ew **O**rleans is the **w**ashing of the **t**ombs. Since the city was built on the **b**ayou, the land is quite swampy. Thus most of the **c**ity's dead have, over the years, been buried in above-ground vaults. On **A**ll **S**aints' **D**ay these vaults are cleaned, whitewashed, and decorated with flowers and wreaths. The favored flower is the **c**hrysanthemum. Despite all of the work going on, the atmosphere has been described as quite festive. Vendors do quite well peddling food, balloons, and even miniature skeletons.

GROUP ACTIVITY

Both exercises in this chapter lend themselves to group activity. Have students respond to exercises individually, and then compare their responses with those of other group members. When the inevitable disagreement occurs, students will have to consult the handbook. Once they become accustomed to using the chapter, they'll likely continue to refer to it as they edit their papers.

TEACHING IDEAS

It would be wise to call attention to underlining as the typewritten equivalent of italics. You may also want to remind students that writing a word in italics is *not* equivalent to putting it in quotation marks.

TEACHING IDEAS

You may want to call attention to the word *need* in the heading for 30e. As the note states, overreliance on typographical means of emphasis suggests that the writer's command of the language is weak.

30e Underline or italicize words if they need a specific emphasis.

Words that you underline or set in italics are given particular emphasis. As a stylistic tool, italicizing will work well only if you do not overuse it.

> Cultural relativity does *not* mean that a behavior appropriate in one place is appropriate everywhere.

Italicized words can be useful to create emphasis and change meaning in sentences, especially when writing attempts to duplicate the emphasis of speech.

> "*You're* going to the movies with him?" [Why you and not Susan?]
> "You're going to the movies with *him*?" [Why would you go with him?]
> "You're going to the *movies* with him?" [Why aren't you going to the theater?]

NOTE: The best way to create emphasis in your writing is not to simulate emotion with punctuation or with typeface, but to make your point with words. Italics should be saved for rare occasions and for a specific purpose. Overuse devalues the emphasis of italics and makes your writing appear overexcited and unconvincing.

OVERUSED The Phoenicians were *masters* of the sea and with the cities they founded, like Tyre and Carthage, they became commercial *giants.* But Rome *envied* the Phoenician wealth. The angry prophet Isaiah called the Phoenicians *sinners,* and the heroic poet Homer thought they were *sly.* Ultimately, these many hatreds *crushed* the Phoenicians.

REWORDED During the hundreds of years that they dominated the seas, the Phoenicians made enemies, the sort of enemies that are inevitable when you are commercially successful. Homer's heroic poems described the Phoenicians as slippery and as swindlers. Isaiah called Tyre a whore. The Romans depicted the Carthaginians as treacherous. In the end, the Phoenicians and Carthaginians lost to those enemies and were completely crushed, militarily and culturally.

30f Underline or italicize words, letters, and numbers to be defined or identified.

1 Use italics for words to be defined.

Words to be defined in a sentence are usually underlined or set in italics. Occasionally, such a word is set in quotation marks.

OPTION The *operating system* runs a computer as a sort of master organizer that can accept commands whenever no specific program is running.

Option The remarkable permanence of color in certain statues at the Acropolis is due, partly, to the technique of "encaustic," in which pigment is mixed with wax and applied to the surface while hot.

2 Use italics for expressions recognized as foreign.

Underline or italicize foreign expressions that have not yet been assimilated into English but whose meanings are generally understood. The following is a brief sampling of such words.

amore [Italian]
enfant terrible [French]
e pluribus unum [Latin]
goyim [Hebrew]
pâté [French]
Doppelgänger [German]
esprit de corps [French]
hombre [Spanish]
post hoc [Latin]

No underlines or italics are used with foreign expressions that have been assimilated into English. The following is a brief sampling of such words.

alter ego [Latin]
ex post facto [Latin]
hoi polloi [Greek]
guru [Sanskrit]
kibitz [Yiddish]
maestro [Italian]
blitz [German]
fait accompli [French]
fellah [Arabic]
kayak [Eskimo]
machete [Spanish]
memorabilia [Latin]

3 Use italics to designate words, numerals, or letters referred to as such.

Underline or italicize words when you are calling attention to them as words.

Many writers have trouble differentiating the uses of *lie* and *lay*.

The word *the* is not capitalized in a title, unless it is the first word of the title or follows a colon or semicolon.

Italicize letters and most numerals when they are referred to as letters or numerals.

She crosses the *t* in *top*.

Shall I write a *1* or a *2*?

The combination of italics (or underlining) and an apostrophe with the letter *s* is used to make numbers and letters plural.

Cross your *t*'s and dot your *i*'s.

We saw *1*'s on the scoreboard each inning—a good sign.

TEACHING IDEAS

ACROSS THE CURRICULUM Many students will have difficulty determining whether or not a foreign word or phrase is indeed common in English. In particular, as they take courses in different disciplines, they'll encounter foreign terms that are common within the discipline but have not been assimilated into lay English. They should be advised to consult their instructors with regard to how to treat such terms.

LOOKING BACK

Students often become confused over which titles to underline and which to place in quotation marks. Refer students to 28b-3 for the appropriate presentation of short works.

30g Use underlining or italics for titles of book-length works separately published or broadcast, as well as for individually named transport craft.

1 Use italics for books, long poems, and plays.

Love in the Ruins [novel]
A Discovery of the Sea [book]
Antigone [play]
The Rime of the Ancient Mariner [long poem]
The Joy Luck Club [novel]
Twelfth Night [play]
The Odyssey [long poem]

The titles of sacred documents (and their parts) as well as legal or public documents are frequently capitalized (see 30d) but are not set in italics.

the Bible
the Magna Carta
the Koran
the New Testament
the Bill of Rights
Book of Exodus

2 Use italics for newspapers, magazines, and periodicals.

the *Boston Globe*
Brookline *Citizen*
the *Georgia Review*
the *New York Times*
Time
Archaeology

With newspapers, do not capitalize, underline, or set in italics the word *the,* even if it is part of the newspaper's title. Italicize or underline the name of a city or town only if it is part of the newspaper's title. Titles of particular selections in a newspaper, magazine, or journal are set in quotation marks.

3 Use italics for works of visual art, long musical works, movies, and broadcast shows.

Rodin's *The Thinker*
Van Gogh's *The Starry Night*
Mozart's *The Magic Flute*
The Last Judgment
the *Burghers of Calais*
the *German Requiem*

NOTE: Underline or set in italics the article *the* only when it is part of a title.

Movies and television or radio shows are italicized.

As the World Turns
Late Show with David Letterman
Apollo 13
A Prairie Home Companion
All Things Considered
Dead Man Walking

4 Use italics for individually named transport craft: Ships, trains, aircraft, and spacecraft.

USS *Hornet* (a ship)	*Atlantis* (a spacecraft)
HMS *Bounty* (a ship)	the *Montrealer* (a train)
Apollo X (a spacecraft)	*Spirit of St. Louis* (an airplane)

Do not underline or italicize USS or HMS in a ship's name.

EXERCISE 2

Correct the use of italics in these sentences. Circle words that should not be italicized. Underline words that should be italicized. Place a check beside any sentence in which italics are used correctly.

Example: The most important tool of the navigator is an *accurate, current chart*, without which it is virtually impossible to navigate successfully.

1. Navigation is the art of staying *out* of trouble.
2. You can keep your charts as current as possible by subscribing to Local Notices to Mariners, a weekly publication of the U.S. Coast Guard.
3. The key to successful navigation is to navigate *continuously,* that is, *always* be able to determine the position of your boat on the chart.
4. *Landmarks* (smokestacks, water towers, buildings, piers, *etc.*) and *aids to navigation* (beacons, lighthouses, buoys) help relate what you see from your boat to items found on the chart.
5. Aids to navigation are installed and maintained by the Coast Guard *specifically* to help you relate your surroundings to the appropriate symbols on the chart.
6. A *beacon* will be denoted on the chart by a triangle and the letters *Bn.*

EXERCISE 2

1. circle: *out*
2. underline: Local Notices to Mariners
3. circle: *continuously, always*
4. circle: *Landmarks, aids to navigation*
5. circle: *specifically*
6. Correct

CHAPTER 31

Abbreviations and Numbers

KEY FEATURES

Depending on the discipline for which students are writing, understanding abbreviations and numbers can be either marginally relevant or absolutely crucial. From the beginning, this chapter makes it clear that different standards apply in different disciplines, cautioning students to become aware of the requirements of any unfamiliar discipline. However, the chapter does cover an extensive array of possible uses, alerting students to cases in which options are available. Coverage of abbreviations includes such topics as titles, measurements, and acronyms; numbers topics include conventional use of figures, numbers beginning sentences, and consistency in using written numbers or figures. Examples are plentiful, and exercises provide valuable practice in using numbers and abbreviations.

REFERENCES

The following style sheets provide advice on using abbreviations and numbers:

The Chicago Manual of Style. 14th ed. Chicago: U of Chicago P, 1993.

GIBALDI, JOSEPH. *MLA Handbook for Writers of Research Papers.* 4th ed. New York: MLA, 1995.

The root word of *abbreviation* is the Latin *breviare,* from which comes the familiar *brief, briefing,* and *brevity.* We use an **abbreviation**—the shortened form of a word followed (for the most part) by a period—only in restricted circumstances, as discussed below. Writers working in an unfamiliar discipline should consult the standard manuals of reference, style, and documentation for guidance in using abbreviations and numbers in the field. Many such reference works are listed in Chapter 36, Documenting Research, with conventions shown in Chapters 37–39 on writing in each of the major discipline areas.

ABBREVIATIONS

31a Abbreviating titles of rank both before and after proper names

The following titles of address are usually abbreviated before a proper name.

Mr. Mrs. Ms. Dr.

Though not an abbreviation, *Ms.* is usually followed by a period.

Abbreviations for titles of rank or honor are usually reserved for the most formal references and addresses in connection with a person's full name and title. Mention of a person's title or rank in a less formal context does not call for an abbreviation. Typically, the abbreviations *Gen., Lt., Sen., Rep.,* and *Hon.* precede a full name—first and last.

FAULTY	Gen. Eisenhower	Sen. Kennedy
REVISED	General Eisenhower	Senator Kennedy
REVISED	Gen. Dwight D. Eisenhower	Sen. Ted Kennedy

The following abbreviated titles or designations of honor are placed *after* a formal address or listing of a person's full name.

B.A. M.A. M.S. Ph.D. C.P.A.
Jr. Sr. M.D. Esq.

Place a comma after the surname, then follow with the abbreviation. If more than one abbreviation is used, place a comma between abbreviations.

Lawrence Swift Jr., M.D.

Abbreviations of medical, professional, or academic titles are *not* combined with the abbreviations *Mr., Mrs.,* or *Ms.*

FAULTY	Ms. Joan Warren, M.D.	Ms. Mindy Lubber, Ed.D.
REVISED	Dr. Joan Warren *or* Joan Warren, M.D.	Mindy Lubber, Ed.D. *or* Dr. Mindy Lubber

Other than for direct reference to academic titles such as *Ph.D.* (Doctor of Philosophy), *M.A.* (Master of Arts), and *M.S.* (Master of Science), do not use freestanding abbreviated titles that have not been paired with a proper name in a sentence.

ACCEPTABLE Jane Thompson earned her Ph.D. in biochemistry. [A degree is referred to separately.]

FAULTY Marie Lew is an M.D. [The degree should either be referred to separately or attached to the person's title.]

REVISED Marie Lew is a physician.

REVISED Marie Lew was awarded an M.D. degree from Harvard.

FAULTY John Kraft is a C.P.A.

REVISED John Kraft is a certified public accountant.

REVISED John passed the C.P.A. examination yesterday.

31b Abbreviating specific dates and numbers

With certain historical or archaeological dates, abbreviations are often used to indicate whether the event occurred in the last two thousand years.

Ancient times (prior to two thousand years ago)

B.C. (before the birth of Christ)

B.C.E. (before the common era)

Both abbreviations follow the date.

Modern times (within the last two thousand years)

C.E. (of the common era)

A.D. (*Anno Domini,* "in the year of the Lord," an abbreviation that precedes the date)

Augustus, the first Roman Emperor, lived from 63 B.C. (*or* B.C.E.) to A.D. 14 (*or* C.E.).

When the context of a paragraph makes clear that the event occurred in the last two thousand years—suppose you are writing on the Industrial Revolution—it would be redundant, even insulting, to write "A.D. 1820."

TEACHING IDEAS

For an interesting account of the history and use of abbreviations, you may want to refer students to Tom McArthur's *Oxford Companion to the English Language* (Oxford: Oxford UP, 1992). McArthur traces the practice of abbreviation back to the ancient Egyptians.

Clock time, indicated as prior to noon or after, uses abbreviations in capitals or in lowercase.

5:44 P.M. (or p.m.)

5:44 A.M. (or a.m.)

When typeset, A.M./P.M. often appear in a smaller type size as capital letters: 5:44 P.M.

When numbers are referred to as specific items (such as numbers in arithmetic operations or as units of currency or measure), they are used with standard abbreviations.

No. 23 or no. 23	2 + 3 = 5
$23.01	99 bbl. [barrels]
54%	

Abbreviations for time, numbers, units, or money should be used only with reference to specific dates or amounts.

Numerical concepts must be fully written out as part of a sentence, not given shortened treatment with abbreviations, unless they are attached to specific years, times, currencies, units, or items.

FAULTY We'll see you in the A.M.

REVISED We'll see you in the morning.

FAULTY Let's wait until the nos. are in before we make a decision.

REVISED Let's wait until the numbers are in before we make a decision.

FAULTY This happened in the B.C. era.

REVISED This happened almost three thousand years ago.

FAULTY Please tell me the % of dropouts for the year.

REVISED Please tell me the percentage of dropouts for the year.

FOR DISCUSSION

Deciding which acronyms and uppercase abbreviations are common enough to use in writing can be difficult. You may want to ask your students to add their own examples to the list here. The class can then decide on an extended list of common acronyms and abbreviations. (You might start them off with examples such as UNICEF, FBI, and DAR.)

31c Using acronyms, uppercase abbreviations, and corporate abbreviations

An **acronym** is the uppercase, pronounceable abbreviation of a proper noun—a person, organization, government agency, or country. Periods are not used with acronyms. If there is any chance that a reader might not be familiar with an acronym or abbreviation, spell it out on first mention, showing the acronym in parentheses.

Medical researchers are struggling to understand the virus that causes Acquired Immune Deficiency Syndrome (AIDS).

The following are some familiar acronyms.

NATO North Atlantic Treaty Organization

MADD Mothers Against Drunk Driving

NASA National Aeronautics and Space Administration

NOW National Organization for Women

Helping Readers to Understand Acronyms

Unless an acronym or uppercase abbreviation is common knowledge, courtesy obligates you to write out the full word, term, or organizational name at its first mention. Then, in a parenthetical remark, you give the abbreviation. In subsequent references to the person, word, or organization, use the abbreviation—as is illustrated in the beginning of this article from the journal *Archaeology.*

> To the end of the Early Intermediate Period (EIP), the appearance of stunning, elaborately decorated ceramics . . . suggests that tribal leaders possessed and exchanged prestige items as a way of consolidating their claims to political power.

In lengthy documents where you will be using many uppercase abbreviations and acronyms, consider creating a glossary in addition to defining abbreviations the first time you use them. The glossary, which is placed at the end of the paper as an appendix, provides one convenient place to make identifications, sparing readers the trouble of flipping through pages and hunting for an abbreviation's first defined use.

Other uppercase abbreviations use the initial letters of familiar persons or groups to form well-known "call letter" designations conventionally used in writing.

JFK John Fitzgerald Kennedy

SEC Securities and Exchange Commission

ISBN International Standard Book Number

NAACP National Association for the Advancement of Colored People

MVP Most Valuable Player

VFW Veterans of Foreign Wars

USA (or U.S.A.) United States of America

Abbreviations used by companies and organizations vary according to the usage of the organization. When referring directly to a specific organization, use its own preferred abbreviations for words such as *Incorporated (Inc.), Limited (Ltd.), Private Corporation (P.C.),* and *Brothers (Bros.).* Some companies will abbreviate the name of a city or state or the words *Apartment (Apt.), Post Office (P.O.) Box, Avenue (Ave.), Street (St.),* and *Boulevard (Blvd.)* in their formal return addresses; others will not. In a sentence that does not refer directly to a specific corporation, do not abbreviate such terms, but spell out all the pronounceable words.

ADDITIONAL EXERCISE A

ACROSS THE CURRICULUM Examine the textbooks you use in all of your courses for evidence of the abbreviations listed in 31d. Make a list of the abbreviations you find, and compare your list to the ones in the book. Are all of the abbreviations you found covered here? If not, ask the appropriate instructor to explain the meaning of the abbreviation to you.

FAULTY I mailed it to a corp. out on the blvd.

REVISED I mailed it to a corporation on the boulevard.
I mailed it to The Impax Corp., Zero Wilshire Blvd.

31d Using abbreviations for parenthetical references

From Latin, the traditional language of international scholarship, we have inherited conventional expressions used in research to make brief references or explanations. These are conventionally used in footnotes, documentation, and sometimes in parenthetical comments. All of these Latin expressions should be replaced in a main sentence by their English equivalents.

e.g. (*exempli gratia*)	for example
et al. (*et alii*)	and others
i.e. (*id est*)	that is
N.B. (*nota bene*)	note well
viz. (*videlicet*)	namely
cf. (*confer*)	compare
c. or ca. (*circa*)	about
etc. (*et cetera*)	and such things; and so on

The extremely vague abbreviation *etc.* should be avoided unless a specific and obvious sequence is being indicated, as in *They proceeded by even numbers (2, 4, 6, 8, etc.).* Even here the phrase *and so on* is preferable. When used in parenthetical or bibliographical comments, these Latin abbreviations are not underlined or italicized since they are commonplace in English. Typically, these expressions introduce a parenthetical remark in an informal aside.

INFORMAL A growing portion of our National Income is composed of government transfer payments (e.g., welfare payments).

FORMAL A growing portion of our National Income is composed of government transfer payments (for example, welfare payments).

Bibliographical abbreviations are commonly used in documentation to provide short forms of reference citations, but they should not be used in sentences of a paragraph. The following are some of the most frequently used abbreviations.

p.	page	Jan.	January
pp.	pages	Feb.	February
ed./eds.	editor(s)	Mar.	March
f./ff.	the following (pages)	Apr.	April
n.d.	no date (for a publication lacking a date)	Aug.	August
		Sep./Sept.	September
ch./chs.	chapter(s)	Oct.	October
ms./mss.	manuscript(s)	Nov.	November
col./cols.	column(s)	Dec.	December
vol./vols.	volume(s)		

Each discipline has specific conventions for abbreviations in documentation. For example, the months May, June, and July are not abbreviated in MLA style; other conventions are discussed in Chapter 36.

Writing in the Disciplines

Conventions differ in the disciplines about when and how much writers should use abbreviations—and about which abbreviations are common knowledge and need not be defined. Across disciplines, abbreviations are avoided in titles. For specific abbreviations lying beyond common knowledge, writers follow the convention of defining the abbreviation on first use. As a demonstration, a sketch of conventions for abbreviating in some of the science disciplines is provided here. For detailed information about conventions in a specific discipline, see the style manuals recommended in 37f, 38e, and 39e, or consult your professor.

- In scientific writing, courtesy dictates that writers define words that are later abbreviated.

  Some 800 species of bats live in diverse habitats and vary greatly in behavior and physical characteristics. Their biosonar pulses also differ, even among species within the same genus. Nevertheless, these pulses can be classified into three types: constant frequency (CF), frequency modulated (FM), and combined (CF-FM).

- Units of measure are generally abbreviated when they are paired with specific numbers. When not thus paired, the units are written out.

  In the next stage, 14 g were added.
  Several grams of the material were sent away for testing.

- Abbreviations of measurements in scientific writing need not be defined on first use.
- Symbol abbreviations are standardized, and you will find lists of accepted abbreviations in the *CBE Style Manual* published by the Council of Biology Editors. Generally, the use of abbreviations in titles is not accepted in science writing. Limited abbreviations—without definition—are accepted in tables.

LOOKING AHEAD

Students can find a wealth of information on writing guidelines for specific disciplines in Chapters 37 (Writing and Reading in the Humanities), 38 (Writing and Reading in the Social Sciences), and 39 (Writing and Reading in the Sciences). You may want to encourage students to get to know the chapter most relevant to their major.

31e Revise to eliminate all but conventional abbreviations from sentences.

In sentences, no abbreviations are used for the names of days or months, units of measure, courses of instruction, geographical names, and page/chapter/volume references. These abbreviations are reserved for specific uses in charts and data presentations that require abbreviated treatment in each discipline.

FAULTY Come see me on the first Mon. in Aug.

REVISED Come see me on the first Monday in August.

Faulty He weighed 25 lbs.

Revised He weighed 25 pounds.

Exception: Abbreviations of standard, lengthy phrases denoting measurement are common in formal writing: miles per hour (mph or m.p.h.) and revolutions per minute (rpm or r.p.m.).

Faulty We enrolled in bio. and soc. next semester.

Revised We enrolled in biology and sociology next semester.

Faulty NYC is a haven for writers.

Revised New York City is a haven for writers.

Faulty The reference can be found in Vol. 6, sec. 5, p. 1. [These are used in bibliographies and documentation only.]

Revised The reference can be found in Volume 6, section 5, page 1.

EXERCISE 1

Correct the use of abbreviations in these sentences. When appropriate, write out abbreviations.

Example: You can create your own home pg. on the World Wide Web—just consult the appropriate chap. In a self-help manual.

You can create your own home page on the World Wide Web—just consult the appropriate chapter in a self-help manual.

1. The World Wide Web was developed mostly at the European Laboratory for Particle Physics, near Geneva, Switz.
2. The Web project was really a spin-off of Apple Comp. Corp.'s HyperCard program.
3. Netscape, which some users claim is the most popular Web browser, has versions for both Windows and Mac. users.
4. Even if you don't have access to a Web browser, you can type in an e-mail address that will do the job; for example, you can tap into the system at Univ. of Kansas.
5. Best of all, you don't have to be a pHd. To figure out how to do some exciting Web browsing.

GROUP ACTIVITY

Both exercises in this chapter lend themselves to group activity. Have students respond to exercises individually, and then compare their responses with those of other group members. When the inevitable disagreement occurs, students will have to consult the handbook. Once they become accustomed to using the chapter, they'll likely continue to refer to it as they edit their papers.

EXERCISE 1

1. The World Wide Web was developed mostly at the European Laboratory for Particle Physics, near Geneva, Switzerland.
2. The Web project was really a spin-off of Apple Computer Corporation's HyperCard program.
3. Netscape, which some users claim is the most popular Web browser, has versions for both Windows and Mac users.
4. Even if you don't have access to a Web browser, you can type in an e-mail address that will do the job; for example, you can tap into the system at University of Kansas.
5. Best of all, you don't have to be a Ph.D. to figure out how to do some exciting Web browsing.

NUMBERS

31f Write out numbers that begin sentences and numbers that can be expressed in one or two words.

One to ninety-nine

nineteen	seventy-six
twenty-six	ninety-nine

Fractions

five-eighths		three-fourths
two and three-quarters		seven-sixteenths

Large round numbers

twenty-one thousand		fifteen hundred

Decades and centuries

the sixties	or	the '60s
the twenty-first century	or	the 21st century

Numbers that begin sentences should be written out.

FAULTY 57 percent of those attending the meeting fell asleep.

REVISED Fifty-seven percent of those attending the meeting fell asleep.

REVISED Of those attending the meeting, 57 percent fell asleep.

When it is awkward to begin a sentence by writing out a long number, rearrange the sentence.

AWKWARD Forty-two thousand eight hundred forty-seven was the paid attendance at last night's game.

REVISED The paid attendance at last night's game was 42,847.

31g Use figures in sentences according to convention.

Numbers longer than two words

1,345 2,455,421

Units of measure

RATES OF SPEED	TEMPERATURE	LENGTH
60 mph	32° F	17.6 nanometers
33 rpm	0° C	24¼ in.

WEIGHT	MONEY
34 grams	\$.02 2¢
21 pounds	\$20.00
	\$1,500,000 \$1.5 million

Amounts of money that can be written in two or three words can be spelled out.

two cents
twenty dollars
one and a half million dollars

TEACHING IDEAS

You may want to remind students of the need for consistency in representing amounts of money. You can call attention to the fact that the symbol $ can be combined with a written amount only to denote excessively large sums (as in the example, $1.5 million). The symbol ¢ is virtually never combined with a written amount.

TEACHING IDEAS

On occasion, addresses will be written out without numerals—the numbers zero and one, for example, are often written out. And formal wedding invitations frequently spell out the numerical portion of the street address. You may want to alert students to these exceptions.

Scores, statistics, ratios

The game ended with the score 2–1.

In the past presidential election, less than 50 percent of the eligible population voted.

The odds against winning the weekly lottery are worse than 1,000,000 to 1.

A mean score of 72 can be expected on the exam.

Addresses

Apartment 6
231 Park Avenue
New York, New York 10021

2nd Avenue
East 53rd Street

Telephone numbers

301-555-1212

Volume, page, and line references

Volume 6 act 1 scene 4 line 16
page 81 pages 120–133

Military units

the 41st Tactical Squadron the 6th Fleet

Dates

70 B.C. A.D. 70
from 1991 to 1992 1991–1992
1991–92

Time

Write out numbers when using the expression *o'clock.*

10:00 a.m. but ten o'clock in the morning
10:02 p.m. but two minutes past ten in the evening

31h Edit to eliminate numbers and figures mixed together in one sentence, unless these have different references.

FAULTY A spacecraft orbiting Earth travels at seventeen thousand miles per hour; but because of the craft's distance from the planet, the images of continents and oceans seen through its window appear to be moving not much faster than images seen through the windshield of a car traveling 60 mph.

REVISED A spacecraft orbiting Earth travels at 17,000 mph; but because of the craft's distance from the planet, the images of continents and oceans seen through its window appear to be moving not much faster than images seen through the windshield of a car traveling 60 mph.

ACCEPTABLE For two months before its closing, the U-Trust Savings and Loan advertised wildly fluctuating interest rates in an effort to secure new cash: 9 percent one month and 15 percent the next. [Both numbers referring to advertised rates are presented as figures; the numbers *two* and *one,* referring to measures of time, are written out.]

EXERCISE 2

Correct the use of numbers in these sentences. Write out numbers in some cases; use figures in others.

Example: On August thirty-first, 1995, Bass PLC sold its distribution network to Tradeteam.

On August 31, 1995, Bass PLC sold its distribution network to Tradeteam.

1. An enterprising British brewery has decided to try out home delivery on its customers with the claim that at least 24 cans of beer will be on the customer's doorstep within forty-eight hours once the order has been placed.
2. 3 cities have been targeted for the service so far—London, Nottingham, and Birmingham.
3. Customers must order a minimum of one crate (24 cans), and they can expect to pay 17.99 pounds with a delivery charge of 1.99£ added on.
4. The service will be tested for 3 months and then evaluated for profitability and consumer satisfaction.
5. Nottingham and Birmingham beer drinkers don't have much of a choice of brands—only one is available—but Londoners can choose from among 8 premium beers.

EXERCISE 2

1. An enterprising British brewery has decided to try out home delivery on its customers with the claim that at least twenty-four cans of beer will be on the customer's doorstep within forty-eight hours once the order has been placed.
2. Three cities have been targeted for the service so far—London, Nottingham, and Birmingham.
3. Customers must order a minimum of one crate (24 cans), and they can expect to pay 17.99£ with a delivery charge of 1.99£ added on.
4. The service will be tested for three months and then evaluated for profitability and consumer satisfaction.
5. Nottingham and Birmingham beer drinkers don't have much of a choice of brands—only one is available—but Londoners can choose from among eight premium beers.

CHAPTER 32

Hyphens

KEY FEATURES

This chapter approaches hyphens from the perspective of clarity: pointing out that lack of hyphenation or improper hyphenation can obscure meaning. The chapter goes on to explain the two primary uses of the hyphen. The coverage is extensive and the approach practical, with the section on compound words covering everything from compound adjectives to compounds formed by prefixes and suffixes. Treatment of hyphenation to divide a word at the end of a line is equally thorough—rules range from dividing compound words to eliminating misleading hyphenation. Examples make clear the rules and conventions covered in the chapter, and exercises provide students with ample practice in using hyphen-ation.

ESL CUE

Spanish speakers frequently use hyphens rather than indentation to signal new paragraphs.

A small but important mark, the **hyphen** (-) has two uses: to join compound words and to divide words at the end of lines. You will find advice on word divisions in any dictionary, where each entry is broken into syllables. If you write on a computer, your word-processing software will probably suggest word divisions. As for compounds, these will require more discernment on your part, for relocating a simple hyphen can alter meanings entirely.

32a Using hyphens to make compound words

Compound words are created when two or more words are brought together to create a distinctive meaning and to function grammatically as a single word. Many compounds occur together so often that they have become one word, formed without a hyphen.

sandbox outline casework aircraft

Many words appearing in pairs remain separate. Two-word compounds may become one word over time, so consult a current dictionary when you are uncertain about spelling.

sand toys out loud case study air conditioning

Use a hyphen to link words when a compound expression would otherwise confuse a reader, even if only momentarily.

CONFUSING Helen's razor sharp wit rarely failed her. [Helen's *razor* is not the subject; Helen's *wit* is.]

CLEAR Helen's razor-sharp wit rarely failed her. [With the hyphen, meaning is clear.]

Small as they are, hyphens make a difference. Each of the following sentences has a distinct meaning.

The cross reference helped me to understand the passage.

The cross-reference helped me to understand the passage.

The first sentence concerns a literary reference to a *cross;* the second, a note that refers readers to some other page in an article or text. The conventions for forming compounds with hyphens are as follows.

1 Form compound adjectives with a hyphen to prevent misreading when they precede the noun being modified.

The following hyphenations make compound or multiple-word modifiers out of words that might otherwise be misread.

low-interest loan   state-of-the-art technology   hoped-for success

Note that when a **compound adjective** is positioned *after* the noun it modifies, it does not need hyphenation. Placed after a noun, the first word of the adjective does not compete for the reader's attention as the subject or object in the sentence.

Helen's wit was razor sharp.

A compound modifier is not hyphenated when its first word ends with the distinctive suffix of a modifier.

Helen's impressively sharp wit rarely failed her.

Because of its ending, the first word in this compound modifier is not misread. In this case, the *-ly* suffix marks *impressive* as an adverb, and the reader knows that *impressively* will not function as the subject. Thus, the suffix in effect instructs the reader to move forward in search of the sentence's first noun—*wit,* which is in fact the subject. Because there is no possibility of misreading, no hyphen is used. The same analysis holds when the first word of the compound is a modifier ending with a comparative or superlative suffix *-er* or *-est* form (see 11e). In the following examples, the reader knows that *least* and *sweetest* are modifiers because of their endings.

The least expensive item in that store cost more than I could afford.
The sweetest sounding voice in the choir belonged to a child of ten. [*By contrast:* The sweet-sounding voice belonged to a child of ten.]

2 Form compound nouns and verbs with a hyphen to prevent misreading.

Use a hyphen with **compound nouns** and **compound verbs** when the first word of the compound invites the reader to regard that word, alone, as a noun or verb. Hyphenated nouns and verbs are marked as such in a dictionary.

cross-reference (n)   cross-examine (v)   runner-up (n)   shrink-wrap (v)

Hyphenating the compound forms makes reading the following sentence easier.

CONFUSING   The runner up staged a protest. [What is intended: *runner-up* or *up-staged*?]

REVISED   The runner-up staged a protest.

REFERENCES

The following style sheets provide advice on hyphenation:

The Chicago Manual of Style. 14th ed. Chicago: U of Chicago P, 1993.

GIBALDI, JOSEPH. *MLA Handbook for Writers of Research Papers.* 4th ed. New York: MLA, 1995.

TEACHING IDEAS

Tom McArthur's *Oxford Companion to the English Language* (Oxford: Oxford University Press, 1992) contains some interesting historical information on the hyphen, tracing its use back to the sixteenth century. You may want to call students' attention to this reference.

ADDITIONAL EXERCISE A

Using the rules in this section (or a dictionary), write the following compound words correctly:

1. under + ground
2. anti + American
3. shell + like
4. anti + war
5. band + wagon
6. high + school

Answers:

1. underground
2. anti-American
3. shell-like
4. antiwar
5. bandwagon
6. high school

3 Use hanging hyphens in a series of compound adjectives.

Hang—that is, suspend—hyphens after the first word of compound adjectives placed in a parallel series. In this usage, observe that the second word of the compound as well as the noun being modified is mentioned *once.*

> The eighth-, ninth-, and tenth-grade classes went on the trip. [The second word of the compound, *grade,* and the noun modified, *classes,* are mentioned once.]

4 Follow conventions in hyphenating numbers, letters, and units.

Hyphenate fractions and the numbers twenty-one through ninety-nine.

Place a hyphen between the numerator and denominator of a fraction, unless one of these (or both) is already hyphenated.

one-fourth   seven-thousandths   seven one-thousandths
forty-six   seventy-one

Hyphenate figures and letters joined with words to form nouns or modifiers.

4-minute mile   B-rated   U-turn

Hyphenate units of measure.

light-year   kilowatt-hour

5 Hyphenate compounds formed by prefixes or suffixes according to convention.

Use a hyphen with the prefixes *ex, quasi,* and *self,* with the suffix *elect,* and with most uses of *vice.* (Consult a dictionary for specifics.)

ex-President   quasi-serious   self-doubt

Use a hyphen with the prefixes *pro, anti,* and *pre* only when they are joined with proper nouns.

No hyphen	*Hyphen with proper noun*
prochoice	pro-Democracy
antimagnetic	anti-Maoist

But use a hyphen with a prefix or suffix that doubles a vowel or that triples a consonant.

No hyphen	*Hyphen with doubled or tripled letters*
antiseptic	anti-intellectual
childlike	bell-like

Hyphenate to avoid misreading.

re-form (to form an object—such as a clay figure—again)
reform (to overhaul and update a system)

32b Using hyphens to divide a word at the end of a line

To the extent possible, avoid dividing words at the end of a line. When you must divide words, do so only at syllable breaks (as indicated in a dictionary). Even when given suggestions for hyphenation by word-processing software, you often face a choice concerning hyphenation that could make a difference in clarity. The following conventions improve comprehension.

Divide compound words at the hyphen marking the compound.

When hyphens join compound words, it is unnecessary and confusing to divide the word at any place other than the compound. (See the discussion on writing compounds in 32a.)

UNNECESSARY The mouthparts of many insects are exquisitely adapted to the nectaries (*nectar-hold-ing* organs) of special flowers.

CLEARER The mouthparts of many insects are exquisitely adapted to the nectaries (*nectar-holding* organs) of special flowers.

Divide words at a prefix or suffix.

Hundreds of words are formed in English by adding prefixes and suffixes to root words (see 22d-2, 3). Divide these words, when possible, between prefix and root word or between suffix and root word. Thus, *un-necessary* would be preferable to *unnec-essary.*

A number of prefixes—such as *pro, anti, quasi, vice,* and *ex*—require the use of a hyphen. Divide these words at the hyphen.

AWKWARD In the election of 1848, the "Free-Soil" party nominated Charles Francis Adams for *Vice-Presi-dent.*

REVISED In the election of 1848, the "Free-Soil" party nominated Charles Francis Adams for *Vice-President.*

Eliminate hyphenations that hang a single letter at the beginning or end of a line.

To avoid misleading your readers, you would not divide these words: *e-nough* (it is misleading) or *tast-y.*

CONFUSING Inflation creates fractures in the implicit and explicit *a-greements* that bind people together.

TEACHING IDEAS

Dividing words at the end of a line is often a problem for students. You may want to ask students to memorize the basic rules listed in the headings of this section. Or you may want to remind them that the correct answer to hyphenation questions is as close as the nearest dictionary.

REVISED Inflation creates fractures in the implicit and explicit *agreements* that bind people together.

Eliminate misleading hyphenations.

The first syllable of a word is sometimes itself a word (for instance, *break-fast, arch-angel, in-stall, match-less*). Confusion results when the first syllable, left hyphenated at the end of a line, fits a sentence's content and suggests one meaning while the full, undivided word suggests another.

Single-syllable words are never hyphenated.

To prevent misleading the reader, you would not, for example, divide any of these words: *ceased, doubt, friend, freeze, though.*

Abbreviations, contractions, or multiple-digit numbers are not hyphenated.

Abbreviations (*apt., IBM, NATO*) and contractions (*can't, won't, they're*) are already shortened forms. To shorten them further by a word division will confuse your readers. A multiple-digit number divided at the end of a line is also confusing.

EXERCISE 1

Use hyphens in the sentences that follow to form compound adjectives; to mark prefixes or suffixes; to note fractions, numbers less than one hundred, or words formed with figures; and to prevent misreading. Place a check beside any sentence in which hyphens are used correctly.

Example: Following WWII, Pepsi Cola Company succeeded in recruiting Alfred N. Steele, a tough talking, two fisted, pin-striped warrior with a unique grasp of the mood of the fifties.

Following WWII, Pepsi-Cola Company succeeded in recruiting Alfred N. Steele, a tough-talking, two-fisted, pin-striped warrior with a unique grasp of the mood of the fifties.

1. Steele was uniquely qualified to lead the Pepsi Cola Company when it began to falter because of its outdated marketing campaign; he had been educated at the world's greatest soft drink institution—the Coca-Cola Company.
2. Beginning his career running a circus, he moved into advertising and then jumped to a vice presidency at Coca Cola.
3. Subsequently, Steele accepted the more lucrative offer from Pepsi-Cola, though in his first quarter at the company it lost $100,000 as Coca-Cola pulverized the entire industry with a 67% stranglehold on the soft drink market.
4. Coca Cola was the darling of the ever expanding middle class, while Pepsi was a favorite of the downtrodden who couldn't afford to sacrifice Pepsi's extra ounces for Coke's prestige.
5. Thus, Steele set his sights on getting Pepsi into America's living rooms, and to that end redesigned Pepsi's standard 12 ounce bottle.

GROUP ACTIVITY

The exercise in this chapter lends itself to group activity. Have students respond to the exercise individually and then compare their responses with those of other group members. When the inevitable disagreement occurs, students will have to consult the handbook. Once they become accustomed to using the chapter, they'll likely continue to refer to it as they edit their papers.

EXERCISE 1

1. Steele was uniquely qualified to lead the Pepsi-Cola Company when it began to falter because of its outdated marketing campaign; he had been educated at the world's greatest soft-drink institution—the Coca-Cola Company.
2. Beginning his career running a circus, he moved into advertising and then jumped to a vice-presidency at Coca-Cola.
3. Subsequently, Steele accepted the more lucrative offer from Pepsi-Cola, though in his first quarter at the company it lost $100,000 as Coca-Cola pulverized the entire industry with a 67% stranglehold on the soft-drink market.
4. Coca-Cola was the darling of the ever-expanding middle class, while Pepsi was a favorite of the downtrodden who couldn't afford to sacrifice Pepsi's extra ounces for Coke's prestige.
5. Thus, Steele set his sights on getting Pepsi into America's living rooms, and to that end redesigned Pepsi's standard 12-ounce bottle.

PART IX
WRITING THE RESEARCH PAPER

CHAPTER 33

Understanding the Research Process

Research begins with a question, with a need to *know.* You will enjoy your work as a researcher more if you can manage to take an assignment from your teacher and make it your own by formulating a question that you, personally, want to answer. Then, you will spend your time locating and examining sources because you are truly interested in your topic, not simply because you are fulfilling an assignment.

This is the first of four chapters devoted to research. This chapter provides the basic strategies for posing the questions that launch research and for seeking information, both inside and outside the library, that will help you to answer your questions in the form of a research paper. Chapter 34 discusses the ways you will actually *use* the source materials you find: by taking notes, summarizing, paraphrasing, and quoting. Chapter 35 provides guidance on arranging materials and writing your paper. And Chapter 36 acquaints you with the process of documenting sources—acknowledging in your papers that you have drawn on the work of others.

33a Making your research worthwhile

1 Personal interest justifies effort.

The process of conducting research takes time. If you are like most students, you are busy; so for a research project to be worthwhile, you're going to have to justify it as a reasonable investment of time and effort. What will make the investment worthwhile? In a word, *interest.* Any efforts you make at the beginning and through the early stages of the process to become truly interested in your work will pay handsome dividends; when you are interested, your hours spent gathering, reading, and synthesizing sources will be productive.

KEY FEATURES

In Part IX, students will watch a fellow student research and write a paper on the question, What do Americans want at the mall? The process of research demonstrated here is a realistic one, illustrating the looping, recursive process of writing. The writer begins with one research question and a tentative thesis; he discovers from his source materials that his question was incomplete, as was his initial thesis. He revises both—and in the process of further reading revises yet again. Student readers will find that this section on the research process disabuses them of the notion that research paper writing is a straight-line process, from question to thesis to supporting sources to completed paper. As the student example shows, the process is more complicated than that; the process is about discovery and revising one's views in the face of new, compelling evidence.

Chapter 33 presents a current, authoritative overview of electronic sources: what the various possibilities are (WAIS, WWW, gopher, etc.); how one accesses electronic sources; and what the relative degrees of reliability are across source types. Also included is a discussion on the logic of search engines and keyword searches. Many students will be able to use the materials here to launch their own electronic searches.

(continued)

Throughout the discussion, this chapter emphasizes the self-generating nature of the research process, encouraging students to follow leads for their own satisfaction as well as for the benefit of the assignment. Extensive examples illustrate key points.

TEACHING IDEAS

Embarking on the dreaded research paper journey can be daunting for many students, and downright paralyzing for some. It's possible, however, to help students maintain a positive attitude about the process. You can do this by telling them something about your own research—including your fears. Sharing your stories with students can help them in two ways. First, it lets them see that even professionals approach research with a certain amount of trepidation, and second, it treats student research seriously as an initial step into the literate community. Students will care more about their research if they see that their professors care.

REFERENCES

BAZERMAN, CHARLES. *The Informed Writer: Using Sources in the Disciplines.* 2nd ed. Boston: Houghton, 1985. Chapters 11–15. A complete description of how the disciplines go about conducting research.

EMIG, JANET. "Writing as a Mode of Learning." CCC 28 (1977): 122–28. Writing is learning; researching, writing, and learning are interconnected.

FLYNN, ELIZABETH A. "Composing 'Composing as a Woman': A Perspective on Research." CCC 41 (1990): 83–89. Feminist theory leads one to discuss students' writing and research in new, more fruitful ways.

LUTZKER, MARILYN. *Research Projects for College Students: What to Write across the Curriculum.* Westport, CT: Greenwood, 1988. This librarian challenges teachers to design projects that are intellectually stimulating and eminently teachable (includes list of research topics and of periodical resources).

MCCARTNEY, ROBERT. "The Cumulative Research Paper." *Teaching English in the Two-Year College* 12 (1985): 198–202. Presents a way for

Motivation is easy to talk about in theory. In practice, generating personal interest in a research topic may be more difficult. Let's assume that you have been given an assignment on shopping malls, which is the topic of the student research paper you'll see developed throughout this section of the book. You've gone to malls. Everyone has. Beyond that, what's to know? People arrive, shop, and go home. Why write about *this* topic? Such a response is legitimate; but given that a teacher expects you to write a research paper, you will have work to do, and you may as well enjoy it by finding something interesting about which to write. And, as will be discussed below, *interested* writers generate more successful papers. To generate interest where none (or little) exists, try the strategies listed in the box.

Tips for Generating Personal Interest

If you are given complete freedom to choose your research area, obviously you should choose a topic that interests, even fascinates, you. If this is not an option, choose a topic of general (even if lukewarm) interest. With a bit of effort, you can discover enthusiasm for many, if not all, topics.

- **If you find the topic interesting:** If you are drawn to the topic, so much the better. Divide it into several well-defined parts. Ask: Which part do I want to learn more about? Use your answer to locate general sources. Then read (see below).
- **If you are repelled by the topic:** If you *don't* like an assigned topic, devote some effort to understanding your negative response. Strong negative reactions, as well as positive ones, can lead to an effective paper. Again, divide the topic into well-defined parts. Ask: What new information could help me to understand my reaction? Use your answer to locate general sources. Then read (see below).
- **If the topic leaves you feeling neutral:** Immediately liking or disliking a topic can launch a research project by sparking in you a need to know. Neutrality, on the other hand, can be a challenge. If the topic leaves you feeling completely uninspired, try reading—just a bit. At the beginning stages, you may not know enough about a topic to be interested; when you learn even a little about the topic, you may discover possibilities. So go to a general source—an encyclopedia or an introductory book—or try a general index (for example, the *Readers' Guide to Periodical Literature*) to locate two or three promising articles.
- **Read:** Try these strategies for increasing your level of interest:
  1. Based on your reading, identify as many angles of approach to the topic as you can. Discovering that there are approaches you never thought existed may be enough to spark your interest.
  2. Generate as many questions as you can, based on what you read. Perhaps one of these questions will become your research focus.
  3. Read in "hyper-alert" mode. Actively respond to multiple points in the article. Perhaps one response will become your research focus.

2 Personal interest motivates critical thinking and reading.

You can use your personal motivation to increase your alertness through all stages of the research process. Fundamentally, you want to be an *active reader.* An active reader becomes alert to *differences* or inconsistencies in the material; for example, you may notice some interesting discrepancies between two or more textual treatments of General Grant or between one author's comments on schizophrenia and your own direct knowledge. As an active reader, you *challenge* your text or your subject (see 1b-1); for example, considering the conflicting interpretations of this historical event, where does the truth lie? What are the reasons for this problem? How extensive is it? Has the author fairly represented the situation? You would also ask questions of yourself (see 1b-2); for example, what do *I* believe about this issue? What do *I* think should be done?

Before you can answer such questions, you need to locate and critically review more information than you currently have. As an active reader, you try to set issues in a *broader context* (see 1c); for example, how is the problem of discovering a cure for AIDS tied up with the broader question of funding for disease research?

You form *opinions* and try to support them (see 1d); for example, does evidence support the conclusion that dropping the atomic bomb on Japan was not necessary to bring about a Japanese surrender? As you initially gather and read sources, expect to take a position—but understand that you may later want to change or modify the position as new materials become available. Further reading will enable you to challenge the assumptions of others, as well as your own assumptions. And you devise *action plans*—in this case, research strategies.

As your research progresses, you will *critically read* your sources. You will attempt to *understand* what others have said (see 1e), and you will *respond,* through questions and answers, to what they have said (see 1f). You will *evaluate* your sources, attempting to separate fact from opinion and to identify and take into account underlying assumptions (see 1g). Finally, you will *synthesize* the information and ideas that you have researched in ways that support your thesis—the statement that serves as your answer to your primary research question (see 1h). As you go through this process you will sift through all your questions, rearranging your research priorities until you have discovered the one key question that motivates you to find the most comprehensive and satisfying answer for your concerns. This may become the "burning question" for your research.

3 Personal interest improves writing.

Your success in all this activity is directly related to your motivation. The best writing invariably comes from those who are interested in their work; research *is* work, but that work can be more or less enjoyable. And enjoyment is not the only benefit of motivation. Motivated research and writ-

students to thoroughly investigate one topic through several assignments.

TOBIN, LAD. "Bridging Gaps: Analyzing Our Students' Metaphors for Composing." CCC 40 (1989): 444–58. Understanding students' metaphors for composing leads to less frustration in teaching the composing process.

WILLIAMS, NANCY. "Research as a Process: A Transactional Approach." *Journal of Teaching Writing* 7 (1988): 193–204. Discusses a set of assignments that illustrates the benefits of the research process.

LOOKING BACK

Not only will another examination of Chapters 1–3 help students see the connections between research and critical thinking/essay writing, but it can also serve to allay some of the fears students may be harboring about research. There's nothing like the familiar to ease one's mind. You may want to ask students to review these early chapters, and then discuss in class what they recall that might be relevant in the research process.

REFERENCES

LANGER, JUDITH A. "Learning through Writing: Study Skills in the Content Areas." *Journal of Reading* 29 (1986): 400–06. Learning content is achieved best through writing, not through note-taking and answering test questions.

STRICKLAND, JAMES. "The Research Sequence: What to Do Before the Term Paper." CCC 37 (1986): 233–36. A set of assignments starting with the generalized opinion paper—to which researched material may be added—ends with a thoroughly researched argument.

ing is actually *better* and more insightful than unmotivated efforts. Evaluating individual sources and, especially, synthesizing multiple sources requires determined effort and creativity.

- Motivated writers are willing to work hard with their sources, staying with each one long enough to form a definite, critical response. By understanding and distinguishing the views of source writers, student writers can identify their own views more precisely.
- Motivated writers are willing to return to a library or make an additional call to locate promising sources. The resulting paper will be more fully developed.
- Motivated writers are willing to tinker with the various ways in which sources might be related. These relationships can provide critical, original insights in the final paper.

The investment of personal interest, then, pays two types of dividends: you are able to enjoy and actively learn from the process of research, and you produce higher quality work.

4 Using essay writing as a foundation for research writing

The process of writing a research paper is similar to that of writing an essay. Both require that you think critically, not only about the sources you read but also about the positions you take as you develop your ideas.

In Chapter 3, you will find a diagram that models the writing process (see 3a-1). This illustration shows writing and thinking as circular, recursive activities. *Recursive* means looping back on itself. That is, while the writing process has identifiable stages, you will *not* work through these stages in a linear fashion. You will devote time to each of the following stages, but not necessarily in this order and not necessarily one stage at a time. You will—

- define your purpose and audience;
- generate ideas and organize information;
- write a draft; and
- revise the draft.

A personal commitment to your topic will motivate you not only to challenge your sources but also to challenge yourself. Each new source will prompt you to go back over your ideas, testing their validity. At times, sources will prompt you to change your ideas, sometimes because they convince you that you were wrong; sometimes because they reveal that your initial thinking did not take into account certain information—which was the case with student researcher Jason Koman. As he read more on the topic of shopping malls, he discovered that his sources wouldn't "give" him the paper he thought he was going to write. Moreover, his sources prompted him to refine his original research question.

Initially, Jason asked, What *is* a shopping mall? His initial answer: Malls are our modern equivalent of the medieval market. As he learned through research, and as you will see demonstrated in his paper, this is only partially true. As Jason read further on his topic, he came to a new, revised question: *What do we want at the mall?* It was in response to this revised question that Jason was able to complete his research and write a successful paper.

Your original ideas are essential.

Writing a research paper involves a process of drafting and revision, in much the same way that writing an essay does—but with a difference: in research writing, you not only have the process itself to help clarify your thinking, but also you have source materials, each of which will help you test the soundness of your ideas as they evolve. Writing a research paper is *not* a process of locating a certain number of sources and then stitching them together mechanically. The process requires original, active thinking on your part, thinking that continually tests its own validity. The successful paper must be based on an original idea: *your* idea.

For more information on the process of writing, see Chapter 3. For an in-depth look at revising and rethinking, see Chapter 4.

EXERCISE 1

Interview two of your instructors. Ask what kinds of research they do and why their research interests them personally. Ask what, if any, "burning questions" have directed their research. Why do these questions burn for them? Take notes during the interviews. Then review these notes and write three paragraphs: two paragraphs devoted to summarizing the interviews; and one paragraph in which you make observations about the research your instructors do and their personal relationships to that research.

33b Determining the scope of your paper and identifying a research question

1 Determining the scope of your paper

In order to avoid the frustrating experience of squeezing a great deal of research into a paper, only to feel that you've treated the material superficially, or, conversely, the experience of trying to pump extra material into a paper for which the topic seems too slight, you will need to understand several factors that affect the scope of your work: assignment, audience, topic, and intended level of detail.

- Your *assignment* helps to set the scope of your project: specific tasks, length, and number and variety of sources expected. In 41b, you will find a list of key verbs associated with essay questions. These same verbs—such as *compare, discuss,* and *justify*—will be found in typical research assignments, so you should be aware of them and their definitions.

EXERCISE 1

Individual responses

FOR DISCUSSION

This exercise can foster valuable discussion about the research process. Select several students to read their paragraphs aloud to the class. (You can either rely on volunteers or read through responses and choose the most meaningful samples yourself.) As they hear different instructors' reflections on research, students can begin to articulate their own questions about what research means (or will come to mean) to them. Discussing what research means to their instructors can help students take their own research more seriously.

REFERENCES

HORNING, ALICE S. "Advising Undecided Students through Research Writing." *CCC* 42 (1991): 80–84. Explains a course designed around researching post-graduate options through writing experiences that move from self-exploration to career exploration.

LARSON, RICHARD L. "The 'Research Paper' in the Writing Course: A Non-Form of Writing." *CE* 44 (1982): 811–16. Rpt. in *The Writing*

(continued)

Teacher's Sourcebook. 3rd ed. Ed. Gary Tate and Edward P. J. Corbett. New York: Oxford UP, 1994. 180–85. Argues against teaching "the generic 'research paper' " as a form of writing, advocating instead that students cultivate their experiences as ways to inform the ideas they wish to develop.

PAGE, MIRIAM DEMPSEY. " 'Thick Description' and a Rhetoric of Inquiry: Freshmen and the Major Fields." Urbana: ERIC Clearinghouse on Reading and Communication Skills, 1987. ERIC ED 279 020. Uses Clifford Geertz's theories to show the benefits of asking students to research career choices in the same way that anthropologists go about researching an unknown culture.

PETERSON, BRUCE T., and JILL N. BURKLAND. "Investigative Reading and Writing: Responding to Reading with Research." *CE* 37 (1986): 236–40. Research is a way of thinking about our experiences with all texts; students can conduct research by tapping into their personal responses to texts.

REFERENCES

CAPOSSELA, TONI-LEE. "Students as Sociolinguists: Getting Real Research from Freshman Writers." *CCC* 42 (1991): 75–79. Research in sociolinguistics emphasizes aspects of language in which students are most expert and encourages students to engage in "real-life" issues.

COON, ANNE C. "Using Ethical Questions to Develop Autonomy in Student Researchers." *CCC* 40 (1989): 85–89. A set of assignments asks students to research an ethical problem, look at it in various ways, and then advance a hypothesis about it.

DELLINGER, DIXIE G. "Alternatives to Clip and Stitch: Real Research and Writing in the Classroom." *English Journal* 78 (1989): 31–38. Students may use different methods of inquiry (surveys, interviews, experiments) to generate their own research and to become engaged in writing about their results.

FORD, JAMES E. et al. "Research Paper Instruction: Comprehensive Bibliography of Periodical Sources, 1023–1980." *Bulletin of Bibliography* 39 (1981): 84–98. Provides resources and ideas for using sources and writing the research paper.

Example: Consider the following assignment. How would you devise an action plan that would lead to a research paper?

> In recent years, much attention has been focused on the ethical aspects of business decisions. Research and discuss a particular business practice that has raised significant ethical questions. Show, by means of case studies, the kinds of controversies and problems that have arisen as a result of such practices, and discuss and evaluate some of the recommended solutions to these problems.

The key verbs in this assignment are: *research, discuss, show,* and *evaluate.* The order of these verbs in the assignment suggests a structure for the paper. In the first section, "research and discuss" indicate that you'll need to define a specific business practice and present the ethical questions associated with it. In the second section, "show, by means of case studies" asks you to find two or, if length permits, three cases that raise the questions and illustrate the concerns you addressed in the first section. In the third and final section, "discuss and evaluate" asks you to identify and then assess the validity of solutions to the ethically troubling practices you've defined. The assignment itself, then, clearly sets out the scope of the paper to be written. But you have other factors to consider as well.

- Your *audience* will determine key elements of your paper, ranging from tone, to vocabulary, to structure. Who is your audience? Will you be writing for specialists or nonspecialists? For college students or readers of the OP-ED page? Are your readers likely to agree with you or not? See 3a-3 for specific questions to help you analyze your audience and its needs and to make subsequent decisions in your paper.

  Example: Again, consider the example assignment. If your instructor asked you to write the paper as an article that you would submit to a weekly, general news magazine, you would avoid the use of specialized vocabulary for readers who, presumably, had no special expertise in business and, particularly, in business ethics. You would also need to provide full background information for the case studies. By contrast, your instructor might have asked you to write the paper as an in-house memo for executives at a corporation concerned with its image problems, arising out of some ethically dubious practices. You could use specialized terms freely and present the background for the cases in a more shorthand way (assuming that your readers were familiar with the details). *Who* is reading your work will determine *how* and *what* you write.

- Your *topic,* and the ways in which you can divide it into subtopics, will also help to define the scope of your paper. Almost immediately on beginning your research, you will learn enough about your topic to define several component parts. In your research paper, you will need to decide how many parts to work with. Your decisions will affect the scope of your paper.

  Example: Periodically, the government forces manufacturers to recall their products. Manufacturers are sometimes aware of certain product "deficiencies," but do not issue recalls voluntarily. Your reading on the topic quickly reveals that the issue of what manufacturers know or don't know about their potentially dangerous products exists across numerous industries: automobiles, toys, bedding, and home appliances, to name a few. As a writer, you have a decision to make concerning the scope of your paper: Will you write about the issue of safety recalls in one or more industries? Why would you choose one approach over the other? How would your decision affect the length of your paper? How would it affect the impact of your paper? There are no right or wrong answers, here—merely decisions that will affect the scope of your work.

- Your *intended level of detail* for the paper will also affect the scope of your work and your selection of topics (or subtopics). A single topic can be discussed in minute detail, at great length, or briefly in a quick overview. Be clear about the level of detail you will be bringing to your paper, or to specific sections of the paper.

  Example: The research assignment asks you to discuss cases that illustrate a business practice and the ethical questions associated with it. In writing this paper, you would have to decide how many cases to discuss. Clearly, that number will be a function of the paper's length: the briefer the paper, the fewer the cases. But given a fixed length, you could decide to discuss two cases in greater detail or three (or even four) cases in lesser detail. Again, there is no one correct approach, but you will need to make these decisions consciously.

  The scope of your research paper—the topic you choose and the extent to which you write—largely depends on four interrelated elements: assignment, audience, topic, and level of detail. By understanding these elements and consciously making decisions concerning them as you write, you will produce papers appropriate for the occasion.

2 Identifying your key research question

As you continue to read about your topic, you will sift through your questions and eventually arrive at one that interests you most—the question that you will answer by conducting still more research. You are working toward a question that, to the best of your knowledge, will sustain you through the days of research that lie ahead; so you have a great deal to gain from making a good choice. How can you tell if your research question is a good one?

Realize that the question you select as your key research question sets limits for your reading. Be aware of the dangers of seizing on a research question too quickly. Even if you think you have a good question, one that clearly interests you and satisfies the criteria above, don't commit yourself to that question if you are still at an early stage in the research process. Otherwise, you may overlook aspects that you would have found particularly interesting. Preliminary research could involve reading an encyclopedia or magazine article, a section of a textbook, or possibly even a short book on the subject. Such reading may raise particular questions in your mind that you feel compelled to pursue.

After doing some preliminary reading, you will be in a better position to restrict your focus—and you will do this primarily by searching your sources to discover the answer to one primary *research question.* This research question may be the one you began with, or it may be another question that

GROUP ACTIVITY

Consider asking students to explore their paper ideas in groups. As they discuss the relevance of the many questions raised here, they should begin to find themselves drawn to some area of inquiry. Even a ten- to fifteen-minute group session can do wonders to spur individual students to action in the exercise.

was raised in the course of your preliminary reading. The advantage of working with a question, as opposed to a thesis, at this point, is that you are acknowledging that you still have to discover the answer(s), rather than just find evidence to support a prematurely established conclusion.

Do You Have a Good Research Question?

As you reflect on what you think will be your main research question, consider the following:

- Have any of your sources answered the question completely and, in your view, comprehensively? If *no,* your question is a good one—a real one in that your research efforts will provide an answer that does not yet exist. *Caution:* If your sources have completely and comprehensively answered your research question, try to find some aspect of the question that is *not* yet answered, to ensure that your efforts are original.
- Does your question linger with you? Do you find yourself thinking about this question at odd times—on the way to the mailbox or the cafeteria? If *yes,* stay with your question: it has engaged you. Frequently, it is in these "off" hours, when you are not formally working, that important insights occur.
- Does investigating your question give you opportunities to make connections from one source to another—connections that the sources themselves don't seem to be making? If *yes,* stay with your question: it is prompting efforts of *synthesis*—you are piecing elements of a puzzle together, which is what researchers do.

LOOKING AHEAD

ACROSS THE CURRICULUM The examples provided here represent assignments from several different disciplines. You may want to inform students at this point that they can find extended discussion of writing requirements in various disciplines in Chapters 37 (Writing and Reading in the Humanities), 38 (Writing and Reading in the Social Sciences), and 39 (Writing and Reading in the Sciences).

FOR DISCUSSION

ACROSS THE CURRICULUM This would be an ideal time to pause and ask students to consider the nature of disciplines. Many students have the idea that there's little connection between fields within a larger discipline, much less between the larger disciplines them-

3 Assignments and initial questions across disciplines

As you move from one discipline to another, the questions you pose as a researcher, your strategies for arguing, and your uses of evidence will change—and you should be aware of differences across disciplines when you write your papers. Topics, too, will change. For instance, a paper on the incidence of alcoholism among student athletes would be suitable for a sociology course, but not for a literature or business course. A paper on the genetic factor in crack cocaine addiction would be suitable for a biology course, but not for a sociology course. The following examples show some representative research assignments in the major disciplinary areas; they concern general topics that can be adapted to a wide variety of particular subjects.

Social science: Writers in business and in the social sciences (as described in 38a), often try to present significant social or economic patterns and to make arguments as to why those patterns are significant. Here's a typical example of a research assignment:

> Describe and discuss a particular behavioral pattern or syndrome among a definable social group. The group may be defined by social class, ethni-

city, gender, occupation, age, or some other factor. You may also wish to compare the behaviors of this group with corresponding behaviors of one or more other groups.

Humanities: As you will see in 37a, writers in the humanities make statements of interpretation about texts in all their variety, including stories, dramas, movies, sacred literature, correspondence, personal or government records, and the work of others (in the humanities). Textual materials become evidence in interpretive arguments; the goal is to persuade others that interpretations are valid. Here's a typical example of a research assignment:

> Examine several works by a particular playwright or novelist, focusing on a single feature or device characteristic of this artist. Explain how and why this feature manifests itself in different forms in various works and perhaps how it develops over the artist's career. Draw on the interpretations of critics and literary scholars to help illuminate your discussion.

Science: As you will see in 39a-2, writers in the sciences often make arguments that involve two claims. The first: *X is a problem,* or *X is puzzling.* The second claim takes this form: *X can be explained as follows.* Here's a typical example of a research assignment:

> Scientists frequently find themselves drawn into controversies when their research tends either to support or to refute the views of particular groups or of social critics. For example, Darwin and his followers were embroiled in conflicts with creationists; physicists have been involved in controversies over the safety of nuclear power plants. Select a particular scientific discovery or line of research and explore the ways in which it has generated controversy among scientists and nonscientists alike.

Understand strategies for writing arguments in different disciplines.

Writing a research paper in one discipline or another involves arguing and using evidence in ways that are appropriate to that discipline. Your success in these papers depends on the extent to which you can demonstrate that you think like a researcher in a particular discipline. Are you asking questions and providing evidence like a sociologist or a biologist? like a historian or an engineer? Conventions for constructing arguments change from one discipline to the next, and you should be aware of these conventions while writing your research papers. You will find discussions in this book that will help: see Chapters 37, 38, and 39 for details on writing arguments in the humanities, the social sciences, and the sciences.

EXERCISE 2

Working with roommates, classmates, or friends, generate a collection of assignments from different disciplines that call for writing. Examine the wording of these assignments with care, and answer these questions: What are the key verbs in each assignment? How do these verbs set an action plan for the writer? Does the role of the writer as originator of ideas change

selves. Here, however, they have an example of an issue that can be researched from a variety of perspectives. You may want to ask students to think of other issues that might lend themselves to a multi- or interdisciplinary approach. Students in different disciplines can then speculate on the direction research would take within those disciplines. (You may want to start the discussion off with a relatively general and easy topic to deal with, such as war.)

FOR DISCUSSION

Some students probably have a successful method for generating ideas for research papers; now is the time to let them speak to the rest of the class. You may want to begin a discussion of how to generate ideas by stressing the idea that critical thinking begins as soon as the writer begins contemplating a writing task. Ask students what they do when they begin a research project, and why they begin that way. As different students offer their strategies, encourage others to comment on and compare them to their own strategies. You may even offer some of your own or your colleagues' strategies to further the discussion.

EXERCISE 2

Individual responses

from one assignment to the next? What is discipline-specific about the assignment: its topic? method of analysis? presentation of findings?

33c Generating ideas for the paper

Perhaps you have selected a broad subject, which you may have already begun to restrict and focus. Or you may have started with a question and have begun to follow it up with additional questions. Here, we consider ways of further focusing your work and of searching for information sources about your topic (see 3a-1). Specifically, we will consider (1) how to keep an ongoing research log of your ideas; (2) how to develop a search strategy for preliminary reading; and (3) how to develop a search strategy for more focused reading, leading toward the development of your working thesis.

1 Keep a research log.

Many students find it valuable to keep track of their ideas in a research log. They write down their initial questions in this log and update it as often as possible. The log becomes a running record of all their inspirations, false starts, dead ends, second thoughts, breakthroughs, self-criticisms, and plans.

One technique that is particularly useful at the outset of a project is called *nonstop writing*. Nonstop writing (sometimes called *brainstorming* or *freewriting*) requires you to put pen to paper, consider your topic, and write down anything that occurs to you. Do not stop to revise, fix punctuation or spelling, or cross out bad ideas. Do not even stop to think what to say next—just write. The goal is to generate as many ideas as you possibly can within a limited period of time—say, ten or fifteen minutes. At the end of a session of nonstop writing, you may (or may not) have some useful ideas that you want to pursue.

Here, for example, are some initial ideas generated by brief brainstorming sessions about shopping malls. Note the difference in personal styles: the first is a stream-of-consciousness entry; the second is a list.

1. shopping malls—building these huge places, the bucks, the hype in the community, hanging out, going to buy, being part of the excitement. How similar is it to what people used to do—hundreds of years ago? Could be very much the same. Go to market, see the people, buy the goods. Is the mall the old market, updated?
2. shopping malls
cost of building: how are they financed? who owns them?
design—outside and inside: what are the concerns?
suburban vs. urban malls: differences & similarities
modern mall vs. old-world market: same? different?

Even though these ideas are in crude form, you can see papers beginning to take shape here. As you proceed with your research, keep your log updated.

REFERENCE

Quantic, Diane. "Insights into the Research Process from Student Logs." *Journal of Teaching Writing* 6 (1986): 211–25. Suggests methods for helping students overcome writing blocks resulting from research paper assignments.

ADDITIONAL EXERCISE A

As you begin your research, get yourself a notebook and start keeping the research log. When you first start out, follow the guidelines listed here as if they were rules; doing that will keep you on track. Remember, however, not to worry about whether everything in the log will be relevant to your paper; the purpose of the log is for you to get *everything* down so that you can decide later what's relevant and what isn't. Once you become comfortable with the log, you can treat the guidelines as suggestions rather than rules.

You will want to do this not just to preserve a record of your research (often valuable in itself), but also to allow you to return to initially discarded ideas, which, at a later stage in the paper, may assume new relevance or importance.

Researchers use a log for other purposes, as well.

1. To jot down *sources* and possible sources—not only library sources, but also names and phone numbers of people to interview.
2. To freewrite their *reactions* to the material they are reading and to the people they are interviewing; these reactions may later find their way into the finished paper.
3. To jot down *questions* that occur to them in the process of research, which they intend to pursue later. (For example, when were the first malls built—in the United States, in Europe? What came before the mall? Markets have been around for a long time. What were the first ones like?)
4. To try out and revise ideas for *theses* as their research progresses.

Avoid using your log for actually taking notes on your sources; it is best to do this on notecards or on your computer, so that you can freely rearrange notes as you prepare to write your first draft.

Generating Ideas for Your Paper

The following are three additional strategies for generating ideas. Each will help you consider ways in which to divide a broad topic into smaller, more manageable parts. You will probably be more specific and imaginative in thinking about *parts* of a topic than you will be in thinking about the topic as a whole.

- **Reading:** Read general works that survey your topic. The survey will suggest subdivisions.
- **Brainstorming:** Place your topic at the top of a page and, working for five or ten minutes continuously, list any related phrases or words that come to mind. After generating your list, group related items. Groups with the greatest number of items indicate areas that should prove fertile in developing your paper.
- **Listing attributes:** In a numbered list, jot down all of the attributes, or features, that a broad topic possesses. Then ask of every item on your list: What are its uses? What are its consequences?

2 Talk with your instructor or with other authorities.

Before you start your research, do not neglect another important resource: your instructor. Schedule a conference or visit your instructor during office hours. Your conference may turn into a kind of verbal freewriting ses-

GROUP ACTIVITY

At this stage it would be helpful for students to have a sounding board for their ideas. In groups of three or four, have students discuss their research so far. They can comment on what they've discovered, mention the sources they've consulted, and articulate several of the questions they've come up with. They may even want to read one or two freewriting entries from their logs. Other members of the group can then offer questions and observations of their own, helping individual writers come to terms with their material—at least enough to generate a tentative thesis. This discussion may also alert students to areas in need of further research.

sion, with several unresolved questions remaining at the end of the session —one of which may become the focus of your paper.

3 Focus your ideas.

You have now focused on one or more research questions; you have done some preliminary reading and perhaps have talked to one or two authorities on the subject; and you have begun generating some written ideas. At this point, you have followed the basic writing process by focusing on a topic (3a-1) and have given some thought to your purpose and audience (3a-2, 3).

Based on what you have learned thus far, try refining your research question if you have not already done so. You might even have begun to frame some informed opinions in response to this question. If you attempted to do this earlier, you might not have been ready. You might have reached a conclusion that could not be supported by additional research. Or you might have proceeded to assemble a mass of supporting material without being sufficiently aware of whether you were missing sources in related areas that could enhance (or even refute) your thesis. On the other hand, do not wait too long to formulate a key question and some possible answers. If you wait, your research is likely to be unfocused, and your supporting material may not provide a coherent answer to your central research question. Remember that having selected a research question, you are under no obligation to zealously guard it against all changes. Quite possibly, you will need to adjust your focus—and therefore your key question—as your research and your thinking on a subject develop.

EXERCISE 3

Choose a subject and develop some ideas about it, using one or more of the strategies discussed in this section. Read at least two relevant sources, and then develop a research question for a paper on the subject.

EXERCISE 3

Individual responses

33d Developing a strategy for preliminary research

Beginning systematic research

Research logs and other strategies can help you to record on paper any ideas and information you already have. Conferences with your instructor or experts can also stimulate your thinking on your subject. Still, until you begin a systematic search for sources, your familiarity with the topic will be limited.

Effective search strategies often begin with the most general reference sources: encyclopedias, bibliographic listings, biographical works, and dic-

ESL CUE

Latin American, Asian, Middle Eastern, and African students will not have had the same experience with libraries that American or European students will have had. For many, a library paper means copying from a text without questioning the authority of that text. Most of these students will need an explanation of the concept of the college library paper and careful instruction about plagiarism and how to avoid it. Such concepts may be totally new for some of them, and even the more acculturated might assume that a bibliography

tionaries. These general sources are designed for people who want to familiarize themselves relatively quickly with the basic information about a particular subject. Authors of general sources assume that their readers have little or no prior knowledge of the subjects covered and of the specialized terminology used in the field. If they use specialized terms, they will define them. General sources are also comprehensive in their coverage. But at the same time, by design, they review a subject in less depth than do specialized sources. So you'll want to read the more general sources relatively early in your search.

Consult librarians as a resource.

We list "librarians" as a primary source, because they are a *major* resource too frequently overlooked both by harassed students *and* by instructors. As one of our colleagues has remarked, "Librarians—especially reference librarians—are *essential.*" Librarians have made it their career to know how to find information quickly and efficiently. This does not mean that they will do your research for you. It means they will be happy to direct you to the tools with which to do your own research. Frequently, the key to getting the information you need is simply knowing where to look. The next sections will provide some assistance in this area. Your reference librarian will be able not only to supplement our list of sources (see 33-f), but also to tell you which ones are best for your purposes.

The diagram on the next page suggests an approach for conducting systematic research. Certainly, there are other avenues into the source materials you will discover. Whatever strategy you follow, try to be systematic. Your efforts at this stage will help you to focus your topic, restricting it to a manageable scope.

Having focused your subject, you can then locate additional information, both from (1) periodicals and newspapers, which you locate through indexes and abstracts and/or computer search; and (2) books, which you locate through the card catalog and/or computer searches. During this part of your search, you may further refine your topic, and you can consult additional books and articles as necessary, along with additional reference sources such as biographical dictionaries, specialized dictionaries, and book reviews.

The second diagram, on page 541, illustrates the focusing and selection process of student researcher Jason Koman in his search for materials on shopping malls. The broadest possible related subject search is "retail sales." Clearly, this is too broad a topic for an eight- to ten-page paper, so the search is focused to sales originating at mail-order houses and stores. Again, more selection and focusing brings Jason to his initial topic of shopping malls. Having read a general source on the topic, he quickly sees the need to restrict the topic still more; guided by additional reading, he identifies four elements of interest, all related to shopping malls: competition, history, role in the U.S. economy, and construction. Any of these areas would provide an appropriate scope for an eight- to ten-page paper. Jason chooses history as his focus. Continued reading in this more specialized area yields a wealth of information that he can work with, comfortably, in an eight- to ten-page paper.

is a license to borrow indiscriminately from sources. The idea of a personal thesis for such a paper will seem strange, as will the idea of evaluating and judging sources. Such practices are culturally determined and should not be considered universal practices to be taken for granted.

Many ESL students come from cultures where students customarily work together on assignments, and some Asians and Middle Easterners in particular have a tradition of the stronger students helping the weaker, with no stigma attached and with no shame at identical answers. Consequently, all forms of plagiarism must be made quite clear and the American attitude toward plagiarism repeated and reinforced or it may not be observed.

TEACHING IDEAS

Students might find it reassuring to use this diagram as a map of their writing process. You may want to ask them to either photocopy the diagram or draw it in their research logs. They can then mark the diagram in much the same way as layout maps for large buildings or malls are marked, with a "you are here" symbol. As that symbol moves through the diagram, students will get the reassurance they need that they are indeed accomplishing something, even though they're far from ready to start the paper. (In fact, they'll also find themselves going back in the diagram on occasion; this can serve as a reminder that research—as all writing—is a recursive process.)

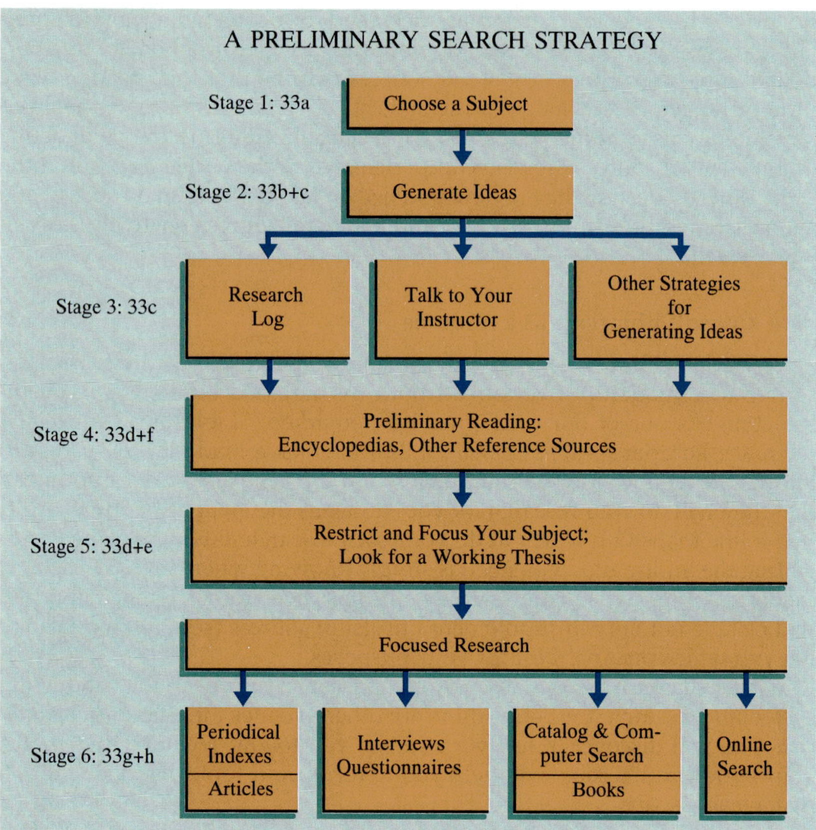

2 Refining your thinking with systematic research

Systematic reading can help you to refine your thinking about a topic. New sources can lead you to a revised research question. Again, Jason Koman's experience provides a good illustration.

A bit too early in the process, Jason settled on his research question: *What is a mall?* Before consulting most of the sources that he would end up using in his paper, he hazarded an answer: *The shopping mall is our modern equivalent of the ancient marketplace.* As Jason continued to read, he found his answer to be premature and, indeed, his question to be limiting. Further reading in detailed sources revealed that the modern mall is *not* an exact equivalent of the ancient markets, in at least one crucial respect. This key difference, Jason realized, could provide the final focus for his paper. He determined to focus on similarities and differences in the context of a newly refined question: *What do we want at the mall?* This new question enabled him to explore people's motivations for gathering in marketplaces—both modern and ancient.

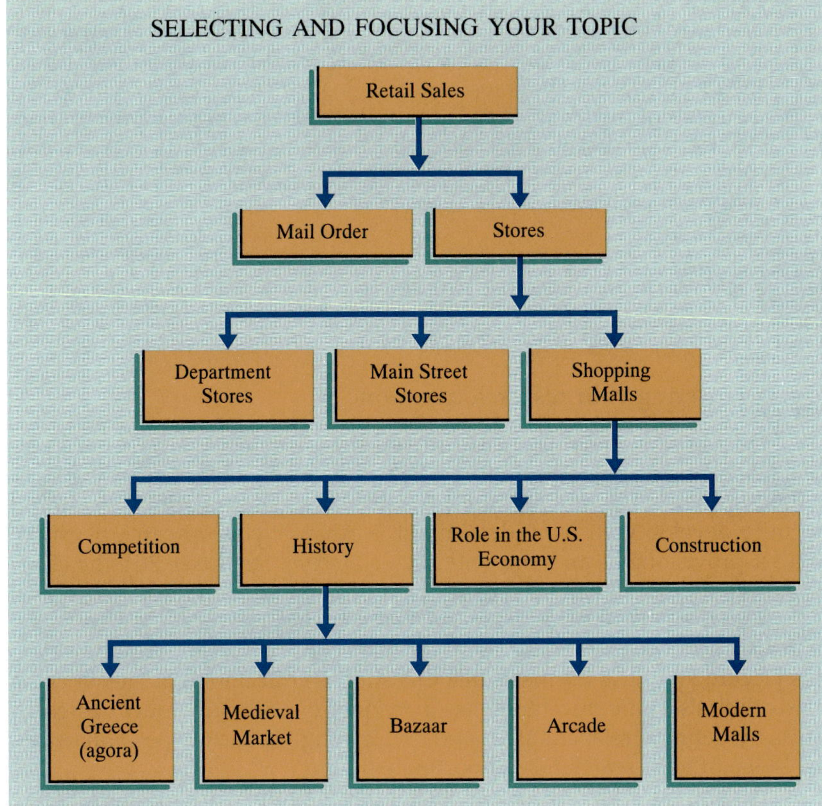

3 Bringing your research to an end

You should recognize that any diagram of the search strategy or of the focusing procedure makes these processes look neater than they generally are. In practice, they are often considerably less systematic, because writing is such a recursive process—as shown in 3a-1 and 3d-3. It is crucial to keep in mind the kinds of resources and procedures that are available to you, and—given the constraints on your time—to use as many as you can.

As you proceed, you will discover that research is to some extent a self-generating process. That is, one source will lead you—through references in the text, citations, and bibliographic entries—to others. Authors will refer to other studies on the subject; and frequently, they will indicate which ones they believe are the most important, and why. At some point you will realize that you have already looked at most of the key research on the subject. This is the point at which you can be reasonably assured that the research stage of your project is nearing its end.

REFERENCES

FORD, JAMES E. "The Research Loop: Helping Students Find Periodical Sources." *CCC* 37 (1986): 223–27. Offers a "research loop" that takes students (and their instructors) through a systematic research process.

KLEINE, MICHAEL. "What Is It We Do When We Write Papers Like This One—and How Can We Get Students to Join Us?" *The Writing Instructor* 6 (1987): 151–61. Advances a "hunting and gathering" metaphor for the research process, affirming that writing the research paper is a discovery process that works best in a community of peers.

SCHMERSAHL, CARMEN B. "Teaching Library Research: Process, Not Product." *Journal of Teaching Writing* 6 (1987): 231–38. A set of assignments introduces students to how the library may be used for researching writing projects.

SCHWEGLER, ROBERT A., and LINDA K. SHAMOON. "The Aims and Processes of the Research Paper." *CE* 44 (1982): 817–24. All research papers (academic and student) first "review" the research and then develop one of three patterns: work with a theory; "refute, refine, or replicate prior research"; or challenge a hypothesis.

TRYZNA, THOMAS N. "Research Outside the Library: Learning a Field." *CCC* 37 (1986): 217–23. A great deal of important, current information may not be discovered in using traditional library sources (provides useful lists of sources).

EXERCISE 4

Individual responses

TEACHING IDEAS

Select one of the four disciplines for which examples of narrowed topics are given. Discuss further narrowing of the topics. For example, when considering the safety of genetically altered foods, discuss criteria by which "safety" is defined. As practice for articulating their view on a question of importance, ask students to brainstorm, write down, and discuss a working thesis about each narrowed topic.

EXERCISE 4

Working with your topic, begin preliminary research. Start keeping a research log. Read one or two general reference sources; from these, try restricting the focus of your topic. As you do so, identify several sources that more specifically address your research needs. Having read one or more of these sources, can you refine your research question? Check on your success in focusing your topic by creating a diagram similar to the one on the preceding page.

33e Devising a working thesis

1 Answering your research question

During your preliminary reading you began to focus on a *research question.* Jason Koman's question was: What do people want when they go to a shopping mall? As you continue to read about your subject, you should begin to develop your own ideas about it. Answer your research question, at least provisionally, and you will have a *working thesis* (see 3d): the clearest, most succinct statement thus far of your paper's main idea.

This thesis is *provisional:* it is subject to change as you come across new material and as your thinking about the subject develops. For now, however, this working thesis is the main idea that shapes your thinking. The working thesis will also influence the focused reading of your subsequent research since, by defining relevant areas and eliminating irrelevant ones, it narrows the scope of your search for supporting evidence.

For the sake of convenience, let's examine four working theses. Here are four discipline areas, and four narrowed topics:

For a paper in the *humanities,* the topic is nineteenth century literature about the potential excesses of science, for example, in *Frankenstein* and *Dr. Jekyll and Mr. Hyde.*

For a paper in *business,* the issue is who owns the information contained in genetic algorithms.

For a paper in the *social sciences,* the topic is social and ethical issues in technological intervention in human reproduction.

For a paper in *science,* the topic is whether genetically altered food products are safe.

2 Taking a stand: The working thesis as a statement to be proven

So far, these are only *topics*—not theses. To develop a working thesis from each of these topics, you will need to make a *statement* about the topic (after surveying a good deal of source material). Here are four statements that can be used as working theses:

Humanities: Frankenstein was perhaps the first in a long line of books to exploit people's nervousness about scientific progress.

Business: Companies employing genetic engineers try to be diligent about patenting their discoveries.

Social Science: Safeguards need to be strengthened to protect infertile couples being promised "miracle cures" from the latest expensive medical procedure.

Science: Biotechnology promises to improve the *quantity* of food, but quantity will mean little unless we can guarantee the safety of genetically altered foods.

Note that while each thesis requires that the writer support his or her opinion, the first two theses tend to be *informative,* whereas the second two tend to be *argumentative.* That is, in each of the first two cases, the thesis itself is not a particularly controversial one; it is not a proposition that normally generates strong emotions. In the latter two cases, however, the writer will argue one side of a fairly controversial issue. These are issues on which it is sometimes difficult to get people to change their minds, even after considering the evidence, because they have strong underlying feelings about them. The stand you take in the thesis may depend on your ambition for the paper (see 3d-3), as well as on the materials available and the conditions that apply to your argument (see 6d-1, 2, 3).

EXERCISE 5

Based on your preliminary reading in general sources (Exercise 4), develop two working thesis statements about your topic: an *informative thesis* and an *argumentative thesis.* Make sure that each thesis takes the form of a *statement* about the topic.

33f Doing preliminary research and reading

If you follow the strategy for preliminary research presented earlier, you will begin your research efforts with a systematic review of general sources. In this section, we will review some of the most useful general sources.

1 Encyclopedias, bibliographies, dictionaries

Encyclopedias

A general encyclopedia is a comprehensive, often multivolume work that covers events, subjects, people, and places across the spectrum of human knowledge. The articles, usually written by specialists, offer a broad overview of the subjects covered. From an encyclopedia you may discover a particular aspect of the subject that interests you and see how that aspect relates

EXERCISE 5

Individual responses

ADDITIONAL EXERCISE B

Having developed a tentative thesis, you're now ready to do some serious research. Bring your thesis and a few notes from your research log to the library and seek out a reference librarian. (If your library is a small one, you may want to call ahead and find out when the reference librarian is available.) Ask the librarian to help you decide where to look to find more information about your topic. Make sure to take notes in your research log so that you won't forget the directions you've received.

TEACHING IDEAS

Some students will have to be reminded more than once that encyclopedias should be used to provide background material only. Many students have been able to cite encyclopedias as sources in high school reports, and most students will be familiar with the ads for encyclopedias on MTV and VH1—ads that clearly present encyclopedias as the only source you'll need for a lengthy report.

to the subject in general. Encyclopedia entries on major subjects frequently include bibliographies.

Keep in mind that encyclopedias—particularly general encyclopedias—are frequently not considered legitimate sources of information for college-level papers. Thus, while you may want to use an encyclopedia article to familiarize yourself with the subject matter of the field and to locate specific topics within that field, you probably should not use it as a major source, or indeed, for anything other than background information.

One disadvantage of encyclopedias is that since new editions are published only once every several years, they frequently do not include the most up-to-date information on a subject. Naturally, this is of more concern in some areas than others: if you are writing on the American Revolution, you are on safer ground consulting an encyclopedia than if you are writing on whether doctors consider alcoholism a disease. Still, the nature of scholarship is that *any* subject—including the American Revolution—is open to reinterpretation and the discovery of new knowledge, so use encyclopedias with due caution.

Following are some of the most frequently used general encyclopedias:

American Academic Encyclopedia
Collier's Encyclopedia
Columbia Encyclopedia
Encyclopedia Americana
Encyclopædia Britannica

Biographical sources

Frequently, you have to look up information on particular people. Note that some biographical sources are classified according to whether the person is living or dead. The following are some of the most common biographical sources:

FOR PERSONS STILL LIVING

American Men and Women of Science
Contemporary Authors: A Biographical Guide to Current Authors and Their Works
Current Biography
Directory of American Scholars
International Who's Who

FOR PERSONS LIVING OR DEAD

American Novelists Since World War II
Biography Almanac
American Poets Since World War II
Contemporary American Composers: A Biographical Dictionary

McGraw-Hill Encyclopedia of World Biography
National Academy of Sciences, Biographical Memoirs
Webster's Biographical Dictionary

Dictionaries

Dictionaries enable you to look up the meaning of particular terms. As with encyclopedias, dictionaries may be either general or specialized in scope. Some of the more common dictionaries are listed in 22b-1.

2 Other print sources of information

In addition to encyclopedias, biographical sources, and dictionaries, you may find the following sources useful.

Guides to the literature enable you to locate and use reference sources within particular disciplines. Here are five examples:

Reference Books: A Brief Guide
How and Where to Look It Up: A Guide to Standard Sources of Information
Sources of Information in the Social Sciences
Guide to Historical Literature
Business Information Sources

Handbooks provide facts and lists of data for particular disciplines. Here are several examples:

Handbook of Chemistry and Physics
The Allyn & Bacon Handbook (covers grammar and style)
Handbook of Basic Economic Statistics
Statistical Abstract of the United States
Gallup Poll: Public Opinion

Almanacs also provide facts and lists of data, but are generally issued annually:

Information Please Almanac (general)
The World Almanac (general)
Almanac of American Politics
Congressional Quarterly Almanac
Dow Jones Irwin Business Almanac

Yearbooks, issued annually, update data already published in encyclopedias and other reference sources:

Americana Annual
Britannica Book of the Year
Statesman's Yearbook

ADDITIONAL EXERCISE C

ACROSS THE CURRICULUM As stated earlier in the chapter, among the best sources of information available to you as you write research papers are instructors in the disciplines. Seek out an instructor in a discipline related to your research interests and ask him or her about the standard reference tools used by professionals in that field. Make note of the references and check them against the list in the handbook, compiling your own personal list of reference works.

TEACHING IDEAS

For a comprehensive, "user-friendly" reference book for general research (including some academic research), refer students to *The New York Public Library Book of How and Where to Look It Up*, edited by Sherwood Harris (Stonesong Press, 1992).

Atlases and gazetteers provide maps and other geographical data:

National Atlas of the United States of America
Times Atlas of the World

Citation indexes indicate when and where a given work has been cited *after* its initial publication; these are useful for tracing the influence of a particular work:

Social Science Citation Index
Humanities Citation Index
Science Citation Index

Book review indexes provide access to book reviews; these are useful for evaluating the scope, quality, and reliability of a particular source:

Book Review Digest (includes excerpts from reviews)
Book Review Index

Government publications are numerous and frequently offer recent and authoritative information in a particular field:

American Statistics Index
Congressional Information Service
The Congressional Record
Government Manual
Guide to U.S. Government Publications
Information U.S.A.
Monthly Catalogue of U.S. Government Publications

Consult your librarian for information on guides to the literature, almanacs, and other reference guides relevant to your subject.

Library of Congress Subject Headings

If you are making a systematic search to refine your subject, you should probably check the *Library of Congress Subject Headings.* This is a set of volumes that indicates how the subjects listed according to the Library of Congress System are broken down. For example, drug abuse is broken down into such subtopics as "religious aspects," "social aspects," and "treatment." You can use the *Library of Congress Subject Headings* as you would use encyclopedia entries or the *Bibliographic Index* below. First, you can survey the main aspects of that subject. Second, you can select a particular aspect that interests you. Third, you can focus your subject search (in both the book and periodical indexes) on the particular aspect or subtopic that interests you, since these subtopics indicate the headings to look under in these indexes.

Bibliographic Index

Although we will cover periodical indexes later (see 33g-2), it is appropriate to mention here the *Bibliographic Index* as an excellent research tool both for browsing through some of the subtopics of a subject and for directing you to additional sources. The *Bibliographic Index* is an annual bibliography of bibliographies (that is, a bibliography that lists other bibliographies), arranged by subject. Shown below, for example, is the listing under "Shopping-centers" in the 1993 *Bibliographic Index.*

Each of these listings represents a bibliography that appears in another source—a book, a pamphlet, or an article. In most cases, the bibliography appears as a source of additional readings at the conclusion of the book, the chapter, or the article. In some cases, however, the bibliography stands by itself as an independent publication. If you browse through a few successive years of listings on a subject, you will probably discover some topics that interest you, as well as a source of readings on that topic.

Main heading — **Shopping centers**
See also
Entry under other main heading — Retail trade
Design
O'Neill, M. J. and Jasper, C. R. An evaluation of models of consumer spatial behavior using the environment-behavior paradigm. *Environ Behav* 24:438–40 Jl '92 — Title of periodical; Volume: page number(s)
Subheading — **Design and construction**
Goss, J. The "magic of the mall": an analysis of form, function, and meaning in the contemporary retail built environment. *Ann Assoc Am Geogr* 83:44–7 Mr '93 — Date of periodical
Great Britain
Location
Author — Brown, Stephen. Retail location; a micro-scale perspective. Avebury 1992 p242–310 — Publisher and date

3 General electronic sources

There are two types of electronic database resources: CD-ROM disks and online material. Most periodical indexes that are available in print (such as *Readers' Guide* and *Humanities Index*) are also available on CD-ROM. Since a CD can store several years' worth of indexes, a CD search takes less time and effort than a search through several bound volumes. Many general-reference print materials, such as *The Oxford English Dictionary* and various encyclopedias, are currently available on CD-ROM—a format that allows users to make rapid cross-references and searches.

One important CD index is InfoTrac, which provides access to articles in over 1,000 business, technological, and general-interest periodicals, as well as the *New York Times* and the *Wall Street Journal.* Some specialized reference works on CD-ROM can be particularly interesting and rich in resources, depending on your research topic; a renowned example is the *Perseus* CD-ROM program from Harvard University Press, a large compendium of material on the classical world, including social, archaeological, literary, and linguistic material from classics scholarship.

ADDITIONAL EXERCISE D

If you're still narrowing your topic, use this sample listing in the *Bibliographic Index* to guide you through a search for sources on possible topics for your research paper. Let the subheadings in the index help you narrow your topic, and make notes on sources that seem promising to you.

Consult your librarian, who will have a listing of CD-ROMs that you can use in your research.

Online electronic sources

Electronic online resources are rapidly expanding. Online services usually originate off-campus. You will be able to access information in three ways:

- Your school library will likely subscribe to one or more databases—perhaps including LEXIS/NEXIS or DIALOG. These will give you access to tens of thousands of full-text articles.
- From a dorm room or home you can access online services such as CompuServe, Prodigy, or America Online—all of which provide a broad array of material ranging from entertainment to travel to educational forums to virtual libraries.
- You can access the worldwide network of computers known as the Internet through America Online and other commercial services, through a school account, or through software that you acquire (such as Netscape) and a phone link. Even if you already have a commercial account for which you are paying, in all likelihood you are eligible for a free Internet account through your college or university.

Why use the Internet? The Internet consists of tens of thousands of host computers, located worldwide, that exist to provide information. Whatever your topic, you will likely find some Internet site—a host computer offering a rich database of information—that can provide you with pertinent source materials. Consider some advantages of Internet research:

- The array of available information on the Internet is broad and is accessible to your computer wherever you work. The Internet will greatly expand your research options.
- Unlike print resources, which may not be available when you need them, once you've located an Internet source, it is always "in"—on the shelf, so to speak, available for your immediate use and storage.

While the Internet offers you revolutionary access to information, once you've located and downloaded information you will treat this material as a source, one among many. It is important to keep your main goal as a writer clearly before you: to write an effective, original paper. What you *do* with your sources (e.g., can you reason soundly with them?) matters far more than where you found them—in your college's print library or online, in a database halfway around the world. The wonders of our digital age notwithstanding, the role of the researcher remains central and unchanged: to evaluate individual sources; to read multiple sources on a single topic; and to synthesize those sources into a coherent, original paper.

No one owns or technically even manages the Internet, so you will find it an unruly thicket of information, stored in a wide assortment of formats on computers around the world. When accessing the Internet, you will travel virtually to these computer sites and will (1) browse to locate promising information; (2) locate particular information, which exists as a computer file; and (3) transfer files to your computer (or your user area on your school's mainframe). As you would do with any source, you would then read and evaluate; take notes; and draw connections among sources as you develop a paper.

You will find no comprehensive card catalog or easy way of finding *all* the information you need on the Internet. The good news is that each of the major modes of accessing the Internet has its own way of searching for and retrieving information, so you won't be reduced to random browsing in the hope you'll find useful material. Just as you do in library research, you can undertake methodical and comprehensive searches on the Internet. Search strategies are discussed in 33h-2.

Using General Sources

- Use *encyclopedias* to get a broad overview of a particular subject.
- Use *biographical sources* to look up information about persons living or dead.
- Use *general dictionaries* to look up the meaning of particular terms.
- Use *guides to the literature* to locate reference sources in particular disciplines.
- Use *handbooks* to look up facts and lists of data for particular disciplines.
- Use *almanacs* to look up annually updated facts and lists of data.
- Use *yearbooks* to find updates of data already published in encyclopedias and other reference sources.
- Use *atlases* and *gazetteers* to find maps and other geographical data.
- Use *citation indexes* to trace references to a given work after its initial publication.
- Use *book review indexes* to look up book reviews.
- Use *government publications* to look up recent and authoritative information in a given field.
- Use *bibliographic sources* to locate books and articles on a particular subject.
- Use *electronic sources* to locate large databases and current information.

EXERCISE 6

Use your working thesis to guide your access to one or more of the reference materials listed in this section. Keep a record of the sources used (keep full bibliographic information, including electronic access information if you browse the Internet or use an online service). Take notes on each source.

EXERCISE 6

Individual responses

33g Doing focused research: Print sources and interviews

If you have looked through a number of general sources, you have probably also developed a working thesis. At this point, you have some basic knowledge about your subject and some tentative ideas about it. But there are limits to your knowledge—which correspond to the limits of the kinds of sources you have relied on so far. You need more specific information to pursue your thesis.

1 Looking for specific sources

General sources are not intended to provide in-depth knowledge, nor can they explore more than a few of the often numerous aspects of a subject. Refer back to the diagram on page 541. If you were researching the subject of retail sales, your general sources might be sufficient to get you to the fourth level of the diagram, but the sources' inherent limitations would prevent them from taking you any further. For information about the kind of topics on the fifth level—details on the markets of ancient Greece and medieval Europe, bazaars, arcades, and malls—you would need to do more focused reading. You need a strategy for locating information in articles and books, either online or in the library, or via interviews.

2 Finding print materials in libraries

The following overview of available sources will help you focus on the ones that best address your working thesis. This overview will start with articles in order to emphasize the fact that periodical indexes are often preferable to the library catalog (formerly called the card catalog) as a first step in conducting focused research. Note that the search process for most print sources involves searching by author, title, and subject. For good *subject* topics, refer back to the *Library of Congress Subject Headings,* described in 33f-2.

General periodical indexes: Magazines

Periodicals are magazines and newspapers published at regular intervals—quarterly, monthly, daily. Periodical articles often contain information available from no other source and are generally more up-to-date than books published during the same period. You are probably familiar with the *Readers' Guide to Periodical Literature* as a means of locating magazine articles, but there are numerous other periodical reference guides.

For example, consider *Ulrich's International Periodicals Directory.* This is not a periodical index, but rather a subject guide to periodicals; that is, it directs you to periodicals on a given subject. To find out more about the nature or scope of a particular magazine, check *Katz's Magazines for Libraries.* This reference tool lists the most commonly used magazines and offers basic descriptive and evaluative information about each.

TEACHING IDEAS

The reference room of the library can be an intimidating place for a first-year college student. You may want to arrange a class visit to the library—perhaps even coordinate a guided tour with the reference librarian. Most reference librarians are eager to assist instructors with research assignments. If you provide the librarian with information on the research questions your students are addressing, he or she can develop a personalized workshop to help students find their way through indexes, bibliographies, and the like. The group approach also makes students feel more at ease about asking questions, since they know that questions are expected in sessions like this.

FOR DISCUSSION

Some students will already be familiar with the *Readers' Guide,* having used it since middle school to locate sources. For the benefit of those unfamiliar with this resource, ask students to talk about their experiences with it: How easy or difficult is it to find in the library? How easy or difficult is it to use? What do you do when your topic isn't listed? How do you determine the complete information about the sources you find in the index?

Like encyclopedias, periodical indexes are of two types: *general* and *specialized.* The most commonly used general periodical index is, of course, the *Readers' Guide to Periodical Literature,* which indexes magazines of general interest such as *Time, Newsweek, U.S. News and World Report, The New Republic, Sports Illustrated, Commonweal.* Here, for example, is a recent *Readers' Guide* entry for "shopping" and "shopping centers." The first entry is from the print volume; the one that follows is from the *Readers' Guide* CD-ROM database.

SHOPPING — Main heading

See also

Bargains
Electronic shopping
Haggling (Shopping)
Mail order business
Sales
Secondhand trade
Stores
Warehouse clubs

— Entries under other main headings

4 star shoppers [E. Quaid, A. Harlech, O. Schnabel and K. McMenamy] il pors *Vogue* v185 p334-9 Ap '95

Better shop around? S. K. Hoge. *National Review* v47 p54-5 My 1 '95

Hey, big spender! Are you shopping your way to credit card hell? [young women] M. Joseph. il *Sassy* v8 p66-9 My '95

Health aspects

The healthy shopper. C. Frank. il *Ladies' Home Journal* v111 p72 D '94 — Includes picture

Subheading — **Psychological aspects**

See also

Compulsive shopping

France

Gallic gallerias. C. Carter. il *Condé Nast Traveler* v30 p120-1 My '95

Japan

Bargains, with honor [Tokyo] E. Lederman. il *Condé Nast Traveler* v30 p88+ Mr '95 — Title of periodical

SHOPPING CENTERS

Don't fence him in [Ivan the gorilla, formerly a Tacoma, Wash. shopping center mascot, now lives in Atlanta Zoo] il *People Weekly* v43 p61 Ap 3 '95 — Subject of article, if not clear from title

Shopping with Leslie Wexner [City Center Mall, Columbus, Ohio] il *Forbes* v155 p131 Je 5 '95

What it will take to keep people hanging out at the mall. K. Labich. il *Fortune* v131 p102-6 My 29 '95 — Author; Volume, pages, date of issue

SHOPPING MALLS *See* Shopping centers — Cross-reference

If you had located the last entry on an electronic search, the screen or printout would look like this:

```
READERS' GUIDE TO PERIODICAL LIT              Data Coverage: 1/85 thru 11/30/95
                    Line    1 of    8 Lines                                READY
áááááááááááááááááááááááááááááááááááááááááááááááááááááááááááááááááááááááááááááááá
Multiple subject search (Wilsearch) PRINT MODE        4 of 73 Entries
áááááááááááááááááááááááááááááááááááááááááááááááááááááááááááááááááááááááááááááááá
  #4
      AUTHOR:  Labich, Kenneth
       TITLE:  What it will take to keep people hanging out at the mall
      SOURCE:  Fortune  (ISSN:0015-8259) v 131 p 102-6 May 29 '95
    CONTAINS:  illustration(s)
  SUBJECTS COVERED:
  Shopping centers
```


ADDITIONAL EXERCISE E

Assuming you have a narrowed topic for your research paper, look it up in a newspaper index. Follow the guidelines provided in this section. If your primary interest is the *New York Times* or another indexed newspaper, then use the appropriate index to locate relevant sources. If you're looking for an article in another newspaper, then use the story dates from the index to help you find relevant source material.

TEACHING IDEAS

InfoTrac has become an immensely popular resource for students and faculty alike. But it's so easy to use that sometimes students don't bother to find out about its limitations. The index only lists articles that have appeared roughly within the last three years; thus, students will have to use other sources to find older material. Furthermore, students should be advised to always take down complete information on each relevant listing. Because the index is constantly updated, a three-year-old listing found during an initial search may well have been deleted by the time the paper is in the draft stages and the writer is checking source information.

Another useful general periodical index is the *Essay and General Literature Index,* which indexes (by subject, author, and sometimes by title) articles and essays that have been collected into books. The index is especially useful in that it gives you access to material that might not otherwise have surfaced in your search. These articles and essays generally would be classified under the humanities, but some deal with social science issues as well.

General periodical indexes: Newspapers

Most libraries have back issues of important newspapers on microfilm. The *New York Times Index* may be used to retrieve articles in the *Times* as far back as 1913. There are also indexes for the *San Francisco Chronicle,* the *Los Angeles Times,* and the *Wall Street Journal* (an important source of business news). The *Newspaper Index* lists articles from the *Chicago Tribune,* the *New Orleans Times-Picayune,* the *Los Angeles Times,* and the *Washington Post.* You can print out "hard copies" (from microfilm) of articles you need. If you're looking for articles in newspapers other than these, check dates of stories in the *New York Times Index,* or see whether the newspaper has a search service.

Following is a sample entry on "shopping centers" from the *New York Times Index.* Notice that the entry refers readers to "Retail Stores and Trade," the heading under which most of the articles on shopping centers appear.

SHOPPING CENTERS. See also
Airports, O 2
Food, F 2
Real Estate, Ja 19
Retail Stores and Trade, Ja 5,20,26,28,29, F 3,5,9,16,23, Mr 1,3,5,15,18,22,25,27,29, Ap 1,5,9,12,20,21,26, My 3,10,15, 24,29, Je 14,19,21,28, Jl 5, 12,26,30, Ag 2,9,18,20,21,30 S 13,27,30, O 18,23,25, N 8,15,24,25,27, D 7,10,13

Entries under other headings

Listed under "Retail Stores and Trade" are the entries noted above for August 18–30, 1992:

GE Capital Corp unit buys 47 shopping centers from Resolution Trust Corp for $71 million in cash; shopping centers are in nine states (S), Ag 18,D,4:1

J C Penney Co, GTE Spacenet and Capital Cities/ABC Inc say they are working on formation of joint venture to provide audio, video and data communication services to retailers in shopping malls around country; venture is called Advanced Retail Communications (S), Ag 20,D,4:4

Addis & Dey's, last of big downtown department stores, Syracuse, NY, is set to close despite efforts of city's leaders to rebuild downtown area and store's rent-free use of city-owned building; closure is symbol of inability of large downtown stores to compete with suburban malls; photos (M), Ag 21,B,1:2

Topics of The Times column notes that while New York does not have glorious leaves of New England's autumn, city does have indoor 'autumn,' in its freezingly air-conditioned department stores, Ag 26,A,20:2

Article on gigantic new Mall of America in Bloomington, Minnesota; 4.2-million-square-foot complex includes specialty stores catering to every demographic group, as well as giant movie theater, numerous eateries and Camp Snoopy, world's largest indoor amusement park; photos; developer Nader Ghermezian also built Canada's West Edmonton Mall, still world's largest with 5.2 million square feet (M), Ag 30,IX,5:1

Staten Island Mall begins $50-million expansion that includes renovation and addition of new stores; rendering (S), Ag 30,X,1:1

Relevant stories are listed in chronological order

Date of story, section no., page no., column no.

Major stories in boldface

Description of story

The library catalog

Almost certainly, your library's catalog has been converted to electronic form, allowing you to search for items far more quickly than you could when they were filed on cards. You can search the catalog by *author,* by *title,* or by *subject.* (A typical keyboard command might be "f a Morrison, Toni" (for *find* items by the *author* Toni Morrison). Many library catalog terminals also allow access to magazine and newspaper databases such as MAGS and NEWS. In some cases, you can view (or print out) abstracts or even complete texts of particular items that you locate in such indexes. Electronic catalogs are much more current than print indexes, since they are updated far more frequently. In addition, electronic magazine and newspaper catalogs generally allow you to search more publications at once than their print counterparts, and they almost always cover a greater period of time—usually several years. The disadvantage is that electronic databases generally don't include information more than ten years old. Thus you would still have to rely largely on print indexes for information about—for example—the Watergate scandal of the 1970s.

Browsing through some of the subject entries is a good way of locating books on your topic; but before you do this, you should have at least begun to narrow your subject. Otherwise, you could be overwhelmed with the sheer number of books available. (There may be several hundred books on various aspects of shopping centers.)

Notice the call number in the upper left-hand corner of the entry. One or more letters preceding the number indicates that the book has been cataloged according to the Library of Congress System, the most common cataloging system for larger libraries. Smaller libraries use the Dewey Decimal System, which always begins with a number. If, for example, you are doing literary research in a library that uses the Library of Congress System, most of the books you will need will likely have call numbers beginning with "PR" (English literature) or "PS" (American Literature); if you are working on a political science paper, you will probably be looking in the "E" section. In a library using the Dewey Decimal System, literary books are in the 800 series and political science books are in the 300 series. Check the reference desk at your library for a key to the cataloging system. The reference desk should also have a library map or shelving guide that will enable you to locate the books or bound periodicals that you need. Be certain that you accurately copy down the call numbers; a missing or incorrect letter or number may send you to the wrong section.

Shown below are an online catalog entry (or screen) and a card catalog (author) card for *The Malling of America: An Inside Look at the Great Consumer Paradise* by William S. Kowinski. One advantage of using the computer catalog is that the displayed item may provide circulation information—whether the book is on the shelf, checked out (and if so, when it is due back), or on reserve.

The convenience of electronic catalog searching should not blind you to the old-fashioned advantages and pleasures of going into the stacks and browsing among the shelves in your area of interest. Browsing is not an ef-

ADDITIONAL EXERCISE F

Whether your library has a computerized cataloging system or a card catalog, this exercise should help you become familiar with the library. Record the call numbers and complete publishing information for the books listed under your topic. (You will probably find that most books share similar call numbers.) Now use the library's map or shelving guide to find the stacks where the books are located. After you have found the books you're interested in, browse the shelves for others that may be relevant. Make sure to take down all essential information on books you may use in your research.

FOR DISCUSSION

Not all students are aware of the reasons for searching by subject, author, or title. Ask the class to comment on situations in which each of these searches might be undertaken. Those students more comfortable with library research can enlighten less experienced students regarding the usefulness of the three categories.

ficient or comprehensive substitute for methodical catalog searching: some important books may be checked out or shelved in another area. But opening promising titles and examining the contents may reveal valuable sources that you might otherwise have overlooked.

Computer display

```
AUTHOR         Kowinski, William Severini.
TITLE          The malling of America: an inside look
               at the great consumer paradise / William
               Severini Kowinski.
EDITION        1st ed.
IMPRINT        New York : W. Morrow, c 1985
DESCRIPT       415 p. : ill. ; 25 cm.
NOTE           Includes index.
ISN/MUSIC#     0688041809.
SUBJECT        Shopping malls -- United States.

LOCATION            CALL NO.              STATUS
1>Mugar             HF5430.3.K68 1985
```

Catalog (author) card

```
HF
5430.3      Kowinski, William Severini.
K68         The malling of America: an inside
1985        look at the great consumer paradise /
            William Severini Kowinski. -- 1st ed.
            -- New York: W. Morrow, c 1985.
            415 p.: ill.; 25 cm.
            Includes index.
            ISBN 0-688-04180-9

            1. Shopping malls -- United States.
           I. Title
MBNU                         NEDDuc86-114508r872
```

Book Review Digest

An invaluable source for determining the quality of books is the *Book Review Digest.* This publication, collected into annual volumes, indexes many of the most important books published during a given year by author, title, and subject. More important, it provides lists of reviews of those books, as well as brief excerpts from some of the reviews. Thus, you can use the *Book Review Digest* to quickly determine not only the scope of a given book (each entry leads off with an objective summary) but also how well that book has been received by reviewers. If the reviews are almost uniformly good, that book will be a good source of information. If they are almost uniformly bad, stay away. If the reviews are mixed, proceed with caution.

Trade bibliographies and bibliographies of books

For books too recent to have been acquired by your library or that the library does not have, you may wish to consult *Books in Print* and *Paperbound Books in Print.* These volumes, organized by author, title, and subject, are available in some libraries and in most bookstores. For books that your library does not have, but that may be in other libraries, consult the *Cumulative Book Index* and the *National Union Catalog.*

Focused Reading for Print Material

- To locate articles in general-interest magazines, use the *Readers' Guide to Periodical Literature,* the *Readers' Guide CD-ROM Index, InfoTrac,* or another database index.
- To locate articles in newspapers, use the *New York Times Index* or other indexes for particular newspapers.
- To identify periodicals specializing in a given subject, use *Ulrich's International Periodicals Directory.*
- To determine the scope of a particular magazine, use *Katz's Magazines for Libraries.*
- To locate books and government publications, use the *library catalog.*
- To determine how a given subject is subclassified in the library catalog, use the *Library of Congress Subject Headings Index.*
- To locate reviews of books, see the *Book Review Digest.*

EXERCISE 7

Researching either the topic you have been working on or some other topic, locate at least five books and ten articles on the subject. Provide complete bibliographic information for these sources (see 34b). Locate several reviews of at least one of the books, and summarize the main responses in a paragraph.

TEACHING IDEAS

Students engaged in literary research will find yet another use for *Book Review Digest.* You may want to remind them that frequently book reviews, especially the extensive reviews found in the *New York Times,* the *Times Literary Supplement,* and the *New York Review of Books,* are at least in part literary analyses. Particularly with regard to contemporary works, students should not overlook the value of *Book Review Digest* as a resource for literature research papers.

FOR DISCUSSION

As students begin their research projects, it will be helpful to them (and to you in the long run) to review their progress periodically. A discussion of the value of the items in the box will allow students to assess their progress so far, to help one another with problem sources, and to fill in gaps in their research. Such a discussion will also alert you early on regarding potential problems in particular students' projects.

EXERCISE 7

Individual responses

TEACHING IDEAS

You may want to add some of your own guidelines for evaluating sources, such as finding sources that represent a variety of viewpoints, checking to see if an author has a vested interest in one side of an argument, and checking up on other pieces the author has written.

GROUP ACTIVITY

You may want to offer students the opportunity to take a "dry run" before they conduct their actual interviews. After students have prepared interview questions on a given topic (either their own or one you've assigned), divide the class into groups of three. One person in the group will be the interviewer, one the subject, and one the evaluator. As the interview is conducted, the evaluator will take notes on what seems to work well and what problems seem to have emerged during the session. After all three students have had the opportunity to do an interview, the group can discuss the strengths and weaknesses of each interview. This exercise should prepare students for the actual interviews they'll conduct during their research project.

TEACHING IDEAS

You may want to suggest that students prepare for interviews by watching a "master" at work. The library will probably have videotapes of some of Bill Moyers's interviews with Joseph Campbell (*The Power of Myth* series) or with various American figures (*A World of Ideas* series). Ask students to pay particular attention to the types of questions Moyers asks, as well as to his obvious preparation.

3 Finding material through interviews and surveys

Although you will probably conduct most of your research in the college library, remember that professional researchers do most of their work *outside* the library—in the field, in labs, in courthouses, and in government and private archives. Consider the possibilities of conducting original research for your own paper, by interviewing knowledgeable people and devising and sending out questionnaires. (Many subjects have been extensively discussed by experts on television news programs, talk shows, and documentaries. It may be possible to borrow videocassettes or to obtain printed transcripts of such programs.)

Interviews

Interviews allow you to conduct primary research and to acquire valuable information unavailable in print sources. By recounting the experiences, ideas, and quotations of people who have direct knowledge of a particular subject, you add considerable authority and immediacy to your paper. You can conduct three types of interviews: (1) by phone, (2) by e-mail, or (3) in person.

Those you select to interview may include businesspeople, government officials, doctors, professors, community activists, or your own grandparents. If you would like to talk to a business executive or a government official but do not have a particular individual in mind, call the public relations office (in a business) or the public information office (in a government agency) and ask for the names of possible interviewees. Then, call the individual and try to schedule an appointment. Even busy people can usually find some time to give an interview; many will be glad to talk to someone about their experiences. But if you are turned down, as sometimes happens, try someone else.

It is important to prepare adequately for your interview. Devise most of your questions in advance; you can improvise with other questions during the interview, according to the turns it takes. Avoid *leading* questions that presume certain conclusions or answers:

> Why do you think that American workers are lazier today than they were a generation ago?
>
> What do you think of the fact that the present administration wants to burden small businesses with added health-care costs?

Instead, ask *neutral* questions that allow the interviewee to express his or her own observations:

> What changes, if any, have you noticed in the work habits of your present employees from those who worked here in the 1960s?
>
> To what extent has government funding of genetic research changed during the present administration?

Also avoid *dead-end* questions that require yes/no answers or *forced choice* questions that impose a simplistic choice on the interviewee:

> Do you think that this was an important experiment? (dead end)
>
> What should take priority, in your view: jobs or the environment? (forced choice)

Instead, ask *open-ended* questions that allow the interviewee to develop her or his thoughts at some length:

> In what way was this an important experiment for you?
>
> How do you think it is possible to deal with the seemingly conflicting needs of jobs and the environment?
>
> What were your impressions of Robert Kennedy when you met him?

Factual questions can be useful for eliciting specific information:

> When did your restaurant begin offering a salad bar?
>
> How many parade permits has the city denied during the past year?

Ask follow-up questions when appropriate, and be prepared to lead your respondent through promising, though unplanned, lines of inquiry. Throughout the interview show your interest in what your respondent is saying. On the other hand, keep in mind that your own reactions may unintentionally create cues that affect your subject's responses. Your subject, for instance, may begin to tell you what he or she thinks you want to hear (even if it is not quite accurate), based on how you have previously reacted. For this reason, trained interviewers try not to specifically respond to the interviewee's answers.

Surveys

Surveys are useful when you want to measure behavior or attitudes of a fairly large, identifiable group of people—provided that both the group and the measurements are carefully specified. An identifiable group could be freshmen on your campus, Democrats in town, Asian Americans in a three-block area, or autoworkers in two factories; measuring attitudes or behavior could mean obtaining records and comparing the frequency of responses made to specific and carefully worded questions. On the basis of measured comparisons among the responses to questions, a researcher might venture some broad claims about patterns of response as indicators of attitudes or behaviors within the population measured (it is not safe to generalize beyond the group actually measured without rigorous statistical procedures). Such generalizations are usually made in quantitative terms: "Fewer than two-thirds of the respondents said they feel threatened by the possibility of contracting AIDS."

To get honest answers to your questions, it is essential to guarantee your respondents' anonymity. Most frequently, questions and answers to surveys are written, though occasionally they may be oral (as when, for exam-

TEACHING IDEAS

ACROSS THE CURRICULUM Students interested in using surveys in their research can be encouraged to seek advice from faculty in the social sciences, particularly psychology and sociology.

Checklist for Interviews

- Determine what kind of information you need from the person, based on the requirements of your paper and its thesis.
- Make an appointment, telling the person what your paper is about and how long the interview will take.
- Become knowledgeable about the subject so that you can ask informed questions. If the person has written a relevant article or book, read it.
- Prepare most of your questions in advance.
- Take pen, pencil, and a hardback notebook to the interview. If you take a tape recorder, ask the person's permission to record the interview. Even if you do record the conversation, take notes on especially important comments.
- At the end of the interview, thank the person for his or her time. Promise to send a copy of the finished paper. Soon afterward, send a follow-up thank you note.

ple, you ask students entering the library for their attitudes on American military activities in the Middle East). When devising questions for a survey, some of the same considerations apply as for interviews. For example, do not ask *loaded* questions that lead the respondent toward a particular answer ("Do you think that the money the university is spending to upgrade the president's residence would be better spent to reduce class size?"). For surveys, short-answer questions are better than open-ended questions, which are difficult to compare precisely or to quantify. It is relatively easy to quantify yes/no responses or responses on a five-point scale ("How concerned do you feel about the threat of AIDS? 5—extremely concerned; 4—very concerned; 3—moderately concerned; 2—somewhat concerned; 1—unconcerned").

33h Doing focused research: Electronic sources

There are two types of electronic sources: *online* information and *CD-ROM* disks. Recently, professional researchers have been classifying online information as "changeable" and CD-ROM information as "unchangeable" or "portable." This distinction acknowledges that online information, accessed through the Internet or commercial online services, is subject to change or even extinction. Thus, information that you find on an online service one day may be revised or even deleted the next. Information on a CD-ROM, on the other hand, always remains the same. Of course, a new edition of a CD-ROM, like the new edition of a book, will be different from the earlier edition. See 33f-3 for more information on CD-ROMs.

Access to the Internet (a global network of computers and computer users) is often free to anyone with a phone (or modem) link to an Internet provider. Your school may provide you with such access, or you may need to sign up with a local Network Service Provider. Commercial services, such as America Online, also provide Internet access.

BACKGROUND

The material from here to the end of the chapter was developed by Rick Branscomb of Salem State College, Salem, Massachusetts. This introduction should help significantly in demystifying the Internet, both for teachers and students. There is more than enough information here for would-be net surfers to begin exploring.

1 Getting online

If you don't already know how to log on to a computer, seek out your school's computer services department, which will likely offer "get acquainted" sessions—teacher-led or self-paced tutorials that will introduce you to online computing. From these sessions, you will learn how to access the Internet through a computer account. When you locate information and wish to retrieve it for later use, you will either type commands or use a mouse to click on icons, depending on your school's computer system, to download the information. You can download information to one of two places: to your user area on your school's mainframe computer or to your personal computer.

- *Your school's mainframe computer:* When you use your school computer account to access the Internet, both the terminal that you operate at the library and the computer you operate in your room function as "dumb" terminals. That is, your keystrokes direct the computer to carry out your search. Any files that you locate will be downloaded to your user area on the school's mainframe. At designated terminals, you can print paper copies or download the material yet again to a floppy disk for later use (say, in a word-processing program).
- *Your personal computer:* When you use a commercial service such as America Online, or software such as Netscape through a local Internet access provider, you are directing your computer, via a modem and phone link, to search various Internet sites. When you locate promising material, you will download files directly to your computer's hard drive.

Extending your print-based research strategies

Many of the same strategies you have used for researching print materials in your school's library will serve you well when conducting Internet searches. You may begin by investigating broad topics. Your search will turn up Internet sites, some of which will strike you as immediately promising. As you browse these sites, you may electronically link to other, related sites. Along the way, you will collect pertinent material—in this case not by photocopying articles or checking books out from the library, but by downloading computer files—again, either to your user area on the school's mainframe computer or to the hard drive on your personal computer. For more on downloading files, see 33h-3.

Bear in mind that whether you conduct research in print libraries or online, in digital libraries, you are engaging in processes that will focus your attention. As you identify particular sources useful to your emerging paper, you will find authors beginning to "talk" to each other by making reference to similar events, information, and ideas. You will join in this conversation and, ultimately, you will use both print and digital research for a single purpose: to advance *your* ideas in an engaging, well-written paper.

The Internet Domain Name System

Accuracy in typing an Internet address is essential: a missed period or transposed letters will frustrate your efforts. To appreciate *why* this is so, read about the Domain Name System.

The naming system

The Domain Name System allows for each computer on the Internet to have its own address, much like the post office's system of states, cities, streets, and house numbers allows each building to have its own unique address. Internet addresses are composed of units separated by the symbol "." (pronounced "dot") and read hierarchically from left to right, from most specific to most general. The Internet address "www.gsfc.nasa.gov" is read as follows:

- The abbreviation "gov" means this Internet site is located at a government agency;
- The particular agency is "nasa";
- The particular computer where the Internet service resides is named "gsfc"; and
- The service provided is particular to the World Wide Web ("www").

World Wide Web sites, of which this NASA site is one, are located on the Internet according to the following convention: the technical protocol by which the domain is to be accessed, followed by the characters "://" followed by the Domain Name. This is called the site's URL (Universal Resource Locator). For example, the URL "http://www.gsfc.nasa.gov" directs a user to access the site "www.gsfc.nasa.gov" by using "HyperText Transport Protocol" (http).

E-mail addresses

Electronic mail (e-mail) accounts reside on your school's computer (or on the computer of a commercial service such as Prodigy). Each account, or "address," has its own naming protocol that includes the account holder's user ID (often a first initial plus a last name: for example, hkissinger), followed by the "@" sign (read "at"), and the particular Domain Name of the person's e-mail account. Aside from "gov," common top-level domains include "edu" (an educational institution: harvard.edu), "com" (a commercial institution: "aol.com"), "net" (a network: city.net), and "org" (another kind of organization: nysernet.org). Note the lack of uppercase letters. To e-mail one of the authors of this book, for instance, type the following address in your electronic mail program:

lrosen@fas.harvard.edu

Finding the right electronic sources online

Commercial and professional information services

Libraries often subscribe to professional and commercial information services. One of the largest of these is DIALOG, which provides access to more than 300 million items in over 400 separate databases in the humanities, the social sciences, the natural sciences, and business. Specialized databases include NEXIS and LEXIS, used for locating news and legal or government publications; PsycINFO, which references items in psychological journals; ERIC, which references educational journals; and Arts and Humanities Search. An especially useful commercial service is WILSONLINE, which provides electronic access to the printed indexes published by H. W. Wilson Co., including *Readers' Guide to Periodical Literature, Education Index,* and *Social Science Index.* If your school subscribes to these services, you will find them on a computer in your library's reference area.

What's on the Internet?

The Internet provides researchers with both *communication* and *information* tools:

Communication tools

Electronic mail (or "e-mail") allows you to contact people all over the world via your computer.

Usenet discussion groups and discussion lists (often called "listservs") allow you to join in academic (and sometimes not-so-academic) discussions in a particular area of interest via the Internet.

Telnet allows you to use the computer where you are sitting as a remote terminal to another computer. Some services—library catalogs, for instance—are available to the public through telnet. You can sit at your own computer and telnet to the online catalog of a library in England, for example. Or, if you are traveling and you have access to an Internet account, you can telnet back to your own account at school and use it as if you were there.

Information tools

anonymous ftp WAIS gopher

the World Wide Web (often called "WWW" or simply "the web")

These information tools allow you to find and retrieve information stored on computers nearly anywhere in the world. Each of these tools generally has one or more search engines associated with it for finding and retrieving information. Details on these information and communication tools follow.

E-mail

Definition. If you've used the Internet at all, it has probably been with e-mail—sending and receiving messages to and from friends and family. But

BACKGROUND

Each of the headings in this section is given a threefold treatment: definition, reliability, and access. Student users will need to know *what* the particular online resource is; they will need to know *how reliable* that resource is, given the wide ranges of reliability among electronically posted materials; and students will need to know *how* to tap into the resource. The text provides an overview of each key point.

ADDITIONAL EXERCISE G

For each of the Internet resources discussed in this section of Chapter 33, find time to log on and peruse available information. If possible, conduct brief searches on the topic you are researching.

e-mail can benefit you as a researcher as well. More and more authorities (university and private researchers, journalists, government officials) have and regularly use e-mail. Many (not all, of course) would welcome an inquiry from a student and would respond with an informed and authoritative reply. Don't overlook the research potential of e-mail. Through e-mail you can do the following:

- Conduct interviews.
- Exchange computer files that are not available to the general Internet user (text, graphics, charts, statistics, and so forth) with people who have such information to share.
- Read the current draft of a new project or an old unpublished conference paper that the scholar would be willing to share with you.

Reliability. Judge the reliability of an e-mail source as you would that of any person you've interviewed. When referring to this source in your paper, provide some background context. Who is this person? What is his or her area of expertise? Why is he or she qualified to speak on your topic? If possible, use an attributive phrase (see 34f-4) to establish the credibility of your source *in* the paper.

Access. How do you find e-mail addresses of people with whom you would like to correspond?

- Simply ask them. There should be an e-mail phone book for the Internet, but there isn't, at least not yet.
- You will find that the e-mail addresses of people who contribute to newsgroups and discussion lists are included in the headers of the messages they send. Save one or two messages and you will have their addresses.
- Keep your own list of e-mail addresses of people with whom you may wish to correspond.

Usenet Discussion Groups or "Newsgroups"

Definition. The easiest way to visualize a newsgroup is to think of a standard cork bulletin board hanging on a wall. Anyone can walk by and tack up a message, and anyone else can come by and read the message, respond to it, or put up a new message. Newsgroups on the Internet are electronic versions of that cork bulletin board. Anyone with an Internet account can use a newsreader to follow a continuing discussion, read the current messages, and post a reply or a new message. Newsgroups can provide an excellent forum for trying out your ideas on others before you commit to these ideas in your paper.

Reliability. Because they are a radically democratic forum in which everyone—the unknowing and the expert—can offer an opinion, newsgroups vary in reliability. Use material gathered from this resource with caution. If you want to refer to a newsgroup posting in a paper, first try to confirm from other sources the reliability of that information. You may also want to interview the person who posted the message by e-mail.

Access. If your school subscribes to a newsfeed, a central computer where all the messages are stored and fed to other providers, you will have access to a newsreader of some kind and you will be able to choose which newsgroups to follow (remember, there are well over 10,000). Newsgroup addresses read hierarchically, much like Domain Names, in a series of units separated by dots (see the box at 33h-1). For example, the newsgroup address "rec.music.bluenote.blue" is read as follows:

Its type is "recreation."

Its subtype is "music."

Its particular category is "bluenote."

Its topic is "blue."

That is, "rec.music.bluenote.blue" is a discussion group about blues music. When you join in on the conversation of a newsgroup, you will be able to read and reply to messages, just as you can with e-mail. Remember that in newsgroup posts what you write is public.

Discussion Lists or "Listservs"

Definition. Academic discussion lists are similar to newsgroups, with one significant difference: you must actively subscribe to the list, and then you receive the messages directly as individual e-mail messages. The mailing of the discussions is essentially managed by automated computer programs that receive all incoming messages and immediately forward them to everyone who subscribes to the list; one of the most common of these automated programs is called "Listserv."

Reliability. Lists usually stick to their stated topics; although theoretically anyone can subscribe to any discussion list, usually contributors are serious about their commitment to the topic. They tend to be knowledgeable —though, as with any source, you will want to verify information before citing it as credible. The mere appearance of information on a discussion list does not ensure its reliability.

Access. To find a listing of currently active academic listservs, use your WWW browser to access the URL http://www.liszt.com (see below for accessing WWW sites). If you find a list to which you would like to subscribe, address an e-mail message *to the listserv* (the machine that manages the list), not to the list itself. The machine will ignore the "subject" line of the e-mail box and read only the message, which must contain the following information:

- Type the word "subscribe". Don't use the quotation marks. Simply type the word as the first word in an e-mail message.
- Next, type the name of the list to which you want to subscribe.
- Finally, type your first name, followed by your last name.

The message must contain absolutely nothing else. (Added words can confuse the machine.) For example, if your name were Mary Rose, you would send the basic message "subscribe deos-l Mary Rose" (again, no quotation marks) to the listserv's address to subscribe to the Distance Education list. After you have subscribed, you will receive further instructions about using the list and posting to it.

Generally it's a good idea to "lurk" (i.e., read all the messages without contributing anything) for a few weeks, to ensure that you don't break any of the rules of "netiquette," the unwritten rules of the particular list's culture. Most lists have available their "FAQs" or "frequently asked questions," a compilation of questions about the intent and operation of the list.

Many lists maintain archives of all their discussions, so that if you want to review what was written on the list previously about a particular topic, you can search the archives. Instructions on how to do this are provided when you subscribe.

Anonymous FTP

Definition. "FTP" stands for "File Transfer Protocol." It's the standard method of transferring files (text documents, graphics, computer software) over the Internet. Normally, if you find a file you want to transfer to your own computer for viewing, you need to be able to access the computer where the information resides, in which case you would theoretically need an account on that computer and a password. However, many computer systems worldwide have been made at least partially accessible to "anonymous" users, people who don't have accounts. Hence, anonymous ftp provides a means for you to retrieve files from computers you normally wouldn't have access to.

Reliability. Information gathered through anonymous ftp is usually as reliable as print information in a library. Often it will consist of government documents, research reports, statistical tabulation of data, and so on. You may actually access visual and graphical information: pictures from the Hubble Space Telescope are available from NASA by anonymous ftp, for example.

Access. The search engine for ftp is called "archie," short for "archiver." Archie servers scour the Internet at regular intervals, looking for anonymous ftp sites and cataloging what they find. With archie, you perform keyword searches for *titles of files:*

- Give archie a file name (if you know it); or
- Give archie a "substring" or section of a file name, and instruct it to search its accumulated catalog, looking for ftp sites with files whose names contain the string of letters you've supplied.
- Once it finds all the sites, archie presents you with a list. You then begin the anonymous ftp process, instructing your computer to transfer the desired file from the remote computer where archie has indicated it exists.

The limitation of archie is its inability to look for subjects or words within files, and often file names are not at all descriptive of their contents.

Retrieving files by anonymous ftp can be arduous. However, using a software program called "Fetch" can make transferring files easy. If "Fetch" or similar software is unavailable, consult your computer services department for specific guidance. Fortunately, newer Internet tools such as gopher and WWW (see below) as well as graphical/PPP ftp applications such as Anarchie (for the Macintosh) can perform anonymous ftp simply and transparently.

WAIS

Definition. WAIS (pronounced "waze") stands for Wide Area Information Server. An indexing package developed by Apple Computer, Dow Jones, and Thinking Machines, Inc., WAIS is a standardized way of indexing large databases so that they can be accessed by any computer over the Internet, regardless of type. WAIS is both an interface (a way of organizing and presenting data) and its own search engine. That is, finding and retrieving information in WAIS are one and the same operation.

Reliability. Much like the documents obtainable through anonymous ftp, WAIS-found documents tend to be substantial and trustworthy.

Access. You can either install a WAIS program on your computer or telnet to one: a common one is found at "bbs.oit.unc.edu." Follow instructions, which will vary depending on the software you're using and the WAIS site you've accessed. You first need to do a keyword search to find the actual databases that you want to search. Once you've located the databases, you do a second keyword search to find the documents contained in the databases that are relevant to your topic.

Gopher

Definition. Until the advent of the World Wide Web and its graphical interface browsers, gopher had been the tool of choice for locating and retrieving information on the Internet. Gopher is a text-based tool (with some exceptions). It presents an easy-to-use, standardized menu interface, allowing you to make selections from a list or menu of choices rather than having to memorize computer commands. The menus you find will list available documents, which you select and display simply by using arrow keys and the enter key. Gopher has the further advantage of being able to perform WAIS and ftp searches and retrievals, all in the background and unknown to you, the user. Gopher essentially supersedes the earlier WAIS and ftp modes.

Reliability. Owing to the enormous popularity of gopher and its widespread use, gopher is prone to turn up massive amounts of information, from archived listservs and newsgroups to valuable research documents. You must evaluate your material carefully.

Access. Gopher's search engine is called "veronica," and although veronica sites worldwide are limited and you will often get an "unable to connect" message because of high usage, it is simple to use.

- Connect to gopher at one of your school's mainframe terminals or at your own computer, which will act as a terminal. (Ask computer services at your school or an experienced net surfer for help.)
- Transfer to one of the veronica sites.
- When prompted, enter your keywords. Veronica supports fairly complex searches, so that if you're interested in O. J. Simpson's football career but don't want to read hundreds of articles about the trial, for example, you can tell veronica to find "O. J. Simpson" but exclude any article containing the word "trial."
- After you initiate the search, veronica presents you with a menu (up to 12 pages worth) of items it found containing the keywords you designated. To

read any of them, select with the moving highlighter using the arrow keys and press enter. Gopher will retrieve the document and display it, if it's text.

- Gopher does not have the capability of displaying nontext documents (graphics). It will ask you if you'd like to download any nontext file that may be attached. Remember that, depending on the software you use, downloading may mean bringing the file to your college's mainframe *or* to your own computer.

World Wide Web

Definition. Currently the most popular way of browsing and searching the Internet is via the World Wide Web. Its popularity derives both from its hypertext interface (clicking on the screen brings you to a new page of information) and its ability to display color and graphics. In addition, like its predecessor gopher, the web has subsumed all previous Internet modes: search engines on the web can do gopher, WAIS, and ftp. Here are some key terms worth knowing:

- *Webservers:* specially configured computers, worldwide, on which information for the WWW is stored.
- *Webpage or home page* (or simply page): individual documents on the WWW.
- *Website or site:* a collection of pages.
- *Hypertext:* links from information on one webpage to related information on another webpage—perhaps located on another webserver in a different school, country, or continent. Hypertext links are usually underlined in blue. If you see something on a webpage that you'd like to explore further and it's underlined in blue, click your mouse or press the appropriate key —and you're there.
- *Browsing:* linking from one web document to another, following your interests.
- *Search engines:* The web has many different search engines, but all work on the keyword search principle. Some of the most popular engines are Alta Vista (http://www.altavista.digital.com), Webcrawler (http://webcrawler.com), Yahoo (http://www.yahoo.com), Lycos (http://www.lycos.com), InfoSeek (accessible by the "Net Search" button in Netscape), and (the newest and perhaps most comprehensive) HotBot (http://www.hotbot.com). Some sites can collect three to four of the most popular engines on one page and allow you to use any or all of them. One such site in Switzerland is W3 Search Engines (http://cuiwww.unige.ch/meta-index.html).

Reliability. The quality and reliability of information you find on the web will vary considerably. Individuals, commercial operations, and organizations create their own websites. So, while you may find research reports and government documents and online medical journals, you may also find unsubstantiated opinion, self-serving advertisements, and propaganda. Judge your materials carefully.

Access. Most likely you will gain access to the web through a graphical browser. "Graphical" in this sense means that you will click your mouse on icons, rather than typing computer commands, to access information. You will move from document to document on the web by following hypertext links (again, underlined in blue). If the trail you follow begins to seem fruitless, you can back out of it by clicking the mouse on the left-pointing arrow near the top of the screen in Netscape (or find similarly functioning icons in other browsers). With enough backward steps like this, eventually you'll return to where you started, for a fresh start.

Keyword searching

One of the most valuable and important skills for searching the Internet—as well as for searching your school library's electronic catalog—is the keyword search. Using the right keyword can mean the difference between a successful search and an unsuccessful one. You want a keyword that is neither too broad nor too narrow. A keyword that is too broad will yield search results with too much information, much of which is irrelevant to you. A keyword that is too narrow will yield search results with too little—or no—information. How do you select the right keywords?

The engineers who write the software code for search engines set up specific, logical rules for their engines, which you should understand. The following questions will help you to identify an engine's basic characteristics:

What Boolean operators—that is, what combination of "AND," "OR," and "NOT" searches—will the engine allow?

An "AND" search (in Webcrawler, the option marked "all") will identify only those documents that contain each and every keyword you've entered. Thus, if you entered "shopping" and "malls" as keywords, Webcrawler would identify only those documents that contain *both* words.

An "OR" search (in Webcrawler marked "any") will identify documents that contain either of two terms or phrases that you define. If you wanted to find information on the largest city in Russia, you could enter the phrase "St. Petersburg Leningrad" and, in Webcrawler, select "any." This command would instruct the engine to find any document containing "St.," "Petersburg," or "Leningrad," thus ensuring that you would find all relevant documents. (Unfortunately, it will also return any document containing "St." as well, so you will be faced with references to "St. Louis" and "St. Jerome" and "Main St.")

A "NOT" search, very useful but not always available, allows you to construct fairly elaborate searches. You can use "AND" or "OR" with a "NOT" search, as in this example: You could enter the keywords "Queen AND Elizabeth NOT ship". This search would allow you to concentrate on the Queen herself without sifting through material about the ship named after her.

Some "adjacency" operators, or commands, allow you to require that "St. Petersburg" be taken as adjacent terms. Using this instruction, the search engine would only return documents in which "St." was followed by "Petersburg."

Exactly what information does the engine scan when you enter a search?

Some possibilities: the whole text of every document searched; the titles of every document; or a list of keywords supplied by the author or indexer of the document.

What are the engine's default (or initial) settings?
Webcrawler, for instance, automatically conducts "AND" searches. For an "OR" search, you would need to select "any" as a search option.

Does the search engine allow substring and wildcard searches?
That is, can you enter "Engl" or perhaps "Engl*" and find documents with the words "England," "England's," and "English"? Most search engines do allow this.

Does your use of upper- and lowercase letters matter in the keyword?
Most search engines ignore case, so it's immaterial whether you enter "gloria steinem," "Gloria Steinem," or "gLoria steiNEM." Still, check for rules on case.

A sample keyword search

Using Netscape, click on the "Enter" button, and type in the URL for Webcrawler (http://webcrawler.com). You'll be presented with the following screen:

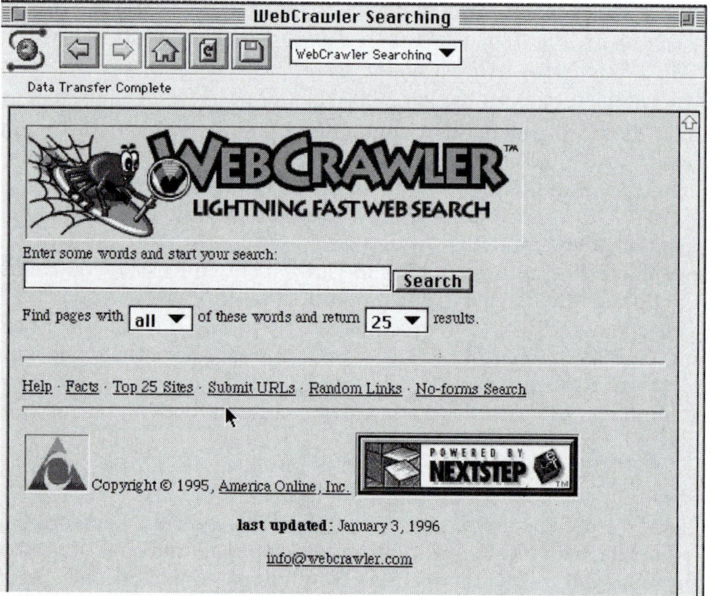

Then type in the three keywords you want to search on. Notice that "all" is selected, making this an "AND" Boolean search. Only documents containing *all three words* will be found.[1]

[1]Actually, this is not literally true. Webcrawler, and a few of the other search engines, will project a possible relevance for each of the documents it finds. If, for example, it can't find *any* documents with all three words, it will find the next best combination, and after performing some mathematical computations, will return to you a rank-ordered list of documents it does find, telling you how closely they match your keyword criteria.

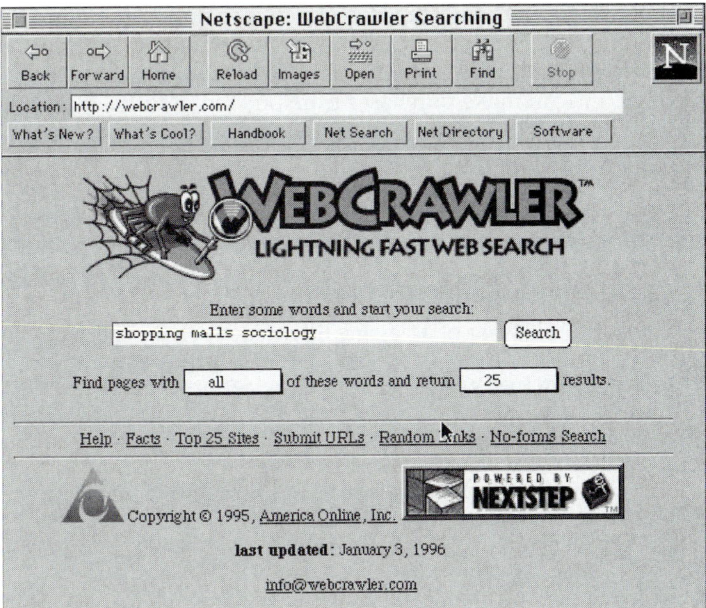

The results of the search are as follows:

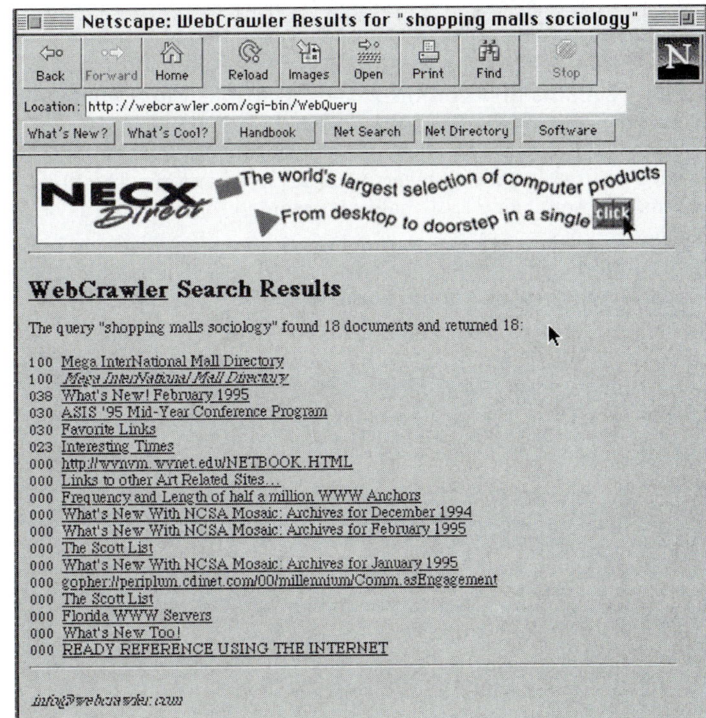

Webcrawler found eighteen documents containing the words "mall" and "shopping" and "sociology." None of the documents seems especially promising: most seem to be related to the virtual shopping malls on the Internet, where one can make purchases from one's computer. You could now click on any or all of the documents listed, and explore each one in turn. Probably, your search was too narrow.

Starting Your Internet Search

There are four basic ways of accessing information on the Internet: WAIS, ftp, gopher, and the World Wide Web. To begin your research, you may want to begin with the WWW. The search engines are more accessible and sophisticated than the engines available in other modes. And since the web is the fastest-growing part of the Internet, you're more likely to find information of interest fairly quickly. Starting your digital search on the web is like starting a print-based search in a large university library first, rather than beginning in a small-town public library.

Web Search

1. Start with an elementary, well-constructed keyword search (see page 567) in one of the simple web search engines: Webcrawler (http://webcrawler.com) is comprehensive, fast, and easy to use, though it does not offer many possibilities for complex AND/OR/NOT searches.
2. Try hypertext linking (by clicking on blue-underlined words or images) to the sites listed in the documents generated by your search.
   a. Start with the first sites displayed. Each "hit" discovered by Webcrawler and most other search engines is given a numeric rating, based on a complex mathematical formula that describes how closely and accurately the site meets your keyword criteria. The first-listed hits are most likely to be helpful, provided your keywords are well chosen.
   b. Browse the Internet by clicking on underlined items in your first document to related information in other documents.
3. To create a more focused initial listing of documents (from which you can also link), try one or two other web search engines that allow for more complex AND/OR/NOT searches than are possible with Webcrawler. For example, try Alta Vista: "http://altavista.digital.com".

Gopher Search

4. Next, try a veronica search in gopher to look for more specialized sources, and perhaps different sources.

Other Searches

5. Finally, try an archie search for ftp documents. Also, a WAIS search may yield a valuable, specialized source.

Storing online sources: Record-keeping and notetaking

It is possible to save a copy of what's on your screen onto a disk. You could save copies of every document you retrieve during your Internet research. However, as with print materials, there is the question of whether you should download and permanently save a copy of an entire document (analogous to photocopying an entire periodical article) or simply take notes. With each new document, you will ask: *How much should I download?*

Reasons to download

- Downloading electronic files is easier and cheaper than photocopying written pages.
- Downloading can usually be accomplished with a click of the mouse or a simple typed command.
- Downloading is free, unless you're paying an hourly fee for your Internet account.
- Downloading offers you the convenience of saving an entire document for later perusal, perhaps even printed out if you're not comfortable reading on-screen text.
- The investment in disk storage space on your computer is minimal, unless the material you're downloading contains graphics.
- Remaining online to do your reading can tie up the connections (especially if you're calling in by modem and phone lines), preventing other students from accessing material as well. You can download a three- or four-page text article in a few seconds; to read that article while you're online may take many minutes.
- Having a text file stored on your computer makes it possible to "cut and paste" exact quotations from the document into your paper (if you have that capability on your computer), thus saving you some typing.

Reasons not to download

- Some files on Internet and elsewhere are enormous. An entire book, for example, or files involving graphics may use huge amounts of memory and take precious time to download or may exceed the storage capacity of a floppy disk.
- Storing such bulky material may make it difficult to locate the material relevant to your purpose, unless you take notes and mark the material appropriately.
- Remember that notetaking is a valuable part of research, forcing you to consider the relevance of raw material to your paper. Taking notes rather than simply copying or downloading whole documents requires you to synthesize and evaluate sources, to be an active researcher rather than a passive collector of information.

Regardless of whether you take notes online or download material, remember to keep a research log. Record the electronic addresses of *all* sources for the information you're gathering—an especially critical consideration for Internet material that may be difficult to relocate. Sites come and go on the web, so you'll want a record of where you've located materials.

CHAPTER 34

Using Sources

KEY FEATURES

This chapter provides students with essential information on the various activities involved in using sources. All of the standard advice is here: reading sources carefully; keeping bibliography and notecards; recording quotations and summarizing/paraphrasing information; and integrating quotations into their own text. The chapter, however, goes beyond the mandatory coverage to offer students genuinely helpful advice on how to make the research process run more smoothly. Students will learn simple tricks like assigning code numbers to bibliography cards in order to save themselves from recopying publishing information on each notecard; they'll also learn more complex skills involved in working sources into their papers. The distinctions among quoting, summarizing, and paraphrasing are explained in detail, and careful attention is paid to plagiarism. In addition, students are not simply urged to integrate quotations into their own texts, but are given a list of words that can be used to introduce quotations. These and other features of this chapter should make it an invaluable resource for students as they work their way through this stage of the research process.

This chapter will offer you strategies for using sources with care. To keep matters in perspective, realize that you will present sources in a paper for one reason only: to support and advance your original thinking. Without your guiding, independent purpose, a research paper has no reason for existing. Clearly, a paper that stitches together the words and ideas of others, but that is guided by no original effort, cannot be called research.

34a Finding sources for authoritative opinions, facts, and examples

How convinced are you by the following?

> Critics of the modern shopping mall make the argument that marketplaces have traditionally been spaces of business as well as community; malls today are places of business, only; and American shoppers are the poorer for it.
>
> Women are underrepresented in the sciences.

In both cases, the writers ask us to accept a statement as true. Should we believe them? If we know relatively little or nothing about a topic, how are we to judge the accuracy of statements made about it? Read the following expanded versions of the example sentences.

> Critics of the modern shopping mall make the argument that marketplaces have traditionally been spaces of business as well as community; malls today are places of business, only; and American shoppers are the poorer for it. Industry specialists heartily agree—at least with the second point: "Malls are designed to maximize profits," says the Chairman of the Environmental Subcommittee for the International Council of Shopping Centers. "They were not built as a replacement for Main Street. If intimacy encourages sales, there will be intimacy" (Marks). One mall executive makes the point with particular bluntness: "We don't want the mall to be a community in any real sense because we'll attract people we don't want to. People who are not here to shop but are coming for some other purpose. It would upset our tenants who want to make money" (qtd. in Lewis 123). [See the citations for Marks and Lewis in "Works Cited," 35h.]
>
> Women are underrepresented in the sciences. For instance, during the 1992–93 academic year (the most recent year for which figures are available), women earned little more than one-third of bachelor degrees in computer science, compared to their earning 54 percent of all bachelor degrees

awarded (U.S. Dept. of Ed. 174). [See this source citation in "Works Cited," 4f.]

With the sources added, each is more convincing than the original, sourceless version, because each is now supported. Carefully used sources can provide authoritative opinions, facts, and examples that will advance the ideas of your research papers.

1 Authoritative opinions

When linking the words of experts to your own words, you shift the basis on which you ask readers to accept key statements. Without authoritative support, you ask readers to take you at your word—which some may be willing to do. But skeptical readers will want proof. By offering authoritative opinions, you ask readers to accept your view because experts also believe it to be true. Student writer Jason Koman illustrates this strategy in the example on shopping malls above (see Jason's paper on shopping malls in Chapter 35).

2 Facts

Certain statements about the world exist in the category of things that are demonstrably true or false. Either the aurora borealis is caused by sunspots or it is not; either London is a more northerly city than New York or it is not. When you make statements such as these, readers want assurance that the statements are accurate. You can provide this assurance by turning to sources for factual support. In the second example above, student writer Lou Cassetta asks us to accept as true the statement that "women are underrepresented in the sciences." Are they? Should we accept that they are because Lou says so? Obviously not. By presenting a statistic from the United States Department of Education, a reliable source, Lou assures the reader of the statement's accuracy. (See Lou's essay on gender and technology in Chapter 4.)

3 Examples

Turn to sources for examples that clarify and support your points. Indeed, it is often *through* a well-chosen example, which your source materials can provide, that readers remember your point. Consider this paragraph from a discussion of nervousness during college interviews. The writer, Anthony Capraro, III, directs a college counseling service:

> **Nervousness** . . . is absolutely and entirely normal. The best way to handle it is to admit it, out loud, to the interviewer. Miles Uhrig, director of admission at Tufts University, sometimes relates this true story to his apprehensive applicants: One extremely agitated young applicant sat opposite

him for her interview with her legs crossed, wearing loafers on her feet. She swung her top leg back and forth to some inaudible rhythm. The loafer on her top foot flew off her foot, hit him in the head, ricocheted to the desk lamp and broke it. She looked at him in terror, but when their glances met, they both dissolved in laughter. The moral of the story—the person on the other side of the desk is also a human being and wants to put you at ease. So admit to your anxiety and don't swing your foot if you're wearing loafers! (By the way, she was admitted.)[1]

LOOKING BACK

This section relies heavily on material from Chapter 1. If you haven't already covered that chapter in class, you may want to do so now. Otherwise, students should review the chapter to help them work with their sources. Specifically, see the discussions on reading to understand, evaluate, and synthesize (1e, 1g, 1h). See also corresponding sections in Chapter 2 on writing summaries, evaluations, and syntheses (2a, 2b, 2d).

34b Classifying sources: Primary and secondary

When attempting to determine the value and quality of a source, keep in mind the distinction between *primary* and *secondary* sources. Primary sources are written by people who have *direct* knowledge of the events or issues under discussion: they were participants in or observers of those events. Examples of primary sources are letters, diaries, autobiographies, oral histories, historical records or documents, and works of literature. Here is a primary source—an announcement for a Fourth of July celebration in 1871 on the Kansas frontier:

> A great 4th of July at Douglas, 1871, everybody is invited to come and bring filled baskets and buckets. There will be a prominent speaker present, who will tell of the big future in store for southern Kansas. Grand fire works at night! Eighteen dollars worth of sky rockets and other brilliant blazes will illuminate the night! There will also be a bunch of Osage Indians and cowboys to help make the program interesting. After the fire works there will be a big platform dance, with music by the Hatfield Brothers.
>
> —qtd. in JOANNA L. STRATTON, *Pioneer Women: Voices from the Kansas Frontier* (New York: Touchstone, 1981) 135.

FOR DISCUSSION

To help students understand fully the distinction between primary and secondary sources, you may want to engage them in a discussion. Ask them to suggest possible primary and secondary sources for a given topic (Japanese-American internment camps, for example, or the psychological effects of growing up in a religious cult). As you list the sources on the board, ask students to explain why each source is classified as primary or secondary, and encourage discussion of questionable responses.

Authors of secondary sources have *indirect* knowledge, only. They rely on primary or other secondary sources for their information. Examples of secondary sources include biographies, textbooks, historical surveys, and literary criticism. A historian studying nineteenth century Wild West shows in America and Europe might use the Independence Day announcement as a source. Working with the question "How would 'a bunch of Osage Indians and cowboys . . . help make the program interesting'?" the historian might investigate what attitudes are revealed about Native Americans in this and similar announcements from the era. If you were writing a research paper on Wild West shows of the nineteenth century, such a historical study would be a secondary source. The original announcement would remain a primary source.

[1]Anthony F. Capraro, III, "The Interview." *Barron's Profiles of American Colleges.* 19th ed. Hauppauge, New York: Barron's Educational Series, 1992. 12.

Can a source be both primary and secondary?

A source can be considered both primary and secondary, depending on how it is used. Consider the historical study of Wild West shows—for your purposes a secondary source, assuming you were writing a paper on this topic. Now imagine a second writer (Writer B) who has begun a research project on the ways in which historians gather evidence. The same historical study of Wild West shows would become for Writer B a *primary* source. Writer B's interest would not concern the shows themselves but rather the ways in which evidence was used and a story was told. Presumably, in Writer B's project, other historical accounts would be treated as primary sources. In certain contexts, then, a secondary source can be approached as a primary source. How that source is used determines the classification.

Advantages and disadvantages of primary and secondary sources

Primary sources are not necessarily superior (or inferior) to secondary sources, but it is good to recognize the strengths and limitations of each.

Primary sources—

- provide facts and viewpoints that are not generally available from other sources;
- often have immediacy and drama; but
- may be colored by the bias of the authors, who want to inflate their own importance or to justify questionable decisions.

Secondary sources—

- may offer a broader perspective, with their distance from original events;
- tend to be less affected by intense passions of the moment than those who participated in those events; but
- may write with a strong, interpretive bias that you will need to evaluate carefully.

Source by source, you will need to make your decisions on reliability, determining whether you consider the material to be primary or secondary.

34c Reading sources critically

Your ability to write a research paper depends on your being able to use sources with care. And your ability to use sources, the subject of this chapter, depends *entirely* on your being able to read well. Because effective reading is a foundational skill on which the success of all research rests, you should turn to Chapter 1 if you are not fully comfortable with the prospect of reading to understand, respond, and forge relationships. Careful, strategic reading is a skill you can teach yourself; once learned, it will serve you well.

Consider how the strategies for critical reading described in Chapter 1 might help as you work with source materials for your research papers.

FOR DISCUSSION

CRITICAL THINKING It is essential that students embarking on research understand the different types of reading discussed in this section. Spending class time on this material now may well ease student anxiety and instructor frustration later in the research process. Ask students to explain in their own words what they understand by reading to understand, to respond, to evaluate, and to synthesize. Allowing for as much free discussion as possible, be sure to lead students away from meaningless generalizations and toward clearer comprehension of the critical reading process.

1 Reading to understand and respond

Your main goal during this stage is to familiarize yourself with your sources and to determine their *relevance* for your research project.

- *Understand.* Preview the source by skimming its contents. Read the table of contents, the introduction or preface, the conclusion, headings, and selected topics.
- *Respond.* Read your source carefully enough to *react* and to *ask questions.* Check the credentials of the author and the critical reception of his or her work (see 33f-2). Does the author's background or professional affiliation suggest to you the point of view he or she will take? (For example, can you predict the likely viewpoint of an officer of the National Rifle Association on handgun control?) Identify the author's stance on the subject: Is she or he pro, con, or neutral? relatively detached or passionately involved (or something in-between)? Is the tone angry, cynical, witty, solemn, or earnest? Does the author have a personal stake in the issue under discussion? If so, how might this affect your acceptance of her or his arguments?

Highlight important questions, particularly those most relevant to your research question, and make notes in the margins. Take notes, looking for important quotations that you might be able to use in the paper. Identify arguments and the positions of people involved. Finally, be alert to *differences* and *similarities* among sources. After critical reading and additional research, you will probably want to discuss such differences.

2 Reading to evaluate and synthesize

Your goal during this stage of critical reading is to clearly assess each source and to consider your sources together, so that you can begin to find patterns of meaning that emerge (see 33c-3, 33d, e). As you continue to read with your research question in mind, you will begin to develop a thesis for your paper.

- *Evaluate.* Determine the *reliability* of your sources. This involves attempting to separate fact from opinion in the source; identifying and assessing the author's assumptions; and evaluating both the evidence offered by the author in support of his or her argument and the logic by which the conclusions are reached (see 6h).

Consider the source. Reading to evaluate also involves considering the source of publication for an article or book. Was the article published in a popular magazine (intended for a general audience) or an academic or professional journal (intended for a specialized audience)? Articles in journals will probably be more difficult to read, but will tend to carry more authority and credibility. Is the book or pamphlet published by a commercial or academic publisher, or by a publisher with a special interest (a chemical company, for example, or a nonprofit agency such as the pro-environmental

Earth First! or the American Civil Liberties Union)? Special-interest publications should not necessarily be discounted, but you should consider the source and be aware of potential biases. For more specific advice, see the box in 6d-2, "Appealing to Authority."

- *Synthesize.* Determine how the evidence from one source is related to evidence from other sources. You must compare what you find in your sources, evaluate the information and assumptions in each, and form your own ideas about the most important relationships among them. The skills for doing this are demonstrated in detail in Chapters 1 and 2 (see 1h and 2d). Your discussion will require cross-references among sources, noting where one author refers to ideas discussed by any others. When possible, establish a relationship among them through comparing, contrasting, defining concepts or examples, or making connections by process or cause and effect. In this way you *synthesize* the sources to let them support your answers to the research question and your argument for the paper's provisional thesis.

3 Evaluating electronic sources

In 33h, you will find an extensive discussion on locating, accessing, and evaluating the reliability of electronic sources. When you draw on these sources, be very careful to assess their validity and credibility, keeping the following considerations in mind:

- Reliability of evidence varies considerably across electronic sources, so judge each source on its merits—as you would any source.
- Sources gained through anonymous ftp and WAIS tend to have the same status as print information in the library.
- Information gained from newsgroups, web pages, and gopher searches can be helpful but also unreliable. Any person or organization can create and post documents on the Internet. The material you find may have been produced for an expressly commercial, political, racial, or religious motive. Carefully consider each source.

ADDITIONAL EXERCISE A

Before you begin taking notes on your sources, make sure that you have all of the necessary information on your notecards. If anything is missing, find it now rather than waiting until the end of the research process. You'll probably be far more pressed for time then, and the source may no longer be readily available.

34d Creating a working bibliography

Your **working bibliography** is a list of all of the sources you locate in preparing your paper. This includes books, articles, entries from biographical sources, handbooks, almanacs, electronic sources, and the various other kinds of sources cited in 33f–h. The bibliography should also include sources you locate in indexes that you intend to check later. Your working bibliography differs from your **final bibliography** in that it is more comprehensive: the final bibliography consists only of those sources that you actually use in writing the paper.

It is absolutely essential that you prepare your working bibliography *at the same time* that you are compiling and consulting your sources. That way you can be sure to have accurate and complete information when the time comes to return to your sources to obtain more information or to double-check information, and to compile your final bibliography. It is enormously frustrating to be typing your list of references (quite possibly, the night before your paper is due!) and to suddenly realize that your notes do not contain all the information you need.

Making bibliographic notes

We recommend that you compile a working bibliography on 3″ x 5″ index cards or by computer record. What you take notes on is less important than your ability to quickly and effortlessly alphabetize entries or to arrange them in any other order (such as by topic and subtopic order, or by sources you have already examined and ones you have not) that is most useful to you during the research and writing process. As you consult each new source, carefully record key information:

1. full name of author (last name first),
2. title (and subtitle),
3. publication information:
   a. place of publication
   b. name of publisher
   c. date of publication
4. inclusive page numbers

In case you have to relocate the source later, indicate the library call number (in the upper right-hand corner) and the name and date of the index where you located the source (at the bottom). It is also a good idea to include a brief annotation (either below the publication information or on the back of the card), in which you describe the contents of that source or the author's main idea, and indicate your reaction to the source and how you might use it in your paper. By surveying your annotations as you proceed with your research, you will quickly be able to see how much you have already found on your subject and what else you still need to look up. Your annotations may also prevent you from wasting time looking up the same sources twice. Finally, you should assign a code number to each bibliographic entry. Then, when you are taking notes on the source, you can simply put that code number in the upper right-hand corner of the note, rather than recopying the complete bibliographic information.

Using your records to create a final bibliography

When the time comes to prepare your final bibliography, you can simply arrange the cards for the sources you used in alphabetical order and type up the pertinent information as a list. If your records are on a computer, you may use "sort" (for database) or "Find" and "cut and paste" functions to alphabetize the entries. Here's a sample bibliography record for a book:

⑤ *Geist, Johann F. Arcades: The History of a Building Type. Trans. Jane O. Newman and John H. Smith. Cambridge: MIT, 1983.* *NA 6218 .G4313x 1983*

First chapter, 3–58: "The Architectural History of the Arcade." Markets, bazaars, arcades—design features and their social significance.

Here is a sample bibliography record for an article:

⑧ *Lewis, George H. "Community Through Exclusion and Illusion: The Creation of Social Worlds in an American Shopping Mall." Journal of Popular Culture 24.2 (1990): 121–36.*

Investigates what sorts of communities, if any, exist in the mall; based conclusions on observations at Mall of New England. Aside from teenagers and elders, no communities exist.

Creating an annotated bibliography

Some instructors may ask for an **annotated bibliography** as an intermediate step between your working bibliography notes and the final bibliography. In effect, an annotated bibliography is a fully annotated working bibliography in manuscript form; it records the same information demonstrated above in card form, presenting it in alphabetical sequence on manuscript sheets for your review and for suggestions from collaborators, peers, or your instructor.

A note on photocopying: Most periodicals and reference books can't be checked out of the library. Therefore, you may find yourself photocopying articles or book chapters. Remember to photocopy or record all pertinent bibliographic data. You will find it handy to photocopy the title page of a book or a periodical's contents page (or whichever page has dates, volume numbers, and other publication information). Two additional reminders may save you hours of retracing your steps late in the writing process:

- Check to see that you've photocopied *all* relevant words on each page. (You'll save yourself the frustration of discovering at a later time that the machine has missed the first five letters of each line.)
- For books that have endnotes, photocopy the corresponding notes at the end of the chapter or end of the book. This way, you won't have to find the source again if you have to track down a reference.

TEACHING IDEAS

Another way to reduce the stress that inevitably accompanies the final stages of the research process is to ask students to present you with an annotated bibliography. This exercise provides students with the necessary incentive to get moving, and allows you the opportunity to evaluate not only their progress but their understanding of the research process as well. Requiring an annotated bibliography at this time might well prevent trouble later on.

TEACHING IDEAS

It is important for students to understand the difference between working and final bibliographies. To make the distinction clearer, you may want to use the analogy of the working and final theses for essays. By now students should have a clear sense of the tentative nature of the working thesis; it may help if they think of the working bibliography in the same way.

EXERCISE 1

Individual responses

TEACHING IDEAS

It's an unfortunate fact of academic life that some people have no scruples about marking up library books, or stealing all or parts of periodicals. Depending on the situation at your college, you may want to admonish students to treat library materials with respect. In addition, students everywhere should be encouraged to report missing pages or complete works—if the library doesn't know they're gone, no replacements will be ordered.

GROUP ACTIVITY

It's almost impossible for one instructor to check on the progress of each student at every stage of the research process. This doesn't mean, however, that students need be without valuable feedback. Ask students to bring in their notecards, and divide the class into groups of three or four. Within groups, students will read each other's cards and then discuss the similarities and differences between them. As they compare their efforts, they should come to a better understanding of the function of notecards in the research process.

EXERCISE 1

Compile a working bibliography—both books and articles—of twenty to twenty-five items for one of the subjects you have been researching for Chapter 33. Or if you prefer, research a new subject. Record key information (as indicated above) on 3″ x 5″ cards or in your electronic database (if the latter, you will need a printout). Include content annotations for at least five items.

34e Taking notes: Summarizing and paraphrasing

Use your computer's notetaking software or 4″ x 6″ cards for taking notes. Again, any system will work as long as you are able to (1) clearly identify the source from which the note is taken and (2) sort through and rearrange notes with ease.

Researchers use various formats for recording their notes, but the following elements are most important:

1. a *code number* corresponding to the code number on your bibliography record *or* the bibliographic reference itself;
2. a *topic* or *subtopic* label (these enable you to easily arrange and rearrange your records in topical order);
3. the *note* itself; and
4. a *page reference.*

Do not attempt to include too much information in a single note record. For example, do not summarize an entire article or chapter in one record, particularly if you are likely to use information from a single record in several places throughout your paper. By limiting each note to a single point or illustration, you make it easier to arrange the records according to your outline, and to rearrange them later if your outline changes. A sample note for *Arcades: The History of a Building Type,* by Johann Geist, appears below. (For comparison's sake, it is placed directly after the bibliography record for that source.)

> (5) *Geist, Johann F. Arcades: The History of a Building Type. Trans. Jane O. Newman and John H. Smith. Cambridge: MIT, 1983.* — *NA 6218 .G4313x 1983*
>
> *First chapter, 3–58: "The Architectural History of the Arcade." Markets, bazaars, arcades—design features and their social significance.*

Design features of arcades 

Physical features of the arcade isolate shoppers from outside world and keep them moving along. Arcades built with skylights, and no windows, so rooms—lit from above—could be otherwise totally enclosed. The effect: to avoid distractions from outside + keep shoppers' minds and eyes on the merchandise. (20)

There are three methods of notetaking: *summarizing, paraphrasing,* and *quoting*. These methods can be used either individually or in combination with one another.

1 Summarizing sources

A *summary* is a relatively brief, objective account, in your own words, of the main idea in a source passage. You summarize a passage when you want to extract the main ideas and use them as background material in your own paper. For details on the process of writing summaries, see 2a. Here is a section of an article by David Guterson, which Jason Koman refers to in his research paper on malls:

> There is, of course, nothing naturally abhorrent in the human impulse to dwell in marketplaces or the urge to buy, sell, and trade. Rural Americans traditionally looked forward to the excitement and sensuality of market day; Native Americans traveled long distances to barter and trade at sprawling, festive encampments. In Persian bazaars and in the ancient Greek agoras the very soul of the community was preserved and could be seen, felt, heard, and smelled as it might be nowhere else. All over the planet the humblest of people have always gone to market with hope in their hearts and in expectation of something beyond mere goods—seeking a place where humanity is temporarily in ascendance, a palette for the senses, one another.
>
> —David Guterson, "Enclosed. Encyclopedic. Endured.: One Week at the Mall of America." *Harper's* Aug. 1993: 51.

Here is a sample summary of this source:

> David Guterson claims that marketplaces have traditionally been places of business as well as social centers. People throughout the ages, from the ancient Greeks to rural Americans, have gone to market in search of goods or profit; but they have also gone for something more: to see, and be part of, the vibrant center of community life (51).

REFERENCE

Sherrard, Carol. "Summary Writing: A Topographical Study." *Written Communication* 3 (1986): 324–43. Inexperienced writers tend to copy when briefly summarizing a passage, but use more of their own words when writing longer summaries.

REFERENCES

ARRINGTON, PHILIP. "A Dramatistic Approach to Understanding and Teaching the Paraphrase." CCC 39 (1988): 185–97. Uses Kenneth Burke's notion of "ratios" to show how paraphrase can illustrate a passage's different ratios and thus interpret its message.

D'ANGELO, FRANK J. "The Art of Paraphrase." CCC 30 (1979): 255–59. Offers strategies for teaching effective paraphrase and provides examples of effectively paraphrased literary works.

NOTE TO THE INSTRUCTOR Formulating their own thesis can help students appreciate the value and purposes of paraphrasing.

EXERCISE 2

Individual responses

2 Paraphrasing sources

A paraphrase is a restatement, in your own words, of a passage of text. Paraphrases are sometimes the same length as the source passage, sometimes shorter. In certain cases, particularly if the source passage is written in densely constructed or jargon-laden prose—the paraphrase may even be longer than the original.

You paraphrase a passage when you want to preserve all (or virtually all) the points of the original, major and minor, and when—perhaps for the sake of clarity—you want to communicate the ideas in your own words. Keep in mind that only an *occasional* word (but not whole phrases) from the original source appears in the paraphrase, and that the paraphrase's sentence structure does not reflect that of the source. The following paragraph appears in an article written by a sociologist who has studied shopping malls. Jason Koman refers to this article in his paper.

Original passage:

> What emerged from the initial observations and interviews, then, was a picture of mall shoppers as a *collectivity,* located in one enclosed space, but utilizing the mall primarily for their own self-defined and rational economic transactions. They may well shop with a friend, or the family may come to the mall, but they are *not* there for the face to face primary interactive relations that are the core of community.
>
> —GEORGE H. LEWIS, "Community Through Exclusion and Illusion: The Creation of Social Worlds in an American Shopping Mall." *Journal of Popular Culture* 24.2 (1990): 125.

Paraphrase:

> Lewis observes that while mallgoers can be said to form a collection of people under one roof, they do not constitute a community: they do not search out the types of interpersonal contacts on which communities are built. Even if they go shopping with a friend or family member, they remain isolated consumers during their time at the mall, looking to buy what they need at prices they can afford (125).

This paraphrase is as long as Lewis's original passage, with roughly the same level of detail. Significantly, the paraphrase eliminates the original's difficult, sociological language: the writer can now take advantage of Lewis's insights, but in a way that does not disrupt the tone of the research paper.

EXERCISE 2

Write a 250–400 word summary of one of the sources you have located for your working bibliography (Exercise 1). Then write a paraphrase of several sentences from a section of text in the same source.

34f Quoting sources

You may decide to quote from a passage when the author's language is particularly well chosen, lively, dramatic, or incisive, and when you think you could not possibly express the same idea so effectively. Or you may decide to quote when you want to bolster the credibility of your argument with the reputation of your source. By the same token, you may occasionally decide to discredit an opposing argument by quoting a discredited or notorious source.

1 Avoiding overquoting

Knowing how much to quote is an art in itself. If you underquote, your paper may come across as dry and secondhand. If you overquote, your paper may come across as an anthology of other people's statements ("a cut-and-paste job"), rather than an original work. Some instructors have developed rules of thumb on quoting. One such rule is that for a ten-page paper, there should be no more than two extended quotations (i.e., indented quotations of more than 100 words); and each page should contain no more than two short quotations. If this rule of thumb makes sense to you (or to your instructor), adopt it; otherwise, modify it to whatever extent you think reasonable.

2 Deciding how to quote

When you quote a source, you need to record the author's wording *exactly;* the conventions for altering quotations with ellipses and with bracketed words (that you provide) are discussed below and in 29e.

In researching his paper on shopping malls, Jason Koman discovered several helpful books on arcades from which he learned that the arcade, both in design as well as in social and psychological impact on the consumer, was the predecessor of the mall. Here is a passage from Margaret MacKeith, *The History and Conservation of Shopping Arcades* (London: Mansell, 1986) 16. The "success" mentioned in the first sentence refers to the commercial success of the first arcades.

> Once the success of such a venture had been established others quickly followed. These were sited where a growing population coincided with a shortage of shops, availability of land, finance and an entrepreneur. The absence of any one of these factors could prejudice commercial success. The pattern of the development of the arcade in Britain shows a move from the South to the North. First the capital, then the major port and the fashionable holiday resorts were overtaken by the expanding industrial cities. Only two arcades were built in London between 1818 and 1879, and per-

GROUP ACTIVITY

Workshops can be useful for checking students' command of summaries, paraphrases, and quotations. Ask students to choose one or two samples of each from their papers, and to provide members of the group with copies of the original sources. Students can then analyze the summaries, paraphrases, and quotations according to the guidelines presented in the previous chapter. If two students read each writer's material, chances are at least one of them will pick up problems. The students can then discuss the problems, clarifying the rules for using sources for those who are confused.

TEACHING IDEAS

Remind students to copy the *exact* call number of every book they record on bibliography cards. They may not be aware of what will await them if they try to remember the number.

haps this was due in part to a parallel and equally diverting means of shopping which went under the name of "bazaar." This despite some contemporary Parisian examples is essentially an English development. The term was chosen not to suggest an exotic environment but to alert the shopper to the extraordinary variety of goods for sale. The segregation of crafts into individual premises and thence into whole streets such as Butcher's Row or Mercer's Street, was a mediaeval method of trade protection which had no relevance by the mid-nineteenth century.

GROUP ACTIVITY

All of the exercises in this chapter lend themselves to group activity. After students have completed each exercise, have them meet in small groups to check each other's work. Each "editor" should check the writer's responses according to the guidelines in the chapter. Those who are better at working with sources will be able to help those who need it, and the inevitable discussion of situations that call for judgment will help all students learn the research process.

LOOKING BACK

You may want to refer students to Chapter 28 (Quotation Marks) for additional advice on using quotation marks.

What you consider to be quotable depends on the purpose of your research. Jason Koman read this section of MacKeith's book to investigate the ways in which the modern mall was descended from the arcade of the nineteenth century. For his purposes, the following quotation was most useful:

```
                Determining location for arcades
"These were sited where a growing population coincided with a
shortage of shops, availability of land, finance and an
entrepreneur." (16)
```

Sometimes you may wish to quote a passage that has itself been quoted by the source author. Generally, you should try to locate the original author when you want to quote. However, this won't always be practical: the original source may not be available at your library or may not be available at all (if the original source was quoted from an unpublished interview or from a lecture). The following passage appears in George Lewis's article on shopping malls. We reprint his footnote to explain why Jason Koman had to quote the source *through* Lewis:

> [T]he high turnover, volume of persons, and transiency that is a designed part of most malls works *against* the development and emergence of community within their walls.
>
> This is understood by mall managers and developers. As one put it: "Having the *perception* of community feeling does not mean that it actually exists. It is not the same thing. Perception is not necessarily reality."[11] So the important thing, from a marketing perspective, is to create the warm *illusion* of community, while at the same time quietly stacking the deck against its actual development. "We don't want the mall to be a community in any real sense because we'll attract people we don't want to. People who are not here to shop but are coming for some other purpose. It would upset our tenants who want to make money. We don't want anything to upset our tenants."
>
> [11]Interview with mall marketing director, 1986.

If you decided to use only the quotation by the marketing director (and not Lewis or Lewis's commentary), your notecard would appear as follows. (The single quotation marks *within* double quotation marks show a quotation within a quotation.)

Community as an illusion in the mall

[Note #8]

Mall marketing director (no name given), interviewed by Lewis in 1986:
"'We don't want the mall to be a community in any real sense because we'll attract people we don't want to. People who are not here to shop but are coming for some other purpose. It would upset our tenants who want to make money. We don't want anything to upset our tenants.'" (qtd. in Lewis 123)

These are the *exact* words from the original. The student writer has added nothing, omitted nothing, and changed nothing.

3 Using brackets and ellipses in quotations

Sometimes for the sake of clarity, conciseness, or smoothness of sentence structure, you will need to make additions, omissions, or changes to quotations. For example, suppose you wanted to quote a passage beginning with the following sentence: "In 1979, one week after receiving a 13.3% pay raise, she was called on the carpet." To clarify the pronoun *she,* you would need to replace it with the name of the person in question enclosed in a pair of brackets: "In 1979, one week after receiving a 13.3% pay raise, [Virginia Rulon-Miller] was called on the carpet." (See 29d.)

Suppose you also decided that the 13.3% pay raise was irrelevant for your purpose in quoting the material. You could omit this phrase, and indicate the omission by means of an *ellipsis*—three spaced periods: "In 1979 . . . [Virginia Rulon-Miller] was called on the carpet." (See 29e.) Note that when using brackets, you do not need to use the ellipsis to indicate that the pronoun (*she*) has been omitted; brackets surrounding proper nouns imply that one word (or set of words) has replaced another. For more on altering quotations with ellipses and brackets, see Chapters 28 and 29, especially 29d–e.

Sometimes you need to change a capital letter to a lowercase one in order to smoothly integrate the quotation into your own sentence. For example, suppose you want to quote the following sentence: "Privacy today matters to employees at all levels, from shop-floor workers to presidents." You could smoothly integrate this quotation into your own sentence by altering the capitalization, as follows.

> The new reality, as John Hoerr points out, is that "[p]rivacy today matters to employees at all levels, from shop-floor workers to presidents."

LOOKING BACK

You may want to refer students to Chapter 29 (Other Marks) for additional advice on using brackets (29d), and ellipses (29e).

Smoothly integrating quotations into your sentences

Using attributive phrases to introduce quotations

Whether or not you alter quotations by means of ellipses or brackets, you should strive to smoothly integrate them into your own sentences. Use attributive phrases (phrases that attribute, or point to the origin of, the quoted source). Here is a quotation from Jason Koman's interview with Richard Marks, the Chairman of the Environmental Subcommittee for the International Council of Shopping Centers.

> Malls are designed to maximize profits. They were not built as a replacement for Main Street. If intimacy encourages sales, there will be intimacy.

The quotation can be integrated in the text of a paper in any of several ways.

1. According to the Chairman of the Environmental Subcommittee for the International Council of Shopping Centers, "Malls are designed to maximize profits. They were not built as a replacement for Main Street. If intimacy encourages sales, there will be intimacy" (Marks).[2]
2. "Malls are designed to maximize profits," according to Richard Marks.
3. "If intimacy encourages sales," says Richard Marks, "there will be intimacy."
4. Richard Marks, Chairman of the Environmental Subcommittee for the International Council of Shopping Centers, is perfectly candid: "Malls are designed to maximize profits."
5. "Malls are designed to maximize profits," says the Chairman of the Environmental Subcommittee for the International Council of Shopping Centers. "They were not built as a replacement for Main Street" (Marks).
6. According to Richard Marks, malls "were not built as a replacement for Main Street."

An attributive remark ("According to . . .) can be shifted around in a sentence from beginning to end. Place a comma after the remark when it introduces a sentence; place a comma before the remark when it ends a sentence; place a *pair* of commas around the remark when it interrupts the quoted sentence. In the fourth example, a sentence (not a phrase) introduces the

CRITICAL THINKING

Which of these six versions of Marks's comment makes it appear *most* authoritative? Explain. Reformulate the sentence so that it seems even more unarguable.

NOTE TO THE INSTRUCTOR This exercise will help students to understand that the way quotes are used can greatly affect their credibility.

GROUP ACTIVITY

No matter how many admonitions you give students regarding integrating quotations, some simply can't figure out what they're supposed to do. It's relatively easy to have students work in groups to highlight quotations that need to be integrated. All the readers need do is call the writer's attention to the offending quotation, and then it's up to the writer to take care of the problem.

---

[2]Because the source of the quotation is an unpublished interview, *not* a published article or book, there are no page references set in the parenthetical citation. Most sources do have page references associated with them, however, and the parenthetical citation form for them is as follows: "Malls offer no community" (Jones 8).

When the source of this quotation *is* mentioned in the sentence, no citation at all follows, since the name itself will steer readers to the proper entry in the Works Cited list. (See the actual entry for this citation on page 626.) For an extended discussion of citation form, see Chapter 36.

quotation, so a colon is the appropriate punctuation (to avoid a comma splice or a run-on).

Using statements with present-tense verbs to introduce quotations

Notice that in example 4 above, the quotation is introduced by a sentence. In examples 3 and 5, the quotation is woven into the structure of a sentence. In these cases, the convention is to use a main sentence verb in the *present* tense (see 9e-1). Even though your source has already been written (and so technically, the author has already declar*ed* or stat*ed* or conclud*ed*), when quoting sources you should use the present tense (declares, states, concludes). This applies even if you are discussing a literary work; thus you would say that Hamlet ponders: "To be or not to be. . . ." The only exception to the use of the present tense would be if you were reporting the historical progress of some development or debate and you wished to emphasize that certain things were said at a particular point in time. ("The Senator assert*ed*: 'I do not intend to dignify these scurrilous charges by responding to them.' ")

Verbs That Help You Attribute Quotations

Attributive phrases use verbs in the present tense. To vary attributive phrases, you might consider verbs such as these:

adds	denies	relates
agrees	derides	reports
argues	disagrees	responds
asks	disputes	reveals
asserts	emphasizes	says
believes	explains	sees
claims	finds	shows
comments	holds	speculates
compares	illustrates	states
concedes	implies	suggests
concludes	insists	thinks
condemns	maintains	warns
considers	notes	writes
contends	observes	
declares	points out	
defends	rejects	

5 Using block quotations

You should integrate most quotations into your own text, using quotation marks. If a quotation runs longer than four lines, however, you should set it apart from the text by indenting it ten spaces from the left margin. Quo-

CRITICAL THINKING

Ask students to rank order the verbs for attributing quotations with #1 being the most authoritative and #45 being the one that least supports the quoted words.

TEACHING IDEAS

Assign students to bring to your next class a copy of a paragraph from a text in another of their courses. This paragraph should contain a quote that they feel is especially persuasive on a debated subject. Join them in discussing exactly where the persuasive strength resides: which words, phrases, and sequencing *build* the persuasiveness?

tation marks are not required around block quotations. Block quotations should be double spaced, like the rest of the text (see 28a).

The following box reviews the discussion on summarizing, paraphrasing, and quoting sources.

GROUP ACTIVITY

This exercise lends itself ideally to group work. After dividing the class into groups of three, ask students to read and comment on each other's use of sources. As they discuss the similarities and differences between their papers, they can work through issues such as the summary/paraphrase/quote decision, accurate representation of quotations, and smooth integration of quotations into the text.

When to Summarize, Paraphrase, or Quote a Source

Summarize

- to present the main points from a relatively long passage
- to condense information essential to your discussion

Paraphrase

- to clarify complex ideas in a short passage
- to clarify difficult language in a short passage

Quote

- when the language of the source is particularly important or effective
- when you want to enhance your credibility by drawing on the words of an authority on the subject

EXERCISE 3

Individual responses

EXERCISE 3

Write a short section of a paper based on several of the sources you have located for exercises in the last two chapters. Summarize, paraphrase, and quote your sources. In particular, carefully select material that you believe deserves quotation, rather than summary or paraphrase. Your quotations should be of varying lengths: perhaps one block quotation, some sentence-length quotations, and others of phrase or clause length. In one or two cases, use ellipses and brackets to modify the quoted material. In all cases, smoothly integrate quotations into your own text, using a variety of attributive phrases.

TEACHING IDEAS

Integration of a quotation, summary, or paraphrase into the context of a paragraph is often troublesome for students. The strategy provided here offers a technique for seamlessly integrating sources. The key is to have students organize their papers by idea, not by source. With an organization by idea, the student can prepare the context for a source, then steer the reader to the source. The "Cycles of Development" technique can quickly give students confidence in using source materials. Once students become comfortable with the process, they will want to vary the technique.

34g Weaving summaries, paraphrases, and quotations into your paragraphs

You have seen that sources can help you to advance the points you wish to make by providing authoritative opinions, facts, and examples. You have also seen how to prepare summaries, paraphrases, and quotations. And you have seen how to use attributive phrases and sentences with present-tense verbs to integrate quotations with sentences. To complete the integration of source materials into your paper, devote your attention to the paragraph level, where ideas are developed *across* sentences. The following approach can help you to integrate summaries, paraphrases, and quotations into the overall scheme of your paper. You will want to vary the approach, but here are the basics:

Sources and Cycles of Development

- Introduce your idea into a paragraph before you introduce a source. Working with your paragraph's idea, create a context into which you can fit the source.
- Having created the context, steer the reader directly to your source using an attributive phrase or a sentence with a present-tense verb.
- Quote, summarize, or paraphrase the source.
- *Use* the source by commenting on it, responding to it, or explaining its significance.

When you apply these principles to individual paragraphs, you create what can be called a "cycle of development" for using source materials. A full cycle will ensure that your reader is properly prepared for the source and that the source will advance your paragraph's idea, which originates with you, without overwhelming that idea. The important concept is that your idea comes first; then you follow with, and integrate, your sources. These principles are illustrated below, using labeled paragraphs from Jason Koman's research paper.

Cycle of development with a quotation

Paragraph's idea + context for source | Steers readers to the quotation | Quotation | Comment

The suburban mall is similar in important respects to the urban arcade, which it replaced when people moved out of the city. Historians tell us that as early as the first decades of the nineteenth century arcades were built "where a growing population coincided with a shortage of shops, availability of land, finance and an entrepreneur" (MacKeith 16). Today, malls are located according to exactly these same criteria.

Cycle of development with a paraphrase

Paragraph's idea + context for source | Steers readers to the paraphrase | Paraphrase

Sociologist George Lewis agrees that malls do not offer community; but, unlike Guterson, he believes that shoppers do *not* seek community at the mall. What they want, he says, is to go shopping in a safe, secure place. As part of a larger study in popular culture, Lewis observed that while mallgoers can be said to form a collection of people under one roof, they do not constitute a community: they do not search out the types of interpersonal contacts on which communities are

ADDITIONAL EXERCISE B

Ask students to take a single source, at least one paragraph in length, and to weave that source into three different paragraphs they write. First, ask students to write a paragraph with a quotation; next, a paragraph with a summary; finally, a paragraph with a paraphrase. In each case, the students should follow the recommendations in the box "Sources and Cycles of Development."

built. Even if they go shopping with a friend or family member, they remain isolated consumers during their time in the mall, looking to make what Lewis calls "self-defined and rational economic transactions" (125). The shoppers Lewis observed showed no evidence of going to the mall with "hope in their hearts" of finding community, which Guterson believes has always characterized people's trips to market (51).

Paraphrase continues

Comment

Cycle of development with a summary

Paragraph's idea + context for source

Steers readers to the summary

Going to the mall has become a routine experience for many Americans. . . . Malls come in a variety of sizes: local strip malls can have as few as a dozen stores, usually including a supermarket. Shoppers in need of greater variety may drive hours to regional or super regional malls, where up to a million square feet of retail space awaits those ready to shop 'till they drop. The most demanding of shoppers have driven five or more hours, climbed aboard buses, and crossed continents and oceans (literally) to shop at the nation's premier mega-mall: the Mall of America in Minnesota (American Survey; Guterson 50).

Summary

Comment (begins a new ¶ in this case)

What are shoppers looking for when they travel to this colossally huge retail space of 4.2 million square feet?

TEACHING IDEAS

Plagiarism is never a pleasant subject to discuss, but as more and more students fall prey to unintentional plagiarism, it becomes crucial for instructors to address the issue. You may want to build a file of unintentionally plagiarized passages, and distribute samples to the class. Ask students first to explain what they see wrong, and then discuss in detail precisely why the passages are unacceptable. Half an hour of class time on this exercise may well result in significantly less unintentional plagiarism in the finished research papers. (You may want to use a similar exercise for imprecise quotation.)

34h Avoiding plagiarism

Plagiarism is an unpleasant subject, but one that must be confronted in any discussion of research papers. In its most blatant form, **plagiarism** is an act of conscious deception: an attempt to pass off the ideas or the words of another as your own. To take an extreme example, a student who buys a research paper from a commercial "paper mill" or borrows a paper written by someone else and turns it in for academic credit is guilty of the worst kind of plagiarism. Only slightly less guilty is the student who copies into his paper passages of text from his sources without giving credit or using quotation marks.

The penalties for plagiarism can be severe—including a failing grade in the course or even a suspension from school. Graduate students guilty of plagiarism have been dropped from advanced degree programs. Even professionals no longer in school can see their reputations damaged or destroyed by charges of plagiarism. During the 1988 presidential campaign, a Democratic candidate was forced to drop out of the race when it was revealed that some of the material in his campaign speeches was copied from a speech by a prominent British politician.

Much plagiarism is unintentional; but unintentional or not, the effect of plagiarizing is the same, so you'll want to avoid the problem. Here are two general rules to help you avoid unintentional plagiarism:

1. Whenever you *quote* the exact words of others, place these words within quotation marks and properly cite the source.
2. Whenever you *paraphrase* or *summarize* the ideas of others, do not use whole phrases, or many of the same words, or sentence structures similar to the original. You must identify the source of the paraphrased or summarized material. Do not assume that you are under no obligation to credit your source if you simply change the wording of the original statement or alter the sentence structure.

1 Determining what is common knowledge

The only exception to the second rule stated above is if the information summarized or paraphrased is considered common knowledge. For example, you need not cite the source of the information that General Lee commanded the Confederate forces during the Civil War, or the fact that Mars is the fourth planet from the sun, or the fact that Ernest Hemingway wrote *The Sun Also Rises.* If, on the other hand, you are summarizing one particular theory of why Lee's forces faced almost certain defeat, or the geological composition of the Martian surface, or how the critical assessment of Hemingway's *The Sun Also Rises* has shifted over the years, then you are obliged to cite the sources of your information or ideas, whether or not you quote them directly.

The key issue underlying the question of common knowledge is the likelihood of readers mistakenly thinking that a certain idea or item of information originated with you when, in fact, it did not. If there is *any* chance of such a mistake occurring, you should cite the source.

Your decision regarding what to consider common knowledge depends, partly, on audience. Suppose you are writing on a technical subject, computer software, for an audience of engineers. There's a great deal of technical information you might find in your sources, perhaps about computer languages, that you might reasonably decide would be common knowledge for readers who are specialists. They would clearly know that the information in question did *not* originate with you. Writing on the same topic for nonspecialists, however, you would want to cite the source of that same information, given the likelihood that your technically less sophisticated readers could reasonably mistake the information as yours.

The obligation is yours, then, *with every new research project,* to anticipate what your audience knows and what assumptions they will make about your knowledge. Let a spirit of honesty and fairness guide you, and you will make the right decisions. Jason Koman wrestled with the common knowledge issue in his paper. See the first paragraph of his paper, as well as the comment on the facing page (see 35h, paragraph A).

REFERENCES

DRUM, ALICE. "Responding to Plagiarism." *CCC* 37 (1986): 241–43. The educational implications as well as the legal aspects of plagiarism should be stressed as a way to forestall the practice.

KROLL, BARRY M. "How College Freshmen View Plagiarism." *Written Communication* 5 (1988): 203–21. In an extensive survey, 150 first-year students conceded that plagiarism is a grievous offense to "truthfulness, fidelity, and trust."

ST. ONGE, KEITH R. *The Melancholy Anatomy of Plagiarism.* Lanham, MD: UP of America, 1988. A "handbook on plagiarism" provides advice on how to avoid plagiarism and how to handle situations involving plagiarism.

ADDITIONAL EXERCISE C

Once you've written a draft in which you've incorporated source material, it's time to evaluate the paper for plagiarism. Using the material in this section as a guide, ask yourself whether or not you've incorrectly assumed an idea to be common knowledge, inadvertently copied an author's words without quoting the author, or inadvertently rewritten the material so that it resembles the original too closely. Revise any possibly plagiarized sections of your paper now.

Identifying blatant plagiarism of a source

We will use the sample passage below to illustrate what can happen when source ideas undergo several possible levels of intentional or unintentional plagiarism in the student examples that follow. The passage is from Steven F. Bloom's "Empty Bottles, Empty Dreams: O'Neill's Use of Drinking and Alcoholism in *Long Day's Journey into Night,*" which appears in *Critical Essays on Eugene O'Neill,* edited by James J. Martine (Boston: G.K. Hall, 1984).

> In *Long Day's Journey into Night,* O'Neill captures his vision of the human condition in the figure of the alcoholic who is constantly and repeatedly faced with the disappointment of his hopes to escape or transcend present reality. As the effects of heavy drinking and alcoholism increase, the alcoholic, in his attempt to attain euphoric forgetfulness, is repeatedly confronted with the painful realities of dissipation, despondency, self-destruction, and ultimately, death. This is the life of an alcoholic, and for O'Neill, this is the life of modern man.

Here is a plagiarized student version of this passage.

> *Long Day's Journey into Night* shows O'Neill's vision of the human condition in the figure of the alcoholic who is constantly faced with the disappointment of his hopes to escape. As the effects of heavy drinking and alcoholism increase, the alcoholic, in his attempt to attain forgetfulness, is repeatedly confronted with the painful realities of dissipation, self-destruction, and, ultimately, death. This is the life of an alcoholic, and for O'Neill, this is the life of modern man.

This is the most blatant form that plagiarism can take. The student has copied the passage almost word for word and has made no attempt to identify the source of either the words or the ideas. Even if the author *were* credited, the student's failure to use quotation marks around quoted material would render this version unacceptable.

Avoiding unintentional plagiarism of a source

Here is another version of the same passage.

> The figure of the disappointed alcoholic who hopes to escape reality represents the human condition in *Long Day's Journey into Night.* Trying to forget his problems, the alcoholic, while drinking more and more, is confronted with the realities of his self-destructive condition, and, ultimately, with death. For Eugene O'Neill, the life of the alcoholic represents the life of modern man.

In this version, the writer has attempted (for the most part) to put the ideas in his own words; but the result still so closely resembles the original in sentence structure, in the sequence of ideas, and in the use of key phrases ("confronted with the realities") that it is also unacceptable. Note that this would hold true even if the author *were* credited; that is, had the first sentence begun,

"According to Steven F. Bloom, ..." The student may not have intended to plagiarize—he may, in fact, believe this to be an acceptable rendition—but it would still be considered plagiarism.

4 Making legitimate use of a source

The following use of the source passage is entirely acceptable:

> According to Steven F. Bloom, alcoholism in *Long Day's Journey into Night* is a metaphor for the human condition. The alcoholic drinks to forget his disappointments and to escape reality, but the more he drinks, the more he is faced with his own mortality. "This is the life of an alcoholic," asserts Bloom, "and for O'Neill, this is the life of modern man" (177).

The student has carefully attributed both the paraphrased idea (in the first part of the passage) and the quotation (in the second part) to the source author, Steven Bloom. The student has also taken special care to phrase the idea in her own language.

Of course, you cannot avoid keeping *some* key terms: obviously, if you are going to paraphrase the ideas in this passage, you will need to use words and phrases such as "alcoholic," "heavy drinking," "the human condition," and so on. However, what you say *about* these terms should be said in your own words.

It is crucial that you give your readers no cause to believe that you are guilty either of intentional or unintentional plagiarism. When you are summarizing or paraphrasing a particular passage, you must do more than change a few words. You must fully and accurately cite your source, by means of parenthetical citations or by means of attributive phrases, such as "According to Bloom, ..."

5 Quoting accurately

When you do quote material directly, be certain that you quote it accurately. For example, consider a student quotation of the preceding passage (which follows the student's introduction).

> *Long Day's Journey into Night* is O'Neill's "vision of the human condition," according to Steven F. Bloom:
>
> > As the effects of his heavy drinking and alcoholism increase, the alcoholic, attempting to achieve forgetfulness, is repeatedly confronted with all the painful realities of dissipation, self-destruction, and death. This is the life of an alcoholic for O'Neill and it is also the life of modern man.

At first glance, this quotation may seem to be accurate. But it is not. The student has *omitted* some words that were in the source passage (in the first sentence, "euphoric" and "despondency"; in the second sentence, "and"); has *changed* other words (in the first sentence, "attempting to achieve," instead

FOR DISCUSSION

Students are necessarily skittish about plagiarism: many know that the penalties are dire, but they don't know exactly what the offense is. After students have had the opportunity to read about plagiarism and to check their own drafts, a discussion of the issue might be useful. You can express your own attitude toward plagiarism, and encourage students to ask questions not only about what constitutes plagiarism but also about why it is considered such a grievous offense.

EXERCISE 4

Individual responses

of "in his attempt to attain"; in the second, "it," instead of "this"); has *added* some words that were not in the original (in the first sentence, "all"; in the second sentence, "also"); and has also omitted punctuation (in the second sentence, the comma after "O'Neill").

These changes may seem trivial and may not seem to essentially change the meaning of the passage, but once you place a passage within quotation marks (or indent it if it is a block quotation), you are obligated to copy it *exactly*. Deleted material should be indicated by an ellipsis (. . .); your own insertions should be indicated by brackets ([ ]). Otherwise, the material within your quotation marks must be word for word, punctuation mark for punctuation mark, *identical* to the original.

With a spirit of honesty and careful attention to accuracy, you will avoid problems with unintentional plagiarism. Develop the habit of proofreading your papers when they are all but final. Compare your typed copy of all quotations, paraphrases, and summaries with your original notes and with photocopies of sources (if you have these). Then enjoy the accomplishment of having used your sources well to advance the ideas of your paper.

EXERCISE 4

Paraphrase a short passage from one of the sources you have located during your research. Then write a short paragraph explaining what you have done to eliminate all possibility of inadvertent plagiarism in your paraphrase.

CHAPTER 35

Writing the Research Paper

The material in this chapter parallels that in Chapters 3 and 4 on planning, writing, and revising the essay. Because the *process* of writing a research paper is in many (but not all) respects similar to that of writing an essay, the discussion of process here will be brief and cross-referenced with earlier sections of the book.

35a Refining the thesis

As you complete your research and prepare to write a paper, you probably have more information than you can possibly absorb. How will you get from the many notes you've taken—on notecards or, perhaps, on computer—to a finished paper? Here is where you must do your work as a critical thinker, synthesizing your sources in ways that advance the single idea at the heart of your paper. At this point in the process, you should be working with a question that interests you, one that motivates you to sift through all your notes in search of a satisfying answer. If you care about your work, the writing and the research will come more easily. With your question in mind, you will work with source materials until you formulate a satisfying answer—a thesis, which will be the core idea of your paper.

In 33e you saw the usefulness of devising a working thesis. *Working,* here, means preliminary. A working thesis offers a provisional idea with which to begin sifting through your notes; with this idea, you can begin to look at new materials in a more focused way. The discussion here will follow the progress of student writer Jason Koman as he works through the process of writing a research paper. After looking through his materials, Jason came up with the following:

INITIAL WORKING THESIS

> America's shopping malls are the modern equivalents of ancient marketplaces.

Listen to your sources: Revise your question and working thesis, if need be.

Sometimes, your sources will in effect "give" you the paper you intended to write from the moment you began your research. At other times, your sources will show that the question you're investigating is more com-

KEY FEATURES

This chapter begins with an acknowledgment of the state many students find themselves in after finishing the "gathering" stage of the research process. Assuring students that this state of "cognitive overload" is natural, the chapter immediately presents students with a strategy for moving forward by returning to the question that spurred the research in the first place. The distinctive features of research as opposed to personal writing are highlighted and covered in depth. Students are advised to consider whether the thesis must be altered to accommodate the direction the research has taken; to facilitate drafting by arranging notecards; and to consider the relative merits of informal, flexible outlines or more rigid formal ones. The chapter acknowledges that moving from gathering material to composing the paper into which that material will be integrated is a daunting task, and that it is tempting to include everything from the notecards, but students are reminded that the paper is *their statement* and not simply a compilation of references. To that end, the chapter recommends that students compose a very rough draft of the paper without reference to any sources, and use that draft as a "scaffold" from which to build the fuller paper. This advice is followed by an extensive analysis of voice and audience considerations, allowing students to move through the planning and drafting stages not by adhering to a set of rules, but rather by considering both their purpose in writing the paper and the needs of their readers. At the end of the chapter a complete and extensively annotated student paper is reproduced, providing students with a clear working model for their own research papers.

ESL CUE

Research and writing as a *process* will be an unfamiliar concept to many international students, though teachers in some cultures do in fact "intervene" with help in the stages of composition. Many students, however, may expect instructors to be uninterested in the process, focusing only on the final product. It may be worth explaining clearly (1) what a student's responsibility for original research, writing, and rewriting is supposed to be; (2) what the differing responsibilities of teacher and student entail in the evaluation of sources and the improvement of early drafts; and (3) what degree of dependency on the instructor (or tutors, peer editors, or other readers) is proper. The last point is crucial if plagiarism problems are to be forestalled.

GROUP ACTIVITY

This would be an ideal time for students to work together in small groups. Ask them to bring to the group a copy of their original working thesis, and to be prepared to discuss what their research revealed to them. As each student reads his or her working thesis to the group and highlights the research, others in the group can comment and ask questions to help the student decide whether the thesis needs alteration, and if so, how to alter it. This activity can help students see their research from a different perspective, as well as reminding them of their obligations to their audience.

TEACHING IDEAS

Students will need more than one reminder that some of the notecards they've so carefully prepared won't end up in the final paper. Reassuring them, as this section suggests, that they may indeed need those notecards for a later project should make it a bit easier for students to refrain from forcing irrelevant material into their papers.

FOR DISCUSSION

Ask students to recall the question that ignited their research. Do they still consider it so important? Ask that they explain reasons for a change in their perspective. Has their research led them to think about pursuing the thesis in

Characteristics of a Working Thesis

- The subject of the thesis is *narrow* enough in scope that you can write a detailed paper without being constrained by the page limits of the assignment (3d-1).
- The predicate of the working thesis communicates a relationship you want to clarify about your subject, based on your understanding of the information you have generated (3d-2).
- The main statement of your thesis may involve one or more (but not many more) of the following relationships: sequential order, definition, classification, comparison, contrast, generalization, or causation.
- The thesis clearly suggests the patterns of development you will be pursuing in your paper. (The types of paragraphs you write in your paper will be directly tied to the relationships you develop in your thesis (3d-2, 3).)
- The thesis will clearly communicate your intellectual ambitions for the paper (3d-3).

plicated than you imagined. In this case, the sources will suggest that you revise both your question and your provisional answer to that question.

This is what happened to Jason Koman. His initial question—in what ways do malls resemble ancient marketplaces—assumed that he would find similarities only. As he progressed in his notetaking, he began to gather information on types of marketplaces throughout history: the agora of Greece, the markets of medieval Europe, the bazaars of Islamic countries. The research only partially confirmed the validity of both his question and his working thesis. True, the modern mall reproduced *some* of the functions of the ancient markets—notably, commerce. But his sources were telling him quite directly that the mall differed in an essential respect from older marketplaces: while older markets were places where people gathered in communities, malls are commercial spaces only. People do not go to malls to forge community ties. Moreover, Jason found a word repeated across various sources: *illusion.* Malls presented shoppers with an illusion of community and intimacy. Jason's sources did not give him the paper he expected to write. He continued to work staying with his original idea, of relating malls to older marketplaces, but he refined his thesis to respond to his revised research question: "What do shoppers want at the mall?" Jason answered as follows:

REFINED WORKING THESIS

> Shoppers in the old markets were able to forge community ties and buy merchandise; shoppers today find merchandise only, and at best, just the illusion of community.

A refined working thesis, reflecting as it does your response to at least several of the sources you've collected, is more sophisticated than an initial working thesis. A refined thesis moves you closer to developing a plan for your paper and writing a first draft.

35b Developing a plan

Keeping your refined working thesis in mind, once again review all the notes you've taken, this time consolidating them into categories that will help you create a plan for your first draft.

Organize your notes into groups

If you have been supplying headings for your notecards or computerized records, your task will be considerably easier. Stack the cards, or electronically move your records, into clusters. Jason Koman devised several categories, including "Community in Old-World Markets," "Community in Malls," "Arcades—Design Features," and "Malls—Design Features."

If you have not already written headings on your notecards or computer records, write them as you review your notes with your refined working thesis in mind. There are at least two ways to do this. You can write headings on your notecards, group notes according to headings, and then use these groupings to construct an outline for your first draft. Or you can sketch a first draft by converting sections of the outline as your headings, and then turning to your notes to organize them in a way that fits your outline. Either way (or if you devise some other way), your goal by this point is to have a refined working thesis, a sketch of your first draft, and notes to draw on as you write each section of this draft.

Outlines

Outlines and sketches for a paper come in all shapes and sizes (see 3d-4). A sketch may be a logically arranged map of key topics and their relationships. If your instructor asks for an *informal outline,* it will generally have only two levels: topics and subtopics. For example:

The medieval marketplace
—social functions
—economic functions

Formal outlines have several levels (3d-4). The most common type employs a combination of Roman and Arabic numerals and letters.

I. Major topic
  A. Subtopic
    1. Minor subtopic
      a. sub-subtopic (or illustration)
        (a) illustration, example, explanation
        (b) illustration, example, explanation
    2. Minor subtopic
  B. Subtopic
II. Major topic

more advanced courses? Discuss how the thesis could be part of a career path. This discussion also could work well *among* students in small groups.

LOOKING BACK

It would be a wise idea for students to review Chapter 3 (Planning, Developing, and Writing a Draft) thoroughly at this point. They're probably feeling overwhelmed with the prospect of turning this pile of notecards into a coherent paper, and it will be reassuring for them to realize that the task before them is only a variation of one they've undertaken many times during the course.

LOOKING AHEAD

This "refined" thesis will get reworked again. The new thesis: "Shoppers today do not go to the mall in search of community, as shoppers used to do, but rather to buy in a predictable, safe environment." Notably, as student writer Jason Koman located more sources, he found that evidence required him to alter both his research question and the answer to this question.

TEACHING IDEAS

The information in this chapter is occasionally very explicit, such as this advice to stack notecards into piles. While to experienced researchers directions like this may seem overly specific, many students need such extensive guidance. You may want to supplement this information with advice of your own (or substitute your information) at any stage of the process, but it's probably best not to overload students with options at this point. If they're feeling overwhelmed, what they need is a sense of control, and following explicit directions can provide that sense.

GROUP ACTIVITY

As they develop outlines, students can "test" them on their classmates. Regardless of the format students choose or you require, it will be valuable for students to read each other's outlines. Advise them that they're not *criticizing* the outlines so much in this exercise as

(continued)

giving the writer *feedback* regarding what the outline seems to promise. Encourage students to ask each other questions that will help clarify the outlines, and to be frank about what they'd expect to see in the paper after having read the outline.

TEACHING IDEAS

Another reminder that the paper is at heart the student's own composition may be in order here. Not only is it difficult to let some of the notecards "fall to the cutting room floor," but it's also tempting to let the "experts" take over the paper. The student who turns her paper into a "memory dump" is probably not acting out of laziness so much as lack of confidence. A student who looks at any paper assignment and asks "What can I possibly have to say about this subject?" is all the more likely to slip into that response after researching what a collection of respected writers have to say. A word of encouragement that students have indeed learned a great deal and formed their own opinions through their research is in order here.

REFERENCE

KANTZ, MARGARET. "Helping Students Use Textual Sources Persuasively." *CE* 52 (1990): 74–91. A research paper allows students to synthesize texts and to meet sophisticated writing aims.

LOOKING BACK

Reviewing Chapters 3 and 4 should reassure students that in drafting this paper they can rely on many of the same strategies they've been using throughout the course.

For more information on how to write outlines, see 3d-4 and 18e; for a discussion on how to work from outlines as you write a first draft, see 3e-2.

Make room for changes

No matter how much care you take in assembling an outline or map of the paper *before* you write, it will inevitably change, to a greater or lesser extent, as you write the draft. Don't be discouraged by these changes. They are part of the writing process. With each successive draft beyond the first, your changes will tend to point you in a single direction: to a final thesis and a completed paper.

35c Drawing on your sources to support *your* idea

Sources in a research paper exist to help you to advance a thesis that *you* have defined. One purpose of research is for you to make connections across sources where few or no clear connections currently exist. These connections, and what you have to say about them, are what will make your paper original. No matter how many sources you use, focus on the ways that *you* synthesize them; focus on the points *you* want to make.

Three ways of treating sources

As discussed in Chapter 34, there are three ways of dealing with source materials: summary, paraphrase, and quotation. Avoid writing a paper that stitches these methods together and leaves no room for you. You can do this by continually asking yourself: What is my overall point? How does this particular source serve the purpose of my paper by advancing that point? If you can keep the focus on your ideas and your connections across sources, then you will avoid letting your sources overwhelm you.

Filling in gaps

After you have developed your outline and arranged notecards to correspond to the outline, you will probably discover that in some areas you have more information than you need, while in other areas you do not have enough. In the latter case, go back to the library to fill in the gaps or take another look at material you have already gathered. In the former case (too much information), you will have to make some hard decisions. After accumulating so much material, you may be tempted to use it *all.* Resist that temptation.

If you provide *too* much information, you risk inundating your reader and drowning out your unique point of view in the paper. Both problems can defeat communication. Your job is to sift through source materials, select from among them those elements that will advance your idea, and incorporate them into your paper. Balance is the key: you want to establish key relationships but not overwhelm your reader.

35d Determining your voice

How do you want to come across to your readers? As a student investigating a topic that *fascinates* you? As an authority speaking to specialists? As an authority speaking to nonspecialists? As a critic writing for a magazine? The option you select determines the *voice, tone,* and *register* of your writing. (See 3a-4 and 21e.)

Deciding on tone: Formal vs. informal

Consider, for example, the voice of a passage written by Johann Geist, an architect and historian. Jason Koman quotes this passage in his research paper (see 35h, "Works Cited"):

> The arcade . . . arose at the beginning of high capitalism. The overproduction caused by technological advances made it imperative for the manufacturers of luxury goods to discover new methods of distribution, faster turnover, and easier promotion.

The voice of this passage is serious, academic, systematic, dry, impersonal, and authoritative. The author makes little attempt to entertain his readers. But entertainment is not his purpose. Though the material is dry and the vocabulary is elevated, the passage is clear and precise. Koman uses it in his paper at a key moment to make an important point about arcades.

Now consider an informal tone from a feature newspaper story, titled "It's a Mall, Mall World," by Kim Ode (see 35h, "Works Cited"):

> The Friday night promenade is picking up in Maplewood Mall. Competitors in the BubbleYum Super Blow-Out Contest line up before a man holding giant cardboard calipers to their distended efforts. The elementary sounds of the kid Karaoke contest drift in from the Food Court.

Becoming sensitive to differences in tone

The difference in voice between passages could hardly be greater. Ode's voice is snappy, hip, intelligent, and colloquial. While Ode clearly has a point to make, the language is lively and not at all academic. We see a writer with a point to make, choosing words precisely. By using expressions such as "is picking up," Ode directs this piece to a nonacademic audience, while Geist directs his to an academic one. Each author's voice is appropriate for the intended purpose and audience.

When writing your paper, choose a tone that is appropriate both for your attitudes toward your paper and for *your* audience (see 3a-4). Think of your readers as intelligent people who are interested in the issue on which you are writing, but who still expect to be engaged, as well as informed. A good academic paper should be like one side of an intelligent conversation—a conversation in which both participants take pleasure. (See 3a-4 for more on determining your own voice.)

TEACHING IDEAS

The advice presented here can be of immeasurable assistance to students who feel intimidated or overwhelmed by their sources. If they force themselves to write a rough draft without any sources, they'll discover what they have to say about the subject, and they'll have the framework they need to make sure they don't turn the paper over to the sources.

REFERENCE

DINITZ, SUSAN, and JEAN KIEDAISCH. "The Research Paper: Teaching Students to Be Members of the Academic Community." *Exercise Exchange* 31 (1986): 8–10. Rhetorical concerns such as purpose, audience, and voice should be addressed in writing the research paper.

GROUP ACTIVITY

Although students may be quite comfortable right now with their writing process in general, the thought of writing a draft of a research paper can be intimidating. (Most instructors have faced the same anxiety many times.) You can ease some of the tension after the students have reviewed Chapters 3 and 4 by asking groups to discuss the similarities and differences between their drafting processes. First ask students to outline the process they normally use when composing a draft, and then ask them to comment on the alterations they'll make to the process in order to accommodate the research paper. In groups, as they discuss their writing processes, they should come to realize that this writing process is not substantially different from the process they've used throughout the course.

35e Writing a draft

Sections 3b–e and 5a provide detailed discussions of strategies that will help you to write a first draft. You will need a method for working (or not working) from your outline, for writing a group of related paragraphs at a single sitting, and for recognizing and responding to obstacles as they arise.

You are finally ready to write. You have conducted systematic research on a subject in which you are interested; you have accumulated a stack of notes, in which you have summarized, paraphrased, and quoted relevant material; you have developed and revised a thesis; and you have prepared a careful sketch or an outline, on the basis of which you have organized your notes: in short, you have become something of an expert on the subject. There is no reason to be anxious at this point. You are not writing the final draft; you are simply preparing a rough draft that will be seen by no one but yourself (and possibly some friends whose advice you trust). You will have plenty of opportunity to revise the rough draft.

Writing a skeleton draft and incorporating sources

To avoid overreliance on sources, as well as to clarify the main lines of a paper's argument, some researchers write their first drafts referring only to their outlines—and not to their source notes. As they write, they mark the places where source material (in summarized, paraphrased, or quoted form) will later be inserted. Drafts written in such a manner are simply skeletons or scaffolds. But by examining the skeleton, you can see whether the logic of your paper is sound. Does the argument make sense to you? Does one part logically follow from another? It should, even without the material from your notes. Remember your purpose and your audience: tell readers, as if you were having a conversation, what they should know about your subject and why you believe as you do.

At some point you will turn to your notes and consider how sources can help advance your ideas. Here are some considerations:

- Try arranging source notes in the order in which you intend to use them, but avoid simply transcribing your notes onto your rough draft.
- If you think you have made your point, move on, and skip any additional, unused notes on the topic or subtopic.
- Once you have completed a draft, you can revisit your notes and decide to substitute particularly effective unused notes for less effective ones used in the draft.

To avoid having to transcribe lengthy quotations or notes onto your draft, consider taping or stapling these notes (or photocopies of the quotations) directly onto the appropriate spots on the draft. When you do incorporate sources, remember to transfer bibliographic codes and page numbers, so that later you can enter the correct citations.

Starting in the middle

Many writers skip the introduction on the rough draft and get right into the body of the paper, believing that they are in a better position to draft the introduction later—when they know exactly what they are introducing. If you believe that you must begin at the beginning and work systematically all the way through, then do that. Whichever approach you take (and neither one is inherently preferable), remember that this is only a *rough* draft; nothing at this stage is final.

35f Revising and editing

In 4a–d, you will find a discussion on revising and editing. Keep in mind that revision literally means "re-seeing." You should not consider revision simply a matter of fixing punctuation and spelling errors and improving a word or phrase here and there. Revision is, rather, a matter of looking at the whole paper from top to bottom and trying to determine whether you have presented material effectively.

Some writers think of revision as a twofold process: *Macro revision* concerns the essay as a whole (its purpose, its voice, its structure), including its larger component units—the section and the paragraph. *Micro revision* concerns sentence structure, grammar, punctuation, and mechanics.

Others consider revision to be a four-stage process, in which writers revise (1) the essay as a whole; (2) individual paragraphs; (3) individual sentences; and (4) individual words.

These strategies are means to the same goal: ensuring that you consider *every* component of your essay, from largest to smallest, as you work to improve it. You will see one page in Jason Koman's revision process—two first-draft paragraphs substantially revised, facing the final-draft version at paragraph H (35h). Such revisions, which represent a fairly major reworking, helped Jason to clarify his thoughts and to state them succinctly.

Arriving at a final thesis

Before writing a draft, you start with a rough working thesis, which provides enough focus to help you sift through the materials you've gathered. More thinking about your sources may require you to refine your thesis. The act of writing a draft will help you to refine and focus still more. Ask yourself these questions as you reread your work:

- What is the main question of this research project?
- Is the question suitably complex for the subject I've defined?
- Is my answer to this question—my thesis—clear?
- Have I stated my thesis clearly in the draft?

GROUP ACTIVITY

You can formalize the process of getting feedback by arranging peer editing groups to facilitate revision of first drafts. Decide first on a framework for the editors to use—either one of the two processes outlined in this section, or a process you devise yourself. You may even want to restrict the focus of peer editing to macro revision. As students respond to each other's papers, they may need to be reminded once again that their job is not to be cheerleaders but coaches, helping the writer do the best job he or she possibly can. They can look to the "marked up" section in the sample paper in 35h for guidance.

TEACHING IDEAS

An ideal setting for receiving feedback from peers is the Writing Center. If your college has one, you may want to recommend it to your students. Some centers even offer group workshops for specific assignments—check to see what services your center offers.

LOOKING AHEAD

See Appendix A, Writing with a Computer, where you will find information regarding collaborative work via disk or network.

Responding to these questions, and making corresponding adjustments in your paper, will help to guide your revision. These questions helped Jason Koman devise a final thesis.

FINAL THESIS

> Shoppers today do not go to malls in search of community, as shoppers used to do, but rather to buy in a predictable, safe, and anonymous environment.

Jason's earlier thesis concentrated only on the fact that shoppers do not go to malls in search of community. Through the process of writing and revising, Jason decided to concentrate, as well, on what shoppers *do* want. Jason found that the act of writing helped his paper to become clear as well as more ambitious. In the final draft of his essay, you will see that this single addition to the thesis contributes directly to the overall structure of the paper. Jason organizes sections of the paper in the following manner. First, he poses the question, "What do we want at the mall?" Then, drawing on sources, he offers three conflicting answers. Finally, he uses these differences to propel himself *and* the reader into a historical review of marketplaces. He uses this review to help answer his initial question.

Working with feedback from readers and peer editors

When revising your paper, get as much feedback as possible from others. It is difficult even for professional writers to get perspective on what they have written immediately after they have written it. You are likely to be too close to the subject, too committed to your outline or to particular words to be very objective at this point. Show your draft to a friend or classmate whose judgment you trust and to your instructor. Obtain reactions on everything from the essay as a whole to the details of word choice.

TEACHING IDEAS

To sharpen students' appreciation of the reasons for documenting their sources, lead them in discussing situations when work that *they* have done has not been appreciated or acknowledged. (This topic also might work well as a short writing assignment, perhaps after a discussion among students in small groups. Each group could make a list of three such occasions and then present it to the whole class for comment.)

35g Understanding the elements of documentation

Writers can use several systems of documentation to credit their sources (see Chapter 36). The system used depends on the discipline in which they are writing—social sciences, humanities, science and technology, or business—or on the preferences of the audience.

Documenting sources is a two-part process:

1. Cite the source *in your paper* to identify it and give credit immediately after its use. This is called an *in-text* citation.
2. Cite the source *at the end of your paper,* in the form of a list of references that readers can pursue in more detail.

For three of the four documentation systems reviewed in Chapter 36—MLA, APA, and CBE—in-text citations are usually placed within parentheses. For the CMS—footnote and endnote—system, you make in-text citations with a small superscript numeral, and references are listed in notes.

Use Documentation to Give Fair Credit and to Assist Your Reader

Why go to the trouble of documenting your sources?

- *To give credit where it is due.* Ethics demands that the originators of ideas and information be credited.
- *To allow readers to gauge the accuracy and reliability of your work.* Any research paper will stand or fall according to how well (how perceptively, accurately, or selectively) you use sources.
- *To avoid charges of plagiarism.* You certainly do not want to give your readers the impression that you are claiming credit for ideas or words that are not yours.
- *To allow interested readers to follow up on a point.* Readers will sometimes want to pursue a point you have raised by going to your sources. Therefore, give readers the clearest possible directions for where to look.

All information and ideas should be documented—not just the sources that you quote directly. Summaries or paraphrases also require acknowledgment. The only exception to this rule is that *common knowledge*—as determined in part by the nature of your audience's level of expertise—need not be documented. (See 34g-1 for a discussion of what counts as common knowledge; and see paragraphs A and I in the sample paper.) For detailed information on documentation styles, see Chapter 36.

35h A sample research paper: "What Do We Want at the Mall?"

The following research paper demonstrates the process of research and writing discussed in these chapters. The student writer, Jason Koman, chose to direct his efforts toward answering a key research question: "What do Americans want at the mall?" This key research question (see 33b-2) led to a working thesis (see 33e-1) and then to a refined thesis (see 35a), but Jason retained the question as the focal point for the paper. Jason describes his motivation for this project as follows:

> My friends and I have always gone to the mall to shop or spend time. Everybody ends up at the mall at some point. Some people (like my grandmother) love to shop. Some old people just sit. Kids hang out. I was interested in why people go to the mall. The whole question of the shopping mall's history and what a mall is—and is not—fascinated me.

Koman's paper conforms to Modern Language Association (MLA) documentation style.

TEACHING IDEAS/LOOKING AHEAD

This paper is consistent, in both form and content, with the typical research paper for a first-year composition course. You may want to refer students to it as a working model for their own papers. For additional sample papers, students can refer to Chapters 37 (a literature paper), 38 (a sociology paper), and 39 (a chemistry lab report).

REFERENCE

JESKE, JEFF. "Borrowing from the Sciences: A Model for the Freshman Research Paper." *The Writing Instructor* 6 (1987): 62–67. Advocates a research paper form based on that of the sciences, including "Materials and Methods," "Results," and "Discussion" sections.

COVER-PAGE FORMAT

What Do We Want at the Mall?

by

Jason Koman

English 160, Section 8
Professor Kelley
3 May 1996

Cover page: Center the title of your paper approximately one-third down the page. Skip four lines and center the preposition *by*. Skip another two lines and center your name. Skip approximately ten lines and center your course number and section. Then follow with your instructor's name and the date submitted, as shown.

NOTE: The fourth edition of the MLA handbook no longer recommends using a cover page. Check with your instructors to determine their preferences on this matter.

Binding: Instructors reading a stack of papers often find transparent folders to be a nuisance. Use a staple or paper clip to bind your paper at the upper-left corner.

TEACHING IDEAS

If you agree with the comment about transparent folders being a nuisance (not to mention a threat to the environment), then you may want to spell out clearly your attitude toward fancy packaging. Some students must be convinced that simpler is actually better. Regardless of your preferences, however, students do need to know exactly what is expected—and written guidelines are the best way to make your expectations clear.

ADDITIONAL EXERCISE A

Use this sample first page and the page shown in Appendix B2 as a model for your paper, and complete the following checklist:

____ Name
____ Instructor's name (spelled correctly)
____ Course / section
____ Date
____ Page number and name
____ Title

FIRST-PAGE FORMAT FOR A PAPER WITHOUT A COVER PAGE

Koman 1

Jason Koman
Professor Kelley
English 160, Section 8
3 May 1996

What Do We Want at the Mall?

Going to the mall has become a routine experience for many Americans. The country's first completely enclosed shopping center--what we commonly refer to as a mall--was built in Edina, Minnesota in 1956. Over the next forty years, developers added 40,000 more shopping centers to the American retail landscape (International 15), which is now saturated with one-stop shopping spaces that invite consumers to buy anything from grapefruit to washing machines. Malls come in a variety of sizes (though usually in a fixed number of shapes--L's, T's, and H's): local strip malls can have as few as a dozen stores, usually including a supermarket. Shoppers in need of greater variety may drive hours to regional or super regional malls, where up to a million square feet of retail space awaits those ready to shop 'till they drop. The most demanding of shoppers have driven five or more hours, climbed aboard buses, and crossed continents and oceans (literally) to shop at the nation's premier mega-mall: the Mall of America in Minnesota (American Survey; Guterson 50).

First page: See page 610 for the first-page format of a paper *with* a cover page. You will see that while the first page is numbered in the upper-right corner, no name appears. Your name and the page number appear beginning with page 2. Use your word processor to run "headers" on every page.

First-page format: Here is the first-page format for a paper *without* a cover page. Provide double-spaced information, flush with the left margin, as shown. (See Appendix B2 for exact measurements and margins.) Skip one double-space and center your title. Skip another double-space and begin your paper. On the first page of the paper, begin numbering your pages, *with* your name, in the upper-right corner as shown. Do *not* use an abbreviation for "page," and do not use a comma. (If you are working with a computer, your word processing program can probably run "headers," which will relieve you of some tedium. Consult your user's manual.)

Outline (pages 608 and 609): Some instructors will ask you to submit a formal outline with your completed paper—for two reasons. For instructors, the outline is a previewing tool. They will be able to read it and quickly get a sense of your paper's scope and direction. For you, writing a formal outline after you *believe* you have written a final draft serves as a final check that your paper is unified and coherent. Papers that do not outline easily may suffer from organizational problems. When outlining what he thought was his final draft, Jason Koman saw a need to revise. Subsequent cuts and mergers in revision (35f) enabled him to eliminate one long paragraph from his essay.

Outline placement and form: Papers with outlines should begin with a cover page. Place the outline immediately after the cover page. Number the outline in the upper-right corner with lowercase roman numerals, beginning with *i.*

Outline in sentences: The example outline is written in sentences. If you choose not to write in sentences, your entries should be parallel (see Chapter 18). Begin the outline with a statement of your thesis, regardless of where the thesis actually appears in the paper. (In the example paper—an argument with an inductive arrangement—the thesis appears at the end, with the conclusion.) Follow the thesis with major section headings (I, II), subsections (A, B), and supporting points (1, 2).

FOR DISCUSSION

A discussion of how students have used outlines in the past may be useful here. Ask students to comment on what kinds of outlines they've used, at what point during the writing process they usually write their outlines, how often they revised them, and what impact they think the outline has had on their papers. Those who have never used outlines profitably in the past may gain a better appreciation for their function.

GROUP ACTIVITY

Ask groups to evaluate this outline the way an instructor might—that is, to use it to get a sense of what to expect in the paper. When all groups have finished their evaluations, representatives from each will report to the class. If there are differences among groups' expectations, class discussion can clarify the reasons.

TEACHING IDEAS

If you wish students to turn in a non-sentence outline, then it might be worthwhile to have them practice on this sample. Ask students to transform this outline into one using parallel non-sentence structures (see 18e-2).

Koman i

Outline

Thesis statement: Shoppers today do not go to malls in search of community, as shoppers used to do, but rather to buy in a predictable, safe, and anonymous environment.

I. Shopping at malls has become routine for many Americans.
   A. Malls are completely enclosed shopping centers.
   B. Malls vary in size.
      1. Strip malls have as few as a dozen stores.
      2. Regional malls are larger, with as much as one million square feet of retail space.
      3. The Mall of America is the nation's mega-mall and a colossal entertainment center.

II. Why do Americans go shopping at malls?
   A. Sociologist Jerry Jacobs believes American shoppers are seeking escape from everyday life. Shoppers want "nothing unusual" to happen. They want the predictable.
   B. David Guterson believes that shoppers go to malls to fulfill a need for community and an "eternal desire for discourse and intimacy."
      1. Malls do not fulfill these needs. They take shoppers' money without respecting their "communal requirements."
      2. Mall management agrees: malls are built to make a profit, not to provide a community.
   C. Sociologist George Lewis agrees that malls do not offer community; but, unlike Guterson, he believes that shoppers do not seek community at the mall. What they want, he says, is to go shopping in a safe, secure place.

III. If the modern marketplace (the mall) does not foster community, and if older marketplaces did, when and why did the change take place?
   A. The Greek market, or agora, had both a social and a commercial function. Later, so did the medieval market and the bazaar.

- B. The social and economic factors that gave the Greek market, medieval market, and bazaar their special character changed with the Industrial Revolution.
  1. By 1800, where people lived, how they earned money, and how they spent money began to change.
  2. The changes altered buying patterns and expectations.
- C. The changes accompanying the Industrial Revolution gave rise to a new type of market: the arcade, the predecessor of the mall.
  1. The arcade arose at a time of "high capitalism," when many luxury goods were available for sale. The arcade brought buyers together with merchandise.
  2. The <u>single</u> purpose of the arcade was to earn a profit. The community function of the marketplace was abandoned.
  3. Modern malls are similar to arcades in several respects.

IV. Conclusion: Shoppers today do not go to the mall in search of community; they go to shop in a predictable, safe, anonymous environment. This purpose for shopping represents a change from the past, when people would go to market both to buy <u>and</u> to meet with others.

- A. It is a mistake to suggest that malls serve the same function in our culture that markets and bazaars did in earlier times.
- B. Shoppers today will not find a community at the mall; but seeking out communities in other places is nonetheless important.
  1. Do communities still exist in America?
  2. If not in the mall, where do we go to find a community?

1

What Do We Want at the Mall?

Going to the mall has become a routine experience for many Americans. The country's first completely enclosed shopping center--what we commonly refer to as a mall--was built in Edina, Minnesota in 1956. Over the next forty years, developers added 40,000 more shopping centers to the American retail landscape (International 15), which is now saturated with one-stop shopping spaces that invite consumers to buy anything from grapefruit to washing machines. Malls come in a variety of sizes (though usually in a fixed number of shapes--L's, T's, and H's): local strip malls can have as few as a dozen stores, usually including a supermarket. Shoppers in need of greater variety may drive hours to regional or super regional malls, where up to a million square feet of retail space awaits those ready to shop 'till they drop. The most demanding of shoppers have driven five or more hours, climbed aboard buses, and crossed continents and oceans (literally) to shop at the nation's premier mega-mall: the Mall of America in Minnesota (American Survey; Guterson 50). **A**

What are shoppers looking for when they travel to this colossal retail space of 4.2 million square feet? Clearly, no one in a day's outing can visit "four department stores, over 400 specialty stores, a seven-acre amusement park complete with roller-coasters, a 14-screen movie complex, 45 restaurants, nine nightclubs, a wedding chapel, a LEGO play center, and an 18-hole miniature golf course" (Labich 105).

Social scientist Jerry Jacobs believes that Americans attempt to escape the boredom of ordinary life by visiting malls. Unlike life on the outside, mall life represents a relief for the average consumer in that it offers an environment carefully controlled for physical comfort and security as well as offering abundant opportunities to buy. Fellow sociologist Joan Emerson finds that, socially speaking, "nothing unusual is happening" in the **B**

Paragraph A (Common knowledge): The entire question of what information and ideas count as common knowledge and what should be attributed to a source is complicated. Partly, the issue depends on audience. A great deal of technical information could be considered to be common knowledge, if you are addressing an expert audience. For an audience of nonspecialists, who might think you have presented the information you're *not* citing as if those were your ideas, you would need to cite the source.

Consider the case of Southdale Center, America's first mall, which Jason Koman refers to in paragraph A. Jason decided that Southdale's status as "first" should be considered common knowledge. Identical information identifying Southdale as first appeared in three sources, and none of those sources cited their information. Jason believed that this fact of mall history, even though unknown to his audience, could justifiably be considered common knowledge. By contrast, see paragraph I, where Jason attributes a key idea in his paper to two sources.

Paragraph A (Reference to a one-page source): When referring to a one-page source, as Jason does in the first of two sources cited at the end of paragraph A, there is no need to cite a page number. Readers will find the information in the Works Cited list.

Paragraph B (Citing an entire work): Sentence one of paragraph B makes a summarizing statement about an entire work. Note that the writer does not, in this instance, cite the work by Jacobs or any page numbers, since the reference is to Jacobs's *entire* book. In such cases, be sure to include a full entry for the reference in the Works Cited. Here is that entry for Jacobs. (You'll see that Jason Koman is rewording, with an addition, the subtitle to Jacobs's book.)

Jacobs, Jerry. *The Mall: An Attempted Escape from Everyday Life.* Prospect Heights, IL: Waveland, 1984.

FOR DISCUSSION

Deciding on a block quotation involves more than just counting lines: the reason for quoting at length must be valid. Ask students to comment on Koman's use of a block quotation here. Do they think the quotation is effective? Would a briefer quotation work as well? a paraphrase or a summary?

Koman 2

mall (qtd. in Jacobs 13). Shoppers who want to avoid potentially upsetting or dangerous people, like the homeless or panhandlers or pamphleteers, can go to the mall with the confidence that the security staff will keep undesirables on the outside. The mall in this way becomes an island, a safe haven with tropical plants, piped-in muzak, and fellow shoppers who can be trusted to do nothing extreme or unsettling. The mall becomes an escape from the threats, and the routine, of everyday life. **B**

David Guterson believes that what Americans secretly go searching for at the mall is community--a connection with humans in a world that is otherwise isolating. Guterson expresses this view in an essay for Harper's, and his criticism echoes the reservations of others (Gumpert and Drucker 188-89; Ode). Having spent a week at the Mall of America in 1993, Guterson reports on the disorienting experience of "[g]etting lost, feeling lost, and being lost" (50). Malls, he says (he regards the Mall of America as an emblem for all malls), take our money without returning even the hint of intimacy and community: **C**

> Here we are free to wander endlessly and to furtively watch our fellow wanderers, thousands upon thousands of milling strangers who have come with the intent of losing themselves in the mall's grand, stimulating design. . . . The mall exploits our acquisitive instincts without honoring our communal requirements, our eternal desire for discourse and intimacy, needs that until the twentieth century were traditionally met in our marketplaces but that are not met at all in our shopping malls. (50)

Guterson's argument is that marketplaces have traditionally been places of business as well as community; malls today are places of business, only; and American shoppers are the poorer for it. Industry specialists heartily agree--at least with the second of Guterson's points: "Malls are designed to maximize profits," says **D**

Paragraph B (Citing indirect sources—the words of one source quoted in another): Koman wants to use Joan Emerson's phrase "nothing unusual is happening," which Jerry Jacobs has quoted. Since Koman is quoting only Emerson, the words get double quotation marks and the lead-in phrasing attributes the quotation to Emerson. Note that the parenthetical citation begins with *qtd. in,* for *quoted in,* and then follows with standard information.

If Koman had introduced Emerson's words while quoting Jacobs's sentence, he would have placed double quotation marks around Jacobs's words—including Jacobs's citation of Emerson—and single quotation marks around Emerson's words:

> "Mall social life," writes Jacobs, "is generally characterized by 'nothing unusual . . . happening' (Emerson, 1969)" (13).

Finally, if Koman had elected to introduce a block quotation at this point, the quotation marks around Emerson's words would again become double marks, since block quotations themselves receive no quotation marks:

> Jacobs claims that shoppers in the suburbs do not have the same experience as shoppers in urban centers:
>
> > This is not only so because of the deja vu sensation generated by the same stores, same signs, or architectural or design similarities, but also because of the nature of interaction on malls and the persons engaged in them. Mall life is generally characterized by "nothing unusual is happening" (Emerson, 1969). (13)

NOTE: Use an original source when you want to quote. When sources are unavailable or difficult to find, then you should rely on the indirect quotation. In the example, Emerson's remarks were delivered orally at a conference. Koman had no choice but to quote Emerson via Jacobs.

Paragraph C (A reference to two sources in a single citation): When you want to refer to two sources in a single citation, place a semicolon between the citations and treat them as you would any citation. The first entry (Gumpert and Drucker) refers to particular pages of the cited source. The second entry (Ode) refers to the entire source. (You will find a similar double reference in paragraph A.)

Paragraph C (Using brackets and ellipses to alter a quotation): In paragraph C, Koman quotes Guterson twice: once by running a phrase of Guterson's into his own sentence and once by quoting at length, in a block. When Koman changes capitalization of a letter, he shows his alteration with a bracket. When he deletes an entire sentence from the block quotation, he shows the deletion with ellipses.

Paragraph D (Deciding how to introduce a quotation): Paragraph D presents two examples of how to lead into a quotation. In the first case, the source is presented as a title—Chairman of the Environmental Subcommittee for the International Council of Shopping Centers. The decision is based

the Chairman of the Environmental Subcommittee for the International Council of Shopping Centers. "They were not built as a replacement for Main Street. If intimacy encourages sales, there will be intimacy" (Marks). One mall executive makes the point with particular bluntness: "We don't want the mall to be a community in any real sense because we'll attract people we don't want to. People who are not here to shop but are coming for some other purpose. It would upset our tenants who want to make money" (qtd. in Lewis 123). **D**

Sociologist George Lewis agrees that malls do not offer community; but, unlike Guterson, he believes that shoppers do <u>not</u> seek community at the mall. What they want, he says, is to go shopping in a safe, secure place. As part of a larger study in popular culture, Lewis observed that while mallgoers can be said to form a collection of people under one roof, they do not constitute a community: they do not search out the types of interpersonal contacts on which communities are built. Even if they go shopping with a friend or family member, they remain isolated consumers during their time in the mall, looking to make what Lewis calls "self-defined and rational economic transactions" (125). The shoppers Lewis observed showed no evidence of going to the mall with "hope in their hearts" of finding community, which Guterson believes has always characterized people's trips to market (51). **E**

What, then, do Americans want at the mall? To escape everyday life? To find community? To shop in a safe, secure place? It is unlikely that all three answers are right. Inasmuch as the mall is a marketplace and exists in a long tradition of marketplaces, a brief historical review might shed some light on the puzzle. With the observations of Jacobs, Guterson, and Lewis in mind, we can turn to history with two questions: Did marketplaces ever foster community? If they did, and the modern mall does not, when and why did the change take place? **F** on Koman's sense that the name and the affiliation of the source is important and lends credibility to the quotation. The particular person, in this context, is less important and is noted parenthetically.

NOTE: Koman cites no page number for this source because, as you will see in the Works Cited, the source was a personal interview.

The "mall executive" in the sentence that follows is never named. The writer's decision is that this name is less important and might even distract from the quoted material, which powerfully illustrates the point about community not being welcome in the mall. In both cases, the in-text citation tells the reader exactly where to find the quoted material.

NOTE: Koman discovered in Lewis's reference list that the origin of this quotation was an interview; Koman therefore had no choice but to quote via Lewis. When you feel that an author's name is important and should be more visible, lead into the quotation with a sentence that includes the name, as in paragraph C.

Paragraph E (Paraphrase): In an early draft, Koman quoted a long passage from George Lewis. On rereading the draft, he decided that the material had too many specialized terms; he therefore decided to write a paraphrase, keeping Lewis's main points but casting them in more commonplace language. At the very end of the paraphrase, Koman retains one brief phrase from the original. This gives readers a feel for Lewis's language. Note that the paraphrase is roughly the same length as the original.

ORIGINAL PASSAGE

> What emerged from the initial observations and interviews, then, was a picture of mall shoppers as a *collectivity,* located in one enclosed space, but utilizing the mall primarily for their own self-defined and rational economic transactions. They may well shop with a friend, or the family may come to the mall, but they are *not* there for the face to face primary interactive relations that are the core of community. (125)

PARAPHRASE

> Lewis observed that while mallgoers can be said to form a collection of people under one roof, they do not constitute a community: they do not search out the types of interpersonal contacts on which communities are built. Even if they go shopping with a friend or family member, they remain isolated consumers during their time in the mall, looking to make what Lewis calls "self-defined and rational economic transactions" (125).

Paragraph F (Key transition): This paragraph functions as a "hinge" in the paper, a key transition that summarizes what has come before: the paper's main question ("What do we want at the mall?") answered differently by three sources. Koman wants to create a motivation for readers to follow him into the next section of the paper, his historical review. He does this by observing an inconsistency (his sources answer his question differently); by stating that malls are linked historically to older markets; and by suggesting that a brief study of history can clarify the confusion.

Koman 4

The ancient agora of Greece, the medieval markets of Europe, and the bazaars of the Orient, from which the mall is descended, did in fact serve important social functions. As early as the sixth century BC, the Greek market, or agora, offered a wide variety of goods in one convenient location. A contemporary described the scene this way:

> In one and the same place you will find all kinds of things for sale together at Athens: figs--Policemen!
> Grapes, turnips, pears, apples--Witnesses! Roses, medlars, porridge, honey-comb, peas--Lawsuits!
> Milk, curds, myrtle-berries--Allotment-machines! Bulbs, lamps--Water clocks, laws, indictments! (qtd. in Thompson)

G

The variety of goods and the suggestion of legal entanglements to be found in the agora suggest the hubbub of a modern shopping center. Significantly, historians describe the space in terms of its commercial <u>and</u> its social functions: "As [Greek] commerce and government expanded, the agora became the focus of business, the market-place, as well as the place of assembly." It was a place "where people met, talked, and conducted business and civic activities" (Rubenstein 2).

The economic and community functions of the agora extended forward in time, both to the marketplaces of Europe and to the bazaars of the Orient. In the medieval towns of Europe, market days were held once each week. Since "nearly everybody lived in the country and earned their living in some way from the land" (Harrison 10), a trip to the market became a much-anticipated social event as well as an opportunity to buy or barter. Bazaars also had a double function, social and economic. Medieval Islamic cities consisted of separate "familial clans, each with its own housing units" that faced inward, to courtyards (Geist 5). The <u>single</u> community space, according to

H

Paragraph G (In-text citation for a source without page numbers): Ordinarily, the in-text citation for the block quotation would refer the reader to a specific page. In this case, the source was a pamphlet that had no pagination, so no reference could be given. Since in-text citations work in conjunction with the Works Cited, the incomplete reference here is explained at the end of the paper, where the reader sees this entry. ("N. pag." is an abbreviation for "no pagination given.")

Thompson, Dorothy Burr. *An Ancient Shopping Center: The Athenian Agora.* Princeton: American School of Classical Studies at Athens, 1971. N. pag.

Paragraph G (Bracketed addition to quoted passage): In its original context, the quoted passage clearly identified *which* nation's commerce and government were expanding. Koman felt that, incorporated into the context of this sentence, the reference was not entirely clear. So he added the word *Greek* to the quotation, placing the addition in brackets.

Paragraphs F, G, and H (Section coherence): These paragraphs fill out section III, paragraph A, in Jason Koman's formal outline of his paper. Here is this part of the outline:

III. If the modern marketplace (the mall) does not foster community, and if older marketplaces did, when and why did the change take place?

A. The Greek market, or agora, had both a social and a commercial function. Later, so did the medieval market and the bazaar.

Notice in paragraphs F, G, and H the number of times Koman uses the words *community* and *social* and then *economic* and *commercial.* His careful repetition in these paragraphs helps to establish the idea that the agora, the medieval market, and the bazaar shared an important *double* function.

Revising the Paper

In revision, the following two paragraphs were combined to yield the final paragraph (H):

The economic & community functions of the agora extended forward in time, both to the marketplaces of Europe & to the bazaars of the Orient.

In the medieval towns of Europe, market days were held once each week. Since "nearly everybody lived in the country and earned their living in some way from the land" (Harrison 10), a trip to the market *became* ~~was~~ a *much-anticipated* social event, *as well as an opportunity to buy or barter.* ~~People who lived at some distance from one another would meet and barter their excess goods, all produced at home. The king or local lord strictly controlled what was sold and where in the market it was sold (Harrison 11).~~ As in ancient times, the market ~~served~~ a ~~social, as well as commercial, function.~~ People who ventured occasionally great ~~distances over poor~~ roads would understand~~ably want~~ to linger, talk, as well as barter at ~~their destina-~~

TEACHING IDEAS

Before commenting on the revisions that produced this page, you may want to ask students to evaluate the writer's style. These paragraphs illustrate the smooth, clear, vivid writing discussed in Chapter 5 and Part V. You may want to ask students what specific components of effective paragraphs and sentences are illustrated in this section of the paper.

GROUP ACTIVITY

After dividing the class into groups, ask each group to compare Koman's draft to his revision. On what basis did he seem to make his decisions? How closely does his revising process mirror those of students in the group? How effective does the group consider his revision to be?

Koman 5

architect and historian Johann Geist, was a collection of buildings that included a bazaar, as well as a mosque and school (5). From the fifth century BC through the eighteenth century AD, markets and bazaars served important economic <u>and</u> community functions. H

The social and economic factors that gave the old markets their special character changed with the Industrial Revolution. Today, far more people live in cities than in the country--a direct reversal of older population patterns; people no longer need to wait for market days to go shopping; a trip to the market is no longer a difficult, dangerous outing over poorly maintained roads; and a trip to the market is no longer the principal means by which people expect to meet others. These changes did not occur all at once. They began with the Industrial Revolution (around 1800)--which at first gradually and then more rapidly raised standards of living throughout Europe and America ("Industrial"). Wealth was created, and for the first time in history a whole class of people could afford luxuries.

Changed economic and social conditions encouraged the rise of a new type of marketplace: the arcade, which is the direct predecessor of the mall (Jacobs 1-2; Kowinski 119). Johann Geist describes the reasons for the arcade's coming into existence:

> The arcade . . . arose at the beginning of high capitalism. The overproduction caused by technological advances made it imperative for the manufacturers of luxury goods to discover new methods of distribution, faster turnover, and easier promotion. The success of the arcade resulted from the combination of two factors: a supply of goods in department-store variety and a supply of public space for undisturbed promenading, window shopping, and display of merchandise. (35) I

~~tion. In town, other than on market days, goods were available from the artisans who made them--armor, leather goods, cloth, and so on. Direct exchange with people responsible for production of these goods encouraged a social exchange.~~

also had a double function, *and*

~~The~~ bazaars ~~of the Islamic world had an expressly~~ social ~~as well as~~ economic ~~purpose~~. ~~The~~ medieval Islamic cit*ies* ~~y~~ consisted of *separate* ~~a "loose community of~~ "familial clans, each with its own housing units" that faced inward, to courtyards (Geist 5). The ~~one~~ *single* community space, according to architect and historian Johann Geist, *was a collection of buildings that included a bazaar as well as a mosque and school (5). From the fifth century BC through the eighteenth century AD, markets and bazaars served important economic and community functions.* ~~"was a building complex consisting of a mosque, madrasa (school), bazaar (for retail trade), chan (for wholesale trade), bath, and other smaller institutions" (5).~~ ~~Trade was strictly controlled and transacted in sometimes enormous and elaborate covered buildings. For example, the Great Bazaar of Istanbul, built in 1461, covered 200,000 square meters--the rival of many modern malls.~~

Paragraph I (Citing the origin of an idea, if it is not yours): The double in-text citation to Jacobs and Kowinski is important, for Koman is here acknowledging that an idea in his paper was not his but one found in a pair of sources. For his argument to succeed, Koman needs to convince readers that the mall is the direct descendant of the arcade. Koman wants help in making this point clear; even though he does not quote or paraphrase Jacobs or Kowinski, he is careful to locate the authority for this idea in their books. Here are brief excerpts from those books.

From Jacobs

> A forerunner of the enclosed shopping mall was the development and expansion of arcades in the 19th century. These were built as a way to deal with the increasingly hostile public environments of urban centers. Enclosed shopping centers of this kind were preceded by the agora of Athens, Roman forums and oriental bazaars (Gruen, 1973). (1–2)

From Kowinski

> The solution [to the weather problem facing the builders of Southdale, which would be the first mall] was, of course, complete enclosure. Gruen [the project's architect] saw it immediately and went to the Dayton-Hudson hierarchy [the developers] with his proposal. He told them about the covered pedestrian arcades in Europe, especially the Galleria Vittorio Emanuele in Milan, Italy, with its arcades rising four stories to a glass barrel vault and a central glass cupola 160 feet high. (119)

Relying on these sources enabled Koman to feel confident about a key claim in his essay: that the arcade was the direct predecessor of the mall. For an example of information that Koman found in several sources but decided not to cite (because he felt the information was common knowledge), see the facing-page note at paragraph A.

The Industrial Revolution fundamentally changed the relationship between those who bought and sold--and, significantly, between buyers themselves (Gumpert and Drucker 188). The _single_ purpose of the new marketplace, the arcade, was to make money. _Community_ was abandoned.

The suburban mall is similar in important respects to the urban arcade, which it replaced when people moved out of the city. Historians tell us that as early as the first decades of the nineteenth century arcades were built "where a growing population coincided with a shortage of shops, availability of land, finance and an entrepreneur" (MacKeith 16). Today, malls are located according to exactly these same criteria. Like the modern mall, the arcade presented an illusion of outdoor space in an indoor space, with pedestrian walkways that wound through rows of store fronts (Geist 4). Though the arcade was privately owned, it presented the illusion of being a public place, and it became a destination for people in search of activity--much as the Mall of America and other malls today are destinations for both shoppers and tourists.

The arcade and mall also share two other important features. Both create indoor streets in which shoppers prefer to be anonymous (Geist 17). And in malls, just as in earlier arcades, shoppers avoid engaging with others. They prefer their own company (Lewis 124). Finally, the arcade was designed for selling and for keeping people moving. The layout of the walkways and even the overhead lighting (as opposed to the use of windows) discouraged customers from stopping to chat about any business unrelated to buying (Geist 20). It appears that arcades were specifically designed to discourage the personal exchanges that foster community. Modern malls are similarly designed. In observing the New England Mall, George Lewis noted that "the high turnover, volume of persons, and transiency that is a designed part of most malls works _against_ the development and emergence of community" (123).

J

Synthesis: Incorporating Notes into Your Paper

Paragraph J: Jason Koman has previously made the point that the arcade directly preceded the mall. In this paragraph, he uses notes filed under the category "Design Features." Two sets of cards follow, two bibliography cards and a notecard for each. Observe how Koman links these notes from separate sources in the paper, finding a key similarity that illustrates his larger point.

---

(5) Geist, Johann F. *Arcades: The History of a Building Type.* Trans. Jane O. Newman and John H. Smith. Cambridge: MIT, 1983.

NA
6218
.G4313x
1983

First chapter, 3-58: "The Architectural History of the Arcade." Markets, bazaars, arcades—design features and their *social* significance.

Design features of arcades 

Physical features of the arcade isolate shoppers from outside world and keep them moving along. Arcades built with skylights, and no windows, so rooms—lit from above—could be otherwise totally enclosed. The effect: to keep shoppers' minds and eyes on the merchandise. (20)

---

(8) Lewis, George H. "Community Through Exclusion and Illusion: The Creation of Social Worlds in an American Shopping Mall." *Journal of Popular Culture* 24.2 (1990): 121-36.

Investigates what sorts of communities, if any, exist in the mall; based conclusions on observations at Mall of New England. Aside from teenagers and elders, no communities exist.

Design features of malls 

Lewis argues that mall developers purposely design malls to discourage community. "In short, the high turnover, volume of persons, and transiency that is a designed part of most malls works *against* the development and emergence of community within their walls." (123)

FOR DISCUSSION

After having students read Koman's paper through, ask them to comment on his choice of placement for the thesis. Is the delay effective? Why, or why not? How would a different placement have altered the effect of the essay?

CRITICAL THINKING

Ask students to identify and list Koman's conclusions. How does he support his conclusions: with fact? assumptions? analysis? Ask students to write out or explain their responses and, in doing so, to refer to specific sentences in Koman's paper when evaluating his persuasiveness.

TEACHING IDEAS

This discussion allows students to see first-hand the purpose of a research paper—not to rehash the ideas of all the sources, but instead to use those ideas to further the writer's own purpose. You may want to lead the class through an analysis of this section of the paper, pointing out specifically how Koman is able to make the material his own.

Koman 7

Keeping the eyes and minds of buyers on the merchandise: this was the single most important design goal for the arcade, and it remains the paramount goal of mall developers (Lagerfeld 115).

Marketplaces have evolved over the centuries, with a crucial turning point coming with the rise of the Industrial Revolution. This historical perspective sheds light on the unexpectedly puzzling question, what do Americans want at the mall? In brief, the answer is this: Shoppers today do not go to malls in search of community, as shoppers used to do, but rather to buy in a predictable, safe, and anonymous environment. K

Unlike in the past, mallgoers want nothing unusual to happen--as Jacobs suggests. Modern life is so uncertain that going to a predictable, if bland, mall seems a relief. By contrast, those who traveled to the medieval market or who ventured into the Islamic bazaar probably lived lives that were so tedious and predictable in their heavy labors that they looked forward to the unusual, or at least the unexpected. Deprived of much new company during the week, marketgoers likely looked forward to meeting others on market days.

Unlike in the past, shoppers today do <u>not</u> seek community at the market. The Industrial Revolution changed the key social and economic facts that gave the old markets their character. For clear historical reasons that led to the development of arcades around 1800, the character of the marketplace changed. <u>Community</u> was abandoned; <u>profit</u> became the chief function of the market, and it remains so today. In this environment, shoppers changed their expectations of shopping so that today, as George Lewis suggests, they approach markets as individuals, <u>not</u> as part of a community; and they appreciate markets that are safe and secure.

The desire for an older type of market, one that encourages direct contact and intimacy, is understandable; but that desire is appropriate for a marketplace that no

Paragraph K (First explicit mention of thesis): Up to this point in the paper, Koman has presented his research question: "What do Americans want at the mall?" He has called on three sources to answer the question, and each does—differently. In an effort to resolve what he calls a "puzzle," he turns to history and examines old marketplaces, the arcade, and the mall. Having done all this, he is in a position to present his thesis: "Shoppers today do not go to malls in search of community, as shoppers used to do, but rather to buy in a predictable, safe, and anonymous environment."

In the three paragraphs that follow, Koman returns to his three sources—Jacobs, Lewis, and Guterson—and links their individual insights with the insights gained in the historical section of the paper. Koman accepts the conclusions of Jacobs and Lewis; he rejects (although sympathetically) the conclusions (on the need for community) advanced earlier by Guterson.

Koman 8

longer exists. For two hundred years, the community functions of the marketplace have been splitting away from the commercial functions, and today we bear the burden--and the fruits--of this change. The modern mall will never be our agora; we will not find community there. Still, we are social creatures, and concerns about community are important. It is fair to ask: In what public spaces do we gather, anymore, to be sociable and to discuss important issues? Is America any longer a nation of communities, national or local? Can we be a nation without communities? These are open questions, and important ones. If not in the mall, where do we look for and take comfort in the company of others? L

Koman 9

Works Cited

"American Survey: Decline and Mall." Economist 29 Aug. 1992: 25.

Geist, Johann F. Arcades: The History of a Building Type. Trans. Jane O. Newman and John H. Smith. Cambridge: MIT, 1983.

Gumpert, Gary, and Susan J. Drucker. "From the Agora to the Electronic Shopping Mall." Critical Studies in Mass Communication 9 (1992): 186-200.

Guterson, David. "Enclosed. Encyclopedic. Endured.: One Week at the Mall of America." Harper's Aug. 1993: 49-56.

Harrison, Molly. People and Shopping: A Social Background. London: Ernest Benn, 1975.

"Industrial Revolution." Concise Columbia Encyclopedia. Microsoft Bookshelf. 1994 ed. CD-ROM. Redmond: Microsoft, 1994.

International Council of Shopping Centers. Scope of the Shopping Center Industry in the United States. New York: ICSC, 1995.

Paragraph L (Conclusion): A common strategy for conclusions is to open the discussion up to wider issues—to broaden the context. (See 5f-2 for a discussion of other strategies.) Koman does exactly this. While Guterson is the one source whose conclusions he has rejected, Koman nonetheless concludes with a sympathetic bow to Guterson, saying that concern for community is important. This broadens the context of the paper.

A note on inductive and deductive strategies

This is an inductively arranged paper: Koman has delayed presenting the thesis until *all* the evidence has been presented to the reader. Then, he offers the thesis at the end of the paper, basically in the same location as the conclusion. Inductive strategies work well when you suspect the reader might resist accepting your conclusion; or, as in this case, when you want to demonstrate that a problem or question is more complex than the reader may have thought, before offering your observations. The goal of induction is to build the reader's thinking about an issue step by step. If the reader takes these steps with you, accepting your logic and evidence, then the reader is likely to accept your conclusions.

A deductively arranged paper states the thesis early on and then devotes its energies to supporting it. You give away some of your paper's drama in this arrangement; but you also give your reader the advantage of seeing the larger picture from the start. With a deductive arrangement, readers are less likely to say, "hurry up and get to the point."

Format for the list of references (Works Cited): See Chapter 36 for explanations and examples of the proper form for each entry. The entries are alphabetical and double-spaced; the heading is centered an inch from the top of the page. Each new entry begins at the left margin; subsequent lines in the entry are indented five spaces.

Note, especially, the following entries in the Works Cited:

- Three sources with an anonymous author: see "American Survey" (magazine); "Industrial" (encyclopedia entry); and "International" (book with corporate author).
- Three electronic sources: see "Industrial," "Lagerfeld," and "Ode"—which illustrate a CD-ROM search, an America Online search, and a Nexis search.
- One source with two authors: see "Gumpert and Drucker."
- Two journals: see "Gumpert and Drucker," which appears in a journal that is paginated consecutively throughout the publication year; see "Lewis," which appears in a journal that paginates each issue separately.
- Three magazine entries, with differing citation forms: see "Guterson," which appears in a magazine that is issued monthly; see "Labich," which appears in a magazine that is issued bi-weekly (twice a month); see "American," which appears in a magazine that is issued weekly.
- One interview (personal): see "Marks."
- Eight books: see "Geist," "Harrison," "International," "Jacobs," "Kowinski," "MacKeith," "Rubenstein," and "Thompson."

Jacobs, Jerry. The Mall: An Attempted Escape from Everyday Life. Prospect Heights, IL: Waveland, 1984.

Kowinski, William Severini. The Malling of America: An Inside Look at the Great Consumer Paradise. New York: William Morrow, 1985.

Labich, Kenneth. "What It Will Take to Keep People Hanging Out at the Mall." Fortune 29 May 1995: 102-06.

Lagerfeld, Steven. "What Main Street Can Learn from the Mall." Atlantic Nov. 1995: 110-16. Online. AOL. 25 Jan. 1996.

Lewis, George H. "Community Through Exclusion and Illusion: The Creation of Social Worlds in an American Shopping Mall." Journal of Popular Culture 24.2 (1990): 121-36.

MacKeith, Margaret. The History and Conservation of Shopping Arcades. London: Mansell, 1986.

Koman 10

Marks, Richard. International Council of Shopping Centers. Personal interview. 26 Jan. 1996.

Ode, Kim. "It's a Mall, Mall World." Star Tribune 2 Aug. 1992: 6sm. Online. Nexis. 24 Jan. 1996.

Rubenstein, Harvey M. Pedestrian Malls, Streetscapes, and Urban Spaces. New York: Wiley, 1992.

Thompson, Dorothy Burr. An Ancient Shopping Center: The Athenian Agora. Princeton: American School of Classical Studies at Athens, 1971. N. pag.

CHAPTER 36

Documenting Research

Any time you use material derived from specific sources, whether quoted passages or summaries or paraphrases of fact, opinion, explanation, or idea, you are ethically obligated to let your reader know who deserves the credit. Further, you must tell your readers precisely where the material came from so that they can locate it for themselves. Often readers will want to trace the facts on which a conclusion is based, or to verify that a passage was quoted or paraphrased accurately. Sometimes readers will simply want to follow up and learn more about your subject.

There are basically two ways for a writer to show a "paper trail" to sources. The most widely used format today is the parenthetical reference, also called an *in-text citation.* This is a telegraphic, short-hand approach to identifying the source of a statement or quotation. It assumes that a complete list of references appears at the end of the paper. Each entry in the list of references includes three essential elements: authorship, full title of the work, and publication information. In the references, entries are arranged, punctuated, and typed to conform to the bibliographic style requirements of the particular discipline or of the instructor. With this list in place, the writer is able to supply the briefest of references—a page number or an author's name—in parentheses right in the text, knowing that the reader will be able to locate the rest of the reference information easily in the list of references. The second method for showing a paper trail is the footnote style—which is less often used today than the parenthetical system.

For more detailed information on the conventions of style in the humanities, social sciences, business disciplines, and sciences, refer to these style manuals:

- Gibaldi, Joseph. *MLA Handbook for Writers of Research Papers.* 4th ed. New York: MLA, 1995.
- *Publication Manual* (of the American Psychological Association). 4th ed. Washington, DC: APA, 1994.
- *Chicago Manual of Style.* 14th ed. Chicago: University of Chicago Press, 1993.
- *CBE Style Manual.* 5th ed. Bethesda, MD: CBE, 1983.
- Li, Xia, and Nancy B. Crane. *Electronic Styles: An Expanded Guide to Citing Electronic Information.* Westport: Meckler, 1996.

36a Using the MLA system of documentation

The Modern Language Association (MLA) publishes a style guide that is widely used for citations and references in the humanities. This section

KEY FEATURES

Documentation is approached in this chapter as a matter of ethics: the writer is obliged to give credit to sources of information and to provide readers with sufficient information to find sources. In order to facilitate its use, the chapter begins with a brief explanation of major forms of documentation, and provides an overview of the four systems to be presented: MLA (Modern Language Association) for most humanities papers; APA (American Psychological Association) for most social science papers; the footnote (or Chicago Manual) style, used in the humanities, social sciences, and some business-related disciplines; and CBE (Council of Biology Editors) for most science papers. New to this section is detailed guidance for citing electronic sources. Each section begins with a detailed index of what can be found in the section, making the chapter much easier to negotiate than the standard documentation chapter. Also in the beginning of each section is an explanation of the rationale behind the documentation system (in social and pure sciences, for example, the date is essential and therefore is emphasized more than in humanities), and detailed examples of standard in-text citations, including advice on placement and punctuation. In general, the chapter emphasizes using common sense as a guide. Students should find this chapter invaluable in documenting their papers in many disciplines.

gives detailed examples of how the MLA system of parenthetical references provides in-text citation. In addition, a later section (36c) will show how to use the Chicago Manual of Style (CMS) system of documentation (formerly used in MLA publications), where complete information on each source is given every time a source is cited.

TEACHING IDEAS

Students are sometimes baffled by the need to document sources. You may want to emphasize the ethical appeal here, perhaps by simply appealing to the human desire to be acknowledged for work accomplished. Students should also be encouraged to survey the overview presented here—the numerous entries in the chapter can be very confusing if students don't have a sense of the major systems. In fact, students may want to mark off this page for future reference.

REFERENCES

FULKERSON, RICHARD. "Oh, What a Cite! A Teaching Tip to Help Students Document Researched Papers Accurately." *The Writing Instructor* 7 (1988): 167–72. Presenting students with a research paper without citations can help them figure out what requires documentation.

HOWELL, JOHN BRUCE. *Style Manuals of the English-Speaking World.* Phoenix: Oryx, 1983. Information on a variety of style manuals.

TEACHING IDEAS

Advise students to ask their instructors—in any course—what form of documentation is preferred. In fact, students can be encouraged to bring the handbook to their instructors for verification of particular citation forms. The index provided at the beginning of each section will be invaluable to students, freeing them from searching through an endless array of headings and examples. Encourage students to familiarize themselves with the index now.

An Overview of the Four Documentation Systems Presented in This Chapter

In a research paper, either of these systems of source citation is followed at the end by a list of references. In the MLA system, the list of references is called "Works Cited." Keep in mind that the complete information provided in the list of references will be the basis of your in-text citations. The parenthetical form provides minimal information and sends the reader to the list of references to find the rest. By contrast, the footnote or endnote system virtually duplicates the information in the list of references but uses a slightly different arrangement of the elements in the entry. Following is an index to this section on the MLA system of documentation.

REFERENCE

GIBALDI, JOSEPH. *MLA Handbook for Writers of Research Papers.* 4th ed. New York: MLA, 1995. Extensive advice on documenting sources.

TEACHING IDEAS

You may want to emphasize the "common sense" rule here: if the author is named in the text, then there's no need to name the author in the parenthetical reference. The remaining information in this section also calls for common sense.

TEACHING IDEAS

ACROSS THE CURRICULUM Assign students to bring to class a secondary source text relating to the subject matter of their own research papers. Ask them to identify and point out the citations on a selected page and to indicate how they are helpful to researchers who wish further to explore the subject.

1 Making in-text citations in the MLA format

When you make a parenthetical in-text citation, you assume that your reader will look to the list of "Works Cited" for complete references. The list of references at the end of your paper will provide three essential pieces of information for each of your sources: author, title, and facts of publication. Within your paper, a parenthetical citation may point to a source considered as a whole or to a specific page location in a source. Here is an example of an MLA in-text citation referring to a story as a whole.

```
In "Escapes," the title story of one contemporary author's book
of short stories, the narrator's alcoholic mother makes a public
spectacle of herself (Williams).
```

The next example refers to a specific page in the story. In the MLA system, no punctuation is placed between a writer's last name and a page reference.

```
In "Escapes," a story about an alcoholic household, a key moment
occurs when the child sees her mother suddenly appear on stage at
the magic show (Williams 11).
```

Here is how the references to the Williams story would appear as described in the list of references or "Works Cited."

```
Williams, Joy. "Escapes." Escapes: Stories. New York: Vintage,
    1990. 1-14.
```

Deciding when to insert a source citation and what information to include is often a judgment call rather than the execution of a mechanical system. Use common sense. Where feasible, incorporate citations smoothly into the text. Introduce the parenthetical reference at a pause in your sentence, at the end if possible. Place it as close to the documented point as possible, making sure that the reader can tell exactly which point is being documented. When the in-text reference is incorporated into a sentence of your own, always place the parenthetical reference *before* any enclosing or end punctuation.

```
In Central Africa in the 1930s, a young girl who comes to town
drinks beer with her date because that's what everyone does
(Lessing 105).
```

```
In a realistic portrayal of Central African city life in the
1930s (Lessing), young people gather daily to drink.
```

When a quotation from a work is incorporated into a sentence of your own, the parenthetical reference *follows* the quotation marks, yet precedes the enclosing or end punctuation.

```
At the popular Sports Club, Lessing's heroine finds the "ubiqui-
tous glass mugs of golden beer" (135).
```

EXCEPTION: When your quotation ends with a question mark or exclamation point, keep these punctuation marks inside the end quotation marks, then give the parenthetical reference, and end with a period.

```
Martha's new attempts at sophistication in town prompted her to
retort, "Children are a nuisance, aren't they?" (Lessing 115).
```

Naming an author in the text

When you want to emphasize the author of a source you are citing, incorporate that author's name into your sentence. Unless you are referring to a particular place in that source, no parenthetical reference is necessary in the text.

```
Biographer Paul Mariani understands Berryman's alcoholism as one
form of his drive toward self-destruction.
```

Naming an author in the parenthetical reference

When you want to emphasize information in a source but not especially the author, omit the author's name in the sentence and place it in the parenthetical reference.

```
Biographers have documented alcohol-related upheavals in John
Berryman's life. Aware, for example, that Dylan Thomas was in an
alcohol-induced coma, dying, Berryman himself drank to escape his
pain (Mariani 273).
```

When you are referring to a particular place in your source and have already incorporated the author's name into your sentence, place only the page number in parentheses.

```
Biographer Paul Mariani describes how Berryman, knowing that his
friend Dylan Thomas was dying in an alcohol-induced coma, himself
began drinking to escape his pain (273).
```

Documenting a block quotation

For block quotations, set the parenthetical reference—with or without an author's name—*outside* of the end punctuation mark.

```
The story graphically portrays the behavior of Central African
young people gathering daily to drink:
          Perry sat stiffly in a shallow chair which looked
          as if it would splay out under the weight of his big
          body . . . while from time to time--at those moments
          when laughter was jerked out of him by Stella--he
          threw back his head with a sudden dismayed movement,
          and flung half a glass of liquor down his throat.
          (Lessing 163)
```

A work by two or three authors

If your source has two or three authors, name them all, either in your text or in a parenthetical reference. Use last names, in the order they are given in the source, connected by *and.*

```
Critics have addressed the question of whether literary artists
discover new truths (Wellek and Warren 33-36).
```

```
One theory claims that the alcoholic wants to "drink his environ-
ment in" (Perls, Hefferline, and Goodman 193-94).
```

A work by four or more authors

For a work with four or more authors, name all the authors, or use the following abbreviated format with *et al.* to signify "and others."

```
Some researchers trace the causes of alcohol dependence to
"flawed family structures" (Stein, Lubber, Koman, and Kelly 318).
```

Some researchers trace the causes of alcohol dependence to "flawed family structures" (Stein et al. 318).

Stein and his coeditors trace the causes of alcohol dependence to "flawed family structures" (318).

Reference to two or more sources with the same authorship

When you are referring to two or more sources written by the same author, include in your in-text citation a shortened form of each title so that references to each text will be clear. The following example discusses how author Joy Williams portrays the drinking scene in her fiction. Note that a comma appears between the author's name and the shortened title.

She shows drinking at parties as a way of life in such stories as "Escapes" and "White Like Midnight." Thus it is matter of course that Joan pours herself a drink while people talk about whether or not they want to survive nuclear war (Williams, "White" 129).

Distinguishing two authors with the same last name

Use one or more initials to supplement references to authors with the same last name.

It is no coincidence that a new translation of Euripides' The Bacchae should appear in the United States (C. K. Williams) at a time when fiction writers portray the use of alcohol as a means of escape from mundane existence (J. Williams).

Two or more sources in a single reference

Particularly in an introductory summary, you may want to group together a number of works that cover one or more aspects of your research topic. Separate one source from another by a semicolon.

Studies that confront the alcoholism of literary figures directly are on the increase (Mariani; Dardis; Gilmore).

A corporate author

A work may be issued by an organization or government agency with no author named. Cite the work as if the name given is the author's. Since the name of a corporate author is often long, try incorporating it into your text rather than using a parenthetical note. In this example the corporate author of the book is Alcoholics Anonymous. The book will be listed alphabetically under "Alcoholics" in Works Cited.

Among publications that discuss how to help young people cope with family problems, Al-Anon Faces Alcoholism, put out by Alcoholics Anonymous, has been reissued frequently since 1974 (117-24).

A multivolume work

When citing a page reference to a multivolume work, specify the volume by an arabic numeral followed by a colon, a space, and the page number. The Trevelyan history is in four volumes.

Drunkenness was such a problem in the first decades of the eighteenth century that it was termed "the acknowledged national vice of Englishmen of all classes" (Trevelyan 3: 46).

A literary work

Well-known literary works, particularly older ones now in the public domain, may appear in numerous editions. When referring to such a work or a part of one, give information for the work itself rather than for the particular edition you are using, unless you are highlighting a special feature or contribution of the edition.

For a play, supply act, scene, and line number in arabic numerals, unless your instructor specifies using Roman numerals for act and scene (II. iv. 118–19). In the following example, the title of the literary work includes numerals referring to the first of two plays that Shakespeare wrote about Henry IV, known as parts 1 and 2.

Shakespeare's Falstaff bellows, "Give me a cup of sack, rogue. Is there no virtue extant?" (1 Henry IV 2.4.118-19).

To cite a modern editor's contribution to the publication of a literary work, adjust the emphasis of your reference. The abbreviation *n* stands for *note.*

Without the editor's footnote in the Riverside Shakespeare explaining that lime was sometimes used as an additive to make wine sparkle, modern readers would be unlikely to understand Falstaff's ranting: "[Y]et a coward is worse than a cup of sack with lime in it. A villainous coward!" (1 Henry IV 2.4.125-26n).

Material quoted in your source

Often you will want to quote and cite material that you are reading at second hand—in a work by an intermediate author. Quote the original material and refer to the place where you found it.

Psychoanalyst Otto Fenichel included alcoholics within a general grouping of addictive personalities, all of whom use addictive substances "to satisfy the archaic oral longing, a need for security, and a need for the maintenance of self-esteem simultaneously" (qtd. in Roebuck and Kessler 86).

An anonymous work

A work with no acknowledged author will be alphabetized in a list of references by the first word of its title. Therefore cite the anonymous work in the same way in your parenthetical reference. The title in this example is *The Hidden Alcoholic in Your Midst.*

People who do not suffer from addiction often can be thoughtless and insensitive to the problems of those around them. That is the message of an emotional and thought-provoking pamphlet (Hidden), whose author writes anonymously about the pain of keeping his alcoholism secret.

Page locations for electronic sources

You will find that some electronic sources and documents from the Internet have page numbers; others have paragraph numbers; many have neither. Since you need to provide specific information to show readers where to locate and examine sources, you can follow these general guidelines—an extension of those developed by the Modern Language Association for print sources. Examples are hypothetical.

- Begin the parenthetical citation by referring to the author or title of the source, as you would with any other in-text citation (provided these are not previously mentioned in your sentence).
- Refer to a page number in the electronic source, if provided.

  Leading scientists have called for a moratorium on the release of genetically engineered organisms into the environment (Weiss 12).

- If the electronic source has no page numbers, refer to paragraph numbers (if provided). If your citation begins with the author's name or a title, place a comma and follow with the abbreviation *par.* or *pars.,* and indicate the paragraph(s) used.

  Hardy reports that many geneticists object to the idea of a moratorium and have formed their own lobbying groups to fight such moves (par. 14).

- If no pagination or paragraph numbering is provided, you can use abbreviations like those used for classic literary works to refer to a structural division within the source: "pt." for part; "sec." for section; "ch." for chapter; "vol." for volume.

```
In the absence of agreement within the scientific community,
Norman Stein, director of Genetics Watch, has called for a
"sensible government policy" (qtd. in Lubber sec. 5).
```

- If the electronic source provides no pagination, no paragraph numbering, and no internal structural divisions, cite the source by name only. At the Works Cited page, readers will see that the electronic source was not paginated.

```
Scientists prefer to govern themselves; historically, the
threat of government intervention has prompted voluntary re-
straints from scientific organizations (Wesley).
```

- Finally, when you are citing a one-page electronic source or an electronic source in which entries are arranged alphabetically (such as a CD-based or online encyclopedia), no in-text reference to a page or paragraph is needed. The following reference is to a "Works Cited" list that names an anonymously written article in an online encyclopedia.

```
For centuries, farmers have manipulated "genetic materials
to achieve desired changes in plants and animals" ("Genetic
Engineering").
```

Following MLA parenthetical style, these in-text citations of electronic sources refer readers to detailed entries in the Works Cited list. See 36a-3 for guidelines on creating these detailed entries.

2 Preparing a list of references in the MLA format

In research papers following MLA format, the list of references is called "Works Cited" when it includes those sources you have referred to in your paper. Be aware that some instructors request a more comprehensive list of references—one that includes every source you consulted in preparing the paper. That list would be titled "Bibliography."

The examples in this section show how entries in the "Works Cited" list consist of three elements essential for a list of references: authorship, full title of the work, and publication information. In addition, if the work is taken from an electronic (online) source, consult 36a-3. The basic format for each entry requires the first line to start at the left margin, with each subsequent line to be indented five typed spaces from the left margin.

Not every possible variation is represented here. In formatting a complicated entry for your own list, you may need to combine features from two or more of the examples.

The MLA "Works Cited" list begins on a new page, after the last page of your paper, and continues the pagination of your paper. Entries in the list are alphabetized by the author's last name. An anonymous work is alphabetized by the first word in its title (but disregard *A, An,* and *The*).

Listing books in the MLA "Works Cited" format

The MLA "Works Cited" list presents book references in the following order:

1. Author's name: Put the last name first, followed by a comma and the first name (and middle name or initial) and a period. Omit the author's titles and degrees, whether one that precedes a name (Dr.) or one that follows (Ph.D.). Leave two typed spaces after the period.
2. Title of the book: Underline the complete title. If there is a subtitle, separate it from the main title by a colon and one typed space. Capitalize all important words, including the first word of any subtitle. The complete title is followed by a period and two typed spaces.
3. Publication information: Name the city of publication, followed by a colon and one typed space; the name of the publisher followed by a comma; the date of publication followed by a period. This information appears on the title page of the book and the copyright page, on the reverse side of the title page.

If the city of publication is not well known, add the name of the state, abbreviated as in the zip code system. Shorten the name of the publisher in a way that is recognizable. "G. P. Putnam's Sons" is shortened to "Putnam's." For university presses use "UP" as in the example "U of Georgia P." Many large publishing companies issue books under imprints that represent particular groups of books. Give the imprint name first, followed by a hyphen and the name of the publisher: Bullseye-Knopf.

Any additional information about the book goes between author and title or between title and publication data. Observe details of how to organize, abbreviate, and punctuate this information in the examples below.

A book with one author

The basic format for a single-author book is as follows:

Mariani, Paul. Dream Song: The Life of John Berryman. New York: Morrow, 1990.

A book with two or three authors

For a book with two or three authors, follow the order of the names on the title page. Notice that first and last name are reversed only for the lead author. Notice also the use of a comma after the first author.

Roebuck, Julian B., and Raymond G. Kessler. The Etiology of Alcoholism: Constitutional, Psychological and Sociological Approaches. Springfield: Thomas, 1972.

A book with four or more authors

As in the example under in-text citations (see 36a-1), you may choose to name all the authors or to use the abbreviated format with *et al.*

Stein, Norman, Mindy Lubber, Stuart L. Koman, and Kathy Kelly. Family Therapy: A Systems Approach. Boston: Allyn, 1990.

Stein, Norman, et al. Family Therapy: A Systems Approach. Boston: Allyn, 1990.

A book that has been reprinted or reissued

In the following entry, the date 1951 is the original publication date of the book, which was reprinted in 1965.

Perls, Frederick, Ralph F. Hefferline, and Paul Goodman. Gestalt Therapy: Excitement and Growth in the Human Personality. 1951. New York: Delta-Dell, 1965.

A dictionary or encyclopedia

If an article in a reference work is signed (usually by initials), include the name of the author, which is spelled out elsewhere in the reference work (usually at the beginning). The first example is unsigned. The second article is signed (F.G.H.T.).

"Alcoholics Anonymous." Encyclopaedia Britannica: Micropaedia. 1991 ed.

Tate, Francis G. H. "Rum." Encyclopaedia Britannica. 1950 ed.

A selection from an edited book or anthology

For a selection from an edited work, name the author of the selection and enclose the selection title in quotation marks. Underline the title of the book containing the selection, and name its editor(s). Give the page numbers for the selection at the end of your entry.

Davies, Phil. "Does Treatment Work? A Sociological Perspective." The Misuse of Alcohol. Ed. Nick Heather et al. New York: New York UP, 1985. 158-77.

When a selection has been reprinted from another source, include that information too, as in the following example. State the facts of original publication first, then describe the book in which it has been reprinted.

Bendiner, Emil. "The Bowery Man on the Couch." The Bowery Man. New York: Nelson, 1961. Rpt. in Man Alone: Alienation in Modern Society. Ed. Eric Josephson and Mary Josephson. New York: Dell, 1962. 401-10.

Two or more works by the same author(s)

When you cite two or more works by the same author(s), you should write the author's full name only once, at first mention, in the reference list. In subsequent entries immediately following, substitute three hyphens and a period in place of the author's name.

Heilbroner, Robert L. The Future as History. New York: Harper Torchbooks-Harper, 1960.

---. An Inquiry into the Human Prospect. New York: Norton, 1974.

A translation

When a work has been translated, acknowledge the translator's name after giving the title.

Kufner, Heinrich, and Wilhelm Feuerlein. In-Patient Treatment for Alcoholism: A Multi-Centre Evaluation Study. Trans. F. K. H. Wagstaff. Berlin: Springer, 1989.

A corporate author

If authorship is not individual but corporate, treat the name of the organization as you would the author. This listing would be alphabetized under "National Center."

National Center for Alcohol Education. The Community Health Nurse and Alcohol-Related Problems: Instructor's Curriculum Planning Guide. Rockville: National Institute on Alcohol Abuse and Alcoholism, 1978.

Signaling publication information that is unknown

If a document fails to state place or date of publication or the name of the publisher, indicate this lack of information in your entry by using the appropriate abbreviation.

Missing, Andrew. Things I Forgot or Never Knew. N.p.: n.p., n.d.

In the above example, the first *n.p.* stands for "no place of publication." The second *n.p.* means "no publisher given," and *n.d.* stands for "no date."

An edition subsequent to the first

Books of continuing importance may be revised substantially before reissue. Cite the edition you have consulted just after giving the title.

Scrignar, C. B. Post-Traumatic Stress Disorder: Diagnosis, Treatment, and Legal Issues. 2nd ed. New Orleans: Bruno, 1988.

A book in a series

If the book you are citing is one in a series, include the series name (no quotation marks or underline) followed by the series number and a period before the publication information. You need not give the name of the series editor.

Schuckit, Marc A., ed. Alcohol Patterns and Problems. Series in Psychological Epidemiology 5. New Brunswick: Rutgers UP, 1985.

An introduction, preface, foreword, or afterword

When citing an introductory or concluding essay by a "guest author" or commentator, begin with the name of that author. Give the type of piece—Introduction, Preface—without quotation marks or underline. Name the author of the book after giving the book title. At the end of the listing, give the page numbers for the essay you are citing. If the author of the separate essay is also the author of the complete work, repeat that author's last name, preceded by *By*, after the book title.

Fromm, Erich. Foreword. Summerhill: A Radical Approach to Child Rearing. By A. S. Neill. New York: Hart, 1960. ix-xiv.

In this book, the editors also wrote the introduction to their anthology.

Josephson, Eric, and Mary Josephson. Introduction. Man Alone: Alienation in Modern Society. Ed. Josephson and Josephson. New York: Dell, 1962. 9-53.

An unpublished dissertation or essay

An unpublished dissertation, even of book length, has its title in quotation marks. Label it as a dissertation in your entry. Naming the university and year will provide the necessary publication facts.

Reiskin, Helen R. "Patterns of Alcohol Usage in a Help-Seeking University Population." Diss. Boston U, 1980.

Listing periodicals in the MLA "Works Cited" format

A *periodical* is any publication that appears regularly over time. A periodical can be a daily or weekly newspaper, a magazine, or a scholarly or professional journal. As with listings for books, a bibliographical listing for a periodical article includes information about authorship, title, and facts of publication. Authorship is treated just as for books, with the author's first and last names reversed. Citation of a title differs in that the title of an article is always enclosed in quotation marks rather than underlined; the title of the periodical in which it appears is always underlined. Notice that the articles *a, an,* and *the,* which often begin the name of a periodical, are omitted from the bibliographical listing.

The facts of publication are the trickiest of the three elements because of the wide variation in how periodicals are dated, paginated, and published. For journals, for example, the publication information generally consists of journal title, the volume number, the year of publication, and the page numbering for the article cited. For newspapers, the listing includes name of the newspaper, full date of publication, and full page numbering by both section and page number(s) if necessary. The following examples show details of how to list different types of periodicals. With the exception of

May, June, and July, you should abbreviate the names of months in each "Works Cited" entry (see 31d).

A journal with continuous pagination through the annual volume

A continuously paginated journal is one that numbers pages consecutively throughout all the issues in a volume instead of beginning with page 1 in each issue. After the author's name (reversed and followed by a period and two typed spaces), give the name of the article in quotation marks. Give the title of the journal, underlined and followed by two typed spaces. Give the volume number, in arabic numerals. After a typed space, give the year, in parentheses, followed by a colon. After one more space, give the page number(s) for the article, including the first and last pages on which it appears.

Kling, William. "Measurement of Ethanol Consumed in Distilled Spirits." Journal of Studies on Alcohol 50 (1989): 456-60.

In a continuously paginated journal, the issue number within the volume and the month of publication are not included in the bibliographical listing.

A journal paginated by issue

Latessa, Edward J., and Susan Goodman. "Alcoholic Offenders: Intensive Probation Program Shows Promise." Corrections Today 51.3 (1989): 38-39+.

This journal numbers the pages in each issue separately, so it is important to identify which issue in volume 51 has this article beginning on page 38. The plus sign following a page number indicates that the article continues after the last-named page, but after intervening pages.

A monthly magazine

This kind of periodical is identified by month and year of issue. Even if the magazine indicates a volume number, omit it from your listing.

Waggoner, Glen. "Gin as Tonic." Esquire Feb. 1990: 30.

Some magazines vary in their publication schedule. *Restaurant Business* publishes once a month or bimonthly. Include the full date of publication in your listing. Give the day first, followed by an abbreviation for the month.

Whelan, Elizabeth M. "Alcohol and Health." Restaurant Business 20 Mar. 1989: 66+.

A daily newspaper

In the following examples, you see that the name of the newspaper is underlined. Any introductory article (*a, an,* and *the*) is omitted. The complete date of publication is given—day, month (abbreviated), year. Specify the edition if one appears on the masthead, since even in one day an article may be located differently in different editions. Precede the page number(s) by a colon and one typed space. If the paper has sections designated by letter (A, B, C), include the section before the page number.

If the article is unsigned, begin your entry with the title, as in the second example ("Alcohol Can Worsen . . . ").

Welch, Patrick. "Kids and Booze: It's 10 O'Clock--Do You Know How Drunk Your Kids Are?" Washington Post 31 Dec. 1989: C1.

The following entry illustrates the importance of including the particular edition of a newspaper.

"Alcohol Can Worsen Ills of Aging, Study Says." New York Times 13 June 1989, natl. ed.: 89.

"Alcohol Can Worsen Ills of Aging, Study Says." New York Times 13 June 1989, late ed.: C5.

A weekly magazine or newspaper

An unsigned article listing would include title, name of the publication, complete date, and page number(s). Even if you know a volume or issue number, omit it.

"A Direct Approach to Alcoholism." Science News 9 Jan. 1988: 25.

A signed editorial, letter to the editor, review

For these entries, first give the name of the author. If the piece has a title, put it within quotation marks. Then name the category of the piece—Letter, Rev. of (for Review), Editorial—without quotation marks or underline. If the reference is to a review, give the name of the work being reviewed with underline or quotation marks as appropriate.

Fraser, Kennedy. Rev. of Stones of His House: A Biography of Paul Scott, by Hilary Spurling. New Yorker 13 May 1991: 103-10.

James, Albert. Letter. Boston Globe 14 Jan. 1992: 61.

Stein, Norman. "Traveling for Work." Editorial. Baltimore Sun 12 Dec. 1991: 82.

Listing other sources in the MLA "Works Cited" format

An abstract of an article

Libraries contain many volumes of abstracts of recent articles in many disciplines. If you are referring to an abstract you have read rather than to the complete article, list it as follows.

Corcoran, K. J., and M. D. Carney. "Alcohol Consumption and Looking for Alternatives to Drinking in College Students." Journal of Cognitive Psychotherapy 3 (1989): 69-78. Abstract. Excerpta Medica Sec. 32 Vol. 60 (1989): 40.

A government publication

Often, a government publication will have group authorship. Be sure to name the agency or committee responsible for writing a document.

United States. Cong. Senate. Subcommittee to Investigate Juvenile Delinquency of the Committee on the Judiciary. <u>Juvenile Alcohol Abuse: Hearing</u>. 95th Cong., 2nd sess. Washington: GPO, 1978.

An unpublished interview

A listing for an unpublished interview begins with the name of the person interviewed. If the interview is untitled, label it as such, without quotation marks or underlining. Name the person doing the interviewing only if that information is relevant. An interview by telephone or e-mail can be noted as part of the interview citation.

Bishop, Robert R. Personal interview. 5 Nov. 1987.

Bly, Robert. Telephone interview. 10 Dec. 1993.

An unpublished letter

Treat an unpublished letter much as you would an unpublished interview. Designate the recipient of the letter. If you as the writer of the paper were the recipient, refer to yourself as "the author."

Bishop, Robert R. Letter to the author. 8 June 1964.

If a letter is housed in a library collection or archive, provide full archival information.

Bishop, Robert R. Letter to Jonathan Morton. 8 June 1964. Carol K. Morton papers. Smith College, Northampton.

A film or videotape

Underline the title, and then name the medium, the distributor, and the year. Supply any information that you think is useful about the performers, director, producer, or physical characteristics of the film or tape.

<u>Alcoholism: The Pit of Despair</u>. Videocassette. Gordon Jump. AIMS Media, 1983. VHS. 20 min.

A television or radio program

If the program you are citing is a single episode with its own title, supply the title in quotation marks. State the name and role of the foremost participant(s). Underline the title of the program, identify the producer and list the station on which it first appeared, the city, and the date.

"Voices of Memory." Li-Young Lee, Gerald Stern, and Bill Moyers. <u>The Power of the Word with Bill Moyers</u>. Exec. prod. Judith

Davidson Moyers and Bill Moyers. Public Affairs TV. WNET, New York. 13 June 1989.

An interview that is broadcast, taped, or published

Treat a published interview as you would any print source. A broadcast or taped interview can be treated as a broadcast program.

"The Broken Cord." Interview with Louise Erdrich and Michael Dorris. Dir. and prod. Catherine Tatge. A World of Ideas with Bill Moyers. Exec. prod. Judith Davidson Moyers and Bill Moyers. Public Affairs TV. WNET, New York. 27 May 1990.

A live performance, lecture

Identify the "who, what, and where" of a live performance. If the "what" is more important than the "who," as in a performance of an opera, give the name of the work before the name of the performers or director. In the following example, the name of the speaker, a cofounder of AA, comes first.

Wilson, Bill. "Alcoholics Anonymous: Beginnings and Growth." Presented to the NYC Medical Society. New York, 8 Apr. 1958.

A work of art

Underline the title of a work of art referred to, and tell the location of the work. The name of the museum or collection is separated from the name of the city by a comma.

Manet, Edouard. The Absinthe Drinker. Ny Carlsberg Glyptotek, Copenhagen.

Computer software

Like a printed book, computer software has authorship, a title, and a publication history. Include this in any bibliographical listing, along with relevant information for your reader about the software and any hardware it requires. Underline the title of the program. Identify the title as computer software. In the example, the name of the author and the location of the company would be added if they were known.

Alcohol and Pregnancy: Protecting the Unborn Child. Computer software. Student Awareness Software, 1988. 48K Apple II and 256K IBM PC.

A separately issued map, chart, or graph

Even a freestanding map or poster generally tells something about who published it, where, and when. Give the title, underlined, and any identifying information available. Use the abbreviation *n.d.* any time a date is lacking in publication information.

Roads in France. Map. Paris: National Tourist Information Agency, n.d.

Listing electronic sources in the MLA "Works Cited" format

Electronic source materials are available to writers in a variety of delivery systems; the Modern Language Association (MLA) system for citing electronic sources varies slightly, depending on whether the material is delivered via

- a CD-ROM that is published periodically (like a journal);
- a CD-ROM that is published once (like a book);
- a diskette;
- a computer service (such as AOL or Prodigy); or
- the Internet.

The guidelines here are presented in sections that correspond to these delivery systems—a presentation derived from the *MLA Handbook for Writers of Research Papers,* fourth edition. As electronic media evolve, conventions for listing digital sources in a "Works Cited" list will also change. However the details of citation may evolve, researchers will always need to give clear, consistent, and specific directions for locating every source used in a paper.

Electronic sources delivered via CD-ROM

When citing a source located on a CD-ROM, you will need to determine if the CD-ROM was published once (like a book) or is updated periodically (like a journal).

CD-ROMs updated periodically with *a print equivalent*

Present the following information in the order listed. Note that some information may be unavailable or not relevant to the Works Cited entry you are preparing: (1) author's name; (2) information for print equivalent (article title in quotation marks, journal or magazine underlined, volume and page, date printed). Following this information, list (3) the database name (underlined), (4) CD-ROM, (5) database provider or "vendor" (if given), and (6) date of CD-ROM publication.

Bureau of the Census. "Exports to Germany, East: Merchandise Trade-Exports by Country." National Trade Statistics (1995): 85-96. National Trade Databank. CD-ROM. U.S. Bur. of Census. 1 Aug. 1995.

CD-ROMs updated periodically with no *print equivalent*

Present the following information in the order listed. Note that some information may be unavailable or not relevant to the Works Cited entry you are preparing: (1) author's name; (2) article title in quotation marks, as well as the article's original date. Following this information, list (3) the database name (underlined), (4) CD-ROM, (5) database provider or "vendor," and (6) date of CD-ROM publication.

Gillette. "Gillette Co.: Balance Sheet, 12/31/93-9/30/95." Compact Disclosure. CD-ROM. Digital Library Systems, Inc. Oct. 1995.

CD-ROMs or diskettes issued as a single publication (analogous to publication of a book)

Present the following information in the order listed. Note that some information may be unavailable or not relevant to the Works Cited entry you are preparing: (1) author's name; (2) title underlined or in quotation marks. Follow with (3) product title (underlined); (4) version/release information; (5) CD-ROM *or* diskette; (6) publication information—city, publisher's name, year.

"Industrial Revolution." Concise Columbia Encyclopedia. Microsoft Bookshelf. 1994 ed. CD-ROM. Redmond: Microsoft, 1994.

Miller, Arthur. The Crucible. CD-ROM. New York: Penguin, 1994.

Pirsig, Robert M. Zen and the Art of Motorcycle Maintenance and Lila: An Inquiry into Morals. Voyager Expanded Book. Diskette. New York: Voyager, 1992.

Online sources: Computer services (AOL, Nexis, etc.)

The development of commercial, online providers such as America Online, Prodigy, New York Times Online, Nexis, and Lexis has provided researchers with a wealth of electronic sources. For citing commercial online services, follow these conventions:

Online sources with *a print equivalent*

Present the following information in the order listed. Note that some information may be unavailable or not relevant to the Works Cited entry you are preparing: (1) author's name; (2) information for print equivalent, including the article title in quotation marks; journal, newspaper, or magazine underlined; the date originally printed. Following this information, list (3) the database name (underlined), (4) Online, (5) computer service (Nexis, AOL, etc.), and (6) date of your electronic access.

Tyler, Patrick E. "Taiwan's Leader Wins Its Election and a Mandate." New York Times 24 Mar. 1996: A1. New York Times Online. Online. AOL. 27 Mar. 1996.

Jager, Peter de. "Communicating in Times of Change; Communication in Management." Journal of Systems Management 45.6 (1994): 28. Online. Nexis. 26 Mar. 1996.

Online sources with no *print equivalent*

Present the following information in the order listed. Note that some information may be unavailable or not relevant to the Works Cited entry you are preparing: (1) author's name; (2) information for electronic posting—title of article in quotation marks, and the date of posting if available. Following this information, list (3) the database name (underlined), (4) Online, (5) computer service (Nexis, AOL, etc.), and (6) date of your electronic access.

Mallory, Jim. "Senior Citizens Need Computing Too." 18 Mar. 1996. Newsbytes. Online. AOL. 24 Mar. 1996.

Online sources: Internet

The citation forms presented here follow specifications set out in the *MLA Handbook for Writers of Research Papers,* fourth edition. The *MLA Handbook* advises that listing an Internet source's electronic address is optional. Because an electronic address enables researchers to revisit any source that is still available on Internet servers (see 33f), we have provided the electronic address for the examples below, following conventions recommended by the Alliance for Computers and Writing (its home page is http://english.ttu.edu/acw/). See the ACW page for a slight variation from MLA on citing Internet sources.

Preparing Works Cited entries

Present the following information in the order listed. Again, note that for any given source, not all of the information listed below will be available or will be relevant. Provide what information you can: (1) author's name; (2) print information or, if the material accessed has been posted electronically only, information on the posting:

- the underlined title of the larger work area—e.g., electronic journal, newsletter, or conference;
- any identifying reference numbers (e.g., volume or issue);
- in parentheses, date of electronic posting;
- number of pages or paragraphs (if provided, or n. pag. for no pagination). Use the abbreviations "pp." for "pages" and "par." or "pars." for "paragraph(s)."

Continue the entry with (3) Online; (4) the electronic database or "repository" holding the information, if relevant; (5) computer network; and (6) date of your access. Most Internet users consider it necessary to provide an electronic address of a source, introduced with the word *Available.* Follow with (7) the Internet address with protocol, plus (8) the path locators used for access.[1]

[1]See the box at 33h-1, "The Internet Domain Name System," for an explanation of Internet addresses. See 33h-2 for a discussion of using ftp, telnet, Gopher, and the World Wide Web for your research.

FTP (File Transfer Protocol) sites

Tompkins, David P. "Thucydides Constructs His Speakers: The Case of Diodotus." Electronic Antiquity 1.1 (1993): 5 pp. Online. Internet. 4 Nov. 1995. Available FTP: into.utas.edu.au departments/classics/antiquity/1,1-June1993/ (4)Articles/Tompkins-Thucydides

Gopher sites

Cooper, Wendy. "Virtual Reality and the Metaphysics of Self, Community, and Nature." (14 Mar. 95): n. pag. Online. Internet. 26 May 1996. Available Gopher: apa.oxy.edu 12.International Philosophy Preprint Exchange 5.Preprints 6.Metaphysics 1.Cooper VR_and_the_Metaphysics_of_Self 5.VR_MUD._TXT

WWW (World Wide Web) sites

Welty, Eudora. "Place in Fiction." Collected Essays. New York: Harcourt, 1994. Online. Electronic Text Center. Internet. 24 Mar. 1996. Available http://darwin.clas.virginia.edu/ %7etsawyer/DRBR/welty.txt

Telnet sites

Cohen, Linda. "Wafer Production: Data Gathering and Analysis." Semiconductors Today (9 Feb. 1996): n. pag. Online. Internet. 16 Aug. 1996. Available Telnet: semi.ceres.freq.nit.com_73412

Synchronous communications (MOOs, MUDs, IRCs)

Jan D-Guest. Online synchronous interview. Online. Internet. 15 May 1996. Available Telnet: wisdom.sensimedia 4567

E-mail and listserv citations

Andrews, Tamsey. "Remote Teachers and Engaged Learners." Personal e-mail. Online. Internet. 6 Feb. 1996.[2]

Nostroni, Eric. "Collaborative Learning in a Networked Environment." Electronic Forum (8 Sept. 95): n. pag. Online. Internet. 12 Apr. 1996. Available: eforum@cgu.edu

---

[2]You may omit personal e-mail addresses, if you choose.

36b Using the APA system of documentation

The American Psychological Association's *Publication Manual* has set documentation style for psychologists. Writers in other fields, especially those in which researchers report their work fairly frequently in periodicals and edited collections of essays, also use the APA system of documentation. Whichever style of documentation you use in a given research paper, use only one; do not mix features of APA and MLA (or any other format) in a single paper.

APA documentation is similar to the MLA system in coupling a brief in-text citation, given in parentheses, with a complete listing of information about the source at the end of the paper. In the APA system this list of references is called "References." In the in-text citation itself, APA style differs by including the date of the work cited. The publication date is often important for a reader to have immediately at hand in psychology and related fields, where researchers may publish frequently, often modifying conclusions reached in prior publications. Date of publication also serves to distinguish readily among publications for authors who have many titles to their name. Following is an index to this section on the APA system of documentation.

TEACHING IDEAS

As with MLA format, students should be encouraged to check with individual instructors regarding documentation requirements. You may also want to point out the rationale behind highlighting the publication date—this explains one of the differences between MLA and APA formats.

REFERENCE

Publication Manual (of the American Psychological Association). 4th ed. Washington, DC: APA, 1994. Extensive advice on documenting sources.

1 Making in-text citations in the APA format

For every fact, opinion, or idea from another source that you quote, summarize, or otherwise use, you must give credit. You must also give just enough information so that your reader can locate the source. Whether in the text itself or in a parenthetical note, APA documentation calls for you to name the author and give the date of publication for every work you refer to. When you have quoted from a work, you must also give the page or page numbers (preceded by *p.* or *pp.,* in APA format). When you summarize or paraphrase, as well, it is often helpful to supply exact location of the source material by page number as part of the parenthetical reference. Supply the page number(s) immediately following a quotation or paraphrase, even if the sentence is not at a pause point.

In the sample paragraphs that follow, you will find variations on using APA in-text citation. Notice that, wherever possible, reference information is incorporated directly into the text and parentheses are used as a supplement to information in the text. Supply the parenthetical date of publication immediately after an author's name in the text. If you refer to a source a second time within a paragraph, you need not repeat the information if the reference is clear. If there is any confusion about which work is being cited, however, supply the clarifying information. If in your entire paper you are citing only one work by a particular author, you need give the date only in the first reference. If the page number for a subsequent reference differs from the earlier page number, supply the number. Separate items within a parenthetical reference by commas.

Dardis's study (1989) examines four twentieth-century American writers--three of them Nobel Prize winners--who were alcoholics. Dardis acknowledged (p. 3) that American painters too include a high percentage of addicted drinkers. Among poets, he concludes (p. 5) that the percentage is not so high as among prose writers.

However, even a casual reading of a recent biography of poet John Berryman (Mariani, 1990) reveals a creative and personal life dominated by alcohol. Indeed, "so regular had [Berryman's]

```
hospital stays [for alcoholism] become . . . that no one came to
visit him anymore" (Mariani, p. 413). Berryman himself had no il-
lusions about the destructive power of alcohol. About his friend
Dylan Thomas he could write, "Dylan murdered himself w. liquor,
tho it took years" (qtd. in Mariani, p. 274). Robert Lowell and
Edna St. Vincent Millay were also prominent American poets who
had problems with alcohol (Dardis, p. 3).
```

A work by two authors

To join the names of two authors of a work, use *and* in text but use the ampersand (&) in a parenthetical reference. Notice how the parenthetical information immediately follows the point to which it applies.

```
Roebuck and Kessler (1972) summarized the earlier research
(pp. 21-41).
```

```
A summary of prior research on the genetic basis of alcoholism
(Roebuck & Kessler, 1972, pp. 21-41) is our starting point.
```

Two or more works by the same author

If the work of the same author has appeared in different years, distinguish references to each separate work by year of publication. If, however, you refer to two or more works published by the same author(s) within a single year, you must list the works in alphabetical order by title in the list of references, and assign each one an order by lowercase letter. Thus,

```
(Holden, 1989a)
```

could represent Caroline Holden's article "Alcohol and Creativity," while

```
(Holden, 1989b)
```

would refer to the same author's "Creativity and Craving," published in the same year.

A work by three to five authors

Use names of all authors in the first reference, but subsequently give only the first of the names followed by *et al.* Use the *et al.* format for six or more authors.

```
Perls, Hefferline, and Goodman (1965) did not focus on the addic-
tive personality. Like other approaches to the study of the mind
in the '50s and '60s, Gestalt psychology (Perls et al.) spoke of
addiction only in passing.
```

A work by a corporate author

Give a corporate author's whole name in a parenthetical reference. If the name can be readily abbreviated, supply the abbreviation in brackets in the first reference. Subsequently, use the abbreviation alone.

Al-Anon Faces Alcoholism (Alcoholics Anonymous [AA], 1974) has been reissued many times since its initial publication.

One of the books most widely read by American teenagers (AA, 1974) deals with alcoholism in the family.

Distinguishing two authors with the same last name

Distinguish authors with the same last name by including first and middle initials in each citation.

(J. Williams, 1990)

(C. K. Williams, 1991)

Two or more sources in a single reference

Separate multiple sources in one citation by a semicolon. List authors alphabetically within the parentheses.

We need to view the alcoholic in twentieth-century America from many perspectives (Bendiner, 1962; Dardis, 1989; Waggoner, 1990) in order to understand how people with ordinary lives as well as people with vast creative talent can appear to behave identically.

TEACHING IDEAS

You may want to inform students that some instructors prefer that the more comprehensive list of references be called "Works Consulted." Students should always ask the instructor for the preferred reference form.

2 Preparing a list of references in the APA format

In research papers following the APA system, the list of references (which is alphabetized) is called "References." Within an entry, the date is separated from the other facts of publication. The APA list of references includes only those works referred to in your paper.

Listing books in the APA format

Leave two typed spaces to separate items in an entry. Double-space the list throughout. Start each entry at the left margin; if the entry runs beyond one line, indent subsequent lines three spaces. (Note that these formatting instructions are for preparing student papers for an APA reference to be read in its final form. If you are preparing a paper for a journal for publication, refer to the APA manual for guidelines.) The following order of presentation is used:

1. Author's name(s): Put the last name first, followed by a comma. Use first—and middle—initial instead of spelling out a first or middle name.
2. Date: Give the year of publication in parentheses followed by a period. If your list includes more than one title by an author in any one year, distinguish those titles by adding a lowercase letter (a, b, etc.) to the year of publication (as in 1989a and 1989b).
3. Title of the book: Underline the complete book title. Capitalize only the first word in a title or subtitle, in addition to proper names.
4. Publication information: Name the city of publication, followed by a colon. Give the full name of the publisher, but without the "Co." or other business designation.

Dardis, T. (1989). The thirsty muse: Alcohol and the American writer. New York: Ticknor & Fields.

A book with two authors

Invert both names; separate them by a comma. Use the ampersand (&).

Roebuck, J. B., & Kessler, R. G. (1972). The etiology of alcoholism: Constitutional, psychological and sociological approaches. Springfield, IL: Charles C. Thomas.

A book with three or more authors

List *all* authors, treating each author's name as in the case of two authors. Use the ampersand before naming the last. (This book was first published in 1951, then reissued without change.)

Perls, R., Hefferline, R. F., & Goodman, P. (1951/1965). Gestalt psychology: Excitement and growth in the human personality. New York: Delta-Dell.

A selection from an edited book or anthology

Underline the title of the book. The selection title is not underlined or enclosed in quotation marks. (In APA style, spell out the name of a university press.)

Davies, P. (1985). Does treatment work? A sociological perspective. In N. Heather (Ed.), The misuse of alcohol (pp. 158-177). New York: New York University Press.

A corporate author

Alphabetize the entry in the references list by the first significant word in the name, which is given in normal order.

National Center for Alcohol Education. (1978). The community health nurse and alcohol-related problems: Instructor's curriculum planning guide. Rockville, MD: National Institute on Alcohol Abuse and Alcoholism.

An edition subsequent to the first

Indicate the edition in parentheses, following the book title.

Scrignar, C. B. (1988). Post-traumatic stress disorder: Diagnosis, treatment, and legal issues (2nd ed.). New Orleans: Bruno.

A dissertation

In contrast with MLA style, the title of an unpublished dissertation or thesis is underlined.

Reiskin, H. R. (1980). Patterns of alcohol usage in a help-seeking university population. Unpublished doctoral dissertation, Boston University.

If you are referring to the abstract of the dissertation, the style of the entry differs because the abstract itself appears in a volume (volume number underlined).

Reiskin, H. R. (1980). Patterns of alcohol usage in a help-seeking university population. Dissertation Abstracts International, 40, 6447A.

Listing periodicals in the APA format

A journal with continuous pagination through the annual volume

The entry for a journal begins with the author's last name and initial(s), inverted, followed by the year of publication in parentheses. The title of the article has neither quotation marks nor underline. Only the first word of the title and subtitle are capitalized, along with proper nouns. The volume number, which follows the underlined title of the journal, is also underlined. Use the abbreviation *p.* or *pp.* when referring to page numbers in a magazine or newspaper. Use no abbreviations when referring to the page numbers of a journal.

Kling, W. (1989). Measurement of ethanol consumed in distilled spirits. Journal of Studies on Alcohol, 50, 456-460.

A journal paginated by issue

In this example, the issue number within volume 51 is given in parentheses. Give all page numbers when the article is not printed continuously.

Latessa, E. J., & Goodman, S. (1989). Alcoholic offenders: Intensive probation program shows promise. Corrections Today, 51(3), 38-39, 45.

A monthly magazine

Invert the year and month of a monthly magazine. Write the name of the month in full. (For newspapers and magazines use the abbreviations *p.* and *pp.*)

Waggoner, G. (1990, February). Gin as tonic. Esquire, p. 30.

A weekly magazine

If the article is signed, begin with the author's name. Otherwise, begin with the article's title. (You would alphabetize the following entry under *d.*)

A direct approach to alcoholism. (1988, January 9). Science News, p. 25.

A daily newspaper

Welch, P. (1989, December 31). Kids and booze: It's 10 o'clock--Do you know how drunk your kids are? The Washington Post, p. C1.

A review or letter to the editor

Treat the title of the review or letter as the title of an article, without quotation. Use brackets to show that the article is a review or letter. If the review is untitled, place the bracketed information immediately after the date.

Fraser, K. (1991, May 13). The bottle and inspiration [Review of the book Stones of his house: A biography of Paul Scott]. The New Yorker, pp. 103-110.

Two or more works by the same author in the same year

If you refer to two or more works published by the same author(s) within a single year, list the works in alphabetical order by title in the list of references, and assign each one an order by lowercase letter.

Chen, J. S., & Amsel, A. (1980a). Learned persistence at 11-12 days but not at 10-11 days in infant rats. Developmental Psychobiology, 13, 481-492.

Chen, J. S., & Amsel, A. (1980b). Retention under changed-reward conditions of persistence learned by infant rats. Developmental Psychobiology, 13, 469-480.

Listing other sources in the APA format

An abstract of an article

Show where the abstract may be found, at the end of the entry.

Corcoran, K. J., & Carney, M. D. (1989). Alcohol consumption and looking for alternatives to drinking in college students.

Journal of Cognitive Psychotherapy, 3, 69-78. (From Excerpta Medica, 1989, 60, Abstract No. 1322)

A government publication

U.S. Senate Judiciary Subcommittee. (Hearing, 95th Congress, 2nd sess.). (1978). Juvenile Alcohol Abuse. Washington, DC: U.S. Government Printing Office.

A film or videotape

For nonprint media, identify the medium in brackets just after the title.

Jump, G. (Producer). (1983). Alcoholism: The pit of despair [Videocassette, VHS and Beta]. New York: AIMS Media.

A television or radio program

Erdrich, L., & Dorris, M. (Interviewees). (1990, May 27). The broken cord. A world of ideas with Bill Moyers [Television program]. New York: Public Affairs TV. WNET.

An information service

Weaver, D. (1988). Software for substance abuse education: A critical review of products (Report No. NREL-RR-88-6). Portland, OR: Northwest Regional Educational Lab. (ERIC Document Reproduction Service No. ED 303 702)

Computer software

Begin your reference to a computer program with the name of the author or other primary contributor, if known.

Cohen, L. S. (1989). Alcohol testing: Self-help [Computer program]. Baltimore, MD: Boxford Enterprises.

Listing electronic sources in the APA format

Conventions for citing electronic sources in APA format begin with the same information on author, title, and date as citations for print sources. Following this initial information and as part of the title (that is, before the period or comma), list *Online* or *CD-ROM* in brackets as the medium of electronic transmission. For online sources, APA requires that the writer end with the word *Available* and a clear path by which the reader can locate the source. For CD-ROM-based information, APA requires clear bibliographic information. For a more complete review of referencing electronic sources in APA format, see the *Publication Manual of the American Psychological Association,* fourth edition. See also APA guidelines in Li and Crane (1996), *Elec-*

tronic Styles: An Expanded Guide to Citing Electronic Information. For a preview of Li and Crane, you can access their Web page (http://www.uvm.edu/-xli/reference/styles.html).

Because of the rapid evolution in electronic media, forms of citation will also evolve. Whatever final standards emerge, they will give readers clear access to electronic sources referenced in a work.

Reference to work on CD-ROM

NCTE. (1987). On writing centers [CD-ROM]. Urbana: ERIC Clearinghouse for Resolutions on the Teaching of Composition. Silver Platter.

Spiegelman, A. (1994). The complete Maus [CD-ROM]. New York: Voyager.

Reference to part of a work on CD-ROM

Peterson, C. L. (1995). Further liftings of the veil: Gender, class, and labor in Frances E. W. Harper's Iola Leroy. In New essays in feminist criticism [CD-ROM]. Silver Platter.

Reference to an online database

Tyler, P. E. (1996, March 24). Taiwan's leader wins its election and a mandate. New York Times [Online], p. A1. Available: NEXIS/NEWS/NYT

Reference to an Internet source

Tompkins, D. P. (1993, June). Thucydides constructs his speakers: The case of Diodotus. Electronic Antiquity [Online], 1 (1). Available FTP: into.utas.edu.au departments/classics/antiquity/1,1-June1993/(4)-Articles/Tompkins-Thucydides

36c Using the CMS style of documentation

The parenthetical reference mode of in-text citation is neat and easy to use. The physical and biological sciences, as well as many social sciences, have used it for decades. However, in many of the humanities (including history, philosophy, and art history), in some social sciences (including economics, communication, and political science), as well as in most business-related disciplines, many writers have long preferred the system of endnotes or footnotes developed in *The Chicago Manual of Style,* fourteenth edition, and the closely related system that is offered as an alternate system in the

MLA Handbook for Writers, fourth edition. (The MLA footnote/endnote system differs from CMS in some details of punctuation and spacing as noted below.) To use footnotes or endnotes, signal a citation in the text by a raised numeral (superscript) at the appropriate point, preferably after a comma or period. The citation information signaled with this numeral is placed in a separate note numbered to match the one in the text. Both CMS and MLA systems prefer citation information to be collected as *endnotes* at the end of your paper, though some publications continue to use *footnotes* placed at the bottom of pages where in-text citations are signaled.

Place endnotes in double-spaced form at the end of your paper on a separate page, with the heading "Notes" appearing before any listed Bibliography. Indent the start of each note three spaces (the MLA convention asks for five spaces), and continue the note on subsequent lines with a return to the left margin. The number preceding each endnote should be the same size and alignment as its text (not a superscript), followed by a period and a space. Here is an endnote or footnote in the recommended CMS format (the MLA format omits the comma before page numbers):

3. Paul Mariani, <u>Dream Song: The Life of John Berryman</u> (New York: Morrow, 1990), 45-49.

If footnotes are used, they are placed at the bottom of a page, four line spaces below the text, in single-space format, with a double space to separate footnotes on the same page. While CMS recommends numbering footnotes in the same manner as endnotes, the old MLA style and other traditional formats specify that they be numbered with superscript numerals like those in the text. Many word processing programs are able to handle these formatting conventions automatically, along with the placement of footnotes at the bottoms of pages. A citation note in the CMS style contains essentially the same information—author, title, publication facts—as an entry in a list of references in the MLA "Works Cited" format. There are differences in order and punctuation, and the note, unlike an entry in "Works Cited," concludes with a page reference. A note need not tell the span of pages of a source article when that information appears in a bibliography included at the end of the paper.

Here is an index to this section on CMS style:

1 Making the first and subsequent references in CMS notes

The first time you cite a source in a CMS paper, you will give complete information about it. If you refer to that source again, you need give only the briefest identification. Usually, this is the author's name and a page reference.

In the following sample paragraph, the first CMS note refers to an entire book. The second note cites a particular passage in a review, and refers to that page only. The third note refers to a work already cited in note 2.

Alcohol has played a destructive, painful role in the lives of numerous twentieth-century writers. Among poets, Dylan Thomas is often the first who comes to mind as a victim of alcoholism. John Berryman, too, suffered from this affliction.[1] Among novelists who battled alcohol was the great British writer Paul Scott, author of the masterpiece The Raj Quartet. A reviewer of a new biography of Scott faults the biographer for not understanding fully the effect of alcoholism on Scott and his wife and daughters.[2] Scott's own mother, out of a kind of bravado, encouraged Paul to drink gin at the age of six.[3]

1. Paul Mariani, Dream Song: The Life of John Berryman (New York: Morrow, 1990).

2. Kennedy Fraser, review of Stones of His House: A Life of Paul Scott, by Hilary Spurling, New Yorker 13 May 1991, 110.

3. Fraser, 108.

Compare the format of these CMS footnotes with their corresponding entries in the MLA "Works Cited" list.

Fraser, Kennedy. Rev. of Stones of His House: A Biography of Paul Scott, by Hilary Spurling. New Yorker 13 May 1991: 103-10.

Mariani, Paul. Dream Song: The Life of John Berryman. New York: Morrow, 1990.

2 Following the CMS note style

Citing books in the CMS note style

A book with two or three authors

1. Julian B. Roebuck and Raymond G. Kessler, The Etiology of Alcoholism: Constitutional, Psychological and Sociological Approaches (Springfield, IL: Thomas, 1972), 72.

A book with four or more authors

Name each author, or use the *et al.* format.

2. Norman Stein et al., Family Therapy: A Systems Approach (Boston: Allyn, 1990), 312.

A corporate author

3. National Center for Alcohol Education, The Community Health Nurse and Alcohol-Related Problems: Instructor's Curriculum Planning Guide (Rockville: National Institute on Alcohol Abuse and Alcoholism, 1978), 45-49.

A multivolume work

4. G. M. Trevelyan, Illustrated English Social History (Harmondsworth: Pelican-Penguin, 1964), 3:46.

Two sources cited in one note

5. Joy Williams, Escapes (New York: Vintage, 1990), 57-62; C. K. Williams, The Bacchae of Euripides: A New Version (New York: Farrar, 1990), 15.

An edition subsequent to the first

6. C. B. Scrignar, Post-Traumatic Stress Disorder: Diagnosis, Treatment, and Legal Issues, 2nd ed. (New Orleans: Bruno, 1988), 23-28.

A selection in an edited book or anthology

7. Emil Bendiner, "The Bowery Man on the Couch," in Man Alone: Alienation in Modern Society, ed. Eric Josephson and Mary Josephson (New York: Dell, 1962), 408.

An introduction, preface, foreword, or afterword

8. Erich Fromm, foreword to Summerhill: A Radical Approach to Child Rearing, by A. S. Neill (New York: Hart, 1960), xii.

Citing periodicals and other sources in the CMS note style

A journal with continuous pagination through the annual volume

9. William Kling, "Measurement of Ethanol Consumed in Distilled Spirits," Journal of Studies on Alcohol 50 (1989): 456.

A monthly magazine

10. Glen Waggoner, "Gin as Tonic," Esquire, February 1990, 30.

A weekly magazine

11. "A Direct Approach to Alcoholism," Science News, 9 January 1988, 25.

A daily newspaper

12. "Alcohol Can Worsen Ills of Aging, Study Says," New York Times, 13 June 1989, late edition, p. C5.

A dissertation abstract

13. Helen R. Reiskin, "Pattern of Alcohol Usage in a Help-Seeking University Population" (Ph.D. diss., Boston University, 1980), abstract in Dissertation Abstracts International 41 (1983): 6447A.

Computer software

14. Alcohol and Pregnancy: Protecting the Unborn Child, computer software, Student Awareness Software, 1988.

A government document

15. United States Senate Judiciary Subcommittee, Juvenile Alcohol Abuse: Hearing, 95th Cong., 2nd sess. (Washington, DC: GPO, 1978), 3.

36d Using the CBE systems of documentation

The Council of Biology Editors (CBE) systems of documentation are standard for the biological sciences and, with minor or minimal adaptations, are also used in many of the other sciences. You will find many similarities between the CBE styles of documentation and the APA style, which was derived from the conventions used in scientific writing. As in APA and MLA styles, any in-text references to a source are provided in shortened form in parentheses. For complete bibliographic information, readers expect to consult the list of references at the end of the document. Following is an index to this section on the CBE systems for documentation.

TEACHING IDEAS

As with MLA and APA formats, students should be encouraged to check with individual instructors regarding documentation requirements. You may also want to point out the many similarities between CBE and APA formats.

REFERENCE

CBE Style Manual, 5th ed. Bethesda, MD: Council of Biology Editors, 1983. Extensive advice on documenting sources.

Making in-text citations in the CBE formats

The *CBE Style Manual* presents three formats for citing a source in the text of an article. Your choice of format will depend on the discipline in which you are writing. Whatever format you choose, remain consistent within any one document.

The name-and-year system

The CBE convention that most closely resembles the APA conventions is the name-and-year system. In this system a writer provides in parentheses the name of an author and the year in which that author's work was published. Note that, in contrast to the APA system, no comma appears between the author's name and the year of publication.

```
Slicing and aeration of quiescent storage tissues induces a rapid
metabolic activation and a development of the membrane systems in
the wounded tissue (Kahl 1974).
```

If an author's name is mentioned in a sentence, then only the year of publication is set in parentheses.

```
Jacobsen et al. found that a marked transition in respiratory
substrate occurs in sliced potato tissue that exhibits the phe-
nomenon of wound respiration (1974).
```

If your paper cites two or more works published by the same author in the same year, assign a letter designation (a, b, etc.) to inform the reader of precisely which piece you have cited. This form of citation applies both to journal articles and to books.

```
Chen and Amsel (1980a) obtained intermittent reinforcement ef-
fects in rats as young as eleven days of age. Under the same
conditions, they observed that the effects of intermittent rein-
forcement on perseverance are long lived (Chen and Amsel 1980b).
```

When citing a work by an organization or government agency with no author named, use the corporate or organizational name in place of a reference to an individual author. Provide the year of publication following the name as indicated previously.

```
Style guides in the sciences caution that the "use of nouns
formed from verbs and ending in -tion produces unnecessarily long
sentences and dull prose" (CBE Style Manual Committee 1983).
```

The number system

The briefest form of parenthetical citation is the number system, a convention in which only an Arabic numeral appears in parentheses to identify a source of information. There are two variations on the number system. With references *in order of first mention,* you assign a reference number to a source in the order of its appearance in your paper. With references *in alphabetized order,* you assign each source a reference number that identifies it in the alphabetized list of references at the end of the paper.

Citation for a reference list in order of first mention

```
According to Kahl et al., slicing and aeration of quiescent stor-
age tissues induces a rapid metabolic activation and a develop-
ment of the membrane systems in the wounded tissue (1). Jacobsen
et al. found that a marked transition in respiratory substrate
occurs in sliced potato tissue that exhibits the phenomenon of
wound respiration (2).
```

Citation for a reference list in alphabetized order

```
According to Kahl et al., slicing and aeration of quiescent stor-
age tissues induces a rapid metabolic activation and a develop-
ment of the membrane systems in the wounded tissue (2). Jacobson
et al. found that a marked transition in respiratory substrate
occurs in sliced potato tissue that exhibits the phenomenon of
wound respiration (1).
```

These numbered text citations are linked to corresponding entries in a list of references. The reference list may be numbered either in the order of first mention or alphabetically.

Preparing a list of references using CBE systems

In the sciences the list of references appearing at the end of the paper is often called "Literature Cited." If you adopt the name-and-year system for in-text citation (see 36d-1), the entries in your list of references are alphabetized, much as with the APA system, rather than numbered. Like the list of references in the APA system, the "Literature Cited" list is double-spaced; each entry starts at the left margin and the second or subsequent lines are indented three typewriter spaces.

If you adopt one of the numbered systems for in-text citation (see 36d-1), you will either number entries alphabetically or in order of appearance in the paper. A numbered entry, beginning with the numeral, starts at the left margin. Place a period after the number, skip two spaces, and list the author's last name followed by the rest of the entry. For the spacing of the second or subsequent lines of a numbered entry, there are two conventions: either align the second line directly beneath the first letter of the author's last name, or indent the second and subsequent lines five spaces from the left margin. Select a convention depending on the preference of your professor. For style guides in the specific sciences, see 39e. The following are some of the basic formats for listing sources in the CBE systems.

Listing books in the CBE format

In preparing a list of references in the CBE format, leave two typed spaces between each item in an entry. Sequence the items in an entry as follows:

- Number: Assign a number to the entry if you are following a numbered system.
- Author's name: Put the last name first, followed by a comma and the initials of the first and middle names.
- Title of the book: Do not use underlining or italics. Capitalize the first letter of the first word only. End the title with a period. If the work is a revised edition, abbreviate the edition as 2d, 3d, 4th, etc.
- Publication information: Name the city of publication (and state, if needed to clarify). Place a colon and give the full name of the publisher. Place a semicolon, and give the year of publication followed by a period.

If you refer to more than one work published by the same author(s) in the same year, list the works in alphabetical order by title in the list of references, and assign each one a lowercase letter according to its order.

Books by individual or multiple authors

For a book with one author follow the conventions immediately above. For a book with multiple authors, place a semicolon after each coauthor.

1. Beevers, H. Respiratory metabolism in plants. Evanston, IL: Row, Peterson and Company; 1961.

2. Goodwin, T. W.; Mercer, E. I. Introduction to plant biochemistry. Elmsford, NY: Pergamon Press; 1972.

Books by corporate authors

3. CBE Style Manual Committee. CBE style manual. 5th ed. Bethesda, MD: Council of Biology Editors; 1983.

Books by compilers or editors

4. Smith, K. C., editor. Light and plant development. New York: Plenum Press; 1977.

Dissertation or thesis

5. Reiskin, H. R. Patterns of alcohol usage in a help-seeking university population. Boston: Boston Univ.; 1980. Dissertation.

Listing periodicals in the CBE format

Leave two typed spaces between each item in an entry. Sequence the items as follows:

- Number: Assign a number to the entry if you are using a numbered system.
- Author's name: Put the last name, followed by a comma and the initials of the first and middle names. If there are multiple authors, see the convention for books above.
- Title of the article: Do not use underlining or quotation marks. Capitalize the first letter of the first word only.
- Journal name: Abbreviate the name, unless it is a single word, without underlining. For example, The Journal of Molecular Evolution would be abbreviated as J. Mol. Evol.
- Publication information: Put the volume number, followed by a colon, followed by page numbers (use no abbreviations), followed by a semicolon and the year of publication.

Articles by individual and multiple authors

6. Kling, W. Measurement of ethanol consumed in distilled spirits. J. Stud. Alcohol. 50:456-460; 1989.

7. Coleman, R. A.; Pratt, L. H. Phytochrome: immunological assay of synthesis and destruction in plants. Planta 119:221-231; 1974.

Newspaper articles

8. Welch, P. Kids and booze: it's 10 o'clock--do you know how drunk your kids are? The Washington Post. 1989 Dec. 21:C1.

Listing other references in the CBE format

Media materials

9. Jump, G. Alcoholism: the pit of despair [Videocassette]. New York: AIMS Media; 1983. VHS; Beta.

Electronic materials

10. Alcohol and pregnancy: protecting the unborn child [Computer program]. New York: Student Awareness Software; 1988.

PART X
WRITING AND READING IN THE DISCIPLINES

CHAPTER 37

Writing and Reading in the Humanities

The *humanities*—traditionally considered as the disciplines of literature, history, and philosophy—address many puzzles of life and human nature, frequently by posing "large," difficult questions to which there are seldom definite answers. Those who study the humanities ask in distinctive ways such questions as these: Who are we? What are our responsibilities to ourselves? To others? What is a *good* life? How do we know what we know? Difficult questions like these lend themselves to difficult and varied answers, and answers in the humanities change from one culture to the next and from one generation to the next. Even within generations and cultures, answers vary. Ask two philosophers *how do we know what we know?* and you will likely get different responses. The same would hold if you approached two historians about the causes of the Civil War or two critics about the literary merit of Kate Chopin's novel *The Awakening*. Indeed, historians, philosophers, and literary critics may fiercely debate among themselves exactly which "large" questions should be asked and how one should go about investigating them.

Still, whatever their specific character, the large questions remain. Philosophers from Plato in ancient times to Richard Rorty today have continued to ask what it means to be an educated human. Two thousand years ago Homer's *Odyssey* told of a Mediterranean hero's search for identity and fulfillment, while James Joyce set his *Ulysses* on the same theme in modern-day Dublin. Thucydides in ancient Greece and Barbara Tuchman today have asked the historian's questions of how we as humans can interpret the events of the past. Such quests for meaning require readers and writers to judge evidence, to develop responsible opinions, to interpret events, and above all to appreciate the value of multiple perspectives.

Students of humanities are concerned with discovering or recreating relationships among (1) the world as it has been observed by or commented on by someone; (2) a *text* that somehow reflects the facts about or the observer's impressions of that world; and (3) an audience—a reader, listener, or viewer. Texts provide the occasion to learn how others have investigated the large questions and to investigate these questions ourselves. A text could

KEY FEATURES

The first of three chapters on academic writing and reading in the disciplines, this chapter establishes the pattern for the subsequent chapters. It approaches the humanities from the perspective of modes of inquiry, arguing that literature, history, and philosophy are united more by questions than by answers. Humanities are "text-centered" and "reactive" in that they explore questions by analyzing, interpreting, and evaluating sources. The chapter is divided into five major sections: writing, reading, types of assignments, responding to literature, and research papers. Writing in the humanities is addressed in terms of the purposes for writing and the methods of argument employed; in the first section a single text is analyzed for different purposes by a literary critic, a philosopher, and an historian. Reading is covered by considering the nature of sources (primary and secondary). The third section discusses various writing assignments students can expect to receive in these disciplines. Relying heavily on Chapter 2 (Critical Thinking and Writing) for its methodology, clear guidelines for writing analyses are presented. Section four guides the student through the process of responding to and writing about literature. Section five reproduces a heavily annotated sample research paper, a literary analysis of Kate Chopin's "A Shameful Affair" (the complete story appears in the chapter). The chapter ends with a comprehensive list of reference materials in the humanities.

be a novel, a philosophical treatise, a letter, a film, a symphony, a song, a poem, a sculpture, or a painting—any creation that records one person's response to or accounting of what is seen and that, later, can be read, viewed, or listened to by someone else.

In this formulation, history is the discipline in which readers question texts to learn what is revealed about a past event and what about that event might be pertinent to the present. Philosophy is the discipline in which readers study the articles and books (the *texts*) of those who, with rigorous and careful reasoning, have reflected on ideas important to understanding human nature. Literature is the discipline in which readers read a work of drama, poetry, or fiction to gain entry into an imaginative world and to learn how this text and its world is constructed, how it might reflect circumstances of the author's experience, and how it might comment on and force questions about the *reader's* experience. For the historian, philosopher, and student of literature, texts are the point of entry into the three-way relationship of text, creator/author, and audience. For a student in the humanities there is always the relationship; there is always the implicit understanding that texts are important and that as we read, view, listen to, and write about them, we create meaning ourselves. In the humanities, we *create* new texts as we study older ones. We carry on a tradition of raising and investigating difficult questions and, through our efforts, seek to grow more aware of who we are and what we have done (Frankel 8–9).*

37a Writing in the humanities

1 Expressing and informing in the humanities

Students in the humanities write for many purposes, two of which are to inform and to express. Expressive writing, often beginning as a personal response to an individual text, discusses questions like these: What do I feel when reading this material? Why do I feel this way? How am I changed in response to this text? How can I account for differences I have observed between this text and others, or between this text and my own experience? Readers may find themselves so involved with a text that they want to respond in writing. You might consider keeping a reading journal in which you record responses to texts and, based on your entries, develop ideas for papers. Much of what is best about writing in the humanities begins as a personal response.

All writing in literature, history, and philosophy courses is, at least in part, informative. Working as an historian, you may need to sift through documents in order to establish a *sequence* to events on which to base a narrative—perhaps the story of how your grandparents came to this country. As

* In-text citations in this chapter refer to the Works Cited list at the end of the book.

ADDITIONAL EXERCISE A

Interview a professor of history, literature, or philosophy on the subject of the writing he or she does in the profession. Pose questions such as the following: What kinds of text do you study? What kinds of questions do you ask about texts? What forms does your writing usually take? What is your purpose in writing in these forms? What kind of audience do you usually address? Try to think of some additional questions as well. Use your notes from the interview to write a paragraph describing the nature of writing in this particular discipline.

LOOKING BACK

Students may want to review patterns of development in Chapter 3 as they study this material. It's important that they recognize how the patterns of development cross disciplinary lines.

a student of literature, you may *compare* and *contrast* works of the same author, responding to assignments such as this: *Choose two of Hawthorne's short stories and discuss his treatment of the origins and consequences of sin.* In a philosophy course, you might be asked to *classify* discussions on a topic, such as education, according to the types of arguments authors are making. In informing readers, you will often *define* and illustrate a term by referring to specific passages in a text.

2 Making arguments

Frequently in the humanities, you will use informative writing to make arguments. The purpose of making arguments in literature, history, and philosophy is to *interpret* texts and to *defend* interpretations as reasonable.[1] No one will expect your arguments to end all discussion of a question, but as in any discipline, your arguments should be compelling and well supported. The purpose of reading stories, of retelling the past, or of puzzling through large questions is not to arrive at agreement (as in the sciences), but to deepen individual perception and to realize that we are part of a larger human community. The goal of an argument in the humanities is reached when readers can make this or a similar acknowledgment: "I understand your point of view, and I find it reasonable." You should therefore not expect to read—or write—a single, correct interpretation of a play. History professors will urge you to reject single, apparently definitive versions of the past. Philosophy professors will urge you to reject the notion that any one answer to the question *What is a good life?* could satisfy all people.

Consensus is not the goal of arguments in the humanities. But this is not to say that all arguments are equally valid. Arguments must be supported and well reasoned. They can be plainly wrong and they can be irresponsible, as when someone insists: "Since discussions in this course are based on personal opinions, my opinion is as good as anyone else's." Not true. One interpretation, argued well, can be clearly superior to and more compelling than another. In each of the humanities this is so, notwithstanding the fact that students of literature, history, and philosophy pose different questions and examine texts using different methods. As a student of literature, you might investigate living conditions during the Great Depression by reading novels like *The Grapes of Wrath.* In a history class, you might work with oral accounts such as the one compiled by Studs Terkel in *Hard Times: An Oral History of the Great Depression.* In a philosophy course, you might read and debate discussions of a society's obligations to its poor. You would in every case be arguing for an interpretation, and in every case your argument would be more or less convincing, in light of the conventions for ar-

[1] This discussion is based directly on the work of Stephen Toulmin, Richard Rieke, and Allan Janik in *Introduction to Reasoning* (New York: Macmillan, 1979). See Chapter 12, their "Introduction" to fields of argument, 195–202; and Chapter 15, "Arguing about the Arts," 265–82. For a related discussion, see Richard D. Rieke and Malcolm O. Sillars, *Argumentation and the Decision Making Process,* 2nd ed. (Glenview: Scott, Foresman 1984).

REFERENCES

BARTHOLOMAE, DAVID. "Inventing the University." *When a Writer Can't Write.* Ed. Mike Rose. New York: Guilford, 1985: 134–65. Essential to being a college student is the mastering of discipline-specific discourses, but such achievement is the result of a gradual process with multiple stages.

BEYER, BARRY K. "Using Writing to Learn in History." *The History Teacher* 13 (1980): 167–78. Writing may be used not only as an aid to students seeking information, but also as a method for their developing "historical-mindedness."

MARTIN, BRUCE K. "Teaching Literature as Experience." *CE* 51 (1989): 377–85. While it may be disturbing, recent renunciations of the formalist tendency to find single, determinate meanings of literary texts may actually liberate teachers who wish to discuss literature openly with their students.

MCLEOD, SUSAN D. "Writing Across the Curriculum: The Second Stage, and Beyond." *CCC* 40 (1989): 337–43. Overview of the changes in WAC that argues for continued reform in thinking, learning, and writing across the disciplines.

RUSSELL, DAVID R. "Writing Across the Curriculum in Historical Perspective: Toward a Social Interpretation." *CE* 52 (1990): 52–73. Looks at WAC in its historical, social context, arguing that such a perspective will provide new ways of "integrating students, instead of excluding them."

YOUNG, ART, and TOBY FULWILER, eds. *Writing Across the Disciplines: Research into Practice.* Upper Montclair, NJ: Boynton, 1986. Collection of essays discussing a writing-across-the-curriculum program, including essays on writing in the humanities.

LOOKING BACK

All of the chapters in this part of the handbook rely heavily on ideas discussed in Chapter 6 (Writing and Evaluating Arguments), especially the material on modes of inquiry in various disciplines. If you haven't yet covered Chapter 6 in class, it would be useful to do so now. Otherwise, students should review the chapter on their own in order to make better use of the information in this part of the handbook.

guing in that discipline. You can help yourself focus on the purpose of argumentation in your humanities classes by posing these questions:

- What sorts of questions will I investigate in this course?
- How do the texts I study help to focus my attention on these questions?
- How do students in this discipline make claims about a text? How do they support these claims?

Claims and evidence

In making a *claim* in the humanities, a writer usually interprets a text. That is, the writer attempts to explain how the text is meaningful—how, for instance, a poem's images direct the reader's attention to certain themes, how an essay confirms or contradicts our understanding of a particular problem, how the content of a letter or diary suggests a revised understanding of some historical event. One much-relied-on process for making and supporting claims in the humanities goes something like this: during the process of reading, you begin to see a pattern emerge—you notice certain details and forge a link between them. (See the discussion of "thesis" at 3d and of "argumentative thesis" at 6b.) At first the pattern may not be well defined; but as you read and reread, the pattern becomes increasingly clear until you can express it as a formal claim. Your claim becomes the basis of an argument that says, in effect: here is one way in which this text is meaningful. You then provide *evidence* for your claim by pointing readers to the same passages in the text that helped you to detect a pattern, explaining why these passages are significant and how they confirm the reasonableness of your claim. The process of claim and support, then, looks like this:

1. Read a text and discover in it certain patterns that help to make the text meaningful (see 37d for hints on detecting patterns in literary works).
2. Reread and confirm that the pattern exists, and then make a claim: a formal statement in which you interpret some element of the text, its relationship to the reader, or its relationship to the writer and the times in which it was written.
3. Refer to the text as evidence for your claim.
4. Comment on or discuss these references (optional).

Consider the following examples of how claims are made and supported in major areas of the humanities.

A literary study. In a paragraph from an essay entitled "The Greatness of *Huckleberry Finn*," the literary critic Lionel Trilling claims that Huck Finn is a character who sympathizes with the misfortunes of others. As you read the paragraph, you will be watching Trilling make his claim *after* he had discovered it for himself. Trilling is persuasive, and you might find yourself thinking "This isn't an interpretation; it's a fact." But Trilling *is* interpreting the novel, and he is trying to convince you that his interpretation is both accurate and useful:

> [Huckleberry Finn's] sympathy is quick and immediate. When the circus audience laughs at the supposedly drunken man who tries to ride the horse, Huck is only miserable: "It wasn't funny to me . . . ; I was all of a tremble to see his danger." When he imprisons the intending murderers on the wrecked steamboat, his first thought is of how to get someone to rescue them, for he considers "how dreadful it was, even for murderers, to be in such a fix. I says to myself, there ain't no telling but I might come to be a murderer myself yet, and then how would I like it?" But his sympathy is never sentimental. When at last he knows that the murderers are beyond help, he has no inclination to false pathos. "I felt a little bit heavy-hearted about the gang, but not much, for I reckoned that if they could stand it I could." His will is genuinely good and therefore he has no need to torture himself with guilty second thoughts.

Notice that Trilling makes two related claims in this paragraph: first, that Huck's "sympathy is quick and immediate," and second, that this "sympathy is never sentimental." He refers the reader to specific passages that support his claims and, after a final quoted passage, makes a comment: "His [Huck's] will is genuinely good and therefore he has no need to torture himself with guilty second thoughts." With this comment, Trilling cements the relationship between the claims he has made and the evidence he has offered. He has made an *argument.* Be assured that Trilling's awareness of Huck's sympathies did not always exist. There must have been some point before which Trilling simply did not think about Huck's "quick and immediate" sympathy. We can assume that Trilling has read the novel many times; we can imagine that on one rereading he began to see a pattern emerging in various passages. We can further imagine that on noticing this pattern, Trilling was able to confirm and refine it by *re*reading various passages. At this point, he was prepared to write: to convert the pattern he had detected (then confirmed) into a claim, which he then used as the basis for an argument.

In one brief paragraph, Lionel Trilling demonstrates the cycle of claim, reference, and comment that is basic to writing about literature. *To make a claim about literature, first find a pattern of meaning in a text. Confirm and refine that pattern and then make a claim. To support this claim, return to the text and discuss specific passages.* An analysis of a literary text is built by linking many such cycles according to an overall plan or thesis. (See 37d for more on writing about literature.)

An historical study. The historian Joanna Stratton supports a claim in the following passage by referring to a source (information from a letter or journal) but does not comment on the source in the same way Trilling does for a literary text. In her book on pioneer women of the American Frontier, Stratton worked with interviews, letters, and journals that her great-grandmother had collected in the 1920s.

> For the most part, the cavelike dugout provided cramped and primitive quarters for the pioneering family. Damp and dark year round, it was practically impossible to keep clean, for dirt from the roof and the walls sifted onto everything. Although its thick earthen walls did afford warm insula-

FOR DISCUSSION

Whether or not your students are familiar with *The Adventures of Huckleberry Finn,* they should be able to follow this discussion with a little guidance. You may want to begin by asking students how this extensive analysis of Trilling's argument is put together. How can one conclude, for example, that "Trilling's awareness of Huck's sympathies did not always exist"? How are Trilling's claims identified? How is it possible to infer his thought processes from reading this paragraph? Discussion may be slow at first, but students should generally begin to see how the paragraph represents critical thinking in literary studies—especially if they have reviewed Chapter 6 prior to the discussion.

TEACHING IDEAS

Students may understand the nature of historical interpretation more clearly if you remind them of the various interpretations of the circumstances surrounding John F. Kennedy's assassination. Popular speculation aside, for over thirty years historians have been arguing about the event, interpreting the medical record, the movements of relevant individuals, the accounts of eyewitnesses, and the historical record of possibly related events.

tion from the cold and strong protection from the wind, in rain the dugout became practically uninhabitable.

"Father made a dugout and covered it with willows and grass," wrote one settler, "and when it rained, the water came through the roof and ran in the door. After the storms, we carried the water out with buckets, then waded around in the mud until it dried up. Then to keep us nerved up, sometimes the bull snakes would get in the roof and now and then one would lose his hold and fall down on the bed, then off on the floor. Mother would grab the hoe and there was something doing and after the fight was over Mr. Bull Snake was dragged outside. Of course there had to be something to keep us from getting discouraged."

JOANNA L. STRATTON, *Pioneer Women*

Often in an historical account the writer wants to maintain focus on the narrative or story, and so withholds immediate comment on a source quotation except in footnotes or in specialized analysis. *To make a claim in history, writers make interpretations of available records from the past and try to reconstruct them into a meaningful pattern.*

Sometimes the presentation of a claim in historical writing may seem not to be an interpretation at all:

[I]n the rain the dugout became practically uninhabitable.

This claim reads as a fact, but actually it is a generalization Joanna Stratton has reached based on available evidence, one example of which she provides with a supporting quotation. Other historians examining the same or different evidence might reach a different conclusion. The importance of an historian's interpretations becomes obvious when you read the conflicting accounts of the events immediately before and after Lincoln's assassination. If these conflicting accounts were based on eyewitness testimony, you would realize that historians must interpret evidence as well as gather it. While Lincoln *was* shot at Ford's Theatre on April 14, 1865, the precise circumstances of and reason for the shooting are subject to historical debate—or interpretation.

GROUP ACTIVITY

There is probably no more profitable way to illustrate the intricacy of philosophical argument than to engage in one. Ask groups to offer their own observations on the meaning of "games." What do they consider games? What essential ingredients are necessary for an activity to be a game? How do physical activity, mental activity, competition, enjoyment, and the like figure into the concept? It's unlikely that group reports to the class will reflect any solid consensus, but that's no problem. The point of the exercise is to highlight the abstract nature of philosophical argument.

A philosophical study. The philosopher Ludwig Wittgenstein makes a claim in the following passage without reference to any written text, but rather to the meaning that is attached to a word and to the patterns of human activity that can be observed in connection with that word. In the process, Wittgenstein himself created a philosophical text, one that later became the subject of interpretation and claim by other philosophers. In this passage, Wittgenstein examines the difficulty of defining the word "game." He does so in the larger context of discussing the complexities of defining "language." Just as "family resemblances" describes the relationship between various games, so too does this term describe what is common to various languages—that is, there is no single feature but rather an array of features.

Consider for example the proceedings that we call "games". I mean board-games, card-games, ball-games, Olympic games, and so on. What is common to them all?—Don't say: "There *must* be something common, or they would not be called 'games' "—but *look and see* whether there is anything

> common to all.—For if you look at them you will not see something that is common to *all,* but similarities, relationships, and a whole series of them at that. To repeat: don't think, but look!—Look for example at board-games, with their multifarious relationships. Now pass to card-games; here you find many correspondences with the first group, but many common features drop out, and others appear. When we pass next to ball-games, much that is common is retained, but much is lost.—Are they all "amusing"? Compare chess with noughts and crosses. Or is there always winning and losing, or competition between players? Think of patience. In ball games there is winning and losing; but when a child throws his ball at the wall and catches it again, this feature has disappeared. Look at the parts played by skill and luck; and at the difference between skill in chess and skill in tennis. Think now of games like ring-a-ring-a-roses; here is the element of amusement, but how many other characteristic features have disappeared! And we can go through the many, many other groups of games in the same way; can see how similarities crop up and disappear.
>
> And the result of this examination is: we see a complicated network of similarities overlapping and criss-crossing: sometimes overall similarities, sometimes similarities of detail.
>
> I can think of no better expression to characterize these similarities than "family resemblances"; for the various resemblances between members of a family: build, features, colour of eyes, gait, temperament, etc. etc. overlap and criss-cross in the same way.—And I shall say: "games" form a family.
>
> —Ludwig Wittgenstein, *Philosophical Investigations*

This passage has generated enormous discussion on the meaning and significance of "family resemblances." For example, some might argue that "amusement" is common to all games and might proceed to define that concept. As a student of philosophy, you will sometimes generate your own evidence for arguments; but more often, you will refer to and build on the work of the philosophers you are studying. Learning to make claims in philosophy can be especially demanding for those with little experience in the discipline. In literature and history, sources and what one writes about them are connected in concrete ways to a story, imagined or actually lived. Philosophy has no elements of story as such. *To support a claim in philosophy, you will focus on ideas and their relation to other ideas.* (Wittgenstein discusses specific games in order to develop his idea of "family resemblance.") Arguments, consequently, can become quite abstract.

The three examples of claims made by Trilling, Stratton, and Wittgenstein do not begin to represent the variety of claims you will encounter in your study of literature, history, and philosophy. These examples are meant to suggest that variety; they suggest, as well, a common concern in the humanities: interpretation. As you read and study in your courses, try to identify the specific types of claims that are made and the methods of evidence used to support them. To aid this process, pose these questions: What sorts of claims (interpretations) do people make in this subject? In what ways do writers use sources (books, films, works of art, or pieces of music) to support their claims?

LOOKING BACK

Students may want to review Chapter 1 (Critical Thinking and Reading) for a general discussion of the subject before reading this section.

TEACHING IDEAS

Since the distinction between primary and secondary sources is an important one, you may want to call students' attention to it here. If they are to make legitimate observations and interpretations of primary sources, then they must spend some time analyzing those sources themselves in addition to evaluating the secondary sources.

REFERENCES

BOOTH, WAYNE C. *The Rhetoric of Fiction.* 2nd ed. Chicago: U of Chicago P, 1983. Study of narration that is indispensable to students of literature.

CHAMBERLAIN, LORI. "Bombs and Other Exciting Devices, or the Problem of Teaching Irony." *CE* 51 (1989): 29–40. Teachers need to emphasize the importance of irony as a device and to encourage its use in student writing, because it establishes a political relationship between writer and reader.

COMMEYRAS, MICHELLE. "Using Literature to Teach Critical Thinking." *Journal of Reading* 32 (1989): 703–7. Studying literature advances critical thinking skills (emphasis is on younger students).

DRAGGA, SAM. "Collaborative Interpretation." *Activities to Promote Critical Thinking: Classroom Practices in Teaching English.* Urbana: NCTE, 1986. 84–87. ED 273 985. Offers a method for creating a student-centered literature classroom based on collaborative learning as an alternative to the traditional teacher-led class.

HOLMAN, C. HUGH, and WILLIAM HARMON. *A Handbook to Literature.* 5th ed. New York: Macmillan, 1986. Complements any classroom discussion of literary criticism, terms, and genres, and offers students accessible discussions concerning the difficulties of approaching literature.

37b Reading in the humanities

When you read a poem, a story, a letter, or an autobiography, you are working with a **primary source.** Of the preceding examples, only the one by Wittgenstein is a primary source. The writings of Trilling and Stratton are examples of **secondary sources,** the work of scholars who themselves have interpreted particular poems, stories, or letters. If you were writing a paper on *Huckleberry Finn,* you might refer to Trilling's interpretations. In doing so, you would need to read with care in order to understand and evaluate his ideas and to distinguish them from your own. In deciding whether to cite Trilling in your paper, you might ask: What point is he making? How well does he make it? Is his observation well grounded in the text that he quotes? On what basis do I agree or disagree with him?

A given source or text in the humanities can be studied from several perspectives within a discipline or across disciplines. Some writers look at a work as a whole, in a broad context of events or ideas surrounding it; others look closely at individual parts of the source, analyzing it independently of its original surroundings. For example, consider how differently Benjamin Franklin's *Autobiography* is studied in the following examples: as a literary expression, as political philosophy, or as an historical event.

Literary critic Joseph Fichtelberg (Fordham University) sees in the *Autobiography* a conscious effort by Franklin to sift through his life's work and beliefs in order to present himself as an "exemplar" to the world, a model of American virtue. The following constitutes one segment of Fichtelberg's argument, which appeared in the journal *Early American Literature.* Numbers in parentheses are page references to sources noted below:

> That the correspondent—the reader—is crucial to Franklin's self-conception is evident throughout the *Autobiography.* Part One, readers have often noted, appears to be a fatherly homily to an ambitious young man. "Now imagining it may be equally agreeable to you to know the Circumstances of *my* Life," Franklin begins, alluding to his spectacular success, "I sit down to write them for you" (I). But as Governor of New Jersey in 1771, William Franklin was successful in his own right, hardly in need of counsel, and, at forty-four, hardly a young man. Rather, Franklin seems to be writing for the "Posterity" he addresses several lines later, indeed, for all American readers, who may find his narrative "suitable to their own Situations, & therefore fit to be imitated" (I). Hence his character, as Mitchell Breitwieser notes, would "liv[e] on in the person of the emulating reader, and . . . gai[n] a wider circulation than it otherwise would have" (265, 270). As he announces his intention to recount the "conducing Means"—the process—by which he achieves eminence, so Franklin's prose emphasizes the reader's own immersion in that process. The fourth sentence in this introductory paragraph (a revision, incidentally, of an earlier draft) is resonantly ungrammatical:
>
> > Having emerg'd from the Poverty & Obscurity in which I was born & bred, to a State of Affluence & some Degree of Reputation in the World, and having

gone so far thro' Life with a considerable Share of Felicity, the conducing Means I made Use of, which with the Blessing of God, so well succeeded, my Posterity may like to know, as they may find some of them suitable to their own Situations, & therefore fit to be imitated. (I)

As Tatham notes, the two dangling participial phrases[2] shift the emphasis from the grammatical subject to "my Posterity," as if "future Americans in general" had taken Franklin's course to affluence and were now eager to understand the "Means," the particular process of their ascent (228).

WORKS CITED [BY FICHTELBERG]

Breitweiser, Mitchell. *Cotton Mather and Benjamin Franklin: The Price of Representative Personality.* Cambridge: Cambridge UP, 1984.

Franklin, Benjamin. *The Autobiography of Benjamin Franklin: A Genetic Text.* Ed. J. A. Leo Lemay and P. M. Zall. Knoxville: U of Tennessee P, 1981.

Tatham, Campbell. "Benjamin Franklin, Cotton Mather, and the Outward State." *Early American Literature* 6 (Winter 1971–72): 223–33.

This analysis focuses on Franklin's *Autobiography* as a work of literature. Joseph Fichtelberg is interested in the relationship between Franklin and the readers he presumably had in mind when composing the *Autobiography.* Fichtelberg begins with a claim that the reader is crucial to the way Franklin thinks of and presents himself in the *Autobiography.* As evidence for this claim, Fichtelberg quotes from the obvious *primary* source, and he refers to *secondary* sources, the work of two literary critics also interested in Franklin. These references, it should be added, place Fichtelberg's own investigation in a tradition of literary criticism. Writers in *every* discipline similarly refer to the work of others in that discipline to benefit from previous research and to become members of a scholarly community. What identifies Fichtelberg's writing as specifically *literary* criticism is not only his references to secondary sources who are themselves literary critics but also his method of arguing: he relies on a cycle of claim and text-based support that is common to literary studies (see 37a-2). Most important, Fichtelberg assumes that the *Autobiography* is a work of literature. He wants to investigate the role that readers played in the creation of a text.

Philosopher Ralph Ketchem approaches the *Autobiography* with an entirely different set of concerns. He sees in Franklin's work an expression of the author's philosophy on the power of individual initiative in politics:

As a public philosopher, Franklin assumed that the traditional personal values have political relevance. He shared the Aristotelian belief that government exists for the sake of the good life and that its powers can be used to that end. A good citizen, guided by the virtues Franklin encour-

[2] Fichtelberg assumes readers will follow the reference here to the following phrases: "Having emerg'd . . . in the World, and having gone so far . . . so well succeeded." The obvious grammatical subject of these phrases is "I"—Franklin is the one who emerged from poverty and who went through life with such success. In the *Autobiography,* however, Franklin dangles these phrases (see 15h) and places "my Posterity" where the grammatical subject, "I," should occur. Both Fichtelberg and the writer he cites (Tatham) find this significant.

SWOPE, JOHN W., and EDGAR H. THOMPSON. "Three R's for Critical Thinking about Literature: Reading, 'Riting, and Responding." *Activities to Promote Critical Thinking: Classroom Practices in Teaching English.* Urbana: NCTE, 1986. 75–79. ED 273 985. Presents assignments that offer alternatives to teaching literature in a lecture format.

FOR DISCUSSION

Students will probably need to talk about this section in order to grasp it. If the chapter is to be understood at all, then students will need to know not only how scholars in different disciplines approach a work, but also how the uses to which a source is put influence the ways in which it is interpreted. You may want to begin by writing the names of the three disciplines on the board and asking students to describe how, based on this example, each discipline approaches a text. If students are able to work through this discussion, you may then want to ask what the text *represents* to scholars in the different disciplines. The discussion should clarify for students many of the points covered in the chapter.

> aged in *Poor Richard's Almanack* and in his *Autobiography,* would undertake civic improvement and participate disinterestedly in government. In an expanding country filled with opportunity, Franklin saw individual initiative as the essential engine of progress, but he did not hesitate to seek whatever seemed required for the public good through government. His confidence in the virtue of the citizens of the United States caused him to favor government by consent, but he was not a simple democrat who believed majority will should be omnipotent. He accepted democracy because he thought it would yield good government; if it did not, he readily rejected it.

Ketchem shows how the *Autobiography* was part of Franklin's overall ambition to promote the role of the individual and of personal values as a force in political life. He supports his claims by focusing on Franklin's ideas about individual values in relation to other ideas about the role of government.

Still another viewpoint, from Franklin's biographer Carl Van Doren, looks at how parts of the *Autobiography* were written and read in their own time and afterward. While literary or philosophical analysts see the work as a self-contained expression of current or ongoing American ideas, the historian looks at the concrete events of the work's arrival and reception.

> The two copies went off to England and France to set in train the complex textual history of this simple book: of which three parts appeared first in French, and of which the earliest English editions were retranslations from the French, and of which [the author's son] Temple Franklin published as authorized in 1818, the copy sent to Le Veillard instead of Franklin's original, which was not published entire, as Franklin wrote it, till 1868. At some time after the copies [of the original manuscript] were made, Franklin, in the six painful months left to him, wrote the fragmentary fourth part and then broke off. It seems likely that he himself had made the revisions which in the copy tamed the original. He could no longer trust his taste and could now and then prefer round academic phrases to his own natural sharp, homely ones. He had lived too long, and put off writing too late, to be able to do justice to himself in a book. His greatest years would have to stay unwritten. He might truly have reflected that this was not altogether the loss it seemed. Plenty of other men could find materials for the story of his latest years. Only he had known about his obscure youth, which could never again be obscure. (767–68)

Van Doren's claims and interpretations try to establish how and where the work came into existence, and the extent to which it reflected Franklin's public versus private personality. The argument follows the pattern of interpreting records to reconstruct a meaningful pattern of events for Franklin's life.

Fichtelberg, Ketchem, and Van Doren interpret a single text differently, according to their separate disciplinary perspectives. Each makes a claim—a statement that expresses the pattern of meaning each author had found in the work he was examining.

FICHTELBERG That the correspondent—the reader—is crucial to Franklin's self-conception is evident throughout the *Autobiography.*

Ketchem   As a public philosopher, Franklin assumed that the traditional personal values have political relevance.

Van Doren   [The *Autobiography* has a] complex textual history.

If all three writers were literary critics, philosophers, or historians, they might just as likely offer different interpretations, since each of the humanities has its subdisciplines or subfields, each of which in turn is guided by a unique perspective. (For examples of this variety in literary studies, see 37d-4.) The more experienced you become in any of these disciplines, the more you will differentiate among perspectives *within* disciplines. *Perspective* determines how you will read, what questions you will pursue, and what interpretations you will make—both between and within disciplines.

37c Types of writing assignments in the humanities

The writing assignments that you will most often encounter in your humanities courses—close analyses of texts, research papers, and book reviews—have in a general way been addressed in Chapter 2, "Critical Thinking and Writing." The discussion here will introduce the special requirements of these assignments in the humanities and will refer you to pertinent sections in Chapter 2.

1 The analysis

An **analysis** is an investigation that you conduct by applying a principle or definition to an activity or to an object in order to see how that activity or object works, what it might mean, or why it might be significant. As a writer, your job is to identify and discuss particular parts, or features, of the text that you feel are especially meaningful. In analyzing a short story or novel, for instance, you might focus on characters, themes, plot, or structure. You might analyze a poem for its rhymes, meter, or symbols (see 37d). These features, which are mutually reinforcing, give literary texts their meaning—though the meaning of a work will never be a simple sum of its analyzed parts. Good literature invites and can sustain multiple analyses without ever being "explained away."

Historical events similarly invite a variety of analyses. As one teacher of history has put it, "[H]istorians like to argue [for differing interpretations of events]. In fact, they disagree to a greater or lesser extent in their views of personalities and events in every major period in United States History, from Captain John Smith to William Westmoreland, from the American Revolution to the computer revolution" (O'Reilly 281). Historians present conflicting interpretations in order to understand as fully as possible the causes of events. These causes are usually complex and resist (as mature works of literature resist) a single, definitive explanation.

TEACHING IDEAS

Students will need to be reminded that these guidelines are a *general pattern,* not a blueprint, for writing analyses. Encourage them to follow closely any specific guidelines from their instructors, or to ask for such guidelines if necessary.

CRITICAL THINKING

Distribute photocopies of a page from an analytical article in one of the disciplines. Ask students to list the main points of the article and to identify a paragraph where the author brings them together to make a claim.

As a student of literature, philosophy, and history, you will use features specific to these disciplines in conducting your analyses. You have seen previously (in 37b) that one text can be analyzed as a work of literature, philosophy, or history, depending on a writer's perspective. Perspective determines the way in which a writer divides a text into analyzable parts. The more you study in a discipline, the more you will learn which features of a text are important to that discipline and, hence, which are worth analyzing.

The following general pattern serves as a model for writing an analysis, regardless of discipline. Placement of one or more of these elements in a paper may vary according to discipline; but when writing an analysis you can expect to touch on the following:

- Introduce the work being analyzed and the interpretation you will make (your claim).
- Introduce the features you will use to analyze the text. Your choice of features will depend on the discipline in which you are writing.
- Conduct your analysis by discussing one feature of a text (or idea) at a time. For literary texts, quote specific passages and *comment* on the ways the passage supports your interpretation (see 37a-2).
- Conclude by summing up the evidence for your interpretation. Show how the features you have discussed separately reinforce one another in creating the effect or quality you have argued for.

Section 2c discussed analysis as an investigation conducted by systematically applying a set of *principles.* In introductory courses to literature, this set of principles will be general if you are interpreting a poem or story according to standard features such as *theme.* (Other standard features are suggested in 37d-4.) In advanced literature courses, and also in philosophy and history courses, you may be asked to analyze a text or some situation by applying a much-discussed theory. In a philosophy course, for example, you might be asked to apply Wittgenstein's notion of "family resemblances" to some activity other than games. In this instance, your professor would be asking that you analyze a situation, based on principles laid out in a specific source.

2 The book review

You may be asked to read and review a book for your courses, both inside and outside of the humanities. The purpose of a review is to make a judgment about the worth of a text and to communicate and justify that judgment to a reader. See 2b for an extended discussion on preparing and writing a review (which in 2b is called an *evaluation*). Before writing to evaluate you should *read* to evaluate. That is, you should understand what an author has written so that you can summarize main points; you should distinguish an author's facts from opinions; and you should distinguish your assumptions from those of the author. Your overall assessment of a book will rest largely on the extent to which you and the author share assumptions about the subject being discussed.

3 The research paper

A research paper calls on you to investigate some topic, using both primary and secondary sources. Often, a research paper in the humanities is an analysis (see 37c-1) that you set in a broader context. In writing an analysis, you typically read and interpret a single text—in the paper that follows, it is a short story ("A Shameful Affair") by Kate Chopin. Broadening your effort into a research paper, you would analyze the story and also draw on available scholarship as an aid to your analysis. A second reason to draw on available scholarship is to provide a context for your thesis. By reviewing the literature on your topic, you tap into the conversation that has taken place concerning it. Aware of what others have written, you can add your voice (through your paper) and contribute to the conversation.

For her paper on "A Shameful Affair," Brandy Brooks turned to the work of two Chopin scholars, Joyce Dyer and Martin Simpson. In a research paper, you remain responsible for developing and supporting an interpretation. You draw on sources, as needed, to help make your points.

Gathering sources on a topic and using them judiciously, according to a plan, is the activity central to writing a research paper. In 2d you will find a discussion on writing a synthesis based on multiple sources. To write an effective research paper in the humanities, you must be able to read multiple sources on a topic, understand the main points of each, and then link these points to one another and to your own guiding interpretation, or thesis. In short, you must read source materials effectively. (See Chapter 1, "Critical Thinking and Reading.") If you are uncertain of your ability to draw on and refer to multiple sources, also see Chapters 33, 34, and 35 on the research process. In Chapter 36, you will find a discussion on how to cite sources when writing a paper. In the humanities, you will generally follow the MLA form for documenting sources.

37d Writing about literature[3]

To write knowledgeably about a literary work—about a poem, a play, a short story, or a novel—you need to understand, generally, how arguments are made in the humanities. In 37a-2 you saw that arguments in the humanities depend on a cycle of claim, reference to a text, and comment. In that same discussion and in 37b you found examples of such arguments about literary texts (about *Huckleberry Finn* and Franklin's *Autobiography*). The cases illustrated a cycle of claim, reference, and comment. If you have not already

[3] In this discussion, the term *literature* refers to works of art *in writing:* poems, plays, and fiction. The expression "review of the literature," common in the humanities, social sciences, and sciences, refers to a writer's presentation of prior research on a topic. Such a presentation is usually meant to set a broader context for a paper and to demonstrate the need for additional research.

TEACHING IDEAS

If you are using this handbook in conjunction with a literature anthology, the guidelines listed here can be of great help to students as they plan their papers. You may want to emphasize that the guidelines offer questions designed only to suggest a focus for a literary analysis, and that only one or two questions from each section would be included in a single paper. Nevertheless, these questions can help students through the often difficult steps of getting started on an analysis.

done so, read these sections of the chapter. The discussion here assumes your familiarity with the terms *claim, text, refer/reference,* and *comment.*

1 First reading: Respond

On a *first* reading, respond to the text.

Personal response is fundamental to the critical reading of *any* text. See Chapter 1 for a discussion of critical reading, generally, and of the importance of responding. Pose these questions to a text: *What can I learn from this selection? What is my background on the subject that this selection concerns? What is the origin of my views on the topics of this text? What new interest, or what new question or observation, does this text spark in me?* These questions, which you can ask of any text, can be refined somewhat when applied to literary texts.

Developing a personal response requires that you read a text closely, in such a way that you are alert to details that make the text meaningful. At the risk of stating the obvious, you should prepare for a close reading by finding a block of uninterrupted time when you are feeling alert and able to concentrate on what you read. Realize that close reading involves *multiple* readings. Expect that you will read a full text twice and selected parts of the text three or more times. On your first reading, disregard for the moment the paper you intend to write and read to be engaged, even moved. Read for the same reasons people have read or listened to stories and poetry or watched dramas for centuries: to be fascinated, to learn something of other lives, to wonder, and to question. Writing about literature is premised on the belief that the text you are examining *is* worthy of your extended reflection. If you have not thought about what you have read, if you have not responded to it personally, you can hardly expect to write about it with conviction.[4]

TEACHING IDEAS

Students sometimes think that once a literary work is subjected to analysis, then all the joy is drained from it. An analogy between reading literature and performing in sports or dance might help students see the fallacy of this line of thinking. Any student who has played a sport seriously or who has danced competitively knows the pure joy of the activity. But he or she also knows that both activities are often difficult; excellence takes practice and hard work. Furthermore, analysis of a batter's or a ballerina's stance, far from draining the performance of beauty, actually enhances its aesthetic value. This analogy may help students approach the study of literature more receptively, and therefore make it easier for them to develop an appreciation for writing about literature.

TEACHING IDEAS

Students can be encouraged at this point to keep a response journal for their reading. As the Brooks example (on page 686) illustrates, the purpose of the journal is not to engage in deep literary analysis, but rather to *react* to a work. Not only will the journal help students articulate their responses to a work, but also it will provide a quick memory refresher when the class begins discussing the work.

---

[4] Which specific features of a text merit our calling it *literature* is a matter of some controversy. There is the traditional "canon," the body of works that for generations scholars (and an obedient public) have regarded as important texts in Western culture: Shakespeare, Keats, Brontë, Shelley, Melville, and many more. But a difficulty arises: Given that authors are forever creating new texts, why are some texts added to the canon, the "important" list worthy of study, while other texts are excluded? Applied historically, this same question has caused a revolution in literary studies: What makes Shakespeare, Shelley, and the others canonical—that is, examples of what we call literature? Why were *they* included in the canon and not more women writers, more minorities, or more representatives of less industrial nations? Who made, and who makes, decisions about what texts are to be called literature? What assumptions about art and culture guide these decision makers, and might not different assumptions lead us to create a different canon? These explosive questions may well become guiding concerns in one of your literature courses. Suffice it to say that what counts as "literature" is under intense scrutiny at the moment.

Questions to prompt a personal response on a first reading

- What do I feel when reading this material? Why do I feel this way?
- Does this text make me *want* to read? Why or why not?
- What about this text is worth reading a second time?
- How am I challenged by or changed in response to this text?
- With what questions does this text leave me?
- What differences do I see between the author's observations of the world and my observations? How can I explain these differences?

Personal responses based on these and related questions can make you want to know more about what you have read. For instance, if on completing a story, drama, or poem you find yourself *moved, offended, challenged, saddened, confused, needled,* or *intrigued,* you will have an immediate and even pressing reason to return for a second reading. And it is the second reading in which you will discover the patterns that will enable you to write a worthwhile paper. Sometimes, you may need to brainstorm after a first reading in order to understand your particular response to a text (see 3b-2). What follows is a demonstration of such a brainstorming session. Brandy Brooks, whose paper you will read in 37e, spent five minutes writing out her responses to "A Shameful Affair," a short story by Kate Chopin. Read Chopin's story here, along with Brooks's marginal notes from her first reading:

"A Shameful Affair"

KATE CHOPIN

Kate Chopin (1851–1904) is a much-admired nineteenth-century American writer known widely for her novel *The Awakening* (1899) and for two collections of short stories, *Bayou Folk* (1894) and *A Night in Arcadie* (1897). Chopin began her career as a published writer when she was thirty-eight years old, after her husband died and she was left to care for six children.

1 Mildred Orme, seated in the snuggest corner of the big front porch of the Kraummer farmhouse, was as content as a girl need hope to be.

2 This was no such farm as one reads about in humorous fiction. Here were swelling acres where the undulating wheat gleamed in the sun like a golden sea. For silver there was the Meramec—or, better, it was pure crystal, for here and there one might look clean through it down to where the pebbles lay like green and yellow gems. Along the river's edge trees were growing to the very water, and in it, sweeping it when they were willows.

Beautiful. I can see the river

3 The house itself was big and broad, as country houses should be. The master was big and broad, too. The mistress was small and thin, and it was always she who went out at noon to pull the great clanging bell that called the farmhands in to dinner.

FOR DISCUSSION

After reading the example of Brooks's marginal notes, you might initiate a discussion of annotating a text. Ask students what they think of the notes she makes—do they sound like the musings of a literary scholar? How similar are they to notes students in the class make? Why do students think she commented as she did? What other notes would members of the class make?

4 From her agreeable corner where she lounged with her Browning or her Ibsen, Mildred watched the woman do this every day. Yet when the clumsy farmhands all came tramping up the steps and crossed the porch in going to their meal that was served within, she never looked at them. Why should she? Farmhands are not so very nice to look at, and she was nothing of an anthropologist. But once when the half dozen men came along, a paper which she had laid carelessly upon the railing was blown across their path. One of them picked it up, and when he had mounted the steps restored it to her. He was young, and brown, of course, as the sun had made him. He had nice blue eyes. His fair hair was dishevelled. His shoulders were broad and square and his limbs strong and clean. A not unpicturesque figure in the rough attire that bared his throat to view and gave perfect freedom to his every motion.

The young man gets M's attention, and mine

5 Mildred did not make these several observations in the half second that she looked at him in courteous acknowledgment. It took her as many days to note them all. For she singled him out each time that he passed her, meaning to give him a condescending little smile, as she knew how. But he never looked at her. To be sure, clever young women of twenty who are handsome, besides, who have refused their half dozen offers and are settling down to the conviction that life is a tedious affair, are not going to care a straw whether farmhands look at them or not. And Mildred did not care, and the thing would not have occupied her a moment if Satan had not intervened, in offering the employment which natural conditions had failed to supply. It was summer time; she was idle; she was piqued, and that was the beginning of the shameful affair.

6 "Who are these men, Mrs. Kraummer, that work for you? Where do you pick them up?"

7 "Oh, ve picks 'em up everywhere. Some is neighbors, some is tramps, and so."

8 "And that broad-shouldered young fellow—is he a neighbor? The one who handed me my paper the other day—you remember?"

9 "Gott, no! you might yust as vell say he was a tramp. Abet he vorks like a steam ingine."

10 "Well, he's an extremely disagreeable-looking man. I should think you'd be afraid to have him about, not knowing him."

11 "Vat you vant to be 'fraid for?" laughed the little woman. "He don't talk no more un ven he vas deef und dumb. I didn't t'ought you vas sooch a baby."

12 "But, Mrs. Kraummer, I don't want you to think I'm a baby, as you say, a coward, as you mean. Ask the man

if he will drive me to church tomorrow. You see, I'm not so very much afraid of him," she added with a smile.

13 The answer which this unmannerly farmhand returned to Mildred's request was simply a refusal. He could not drive her to church because he was going fishing.

14 "Aber," offered good Mrs. Kraummer, "Hans Platzfeldt vill drive you to church, oder verever you vants. He vas a goot boy vat you can trust, dat Hans."

15 "Oh, thank him very much. But I find I have so many letters to write tomorrow, and it promises to be hot, too. I shan't care to go to church after all."

16 She could have cried for vexation. Snubbed by a farmhand! a tramp, perhaps. She, Mildred Orme, who ought really to have been with the rest of the family at Narragansett—who had come to seek in this retired spot the repose that would enable her to follow exalted lines of thought. She marveled at the problematic nature of farmhands.

17 After sending her the uncivil message already recorded, and as he passed beneath the porch where she sat, he did look at her finally, in a way to make her positively gasp at the sudden effrontery of the man.

18 But the inexplicable look stayed with her. She could not banish it.

II

19 It was not so very hot after all, the next day, when Mildred walked down the long narrow footpath that led through the bending wheat to the river. High above her waist reached the yellow grain. Mildred's brown eyes filled with a reflected golden light as they caught the glint of it, as she heard the trill that it answered to the gentle breeze. Anyone who has walked through the wheat in midsummer-time knows that sound.

Again I can see this. M into the wheat

20 In the woods it was sweet and solemn and cool. And there beside the river was the wretch who had annoyed her, first, with his indifference, then with the sudden boldness of his glance.

21 "Are you fishing?" she asked politely and with kindly dignity, which she supposed would define her position toward him. The inquiry lacked not pertinence, seeing that he sat motionless, with a pole in his hand and his eyes fixed on a cork that bobbed aimlessly on the water.

22 "Yes, madam," was his brief reply.

23 "It won't disturb you if I stand here a moment, to see what success you will have?"

24 "No, madam."

25 She stood very still, holding tight to the book she had brought with her. Her straw hat had slipped disreputably to one side, over the wavy bronze-brown bang that half covered her forehead. Her cheeks were ripe with color that the sun had coaxed there; so were her lips.

26 All the other farmhands had gone forth in Sunday attire. Perhaps this one had none better than these working clothes that he wore. A feminine commiseration swept her at the thought. He spoke never a word. She wondered how many hours he could sit there, so patiently waiting for fish to come to his hook. For her part, the situation began to pall, and she wanted to change it at last.

27 "Let me try a moment, please? I have an idea."

28 "Yes, madam."

29 "The man is surely an idiot, with his monosyllables," she commented inwardly. But she remembered that monosyllables belong to a boot's equipment.

30 She laid her book carefully down and took the pole gingerly that he came to place in her hands. Then it was his turn to stand back and look respectfully and silently on at the absorbing performance.

31 "Oh!" cried the girl, suddenly, seized with excitement upon seeing the line dragged deep in the water.

32 "Wait, wait! Not yet."

33 He sprang to her side. With his eyes eagerly fastened on the tense line, he grasped the pole to prevent her drawing it, as her intention seemed to be. That is, he meant to grasp the pole, but instead, his brown hand came down upon Mildred's white one.

34 He started violently at finding himself so close to a bronze-brown tangle that almost swept his chin—to a hot cheek only a few inches away from his shoulder, to a pair of young, dark eyes that gleamed for an instant unconscious things into his own.

35 Then, why ever it happened, or how ever it happened, his arms were holding Mildred and he kissed her lips. She did not know if it was ten times or only once. *The moment! Kiss*

36 She looked around—her face milk white—to see him disappear with rapid strides through the path that had brought her there. Then she was alone.

37 Only the birds had seen, and she could count on their discretion. She was not wildly indignant, as many would have been. Shame stunned her. But through it she gropingly wondered if she should tell the Kraummers that her chaste lips had been rifled of their innocence. Publish her own confusion? No! Once in her room she would give calm thought to the situation, and determine then how to act. The secret must remain her

own: a hateful burden to bear alone until she could forget it.

III

38 And because she feared not to forget it, Mildred wept that night. All day long a hideous truth had been thrusting itself upon her that made her ask herself if she could be mad. She feared it. Else why was that kiss the most delicious thing she had known in her twenty years of life? The sting of it had never left her lips since it was pressed into them. The sweet trouble of it banished sleep from her pillow.

39 But Mildred would not bend the outward conditions of her life to serve any shameful whim that chanced to visit her soul, like an ugly dream. She would avoid nothing. She would go and come as always.

40 In the morning she found in her chair upon the porch the book she had left by the river. A fresh indignity! But she came and went as she intended to, and sat as usual upon the porch amid her familiar surroundings. When the Offender passed her by she knew it, though her eyes were never lifted. Are there only sight and sound to tell such things? She discerned it by a wave that swept her with confusion and she knew not what besides.

41 She watched him furtively, one day, when he talked with Farmer Kraummer out in the open. When he walked away she remained like one who has drunk much wine. Then unhesitatingly she turned and began her preparations to leave the Kraummer farmhouse.

42 When the afternoon was far spent they brought letters to her. One of them read like this:

43 "My Mildred, deary! I am only now at Narragansett, and so broke up not to find you. So you are down at the Kraummer farm, on the Iron Mountains. Well! What do you think of that delicious crank, Fred Evelyn? For a man must be a crank who does such things. Only fancy! Last year he chose to drive an engine back and forth across the plains. This year he tills the soil with laborers. Next year it will be something else as insane—because he likes to live more lives than one kind, and other Quixotic reasons. We are great chums. He writes me he's grown as strong as an ox. But he hasn't mentioned that you are there. I know you don't get on with him, for he isn't a bit intellectual—detests Ibsen and abuses Tolstoi. He doesn't read 'in books'—says they are spectacles for the shortsighted to look at life through. Don't snub him, dear, or be too hard on him; he has a heart of gold, if he is the first crank in America."

44 Mildred tried to think—to feel the intelligence which this letter brought to her would take somewhat of the sting from the shame that tortured her. But it did not. She knew that it could not.

45 In the gathering twilight she walked through the wheat that was heavy and fragrant with dew. The path was very long and very narrow. When she was midway she saw the Offender coming toward her. What could she do? Turn and run, as a little child might? Spring into the wheat, as some frightened four footed creature would? There was nothing but to pass him with the dignity which the occasion clearly demanded.

46 But he did not let her pass. He stood squarely in the pathway before her, hat in hand, a perturbed look upon his face.

47 "Miss Orme," he said, "I have wanted to say to you, every hour of the past week, that I am the most consummate hound that walks the earth." *(He's no farm hand)*

48 She made no protest. Her whole bearing seemed to indicate that her opinion coincided with his own.

49 "If you have a father, or brother, or any one, in short, to whom you may say such things—"

50 "I think you aggravate the offense, sir by speaking of it. I shall ask you never to mention it again. I want to forget that it ever happened. Will you kindly let me by."

51 "Oh," he ventured eagerly, "you want to forget it! Then, maybe, since you are willing to forget, you will be generous enough to forgive the offender some day?"

52 "Some day," she repeated, almost inaudibly, looking seemingly through him, but not at him—"some day—perhaps; when I shall have forgiven myself."

53 He stood motionless, watching her slim, straight figure lessening by degrees as she walked slowly away from him. He was wondering what she meant. Then a sudden, quick wave came beating into his brown throat and staining it crimson, when he guessed what it might be. *Why crimson?*

Brandy Brooks wrote for several minutes on completing "A Shameful Affair." Here is her response:

I'm impressed by how vivid the images are involving colors in this story. In any passage where Chopin uses color to describe a scene or a character, the mental picture that I developed was bright and clear. It seems like Chopin's color descriptions act as a highlighter to focus me on an event or passage and signal its importance. Her use of color adds drama and evokes emotion--like when Mildred's walking through the wheat. That's a beautiful spot, and Chopin for the first time lets us see Mildred.

2 Second reading: Analyze the text—find patterns of meaning in it based on your response.

> Ask *why* or *how* of your personal response, and you will have a specific, guiding question to lead you through a second reading. Your goal with this question is to understand your response by finding a pattern that makes the text meaningful.

In Chapter 2, you will find an extended discussion on the ways in which thoughtful writing is based on a close, critical reading of a text. Certainly, thoughtful writing about literature is based on your reading of the literary work. *Response* is the first component of this reading; *analysis,* based on that response, is the second. See 2c for a general discussion on writing analyses. The principles established there apply to this discussion as well.

You can approach a second reading of a text by working with the response that most interested you in your first reading. Convert that response into a pointed question by asking *Why? How? What are some examples?* Guided by this question, return to the text and analyze it (see 2c-2). If your analysis succeeds, it will yield insights into how the text works, how you think it achieves its meaning in one particular way (with respect to your question). As you read a second time, make notes in the margin wherever you feel the text provides details that can help you answer your guiding question. These notes, considered in light of your question, can suggest a pattern that makes the text meaningful. You can write a successful paper by presenting this same pattern to your reader.

Following is an illustration of a second reading—selected paragraphs from the section of "A Shameful Affair" in which Mildred walks through the wheat field in search of Fred Evelyn. The excerpt is accompanied by Brandy Brooks's margin notes. The question she used to guide her second reading was as follows: *How does Chopin use colors in this story to communicate Mildred's emotions and her growing awareness?* Note how the question builds directly on the response she made in her five-minute brainstorming session, in which her main concern was with color. Observe how she uses her question to tease out details in the story that will, subsequently, provide her with material for a paper. If you have trouble deciding on a question to guide your second reading, reflect again on your response to the text. See also 37d-4 for a discussion of how you can pose specific questions based on one or another theory of literary criticism.

19 It was not so very hot after all, the next day, when Mildred walked down the long narrow footpath that led through the bending wheat to the river. High above her waist reached the yellow grain. Mildred's brown eyes filled with a reflected golden light as they caught the glint of it, as she heard the trill that it answered to the

M in the wheat—a setting filled w/ Nature's color

FOR DISCUSSION

In this discussion students will continue their commentary on annotating a text. Questions to consider now include the following: How did Brooks come up with her controlling question? How is the question reflected in her annotations? Do students see anything else in the selection that is relevant to the question?

gentle breeze. Anyone who has walked through the wheat in midsummer-time knows that sound.

20 In the woods it was sweet and solemn and cool. And there beside the river was the wretch who had annoyed her, first, with his indifference, then with the sudden boldness of his glance.

21 "Are you fishing?" she asked politely and with kindly dignity, which she supposed would define her position toward him. The inquiry lacked not pertinence, seeing that he sat motionless, with a pole in his hand and his eyes fixed on a cork that bobbed aimlessly on the water.

22 "Yes, madam," was his brief reply.

23 "It won't disturb you if I stand here a moment, to see what success you will have?"

24 "No, madam."

25 She stood very still, holding tight to the book she had brought with her. Her straw hat had slipped disreputably to one side, over the wavy bronze-brown bang that half covered her forehead. Her cheeks were ripe with color that the sun had coaxed there; so were her lips.

Now M has color—hair, cheeks, lips. She's part of Nature!

26 All the other farmhands had gone forth in Sunday attire. Perhaps this one had none better than these working clothes that he wore. A feminine commiseration swept her at the thought. He spoke never a word. She wondered how many hours he could sit there, so patiently waiting for fish to come to his hook. For her part, the situation began to pall, and she wanted to change it at last.

27 "Let me try a moment, please? I have an idea."

28 "Yes, madam."

29 "The man is surely an idiot, with his monosyllables," she commented inwardly. But she remembered that monosyllables belong to a boot's equipment.

30 She laid her book carefully down and took the pole gingerly that he came to place in her hands. Then it was his turn to stand back and look respectfully and silently on at the absorbing performance.

31 "Oh!" cried the girl, suddenly, seized with excitement upon seeing the line dragged deep in the water.

32 "Wait, wait! Not yet."

33 He sprang to her side. With his eyes eagerly fastened on the tense line, he grasped the pole to prevent her drawing it, as her intention seemed to be. That is, he meant to grasp the pole, but instead, his brown hand came down upon Mildred's white one.

A touch—the moment, & described in colors

34 He started violently at finding himself so close to a bronze-brown tangle that almost swept his chin—to a hot cheek only a few inches away from his shoulder, to

a pair of young, dark eyes that gleamed for an instant unconscious things into his own.

35 Then, why ever it happened, or how ever it happened, his arms were holding Mildred and he kissed her lips. She did not know if it was ten times or only once.

36 She looked around—her face milk white—to see him disappear with rapid strides through the path that had brought her there. Then she was alone. *Color drains out of M's face*

3 Construct a pattern of meaning: Making claims and providing evidence

Refine the pattern you have found and make a claim. Locate passages in the text that support this claim.

Based on your first and second readings of a text, you are ready to make a claim: to state for your readers the pattern you have found and your reasons for believing this pattern is worth your time pursuing and your reader's time considering. With her first and second readings of Chopin's "A Shameful Affair," in mind, Brandy Brooks developed this claim:

```
In "A Shameful Affair," Kate Chopin communicates Mildred Orme's
sexual awakening through descriptions of a farm and, particu-
larly, through the colors one finds there.
```

Brooks has found a pattern that helps make Chopin's story meaningful to her, and she formally expresses this pattern as a claim. That Brooks found this pattern and not another should not suggest that other patterns do not exist. Many do. "A Shameful Affair" is a story rich with meaning and, like any literary work, lends itself to countless interpretations. The point to remember is that whatever pattern a student of literature finds in a text, she or he is obliged to show readers why, given all the patterns that *could* be found, this one is reasonable and worth the reader's consideration. A writer demonstrates the worthiness of a pattern, or claim, by repeatedly referring the reader to the text—a primary source, and when pertinent, to secondary sources. (See 37a and b.) Again, you have seen in examples in this chapter (37a-2) how claims in the humanities in general, and claims about literary texts in particular, are supported. Often, before planning an argument in support of a claim, the writer will prepare a sketch. Here's how Brooks planned to support the claim above, based on both her reading of the text and her reading of two secondary sources.

```
Intro
  Chopin: sexual awakening, symbolism, importance of location
  Claim
```

TEACHING IDEAS

This section provides an ideal opportunity for you to discuss another mistaken notion about literary analysis: that it's all opinion, and therefore everybody's opinion counts. The care with which Brooks chooses and plans to support her claim indicates that she is not merely offering an opinion. Instead, she is making a claim whose worthiness will be demonstrated by her careful reference to primary and secondary sources. The sketch she uses can become a model for students, keeping them from making unsubstantiated claims about the works they're studying.

```
Plot summary
1st demonstration of color being important--farm setting
   Reference to Joyce Dyer--symbolism of farm, nature
2nd demo of color--intro of Fred Evelyn
3rd demo of color--Mildred into the wheat, to see Fred
4th demo of color--but color not used (after kiss)
5th demo of color--re-introduced at key point, the end
Conclusion
   Reference to Martin Simpson
```

When you read the paper in 37e, you will see that Brooks used this sketch as a guide to selecting passages in "A Shameful Affair" and in secondary sources that helped her to support her claim about Chopin's use of color. You will find on reading the paper that Brooks adheres closely to her sketch; that her sketch is built directly from the notes she made in her second reading; and that her second reading followed directly from the question that evolved from her first, personal response to the story.

TEACHING IDEAS

You may want to emphasize here that the plot summary is presented for a specific purpose and not as an end in itself. Brooks only includes enough of the plot to allow the reader to follow her argument. And she certainly doesn't attempt to pass off a plot summary as a literary analysis.

REFERENCE

LYNN, STEVEN. "A Passage into Critical Theory." *CE* 52 (1990): 258–71. Illustrates various critical approaches (from formalism to feminism) by submitting a sample text to analysis.

Plot summaries

Brooks's planned use of the plot summary should be noted here because it is a feature common to so many papers written about literature. A **plot summary** is a brief description of characters and events that provides readers, some of whom may be unfamiliar with the story, context enough to follow a discussion. Plot summaries are written in the historical present tense. Consider these sentences from Brooks's paper (present-tense verbs are underlined):

Mildred Orme <u>is</u> a 20-year-old sophisticated beauty who <u>seeks</u> simple country life for a summer of quiet reading and reflection. . . . Mildred <u>sees</u> the farm hands every day as she <u>sits</u> reading on the Kraummer's porch.

Variations from the present tense may be needed from time to time to clarify sequences of events; but plot summaries are written predominantly in the present tense because the events of a text are always present to a reader—the same actions occur in the same order in the text no matter how many times that text is read. Remember that the purpose of the plot summary is to allow the writer to refer to a text and in this way support a claim. Typically, the writer's observation about the text immediately follows the plot summary, sometimes in the same sentence:

As of yet, Mildred's chosen farmhand is without a name; but like the retouched color rose in a black and white photograph, this young man stands apart from the farmhands that cross Mildred's path, none of whom have been described in terms of color.

The clause beginning "but like the retouched color rose" is not part of Brooks's summary but is rather one of her observations about the story, an observation that supports her claim and that follows from her guiding question *(How does Chopin use colors in this story to communicate Mildred's emotions and her growing awareness?).* To ensure that readers can follow her discussion, Brooks summarizes portions of "A Shameful Affair" throughout her paper so that her observations will have a specific reference and will make sense to her readers.

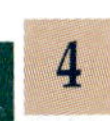

4 Literary criticism: More formal readings of texts

What counts as a detail worth noting in a poem, story, or play? What counts as a pattern of details worth discovering? Answers depend on the questions a reader poses. You will see (in 37d-5) that Brandy Brooks observed details of "A Shameful Affair" and fit them together in a pattern based on a question built from her *personal response* to the story. There are other, more formal questions that can be put to a literary text, and these are based on the philosophies of various "schools" of literary criticism, each of which regards texts differently and, based on its approach, poses distinctive questions.

Scholars who write professionally about and teach poetry, plays, and fiction are called *literary critics;* and critics affiliate themselves with one of several approaches to literature. Some critics read *Moby Dick,* for instance, and ask: What is the psychological basis of the relationship between Ishmael and Queequeg? Some read the novel with this question: What echoes can we find of Melville's years at sea? Some look at the public's initial reaction to the novel (they disliked it) and ask: Why and when did this work come to be regarded as an American classic? The possible angles from which to study a literary work are many; and each angle suggests its own set of questions, its own set of problems worth investigating, and its own rules about what counts as acceptable evidence in support of an argument. Fundamentally, readers find in a text what they look for: pose one question, and you will focus on the relationship between Ishmael and Queequeg; pose another, and you will concern yourself with the readers' changing responses to *Moby Dick* over the years.

The questions that guide your reading, then, are of paramount importance. People who make a profession of literary studies insist that their questions be based on sound, carefully thought through philosophical principles. From one school to the next, these principles differ. Differences notwithstanding, all literary critics believe in the abiding value of literature, and believe that we can learn about ourselves and others by reading it. All critics and all teachers of literature accept as a general model of argumentation the cycle of claim, reference to a text, and comment.

It is impossible to say that one approach to a literary text is ultimately correct. There are *many* approaches, and each can show us patterns of meaning in a text that make the text more understandable. If you major in literature, and especially if you go on to graduate school, you will learn about schools of literary criticism. For the moment, even without the benefit of a literary critic's carefully prepared questions (some of which will be presented below), you can gain lasting insights into a poem, play, or work of fiction by finding in it a pattern based on your own personal responses.

Posing more formal questions for a second reading

You may find yourself writing papers for literature courses in which you approach the study of literature according to the viewpoints of various schools of literary criticism. Without naming these schools here and introducing you to complicated terminologies and methods, following are some additional questions you might pose to a text. These questions assume that you have already completed a first close reading.

- What circumstances of the author's life does the text reflect?
- In what ways does the text exist in a relationship with other texts by the same author and with other texts from the same time period?
- How might the text shift its meaning from one reader to the next? from one audience to the next, over time?
- What is the reader's role in making this text meaningful?
- How does the text reflect certain cultural assumptions (about gender or culture, for instance) in the author's and the readers' times?
- What psychological motives underlie the characters' actions?
- What are the economic or power relationships among the characters?

When you want to maintain your focus on a poem, play, or work of fiction itself (as opposed to considering the readers' responses or various influences on the author), then you can pose the following questions, arranged by category. These questions are often appropriate for introductory survey courses in literature.

Characterization Who are the main characters? What are their qualities? Is each character equally important? Equally well developed?

Language What devices such as rhyme (identical sounds), meter (carefully controlled rhythms), and pauses does the author use to create special emphasis? How does the author use metaphors and choose words to create visual images? In what ways are these images tied to the meaning of the text?

Narrator, Point of View Who is speaking? What is the narrator's personality and how does this affect the telling? Is the narrator omniscient in the sense that he or she can read into the thoughts of every character? If not, how is the narrator's vision limited?

Plot How does the writer sequence events so as to maintain the reader's attention? Which actions are central? How are other, subsidiary actions linked to the central ones? What patterning to the plot do you see? Are there ways in which the plot's structure and theme are related?

Structure In what ways can you (or does the author) divide the whole poem or story into component parts—according to theme? plot? setting? stanza? How are these parts related?

Setting Where does the story take place? How significant is the setting to the meaning of the text?

Symbolism Are any symbols operating, any objects that (like a flag) create for readers emotional, political, religious, or other associations? If so, how do these symbols function in the poem, story, or play?

Theme What large issues does this text raise? Through which characters, events, or specific lines are the questions raised? To what extent does the text answer these questions?

5 Write the paper: Synthesize the details you have assembled.

> Demonstrate the reasonableness of your claim by making observations about the text; if appropriate, refer to secondary sources and the observations of others. Synthesize these observations into a coherent argument.

The goal of a paper in a literature course is to show that your interpretation, the pattern of meaning you have found, is reasonable and can help others understand the text. Your observations about the text and, if you use them, the observations of others, are the details that you will *synthesize* into a coherent argument. See 2d for a discussion on writing syntheses. The principles reviewed there apply here.

LOOKING BACK

As students prepare to write literary analyses, it might be worthwhile to review Chapter 2 in class, especially the material on synthesis (2d).

37e Sample student paper: "The Role of Color in Kate Chopin's 'A Shameful Affair' "

In the following paper, Brandy Brooks examines the ways in which Kate Chopin uses colors and descriptions of nature to suggest the sexual awakening of the character Mildred Orme. Throughout the paper, you will find Brooks following the pattern of claim and support common in literary criticism: Brooks makes a claim, refers to a passage, and then comments on the passage in order to cement its relationship to the claim. She carefully develops an interpretation of the story and, when she finds the need, draws on secondary sources.

TEACHING IDEAS

The sample research paper presented here is heavily annotated so that students can use it as a guide in writing their own research papers. You may want to call particular attention to specific features peculiar to humanities papers—arrangement, documentation, method of supporting claims, and the like.

GROUP ACTIVITY

Ask students to read Brooks's paper in its entirety, and then divide the class into groups of three or four. Each group will then analyze the effectiveness of Brooks's argument based on the material presented in the chapter. You may want to offer the following guidelines for the analysis:

- How clearly does Brooks state her claim?
- How do her references to the text support her claim?
- How does she use secondary sources to support her claim?
- How effectively does she synthesize her observations?

1"

1/2"

Brooks 1

Brandy H. M. Brooks

Dr. Glenn Adelson

English 16

25 October 1996 — Double space

The Role of Color in Kate Chopin's "A Shameful Affair"

Indent 5 spaces

1"

Kate Chopin is a writer of self-discoveries--of characters who awaken to desires buried deep within and only dimly understood (if understood at all). In leading the reader through a character's discovery, Chopin often prefers powerful descriptive images to explicit speeches or action. The setting in which a character finds herself, for instance, can reflect or influence her development of self-awareness. In "A Shameful Affair," Chopin communicates Mildred Orme's sexual awakening through descriptions of a farm and, particularly, through the colors one finds there.

The thesis

Mildred Orme is a twenty-year-old sophisticated beauty who seeks simple country life for a summer of quiet reading and reflection. With the rest of her family vacationing at Narragansett Bay, Mildred arrives at Kraummer's farm as a mature young woman who's temporarily free of her parents' restrictions and fully aware that she's placed herself in the company of strong, young men. Mildred sees the farmhands every day as she sits reading on the Kraummer's porch. While at first "she never look[s] at them" (682), one day one of the men returns a slip of paper blown from her side by a gust of wind.[1] She notices him. And "that," writes Chopin, is "the beginning of the shameful affair" (682).

Plot summary (present tense)

At the farm, Mildred finds herself immersed in a rich, fertile natural world that distracts her

1"

[1]Page references are to "A Shameful Affair" as reprinted in *The Allyn & Bacon Handbook,* on pages 681–86.

1/2"

1"

Brooks 2

1"

from the "exalted lines of thought" (683) she had intended to pursue during her visit. The pull of nature is strong and sensual:

Indent 10 spaces

> Here were swelling acres where the undulating wheat gleamed in the sun like a golden sea. For silver there was the Meramec--or, better, it was pure crystal, for here and there one might look clean through it down to where the pebbles lay like green and yellow gems. Along the river's edge trees were growing to the very water, and in it, sweeping it when they were willows. (681)

1st demonstration of color in the story

1"

These colors are bright and gleaming. There is a "golden sea," a river described as "silver" or "pure crystal," and pebbles that sparkle like gemstones. With her use of color, Chopin draws our attention to the farm and its natural setting, to its physical beauty as a place into which Mildred, ready for sexual awakening, has stepped. According to critic Joyce Dyer, the farm is a symbol "of natural growth and fertility . . . that will help us understand the force that drives Mildred toward Fred Evelyn" (448).

Reference to a secondary source in support of the thesis

Chopin continues to control the use of color when introducing Mildred's young man. We learn that Fred "was young, and brown"; "[h]e had nice blue eyes. His fair hair was dishevelled" (682). As of yet, Mildred's chosen farmhand is without a name; but like the retouched color rose in a black and white photograph, this young man stands apart from the farmhands that cross Mildred's path, none of whom have been described in terms of color. Chopin gives to Fred the "brown" of the earth and the "blue" of the sky, making him as much a part of the natural ripeness of the Kraummer farm as the "swelling acres . . . [of] undulating wheat" (681).

2nd demonstration of color in the story

1"

TEACHING IDEAS

This page provides some excellent examples of the use of quotations. You may want to call attention to such features as the use of ellipses, the smooth integration of quotations into the text, and the appropriate use of parenthetical references.

Brooks 3

Indirectly, through Mrs. Kraummer, Mildred asks Fred to drive her to church the next day--Sunday. Fred won't because he has plans to go fishing. The refusal stings Mildred. On Sunday she abandons her plans for church and decides, instead, on a walk. And where should she go but to the river. For reasons Mildred does not yet understand but that nonetheless compel her, she must be near Fred Evelyn. The scene into which she plunges is rich with the colors of ripe, fertile nature:

> High above her waist reached the yellow grain. Mildred's brown eyes filled with a reflected golden light as they caught the glint of it, as she heard the trill that it answered to the gentle breeze. (683)

And Mildred herself takes on color as she works her way toward the river, drawing closer to the man she unconsciously desires:

> Her straw hat had slipped disreputably to one side, over the wavy bronze-brown bang that half covered her forehead. Her cheeks were ripe with color that the sun had coaxed there; so were her lips. (684)

Mildred's "brown eyes" reflect "golden light"; her "bronze-brown bang" covers her forehead; her cheeks and lips are "ripe" with color. She, the wheat fields, the stream, and Fred Evelyn are all <u>alive</u> with natural energy, as communicated by Chopin through the use of color. Without ever stating explicitly that Mildred is on the threshold of discovering her sexuality, Chopin prepares us for the moment.

At the river, Fred Evelyn is fishing. Mildred asks if she can try--and promptly catches a fish. In the excitement that follows, Fred's "brown hand [comes] down upon Mildred's white one" (684). The contrast of colors increases our tension: after the

Sentences of plot summary (present tense)

3rd demonstration of color in the story

Sentences of plot summary (present tense)

Brooks 4

long build-up, two people (two colors), touch. What will happen? Fred cannot restrain himself, so close is he "to a bronze-brown tangle that almost swept his chin . . . to a pair of young, dark eyes that gleamed for an instant unconscious things into his own" (684). Without thinking, he reaches for Mil-dred and kisses her lips.

Just as Chopin uses color in this story to prepare us for her character's fulfillment of sex-ual desire, she uses the <u>absence</u> of color to sug-gest the dampening effect of society on that desire. Immediately after the kiss, color drains from Mildred's once-ripe cheeks. She turns, "her face milk white" (684), to watch Fred run back to the farm. Confusion sweeps over her: she stares blankly, with shock and shame. She cries that night, wanting to forget the kiss but cannot--and is frightened that it was "the most delicious thing she had known in her twenty years of life" (685).

4th demonstration of color; this time, color <u>not</u> used

During and following this emotional ordeal, Chopin stops using color in the story. All the lus-cious ripeness of nature is gone while Mildred struggles with the social consequences of her act. Color returns when she meets Fred a final time in the wheat field. Before this meeting, we gain a crucial piece of information: in a letter from her family, Mildred learns that Fred belongs to her same social class. He has come to do farm work in an effort "to live more lives than one kind" (685). Suddenly, he is no longer a rough farmhand to whom she was drawn physically, but an adventurer and a potential partner--someone who might gain the ap-proval of her parents. Her next meeting with him, the last of the story, promises a final drama: not only might they discuss their kiss, they might dis-cuss their future.

Brooks 5

But the young woman and man awkwardly stammer their words. Fred apologizes (in language very unlike that of a farmhand): "I have wanted to say . . . that I am the most consummate hound that walks the earth" (686). Responding to a request that she forgive him, Mildred says: "[S]ome day--perhaps; when I shall have forgiven myself" (686). Fred ponders her meaning. "Then a sudden, quick wave came beating into his brown throat and staining it crimson, when he guessed what it might be" (686).

Final demonstration of color in the story

Color--the blood-red color of animal life--returns at precisely the moment a physical, natural connection between the young woman and man once again becomes possible. Through her use of color in the final moment of the story, Chopin pulls us away from social worries about kissing and thrusts us back into nature, into the world of "undulating wheat." Mildred's "some day" suggests that she may not simply wish to forget Fred. The moment he understands this, color floods him. Where color is present in this story, sexual fulfillment is possible.

Conclusion

In "A Shameful Affair," Kate Chopin uses vivid description to trace the path of Mildred Orme's sexual awakening. In a few brief pages, we watch her "drawn out of the world of sheltered social convention and into a natural world that is rich with sensuous physical surroundings" (Simpson 59). Chopin carefully, and subtly, uses color to heighten the drama of each moment in which Mildred grows in sexual awareness.

Reference to a secondary source in support of the thesis

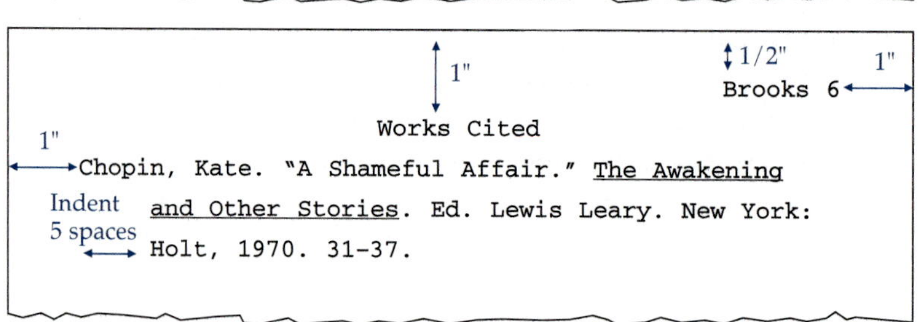

Brooks 6

Works Cited

Chopin, Kate. "A Shameful Affair." The Awakening and Other Stories. Ed. Lewis Leary. New York: Holt, 1970. 31-37.

Dyer, Joyce. "Symbolic Setting in Kate Chopin's 'A Shameful Affair.'" Southern Studies: An Interdisciplinary Journal of the South 20 (1981): 447-52.

Simpson, Martin. "Chopin's 'A Shameful Affair.'" The Explicator 45.1 (1986): 59-60.

37f Reference materials in the humanities

Style guides

The following sources offer discipline-specific guidance for writing in the humanities.

Barnet, Sylvan. *A Short Guide to Writing About Literature.* 5th ed. Glenview: Scott, 1985.

Blanshard, Brand. *On Philosophical Style.* Bloomington: Indiana UP, 1954.

Daniels, Robert V. *Studying History: How and Why.* 3rd ed. Englewood Cliffs, NJ: Prentice, 1981.

Specialized references

The following specialized references will help you to assemble information in a particular discipline or field within a discipline.

Encyclopedias provide general information useful when beginning a search.

Cassell's Encyclopedia of World Literature rev. ed.
Encyclopedia of American History
Encyclopedia of Art
Encyclopedia of Bioethics
Encyclopedia of Dance and Ballet
Encyclopedia of Philosophy
Encyclopedia of Religion and Ethics
Encyclopedia of World Art
An Encyclopedia of World History: Ancient, Medieval, and Modern
International Encyclopedia of Film
International Standard Bible Encyclopedia
The New College Encyclopedia of Music
Oxford Companion to Art
Oxford Companion to Film

REFERENCES

BIDDLE, ARTHUR W., and TOBY FULWILER, eds. *Reading, Writing, and the Study of Literature.* New York: Random, 1989. An introduction to different ways students may approach literature (includes chapters, with bibliographies, authored by different scholars on genres and literary criticism).

CULLER, JONATHAN. *The Pursuit of Signs: Semiotics, Literature, Deconstruction.* Ithaca: Cornell UP, 1981. Important discussion about the influence of poststructuralist criticism on the interpretation of literary texts.

EAGLETON, TERRY. *Literary Theory: An Introduction.* Minneapolis: U of Minnesota P, 1983. Surveys and critiques twentieth-century literary theory (the chapter "The Rise of English" is indispensable to anyone involved in literary study).

GOULD, CHRISTOPHER. "Literature in the Basic Writing Course: A Bibliographic Survey." *CE* 49 (1987): 558–74. Integrates theory and practice for teachers of basic writing who want to use literature in their classes (includes list of helpful texts).

LENTRICCIA, FRANK, and THOMAS MCLAUGHLIN, eds. *Critical Terms for Literary Study.* Chicago: U of Chicago P, 1990. Collection of essays that provides current, clear, and comprehensive discussions of twenty-two common terms such as "author," "figurative language," and "structure."

LYNN, STEVEN. "A Passage into Critical Theory." *CE* 52 (1990): 258–71. Illustrates various critical approaches (from formalism to feminism) by analyzing a sample text.

(continued)

REILLY, JILL M., et al. "The Effects of Prewriting on Literary Interpretation." ERIC, 1986. ED 276058. Presents results of a study that show how focused prewriting exercises lead students to compose more effective analytical papers.

TOMPKINS, JANE P., ed. *Reader-Response Criticism: From Formalism to Post-Structuralism.* Baltimore: Johns Hopkins UP, 1980. Selection of representative essays on poststructuralist criticism (Tompkins's introduction includes insightful discussion of reader-response criticism).

TUCHMAN, BARBARA W. *Practicing History: Selected Essays.* New York: Knopf, 1981. Provides recommendations for the analysis of works in history.

Oxford Companion to Canadian Literature (there are also *Oxford Companion* volumes for Classical, English, French, German, and Spanish Literature)

Oxford Companion to Music

Penguin Companion to American Literature (there are also *Penguin Companion* volumes for English, European, Classical, Oriental, and African Literature)

Princeton Encyclopedia of Poetry and Poetics

Dictionaries provide definitions for technical terms.

A Handbook to Literature
Concise Oxford Dictionary of Ballet
Dictionary of American History
Dictionary of Films
Dictionary of Philosophy
Harvard Dictionary of Music
Interpreter's Dictionary of the Bible
McGraw-Hill Dictionary of Art
New Grove Dictionary of Music and Musicians

Periodical indexes list articles published in a particular discipline over a particular period. *Abstracts,* which summarize the sources listed and involve a considerable amount of work to compile, tend to be more selective than indexes.

Abstracts of English Studies
America: History and Life
Art Index
Arts and Humanities Citation Index
British Humanities Index
Cambridge Bibliography of English Literature and New Cambridge Bibliography of English Literature
Essay and General Literature Index
Film Literature Index
Historical Abstracts
Humanities Index
Index to Book Reviews in the Humanities
International Index of Film Periodicals
MLA International Bibliography of Books and Articles on Modern Languages and Literatures
Music Index
New York Times Film Reviews
Philosopher's Index One: Periodicals
Religion Index
Year's Work in English Studies

CHAPTER 38

Writing and Reading in the Social Sciences

Herbert Spencer, a nineteenth-century pioneer of social science, observed, "Socially, as well as individually, organization is indispensable to growth" (59).* Today, the inheritors of that view—psychologists, sociologists, economists, political scientists, and anthropologists—attempt to discover patterns in human behavior that illuminate the ways in which we behave as members of groups: as members of family or community groups; as members of racial, ethnic, or religious groups; and as members of political or economic groups.

The belief that behavior is patterned suggests that a person's actions in his or her social setting are not random but instead are purposeful—whether or not the actor explicitly understands this. Social scientists do not claim that human behavior can be known absolutely—that, for instance, given enough information we can plot a person's future. They speak, rather, in terms of how and why a person or group is likely to behave in one set of circumstances or another. Social science is not mathematically precise in the manner of the natural sciences, and yet it is similar to those disciplines in the way that claims are based on what can be observed. Social scientists share the following broad theories:

- Human behavior is patterned, rule-governed behavior that can be described and explained.
- Individuals exist in a complex array of social systems, large and small. Individuals within systems interact; systems themselves interact and are dynamic, evolving entities.
- Individuals and social systems evolve—they change over time. Present behaviors can be traced to prior causes.

At any given moment, each of us exists in a broad constellation of systems: economic, political, cultural, psychological, and familial. The fabric of our lives is so complex that, in order to speak meaningfully and in detail about how we interact, social scientists carve up the social world according to the separate systems that constitute it. But no one of the social sciences is dominant: each contributes a partial understanding to what we know of human society.[1]

KEY FEATURES

While the humanities ask questions about the meaning of human existence, the social sciences seek to find patterns to help explain human behavior. This chapter approaches the social sciences from the perspective of common underlying theories of human behavior as well as distinctive modes of inquiry. Like the preceding chapter on the humanities, this chapter is divided into four major sections: writing, reading, types of assignments, and research papers. Writing in the social sciences is addressed in terms of patterns of informative writing and methods of argumentative writing; in this section the two primary methods of investigation, the laboratory experiment and the field (or case) study, are represented. Reading is addressed by considering the difference between quantitative and qualitative reports. The third section discusses various writing assignments students can expect to receive in these disciplines, relying on Chapter 2 (Critical Thinking and Writing) and Chapter 39 (Writing and Reading in the Sciences) for methodology; clear guidelines for manuscript form and contents of reports are presented in this section. Section four reproduces an annotated sample research paper, a sociological study of women alcoholics. The chapter ends with a comprehensive list of reference materials in the social sciences.

---

* In-text citations refer to the Works Cited list at the end of the book.

[1] To the extent that historical inquiry is based on an interpretation of texts, history is regarded as one of the humanities. Many historians, though, consider themselves to be social scientists in that they use procedures such as statistical analysis to find meaningful patterns in the past. In this book, history is discussed as one of the humanities. See Chapter 37.

CRITICAL THINKING

This is a short research and in-class writing assignment. Assign students to bring to class a photocopy of a page from a text in another course; they should consider this page to be a model of *informative* writing. Have them bring a page of their own recent writing also. Ask that they be prepared to discuss how each page functions (how much and what kinds of evidence it contains; how the facts, inferences, and opinions are arranged, etc.), and to comment in an evaluative paragraph on ways in which *each* page could be improved in its diction, phrasing, content, and organization.

ADDITIONAL EXERCISE A

Interview a professor of psychology, sociology, political science, economics, or anthropology on the subject of the writing he or she does in the profession. Pose questions such as the following: What phenomena do you study? What kinds of investigations do you conduct? What forms does your writing usually take? What is your purpose in writing in these forms? What kind of audience do you usually address? Try to think of some additional questions as well. Use your notes from the interview to write a paragraph describing the nature of writing in this particular discipline.

LOOKING BACK

Students may want to review the appropriate sections of Chapter 3 as they study this material. It's important that they recognize how the patterns of development cross disciplinary lines.

LOOKING BACK

All of the chapters in this part of the handbook rely heavily on ideas discussed in Chapter 6 (Writing and Evaluating Arguments), especially the material on modes of inquiry in various disciplines. If you haven't yet covered Chapter 6 in class, it would be useful to do so now. Otherwise, students should review the chapter in order to make better use of the information in this part of the handbook.

38a Writing in the social sciences

1 Writing to inform

Before significance can be found in social behavior, behavior must be accurately described and, when appropriate, objectively measured. A great deal of what social scientists do when they write is to *inform* readers with precise descriptions. Consider, for instance, an anthropologist's account of ritual drug-taking among the Yanomamo Indians of Venezuela and Brazil.

> Another useful plant provided by the jungle is the *ebene* tree. The inner bark of this tree is used in the manufacture of one kind of hallucinogenic drug. The bark is scraped from the trunk after the exterior layer of bark is removed, or is scraped from the inside of the bark surface itself. This material, which is fairly moist, is then mixed with wood ashes and kneaded between the palms of the hands. Additional moisture is provided by spitting periodically into the pliable wad of drug. When the drug has been thoroughly mixed with saliva and ashes, it is placed on a hot piece of broken clay pot and the moisture driven out with heat. It is ground into a powder as it dries, the flat side of a stone axe serving as the grinding pestle. The dried, green powder, no more than several tablespoons full, is then swept onto a leaf with a stiff feather. The men then gather around the leaf containing the drug, usually in the late afternoon, and take it by blowing the powder into each other's nostrils.

As in other disciplines, informative writing in the social sciences is built on recognizable patterns, one such pattern being a *process* by which some activity takes place. Napoleon Chagnon's account of the process by which a hallucinogenic drug is prepared is precise and authoritative—in a word, informative. Similarly informative accounts can be found in any of the disciplines in the social sciences. A psychologist, for instance, might *compare* and *contrast* the different motivations people have for joining groups. In the course of this discussion, the psychologist might *classify* types of people according to their need for group identity. Such a discussion might begin or end with an attempt to *define* the term *group*. All of the techniques discussed in Chapter 3 for informing writers are put to use in social science writing.

2 Making arguments

When social scientists report their findings in journals, they make arguments. Achieving general agreement about the causes of human behavior may be a distant goal of researchers, but achieving this goal is unlikely inasmuch as the subjects that social scientists study—humans—are willful beings whose behavior is determined by numerous, overlapping causes. Researchers acknowledge the complexity of human behavior by avoiding cause-and-effect explanations. They prefer, instead, to express findings in terms of their *probability* of being correct—in terms of their "significance level." A level of .05, for instance, signifies that there is a less than 5 out of 100 possibility that the researcher's findings occurred by chance.

Arguments are the means by which knowledge is built in the social sciences. Various subdisciplines within each discipline carry on these arguments, and each one frames questions differently, uses distinctive methods, and subscribes to different theories. For instance, the discipline of anthropology is broadly understood as the study of humankind in its physical and cultural setting. There are two broad divisions of anthropology: physical anthropology and cultural anthropology. Physical anthropologists study humans as a biological species that evolved in certain environments from earlier forms (such as *Australopithecus*) to its present form (*Homo sapiens*). Cultural anthropologists investigate the artifacts of civilization in an effort to understand how various peoples have organized their lives socially, economically, technologically, or linguistically. Ethnographers, ethnologists, geographers, linguists, archaeologists, and other specialists in the discipline can all be termed anthropologists in that they share basic assumptions—for instance, about the value of studying the physical and/or cultural development of humankind. Nonetheless, both within and between subfields of anthropology, researchers will disagree on how to study human culture or biology. As a student in one of the social sciences, you will learn to read, think, and write in the context of arguments made in a particular field. The more courses you take in a discipline, the more you will learn how to produce arguments and to think like researchers in that discipline.

Claims and evidence

A *claim* is an arguable statement that a writer is obliged to support with evidence. *Claims in the social sciences will often commit you to observing the actions of individuals or groups and to stating how these actions are significant, both for certain individuals and for the people responding to them* (Braybrooke 11). The variety of human behavior is, of course, vast, and researchers have developed methods for gathering data both in controlled laboratory settings and in field settings. The interview and the survey are two widely used techniques that allow researchers to observe aspects of behavior that remain largely invisible such as attitudes, beliefs, and desires. Researchers carefully develop questionnaires, trying not to skew responses by the way questions are framed. If successfully developed and administered, questionnaires yield information about behavior that can be quantified and grouped into categories. These categories, in turn, can be analyzed statistically so that logical and reliable comparisons or contrasts can be drawn. Statistics can then be used as *evidence* in social scientific arguments to show whether a proposed connection between behaviors is significant.

The logic by which social scientists argue and connect evidence to claims (see 3d and 6d-1) will also depend on the method of investigation. Following is a sketch of two social scientific arguments, excerpts of which you will read in 38b-1. You will see in each the interplay of method of observation, type of evidence, and logic that connects evidence to a claim.

TEACHING IDEAS

Students unfamiliar with writing outside the humanities may need to spend some time sifting through this material. While critical approaches differ within the humanities, the essential method of investigation—analyzing a text—remains the same. This is not so in the social sciences. You may want to reinforce the material here by cautioning students to be aware of the connections between type of claim and method of investigation. (The two sample arguments outlined below should help students see the difference between methods.)

REFERENCES

DAEMMRICH, INGRID. "A Bridge to Academic Discourse: Social Science Research Strategies in the Freshman Composition Course." CCC 40 (1989): 343–48. Presents three strategies (family stories, observation reports, and case studies) that introduce inexperienced writers to the methodological and discourse conventions of the social sciences.

GRIFFIN, C. W., ed. *New Directions for Teaching and Learning: Teaching Writing in All Disciplines.* San Francisco: Jossey-Bass, 1982. Collection of essays that examines how writing may lead students to learn about the content of the various disciplines.

YOUNG, ART, and TOBY FULWILER, eds. *Writing Across the Disciplines: Research into Practice.* Upper Montclair, NJ: Boynton, 1986. Collection of essays discussing a writing-across-the-curriculum program, including essays on writing in the social sciences.

REFERENCES

ABRAHAMSON, MARK. *Social Research Methods.* Englewood Cliffs, NJ: Prentice, 1983. Discusses research methods in the social sciences, including surveys and interviews.

BEERS, SUSAN E. "Questioning and Peer Collaboration as Techniques for Thinking and Writing About Personality." *Teaching of Psychology* 13 (1986): 75–77. Describes an assignment sequence that leads students to inquire and to write about the topic of personality.

MACDONALD, SUSAN PECK. "Problem Definition in Academic Writing." *CE* 49 (1987): 315–33. Argues that different ways of composing are demanded by the different disciplines of the college or university.

PITTENDRIGH, ADELE S., and PATRICK C. JOBES. "Teaching Across the Curriculum: Critical Communication in the Sociology Classroom." *Teaching Sociology* 11 (1984): 281–96. Discusses a set of writing assignments designed to help students develop the critical thinking and communications skills required in the sociology profession.

SHAMOON, LINDA K., and ROBERT A. SCHWEGLER. "Sociologists Reading Student Texts: Expectations and Perceptions." *The Writing Instructor* 7 (1988): 71–81. Asserts that there are significant differences in the ways sociology and composition instructors perceive the features of a paper.

SNODGRAS, SARA E. "Writing as a Tool for Teaching Social Psychology." *Teaching of Psychology* 12 (1985): 91–94. Argues that implementing writing assignments (journals, analyses of published articles, observational studies, and formal research reports) enhances students' learning of social psychology.

Study 1: "Factors Influencing the Willingness to Taste Unusual Foods"

PURPOSE Psychologist Laura P. Otis investigates the factors that influence a person's willingness to taste unusual foods.

METHOD Laboratory experiment—Otis showed students at a Canadian university various unusual foods (e.g., octopus), which they were led to believe they might eat. At various points during the experiment, subjects responded to questionnaires.

EVIDENCE Statistical, based on frequency of responses to a questionnaire.

LOGIC An argument from correlation or sign (see 6d-1); one pattern of responses is shown to be closely associated with another pattern—one pattern indicates the presence of another.

CLAIM The older a person is, the more likely it is that he or she will experiment with unusual foods. Food preference is generally unrelated to an individual's willingness to engage in novel or risky activities.

Study 2: "The Story of Edward: The Everyday Geography of Elderly Single Room Occupancy Hotel Tenants"

PURPOSE Ethnographer Paul A. Rollinson "seeks to provide a rich description of the everyday geography of an often overlooked population in contemporary urban America: elderly tenants of Single Room Occupancy Hotels" (188).

METHOD Participant observation—Rollinson spends extended periods of time visiting run-down hotels in a section of Chicago where elderly tenants rent rooms. He tape records his conversations with tenants and forms a close and trusting relationship with one such man, 62-year-old Edward.

EVIDENCE Personal observations

LOGIC An argument from generalization (see 6d-1); the observations made are shown to form a pattern. The observer suggests that this pattern may form a general principle describing conditions for other individuals in similar circumstances.

CLAIM "The problems faced by elderly tenants of SRO hotels are numerous and often life-threatening. Their treasured independence is encumbered by their poverty-level incomes, their wide range of chronic disabilities, and their inappropriate housing environments." [The generalization of this particular field study extends only to elderly tenants in SRO hotels. While still a generalization, the claim is kept relatively narrow. As you will see, Rollinson is seeking to inform with his discussion as much as to argue.]

These two studies, excerpts of which follow, represent two distinct strains of social scientific research—one quantitative (a researcher's number-based analysis of experiments in a laboratory setting) and the other qualitative (a researcher's perceptions of life lived in its natural social setting).

Social scientists have developed methods for investigating human behavior and, accordingly, many types of evidence are used in a variety of arguments. You can help orient yourself to your courses in the social sciences by understanding the special characteristics of arguments. Pose these questions in each of your courses:

- What questions about human behavior are studied in this discipline?
- What methods of investigation do researchers in this discipline use to study these questions?
- How are claims that researchers make related to methods of investigation?
- In this discipline, what types of information count as evidence in support of a claim?

Expect a variety of answers to these questions, even when you ask them of a single discipline. Given the many subspecialties in the social sciences, you are likely to find researchers using several methods to investigate a particular question. For instance, sociologists wanting to clarify the relationship between violence on television and the activities of children might set up several studies. One might be a lab experiment in which a group of children, closely monitored for their reactions, watch violent and nonviolent programs; a second study might take researchers into the field to videotape children watching television programs at home; a third study might collect, analyze, and draw conclusions about the state of published research on television violence and behavior of children (Rieke and Sillars 245–46). Each of these studies would properly be described as "sociological," but each would have its own distinct method and would, accordingly, lead to different claims and different sorts of evidence offered in support of these claims.

38b Reading in the social sciences

The sources you read in the social sciences will represent the variety of investigations carried out by researchers. Aside from textbooks and other general surveys of the disciplines, you will read reports of carefully controlled laboratory experiments as well as field and case studies. These two broad categories of source types parallel two major strategies for generating information in the social sciences: quantitative (number-based) and qualitative (observation-based) research.

Experimental (quantitative) reports

One method that social scientists have developed for studying human behavior is to conduct controlled experiments in a laboratory. Experimental researchers seek evidence for their claims by making careful observations and measurements in a lab. Based on statistical evidence (often questionnaire responses represented numerically), researchers are able to argue that the relationships they claim exist among various behaviors in fact *do* exist and are very likely not due to chance. Equally important can be the finding

LOOKING BACK

Students may want to review Chapter 1 (Critical Thinking and Reading) for a general discussion of the subject before reading this section. While Chapter 1 focuses primarily on reading texts other than reports, the general principles are still relevant.

TEACHING IDEAS

The distinction between experimental (quantitative) reports and field (qualitative) studies is an important one for students to understand. You may want to advise students to read the two sample reports closely, determining for themselves the differences, in order to ensure that they understand the material.

that no relationship exists between variables. For example, in the following report of a laboratory experiment, psychologist Laura Otis makes the claim displayed previously in Study #1 (38a-2).

Otis began her study with a specific question about human behavior: "Why do some people apparently prefer to eat novel or unusual foods?" Her report represents a particular instance of a social scientist observing the actions of individuals and stating how these actions are significant. Note that whenever Otis makes a direct statement concerning preferences for food, she reviews the literature—that is, she reviews previous research and theories—and thereby situates herself in a tradition of experimental research. Her opening section and the Methods section are reproduced entirely. Most of her highly technical Results and Discussion section has been omitted (as well as her References section), although it is in this technical discussion that Otis conducts her statistical analysis, which she then uses as evidence in support of her claims.

FOR DISCUSSION

You may want to initiate a class discussion of this model, particularly the opening summary. Some students may have declared social science majors already and understand quantitative reports; others will need the format explained to them. If students can discuss the features of the report themselves, they are more likely to understand the chapter.

Factors Influencing the Willingness to Taste Unusual Foods

LAURA P. OTIS

York University

Summary.—Factors associated with willingness to taste 12 unusual foods were examined among 42 mature university students in a realistic taste testing situation. Low or nonsignificant correlations were found between subjects' willingness to taste the different foods and their scores on personality measures of sensation seeking as well as their ratings of familiarity with each food. Unexpectedly, age was a significant factor, with the older subjects being somewhat more willing to taste the unusual foods. Only a scale of items dealing specifically with food habits was highly correlated with subjects' willingness to try the unusual foods. The results suggest that food adventurousness is best accounted for by highly specific attitudes about food rather than general personality measures.

Context-setting introduction.

Both humans and animals have strong preferences for familiar rather than novel foods (Barnett, 1956; Domjan, 1977; Hall & Hall, 1939; Hill, 1978; Maslow, 1933, 1937; Meiselman & Waterman, 1978; Peryam, 1963; Pliner, 1982; Rozin, 1976). Typically, the animal research on this topic has been interpreted in terms of the "learned safety" hypothesis (Kalat & Rozin, 1973) while research with humans has been interpreted in terms of the "familiarity breeds liking" hypothesis (Zajonc, 1968).

Review of the literature—of existing research and theories on the topic.

However, neither hypothesis is sufficient to explain the full range of human selection of food. For example, why do some people apparently prefer to eat novel or unusual foods? One possibility is that the desire for novelty in food is a consequence of the negative effects of monotony (Balintfy, Duffy, & Sinha, 1974; Brickman & D'Amato, 1975; Kamen & Peryam, 1961; Siegel & Pilgrim, 1958). Further, it may be that preference for unfamiliar food is a reflection of some personality trait which predisposes some people toward novelty or sensation seeking. In fact, the item "I like to try new foods that I have never tasted before" is included in Zuckerman's Sensation Seeking Scale (Zuckerman, Kolin, Price, & Zoob, 1964) on the assumption that trying new foods reflects a general preference for engaging in risky and exciting kinds of activities.

All statements supported with references to social science literature.

Only a very few studies have actually investigated the relationship between sensation seeking and food preferences. Kish and Donnenwerth (1972) found a significant, although very modest relationship between sensation seeking and preference for sour, crunchy, and spicy foods. Similarly, Brown, Ruder, Ruder, and Young (1974) report a low but significant correlation between scores on the Change Seeker Index and preference for spicy food. But Rozin and Schiller (1980) conclude that sensation seeking is not related to preference for hot chili pepper. The only other evidence of a relationship between sensation seeking and food preference is provided by Back and Glasgow (1981) who noted that self-proclaimed gourmets scored significantly higher than vegetarians on measures of the General Sensation Seeking Scale and the Experience Seeking subscale of the Sensation Seeking Scale.

Gaps in existing research leave room for additional research.

It is difficult to draw any clear conclusions regarding the relationship between sensation seeking and food preferences from the existing literature. An obvious omission in the research to date is that no study has looked specifically at the relationship between sensation seeking and preference for *novel* foods. The purpose of the present study was to look specifically at the relationship between personality measures of sensation seeking and preference for unfamiliar and unusual foods. Also, since most previous studies used only verbal measures of acceptance of food, the present study employed a realistic food-choice situation. Finally, the Neary-Zuckerman Sensation Seeking and Anxiety State Scale (Zuckerman, 1979) was included to assess the contribution of situational reactions to preference for unusual foods.

Present study designed to address gaps in existing research.

TEACHING IDEAS

Although the format may seem intimidating to students accustomed to writing in the humanities, the practice of spelling out method actually makes for a clear, forthright presentation. You may want to ask students to compare this material to the types of writing they're accustomed to reading. Which seems easier to comprehend? Why?

Method

Subjects

The subjects were 42 students enrolled in a summer session Introductory Psychology class at Glendon College, York University, Toronto. Their ages ranged from 17 to 50 yr., with a mean age of 30 yr. Many of the subjects were public school teachers.

Questionnaire described—research results to be based on data obtained from questionnaire.

Materials and Procedures

As part of a special class exercise, students were given a brief introduction to the present study which was described as research about attitudes towards foods. Questionnaires were distributed and students were asked to fill in the first two sections of the questionnaire. Section one, entitled "General Interest and Preference Survey" was made up of three subscales of Zuckerman's Sensation Seeking Scale (Form V), the Experience Seeking subscale, the Boredom Susceptibility subscale, and the Thrill and Adventure Seeking subscale (Zuckerman, 1979). The second section, entitled "Food Preference Survey" was made up of 13 items dealing specifically with attitudes towards trying new foods.

These items were developed and pretested in an earlier pilot study. The survey included statements such as "I consider myself an adventurous eater," "I don't like eating unusual food because it might upset my stomach," and "I often try new brands of food on the chance of finding something different or better." Each statement was answered on a five-point scale going from 1 (not at all) to 5 (very much) according to how much each statement reflected the respondent's own eating habits.

Physical setting of experiment.

While these sections of the questionnaire were being completed, the food display table in the front of the room was set up. Bite-size pieces of 12 different foods (octopus, hearts of palm, seaweed, soya bean milk, blood sausage, Chinese sweet rice cake, pickled watermelon rind, raw fish, quail egg, star fruit, sheep milk cheese, and black beans) were placed on separate paper plates. Each plate was clearly labeled and the product container or intact fresh example of the product was placed beside the food sample plate. When students had finished the Sensation Seeking Scale and the Food Preference Survey they were instructed to leave their seats and walk around the display table where they were to look at but not yet taste the different foods. Students were led to believe that they would be tasting some of the samples at a later time. They were asked not to talk or communicate their feelings about the foods in any way. Students then returned to their seats and completed the third section of the questionnaire, the Sensation Seeking and Anxiety State Scale. The last section of the questionnaire asked students for three kinds of food evaluation. First, they actually ate and then rated the appearance, taste, and preference for an unfamiliar Japanese snack food. Next, they indicated their willingness to try each of the 12 different food items. These two evaluations were made on a five-point scale going from 1 (not at all) to 5 (very much). They then rated their familiarity with each of the 12 foods on a five-point scale from 1 ("I have never heard of it or seen it before") to 5 ("I have tasted it often"). Finally, students were asked to indicate their age, sex, and whether or not they followed any special diet. At the end of the study, students were given a complete explanation of the purpose of the research and were told that they would not be required actually to eat any of the food samples. Of the 42 participants in the study, 32 indicated at this point that they fully believed that they would be expected to taste some of the food items.

Results and Discussion

Various statistical tests conducted (discussion omitted here).

The data are discussed in terms of the relationship between each of the main predictor variables (familiarity, trait and state measures of Sensation Seeking, the Food Preference Survey, and age) and the subjects' willingness to taste the unusual foods. A multiple regression analysis showing the relative contribution of each of these factors is also described.

• • •

Conclusions

Conclusion, based on statistical evidence, is presented and set in context of existing research.

In exploring a number of factors associated with food adventurousness, several surprises were found. An expected positive relationship between familiarity and food adventurousness was not confirmed. On the other hand, an unanticipated positive relationship between food adventurousness and age was noted. Consistent with previous research, personality measures did not appear to play a very significant role in individual food selections. In conclusion, this study suggests that willingness to taste unusual foods is best predicted by specific attitudes about food and is largely unrelated to preferences for engaging in other kinds of novel or risky activities.

Field (qualitative) studies

Quite different from experimental research, which takes place in the controlled conditions of a laboratory and generates quantifiable data, field studies situate researchers among people in a community in order to observe life as it is lived in its natural social context. The result is a *qualitative* study built on an observer's descriptions and interpretations of behavior. Based on observations, the field worker writes reports and discusses the possible general significance of the behavior he or she has seen, offering what in many cases is a fascinating glimpse into exotic cultures both foreign and local.

Following are excerpts from a field study of an elderly population living in Single Room Occupancy (SRO) hotels in Chicago. You will notice that author Paul Rollinson bases his claims either on prior participant-observer research or on his own observations. Rollinson maintains a distance from his subject that allows him an analytical stance, yet at the same time he is able to enter into the lives of the population he has observed. His report is qualitative, based on personal observations that he then interprets in the context of scholarly work in his discipline. (The References section has been omitted here.) As testament to the impact field studies can have on a researcher, Rollinson dedicates his article to the principal subject of his study, Edward, who (says Rollinson) "taught me infinitely more valuable lessons than my formal academic training."

GROUP ACTIVITY

In order to help students better understand the concept of a field study, divide the class into groups to discuss the purpose of such studies. Each group will come up with several examples of reasons for conducting field studies and populations on which the studies can be conducted. (Example: to determine how the threat of AIDS has affected certain populations, study college students living away from home.)

The Story of Edward

The Everyday Geography of Elderly Single Room Occupancy (SRO) Hotel Tenants

PAUL A. ROLLINSON

This article seeks to provide a rich description of the everyday geography of an often overlooked population in contemporary urban America: elderly tenants of Single Room Occupancy (SRO) hotels. The term SRO is a recent one, originally coined to describe apartment dwellings that had been subdivided into single rooms in New York City (Shapiro 1966). SRO's have also been described as "flophouses" and "fleabag hotels" (Eckert 1979). These buildings, originally designated as transient facilities, have evolved into largely permanent residences for the single poor of all ages. Today, SRO hotels, which are typically located in dilapidated and deteriorating inner city areas, have been characterized as the nation's least desirable housing (Kasinitz 1984).

• • •

FOR DISCUSSION

Social science writing, especially the field study report, is sometimes erroneously considered dry and objective. You may want to initiate a discussion to dispel this notion by asking the class to characterize Rollinson's attitude toward his subjects, based on the introduction to his study. Ask students to explain their characterizations and to comment on how they think Rollinson's attitude affects his work.

The problem to be studied is defined and set in context of existing research.

The scope of the problem facing the elderly living in these SRO hotels throughout the nation is great; at least 400,000 are estimated to live in such accommodations (Eckert 1983). Previous ethnographic studies have brought attention to the unique sociodemographic characteristics of this population. Elderly tenants of SRO's are overwhelmingly single males (Eckert 1980; Mackelman 1961; Stephens 1976) who exist in a state of poverty (Tissue 1971). They are not newcomers to the inner city (Erickson and Eckert 1977; Lally et al. 1979), and Shapiro (1971), Siegal (1978), and Sokolovsky et al. (1978) have all found evidence to suggest the presence of considerable ties among elderly SRO tenants. However, little attention has been paid to this population's involvement in the built environment, their geographical movement, the places that are vital to these men and women, and the barriers that constrain them (Stutz 1976). It is the purpose of this description to pay attention to the elderly tenants' involvement in the built environment within a framework of the geography of everyday experience, defined as "the sum total of a person's first-hand involvements with the geographical world in which he or she typically lives" (Seamon 1979, 15–16). The primary focus of this framework is on understanding and conveying the everyday geographical experience in a "lived" form with as little a priori structuring as possible (Reinharz and Rowles 1988). SRO hotels have, in the past, been portrayed romantically as allowing this population to live independent lives (Eckert 1979; Stephens 1976). In reality, the findings of this exploration suggest that these hotels offer anything but independence. The elderly men and women in this study were caught in an environment that exacerbated their isolation and withdrawal from society. In this research, I portray this unique and vulnerable elderly population's everyday geography.

Purpose of present research.

Framework (or point of view) from which observations will be made.

Methods

Method of observation set in context of a tradition of observation.

The methodology I used aligns itself with a lengthy tradition of participant-observation studies in exploratory social science research (Clark 1965; Gans 1962; Hill 1986; Jackson 1980; Ley 1974; Rowles 1978; Suttles 1968; Whyte 1943; Zorbaugh 1929).

• • •

The Everyday Geography of Edward

This is the story of Edward, an elderly SRO tenant. I compare Edward to the other elderly tenants in the study, briefly describe his life history, how he viewed the SRO hotel and the neighborhood environment, and I discuss his everyday geography and concerns about the future. I met Edward in the lobby of one of the four hotels in August of 1985. Initially, he simply agreed to answer some of my questions. Later, he invited me to his room and subsequently to spend time with him traveling around the neighborhood.

Description of the subject in the subject's world.

Edward was similar to the majority of the elderly SRO tenant population I saw. The elderly SRO tenant population in the study had a mean age of 70 years, was predominantly white (92%), and male (58%). Edward was a 62-year-old white male. Overall, the elderly tenants had a low educational attainment; almost three-quarters (73%) had achieved education levels of high school or lower. Edward, in contrast, had completed two years of college. Elderly SRO tenants were extremely poor; Edward's yearly income ($4,620 in 1986) was even less than the mean of the elderly tenants in the study ($5,559) and well below the mean poverty level ($5,360). Accompanying his low income was a higher than average rent burden of 69% (compared to the already high mean of 46% for all those I interviewed), which exacerbated the tenuousness of Edward's already critical financial status. Nationally, the accepted normal rent-to-income ratio was 30%. Like 62% of his fellow elderly tenants, Edward received most of his income from Social Security. He was fortunate in that he had some savings to rely upon in times of financial need, as only 10% of all the elderly tenants interviewed had any savings.

• • •

Conclusions

Graphic review of conditions observed.

The elderly tenants of SRO hotels had few resources or alternatives, and they lived there out of necessity. The SRO hotel environments were largely unsuited to the needs of this population. These hotels were deteriorating, dirty, and dangerous. In the winter, the heating systems were nonfunctional for days at a time. In the summer, the hotels were unbearably hot. The rooms, bathrooms, hallways, and elevators were not designed to accommodate the functionally impaired elderly tenants. It is very important to remember that the hotels in this study represented the least dilapidated and more conscientiously managed of the hotels, both in the study neighborhood and in the city of Chicago. The elderly tenants were overlooked by social scientists, social service providers, and planners because the majority were trapped inside their hotels and not visible to the wider society. This isolation should not be confused with independence. . . .

Claims made based on observations.

The problems faced by elderly tenants of SRO hotels are numerous and often life-threatening. Their treasured independence is encumbered by their poverty-level incomes, their wide range of chronic disabilities, and their inappropriate housing environments. Their desire to make choices and remain independent is all-important to these men and women. Their residence in the

GROUP ACTIVITY

Students should be able to appreciate the reasoning involved in this study through the following activity. Ask groups to point to evidence from the study that would lead to the author's conclusions. How compelling do they find the evidence? How credible is its presentation?

SRO hotels was not a genuine choice. Policymakers and social service agencies must strive to create a genuine choice for these men and women and they must also honor the right of this population to choose their unique and independent life-style. Given the fact that this elderly population had few resources and alternatives, the current and rapid decline in the SRO housing stock poses a serious threat to their ability to secure shelter. SRO hotels were inappropriate to the needs of the elderly tenants, but they did provide shelter at a time when homelessness was on the rise throughout the nation. Tenants of SRO hotels are labelled both deviant and undesirable, as "bums" or "derelicts." These men and women suffer greatly as a result of these inaccurate labels and they are consequently left in isolation, and the hotels are allowed to be removed from the housing stock. Edward noted: "[To] whoever is out there I'd like to say that one day you are going to be old. You will never know what it's like until it happens. A lot of us thought that there would always be someone to look out for us. It's a shock to us all to be in this situation."

38c Types of writing assignments in the social sciences

The assignments you will most often be given in your social sciences courses have in a general way been addressed in Chapter 2, "Critical Thinking and Writing," as well as in other chapters. The discussion here will introduce the special requirements of assignments in the social sciences and will provide references to other sections of the book.

TEACHING IDEAS

Students will need to be reminded that the guidelines here are a *general pattern,* not a blueprint, for writing lab reports. Encourage them to follow closely any specific guidelines from their instructors, or to ask for such guidelines if necessary.

1 The lab report (quantitative research)

Experimental researchers in the social sciences have patterned their writing of lab reports on those done in the sciences. Section 39c-1 discusses the general requirements of each section of the standard lab report: introduction, methods, results, and discussion. In the social sciences, you will encounter more variability than in the sciences in titling the various sections of a research report.

The opening

Depending on the conventions in a discipline (check with your professor), a paper's first section may be titled "Introduction," "Theoretical Background," or "Previous Work," or may appear with no heading at all, as is the case of the example report you read by Laura Otis in 38b. Whatever you call your introduction, make sure it orients your reader to the perspective from which you are conducting research and that it situates your thesis, or claim, in relation to the claims of other scholars. You will need to review the litera-

Manuscript Form for Research Reports in the Social Sciences

- A research paper should have its own (unnumbered) title page. One-third of the way down the page, center your title. Do *not* place it in quotation marks. Center a line below the title and then center your name: first name, middle initial, last name. Below your name, center the name of the department in which you are taking the course. On the next line, center the name of your college or university. On the next line, center the address of your college or university (Solomon 19, 31).
- Give the abstract its own numbered page following the title page. (The abstract is the first numbered page of the report.) Center the word Abstract, skip a line, and begin, writing the abstract as a single paragraph.
- The heading, Method, is given its own line and is centered. Skip a line to begin the first subsection, Subjects. Each subheading—such as Subjects, Measures, Apparatus, Procedure, and Design—is given its own line, is underlined, and is placed flush to the left margin.
- Each table or figure should be numbered and titled and placed on its own page at the end of the report, after the Reference list. (In a published article, tables and figures appear in the body of the report.) When referring in your report to a particular table or figure, capitalize the *T* and *F*.
- Observe APA (American Psychological Association) citation form. (See 36b, and see 36a and 36d for citation forms in the humanities and sciences, respectively.)

ture on your topic to suggest gaps in existing research and to provide a rationale for your own study. This can be done by reviewing the history of the question you are investigating and by citing pertinent sources.

Methods

This section describes how you conducted your study. In the social sciences, the Methods section is divided into subsections as needed to provide a full and accurate accounting of an experiment. Standard subsections include "Subjects," "Measures," "Apparatus," "Procedures," and "Design." In the Methods section, the researcher discusses any instruments that were used, such as questionnaires, in generating data for the experiment.

Results

This section presents the data generated by your research. If you have used surveys in your research, you will probably compress your results numerically and run one or more statistical programs, the results of which will provide the evidence for whatever claims you are making.

TEACHING IDEAS

The guidelines for manuscript form will be invaluable to students preparing lab reports in their social science classes. Students should be encouraged to mark this page for future reference.

Discussion

This section calls a reader's attention to significant patterns that emerge from your statistical analysis. Your discussion will interpret your results for the reader and lead to a statement of your claims. The discussion will often end with a note on the significance of your research and, if appropriate, suggestions for future research.

2 The field report and case study (qualitative research)

Many inquiries in the social sciences do not lend themselves to statistical analysis but rather to observations of social interactions in the communities where they occur. Researchers who conduct qualitative research go into the "field," a closely defined area of study that may be as exotic as the Trobriand Islands or as commonplace as an urban pool hall. The investigator, informed by a particular disciplinary point of view, collects data by directly observing and in many cases participating in social life. Then the researcher sifts through notes and conducts an analysis (see 2c). At the beginning of research, an observer or participant-observer may purposely try *not* to make predictions, as quantitative researchers do, so as to approach the novel social environment with as few preconceived ideas as possible (Richlin-Klonsky and Strenski 90–91; Rollinson 189). One outcome of field research is the field report, which provides a rich and detailed description of the behaviors observed as well as an analysis that discusses the possible significance of those behaviors. In Paul Rollinson's "Story of Edward," you read a field report—which is also called an *ethnography.*

A set of field observations may be put to other uses. When they concern a "relatively short, self-contained episode or segment of a person's life," field notes may be used in a *case study,* a focused narrative account that becomes the occasion for an analysis (Bromley 1). The case may provide the basis for making a recommendation: for example, concerning the placement of a drunk driver in a rehabilitation program (as opposed to jail) or concerning the placement of a child in an appropriate class. You will find case studies used as the basis of recommendations in most disciplines, but especially in the social sciences and the business and medical professions. You may also be given cases to analyze. In this instance, your professor will present a snapshot narrative of some behavior in its social context: perhaps observations of a child in a daycare setting or observations about employee morale at a business. Your job will be to sort through the information presented just as if you had made and recorded the observations yourself. Then you select the most important information to include in your case analysis, based on a theoretical approach recently read or reviewed in class.

If you go into the field to conduct research, you will keep a notebook or journal in which to record observations. Your professor will review particular methods for observing and making field notes. One challenge of writing your report will involve choosing and organizing the particular observations you want to discuss. The following categories of information often appear in case or field reports, and the categories can be useful for note-taking. (In brief reports, the researcher may not write on each of these categories.)

- An introduction that sets the question or problem you have studied in a context of prior research and that establishes your question or problem as *worthy* of research
- Information on the subjects studied and the environment in which you observed them
- Your theoretical perspective
- Your method of making observations
- Your analysis of significant behaviors
- Your conclusions

3 The library research paper

Just as in other disciplines, your library research paper in the social sciences should be guided by a central "burning" question. (See 33a-1 and, generally, Chapter 33, "Understanding the Research Process.") You will base your library research on secondary sources of the sort you found illustrated in 38b. Depending on your topic, you will read journal articles and books that are both qualitative and quantitative in their method. As you choose a topic, be aware that you will need to narrow it so that you can reasonably manage your discussion in an allotted number of pages. Also, be aware that professors will want you to use sources to support a thesis, or claim, of your own design. In a research paper, you will read sources and relate them to each other and to your thesis. As you synthesize material, try to arrange your discussion by *topic* or *idea,* not by source (see 2d). If you need help in conducting your library research, consult Chapters 33, 34, and 35 on writing research papers. For suggestions of discipline-specific sources you might turn to when conducting library research, see 38e. And for the conventions of documenting sources in the social sciences, see 36b.

38d Sample student paper: "Women Alcoholics: A Conspiracy of Silence"

The following library research paper, written by a student for her sociology class, investigates why women alcoholics in this country are largely an unrecognized population. Kristy Bell read several sources in order to support her thesis that the denial surrounding the problems of women alcoholics "amounts to a virtual conspiracy of silence and greatly complicates the process of diagnosis and treatment." Notice that Bell organizes her material by *idea,* not by source—one clear indication of which is her use of headings in the paper. Each heading develops one part of her thesis. Notice as well her use of the American Psychological Association's (APA's) format for documenting sources.

REFERENCES

BARTHOLOMAE, DAVID. "Inventing the University." *When a Writer Can't Write.* Ed. Mike Rose. New York: Guilford, 1985. 134–65. Essential to being a college student is the mastering of discipline-specific discourses, but such achievement is the result of a gradual process with multiple stages.

MCLEOD, SUSAN H. "Writing Across the Curriculum: The Second Stage, and Beyond." *CCC* 40 (1989): 337–43. Overview of the changes in WAC that argues for continued reform in thinking, learning, and writing across the disciplines.

RUSSELL, DAVID R. "Writing Across the Curriculum in Historical Perspective: Toward a Social Interpretation." *CE* 52 (1990): 52–73. Looks at WAC in its historical, social context, arguing that such a perspective will provide new ways of "integrating students, instead of excluding them."

YOUNG, ART, and TOBY FULWILER, eds. *Writing Across the Disciplines: Research into Practice.* Upper Montclair, NJ: Boynton, 1986. Collection of essays discussing a writing-across-the-curriculum program, including essays on writing in the humanities.

TEACHING IDEAS

The sample research paper presented here is fully annotated so that students can use it as a guide in writing their own research papers. You may want to call particular attention to specific features peculiar to social science papers—arrangement, documentation, method of supporting claims, and the like.

Women Alcoholics: A Conspiracy of Silence

Kristy Bell
Behavioral Sciences Department
Bentley College
Waltham, Massachusetts
November 4, 1991

Information centered on title page

Bell 1

Currently, in the United States, there are at least two million women alcoholics (Unterberger, 1989, p. 1150). Americans are largely unaware of the extent of this debilitating disease among women and the problems it presents. Numerous women dependent on alcohol remain invisible largely because friends, family, coworkers, and the women themselves refuse to acknowledge the problem. This denial amounts to a virtual conspiracy of silence and greatly complicates the process of diagnosis and treatment.

Introduction: women alcoholics will be studied in their social context.

Thesis

Silence: The Denial of Family, Friends and Employers

Although the extent of the problem of alcoholism among women is slowly being recognized, a tremendous stigma still accompanies the disease for women. The general public remains very uncomfortable in discussing the topic. A primary reason that women alcoholics remain invisible is that they are so well protected. Family and friends, even if aware of the seriousness of the addiction, suffer pain and embarrassment and generally protect their loved one rather than suggesting that she seek professional counseling. By not confronting the issue, family and friends hope the problem will correct itself. According to Turnbull (1988), "The initial response of those close to the alcoholic woman is usually to deny the problem right along with her" (p. 366). Spouses, friends, relatives and even employers tend to protect the alcoholic rather than help her initiate treatment. "A husband will nervously protect his wife's illness from friends and neighbors" (Sandmaier, 1980, p. 8). Family and friends experience a great deal of guilt and responsibility that, in turn, causes them to deny or hide the problem (Grasso, 1990, p. 32).

Denial by others.

Claims supported by references to social science literature.

APA format for documenting sources.

TEACHING IDEAS

You may want to call students' attention to the difference between in-text citations in APA and MLA styles. Note the importance of the date of publication in APA style.

FOR DISCUSSION

Just as Rollinson does in his study of Edward, Bell allows her own attitude to come through in her writing. You may want to ask students to point out evidence of her sympathies in the paper, and explain how her writing reflects her feelings in addition to laying out her reasoned argument.

Bell 2

The needs of women dependent on alcohol are also ignored by employers, who are unable to confront the problem, in part, due to their having no prior experience with alcoholic women. The conspiracy of silence thus extends to the workplace. Employers tend generally to dodge confrontation by simply firing the alcoholic woman on an unrelated charge rather than steering her to an employee assistance program (Sandmaier, p. 131).

Silence: Self-Denial Among Women Alcoholics

Women not only fail to seek treatment because they are ignored and abandoned, but also because they deny the extent of the problem themselves. Sandmaier believes that in "responding to survey questions, women may be more likely than men to minimize alcohol-related problems because of more intense guilt and shame" (p. 73). Thus, statistics published concerning women's dependence upon alcohol understate the extent of the problem. Once again, guilt and pain can be directly related to unfamiliarity with the issue--this time the woman alcoholic's own awareness that alcoholism among women is a debilitating and growing problem. Women alcoholics suffer from the same feelings of guilt and embarrassment felt by family members and friends. Obviously, these feelings are incredibly more intense in the actual alcoholic and tend to force the woman to be driven underground by her drinking problem. Unterberger observes that "[m]ore often than men, female alcoholics turn their anger on themselves rather than others, with anxiety and guilt being the result" (p. 1150).

Denial by alcoholic, herself.

At second and subsequent references to an author, no date needed in citation.

A common feeling among women alcoholics is that they are disrupting their lives and that any wrongdoing is their fault. More so than the male, claims Sandmaier, they tend to feel guilty about their

Bell 3

drinking habits because they realize the effects it can have on family, home, and career: "Both recovered alcoholic women and treatment specialists attest to the intense guilt and self-hatred borne by alcoholic women because of society's judgment that they have failed as wives and mothers" (p. 17). Specialists in the field of alcoholism believe that there is an inherent trait among women to ignore the value of their own lives. Unfortunately, a woman today is rarely taught nor is she able to properly take care of herself first (Grasso, p. 40). As soon as she marries, in most cases, she is expected to "take care" of her husband. With the arrival of children she is required to take care of them. Often, if parents are aged, she will feel responsible for their well-being. Grasso firmly believes that women not only ignore and deny their problem, but never really think enough about themselves to realize that they are in trouble with and becoming very dependent on alcohol. Sandmaier says this feeling is especially true among housewives due to the close identification with their dual roles of wife and mother.

Examination of reasons alcoholic women deny their problems

Difficulties in Treatment and Diagnosis

Many women avoid treatment because of concern for the well-being of their children. A rehabilitation program including hospital care cannot be considered because the woman is unable to be absent from home for an extended period. Feelings of obligation to a husband and children are extremely powerful for a woman, especially one whose emotions are intensified by alcohol. Turnbull (1988) believes that "child-care services need to be provided to allow women to seek and remain in treatment" (p. 369). Treatment would be considerably easier and progress much more quickly if the

New heading signals development of second part of thesis

Date continues to be cited in this reference since Turnbull has written two articles that are referred to in this paper

FOR DISCUSSION

While these chapters spend a good deal of time emphasizing the differences in writing and thinking between disciplines, this section of Bell's paper illustrates similarities. Ask students to analyze how Bell supports her argument in this section, and to compare her use of outside sources to those used by Brooks in the previous chapter.

Bell 4

woman was confident that her children would receive proper care.

Professionals in the field of social work are not yet experienced enough to recognize alcoholism by its preliminary characteristics. Because female alcoholism has never really been a well-defined problem, health specialists do not have the experience needed to detect it when a woman approaches them with an alcohol-related problem. Frequently, the alcoholic woman is dismissed as being "just depressed" or under stress (Turnbull, 1989, p. 291). Moreover, she is not likely to announce the problem directly:

> An alcoholic woman is unlikely to come into her doctor's office announcing her drinking problem, but she is apt to seek medical attention for a wide range of problems commonly associated with alcohol abuse, including depression, anxiety, stomach trouble, and injuries from alcohol-related accidents or physical abuse. (Sandmaier, p. 207)

On numerous occasions, many alcoholic women have had personal contacts with health professionals during which opportunities for intervention went unobserved or ignored (Turnbull, 1988, p. 369).

Conclusion

Society is now realizing that there is and has been a definite alcohol problem among women. The problem now lies in learning to recognize the symptoms and help women to seek treatment. Many believe that women should be screened routinely at the onset of any kind of treatment program. This would allow for identification of alcohol problems much earlier and would facilitate treatment before problems grow out of control. Social workers, as well,

Social work professionals need help in detecting alcoholism among women.

Extended block quotation

Conclusion: the paper *has* established that a problem exists.

TEACHING IDEAS

You may want to call attention to a similarity and a difference between social science and humanities: the block quotation is treated in essentially the same way in both disciplinary styles, while the conclusion is highlighted in social science writing.

Bell 5

should include screening for drinking problems in all female clients. Some specialists believe that routine screening for substance abuse should become a mandatory part of all gynecological examinations as well as job orientations (Turnbull, 1988, pp. 366-68).

Two solutions explored

As the recognition of alcoholism among women grows, changes are being initiated to help make these women more visible to themselves, to health care professionals, and to society at large. "Public education programs must be strengthened to counter the fear of social stigma that inhibits women from seeking treatment" (Turnbull, 1988, p. 369). The public must be made aware of the severity of the problem of alcoholism.

Self-perception of women alcoholics encouraged

Bell 6

References

Grasso, A. (1990). Special treatment needs of the chemically dependent woman. Syracuse: Crouse-Irving Memorial School of Nursing.

Sandmaier, M. (1980). The invisible alcoholics. New York: McGraw-Hill.

Turnbull, J. (1988). Primary and secondary alcoholic women. Social Casework: The Journal of Contemporary Social Casework, 36, 290-298.

Turnbull, J. (1989). Treatment issues for alcoholic women. Social Casework: The Journal of Contemporary Social Casework, 47, 364-370.

Unterberger, G. (1989, December 6). Twelve steps for women alcoholics. The Christian Century, pp. 1150-1152.

FOR DISCUSSION

It would be helpful for students to recognize the differences in format between APA and MLA style with regard to references. Ask students to note the differences, and to explain why they think the date is highlighted in APA style.

TEACHING IDEAS

Students who plan to major or minor in the social sciences should be encouraged to consult faculty in their chosen discipline regarding the preferred style guide. With so many from which to choose, it is important that students know which guide their instructors use.

38e Reference materials in the social sciences

Style guides

The following sources offer general or discipline-specific guidance for writing in the social sciences.

Bart, Pauline, and Linda Frankel. *The Student Sociologist's Handbook.* 4th ed. New York: Random House, 1986.

Becker, Howard S., with a chapter written by Pamela Richards. *Writing for Social Scientists: How to Start and Finish Your Thesis, Book, or Article.* Chicago: University of Chicago Press, 1986.

Cuba, Lee J. *A Short Guide to Writing About Social Science.* Glenview: Scott, Foresman, 1988.

Jolley, Janina M., Peter A. Keller, and J. Dennis Murray. *How to Write Psychology Papers: A Student's Survival Guide for Psychology and Related Fields.* Sarasota: Professional Resource Exchange, 1984.

McCloskey, Donald. *The Writing of Economics.* New York: Macmillan, 1987.

Publication Manual of the American Psychological Association. 4th ed. Washington: American Psychological Association, 1994.

Richlin-Klonsky, Judith, and Ellen Strenski, coordinators and eds. *A Guide to Writing Sociology Papers.* New York: St. Martin's, 1986.

Specialized references

The following specialized references will help you to assemble information in a particular discipline or field within a discipline.

Encyclopedias provide general information that is useful when beginning a search.

Editorial Research Reports (current events)
Encyclopedia of Crime and Justice
Encyclopedia of Education
Encyclopedia of Human Behavior
Encyclopedia of Psychology
Encyclopedia of Social Work
Encyclopedia of Sociology
Guide to American Law
International Encyclopedia of Higher Education
International Encyclopedia of Psychiatry, Psychology, Psychoanalysis and Neurology
International Encyclopedia of the Social Sciences

Dictionaries provide definitions of technical terms.

Black's Law Dictionary
Dictionary of the Social Sciences
McGraw-Hill Dictionary of Modern Economics: A Handbook of Terms and Organizations
The Encyclopedic Dictionary of Psychology
The Prentice-Hall Dictionary of Business, Finance and Law

Periodical indexes and abstracts list articles published in a particular discipline over a particular period. *Abstracts,* which summarize the sources listed and involve a considerable amount of work to compile, tend to be more selective than indexes.

Abstracts in Anthropology
Current Index to Journals in Education (CIJE)
Education Index
Key to Economic Science
Psychological Abstracts
Public Affairs Information Service (PAIS)
Social Sciences Citation Index
Social Science Index
Social Work Research and Abstracts
Sociological Abstracts
Women's Studies Abstracts

CHAPTER 39

Writing and Reading in the Sciences

KEY FEATURES

Questioning in the sciences encompasses not just human nature, but all of nature; scientists question the origins, makeup, and distinctive features of things. This chapter approaches the sciences from the perspective of the empirical nature of scientific inquiry. Like the preceding chapters on the humanities and the social sciences, this chapter is divided into four major sections: writing, reading, types of assignments, and research papers. Coverage of writing in the sciences focuses on precision, quantifiable evidence, and collaboration; in this section an extensive example of inquiry about the frost-resistance of certain plants provides a clear, accessible illustration of scientific inquiry. The reading section explores textbooks and scientific journals, with extensive discussion of the pattern of arrangement for journal articles. The third section discusses various writing assignments students can expect to receive in these disciplines, focusing on lab reports and literature reviews; clear guidelines for manuscript form and contents of reports are presented in this section. Section four reproduces a heavily annotated sample lab report on the fermentation of wine. The chapter ends with a comprehensive list of reference materials in the sciences, completing its thorough and accessible introduction to the sciences.

FOR DISCUSSION

The concepts of empirical evidence and hypothesis may be difficult for your students to grasp. You may want to ask them to distinguish between empirical evidence and the kind of evidence they've studied in humanities and/or social science arguments. It's likely that one or two students in the class have some scientific background; if they can articulate the

Scientists work systematically to investigate the world of nature—at scales so small that they are invisible to the naked eye and at scales so vast that they are equally invisible. A scientist's investigations are always built on observable, verifiable information, known as *empirical evidence.* Scientific investigations often begin with questions like these:

- What kinds of things are there in the world of nature?
- What are these things composed of, and how does this makeup affect their behavior or operation?
- How did all these things come to be structured as they are?
- What are the characteristic functions of each natural thing and/or its parts? (Toulmin, Rieke, and Janik 231)*

At one point or another, we have all asked these questions and speculated on answers. Scientists do more than speculate. They devise experiments in order to gather information and, on the basis of carefully stated predictions, or **hypotheses,** they conduct analyses and offer explanations. All scientists share two fundamental assumptions about the world and the way it works: that "things and events in the universe occur in consistent patterns that are comprehensible through careful, systematic study" and that "[k]nowledge gained from studying one part of the universe is applicable to other parts" (American Association 25). On the strength of these assumptions, scientists pose questions and conduct experiments in which they observe and measure. Then they make claims (usually) of fact or definition, about *whether* a thing exists and, if it does, *what* it is or *why* it occurs. Questions that cannot be answered by an appeal to observable, quantifiable fact may be important and necessary to ask (for example, "What makes *Moby Dick* a great novel?" or "What are a society's responsibilities to its poor?"), but these are not matters for scientific investigation.

39a Writing in the sciences

1 Writing to inform

A major function of scientific writing is to *inform;* and scientists try to be precise in their descriptions of the world, writing, when possible, with

*In-text citations in this chapter refer to the Works Cited list at the end of the book.

mathematical or *quantifiable* precision. A researcher would report the temperature of water as 4°C, not as "near freezing"—an inexact expression, the meaning of which would change depending on the observer. Precise measurements taken from a thermometer or some other standard laboratory instrument help readers of scientific literature to know exactly what has been observed or what procedures have been followed so that, if necessary, experiments can be repeated.

As in other disciplines, informative writing in science is built on recognizable patterns. One of the ways in which a scientist may inform is by writing a precise *description*—for example, of experimental methods and materials or of observations made in the lab or field. A description may involve presenting a *sequence* of events—perhaps the sequence by which volcanic islands are born. Presenting information can also take the form of a *comparison and contrast*—for example, between the organization of the human brain and that of a computer. Scientists also *classify* the objects they study. When entomologists report on newly discovered insects, they identify each discovery with respect to a known species of insect. If no closely related species exists, researchers may attempt to *define* a new one.

When contributors bring different specialties to a project, researchers very often work and write collaboratively. Look in any journal and you will find a number of multiauthored articles. The great advantage of working collaboratively is that researchers can put the power of several minds to work on a particular problem. The challenge in writing collaboratively is to make a final report read as though *one* person had written it, even if several people have had a hand in its creation. If you are part of a group assigned to write a paper, be sure to meet with group members before any writing takes place. Agree on a structure for the document and then assign parts to individual group members. (See 3e for details on how to manage the logistics of collaborative writing.)

2 Arguing in the sciences

A scientist's efforts to inform readers are very often part of a larger attempt to *persuade*. In every discipline arguments are built on claims, evidence, and the logical relationships that connect them. But the characteristics of these elements change from one discipline to the next and also *within* disciplines as theoretical perspectives change.[1] Geneticists working on techniques of tissue analysis argue differently from astronomers. Each discipline uses different methods and different tools of investigation. Each asks different questions and finds meaning in different sorts of information. Within any one discipline you will find that multiple perspectives give rise to competing communities or schools of thought. Within any one scientific community

[1] This discussion is based directly on the work of Stephen Toulmin, Richard Rieke, and Allan Janik in *Introduction to Reasoning* (New York: Macmillan, 1979). See Chapter 12, their "Introduction" to fields of argument, 195–202; and Chapter 14, "Argumentation in Science," 229–63. For a related discussion, see Richard D. Rieke and Malcolm O. Sillars, *Argumentation and the Decision Making Process,* 2nd ed. (Glenview: Scott, Foresman, 1984).

nature of scientific argument, while other students articulate humanistic or social scientific arguments, the class should be better able to distinguish between different types of arguments.

ADDITIONAL EXERCISE A

Interview a professor of biology, chemistry, or physics on the subject of the writing he or she does in the profession. Pose questions such as the following: What kinds of questions do you ask? What kinds of investigations do you conduct? What forms does your writing usually take? What is your purpose in writing in these forms? What kind of audience do you usually address? Try to think of some additional questions as well. Use your notes from the interview to write a paragraph describing the nature of writing in this particular discipline.

LOOKING BACK

Students may want to review the appropriate sections of Chapter 3 as they study this material. It's important that they recognize how the patterns of development cross disciplinary lines.

TEACHING IDEAS

Students unfamiliar with writing outside the humanities may need to spend some time sifting through this material. In particular, the concept of replication may be difficult for students to grasp. Why would anyone want to repeat an experiment that's already been done? You may want to actually "walk students through" this section of the chapter.

LOOKING BACK

All of the chapters in this part of the handbook rely heavily on ideas discussed in Chapter 6 (Writing and Evaluating Arguments), especially the material on modes of inquiry in various disciplines. If you haven't yet covered Chapter 6 in class, it would be useful to do so now. Otherwise, students should review the chapter in order to make better use of the information in this part of the handbook.

REFERENCES

BARTHOLOMAE, DAVID. "Inventing the University." *When a Writer Can't Write.* Ed. Mike Rose. New York: Guilford, 1985. 134–65. Essential to being a college student is the mastering of discipline-specific discourses, but such achievement is the result of a gradual process with multiple stages.

MCLEOD, SUSAN H. "Writing Across the Curriculum: The Second Stage, and Beyond." *CCC* 40 (1989): 337–43. Overview of the changes in WAC that argues for continued reform in thinking, learning, and writing across the disciplines.

RUSSELL, DAVID R. "Writing Across the Curriculum in Historical Perspective: Toward a Social Interpretation." *CE* 52 (1990): 52–73. Looks at WAC in its historical, social context, arguing that such a perspective will provide new ways of "integrating students, instead of excluding them."

YOUNG, ART, and TOBY FULWILER, eds. *Writing Across the Disciplines: Research into Practice.* Upper Montclair, NJ: Boynton, 1986. Collection of essays discussing a writing-across-the-curriculum program.

the purpose of argument will be to achieve agreement about the way in which some part of the universe works.

The process of scientific inquiry generally goes like this: once investigators make their observations in a laboratory or in a natural setting, they report their findings to colleagues in articles written for scientific and technical journals. The scientific community will not accept these reports as dependable until independent researchers can recreate experiments and observe similar findings. As scientists around the world try to replicate the experiments and confirm results, a conversation—an argument—develops in which researchers might publish a challenge or addition to the original findings. In this way, a body of literature—of writing on a particular topic—grows.

As in other disciplines, debates in science can grow heated—for instance, when one person attempts to demonstrate why a particular theory is flawed and should be replaced. Revolutions in scientific thinking may upend whole schools of thought and threaten careers of those who have built reputations on outmoded theories. At any one moment, agreement (if it exists) is provisional and will last only until some new challenge is put to conventional thinking—perhaps by a researcher who has observed some new fact that cannot be explained by existing knowledge. As an undergraduate student in the sciences, you will be introduced to scientific thinking and to the ways in which scientists argue. In each of your science classes, try to identify the purposes of argumentation. Pose these questions:

- In this area of science, what are the particular issues on which researchers seek to gain agreement?
- What questions do researchers pose and why are these questions useful?

Claims

Scientific arguments often involve two sorts of claims. The first takes the form *X is a problem* or *X is somehow puzzling.* This claim establishes some issue as worthy of investigation, and it is on the basis of this claim (which must be supported) that experiments are designed. Recognizing what counts as a problem or a puzzle requires both experience and creativity. Assume it is early October. One evening the temperature drops and you have the first hard frost of the season. The following day you notice that most of the flowers and vegetables in your garden have wilted—but one particular grouping of flowers (your mums) and one vegetable (your turnips) seem as healthy as ever. You and your neighbor both notice this fact. Your neighbor passes it by with a shrug, but you wonder *why.* You have noticed a *difference,* an anomaly (see 1a). If you were scientifically inclined, you might begin an investigation into why a certain plant or flower is frost resistant.

Recognizing a difference or anomaly often begins the process of scientific investigation. The process continues when you make a second claim that attempts to explain the anomaly. Such a claim takes this form: *X can be explained as follows.* If in a book on horticulture you did not find an answer to your puzzle about frost heartiness, you might conduct a study in which you

Tense in Scientific Writing

There is one special convention of writing scientific papers that is very sticky. It has to do with *tense,* and it is important because proper usage derives from scientific ethics.

When a scientific paper has been validly published in a primary journal, it thereby becomes knowledge. Therefore, whenever you quote previously published work, ethics requires you to treat that work with respect. You do this by using the *present* tense. It is correct to say "Streptomycin inhibits the growth of *M. tuberculosis* (13)." Whenever you quote or discuss previously published work, you should use the present tense; you are quoting established knowledge.

Your own present work must be referred to in the *past* tense. Your work is not presumed to be established knowledge until *after* it has been published. If you determined that the optimal growth temperature for *Streptomyces everycolor* was 37°C, you should say "*S. everycolor* grew best at 37°C." If you are citing previous work, possibly your own, it is then correct to say "*S. everycolor* grows best at 37°C."

In the typical paper, you will normally go back and forth between the past and present tenses. Most of the Abstract should be in the past tense, because you are referring to your own present results. Likewise, the Materials and Methods and the Results sections should be in the past tense, as you describe what you did and what you found. On the other hand, most of the Introduction and much of the Discussion should be in the present tense, because these sections usually emphasize previously established knowledge.

Source: Robert Day, *How to Write and Publish a Scientific Paper,* 3rd ed. (Phoenix: Oryx Press, 1988) 158–59.

examined the leaf and root structures of the various plants in your garden. Based on your research you might develop an educated guess, or hypothesis, to explain why certain plants are frost resistant. To test your hypothesis you might design an experiment in which you exposed several plants to varying temperatures. Based on your results, you might claim that frost resistance in plants depends on two or three specific factors. Generally, when you are reading or writing in the sciences, these questions will help you to clarify how arguments are made:

- What is the question being investigated? What problem or anomaly is said to exist?
- What explanation is offered in response to this problem or anomaly?

Logic and evidence

As in any discipline, writers in science use various principles of logic to examine raw data and to select *particular* information as significant. The variety of logical principles that scientists have available to them in trying to

LOOKING BACK

If students have difficulty understanding this discussion of tense, you may want to refer them to the treatment of "historical present tense" in 9e-1.

REFERENCES

AMBRON, JOANNA. "Writing to Improve Learning in Biology." *Journal of College Science Teaching* 15 (1987): 263–66. Discusses three writing assignments (journals, freewriting, short essays [microthemes]) that develop analytical skills and improve learning biology.

GOODMAN, W. DANIEL, and JOHN C. BEAN. "A Chemistry Laboratory Project to Develop Thinking and Writing Skills." *Journal of Chemical Education* 60 (1983): 483–84. Discusses a way to integrate laboratory projects and research writing in a collaborative setting, the end result being the approximation of a professional research paper.

MALACHOWSKI, MITCHELL R. "Honing Observational Skills by the Use of Writing Exercises." *Journal of Chemical Education* 63 (1986): 497. Assigning short, in-class writing assignments helps students to consolidate their chemistry lab findings.

MOGER, SUSAN, and ROBERT G. WLEZIEN. "Using Current Technological Issues in a Writing Course for Engineers." *Engineering Education* 73 (1983): 316–18. Offers an alternative approach to teaching traditional technical writing by designing employment-related and socially important topics and by emphasizing revision and collaboration.

NAHRGANG, CYNTHIA L., and BRUCE T. PETERSEN. "Using Writing to Learn Mathematics." *Mathematics Teacher* 79 (1986): 461–65. Describes how journal writing assists students in organizing their thoughts about mathematics and improves their writing ability.

OLMSTED, JOHN III. "Teaching Varied Technical Writing Styles in the Upper Division Laboratory." *Journal of Chemical Education* 61 (1984): 798–800. Discusses in detail twelve types of reports, each with a different style, that students must write on experiments they conduct.

(continued)

POTVIN, JANET H., and ROBERT L. WOODS. "Technical Communication and the Non-Native Speaker." *Engineering Education* 74 (1983): 171–73. Argues that teaching communication skills in the technological disciplines must entail sensitivity to linguistic, stylistic, and grammatical differences of non-native speakers.

STRAUSS, MICHAEL J., and TOBY FULWILER. "Interactive Writing and Learning Chemistry." *Journal of College Science Teaching* 15 (1987): 256–62. Informal writing deposited into "Questions/Concerns/Critiques" boxes at the exits of a lecture hall led students to work through their chemistry problems in writing, thereby beginning the process of solving them.

VARGAS, MARJORIE FINK. "Writing Skills for Science Labs." *The Science Teacher* (1986): 29–33. Discusses a classroom exercise to show students how choices in voice are predicated on the demands of report writing.

WINSOR, DOROTHY A. "Engineering Writing/Writing Engineering." CCC 41 (1990): 58–70. Attempts to show what engineers' writing looks like through the lens of "contemporary views about the textual shaping of knowledge," suggesting that such writers reveal "both their knowledge and themselves."

make sense of their research is vast and complex, and if you major in a science it will be the purpose of your entire undergraduate career to train you to understand which principles of logic are appropriately applied in which circumstances. For purposes of demonstration, observe the application of one common logical principle—concerning *types.* Watch how certain kinds of evidence are assembled on the basis of this logic.

> *Investigations begin with a puzzle or anomaly.*
> All the flowers and vegetables in my garden—except for mums and turnips—have wilted after the first hard frost. Why weren't these harmed?
>
> *A variety of information is available.*
> This is an above-ground garden, 3 feet deep, 5 feet wide, and 10 feet long. The garden gets full morning sun but is largely shaded each afternoon. I grow tomatoes, beans, peas, cucumbers, turnips, table flowers, geraniums, mums, and morning glories. The soil tests slightly acidic, and it is well fertilized. Turnips are my sweetest crop, high in sugar. All the plants except the turnips grow above ground. The mums differ from the other above-ground plants in that their crown is located below ground. I water the garden twice daily, morning and evening.
>
> *The investigator applies a logical principle as an aid to sifting through the available information.*
> A frost-resistant plant is a type of plant that exhibits two or three of these features: (1) The plant is high in sugar content; solutions high in sugar resist freezing. (2) The cell walls of the leaves are thick and fibrous and are not easily punctured by ice crystals. (3) The crown—the portion of the plant from which the above-ground plant grows—is located below ground and is not harmed until the temperature drops to 25°F.
>
> *The investigator uses the principle to distinguish meaningful information—potential evidence—from meaningless information.*
> Based on the principle above, I see that mums exhibit features 2 and 3, while turnips exhibit features 1 and 3.
>
> *Working with an inference and carefully selected evidence, a writer can support a claim (or conclusion).*
> Of all the *types* of plants in my garden, only mums and turnips can be classified as frost resistant in that only they exhibit two of the three features characteristic of frost-resistant plants.

Each different logical pattern an investigator might use prompts him or her to look for a certain patterning among available information. You can better understand the workings of a science by identifying the varieties of logical principles researchers use in making arguments. As a student reading or writing in a scientific discipline, pose these questions:

- What logical principles are used in this discipline to make meaningful, supportable connections between observed facts and claims?
- What observable, measurable evidence can help to support a scientific claim?

39b Reading in the sciences

Scientists work with written sources all the time. Accurate written records of experiments are essential in the process of reaching consensus about questions of scientific interest. As a student of science, you will read journal articles and textbooks, and you will do well to establish a strategy for reading both. First of all, adopt the general strategies suggested in Chapter 1 of this book, especially in 1e, "Reading to understand."

Journal articles

Journal articles are written by researchers for colleagues, not for students, and you can expect the language, concepts, and methodologies in journals to be challenging. The use of equations and sophisticated statistical techniques in a study's results section may leave you baffled. But you can still develop a general, useful understanding of an article (if not a critical response to the author's research methodology) by reading as follows. Read the article's Abstract, the Introduction, and the Discussion—in this order. If these sections prove interesting, then read the middle sections (the Materials and Methods, and the Results), which will probably contain the article's most technical elements. As you read, pose these questions:

- What is the purpose of this study?
- What is the researcher's perspective—for instance, biologist, chemist, or electrical engineer—and how does this influence the study?
- What is the researcher's claim or conclusion?
- What seems significant about this research?

The following Abstract, Introduction, and Discussion are sections of a scientific report on mummified human tissue. The authors employ a sophisticated DNA analysis in their study—techniques far too complicated for anyone but specialists to follow. But by reading selected sections of the article, any persistent reader can gain a good sense of how the study develops and why the authors think their work is significant. Written by Ingolf Thuesen and Jan Engberg, "Recovery and Analysis of Human Genetic Material from Mummified Tissue and Bone" appeared in the *Journal of Archaeological Science* 17 (1990): 679–89.

ABSTRACT

Using sensitive techniques of molecular biology, we have been able to demonstrate the presence of genomic material of human origin in samples of mummified human tissue and bone from selected archaeological sites in Greenland. This result has far-reaching consequences for both evolutionary and archaeological studies of past human populations.

INTRODUCTION

Using sensitive techniques of molecular biology, we have investigated the possibility of recovering and analyzing genetic materials (deoxyribonucleic

LOOKING BACK

Students may want to review Chapter 1 (Critical Thinking and Reading) for a general discussion of the subject before reading this section. While Chapter 1 focuses primarily on reading texts other than reports, the general principles are still relevant.

TEACHING IDEAS

Students accustomed to reading through a journal article from start to finish may have trouble understanding the advice given here. If you focus on the questions listed and ask students where in the sample those questions are answered, you should be able to reinforce the advice to read the middle sections of scientific reports last.

FOR DISCUSSION

Some of your students will probably be enrolled simultaneously in introductory science classes. Ask them to bring their textbooks to class and to comment on how they differ from texts in humanities and social sciences. With a little prodding from you, this activity should lead to a class discussion on the different purposes and expectations of textbooks in various disciplines.

acid, DNA) from mummified human tissue and bone from selected archaeological sites in Greenland. Simple extraction procedures of both skin and bone samples yielded DNA material in purified form. Using human specific probes, we demonstrated that a minor, but distinct, portion of the purified DNA material was of human origin. Further analysis showed the remaining portion of the isolated DNA to consist mainly of DNA of fungal origin. The findings of DNA of human origin in mummified skin and bone samples, in particular, opens up the possibility for detailed anthropological genetic studies.

Discussion

Recovery and analysis of ancient tissue and bone of human origin has long been intensively investigated. With the rapid advances within molecular biology in recent years, we have seen the first successful extraction of DNA from archaeological and anthropological materials (Higuchi *et al.* 1984; Pääbo 1985*a, b*; Doran *et al.* 1986). The perspective arising from those results and results of the reported work are indeed fascinating. The potential in establishing libraries of ancient DNA is obvious and prepares the road not only for the study of biological evolution (Thomas *et al.* 1989), but also for research into human cultural history.

Within the archaeological discipline the information that may be recovered from survived fragments of DNA may concern inherited diseases, ethnic or racial associations and even sex and lineage. With the successful extraction of DNA from bones, we are also stabilizing and expanding the interpretative basis of the method. Bones are much more abundant in museum magazines and excavations than soft tissue fragments whether from artificially or naturally mummified bodies. According to our results bones are not contaminated in the same way as is skin tissue. An example of future research topics generated by the present project would be a search for the Eskimo–Norseman ethnic relationship and/or the occurrence of inherited diseases, based on successful extraction of DNA from bone material, which is abundantly available in the collections.

Despite being a time-consuming task, the extraction and identification of relevant fragments of ancient DNA should be a challenge for many anthropologists or evolutionists. In particular, after the appearance of the PCR technique, this task no longer seems out of reach (Pääbo and Wilson, 1988). The study of ancient DNA has already been suggested as a subdiscipline to paleoanthropology (Perizonius *et al.* 1989). As a curiosity we may mention, that during our work, which has also involved other mummified tissues such as Danish bog people, Nubian cemetery samples (natural mummification) and artificially mummified Egyptians, the project was nicknamed GAP, Genetic Archaeology Project.

The lengthy and highly technical Materials and Methods section, and Results section (omitted here) are detailed, and other molecular biologists could repeat the authors' DNA analysis. As a student in an introductory course, surely replication will not be your purpose for reading journal articles. Read for other reasons: to see issues important to particular scientists raised and addressed from a particular perspective; to see the process of scientific inquiry at work; and to share in a researcher's excitement.

Textbooks

In introductory courses your reading will be primarily in textbooks, where the writing is directed to students and should, therefore, be more accessible than the writing in journal articles. In the sciences, textbooks play a special role in synthesizing available knowledge in an area and presenting it, with explanations, to students. The material in texts will grow increasingly technical as you move from introductory to specialized courses. Read your texts in science courses closely (see 1e), monitoring your progress frequently to ensure that you understand the material. Highlight any concepts or terms that confuse you, and seek clarification from classmates or a professor.

39c Types of writing assignments in the sciences

As an undergraduate, you will most often be assigned two kinds of writing: a report of a laboratory experiment and a literature review. The purpose of writing in both cases will be to introduce you to methods of scientific thinking and ways that scientists argue.

The lab report

A laboratory experiment represents a distinct (empirical) strategy for learning about the world. Experimental researchers agree on this basic premise: that research must be *replicable*—that is, repeatable. Knowledge gained through experiment is based on what can be *observed*; and what is observed, if it is going to be accepted universally as a fact, must be observed by others: hence the need for *reporting on* and *writing* original research. Reports of experimental research usually consist of four parts: Introduction, Methods, Results, and Discussion. Even when scientific papers do not follow this structure, they will mirror its problem-solution approach. Robert A. Day, author of a highly readable and authoritative guide to writing scientific papers, characterizes the logic of the four-part form this way:

> What question (problem) was studied? The answer is the Introduction. How was the problem studied? The answer is the Methods. What were the findings? The answer is the Results. What do these findings mean? The answer is the Discussion. (7)

Introduction

The Introduction of a scientific paper should clearly define the problem(s) or state the hypothesis you are investigating, as well as the point of view from which you will be investigating it. Establishing your point of view will help readers to anticipate the type of experiment you will be reporting

TEACHING IDEAS

Students will need to be reminded that the guidelines here are a *general pattern,* not a blueprint, for writing lab reports. Encourage them to follow closely any specific guidelines from their instructors, or to ask for such guidelines if necessary.

FOR DISCUSSION

You may want to ask students to explain why they think these guidelines are necessary for a laboratory notebook. Those who have already taken laboratory science courses may be able to help the uninitiated understand the purpose of the notebook.

Keeping a Laboratory Notebook

The notebook should reflect a daily record of work. It is best to make entries explaining the results expected from each stage of the investigation. Entries should be in chronological order, and so thorough and comprehensive that they can be understood by the corroborating witnesses. Each page should be signed by the inventor or researcher below the last entry, and by one or preferably two witnesses. Full names should be used and the signatures dated.

• • •

1. Use a *bound* notebook, if possible.
2. If a loose leaf notebook is preferred, the pages should be numbered in advance and a record kept of the numbered pages given to each laboratory worker. The point is to rebut any inference that a worker may have inserted a page at a later date.[1]
3. Do not remove any pages or any part of a page. Pages missing from a notebook will seriously weaken a case in the Patent Office, or in cases that go to court for litigation.
4. Record all entries directly and legibly in solvent-resistant black ink.
5. Define the problem or objective concisely. Make entries consistently as the work is performed.
6. All original work, including simple arithmetical calculations, should be performed in the notebook. If you make a mistake, recalculate—**do not erase.**
7. Never use correction fluid or paste-overs of any kind. If you decide to correct an error, place a single line through the mistake, sign and date

(continued)

on, as well as your conclusions. Your Introduction should also state clearly your reasons for investigating a particular subject. This is common practice in journal articles, where researchers will cite pertinent literature in order to set their current project in a context. In referring to prior work in which the same or similar problems or processes have been reported, you will cite sources. (See 36d for the conventions on citing and documenting sources in the sciences.) These references will help you to establish a context as well as a need for the present experiment.

Materials and methods

The Methods section of the lab report is given slightly different names in different discipline areas: Experimental Details, Experimental Methods, Experimental Section, or Materials and Methods (American Chemical Society [ACS] 6); and Subjects, Materials, and Methods (CBE 21). Whatever

Keeping a Laboratory Notebook *(continued)*

the correction, and give a reason for the error. Take care the underlying type can still be read. However, even the practice of drawing a line through numbers entered in error is discouraged in many companies. Instead, workers are asked simply to make a new entry, correcting the error when possible.

8. Do not leave blank spaces on any page. Instead, either draw diagonal lines or a cross through any portion of the page you don't use.
9. Date and sign what you have written on the day of entry. In addition, have each notebook page read, signed, and dated by a qualified witness—someone who is not directly involved in the work performed, but who understands the purpose of the experiment and the results obtained.
10. Extra materials such as graphs and charts should be inserted, signed, and witnessed in the same way as other entries.
11. All apparatus should be identified. Schematic sketches should be included.
12. Head each entry with a title. If you are continuing on the next page, say so at the bottom of the page before you continue.

These rules have received a popular formulation as, "Record it. Date it. Sign it. Have it witnessed."

[1]1976 Patent Institute. "A Continuing Seminar of New Developments in Law and Practice," College of Business Administration, Fairleigh Dickinson University, Madison, NJ.

Source: Anne Eisenberg, "Keeping a Laboratory Notebook," *Journal of Chemical Education* 59 (1982): 1045–46.

heading your instructor prefers, it is in the Materials and Methods section that you provide readers with the basis on which to reproduce your experimental study. Unless you have some reason for not doing so, describe your experimental methods chronologically. When reporting on the Materials and Methods of *field studies* (investigations carried out beyond the strictly controlled environment of the lab), describe precisely *where* you conducted your study, *what* you chose to study, the *instruments* you used to conduct the study, and the *methods of analysis* you employed.

As you set up and conduct your experiment, keep detailed records that will allow you to report precisely on your work when the time comes for writing. Both student and professional experimenters keep a *lab notebook* for this purpose. Even though you may be tempted to make quick, shorthand entries, write in precise and complete sentences that will allow you to retrace your steps. The notebook should be complete, containing the information necessary to write your lab report.

Results

The Results section of your paper should precisely set out the data you have accumulated in your research. The statements you make in this section will provide the basis on which you state conclusions in the Discussion section to follow; your presentation of results, therefore, must be both clear and logically ordered. (Instructors will usually review in class what constitutes clear and logical ordering of results in their disciplines.) As in the Materials and Methods section, when your discussion of results is lengthy, use subheadings to organize the presentation.

GROUP ACTIVITY

In order to help students better understand the purpose of the Discussion section of a laboratory report, divide the class into groups and ask them to list several modern scientific endeavors (e.g., the discovery of a polio vaccine or the race to find a cure for AIDS). Then they can talk about the history of those discoveries: what scientists had thought previously, how certain experiments changed scientific thinking, and how society was affected by the discoveries. The Discussion section of laboratory reports invites other scientists to replicate the study or to carry it further.

FOR DISCUSSION

You may want to engage students in a discussion of the advantages of abstracts. Ask students about their own research experience, particularly with titles of sources that seemed relevant but on inspection turned out to be useless. The abstract alleviates this problem considerably. You may even want to note that general databases such as InfoTrac contain a number of abstracts.

Discussion

The purpose of the Discussion section in your report is to interpret experimental findings and to discuss their implications. In the Discussion, your main task is to address the *So what?* question. Readers should know, clearly, what you have accomplished (or failed to accomplish) and why this is significant. Directly address the question or problem that prompted the experimental study, and state the extent to which your data adequately answer the initial question(s). If you believe your research findings are significant, say so and give your reasons. If appropriate, suggest directions for future study. As in the Introduction, set your experimental findings in a context by relating them to the findings of other experiments. When your results differ from those you expected or from results reported by others, explain the difference.

The Abstract

The Abstract is the *briefest possible* summary of an article (see 2a). In some journals, articles conclude with a Summary (marked as such). It is more common to find the Abstract appearing at the beginning. An article published in a scientific journal will usually have the complete text of its Abstract reproduced on an electronic database. Researchers scanning the database will read the Abstract to determine whether an article is related to their own work and, thus, worth retrieving in its entirety. Abstracts must therefore be concise and self-contained. Typically, they include the following:

- The subject of the paper, its purpose and objectives
- The experiment's materials and methods, including the names of specific organisms, drugs, and compounds
- Experimental results and their significance

Most often, the Abstract excludes the following:

- References to literature cited in the paper
- Any reference to equations, figures, or tables (AIP 5; CBE 20)

When writing the Abstract of your lab report, consider devoting one sentence of summary to each of the major headings (Introduction, Materials and Methods, Results, and Discussion). If necessary, follow your four-sentence Abstract with a concluding sentence.

Title page and manuscript form

Every research report should have a precise, descriptive title. The title, along with the Abstract, will be read first, so if you want to pique interest, this is the place to begin. Check with your instructor about the form your lab report should take. All text—including the Abstract, footnotes, and the reference list—should be double spaced. Generally, all pages of a manuscript are numbered consecutively, *beginning* with the title page. The Abstract page follows, then the body of your report. Each major heading—Introduction, Materials and Methods, Results, and Discussion—should be centered on its own line. (Some instructors will want to see each major section begin on a new page.) Subheadings should be placed flush to the left margin; after each, skip one line and begin your text. Place the reference list at the end of the report and follow with your tables and figures if you do not incorporate them into the text of your paper. Each table and figure should be titled and placed on a separate page.

2 The Literature Review

The Literature Review, a prominent and important form of writing in science, synthesizes current knowledge on a topic. Unlike a term paper, which draws on a limited number of sources in order to support a thesis, a Literature Review covers and brings coherence to the range of studies on a topic. A review may also evaluate articles, advising readers pressed for time about which articles merit attention. While every experimental report begins with a review of pertinent literature, only the Literature Review makes this discussion its main business.

Instructors assigning review papers will not ask that you conduct an exhaustive search of literature on a topic. Your search should be limited in such a way that it will both introduce you to a topic and acquaint you with scientific ways of thinking. Your topic should not be so broad that you overwhelm yourself with vast amounts of reading material. For general advice on the skills necessary for conducting a Literature Review, see "Reading to evaluate" (1g), "Reading to synthesize" (1h), and "Writing a synthesis" (2d). (These same principles apply to writing Literature Reviews in the social sciences and the humanities. In both discipline areas, scholars periodically write articles in which they bring their colleagues up to date on research concerning one topic.)

LOOKING BACK

Students preparing to write a Literature Review would do well to review thoroughly the sections of Chapters 1 and 2 mentioned here. Proper evaluation of a source is crucial to the Literature Review, as is making inferences about relationships among sources and synthesizing a number of sources in one paper.

Writing the paper

Writing a Literature Review in the sciences involves several steps. Once you have a topic in mind, you will need to read widely so as to learn enough that you can ask a pointed question and can begin to conduct more focused library research. Reading scholarly review articles is an excellent place to begin, since by definition they survey a great many potential sources for you and, better still, point out themes and raise questions that you can take up in your own review. Review articles are published for most of the sciences. Locate them by searching for the word *review* in the various publications that abstract and index journal articles, such as *Microbiological Abstracts, Chemical Abstracts, Engineering Index Annual, Physics Abstracts,* and *Science Abstracts.*

If you are unfamiliar with the process of conducting research, then before attempting a Literature Review you might skim Chapter 33, where you will find general strategies for writing a research paper. A Literature Review, like any good synthesis or research paper, is usually organized by *ideas,* not by sources. (See the discussion in 2d, on "Ensuring that your voice is heard.") In Literature Reviews, you will not find a simple listing of summaries: these are the substance of annotated bibliographies, which are themselves useful tools to researchers. The review should represent your best effort at inferring themes, problems, trends, and so on. When referring to sources, use the citation form appropriate to your discipline. See 36d for information on citing and documenting sources in the sciences.

TEACHING IDEAS

Students should pay close attention to the difference among styles with regard to title pages. CBE style calls for more information than either MLA or APA.

TEACHING IDEAS

The sample lab report presented here is heavily annotated so that students can use it as a guide in writing their own reports. You may want to call particular attention to specific features peculiar to lab reports—format, presentation of results, use of tables and graphs, and the like.

39d Sample student paper: "Comparison of Two Strains of Wine-Producing Yeasts"

Following is a lab report on the fermentation of wine. The microbiological processes involved in wine production have been known for nearly 150 years, and the student writing this report has added no new knowledge to our understanding of how wine is made. But creating new knowledge was not the purpose of the assignment. Clarence S. Ivie met his professor's objectives by successfully planning and carrying out an experiment, by making careful observations, and by thinking and writing like a biologist.

Here are several features you might look for when reading Clarence Ivie's paper.

- The writer assumes an audience of experts, and it is clear that the occasion for writing is formal. Ivie does not define scientific terms—he assumes his readers will understand all references. (This same observation accounts for the difficulty you might have in reading the paper.)
- The writer demonstrates the logic of a scientific investigation. Ivie bases claims on measurable observations—with an important exception at the end of the paper, in which he makes what he calls "subjective observations" of the two wines he is comparing. In the context of a laboratory experiment, Ivie is careful to distinguish subjective impressions from objective measurements. He follows a standard format for reporting lab results.
- The writer uses graphs and a table to show the relationship among three different sets of information. For those who can read graphs and tables (the assumed reader *can*), these are useful tools for communicating experimental results.
- In sections of the paper where technical language is not needed, the writer avoids such language. See especially the Introduction (the first paragraph) and the Discussion.

Comparison of Two Strains of
Wine-Producing Yeasts

Clarence S. Ivie III

Microbiology 314
Department of Biological Sciences
University of South Alabama
Mobile, Alabama 36688
Professor Burke Brown
4 March 1995

TEACHING IDEAS

You may want to ask students to read the abstract carefully and comment on how it fulfills the function of the abstract described earlier in the chapter.

1

Comparison of Two Strains of
Wine-Producing Yeasts

The purpose of this experiment was to determine which strain of yeast produced the most favorable wine. Wine yeast, _Saccharomyces cerevisiæ_ var. _ellipsoideus_ and Fleischmann's baker's yeast, _Saccharomyces cerevisiæ_, were used to make two samples of wine. The wines were then compared with one another to determine which yeast created the best wine based on smell, taste, and alcohol content. The results of the experiment indicated that the wine yeast produced a better wine.

The abstract consists of one-sentence summaries of the report's major sections.

Fermentation is a process whereby a strain of yeast metabolizes sugar to produce alcohol. Wine is most commonly produced from grape juice by the process of fermentation. Grapes are crushed to acquire the juice. Sugar is then added to the grape juice. The grape juice, or _must_, is then inoculated with yeast and allowed to ferment, a process that takes around fourteen days. The end product is an alcoholic beverage which has been valued for centuries. It is not known when the first wines were created. However, throughout the history of wine making, people have constantly made attempts at improving the quality of the wine (2). In this experiment, the strain of yeast that produced the best wine was determined on the basis of smell, taste, and alcohol content.

In some disciplines, "Introduction," as a heading, is omitted from the lab report.

The introduction sets the study in a larger context and establishes the research perspective: microbiology.

Materials and Methods

Two 1.9L bottles were used in this experiment. Each bottle contained 1.7L of grape juice. Two hun-

The author provides exact information so that readers can replicate the study.

Ivie 2

dred thirty (230) grams of table sugar was added to each bottle of grape juice. Bottle #1 was then inoculated with one package of Saccharomyces var. ellipsoideus. Bottle #2 was inoculated with one package of Fleischmann's baker's yeast. The mixtures were then shaken to dissolve their contents. Initial measurements were immediately taken, including: pH, specific gravity, and temperature. Subjective observations, such as the mixture's color, were also made. A pH meter was used to measure pH, a hydrometer was used to measure specific gravity, and a thermometer was used to measure temperature. After the initial measurements were taken, both bottles were then sealed and allowed to ferment. Periodically CO_2 gas production rates were measured for each experimental wine fermentation procedure. This was done by measuring the volume of displacement, due to the gas production. As the wine continued to ferment, these measurements were made daily throughout the 20 day duration of the experiment. On the eighteenth day of the experiment, both bottles were inoculated with a bisulphite to stop the fermentation process.

Results

After the fermentation process was halted, the specific gravity changes of bottles 1 and 2 were compared. The specific gravities of both wine experiments decreased, but the most substantial decrease occurred in bottle #1. These results indicated that the wine yeast metabolized the sugar more efficiently than the Fleischmann's baker's yeast (Fig. 1).

The results of the pH change, in each case, fluctuated daily. There was, however, an overall increase in both samples.

The author provides a specific criterion, or test, by which to analyze the two samples.

FOR DISCUSSION

Students should recognize immediately the stylistic differences between a scientific lab report and a social science field study report. Even more striking should be the differences between a lab report and a literary analysis. Ask students to cite the differences among the discipline-specific forms of writing, explaining why they think such differences exist.

FOR DISCUSSION

After they have read the entire lab report, students should discuss the function of the graphs. What purpose do the graphs serve? How do they support the narrative portion of the report? What effect would you expect them to have on an audience of scientists? How would the impact of the report be altered if the graphs were eliminated?

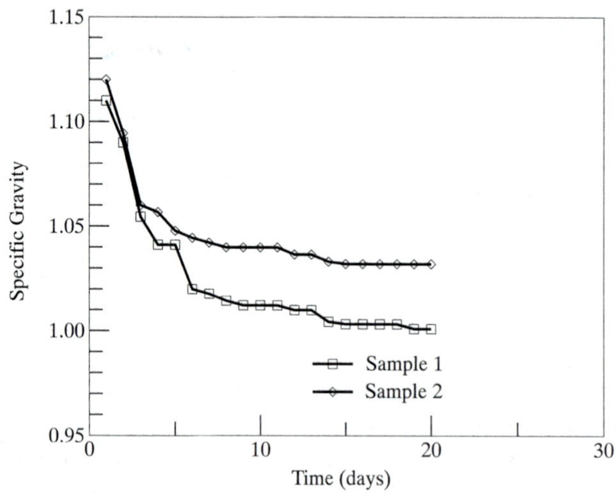

The graph is given a title; its elements are clearly labeled; its information is self-contained.

Fig. 1. Comparison of specific gravity versus time between Saccharomyces var. ellipsoideus, the wine yeast, and Saccharomyces cerevisiæ, the baker's yeast.

The temperatures of both samples remained more or less constant at 22.5 degrees Celsius throughout the entire fermentation process.

The author provides three additional criteria by which to analyze the samples.

The gas production measurements showed that the wine yeast produced more carbon dioxide than the baker's yeast. Gas production is directly related to yeast growth. Because of this fact, it was not a surprise to find that the graph of the gas production rate of the yeast was quite similar to a typical growth curve (Fig. 2).

To calculate the % alcohol content of wine, data from table 1 was used in the following equation (1): % alc. = (Initial % potential alc.) - (Final % potential alc.)

The wine produced from Saccharomyces var. ellipsoideus was 14.9% alcoholic, while the wine produced from Saccharomyces cerevisiæ was only 12.3% alcoholic.

Ivie 4

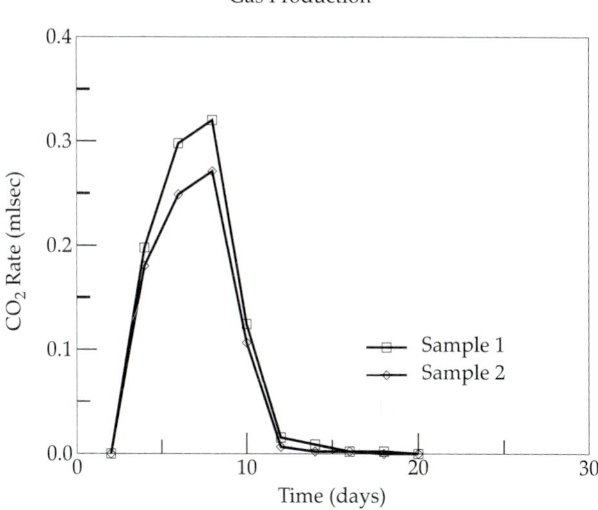

Fig. 2. Comparison of CO_2 production between <u>Saccharomyces</u> var. <u>ellipsoideus</u> and <u>Saccharomyces cerevisiæ</u>.

The graph is given a title; its elements are clearly labeled; its information is self-contained.

<u>Subjective observations of smell and taste favored the wine yeast</u>. The wine made from the baker's yeast smelled like bread and tasted bitter. The wine made from the wine yeast smelled like wine and tasted sweet.

Subjective observations are clearly distinguished from objective measurements.

Discussion

Wine is the product of yeast fermentation. The purpose of this experiment was to determine which type of yeast produced the best wine. The basis by which the wines made in the experiment were judged included taste, smell, and alcohol content. It was clearly evident that the wine yeast created a more pleasant smelling and tasting wine than did the baker's yeast. The wine produced by the baker's yeast had a harshly overpowering smell which resembled the smell of bread. Its taste was extremely bitter. Overall, on the basis of taste and smell,

The discussion does more than merely repeat results: it reviews the purpose of the experiment, sets the results in relation to the purpose, and succinctly states a conclusion.

TEACHING IDEAS

You may want to ask students to read the Discussion carefully and comment on how it fulfills the function of the Discussion described earlier in the chapter.

Table 1. Relations between specific gravities and % potential alcohol

Specific Gravity	% Potential Alcohol
1.000	0
1.010	0.9
1.020	2.3
1.030	3.7
1.040	5.1
1.050	6.5
1.090	7.8
1.080	10.6
1.090	12.0
1.100	13.4
1.110	14.9
1.120	16.3
1.130	17.7

The information in the table is clearly displayed and is self-contained. The table provides the standards by which alcohol percentages are determined in the experiment.

the baker's yeast created an undesirable wine while the wine yeast created a pleasant smelling and more desirable tasting wine. On the basis of alcohol content, it is clearly seen from the results of this experiment that the wine yeast produced a more alcoholic wine than the baker's yeast. The wine yeast proved to be more efficient in the metabolism of sugar than the baker's yeast. Evidence of this is seen in the specific gravity measurements. The wine yeast also achieved a greater rate of fermentation as seen in the gas production measurement. From this experiment, it can be concluded that the use of wine yeast, *Saccharomyces* var. *ellipsoideus*, is far more advantageous than the use of baker's yeast in making wine.

Each of the author's claims is supported by evidence gathered during the experiment.

Ivie 6

Literature Cited

1. Case, J.; Johnson, L. Laboratory experiments in microbiology. Reading, MA: The Benjamin/ Cummings Publishing Company; 1984.
2. Prescott, A.; Harley, J.; Klein, P. Microbiology. Dubuque, IA: Wm. C. Brown Publishers; 1990.
3. Stryer M.; Lubert, A. Biochemistry. New York: W. H. Freeman and Company; 1988.

39e Reference materials in the sciences

Style guides

A source of excellent general advice for writing papers in the sciences is Robert Day's *How to Write and Publish a Scientific Paper,* 3rd ed. (Phoenix: Oryx Press, 1988). For discipline-specific advice on writing, consult the following works:

AIP [American Institute of Physics] Style Manual. 4th ed. New York: AIP, 1990.

CBE [Council of Biology Editors] Style Manual. 5th ed. Bethesda: CBE, 1983.

Dodd, Janet S., et al. *The ACS [American Chemical Society] Style Guide: A Manual for Authors and Editors.* Washington: ACS, 1986.

Michaelson, Herbert B. *How to Write and Publish Engineering Papers and Reports.* 2nd ed. Philadelphia: ISI Press, 1986.

Specialized references

The following specialized references will help you to assemble information in a particular discipline or field within the discipline.

Encyclopedias provide general information useful when beginning a search.

Cambridge Encyclopedia of Astronomy
Encyclopedia of Biological Sciences
Encyclopedia of Chemistry
Encyclopedia of Computer Science and Engineering
Encyclopedia of Computer Science and Technology
Encyclopedia of Earth Sciences
Encyclopedia of Physics
Grzimek's Animal Life Encyclopedia

FOR DISCUSSION

It would be helpful for students to recognize the differences in format among CBE, APA, and MLA style with regard to references—in particular the order of references in CBE style.

TEACHING IDEAS

Students who plan to major or minor in the sciences should be encouraged to consult faculty in their chosen discipline regarding the preferred style guide. With so many from which to choose, it is important that students know which guide their instructors use.

Grzimek's Encyclopedia of Ecology
Harper's Encyclopedia of Science
Larousse Encyclopedia of Astronomy
McGraw-Hill Encyclopedia of Environmental Science
McGraw-Hill Yearbook of Science and Technology
Stein and Day International Medical Encyclopedia
Universal Encyclopedia of Mathematics
Van Nostrand's Scientific Encyclopedia

Dictionaries provide definitions of technical terms.

Computer Dictionary and Handbook
Condensed Chemical Dictionary
Dictionary of Biology
Dorland's Medical Dictionary
Illustrated Stedman's Medical Dictionary
McGraw-Hill Dictionary of Scientific and Technical Terms

Periodical indexes list articles published in a particular discipline over a particular period. *Abstracts,* which summarize the sources listed and involve a considerable amount of work to compile, tend to be more selective than indexes.

Applied Science and Technology Index
Biological Abstracts
Biological and Agricultural Index
Cumulative Index to Nursing and Allied Health Literature
Current Abstracts of Chemistry and Index Chemicus
Engineering Index
General Science Index
Index Medicus
Index to Scientific and Technical Proceedings
Science Citation Index

Computerized periodical indexes are available for many specialized areas and may be faster than leafing through years of bound periodicals. Access to these databases may be expensive.

Science and Technology Databases
Agricola (agriculture)
Biosis Previews (biology, botany)
CA Search (chemistry)
Compendix (engineering)
NTIS (National Technical Information Search)
ORBIT (science and technology)
SciSearch
SPIN (physics)

PART XI

WRITING FOR SPECIAL OCCASIONS

CHAPTER 40

Writing in a Business Environment

In a business environment, much is accomplished—meetings are attended, information is shared, agendas are set, arguments are settled—based on writing alone. When you enter this environment by writing a letter or memo, you must understand that people are not obligated to answer you (rude as this might seem). Businesspeople have many demands placed on them simultaneously. When reading, they must know a writer's purpose and they must be given a motivation for continuing to read. Lacking either of these qualities, a document will not represent itself as *important* enough to merit attention, and the reader will simply turn to more pressing concerns.

You will significantly improve your chances of readers acting on your letters and memos if you begin by appreciating the constraints on their time. Think of your readers as busy people inclined to help if your writing is direct, concise, and clearly organized. A *direct* letter or memo will state in its opening sentence your purpose for writing. A *concise* letter or memo will state your exact needs in as few words as possible. A *well-organized* letter or memo will present only the information that is pertinent to your main point, in a sequence that is readily understood.

The writing process in a business environment

Direct, concise, and clearly organized writing takes time, of course, and is seldom the effort of a single draft. Writing a document in a business setting involves a process, just as your writing a research paper in an academic setting involves a process. It may seem counterintuitive, but you will spend less time writing a letter twice (producing both rough and revised drafts) than you will trying to do a creditable job in a single draft. Generally, you will do well to follow the advice in Chapters 3 and 4 on planning, developing, drafting, and revising a paper. For every document that you write,

KEY FEATURES

In discussing the various types of business writing, this chapter maintains the emphasis introduced in the first chapters of the handbook: good writing takes into consideration both the purpose of the document and the audience to which it is addressed. In business this translates into the importance of getting to the point in an environment where time is of the essence. Business writing is characterized in the chapter as being direct, concise, and clearly organized. Referring to Chapters 3 and 4, this chapter presents a "distilled" process of preparation, drafting, and revision. Many forms of business writing are covered, including letters, résumés, and memoranda. Students are advised on matters of form and content, and are provided with clearly annotated examples.

LOOKING BACK

Most students should be able to appreciate the audience concerns expressed in this chapter. Nevertheless, you may want to ask them to review Chapter 3 on audience awareness.

aside from the simplest two- or three-line notes, you should prepare to write, write a draft, and then revise.

LOOKING BACK

The admonition that writing twice actually saves time recalls similar advice offered about critical reading in Chapter 1. Students should also review Chapters 3 and 4 on the process of moving from general idea to finished product; Chapter 17 on clarity, conciseness, and directness; and Chapters 18–20 on sentence style.

ADDITIONAL EXERCISE A

Interview someone in business on the subject of the writing he or she does on the job. Pose questions such as the following: What kinds of writing are you required to do? What are the purposes for your writing? What audiences do you usually address? How do purpose and audience determine the form your writing takes? How much of your time is spent writing? Try to think of some additional questions as well. Use your notes from the interview to write a paragraph describing the role of writing in business.

40a Standard formats, spacing, and information in a business letter

Standard formats

Use unlined, white bond paper (8½ × 11 inches) or letterhead stationery for your business correspondence. Prepare your letter on a typewriter or word processor, and print on one side of the page only. Format your letter according to one of three conventions: full block, block, and semi-block—terms describing the ways in which you indent information. The six basic elements of a letter—return address, inside address and date, salutation, body, closing, and abbreviated matter—begin at the left margin in the *full block* format. Displayed information such as lists begins five spaces from the left margin. In the *block* format, the return address and the closing are aligned just beyond the middle of the page, while the inside address, salutation, new paragraphs, and abbreviated matter each begin at the left margin. (See the "Letter of Inquiry" in 40b for an example of block format.) The *semi-block* format is similar to the block format except that each new paragraph is indented five spaces from the left margin and any displayed information is indented ten spaces. (See the "Letter of Application" in 40d for an example of a semi-block format.)

Standard spacing

Maintain a one-inch margin at the top, bottom, and sides of the page. Single-space the document for all but very brief letters (two to five lines), the body of which you should double-space. Skip one or two lines between the return address and the inside address; one line between the inside address and the salutation (which is followed by a colon); one line between the salutation and opening paragraph; one line between paragraphs; one line between your final paragraph and your complimentary closing (which is followed by a comma); four lines between your closing and typewritten name; and one line between your typewritten name and any abbreviated matter.

Standard information

RETURN ADDRESS AND DATE

Unless you are writing on letterhead stationery (on which your return address is preprinted), type as a block of information your return address—street address on one line; city, state, and zip code on the next; the date on a third line. If you are writing on letterhead, type the date only, centered one or two lines below the letterhead's final line.

Inside address

Provide as a block of information the full name and address of the person to whom you are writing. Be sure to spell all names—personal, company, and address—correctly. Use abbreviations only if the company abbreviates words in its own name or address.

Salutation

Begin your letter with a formal greeting, traditionally *Dear* ____: Unless another title applies, such as *Dr.* or *Senator,* address a man as *Mr.* and a woman as *Miss* or *Mrs.*—or as *Ms.* if you or the person addressed prefer this. When in doubt about a woman's marital status or preferences in a salutation, use *Ms.* If you are not writing to a specific person, avoid the gender-specific and potentially insulting *Dear Sirs.* Many readers find the generic *Dear Sir or Madam* and *To whom it may concern* to be equivocal, and you may want to open instead with the company name, *Dear Acme Printing,* or with a specific department name or position title: *Dear Personnel Department* or *Dear Personnel Manager.* See the discussion at 31a for the conventions on abbreviating titles in a salutation or an address.

Body of the letter

Develop your letter in paragraph form. State your purpose clearly in the opening paragraph. Avoid giving your letter a visually dense impression. When your content lends itself to displayed treatment (if, for instance, you are presenting a list), indent the information. You may want to use bullets, numbers, or hyphens. (See, for example, the "Letter of Inquiry" in 40b.)

Closing

Close with some complimentary expression such as *Yours truly, Sincerely,* or *Sincerely yours.* Capitalize the first word only of this closing remark and follow the remark with a comma. Allow four blank lines for your signature, then type your name and, below that, any title that applies.

Abbreviated matter

Several abbreviations may follow at the left-hand margin, one line below your closing. If someone else has typed your letter, abbreviate initials as follows. Capitalize your initials, place a slash, then place the typist's initials in lowercase—*LR/hb.* If you are enclosing any material with your letter, type *Enclosure* or *Enc.* If you care to itemize this information, place a colon and align items as in the example letter in 40d. If you are sending copies of the letter to other readers (known as a *secondary audience*), write *cc:* (for *carbon copy*) and list the names of the recipients of the copies, as in the example letter in 40f.

The second page

Begin your letter's second page with identifying information so that if the first and second pages are separated the reader will easily be able to match them again. The blocked information should consist of your name, the date, and the page number presented in a block at the upper left-hand corner of the page.

REFERENCES

Barnett, Marva T. *Writing for Technicians.* Albany: Delmar, 1982. Includes chapters on types of letters, résumés, and application inquiries.

Keene, Michael L. "Technical Information in the Information Economy." Rpt. in *Perspectives on Research and Scholarship in Composition.* Ed. Ben W. McClelland and Timothy R. Donovan. New York: Modern Language Association, 1985. A look at recent scholarship in business communication.

Lanham, Richard A. *Revising Business Prose.* New York: Scribner's, 1981. Offers writers the successful methods for business writing (including his plea for writing in plain English) he developed for academic writing in *Revising Prose.*

Mendelson, Michael. "Business Prose and the Nature of the Plain Style." *Journal of Business Communication* 24 (Spring 1987): 3–18. Students should be oriented to various stylistic possibilities as a way of making their content more persuasive.

Odell, Lee, and Dixie Goswami, eds. *Writing in Nonacademic Settings.* New York: Guilford, 1986. Essays by Paul V. Anderson and Janice C. Redish. Indispensable collection of essays for teaching writing in business.

Shenk, Robert. "Ghost-Writing in Professional Communities." *Journal of Technical Writing and Communication* 18 (1988): 377–87. Writers can effectively compose materials to which their department heads may attach signatures.

Sterkel, Karen S. "The Relationship between Gender and Writing Style in Business Communication." *Journal of Business Communication* 25 (Fall 1988): 17–38. An evaluation of business letters written by students of both sexes revealed "no significant [gender] differences"; students do not write as themselves.

40a

FOR DISCUSSION

Some of your students probably have had experience with business letters; some may work in the business world, some may have taken business courses, and some may have written letters of inquiry or complaint. Ask these students to discuss the reasons why the guidelines for business letters are so precise. What purpose does the letter serve in business communications?

```
Jon Lipman
January 7, 1995
Page 2

and in the event of your coming to Worcester, I would
be happy to set up an interview with you here. Perhaps
the week of May 20 would be convenient, since I will be
traveling to eastern Massachusetts.
```

Envelope

Single-space all information. If you are not using an envelope with a preprinted return address, type your return address at the upper left-hand corner. Center between the right- and left-hand sides the name and address of the person to whom you are writing. Vertically, type the address just below center.

```
Jon Lipman
231 Gray Street
Worcester, Massachusetts 01610


                    Ms. Hannah Marks
                    Equipment Design, Inc.
                    1254 Glenn Avenue
                    Arlington, Massachusetts 02174
```

40b Letters of inquiry

A letter of inquiry is based on a question you want answered. Presumably, you have done enough research to have identified a person knowledgeable in the area concerning you. Do not ask for too much information or for very general information that you could readily find in a library. Avoid giving your reader the impression that you are asking him or her for basic information that you should have managed to locate yourself. If you are inquiring about price or product information, simply ask for a brochure.

- Begin the letter with a sentence that identifies your need. State who you are, what your general project is (if the information is pertinent), and the reason for your writing.
- Follow with a sentence devoted to how you have learned of the reader or the reader's company and how this person or company could be of help to you.
- Pose a few *specific* questions. Frame these questions in such a way that you demonstrate you have done background research.
- State any time constraints you may have. Do not expect your reader to respond any sooner than two or three weeks.
- Close with a brief statement of appreciation. If you feel it would expedite matters, you might include a self-addressed, stamped envelope.

ESL CUE

American-style business writing is not standard internationally. In many places a typed letter indicates an impersonal lack of concern while a handwritten letter indicates an attempt to make personal contact and to show personal consideration.

By the standards of most cultures, American-style business letters are rude; they get down to business too quickly and they don't take time for the amenities. For example, a Japanese business letter must make some comment about the beauty of the season: "It is cherry-blossom time in Tokyo today," and introduce the serious business concerns with a casual "by the way . . . " Latin American, Greek, and Arab writers might ask about the reader's family or health, and their greetings will be much more effusive and "flowery" by our standards than our simple "Dear Sir." In many cultures personal statements and questions (about health, family, etc.) provide a friendly, personal touch before getting down to business.

ADDITIONAL EXERCISE B

Following the guidelines provided in this chapter, write a letter of inquiry, complaint, or application. Use either full block, block, or semi-block format as illustrated in the sample letters.

GROUP ACTIVITY

Ask students to use the model business letter as a guide for this activity. In groups of three, have students give each other editorial advice (on both form and content) on the letters composed for Additional Exercise B. Then ask students to discuss the comments and make revisions based on their readers' advice.

Block Format

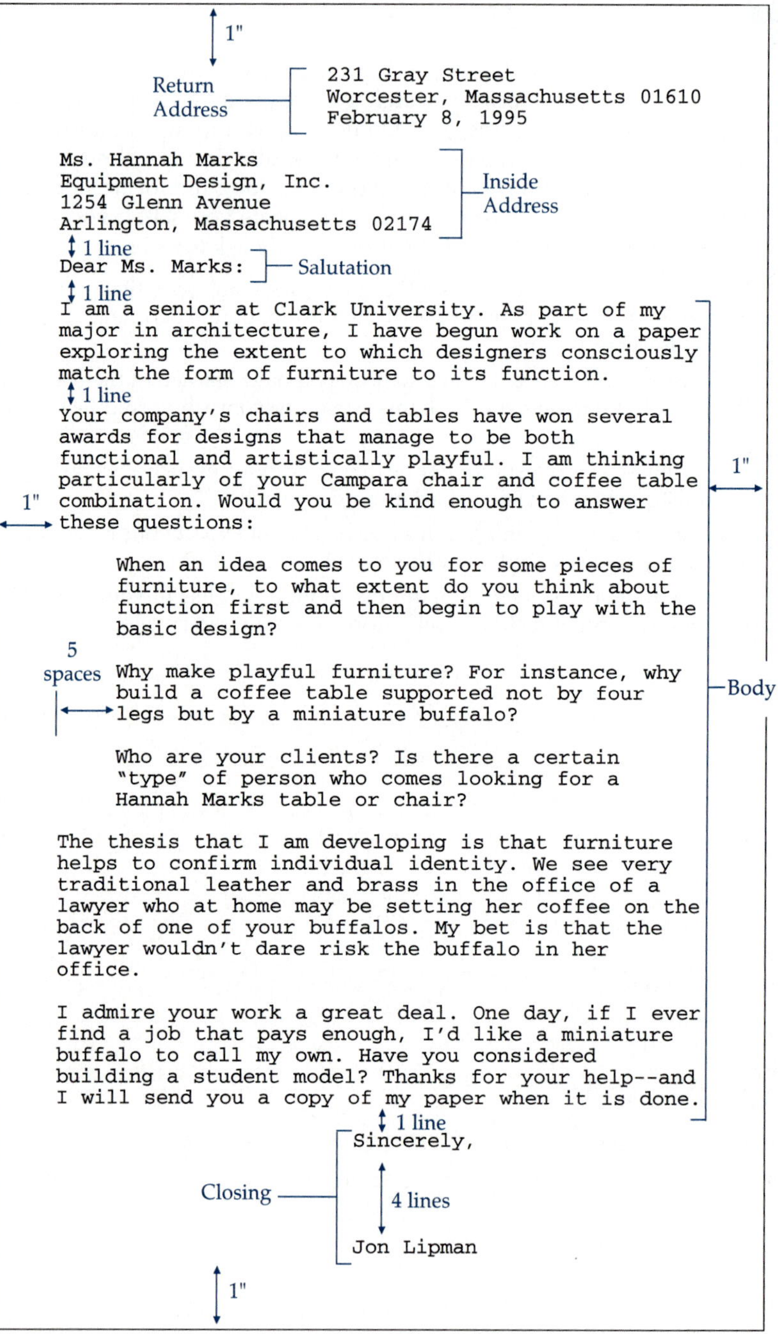
231 Gray Street
Worcester, Massachusetts 01610
February 8, 1995

Ms. Hannah Marks
Equipment Design, Inc.
1254 Glenn Avenue
Arlington, Massachusetts 02174

Dear Ms. Marks:

I am a senior at Clark University. As part of my major in architecture, I have begun work on a paper exploring the extent to which designers consciously match the form of furniture to its function.

Your company's chairs and tables have won several awards for designs that manage to be both functional and artistically playful. I am thinking particularly of your Campara chair and coffee table combination. Would you be kind enough to answer these questions:

When an idea comes to you for some pieces of furniture, to what extent do you think about function first and then begin to play with the basic design?

Why make playful furniture? For instance, why build a coffee table supported not by four legs but by a miniature buffalo?

Who are your clients? Is there a certain "type" of person who comes looking for a Hannah Marks table or chair?

The thesis that I am developing is that furniture helps to confirm individual identity. We see very traditional leather and brass in the office of a lawyer who at home may be setting her coffee on the back of one of your buffalos. My bet is that the lawyer wouldn't dare risk the buffalo in her office.

I admire your work a great deal. One day, if I ever find a job that pays enough, I'd like a miniature buffalo to call my own. Have you considered building a student model? Thanks for your help--and I will send you a copy of my paper when it is done.

Sincerely,

Jon Lipman

40c Letters of complaint

When you have a problem that you want remedied, write a letter of complaint. No matter how irate you may be, keep a civil but firm tone and do not threaten. If the time comes to take follow-up action, write a second letter in which you repeat your complaint and state your intentions. Your letter of complaint should be clear on the following points:

- Present the problem.
- State when and where you bought the product in question (if this is a consumer complaint). Provide an exact model number. If this is a complaint about poor service or ill treatment, state when and where you encountered the unacceptable behavior.
- Describe precisely the product failure or the way in which a behavior was unsatisfactory.
- Summarize the expectations you had when you bought the product or when you engaged someone's services. State succinctly how your expectations were violated and how you were inconvenienced (or worse).
- State exactly how you want the problem resolved.

40d Letters of application

Whether you are applying for summertime work or for a full-time job after graduation, your first move probably will be to write a letter of application in which you ask for an interview. A successful letter of application will pique a prospective employer's interest by achieving a delicate balance. On the one hand you will present yourself as a bright, dependable, and resourceful person while on the other you will avoid sounding like an unabashed self-promoter. Your goal is to show a humble and earnest confidence. As you gather thoughts for writing, think of the employer as someone in need of a person who can be counted on for dependable and steady work, for creative thinking, and for an ability to function amiably as a member of a team. Avoid presenting yourself merely as someone who has a particular set of skills. You are more than this. Skills grow dated as new technologies become available. You want to suggest that your ability to learn and to adapt will never grow dated.

- Keep your letter of application to one typewritten page.
- Open by stating which job you are applying for and where you learned of the job.
- Review your specific skills and work experience that make you well suited for the job.
- Review your more general qualities (in relation to work experience, if appropriate) that make you well suited for the job.

ESL CUE

The letter of complaint was unimaginable and is still relatively unknown in Russia and former USSR nations; students from those areas will not understand the rationale for them and will have no models or standards for such a letter other than the ones provided in the text or by the instructor. Indonesians and other Asians from a similar tradition will understand the concept, but will instinctively be more indirect and polite in such letters because of their culture's emphasis on avoiding direct confrontation.

REFERENCES

ANDERSON, W. STEVE. "The Rhetoric of the Résumé." ERIC, 1984, ED 249 537. Applies James Kinneavy's communication triangle and asserts that students need to attend to the relationship of the writer, text, and reader in order to compose effective résumés.

HALL, DEAN G., and BONNIE A. NELSON. "Initiating Students into Professionalism: Teaching the Letter of Inquiry." *Technical Writing Teacher* 14 (Winter 1987): 86–89. Argues for using the letter of inquiry in a set of assignments that may include a current research topic or a career option.

NORMAN, ROSE. "Résumés: A Computer Exercise for Teaching Résumé-Writing." *Technical Writing Teacher* 15 (1988): 162–66. Offering questions may lead students to discover ways for revising résumés; the computer can illustrate how stylistic changes affect résumés.

- Express your desire for an interview and note any constraints on your time: exams, jobs, and other commitments. Avoid statements like "you can contact me at. . . ." You will provide your address and phone number on your résumé.
- Close with a word of appreciation.

When you have written a second draft of your letter, seek out editorial advice from those who have had experience applying for jobs and particularly from those who have been in a position of reading letters of application and setting up interviews. Here are a few questions you can put to your readers: What sort of person does this letter describe? Am I emphasizing my skills and abilities in the right way? How do you feel about the tone of this letter? Am I direct and confident without being pushy? Based on editorial feedback, revise. Proofread two or three times so that your final document is direct, concise, well organized, and letter-perfect with respect to grammar, usage, and punctuation. Write your letter in a block or semi-block format on bond paper that has a good, substantial feel to it. Use paper with at least a twenty-five percent cotton fiber content, which you will find at any stationery store. Use an envelope of matching bond paper.

Semi-Block Format

231 Gray Street
Worcester, Massachusetts 01610
March 30, 1995

Ms. Hannah Marks
Equipment Design, Inc.
1254 Glenn Avenue
Arlington, Massachusetts 02174

Dear Ms. Marks:

5 spaces

⟷ I would like to apply for the marketing position you advertised in Architectural Digest. As you know from our previous correspondence, I am an architecture major with an interest in furniture design. As part of my course work I took a minor in marketing, with the hope of finding a job similar to the one you have listed.

For the past two summers I have apprenticed myself to a cabinet maker in Berkshire County, Massachusetts. Mr. Hiram Stains is 70 years old and a master at working with cherry and walnut. While I love working in a shop, and have built most of the furniture in my own apartment (see the photographic enclosures), I realize that a craftsman's life is a bit too solitary for me. Ideally, I would like to combine in one job my woodworking skills, my degree in architecture, and my desire to interact with people.

Your job offers precisely this opportunity. I respect your work immensely and am sure I could represent Equipment Design with enthusiasm. Over time, if my suggestions were welcomed, I might also be able to contribute in terms of design ideas.

I would very much like to arrange an interview. Final exams are scheduled for the last week of April. I'll be preparing the week before that, so I'm available for an interview anytime aside from that two-week block. Thank you for your interest, and I hope to hear from you soon.

Sincerely,

Jon Lipman

Jon Lipman

enc.: photographs
writing sample

Align itemized enclosures

ADDITIONAL EXERCISE C

This exercise will help students fine-tune their evaluation skills. In groups of three or four, students should evaluate the effectiveness of the model letter, based on the material covered in the book. Ask students to consider such issues as the intended audience of the letter, its tone, the personality of the writer, and the clarity of the content.

TEACHING IDEAS

Students can benefit from seeing a variety of résumés. Gather a collection—from business writing texts, from friends in business, or from other sources—to distribute to students. In comparing the effectiveness of various forms, students will get a better idea of how to prepare their own résumés.

40e Résumés

A résumé highlights information that you think employers will find useful in considering you for a job. Typically, résumés are written in a clipped form. Although word groups are punctuated as sentences, they are, strictly speaking, fragments. For instance, instead of writing "I supervised fund-raising activities" you would write "Supervised fund-raising activities." Keep these fragments parallel. Keep all verbs in either the present or the past tense; begin all fragments with either verbs or nouns.

NOT PARALLEL Supervised fund-raising activities. Speaker at three area meetings on the "Entrepreneurial Side of the Art World." [The first fragment begins with a verb; the second begins with a noun.]

PARALLEL Supervised fund-raising activities. Spoke at three area meetings on the "Entrepreneurial Side of the Art World." [Both fragments begin with a verb in the past tense.]

A résumé works in tandem with your job application. The letter of application establishes a direct communication between you and your prospective employer. Written in your voice, the letter will suggest intangible elements such as your habits of mind and traits of character that make you an attractive candidate. The résumé, by contrast, works as a summary sheet or catalog of your educational and work experience. The tone of the résumé is neutral and fact-oriented. The basic components are these:

- Your name, address, and telephone number—each centered on its own line at the top of the page.

Provide headings, as follows:

- *Position Desired* or *Objective.* State the specific job you want.
- *Education.* Provide your pertinent college (and graduate school) experience. List degrees earned (or to be earned); major; classes taken, if pertinent; and your grade point average, if you are comfortable sharing this information.
- *Work Experience.* List your jobs, including titles, chronologically, beginning with your most recent job.
- *Related Activities.* List any clubs, volunteer positions, or activities that you feel are indicative of your general interests and character.
- *References.* Provide names and addresses if you expect the employer to contact references directly. If you are keeping references on file at a campus office, state that your references are available upon request.

Jon Lipman
231 Gray Street
Worcester, Massachusetts 01610
508-555-8212

Objective:	Marketing position in an arts-related company
Education:	Clark University, Worcester, Massachusetts Bachelor of Arts in Architecture, May 1995 Minor in Marketing, May 1995 Grade point average (to date) 3.3/4.0
Work Experience:	September 1994-present: Directed marketing campaign for campus-based artists' collective and supervised fund raising. Spoke at three area meetings on the "Entrepreneurial Side of the Art World." Generated community interest in the work of campus artists by organizing a fair and a direct mail program. May 1994-August 1994: Studied cabinet making with Hiram Stains, master cabinetmaker in Berkshire County, Massachusetts. Prepared wood for joining, learned dove-tail technique, and applied design principles learned in school to cabinet construction. September 1993-April 1994: Organized artists' collective on campus and developed marketing plan. May 1993-August 1993: Studied cabinet making with Hiram Stains. Learned tool use and maintenance.
Related Activities:	Supervised set design for theater productions on campus. Donated services as carpenter to local shelter for the homeless. Designed and built virtually all furniture in my apartment.
References:	Mr. Hiram Stains Route 16 Richmond, Massachusetts 01201 Ms. Amanda Lopez Center Street Shelter Worcester, Massachusetts 01610 Dr. Edward Bing Department of Architecture Clark University Worcester, Massachusetts 01610

ADDITIONAL EXERCISE D

Using this résumé as a model, compose one of your own. Be sure that you emphasize your skills and that you pay close attention to layout. Ask for editorial advice from other students, and revise your résumé accordingly.

40f Memoranda

Memoranda, or memos, are internal documents written from one employee to another in the same company. The reasons for writing memos are many: you may want to announce a meeting, summarize your understanding of a meeting, set a schedule, request information, define and resolve a problem, argue for funding, build consensus, and so on. Because they are written "in-house," memos tend to be less formal in tone than business letters; still, they must be every bit as direct, concise, and well organized, or readers will ignore them. When writing a memo longer than a few lines, follow the process discussed earlier of preparing to write, writing, and revising. A memo will differ from a business letter in the following ways:

- The memo has no return address, no inside address, and no salutation. Instead, the memo begins with this information:

  (Date)
  To:
  From:
  Subject:
- The memo follows a full block format, with all information placed flush to the left margin.
- The memo is often divided into headings that separate the document into readily distinguished parts.
- Portions of the memo are often displayed—that is, set off and indented when there are lists or other information lending itself to such treatment.
- Some companies highlight the information about distribution of memo copies to others, either placing the *cc:* line under the *To:* line or adding a subsection titled *Distribution:* with the opening section.

If your memo is three-quarters of a page or longer, consider highlighting its organization with headings, as in the example memo below. Headings work in tandem with the memo's subject line and first sentence to give readers the ability to scan the memo and quickly—within thirty seconds—understand your message. Once again, realize that your readers are busy; they will appreciate any attempt to make their job of reading easier.

ADDITIONAL EXERCISE E

Following the guidelines in this chapter, write a "summary of understanding" memorandum to one of your instructors regarding the deadlines for assignments throughout the semester. Be sure to use the format illustrated in the sample memo.

GROUP ACTIVITY

Ask students to give each other editorial advice (on both form and content) on the memos composed for Additional Exercise E. If students meet in groups of three, each writer will receive feedback from two readers. Ask students to revise their memos based on readers' advice.

ADDITIONAL EXERCISE F

Assuming you received no response to the letter you wrote for Additional Exercise B, write a *second* letter. Assuming you received no response to a follow-up you wrote to the memo for Additional Exercise E, write a *third* memorandum (with a copy to the appropriate department chair). Follow the guidelines in this chapter.

GROUP ACTIVITY

Ask students to give each other editorial advice (on both form and content) on the letters and memos composed for Additional Exercise F. If students meet in groups of three, each writer will receive feedback from two readers. Ask students to revise their letters and memos based on readers' advice.

February 14, 1995

TO: Linda Cohen

FROM: Matthew Franks

SUBJECT: Brochure production schedule

Thanks for helping to resolve the production schedule for our new brochure. Please review the following production and distribution dates. By return memo, confirm that you will commit your department to meeting this schedule.

Production dates

Feb. 19	1995	First draft of brochure copy
March 1	1995	First draft of design plans
March 8	1995	Second draft of brochure copy and design
March 15	1995	Review of final draft and design
March 17	1995	Brochure to printer

Distribution dates

April 4	1995	First printing of 10,000 in our warehouse
April 11	1995	Mailing to Zone 1
April 14	1995	Mailing to Zone 2
April 17	1995	Mailing to Zones 3 and 4

Please let me hear from you by this Friday. If I haven't, I'll assume your agreement and commitment. It looks as though we'll have a good brochure this year. Thanks for all your help.

cc: Amy Hanson

ADDITIONAL EXERCISE G

This exercise will help students further fine-tune their evaluation skills. In groups of three or four, students should evaluate the effectiveness of the model memo, based on the material covered in the book. Ask students to consider such issues as the purpose of the memo, the clarity of information presented, and the layout.

CHAPTER 41

Writing Essay Exams

KEY FEATURES

This chapter advises students to apply the basic principles of reading and writing presented in Chapters 1 through 4 when they write essay exams. Focusing on the importance of critical thinking in preparing for and writing essay exams, the chapter advises students to begin with notes and general ideas, and to move through a compressed writing process as they compose their responses. Reference is also made to Chapters 37 through 39 in advising students to be aware of the specific requirements of different disciplines. Strategies for managing time, for reading exam questions, and for drafting and revising responses are explained in detail. A list of key verbs found in essay questions is reproduced at the end of the chapter, providing students with a valuable reference to guide them in formulating responses.

Increasingly, professors across the curriculum are using essay exams to test student mastery of important concepts and relationships. A carefully conceived exam will challenge you not only to recall and organize what you know of a subject but also to extend and apply your knowledge. Essay exams will require of you numerous responses; but the one response to *avoid* is the so-called information dump in which at first glimpse of a topic you begin pouring onto the page *everything* you have ever read or heard about it. A good answer to an essay exam question requires that you be selective in choosing the information you discuss. What you say about that information and what relationships you make with it are critical. As is often the case with good writing, less tends to be more—provided that you adopt and follow a strategy.

41a A strategy for taking essay exams

Prepare

Ideally, you will have read your textbooks and assigned articles with care *as* they were assigned during the period prior to the exam. If you have read closely, or "critically" (see 1e–1h), your preparation for an exam will amount to a *review* of material you have already thought carefully about. Skim assigned materials and pay close attention to notes you have made in the margins or have recorded in a reading log. Take new notes based on your original notes: highlight important concepts from each assignment. Then reorganize your notes according to key ideas that you think serve as themes or focus points for your course. List each idea separately, and beneath each, list any reading that in some way comments on or provides information about that idea. In an American literature course this idea might be "nature as a character" or "innocence lost." In a sociology course the idea might be "social constructions of identity." Turn next to your class notes (you may want to do this *before* reviewing your reading assignments), and add information and comments to your lists of key ideas. Study these lists. Develop statements about each idea that you could, if asked, support with references to specific information. Try to anticipate your instructor's questions.

Read the entire exam before beginning to write.

Allot yourself a certain number of minutes to answer each essay question, allowing extra time for the more complex questions. As you write, monitor your use of time.

Adopt a discipline-appropriate perspective.

Essay exams are designed in part to see how well you understand particular ways of thinking in a discipline. If you are writing a mid-term exam in chemistry, for instance, appreciate that your professor will expect you to discuss material from a chemist's perspective. That is, you will need to demonstrate not only that you know your information but also that you can *do* things with it: namely, think and reach conclusions in discipline-appropriate ways.

Adapt the writing process according to the time allotted for a question.

Assuming that you have thirty minutes to answer an essay question, spend at least five minutes of this allotted time in plotting an answer.

- Locate the assignment's key verb and identify your specific tasks in writing. (See the box that follows.)
- Given these tasks, list information you can draw on in developing your answer.
- Examine the information you have listed and develop a thesis (see 3d), a statement that directly answers the question and that demonstrates your understanding and application of some key concept associated with the essay topic.
- Sketch an outline of your answer. In taking an essay exam, you have little or no time for writing to discover. Know before you write what major points you will develop in support of your thesis and in what order.

Spend twenty minutes of your allotted time on writing your answer. When you begin writing, be conscious of making clear, logical connections between sentences and paragraphs. Well-chosen transitions (see 5d-3) not only will help your professor follow your discussion but also will help you to project your ideas forward and to continue writing. As you do in formal papers, develop your essay in sections, with each section organized by a section thesis (see 5a). Develop each section of your essay by discussing *specific* information.

Save five minutes to reread your work and ensure that its logic is clear and that you address the exam question from a discipline-appropriate point of view. Given the time constraints of the essay exam format, professors understand that you will not submit a polished draft. Nevertheless, they will expect writing that faces the question and that is coherent, unified, and grammatical. Again, avoid an information dump. Select information with care and write with a strategy.

41b The importance of verbs in an essay question

In reading an essay assignment, you will need to identify a specific topic and purpose for writing. Often, you can identify exactly what an in-

LOOKING BACK

Advice in this chapter relies on a number of previous chapters in the handbook. In particular, students should refer to Chapters 1–2 on critical reading and writing, Chapters 3–4 on the writing process, Chapter 5 on paragraphs, and Chapters 37–39 on writing in the disciplines.

REFERENCES

Bartholomae David, and Anthony Petrosky. *Facts, Artifacts, and Counterfacts: Theory and Method for a Reading and Writing Course.* Upper Montclair, NJ: Boynton, 1986. Discusses the implications of essay examinations in a process-oriented writing course, cautioning that the emphasis may shift from global to local concerns.

Berlin, James A. *Rhetoric and Reality: Writing Instruction in American Colleges, 1900–1985.* Carbondale and Edwardsville, IL: Southern Illinois UP, 1987. Provides history of the essay examination, arguing that it proliferated as a result of a shift in emphasis from rhetoric to poetics.

Biddle, Arthur W., and Toby Fulwiler, eds. *Reading, Writing, and the Study of Literature.* New York: Random, 1989. Useful chapter discussing the writing of essay exams (includes bibliography).

Greenberg, Karen, Harvey S. Weiner, and Richard A. Donovan, eds. *Writing Assessment: Issues and Strategies.* New York: Longman, 1986. Collection of twelve essays on assessment (includes annotated bibliography).

Ottens, Allen J. *Coping with Academic Anxiety.* New York: Rosen Pub. Group, 1984. Provides suggestions for overcoming "test anxiety."

ESL CUE

Native speakers have grown up interpreting the terms standard to class assignments; nonnative speakers have not. They will benefit from the explanatory list in this section and from practice interpreting assignment requirements. For example, what do you *do* when you "discuss" or "evaluate" on an essay exam? European exams reward eloquent style and more abstract and philosophical language over specificity.

REFERENCES

BRUCE, BERTRAM, SARAH MICHAELS, and KAREN WATSON-GEGEO. "How Computers Can Change the Writing Process." *Language Arts* 62 (1985): 143–49.

COSTANZO, WILLIAM. "Language, Thinking, and the Culture of Computers." *Language Arts* 62 (1985): 516–23.

KIEFER, KATHLEEN. "Revising on the Word-Processor: What's Happened, What's Ahead." *ADE Bulletin* 87 (1987): 24–27.

———. "Writing: Using the Computer as Tool." *Computer-Aided Instruction in the Humanities.* Ed. Solveig Olsen. New York: MLA, 1985.

MARCUS, STEPHEN. "Computers and English: Future Tense, Future Perfect?" *English Journal* 76 (1987): 88–90.

OLSEN, SOLVEIG. *Computer-Aided Instruction in the Humanities.* New York: MLA, 1985.

ROSS, DONALD, and LILLIAN S. BRIDWELL. "Computer-Aided Composing: Gaps in the Software." *Computer-Aided Instruction in the Humanities.* Ed. Solveig Olsen. New York: MLA, 1985.

structor expects by locating a key verb in the assignment such as *illustrate, discuss,* or *compare.* Following is a guide to students on "Important Word Meanings" in assignments. Developed by the History Department at UCLA, this guide was intended to help students develop effective responses to essay questions. The guide will serve you well in any of your courses.

Important Word Meanings

Good answers to essay questions depend in part upon a clear understanding of the meanings of the important directive words. These are the words like *explain, compare, contrast,* and *justify,* which indicate the way in which the material is to be presented. Background knowledge of the subject matter is essential. But mere evidence of this knowledge is not enough. If you are asked to *compare* the British and American secondary school systems, you will get little or no credit if you merely *describe* them. If you are asked to *criticize* the present electoral system, you are not answering the question if you merely *explain* how it operates. A paper is satisfactory only if it answers directly the question that was asked.

The words that follow are frequently used in essay examinations:

summarize sum up; give the main points briefly. *Summarize the ways in which man preserves food.*

evaluate give the good points and the bad ones; appraise; give an opinion regarding the value of; talk over the advantages and limitations. *Evaluate the contributions of teaching machines.*

contrast bring out the points of difference. *Contrast the novels of Jane Austen and William Makepeace Thackeray.*

explain make clear; interpret; make plain; tell "how" to do; tell the meaning of. *Explain how man can, at times, trigger a full-scale rainstorm.*

describe give an account of; tell about; give a word picture of. *Describe the Pyramids of Giza.*

define give the meaning of a word or concept; place it in the class to which it belongs and set it off from other items in the same class. *Define the term "archetype."*

compare bring out points of similarity and points of difference. *Compare the legislative branches of the state government and the national government.*

discuss talk over; consider from various points of view; present the different sides of. *Discuss the use of pesticides in controlling mosquitoes.*

criticize state your opinion of the correctness or merits of an item or issue; criticism may approve or disapprove. *Criticize the increasing use of alcohol.*

justify show good reasons for; give your evidence; present facts to support your position. *Justify the American entry into World War II.*

trace follow the course of; follow the trail of; give a description of progress. *Trace the development of television in school instruction.*

(continued)

Important Word Meanings (continued)

interpret make plain; give the meaning of; give your thinking about; translate. *Interpret the poetic line, "The sound of a cobweb snapping is the noise of my life."*

prove establish the truth of something by giving factual evidence or logical reasons. *Prove that in a full-employment economy, a society can get more of one product only by giving up another product.*

illustrate use a word picture, a diagram, a chart, or a concrete example to clarify a point. *Illustrate the use of catapults in the amphibious warfare of Alexander.*

Source: Andrew Moss and Carol Holder, *Improving Student Writing: A Guide for Faculty in All Disciplines* (Dubuque, IA: Kendall/Hunt, 1988) 17–18.

PART XII
ESL REFERENCE GUIDE

The next three chapters are designed to supplement the rest of the *Handbook.* They provide basic information on structural and idiomatic features of the English language that students from an English as a Second Language (ESL) background may need for reference.

These chapters assume that ESL students are now working in a basic English composition course alongside native speakers, and that they have already completed a college-level course of instruction (or its equivalent) in using English as a Second Language. The role of this material is not to provide primary ESL instruction but to give students help in three ways: (1) to identify key topics and problems that persistently cause difficulties for ESL students from many different backgrounds; (2) to propose standard usage guidelines and remedies for such problems (with the assistance of exercises); and (3) to refer ESL students to sections of Chapters 1–41 that will give particular help with difficult language and usage issues in English. Students should also notice that Chapters 7–33 have been furnished with topical "ESL Note" references, which briefly describe key issues and refer readers to pertinent sections of these supplementary chapters.

The following chapters cover topics in the three functional areas of English language usage: Chapter 42—nouns and noun-related structures (including articles and determiners); Chapter 43—verbs, verbals, and related structures (including particles with phrasal verbs); and Chapter 44—usage for modifiers and modifying structures. Prepositions—perhaps the most troublesome feature of English—are treated in connection with the structures that determine them in each chapter of this part. (Prepositions determined by nouns are discussed in 42c; those determined by phrasal verbs are discussed in 43f; and those governed by adjectives are discussed in 44b.)

CHAPTER 42

Using English Nouns, Pronouns, and Articles

42a Using the different classes of English nouns

English nouns name things or people that are considered either countable or not countable in English. English also distinguishes whether a noun names a person or thing that is specific, or something that is generic.

1 Identifying and using count nouns

In English, **count nouns** name things or people that are considered countable. They identify one of many possible individuals or things in the category named. Count nouns have three important characteristics.

- Singular count nouns can be preceded by *one,* or by *a/an*—the indefinite articles that convey the meaning "one (of many)."

  one car a rowboat a truck an ambulance

Singular count nouns can also be preceded by demonstrative pronouns (*this, that*), by possessive pronouns (*my, your, their*), and often by the definite article (*the*).

- Plural count nouns can be preceded by expressions of quantity (*two, three, some, many, a few*) and can use a plural form.

  two cars some rowboats many trucks a few ambulances

- A count noun used as a singular or plural subject must agree with a singular or plural verb form.

  This *car stops* quickly. [A singular subject and verb agree.]
  Other *cars stop* slowly. [A plural subject and verb agree.]

  (See 10a for guidelines on subject–verb agreement.)

2 Forming plurals with count nouns

Plural count nouns are either regular or irregular. Regular nouns form the plural with *-s* or *-es.* Irregular plural forms—such as *man/men, tooth/teeth, wolf/wolves, medium/media*—follow the models shown in 23e. (See rules for plural forms in 10a and in the spelling sections in 23e-1, 3, and 5.)

KEY FEATURES

Teaching ESL students to write well in English in the face of grammatical and cultural interference complicates the already difficult task of the writing instructor, but can also bring unanticipated pleasures and rewards. The former involve helping students face a monumentally difficult task; the latter come from new understandings by the instructor of grammar and rhetoric derived most effectively from contrasts with a radically different system. The ESL Cues in this Instructor's Edition are based on teacher experiences with students at particular schools, and are backed by panels of native speakers at those schools. A caveat is necessary: that all such experiences are shaped and distorted by individual differences and differences *within* cultures. *Your* Chinese students may not experience the problems described in these notes. The task of an ESL teacher, however, is not to lay down certitudes, but rather to generate explanations and "rules" in response to student difficulty.

Identifying and using noncount (mass) nouns

In English, **noncount (mass) nouns** name things that are being considered as a whole, undivided group or category that is not being counted. Noncount (mass) nouns name various kinds of individuals or things that are considered as group categories in English, such as these:

abstractions: courage, grammar
fields of activity: chemistry, tennis
natural phenomena: weather, dew, rain
whole groups of objects: rice, sand, oxygen, wood, oil

Objects that are considered too numerous or shapeless to count are often treated as noncount nouns, as with the word *rock* in this sentence.

We mined dense rock in this mountain.

As such objects become individually identifiable, the same word may be used as a count noun.

Four *rocks* fell across the road.

Some nouns name things that can be considered either countable or noncountable in English, depending on whether they name something specific or something generic.

COUNTABLE (AND SPECIFIC)	A *chicken* or two ran off. A *straw* or two flew up.
NONCOUNTABLE (AND GENERIC)	*Chicken* should be cooked well. *Straw* can be very dry.

Nouns that name generalized or generic things often occur in noncountable form, but may also occur in singular form in scientific usage (see 42a-5).

Three characteristics distinguish noncount (mass) nouns:

- Noncount nouns never use the indefinite article *a/an* (or *one*). (Articles are discussed in detail in 42b.)
- Noncount nouns are never used in a plural form.
- Noncount nouns always take singular verbs. (See 10a for guidelines on subject–verb agreement.)

Using expressions of quantity with count and noncount nouns

Expressions of quantity—such as *many, few, much, little, some,* and *plenty* —are typically used to modify nouns. Some expressions are used to quantify count nouns; some are used with noncount nouns; and others are used with both kinds of nouns.

Count nouns	Noncount nouns	Both count and noncount nouns
many potatoes	*much* rice	*lots of* potatoes and rice
few potatoes	*little* rice	*plenty of* potatoes and rice
		some, any potatoes and rice

When the context is very clear, these expressions can also be used alone as pronouns.

Do you have *any* potatoes or rice?
I have *plenty* if you need *some.*

5 Using nouns in specific and generic senses

English nouns show differences in usage between nouns that name specific things or people and nouns that name generalized or generic things.

A definite noun The whale migrated thousands of miles.
The whales migrated thousands of miles. [When a noun names something very specific, either singular or plural, it is preceded by the **definite article** (or by demonstrative pronouns *this/that*).]

An indefinite noun A whale surfaced nearby; then several whales surfaced. [When a noun names something indefinite but countable, the **indefinite article** is used.]

Generic usage Whales are migratory animals.
A whale is a migratory animal. [When the reference is to a general group, nouns often use either the **plural with no article** or the **singular with an indefinite article.**]

Scientific usage The whale is a migratory animal.
Whales are migratory animals. [A generic noun may also be singular or plural with a definite article (see 42b-2).]

6 Distinguishing pronouns in specific and indefinite or generic uses

Most pronouns, including personal pronouns, rename and refer to a noun located elsewhere that names a specific individual or thing. However, indefinite pronouns, such as *some, any, one, someone,* or *anyone,* may refer to a noun in an indefinite or generic sense.

Personal pronoun Where are my pencils? I need *them.* [Meaning: I need specific pencils that are mine.]

Indefinite pronoun Where are my pencils? I need *some.* [Meaning: I need generic, indefinable pencils; I will use any I can find.]

(The list in 7a-7 gives terms that describe various classes of pronouns.)

ESL CUE

Some languages, such as Russian, Korean, and Japanese, have no articles, so the concept of the article, not just our distinction between definite and indefinite, will need explanation. Some languages that do have articles do not make the general/specific distinction English speakers make. Because of Spanish and Italian pronunciation of "*i*," speakers of those languages may confuse "this" and "these."

42b Using articles with nouns

Articles are the most important class of words used in English to show whether nouns are being used as count or noncount nouns, or as specific or generic nouns. There are three articles in English: *a, an,* and *the. Some,* the indefinite pronoun, is occasionally used as if it were an indefinite article.

1 Nouns sometimes take the indefinite articles *a* and *an.*

The indefinite articles *a* and *an* are grammatically the same. They are singular indefinite articles that mean "one (of many)," and they are used only with singular count nouns. Pronunciation determines which to use. *A* precedes a noun beginning with a consonant or a consonant sound (a bottle, a hotel, a youth, a user, a xylophone). *An* precedes a noun beginning with a vowel or vowel sound (an egg, an hour, an undertaker).

A is sometimes used with the quantifiers *little* and *few.* Note the differences in the following examples.

Example	Meaning
a little, a few a few onions a little oil	a small amount of something
little, few few onions little oil	a less-than-expected amount of something

A and *an* are rarely used with proper nouns, which usually identify a unique individual rather than one of many. The indefinite article occasionally appears with a proper noun in a hypothetical statement about one of many possible persons or things in the category named, as in this sentence.

> Dr. King dreamed of *an America* where children of all colors would grow up in harmony. [We may dream of more than one possible "America."]

2 Nouns sometimes take the definite article *the.*

Use *the* with specific singular and plural count nouns and with noncount nouns.

Specific nouns

> I need *the tool* and *the rivets.* [one singular and one plural noun]
>
> I need *the equipment.* [a noncount noun]
>
> I need *the tool* on *the top shelf.*
> I need *the tools* that are painted orange.
> I need *the smallest tool* on *that shelf.*
>
> [Note the modifiers, clauses, and phrases that make the nouns specific.]

GENERIC NOUNS

I need tools for that work. [In this case, no article is used.]

(For varieties of usage with generic nouns, see 42a-5.)

Use *the* in a context where a noun has previously been mentioned, or where the writer and the reader both know the particular thing or person being referred to.

I saw a giraffe at the zoo. *The giraffe* was eating leaves from a tree.

I stopped at an intersection. When *the light* turned green, I started to leave. [The sentence assumes the existence of a particular traffic light at the intersection.]

Other uses of the definite article

- Use *the* with items that are to be designated as one of a kind (*the* sun, *the* moon, *the* first, *the* second, *the* last).
- Use *the* with official names of countries when it is needed to give specific meaning to nouns like *union, kingdom, state(s), republic, duchy,* and so on (*the* United States, *the* Republic of Cyprus, *the* Hashemite Kingdom of Jordan). No article is needed with certain other countries (Cyprus, Jordan, Japan, El Salvador).
- Use *the* when a noun identifies institutions or generic activities *other than sports,* and in certain usages for generic groups (see 42a-5).

  We called *the* newspapers, *the* radio, and *the* news services.

  Sergei plays *the* piano, *the* flute, and *the* guitar.

  The whales are migratory animals. *The* birds have feathers.

  WITHOUT AN ARTICLE Nadia plays basketball, hockey, and volleyball.
- Use *the* with names of oceans, seas, rivers, and deserts.

  the Pacific *the* Amazon *the* Himalayas *the* Sahara

  WITHOUT AN ARTICLE Lake Michigan Mt. Fuji
- Use *the* to give specific meaning to expressions using the noun *language,* but not for the proper name of a language by itself.

  He studied the Sanskrit language, not the Urdu language.

  WITHOUT AN ARTICLE He studied Sanskrit, not Urdu.
- Use *the* with names of colleges and universities containing *of.*

  He studied at *the* University *of* Michigan.

  WITHOUT AN ARTICLE (TYPICALLY) He studied at Michigan State University.

3 Nouns sometimes take no article.

Typically no article is needed with names of unique individuals, because they do not need to be made specific and they are not usually counted as one among many. In addition, nouns naming generalized persons or things in a generic usage commonly use no article: *Managers often work long hours. Whales are migratory animals.* (See 42a-5.)

Some situations in which no article is used are shown in 42b-2. Here are some others.

- Use no article with proper names of continents, states, cities, and streets, and with religious place names.

  Europe Alaska New York Main Street heaven hell

- Use no article with titles of officials when accompanied by personal names; the title effectively becomes part of the proper noun.

  President Truman King Juan Carlos Emperor Napoleon

- Use no article with fields of study.

  Ali studied literature. Juan studied engineering.

- Use no article with names of diseases.

  He has cancer. AIDS is a very serious disease.

- Use no article with names of magazines and periodicals, unless the article is part of the formal title.

  Life *Popular Science* *Sports Illustrated*

  BUT: *The New Yorker* [The article is part of the proper name.]

42c Using nouns with prepositions

Some of the complex forms of prepositions in English are determined by their use with nouns. Nouns that follow prepositions are called **objects of prepositions** (see 7a-8 and 8b-1); this grouping forms a modifying **prepositional phrase** (7d-1). The distinctive function of such modifying phrases often determines which preposition to choose in an English sentence.

1 Using the preposition *of* to show possession

The preposition *of* is often widely used to show possession as an alternative to the possessive case form (*I hear a man's voice. I hear the voice of a man*). It is also widely used to show possession for many nouns that do not usually take a possessive form. For example, many inanimate nouns, as well as some nouns naming a large group of people (*crowd, mob, company*) or a location (*place, center*), are not typically used with a possessive case form, and are likely to show possession with the preposition *of.*

FAULTY I washed the *car's hood.*

CORRECT I washed the *hood of her car.*

FAULTY *The Information Center's* location is unknown.

CORRECT The location *of the Information Center* is unknown.

The preposition *of* is not used with proper nouns.

ESL CUE

There is little logic to English speakers' use of prepositions, and such use differs in British and American English. In fact, American usage can vary as well ("stand on line"—East Coast; "stand in line"—other regions). ESL students may *never* master English prepositions completely and *should not be expected to.* There are some rules to help with prepositions of location, but even a seemingly bilingual student can be recognized as a nonnative speaker by occasional preposition misuse.

Occasionally, a helpful rule can be invented; for instance, most English words beginning with "co-," "col-," "com-," "con-," or "cor-," take the preposition "with," as in "cooperate with," "collaborate with," "communicate with," "connect with," "correspond with," because this prefix carries the idea of "together." "On" used for location frequently refers to the surface and "in" to the interior as in "on the desk" as opposed to "in the desk." You use "on" if you must step up to board ("get on a bus," "get on a train," "get on a large ship") but "in" if you must step down ("get in a small boat," "get in a car"). Contrast "*in* a canoe" with "*on* a raft." The best rule for "on" and "in" contrasts "touching" and "enclosed": "Those who ride *on* the back of a tiger are in danger of ending up *in* the tiger" (with apologies to J. F. Kennedy).

Multiword prepositions will be the hardest ones for nonnative speakers to recognize as prepositions, and prepositions used in two- and three-part verbs—called *particles* (see 43f)—will confuse every nonnative speaker of English.

FAULTY I washed the *car of Luisa.*

CORRECT I washed *Luisa's car.*

2 Using prepositions in phrases with nouns or pronouns

The distinctive function of a modifying prepositional phrase often determines which preposition to choose in an English sentence. Here are a few typical functions for prepositional phrases, with distinctive prepositions in use.

Function	*Preposition*	*Example/Explanation*
Passive voice (9g)	*by* the cook	He was insulted *by* the cook.
	with a snowball	I was hit *with* a snowball.
Time expressions	*on* January 1	use for specific dates
	on Sundays	use for specific days
	in January	use for months
	in 1984	use for years
	in spring	use for seasons
	at noon, *at* 5 P.M.	use for specific times
	by noon, *by* 5 P.M.	use to indicate *before* a specific hour
	by April 15	use to indicate *before* a specific date
Locations	*at* 301 South Street	use for an address
	in the house	
	on the floor	
Directions	*onto* the floor	
	beside the library	
	through the window	
	into the air	

For information on verbs with prepositions, see 43f; for information on adjectives with prepositions, see 44b.

EXERCISE 1

Complete the following sentences with *a, an, the,* or *some,* or write *X* for no article.

1. Please pass me ____ butter. I usually eat ____ bread with lunch.
2. Today we watched ____ policeman arguing with ____ driver. ____ driver didn't understand ____ English.
3. You need ____ furniture. You should buy ____ chair and borrow ____ round green table in my house.

Choose the correct form.

4. He admired (Sam's motorcycle) (the motorcycle of Sam) where it stood in the (driveway's center) (center of the driveway).
5. Meet me (on) (in) (at) March 15 (on) (at) the theater (on) (in) (at) six o'clock.

EXERCISE 1

1. the; X
2. a; a; The; X
3. some; a; the
4. Sam's motorcycle; center of the driveway
5. on; at; at

CHAPTER 43

Using English Verbs

43a Distinguishing different types of verbs and verb constructions

A verb, the main word in the predicate of an English sentence, asserts the action undertaken by the subject or else the condition in which the subject exists. The four types of verbs include transitive verbs (which take direct objects), intransitive verbs (which do not take direct objects), linking verbs, and helping or auxiliary verbs (which show tense or mood). Although only transitive verbs can show passive voice, most verbs can show various tenses and mood. (See Chapter 9 for a discussion of verb usage.)

1 Transitive and intransitive verbs work differently.

A **transitive verb** can take an object. Examples of transitive verbs include *throw* and *take.*

subject	verb	object	subject	verb	object
He	throws	a pass.	They	took	the ball.

Because transitive verbs can take an object, most of them can operate in both the active and passive voices.[1] The active and the passive forms of the verb may be similar in meaning, but the emphasis changes with the rearrangement of the subject and object, as well as with changes in the verb form (to the past participle with *be*).

subject	verb	object	subject	verb	modifiers
Workers in Ohio	make	Hondas.	Hondas	are made	(by workers) in Ohio.
active voice			passive voice		

Notice how the active-voice object *Hondas* in the first sentence becomes the passive-voice subject in the second. In a passive-voice sentence the original performer of the action (*workers* in the example) is not emphasized and may even be omitted. (See 9g on the uses of passive constructions.)

By contrast, an **intransitive verb** never takes an object and can never be used in the passive voice. Examples of intransitive verbs include *smile* and *go.*

subject	verb	subject	verb
The politician	smiled.	He	went into the crowd.

---

[1]**Exceptions:** Transitive verbs *have, get, want, like,* and *hate* are seldom used in passive voice.

2 Linking verbs are used in distinctive patterns.

Linking verbs, the most common example of which is *be*, serve in sentences as "equals signs" to link a subject with an equivalent noun or adjective. Some other linking verbs are *appear, become,* and *seem.* (See 11d for a full list and description of linking verbs; see also 7b, Pattern 5.)

Things *seem* unsettled.
Shall I *become* a doctor?

Expletives

Linking verbs also serve in a distinctive English construction that uses changed word order with an **expletive** word, *there* or *it*. Expletives are used only with linking verbs, as in these sentences.

It *is* important to leave now. It *appears* unnecessary to do that.
There *seems* to be a problem. It *seems* important.

There and *it* form "dummy subjects" or filler words that occupy the position of the subject in a normal sentence; the true subject is elsewhere in the sentence, and the verb agrees with the true subject (see 10a-8).

Expletive in subject position	True subject
There is a cat in that tree.	*A cat* is in that tree.
There are some cats in the tree.	*Some cats* are in the tree.
It is convenient to use the train.	*To use the train* is convenient.

The expletive *it* also has a unique role in expressing length of time with *take* followed by an infinitive.

It takes an hour to get home by car. *It took* us forever.

Expletive constructions are important and useful for length-of-time expressions and for short or emphatic statements.

It is a tale of great sorrow. There were no survivors.

However, in complex and formal English sentences, the "dummy subject" expletive becomes an unnecessary word obscuring the true subject. The expletive also encourages using linking verbs instead of more direct, active verbs—transitive or intransitive verbs. To eliminate wordiness and promote the clear, direct style that is preferred in English academic prose, try to avoid expletives; revise sentences to restore normal word order (see 17a-3).

ESL CUE

A general distinction between the expletive "there" and the expletive "it" is that "there" is normally followed by a noun while "it" is normally followed by an adjective, except in cases of identification, time, and distance.

43b Changing verb forms

Verb forms express *tense,* an indication of when an action or state of being occurs. The three basic tenses in English are the past, the present, and the future. (See 9a for a discussion of the forms of English verbs, and 9e-1, 2 for a basic discussion of tenses.)

1 Not all verbs use progressive tense forms.

Each of the three basic tenses has a progressive form, made up of *be* and the present participle (the *-ing* form of the verb). The progressive tense emphasizes the *process* of doing whatever action the verb asserts. The tense is indicated by a form of *be:* present progressive (I *am going*), past progressive (I *was going*), past perfect progressive (I *had been going*), future progressive (I *will be going*). For examples, see 9e and 9f.

Certain verbs are generally *not* used in the progressive form; others have a progressive use only for process-oriented or ongoing meanings of the verb.

Words that are rarely seen in a progressive form

Think (in the sense of "believe"): "I think not."

EXCEPTION: The progressive form can be used for a process of considering something.

FAULTY I *am thinking* it is wrong.

CORRECT I *am thinking* about changing jobs. [considering]

Believe, understand, recognize, realize, remember: "You believe it."

EXCEPTION: The last four can sometimes use the progressive form if a process of recognition or recollection is meant: "He is slowly realizing the truth." "He is gradually remembering what happened."

Belong, possess, own, want, need: "We want some." "We once owned it."

Have: "You have what you need."

EXCEPTION: The progressive form can be used in the sense of "experiencing."

FAULTY Maria *is having* a car.

CORRECT Mary *is having* a baby. [experiencing childbirth]

Maria *is having* success in her project.

Be, exist, seem: "This seems acceptable."

EXCEPTION: The progressive form is used only with an abstract emphasis on a process of "being" or "seeming": "Just existing from day to day is enough."

Smell, sound, and **taste** as intransitive verbs, as in "It smells good"; "it sounds funny"; "it tastes bad."

Appear in the sense of "seem": "It appeared to be the right time."

EXCEPTION: Sometimes the progressive form is used in the sense of presenting itself/oneself over a time period. "She's appearing nightly as the star actress."

See: "I can never see why you do it."

EXCEPTION: The progressive form is used in the sense of interviewing someone or witnessing or experiencing something.

FAULTY I *am seeing* an airplane now.

REVISED I *am seeing* a new patient. [interviewing]

Surprise, hate, love, like: "It surprises me"; "I hate lima beans."

Using the perfect forms

The perfect tense is made up of *have* and the past participle (the *-ed* form of the verb). The form of *have* indicates the tense: present perfect (*has* worked), past perfect (*had* worked), and future perfect (*will have* worked). (See 9e and 9f; also 9b, irregular past participles.)

Sometimes students confuse the use of the simple past with the use of the present perfect. The present perfect is used when an action or state of being that began in the past continues to the present; it is also used to express an action or state of being that happened at an indefinite time in the past.

PRESENT PERFECT Linda has worked in Mexico since 1987.

PRESENT PERFECT Ann has worked in Mexico. [The time is unspecified.]

By contrast, the simple past is used when an action or state of being began *and ended* in the past.

SIMPLE PAST Linda worked in Mexico last year. [She no longer works there.]

Since or *for* with perfect tenses in prepositional phrases of time

A phrase with *since* requires using the present perfect (*has worked*) or past perfect tenses (*had worked*); it indicates action beginning at *a single point in time* and still continuing at the time shown by the verb tense.

She [has/had worked] *since* noon
since July
since 1991
since the end of the school year
since the last storm
since the baby was born

A time phrase with *since* cannot have a noun object that shows plural time; *since* phrases must indicate a single point in time.

FAULTY He lived here since three months.
I am here since May.

REVISED He has lived here *for* three months.
I have been here since May.

Also, a time phrase with *since* cannot modify a simple past tense or any present tense.

ESL CUE

ESL students may need help distinguishing between "since," which takes a specific initial time (since 3 P.M.; since July 3) and "for," which takes a length or period of time (for two hours; for 10 days).

Faulty He lived here since three months.
I am here since May.

Revised He *had lived* here since February.
I *have been* here since May.

The perfect tenses can have a time modifier with a prepositional phrase formed either with *since* or *for.*

He has worked since noon.
He had worked for a month.

A modifying phrase with *for* indicates action *through a duration of time.*

He [has/had worked] *for* three hours
for a month and a half
for two years
for a few weeks

When a phrase uses a plural noun, thus showing duration of time, this signals that the preposition in the modifier must be *for,* not *since.*

Faulty I had worked on it since many years.

Revised I had worked on it for many years.

3 Using the varied forms of English future tenses

The following list shows different ways of expressing the future.

Verb form	Explanation
She *will call* us soon. She *is going to* call us soon.	These examples have the same meaning.
The movie *arrives* in town tomorrow. The next bus *leaves* in five minutes. The bus *is leaving* very soon.	The simple present and the present progressive are used to express definite future plans, as from a schedule.
Your flight *is taking off* at 6:55. The doctor *is operating* at once. I *am calling* them right now.	The present progressive is sometimes used to make strong statements about the future.
Hurry! The movie *is about to* begin. Finish up! The bell *is about to* ring.	The "near" future is expressed by some form of *be* plus *about to* and a verb.
It's cold. *I'm going to* get a sweater. It's cold. *I'll lend* you a sweater.	This suggests a plan. This suggests a willingness.

Verbs expressing thoughts about future actions, such as *intend* and *hope,* are not used in any future tense, and the verb *plan* uses a future tense only in the idiomatic *plan on* (to make or follow a plan).

Faulty I will intend to meet my friends tomorrow.

Revised I intend to meet my friends tomorrow.
I plan to attend college.

See 43b-5 for guidelines on expressing future time in conditional sentences.

4 Using verb tenses in sentences with a sequence of actions

In complex sentences that have more than one verb, it is important to adjust the sequence of verb tenses to avoid confusion. See the discussion on verb tense combinations in 9f.

Verb tenses with reported speech

Reported speech, or indirect discourse, is very different from directly quoted speech, which gives the exact verb tense of the original.

Direct speech Ellie said, "He is taking a picture of my boat."

Indirectly quoted speech may occasionally be reported immediately.

Reported speech Ellie just said [that] he is taking a picture of her boat.

Some kinds of reported speech can be summarized with verbs like *tell, ask, remind,* and *urge,* followed by an infinitive:

Reported speech Ellie asked him to take a picture of her boat.

Most often, however, reported speech has occurred sometime before the time of the main verb reporting it. In English, the indirect quotation then requires changes in verb tense and pronouns.

Reported speech She said [that] he had taken a picture of her boat.

In this situation, the reported speech itself takes the form of a *that* noun clause (although the word *that* is often omitted); its verb tense shifts to past tense, following the guidelines shown in 9f-1 for tense sequences.

The following table shows the patterns for changing verb tenses, verb forms, and modal auxiliaries in reported speech or indirect discourse.

Direct Speech		*Reported Speech*
Tenses:		
present Ellie said, "I like horses."	→	**past** Ellie said [that] she liked horses.
past Ellie said, "I rode the horse."	→	**past perfect** Ellie said [that] she had ridden the horse.
present progressive Ellie said, "I'm going riding."	→	**past progressive** Ellie said [that] she was going riding.

(continued)

Direct Speech	Reported Speech
Tenses:	
present perfect	→ **past perfect**
Ellie said, "I have ridden there."	Ellie said [that] she had ridden there.
past progressive	→ **past perfect progressive**
She said, "I was out riding."	She said [that] she had been out riding.
***past perfect**	→ **past perfect**
She said, "I had ridden there."	She said [that] she had ridden there.
Auxiliary verbs:	
can	→ **could**
She said, "I can show him."	She said [that] she could show him.
will	→ **would**
She said, "I will ride again."	She said [that] she would ride again.
***could**	→ **could**
She said, "I could ride."	She said [that] she could ride.
***would**	→ **would**
She said, "I would go."	She said [that] she would go.

Note: The asterisked verbs do not change form as they undergo tense shifts.

Conventions for maintaining consistency with direct and indirect discourse in English are discussed in 16d; punctuation is discussed in 28a-1.

5 Using verb tenses in conditional and subjunctive sentences

Conditional sentences talk about situations that are either possible in the future or else unreal or hypothetical (contrary to fact) in the present or past. Conditional sentences typically contain the conjunction *if* or a related conditional term (*unless, provided that, only if, (only) after, (only) when,* etc.). The following are guidelines for using verb forms in conditional sentences.

Possible or real statements about the future

Use the present tense to express the condition in possible statements about the future; in the same sentence, use the future to express the result of that condition.

	conditional + present	future (*will* + base form)
REAL STATEMENT	*If I have* enough money,	*I will go* next week.
	When I get enough money,	*I will go.*
	[**Meaning:** The speaker may have enough money.]	

Hypothetical or unreal statements about the future

Use the past subjunctive form (which looks like a past tense) with sentences that make "unreal" or hypothetical statements about the future; in the same sentence, use the past form of a modal auxiliary (usually *would, could,* or *might*) to express an unreal result of that stated condition.

	***If* + past**	**past form of modal (*would*)**
UNREAL STATEMENT	*If you found* the money,	*you would go* next week.
	[**Meaning:** The speaker now is fairly sure you will not have the money.]	

Hypothetical or unreal statements about the past

Use the subjunctive with appropriate perfect tense verb forms with sentences that make hypothetical or unreal statements about the past. Use the past perfect tense for the unreal statement about the past. In the same sentence, use the past form of the modal auxiliary plus the present perfect to express the unreal result.

	***If* + past perfect (*had made*)**	**past modal + present perfect (*would*) (*have gone*)**
UNREAL STATEMENT	*If I had made* money,	*I would have gone* last week.
	[**Meaning:** At that time the speaker did not have the money.]	

For more on the subjunctive, see 9h-1; for more on modal auxiliaries, see 43d.

6 Expressing a wish or suggestion for a hypothetical event

In stating a wish in the present that might hypothetically occur, use the *past subjunctive* (which looks like the past tense) in the clause expressing the wish. (The object of the wish takes the form of a *that* clause, although the word *that* is often omitted.)

present	**[that]**	**past subjunctive (like past tense)**
He *wishes*	[that]	she *had* a holiday.
I *wish*	[that]	I *were* on vacation.

The auxiliaries *would* and *could* (which have the same form in the present and past tenses) are often used to express the object of a wish.

present	**[that]**	***would/could* + base form**
I *wish*	[that]	she *would stay.*
We *wish*	[that]	we *could take* a vacation day.

In stating a wish made in the past or present for something that hypothetically might have occurred in the past, use the past perfect in the *that* clause. (The verb *wish* may be expressed either in the past or in the present tense.)

present OR past	**[that]**	**past perfect *[had worked]***
I wished	[that]	I *had* not *worked* yesterday.
I wish	[that]	it *had been* a holiday.

See 9h-4 for guidelines on using the subjunctive mood with *that* clauses.

Expressing a recommendation, suggestion, or urgent request

In stating a recommendation, suggestion, or urgent request, use the *present subjunctive*—the base form of the verb (*be, do*)—in the *that* clause (see 9h).

present	[that]	present subjunctive = base form
We *suggest*	[that]	he *find* the money.
We *advise*	[that]	you *be* there on time.

(See 9h-4 for comments on the subjunctive in this form.)

EXERCISE 1

1. wanted
2. smelled
3. heard
4. had wanted; would have gotten
5. could do

EXERCISE 1

Circle the appropriate verb form.

1. Sam insisted that she (wants/wanted) something to drink.
2. For some reason it (smelled/was smelling) very strange.
3. Many years ago I (heard/have heard) an unusual story.
4. Perhaps if you (had wanted/would have wanted) the job, you (would have gotten/had gotten) some money.
5. She wishes that she (could do/can do) a good job.

43c Changing word order with verbs

1 Invert the subject and all or part of the verb to form questions.

The subject and verb are inverted from normal order to form questions. The following patterns are used with the verb *be,* with modal auxiliaries, with progressive forms, and with perfect forms.

	Normal Statement Form	*Question Form*
Be	He *is* sick today.	*Is he* sick today?
Modals	She *can* help us.	*Can she* help us?
Progressive	They *are* studying here.	*Are they* studying here?
Perfect	It *has* made this sound before.	*Has it* made this sound before?

Questions (and negatives) with the auxiliary *do/does*

Verbs other than those shown above use the auxiliary verbs *do/does* to form questions, and also to form negatives with *not.* In this form, when the auxiliary verb *do/does* is added, the verb changes to the base form (the dictionary form). Use this pattern for the simple present and simple past:

Question Form / Negative Form: Do + Base Form

STATEMENT He *gets on* this bus.

QUESTION *Does* he *get on* this bus?

NEGATIVE	He *does not get on* this bus.
AVOID	Does he *gets on* this bus? [Needs a base form.]
STATEMENT	She *finishes* at noon.
QUESTION	*Does* she *finish* at noon?
NEGATIVE	She *does not finish.*
AVOID	Does she *finishes* at noon? [Needs a base form.]
STATEMENT	It *ran* better yesterday.
QUESTION	*Did* it *run* better yesterday?
NEGATIVE	It *did not run* better.
AVOID	Did it *ran* better yesterday? [Needs a base form.]
STATEMENT	They *arrived* at noon.
QUESTION	When *did* they *arrive?*
NEGATIVE	They *did not arrive.*
AVOID	When do they *arrived?* [Needs a base form.]

For more on auxiliary verbs, see the listings in 9c and in 43d.

2 Invert the subject and verb in some emphatic statements.

The question form is also used with auxiliaries or expletives in some emphatic statements that begin with adverbs such as *never, rarely,* and *hardly,* producing a negative meaning.

NORMAL	EMPHATIC
There is never an easy answer.	Never *is there* an easy answer to that.
They have rarely come to check.	Rarely *have they* come to check the work.

43d Using the helping verbs: Auxiliaries and modal auxiliaries

1 Auxiliary verbs, or helping verbs, are part of basic grammar.

The basic auxiliary verbs (*be, will, have, do*) are used to show tense, to form questions, to show emphasis, and to show negation.

To show tense, or aspect (*be, will, have*): He is driving. She has driven.
To form questions (*do/does*): Do they drive? Why do you drive?
To show negation (*do + not*): I do not drive there.
To show emphasis (*do/does*): She does drive sometimes.

Use modal auxiliaries for a wide range of meanings.

Modal auxiliaries include *can, could, may, might, should, would,* and *must,* as well as the four modals that always appear with the particle *to: ought to, have to, able to,* and *have got to.* The base form of the verb (the dictionary form) is always used with a modal auxiliary, whether the time reference is to the future, present, or past. For a past time reference, use the modal plus the past perfect (*have* + the past participle).

Meaning Expressed	*Present Time or Past Time*	*Modal + Past Perfect*
ability and permission	She can drive.	
	She could drive.	She could have driven.
possibility	She may drive.	
	She might drive.	She might have driven.
advisability	She should drive.	She should have driven.
	She ought to drive.	She ought to have driven.
	She had better drive.	
necessity	She must drive.	
	She has to drive.	She had to drive.
negative necessity	She does not have to drive. [she need not]	
versus prohibition*	She must not drive. [she is not allowed]	

*Note that the two negatives above have very different meanings.

Some idiomatic expressions with modals

Some other idiomatic expressions with modals are expressed in the following list.

EXAMPLE	MEANING
I *would rather* drive than fly.	I prefer driving to flying.
We *would talk* for hours.	We always talked for hours then.
She has car keys, so she *must* drive.	[must = probably does]
Shall we dance again?	I'm inviting you to dance again.
Would you mind turning the heat up?	[would you mind = would you object to]
Do you mind turning it off?	Please turn it off.

Choosing gerunds and infinitives with verbs

There are three types of verbals: infinitives, gerunds, and participles (see 7a-4).

Using infinitives and gerunds as nouns

Use an infinitive or a gerund to function either as a subject or as an object.

As subjects	*To be one of the leaders here* is not really what I want. *His being one of the leaders here* is unacceptable.
As objects	I don't really want *to be one of the leaders here.* I don't accept *his being one of the leaders here.*

Note: The possessive case is used with gerunds; see 8c-2. (See 7a-4 and 7d-2, 3 for basic definitions and examples of verbals. See 44a-1 for participles that function as modifiers, and 43b-1 for participles in the progressive form of English verbs.)

2 Learning idiomatic uses of verb/verbal sequences

Sometimes it is difficult to determine which verbs are followed by a gerund, which are followed by an infinitive, and which can be followed by either verbal. This usage is idiomatic and must be memorized; there are no rules to govern these forms. Note in the following examples that verb tense does not affect a verbal.

Verb + Gerund	*Verb + Infinitive*	*Verb + Either Verbal*
enjoy I enjoy swimming.	**want** I want to swim now.	**begin** Today I begin swimming. Today I begin to swim.
go I went swimming.	**agree** I agreed to swim.	**continue** I continued swimming. I continued to swim.
enjoy + gerund	want + infinitive	begin + either verbal
go + gerund	agree + infinitive	continue + either verbal
finish + gerund	decide + infinitive	like + either verbal
recommend + gerund	need + infinitive	prefer + either verbal
risk + gerund	plan + infinitive	start + either verbal
suggest + gerund	seem + infinitive	love + either verbal
consider + gerund	expect + infinitive	hate + either verbal
postpone + gerund	fall + infinitive	can't bear + either verbal
practice + gerund	pretend + infinitive	can't stand + either verbal

Note: There is no difference in meaning between *I begin to swim* and *I begin swimming.* However, sentences with other verbs differ in meaning depending on whether a gerund or an infinitive follows the verb. This difference in meaning is a function of certain verbs. See the following examples.

Example	Meaning
I always remember *to lock* the car.	I always remember to do this.
I remember *locking* the car.	I remember that I did this.
They stop *to drink* some water.	They stopped in order to drink.
They stopped *drinking* water.	They didn't drink anymore.

Information on idiomatic usage is provided in ESL dictionaries such as the *Longman Dictionary of American English: A Dictionary for Learners of English,* 1983.

ESL CUE

Students should be reminded that because gerunds serve the function of nouns and may appear wherever a noun appears, one gerund equals one noun and therefore takes a singular verb. Gerunds often, though not always, refer to action in the past or action from the past to the present (in contrast to infinitives, which refer to the future). When gerunds are placed as objects of the verb, this distinction is vital to clear communication, as in the following.

He stopped seeing her. / He stopped to see her.
He remembered going there. / He must remember to go there.

Also, gerunds take the possessive pronoun:

his book / his having done that.

Another helpful rule is that two- and three-part verbs always take a gerund instead of an infinitive object: "look forward to going" not "look forward to go."

Recognizing gerund and infinitive subjects may be difficult for ESL students, who might benefit from practice underlining subjects, as in "*Getting to know you* will be fun" and "*To be or not to be* was Hamlet's question."

EXERCISE 2

1. have to
2. to do
3. walking
4. get
5. doing

ESL EXERCISE

Write down as many two- and three-part verbs as you can using:

1. get 2. check 3. look.

Go over these in class, discussing the way the preposition or particle changes the meaning.

ESL students can *never* get enough practice with these forms, and not knowing them or misusing them can create confusion and misunderstanding.

EXERCISE 2

Circle the appropriate verb form.

1. I am certain that you (have to/might) walk to town.
2. They all need (doing/to do) some daily exercise.
3. You might consider (walking/to walk) to town.
4. Doesn't she (get/gets) angry sometimes?
5. We can postpone (doing/to do) the hard work till later.

43f Using two- and three-word verbs, or phrasal verbs, with particles

Phrasal verbs consist of a verb and a *particle.* Note that a particle can be one or more prepositions (off, up, with) or an adverb (away, back). English has many phrasal verbs, often built on verbs that have one basic meaning in their simple one-word form, but different meanings when particles are added.

The coach *called off* the game because of the storm.
He *left out* some important details.

The meaning of a phrasal verb is idiomatic; that is, the words as a group have a different meaning from each of the words separately. Most of these varied meanings are found in a standard English dictionary. Here are some examples of sentences with two-word and three-word verbs.

I *got ready* for work.
She didn't go to the party because she didn't *feel up to* it.
The doctor told him to *cut down on* red meat.
They *did without* a television for a few years.

1 Some phrasal verbs are separable.

With separable phrasal verbs, a noun object either can separate a verb and particle or follow the particle.

CORRECT I *made out* a check (noun object) to the IRS. I *made* a check (noun object) *out* to the IRS.

However, a pronoun object always separates the verb and the particle. A pronoun never follows the particle.

FAULTY I *made out* it (pronoun object) to the IRS.

REVISED I *made* it *out* to the IRS.

Other separable phrasal verbs include the following:

call off	hand out	prevent from
check out	leave in, out	set up
divide up	look up [research]	sign on, up
find out	pick up	start over, up

fill in	put over [present deceptively]	take on
fit in	put up to [promote]	throw out
give back, up	put back	turn on, off, up, down
hang out, up [suspend: trans.]	put off	wake up
		write down

2 Some phrasal verbs are nonseparable.

With nonseparable phrasal verbs, a noun or pronoun object always follows the particle. For these verbs it is not possible to separate the verb and its particle with a noun or pronoun object.

	noun object		pronoun object
FAULTY	I ran Mary into.	FAULTY	I ran her into.
REVISED	I ran into Mary.	REVISED	I ran into her.

Other nonseparable phrasal verbs include the following:

bump into	call on	do without
get into	get over	get through
keep on	keep up with	hang out [= stay]
refer to	see about	stop by

Several verbs in their basic form are intransitive, but can become transitive phrasal verbs when a nonseparable prepositional particle is added to them.

INTRANSITIVE The politician *smiled* sheepishly, then quickly *apologized.*

TRANSITIVE He *smiled at* me sheepishly, then *apologized* quickly *for* being late.

Other examples of this kind of verb include the following:

complain about	laugh at	participate in
feel up to	look at, into	run into
insist on	object to	walk around, down, up, into, etc.

NOTE: An adverb, but not a noun or pronoun, may separate the verb from its particle.

He *apologized* quickly *for* being late.

The following are nonseparable two-word verbs that are intransitive, but that can be made transitive if still another particle is added to them:

run around with	*get ready* for	*get by* with
get away with	*drop out* of	*look out* for
read up on		

3 Some phrasal verbs can be either separable or nonseparable.

Some phrasal verbs can be either separable or nonseparable. The meaning of a phrasal verb will change, depending on whether or not the phrase is separated by an object. Note the difference in meaning that appears with the placement of the object in the similar verbs below.

EXAMPLES	MEANING
I *saw through* it. [nonsep.]	I found it transparent.
I *saw* it *through.* [sep.]	I persisted.
She *looked over* the wall. [nonsep.]	She looked over the top of it.
She *looked* the wall *over.* [sep.]	She examined or studied it.
I *turned on* him. [nonsep.]	I turned to attack him.
I *turned* it *on.* [sep.]	I flipped a switch.
I *turned* him *on.* [sep.]	I aroused his passion.
They *talked to* us. [nonsep.]	They spoke to us.
They *talked* us *into* staying. [sep.]	They convinced us to stay.

NOTE: Standard dictionaries usually list verbs with the meanings of most particles (indicating whether or not they are transitive), but they usually do not indicate whether a phrasal verb is separable or nonseparable. However, this information is provided in ESL dictionaries such as the *Longman Dictionary of American English: A Dictionary for Learners of English,* 1983.

EXERCISE 3

1. fit it in
2. call on her
3. wake her up
4. left it out
5. set him up

EXERCISE 3

Circle the appropriate verb form.

1. Can you (fit in it/fit it in) to your busy schedule?
2. If you (call on her/call her on), she may not be home.
3. We may want to (wake up her/wake her up) early today.
4. I forgot to tell you something; I (left out it/left it out) of my note yesterday.
5. Will you (set up him/set him up) to do the job?

CHAPTER 44

Using Modifiers and Connectors in English Sentences

Modifiers expand sentences in a variety of ways. The two types of modifiers are adjectives and adverbs, as well as phrases and clauses that function as adjectives or adverbs. There are two types of adverbs, descriptive and conjunctive. For basic discussions of the types of modifiers, how they function, and how they are placed or located in sentences, see 7a-5 and 6, and 7c. (For more on adjectives, see 11a-1 and 11e. For more on descriptive adverbs, see 11e and f. For more on conjunctive adverbs, see 19a-3.)

44a Using single-word adjectives and nouns as modifiers of nouns

A modifier of a noun must be placed as close to the noun modified as possible (11a-1; 15a). Single-word adjectives are normally placed before a noun or after a linking verb.

BEFORE A NOUN	The *bored student* slept through the *boring lecture.*
AFTER A LINKING VERB	Jack *is bored.* The lecture he heard *was boring.*

1 Using the present and past participle forms of verbs as adjectives

The present participle and the past participle forms of verbs are often used as single-word adjectives. The choice of form has an important impact on meaning. In the following examples, notice that these forms can be very different—almost opposite—in meaning.

PAST PARTICIPLE	MEANING
a tired student	Something tired this student.
damaged buildings	Something damaged these buildings.
a frightened passenger	Something frightened this passenger.
excited tourists	Something excited the tourists.
an accredited school	Some group accredited the school.

PRESENT PARTICIPLE	MEANING
a tiring lecture	The lecture causes a feeling of being tired.
a damaging explosion	The explosion caused the damage.
a frightening storm	The storm causes the fright.
an exciting tour	The tour caused excitement.
an accrediting board	This group gives accrediting status.

2 Using nouns as modifiers

When two nouns are combined in sequence, the last is considered to be the noun modified; the first is the modifier. (This follows the pattern for single-word adjectives mentioned earlier.) The importance of sequence is evident in the following examples, where the same nouns are combined in different order to produce different meanings.

MODIFIER	+ NOUN MODIFIED	MEANING
a car	company	a company whose business involves cars
a company	car	a car provided to someone by the business
a light	truck	a small truck
a truck	light	a light attached to a truck
a game	parlor	a place where indoor games are played
a parlor	game	a type of game, such as chess, played indoors

When more than two nouns are combined in sequence, it is increasingly difficult to determine which noun is modified and which is a modifier; see 44f-2. For this reason, it is best to avoid overusing nouns as modifiers (see 11g).

ESL CUE

There is little logic to English speakers' use of prepositions, and such use differs in British and American English. See the comments at 42c.

44b Using adjectival modifiers with linking verbs and prepositions

Adjectives and past-participle adjectives in sentences with linking verbs are often followed by a modifying prepositional phrase.

We are *ready*. We are *ready for* the next phase of training.
Jenny seems an *involved* person. She is *involved with* a boyfriend.

The preposition to be used in such phrases is determined by the adjective or participle adjective. With each such adjective, the choice of preposition is idiomatic, not logical; therefore, adjective/preposition combinations must be memorized. Sometimes the same adjective will change its meaning with different prepositions, as in this example.

Jenny was *involved in* planning from the start. Meanwhile, she was *involved with* a new boyfriend.

Past-participle adjective examples include the following:

excited about	acquainted with	divorced from
composed of	opposed to	scared of/by
involved in	interested in	cautioned to/against
exhausted from	done with	angry at/with

Single-word adjective examples include the following:

absent from	afraid of	mad at
bad for	clear to	sure of
crazy about	familiar with	cruel to
excited about	capable of	accustomed to
guilty of	responsible for	

NOTE: Standard dictionaries may not indicate which preposition is typically used with a given adjective. However, this information is provided in ESL dictionaries such as the *Longman Dictionary of American English: A Dictionary for Learners of English,* 1983.

44c Positioning adverbial modifiers

1 Observe typical locations for adverbs in English sentences.

Adverbs have typical or standard locations in English sentences, although these patterns can be varied for special emphasis. Adverbs are typically located immediately before a transitive or intransitive verb.

FAULTY She finishes cheerfully her homework.

REVISED She cheerfully finishes her homework.

EMPHATIC She finishes her homework—cheerfully.

Common adverbs expressing frequency or probability typically come after the verb *be* and helping verbs. In questions, such adverbs can come after the subject.

He was frequently at the gym on Fridays.
She may often discuss politics.
Does she often come here?

However, when sentences are inverted for negatives, these adverbs are usually placed before the helping verb.

FAULTY They don't frequently talk. It doesn't sometimes matter.

REVISED They frequently don't talk. It sometimes doesn't matter.

ESL CUE

Adverb placement is not treated clearly in most ESL texts; such texts do not explain well the shifts in meaning and emphasis possible through shifts in placement, so the examples in this section require close attention. Students may have trouble with placement of adverbs in three-part verbs: frequency/time between the first two parts, and manner/degree between the last two, as in "She had *rarely* been so *completely* enchanted" or "*Yesterday* she had *nearly* been *completely* convinced." This is because native speakers have an instinctual sense of when a variation of this standard pattern is necessary, as in "She has *recently* been advancing *more slowly,*" but cannot always articulate clearly why this variation must occur (in this case the extra word makes the two final words a phrase of manner and phrases of manner follow the verb just as phrases of frequency follow phrases of manner: "I understand him more and more fully each time I see him").

2 Limiting modifiers cannot move without changing meaning.

Although many adverbs can be located at a number of different places in a sentence without changing the meaning, positioning is quite critical with certain **limiting modifiers** such as *only, almost, just, nearly, even, simply* (see 15b).

No change in meaning	Significant change in meaning
Generally it rains a lot in April.	*Only* Leonid sings those songs.
It *generally* rains a lot in April.	Leonid *only* sings those songs.
It rains a lot in April, *generally.*	Leonid sings *only* those songs.
	[OR . . . sings those songs *only.*]

See 15a–g more on positioning modifiers. See also 43c-2 for inverted word order with adverbs—such as *rarely, never, seldom*—located at the beginning of a sentence.

44d Using phrases and clauses to modify nouns and pronouns

See the guidelines for modifier placement in 15a–h.

1 Positioning adjective phrases and clauses

Unlike single-word adjective modifiers (which are placed before a noun and after a linking verb; 44a), clauses and most phrases functioning as adjectives must immediately *follow* the noun or pronoun they modify in order to avoid confusion with adverbial modifiers in the sentence.

Faulty I brought the tire to the garage *with the puncture.*
I brought the tire to the garage *that had a puncture.*
[The modifier next to *garage* is very confusing.]

Revised I brought the tire *with the puncture* to the garage.
I brought the tire *that had a puncture* to the garage.

If two or more adjective phrases or clauses modify the same noun, typical patterns of sequence operate, as shown in 44f-1. (See 25d-1–3 for rules on punctuating adjective clauses.)

2 Avoid adding unnecessary pronouns after adjective clauses.

The subject in an English sentence can be stated only once; pronouns in the sentence refer to the subject (or to other nouns) but they do not repeat it. When a lengthy adjective clause follows the subject as a modifier, it is important not to repeat the subject with an unnecessary pronoun before the verb.

ESL CUE

ESL students may need to note how single or phrasal participles may be placed before or after the noun they describe. Adjective clauses are less versatile and must always go directly after the noun and preferably immediately adjacent to the noun. Note the contrast:

"Seeing the problem, the women agreed to . . ." and
"The women, seeing the problem, agreed to . . ."

in contrast to

"The women, who saw the problem, agreed to . . ."

but never

"Who saw the problem, the women agreed . . ."

nor

"The women, standing near us, who saw the problem, agreed . . ."

FAULTY The *person* who works in office #382 *she* decides. [The subject is repeated with an unnecessary pronoun.]

REVISED The person who works in office #382 decides.

This error is likely to occur because of a failure to observe the steps in forming a dependent clause. Here is the process for forming an adjective clause, using *who, which,* or *that* to replace the noun or pronoun of the dependent clause:

TWO SENTENCES	The person decides. *She* works in office #382.
TRANSFORM TO A CLAUSE	[*she* = *who*] *who* works in office #382
PLACE THE CLAUSE	The person *who works in office #382* decides.

The correct form for the relative pronouns *who* or *whom* in a dependent clause is discussed in 8f-2.

3 Use the relative pronoun *whose* for a clause showing possession.

An adjective clause is often constructed using the relative pronoun *whose* to show possession by the person or thing modified. Students sometimes omit a step in transforming a separate possessive statement into an adjective clause with *whose.*

FAULTY The person whom her office was locked called security.

REVISED The person whose office was locked called security.

Here is the pattern for transforming a sentence showing possession to a relative clause showing possession, using *whose* to replace the possessive noun or pronoun.

TWO SENTENCES	The person called security. *Her* office was locked.
REPLACE POSSESSIVE SUBJECT WITH *WHOSE*	*whose office was locked* [Her = *whose*]
PLACE THE CLAUSE	The person *whose* office was locked called security.

The same process is used for a clause showing possession of a thing.

TWO SENTENCES	The government made a protest. *Its* ambassador was insulted.
TRANSFORM: REPLACE WITH *WHOSE*	[*its* = *whose*] ambassador was insulted
PLACE THE CLAUSE	The government *whose* ambassador was insulted made a protest.

44e Combining phrases and clauses with connecting words

As writers combine phrases and clauses, they choose between two basic relationships: a coordinate or a subordinate connection. Elements that have a *coordinate* connection emphasize a balance or equality between elements. (See 19a for a discussion of coordinate relationships.) Elements can also have a subordinate or dependent connection that emphasizes that the elements are unequal, with one having a dependent link to another. (See 7e and 19b for a discussion of subordinate relationships.)

Phrases and clauses are often logically linked with connecting words, **conjunctions** and **conjunctive adverbs,** that require careful consideration of the kind of connection students wish to establish.

1 Choose the right connecting word for coordinate structures.

Connecting words for a coordinate, or balanced, relationship include **coordinating conjunctions** (*and, but, or, nor, so, for, yet*), **correlative conjunctions** (*either/or, neither/nor, both/and, not only/but, whether/or, not only/but also*), and many **conjunctive adverbs** (*however, nevertheless, accordingly, also, besides, afterward, then, indeed, otherwise*). These words show relationships of contrast, consequence, sequence, and emphasis; they are discussed in 19a-1–3.

After deciding on the desired relationship among sentence parts, select a *single set of connecting words.* Avoid a mixture of words that may cancel out the meaning.

MIXED They were *both* competitive, *but however* they were well matched. [The mixed connecting words show similarity and contrast at the same time.]

BALANCED They were *both* competitive, *and* they were well matched. They were competitive; *however,* they were well matched.

See 25a-1 and 25f-1 for appropriate rules on punctuation.

2 Choose the subordinating conjunction that establishes the desired dependent relationship.

Subordinating conjunctions establish different relationships, including conditional relationships and relationships of contrast, cause and effect, time and place, purpose, and outcome (see Chapter 19). In your writing, choose a single coordinating conjunction, and avoid combinations that are contradictory or confusing.

MIXED *Because* she was sick, *so* she went to the clinic. [A relation of cause and effect is confusingly combined with one of purpose or outcome.]

CLEAR *Because* she was sick, she went to the clinic. [cause/effect]
She was sick, *so* she went to the clinic. [outcome]

See 19b for a full discussion on establishing clear subordinate relationships among sentence parts. See 25a-1 and 25f-1 for rules on punctuation.

44f Arranging cumulative modifiers

1 Observing typical order of cumulative adjectives

Single-word adjective modifiers are placed close to a noun, immediately before a noun, or after a linking verb (44a).

Cumulative adjectives are groups of adjectives that modify the same noun. There is a typical order of modifiers and cumulative adjectives in an English sentence. A major disruption of typical order can be confusing.

FAULTY	a beach French gorgeous tent	red light my small bulb
REVISED	a gorgeous French beach tent	my small red light bulb

Although some stylistic variations from typical order in the location of cumulative adjectives are possible for emphasis, typical locations in an English sentence provide a very strong normal pattern. Here are some guidelines.

Possessives precede numbers. Ordinal numbers follow cardinal numbers.

Jill's first car   my first nine drafts

The typical order of descriptive adjectives is shown below:

(1) Opinion	*(2) Size*	*(3) Shape*	*(4) Condition*	*(5) Age*	*(6) Color*	*(7) Origin*	*(8) Noun*
ugly		round			green		fenders
	huge		muddy				spots
lovely				old	red	Turkish	slippers
comfortable			sunny				room

2 Arranging cumulative phrases, clauses, or noun modifiers*

A single phrase or clause functioning as an adjective immediately follows the noun or pronoun it modifies to avoid confusion with any adverbial phrases in the same sentence (44b).

When accumulated adjective phrases or clauses modify the same noun, their flexible emphasis creates an extremely varied sequence, especially for issues of opinion. In a neutral context some of the same typical sequences

*We owe this discussion on order of modifiers to Jean Praninskas, *Rapid Review of English Grammar* (Englewood Cliffs, NJ: Prentice-Hall, 1975).

ESL CUE

For Americans, correct adjective order is intuitive; for ESL students it must be learned consciously. Both Marcella Frank's *Modern English, Part I* and Betty Azar's *Understanding and Using English Grammar* have excellent charts detailing the logic behind our adjective order system.

Spanish, Korean, and Vietnamese, as well as a number of other languages, place the adjective after the noun: *the house red.* This accounts for what may seem to be peculiar constructions, even in highly fluent students who occasionally "forget" and revert to the deep structure of the mother tongue. The surface error rarely causes confusion except in one of the few cases of English reversible adjectives and nouns: house cat/cat house, ice free/free ice, etc.

Another troubling adjective problem is with number. Many languages make nouns and adjectives agree in number, while English adjectives take only the singular or nonnumbered form; thus the fairly common habit of Spanish speakers writing in English of adding a number inflection to adjectives: the reds houses.

may be observed as for single-word adjectives (above), except that the modifying phrases follow the noun.

I found *spots* that are *huge* and that are also very *muddy.*

We saw that the *rooms* were very *narrow* and yet they seemed *bright.*

When two adverbial phrases or clauses are accumulated, place phrases typically precede time phrases.

NOT TYPICAL They lived in the 1970s in Japan.

TYPICAL They lived in Japan in the 1970s.

Two-word modifiers of nouns

Three nouns are often combined, with the first two forming a two-word modifier for the last noun. When this happens, nouns fall into a typical arrangement somewhat comparable with that of adjectives.

NOT TYPICAL a file steel cabinet

TYPICAL a steel file cabinet

The sequence of two nouns to modify a third noun may be classified and arranged in this sequence.

Material, Number, or Location	*Origin, Purpose, or Type*	*Noun Modified*
chapter	review	questions
two-word	noun	modifier
slate	roofing	tile
steel	file	cabinet

However, the categories of meaning for nouns are less clear than for adjectives and the opportunity for confusion is much greater. Students are therefore advised to avoid accumulating noun modifiers beyond this limit, and to rewrite combinations as phrases and clauses (see 11g).

EXERCISE 1

1. exciting; interested
2. of; to
3. usually walks; even when
4. who spoke
5. beautiful yellow; large Japanese

EXERCISE 1

Circle the correct form.

1. The girls thought the ride was (excited/exciting) and they were (interested/interesting) in the things they saw.
2. These gang members seemed capable (of/in) any kind of violence and were cruel (at/to) their enemies.
3. Luisa (walks usually/usually walks) to her studio (even when/when even) she feels tired.
4. The famous preacher (he spoke/who spoke) at our meeting was inspiring.
5. I have lost my (yellow beautiful/beautiful yellow) umbrella with the (large Japanese/Japanese large) designs.

APPENDIX A

Writing with a Computer

If a computer's word processing software only relieved writers of tedium, this benefit in itself would be enormous. In the bad old days, only fifteen years ago, a student would need to retype an entire page for the sake of some small correction, such as a spelling error. Today, only a few keystrokes are needed to enter changes and command a printer to reproduce a corrected page. Of greater significance than this ease of correction is the help a computer can offer in the composing and revising process.

With a little patience you can learn simple word processing techniques that will eradicate difficulties that used to plague writers. Whether you own a computer, a word processor, or simply have access to a computer at school or work, this tool exists to make life easier for you at every stage of the writing process. It makes sense to take advantage of it.

A1 Some basic terminology

Making files

Your word processor will have specific commands that will tell you how to "open" a file—which means a specially designated blank screen where you can put down your words—and then how to "save" your file when finished. If you don't save your file, it might get erased automatically the moment you "exit" your word processing program.

> It's vitally important that you save your work frequently, about every fifteen minutes, and not just at the end of a session! If you accidentally exit the program, or if there's a power surge, you'll still have most of your work saved.

You'll also have to title your file. The computer will usually ask you to do this the first time you save your text. The purpose of a file name is to enable you to differentiate among many different texts located in the same "directory"—that is, on the same disk or on the same hard drive. Let's say you've completed the first draft for an art history paper on Jackson Pollock. You wouldn't want to title your file "DRAFT," since this will be too general.

Rather, you could type "POLLOCK.1" or "Pollock Essay, Version 1" (depending on whether you're working with an IBM-compatible machine, which allows only for shorter titles, or a Macintosh, which permits longer titles).

Entering text

This is a simple process: just start typing. Your text will appear wherever the cursor happens to be, and you can move that cursor by using either the arrow keys or the mouse. There's an automatic wraparound feature in all word processing programs, so you won't have to hit a carriage return at the end of each line, only when you wish to begin a new paragraph.

Changing text

With a typewriter, errors, deletions, or changes have to be made with white-out or erasable ribbon; with a computer, all you need do is position your cursor immediately following the part you want to erase, and hit the backspace key.

Working with blocks of text

By "blocking" off parts of your text, either with the arrow keys or the mouse, you can select large portions of your text to work with. This is one of the most valuable features of any word processing program.

When you block text—say an entire paragraph—and "cut" it, it disappears, but it is saved in what is sometimes called a "clipboard." If you want to insert that paragraph somewhere else in your paper, move the cursor to the new spot and hit "paste." The excerpted paragraph will instantly reappear.

At other times you might want to "copy" a portion of the text, perhaps so that an extra copy of it may be kept in another file. In this case you would simply hit "copy" instead of "cut," and your computer would save a copy of that excerpted passage.

Finally, blocking text allows you to reformat that text. You can block an entire essay, for example, and then tell the computer to change the font size or typeface. Or, you can block a word or sentence and have it changed to boldface or italics.

A2 Computers and the writing process

1 Preparing to write

The computer can be enormously helpful in preparing to write. As you read a writing assignment, focus on two key questions: What do you know about your topic? What do you want to say to your audience? Subsequent decisions will depend on your answers, and you can use the power of word processing to make flexible entries and notes that can be rearranged to suit your changing purpose.

Generating ideas and organizing your thoughts

If you use the computer to generate ideas and to keep notes, you can put your word processing software to work by creating an outline of your paper and then moving into that outline all the pertinent information you have generated or collected. With the computer's *block move* or *cut/paste* commands you can rearrange material and sketch your paper in any number of ways, allowing you to compare possible strategies. The more flexible you are in experimenting with different outlines, the more likely it is you will arrive at one that represents a strong, creative synthesis of possible approaches.

Writing collaboratively

If your computer is hooked into a network, you can share your ideas for a paper with classmates and friends. Send them an electronic letter in which you describe the general approach you want to take in the paper and ask for reactions. As you work through the writing process, use a network for conducting research, revising, and editing. (See A2-4.)

Conducting library research

If you are writing a research paper, you can take your "to do" list with you to the library as you begin the general search process (see Chapter 33). If your computer is hooked into a network, you may not need to travel to the library to check its holdings since these may exist on file in the college's main computer, which you can access over the phone lines. Many colleges have general references on a mainframe computer, and you will be able to peruse these and do your initial reading while seated at your own computer. If you surf the Internet (see 33f-3, 33h-1, 33h-2), you can locate an astonishingly wide array of sources from Internet sites around the world and then download them onto your computer. Take notes at the computer, too. When the time comes for sketching a plan for your paper, you can print out your notes, laying before you all the information that you have to work with.

2 Writing a first draft

Some people need the physical connection of hand to pen to paper when writing. Some can draft certain sorts of documents—say, business correspondence—on a computer but must write longer efforts by hand. Whatever your preferences, remember that the purpose of a first draft is to get a version of your document written—quickly. If you can work on a computer, all the better. Even if you are a poor typist, a computer keyboard encourages speed. Once you are open to the idea of writing a first draft, making large and small refinements later, you free yourself to write quickly, even furiously. The clear advantage of working on a computer at this stage is having your draft on file, ready and waiting for the work of revision.

3 Revising

Whether you're going to write only one first draft or (ideally) a series of intermediary drafts, there's one thing you ought to do after each one: print out a hard copy, read it, and make changes on that copy. Once you're satisfied with your changes, transfer them into your latest draft along with any other major and minor revisions.

There are several reasons to periodically print out and read hard copies of your work. For one, your eye will catch mistakes on paper that it will miss on the screen. (Incidentally, it's a great idea to read your work out loud as well, so that your ear will catch errors your eye might not see.) Also, there's a definite advantage to seeing the entire text on a piece of paper as opposed to visualizing your paper only through the keyhole of the computer screen. After all, chances are your final text will be presented to an audience in hard copy format, so it would be wise to familiarize yourself with what such a printout looks like at phases throughout the revising process.

Proofreading

You have worked too hard on your paper to let trivial errors of spelling, doubled words, or inadvertently used homonyms mar the end product. Now is the time to engage your word processor's *spell check program.* If your software package does not include such a program, you are sure to find a reasonably priced one at a local retailer's or in a catalog of public domain software. With its dictionary of 200,000 words or more, a spell checker compares every word of your paper against the words in its memory. The best a computer can do is call attention to apparent inconsistencies between its word database and what is shown on the screen. No computer will highlight as incorrect the contraction *it's,* even when the context of your sentence requires using the possessive pronoun *its.* Once again, rely on your good judgment as a writer.

Printing

When you have proofread your document, print two final copies: one for you and one for your instructor. Make sure the format—in the line spacing, font, and margins—meets the requirements of your audience. It may be necessary to print out several copies before all of these final details are in order.

You should save at least some of the various drafts you've worked on prior to this point; in some cases an instructor might wish to see them to gauge your progress as a writer. While it's not always necessary to print your final paper out on a laser printer, which in some computer labs might require a fee, at least make sure that your text is dark and readable. Dot matrix printouts are sometimes hard to read, which is why some instructors don't permit them. Finally, remember to recycle any unnecessary copies you may have printed out.

4 Computers and collaboration

Writing with a computer facilitates the author/editor relationship in major ways. If you are working with a group on a single project, you can easily swap drafts by exchanging disks, thereby saving considerable time during the revision process. Or, if you're working on your own paper, you can still send your drafts to others over a network within seconds; then they can respond rapidly with feedback. In fact, with a network, you can reach readers virtually all over the world.

Disk swapping techniques

Once you have a complete draft of your paper, consider giving a hard copy of it as well as an electronic copy on floppy disk to a friend for peer review; this will then allow him or her to either make annotated comments on the hard copy, or to make detailed revisions directly on the disk. The speed of the computer allows your reader to make more revisions than might otherwise be possible, and you can keep or modify those suggestions that make sense to you while disregarding the others. (Some word processing programs have a feature that allows an editor to suggest deletions and additions without destroying any of your text. When your editor returns the document, the suggestions will show up on your screen either shaded or underlined.)

NOTE: Make sure that, prior to giving anyone a copy of your work, you have made a second copy of your original draft on another disk in your possession. That way, you can compare your version of the draft with that of your peers, and also have a backup copy in case your reader loses or damages your disk. It is a good idea to have anyone who is going to alter your text place the modified draft into a separate file with the date of the changes. This way, if there are several people rewriting the same draft over a period of time, each person will have a dated record of every version of the paper. This can be a tremendous service should you wish to review the progress of a paper, and also if your instructor ever asks to see earlier versions of the assignment.

Using networks

There are software programs available now that allow multiple writers to work simultaneously on a single text, whether they are all congregated at linked terminals in a computer lab or working at remote sites and connected via telephone lines. Such software typically works like this: as you write a sentence or paragraph, those words will appear almost simultaneously on everyone else's screen, just as their words will be materializing on your screen. With such software you can have everyone write separate paragraphs and thus work on separate sections of the text, or you can all work simultaneously within the same paragraph. And, rather than waiting a period of time in order to get feedback before revising a text, editing decisions can be made during the same session in which a first draft is created: that is, all writers are free to return to any part of the text and change it.

Usually the procedure for doing this is to use small dialogue boxes off to one side of the screen, where you can converse with the other writers about any editorial changes prior to making them, thereby avoiding stepping on the toes of other writers and ensuring that your collaborative writing session does not degenerate into chaos. This can be a fascinating way to work with other writers, for you get to see not only what other people write in response to your words, but also the idiosyncrasies of their writing processes as the words "magically" appear and undergo changes on your screen.

Chances are good that sooner or later you'll be in a situation where you can benefit greatly from collaborating with another writer via a computer, whether your career takes you into business, medicine, law, education, the arts, or any other area. Consequently, it will be to your advantage to get a taste of what computer collaboration might entail now, so that transitions to future technologies will be easier.

APPENDIX B

Manuscript Form and Preparation

Before readers register a word of your writing, they form an impression based on your paper's appearance. If you are committed enough to a paper to have revised it several times, surely you will want to give it a crisp appearance. A clean, well-prepared, typed manuscript is a sign of an attentive attitude taken toward all the stages of writing. Careful manuscript preparation implicitly shows respect for your readers, who will certainly appreciate any efforts to make their work easier.

Style guides in the disciplines recommend slightly different conventions for preparing manuscripts, and you should consult the specialized guides listed in 37f, 38e, and 39e when writing in the humanities, social sciences, and sciences. Consult your professor as well. The recommendations here follow the guide commonly used in the humanities, the *MLA [Modern Language Association] Handbook for Writers of Research Papers,* 4th ed.

B1 Paper and binding

Prepare your work on plain white, twenty-pound paper that measures 8-1/2 × 11 inches. For economy's sake, you might consider buying a ream (500 sheets) if you are typing the manuscript or are preparing it on a laser printer. If you are working with a dot matrix printer, buy a box of 500 or 1000 sheets of fanfold paper. Unless your instructor advises otherwise, avoid onion skin or erasable paper, both of which will easily smudge. (For ease of preparation, though, you might type your work on erasable paper and submit a photocopy, which will not smudge.) Make a copy of your final paper to keep for your files, and submit the original to your instructor. In binding pages, affix a single paper clip to the upper left-hand corner. To ease your reader's handling of your paper, do *not* place multiple staples along the left margin, and avoid plastic folders unless otherwise directed.

B2 Page layout

Whether you adopt conventions for page layout suggested by the *MLA Handbook* or by other style guides, maintain consistent margins and spacing.

Your paper's first page, subsequent pages, and reference-list page(s) should be designed according to standard practice in a discipline.

Margins and line spacing

Type on one side of a page, double-spacing all text (including footnotes and endnotes). Maintain double-spacing between paragraphs and between lines of text and any displayed quotations. Leave a one-inch margin on the top and bottom of a page and a one-inch margin on both sides of a page. If you are working on a computer, set the margins as well as the running head (your last name and a page number) automatically. With each new paragraph, indent five spaces (on a computer, press the Tab key). For displayed quotations (see 28a-4), indent ten spaces and maintain that indentation for the length of the quotation.

Design of first page

Following the MLA format, you do not need to prepare a separate title page for your research papers. (This convention differs in the sciences and social sciences. See the box on page 713 as well as the example research paper on page 737.) Observe the spacing of headings and title in the following example.

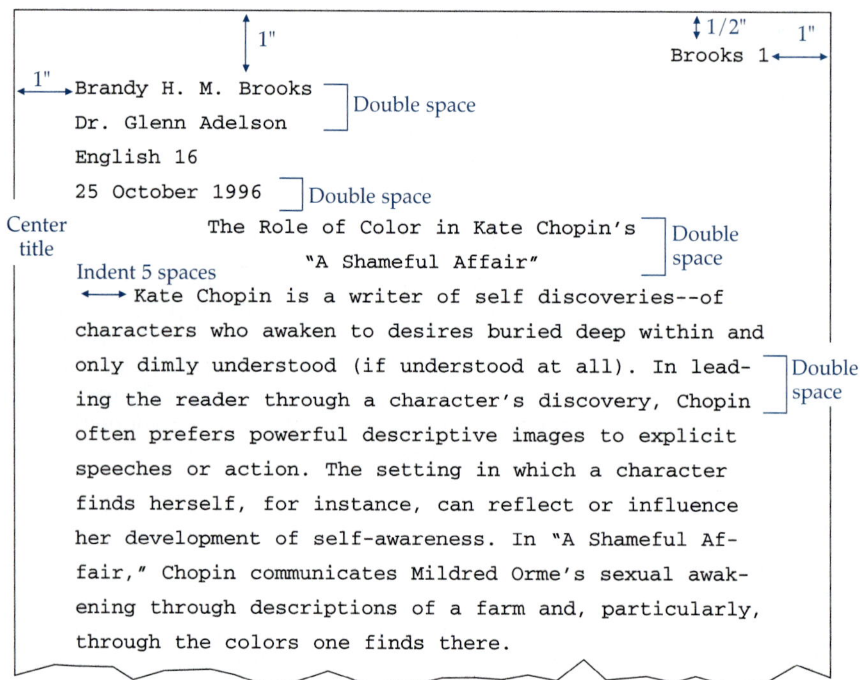
1"
1/2"
1"
Brooks 1
1"
Brandy H. M. Brooks
Dr. Glenn Adelson
English 16
25 October 1996
Double space
Double space
Center title
The Role of Color in Kate Chopin's "A Shameful Affair"
Double space
Indent 5 spaces
Kate Chopin is a writer of self discoveries--of characters who awaken to desires buried deep within and only dimly understood (if understood at all). In leading the reader through a character's discovery, Chopin often prefers powerful descriptive images to explicit speeches or action. The setting in which a character finds herself, for instance, can reflect or influence her development of self-awareness. In "A Shameful Affair," Chopin communicates Mildred Orme's sexual awakening through descriptions of a farm and, particularly, through the colors one finds there.
Double space

Design of subsequent pages

Observe the position of the running head and the first line of text on a paper's second or subsequent page.

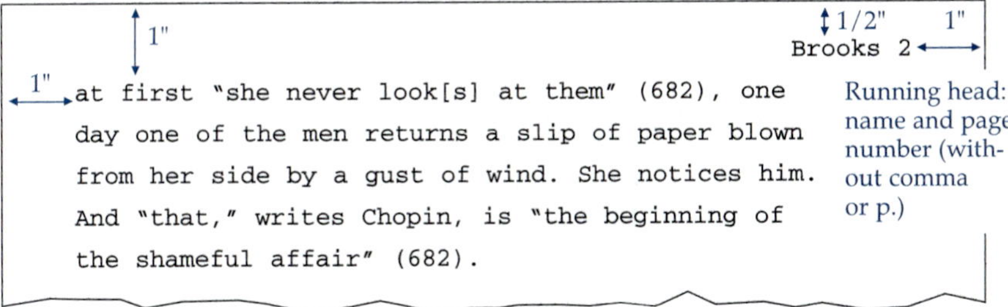

1/2" 1"
Brooks 2

1" 1"

at first "she never look[s] at them" (682), one day one of the men returns a slip of paper blown from her side by a gust of wind. She notices him. And "that," writes Chopin, is "the beginning of the shameful affair" (682).

Running head: name and page number (without comma or p.)

Design of "Works Cited" page

Observe the position of the running head, the title "Works Cited," and the indentation of the reference entry's second line.

1" 1/2" 1"

Brooks 8

Works Cited — Double space

1"

5 spaces

Chopin, Kate. "A Shameful Affair." The Awakening and Other Stories. Ed. Lewis Leary. New York: Holt, 1970. 31-37.

Dyer, Joyce. "Symbolic Setting in Kate Chopin's 'A Shameful Affair.'" Southern Studies: An Interdisciplinary Journal of the South 20 (1981): 447-52.

Simpson, Martin. "Chopin's 'A Shameful Affair.'" The Explicator 45.1 (1986): 59-60.

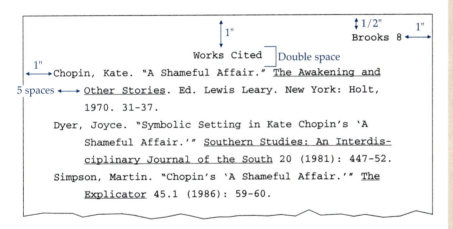

B3 Text preparation

Printing a manuscript on a word processor

Print on one side of the page and, if possible, use a laser printer. If none is available, use a dot matrix printer with a fresh enough ribbon that readers will have no trouble reading your text. Keep the right-hand edge of your text ragged, or *un*justified. If your dot matrix machine is printing a light page, you may be able to improve the product by photocopying the page with the photocopier adjusted to a darker than normal setting.

Printing a manuscript on a typewriter

Type on one side of a page with standard typewriter fonts. Avoid typefaces giving the appearance of script, since these are difficult to read. Use a fresh ribbon with black ink.

Handwriting a manuscript

Very few professors accept handwritten papers. If yours does, use lined, white 8-1/2 × 11 inch paper. Do not use spiral-bound notebook paper with its ragged edges. Write neatly and legibly in pen, on one side of the page, using dark blue or black ink. Consult your professor, who may ask you to skip every other line to allow room for editorial comments.

Alterations

In a final review of your paper, when you are working away from your typewriter or word processor, you may find it necessary to make minor changes to your text—perhaps to correct a typographical error or to improve your wording. Make corrections *neatly.* When striking out a word, do so with a single line. Use a caret (^) to mark an insertion in the text, and write your correction or addition above the line you are altering. If time permits and you have worked on a word processor, enter the changes into your file and reprint the affected pages. Retype or reprint a page when you make three or more handwritten corrections on it. If your typewriter or computer keyboard lacks a particular symbol or mark that you need, handwrite that symbol on the page.

```
                                                   nonetheless
For reasons Mildred does not yet understand but that^ compel
her, she must be near Fred Evelyn.
```

Punctuation and spacing

Observe the following standard conventions for spacing before and after marks of punctuation.

ONE SPACE BEFORE

beginning parenthesis or bracket

beginning quotation mark

period in a series denoting an omission—see ellipses, 29e

NO SPACE BEFORE (EXCEPT AS NOTED)

comma	question mark	semicolon
period[1]	apostrophe	end quotation mark
exclamation point	colon	hyphen or dash

No space after (except as noted)

hyphen[2] or dash

beginning parenthesis or bracket

apostrophe[3]

One space after (except as noted)

comma

semicolon

colon[4]

apostrophe denoting the possessive form of a plural

end parenthesis or bracket that does not end a sentence

end quotation within a sentence

period in a series denoting an omission—see ellipses, 29e

period marking an abbreviated name or an initial

Two spaces after the following marks when they conclude a sentence

period	closing quotation
question mark	end parenthesis or bracket
exclamation	

Exceptions (as noted above)

[1]Unless the period occurs in a series denoting omission—see 29e.

[2]Unless the hyphen denotes one in a pair or series of delayed adjectives, as in *a first-, second-, or third-place finish.*

[3]Unless the apostrophe denotes the possessive form of a plural, as in *boys'*, in which case skip one space.

[4]Unless the colon denotes a ratio, as in *3:2.*

APPENDIX C

The Visual Design of Documents

Your goal in writing is to communicate a particular content. If your content is clear, readers will understand—and your efforts will have succeeded. Everything you have read in this book encourages you to communicate clearly, through words. Here we consider how document design—the use of art, graphics, typeface, and format—can make your content more accessible to readers. A single principle underlies this discussion:

> Every design element in a document should help readers to understand the content.

Without content, you have no reason for writing. Therefore, understand your content first. Articulate it as clearly as you can, with words; then look to the ways effective design can help you to deliver that content.

C1 Design elements and the audiences for your documents

When you write for traditional academic audiences—when you write papers for your college courses, for instance—look for design conventions in Appendix B, "Manuscript Form" and also in the example student papers for the humanities, social sciences, and sciences in Chapters 37, 38, and 39. There you will find discussions and illustrations of basic visual elements of academic writing:

- Titles—to focus attention on your topic and argument
- Headings—to provide summary organizers for sections of a paper
- Displayed (or "block") quotations—to emphasize key words of others
- Graphs, charts—to synthesize often complex data into visual form

Design elements for nonacademic audiences

When you address readers in the world of business, government, or technical fields beyond academic settings, it is especially important to make the unity and coherence of your writing accessible, and a well-planned design can help. The following types of documents will benefit from carefully designed visual elements:

- Presentation pieces intending to educate, technically train, or persuade business or government audiences. This text is an example of one kind of instruction and presentation material.
- Special reports, especially proposals in the science and business worlds, which need to emphasize clear and persuasive problem-solution structures. The science research paper in 39d develops some of the conventions common in this type of presentation.
- Promotional, public relations, and marketing pieces designed to attract and persuade specific audiences.
- Newsletters and public information bulletins in print and on electronic media.

Readers of these types of documents have many demands on their time. They will first skim articles and reports to determine if there is anything of use to them; only then will they read sections (if not an entire piece) slowly and carefully. You must therefore try to focus the attention of these readers, capturing their interest so that they will give your document consideration. You can focus attention by using techniques found in conventional, academic writing (titles, headings, block quotations, and graphs and charts). You can also focus attention in more visually exciting ways.

- Emphatic type—to highlight key words and phrases
- Art and photos—to express information, mood, and ideas
- Layout and use of white space—to ensure a balanced, open look

The magazines you read, along with advertisements, promotional materials, newspapers, and electronic communications (web pages, for instance), can provide visually stimulating and sophisticated examples, many of them prepared by specialists well-versed in type design, art, and layout. This Appendix can help you look for basic ways to ensure that visual interest and clarity are part of your writing; you also can consult a number of books for detailed help on document design for business and technical communication. Some recent books include K. W. Houp et al., *Reporting Technical Information*, 8th edition; M. J. Killingsworth, *Information in Action: A Guide to Technical Communication*; or P. W. Agnew et al., *Multimedia in the Classroom* (all Boston: Allyn & Bacon, 1996).

C2 Effective headings and typography emphasize content

Begin with clear, concise writing. Well-chosen typography will improve readability and reduce confusion. Clearly worded, brief headings will communicate the logic of your document's organization. The combination of clear typeface and carefully worded headings will bring a visual coherence to your work that suggests coherent ideas.

Typeface

A type "face" is the name given to the distinctive design and shape of a family of lettering used for text. A face or design usually includes several "fonts," or lettering of different sizes and styles, including italics or boldface. As a general principle, the fewer the typefaces in one document, the better.

Assigning different typefaces to specific functions

Sometimes, when you need to distinguish one kind of text function from another, a distinctive typeface can be assigned for each function, adding coherence as well as visual interest to a document. As a second principle, when you introduce a different typeface, assign each face a single function.

The typography of this textbook illustrates the point. Notice that the book has only three typefaces or designs (though it uses different fonts and type sizes); each clearly signals that a different category of information is being presented.

You are now reading the regular typeface used for the text. When you read the color-printed headings, you see a slightly different, thicker font used only for these emphatic headlines. When student writing is shown, as in the papers for Chapters 37 to 39, you see the student text in a very different face (called Courier, seen in typewriters or in e-mail) to show a distinctive kind of writing.

Word processing typefaces

If you write with a word processor, you will likely have many choices of typefaces. Your most basic consideration, for anything simpler that an advertising brochure, is whether to use a typeface that features "serif" lettering, or "sans serif" lettering. Serif lettering, as used throughout this book, is the family of typefaces most commonly seen in North America for basic text. If you closely observe the two samples below, you will notice an important difference. The text sample on the left features fine horizontal lines, called "serifs," at the top and bottom of each vertical stroke in the lettering. But the sample on the right, lacking these horizontal serifs, has a plainer look and (using the French term for "without") is called a "sans serif" or sometimes "gothic" family of lettering.

This is serif lettering.   [This is sans serif lettering.]

For most North American readers the difference is more than stylistic; the serifs are thought to act like a horizontal ruler, leading the eye smoothly across a long line of type on a page. For this reason serif type is commonly considered effective for lengthy documents featuring long lines of text. Sans serif, with its clean, emphatic appearance, is often considered useful for headings or brief messages presented in short lines.

Type size

Your word processor will be able to vary emphasis and readability by expanding or contracting type sizes. These sizes are commonly designated with numbers from as low as 6 or 8 "points" (a typesetter's unit of measure) to 10, 11, or 12, commonly seen for basic text in books or magazines, up to point sizes as large as the 30-, 40-, or even 50-point headings seen in advertising.

If you vary type size in your document, again bear in mind the principle of orderliness. Assign specific type sizes to specific functions. Relative to the size of the standard type size you are using in your document, you may want to assign section headings a larger size and chapter titles an even larger size, while footnotes and index entries might receive a smaller size. You can see several varieties of type sizes in this book, each for a distinct purpose.

Formatting the margins

If you work with a word processor, another decision you need to make for basic text is how to treat the margins. It is standard to see the left margin in straight alignment for documents other than advertising brochures, where centering or right-alignment of type is sometimes used. The left-aligned convention helps the eye begin each line at the same place on the page.

For the right margin you need to decide whether or not to "justify"—that is, to align letters on both left and right exactly in a vertical line. Right-justified documents are common in professionally prepared documents and are possible with most word processors, often without complex hyphenation for line breaks. (Hyphenation, available on many word processors, is often avoided because it slows scrolling and processing.) Unless the software is very sophisticated, right-justified documents without hyphenation may create uneven spacing, or "holes" on the page, making reading erratic and difficult. To avoid this, and to help readers follow individual lines more smoothly without hyphenation, many professional documents prefer to show the typewriter's standard "ragged right" format, with which most readers are quite comfortable.

Highlighting with boldface, italics, and boxes

Again, the principle of restraint holds: less is usually more. If you want boldfaced, italicized, or boxed words and phrases to receive special emphasis, then use these tools sparingly. Maintain a "base" of plain text that contrasts clearly with any emphatic type, and try to establish a convention for its use. For instance, you could reserve boldfaced words for headings; you could reserve italics for words that are being defined; you could draw a box around material that you consider crucially important. Overuse of these tools will quickly diminish their effectiveness and disorient your readers with a cluttered document.

In this text, italicized words are used only to emphasize important terms, to identify key words in examples, and for conventional usage in titles. Boldface type is restricted to terms that are included in the glossary; boxed information appears only with the stepwise procedures in 37d and the one key principle in this appendix:

Every design element in a document should help readers to understand the content.

Overall format and heading structure

A coherent, overall plan

Plan an overall structure for your document in such a way that its internal logic, and its key points, are quickly communicated to anyone who takes a few minutes to scan the pages. To communicate structure and idea, divide your content into well-connected chunks of varying sizes: major units, sections, subsections, paragraphs. Communicate these chunks of material with format elements like these:

- Table of contents—For longer, formal presentations, a listing of titles or topics can provide a map and overview of your document's plan. Schematic overviews or charts can also be used—as on the endpapers of this book.
- Unit or chapter titles—Units that begin on new pages will focus attention on the main elements of your presentation.
- Unit or chapter openings—Brief overviewing paragraphs can set out the unit's plan—as typified by the opening of Chapter 29 in this book.
- Section titles—Headings at different levels of emphasis can focus the reader's attention on broad ideas and specifics. (See the next section.)
- Unit summaries—When clearly marked and located at the end of a unit, or possibly at the opening of a chapter and called an "abstract" (see 38b or 39b, c), summary restatements can distill key points.

When you choose format elements for your document, be consistent in structure, heading scheme, and typeface. Readers will understand these visual elements and will come to depend on them as cues to your content.

Headings

Headings—words or brief phrases or sentences—announce the content of your presentation. An effective scheme for headings will communicate your overall idea to readers who scan a long document, but a clear scheme is also important for newsletters, brochures, or web pages. By assigning a particular typestyle and heading structure to each element of your document, you can enhance its clarity, interest, and visual coherence.

The wording of headings should forecast the main issues or thesis ideas to come in each section. Frame your headings with enough white space to give the full visual emphasis you desire. Here is a checklist of questions to help you to plan a heading scheme:

- How many levels of heads will you use? Consult your outline and try to reduce the number of hierarchical levels to a simple scheme.

- Will you number the heads? Numbering is normally to be avoided except in complex reference or technical works, where numbered heads make it easy to cross-reference, as in this book.
- What typographical emphasis will you give the hierarchy of headings? For each level, make a consistent scheme for distinctive treatment of size, typeface, boldface, italics, or color, with all headings made distinct from your text.
- Will you use color in headings or in type? If so, keep the color scheme simple. Too many colors used unsystematically may confuse readers and make your scheme harder to follow. This book's system uses one color (black) for chapters and minor subheads, another color (blue) for text headings at three levels, and a third (green) for special features.
- In addition to heads, will you use software to make "headers" or "footers"—brief identifying phrases that appear at the top or bottom of pages, usually on the line with page numbers? If yes, use these as brief locating labels, not as a way to convey detailed information. Will headers and footers be different on the left and right pages? If so, it is common for the left header or footer to give a brief version of the unit or chapter heading, and for the right side to give a label for lesser sections or subsections.

A WARNING: When your final document is laid out in pages, survey it to make sure that headings at the bottom of a page are not left alone ("widowed"), but have at least two or three lines of text following. If need be, break pages to run a short page and push the lone heading to the top of a new page.

Itemized lists

Lists, outlines, and bullet points are effective visual tools for concentrating the reader's attention on the content you deem important. A list of brief items can compress ideas and connect them in a series that forecasts a direction or a pattern you want readers to see. Many examples of listed and bulleted items appear in this appendix, but lists are a frequent feature of newsletters, brochures, and web pages. For lists and bullet points, bear these considerations in mind:

- List items that you can express in a sentence or two.
- Use a bullet (•), a dash (—), or an asterisk (*) for briefer material that you can express in one or two indented lines.
- Keep listed and bulleted items grammatically parallel. The rules of parallelism for outlining apply especially to lists, and often to a series of headings as well. (See 18e-1, 2.)
- Indent the listed numbers or bullet points to set them off from your text.
- Use bullet points if the order of items is unimportant; otherwise, use numbers.
- For the left margins of lists, either use the list format on your word processor, or else the "hanging indent" form, with second and subsequent lines indented back from the initial word, number, or bullet, and aligned as in this example.

If your list or your bullet points run longer than seven or eight items, consider regrouping material and presenting two lists or sets of bullet points, each with its own heading. As with other formatting elements, it is important to make a consistent plan for functional use of itemized or bulleted lists, avoiding visual confusion from inconsistency or overuse.

Using white space

Too much text on a page tires readers' eyes as they scan the page looking for important information. Some experts on page design (especially for documents intended for nonacademic audiences) suggest that writers devote no more than 60 percent of a page to text. The remainder of the page should consist of graphical elements and white space. The use of white space on a page creates a frame for information you have already highlighted with type styles, and thus doubly emphasizes it. For examples of white space strategically used, see the following sections of this book: 39d, a scientific report with graphs; 40b, a business letter; 40f, a memorandum.

C3 Graphic material in reports, presentations, or proposals

The documents you write are intended to convey a meaning and to leave a message with readers. Along with creative, functional, and simple use of headings and typography, graphics can add considerable interest to a document. Quite aside from the visual variety graphics contribute to a document, flowcharts, tables, charts, graphs, photographs, and art can actually be "worth a thousand words" as the clearest and most compact way of delivering information. As with your use of headings and typography to focus a reader's attention, you should strive in your use of graphics for a simple, consistent, and clean design framed by plenty of white space.

Graphic elements and their functions

Ideally, your use of graphics will complement—but not repeat—the material you've already written. To achieve an effective visual balance in your documents, plan the document's layout in advance. Understand in broad terms the balance you want to achieve between text and graphics. When you do incorporate graphical elements, refer in your text to these elements at the earliest opportunity. Try to not wait until your reader has completed reading your text to present related graphics. Consider using these graphical forms for the following specific purposes:

TO review, preview, emphasize, or prioritize	USE a flowchart, table list, outline list
TO orient readers in terms of space or sequences	USE a chart, diagram, map, photo views

TO show flow of functions or actions	USE a flowchart, diagram, photo
TO add emphasis to key relationships	USE a bar graph, pie chart, simple table
TO analyze or summarize key data	USE a complex graph, table, diagram
TO illustrate original data and sources	USE a facsimile recreating your source
TO help motivate	USE a photo, image, drawing, cartoon

For a detailed look at how to organize and present the types of graphical materials just mentioned, see the following recent texts: K. W. Houp et al., *Reporting Technical Information*, 8th edition, Chapter 11, "Graphical Elements" and M. J. Killingsworth, *Information in Action: A Guide to Technical Communication*, Chapter 3, "Developing Purposeful Graphics" (both Boston: Allyn & Bacon, 1996).

Tables, charts, graphs

Tables present data that usually shows a relationship between at least two sets of varying quantities, listed in columns. To show a table's relationships clearly, each set of quantities in each column or section of data is labeled, as shown in the example at the end of the paper in 39d. The often dense, complex data in tables needs simple, direct labels. Any qualifying or complex elements should be explained in footnotes.

Tables are the best vehicle for displaying large blocks of dense quantitative data. When you need a vivid display of critical changes or patterns of relationships in the table, a graph is the next option. The student paper in 39d shows similar data displayed both in tabular and graphed form. Using software packages, you can convert tabular data into line, bar, or circle graphs.

Consider the following examples showing similar material displayed in a line graph, a bar graph, and a circle graph. All three graphs compress a great deal of numerical information into a readily understood visual format. While the graphs show similar material relating to Medicare/Medicaid finances, each type offers a different emphasis and different options for the presentation best suited to your data and the points you wish to emphasize.

Note that in all three presentations there is a brief label, similar to those for tables, that identifies the significance of the quantities in each dimension of the graph. In constructing line or bar graphs, it is very important to plan the proportions you attach to the vertical and horizontal scale of quantities being displayed. If either dimension appears too short or too long, readers are likely to challenge the relationship you are showing between the graphed quantities, especially if the graph looks steeper or flatter than seems warranted by the data.

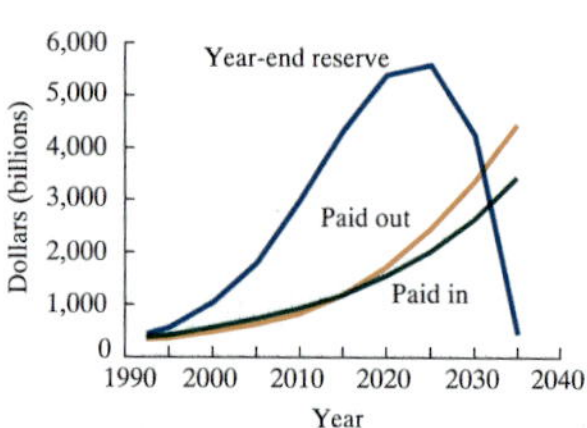

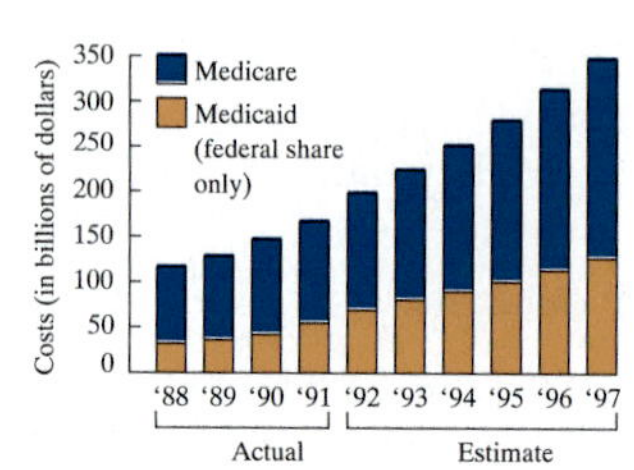

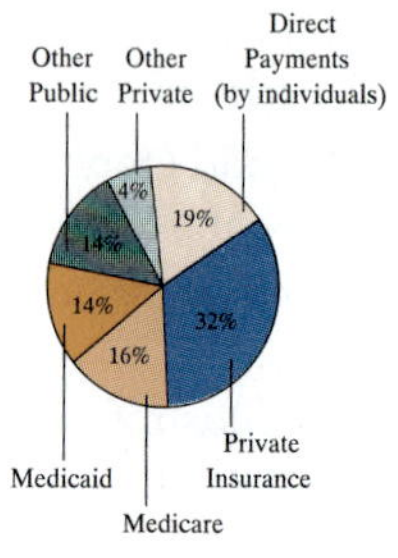

A line graph can show complex relationships, trends, and changes over space or time—in this case money paid into and out from federal Medicaid / Medicare funds, with surpluses and projected deficits shown. The scales on both axes of the graph are proportionally chosen to represent the abruptness of change.

When your message consists of simpler, less dense information, consider converting line graphs to bar graphs or pie charts. A bar graph emphasizes simple contrastive relationships among distinct units being compared, rather than the continuous trend relationships of line graphs. A pie chart is good for showing proportional parts of a whole entity—especially percentages.

Diagrams and images

Use diagrams, photographs, and images to help readers focus on your content and to amplify its meaning. For example, this book's "Thinking and Writing Wheel" graphic in Chapter 3 (see particularly 3a and 3b), is a schematic diagram that complements the text in those sections, giving readers a conceptual "map" and overview of a complex process. Use graphical elements with care, positioning them where you think they will best enhance the reader's understanding of your content.

Writers working on computers now have thousands of images available for use from clip-art programs. Here are three much-used examples:

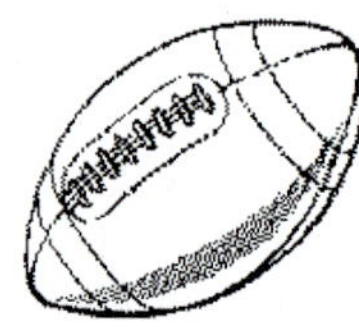

Clip-art images can sometimes direct a reader's attention effectively and thus have a place in document design. But take care to match clip-art images with your content. Do not decorate documents with images that can't be justified on the basis of content.

C4 Designing newsletters and web pages

You may find yourself working in organizations that produce pamphlets, brochures, newsletters, or their electronic cousin—web pages. For all of these formats, the basic principles from preceding sections for typography, headings, organizing schemes, and graphic elements are even more important than for reports and technical documents. If your job description calls for you to produce these types of documents, the success of which depends heavily on good visual design, then you should consult a specialized book such as K. C. McAdams and J. J. Elliott, *Reaching Audiences: A Guide to Media Writing* (Boston: Allyn & Bacon, 1996).

Newsletters

Organizations of all sorts use newsletters to disseminate information both internally, to employees, and externally, to the public. The newsletter is often presented in an 8-1/2 × 11 inch format that takes advantage of the various design tools discussed in this appendix. One distinctive feature is the newsletter's newspaper-like column width for text, which you see in the example on page 814 from the Massachusetts Cultural Council, a state agency for the arts. Notice the use of photographs, type style and size, headers, a box, white space, ruled lines of varying thickness, and clip-art images to achieve unity, balance, and proportion. Attractively designed, this first page of the newsletter invites readers to continue reading inside.

Web pages

With the explosive development of the Internet, especially the World Wide Web, web pages have become a popular medium for disseminating information. Receivers of web pages depend on one of several commercially available software "browsers" to deliver material on screen in semi-standardized formats. (See 33f, h.) In addition to their ability to display useful and interesting graphic images, web pages have further revolutionized document design through "hyperlinking"—attaching "hot buttons" to words or images and allowing readers to choose whether they will "jump" to new sections of a document or to other documents that the author feels are related. Audiences for web pages expect to be given options and choices about what to read and what to pursue.

Businesses use web pages for advertisements and sales; federal, state, and municipal governments publish announcements, reports, research results, and much-used forms on web pages; schools use web pages for course work and to provide library access. As the uses of the web expand, you may want to design a web page (or may be required to as part of a school or job assignment).

Creating a complete web page involves your writing coded computer instructions that are "wrapped around" individual text and graphic elements (likely with the help of a software package) and thus delivered to the web

C4

Massachusetts

CULTURAL COUNCIL

SUPPORTING PUBLIC PROGRAMS IN THE ARTS, HUMANITIES & SCIENCES

Summer 1994 Volume 3, Issue 2

NEA EXPLORES ARTS IN THE 21ST CENTURY

In April, National Endowment for the Arts Chair June Alexander convened ART-21, the first national conference in the federal agency's 29-year history. The purpose of ART-21 was to help the NEA prepare to redefine and restructure its services and financial resources to meet changing needs.

Over three days in Chicago more than 1,000 of the nation's artists, art administrators, educators, funders, community leaders, business leaders, and politicians participated in lectures, performances and hearings that focused on four major topics: The Artist in Society; The Arts and Technology; Expanding Resources for the Arts, and Lifelong Learning Through the Arts.

The following are excerpts from three of the inspiring keynote addresses delivered at ART-21, preceded by an introduction given by Chair Alexander. For a copy of the complete transcripts, please contact the MCC. Enjoy them as part of your summer reading!

WELCOMING REMARKS
Given by Jane Alexander, Chair of the National Endowment for the Arts

This conference emerged out of a sense of necessity. We are at a turning point in the history of public funding for the arts. As government re-invents itself, we, too, look to new inventions for a lively NEA. In the face of fiscal restraints, we depend more than ever on each other for our mutual survival. In the wake of attacks, we longed for a way out of tough times. We reach out now, not to the past, but to each other in the promise of a new century and a new beginning. As the President said, "Support of the arts is part of a broader social agenda that speaks to our very essence as Americans" . . .

In listening to the many voices in my travels across the country, in reading reports such as those from Wingspread last summer, in speaking with an eager and enthusiastic staff at the Endowment, I became convinced we can re-capture the spirit that created the Endowment 29 years ago. Those were days of energy and enthusiasm, when passionate men and women of vision worked together to create a new service agency dedicated to the cultural life of this country. Those passionate men and women of vision have new faces, but they exist today in all parts of this country, in all kinds of arts venues. They are great reason for hope, and you will hear some of their stories in the next few days.

THE ARTIST IN SOCIETY
Excerpt of keynote address given by Thulani Davis

Thulani Davis is a distinguished writer whose work includes fiction, theater, poetry, and journalism. Among her written works are the novel "1959," and "Malcolm X, The Great Photographs." Davis wrote the libretto for the acclaimed opera, "X, The Life and Times of Malcolm X," by Anthony Davis, the recording of which was nominated for a Grammy. Davis has been awarded several fellowships.

What does the artist do in society?

I looked up what a few artists have to say about that. Paul Gauguin said the artist is a person who shuts his eyes to see. Paul Klee said the objective of art "is not to reflect the visible but to make visible." Picasso said, "art is the lie that enables us to realize the truth."

I think of the artist as the person who is asked to express the inexpressible. I say the artist is asked to do this because it was my first experience of artists that he or she was often the person in my community who was called upon at the awkward moment before an important ritual to find the words for a union, a birth, or a separation from life. The poet was asked to find the poem to say what cannot be said about life's meaning. The singer is asked to give "Amazing Grace" or to make a wedding

continued on page 3

INSIDE THIS ISSUE

system on your own or your school's computer. If you are planning to create a web page, you might bear these considerations in mind:

- Be aware that not every web page will appear the same on every browser, since different browsers may decode markup elements differently.
- Be aware that, while simple images transport easily on most browser software, some web browser software will not be able to decode complex

graphics, audio, or video. Even with the right software, these complex files can be bulky and time consuming to deliver, as well as to create.

A review of other pages will help you determine what kinds of elements are simplest and most effective.

To create an effective web page, you will need instruction in an appropriate software package or a current web-page manual (available in most bookstores). Some basic information about the process can be gleaned from general books, such as P. W. Agnew et al., *Multimedia in the Classroom,* "Appendix: Multimedia Publication on the Internet's WWW" (Boston: Allyn & Bacon, 1996) or G. Pfaffenberger, *Publish It on the Web* (New York: McGraw, 1995).

Here is an example of a web page showing the "home page" that serves as a starting point or headline page. On this page, graphical elements are used as a menu device to reach various materials available at this web location. To achieve the effect shown, raw text elements are coded with a markup language and graphical or media elements are added in special computer files, some linked by images or "hot button" hypertext to other locations. Internet users reach this site by specifying the address elements that appear in the "location" bar at the top of the page.

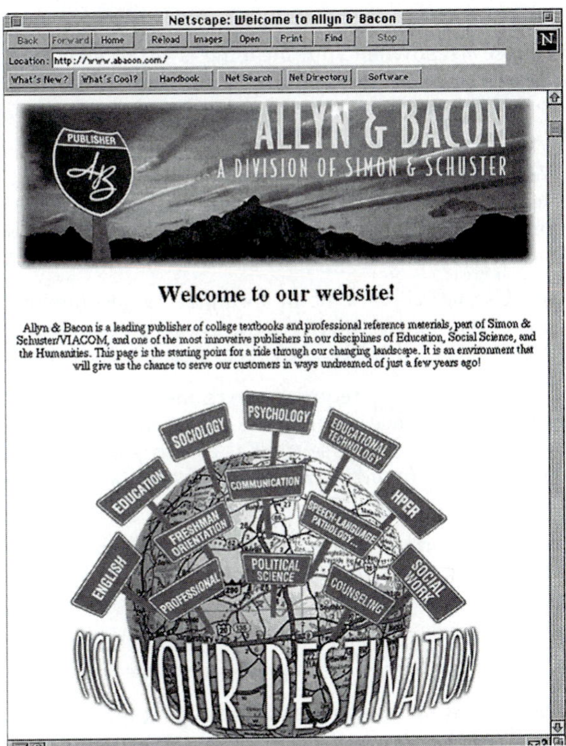

Glossary of Usage

This glossary is intended to provide definitions and descriptions of selected word usages current in formal academic writing. In consulting this kind of glossary, writers should be prepared to make informed decisions about the meaning and the level of diction that is most appropriate to their writing project.

Many entries in this glossary consist of commonly confused homonyms —words that are pronounced almost alike but have different meanings and spellings. A comprehensive listing of often-confused homonyms appears in 23a-1 in the spelling chapter.

a, an Use *a* when the article precedes a noun beginning with a consonant. For example, *At last we found a hotel.* Use *an* when the article precedes a word beginning with a vowel or an unpronounced *h. It was an honor to receive an invitation.* (See 7a.)

accept, except Use *accept* when your meaning is "to receive." Use *except* when you mean an exception, as in *He invited everyone except Thuan.* You can also use *except* as a verb that means "to leave out," as in *The report excepted the two episodes of misconduct.*

adverse, averse Use *averse* when you mean a person's feelings of opposition. Use *adverse* when you refer to a thing that stands in opposition or is opposed to someone or something, as in *I was not averse to taking the roofing job, but the adverse circumstances of a tight deadline and bad weather almost kept me from it.*

advice, advise Use *advice* as a noun meaning "a recommendation," as in *Longfellow gave excellent military advice.* Use *advise* as a verb meaning "to recommend," as in *Many counselors advise students to declare a double major.*

affect, effect If your sentence requires a verb meaning "to have an influence on," use *affect.* If your sentence requires a noun meaning "result," use *effect. Effect* can also be a verb, however. Use *effect* as a verb when you mean "to make happen," as in *He was able to effect a change in how the city council viewed the benefits of recycling.*

aggravate, irritate In formal writing, use *aggravate* when you mean "to make worse," as in *The smoke aggravated his cough.* Use *irritate* when you mean "to bother," as in *He became irritated when the drunken driver said the accident was not her fault.*

ain't Do not use *ain't* in formal writing. Use *is not, are not,* or *am not* instead.

all ready, already Use *all ready* when you mean "prepared" as in *He was all ready for an expedition to Antarctica.* Use *already* when you mean "by this time," as in *The ushers at Symphony Hall will not seat you if the concert has already started.*

all right Do not use *alright.* It is simply a misspelling.

all together, altogether Use *all together* when you mean "as a group" or "in unison," as in *Once we got the family all together, we could discuss the estate.* Use *altogether* when you mean "entirely," as in *Some of the stories about Poe's addictions and personal habits are not altogether correct.* (See 23a.)

allude, elude Use *allude* when you mean "to refer indirectly to." Use *elude* when you mean "to avoid or escape."

allusion, illusion Use *allusion* when you mean "an indirect reference," as in *The children did not understand the allusion to Roman mythology.* Use *illusion* when you mean "false or misleading belief or appearance," as in *Smith labored under the illusion that he was a great artist.*

a lot Do not use *a lot* in formal writing. Use a more specific modifier instead. When you use *a lot* in other contexts, remember that it is always two words.

among, between Use *between* when you are expressing a relationship involving two people or things, as in *There was general agreement between Robb and Jackson on that issue.* Use *among* when you are expressing a relationship involving three or more separable people or things, as in *He failed to detect a link among the blood cholesterol levels, the red blood cell counts, and the T-cell production rates.*

amongst Do not use *amongst* in formal writing. Instead, use *among.*

amount, number Use *amount* when you refer to a quantity of something that cannot be counted, as in *The amount of effort put into finding the cure for AIDS is beyond calculation.* Use *number* when you refer to something that can be counted, as in *The number of people who want to run the Boston Marathon increases yearly.*

an, and Use *an* when the article precedes a noun beginning with a vowel or an unpronounced *h.* Use *and* when your sentence requires a conjunction that means "in addition to."

and etc. Avoid using *etc.* in formal writing. When you must use *etc.* in nonformal writing, do not use *and. Et cetera* means "and so forth"; therefore, *and etc.* is redundant.

and/or Use *and* or *or,* or explain your ideas by writing them out fully. But avoid *and/or,* which is usually too ambiguous to meet the demands of formal writing.

anxious, eager Use *anxious* when you mean "worried" or "nervous." Use *eager* when you mean "excited or enthusiastic about the possibility of doing something."

anybody, any body; anyone, any one Use *anybody* and *anyone* when the sense of your sentence requires an indefinite pronoun. Use *any body* and *any one* when the words *body* and *one* are modified by *any,* as in *The teacher was careful not to favor any one student* and *Any body of knowledge is subject to change.*

any more, anymore Use *any more* to mean "no more," as in *I don't want any more of those plums.* Use *anymore* as an adverb meaning "now," as in *He doesn't work here anymore.*

anyplace Do not use *anyplace* in formal writing. Use *anywhere* instead.

anyways, anywheres Do not use *anyways* and *anywheres* in formal writing; use *anyway* and *anywhere* instead.

apt, likely, liable Use *apt* when you mean "having a tendency to," as in *Khrushchev was apt to lose his temper in public.* Use *likely* when you mean "probably going to," as in *We will likely hear from the Senator by Friday.* Use *liable* when you mean "in danger of," as in *People who jog long distances over concrete surfaces are liable to sustain knee injuries.* Also use *liable* when you are referring to legal responsibility, as in *The driver who was at fault was liable for the damages.*

as, like Use *as* either as a preposition or as a conjunction, but use *like* as a preposition only. If your sentence requires a preposition, use *as* when you are making an exact equivalence, as in *Edison was known as the wizard of Menlo Park.* Use *like* when you are referring to likeness, resemblance, or similarity, as in *Like Roosevelt, Reagan was able to make his constituency feel optimism.*

as, than When you are making a comparison, you can follow both *as* and *than* with a subjective- or objective-case pronoun, depending on meaning. For example, *We trusted O'Keeffe more than him [we trusted Smith]* and *We trusted O'Keeffe more than he [Jones trusted O'Keeffe]. O'Keeffe was as talented as he [was talented]* and *We found O'Keeffe as trustworthy as [we found] him.* (See 8g.)

as to Do not use *as to* in formal writing. Rewrite a sentence such as *The president was questioned as to his recent decisions in the Middle East* to read *The president was questioned about his recent decisions in the Middle East.*

assure, ensure, insure Use *assure* when you mean "to promise" as in *He assured his mother that he would return early.* Use *ensure* when you mean "to make certain," as in *Taking a prep course does not ensure success in the SATs.* Use *insure* when you mean "to make certain" in a legal or financial sense, as in *He insured his boat against theft and vandalism.*

at Do not use *at* in a question formed with *where.* For example, rewrite a sentence such as *Where is the class at?* to read *Where is the class?*

a while, awhile Use *awhile* when your sentence requires an adverb, as in *He swam awhile.* If you are not modifying a verb, but rather want a noun with an article, use *a while,* as in *I have not seen you in a while.*

bad, badly Use *bad* as an adjective, as in *Bad pitching changed the complexion of the game.* Use *badly* as an adverb, as in *The refugees badly needed food and shelter.* Use *bad* to follow linking verbs that involve appearance or feeling, as in *She felt bad about missing the party.* (See 11d.)

being as, being that Do not use either *being as* or *being that* to mean "because" in formal writing. Use *because* instead.

beside, besides Use *beside* as a preposition meaning "next to." Use *besides* as an adverb meaning "also" or "in addition to" as in *Besides, I needed to lose the weight.* Use *besides* as an adjective meaning "except" or "in addition to," as in *Rosa Parks seemed to have nothing besides courage to support her.*

better, had better; best, had best Do not use *better, had better, best,* and *had best* for *should* in formal writing. Use *ought* or *should* instead.

between, among See *among, between.*

breath, breathe Use *breath* as a noun; use *breathe* as a verb.

bring, take Use *bring* when you are referring to movement from a farther place to a nearer one, as in *The astronauts were asked to bring back rock samples.* Use *take* for all other types of movement.

broke Use *broke* only as the past tense, as in *He broke the Ming vase.* Do not use *broke* as the past participle; for example, instead of writing *The priceless vase was broke as a result of careless handling,* write *The priceless vase was broken as a result of careless handling.*

bunch Use *bunch* to refer to "a group or cluster of things growing together." Do not use *bunch* to refer to people or a group of items in formal writing.

burst, bust Use *burst* when you mean "to fly apart suddenly," as in *The pomegranate burst open.* (Notice that the example sentence doesn't say *bursted;* there is no such form of the verb.) (See 9b.)

but however, but yet When you use *however* and *yet,* do not precede them with *but* in formal writing. The *but* is redundant.

but that, but what When you use *that* and *what,* do not precede them with *but* in formal writing. The *but* is unnecessary.

calculate, figure, reckon If your sentence requires a word that means "imagine," use *imagine.* Do not use *calculate, figure,* or *reckon,* which are colloquial substitutes for "imagine."

can, may Use *can* when you are writing about the ability to do something, as in *He can jump six feet.* Use *may* when you are referring to permission, as in *He may rejoin the team when the period of probation is over.*

can't, couldn't Do not use these contractions in formal writing. Use *cannot* and *could not* instead.

can't hardly, can't scarcely See *not but, not hardly, not scarcely.*

can't help but Use *can't help* by itself; the *but* is redundant.

censor, censure Use *censor* when you mean editing or removing from the public eye on the basis of morality. Use *censure* when you mean "to give a formal or official scolding or verbal punishment."

center around Do not use *center around* in formal writing. Instead, use *center on.*

chose, choose Use the verb *choose* in the present tense for the first and second person and for the future tense, as in *They choose [or will choose] their teams carefully.* Use *chose* for the past tense, as in *The presidential candidate chose a distinguished running mate.*

compare to, compare with Use *compare to* to note similarities between things, as in *He compared the Chinese wine vessel to the Etruscan wine cup.* Use *compare with* to note similarities and contrasts, as in *When comparing market-driven economies with socialist economies, social scientists find a wide range of difference in the standard of living of individuals.*

complement, compliment Use *complement* when you mean "something that completes," as in *The wine was the perfect complement for the elegant meal.* Use *compliment* when you mean "praise," as in *The administrator savored the compliment on her organizational skills.*

conscience, conscious Use *conscience* when your sentence requires a noun meaning "a sense of right or wrong." Use *conscious* as an adjective to mean "aware of" or "awake."

consensus of opinion Do not use *consensus of opinion* in formal writing. Use *consensus* instead to avoid redundancy.

continual, continuous Use *continual* when you mean "constantly recurring," as in *Continual thunderstorms ruined their vacation days at the beach.* Use *continuous* when you mean "unceasing," as in *The continuous sound of a heartbeat, unceasing and increasing in volume, haunted the narrator.*

could of, would of, should of, might of, may of, must of In formal writing, avoid combining modal auxiliaries (*could, would, should, might, may,* and *must*) with *of.* Instead, write *could have, would have, should have, might have, may have,* and *must have.*

couple, couple of Do not use *couple* or *couple of* to mean "a few" in formal writing. Instead, write *a few.*

criteria Use *criteria* when you want a plural word referring to more than one standard of judgment. Use *criterion* when you are referring to only one standard of judgment.

data Use *data* when you are referring to more than one fact, statistic, or other means of support for a conclusion. When you are referring to a single fact, use the word *datum* in formal writing, or use *fact, figure,* or another term that is specific to the single means of support.

different from, different than Use *different from* when an object or phrase follows, as in *Braque's style is different from Picasso's.* Use *different than* when a clause follows, as in *Smith's position on the deficit was <u>different</u> when he was seeking the presidency <u>than</u> it was when he was president.*

differ from, differ with Use *differ from* when you are referring to unlike things, as in *Subsequent results of experiments in cold fusion differed radically from results first obtained in Utah.* Use *differ with* to mean "disagree," as in *One expert might differ with another on a point of usage.*

discreet, discrete Use *discreet* to mean "respectfully reserved," as in *He was always discreet when he entered the synagogue.* Use *discrete* to mean "separate" or "distinct," as in *The essay was a discrete part of the examination and could be answered as a take-home assignment.*

disinterested, uninterested Use *disinterested* to mean "impartial," as in *An umpire should always be disinterested in which team wins.* Use *uninterested* to mean "bored" or "not interested."

doesn't, don't Do not use *doesn't* and *don't* in formal writing; instead, use *does not* and *do not.* In other contexts, use *don't* with the first and second person singular, as in *I don't smoke* and with the third person plural, as in *They don't smoke.* Use *doesn't* with the third person singular, as in *He doesn't ride the subway.*

done Use *done* when your sentence requires the past participle; do not use done as the simple past. For example, rewrite a sentence such as *Van Gogh done the painting at Arles* to read *Van Gogh did the painting at Arles.*

due to, due to the fact that Use *due to* to mean "because" only when it follows a form of the verb *be,* as in *The sensation of a leg falling asleep is due to pooling of the blood in the veins.* Do not use *due to* as a preposition, however. Also, do not use *due to the fact that* in formal writing because it is wordy. (See 17a.)

eager, anxious See *anxious, eager.*

effect, affect See *affect, effect.*

elicit, illicit Use *elicit* to mean "to draw out," as in *The social worker finally elicited a response from the child.* Use *illicit* to mean "illegal," as in *Illicit transactions on the black market fuel an underground Soviet economy.* (See 23a.)

emigrate, immigrate, migrate Use *emigrate* to mean "to move away from one's country." Use *immigrate* to mean "to move to another country." Use *migrate* to mean "to move to another place on a temporary basis."

ensure, assure, insure See *assure, ensure, insure.*

enthused, enthusiastic Use *enthusiastic* when you mean "excited about" or "showing enthusiasm." Do not use *enthused* in formal writing.

especially, specially Use *especially* when you mean "particularly," as in *Maria Mitchell was especially talented as a mathematician.* Use *specially* when you mean "for a specific reason," as in *The drug was intended specially for the treatment of rheumatism.*

et al., etc. Do not use *et al.* and *etc.* interchangeably. *Et al.* is generally used in references and bibliographies and is Latin for "and others." *Et cetera* is Latin for "and so forth." Like all abbreviations, *et al.* and *etc.* are generally not used in formal writing, except that *et al.* is acceptable in the context of a citation to a source.

etc. Do not use *etc.* in formal writing. Use *and so forth* instead. Or, preferably, be as specific as necessary to eliminate the phrase.

everybody, every body Use *everybody* when you mean "everyone." Use *every body* when you are using *body* as a distinct word modified by *every,* as in *Is every body of water in Canada contaminated by acid rain?*

every day, everyday Use *everyday* when your sentence requires an adjective meaning "common" or "daily," as in *Availability of water was an everyday problem in ancient Egypt.* Use *every day* when you are using the word *day* and modifying it with the adjective *every,* as in *Enrico went to the art gallery every day.*

everywheres Do not use *everywheres* in formal writing. Use *everywhere* instead.

except, accept See *accept, except.*

except for the fact that In formal writing prefer the less wordy *except that.*

explicit, implicit Use *explicit* when you mean "stated outright," as in *The Supreme Court rules on issues that are not explicit in the Constitution.* Use *implicit* when you mean "implied," as in *Her respect for the constitution was implicit in her remarks.*

farther, further Use *farther* when you are referring to distance, as in *He was able to run farther after eating carbohydrates.* Use *further* when you are referring to something that cannot be measured, such as *Further negotiations are needed between the central government and the people of Azerbaijan.*

fewer, less Use *fewer* when you are referring to items that can be counted, as in *There are fewer savings accounts at the branch office this year.* Use *less* when you are referring to things that cannot be counted, as in *The East German people have less confidence in the concept of unification than they had one year ago.* (See 11e.)

figure See *calculate, figure, reckon.*

fixing to Do not use *fixing to* in formal writing. Use *intend to* instead.

former, latter Use *former* and *latter* only when you are referring to two things. In that case, the former is the first thing, and the latter is the second. If you are referring to more than two things, use *first* for the first and *last* for the last.

get Do not overuse *get* in formal writing. Prefer more precise words. For example, instead of *get better,* write *improve;* instead of *get,* write *receive, catch,* or *become;* instead of *get done,* write *finish* or *end.*

gone, went Use *gone* when your sentence requires the past participle of *to go,* as in *They had gone there several times.* Use *went* when your sentence requires the past tense of *to go,* as in *They went to the theater Friday.*

good and Do not use *good and* in formal writing. Use *very* or, preferably, a more precise modifier instead.

good, well Use *good* as an adjective, as in *Astaire gave a good performance, but not one of his best.* Use *well* as an adverb, as in *He danced well.* You can also use *well* as an adjective when you refer to good health, as in *She felt well* or *She is well today.* (See 11d.)

got, have; has/have got to Do not use *got* in place of *have* in formal writing. For example, rewrite a sentence such as *I got to lose weight* to read *I have to [*or *I must] lose weight.*

had better, better; had best, best See *better, had better.*

had ought Do not use *had ought* in formal writing. Use *ought* by itself instead.

half When you refer to half of something in formal writing, use *a half* or *one-half,* but do not use *a half a.* For example, rewrite a sentence such as *He had a half a sandwich for dinner* to read *He had a half sandwich for dinner.*

hanged, hung Use *hanged* for the action of hanging a person, as in *The innocent man was hanged by an angry mob.* Use *hung* for all other meanings, such as *The clothes were hung on the line* and *The chandelier hung from a golden rope.* (See 9b.)

he, she; he/she; his, her; his/her; him, her; him/her When you are using a pronoun to refer back to a noun that could be either masculine or feminine, you might use *he or she* in order to avoid language that is now considered sexist. For example, instead of writing *A doctor must be constantly alert; he cannot make a single mistake* to refer generally to doctors, you could write *A doctor must be constantly alert; he or she cannot make a single mistake.* Or you could recast the sentence in the plural to avoid this problem: *Doctors must be constantly alert; they cannot make a single mistake.* (See 10c and 21g for specific strategies on avoiding gender-offensive pronoun references.)

herself, himself, myself, yourself Use pronouns ending in *-self* when the pronouns refer to a noun that they intensify, as in *The teacher himself could not pass the test.* Do not use pronouns ending in *-self* to take the place of subjective- or objective-case pronouns. Instead of writing, for example, *Joan and myself are good friends,* write *Joan and I are good friends.* (See 7a.)

himself See *herself, himself, myself, yourself.*

his/her See *he/she.*

hisself Do not use *hisself* in formal writing. In a context such as *He hisself organized the picnic,* recast the sentence to read *He himself organized the picnic.*

hopefully Use *hopefully* when you mean "with hope," as in *Relatives watched hopefully as the first miners emerged after the fire.* Avoid using *hopefully* as a modifier for an entire clause or to convey any other meaning. For example, avoid *Hopefully, a cure for leukemia is not far away.*

hung, hanged See *hanged, hung.*

if, whether Use *if* to begin a subordinate clause when a stated or implied result follows, as in *If the court rules against the cigarette manufacturers, [then] thousands of lawsuits could follow.* Use *whether* when you are expressing an alternative, as in *Economists do not know whether the dollar will rebound or fall against the strength of the yen.*

illicit, elicit See *elicit, illicit.*

illusion, allusion See *allusion, illusion.*

immigrate See *emigrate, immigrate, migrate.*

impact Use *impact* when you are referring to a forceful collision, as in *The impact of the cars was so great that one was flattened.* Do not use *impact* as a verb meaning "to have an effect on." Instead of writing *Each of us can positively impact waste reduction efforts,* write *Each of us can reduce waste.*

implicit, explicit See *explicit, implicit.*

imply, infer Use *imply* when you mean "to suggest without directly stating," as in *The doctor implied that being overweight was the main cause of my problem.* Use *infer* when you mean "to find the meaning of something," as in *I inferred from her lecture that drinking more than two cups of coffee a day was a health risk.*

in, into Use *in* when you are referring to location or condition. Use *into* to refer to a change in location, such as *The famous portrait shows a man going into a palace.* (See 23a.) In formal writing, do not use *into* for "interested in." For example, avoid a statement such as *I am into repairing engines.*

incredible, incredulous Use *incredible* to mean "unbelievable," as in *Some of Houdini's exploits seem incredible to those who did not witness them.* Use *incredulous* to mean "unbelieving," as in *Many inlanders were incredulous when they heard tales of white people capturing men, women, and children who lived on the coast.*

individual, person, party Use *individual* when you are referring to a single person and when your purpose is to stress that the person is unique, as in *Curie was a tireless and brilliant individual.* Use *party* when you mean a group, as in *The party of eight at the next table disturbed our conversation and ruined our evening.* The word *party* is also correctly used in legal documents referring to a single person. Use *person* for other meanings.

infer, imply See *imply, infer.*

in regards to Do not use *in regards to* in formal writing. Generally, you can substitute *about* for *in regards to.*

inside of, outside of Use *inside* and *outside,* without *of,* when you are referring to location, as in *The roller blades were stored inside the garage.* In formal writing, do not use *inside of* to replace *within* in an expression of time. For example, avoid a sentence such as *I'll have that report inside of an hour.*

insure, assure, ensure See *assure, ensure, insure.*

irregardless, regardless Do not use *irregardless.* Use *regardless* instead.

is when, is where Do not use *is when* and *is where* when you are defining something. Instead of writing *Dinner time is when my family relaxes,* write *At dinner time, my family relaxes.*

its, it's Use *its* when your sentence requires a possessive pronoun, as in *Its leaves are actually long, slender blades.* (See 8c-1 and 27a-2.) Use *it's* only when you mean "it is." (See 23a.)

-ize Do not use the suffix *-ize* to turn a noun into a verb in formal writing. For example, instead of writing *He is finalizing his draft,* write *He is finishing his draft* or *He is working on his final draft.*

kind, sort, type Do not precede the singular words *kind, sort,* and *type* with the plural word *these.* Use *this* instead. Also, prefer more specific words than *kind, sort,* and *type.* (See 17a.)

kind of, sort of Do not use these phrases as adjectives in formal writing. Instead, use *rather* or *somewhat.*

later, latter Use *later* when you refer to time, as in *I will go to the concert later.* Use *latter* when you refer to the second of two things, as in *The latter of the two dates is better for my schedule.* (See also *former, latter.*)

latter, former See *former, latter.*

lay, lie Use *lay* when you mean "to put" or "to place," as in *She lays the present on the table.* Use *lie* when you mean "recline," as in *She lies awake at night,* or when you mean "is situated," as in *The city lies between a desert and a mountain range.* Also, remember that *lay* is a transitive verb that takes a direct object. (See 9d.)

learn, teach Do not use *learn* to mean "teach." For example, rewrite a sentence such as *Ms. Chin learned us Algebra* to read *Ms. Chin taught us Algebra.*

leave, let Use *leave* to mean "depart." Use *let* to mean "allow." You can use either *leave* or *let* when the word is followed by *alone,* as in *Leave her alone* or *Let him alone.*

less, fewer See *fewer, less.*

liable See *apt, liable, likely.*

lie, lay See *lay, lie.*

like, as See *as, like.*

like, such as Use *like* to make a comparison, as in *Verbena is like ageratum in size and color.* Use *such as* when you are giving examples, as in *Many small flowers, such as verbena, ageratum, and alyssum, can be combined to create decorative borders and edgings.*

likely See *apt, liable, likely.*

lose, loose Use *lose* as a verb meaning "to misplace" or "to fail to win." Use *loose* as an adjective meaning "not tight" or "unfastened." You can also use *loose* as a verb meaning "to let loose," as in *They loosed the enraged bull when the matador entered the ring.* (See 23a.)

lots, lots of Do not use *lots* or *lots of* in formal writing. Use *many, very many, much,* or choose a more precise word instead.

man, mankind Do not use *man* and *mankind* to refer to all people in general. Instead, consider using *people, men and women, humans,* or *humankind.* (See 21g.)

may be, maybe Use *maybe* to mean "perhaps." Use *may be* as a verb (or auxiliary verb), as in *William may be visiting tomorrow.* (See 23a.)

may, can See *can, may.*

may of See *could of, would of, should of, might of, may of, must of.*

media Use a plural verb with *media,* as in *The media are often credited with helping the consumer win cases against large companies. Medium* is the singular form.

might of See *could of, would of, should of, might of, may of, must of.*

migrate See *emigrate, immigrate, migrate.*

moral, morale Use *moral* when you mean "an object lesson" or "knowing right from wrong." *What is the moral to the story?* Use *morale* when you mean "outlook" or "attitude." *The team's morale was high.* (See 23a.)

Ms. Use *Ms.* to refer to a woman when a title is required and when you either know that she prefers this title or you do not know her marital status. An invented title, *Ms.* was intended to address the issue of discrimination or judgment based on marital status. In research writing, use last names alone, without any title, as in *Jenkins recommends. . . .* In this case, do not use a title for either a man or a woman.

must of See *could of, would of, should of, might of, may of, must of.*

myself See *herself, himself, myself, yourself.*

nor, or Use *nor* and *or* to suggest a choice. Use *nor* when the choice is negative; use *or* when the choice is positive. (See 7f.)

not but, not hardly, not scarcely Do not use *not* to precede *hardly, scarcely,* and *but* in formal writing. Because *but, hardly,* and *scarcely* already carry the meaning of a negative, it is not necessary or correct to add another negative.

nothing like, nowhere near Do not use *nothing like* and *nowhere near* in formal writing. Instead, use *not nearly.*

nowheres Do not use *nowheres* in formal writing. Use *nowhere* instead.

number, amount See *amount, number.*

off of Do not use *off of* in formal writing. Use *off* or *from* alone instead, as in *She jumped off the bridge* or *He leaped from the rooftop.*

Ok, okay, O.K. Do not use *Ok, okay,* or *O.K.* in formal writing as a substitute for *acceptable.*

on account of Do not use this as a substitute for *because.* Use *because* instead.

on, upon Use *on* instead of *upon* in formal writing.

or, nor See *nor, or.*

outside of, inside of See *inside of, outside of.*

party, individual, person See *individual, person, party.*

people, persons Use *people* to refer to a general group, as in *The people will make their voices heard.* Use *persons* to refer to a (usually small) collection of individuals, as in *The persons we interviewed were nearly unanimous in their opinion.*

per Do not use *per* in formal writing. For example, instead of writing *The package was sent per your instructions,* it is better to write *The package was sent according to your instructions. Per* is acceptable in technical writing or when used with data and prices, as in *Charging $75 per hour, the consultant earned a handsome salary.*

percent (per cent), percentage Use *percent* (or *per cent*) with a specific number. Use *percentage* with specific descriptive words and phrases, such as *A small percentage of the group did not eat meat.* Do not use *percentage* as a substitute for *part;* for example, rewrite a sentence such as *A percentage of my diet consists of complex carbohydrates* to read *Part of my diet consists of complex carbohydrates.*

person, party, individual See *individual, person, party.*

plenty Do not use *plenty* as a substitute for *quite* or *very.* For example, instead of writing *The Confederate troops were plenty hungry during the winter of 1864,* write *The Confederate troops were hungry [or starving] during the winter of 1864.*

plus Avoid using *plus* as a conjunction joining independent clauses or as a conjunctive adverb. For example, rewrite *Picasso used color in a new way plus he experimented with shape; plus, he brought new meaning to ideas about abstract painting* to read *Picasso used color in a new way and he experimented with shape; moreover, he brought new meaning to ideas about abstract painting.* It is acceptable to use *plus* when you need an expression meaning "in addition to," as in *The costs of day care, plus the costs of feeding and clothing the child, weighed heavily on the single parent's budget.*

practicable, practical Use *practicable* when you mean "capable of putting into practice," as in *Although it seemed logical, the plan for saving the zoo was very expensive and turned out not to be practicable.* Use *practical* when you mean "sensible," as in *Lincoln was a practical young man who studied hard, paid his debts, and dealt with people honestly.*

precede, proceed Use *precede* when you mean "come before," as in *The opening remarks precede the speech.* Use *proceed* when you mean "go forward," as in *The motorists proceeded with caution.*

pretty Do not use *pretty,* as in *pretty close,* to mean "somewhat" or "quite" in formal writing. Use *somewhat, rather,* or *quite* instead.

previous to, prior to Avoid these wordy expressions. Use *before* instead.

principal, principle Use *principal* when you refer to a school administrator or an amount of money. Use *principle* when you are referring to a law, conviction, or fundamental truth. You can also use *principal* as an adjective meaning "major" or "most important," as in *The principal players in the decision were Sue Marks and Tom Cohen.*

quotation, quote Use *quotation* when your sentence requires a noun, as in *The quotation from Nobel laureate Joseph Goldstein was used to lend credence to the theory.* Use *quote* when your sentence requires a verb, as in *She asked Goldstein whether she could quote him.*

raise, rise Use *raise* when you mean "to lift." Use *rise* when you mean "to get up." To help you understand the difference, remember that *raise* is transitive and takes a direct object; *rise* is intransitive. (See 9d.)

rarely ever Do not use *rarely ever* in formal writing. Use *rarely* or *hardly ever* instead.

real, really Use *real* as an adjective and use *really* as an adverb.

reason is because Do not use *reason is because* in formal writing. Rewrite your sentence to say, for example, *The real reason that the bomb was dropped was to end the war quickly* or *The bomb was dropped because Truman wanted to prevent Soviet influence in the Far Eastern settlement.*

reckon See *calculate, figure, reckon.*

regarding, in regard to, with regard to In formal writing that is not legal in nature, use *about* or *concerning* instead of these terms.

regardless, irregardless See *irregardless, regardless.*

respectfully, respectively Use *respectfully* when you mean "with respect," as in *He respectfully submitted his grievances.* Use *respectively* when you mean "in the given order," as in *The chief of police, the director of the department of public works, and the director of parks and recreation, respectively, submitted their ideas for budget cuts.*

right Do not use *right* as an intensifier in formal writing. For example, instead of writing that *The farmer was right tired after milking the cows,* write *The farmer was tired [or exhausted] after milking the cows.*

rise, raise See *raise, rise.*

seen Do not use *seen* without an auxiliary such as *have, has,* or *had.* For example, rewrite a sentence such as *I seen the film* to read *I have seen the film.*

set, sit Use *set* when you mean "to place." *Set* is a transitive verb that requires an object, as in *I set the book on the table.* Do not use *set* to mean "to sit" in formal writing. (See 9d.)

shall, will Use *shall* instead of *will* for questions that contain the first person in extremely formal writing, as in *Shall we attend the meeting?* In all other cases, use *will.*

should of See *could of, would of, should of, might of, may of, must of.*

should, would Use *should* when you are referring to an obligation or a condition, as in *The governor's mansion should be restored.* Use *would* when you are referring to a wish, as in *I would like to see it repainted in its original colors.*

sit, set See *set, sit.*

so Do not use *so* in formal writing to mean "very" or "extremely," as in *He is so entertaining.* Use *very, extremely,* or, preferably, a more specific intensifier instead. Or follow *so* with an explanation preceded by *that,* as in *The reaction to the Freedom Riders was* so *violent* that *Robert F. Kennedy ordered a military escort.*

some Do not use *some* to mean either "remarkable" or "somewhat" in formal writing. For example, rewrite a sentence such as *Babe Ruth was some hitter* to read *Babe Ruth was a remarkable hitter,* or use another more precise adjective to modify *hitter.* Also, rewrite a sentence such as *Wright's mother worried some about the kinds of building blocks her young child used* to read *Wright's mother worried a bit [or was somewhat worried about] the kinds of building blocks her young child used.*

somebody, some body; someone, some one Use the indefinite pronouns *somebody* and *someone* when referring to a person, such as *There is someone I admire.* Use *some body* and *some one* when the adjective *some* modifies the noun *body* or *one,* as in *We will find the answer in some body of information.*

sometime, sometimes, some time Use *sometime* when you mean "an indefinite, later time." Use *sometimes* when you mean "occasionally" or "from time to time." Use *some time* when *some* functions as an adjective modifying *time,* as in *His eyes required some time to adjust to the darkened room.*

sort See *kind, sort, type.*

specially, especially See *especially, specially.*

stationary, stationery Use *stationary* to mean "standing still." Use *stationery* to mean "writing paper."

such Do not use *such* to mean "very" or "extremely" unless *such* is followed by *that.* For example, rewrite a sentence such as *It had such boring lyrics* to read *It had extremely boring lyrics* or *It had* <u>such</u> *boring lyrics* that *I almost fell asleep half way through the song.*

such as, like See *like, such as.*

supposed to, used to Do not use *suppose to* or *use to* in formal writing. Use *supposed to* or *used to* instead.

sure and, sure to; try and, try to Do not use *sure and* and *try and* in formal writing. Instead, use *sure to* and *try to.* For example, rewrite the sentence *Be sure and bring your computer* to read *Be sure to bring your computer.*

sure, surely Use *surely* instead of *sure* when your sentence requires an adverb. For example, rewrite a sentence such as *Robert Fulton was sure a genius* to read *Robert Fulton was surely [or certainly] a genius.*

take, bring See *bring, take.*

than, as See *as, than.*

than, then Use *than* when you mean "as compared with," as in *The violin is smaller than the cello.* Use *then* when you are stating a sequence of events, as in *First, he learned how to play the violin. Then he learned to play the cello.* Also use *then* when you mean "at that time" or "therefore." (See 23a.)

that there See *this here, these here, that there, them there.*

that, which Use *that* or *which* in an essential (or restrictive) clause, or a clause that is necessary to the meaning of the sentence, as in *This is the book that explains Locke's philosophy.* Use *which* in a nonessential (nonrestrictive) clause, or one that is not necessary to the meaning of the sentence, as in *My library just acquired Smith's book on Locke, which is not always easy to find.* (See 14e.)

their, there, they're Use *their* as a possessive pronoun, as in *Their father prevented William and Henry James from being under the control of any one teacher for more than a year.* (See 8c-1.) Use *there* to refer to a place, as the opposite of *here.* Use *they're* to mean "they are." (See 27a-2.)

theirselves Do not use *theirselves* in formal writing. Rewrite a sentence such as *They treated theirselves to ice cream* to read *They treated themselves to ice cream.*

them there See *this here, these here, that there, them there.*

then, than See *than, then.*

these here See *this here, these here, that there, them there.*

these kind See *kind, sort, type.*

this here, these here, that there, them there Do not use *this here, these here, that there,* and *them there* in formal writing. Use *this, that, these,* and *those* instead.

thru Do not use *thru* in formal writing. Use *through* instead.

thusly Do not use *thusly* in formal writing. Use *thus* instead. (*Thus,* which is already an adverb, does not need an *-ly* ending.)

till, until, 'til Do not use *'til* or *till* in formal writing. Prefer *until.*

to, too, two Use *to* as a preposition meaning "toward"; use *too* to mean "also" or "excessively"; and use *two* as a number. (See 23a.)

toward, towards Use *toward* instead of *towards* in formal writing. *Towards* is the British form.

try and, try to See *sure and, sure to; try and, try to.*

type of Do not use *type* in formal writing when you mean "type of." For example, rewrite a sentence such as *He is an anxious type person* to read *He is an anxious type of person.* (See also *kind, sort, type.*)

uninterested, disinterested See *disinterested, uninterested.*

unique Do not modify *unique* in formal writing. Because *unique* is an absolute, you should not write, for example, *most unique* or *very unique.*

until See *till, until,'til; until* is the preferred form in formal writing.

use, utilize When you need a word that means "use," prefer *use. Utilize* is a less direct choice with the same meaning. (See 17a.)

used to See *supposed to, used to.*

very Avoid using *very* as an intensifier. Sometimes you will want to replace more than one word in order to eliminate *very.* For example, in the sentence *It was a very nice painting,* you could substitute more precise language, such as *It was a colorful [or provocative or highly abstract] painting.* (See 17a.)

wait for, wait on Unless you are referring to waiting on tables, use *wait for* instead of *wait on* in formal writing. For example, rewrite *We grew tired as we waited on Sarah* to read *We grew tired as we waited for Sarah.*

ways Do not use *ways* in formal writing to mean "way." Use *way* instead.

well, good See *good, well.*

where at See *at.*

whether, if See *if, whether.*

which, that See *that, which.*

which, who Use *which* when you are referring to things. Use *who* when you are referring to people.

who, whom Use *who* when a sentence requires a subject pronoun, as in *Who can answer this question?* Use *whom* when a sentence requires an object pronoun, as in *Whom did you invite?* (See 8f.)

who's, whose Do not use *who's* in formal writing. Use *who is* instead. (See 27a-2.) Use *whose* to show possession, as in *Whose computer did you use?* (See 8f.)

will, shall See *shall, will.*

-wise Do not attach the suffix *-wise* to nouns or adjectives to turn them into adverbs in formal writing. For example, instead of writing *I am not doing well gradewise,* you could recast the sentence to read *My grades are falling* or *My grades are low.*

would of See *could of, would of, should of, might of, may of, must of.*

would, should See *should, would.*

your, you're Do not use *you're* in formal writing. Use *you are* instead. (See 27a-2.) Use *your* to show possession, as in *Your CD player is broken.* (See 8f.)

yourself See *herself, himself, myself, yourself.*

APPENDIX E

Glossary of Terms: Grammar and Composition

abbreviation The shortened form of a word, usually followed by a period.

absolute phrase See *phrase.*

abstract expression An expression that refers to broad categories or ideas (*evil, friendship, love*).

abstract noun See *noun.*

acronym The uppercase, pronounceable abbreviation of a proper noun—a person, organization, government agency, or country. Periods are not used with acronyms (*ARCO, WAVES*). (See 31c.)

active voice See *voice.*

adjective A word that modifies or describes a noun, pronoun, or group of words functioning as a noun. Adjectives answer the questions: which, what kind, and how many. A single-word adjective is usually placed before the word it modifies. Pure adjectives are not derived from other words. (See 7a-5; Chapter 11.)

adjective clause See *clause.*

adjective forms Adjectives change form to express comparative relationships. The **positive form** of an adjective is its base form. The **comparative form** is used to express a relationship between two elements. The **superlative form** is used to express a relationship between three or more elements. Most single-syllable adjectives and many two-syllable adjectives show comparisons with the suffix *-er* (tall*er*) and superlatives with the suffix *-est* (tall*est*). Adjectives of three or more syllables change to the comparative and superlative forms with the words *more* and *most,* respectively (*more beautiful, most beautiful*). Negative comparisons are formed by placing the words *less* and *least* before the positive form (*less interesting, least interesting*). (See 11e.)

adverb A word that modifies a verb, an adjective, another adverb, or an entire sentence. Adverbs describe, define, or otherwise limit the words they modify, answering the questions when, how, where, how often, to what extent, and to what degree. Adverbs (as words, phrases, or clauses) can appear in different places in a sentence, depending on the rhythm the writer wants to achieve. Most adverbs are formed by adding the suffix *-ly* to an adjective. (See 7a-6; Chapter 11.)

adverb clause See *clause.*

adverb forms The change of form that adverbs undergo to express comparative relationships. The **positive form** of an adverb is its base form. The **comparative form** is used to express a relationship between two elements. The **superlative form** is used to express a relationship among three or more elements. Most single-syllable adverbs show comparisons with the suffix *-er* (*nearer*) and superlatives with the suffix *-est* (*nearest*). Adverbs of two or more syllables change to comparative and superlative forms with *more* and *most,* respectively (*more beautifully, most beautifully*). Negative comparisons are formed by placing the words *less* and *least* before the positive form (*less strangely, least strangely*). (See 11e.)

adverbial conjunctions See *conjunctive adverbs.*

agreement The grammatical relationship between a subject and a verb, and a pronoun and its antecedent. If one element in these pairs is changed, the other must also be changed. Subjects and verbs must agree in number and person; pronouns and antecedents must agree in number, person, and gender. (See Chapter 10.)

analogy A figure of speech that makes a comparison between two apparently unrelated people, objects, conditions, or events in order to clarify a process or a difficult concept. The unknown entity is explained in terms of the more familiar entity. (See 5e-7; 6d-1; 21f-1.)

analysis A close, careful reading of a text in which parts are studied to determine how the text as a whole functions. In a written analysis, in most instances, the author is obliged to support his or her interpretation with direct evidence from a text. (See 37c-1.)

antecedent A noun (or occasionally a pronoun) that a pronoun refers to and renames. A pronoun and its antecedent must agree in number, person, and gender. (See 10b; Chapter 14.)

antonym A word whose denotation (dictionary meaning) is opposite that of another word.

apostrophe A punctuation mark used to show possession, mark the omission of letters or numbers, and mark plural forms. (See Chapter 27.)

appositive A word or phrase that describes, identifies, or renames a noun in a sentence. (See 8e-2.)

appositive phrase See *phrase.*

article The words *a, an,* or *the.* The **indefinite article,** *a* or *an,* introduces a generalized noun. *A* appears before nouns beginning with a consonant; *an* is placed before nouns beginning with a vowel or an unpronounced *h.* The **definite article,** *the,* denotes a specific noun. Also called *determiners.*

assumption A core belief, often unstated, that shapes the way people perceive the world. (See 1g.)

audience The person or people who will be reading a piece of writing. Writing that takes a particular audience's needs and experience into consideration is most effective.

auxiliary verb The verbs *be, will, can, have, do, shall,* and *may,* combined with the base form of another verb, or its present or past participle. Such auxiliary verbs are used to establish tense, mood, and voice in a sentence. Also called *helping verbs.* (See 7a-3; 9c.)

base form The infinitive form of a verb (*to be, to go*) from which all changes are made. Also called the *dictionary form.*

bibliography The list of sources used in writing a paper. An **annotated bibliography** is a fully annotated working bibliography in manuscript form. A **working bibliography** includes all of the sources located in researching a paper. A **final bibliography** consists of only those sources used in the actual writing of a paper. In Modern Language Association (MLA) format, the bibliography is titled *Works Cited;* in American Psychological Association (APA) format, it is called *References;* and in Council of Biology Editors (CBE) format, it is called *Literature Cited.* (See 34d; Chapter 36.)

brackets Punctuation marks used to clarify or insert remarks into quoted material. (See 29d.)

brainstorming A technique of idea generation in which the writer quickly jots down words or phrases related to a broad subject. When the time limit (five or ten minutes) is reached, related items are grouped; groupings with the greatest number of items indicate potential topics for composition. (See 3b-2.)

buzzwords Vague, often abstract expressions that sound as if they have meaning, but do not contribute anything of substance to a sentence. (See 17a-4.)

case The change in form of a noun or pronoun, depending on its function in a sentence. The three cases are the subjective, objective, and possessive forms. Nouns and indefinite pronouns take all three cases, but change form only when they show possession (with the addition of an apostrophe and *s*). Pronouns change form in all three cases. The **subjective case** is used when a pronoun functions as a subject, subject complement, or as an appositive that renames a subject. The **objective case** is used when a pronoun functions as the object of a preposition, as the object or indirect object of a verb, as the object of a verbal, or as the subject of an infinitive. The **possessive case** of a noun or pronoun indicates possession or ownership. (See Chapter 8.)

chronological arrangement A method of organizing a paper in which the writing begins at one point in time and proceeds in sequence, forward or backward, to some other point. (See 5d-1.)

clause A grouping of words that has a subject and a predicate. An **independent clause** (or *main clause*) is a core statement that can stand alone as a sentence. A **dependent clause** (or *subordinate clause*) cannot stand alone as a sentence; it is joined to an independent clause by either a subordinating conjunction or a relative pronoun. There are four types of dependent clauses. **Adverb clauses** begin with subordinating conjunctions (*when, because, although*) and modify verbs, adjectives, and other adverbs. **Adjective clauses** begin with relative pronouns (*which, that, who, whom, whose*) and modify nouns or pronouns. **Noun clauses** are introduced by pronouns (*which, whichever, who, whoever, whom, whomever, whose*) and the words *how, when, why, where, whether,* and *whatever* and function as subjects, objects, complements, or appositives. **Elliptical clauses** have an omitted word or words (often relative pronouns or the logically parallel second parts of comparisons), but the sense of the sentence remains clear. (See 7e; 16e.)

cliché A trite expression that has lost its impact. (See 21f-3.)

coherence The clarity of the relationship between one unit of meaning and another. (See 4b-2.)

collective noun See *noun.*

colloquial Informal, conversational language. (See 21e-3.)

colon A punctuation mark (:) generally used to make an announcement. In formal writing, the colon follows only a complete independent clause and introduces a word, phrase, sentence, or group of sentences. (See 29a.)

comma A punctuation mark (,) used to signal that some element, some word or cluster of related words, is being set off from a main clause for a reason. (See Chapter 25.)

comma splice The incorrect use of a comma to mark the boundary between two independent clauses. (See Chapter 13; 25f-1.)

common noun See *noun.*

comparative form See *adjective forms, adverb forms.*

complement A word or group of words that completes the meaning of a subject or direct object by renaming it or describing it. A **subject complement** follows a linking verb and can be a noun, pronoun, adjective, or group of words substituting for an adjective or noun. An **object complement** typically follows verbs such as *appoint, call, choose, make,* and *show* and can be a noun, adjective, or group of words substituting for a noun or adjective.

complete predicate See *predicate.*

complete subject See *subject.*

complex sentence See *sentence.*

compound adjective Two or more words that are combined to modify a given noun. Often, when a compound adjective precedes a noun it is hyphenated to prevent misreading; when it follows the noun it modifies, it does not need hyphenation. (See 32a-1; 32a-3.)

compound-complex sentence See *sentence.*

compound noun Two or more words that are combined to function as a single noun. Hyphens are used when the first word of the compound could be read alone as a noun (*cross-reference*). (See 32a-2.)

compound predicate Two or more verbs and their objects and modifiers that are joined with a coordinating conjunction to form a single predicate.

compound sentence See *sentence.*

compound subject Two or more nouns or pronouns and their modifiers that function as a single subject.

compound verb Two or more verbs that are combined to function as a single verb. Hyphens are used when the first word of the compound could be read alone as a verb (*shrink-wrap*). (See 32a-2.)

compound words Nouns, adjectives, or prepositions created when two or more words are brought together to form a distinctive meaning and to function grammatically as a single word. (See 32a.)

concrete expression A vivid, detailed expression (*a throbbing headache*).

concrete noun See *noun.*

conjunction A word that joins sentence elements or entire sentences by establishing a coordinate or equal relationship among combined parts, or by establishing a subordinate or unequal relationship. **Coordinating conjunctions** (*and, but, or, nor, for, so, yet*) join complete sentences or parallel elements from two or more sentences into a single sentence and express specific logical relationships between these elements. **Correlative conjunctions** (*both/and, neither/nor, either/or, not only/but also*) are pairs of coordinating conjunctions that place extra emphasis on the relationship between the parts of the coordinated construction. The parts of the sentence joined by correlative conjunctions must be grammatically parallel. **Subordinating conjunctions** (*when, while, although, because, if, since, whereas*) connect dependent clauses to independent clauses. (See 7a-9; 18b; 19a-1, 2.)

conjunctive adverb An adverb (such as *however, therefore, consequently, otherwise,* or *indeed*) used to create a compound sentence in which the independent clauses that are joined share a logically balanced emphasis. Also called *adverbial conjunction.* (See 7a-9; 19a-3; 26b.)

connotation The implications, associations, and nuances of a word's meaning. (See 21a.)

coordinate adjectives Two or more adjectives in a series, whose order can be reversed without affecting the meaning of the noun being modified. Coordinate adjectives are linked by a comma or by a coordinating conjunction (*an intelligent, engaging speaker*). (See 25c-2.)

coordinating conjunction See *conjunction.*

coordination The combining of sentence elements by the use of coordinating and correlative conjunctions and conjunctive adverbs. Elements in a coordinate relationship share equal grammatical status and equal emphasis. (See 19a; 20b-1.)

correlative conjunction See *conjunction.*

count noun See *noun.*

cues Words and phrases that remind readers as they move from sentence to sentence (1) that they continue to read about the same topic and (2) that ideas are unfolding logically. Four types of cues are pronouns, repetition, parallel structures, and transitions. (See 5d-2.)

cut To delete sentences because they are off the point or because they give too much attention to a subordinate point. (See 4b-3.)

dangling modifier A word, phrase, or clause whose referent in a sentence is not clearly apparent. (See 15h.)

dash A punctuation mark (—) used to set off and give emphasis to brief or lengthy modifiers, appositives, repeating structures, and interruptions in dialogue. (See 29b.)

dead metaphor A metaphor that has been used so much it has become an ordinary word.

declarative sentence See *sentence.*

demonstrative pronoun See *pronoun.*

denotation The dictionary meaning of a word. (See 21a.)

dependent clause See *clause.* Also called *subordinate clause.*

descriptive adverb An adverb used to describe individual words within a sentence. (Poverty *almost* always can be eliminated at a higher cost to the rich.)

determiner See *article.*

dialect Expressions specific to certain social or ethnic groups as well as regional groups within a country. (See 21e-2.)

diction A writer's choice of words. (See Chapter 21.)

dictionary form See *base form.*

direct discourse The exact recreation, using quotation marks, of words spoken or written by a person. Also called *direct quotation.* (See 28a-1.)

direct object See *object.*

direct quotation See *direct discourse.*

documentation The credit given to sources used in a paper, including the author, title of the work, city, name of publisher, and date of publication. There are different systems of documentation for various disciplines; three frequently used systems include the Modern Language Association (MLA), American Psychological Association (APA), and the Council of Biology Editors (CBE) systems of documentation. (See Chapter 36.)

double comparative An incorrect method of showing the comparative form of an adverb or adjective by adding both the suffix *-er* to the word and placing the word *more* before the adverb or adjective. Only one form should be used. (See 11f.)

double negative An incorrect method of negation in which two negative modifiers are used in the same sentence. Only one negative should be used. (See 11f.)

double superlative An incorrect method of showing the superlative form of an adverb or adjective by adding both the suffix *-est* to the word and placing the word *most* before the adverb or adjective. Only one form should be used. (See 11f.)

drafting The stage in the composition process in which the writer generates the first form of a paper from a working thesis or outline. (See 3e; 35e.)

editing The stage in the composition process in which the writer examines and, if necessary, alters the work's style, grammar, punctuation, and word choice. (See 4c-1; 35f.)

ellipses Punctuation marks (. . .) consisting of three spaced periods that indicate the writer has deleted either words or entire sentences from a passage being quoted. (See 29e.)

elliptical clause See *clause.*

elliptical construction A shortened sentence in which certain words have been omitted deliberately in order to streamline communication. (See 16g.)

essential modifier A word, phrase, or clause that provides information crucial for identifying a noun; this type of modifier appears in its sentence without commas. The relative pronoun *that* is used only in essential clauses (*who* or *which* may also be used). Also called a *restrictive modifier.* (See 14e-2; 25d-1.)

etymology The study of the history of words. (See 22d.)

euphemism A polite rewording of a term that the writer feels will offend readers.

euphony The pleasing sound produced by certain word combinations.

evaluation A judgment of the effectiveness and reliability of a text in which the writer discusses the extent of his or her disagreement with an author.

exclamation point A punctuation mark (!) used to indicate an emphatic statement or command. (See 24c.)

exclamatory sentence See *sentence.*

expletive A word that fills the space left in a sentence that has been rearranged. The words *it* and *there* are expletives (filler words without meaning of their own) when used with the verb *be* in sentences with a delayed subject.

fact Any statement that can be verified.

faulty parallelism An error in a sentence where elements that should be grammatically equivalent are not. Faulty parallelism is indicated in a sentence when the use of a coordinating conjunction makes part of the sentence sound out of place or illogical. (See 18a.)

faulty predication An error in a sentence indicated when the predicate part of a sentence does not logically complete its subject. Faulty predication often involves a form of the linking verb *be.*

figure of speech A carefully controlled comparison that intensifies meaning. See *simile, analogy,* and *metaphor.*

final thesis See *thesis.*

first person See *person.*

formal English The acknowledged standard of correct English. (See 21e.)

formal register The writing of professional and academic worlds. Formal writing is precise and concise, avoids colloquial expressions, is thorough in content, and is highly structured. (See 3a-4.)

freewriting A technique of idea generation in which the writer chooses a broad area of interest and writes for a predetermined amount of time or in a prescribed number of pages, without pausing to organize or analyze thoughts. In *focused freewriting,* the same process is followed, but a specific topic is prescribed. (See 3b-3.)

fused sentence The joining of two independent clauses without a coordinate conjunction or proper punctuation. Also called a *run-on sentence.* (See Chapter 13.)

gender The labeling of nouns or pronouns as masculine, feminine, or neuter.

gerund The *-ing* form of a verb without its helping verbs; gerunds function as nouns.

gerund phrase See *phrase.*

historical present tense The present tense form used when referring to actions in an already existing work (a book, a movie). (See 9e-1.)

homonyms Words that sound alike or are pronounced alike but that have different spellings and meanings. (See 23a-1.)

hyphen A punctuation mark (-) used to join compound words and to divide words at the end of lines.

hypothesis A carefully stated prediction.

idiom A grouping of words, one of which is usually a preposition, whose meaning may or may not be apparent based solely on simple dictionary definitions. The grammar of idioms is often a matter of customary usage and is often difficult to explain. (See 21b-2.)

imperative mood See *mood.*

imperative sentence See *sentence.*

incomplete sentence A sentence that lacks certain important elements—a word, subject, or predicate.

indefinite pronoun See *pronoun.*

independent clause See *clause.*

indicative mood See *mood.*

indirect discourse The inexact quotation of the spoken or written words of a person. Indirect discourse inserts the writer's voice into the quotation. Also called *indirect quotation.* (See 28a-1.)

indirect object See *object.*

indirect question A restatement of a question asked by someone else. An indirect question uses a period as punctuation, not a question mark.

indirect quotation See *indirect discourse.*

infinitive The base form of a verb, which is often preceded by the word *to.* Also called the *dictionary form.*

infinitive phrase See *phrase.*

informal register The more colloquial, casual writing of personal correspondence and journals. (See 3a-4.)

intensive pronoun See *pronoun.*

interjection An emphatic word or phrase. When it stands alone, an interjection is frequently followed by an exclamation point. As part of a sentence, an interjection is usually set off by commas. (See 7a-10.)

interrogative pronoun See *pronoun.*

interrogative sentence See *sentence.*

intransitive verb See *verb.*

irregular verb A verb that changes its root spelling to show the past tense and form the past participle, as opposed to adding *-d* or *-ed.*

jargon The in-group language of professionals, who may use acronyms and other linguistic devices to take short-cuts when speaking with colleagues. (See 21e-4.)

limiting modifier A word that restricts the meaning of another word placed directly after it (*only, almost, just, nearly, even, simply*).

linking verb See *verb.*

list A displayed series of items that are logically similar or comparable and are expressed in grammatically parallel form.

logical arrangement A method of organizing a paper in which the topic is divided into its constituent parts, and the parts are discussed one at a time in an order that will make sense to readers. (See 5d-1.)

main clause See *clause.*

mapping A visual method of idea generation. The topic (word or phrase) is circled and from the circle are drawn spokes labeled with the "journalist's questions" (*who, what, where, when, how, why*). The answer to each question is then queried with the journalist's questions again. This method groups and subordinates ideas, thus assisting in generating main ideas and supporting information. (See 3b-7.)

mass noun See *noun.*

metaphor A figure of speech that illustrates or intensifies something relatively unknown by comparing it with something familiar. (See 21f-1.)

misplaced modifier A word, phrase, or clause whose position confuses the meaning of a sentence. A misplaced modifier is not placed next to the word(s) it is meant to modify. (See 15a.)

mixed construction A confused sentence structure that begins with a certain grammatical pattern and then abruptly changes direction with another grammatical pattern.

mixed metaphor An illogical comparison of two elements. (See 21f-2.)

modal auxiliary A verb that is paired with the base form of a verb to express urgency, obligation, likelihood, or possibility (*can, could, may, might, must, ought to, should, would*). (See 9c-1.)

modifier An adjective or adverb, in the form of a single word, phrase, or clause, that adds descriptive information to a noun or verb. A single-word adjective is often positioned directly before the noun it modifies. Adverbs can be shifted to any part of a sentence. Depending on its location, an adverb will change the meaning or rhythm of a sentence, so care must be taken to ensure that an adverb modifies the word intended. (See 7c.)

mood The form of a verb that indicates the writer's attitude about an action. The **indicative mood** expresses facts, opinions, or questions. The **imperative mood** expresses commands. The **subjunctive mood** expresses a recommendation, a wish, a requirement, or a statement contrary to fact. (See 9h.)

nonessential modifier A word, phrase, or clause that provides information that is not essential for defining a word. Commas are used to set the clause apart from the sentence in which it appears. The relative pronouns *who* and *which* may be used in nonessential clauses. Also called *nonrestrictive modifier.* (See 14e-2; 25d-2.)

nonrestrictive modifier See *nonessential modifier.*

noun A noun names a person, place, thing, or idea. Nouns change their form to show number; the plural is usually formed by adding *-s* or *-es.* Possession is indicated with the addition of an apostrophe and usually an *s.* **Proper nouns,** which are capitalized, name particular persons, places, or things. **Common nouns** refer to general persons, places, or things. **Mass nouns** denote items that cannot be counted. **Count nouns** denote items that can be counted. **Concrete nouns** name tangible objects. **Abstract nouns** name intangible ideas, emotions, or qualities. **Animate** versus **inanimate nouns** differ according to whether they name something alive. **Collective nouns** are singular in form and have either a singular or plural sense, depending on the meaning of the sentence. (See 7a-2; 10a-5.)

noun clause See *clause.*

noun phrase See *phrase.*

number A change in the form of a noun, pronoun, or verb that indicates whether it is singular or plural. (See 16a.)

object A noun, pronoun, or group of words substituting for a noun that receives the action of a transitive verb (**direct object**); is indirectly affected by the action of a transitive verb (**indirect object**); or follows a preposition (**object of a preposition**). (See 7b.)

object complement See *complement.*

objective case See *case.*

object of a preposition See *object.*

opinion A statement of interpretation and judgment.

outline A logically parallel list with further subdivision and subsections under individual items in the list. (See 18e-2.)

paragraph A group of related sentences organized by a single, controlling idea. (See Chapter 5.)

parallel case An argument that develops a relationship between directly related people, objects, events, or conditions.

parallelism The use of grammatically equivalent words, phrases, and sentences to achieve coherence and balance in writing. (See 5d-2; Chapter 18.)

paraphrase A restatement of a passage of text. The structure of a paraphrase reflects the structure of the source passage. (See 34f-2.)

parentheses Punctuation marks used to enclose and set off nonessential dates, words, phrases, or whole sentences that provide examples, comments, and other supporting information. (See 29c.)

participial phrase See *phrase.*

participle A verb form. The **present participle** (the *-ing* form) functions as a main verb of a sentence and shows continuing action when paired with *be;* functions as an adjective when paired with a noun or pronoun (*the loving parent*); and functions as a noun when used as a gerund (*studying takes time*). (See *gerund.*) The **past participle** (the past tense *-d, -ed, -n,* or *-en* forms) functions as the main verb of a sentence when paired with *have* (*I have studied for days*); forms a passive construction when paired with *be* (*The rock was thrown*); and functions as an adjective when paired with a noun or pronoun (*the contented cow*).

parts of speech The categories into which words are grouped according to their grammatical function in a sentence: nouns, verbs, verbals, adjectives, adverbs, pronouns, prepositions, conjunctions, interjections, and expletives. (See glossary entries for each category and 7a-2–11.)

passive voice See *voice.*

past participle See *participle.*

past tense See *tense.*

period A punctuation mark (.) that denotes a complete stop—the end of a sentence. (See 24a.)

person The form of a pronoun or a noun that identifies whether the subject of a sentence is the person speaking (the **first person**); the person spoken to (the **second person**); or the person spoken about (the **third person**). (See 16a.)

personal pronoun See *pronoun.*

phrase A grouping of words that lacks a subject and predicate and cannot stand alone as a sentence. **Verbal phrases** consist of infinitive phrases, gerund phrases, and participial phrases—all of which are built on verb forms not functioning as verbs in a sentence, along with associated words (objects and modifiers). **Infinitive phrases** consist of the infinitive form, often preceded by *to*; they function as adjectives, adverbs, or nouns. **Gerund phrases** consist of the *-ing* form of a verb and function as nouns—as subjects, objects, or complements. **Participial phrases** consist of the present or past participle of a verb and function as adjectives. **Verb phrases** consist of the combination of an auxiliary and the base form, or present or past participle, of a verb. **Noun phrases** consist of a noun accompanied by all of its modifying words. A noun phrase may be quite lengthy, but it always functions as a single noun—as a subject, object, or complement. **Absolute phrases** consist of a subject and an incomplete predicate; they modify entire sentences, not individual words. **Appositive phrases** rename or further identify nouns and are placed directly beside the nouns they refer to. (See 7d; 12c; 29a-4; 29b-1.) **Prepositional phrases** consist of a preposition combined with a noun (called an *object*), which functions in a sentence as a modifier, such as an adjective or adverb.

plagiarism A conscious attempt to pass off the ideas or the words of another as one's own. (See 34h.)

plot summary A brief description of characters and events that provides readers context enough to follow a discussion. Plot summaries are written in the historical present tense.

popular register The writing typical of most general-interest magazines. The language is more conversational than formal writing, but all conventions of grammar, usage, spelling, and punctuation are adhered to. (See 3a-4.)

positive form See *adjective forms, adverb forms.*

possession Nouns and pronouns indicate ownership, possession, or attachment with a change in case form. Nouns indicate possession with the addition of an apostrophe and usually an *s*. (See 7a-2.)

possessive case See *case.*

predicate A verb and other words associated with it that state the action undertaken by a subject or the condition in which the subject exists. A **simple predicate** consists of the verb and its auxiliaries. A **complete predicate** consists of the simple predicate and its modifiers and objects. A **compound predicate** consists of two verbs and their associated words which are joined with a coordinating conjunction and share the same subject. (See 7a-1.)

prefix A group of letters joined to the beginning of a root word to form a new, derived word. Prefixes indicate number, size, status or condition, negation, and relations in time and space. (See 22d-2; 23c.)

preposition A word (*in, at, of, for, on, by, above, under*) that links a noun, pronoun, or word group substituting for a noun to other words in a sentence—to nouns, pronouns, verbs, or adjectives. (See 7a-8.)

prepositional phrase See *phrase.*

present participle See *participle.*

primary source An original document or artifact that may be referred to in a paper, such as a story, letter, or autobiography.

principal parts The forms of a verb built from the infinitive, from which the tenses are formed: past tense, present participle, and past participle.

pronoun A word that takes on the meaning of and substitutes for a noun (referred to as the pronoun's *antecedent*). Pronouns show number (singular or plural) and change case depending on their function in a sentence. **Personal pronouns** (*I, me, you, us, his, hers . . .*) refer to people or things. **Relative pronouns** (*who, which, that . . .*) introduce dependent clauses that usually function as adjectives. The pronouns *who, which,* and *that* rename and refer to the nouns they follow. **Demonstrative pronouns** (*this, that, these, those*) point to the nouns they replace. **Interrogative pronouns** (*who, which, what, whose*) form questions. **Intensive pronouns** (*herself, themselves*) are formed with the suffix *-self* or *-selves* to repeat and emphasize a noun or pronoun. **Reflexive pronouns** (*herself, ourselves*) are formed with the suffix *-self* or *-selves* and rename or reflect back to a preceding noun or pronoun. **Indefinite pronouns** (*one, anybody*) refer to general or nonspecific persons or things. **Reciprocal pronouns** (*one another, each other*) refer to the separate parts of a plural noun. (See 7a-7; Chapter 8; Chapter 14.)

proofreading The final stage in the composition process in which the writer rereads the final paper to identify and correct misspelled words; words (often prepositions) omitted from sentences; words that have been doubled; punctuation that may have been forgotten; and homonyms. (See 4c-2.)

proper noun See *noun.*

quotation See *direct discourse.*

quotation marks These marks (" ") denote the exact reproduction of words written or spoken by someone else.

reciprocal pronoun See *pronoun.*

redundant phrase An expression that repeats a message unnecessarily.

reflexive pronoun See *pronoun.*

regionalism An expression whose meaning is specific to certain areas of the country. Use of such expressions is inappropriate in formal writing. (See 21e-2.)

register The level of language or tone used in a paper. (See *formal register, informal register, popular register.*)

regular verbs Verbs that change form in predictable ways, taking the suffix *-ed* to show the past tense and the past participle.

relative pronoun See *pronoun.*

restrictive modifier See *essential modifier.*

revision A stage in the composition process in which the writer examines the first draft to clarify the purpose or thesis; rewrites to achieve unity and coherence; and adjusts to achieve balance by expanding, condensing, or cutting material. (See Chapter 4; 35f.)

root word The base form of a word that contains its core meaning. Suffixes and prefixes are added to a root word to form additional words.

run-on sentence See *fused sentence.*

-*s* form The form of a verb that occurs with third-person, singular subjects when an action is in the present. This form (created by adding *-s* or *-es* to a verb) is used with the personal pronoun *he, she,* or *it;* with any noun that can be replaced by these pronouns; and with a number of indefinite pronouns (e.g., *something* or *no one*), which are often considered singular.

second person See *person.*

secondary source The work of scholars who have interpreted the writings of others.

section A grouping of paragraphs that constitutes part of the larger document. (See 5a-1.)

section thesis See *thesis.*

semicolon A punctuation mark (;) used to denote a partial separation between independent elements. (See Chapter 26.)

sentence A fully expressed thought consisting of a complete subject and a complete predicate. A sentence begins with a capital letter and ends with a period, question mark, or exclamation point. The four functional types of sentences include declarative, interrogative, exclamatory, and imperative sentences. A **declarative sentence** makes a statement or assertion about a subject. An **interrogative sentence** poses a question and is formed either by inverting a sentence's usual word order or by preceding the sentence with a word such as *who, which,* *when, where,* or *how.* An **exclamatory sentence** is used as a direct expression of a speaker's or writer's strong emotion. An **imperative sentence** expresses a command. The four structural types of sentences are simple, compound, complex, and compound-complex sentences. A **simple sentence** has a single subject and a single predicate. A **compound sentence** has two subjects and two predicates. A **complex sentence** has an independent clause and one or more dependent clauses. A **compound-complex sentence** has at least two independent clauses and one subordinate, dependent clause.

sentence fragment A partial sentence punctuated as if it were a complete sentence, with an uppercase letter at its beginning and a period, question mark, or exclamation point at its end. A sentence fragment lacks either a subject or a predicate, and sometimes both. It can also be a dependent clause that has not been joined to an independent clause.

sexism In writing, the use of inappropriate gender-specific words (*a biologist in his lab*) that creates biased or inaccurate characterizations linked with a male or female reference. (See 21g.)

simile A figure of speech in which two different things, one usually familiar, the other not, are explicitly compared. The properties of the known thing help to define the unknown thing. Similes often use the words *like* or *as* to set up the comparison. (See 21f-1.)

simple future tense See *tense.*

simple past tense See *tense.*

simple predicate See *predicate.*

simple present tense See *tense.*

simple sentence See *sentence.*

simple subject See *subject.*

slang The informal language peculiar to a culture or subculture; inappropriate for formal writing.

slash A punctuation mark (/) used to separate lines of poetry run in with the text of a sentence; to show choice, as in *either/or;* and to note division in fractions or formulas. (See 29f.)

spatial arrangement A method of organizing a paper in which the subjects are described according to their relative positions; for example, for a photograph, the foreground, middle ground, and background might be described. (See 5d-1.)

split infinitive The insertion of an adverbial modifier between the two parts of an infinitive—the word *to* and the base form—which can disrupt the intended meaning (. . . *to* successfully *attempt*). (See 15f.)

squinting modifier A word, phrase, or clause that ambiguously appears to modify two words in a sentence—both the word preceding and following it.

subject A noun, pronoun, or group of words substituting for a noun, that engages in the main action of a sentence or is described by the sentence. A **simple subject** consists of a single noun or pronoun. A **complete subject** consists of a simple subject and its modifiers. A **compound subject** consists of a multiple subject created by using the coordinating conjunction *and.*

subject complement See *complement.*

subjective case See *case.*

subjunctive mood See *mood.*

subordinate clause See *clause, dependent clause.*

subordinating conjunction See *conjunction.*

subordination A method for linking words, phrases, or clauses that is used to give more emphasis to one idea than to another in a sentence. The words in a dependent (subordinate) clause cannot stand alone as a sentence. (See 19b.)

suffix A group of letters joined to the end of a root word. Suffixes change the grammatical function of words and can be used to indicate tense.

summary A brief, objective account of the main ideas of a source passage.

superlative form See *adjective forms, adverb forms.*

synonym A word that has approximately the same denotation (dictionary meaning) as another word.

synthesis A presentation that draws together material from several sources. (See 2d.)

tag question A brief question attached to a statement, set off by a comma. Tag questions consist of a helping verb, a pronoun, and frequently the word *not* (*He won the match, didn't he?*). (See 25e-5.)

tense The change in form of a verb that shows when an action has occurred or when a subject exists in a certain state of being. Tenses are marked by verb endings and auxiliary verbs. (See 9e, f; 16b-1.) The **simple present tense** indicates an action taking place at the writer's present time. The verb's base form is used for singular or plural first- and second-person subjects, as well as for plural third-person subjects (*I go, you go, they go*). The verb for a third-person singular subject ends with the suffix *-s* (*she goes*). The **simple past tense** indicates an action completed at a definite time in the past. Regular verbs form this tense by adding *-d* or *-ed* to the base form. The **simple future tense** indicates an action or state of being that will begin in the future. All other tenses build on these basic tenses by using auxiliaries. See Chapter 9 for more information on the present, past, and future perfect tenses; the present, past, and future progressive tenses; and the perfect progressive tenses.

thesis A general statement about a topic that crystallizes the main purpose of a writing and suggests its main parts. A **section thesis** explicitly announces the point to be addressed in a section and either directly or indirectly suggests what will be discussed relating to this point. (See 5a-2.) A **working thesis** is a statement that should prove to be a reasonably accurate summary of what will be written. A **final thesis** is an accurate, one-sentence summary of a work that will appear in the final draft. (See 3d; 33e; 35a.)

third person See *person.*

tone The expression of a writer's attitude toward the subject or audience. Tone is determined by word choice and quality of description, verb selection, sentence structure, and sentence mood and voice. The tone of a piece changes depending on the audience. (See 3a-4; 16c.)

topic The subject of a piece of writing. (See 3a.)

topical development The expansion of statements about a topic announced in the opening sentence of a paragraph. After its opening announcement, the topic is divided into two or three parts, each of which is developed at a different location in the paragraph. (See 5e.)

topic sentence A paragraph's central, controlling idea. (See 5c.)

transition A word, sentence, or paragraph devoted to building a smooth, logical relationship between ideas in a sentence, between sentences, between paragraphs, or between whole sections of an essay. (Phrases include *for example, on the other hand, in addition.*) (See 4b-2; 5d-3; 20c-1.)

transitive verb See *verb.*

usage The prevailing, customary conditions describing how, where, and when a word is normally used in speech and writing. Usage labels in a dictionary, such as *colloquial, slang, archaic,* and *dialect,* indicate special restrictions on the conditions for using a particular meaning or form of a word.

verb The main word in the predicate of a sentence expressing an action or occurrence or establishing a state of being. Verbs change form to demonstrate tense, number, mood, and voice. **Transitive verbs** (*kick, buy*) transfer the action from an actor—the subject of the sentence—to a direct object—a person, place, or thing receiving that action. **Intransitive verbs** (*laugh, sing, smile*) show action that is limited to the subject; there is no direct object that is acted upon. (*The rock fell.*) The same verb can be transitive in one sentence and intransitive in another. (*She runs a good business. She runs every day.*) **Linking verbs** (*is, feel, appear, seem*) allow the word or words following the verb to complete the meaning of the subject. (*Joan is a lawyer.*) (See 7a-3; Chapter 9.)

verb phrase See *phrase.*

verbal A verb form that functions in a sentence as an adjective, an adverb, or a noun. Verbals include infinitives, participles, and gerunds. (See *infinitive, participle, gerund;* 7a-4; 7d-2.)

verbal phrase See *phrase.*

voice The form of a transitive verb in a sentence that shows whether emphasis is given to the actor or to the object acted upon. **Active-voice** sentences emphasize the doer of an action. **Passive-voice** sentences emphasize the object acted upon or deemphasize an unknown subject. In passive-voice sentences the words are rearranged so that the object occupies the first position. This construction requires the use of a form of the verb *be* and the preposition *by.* (*The house was designed by Frank Lloyd Wright.*)

working thesis See *thesis.*

REFERENCES *and* WORKS CITED

Chapter 1: Works Cited

All works cited in this chapter are listed in the "Works Cited" section of the student paper by Lou Cassetta in 4f.

Cowan, Ruth Schwartz. "Virginia Dare to Virginia Slims: Women and Technology in American Life." *Technology in Society* Jan. 1979: 51–63.

Healy, Bernardine. "Quotable" column. *The Chronicle of Higher Education* 25 Mar. 1992: B-5.

Chapter 5: References

The illustrative paragraphs in this chapter are attributed in the text as they occur; they are drawn from the following sources:

Bergom, Mike. *Technology, Jazz, and History*. Reprinted by permission of the author.

Capraro, Anthony F., III. "The Interview." *Barron's Profiles of American Colleges*. 19th ed. Hauppage, NY: Barron's Educational Services, 1992.

Carson, Rachel. *Silent Spring*. Boston: Houghton, 1962. 39, 105, 136.

Cheever, Daniel S., Jr. "Higher and Higher Ed." *Boston Sunday Globe* 26 April 1992: 73, 75.

Cornish, Roger, and Violet Ketels. Introduction. *Landmarks of Modern British Drama: The Plays of the Sixties*. Vol. 1. New York: Methuen, 1985: vii–xxxv.

Curtis, Helena. *Biology*. 2nd ed. New York: Worth, 1975. 47.

Dennis, Jerry. "Mates for Life." *Wildlife Conservation* May/June 1993: 70–71, 82.

Farber, Stephen. *The Movie Rating Game*. Public Affairs Press, 1972. Rpt. in *Writing and Reading Across the Curriculum*. 3rd ed. Ed. Laurence Behrens and Leonard Rosen. Glenview: Scott, 1987. 177.

Fagan, Brian M. *Archaeology: A Brief Introduction*. 3rd ed. Glenview: Scott, 1988. 37–38.

Gould, Stephen Jay. "Sex, Drugs, Disasters." *The Winchester Reader*. Ed. Donald McQuade and Robert Atwan. Boston: Bedford, 1991. 816.

"Update on Alzheimer's Disease—Part 1." *Harvard Mental Health Letter* 11.8 (Feb. 1995): 1–2.

Homsy, George. "From Kings to Caddies in Edinburgh—an Offbeat Tour of the City's History." *Boston Sunday Globe* 15 Oct. 1995: B:14 +.

Jones, Rachel L. "What's Wrong with Black English." *Newsweek*, "My Turn," 27 Dec. 1982: 7. Rpt. in *Effective Argument*. Ed. J. Karl Nicholas and James R. Nicholl. Boston: Allyn and Bacon, 1991. 157, 159.

Keller, Helen. *The Story of My Life*. New York: Doubleday, 1954. 35–37.

Kozol, Jonathan. "Distancing the Homeless." *The Winchester Reader*. Ed. Donald McQuade and Robert Atwan. Boston: Bedford, 1991. 175.

Lefton, Lester. "Aging." *Psychology*. 4th ed. Boston: Allyn & Bacon, 1991. 363.

Neuman, Susan B. "A Different Understanding of the Relation Between Media." *Literacy in the Television Age: The Myth of the TV Effect*. Ablex Publishing Corporation, 1991. 194–96.

Pelletier, Michele L. "The Volunteer Army: A Good Idea." Reprinted by permission of the author.

Quindlen, Anna. "A City's Needy." *New York Times* 30 Nov. 1986.

SOURCES FOR NEW EXERCISES AND EXAMPLES

CHAPTER 6

de la Croix, Horst, Richard D. Tansey, and Diane Kirkpatrick. *Gardner's Art through the Ages*. 9th ed. New York: Harcourt, Brace, Jovanovich, 1970.

Morais, Richard C. "Saga of Fire and Ice." *Forbes* 23 Oct. 1995: 162+.

Morris, Betsy. "Executive Women Confront Midlife Crisis." *Fortune* 18 Sept. 1995: 60+.

Weigel, George. "Are Human Rights Still Universal?" *Commentary* 99.2 (Feb. 1995).

West, Cornel. "Why I'm Marching on Washington." *The New York Times Large Type Weekly* 16 Oct. 1995: 20–21.

CHAPTER 7

Sharpe, Lora. "The Right Track." *Boston Sunday Globe*. Special Section "Careers 95" 15 Oct. 1995: 2.

Strauss, Bob. "Rebirth of the Cool." *Boston Sunday Globe*. "Arts Etc." 15 Oct. 1995: 63.

Varma, Devendra P. "The Vampire in Legend, Lore and Literature." *The Vampire in Literature*. Ed. Margaret L. Carter. Ann Arbor: UMI Research Press, 1989. 13–29.

CHAPTER 8

Weinstein, Miriam. "Presenting . . . the Past." *Boston Globe Magazine* 29 Oct. 1995: 26–34.

CHAPTER 9

Carr, Jay. "'Scarlet' Woman" *Boston Sunday Globe*. "Arts, Etc." 8 Oct. 1995: B:21–22.

Fabricant, Florence. "Cradle of an Empire." *New York Times* 22 Oct. 1995: 5:16 +.

Johnston, David Cay. "Building a Better 401 (k)." *New York Times*. "Money & Business" 22 Oct. 1995: 3:1+.

Pedersen, Laura. " My TV, Your VCR: How to Avoid a House Divided." *New York Times* 22 Oct. 1995. 3:10.

Tschihart-Sanford, Linda, and Mary Ellen Donovan. *Women and Self-Esteem*. New York: Penguin, 1985.

CHAPTER 10

Berman, Kenneth. " So You Think O.J. Got Away with Murder." *Boston Sunday Globe* 8 Oct. 1995: A:32.

Winter, Douglas E. *Stephen King: The Art of Darkness*. New York: Signet, 1986.

CHAPTER 11

Wilks, Brian. *The Brontës.* London: The Hamlyn Publishing Group, 1975.

CHAPTER 12

Hansen, Arlen J. "The Imagination Gap." *Newsweek* 25 Jul. 1977: 9.

Leo, John. " A Good Word for Bad Words." *Time* 14 Dec. 1981: 77.

Mueller, John. " From Two-Step to Goose Step." Rev. of *Keeping Together in Time: Dance and Drill in Human History* by William H. McNeill. *New York Times Book Review* 22 Oct. 1995: 22.

Powers, John. "Bitespeak." *Boston Globe Magazine* 15 July 1990: 17–40.

Saltus, Richard. "Getting Organized." *Boston Globe* "Your Health" Special Section. 15 Oct. 1995: 1+.

CHAPTER 13

Miller, Margo. "At Forest Hills Cemetery, the *Gothic* Aesthetic Prevails." *Boston Globe* 26 Oct. 1995: A:1, 6.

Scarry, Elaine. *Resisting Representation.* New York: Oxford UP, 1994.

Wood, Christopher. *The Pre-Raphaelites.* New York: Viking, 1981.

CHAPTER 14

Carruth, Gordon. *The American Encyclopedia of American Facts and Dates.* 9th ed. New York: HarperCollins, 1993. 417.

Flamsteed, Sam. "Where Giants Come from." *Discover* Nov. 1995: 82+.

Pendick, David. "Tornado Troopers." *Earth* Oct. 1995: 40–49.

Tannen, Deborah. "The Power of Talk." *Harvard Business Review* Sept.–Oct. 1995: 138–48.

CHAPTER 15

Drexler, Madeline. "Record Collecting." *Boston Globe Magazine* 29 Oct. 1995: 8–9.

Greenwald, John. "The Battle to Revive the Unions." *Time* 30 Oct. 1995: 64–66.

Langreth, Robert. "Hypermusic!" *Popular Science* Oct. 1995: 61–64.

CHAPTER 16

Bevington, David. *Medieval Drama.* Boston: Houghton Mifflin Company, 1975.

Bratton, Lorna. "The Great Escape." *Boston Sunday Globe* 29 Oct. 1995: B:15+.

Hardaway, Francine. "Foul Play: Sports Metaphors as Public Doublespeak." *College English* 38.1 (Sept. 1976): 78–82.

Roddy, Joseph. "*Marat/Sade* Stuns Playgoers with Sanity from the Asylum." *Look* 22 Feb. 1966: 107–10.

CHAPTER 17

Auerbach, Jon."The Doctor Is On Line." *Boston Sunday Globe* 5 Nov. 1995: 1+.

Raymo, Chet. "To Light the Fire of Science, Start with Some Fantasy and Wonder." *Boston Globe* 21 Dec. 1992, Science Musings. 36.

Rybczynski, Witold. "Downsizing Cities." *Atlantic Monthly* Oct. 1995: 36+.

Sainsbury, Steven J., M.D. "Condoms: Safer But Not 'Safe' Sex." Reprinted by permission of the author.

Shaheen, Jack. *In Search of the Arab.* Bowling Green, OH: Bowling Green State UP, 1984. 7.

Sugarman, Josh. "The NRA Is Right." *Washington Monthly* June 1987: 11–15.

Shushan, Ronnie, and Don Wright. *Desktop Publishing by Design.* 3rd ed. Redmond, WA: Microsoft Press, 1994.

Tschopp, Alison. "Advertising to Children Should Not Be Banned." Reprinted by permission of the author.

Trahar, Jenafer. "Athletes and Education." Student essay. Quoted by permission of the author.

Van Biema, David. "Crime: Murder on the Sunset Limited." *Time Magazine Online.* America Online. 8 Oct. 1995.

Watts, James, and Allen F. Davis, eds. *Your Family in Modern American History.* 2nd ed. New York: Knopf, 1978. Rpt. in *Writing and Reading Across the Curriculum.* Ed. Laurence Behrens and Leonard Rosen. Boston: Little, Brown, 1982. 136.

Wigginton, Eliot. "Furnaces." *Foxfire 5.* New York: Doubleday, 1979. 77–79.

Winn, Marie. "Television and Addiction." *The Plug-in Drug.* Rev. ed., New York: Viking Penguin, 1977, 1985. 23–25.

Yale Daily News Company. *The Insider's Guide to the Colleges, 1994.* New York: St. Martin's Press, 1994. 8–10.

Chapter 6: Works Cited

Berger, Arthur Asa. "Sex as Symbol in Fashion Advertising." *Media Analysis Techniques* (Vol 10, The Sage COMMTEXT Series), 1982. Rpt. in *Reading Culture.* Ed. Diana George and John Trimbur. New York: HarperCollins, 1992. 257.

Carson, Rachel L. "The Obligation to Endure." *Silent Spring.* Rpt. in *The Shape of this Century.* Ed. Diana Wyllie Rigden and Susan S. Waugh. New York: Harcourt, 1990. 393.

Healy, Bernardine. "Quotable" column. *The Chronicle of Higher Education* 25 Mar. 1992: B-5.

Jones, Beau Fly, Annemarie Sullivan Palincsar, Donna Sederburg Ogle, and Eileen Glynn Carr. *Strategic Thinking and Learning: Cognitive Instruction in the Content Areas.* Alexandia: ASCD, 1987. 22–23.

Quindlen, Anna. "A City's Needy." *New York Times* 30 Nov. 1986.

Tuchman, Barbara. "On Our Birthday—America as Idea." *Newsweek* 12 July 1976.

Turbak, Gary. "60 Billion Pounds of Trouble." *American Legion Magazine* Nov. 1989. Rpt. in *Effective Argument.* Ed. J. Karl Nicholas and James R. Nicholl. Boston: Allyn and Bacon, 1991. 135–136.

Chapter 37: Works Cited

Chopin, Kate. "A Shameful Affair," *The Awakening and Other Stories* Ed. Lewis Leary. Rpt. New York: Harcourt Brace, 1979.

Fichtelberg, Joseph. "The Complex Image: Text and Reader in the *Autobiography* of Benjamin Franklin." *Early American Literature* 23.2 (1988): 206.

Frankel, Charles. "Why the Humanities?" *The Humanist as Citizen.* Ed. John Agresto and Peter Riesenberg. Chapel Hill: N. Carolina UP, 1981.

Franklin, Benjamin. *The Autobiography and Other Writings.* New York: Penguin, 1987.

Ketchem, Ralph. "Benjamin Franklin." *Encyclopedia of Philosophy.* Rpt. 1972 ed.

Oates, Joyce Carol. *The Edge of Impossibility: Tragic Forms in Literature.* New York: Vanguard, 1972.

———. *On Boxing.* Garden City: Dolphin, 1987.

———. "Where Have You Been? Where Are You Going?" *The Wheel of Love.* New York: Vanguard, 1970.

O'Reilly, Kevin. "Teaching Critical Thinking in High School History." *Social Education* Apr. 1985: 281.

Rieke, Richard D., and Malcolm O. Sillars. *Argumentation and the Decision Making Process.* 2nd ed. Glenview: Scott, 1984.

Stratton, Joanna L. *Pioneer Women.* New York: Touchstone, 1981.

Toulmin, Stephen, Richard Rieke, and Allan Janik. *An Introduction to Reasoning.* New York: Macmillan, 1979.

Trilling, Lionel. "The Greatness of *Huckleberry Finn.*" *Adventures of Huckleberry Finn.* By Samuel Langhorn Clemens. Ed. Sculley Bradley, et al. 2nd ed. Norton Critical Edition. New York: Norton, 1977.

Van Doren, Carl. *Benjamin Franklin.* New York: Viking, 1938.

Wittgenstein, Ludwig. *Philosophical Investigations.* 3rd ed. Trans. G.E.M. Anscombe. New York: Macmillan, 1968.

Chapter 38: Works Cited

Braybrooke, David. *Philosophy of Social Science.* Prentice-Hall Foundations of Philosophy Series. Englewood Cliffs: Prentice, 1987.

Bromley, D. B. *The Case-study Method in Psychology and Related Disciplines.* Chichester, Great Britain: John Wiley, 1986.

Otis, Laura P. "Factors Influencing the Willingness to Taste Unusual Foods." *Psychological Reports* 54 (1984): 739–45.

Richlin-Klonsky, Judith, and Ellen Strenski, coordinators and eds. *A Guide to Writing Sociology Papers.* New York: St. Martin's, 1986.

Rieke, Richard D., and Malcolm O. Sillars. *Argumentation and the Decision Making Process.* 2nd ed. Glenview: Scott, 1984.

Rollinson, Paul A. "The Story of Edward: The Everyday Geography of Elderly Single Room Occupancy (SRO) Hotel Tenants." *Journal of Contemporary Ethnography* 19 (1990): 188–206.

Skinner, B. F. "Two Types of Conditioned Reflex and a Pseudo-type." *The Journal of General Psychology* 12 (1935): 66–77. Rpt. in B.F. Skinner, *Cumulative Record: A Selection of Papers.* 3rd ed. New York: Appleton, 1972, 479.

———. "How to Teach Animals." *Scientific American* 185 (1951): 26–29. Rpt. in B.F. Skinner, *Cumulative Record: A Selection of Papers.* 3rd ed. New York: Appleton, 1972, 539.

Solomon, Paul R. *A Student's Guide to Research Report Writing in Psychology.* Glenview: Scott, 1985.

Spencer, Herbert. *The Study of Sociology.* Ann Arbor: U of Michigan P, 1961.

Chapter 39: Works Cited

AIP [American Institute of Physics] Style Manual. 4th ed. New York: AIP, 1990.

American Association for the Advancement of Science. *Project 2061: Science for All Americans.* Washington: AAAS, 1989.

CBE [Council of Biology Editors] Style Manual. 5th ed. Bethesda: CBE, 1983.

Day, Robert. *How to Write and Publish a Scientific Paper.* 3rd ed. Phoenix: Oryx Press, 1988.

Gould, Stephen Jay. *Hen's Teeth and Horse's Toes: Further Reflections on Natural History.* New York: Norton, 1983.

Thuesen, Ingolf, and Jan Engberg. "Recovery and Analysis of Human Genetic Material from Mummified Tissue and Bone." *Journal of Archaeological Science* 17 (1990): 679–89.

Toulmin, Stephen, Richard Rieke, and Allan Janik. *An Introduction to Reasoning.* New York: Macmillan, 1979.

CHAPTER 19

Anon. *Creepy Crawlies.* New York: Sterling Publishing Co., 1991.

Bassett, Richard. "Transylvania." *A Guide to Central Europe.* New York: Viking, 1987. 116–25.

Centofanti. M. "Mummified HIV: It's Still Dangerous." *Science News* 28 Oct. 1995: 276.

Luciano, Lani. "Cut College Costs in Half—Or More." *Money* Oct. 1995: 135.

Moers, Ellen. *Literary Women.* New York: Anchor/Doubleday, 1977. 145–46.

Preston-Matham, Rod and Ken. *Spiders of the World.* New York: Blandford P., Ltd., 1984.

Sagan, Carl. *Cosmos.* New York: Random House, 1980. 39.

Smith, Dennis. "The Triangle Fire: New York, 1911." *Dennis Smith's History of Fire Fighting in America.* New York: Dial Press, 1978. 122–25.

Weier, T. Elliot, Ralph Stocking, and Michael G. Barbour. *Botany: Introduction to Plant Biology.* 5th ed. New York: John Wiley & Sons, 1974.

Zeiller, Warren. "Amazonian and West African Manatees." *Introducing the Manatee.* Gainesville: UP of Florida, 1992. 104–05.

Zweig, Stefan. *Marie Antoinette.* New York: Atrium P, Ltd., 1984. 13.

CHAPTER 20

Burton, Elizabeth. *The Pageant of Early Tudor England.* New York: Charles Scribner's Sons, 1976.

Celoria, Francis. *Archeology.* New York: Grosset & Dunlap, 1973.

Coogan, Tim Pat. *The IRA.* Niwot, CO: Roberts Rinehart, Publisher, 1994. 4.

Larsen, Ronald J. *The Puerto Ricans in America.* Minneapolis: Lerner Publications Co. 1989. 19–22.

Snow, Edward Rowe. *Unsolved Mysteries of Sea and Shore.* New York: Dodd, Mead & Co., 1963. 139–41.

Virch, Claus. *Francisco Goya.* New York: McGraw-Hill. 1967.

CHAPTER 21

Dembner, Alice. "Silber's Number One Job: Reading Skills." *Boston Sunday Globe* 5 Nov. 1995: 33–34.

Group for the Advancement of Psychiatry. *The Educated Woman.* New York: Charles Scribner's Sons, 1975. 103.

Mullin, Walter. "Professor Researches Public TV." *The Daily Pennsylvanian* 26 Oct. 1982.

Nilsen, Alleen Pace, et. al. *Sexism and Language.* Urbana, IL: National Council of Teachers of English, 1977. 172.

CHAPTER 24

Marcus, Geoffrey. *The Maiden Voyage.* New York: Viking Press, 1969. 148–49.

Quittel, Frances. *Fire Power.* Berkeley: Ten Speed Press, 1994. 44–45.

CHAPTER 25

Carnes, Mark C. "Hollywood History." *American Heritage* Sept. 1995: 76–84.

Green, Jonathan. *Greatest Criminals of All Time.* New York: Stein & Day, 1982. 193.

Lagerfeld, Steven. "What Main Street Can Learn from the Mall." *Atlantic Monthly* Nov. 95: 110–20.

de Lange, Nicholas. *Atlas of the Jewish World.* New York: Facts on File. 1984: 107+.

Vogel, Shawna. "Has Global Warming Begun?" *Earth* Dec. 1995: 25–34.

CHAPTER 26

Shreeve, James. "The Brain that Misplaced Its Body." *Discover* May 1995: 82–90.

Ullman, James Ramsey. *Americans on Everest.* Philadelphia: J. Lippincott Co., 1964. 6–7.

Woodward, Kenneth L. "Do We Need Satan?" *Newsweek* 13 Nov. 1995: 63–64.

CHAPTER 27

Woodcock, Joanne. *The Ultimate Windows 95 Book.* Redmond, WA: Microsoft Press, 1995.

CHAPTER 30

Cohen, Hennig, and Tristam P. Coffin, Eds. "Washing the Tombs on All Saints' Day." *The Folklore of American Holidays* 31.3 [Original Source: Wayne State University Folklore Archive, 196.]

CHAPTER 31

Dixon, Pam, and Sylvia Tiersten. *Be Your Own Headhunter Online.* New York: Random House, 1995.

Associated Press. "UK Brewer Bass to Offer Home Delivery Service." *Boston Sunday Globe* 12 Nov. 1995: A:125.

CREDITS FOR THE INSTRUCTOR'S EDITION

Carl Becker, excerpt from "Everyman His Own Historian," *American Historical Review,* vol. XXXVII (January 1932) pp. 221–236. Reprinted by permission.

Robert B. Kaplan, "Cultural Thought Patterns in Intercultural Education," *Language Learning* 16 (1966): 1–20. Reprinted by permission of *Language Learning* and Robert B. Kaplan.

Woodruff, David S., and Stephen Jay Gould, "Fifty Years of Interspecific Hybridization: Genetics and Morphometrics of a Controlled Experiment on the Land Snail *Cerion* in the Florida Keys." *Evolution* 41 (1987): 1026.

CREDITS

Bibliographic Index. Entry from *Bibliographic Index,* 1986, p. 21. Copyright © 1985, 1986 by The H.W. Wilson Company. Reprinted by permission of the publisher.

Ruth Schwartz Cowan, excerpt from "Virginia Dare to Virginia Slims: Women and Technology in American Life." Reprinted from *Technology and Society,* Jan. 1979, pp. 51–63: Copyright 1979, with kind permission of Elsevier Science Ltd., The Boulevard, Langford Lane, Kidlington OX5 1GB, UK.

Robert A. Day, "Tense in Scientific Writing." Reprinted from *How to Write and Publish a Scientific Paper,* 3rd ed., pp. 158–159, by Robert A. Day, Oryx Press, 4041 N. Central at Indian School Rd., Phoenix, AZ 85012. Copyright 1988 by Robert A. Day. Used by permission of The Oryx Press.

Anne Eisenberg, "Keeping a Laboratory Notebook." Reprinted by permission from *Journal of Chemical Education,* 59 (1982): 1045–1046.

Joseph Fichtelberg, excerpt from "The Complex Image," *Early American Literary Journal,* Vol. 23, No. 2, 1988. Reprinted by permission.

Jack Gordon, excerpt from "Drug Testing as a Productivity Booster?" Adapted with permission from the March 2, 1987 issue of *Training* Magazine. Copyright 1987, Lakewood Publications, Inc., Minneapolis, MN, (612) 333-0471. All rights reserved.

Bernardine Healy, excerpt from "Quotable" column, *The Chronicle of Higher Education,* March 25, 1992, p. B-5, Reprinted by permission of the author.

Rachel L. Jones, excerpts from "What's Wrong with Black English?" *Newsweek,* "My Turn Column," December 27, 1982. Reprinted by permission of the author.

Andrew Moss and Carol Holder, "Important Word Meaning," *Improving Student Writing: A Guide for Faculty in All Disciplines,* pp. 17–18, originally published by Kendall/Hunt, © Trustees of The California State University. Reprinted by permission.

The New York Times Index. Entry from *The New York Times Index,* 1989. Copyright © 1989 by The New York Times Company. Reprinted by permission.

Laura P. Otis, excerpt reproduced with permission of author and publisher from: Otis, L. P. "Factors Influencing the Willingness to Taste Unusual Foods." *Psycholoqical Reports,* 1984, 54, pp. 739–745. © Psychological Reports 1984.

Josefa Pinto, "Genetic Engineering and Advertising"; student paper by Jose Pinto. Reprinted by permission of the author.

Readers' Guide to Periodical Literature. Entry from *Readers' Guide to Periodical Literature,* 1989, p. 614. Copyright © 1989, 1990 by The H.W. Wilson Company. Reprinted by permission of the publisher.

Paul A. Rollinson, excerpt from "The Story of Edward," *Journal of Contemporary Ethnography,* Vol. 19, No. 2, July 1990, pp. 188–206, © 1990 by Sage Publications, Inc. Reprinted by permission.

Jeffrey Schrank, excerpt from "The Language of Advertising Claims," *Media & Methods,* March 1974, pp. 44–48, 51. Reprinted by permission of the author.

Ingolf Thuesen and Jan Engberg, excerpts from "Recovery and Analysis of Human Genetic Material from Mummified Tissue and Bone," *Journal of Archaeological Science* 17 (1990): 679–689. © 1990 Academic Press Limited. Reprinted by permission.

Alison Tschopp, "Advertising to Children Should Not be Banned." Student paper reprinted by permission of the author.

Ludwig Wittgenstein, excerpt from *Philosophical Investigations,* 3/e, © 1973. Reprinted by permission of Prentice Hall, Upper Saddle River, New Jersey and Blackwell Publishers.

INDEX

REVISION SYMBOLS

The symbols below indicate a need to make revisions in the areas designated. Boldface numbers and letters refer to handbook sections.

ab	abbreviation **31 a–e**
ad	form of adjective/adverb **7c, 11**
agr	agreement **10**
awk	awkward diction or construction **7b, 15, 21**
ca	case form **8**
cap	capitalization **30a–d**
coh	coherence **4b, 5d**
coord	coordination **7f, 18a, 19a**
cs	comma splice **13**
d	diction, word choice **21, 22**
dm	dangling modifier **15h**
dev	development needed **3, 4, 18d**
emph	emphasis needed **19, 20**
frag	sentence fragment **7b, 12**
fs	fused sentence **13**
hyph	hyphen **32**
inc	incomplete construction **7b, 16g–h**
ital	italics **30e–g**
k	awkward diction or construction **7b, 11g, 15, 21**
lc	lowercase letter **30a–d**
log	logic **6, 37a, 38a, 39a**
mm	misplaced modifier **7d, 15**
ms	manuscript form **35h, Appx. B**
mix	mixed construction **16e–f**
no ¶	no paragraph needed **5**
num	number **31f–h**
¶	paragraph **5**
¶ dev	paragraph development needed **5**

ref	unclear pronoun reference **14**
rep	unnecessary repetition **17a**
sp	spelling error **23**
shift	inconsistent, shifted construction **16**
sub	sentence subordination **7e–f, 19b**
t	verb tense error **9e–f**
trans	transition needed **5a, 5d, 5f**
var	sentence variety needed **19, 20**
vb	verb form error **9, 17b**
w	wordy **17a**
ww	wrong word; word choice **10c, 21, 22**
//	faulty parallelism **18**
. ? !	end punctuation **24**
:	colon **29a**
’ (inserted)	apostrophe **27**
—	dash **29b**
( )	parentheses **29c**
[ ]	brackets **29d**
. . .	ellipsis **29e**
/	slash **29f**
;	semicolon **26**
“ ”	quotation marks **28**
, (inserted)	comma **25**
⁀‿	close up
^	insert a missing element
(delete mark)	delete
⊔⊓	transpose order

SPOTLIGHT ON COMMON ERRORS

I. FORMS OF NOUNS AND PRONOUNS **See the SPOTLIGHT (page 208), Chapter 8.**

Apostrophes can show possession or contraction. Never use an apostrophe with a possessive pronoun.

Faulty Forms	Revised
The scarf is *Chris.* It is *her's.*	The scarf is *Chris's.* It is *hers.*
Give the dog *it's* collar.	Give the dog *its* collar.
Its a difficult thing.	*It's* [it is] a difficult thing.

Choose a pronoun's form depending on its use. For pronouns connected by *and,* or with forms of the verb *be (is/are/was/were),* decide which forms to use *(I/he/she/they OR me/him/her/them).*

Faulty Forms	Revised
This is *him.* It was *me.* Is that *her?*	This is *he.* It was *I.* Is that *she?*
The ball landed between *she* and *I.*	The ball landed between *her* and *me.*
Her and *me* practice daily.	*She* and *I* practice daily.

II. VERBS **See the SPOTLIGHT (page 222), Chapter 9.**

Keep verb tenses consistent when describing two closely connected events.

Inconsistent	Revised
She *liked* the work. Still, she *keeps* to herself.	She *likes* the work. Still, she *keeps* to herself.

(a) Choose the right verb forms with an *if* clause expressing an unreal or hypothetical condition. (b) Decide on which of these verb forms to use: *sit* or *set, lie* or *lay, rise* or *raise.*

Faulty Verb Form	Revised
(a) If it *would be* any colder, the pipes *would* freeze.	(a) If it *were* any colder, the pipes *would* freeze.
(b) *Lie* the books here. Then *lay* down.	(b) *Lay* the books here. Then *lie* down.

III. AGREEMENT **See the SPOTLIGHT (page 248), Chapter 10.**

Match subjects with verbs. Make sure both are either singular or plural.

Not in Agreement	Revised
The *reason* she wins *are* her friends.	The *reason* she wins *is* her friends.

Match pronouns with the words they refer to. (a) Words joined by *and* require a plural pronoun and verb. (b) For words joined by *or/nor,* match the pronoun and verb to the nearer word.

Not in Agreement	Revised
(a) My friends **and** Sue *likes her* pizza hot.	(a) My friends **and** Sue *like their* pizza hot.
(b) Neither her friends **nor** Sue *like their* pizza cold.	(b) Neither her friends **nor** Sue *likes her* pizza cold.

IV. SENTENCE STRUCTURE: FRAGMENTS **See SPOTLIGHT (page 275), Chapter 12.**

Recognize sentence boundaries. Mark where sentences should end, usually with a period (or sometimes with a semicolon). Avoid a FRAGMENT—a word group that will not stand alone with a full subject and predicate. See the test for fragments in Chapter 12.

Faulty	Revised
If our cousins arrive today. [Fragment]	Our cousins may arrive today.

V. SENTENCE STRUCTURE: BOUNDARIES **See SPOTLIGHT (page 287), Chapter 13.**

Recognize boundaries. (a) Avoid a FUSED SENTENCE: two sentences with no connecting word or punctuation. (b) Avoid a COMMA SPLICE: two sentences with only a comma between them.

Faulty	Revised
(a) He's here now later he'll go to Iowa. [Fused]	He's here now. Later he'll go to Iowa.
(b) He's here now, later he'll go to Iowa. [Splice]	He's here now; later he'll go to Iowa.